DATE DUE

			PRINTED IN U.S.A.

Literature Criticism from 1400 to 1800

Guide to Gale Literary Criticism Series

For criticism on	Consult these Gale series
Authors now living or who died after December 31, 1959	*CONTEMPORARY LITERARY CRITICISM (CLC)*
Authors who died between 1900 and 1959	*TWENTIETH-CENTURY LITERARY CRITICISM (TCLC)*
Authors who died between 1800 and 1899	*NINETEENTH-CENTURY LITERATURE CRITICISM (NCLC)*
Authors who died between 1400 and 1799	*LITERATURE CRITICISM FROM 1400 TO 1800 (LC)* *SHAKESPEAREAN CRITICISM (SC)*
Authors who died before 1400	*CLASSICAL AND MEDIEVAL LITERATURE CRITICISM (CMLC)*
Authors of books for children and young adults	*CHILDREN'S LITERATURE REVIEW (CLR)*
Dramatists	*DRAMA CRITICISM (DC)*
Poets	*POETRY CRITICISM (PC)*
Short story writers	*SHORT STORY CRITICISM (SSC)*
Black writers of the past two hundred years	*BLACK LITERATURE CRITICISM (BLC)*
Hispanic writers of the late nineteenth and twentieth centuries	*HISPANIC LITERATURE CRITICISM (HLC)*
Native North American writers and orators of the eighteenth, nineteenth, and twentieth centuries	*NATIVE NORTH AMERICAN LITERATURE (NNAL)*
Major authors from the Renaissance to the present	*WORLD LITERATURE CRITICISM, 1500 TO THE PRESENT (WLC)*

ISSN 0740-2880

Volume 48

Literature Criticism from 1400 to 1800

Critical Discussion of the Works
of Fifteenth-, Sixteenth-, Seventeenth-, and
Eighteenth-Century Novelists, Poets, Playwrights,
Philosophers, and Other Creative Writers

Marie Lazzari
Editor

The Gale Group

DETROIT • SAN FRANCISCO • LONDON • BOSTON • WOODBRIDGE, CT

STAFF

Marie Lazzari, *Editor*
Ira Mark Milne, *Associate Editor*
Janet Witalec, *Managing Editor*

Maria Franklin, *Permissions Manager*
Kimberly F. Smilay, *Permissions Specialist*
Kelly A. Quin, *Permissions Associate*
Sandra K. Gore, *Permissions Assistant*

Victoria B. Cariappa, *Research Manager*
Patricia T. Ballard, Tamara C. Nott, Tracie A. Richardson,
Corrine Stocker, Cheryl L. Warnock, *Research Associates*

Gary Leach, *Graphic Artist*
Randy Bassett, *Image Database Supervisor*
Mike Logusz, Robert Duncan, *Imaging Specialists*
Pamela A. Reed, *Imaging Coordinator*

This book is printed on acid-free paper that meets the minimum requirements of American National Standard for Information Sciences—Permanence Paper for Printed Library Materials, ANSI Z39.48-1984.

Library of Congress Catalog Card Number 94-29718
ISBN 0-7876-3263-5
ISSN 0740-2880
Printed in the United States of America

10 9 8 7 6 5 4 3 2 1

Contents

Preface vii

Acknowledgments xi

Preface

L iterature Criticism from 1400 to 1800 (LC) presents critical discussion of world literature from the fifteenth through the eighteenth centuries. The literature of this period is especially vital: the years 1400 to 1800 saw the rise of modern European drama, the birth of the novel and personal essay forms, the emergence of newspapers and periodicals, and major achievements in poetry and philosophy. *LC* provides valuable insight into the art, life, thought, and cultural transformations that took place during these centuries.

Scope of the Series

LC provides an introduction to the great poets, dramatists, novelists, essayists, and philosophers of the fifteenth through eighteenth centuries, and to the most significant interpretations of these authors' works. Because criticism of this literature spans nearly six hundred years, an overwhelming amount of scholarship confronts the student. *LC* organizes this material concisely and logically. Every attempt is made to reprint the most noteworthy, relevant, and educationally valuable essays available.

A separate Gale reference series, *Shakespearean Criticism,* is devoted exclusively to Shakespearean studies. Although properly belonging to the period covered in *LC,* William Shakespeare has inspired such a tremendous and ever-growing body of secondary material that a separate series was deemed essential.

Each entry in *LC* presents a representative selection of critical response to an author, a literary topic, or to a single important work of literature. Early commentary is offered to indicate initial responses, later selections document changes in literary reputations, and retrospective analyses provide the reader with modern views. The size of each author entry is a relative reflection of the scope of criticism available in English. Every attempt has been made to identify and include the seminal essays on each author's work and to include recent commentary providing modern perspectives.

Volumes 1 through 12 of the series feature author entries arranged alphabetically by author. Volumes 13 through 47 of the series feature a thematic arrangement. Each volume includes an entry devoted to the general study of a specific literary or philosophical movement, writings surrounding important political and historical events, the philosophy and art associated with eras of cultural transformation, or the literature of specific social or ethnic groups. Each of these volumes also includes several author entries devoted to major representatives of the featured period, genre, or national literature. With Volume 48, the series returns to a standard author approach, with occasional entries devoted to a single important work of world literature. One volume annually is devoted wholly to literary topics.

Organization of the Book

Each entry consists of a heading, an introduction, a list of principal works, annotated works of criticism, each preceded by a bibliographical citation, and a bibliography of recommended further reading. Many of the entries include illustrations.

- The **Author Heading** consists of the most commonly used form of the author's name, followed by birth and death dates. Also located here are any name variations under which an author wrote, including transliterated forms for authors whose native languages use nonroman alphabets. Uncertain birth or death dates are indicated by question marks. Topic entries are preceded by a **Thematic Heading**, which simply states the subject of the entry. Single-work entries are preceded by the title of the work and its date of publication.

- The **Introduction** contains background information that concisely introduces the reader to the author, work, or topic that is the subject of the entry.

- The list of **Principal Works** is ordered chronologically by date of first publication. The genre and publication date of each work is given. In the case of foreign authors whose works have been translated into English, the title and date (if available) of the first English-language edition is given in brackets following the original title. Unless otherwise indicated, dramas are dated by first performance, not first publication. Lists of **Representative Works** by different authors appear with topic entries.

- Reprinted **Criticism** is arranged chronologically in each entry to provide a useful perspective on changes in critical evaluation over time. The critic's name and the date of composition or publication of the critical work are given at the beginning of each piece of criticism. Unsigned criticism is preceded by the title of the source in which it appeared. All titles by the author featured in the text are printed in boldface type. Footnotes are reprinted at the end of each essay or excerpt. In the case of excerpted criticism, only those footnotes that pertain to the excerpted text are included. Criticism in topic entries is arranged chronologically under a variety of subheadings to facilitate the study of different aspects of the topic.

- Critical essays are prefaced by brief **Annotations** explicating each piece.

- A complete **Bibliographical Citation** of the original essay or book precedes each piece of criticism.

- An annotated bibliography of **Further Reading** appears at the end of each entry and suggests resources for additional study. In some cases, significant essays for which the editors could not obtain reprint rights are included here.

Cumulative Indexes

Each volume of *LC* includes a series-specific cumulative **Nationality Index** in which author names are arranged alphabetically by nationality. The volume or volumes of *LC* in which each author appears are also listed.

Each volume of *LC* includes a cumulative **Author Index** listing all of the authors that appear in a wide variety of reference sources published by The Gale Group, including *LC*. A complete list of these sources is found facing the first page of the Author Index. The index also includes birth and death dates and cross references between pseudonyms and actual names.

LC includes a cumulative **Topic Index** that lists the literary themes and topics treated in the series as well as in *Nineteenth-Century Literature Criticism*, *Twentieth-Century Literary Criticism*, and the *Contemporary Literature Criticism* Yearbook.

Each volume of *LC* also includes a cumulative **Title Index,** an alphabetical listing of all the literary works discussed in the series. Each title listing includes the corresponding volume and page numbers where criticism may be located. Foreign-language titles that have been translated into English followed by the tiles of the translation—for example, *El ingenioso hidalgo Don Quixote de la Mancha (Don Quixote)*. Page numbers following these translated titles refer to all pages on which any form of the titles, either foreign-language or translated, appear. Titles of novels, dramas, nonfiction books, and poetry, short story, or essay collections are printed in italics, while individual poems, short stories, and essays are printed in roman type within quotation marks.

A Note to the Reader

When writing papers, students who quote directly from any volume in the Literary Criticism Series may use the following general format to footnote reprinted criticism. The first example pertains to material drawn from periodicals, the second to material reprinted from books.

Eileen Reeves, "Daniel 5 and the *Assayer*: Galileo Reads the Handwriting on the Wall," *The Journal of Medieval and Renaissance Studies,* Vol. 21, No. 1, Spring, 1991, pp. 1-27; reprinted in *Literature Criticism from 1400 to 1800,* Vol. 45, ed. Jelena O. Krstović and Marie Lazzari, Farmington Hills, Mich.: The Gale Group, 1999, pp. 297-310.

Margaret Anne Doody, *A Natural Passion: A Study of the Novels of Samuel Richardson*, Oxford University Press, 1974, pp. 17-22, 132-35, excerpted and reprinted in *Literature Criticism from 1400 to 1800,* Vol. 46, ed. Jelena O. Krstović and Marie Lazzari. Farmington Hills, Mich.: The Gale Group, 1999, pp. 20-2.

Suggestions Are Welcome

Readers who wish to suggest new features, topics, or authors to appear in future volumes, or who have other suggestions or comments are cordially invited to call, write, or fax the editor:

Editor, *Literature Criticism 1400-1800*
The Gale Group
27500 Drake Road
Farmington Hills, MI 48133-3535
1-800-347-4253
fax: 248-699-8049

Acknowledgments

The editors wish to thank the copyright holders of the excerpted criticism included in this volume and the permissions managers of many book and magazine publishing companies for assisting us in securing reproduction rights. We are also grateful to the staffs of the Detroit Public Library, the Library of Congress, the University of Detroit Mercy Library, Wayne State University Purdy/Kresge Library Complex, and the University of Michigan Libraries for making their resources available to us. Following is a list of the copyright holders who have granted us permission to reproduce material in this volume of *LC.* Every effort has been made to trace copyright, but if omissions have been made, please let us know.

COPYRIGHTED EXCERPTS IN *LC,* VOLUME 48, WERE REPRODUCED FROM THE FOLLOWING PERIODICALS

Ariel: A Review of International English Literature, v. 23, July, 1992 for "The Margins of Sentiment: Nature, Letter, and Law in Frances Brooke's Epistolary Novels" by Barbara M. Benedict. Copyright © 1992 The Board of Governors, The University of Calgary. Reproduced by permission of the publisher and the author.—*Ball State University Forum,* v. 9, Spring, 1968. © 1968 Ball State University. Reproduced by permission.—*Canadian Literature,* n. 86, Autumn, 1980 for "Frances Brooke's Early Fiction" by Lorraine McMullen; n. 133, Summer, 1992 for "The Politics of Romance in 'The History of Emily Montague'" by Robert James Merrett. Both reproduced by permission of the respective authors.—*Canadian Review of Comparative Literature,* v. 20, September-December, 1993. © Canadian Comparative Literature Association 1993. Reproduced by permission.—*The Critical Quarterly,* v. 13, Autumn, 1971. Reproduced by permission of Blackwell Publishers.—*Eighteenth-Century Fiction,* v. 9, April, 1997. Reproduced by permission.—*Eighteenth-Century Studies,* v. 4, Fall, 1970. © 1970 by The American Society for Eighteenth-Century Studies. Reproduced by permission.—*Éire-Ireland,* v. XVIII, 1983. Copyright © 1983 by the Irish American Cultural Institute. Reproduced by permission of the publisher.—*ELH,* v. 46, Spring, 1979. Copyright © 1979 by The Johns Hopkins University Press. All rights reserved. Reproduced by permission.—*Encounter,* v. XXI, October, 1963 for "The Old Last Act: Some Observations on 'Fanny Hill'" by John Hollander. Reproduced by permission of the author.—*English Studies in Canada,* v. VII, Summer, 1981 for "Frances Brooke's 'The History of Emily Montague': A Biographical Context" by Mary Jane Edwards. © Association of Canadian University Teachers of English 1981. Reproduced by permission of the publisher and the author.—*Essays in Criticism,* v. XIV, January, 1964 for "What is 'Fanny Hill'?" by B. Slepian and L. J. Morrissey. Reproduced by permission of Oxford University Press and the authors.—*Essays on Canadian Writing,* v. 51-52, Winter 1993-Spring 1994. © 1994 Essays on Canadian Writing Ltd. Reproduced by permission.—*German Life and Letters,* v. 20, 1966-67. Reproduced by permission of Blackwell Publishers.—*Journal of Canadian Fiction,* v. 21, 1977-78. Reproduced by permission from *Journal of Canadian Fiction,* 2050 Mackay St., Montreal, Quebec H3G 2J1, Canada.—*Quadrant,* v. VIII, April-May, 1964 for "Matters of Sex" by Leonie Kramer. Reproduced by permission of the publisher and the author.—*The Review of English Studies,* n.s. v. XLI, May, 1990 for "Goldsmith's First Vicar" by Richard C. Taylor. © Oxford University Press 1990. Reproduced by permission of Oxford University Press and the author.—*RS-SI: Recherches Semiotiques-Semiotic Inquiry,* v. 14, 1994 for "Signs of Nationalism in 'The History of Montague; Canadians of Old and The Imperialist': Cultural Displacement and the Semiotics of Wine" by Robert James Merrett. © Association canadienne de sémiotique/Canadian Semiotic Association. Reproduced by permission of the publisher and the author.—*Studies in English Literature, 1500-1900,* v. 23, Summer, 1983. © 1983 William Marsh Rice University. Reproduced by permission of *SEL Studies in English Literature, 1500-1900.*—*Studies in Philology,* v. LXXV, October, 1978; v. LXXXI, Spring, 1984. Copyright © 1978, 1984 by the University of North Carolina Press. Both reproduced by permission.—*Studies in the Novel,* v. IV, Fall, 1972. Copyright 1972 by North Texas State University. Reproduced by permission of the publisher.—*Women's Studies: An Interdisciplinary Journal,* v. 12, 1986. © Gordon and Breach Science Publishers, Inc. Reproduced by permission.

COPYRIGHTED EXCERPTS IN *LC,* VOLUME 48, WERE REPRODUCED FROM THE FOLLOWING BOOKS:

Anderson, Howard. From "Structure, Language, Experience in the Novels of Laurence Sterne," in *Essays in Under-*

PHOTOGRAPHS AND ILLUSTRATIONS APPEARING IN *LC,* VOLUME 48, WERE RECEIVED FROM THE FOLLOWING SOURCES:

Thomas Amory

1691(?)-1788

English novelist

INTRODUCTION

Amory is remembered for two highly idiosyncratic works: *Memoirs: Containing the Lives of Several Ladies of Great Britain,* and *The Life of John Buncle, Esq.* Although generally called novels, these works are quite different from the novel form as it is recognized today, and even departed from the novel form that was developing at the time of their appearance. Both works incorporate lively, informed discussion of philosophical, theological, scientific, mathematical, and religious thought within thinly developed, fanciful plots.

Biographical Information

Amory was a reclusive figure, and much of what has been taken as biographical information about him was inferred from his published works. Born in England to an Irish family, Amory lived for many years in Ireland. He may have attended the University of Dublin, but this is not certain. He returned to England as an adult and settled in London. He married and had one son, who occasionally published letters in newspapers and magazines to correct extravagant suppositions made in the press regarding Amory. He died in 1788.

Major Works

Memoirs: Containing the Lives of Several Ladies of Great Britain, published in two volumes in 1755, purports to be an account of the remarkable women whom the narrator—presumably Amory himself—met on his travels. Much of the book, however, is taken up with transcriptions of the "Ladies" discussing Unitarian theology. Is is assumed that Amory used this method to transmit his own religious principles. *The Life of John Buncle, Esq.* was also published in two volumes, the first in 1756, the second ten years later. The uncomplicated plot has the eponymous protagonist meeting and marrying a series of wealthy, beautiful, and scholarly Unitarian women in succession. The narrative is composed primarily of Buncle's descriptions of where and how he meets each woman, and of the long, intellectual talks that constitute their courtship. Amory drew widely, if sketchily, from such important thinkers of the period as John Locke, Isaac Newton, and Voltaire to create the sparkling, informed conversation of Buncle's wives, thus giving readers a selective, though necessarily superficial, overview of English Enlightenment thought.

Critical Reception

Amory's contemporaries were confused by and hostile to the author's published works. The *Critical Review,* for example, called *The Life of John Buncle* "nonsense" and found the book "insufferable." Amory's reputation enjoyed a brief resuscitation during the English Romantic period in the early nineteenth century. Prominent critics such as William Hazlitt, Leigh Hunt, and Charles Lamb, reflecting the preoccupations of English Romanticism, were intrigued by the book's descriptions of natural wonders. Hazlitt even called Amory "the English *Rabelais*" because of his ability to create larger-than-life figures who fuse a life of the mind and spirit with that of the body. With the waning of Romanticism, however, Amory's reputation declined. In the twentieth century his books are little regarded except as curiosities. He has been compared with Laurence Sterne, the author of another eccentric, rambling novel, *Tristram Shandy*. But while Sterne successfully fused the novel's digressions into an overall narrative scheme, critics agree that Amory's books are little more than thinly disguised treatises on his theological and philosophical avocations Most commentators, however, acknowledge the humor and enthusiasm with which Amory created his improbable plots and unlikely characters.

PRINCIPAL WORKS

Memoirs: Containing the Lives of Several Ladies of Great Britain. A History of Antiquities, Productions of Nature and Monuments of Art. Observations on the Christian Religion as Professed by the Established Church and Dissenters of Every Denomination. Remarks on the Writings of the Greatest English Divines: with a Variety of Disquisitions and Opinions Relative to Criticism and Manners and Many Extraordinary Actions (novel) 1755.

The Life of John Buncle, Esq.: Containing Various Observations and Reflections Made in Several Parts of the World and Many Extraordinary Relations (novel) 1756 (vol. I) and 1766 (vol. II)

CRITICISM

The Monthly Review (review date 1766)

SOURCE: Review of *The Life of John Buncle, Esq.,* *Monthly Review,* July 1766, pp. 33-43.

[In the following review of The Life of John Buncle, Esq., *published in 1766, the reviewer finds the narrative absurd and improbable, particularly in comparison with Amory's earlier work. The reviewer, however, praises the book for its imaginativeness as well as its strong advocacy of the principles of Unitarianism.]*

Many of our Readers, no doubt, remember the accounts we gave of this most extraordinary Author's former productions; his **"Memoirs of learned Ladies,"** and the first Volume of his own life: for which see *Review,* Vol. XIII, and XV.

Mr. Buncle is still the same extravagant, visionary, romantic writer; and his adventures, recorded in this new publication, are not in any degree more consistent with nature and probability, nor a whit less absurd, than those which, in his former productions, have so greatly astonished and, we had almost said, confounded his Readers.

Yet, wild and wonderful as are the stories told by this strange adventurer, and monstrous, and even ridiculous as some of his narrations are, they are *splendide mendaces;* and we cannot help admiring the singular turn and capacity of the writer:—Who, whenever he soars above the limits of common sense, is generally elevated into so fine a frenzy, that we willingly suffer him to transport us, in his aerial flights, to 'Thebes, to Athens, or the Lord knows where.'—When, like one of the weird sisters on a broomstick, he scampers away over earth and seas, or desperately plunges into some horrible and untried gulph, we are nothing loth to mount behind and bear him company, though it were down to the centre, or 'beyond the visible diurnal sphere.'—What an amazing mortal is this Buncle! Never, surely, did his equal exist! Nat. Lee is nothing to him; nor even the fiery poet, Lord Flame, who kept the town staring, laughing and hollowing, for near a month together, with his Hurlothrumbo[1]. In fine, he is a perfect *unique,* and, certainly, as much an original, in his way, as Shakespeare or Sam. Richardson; though, possibly, with this difference, that their excellencies proceeded merely from native, uncultivated genius; while our Author's peculiar sublimities seem to be the produce of a genius and imagination over-heated and run to seed in the hot-beds of romance and religious controversy. In all his extravagancies, however, he appears to maintain, with strictest uniformity, the character of an honest man,—earnest in promoting the best interests of his fellow creatures, and zealous to the highest degree, for what he apprehends to be the cause of Truth.—Being, moreover, a scholar, a mathematician, a philosopher, a divine, a physician, an historian and a poet, his books may truly be stiled a most entertaining miscellany, in which Readers of every class will find something for their amusement; and no one, we believe, can be wholly displeased with so various a writer, except those who cannot bear to hear the church of Rome censured, and the doctrine of the Trinity called in question; for, indeed, Mr. Buncle is the warmest advocate for the Reformation, and for the unity of God, that we ever met with. But then he introduces these controverted subjects so often, that, although he frequently says very strong things upon them, yet even those who are in his own sentiments must naturally be tired out with the eternal repetition.

This volume opens with what the Author calls his 'apology for the married state;' and, verily according to his account few men have been better qualified to do justice to the subject: as he had no less than seven wives—but all in due succession to each other; for you are not to imagine, gentle Reader, that Mr. Buncle was a polygamist.

Happily, indeed, did our Author and his amiable (first) wife pass their time at Orton-lodge, where we left them at the close of our account of his former volume; but short as well as sweet was the term of their felicity! The 'soft transporting period' lasted but two years; when 'in came death, when they least expected him, snatched Mr. Buncle's charming partner from him, and (as he expresses it) melted all his happiness into air;' a fever, says he, 'in a few days, snapt the thread of her life, and made me the child of affliction, when I had not a thought of the mourner. Language cannot paint the distress this calamity reduced me to; nor give an idea of what I suffered when I saw her eyes swimming in death, and the throes of her departing spirit. Blest as she was in every virtue that adorns a woman, how inconsolable must her husband be!'—Not absolutely inconsolable, however; for in the very next section we find him in high raptures with a Miss Statia Henley; a delightful young lady, of whom he gives the following description. 'She was at this time just turned of twenty, and had such diffusive charms as soon new fired my heart, and gave my soul a softness even beyond what it had felt before. She was a little taller than the middle size, and had a face that was perfectly beautiful. Her eyes were extremely fine, full, black, sparkling, and her conversation was as charming as her person; both easy, unconstrained and sprightly.'—We give this short description of Miss Henley, as we shall do that of all his wives; because it may gratify the curiosity of the Reader to compare the several pictures with each other, and mark their different and distinguishing beauties: for beauties they all were, and peerless ones too, however extraordinary such a circumstance may seem,—and still more extraordinary that so many divine and glorious creatures (to speak in our Author's own style) should fall to the happy, seven times happy! lot of one man!

He met with this lady at a most delightful romantic spot among the fells of Westmoreland, the happy retirement of her grand father, Charles Henley, Esq; and here, too, he met with some other wonderful things, particularly a curious moralizing skeleton, leaning on a reading desk in the midst of a library.—But we feel ourselves rather attracted by the blooming lady, than by the scare-crow remains of her father: for such it seems were the extraordinary figure at the desk.

Mr. Buncle, though an entire stranger, who had by mere chance rambled to the rural *groves of Basil,* presently got into the good graces of both the old gentleman and his grand daughter. The former soon made him the offer of living with them till Miss Henley should be of age; when she, with a good fortune, might be at our adventurer's service, provided he, in that time, could make his assiduities acceptable to the young lady. This offer was as readily accepted as made; and Mr. Buncle is now superlatively happy with his new friends at Basil groves: where he delightfully passed the winter and spring following. 'The mornings, says he, I generally spent in the library, [a very noble one] reading, or writing extracts from some various MSS. or scarce books; and in the afternoons Miss Henley and I walked in the lawns and woods, or sat down to cards. She was a fine creature indeed, in body and soul—and charmed me to a high degree. Her conversation was rational and easy, without the least affectation from the books she had read; and she would enliven it sometimes by singing, in which she was a great mistress—as to her heart, I found it was to be gained'—

His two years apprenticeship to love, was, however, cut short by the death of the good old Mr. Henley; on which event, the lady somewhat surprized our amorous Author with a declaration in favour of a single life, and a civil intimation that he was at liberty to retire from the *groves of Basil.* This stroke Mr. Buncle had the dexterity to parry; and with what weapon do you think, gentle Readers, did this young gallant ward off the impending flow? Why—with a strange dry speech about *baptism,* the *Abrahamic covenant,* and *circumcision;*—however, he wound up his oration with an earnest persuasive to *marry*——for the sake of keeping up a *succession* in a *regular* and *hallowed* way.——What a method of courting a fine, delicate young lady!—But this was one of Mr. Buncle's *oddities.*

Yet, odd, and uncouth, and rather suitable to the character of some old scholiast, as was our Author's mode of address to Miss Henley, on her intimated resolution to live single, it had power enough to make her change that resolution, and to declare in favour of a *succession.* They were married, lived happily for two years, and then poor Statia died also, and was laid by the side of her predecessor.

Mr. Buncle's sorrow for the loss of his excellent *second* was too violent to last long: he bewailed himself—as long as his grief would hold out; sat with his eyes shut for three days; and at last called for his horse, 'to try what air, exercise, and a variety of objects, could do.'

In the third section, we find our wandering knight on his way to Harrogate Spaw; and of his journey thitherward we have a most romantic account. In a wonderfully pleasant valley in Westmoreland, surrounded by mountains of stupendous height, he met with a religious society of married people; with whom he spent some days: and gives an ample account of their institution; the regularity of their lives; their antipathy to the doctrine of celibacy, and some other popish absurdities; their exemplary devotions, and their rational studies.—Proceeding on his route to Harrogate, he misses his way, (as he generally does wherever he goes, for his horse usually has the direction and choice of the road) and arrives at a beautiful country seat in the northern extremity of Stanmore. Here, without seeing any human creature, he passes the night in a curious sleeping parlour, built in a most enchanting grove: while his servant, O Fin, stays without to take care of the horses, and under a great tree takes as comfortable a nap as his master. Next morning he receives, from a countryman, some account of Miss Antonia Cramer, a charming young lady, Mistress of this delightful abode; and immediately falling in love with her character, he forms a scheme for obtaining her, to fill up the vacancy made at Orton-lodge, by the death of his second wife. Unluckily, however, she was then absent, on a journey, and was not to come home again till the end of twenty days; but this circumstance was nothing to Mr. Buncle, who resolving to wait her return, took up his quarters, at a neighbouring cottage, where he gains intelligence of an extraordinary man, an hermit, whose dwelling was not far off, and to whom our rambling philosopher instantly repairs, to pass away, in the conversation of this Solitary, some of the tedious hours which slowly crept along, during the absence of the divine Antonia. And now comes the episodical story of Mr. Dorick Watson the hermit. He was an English gentleman, who had been bred a Catholic in France, and there married a sister of the famous Abbe le Blanc,—with whose *letters concerning the English nation* we suppose most of our Readers are acquainted.—In Mr. Watson's narrative of his own life, we have a curious detail of his reasons for renouncing the errors of the Romish church; the conversion also of his wife; her death; and his motive for turning Anchorite. In this part of our Author's work, the celebrated *notes* of Cardinal Bellarmine are smartly attacked and exploded. Here, also, is introduced an account of Abbe le Blanc, with some notable strictures on Monsieur de Voltaire: 'That wonderful compound of a man, says he, half infidel, half papist; who seems to have no regard for *Christianity;* and yet compliments *Popery,* at the expence of his understanding[2]; who writes the history of England with a partiality and malevolence almost as great as Smollett's, and pretends to describe the Britannic constitution, tho' it is plain from what he says, that he has not one true idea of the *primary institutions* of it, but taking this nation to be just such another kingdom of slaves as his own country, rails at the REVOLUTION, &c. &c.'—Doubtless Voltaire has given but too much cause for this charge of inconsistency—but to go on with our Author.

On his return to the poor man's cottage, he learns that Miss Cramer, and her Cousin, Miss Vane, who constantly resided with her as her companion, were returned home. The honest cottager, it seems, had already apprized the ladies concerning Mr. Buncle's arrival in those parts; and had mentioned him 'as a traveller who had journeyed into that remote corner of the world, in search of antiquities and curiosities.'—And now, Reader, be-hold in what manner our enamorato contrives to introduce himself to this Sylvan Goddess. 'Immediately, says he, I crossed the water, and as I saw her and the fair Agnes, her cousin, walking in the garden near the *Ha,* leaped it over, broad as it was, [well done, Sir Knight!] and with my hat in my hand made her a low bow, apologized for presuming to introduce myself to her presence in such a manner, and concluded with my being in love with her charming character, before I had the honour and happiness of seeing her.' —All this was very handsome, to be sure; but how did Mr. Buncle manage to distinguish Miss Cramer from her lovely cousin, as he had no one to introduce him?—This query should be resolved in the second edition.

But if Mr. Buncle was so much enamoured before he had seen this heaven-born maid, as he styles her, what must be his situation at this first interview? Why, he tells us that *strange* pleasures filled his soul, and all his talk was love. *Strange,* however, that the pleasure he felt on this occasion should be so *new* to him, who had been twice so violently in love before! but different objects, we must suppose, produce different sensations.—Well! the issue of this introductory address was, that he became so well acquainted with this INNOCENT BEAUTY, that, on taking his leave, he had an invitation to breakfast the next morning. 'I was there, says he, by eight, and really and truly quite charmed with her. She was pretty as it was possible for flesh and blood to be; had a beautiful[3] understanding, and as she had very little notion of men, having seen very few, except the two old servants who lived with her, she had not an idea of any danger that could come from conversing freely with a man she knew nothing of, and who might be an enemy in disguise.'

Every day, for a month together, did he repeat his visits to this pretty little innocent soul; and, before the end of six weeks, he married her.—Surely there must have been something uncommonly attractive about this gentleman, by the force of which he so easily and quickly subdued the heart of every female to whom he paid his addresses! none of them hold out above a month or two.

With this lady, 'who was as good as an angel,' our Author lived in unspeakable felicity, at Orton Lodge, for two years; when she, too, died of the small-pox. Leaving her husband, once more, the most disconsolate of men.'—*Four* days did he now remain, with his eyes shut, on account of this new loss;—and then he left the Lodge once more, 'to *live,* says he, if I could, since my religion ordered me to do so, and see what I was next to meet with in the world.'—As grief sat powerfully on his spirits, and if not dislodged, as he said, 'would have drank them up very soon,' he now resumed his design of visiting Harrogate-wells, to try, in the festivities of that place, to forget his departed wife 'as soon as he could.'

As he has hitherto said nothing of his having any children by so many wives, and does not in the remainder of his history speak of any, he here mentions them once for all. 'I think it sufficient, says he, to observe, that I had a great many, to carry on the *succession;* but as they never were concerned in any extraordinary affairs, nor ever did any remarkable things, that I heard of;—only rise and breakfast, read and saunter, drink and eat, it would not be fair, in my opinion, to make any one pay for *their* history.'

In the fifth section we at length actually find our adventurer at Harrogate, in Yorkshire; where he arrived in 1731. He gives a short description of the place, with a particular account of the nature and qualities of the sulphurous wells, and the various disorders in which they have been found efficacious and salutary. He likewise describes the company he found there; particularly half a dozen Irish gentlemen, some of whose characters may be selected for the amusement of our Readers, and will afford them also some farther light into that of our Author. 'These gentlemen, says he, were Mr. Gollogher, Mr. Gallaspy, Mr. Dunkley, Mr. Makins, Mr. Monaghan, and Mr. O'Keefe, descended from the Irish kings, and first cousin to the great O'Keefe, who was buried not long ago in Westminster abbey. They were all men of large fortunes, and, Mr. Makins excepted, were as handsome, fine fellows as could be picked out in all the world. Makins was a very low, thin man, not four feet high, and had but one eye, with which he squinted most shockingly. He wore his own hair, which was short and bad, and only drest by his combing it himself in the morning, without oil or powder. But as he was matchless on the fiddle, sung well, and chatted agreeably, he was a favourite with the ladies. They preferred ugly Makins (as he was called) to many very handsome men. I will here give the public the character of these Irish gentlemen, for the honour of Ireland, and as they were curiosities of the human kind.'

Of Mr. Makins he gives a farther account, in the following terms: 'Makins was possessed of all the excellent qualities and perfections that are within the reach of human abilities. He had received from nature the happiest talents, and he made singular improvements of them by a successful application to the most useful and most ornamental studies. Music, as before observed, he excelled in. His intellectual faculties were fine, and, to his honour I can affirm, that he mostly employed them, as he did his great estate, to the good of mankind, the advancement of morality, and the spread of *pure theism,* the worship of God *our Saviour,* who raised and sent Christ to be a Redeemer. This gentleman was a zealous Unitarian, and, though but five and twenty, (when we met at Harrogate) a religious man: but his religion was without any melancholy; nor had it any thing of that severity of temper, which diffuses too often into the hearts of the religious, a morose contempt of the world, and an antipathy to the pleasures of it. He avoided the assemblies of fools, knaves, and blockheads, but was fond of good company, and condemned that doctrine which taught men to retire from human society to seek God in the horrors of solitude. He thought the Almighty may be best found among men, where his goodness is most active, and his providence most employed.'

The character of Gallaspy is one of the strangest compounds that ever existed, and probably never did exist, but in these Memoirs: however, as the features of this picture are strongly marked, and the whole is very highly coloured, we are determined to give our Readers an opportunity of forming their own judgment concerning it.

'Gallaspy was the tallest and strongest man I have ever seen, well made, and very handsome. He had wit and abilities, sung well, and talked with great sweetness and fluency, but was so extremely wicked, that it were better for him, if he had been a natural fool. By his vast strength and activity, his riches and eloquence, few things could withstand him. He was the most prophane swearer I have known: fought every thing, whored every thing, and drank seven in a hand; that is, seven glasses so placed between the fingers of his right hand, that in drinking, the liquor fell into the next glasses, and thereby he drank out of the first glass seven glasses at once. This was a common thing, I find from a book in my possession, in the reign of Charles the Second, in the madness that followed the restoration of that profligate and worthless prince. But this gentleman was the only man I ever saw who could or would attempt to do it; and he made but one gulp of whatever he drank; he did not swallow a fluid like other people, but if it was a quart, poured it in as from pitcher to pitcher. When he smoaked tobacco, he always blew two pipes at once, one at each corner of his mouth, and threw the smoke of both out of his nostrils. He had killed two men in duels before I left Ireland, and would have been hanged, but that it was his good fortune to be tried before a judge, who never let any man suffer for killing another in this manner. (This was the late Sir John St. Leger.) He debauched all the women he could, and many whom he could not corrupt, he ravished. I went with him once in the stage-coach to Kilkenny, and seeing two pretty ladies pass by in their own chariot, he swore in his horrible way, having drank very hard after dinner, that he would immediately stop them, and ravish them: nor was it without great difficulty that I hindered him from attempting the thing; by assuring him I would be their Protector, and he must pass through my heart before he could proceed to offer them the least rudeness. In sum, I never saw his equal in impiety, especially when inflamed with liquor, as he was every day of his life, though it was not in the power of wine to make him drunk, weak or senseless. He set no bounds or restrictions to mirth and revels. He only slept every third night, and that often in his cloaths in a chair, where he would sweat so prodigiously as to be wet quite through; as wet as if come from a pond, or a pail of water had been thrown on him. While all the world was at rest, he was either drinking or dancing, scouring the bawdy-houses, or riding as hard as he could drive his horse, on some iniquitous project. And yet, he never was sick, nor did he ever receive any hurt or mischief. In health, joy, and plenty, he passed life away, and died about a year ago at his house in the county of Galway, without a pang or any kind of pain. This was Jack Gallaspy. There are however some things to be said in his favour, and as he had more regard for me than any of his acquaintance, I should be ungrateful were I not to do him all the justice in my power.

'He was in the first place far from being quarrelsome, and if he fought a gentleman at the small-sword, or boxed with a porter or coachman, it was because he had in some degree been ill used, or fancied that the laws of honour required him to call an equal to an account, for any transaction. His temper was naturally sweet.

'In the next place, he was the most generous of mankind, His purse was ever at his friend's service: he was kind and good to his tenants: to the poor a very great benefactor. He would give more money away to the sick and distressed in one year, than I believe many rich pious people do in seven. He had the blessings of thousands for his charities, and, perhaps, this procured him the protection of heaven.

'As to swearing, he thought it was only criminal, when it was false, or men lyed in their affirmations: and for whoring, he hoped there would be mercy, since men will be men while there are women. Ravishing he did not pretend to justify, as the laws of his country were against it; but he could not think the woman was a sufferer by it, as she enjoyed without sinning the highest felicity. He intended her happiness; and her saying no, kept her innocent.

'How far all this can excuse Mr. Gallaspy, I pretend not to determine; but as I thought it proper to give the world the picture of so extraordinary a man, it was incumbent on me, as his friend, to say all I could, with truth, in his vindication.'

Dunkley, Monaghan, and O'Keefe were less extraordinary characters; but Mr. Gollogher, notwithstanding the Gorgon found of his name, was a most engaging fellow. He is thus described:

'Gollogher was a man of learning and extraordinary abilities. He had read very hard for several years, and during that time, had collected and extracted from the best books more than any man I ever was acquainted with. He had four vast volumes of common place, royal paper, bound in rough calf, and had filled them with what is most curious and beautiful in works of literature, most refined in eloquent discourses, most poignant in books of criticism, most instructive in history, most touching and affecting in news, catastrophes, and stories; and with aphorisms, sayings, and epigrams. A prodigious memory made all this his own, and a great judgment enabled him to reduce every thing to the most exact point of truth and accuracy. A rare man! Till he was five and twenty, he continued this studious life, and but seldom went into the mixed and fashionable circles of the world. Then, all at once, he sold every book he had, and determined to read no more. He spent his every day in the best company of every kind; and as he had the happy talent of *manner,* and possessed that great power which strikes and awakens fancy, by giving every subject the new dress and decoration it requires;—could make the most common thing no longer trivial, when in his hand, and render a good thing most exquisitely pleasing;—as he told a story beyond most men, and had, in short, a universal means towards a universal success, it was but natural that he should be every where liked and wished for. He charmed wherever he came. The specific I have mentioned made every one fond of him. With the ladies especially he was a great favourite, and more fortunate in his amours than any man I knew. Had he wanted the fine talents he was blest with, yet his being an extremely handsome man, and a master on the fiddle, could not but recommend him to the sex. He might, if he had pleased, have married any one of the most illustrious and richest women in the kingdom. But he had an aversion to matrimony, and could not bear the thought of a wife. Love and a bottle were his taste. He was however the most honourable of men in his amours, and never abandoned any woman to distress, as too many men of fortune do, when they have gratified desire. All the distressed were ever sharers in Mr. Gollogher's fine estate, and especially the girls he had taken to his breast. He provided happily for them all, and left ninteen daughters he had by several women a thousand pounds each. This was acting with a temper worthy of a man; and to the memory of the benevolent Tom Gollogher I devote this memorandum.'

Having observed that too many men of fortune abandon the girls they have ruined, our Author here gives an instance of the horrid consequences of so base and ungenerous a procedure, in the affecting story of Miss Hunt, an Irish beauty, who was villainously debauched and deserted by one Mr. R—. The catastrophe, with regard to the poor young lady, was most shocking to relate; and our Author has told the story in very moving terms: but we shall not disgust our Readers with such a proof of human depravity. The present article is, moreover, of a sufficient length; and therefore we must defer the sequel of this history to our next month's review.

In the foregoing abstract, we have avoided the more romantic and marvellous parts of Mr. Buncle's narrative; as we suppose the soberest and least wonderful incidents would be most aceptable to the generality of our Readers.—Indeed the present vol. does not afford many such supernatural adventures, such amazing scenes, such astonishing proofs of the Author's prodigious imagination and invention, as are to be met with in the former part of his work. So that, perhaps, on the whole, there will, in the opinion of some Readers, appear to be a great falling off, in the volume now offered to the public.

Notes

[1] See Playhouse Dictionary, Vol. II. art. Johnson, Sam.

[2] He very well supports this charge, by citing Voltaire's own words; to which he has subjoined some lively, spirited animadversions.

[3] Mr. Buncle is not always very nice in his choice of epithets. What idea are we to form of a *beautiful* understanding? Would he say, if a lady whose mental qualities where somewhat inferior to those of Miss Cramer, that she had an *handsome* understanding?

Edmund Gosse (essay date 1891)

"The Life of John Buncle," in *Gossip in a Library,* Heinemann, 1891, pp. 215-226.

[*In the following essay, Gosse acknowledges the odd nature of* The Life of John Buncle, Esq., *but commends its picturesqueness, the wide range of learning Amory displays, the tenderness of its romantic passages, and the author's delight in the beauty and variety of the natural world.*]

In the year 1756, there resided in the Barbican, where the great John Milton had lived before him, a funny elderly personage called Mr. Thomas Amory, of whom not nearly so much is recorded as the lovers of literary anecdote would like to possess. He was sixty-five years of age; he was an Irish gentleman of means, and he was an ardent Unitarian. Some unkind people have suggested that he was out of his mind, and he had, it is certain, many peculiarities. One was, that he never left his house, or ventured into the streets, save "like a bat, in the dusk of the evening." He was, in short, what is called a "crank," and he gloried in his eccentricity. He desired that it might be written on his tombstone, "Here lies an Odd Man." For sixty years he had made no effort to attract popular attention, but in 1755 he had published a sort of romance, called *Memoirs of Several Ladies of Great Britain,* and now he succeeded it by the truly extraordinary work, the name of which stands at the head of this article. Ten years later there would appear another volume of *John Buncle,* and then Amory disappeared again. All we know is, that he died in 1788, at the very respectable age of ninety-seven. So little is known about him, so successfully did he hide "like a bat" through the dusk of nearly a century, that we may be glad to eke out the scanty information given above by a passage of autobiography from the preface of the book before us:—

> "I was born in London, and carried as an infant to Ireland, where I learned the Irish language, and became intimately acquainted with its original inhabitants. I was not only a lover of books from the time I could spell them to this hour, but read with an extraordinary pleasure, before I was twenty, the works of several of the Fathers, and all the old romances; which tinged my ideas with a certain piety and extravagance that rendered my virtues as well as my imperfections particularly mine. . . . The dull, the formal, and the visionary, the hard-honest man, and the poor-liver, are a people I have had no connection with; but have always kept company with the polite, the generous, the lively, the rational, and the brightest freethinkers of this age. Besides all this, I was in the days of my youth, one of the most active men in the world at every exercise; and to a degree of rashness, often venturesome, when there was no necessity for running any hazards; *in diebus illis,* I have descended head-foremost, from a high cliff into the ocean, to swim, when I could, and ought, to have gone off a rock not a yard from the surface of the deep. I have swam near a mile and a half out in the sea to a ship that lay off, gone on board, got clothes from the mate of the vessel, and proceeded with them to the next port; while my companion I left on the beach concluded me drowned, and related my sad fate in the town. I have taken a cool thrust over a bottle, without the least animosity on either side, but both of us depending on our skill in the small sword for preservation from mischief. Such things as these I now call wrong."

If this is not a person of whom we would like to know more, I know not what the romance of biography is. Thomas Amory's life must have been a streak of crimson on the grey surface of the eighteenth century.

It is really a misfortune that the red is almost all washed off.

No odder book than *John Buncle* was published in England throughout the long life of Amory. Romances there were, like *Gulliver's Travels* and *Peter Wilkins,* in which the incidents were much more incredible, but there was no supposition that these would be treated as real history. The curious feature of *John Buncle* is that the story is told with the strictest attention to realism and detail, and yet is embroidered all over with the impossible. There can be no doubt that Amory, who belonged to an older school, was affected by the form of the new novels which were the fashion in 1756. He wished to be as particular as Mr. Richardson, as manly as Captain Fielding, as breezy and vigorous as Dr. Smollett, the three new writers who were all the talk of the town. But there was a twist in his brain which made his pictures of real life appear like scenes looked at through flawed glass.

The memoirs of John Buncle take the form of an autobiography, and there has been much discussion as to how much is, and how much is not, the personal history of Amory. I confess I cannot see why we should not suppose all of it to be invented, although it certainly is odd to relate anecdotes and impressions of Dr. Swift, *à propos* of nothing at all, unless they formed part of the author's experience. For one thing, the hero is represented as being born about thirteen years later than Amory was—if, indeed, we possess the true date of our worthy's birth. Buncle goes to college and becomes an earnest Unitarian. The incidents of his life are all intellectual, until one "glorious first of August," when he sallies forth from college with his gun and dog, and after four hours' walk discovers that he has lost his way. He is in the midst of splendid mountain scenery—which leads us to wonder at which English University he was studying—and descends through woody ravines and cliffs that overhang torrents, till he suddenly comes in sight of a "little harmonic building that had every charm and proportion architecture could give it." Finding one of the garden doors open, and being very hungry, the adventurous Buncle strolls in, and finds himself in "a grotto or shell-house, in which a politeness of fancy had produced and blended the greatest beauties of nature and decoration." (There are more grottos in the pages of Amory than exist in the whole of the British Islands.) This shell-house opened into a library, and in the library a beauteous object was sitting and reading. She was studying a Hebrew Bible, and making philological notes on a small desk. She raised her eyes and approached the stranger, "to know who I wanted" (for Buncle's style, though picturesque, is not always grammatically irreproachable).

Before he could answer, a venerable gentleman was at his side, to whom the young sportsman confessed that he was dying of hunger and had lost his way. Mr.

Noel, a patriarchal widower of vast wealth, was inhabiting this mansion in the sole company of his only daughter, the lovely being just referred to. Mr. Buncle was immediately "stiffened by enchantment" at the beauty of Miss Harriot Noel, and could not be induced to leave when he had eaten his breakfast. This difficulty was removed by the old gentleman asking him to stay to dinner, until the time of which meal Miss Noel should entertain him. At about 10 A.M. Mr. Buncle offers his hand to the astonished Miss Noel, who, with great propriety, bids him recollect that he is an entire stranger to her. They then have a long conversation about the Chaldeans, and the "primævity" of the Hebrew language, and the extraordinary longevity of the Antediluvians; at the close of which (*circa* 11.15 A.M.) Buncle proposes again. "You force me to smile (the illustrious Miss Noel replied), and oblige me to call you an odd compound of a man," and to distract his thoughts, she takes him round her famous grotto. The conversation, all repeated at length, turns on conchology and on the philosophy of Epictetus until it is time for dinner, when Mr. Noel and young Buncle drink a bottle of old Alicant, and discuss the gallery of Verres and the poetry of Catullus. Left alone at last, Buncle still does not go away, but at 5 P.M. proposes for the third time, "over a pot of tea." Miss Noel says that the conversation will have to take some other turn, or she must leave the room. They therefore immediately "consider the miracle at Babel," and the argument of Hutchinson on the Hebrew word *Shephah,* until, while Miss Noel is in the very act of explaining that "the Aramitish was the customary language of the line of Shem," young Buncle (*circa* 7.30) "could not help snatching this beauty to my arms, and without thinking what I did, impressed on her balmy mouth half a dozen kisses. This was wrong, and gave offence," but then papa returning, the trio sat down peacefully to cribbage and a little music. Of course Miss Noel is ultimately won, and this is a very fair specimen of the conduct of the book.

A fortnight before the marriage, however, "the small-pox steps in, and in seven days' time reduced the finest human frame in the universe to the most hideous and offensive block," and Miss Harriot Noel dies. If this dismal occurrence is rather abruptly introduced, it is because Buncle has to be betrothed, in succession, to six other lively and delicious young females, all of them beautiful, all of them learned, and all of them earnestly convinced Unitarians. If they did not rapidly die off, how could they be seven? Buncle mourns the decease of each, and then hastily forms an equally violent attachment to another. It must be admitted that he is a sad wife-waster. Azora is one of the most delightful of these deciduous loves. She "had an amazing collection of the most rational philosophical ideas, and she delivered them in the most pleasing dress." She resided in a grotto within a romantic dale in Yorkshire, in a "little female republic" of one hundred souls, all of them "straight, clean, handsome girls." In this glen

there is only one man, and he a fossil. Miss Melmoth, who would discuss the *paulo-post futurum* of a Greek verb with the utmost care and politeness, and had studied "the Minerva of Sanctius and Hickes' Northern Thesaurus," was another nice young lady, though rather free in her manner with gentlemen. But they all die, sacrificed to the insatiable fate of Buncle.

Here the reader may like to enjoy a sample of Buncle as a philosopher. It is a characteristic passage:—

> "Such was the soliloquy I spoke, as I gazed on the skeleton of John Orton; and just as I had ended, the boys brought in the wild turkey, which they had very ingeniously roasted, and with some of Mrs. Burcot's fine ale and bread, I had an excellent supper. The bones of the penitent Orton I removed to a hole I had ordered my lad to dig for them; the skull excepted, which I kept, and still keep on my table for a *memento mori;* and that I may never forget the good lesson which the percipient who once resided in it had given. It is often the subject of my meditation. When I am alone of an evening, in my closet, which is often my case, I have the skull of John Orton before me, and as I smoke a philosophic pipe, with my eyes fastened on it, I learn more from the solemn object than I could from the most philosophical and laboured speculations. What a wild and hot head once—how cold and still now; poor skull, I say: and what was the end of all thy daring, frolics and gambols—thy licentiousness and impiety—a severe and bitter repentance. In piety and goodness John Orton found at last that happiness the world could not give him."

Hazlitt has said that "the soul of Rabelais passed into John Amory." His name was Thomas, not John, and there is very little that is Rabelaisian in his spirit. One sees what Hazlitt meant—the voluble and diffuse learning, the desultory thread of narration, the mixture of religion and animalism. But the resemblance is very superficial, and the parallel too complimentary to Amory. It is difficult to think of the soul of Rabelais in connection with a pedantic and uxorious Unitarian. To lovers of odd books, ***John Buncle*** will always have a genuine attraction. Its learning would have dazzled Dr. Primrose, and is put on in glittering spars and shells, like the ornaments of the many grottoes that it describes. It is diversified by descriptions of natural scenery, which are often exceedingly felicitous and original, and it is quickened by the human warmth and flush of the love passages, which, with all their quaintness, are extremely human. Amory was a fervid admirer of womankind, and he favoured a rare type, the learned lady who bears her learning lightly and can discuss "the quadrations of curvilinear spaces" without ceasing to be "a bouncing, dear, delightful girl," and adroit in the preparation of toasts and chocolate. The style of the book is very careless and irregular, but rises in its best pages to an admirable picturesqueness.

Ernest A. Baker (essay date 1904)

SOURCE: Introduction to *The Life and Opinions of John Buncle, Esq.,* George Routledge and Sons, 1904, pp. v-xiii.

[*In the following essay, Baker explores the source of the appeal that* The Life of John Buncle, Esq., *has for readers interested in literary curiosities: the book's vigor, frankness, and ability to unfold the title character's nature.*]

The *History of John Buncle* has never been a popular book. It is hardly possible to imagine a period whose standard of taste and culture would render it popular. Yet it is safe to predict that it will always, as in the past, be an object of interest to the connoisseur, the explorer of curious by-paths of literature, and to all who have a liking for the eccentricities of human nature, when conjoined with strength and shrewdness, and with candour of expression. Thrice during the last century was the book disinterred from the obscurity that covered it, and on each occasion by a critic distinguished by this taste for originality. Charles Lamb, in *The Two Races of Men,* hits off the book with delightful humour when he says, "In yonder nook, John Buncle, a widower-volume, with 'eyes closed,' mourns his ravished mate." Hazlitt's enthusiasm led him, ill advisedly, to compare the author with a genius of a far superior order:—

> "The soul of Francis Rabelais passed into John (*sic*) Amory, the author of *The Life and Adventures of John Buncle.* Both were physicians, and enemies of too much gravity. Their business was to enjoy life. Rabelais indulges his spirit of sensuality in wine, in dried neats'-tongues, in Bologna sausages, in botargos. John Buncle shows the same symptoms of inordinate satisfaction in tea and bread-and-butter. While Rabelais roared with Friar John and the monks, John Buncle gossiped with the ladies, and with equal and uncontrolled gaiety. These two authors possessed all the insolence of health, so that their works give a fillip to the constitution; but they carried off the exuberance of their natural spirits in different ways. The title of one of Rabelais' chapters (and the contents answer to the title) is, 'How they chirped over their cups.' The title of a corresponding chapter in *John Buncle* would run thus: 'The author is invited to spend the evening with the divine Miss Hawkins, and goes accordingly; with the delightful conversation that ensued.'"

The essay is so well known and so sententious that it has probably led many a man to take its judgments on trust, and not trouble to peruse the book for himself. Leigh Hunt, on the contrary, in that charming literary *vade mecum* of his, *A Book for a Corner,* entices one to get the book and read it, or rather to roam about in its leisurely and discursive pages. But whoever has been so tempted hitherto must have met with an initial difficulty, the extreme scarcity of the work. Amory published the first volume in 1756, along with a complete edition in four volumes, 12 mo. Another edition appeared in three volumes in 1825, since which date the chances of coming across the book in any form have steadily grown more remote.

What is the peculiar attraction of *John Buncle*? That a book is merely a literary curiosity, or that it contains excellent passages interspersed amid a huge extent of tedious prosing, is certainly not the thing to secure the interest of Lamb, Hazlitt, Leigh Hunt. What fascinates in the book is the vigour and the frankness with which a most exceptional, yet, in a way, a most representative kind of man reveals the whole of his character. For John Buncle is an eccentric only in the sense that he carries very common traits of character to a strange excess. In his love of good living, his sensuality combined with a pharisaic animus against vice, in that blind egotism and portentous arrogance, one might perceive the exaggeration of certain national qualities, with which the author, who was in the first case anonymous, shows his sympathy by exalting them to the degree of absurdity. John Bull, at least one side of him, was caricatured, unintentionally, in *John Buncle.* And the sectarian spirit that is so deeply ingrained in the national character is faithfully portrayed in *John Buncle* the unitarian, with his dogmatism and utter intolerance, and his delight in wordy argument untempered by the slightest capacity for understanding his adversary's point of view.

It is, in fact, such a paradox of a book that it tempts every one to fly into paradoxes. Buncle himself is so hot in denouncing immorality and yet so immoral; condemns sensuality with so much eloquence yet is so shamelessly sensual; is so sincere and yet such a hypocrite; so fervent in his religious zeal, yet degrades religion so unblushingly to consecrate his unholy appetites. "It is impossible," said Leigh Hunt, "to be serious with John Buncle, Esq., jolly dog, Unitarian, and Bluebeard; otherwise, if we were to take him at his word, we should pronounce him, besides being a jolly dog, to be one of a very selfish description, with too good a constitution to correct him, a prodigious vanity, no feeling whatever, and a provoking contempt for everything unfortunate, or opposed to his whims. He quarrels with bigotry, and is a bigot; with abuse, and riots in it. He hates the cruel opinions held by Athanasius, and sends people to the devil as an Arian. He kills off seven wives out of pure incontinence and love of change, yet cannot abide a rake or even the poorest victim of the rake, unless both happen to be his acquaintances. The way in which he tramples on the miserable wretches in the streets is the very rage and triumph of hard-heartedness, furious at seeing its own vices reflected on it, unredeemed by the privileges of law, divinity, and success. But the truth is, John is no more responsible for his opinions than health itself, or a high-mettled racer. He only 'thinks he's thinking.' He does, in reality, nothing at all but eat, drink, talk, and enjoy himself. Amory, Buncle's creator, was in all probability an honest man, or he would hardly have been innocent enough to put such extravagances on paper."

Leigh Hunt also says in the same place: "John's life is not a classic: it contains no passage which is a general favourite: no extract could be made from it of any length to which readers of good taste would not find objections. Yet there is so curious an interest in all its absurdities; its jumble of the gayest and gravest considerations is so founded in the actual state of things; it draws now and then such excellent portraits from life; and, above all, its animal spirits are at once so excessive and so real, that we defy the best readers not to be entertained with it, and having had one or two specimens, not to desire more. Buncle would say, that there is 'cut and come again' in him like one of his luncheons of cold beef and a foaming tankard."

The Life of John Buncle has many of the same merits as the life of Samuel Pepys, not the least of which is the unconscious humour of the book. Buncle himself is utterly devoid of a sense of humour; his heavy seriousness is something unconscionable. But I doubt if there be a more egregious example in literature of the unintentionally comic. The entire plan, or no-plan, of the book, with its aimless narrative and irrelevant digressions (the story seems to exist for the sake of the digressions) is so absurd; and the idea is so comic of the man going out to try his fortune in the world, "not like the Chevalier La Mancha, in hopes of conquering a kingdom, or marrying some great Princess; but to see if I could find another good country girl for a wife, and get a little more money; as they were the only two things united, that could secure me from melancholy, and confer real happiness."

He puts the case with inimitable gravity: "In the next place, as I had forfeited my father's favour and estate, for the sake of christian-deism, and had nothing but my own honest industry to secure me daily bread, it was necessary for me to lay hold of every opportunity to improve my fortune, and of consequence do my best to gain the heart of the first rich young woman who came in my way, after I had buried a wife. It was not fit for me to sit snivelling for months, because my wife died before me, which was, at least, as probable, as that she should be the survivor; but instead of solemn affiction, and the inconsolable part, for an event I foresaw, it was incumbent on me, after a little decent mourning, to consecrate myself to virtue and good fortune united in the form of a woman."

Most diverting of all are the scenes of love-making, a kind of love-making which is, surely, quite unique in literature or in life. What coy maiden was ever wooed after the manner employed to win the "illustrious Statia"? Indelicacy almost ceases to be indelicate when it becomes so elephantine.

> "Ponder, illustrious Statia, on the important point. Consider what it is to die a maid, when you may, in a regular way, produce heirs to that inestimable blessing of life and favour, which the munificence of the Most High was pleased freely to bestow, and which the great Christian mediator, agent, and negociator, republished, confirmed, and sealed with his blood. Marry then in regard to the gospel, and let it be the fine employment of your life, to open gradually the treasures of revelation to the understandings of the little Christians you produce. What do you say, illustrious Statia? Shall it be a succession, as you are an upright Christian? And may I hope to have the honour of sharing in the mutual satisfaction that must attend the discharge of so momentous a duty?"

Needless to say, the lady is not proof against such eloquence; and the nuptials are concluded with a dispatch befitting the urgency of the obligation. The disquisitions on fluxions, geometry, algebra (with diagrammatic illustrations), on the Hebraic covenant, the rite of circumcision, and similarly erudite topics, that take the place of amorous small talk, are equally entertaining in a way that their author never intended. The young ladies are charming in spite of their prodigious learning; but more charming is the force which their personal attractions add to their reasoning. "But is there no other way," asks John Buncle of an accomplished female who has been demonstrating a curious mathematical theorem, "of paying £100 in guineas and pistoles, besides the six ways you have mentioned?" 'There is no other way,' *the fine girl answered.*" There is something most refreshing to hear Buncle, the epicure, the amorous, and the successful, delivering himself gravely on the subject of resignation to the decrees of providence:—

> "This is a summary of my past life; what is before me heaven only knows. My fortune I trust with the Preserver of men, and the Father of spirits. One thing I am certain of by observation, few as the days of the years of my pilgrimage have been, that the emptiness, and unsatisfying nature of this world's enjoyments, are enough to prevent my having any fondness to stay in this region of darkness and sorrow. I shall never leap over the bars of life, let what will happen; but the sooner I have leave to depart, I shall think it the better for me."

"'Tis a very interesting," as Charles Lamb says, "and an extraordinary compound of all manner of subjects, from the depth of the ludicrous to the heights of sublime religious truth. There is much abstruse science in it above my cut, and an infinite fund of pleasantry. John Buncle is a famous fine man, formed in Nature's most eccentric hour." And with all its defects and its offences against good taste, Lamb said emphatically to some one who objected to the epithet so applied, *The Life of John Buncle* is "a healthy book." It is perhaps a tribute to the originality of the book, and no detriment to its real merits, that a Saturday Reviewer called it "a book which nowadays would have been dated from Colney Hatch, or, more likely, suppressed by the care of relatives." And that the *Biographie Universelle* should run it down is, perhaps, testimony as emphatic to its truly English qualities.

John Buncle is virtually a sequel to an earlier book of Amory's published in 1755, entitled, *Memoirs containing the Lives of several Ladies of Great Britain:* "A History of Antiquities, Productions of Nature, and Monuments of Art; Observations on the Christian Religion as professed by the Established Church and Dissenters of every Denomination; Remarks on the Writings of the Greatest English Divines; with a Variety of Disquisitions and Opinions relative to Criticism and Manners; and many Extraordinary Actions." This is another Unitarian romance, as eccentric, rambling and bizarre in style as *John Buncle,* which it resembles in every respect save that it is, perhaps, even less like any other sort of book on record, and has less of the personal element in it. But such episodes as the casual meeting of the author with the beautiful Miss Bruce, in a little mansion set amidst "the finest flowering greens," in a sequestered spot among "the vast hills of Northumberland," a meeting that is, of course, the prelude to a lengthy discourse on Philosophic Deism; such characters as Miss West, Julia Desborough and Charles Benlow, paragons of virtue, wisdom and orthodox Unitarianism; with their adventures in the wilds of northern England, the Hebrides, and a sort of Deistic Utopia in the Cape Verde Islands, might have been taken from the pages of *John Buncle.* A reader of the latter volume might easily fancy himself familiar with such incidents as the two following, taken from the *Memoirs:*—

> "They were riding to Crawford Dyke, near Dunglass, the place I intended for, and by a wrong turn in the road came to Mrs. Benlow's house instead of going to Robin's Toad, where they designed to bait. It was between eight and nine at night when they got to her door; and as they appeared, by the richness of their riding-dress, their servants, and the beautiful horses they rid, to be women of distinction, Mrs. Benlow invited them in, and requested they would lie at her house that night, as the inn they were looking for was very bad. Nothing could be more grateful to the ladies than this proposal. They were on the ground in a moment; and all sat down soon after, with the greatest cheerfulness, to a fine dish of trouts, roasted chickens, tarts, and sparragrass. The strangers were quite charmed with everything they saw. The sweet rural room they were in, and the wild beauties of the garden in view, they could not enough admire; and they were so struck with

Mrs. Benlow's goodness, and the lively, happy manner she has of showing it, that they conceived immediately the greatest affection for her. Felicity could not rise higher than it did at this table. For a couple of hours we laughed most immoderately."

"As I travelled once in the month of September, over a wild part of Yorkshire, and fancied in the afternoon that I was near the place I intended to rest at, it appeared, from a great water we came to, that we had for half a day been going wrong, and were many a mile from any village. This was vexatious; but what was worse, the winds began to blow out-rageously, the clouds gathered, and, as the evening advanced, the rain came down like waterspouts from the heavens. All the good that offered was the ruins of a nunnery, within a few yards of the water, and among the walls, once sacred to devotion, a part of an arch that was enough to shelter us and our beasts from the floods and tempest. Into this we entered, the horses, and Moses, and his master, and for some hours were right glad to be so lodged. But, at last, the storm and rain were quite over, we saw the fair rising moon hang up her ready lamp, and with mild lustre drive back the hovering shades. Out then I came from the cavern, and as I walked for a while on the banks of the fine lake, I saw a handsome little boat, with two oars, in a creek, and concluded very justly, that there must be some habitation not far from one side or other of the water. Into the boat therefore we went, having se-cured our horses, and began to row round, the better to discover. Two hours we were at it as hard as we could labour, and then came to the bottom of a garden, which had a flight of stairs leading up to it. These I ascended. I walked on, and, at the farther end of the fine improved spot, came to a mansion. I immediately knocked at the door, sent in my story to the lady of the house, as there was no master, and in a few minutes was shown into a parlour. I continued alone for a quarter of an hour, and then entered a lady, who struck me into amazement. She was a beauty, of whom I had been passionately fond when she was fourteen and I sixteen years of age. I saw her first in a French family of distinction, where my father had lodged me for the same reason as her parents had placed her there; that is, for the sake of the purity of the French tongue; and as she had a rational generosity of heart, and an under-standing that was surprisingly luminous for her years; could construe an Ode of Horace in a manner the most delightful, and read a chapter in the Greek Testament with great ease every morning; she soon became my heart's fond idol; she appeared in my eyes as something more than mortal. I thought her a divinity. Books furnished us with an occasion of being often together, and we fancied the time was happily spent. But all at once she disappeared. As she had a vast fortune, and as there was a suspicion of an amour, she was snatched away in a moment, and for twenty years from the afternoon she van-ished, I could not see her or hear of her: whether living or dead, I knew not till the night I am speaking of, that I saw come into the room, the lovely Julia Desborough transformed into

Mrs. Mort. Our mutual surprise was vastly great. We could not speak for some time. We knew each other as well as if it had been but an hour ago we parted, so strong was the impression made. She was still divinely fair; but I wondered she could remember me so well, as time and many shaking rubs had altered me very greatly for the worse. See how strangely things are brought about! Miss Desborough was removed all the way to Italy, kept many years abroad that she might never see me more, and in the character of Mrs. Mort, by accident, I found her in solitude in the same country I lived in, and still my friend. This lady told me, she had buried an admirable husband a few years ago, and, as she never had any liking to the world, she devoted her time to books, her old favourites, the education of her daughter, and the salvation of her soul. Miss Mort and she lived like two friends. They read and spun some hours of their time every day away.

"They had a few agreeable neighbours, and from the lake and cultivation of their gardens derived a variety of successive pleasures. They had no relish for the tumultuous pleasures of the town; but in the charms of letters and religion, the philosophy of flowers, the converse of their neighbours, a linen manufactory, and their rural situation, were as happy as their wishes could rise to in this hemisphere. All this to me was like a vision. I wondered, I admired. Is this Miss Desborough with whom I was wont to pass so many hours in reading Milton to her, or Telemaque, or L'Avare de Moliere? What a fleeting scene is life! But a little while and we go on to another world. Fortunate are they who are fit for the remove, who have a clear conception of the precariousness and vanity of all human things, and by virtue and piety so strive to act what is fairest and most laudable, and so pass becomingly through this life, that they may in the next obtain the blessed and immortal abodes prepared for those who can give up their account with joy."

Though his admiration for the female sex was always enthusiastic, it is not until he gets to the sequel that our author begins to show the sincerity of his appreciation by marrying them. When he does begin, his perseverance is limited only by his profound respect for human and divine legislation. John Buncle is a Mormon born out of due time. Had he lived in the day of Joe Smith, he would, beyond all manner of doubt, have proved his belief in a religion so consistent with the dictates of reason and the constitution of man by becoming one of the most distinguished of the Latter-Day Saints. Buncle represents the man who, in Meredith's phrase, has neither rounded Seraglio Point nor doubled Cape Turk; yet his constitutional respect for law, rather the letter than the spirit, is such that he finds a pleasure in restraining his polygamous instincts—and denouncing those of other people. Buncle's conscience was, in truth, a curious faculty. So long as he kept to the strict article of a definite, but somewhat shaky, code of morals, he was never tired of pluming himself upon his virtue, and complimenting those people who agreed with him.

When once he begins to argue with himself or his detractors upon ethical questions, then his unconscious humour becomes most delectable. His apology to such as objected to the brevity of his periods of mourning for his deceased wives and his haste in securing another partner, has been quoted often enough, but I will venture to quote it again:—

"I reply, that I think it unreasonable and impious to grieve immoderately for the dead. A decent and proper tribute of tears and sorrow, humanity requires; but when that duty has been paid, we must remember, that to lament a dead woman is not to lament a wife. A wife must be a living woman. The wife we lose by death is no more than a sad and empty object, formed by the imagination, and to be still devoted to her, is to be in love with an idea. It is a mere chimerical passion, as the deceased has no more to do with this world, than if she had existed before the flood. As we cannot restore what nature has destroyed, it is foolish to be faithful to affliction. Nor is this all, if the woman we marry has the seven qualifications which every man would wish to find in a wife, beauty, discretion, sweetness of temper, a sprightly wit, fertility, wealth, and noble extraction, yet death's snatching so amiable a wife from our arms can be no reason for accusing fate of cruelty, that is, providence of injustice; nor can it authorise us to sink into insensibility, and neglect the duty and business of life. This wife was born to die, and we receive her under the condition of mortality. She is lent but for a term, the limits of which we are not made acquainted with; and when this term is expired, there can be no injustice in taking her back; nor are we to indulge the transports of grief to distraction, but should look out for another with the seven qualifications, as it is not good for man to be alone, and as he is by the Abrahamic covenant bound to carry on the succession in a regular way if it be in his power. Nor is this all, if the woman adorned with every natural and acquired excellence is translated from this gloomy planet to some better world, to be a sharer of the divine favour, in that peaceful and happy state which God hath prepared for the virtuous and faithful, must it not be senseless for me to indulge melancholy and continue a mourner on her account, while she is breathing the balmy air of paradise, enjoying pure and radiant vision, and beyond description happy?"

His other motives for desiring to get married as often as he decently could, and the workings of his very peculiar conscience, are revealed with wonted frankness in the following statement of his mental deliberations when confronted with the responsibility of a choice of brides:—

"Against staying longer than two or three days, I had many good reasons that made it necessary for me to depart: beside the unreasonableness of my being an expense to Mr. Turner in his absence, or confining his sister to the country; there was Orton-Lodge, to which I could not avoid going again: and there was Miss Melmoth, on whom I had promised to wait, and did intend to ask her if she would give me her hand, as I liked her and her circumstances, and fancied she would live with me in any retreat I pleased to name; which was a thing that would be most pleasing to my mind. It is true, if Charles Turner had come home, while I stayed at his house, it was possible I might have got his sister, who was a very great fortune: but this was an uncertainty however, and in his absence, I could not in honour make my addresses to her: if it should be against his mind, it would be acting a false part, while I was eating his bread. Miss Turner to be sure had fifty thousand pounds at her own disposal, and so far as I could judge of her mind, during the three days that I stayed with her at Skelsmore-Vale, I had some reason to imagine her heart might be gained: but for a man worth nothing to do this, in her brother's house without his leave, was a part I could not act, though by missing her I had been brought to beg my bread."

The moral, religious, and speculative digressions that take up by far the greater space in the book are of singularly little interest to us. They contain no original thought, and merely display the extent of their author's erudition. The utmost praise one can give is that now and then he puts a commonplace well, as for instance:—

"How shall we account for such things? By saying, that the world that now is, and the world that is to come, are in the hands of God, and every transaction in them is quite right, though the reason of the procedure may be beyond our view. We cannot judge certainly of the ends and purposes of Providence, and therefore to pass judgment on the ways of God, is not only impious, but ridiculous to the last degree."

Beyond that his science is absurd, his speculations are vain, and his reasoning, in spite of its pompous phrasing, very shallow.

Amory's exaggerated descriptions of scenery, in the **Memoirs,** and the earlier part of **John Buncle,** have drawn upon his head a great deal of ridicule. Perhaps he has been laughed at rather unfairly, and more allowance ought to have been made for the ideas of the time when he wrote. With hardly any exception, the eighteenth century writers who have tried to delineate savage scenery have been afflicted by emotions of nervousness and stupefaction that seem rather absurd nowadays. This is how Pennant describes the scenery of Derwentwater: "Here all the possible variety of Alpine scenery is exhibited, with all the horror of precipice, overhanging rock, or insulated pyramidal hills, contrasted with others whose smooth and verdant sides, swelling into immense aerial heights, at once please and surprise the eye. The two extremities of the lake afford most discordant prospects: the southern is a composition of all that is horrible, an immense chasm opens," and so on. Dr. Brown, in his famous letter, finds that "the full perfection of Keswick consists of

three circumstances, *beauty, horror,* and *immensity* united." "On the opposite shore," says he, "you will find rocks and cliffs of stupendous height, hanging broken over the lake in horrible grandeur, some of them a thousand feet high, the woods climbing up their steep and shaggy sides, where mortal foot never yet approached. On these dreadful heights the eagles build their nests; a variety of waterfalls are seen pouring from their summits, and tumbling in vast sheets from rock to rock in rude and terrible magnificence," etc. At Malham Cove, in Craven, one of the spots, probably, where Buncle encountered an impassable range of unscalable "mountains," the poet Gray found it "safer to shelter yourself close to its bottom" (lest any of the rocks at the summit should give way and overwhelm the spectator), "and trust to the mercy of that enormous mass, which nothing but an earthquake can stir." "I stayed there," he continues, "not without shuddering, a quarter of an hour, and thought my trouble richly paid, for the impression will last for life." West, of Ulverston, the author of the earliest guide to the Lakes, who fell foul of Gray for his hyperbolic descriptions, speaks of "an arrangement of vast mountains, entirely new, both in form and colouring of rock; large hollow craters scooped in their bosoms, once the seeming seats of raging liquid fire, though at present overflowing with the purest water, that foams down the craggy brows." Here we can almost picture the tarns on the hill-tops described by Buncle, their depths communicating with the "abyss." And again we can realize some of his difficulties in travelling when we read of another writer who found the lake of Wastwater "of access most laborious from the nature of its surrounding soil, which is utterly devoid of tenacity." West goes on, "The lower parts are pastured with a motley herd; the middle tract is assumed by the flocks, the upper regions (to man inaccessible) are abandoned to the birds of Jove." Mr. W. P. Haskett Smith quotes Mrs. Radcliffe touching the ascent of Saddleback: "The views from the summit are exceedingly extensive, but those immediately under the eye on the mountain itself so tremendous and appalling that few persons have sufficient resolution to experience the emotions which those awful scenes inspire." "When we had ascended about a mile," says another writer, "one of the party, on looking round, was so astonished with the different appearance of objects in the valley so far beneath us that he declined proceeding. We had not gone much further till the other companion was suddenly taken ill and wished to loose blood and return."

Buncle's romantic pen, sketching freely from memory, and biassed by his constitutional megalomania, went very little farther, after all, when he turned these awe-inspiring fells into ranges of impassable mountains. The lakes, the tarns, the bogs, and the waterfalls are still there, and may have similar effects on people who are prepared by a suitable education to be appalled. Stainmore Forest has always been one of the wildest districts in Britain, and in Amory's day still retained an evil reputation for murders and highway robberies. The burning river may have had its origin in a reminiscence of bog-fires, more plentiful then than now. The adjoining district of Craven possesses genuine marvels enough in the way of caves, pot-holes and underground water-channels, wet and dry, to furnish a Jules Verne with ample materials for romance. Buncle has simply multiplied the existing caverns and magnified their proportions. If we make proper allowance for the attitude of the time as regards natural sublimity, I think Amory is not a much more flagrant offender against truth and probability than the author of *Lorna Doone*.

John Buncle is a personage of definite lineaments whom, once known, we can never forget or confuse with any other personage, real or fictitious: his author, Thomas Amory, is a very vague and unsubstantial being indeed. Yet there is much to be said, if only on internal evidence, for the view that in the creation we may recognize the authentic features of the author himself. There is a certain class of books that convince their reader, although it might be impossible to prove the case by actual reason, that they are autobiographical, in the sense that they express, more or less consciously, the character of their writers. One feels it in reading them, the perception is intuitive and irresistible. Whether it be the accent given to unimportant traits, or the emergence of more intimate peculiarities, or something altogether undefinable and intangible, we feel it, quite independently of external evidence, in reading *David Copperfield, Pendennis,* or *Jane Eyre,* and even minor works like *The Fool of Quality*. We feel it, never more strongly, whilst perusing **The Life of John Buncle,** so strongly that it would require cogent proofs of the contrary to unsettle our convictions. The reader must judge from the following summary of what can be ascertained about Thomas Amory, from the statements of himself, his son, and other persons, whether the validity of the intuitive view is confirmed in the present instance.

A letter appeared in the *St. James's Chronicle* on October 25, 1788, inquiring as to the authorship of **John Buncle,** and it was replied to in a letter, which can be referred to in the *Gentleman's Magazine* (vol. lviii. p. 1062), stating that the unknown author was Thomas Amory, a native of Ireland, who had been bred to some branch of the profession of physic, and was now living as a recluse on a small fortune in Orchard Street, Westminster, with a country house to which he occasionally retired at Bellfont, near Hounslow. The correspondent went on to describe Amory as "A man of a very peculiar Look and Aspect, though at the same time, he bore quite the Appearance of a Gentleman. He read much; and scarce ever stirred, but like a Bat, in the Dark of the Evening; and then he would take his usual Walk; but seemed to be always ruminating on speculative Subjects, even while passing along the most crowded Streets." This elicited a

reply from the son of the mysterious author, Robert Amory, M.D., who controverted certain erroneous statements, and gave a genealogy of the Amorys, whose lineage he traced to Amory de Montford, who married the sister of Henry II., and was created Earl of Leicester. Amory "was not a native of Ireland. His Father, Councillor Amory, attended King William to Ireland, and was appointed Secretary for the forfeited Estates in that Kingdom, and was possessed of very extensive Property in the County of Clare. He was the youngest Brother of Amory or Damer, the Miser, whom Pope calls 'the Wealthy and the Wise'; from whom comes Lord Milton, etc., etc. My Grandfather married the Daughter of Fitzmaurice, Earl of Kerry; Sir William Petty another Daughter; and the Grandfather of the Duke of Leinster another." He goes on to state that Thomas Amory lived on Mill Bank, Westminster, and for a few years rented a house at Bedfont. He never had but one wife, and Robert Amory was himself the only surviving child. At that date, 1788, his father was still living, though now ninety-seven years old. When young he was a very handsome man. He had published many religious and political tracts, poems and songs. He now lived in complete seclusion, not seeing anybody.

This letter was replied to by Louis Renas, who threw doubt and contumely on the alleged genealogy, which he characterized as "an idle tale, void of foundation or probability." The insult drew out a further letter from Dr. Amory, who in an irritated manner reasserted his original statements, and wound up by insinuating that his correspondent's real name was "Mr. Louis the Ass," whence he said it would be easy for the Heralds Office to find out his family connections. This pretty controversy came to an end with a letter from L. Renas, dated April 20, 1790, in which he apologized for a slight error in his previous communications, and admitted that Thomas Amory was indeed the grandson of a lord—Baron Kerry—but reiterated his other contentions. There can be little doubt that Robert Amory, M.D., had inherited some of the eccentricities and a good deal of the temper of his father, who was as fond of a dispute as his hero, John Buncle.

Amory, if not a native of Ireland, seems to have lived in Dublin at some period, and to have been acquainted with Swift. In 1751, on the publication of Lord Orrery's remarks on the life and writings of Dr. Swift, the following advertisement appeared in the *Whitehall Evening Post,* but there is no record that the pamphlet was ever printed: "Soon will be published a Letter to Lord Orrery in answer to what his Lordship says in his late remarks in praise of Swift's Sermon on the Trinity; being an attempt to vindicate the divinity of God the Father Almighty, and to convince his Lordship, if he has a mind open to conviction, that the tritheistic discourse preached by the Dean of St. Patrick's is so far from being that masterpiece my Lord Orrery calls it that it is in reality the most senseless and despicable performance ever produced by orthodoxy to corrupt the divine religion of Jesus Christ. By Thomas Amory, Esq." One would like greatly to read this fulmination by a man who, to judge by the disposition of his fictitious counterpart, was quick to wrath, a good hater, and outdid even that other eccentric of genius, George Borrow, in the violence of his enmity for Roman Catholics, and most other people who disagreed with him. In 1776 appeared an anonymous work entitled *John Buncle, junr., Gentleman,* 12 mo, Dublin, the author of which was a certain Dr. Cogan. An anonymous pamphlet that appeared in the same year as the **Memoirs,** entitled, "A Letter to the Reviewers occasioned by their account of a book called **Memoirs,** etc." was presumably written by Amory. In *Notes and Queries* for January 27, 1855, is quoted a letter from "Amouri," (Thomas Amory) to an unnamed lady, enclosing a copy of verses composed by ten gentlemen, including the writer, in praise of a certain Molly Rowe. The following stanza is signed "T. Amory":—

> "In the dance, through the couples ascudding,
>   How graceful and light does she go!
> No Englishman ever lov'd pudding
>   As I love my sweet Molly Rowe."

The pudding simile is certainly in the vein of John Buncle. The letter is dated from Newton in Yorkshire, July th' 8, 1773. Amory died on November 25, 1788, at the age of ninety-seven.

It is regrettable that the *Dictionary of National Biography* and the latest edition of Chambers's *Cyclopædia of English Literature* should still persist in the statement that the author of **John Buncle** must have been disordered in his intellect, in spite of the indignation with which this charge, advanced in the *General Biographical Dictionary,* in 1798, was repudiated by an able writer in the *Retrospective Review* (vol. vi., 1822). Although it is insinuated that anybody who admires the book must likewise be in want of medical treatment, we can afford to bear the reflection with equanimity in the distinguished company of Lamb, Hazlitt, Leigh Hunt, and other able men who have confessed a liking for this strange book.

John Fyvie (essay date 1906)

SOURCE: *Some Literary Eccentrics,* Archibald Constable and Company, 1906, pp. 1-34.

[*In the following essay, Fyvie contends that the purpose of* The Life of John Buncle, Esq. *was to explicate Unitarian religious principles.*]

In one of his *Round Table* essays, Hazlitt makes some highly eulogistic remarks on a book which is scarcely known, even by name, to the present generation of readers; and, not content with describing it as one of the most singular productions in our language (which without a doubt it really is), this brilliant but paradoxical critic assures us that 'John Buncle is the English Rabelais.' Both Buncle and Rebelais, he contends, were enemies of too much gravity; both had 'the insolence of health'; the business of both was to enjoy life; and, if the one indulged his spirit of sensuality in wine, in dried neats' tongues, in Bologna sausages and botargos, the other showed precisely the same symptoms of inordinate satisfaction in tea and bread-and-butter; as Rabelais roared with Friar John and the monks, so Buncle gossipped with the ladies, with an equal and uncontrolled gaiety. Hazlitt's criticism of old authors is not usually very wide of the mark, and his praise especially is apt to be fine and felicitous; but in this case his comparison is, to say the least of it, peculiar. For the reader who, after much trouble and expense, has at length succeeded in procuring a copy of this rare and curious work will find, to his surprise, that in the so-called English Rabelais there is not one gleam of humour from beginning to end! Notwithstanding the extraordinary exuberance of animal spirits which the author exhibits in a series of amorous adventures, his dominant mood is serious, and even fanatical, and he almost stifles his readers in an atmosphere of rancorous and inconclusive theological controversy. The oddity and absurdity, both of his adventures and his arguments, will, it is true, occasionally raise a smile; but the laugh is invariably against the author, and not with him. Our disappointment in this respect, however, is somewhat tempered by the discovery that, if we have not found an English Rabelais, we have, at any rate, been introduced to a literary curiosity of an absolutely unique character.

Hazlitt calls the book a Unitarian Romance; but it is too strange a medley to fall easily under any classification. It appears to be partly autobiographical, and partly fictitious; and the author states that his object in writing it was—'to serve the interests of truth, liberty, and religion, and to advance useful learning,' while, at the same time, vindicating his character from misrepresentation, and illustrating his previous book of **Memoirs.** The book may perhaps be regarded as a crude anticipation of our modern 'novel with a purpose.' The author's two pet aversions appear to have been, celibacy and the orthodox Trinitarian theology; and **John Buncle** was evidently written with the dual purpose of glorifying marriage, and showing the reasonableness of Unitarianism. His previous work, the **Memoirs of Several Ladies of Great Britain,** notwithstanding that its dedication (with notes!) runs to sixteen pages, and that there are thirteen pages more devoted to an explanation of how and why the **Memoirs** were written, does not help us much toward an understanding either of **John Buncle** or its author. The latter originally set out, it appears, with the intention of writing the lives of no less than twenty 'illustrious' ladies (whose names are duly given), all of great beauty and extraordinary accomplishments, and all zealous Unitarians. But, as the life of only one occupies the whole of this thick octavo volume, we need not be greatly surprised that nothing more was ever heard of the remaining nineteen. Neither in these *Memoirs,* nor in *John Buncle,* however, did the author propose to limit himself to a biographical record; and the reader is informed that he may expect to find also 'a thousand inquiries into other subjects, curious or antiquarian, accounts of men, and things, and books, and philosophical observations.' Many years ago he had begun a work on *The Antient and Present State of Great Britain;* but a learned friend pointed out so many errors in it, that he undertook a further course of reading and travel, in order to qualify himself for a thorough revision of this work, before venturing on publication. He then put together a large quarto volume, which he called a *Preliminary Discourse;* but this was unfortunately burnt while he was reading it in bed, and he narrowly escaped being burnt with it. The *Memoirs* and *John Buncle* we are therefore invited to regard as a sort of salvage from the destroyed *magnum opus.* We may be proportionately thankful for that merciful fire; but, at the same time, the salvage is certainly curious enough to justify an epitomised account of it, although few readers would be able to get through the whole of our author's three stout octavo volumes without weariness—and perhaps disgust.

The story of *John Buncle,* then, is, briefly, as follows. He was born in London, but carried over during his infancy to Ireland, where his father owned considerable estates. From the time he could spell, he became a lover of books; and, before he was twenty, he had read, with extraordinary pleasure, the works of several of the Fathers, and all the old romances—an exercise which he admits to have tinged his ideas with a combination of piety and extravagance. At the age of fifteen he was sent to the University, where he devoted the whole of his time to study. Locke's *Essay on the Human Understanding* was his favourite reading; and he also found algebra so congenial an occupation that he often sat at it all night, without a notion of its being day until the shutters of his room were opened. Walking and music were his only recreations. One morning, during his last term, he went out, before the sun was up, with dog and gun, and, after having travelled over hill and dale, for five hours, without knowing whither he was going, or giving a single thought to his college, he not unnaturally began to feel extremely hungry. Looking around, he espied a mansion at no great distance, towards which he at once bent his steps. In a rotunda or temple in the garden of the house he saw a beautiful young lady, engaged in writing, and occasionally glancing up with a pair of wonderful eyes at a Hebrew Bible. On seeing a visitor, she came to the window, and at the same moment her father, a vener-

able and genial old man, walked up from another part of the grounds. Buncle explained that he had lost his way, and was famished. On this hint, the old gentleman at once conducted him into the house, where the daughter speedily provided him with tea, 'and plenty of fine cream, and extraordinary bread-and-butter.' The young lady spoke so well, and looked so lovely, that Buncle was scarcely less charmed with her mind than he was lost in admiration of her person. He managed to prolong their talk till noon, when, to his joy, the old father reappeared, and insisted that he should stay to dinner, requesting his daughter to entertain the visitor meanwhile. As soon as Buncle was again left alone with Miss Noel, he told her ingenuously that although he could not be certain whether he was in love with her, as he had never experienced the passion before, yet he felt very strange emotions within him, and was sure that he could never be happy without her. This was a little sudden; and Miss Noel begged that she might hear no more on that subject. She would rather, she said, hear his views on the 'primævity' of the Hebrew language. Thus challenged, Buncle proceeded to give, at some length, his reasons for thinking that Biblical Hebrew was the language of Paradise, and that it continued to be spoken by all men until long after the time of Moses. But, to his great surprise, Miss Noel at once controverted this (at equal or even greater length), and, finding all his arguments hopelessly confounded, the young man cried—

> 'Illuminate me, thou glorious girl, in this dark article, and be my teacher in Hebrew learning, as I flatter myself you will be my guide and dirigent of all my notions and my days. Yes, charming Hariot, my fate is in your hands. Dispose of it as you will, and make me what you please.'

Buncle, it will be observed, had none of the embarrassing bashfulness of the ordinary youth, inexperienced in affairs of the heart; but, as we shall see later on, he was to the manner born. Miss Noel smiled, said he was an odd compound of a man, but forbade him to let her hear any more of such romantic flights. She then, by way of diverting his attention, took him to see her grotto, and they stayed admiring its beauties until they were summoned to dinner. After dinner, Mr. Noel, who was over eighty years of age, retired for his evening nap, charging his daughter to make tea for the visitor, whom he had invited to stay the night. Buncle declares that he was as happy over that pot of tea 'as ever with his Statia sat the conqueror of the world.'

> Charming angel! [he burst out] the beauties of your mind have inspired me with a passion that must increase every time that I behold the harmony of your face; and by the powers divine I swear to love you so long as Heaven shall permit me to breathe the vital air. Bid me, then, either live or die, and while I do live, be assured that my life shall be devoted to you only.'

But in vain was all this warmth; for Miss Noel quietly replied that, if he did not talk about something more rational, she must leave the room. 'If you please, then, Madam,' said he at once, 'we will consider the miracle at Babel.' He then owned to being himself of the opinion of Hutchinson on this matter; but Miss Noel summarily confuted poor Hutchinson's theory (the argument occupying some ten pages) with a highly curious and unexpected result. So amazed was I, says Buncle, at so high a degree of intelligence in a female that 'I could not help snatching this beauty to my arms, and without thinking of what I did, impressed on her balmy mouth half a dozen kisses.' His impetuosity seems to have given some offence; and he admits that it was wrong. But when he had begged her pardon, and assured her that the magic of her glorious eyes, added to the bright powers of her mind, had transported him beside himself, she was easily reconciled, and proposed a game at cribbage. Then, seeing the head of his German flute sticking out of his pocket, she asked him to oblige her with a song instead. Of course he readily complied, and proceeded to play one of his own composing; the old father, who had now finished his nap, arriving in time to hear the finish of it, and demanding another. The music so pleased the old gentleman, that he invited Buncle to stay a month if he liked, and to come again as often, and stay as long, as he pleased. After all this, the reader will not be surprised to find that, before many weeks had expired, Buncle was engaged to the lovely Hariot, who was to bring with her a large fortune in ready cash, and be made her father's heir. But there's many a slip between cup and lip, and, just a fortnight before the day fixed for their wedding, Miss Noel died of the small-pox. For the space of two months the bereaved lover scarcely spoke; then he resolved to go home to his father, whom he had not seen for five years. But at home further trouble was in store for him. His father had recently married a young wife, who proved to be antagonistic to her stepson; and the father himself was so enraged when the son (having, since he left home, become a Unitarian) refused to read the orthodox prayers at family worship, that young Buncle was promptly disinherited, and turned out of house and home.

Having nothing on which to start in the world but a vigorous constitution, a purse full of gold, and a £500 bank-note which Miss Noel had left him by will the day she sickened, young Buncle put his trust in Providence, and took ship for England. And Providence almost immediately afforded him the opportunity of saving the life of a young lady, a fellow-passenger on board the ship. On landing at Whitehaven, he and this young lady, Miss Melmoth, put up at the same inn, and for the following three weeks breakfasted, dined, and supped together. Miss Melmoth was fluent in Latin and Greek, and they talked together 'like two critics, or two grammarians, antiquarians, historians, or philosophers,' but (a circumstance which he notes as 'very odd') during the whole of that time there was not one look of love between them. At the end of the three weeks, they travelled together to a point where their roads diverged; she and her servants being bound for Yorkshire, while he was bent on seeking out an old University chum, named Turner, who dwelt somewhere in the wilds of Westmoreland. Before they parted, however, Miss Melmoth burst into tears; and on his inquiring for the cause, she told him her grief was caused by the thought that she might never see him, the gallant preserver of her life, any more. Buncle, as we shall see, did not usually wait for a hint from any lady; but he declares that it was then that, for the first time, he kissed Miss Melmoth, promising to travel on to her house in Yorkshire as soon as he had paid his respects to his friend Turner. After parting with this charming travelling companion, Buncle entered into 'a vast valley, enclosed by mountains whose tops were above the clouds, and soon came into a country that is wilder than the Campagna of Rome, or the uncultivated vales of the Alps and Apennines.' His love of the country, and especially his admiration for wild scenery, is in striking contrast with the indifference shown by most contemporary authors. Dr. Johnson, for instance, made his celebrated tour to the Hebrides in 1763, and he, as we know, declared that a blade of grass was always a blade of grass, whether in one country or another, and that, wherever a traveller might be, the proper study of mankind was Man. Buncle, on the other hand, seems to have been of opinion that the proper study of mankind was Woman; and he liked to picture her (and, what is more remarkable, was perpetually finding her) immersed in the study of theology and mathematics, against a background of wild and wonderful woodland scenery. His descriptions of the country he passes through are always extravagant; but again and again he goes into raptures as he traverses the beautiful country about the fells, riding by the shores of lovely lakes or along the banks of bright running streams, and seeing neither house nor man for eight hours or more at a time. It is characteristic of him, however, that always before nightfall he lights upon some well-placed mansion or sweetly situated cottage, whose owner, whether total stranger or former friend (and it is really astonishing what a number of long-lost friends he thus finds in unexpected places), receives him with delight, promptly places before him a fowl with bacon and greens, or a pound of rump steak and a quart of green peas, together with strong ale and port wine, entertains him likewise with a lengthy discourse on the principles of true Christianity (*i.e.* of course, Unitarianism), and invites him to stay a week, or a month, or as long as he likes.

The first house Buncle sees, at the end of his first day's journey after leaving Miss Melmoth, turns out to be the habitation of an old friend, named Jack Price, who is now married and settled, as he declares, with a wife who 'makes it the sole study and pleasure of her life to crown me every day with the highest satisfactions and comforts.' Jack had formerly been a terrible debauchee; but his Martha had converted him into a 'reasonable Christian,' or, in other words, an enthusiastic Unitarian. 'I shall never forget the lesson,' he confides to Buncle; 'the substance of what she said is as follows'—and then we get a regulation sermon. By and by, Mrs. Price is introduced, and she and her visitor immediately plunge into a conversation on primitive Christianity; the lady having first innings in an argument which takes up eleven pages of the book, and Buncle following on, and victoriously scoring point after point against the orthodox professors of theology, for forty-seven pages more. After a short stay with these estimable friends, Buncle proceeds on his journey, and, having passed through a country whose wild scenery 'harrowed the soul with horror,' he arrived at a place named Burcott Lodge, where he finds a sort of female republic of one hundred souls, presided over by a young paragon whom he calls Azora. This lady, unlike most of those whom Buncle meets on his travels, was not particularly learned; she understood English only, and had but few books; but he found that she could instruct him in his favourite algebra, while on the fundamental points of religion he admits that he was not only out-talked but out-reasoned. And she gave him other valuable instruction as well; for he declares that, if he had set down all that she told him about salads, cucumbers, early cabbages, strawberries, etc., it would have made an octavo volume. Azora founded her female community (which strikes one as a grotesque anticipation of the idea of Tennyson's *Princess*) when her father and all the men of the neighbourhood were swept off by a fever. She had a bodyguard of ten maidens, specially educated in fine needlework, in music, and in mathematics. Buncle, always proud of his head for figures, set these girls a few sums, all of which they did according to improved methods, with surprising quickness; while Azora and her lieutenant, Antonina, speedily showed him that in the higher mathematics they could give him points and beat him easily. Whereupon he observes: 'My whole life has been spent in reading and thinking; and nevertheless I have met with many women in my time who, with very little reading, have been too hard for me on several subjects'; and he concludes that—

'if they had the laboured education the men have, and applied to books with all possible attention for as many years as we do, there would be found among them as great divines as Episcopius, Limborch, Whichcote, Barrow, Tillotson, and Clarke, and as great mathematicians as Maclaurin, Saunderson, and Simpson.'

Some of Buncle's illustrations are a trifle fantastic; but the idea of woman's sphere and mission floating in his mind seems to have been substantially that which we now associate with the name of John Stuart Mill. This female republic, however, was not altogether a thing after Buncle's heart; and he takes care to tell us in a note that, soon after Azora's death, her lieutenant, Antonina, advised the young women to marry some stalwart young men from the neighbouring mountains, so as to increase the number of her people. And, says Buncle, many advantages were found from the presence of men amongst them; the most notable apparently being that 'more than half the women who married had twins the first year!'

In the early part of the eighteenth century, the English Lake District was very little visited; and an adventurous traveller might have allowed considerable licence to his imagination, without much chance of being found out. But it is difficult to believe that the veriest Cockney can ever have been taken in by some of Buncle's extraordinary relations. He has no sooner left the female republic just described than, in one of the numerous happy valleys lying among the hills, which he always represents as Alps, he comes suddenly upon a pretty hermitage which, on entering, he discovers to be inhabited by a solitary skeleton, with its bones picked as clean and white as if from the hands of a surgeon. On a table lies a box, and in the box he finds a paper telling the skeleton's story. His name was John Orton, and this history states him to have been, up to the age of forty, a licentious and abandoned wretch. But he then had a fever, which caused him to sell all his worldly goods and retire to these mountains, where he cultivated his garden, studied his Bible, and piously meditated on his latter end. While Buncle soliloquises over the skeleton, his two boys bring in a wild turkey which they have meantime caught and roasted; so our cheerful philosopher is enabled to sit down to an excellent supper before burying John Orton's bones, making a careful inventory of all the goods in the house, and resolving to settle down in the place, and end his life of adventures. But he soon pines for livelier company than the skull of John Orton, which he has kept for a *memento mori;* and it occurs to him that Miss Melmoth's presence would give the place much more the air of an Earthly Paradise. Moreover, he has not yet succeeded in finding his old college chum, Turner. So he mounts to horse once more, and, after one or two other adventures, which may be passed over, tumbles suddenly through a hole or tunnel in one of those mysterious mountains, plump into a secluded valley which he might never have otherwise discovered; and there, before his eyes, stands the house of his friend. Turner is away in Italy, but Buncle is cordially welcomed by a beautiful young sister of his friend, who, besides being well acquainted with antiquity, history, and geography, has £50,000 at her own disposal; and the now experienced eye of the visitor soon detects that she is very favourably inclined towards him. Being, however, as he assures us, a man of punctilious honour, he could not permit himself to ask her hand in her brother's absence; so, after a few days' stay, he continues his journey towards the home of Miss Melmoth. On arriving at the address she had given him, however, he finds, to his dismay, that the lady of the house has recently died, and that Miss Melmoth, who inherited all her property, has sold it off and gone away. She had left behind her a letter for a gentleman who was expected to call, (presumably himself); but this the caretaker has unfortunately lost. He frantically scours the neighbouring country in search of her for the following three weeks, but, meeting with no success, is just on the point of abandoning the quest, when, as he is one evening standing disconsolately at an inn door waiting for his supper, the lady herself rides up to him. She had heard of his call and the loss of her letter, and for three weeks they had been playing hide-and-seek with one another all over the country. There is never any beating about the bush with Buncle; whether in love or theology, he goes directly for his object like a bull at a gate. So he promptly gives Miss Melmoth what he candidly admits was a rather flowery description of Orton Lodge, and asks if she is willing to share his solitude there. The lady is as downright as the gentleman, and, without hesitation, declares that she would be ready to go with him to Hudson's Bay, while, if she had a hundred thousand pounds, they should be as entirely at his service as is the moderate fortune of four thousand and a little personal estate, which is all she has to offer.

> 'Give me thy hand, then (I said), thou generous girl. You have made me the happiest of men, and in return I swear by that *one, supreme, tremendous Power* I adore, that I will be true and faithful to thee till death dissolves the sacred obligation. Twice do I swear by the *Great Spirit* in whose dread presence I am, with your right hand locked fast in mine across this table, and call on him as witness to our vows, that neither time, nor chance, nor aught but death's inevitable hand shall e'er divide our loves. Miss Melmoth said: *Amen.*'

Forthwith they mounted their horses and galloped off to Orton Lodge, where the best things the house afforded were set on the table, a Roman Catholic Priest of the neighbourhood, whose acquaintance Buncle had already made, was quickly called in to perform the marriage ceremony, and 'man and wife we sat down to supper.' Two years, full of delight, were passed with his Charlotte at Orton Lodge; and then she died, during an epidemic of fever which devastated the district. He describes himself as overwhelmed with sorrow, 'like a traveller in Greenland who has lost the sun'; but this dejection was of short duration, and within a little while he sold off his live stock, locked up the house, and set off on horseback, accompanied by one manservant, not, like the Knight of La Mancha, in hopes of conquering a kingdom and winning a princess, but with this more prosaic, though more attainable object, viz. 'to see if I could find another good country girl for a wife, and get a little more money; as these were the only two

things united that would save me from melancholy, and secure real happiness.' He had not far to seek. Before the end of the first day, he had arrived at a handsome square house, set in a beautiful garden; and, finding nobody to oppose his entrance, he marched straight into a fine spacious room, filled on every side with books, globes, telescopes, etc., where, in a chair, sat a silver-haired old gentleman, nearly a hundred years of age, with a beautiful grand-daughter beside him. In the middle of the room was a reading-desk, on which leaned the skeleton of a man, with an inscription attached, which informed the casual visitor that 'This skeleton was once Charles Henley, Esquire.' The silver-haired old gentleman politely welcomed Buncle, who, being now familiar with skeletons, forbore to ask any questions, and volunteered his own history instead. Next morning, however, he learns the story of the old gentleman's family, including that of the obtrusive family skeleton. The young lady, it appears, is the skeleton's daughter; and her learning and accomplishments are as great as her beauty. Her father has left her his house and estate, together with £10,000 a year; but she is not to inherit or to marry before she is twenty-two years of age; and, meanwhile, the skeleton is always to stand in the middle of the room as a *memento mori*. Statia, says her amiable grandfather, is now only in the second month of her twenty-first year; but if Buncle will be good enough to stay with them until her twenty-second birthday, he shall then marry her. Buncle, like Barkis, is always willing, and agrees to stay the time; though when, seven months afterwards, the old gentleman dies, he proposes as an amendment that they should marry at once. But, to his consternation, the young lady now declares that she is more inclined towards a life of celibacy; and that, as her guardian is no longer with them, it is improper for Buncle to remain in the house. This was an altogether unexpected and staggering development; but our matrimonial philosopher was equal to the occasion, and, collecting all his eloquence, delivered a discourse of such power on the duty of all good Christians to increase and multiply, so as to provide a succession of generations to share in the honours and privileges of the true Church, that the convinced Statia capitulated on the spot. Father Fleming was instantly sent for, and they were promptly married, in spite of the provisions of the skeleton's will. Orton Lodge was decided upon for their honeymoon, and they liked the place so well, that they remained there for two years; at the end of which time another epidemic carried Statia off, and Buncle laid her by the side of Charlotte. 'I sat with my eyes shut for three days,' he solemnly relates, 'but at last called for my horse, to try what air, exercise, and a variety of objects could do.'

On the road towards Harrogate, at which place he proposes to take the waters, Buncle pays a passing visit to a society of married friars, and gives it as his opinion that 'it is really a fine thing to monk it on *this* plan.' They are Socinian frairs, of course; and he treats the reader to forty-six pages concerning their way of life and their theology. Then, proceeding on his journey, he loses his way. After a time, we get to know that, whenever Buncle loses his way, something astonishing or delightful is about to happen. In this instance, he discovers the prettiest little house he ever beheld, and, getting no answer to repeated knocks for admission, roams about the grounds until, finding 'a sleeping parlour similar to that in the gardens at Stowe,' he makes himself comfortable there for the night. Next day he learns that the house belongs to a young lady of great fortune, Miss Cranmer, whose father has been dead about a year, and who is now away from home for a short time. As might be expected of him, he puts up at a neighbouring cottage to wait for this lady's return. To fill up his time in the interval, he goes to visit a hermit who lives a few miles off; and, as a consequence, the reader, as well as this unfortunate man, is treated to more than twenty pages of objections to the theological doctrines of Bellarmine and Le Blanc. Miss Cranmer, on her return three weeks later, proved to be 'as pretty as it was possible for flesh and blood to be'; and 'as she had very little notion of men, having seen very few except the two old servants who lived with her,' our amorous widower induced her to marry him before the expiration of another six weeks. She was as good as an angel, he declares, and they lived together at Orton Lodge 'in unspeakable felicity' until, at the end of two years, she also was carried off by that inevitable epidemic, and had to be laid by the side of Charlotte and Statia. On the occasion of this third bereavement, he sat with his eyes closed for four days, and then, as before, mounted his horse and set out for Harrogate. At this point of the story, it suddenly occurs to him that some readers may wonder that no mention has been made of any children by so many wives; and he therefore explains, once for all, that, though he has a great many to carry on the succession, they have, so far, done nothing but 'rise and breakfast, read and saunter, drink and eat,' and therefore it would not be fair to make anybody pay for their history. During this visit to his favourite Harrogate, he renews acquaintanceship with six Irish gentlemen whom he had formerly known in Dublin. They were all men of large fortunes, and as handsome fine fellows as could be picked out in all the world; but, although he favours us with a character-sketch of each, we must content ourselves here with a few words concerning the most remarkable of the group. This was a Mr. Gallaspy, who was the tallest and strongest man Buncle had ever seen; who never went to bed more often than one night in three, was the most profane swearer ever known, had already killed two men in duels, and, in addition to certain other accomplishments, which Buncle particularises, but which our more modest age will not allow to be mentioned in print, always smoked two pipes at once, one in each corner of his mouth, and blew the smoke of both out of his nostrils, and was

also in the habit of drinking 'seven in a hand,' that is to say, 'seven glasses so placed between the fingers of his right hand that, in drinking, the liquor fell into the next glass, and thereby he drank out of the first glass seven glasses at once.' This episode is the only instance throughout the book of the specifically Rabelaisian type of extravagance; and the quality of it is hardly such as to make us wish for more.

But it was not only Irishmen that Buncle met at Harrogate. He had only been there a day or two, when it was his fortune to dance with Miss Spence, of Westmoreland, a lady 'who had the *head* of Aristotle, the *heart* of a primitive Christian, and the *form* of the Venus de Medicis'; and the reader will be by no means surprised to hear that he was not many hours in her company before he was passionately in love with her. But he anticipates that perhaps some conventionally-minded persons may not heartily agree with his plighting his vows to a fourth girl when the three wives he has already buried are scarcely cold in their graves; so he thinks it well to set out at length his apology for marrying so often.

> 'I think it unreasonable and impious to grieve immoderately for the dead. A decent and proper tribute of tears and sorrow humanity requires; but when that duty has been paid, we must remember that to lament a dead woman is not to lament a wife. A wife must be a living woman. The wife we lose by death is no more than a sad and empty object, formed by the imagination; and to be still devoted to her is to be in love with an idea. It is a mere chimerical passion, as the deceased has no more to do with this world than if she had existed before the Flood. As we cannot restore what Nature has destroyed, it is foolish to be faithful to affliction. Nor is this all. If the woman we marry has the seven qualifications which every man would wish to find in a wife,—beauty, discretion, sweetness of temper, a sprightly wit, fertility, wealth, and noble extraction,—yet death's snatching so amiable a wife from our arms can be no reason for accusing fate of cruelty, that is, Providence of injustice; nor can it authorise us to sink into insensibility, and neglect the duty and business of life. This wife was born to die; and we receive her under the condition of mortality . . . and when this term is expired . . . we should look out for another with the seven qualifications, as it is not good for man to be alone, and as he is by the Abrahamic covenant bound to carry on the succession, in a regular way, if it be in his power.'

There is more, to the same effect, on the general question, and then follows a special application to his own particular case:—

> 'As I had forfeited my father's favour and estate for the sake of Christian Deism, and had nothing but my own honest industry to secure me daily bread, it was necessary for me to lay hold of every opportunity to improve my fortune, and, of consequence,

do my best to gain the heart of the first rich young woman who came in my way after I had buried a wife. It was not for me to be snivelling for months because my wife died before me, which was, at least, as probable as that she should be the survivor.'

Any comment on this callous and fantastic, but apparently perfectly serious, apology being surely superfluous, we hasten on with the story. Miss Spence promises to consider Buncle's proposal, and give him an answer later on at her home in Westmoreland. In the interval, he employs himself in rescuing two young and beautiful heiresses—one aged nineteen and the other twenty, and each entitled to £100,000 on coming of age—from the moated house in which their rascally guardian is keeping them immured. But, as he would not risk marrying one of them (even were Miss Spence out of the question) in case she might die before inheriting her money, he takes them both to Orton Lodge, and leaves them there while he posts off to get his answer from the Lady with the head of Aristotle and the form of Venus de Medicis. Miss Spence was of the age of twenty-four, she possessed a neat and pretty mansion standing in about two hundred acres of charming grounds, and she was one of several ladies Buncle met with in the course of his travels who understood 'the arithmetic of fluxions.' It may, perhaps, go without the saying, that she was also a 'Christian Deist.' On his arrival at her 'neat and pretty mansion,' she is just on the point of starting on a journey to London, accompanied by a maid and a footman, on horseback, and is glad to avail herself of her admirer's escort. By the way, they discuss Leibnitz and Newton, and fluxions; and the reader has the benefit of nearly twenty pages of their conversation, the report of which by no means bears out Buncle's reference to the head of Aristotle. What they saw or did while in London, he unfortunately omits to tell us. He briefly says that, within three weeks of their arrival, they were married; and then, with equal brevity, that before the end of six months she was dead; and that, though he mourned her loss 'with a degree of sorrow due to so much excellence, endearment, and delight,' yet he soon went out into the world again, to relieve his mind, and try his fortune once more. Three months later, Miss Turner, the beautiful sister of his old college chum, and the mistress, as we have seen, of £50,000, rides up to the inn in which Buncle happens to be staying; and, as soon as he hears that her brother is no more, he proposes to her on the spot. She agrees to give him her answer in the course of a few days; but, while playing cards in the evening, it becomes evident to the penetrating eye of this past master of proposals, that she is already all his own; so without waiting for her formal answer, he at once sends his man off for Father Fleming, and they are married on the following morning. It is but three short months since the death of wife number four; but 'a dead woman is no wife,' he exclaims, 'and marriage is ever glorious!' After spending six weeks at the inn were they were married, the happy couple set off for a visit to London; but they had proceeded a very little way on their journey, before their carriage was overturned by the side of a steep hill, and his fifth charmer was killed. 'It was in vain for me to continue lamenting,' he simply remarks, 'she is gone for ever'; so 'her body I deposited in the next churchyard, and immediately after rid as fast as I could up to London.'

On his visit to the great city, he took lodgings in the house of Edmund Curll, the bookseller, a man who is more or less familiar to us from Pope's references to him in the *Dunciad* and elsewhere. Buncle's sketch of this notorious character is by no means flattering. 'Curll was in person,' he says, 'very tall and thin, an ungainly, awkward, white-faced man. His eyes were a light grey, large, projecting, goggle, and purblind. He was splay-footed and baker-kneed.' No man could talk so well on theatrical subjects and theology, we are told; but he printed lewd things and was altogether a lewd fellow, being too fond of drink when he could get it at other people's expense, and behaving so miserly to his staff of miserable Grub Street hacks, that 'his translators in pay lay, three in a bed, at the *Pewter Platter* in Holborn.' Curll introduced Buncle to some of the most infamous dens in London; and it was at Curll's house that he met the two Irish sharpers, who inveigled him into a gambling-hell, and quickly fleeced him out of all the money which he had made by his various fortunate marriages. By way of making amends for this last crushing misfortune, however, the dissolute bookseller put him in the way of running off with the only daughter and heiress of an old and wealthy miser named Dunk. Agnes Dunk, of course, was a young and beautiful and cultivated girl, and she readily agreed to ride off with Buncle to Cumberland to be married. But, on the way, she fell ill of a fever and died; whereupon Buncle sadly put her into a coffin with his own hands, and, after keeping her seven days, according to the old Roman fashion, disconsolately followed her to her grave. And now comes one of the strangest experiences of even his strange life. For, six months later, being driven by stress of weather to take shelter in the house of a Dr. Stowell in Westmoreland, he is staggered to find that the doctor's wife is, without a doubt, no other than this very Miss Dunk, whom he had so carefully buried with his own hands. She does not appear to recognise him, so he discreetly says nothing; but he sets his servant to make inquiries, from which it appears that the doctor had been in the habit of having bodies brought to him from churchyards for purposes of dissection, and that, on one such occasion, just as he was about to use his knife, one of these bodies moved, and, on being resuscitated, it turned out to be so charming a woman, that her preserver lost no time in marrying her. Before long, Buncle hears of another North-country medical man, named Fitzgibbon, who has an only daughter, 'a very divinity'; and, on paying him a visit, is invited to take up his quarters in the house for the purpose of studying physic. He does so; and, at the end of two years, marries the doctor's lovely daughter, Julia. Dr. Fitzgibbon dies a few weeks after his daughter's wedding, leaving Buncle not only his house, his library, and his practice, but a handsome fortune as well. Ten months after marriage, Julia fell into a river that flowed by the end of her garden, and was drowned. This time, Buncle sat with his eyes shut for the length of ten days; reflecting, he says, on the wisdom of God.

> 'And when I had done, I called to my man, Soto ô Fiñ, to bring the horses out immediately, and I would go somewhere or other to see new scenes, and, if I could, get another wife. . . . What man could say he had had enough of wedlock because he had buried seven such wives? I am sure I could not.'

With this notion in his head he determined to make for Orton Lodge, reflecting that one of the two young heiresses he had left in possession there would now be just about of legal age. But, on arrival, he found the place shut up, and a note fastened to the doorkey, informing him that, having heard nothing of him for so long, and learning that their nefarious guardian was now dead, the young ladies had felt free to go away,— but whither he could not even guess. So he settles down for a month in his old home to cogitate; and then a desire comes upon him to 'look once more at that fair curiosity, Miss Dunk that was.' Mrs. Stowell makes no more sign of recognising him than on the occasion of his former visit; and he plunges into a spirited conversation with her husband on 'the wisdom and goodness of God in the production of the Spanish fly for the benefit of man'; but, after talking for a very short time, the good doctor dropped dead from his chair. What followed can only be told in his own words:—

> 'When the beautiful Mrs. Stowell saw her husband was really dead, and had paid that decent tribute to his memory which was due to a man who had left her in his will all his estate, real and personal, to be by her disposed of as she pleased, she sent for me to her chamber the next morning, and, after a long conversation with her, told me she could now own who she was, and, instead of acting any longer by the directions of her head, let me know from her heart that she still had the same regard for me as when we travelled away from her father's house.'

Of course Buncle was ready for another wedding at once; but the lady insisted on going away for three months, for propriety's sake. He remained in possession of the house and property in the meantime; and they were duly married a week after her return. Just at this time he learns that his father is dying, and therefore selects Ireland for his seventh honeymoon. On arriving at the paternal mansion, which he has not seen or heard from since the days of his youth, he is astonished to find that the old gentleman has become as strict a Unitarian as himself; a circumstance which would have given him even more satisfaction than it did if, during his passion for orthodoxy, that stern parent had not alienated his estate, so that now he can leave his son nothing but £100 a year, a little ready money, and a small ship, a sloop of twenty-five tons, then lying at anchor in the bay. The father dies in all the odour of Unitarian sanctity, and Buncle, with Mrs. Buncle the seventh, soon returns to England in the family sloop. Whether the possession of a ship turned his thoughts from matrimony, or whether there were any other cause, he does not inform us. But when, a year later, 'Miss Dunk that was' left him again a widower, he circumnavigated the globe in this cockle-shell, and made it his habitation for nine years. After which he purchased 'a little flowery retreat' within a few miles of London, and there settled down, without (at any rate up to the moment of writing) any further matrimonial inclinations, and yet, he declares, as happy a mortal as can exist on this planet.

The *Life of John Buncle* purports to be an autobiography. Doubtless there are some few grains of fact in this bushel of fiction; but it would be scarcely worth while, even if it were possible, to pick them out; and all that is independently known of the author amounts to very little. In a letter to the *St. James's Chronicle* of 25th October 1788, a correspondent, who had been much struck with the singularities of *John Buncle,* inquired whether anybody knew anything concerning 'an author whose real name has been as studiously concealed from the world as that of the gentleman who wrote the celebrated letters signed *Junius.*' In answer to this, a few days later, another correspondent, signing himself 'X,' informed the public that the real name of the author of *John Buncle* was Amory, and that he had frequently seen, and occasionally exchanged a few words with, this 'very singular person,' whom he believed to be now dead. The letter goes on—

> 'I believe he was a native of Ireland; and I have been informed that he was bred to some Branch of the Profession of Physick. Whether he ever followed that, or any other profession, I have not heard. When I knew him, he lived in a very recluse Way, on a small Fortune; and his residence was in Orchard Street, Westminster. At that time he had a Country Lodging for occasional Retirement, in the Summer, at Belfound [Bedfont], near Hounslow. This was about 30 years ago. He had then a Wife, who bore a very respectable Character; and by whom he had a Son, who, if living, is a Physician somewhere in the North of England.'

'X' appeals to this son to favour the public with a more satisfactory account of his 'learned though very eccentric Father,' who was, he goes on to say—

'a Man of a very peculiar Look and Aspect; though at the same Time he bore quite the Appearance of a Gentleman. He read much; and scarce ever stirred, but like a Bat, in the Dark of the Evening: and then he would take his usual Walk; but seemed to be always ruminating on speculative Subjects, even while passing along the most crowded streets.'

He further declares, that Amory was a zealous Unitarian 'to a most Romantick Degree,' and that it was generally thought that, in the character and adventures of Mr. Buncle, he intended 'at least a sketch of his own Picture,' 'X' venturing his own opinion that 'perhaps the general outline is not unlike.' This communication speedily drew a reply from Amory's son; which is not very illuminating, but which, as an epistolary curiosity, may be given *in extenso.*

> 'In your paper of the 6th of this Month I found some very erroneous statements of my Father (John Buncle), Thomas Amory, Esq. He was not a native of Ireland. His Father, Councillor Amory, attended King William to Ireland, and was appointed Secretary for the forfeited Estates in that Kingdom, and was possessed of very extensive property in the County of Clare. He was the youngest Brother of Amory or Damer, the Miser, whom Pope calls "the Wealthy and the Wise"; from whom comes Lord Milton, etc., etc. My grandfather married the Daughter of FitzMaurice, Earl of Kerry; Sir William Petty another Daughter; and the grandfather of the Duke of Leinster another. My father lived on Millbank, Westminster, and for a few Years rented a house at Bellfont. He never had but one Wife, and I am the only surviving Child; he is yet living, and is now 97 Years old, and when young was a very handsome Man. He has published many political and religious Tracts, Poems, and Songs. I cannot comprehend any Sense in your calling him an "Unitarian to a romantic degree." He worships one God through the Mediation of Jesus Christ. I cannot see any Romance in that. He will not see any Company, nor ever comes out of his Room.— I remain, Sir, Your humble Servant,
>
>   ROBERT AMORY, M.D.
>   'WAKEFIELD, *Nov.* 19, 1788.

> '*P.S.*—I have practised Physic here 27 years. We are lineally descended from Amory de Montford, who married the sister of Henry II., and was created Earl of Leicester. I have three sons, all in the army. My eldest son, Robert, is a miserable Cripple, from an Injury received in the Action under Lord Rodney on the 12th of April; my second Son is a lieutenant in the 71st, and my third an Ensign in the 57th.'

In January 1789, a Mr. Louis Renas, writing in the *Gentleman's Magazine,* gave reasons for doubting Dr. Amory's genealogy; whereupon the irate doctor wrote to 'Mr. Urban,' that his account was taken from his grandfather's papers, and had been confirmed by his father; that the Ignorance and Low Abuse of Renas were beneath contempt, and that this person 'should sign his name *Mr. Louis the Ass,* and then the Herald's Office might easily have found out *his* connections.' In this letter he incidentally mentions that his aged father had died in November of the previous year; but the correspondence is chiefly interesting as showing that Dr. Amory, though without any of his father's literary faculty, at any rate 'carried on the succession' in respect of eccentricity. Buncle desired to be remembered as 'an odd man'; and, so far as Amory is remembered at all, it will only be as an odd writer. His books have not even the interest of marking any transition stage in the evolution of the English novel; for Richardson's *Pamela, Clarissa,* and *Sir Charles Grandison,* Fielding's *Joseph Andrews* and *Tom Jones,* and Smollett's *Roderick Random* had all appeared before the **Memoirs** and **John Buncle.** In neither book is there either plot, or analysis of motives, or delineation of feelings, or discrimination of character. A large proportion of Buncle's adventures are as preposterous as those of Baron Munchausen; and as for the philosophical, scientific, and theological dissertations with which these are interspersed, all that need be said of them is, that they are not above the level of a Sunday orator in Hyde Park. Some books, says the wise Bacon, may be read by deputy; and in this class we may unhesitatingly place Amory's **Memoirs** of 'illustrious' ladies, and the **Life of John Buncle.**

Katherine A. Esdaile (essay date 1940)

SOURCE: "The Real Thomas Amory," in *Essays and Studies,* Vol. XXVI, 1940, pp. 45-72.

[*In the following essay, Esdaile offers an autobiographical interpretation of* The Life of John Buncle, Esq.]

Readers of Lamb and Hazlitt know the name of **John Buncle;** his author, Thomas Amory (1691-1788), is ignored in no serious history of eighteenth-century literature and has his place in the *D.N.B.;* yet no one has troubled to disinter from his pages the autobiographical fragments which, as Leslie Stephen saw, are embedded in it, or to check his references to notable Englishmen or his reactions to the people and to literature of his own day. As his writings are the reflection of his own vivid personality, as his wildest adventures reflect his dreams if not invariably his experiences, it is worth while to attempt a full-length portrait, remembering that his own son equated Amory with his hero Buncle, and that there is nothing the least like his work in the whole vast field of English literature.

> I was born in London and carried as an infant into Ireland, where I learned the *Irish* language, and became intimately acquainted with its original inhabitants; I was not only a lover of books from

the time I could spell them to this hour; but read with an extraordinary pleasure, before I was twenty, the works of several of the fathers, and all the old romances; which tinged my ideas with a certain piety and extravagance, that rendered my virtues as well as my imperfections particularly mine. (Preface to *John Buncle*.)

The *St. James's Chronicle* stated that he was trained for a doctor (Buncle also, as we shall see, took to doctoring); but no profession could long keep him in one place. 'Compelled to be an adventurer when very young', by his own account he was a bundle of incongruous qualities; he developed 'a passion for extraordinary things and places'; was a passionate Unitarian; adored learned ladies; disliked commonplace people; dived from a (low?) cliff for fun, swam out to sea, boarded a ship, and sailed to the next port, leaving his companion to conclude him drowned; and was a good hand with the small sword.

> If oddness consists in spirit, freedom of thought, and a zeal for the divine unity; in honouring women, who were admirable for goodness, letters, and arts; and in thinking, after all the scenes I have gone thro', that everything here is vanity; except that *virtue* and *charity,* which gives us a right to *expect beyond the grave* . . . then may it be written on my stone—Here lies an odd man.

So much for Thomas Amory on himself. His son, Robert Amory, M.D. of Wakefield, tells us that his grandfather went with William III to Ireland and became Secretary of the Forfeited Estates; that he was a considerable landowner in County Clare, his seat being Bunralty Castle; that the family was connected with the de Monforts, Pettys, and Fitzmaurices; and finally that his father lived on Millbank, but being 'now 97 years old . . . will not see any company, nor ever comes out of his room', adding that 'when very young, he was a very handsome man'. This statement will be found in the *Gentleman's Magazine* for 1788 (p. 1062); on November 25th of that year appears among the Obituaries: 'Nov. 25, Aged 97, *Tho. Amory* esq. author of *John Buncle*'.

The younger Amory had rushed into print in consequence of genealogical inaccuracies in an account of his father in the *St. James's Chronicle* for November 6th, 1788, but the personal details there given, evidently in the belief that Amory was dead, Boswellian as they are, are not denied:

> Mr Amory was a man of very peculiar look and aspect; though at the same time he bore quite the appearance of a gentleman. He read much, and scarce ever stirred but like a bat in the dusk of the evening, and then he would take his usual walk, but seemed always to be ruminating upon speculative subjects, even while passing along the most crowded streets.

Public interest in Amory must have been considerable for such details to be acceptable, and it is significant that the Wakefield doctor finds it necessary to protest that his father 'never had but the one wife'; the public clearly thought that Buncle's many 'charmers' reflected his own experiences. But as his son begins his correction with the phrase 'My father (John Buncle) Thomas Amory esq', the public was hardly to blame for the mistake, and may even have drawn the deduction that Buncle's dismissal of his own offspring as thoroughly uninteresting was based on his knowledge of this his one surviving child. For not only was Dr. Robert Amory a dull dog, anxious to assert the dignity of his family indeed, but confused and heavy-handed in his description of his ancestry, but Amory himself was not interested in children, even giving no account of his own childhood, on the ground that it would not be fair to make the public pay for anything so uninteresting. One incident of that childhood indeed he does record, but that is because Steele, in the *Tatler,* had given currency to an inaccurate version of a story which he only knew by hearsay: the public ought to know the facts, which are, in truth, illuminating.

As 'a little boy in Dublin, between seven and eight', Amory knew his father's neighbours Mr. and Mrs. Eustace, the Orlando and Belinda of the 172nd *Tatler;* Belinda indeed, 'a lively prattling thing, by tarts and fruits, encouraged me to run into her parlour as often as I could. . . . As I was a remarker so early in my life' (*Buncle,* iii, p. 3) he adds, he perceived the pride and obstinacy of the one, the vanity and satirical wit of the other, which led to the disaster. Belinda's sister spent a guinea on a fan with Indian figures on it; Belinda admired it, Orlando did not; they quarrelled; Belinda went to bed before him; and when she was asleep, the 'despotic husband' stabbed her, barricaded himself in his house, and was shot by an officer of justice at whom he was taking aim. The body was carried head downward through the city on a cart and the child saw it; 'and of all the faces of the dead I have seen, none ever looked like his. There was an anxiety, a range, a horror, and a despair to be seen in it, that no pencil could depict'. Is it fanciful to see in this tragic incident of Amory's childhood the origin of that quixotic desire to help and justify injured women, always young and always beautiful, which plays so large a part in his books?

The boy was sent to the best school in Dublin, Dr. Sheridan's, who on Swift's authority 'shone in his proper element' as a headmaster; the curriculum seems to have been far from conventional, and of high educational value. The boys acted plays in Greek and English, Amory playing Falstaff in *Henry V* (*Buncle,* i, p. 108), and recalling with delight the holiday joys of 'frolicks and rambles, and merry dancings we had at *Mother Red-Cap's* in Barn-Lane, the hurling matches we have played at *Dolphin's Barn* and the cakes and ale we used to have at the Organ-house on *Arbor Hill'*.

It was either in some Long Vacation or between school and college that he was 'placed in a *French* family of distinction' (Dedication to the **Ladies**), and met the first of his female prodigies; but he was certainly in Dublin by 1706 or 1707, going up to Trinity College at sixteen and spending five years there, devoted to five several subjects, of which Divinity was one. He 'lived in the same chambers' with his tutor, Jack Bruce, the 'bright and excellent', for four years, discussing *inter alia* Divinity: 'Religion', would Jack Bruce say, as we passed an evening over a little bowl of nectar, for he never taught in the dry, sour method—'Religion consists in a steady belief in the Existence of God', &c. and we learn that he placed the virtues of civility and good manners beside those of 'temperance, mercy and charity'.

We shall meet some of Amory's undergraduate friends at Harrogate; meanwhile we may note that the Irish historian MacCurtin (**Ladies**, iii, p. 218) and Bishop Brown of Cork, 'a man of vast learning, exemplary piety and great goodness to the poor', but a Jacobite 'who in hatred to King *William* writ a book against drinking healths to the memory of anyone' (**Ladies**, 1, p. 85) were friends of his, and of another friend, Mrs. Grierson he writes:

> Mr Ballard's account of her in his *Memoirs of some English Ladies* lately published [1752] is not worth a rush. He knew nothing of her. And the imperfect relation he got from *Mrs Barber* is next to nothing. I was intimately acquainted with Mrs Grierson, and have passed a hundred afternoons with her in literary conversation in her own parlour. Therefore, it is in my power to give a very particular and exact account of this extraordinary woman,

which, alas, he never did. Now this passage serves to explain many episodes in **John Buncle.** Not only had Constantia Grierson studied obstetrics at seventeen under Mrs. Pilkington's father, a well-known Dublin doctor, but, according to Mrs. Pilkington herself, was mistress of Hebrew, Greek, Latin, and French, a student of higher mathematics, and an elegant writer in verse and prose. She edited Terence, dedicating her edition in a Greek epigram to her son, afterwards a friend of Dr. Johnson, and her edition of Tacitus [1730] was pronounced by Dr. Harwood, a good judge, 'one of the best edited books ever delivered to the world'; her unpublished annotations of Sallust belonged successively to, and were treasured by, Lord George Germain and John Wilkes. She was an intimate friend of Swift, Dr. Sheridan, and Dr. Delany; and Mrs. Delany, before she became the Dean's wife, speaks appreciatively of 'beginning an acquaintance among the wits Mrs. Grierson, Mrs. Byron and Mrs. Pilkington'

(*Autobiography,* i, p. 301); the society of Mrs. Grierson, then only twenty-five years old, was, that is to say, regarded as an honour by a distinguished and aristocratic Englishwoman visiting Dublin for the first time. As for the contemned Ballard,[1] his praise is so unstinted that one cannot but wonder what Amory could have added to it:

> She was not only happy in a fine imagination, a great memory, an excellent understanding, and an exact judgement, but had all these crowned by virtue and piety; she was too learned to be vain, too wise to be conceited, too knowing and too clear-sighted to be irreligious. As her learning and her abilities raised her above her own sex, so they left her no room to envy any; on the contrary, her delight was to see others excel. She was always ready to advise and direct those who applied to her, and was herself willing to be advised. Lord Carteret [to whom her Tacitus was dedicated] when he was Lord Lieutenant of Ireland, obtained a patent for Mr. Grierson, her husband, to be the King's printer, and to distinguish and reward her uncommon merit, had her life inserted in it.

This gifted and delightful creature died in 1733 at the age of twenty-seven, and when we are tempted to laugh at Amory's many accomplished ladies, always young, always attractive, and always ready to discuss divinity, fluxions, the meaning of Hebrew phrases and the classics, it is well to remember that he had actually known, and known well, a woman who was at least as charming, learned, and accomplished as any Harriot or Statia of them all. In fact, what has been treated by every writer as utterly fantastic turns out to be autobiography, actual reminiscences of days spent in Mrs. Grierson's parlour, and not, as has always been supposed, the dreams of an unbalanced mind.

But before pursuing his adventures as depicted in his novels, we must say something of Amory's relations with Swift. His promised account of him never appeared, any more than did that of Mrs. Grierson, but the long Advertisement contains what he did write, and must be quoted in full. He is protesting against the four recent biographies, by '*Lord Orrery, The Observer on Lord Orrery, Dean*[e] *Swift Esq., and Mrs. Pilkington',* as quite inadequate:

> After all the man is not described. The ingenious female writer comes nearest to his character, so far as she relates; but her relation is an imperfect piece. My Lord, and the Remarker on his Lordship have given us mere critiques on his writings, and not so satisfactory as one could wish.
>
> They are not painters. And as to Mr. Swift, the Dean's cousin, his essay is an odd kind of history of the doctor's family, and vindication of the Dean's high birth, pride, and proceedings. His true character is not attempted.

I knew him well, tho' I was never within side of his house, because I could not flatter, cringe, or meanly humour the extravagancies of any man. I am sure I knew him much better than any of those friends he entertained twice a week at the Deanery; *Stella* excepted. I had him often to myself in his rides and walks, and have studied his soul, when he little thought what I was about. As I lodged for a year within a few doors of him, I knew his times of going out to a minute, and generally nicked the opportunity. He was fond of company upon these occasions, and glad to have any rational to talk to: for, whatever was the meaning of it, he rarely had any of his friends attending him at his exercises. One servant only, and no companion, he had with him, as often as I have met him, or came up with him. What gave me the easier access to him, was my being tolerably well acquainted with our politicks and history, and knowing many places, things, people, and parties, moral and religious of his beloved England. Upon this account he was glad I joined him. We talked generally of factions and religion, states, revolutions, leaders and pieties. Sometimes we had other subjects. Who I was he never knew; nor did I seem to know he was the Dean for a long time, not till one Sunday evening that his Verger put me into his seat at St Patrick's prayers; without my knowing the Doctor sat there. Then I was obliged to recognize the great man, and seemed in a very great surprize. This pretended ignorance of mine as to the person of the Dean, had given me an opportunity of discoursing more freely with and of receiving more information from the Doctor, than otherwise I could have enjoyed. The Dean was proud beyond all other mortals that I have ever seen, and quite another man when he was known.

This may seem strange to many, but it must be to those who are not acquainted with me. I was so far from having a vanity to be known to Dr. *Swift,* or to be seen among the fortunate at his house (as I have heard those who met there called) that I am sure it would not have been in the power of any person or consideration to get me there. What I wanted in relation to the Dean, I had. This was enough for me; I desired no more of him. I was enabled by the means related, to know the excellencies and defects of his understanding; and the picture I have drawn of his mind you shall see, with some remarks on his writings, and on the cases of *Vanessa* and *Stella.*

This passage is reprinted in the second supplementary volume of Hawkesworth's *Swift* with a denial of its accuracy by Deane Swift which cannot be regarded as final: Amory's account is so undramatic that in a man of his perfervid imagination it may be taken as true. Amory's college friends were a lively set, but one at least became a 'glorious penitent' and died owning a Thomas à Kempis (**Buncle**, ii, pp. 51, 57). He had the entrée to the Castle (**Buncle**, iii, p. 304); knew the

Knight of Kerry and the Knight of the Glin; had friends in Tipperary, Kildare, and Galway (iii, pp. 107, 173, 200); spent Christmas of 1715 with the Wolfes of Balineskey, and saw a friend acquitted by Sir John St. Leger, a judge who, he says, would never convict a duellist of murder. Soon after he went down, however, his father, already an old man, married 'an artful cruel servant-maid' who contrived to get him ousted from favour, and turned loose on the world, though with a comfortable sum in his pocket. In his wandering life he 'met with a wonderful deliverance' unnamed (**Buncle**, Preface), and at some time, in the 1720's presumably, went to London, where his friends included 'worthy John Toland—I say worthy from my own knowledge', and another deist 'Unhappy [elsewhere Mad] Tom Woodston, my intimate acquaintance', who was convicted of blasphemy on March 4th, 1729, the day before Buncle (read Amory) set off on the travels which form the subject of *John Buncle.*

A much more dangerous London acquaintance was Edmund Curll the bookseller, with whom Amory as well as Buncle lodged; only personal knowledge could have produced Buncle's description of him and his company. Curll was

> in person very tall and thin, an ungainly, awkward, white-faced man. His eyes were a light grey, large, projecting, gogle and semi-blind. He was splay-footed and baker-kneed. He had a good natural understanding and was well acquainted with more than the title pages of books . . . debauchee to the last degree, and so injurious to society, that by filling his translations with unnecessary notes, forged letters, and bad pictures, he raised the price of a four shilling book to ten. His translators in pay, lay three in a bed, at the *Pewter Platter Inn,* Holborn, and he and they were ever at work to deceive the public.

The subsequent statement regarding 'the holy goggle of his eyes in his public devotions' and his penitence are not impressive, but 'there were men in respect of whom Curll was a cherubim' (vol. iv, p. 151). This passage suggests that Amory knew John Dunton's *Life and Errors.*

Curll took Amory round the town, to the playhouse (he mentions Garrick, iv, p. 294) Sadlers Wells, the night cellars, and that haunt of vice, Tom King's in Covent Garden. The female company was of the worst, but gave him a chance of meeting Carola Bennet, a victim reclaimed by a 'sensible and excellent' young clergyman, who ultimately married her: from a 'charming libertine' she had become 'beautiful and modest'. There is one touching story which probably reflects a real episode, the discovery of a woman whom Amory had known as an innocent girl in the last stages of disease and famine, his carrying her to the house of a good woman, and having her tenderly nursed until her death: the reader will remember Dr. Johnson, whose charity was nobler still because the woman was a stranger.

Amory must have gone abroad again, for his visit to France as a child can hardly have sufficed for his obvious knowledge of Paris. He compares an English wood to the 'venerable' forest of Fontainebleau (iii, p. 116), and had a most remarkable knowledge of French literature from Courayer, Fénelon, Mézeray to Calprenède and Molière, whom he delighted in, and Voltaire, whom he detested. Much more doubtful is his having 'ventured in a light boat copied from the *Indian Praw* from the coast of Norway to a high latitude in West Greenland', which, with his descriptions of the Canary Islands and Brazil, must be ranked as a literary flight; but he certainly knew Scotland (iii, p. 190), St. Donat's in South Wales (iii, p. 64) and the Roman Wall (his one surviving letter proves that he was in Yorkshire in 1773), so that when Buncle 'set out to travel over Britain' he was only doing what his author had done before him.

But *John Buncle* was not Amory's first novel: that honour belongs to

> *Memoirs: concerning the Lives of Several Ladies of Great Britain. A History of Antiquities, Productions of Nature and Monuments of Art. Observations on the* **Christian Religion,** *as preferred by the Established Church, and Dissentors of every Denomination. Remarks on the Writings of the greatest English DIVINES; With a Variety of Disquisitions and Opinions relative to Criticism and Manners: and many extraordinary* **Actions.** 2 vols. 8vo. 1755 (Vol. i reprinted 1769, vol. ii reprinted 1766).

The dedication is 'To Mrs. Monkhouse of Paterdale, on the Banks of the River *Glenkroden,* in *Westmoreland';* the Advertisement already quoted describes the purpose of the book, and mentions a whole series of ladies whose stories—'true histories of amour, distress and relief'—were never published, though allusions in his second and more famous work suggest that they were written. A second part, 'to be published with all convenient speed', never appeared.

The *Memoirs* must have succeeded, since in the following year appeared the far more famous work:

> *The Life of John Buncle Esq:* containing Various Observations and Reflections made in several Parts of the World, and Many extraordinary Relations. In Four Volumes. 1756-66 (reprinted in 12mo, 1770, from which quotations are here given).

The book was a favourite with Lamb, Hazlitt, and Leigh Hunt, and to the extracts given in the latter's 'Book for a Corner', read at the age of twelve, I owe my own introduction to Amory. A year or so later I was puzzling over Hazlitt's description of Buncle as 'the English Rabelais'; a less apt description of Amory's luscious delight in religious controversies, wild scenery, good eating, and the Fair Female Form it would be hard to conceive, but he and Hazlitt has at least the merit of gusto in common.

As the *Memoirs of Several Ladies* was a book for women, so *John Buncle* was a book for men. This 'true history of my life and notions' is dedicated to 'The Critics', and written 'to vindicate my character from misrepresentations and idle stories; and to illustrate my *Memoirs';* it was, indeed, as he admitted, 'requisite to render the Memoirs before-mentioned intelligible'.

The matter of both books is fairly summed up in the title of the first; the manner may be described as the Picaresque in search of the Picturesque, with the important additions that the Picaro is a religious maniac, but a very learned one, and that he contrives to introduce a number of heroines of his favourite type by killing off a series of wives—'to lament a dead woman is not to lament a wife'—and to bring the hero into contact with other ladies, married and single, all as ready to tell their stories as Fielding's Man of the Hill. Running through all this is a singular acquaintance with art, literature, and the Fathers; a passion for caves, ruins, and wild nature; attacks on Popery and the Athanasian Creed; a remarkable appreciation of the social value of the convent system; a detailed acquaintance with birds and botany; and a prodigious gust of life, and you have a picture of the novelist whom his son equated with John Buncle.

On the literary side we note references to *Don Quixote, Astræa* and other romances of the school of Calprenède, *Amadis de Gaule,* the *Pilgrim's Progress,* and *David Simple* (*Buncle,* i, p. 226); an absolute passion for Shakespeare and Milton; an intimate acquaintance with Molière; a use of the word Gothic as a term of admiration in the manner of Browne Willis and Horace Walpole, whose appreciation of gardening he anticipates; and an insistence on the intellectual equality of men and women otherwise unknown before the next century. Even the Dedication to the *Ladies* describes how, when placed as a child with a French family, he met a girl of fourteen who 'could construe an Ode of Horace in a manner the most delightful and read a chapter in the Greek Testament with ease every morning'; he was later to meet with a child of eleven yet more precocious; and the theme is developed when, as a young man, he was inspired by the 'Admirable Maria', for whom we may, as elsewhere, read Constantia Grierson, to write that remarkable passage on the cultivation of the powers of women (*Buncle,* iv, p. 25)[2] to which no parallel can be found for half a century. In his *Transactions and Observations in a Voyage to the Western Islands in the year 1741* (*Ladies,* i, p. 126) he anticipates Dr. Johnson by forty years, and, like Johnson, must have known Martin's books on those islands as a child, since where his own observations differed from Martin's he does not hesitate to say so. Twenty years before Gray had uttered his daring praise of the Lakes, Amory was exalting them, and scenery remoter and more wild, in unmeasured terms, as well as taking notice of inscriptions on Roman cinerary urns and the tombs among twelfth-century ruins. Is it fanciful to suggest that Leigh Hunt, a devoted Buncleite, took the title of his *Men, Women and Books,* from Amory's *Notes relating to Men, and Things, and Books*? This is mentioned in **Buncle,** iii, p. 147, as though it were published and accessible, but in iv, p. 287 as to be 'published as soon as possible'. The word 'Men' must be generic, as a book by Amory omitting all mention of women is unthinkable.

In 1739, he tells us in the **Ladies,** he 'travelled many hundred miles to visit antient monuments and to discover curious things' among the 'vast hills' of Northumberland, and met Marinda Bruce, the daughter with whom he endowed his old friend and tutor of the Dublin days, reciting Shakespeare; she asked him in, and proved to be a painter then engaged on 'finishing an *arcadia* and a *crucifixion',* the first after Poussin, the second (with some difficulty, one fancies) 'uniting the different excellencies' of Rubens and Coypel. 'These pictures got Miss Bruce a husband' in the shape of a Mr. Benbow, whose early death left her in possession of Hali Farm, its ruins, its live eagle in a niche, its grotto, its flower-frescoes 'beyond anything of Baptist' (had Amory visited Montague House?), and its ducks, green peas, and cream. Her companion, Elise Janson, a Huguenot refugee, had translated *Astraea* and herself written a romance entitled 'The history of Florisbella the Good, Queen of the Northern Hills', and both she and another lady, Carola Chawcer, tell the stories of their lives in approved eighteenth-century fashion, not without garnishings of Epictetus (in Greek), German philosophy, and the Council of Trent. So do other ladies whom he met, Miss West and Mrs. Schomberg (*née* Bossuet), the latter

> as beautiful as Lalage, a born mime; she takes off *Warburton* in the greatest exactness; his very voice, and the mien of his visage, as he contemplates, and as he predicates; and when she brings him on with a bit of his *legation* [*The Divine Legation of Moses*] in his mouth, or some scraps of his controversy with *Stebbing,* or *Tilliard,* or *Sykes,* or *Jackson,* one cannot help screeching with laughter. You see all the vanity and self sufficiency of this gentleman, in her face and manner, when she is drest as a parson, and then, like him dictates his fancies, and pronounces all the world, except himself, a *crude writer.* I really believe if the Doctor saw her at this work, he could not forbear laughing.

As for Miss West, her reading of Milton was better than Quin's, reported 'the best reader of the *Paradise Lost* now living'; he was an excellent Comus on the stage,[3] but Miss West could make 'the poet admired and the actors forgotten'.

With regard to the Western Islands, however, it must be remembered that the poets may have sent him there; 'The stormy Hebrides' of *Lycidas*—and Amory was a fanatical admirer of Milton—he would not forget, and the authentic voice of poetry is heard as almost nowhere else at the time in that stanza in the *Castle of Indolence* beginning:

> As when a shepherd of the Hebrid isle,
> Plac'd far amid the melancholy main,

and in the ninth stanza of Collins's *Ode on the Popular Superstitions of the Highlands of Scotland:*

> Unbounded is thy range; with varied skill
> Thy Muse may like those feathery tribes which spring
> From their rude rocks, extend her skirting wing
> Round the moist marge of each cold Hebrid isle,
> To that hoar pile which still its ruins shews:
> In whose small vaults, a pigmy folk is found,
> Whose bones the delver with his spade upthrows,
> And culls them, wondering, from the hallow'd ground:
> Or thither, where beneath the showery west,
> The mighty kings of three fair realms are laid;
> Once foes perhaps, together now they rest,
> No slaves revere them, and no wars invade;
> Yet frequent now, at midnight's solemn hour,
> The rifted mounds their yawning cells unfold,
> And forth the monarchs stalk with sovran power
> In pageant robes and wreathed with sheeny gold—
> And on their twilight tombs aërial council hold.

Since Amory was a bookman first and foremost there is nothing strange in the fact that his passion for travelling, wild scenery, and romance should have led him to the Hebrides, to make accurate notes on the flora and fauna, and people the remote and lonely islands with new wonders of his own.

As Mrs. Schomberg had already in conversation rejected the authority of the Fathers as 'no more true than the splendid fancies of Bunyan the Tinker', and the minds of the other ladies ran on the same lines, it was a fit company that set out together for the Western Islands in the beginning of June 1741 in a ship commanded by Captain Scarlet, whose treatment of Hebridean superstitions was, as we shall see, unlike that of the poet. They spent a few days on the mainland of Scotland with a Mrs. Howel, and added to their number both that lady and her daughter, aged eleven, who discussed Bishop King's *Origin of Evil* and Chubb's *True Gospel Asserted* with modesty and spirit. They saw the Uists and Harris, Mull and Skye, passed the Green Island in the distance, and landed on Troda, whose birds and long-tailed rabbits are described, along with the four poor families who spoke only 'Irish', a convent of Poor Clares, and two old Franciscan friars. MacDuffs, Macphersons, Macleods, O'Connors, O'Rorkes, O'Briens, and O'Kellys peopled the convent; they wore 'the white plaid, that has a few narrow stripes of black, blue and red', with blue sleeves and silver crosses on their arms, the costume, in fact, of the old-fashioned inhabitants of Skye, crosses apart, as described by Martin at the end of the seventeenth century. Miss O'Rorke, of course, told her story, partly in excellent French, and defended 'the things of the Roman Religion' such as the Mass and prayers to the saints as 'figurative and spiritual' in a way which Amory so much admired that he promised her 'a welcome to his home and a comfortable provision'. Miss O'Brien, on the other hand, 'this charming votary', was a mystic on whom he could make no impression, so on June 28th they set sail again, and with a fair gale of wind sailed north-west round the Island of Lewis, coming at last 'to a vast rock' where they set up their tents, and found a solitary ensconced in a natural 'suite of rooms' in the side of a valley, where he had collected books, globes, mathematical instruments, a case of arms, a portrait and an admirable bust of a fair lady, and a gold box lettered *The Heart of Belvidera.* They drank *Great George the Second* after a good supper; the hermit told his story and that of Belvidera Dellon, who was torn from his arms by a ruffian, but happily discovered in a wood near Avignon, whereupon he married her, and, losing her ten years later, placed her heart in a box and retired to his Hebridean rock. The party then sailed to Lewis, where Buncle found some natives with black hair and eyes, though Martin had found 'all red-haired in his time', admired their musical gifts and native songs, and rode over to see a Mr. Bannerman, who wrote Unitarian tracts and escorted them to see some grottoes undescribed by Martin, which 'were really very strange'. The first series contained 'hundreds of rooms' full of stalactites and spars; another 'had a hideous and hollow noise in it', and as their lights were blown out they sat for long 'in an unspeakable horror'; he thought Martin's account of another cave in the *Loch Grace* inadequate, but noted that the animals of Lewis had nothing uncommon 'except their tiny breed of horses and a variety of birds'. He saw what appears to be a genuine Roman inscription to Julia Sorana, a Roman altar to Carausius, the marble urn of a daughter of the Augustan Legate, various Roman coins, and a stone circle which led to a discourse on the Druids and the discovery that it was used for divine service by a good old lady, Mrs. Gordon of Lewis, who presented him with a doctrinal manuscript written in a style suspiciously like his own.

They then set off for St. Kilda, but were swept south by a terrific tempest, probably derived from one of Amory's commonplace books, to the Cape Verde Islands,[4] where they spent a month and a day, and found the black inhabitants generous and good natured, and Zulima, the Governor's niece, exceedingly friendly, and quite ready to be converted to Unitarianism; in fact, with her uncle the noble Abdullah's leave, she sailed for England with them but is never heard of afterwards. They were driven north to the Green Island again, which Martin had only seen at a distance, and the ship's captain expressed his disbelief in the sailors' stories of 'Barbecula the finest glen in the world', where lived 'the *great men,* the souls of the Kings and champions, who lived and ruled in those islands in former times', and who obviously inspired the last lines in Collins's great stanza. The captain, however, promised: 'Be they *great men* or *great women, hoblins* or *goblins, fairies* or *genii,* I will give you a good account of them, ladies', and Buncle set out to find them for himself. What he did find was, in the words of the Postscript to the **Ladies,** 'a Villa Mouseion, a plain conventual retirement for the delights of reading and contemplation', with near twenty acres of garden and a statue of Mercury 'directing the traveller to the Elysian Fields', forty acres of laurels, shrubs, and flowers 'much finer than the Elysium at Stowe'; a statue of Cerberus stood 'on the way to Pluto's seat', and there were also statues of 'eight Greek Philosophers, twelve royal personages (all English except Marcus Aurelius), twenty-three divines, nine poets, eight Fathers, and many ladies'. Twenty ladies were 'sitting round a table, playing and singing', so the party started to sing 'the symphony in the opera of Rowland' to attract attention, and were invited by 'a black in a rich running dress, who came from his lady, *Mrs. Harcourt,* to know who we were'; she of course invited the party to stay; proved to be from the North Riding; had had a learned education; travelled all over Europe; inherited a fine estate, and was of course a Unitarian. A series of notes on Loyola, Mrs. Rowe, Jeremy Taylor, Conyers Middleton, and Dr. Cheyne, who, Amory says, turned to Jacob Behmen, 'the reverend philosopher, and William Law the father of our intellectuals, in his old age, after he had turned vegetarian', interrupt the story, and we may note that as regards Cheyne at least what Amory says is true: 'He carried his vegetarian views to great extremes', says the *D.N.B.,* 'as when he maintains that old age permitted the use of animal food to man only to shorten human life'. His views on this point would hardly have suited Amory, who describes more good eating than any novelist on record; but Cheyne had written on *The Philosophical Principles of Religion* and on Fluxions, and would be dear to him on both accounts.

We then get a statement that Mrs. Harcourt 'died suddenly, at her seat in Richmondshire, the first of December 1743, and not in the year 37, as the world was told in several advertisements in the London *Evening Post* of December 1739, by a gentleman who was imposed on by a false account he received of her death; this statement it has proved impossible to check, as the Burney newspapers are evacuated and the journal is not at Bodley's. We hear that the ladies' statues were removed after Mrs. Harcourt's real death to the 'noble library' of another seat of hers in Richmondshire, though 'all the other statues remain there [in the Hebrides] still'. A beautiful Rotunda, used for religious services, completed the view, and the twelve ladies and 'their eleven eleves' passed the time in music, devotion, riding, and painting, the twelve dressed alike, the others 'wearing what they please, except that *Diabolical innovation, that for ever execrable ensign the impious and unnatural hoop-petticoat*', on the immorality of which Amory agrees with the *Spectator*. Every Saturday every member of the Society had to read 'an essay, observation, or poem of her composing' on the week's studies, the best being entered in a large folio book with the author's name; twelve poor girls who attended on them were, we are told, well educated and well fed. After this it seems superfluous to find an attack on the 'endless and wild imaginations of the Hutchinsonians'.

Near the Elysian Fields were the ruins 'of a once grand abbey of Benedictine nuns of the order of Cluny' covering more than an acre of ground, and a curiously sympathetic account of St. Bernard follows, as well as a list of sepulchral monuments to Charitas de Shareshull (ob. 1220), Caroletta de Shoreditch (ob. 1222), Agnes de Shardeloe (ob. 1225), and many more, the latest of 1464, as well as many inscriptions in Gaelic; this appears to be based on Martin's account of the tombs of Abbots in St. Mary's, Iona, combined with that at St. Ouran's near-by, one of which Martin calls splendid. An interesting passage follows:

> By the way, Jewks, it is very wrong to ridicule nunneries in the manners some protestants do . . . I have had an intimacy with several ladies who had taken the vow and veil in Roman catholic cloisters, and . . . I declare that I never saw the least tendency to levity or indiscretion. . . . As to the stories of *Love in a Nunnery,* they are for the most part idle inventions; and if there be an unfortunate case now and then, it no more affects the church of Rome, than the debauch of a protestant daughter in her father's house . . . can be a blot on the morals of her pious parents.

Very few eighteenth-century polemical writers could have written such a paragraph.

Scalpa, by the way, they visited in a coracle, which he calls a *Nerogue* or *Currogh;* their waterman was called Shoneen, and caught them fish, and roasted eggs for dinner, and the sixty-odd inhabitants of Scalpa welcomed them warmly, setting before them fish, eggs, potatoes, oatcake, goat butter, goat's milk, and whisky or aqua vitae. They attended the Sunday service, 'beautiful in simplicity', in a field, and spent nine days weather bound, getting off at last in the coracle and coming safe to land.

The 'natural cathedral' in the rock, containing a writing table with a manuscript 'Historiae Naturales in the Saxon Hand' signed by '*Morchar the Carmelite* A.D. 1422' is as incredible as Mrs. Harcourt's establishment, but Buncle knew all about the Cashel Psalter, and Martin mentions caves at Arran, in one of which, used as a church, a hundred men could sit, while another had an altar in it. It is more surprising to find that Amory was interested in Egyptology. A minute and scholarly description of two Egyptian mummycases and their contents, and two statues of gods, all sold to Mrs. Harcourt by a Copt 'who might have been honest' might almost come from a current Museum Guide Book, and must have been based on knowledge; scrolls, hieroglyphs, bearded faces, swathing, are vividly described, and no mere reading would have told Amory that polished basalt looks like steel.

One of Mrs. Harcourt's recluses, Mrs. Bathurst, 'a writer in the Hebrew, Greek, and Latin', unexpectedly praises that 'great and beautiful genius Fenelon, Mme Bourignon and Mme Guion, the other illustrious visionary' in terms which leave no doubt that Amory's admiration for them was genuine; it is worth remembering that Wesley's abridgement of the latter was familiar to Dinah in *Adam Bede*. This Postscript also contains a 'description of the *Green Island,* its curiosities, and monuments of antiquity', a brief glimpse of the 'amazing frightful rock' of Scalpa and the 'little wrinkled rumpled woman' of nearly a hundred of whom he says 'I have not elsewhere seen anything for age that comes up to the *Old Woman of Scalpa';* we could have done with more about her. The position of the islands is accurately described, but 'tho everything new and curious, what [sic] had not been observed by other people' was avowedly included, Mrs. Harcourt's establishment, like Belvidera's solitary, remains incredible; we must remember, however, that the accurate Martin saw an old Lay Capuchin on Benbecula, and a chapel whose altar bore a crucifix at St. Kilda.

When we come to **John Buncle,** obvious autobiography and critical opinions, often of great interest, are mixed up with extravagant romance in a fashion which can only be illustrated by a summary—a very brief summary—of the narrative;[5] the two cannot be disentangled, and as a man is said to be known by his dreams, Amory is surely explained by his fantasies. His first 'charming angel' was a Miss Noel, whose reading of Hebrew so surprised him that he sat 'terrified, like the Enchanted Prince in *Amadis of Gaul*'; but she died of smallpox on December 29th, 1724, just before their marriage, so he returned to Dublin to find his father in the toils of his detestable young wife and sadly troubling his son's conscience by using the Prayer Book at Family Prayers; on May 1st, 1725, therefore, he left his father's house, and with fifty Spanish pistoles and a banknote for £500 made for England. The Dean of Derry was on board, but broke down in the gale, whereas Buncle's next 'angel', Miss Melmoth, sat calmly discoursing on the Divine Power with the mate and himself, while a group of officers, 'dismal disturbing howlers', cursed, swore and lost their heads. Miss Melmoth and he went north (the notes on the northern inns are very interesting: coffee, toast, and butter were provided even at 'a little lone house on the edge of Stainmore'), and he ran into an old schoolfellow who hailed him as Falstaff, having himself played the Prince in their performance of *Henry V.* The pair joyfully recalled their schooldays in the passage already quoted; Jack Prince told his story and invited him to stay; but on June 13th, 1725, Buncle left him to wander among the Lakes (which inspire many pages on the Deluge) and ran into Azora, who had a grotto, a garden, and a greenhouse at Burcot Lodge, and was of course a convinced Unitarian, with a father half ruined by a passion for alchemy. Azora understood algebra and had ten pupils, all devoted to her, and with these ladies he stayed until June 18th, 1725 (in the margin July 19th, 1726). His pages show an intimate knowledge of the wild Westmorland country, then wild indeed; he had an affair with highwaymen near Brough; met the 'glorious penitent' already mentioned; and decided to marry 'some sensible good-humoured girl of the mountains', and to encourage his two servants 'to pick up two bouncing females on scripture principles and start a state of his own'. Coming on a building 'more like a small gothic cathedral than a house' called Ulubrae, he was invited in, for once by a party of gentlemen; they discussed the rules of geometry and suggested improvements; 'studied the vegetable world' through the microscope, and a battle between a louse and a flea which the louse won; examined manuscripts and incunabula in the library and the works of great writers from Bellarmine to Scaliger, and noticed a remarkable cornelian portrait of Erasmus, to whom Amory devotes some learned notes (pp. 109-11). Hearing of a notable cave, he had himself lowered into it, getting out with difficulty to find Mr. Harcourt's house, where he met Harriot Eusebia his daughter, later the Mrs. Harcourt of the ***Ladies,*** whose paintings of scenes from the Revelation and whose powers of talking Latin, Spanish, and English were only less admirable than her religious notions. It was after her father's death at Constantinople in 1733 that she returned to England and and started the Hebridean nunnery with which we are already familiar.

He then met the sister of his old friend Charles Turner, and, while waiting his return from Scarborough, came on a country seat with a deep moat: its owner was that very Miss Melmoth whom he had already admired, and he settled down to wedded bliss for two years, for his Charlotte sang divinely, and he was the happiest man on earth till she died of a fever, when he set out, 'not like the Chevalier of *La Mancha,* in hopes of conquering a kingdom, or marrying some great Princess; but to see if I could find another good country girl for a wife, and get a little more money'. His first call was at Basil Grove, where an open door admitted him into a noble library filled with books and scientific instruments and adorned with an object rare in libraries of that or any period: in the middle of the room was a reading-desk, and on it leaned the skeleton of a man bearing the legend '*This skeleton was once Charles Henly, Esq.*'; in its hand was a scroll of parchment exhorting the reader to piety. The explanation came from a second house in the neighbourhood where, under groves and trees, sat an ancient gentleman and his lovely granddaughter, whose father was the skeleton; they were rash enough to ask for Buncle's life history, and got it, after which they asked him to stay the night. The grandfather offered him his granddaughter's hand when she was two-and-twenty, but Statia, 'bright and beautiful as *Aurora*', developed religious scruples after the old man's death which were happily dispersed by Buncle's argument that it was 'cruel to deprive children of their entailed heavenly inheritance', 'a greater sin, in fact, than murder'. The *cri du cœur,* 'Marry then, illustrious Statia, marry and let the blessing of Abraham come upon us Gentiles', melted her, and they spent a year or two in perfect happiness till she died of the small-pox. After sitting with his eyes shut for three days, he set out for Harrogate, 'through scenes, an amazing mixture of the beautiful and terrible', meditating on commencing the 'Married Regular' after meeting with a convent of Ivonites, or married friars, among the fells of Westmorland. This he left on April 8th; 'spent several days in the cottage of a poor fisherman in Bishoprick'; kept an eye on the 'charming Antonia'; and met with Dorick Watson the hermit, a brother-in-law of the famous Abbé le Blanc, whose garden surpassed 'the laboured and expensive gardens of Chiswick, the work of the late Lord Burlington', for, having lost his Adelaide, 'Contemplation was become his *Venus*'. The name of Le Blanc introduces a curious attack on Voltaire, *'half infidel, half pagan',* who 'writes the history of *England* with a *partiality* and malevolence almost as great as *Smollet*'s' and 'like all the Jacobite clerics, prates against the *placing* of the *Prince of Orange* on the *throne*'. Worse still, he 'denies *Shakespeare* almost every dramatic excellence . . . though in his *Mahomet,* he pilfers from *Macbeth* almost every capital scene (Shakespear, who furnishes out more elegant, pleasing, and in teresting entertainment in his plays, than all the other dramatic writers, ancient and modern, have been able to do;

and, without observing any one unity but that of character, for ever diverts and instructs)'. This almost foreshadows Dr. Johnson's famous *Preface*.

After an impassioned defence of the Reformation, he wins his 'innocent beauty', Antonia, who dies of the small-pox after two years, whereupon, after sitting with his eyes shut for four days, he at last gets to Harrogate. It is this chapter which ends with the famous passage on children which explains the odd contempt for his own childhood expressed in the **Ladies**:

> N.B. As I mention nothing of any children by so many wives . . . once for all, I think it sufficient to observe that I had a great many, to carry on the succession, but as they never were concerned in any extraordinary affairs, nor ever did any remarkable things, that I heard of;—only rise and breakfast, read and saunter, drink and eat, it would not be fair, in my opinion, to make anyone pay for their history.

Harrogate, 'a small straggling village on a heath, two miles from Knaresborough', was unique among eighteenth-century watering places; the company was very good, though too often counteracting the action of the waters by self-indulgence (hence an address on 'Temperance! Divine Temperance') but 'the lady of pleasure, the well drest taylor, the gamester are not to be found there', though this statement is counteracted in part by the 'six *Irish* gentlemen who had been my contemporaries at Trinity College, *Dublin* . . . we had been *Sociorums* (a word of *Swift*'s) at the conniving house *Ring's end*, for many a summer evening, and their regard for me was great'. All save Mr. Makins were 'handsome fine fellows', but the ladies 'preferred ugly *Makins,* as he was called, to many handsome men'; a zealous Unitarian of five and twenty 'he had but one eye, with which he squinted most shockingly, wore his own hair, which was short and bad, and only drest by his combing it himself in the morning, without oil or powder'; but he was 'matchless on the fiddle, sung well, and chatted agreeably'; whereas the gigantic Gallaspy was woefully immoral, a drunkard, a duellist, and most unsuitably 'passed life away in health, joy and plenty; dying without a pang for any kind of pain' at his house in Galway about 1753. We are reminded of the Hon. Galahad Threepwood, whose misspent life had left him at fifty-three a rosy little cock-sparrow of a man, whose contemporaries groaned and envied him at Spa and Vichy.

Mr. Duckley prided himself on being all things to all men; Mr. Monaghan knew books and men; Mr. Gollogher, after reading very hard for several years and keeping a common-place book in four vast volumes, 'sold every book he had, determined to read no more, and spent his every day in the best company of every kind', his taste for *Love and a Bottle* resulting in his

leaving nineteen daughters a thousand pounds each. It is sad that biographies of Mr. Gallaspy and 'Mr. O'Keefe, descended from the *Irish* kings and first cousin to the great *O'Keefe* who was buried not long ago in Westminster Abbey' (a fact: the dramatist's tablet is in the Cloisters) are lacking, apparently because Amory was in haste to get on to Miss Spence, 'a lady who had the *head* of Aristotle, the *heart* of a primitive *Christian,* and the *form* of *Venus de Medicis*'; it was the powers of the 'Admirable Maria' which led him (iv, p. 25) to those reflections on the cultivation of the minds of women which anticipate Charlotte Brontë. Maria's discussions of the differential calculus as practised by Newton and Leibnitz, and her refutation of Berkeley formed agreeable subjects of conversation on the ride to London which ended in their marriage, but Maria died in six months, and as he 'would not quarrel with Providence', he set out again to try his fortune, after printing her *Moral Thoughts* at length as a memorial of her.

'At a pleasant village not far from Nottingham' he met over a good supper a couple of invalids, one of them a chemist; Phlogiston—just made fashionable by Dr. Priestley—the properties of minerals, and the virtues of the Middle State formed the subject of their discourse, but next day produced another country house and hospitable host, as ready as usual to tell his story, for once of an unfaithful wife; the day after brought him to 'a lone inn' and Miss Turner. So charming was she that they sent for Father Fleming, Buncle's tame friar, at once, 'to qualify us for the implanted impulse, and sanctify the call', but soon after they had started for London their chariot and four overturned and the charmer was killed, dying with a Latin epitaph upon her lips. He rode on, and at Curll's met Dunk the miser, whom Curll, stationer as well as bookseller, supplied with 'paper, pens, ink, wax and pamphlets'. He had a lovely daughter whom Curll recommended as a wife; 'the charming Agnes' accepted Curll's letter of introduction, which seems rash, and was about to marry Buncle when she died and left him free for adventures in Westmorland, where he met her, disconcertingly, as the wife of one Dr. Stanvil; her body had been dug up and sold to the Doctor for dissection; one incision showed that she was alive, and the Doctor married her ('this case of Mrs Stanvil may be depended on as a fact'). The situation was an uncomfortable one for all parties, but fortunately a neighbour, Dr. Fitzgibbon, recognized Buncle as the man who had saved his son's life in Ireland,[6] and took him as a pupil for two years. As the *St. James's Chronicle* specifically states that Amory was 'bred to some branch of the medical profession', and as Robert Amory did not contradict the statement, we may take it that this is another case of actual experience being fantastically worked into the life of Buncle, who married the doctor's daughter, 'the illustrious Julia', in the beginning of 1734 and took over the practice. Julia was drowned, however, and after he had sat with his eyes shut for ten days, he set out to pay a visit to the Stanvils; after a harangue on the properties of salts, the doctor fell down dead of 'a rarefaction in his stomach'. 'A decent tribute of tears' followed; Mrs. Stanvil agreed to become Mrs. Buncle in earnest; and the pair started for Bagatrogh Castle: but the poor lady died in the beginning of the year 1736, and her disconsolate husband sailed for Brazil via the Canary Islands and Cape Verde, spending nine years in Borneo and Asia and returning 'to a little flowery retreat within a few miles of London' (at Bedfont, in fact, as his son says) to rest from his labours and write the history of his life, with his observations on three continents, 'in a scheme that gives a relief to still-life, and renders it a contrast to the breezy, bustling crowds of men'. Almost on the last page of the fourth volume he alludes to *The Voyages and Travels of Dr Lorimer;* this like the *Notes* (p. 56) has not been traced, but his son the doctor informed Sylvanus Urban that Amory 'published many political and religious tracts, poems, and songs', a statement curiously illustrated by a correspondent in *Notes and Queries* who was the lucky possessor of the only known letter of Amory's and of several more which he did not, unfortunately, publish; true to type, it is addressed to one of a party of ladies during a visit of Amory's to Yorkshire at the age of 82. It was on going through his papers that C. de D. 'found several letters from T. Amory (John Buncle), and very curious ones they are. I send you a copy of one, which you may perhaps think worth preserving in your entertaining and instructive papers [i.e. *Notes and Queries,* vol. i, p. 589].'

My dear Miss——,

I send you a curious paper for a few minutes' amusement to you and the ladies with you. It was written above thirty years ago. Perhaps you may have seen it in the magazines, where I put it; but the history of it was never known till now that I lay it before you.

I am,
Miss——
your faithful, humble servant,
Amouri

Newton Hall [2] 8. 73.

A Song
in praise of Miss Rowe.

Written one night extempore by a club of gentlemen in the county of Tipperary in Ireland. It was agreed that each member should, off-hand, write four lines, and they produced the following verses:

Nota bene.—When by our mutual contributions we had finished our song, we all drank bumpers to Miss Rowe's health, and sang the last verse in grand chorus.

I do not remember, in all my reading or acquaintance, such a thing being done before, and, perhaps, will never be again.

All the composers of this song (except Amory and Miss Rowe) are now in the grave. Here I am, round and sound, by the order of Providence, for some of God's adorable decrees.

Newton in Yorkshire, July th' 8th, 1773.

Amory's own verse must suffice; all the verses are metrical and in much the same manner, and the rhyme scheme is the same, the whole an imitation of Gay's *Molly Mog.*

In the dance, though the couples are scudding,
How graceful and light does she go!
No Englishman even lov'd pudding
As I love my sweet Molly Rowe.

This letter would be in place in the pages of Buncle: no wonder the author's son equated him and Amory. His earlier novel was written when he was well over sixty; the letter shows that this amazing gust of life was equally well marked when he was past eighty. That Amory spent part of his old age at Wakefield is also proved by a letter from a charming young Scots doctor, Thomas Christie, to John Nichols. Christie was making a tour of England, and on July 24th, 1787, writes from Lichfield, 'the birthplace of the glorious Johnson', that Wakefield had proved a disappointment: 'I neither learnt aught from the wisdom of the Rev. Dr. Turner . . . neither saw I Mr. Amory, the author of John Buncle, nor his son Dr. Amory M.D.' (*Lit. Anec.* ix, p. 379). Of Dr. Turner the *D.N.B.* states that 'his Wakefield ministry brought him into close connection with Thomas Amory', a sentence not, unfortunately, elucidated in the article on Amory himself; Unitarianism was clearly the link between them, for Turner and Priestley were intimate friends.

How does Amory stand among eighteenth-century novelists? First, we may note as significant that the only contemporary fiction he alludes to is by a woman, Sarah Fielding's *David Simple,* though his knowledge of seventeenth-century romances is wide and various. Next, he is the first novelist to make scenery play a vital part in his stories, treating the sight of wild Nature as an end in itself, not as an incident. Finally—and we may probably thank his father's library and perhaps Jack Bruce for this—his reading, though deep and wide, is both in form and matter mainly of the past. How he came across Thomas à Kempis and

Madame Bourignon, still more how he came to appreciate the virtues of the conventual life from the time of St. Bernard to his own day, is more mysterious, but his conversion to Unitarianism may well have been due to Toland and Woolston. Two things are certain, he never forgot Mrs. Grierson, though of the character and name of his own wife we have no idea, and when he cast in the novel form his views on divinity, scenery, nuns, antiquities, the education of women, he would at another time have written pamphlets or essays; in the 1750s—and the **Ladies** was written after 1752, since that date occurs in a note—the pressure of the age forced him to use the novel, whatever absurdities it led him into.

What his contemporaries made of him may be gathered from the fact that though both books were translated into German, in 1769 and 1778, a parody, *Geschichte einiger Esel,* appeared in 1782-3, after the publication of Cogan's *John Buncle Junior* (1776), two volumes of letters professedly by

> the youngest son of *John Buncle Gent.* of Marvellous Memory; who leaped Precipices, tumbled through Mountains [an adventure omitted here for lack of space] found *wise* and *good* Men, *beautiful* and *learned* Women.

as the Preface has it. 'My Progenitrix was his seventh consort', Cogan says, and when he comes to an elegant retreat, he cries 'Oh, for the pen of my worthy Sire, to describe this enchanting scene, to do justice to the bread and butter and delicious cream, to raise up some fair, for the loss of which to pour out the tear, and captivate our hearts!' The author quotes Gray's *Elegy,* and banters 'my father of Blessed memory'; but the authentic fire is wanting. There is only one John Buncle, and his name is Amory.

NOTE.—When he created Ulubrae (p. 64) had Amory heard of the inscription over the door of Auchinleck, that 'house of hewn stone, very stately and durable'? Or is this a pure coincidence?

Notes

[1] *Memoirs of the learned Ladies of Great Britain* (1752).

[2] Ballard, in his account of Mrs. Elstob, remarks her guardian objected to her learning other languages 'through a vulgar mistaken notion *that one tongue was enough for a woman'.*

[3] Can this refer to the famous performance of *Comus* for the benefit of Milton's granddaughter in 1750, at the very end of Quin's life, or was the masque acted earlier in the century?

[4] Martin, trying to make St. Kilda's, met a storm which

'almost drove us to the Ocean', and this may have inspired Buncle's more romantic experiences.

[5] It may be worth noting that a certain Mrs. Nally, of Duke Street, near Lincolns Inn Fields, who died in July 1743, had had eight husbands, according to the *Gentleman's Magazine,* 'and was scarce ever sick till a little before her death'.

[6] The episode is narrated in *Buncle,* iv, p. 194: Buncle's skill with the small-sword brought him off victorious but with a broken collarbone.

James R. Foster (essay date 1949)

SOURCE: *History of the Pre-Romantic Novel in England,* Modern Language Association of America, 1949, pp. 94-100.

[*In the following excerpt , Foster examines Amory's* Memoirs *and* The Life of John Buncle, Esq., *emphasizing that both works reflect the author's strong belief in the tenets of eighteenth-century deism.*]

Thomas Amory (1691 or 1697-1788) was less of the mountebank but much more the eccentric. In fact, impartial observers, and at times even his friends, strongly suspected that he was disordered in his intellect. Amory had some Irish in him. His father, who had come to Ireland with William III, owned property in County Clare and was prosperous enough to give his son a good education. Young Amory was sent to Dr. Sheridan's school in Dublin, spent some time living with a family in France to pick up the language, and studied at Trinity College, Dublin. Some of the most inspiring hours of his youth were spent in the parlor of Constantia Grierson, who as a girl of seventeen studied obstetrics under Letitia Pilkington's father, and after dazzling the Dubliners with her brilliance and beauty, died at the age of twenty-seven. She made a deep impression upon Amory; in fact, she was the model for more than one of his fine learned ladies who were so wonderful but so perishable. He promised in his **Memoirs of Several Ladies of Great Britain** (1755) to tell about his relations with Constantia but never did. Neither did he keep his promise to describe his meetings with Swift in Dublin. He declared that although he had often ridden or walked with the Dean, he had never entered his house because he "could not flatter, cringe, or meanly humor the extravagances of any man."

If caution is used some trustworthy information about Amory can be gathered from his writings, for he loved to write about himself. Although he identified himself with the oft-wedded John Buncle, we know that Amory married just once and had but one son, a doctor who practiced in Wakefield and was as odd as his father. There is more truth and less fancy when he writes in the preface of the *Life of John Buncle, Esq.*[1] that as a youth he was active and rash. He had swum to a boat anchored a mile and a half off shore; he had descended a precipitous cliff head foremost, and had taken a cool thrust with a small sword over a bottle. If oddness, he says here, consists in "spirit, freedom of thought, and a zeal for divine unity; in a taste for what is natural, antique, romantic and wild . . . then, may it be written on my stone—Here lies an odd man." In truth, this sentence sums him up rather neatly.

In London he struck up many acquaintances. He knew Curll the printer and associated with the deists. He was on intimate terms with John Toland and Thomas Woolston, especially the latter. Woolston was the unfortunate deist who was indicted for blasphemy and, after serving his term three times over because neither he nor his friends could scrape together thirty pounds to pay his fine, died in King's Bench Prison. The ideas which came from Woolston, Clarke, and Toland set Amory's head awhirl, and he became almost a fanatical believer in the Religion of Nature. The special form which his faith took was Christian deism (Socinianism) or Unitarianism. He was a primitivist and thought that the purity and perfection of the laws of Nature had been spoiled by the Pagan and Christian priests of Rome and by the degeneracy of civilized man. His special hero was Conyers Middleton, whose *Life of Cicero* was translated into French by Abbé Prevost. However, it was not this book but Middleton's latitudinarian *Free Inquiry into Miracles* (1748), which set forth the theory that all post-apostolic miracles were unreal, that aroused Amory's enthusiasm.

He had a tremendous appetite for learning: he read Shaftesbury, Locke, Du Bos, Tindal, Blomberg, and Pontoppidan. Theology and mathematics were not enough; he became an antiquarian and a kind of amateur topographer, making friends of eccentrics like Benjamin Forster, the antiquarian who had but one word, "FUI," inscribed on his tombstone. Forster, who called Amory "John Buncle" after the novel, wrote to Richard Gough on Oct. 20, 1768, and speaking of scenery said, "Do you know that I am become mighty gracious with John Buncle: he repeats to me the wonders of his book, and invites me to accompany him through Craven, after which he would accompany me to spots that had never been visited before, except by here and there a curious traveller, since the times of the Great Romans, of whom he could shew me many very credible remains." In another letter to the same friend we read that Forster had sent a copy of Gough's *Anecdotes of British Topography* to "John Buncle, but he has been ill and kept his chamber, and I have not seen him since. Methinks I could wish some kind of honourable mention had been made of his Reveries,

under the title of Westmoreland, as there is a little of topographical truth amongst his visions."[2] This is a reference to the Westmoreland landscapes in the latter part of *John Buncle.*

Amory must have travelled over England a great deal. At the time of Forster's letter, however, he was getting old and did not often range far from his house in Westminster or the little retreat he had near Hounslow. He was described as always being gentlemanly in appearance but as having a very peculiar look as he wandered idly dreaming through the London streets at night. Like the bat, he only stirred abroad in the dusk of the evening.

His first literary attempt he called *The Antient and Present State of Great Britain.* When a friend pointed out errors in it, he decided to travel and study and then revise the work. But one night while reading the revision in bed, he accidentally set fire to the manuscript and most of it was destroyed. From what was left came the *Memoirs* and *John Buncle.* This account, which is Amory's, may be mere invention, but there is no doubt but that these two books are absolutely unique literary curiosities. They reveal one of the most curious and eccentric personalities ever to write. Whether in the slight disguise of John Buncle or in his own person as narrator, actor, and editor of the letters in the *Memoirs,* Amory makes an impression. He is always the deist who travels to view the wonders of God's great outdoors, who tries to argue people into accepting the religion of nature, and who is not ashamed to admit that he derives pleasure from eating, drinking, smoking, and loving. He is a true fancier of the fair sex. "What a vast variety of beauty do we see in the infinity of nature," rapturously exclaims John Buncle. "Among the sex, we may find a thousand and a thousand perfect images and characters; all equally striking, and yet as different as the pictures of the greatest masters in Italy." "But," cries he, "a pox on streetwhores, chamber-whores, and kept-whores." His women must be chaste, rich, scholarly, and believers in deism. All of his wives are more or less like Miss Spence, his Number Five, who had the head of Aristotle, the heart of a primitive Christian, and the form of Venus. With a wife like Tristram Shandy's mother Buncle would have found it impossible to carry on discussions about Hebrew, the binomial theorem, or the faults of the Athanasian creed.

To his brilliant and charming females Buncle could offer intellectual and physical companionship if not the handsomeness of a youthful romantic lover. Buncle was no *petit-maître* but rough hewn, "natural," unpolished, pretty much in a state of nature. He was a great trencherman and very fond of his pipe and bottle. He confessed that a wife was a physical necessity to him. So when one died, he set out in search of another. After his Number Seven had passed on, he declared that he could still "with rapture take hundreds of them to [his] breast, one after another, and piously propagate the kind." If there is wit in this, it is unintentional. There is no Rabelaisian humor in Amory.

The *Memoirs* were never finished. Amory had planned to extend them to eight volumes and have them include everything new and curious that had happened to him, beginning with 1729, when he began to travel over England just after the trial of his friend, the unhappy "Tom" Woolston. In the two volumes completed the reader meets several interesting women—Marinda, who could read Greek and Latin, pretty Carola Chawcer and Elise Janson, whose head was turned by D'Urfé and La Calprenède—both girls were converted to deism—and the widow Schomberg, who was fond of acting a part in *Tartuffe*. With these and other intellectual charmers Amory sets sail from Crawford Dike for a trip through the Hebrides. They meet a nun who is easily converted to the religion of nature and another with whom they can do nothing because of her mystical enthusiasm. A hermit who lives on a rocky isle and dresses like a Turk tells of his unhappy romance and shows the heart of his dead Belvidere in a box. The ladies become frightened when they lose their way in a great cavern, and they find many Roman monuments and coins. The groves about the Druid temples had been cut down long ago, but the sacred circles are still visible.

Now a mighty storm blows the voyagers through the Straits of Gibraltar, and they are forced to put in at St. Nicholas in the Cape Verde Islands. Here the natives find it easy to embrace deism because it is much more like their old native religion than the Catholicism which had been forced upon them. Sailing back to the north, the voyagers discover Mrs. Harcourt's deistic Utopia on Green Island and listen to the happy ladies of the community sing an oratorio. It is a place of idyllic beauty. Later the party visits the noble peasants in the Black Bay of Scalpa and finds that their religion is of the purest kind and therefore much like deism.

Amory dropped the *Memoirs* at this point. However, *John Buncle* is really a continuation of them, with the difference that the author, instead of being a mere observer, gets right into the middle of things by becoming the chief character and marrying a series of heroines, some of them doubtless ladies whom he had intended to put into the *Memoirs*. This shift brought with it the danger of making Buncle a faithless, heartless widower continually discarding his mourning to don a wedding suit, and losing all too soon after each wife's demise all recollection of his last mate and any idea of being faithful to her memory. This danger the author does not entirely escape. On each sad occasion Buncle shows his sorrow in bizarre fashion by refraining from speaking or by closing his eyes for a long

time, but this is not very convincing. As for the plea that his physical exuberance (and his need for funds) make a new mate necessary—that seems unfeeling, selfish, and unheroic.

Regardless of what the readers might think, in Buncle's hour of need Providence always leads him to a paragon of beauty and learning who is also, *mirabile dictu,* an heiress. Buncle, with his German flute under his arm and his pipe in his mouth, usually approaches her abode from the rear or side, never in the usual formal way. Often he finds the charmer alone. Sometimes she is guarded by an old, gray-haired father—once by a skeleton leaning over a table—but never by a mother who might counsel or warn, or by a male strong enough to stand in the way. In other words, it is a dream world where the ladies are as accessible as houris in the Mohammedan heaven. So Buncle approaches, proposes, is accepted, inherits, husbands it for a while, and then takes his mate to the cemetery.

In general the routine is the same, but the wives differ and so do the circumstances. The case of the heiress Agnes Dunk is the strangest, for she died before Buncle married her and came alive again after he had kept her in her coffin for seven days, according to the custom of the old Romans. Her body was picked up and brought in a hamper to the laboratory of Dr. Stanvil. At the touch of Stanvil's scalpel she revived. Not only that, but the doctor married her, and this put Buncle out a great deal because he had to wait until Agnes became a widow before he could take his turn at marrying her.

There is a typical deistic villain, a false devotee, in the story of the beautiful courtesan, Carola Bennet, with whom Curll made Buncle acquainted while the "splay-footed and baker-kneed" printer was showing his guest the night cellars in the Covent Garden district. The villain is Carola's aunt, a woman who was always meticulous in the observance of all the external practices of religion and often affected the "holy goggle," but who sells Carola to a licentious fellow for £500. After this rascal abandons her, the aunt forces her to become a kept mistress. At heart Carola is really virtuous. She gives alms to the poor and when she can lives chastely. Finally an exceptionally broadminded, forgiving, and wealthy clergyman weds her and takes her to his country seat in Devonshire. Of special interest too are the vivid sketches of Curll[3] and Jack Gallaspy, the Irish rapist who smoked two pipes at once, slept only every third night, "fought everything, whored everything, and drank seven in a hand."

Although most of Buncle's time is taken up in wooing and burying his eight wives, he still finds abundant opportunity for discoursing upon his favorite subjects and describing the scenery of mountain, valley, and lake. All the critics have pointed out the novelty and importance of Amory's landscapes with their mag-nified dimensions and romantic features. Mary Collyer had made a modest start in landscape description, but she made no attempt to magnify proportions. Amory's romanticizing of his landscapes was at least in part due to the examples of awe-inspiring and wonderful scen-ery he found in Bishop Pontoppidan's *Natural History of Norway,* which appeared in English in 1755.[4] Amory, appropriating as much of this Norwegian grandeur as he thought he could make profitable use of, transferred it to the Fell District of England, that is, to the borders of Lancashire, Yorkshire, Westmoreland, Durham, and Cumberland. Instead of reducing the scale to the rela-tively modest proportions of the English mountains, valleys, and lakes, he stretched these to fit the more romantic and magnificent Norwegian model. Thus, almost the first English romantic landscapes are large-ly imitations of Norwegian scenes.

Buncle tells us that beyond the wild scenery which "harrowed the soul with horror" he discovered another deistic Utopia, "a female republic of a hundred souls" led by the beautiful and brilliant Azora. To bring his medley to an end Amory explains how Buncle con-verted his father to deism, and having buried his last wife, sailed for a nine-years' voyage through the West Indies, and then retired to a "little, flowery retreat [he] had purchased within a few miles of London." This was, of course, Amory's place in Hounslow, and is another indication of how closely he identified himself with Buncle.

John Buncle attracted much attention. In his *Anec-dotes and Egoisms* Henry Mackenzie called it "a strange extravagant novel then much admired,"[5] and it helped James Lackington, proprietor of the famous bookshop in Finsbury Square and author of the *Memoirs* (1791), to shake off the shackles of Methodist "enthusiasm." Smollett gave the first volume a nine-page review in the *Critical.* The writer of the article, doubtless Smollett himself, did not like the book, called it a "very surprising performance," twitted Amory for his heterodoxy, and concluded with a parody on his style, which begins: "Mr. *John Buncle,* then, the *lepid rural-ist,* is, *without all peradventure,* the most *doleful* jumble of *miscellany thoughts, replications,* and *hair-ing, staring diabolism* that was ever *posited* in the *sensory* of a man's head."[6] Amory had this article in mind when he wrote in the preface to the second part of *Buncle:* "I imagine, then, that all critics (except the *Critical Review*) will wink at the blemishes of a laud-able writing." Again in the body of the book he assert-ed that Voltaire wrote the history of England with a "partiality and malevolence almost as great as Smol-lett's."[7] In later years Lamb, Hazlitt, and Hunt praised *John Buncle.*

It was more popular than the *Memoirs.*[8] Dr. Thomas Cogan, the freethinking man-midwife, provided John

Buncle with a son in *John Buncle, Junior, Gentleman* (1776), which is purported to be a memoir written by Miss Dunk. The younger Buncle has undergone the influence of Sterne, and as a sentimentalist of the newer mode describes his father as "such a Bigot for *enlarged sentiments,* and so furious for *moderation,* that he would often be tempted to *damn* a man for want of charity." Not much happens to young Buncle on his sentimental journey, the novel unfortunately being chiefly com-posed of moral and philosophical disquisitions.

Notes

[1] Part I was published in 1756 and Part II in 1766.

[2] Forster's letters to Gough are in Nichol's *Illustra-tions of the Literary History of the Eighteenth Century* (1817), v, 314-315.

[3] Amory has Buncle (II, 383) say that Curll "lost his ears for the *Nun in her Smock,* and another thing," and describes him as underpaying the poor Grubstreet hacks who wrote his books, and lodging his translators at the Pewter Platter in Holborn, where they slept three in a bed.

[4] See H. V. Hong, *Thomas Amory: Eccentric Literary Philosopher,* University of Minnesota dissertation (1938).

[5] Ed. H. W. Thompson (London, 1927), p. 81.

[6] *Critical Review,* II (1756), 219-227.

[7] II, 115-116.

[8] The *Memoirs* were reprinted in 1769 and *John Bun-cle* in 1770 and several times in the nineteenth centu-ry. There was a shortened version entitled *The Spirit of Buncle, or the surprising Adventures of that original and extraordinary character, John Buncle, Esq.* pub-lished in 1823. This was reprinted at least four times.

G. L. Jones (essay date 1966-67)

SOURCE: "Lessing and Amory," in *German Life and Letters,* Vol. 20, 1966-67, pp. 298-306.

[*In the following excerpt, Jones presents an overview of* The Life of John Buncle, Esq., *in the context of a larger discussion of German dramatist Gotthold Less-ing's interest in Amory's theological thought.*]

Lessing's interest in Thomas Amory's novel, *The Life of John Buncle, Esq.* (1756, 1766), can be traced back to his early months in Wolfenbüttel. In a letter to his brother Karl, dated November 11th, 1770, he writes that it was Mendelssohn who first drew his attention to this work:

Vor allen Dingen bitte ich Dich, Herrn Moses zu ersuchen, dass er mir die zwei versprochenen Bücher schickt. Wenn er nicht Zeit hat, so lass Dir sie nur von ihm geben, und sende sie mir mit der ersten fahrenden Post. Es ist John Bunckel [*sic*], oder wie er sich schreibt, und Ferguson. Auf den ersten hat er mich gar zu neugierig gemacht, und den andern möchte ich auch gern lieber englisch als deutsch lesen.[1]

Although there are five further references to Amory's novel in Lessing's letters, its significance for him has never been fully considered. Reasons for this neglect are not difficult to find. The fact that Lessing's first reference to **John Buncle** occurs in the same sentence as a reference to Ferguson has probably led many critics to concentrate on the latter at the expense of the former. Perhaps, too, the nature of Amory's novel, its interminable and verbose discussions of almost every conceivable subject, has discouraged many commentators from devoting any time to it. Amory's reputation, his alleged insanity,[2] might also be an explanatory factor in this general neglect. The very fact, however, that Lessing's references to **John Buncle** span almost a decade, should have merited for it some attention. Furthermore, when one considers how decisive these years at Wolfenbüttel were in the development of Lessing's theological thought, this neglect of even a minor work is surprising. Above all, his intention in 1771 to translate Amory's novel, and his subsequent revision of his attitude towards it fully justify an examination of its significance for him.

The hero of Amory's novel is an Englishman who was born in Ireland at the beginning of the eighteenth century. The book is a record of everything he thought worth noticing, 'as men and matters, books and circumstances, came in my way'.[3] Amory stresses the scholarly, ethical and aesthetic aims of his work at the very outset:

> . . . all the relations, the thoughts, the observations, are designed for the advancement of valuable Learning, and to promote whatsoever things are true, whatsoever things are honest, whatsoever things are just, whatsoever things are pure, whatsoever things are lovely, whatsoever things are of good report.[4]

Stylistically, the book has little to recommend it. The many descriptive passages are couched in a language which is both hackneyed and repetitive. The conversations recorded consist mostly of a long oration by one character, followed by an equally long rejoinder by another. Neither Buncle nor his creator is blessed to any great extent with the gift of humour. Hazlitt's praise of Amory as a humorous writer can hardly be borne out by an examination of the novel:

> The soul of Francis Rabelais passed into John Amory [*sic*], the author of *The Life and Adventures of John Buncle* [*sic*]. Both were physicians, and enemies of too much gravity. Their great business was to enjoy life.[5]

If the reader is amused, it will not be by a conscious endeavour on Amory's part to be humorous, but rather by the solemnity with which he allows Buncle to record the most ludicrous of observations. However, it cannot be denied that Amory's hero, though he lacks humour, is decidedly eccentric. In this regard Buncle is obviously patterned on Amory himself, who in the Preface to the novel declares that he would not take exception to the words, 'Here lies an odd man',[6] being written as an epitaph on his grave-stone. It is clear from this Preface that Amory deliberately sought to cultivate this eccentricity and to endow his hero with it.

After completing his studies in Dublin, Buncle returned to his paternal home. There the coldness shown to him by his step-mother and the hostility of his orthodox father to his anti-trinitarian views led Buncle to leave Ireland and set out for England, ostensibly in search of a former schoolfriend. Buncle's ignorance of the latter's precise address enables him to wander for years in the North of England and to make occasional visits to London. In the course of the novel Buncle marries seven times, and each time his nuptial bliss is rudely curtailed by the sudden death of his wife. In between such remarkable matrimonial occurrences Buncle is able to expatiate on innumerable subjects, ranging from algebra to sea-shells. Towards the end of the novel Buncle returns to Ireland and is encouraged to find that though his father is on the brink of death, the old man has changed his views on religion. Thanks to some manuscripts Buncle left at home, his father dies as strict a Unitarian as himself. After voyaging around the world for the next nine years, Buncle eventually settles down to a contented life of rest and reflection in 'a little flowery retreat' near London. There he passed the remainder of his time away in 'rational amusements'.[7]

In spite of Buncle's supposedly high ethical aim in recording his life-history, the inconsistencies between his theoretical views on morals and his own behaviour are very obvious. For a man who can deliver eloquent orations on the vanity of worldly things, Buncle's zest for life is astounding. Shortly after apostrophizing temperance, for example, as the 'preserver and restorer of health, and the protracter of life . . . the maintainer of the dignity and liberty of rational beings',[8] Buncle, waking one morning 'very ill from having drank too hard the preceding night', is obliged to ride a few miles to Oldfield-Spa, as 'I had heard an extraordinary account of its usefulness after a debauch'.[9] Furthermore, throughout the novel he entertains his reader with accounts of the varying repasts he enjoys, usually at the expense of others. Nothing apparently can destroy

Buncle's appetite. Even the presence of two poor wretches, one a dying man and the other a victim of consumption, does not deter him from dispatching with a fine appetite 'a pound of rump steaks, and a quart of green peas; two cuts of bread, a tankard of strong beer, and a pint of port wine'.[10] His inconsistency is most apparent in the explanations he offers for his many marriages. A favourite argument he advances for marriage is that, by procreating, man is fulfilling the divine will. Thus, for instance, he persuades the twenty-year-old Statia Henley to become his second wife by warning her not to commit 'a great crime' against God by hindering 'the regular propagation of a species, which God hath declared to be under his particular inspection and blessing'.[11] A virgin, he argues, who refuses to marry is guilty of murder in so far as she prevents succeeding generations from attaining perfect bliss. Buncle concludes his argument with a proposal of marriage:

> And may I hope to have the high honour of sharing in the mutual satisfaction that must attend the discharge of so momentous a duty?[12]

It is on account of this argument that Buncle, the zealous opponent of monasticism, can admire the Ivonites, a religious society of married people:

> Their days are spent in piety and usefulness; and at night, after the 'completorium', they lie down together in the most heavenly charity, and according to the first great hail, endeavour to increase and multiply. This is a divine life. I am for a cloyster on these terms. It pleased me so much to see these *monks* march off with their smiling partners, after the last psalm, that I could not help wishing for a charmer there, that I might commence the *Married Regular,* and add to the stock of children in this holy house. It is really a fine thing to *monk* it on this plan. It is a divine institution: gentle and generous, useful and pious.[13]

Not content with marrying seven times, Buncle also endeavours to provide suitable wives for others who are less fortunate than himself. Thus, for example, he offers to find for one Avery Moncton, a man whose initial experience of the marital state proved disastrous, 'a primitive Christian of a woman, with all the beauties of body that *Lucian* gives his images'.[14] It need hardly surprise the reader that eventually Buncle turns to him and advises him to marry:

> My dear Reader, if you are unmarried, and healthy, get a wife as soon as possible, some charming girl, or pretty widow, adorned with modesty, robed with meekness, and who has the grace to attract the soul, and heighten every joy continually;—take her to thy breast, and bravely, in holy wedlock, propagate.[15]

Buncle, who confesses that he was born with the 'disease of repletion' (2, p. 483), is so concerned to carry out the divine edict that should he live for ages, and should he lose such partners as he has described, he would, he declares, 'with rapture take hundreds of them to my breast, one after another, and piously propagate the kind'.[16] Consistent with his belief in the divine institution of marriage are his frequent attacks on celibacy and prostitution, both of which he denounces in their varying ways as incompatible with the will of God.

From this religious standpoint Buncle's marriages appear not merely excusable but positively laudable. It soon becomes apparent, however, that he is motivated by something far less awe-inspiring than a profound desire to fulfil the will of God, namely, financial considerations. Soon after the death of his first wife, for instance, Buncle sets out to see if he can find another 'good country girl for a wife, and get a little money'. These two things, he explains, could alone secure him from melancholy and confer on him real happiness. The incompatibility of these two reasons for marrying does not apparently worry him. He can write happily of them at one and the same time (2, pp. 165-6). Indeed, it even seems dubious as to which he deems the more important. On one occasion he does not marry one of the two young ladies whom he has freed from the care of their cruel guardian, because they are minors and 'if such a wife died under age, I could be no gainer, and might have children to maintain without any fortune'.[17]

For a man who is so anxious to ensure the survival of the species, Buncle has scarcely anything to say about his children. This omission is, however, not fortuitous, as he himself hastens to assure us. He has, of course, had a great many children 'to carry on the succession', but does not feel constrained to relate anything about them because they 'never did any remarkable things'.[18] Thus, the reader is left to muse how such an eccentric father could produce such uninteresting offspring.

It would appear from Lessing's initial references to the novel that it was Buncle's eccentricity which first attracted him. Thus Lessing calls him 'the foolish fellow'—'der närrische Kerl'[19]—and a month later he is imploring Nicolai to send the novel to him, stressing that Buncle is the kind of companion he needs in his loneliness.[20] We know that Lessing intended to translate Amory's novel, and yet before the end of the same year (1771) he is already dissuading his brother Karl from attempting such a translation. The change in Lessing's attitude is explained in a letter which he wrote to Nicolai on March 30th, 1779. A translation of Amory's novel had eventually been published by Nicolai in 1778 (*Leben und Meinungen Johann Bunkels*), and had provoked a caustic review by Wieland, entitled *Die Bunkliade oder Die Quintessenz aus Johann*

Bunkels Leben, Bemerkungen und Meinungen (1778), in which he denounced the work as a literary, theological and moral monstrosity. Wieland compared Nicolai's annotated translation to a feast, consisting of numerous indigestible, obnoxious, badly prepared foods; beside the dishes containing these foods were placed packets of powder and glasses of medicine so that the guests could avail themselves at once of the necessary antidote. In defence of his translation Nicolai had written to Lessing and asked whether he could mention the fact that Lessing himself intended to translate Amory's novel in 1771. Lessing, in refusing Nicolai's request, pointed out that such a disclosure would oblige him to explain his position and thus, in all probability, cast a derogatory light on **Buncle**. Lessing then goes on to outline his explanation:

> . . . als ich ihn (*Buncle*) vor zwölf Jahren übersetzen wollte, war ich gutherzig genug zu glauben, dass ich mit Verbreitung des darin enthaltenen Systems der christlichen Religion einen grossen Dienst erweisen könne. So gutherzig bin ich nun nicht mehr; sondern wenn ich ihn noch itzt übersetzen müsste und wollte, würde es gerade in der gegenstehenden Absicht geschehen: um überall in beigefügten Anmerkungen zu zeigen, dass das Arianische System noch unendlich abgeschmackter und lästerlicher ist, als das orthodoxe.[21]

What are Buncle's beliefs, which Lessing came to reject so strongly? The hero of the novel had been sent to the university by his orthodox father in order to become 'a *theologer* . . . and an able defender of the *Creed of St Athanasius*'.[22] Contrary to his father's plan, however, Buncle became in Dublin a 'Christian deist', and thus, on his return home refused to preach the 'mystery' of the Trinity and so 'enflame the people against *reason,* that traitor to God and religion, which our adversaries, the Christian deists, would make Lord and King in opposition to *faith*'.[23] As far as Buncle's orthodox father was concerned, reason was 'a carnal sensual devil', a 'tempter' which had no role to play in religious belief:

> It is the glory of *orthodox Christians,* that their faith is not only contrary to the carnal mind, but even to the *most exalted reason.* In matters of faith, we must renounce our reason, even tho' it be the only thing that distinguishes us from the beasts, and makes us capable of any religion at all.[24]

Buncle himself cannot accept revelation which is incomprehensible to human reason. For him 'an act of faith is an act of reason, and an act of reason an act of faith, in religious matters'.[25]

The most irrational element in orthodox Christianity, so Buncle argues, is belief in the Trinity, 'the dreadful heresy of three Gods' (1, p. 500 n. 44). He is indefatigable in his attacks on 'the horrible *creed of*

Athanasius (2, p. 435), the 'Athanasian jumble' (2, p. 325), 'the miserable invention of divines' (1, p. 379), and on those so-called teachers of Christianity, a thousand of whom he has heard 'on this *holy topic, sweating* and *drivelling* at each *corner* of their mouths with eagerness to convert the world to *their mysteries*' (2, p. 511). Indeed, his detestation of this doctrine is only matched by his hatred of the Church of Rome, 'the licentious whore' (2, p. 116 n. 8), 'the religion of hell' (2, p. 134 n. 10), and of 'all the diabolism of popery' (1, p. 344).

Of what, then, does the religion of John Buncle, Christian deist and unitarian, consist? The most complete statement of his religion is found towards the end of the novel, when Amory, addressing the preachers of his day, writes:

> . . . the *true Christian profession* is, to *pray to God our Father for grace, mercy, and peace, through the Lord Jesus Christ;* without ever mentioning the *Athanasian scheme.* . . . And in the next place, to tell your *flocks* in serious and practical address, that their *main business* is, as the *disciples* of the *holy Jesus,* a *good life;*—to *strive against sin* continually, and be *virtuous* and *useful* to the utmost of our power;—to *imitate* the *purity* and *goodness* of their *great master* (*the Author of eternal salvation to all them* that obey him); and by *repentance* and *holiness of heart, in a patient continuance in well-doing,* make it the labour of their every day, to *live soberly, righteously,* and *godly* in this present world: You must become *partakers of a divine nature, having escaped the corruption* that is in the world through lust, and by acquiring the *true principles* of *Christian perfection,* render yourselves *fit* for the *heavenly bliss.* . . . This, my dearly beloved brethren, is the great design of *Christ* and his *gospel.*[26]

What meaning, however, can such terms as grace, mercy, salvation have in a religion which claims to contain nothing which transcends reason? What role does revelation, and particularly the revelation in Jesus Christ, play in a religion, the moral tenets of which are easily comprehended by human reason, untainted by the Fall? These questions are discussed frequently throughout the novel, and the answer given is always the same. Jesus Christ, it is argued, came into the world to restore and republish the law of nature; revelation restored the dictates of reason which had over the centuries 'been darkened by the clouds of error and a general corruption'. Added to this, the revelation through Jesus Christ 'gives better evidence for the truth and certainty of life and immortality than nature before had given'.[27]

The reader cannot help feeling that, in spite of the distinction which Amory seeks to make between natural religion and Christianity, the difference between the two is negligible. It is probably this identification between revelation and reason which Lessing found most unacceptable in *John Buncle*. He discusses this problem in his comments on Reimarus's *Erstes Fragment: Von der Verschreiung der Vernunft auf den Kanzeln* (1777). Here Lessing contrasts the ease with which those theologians could be answered who attacked reason, with the difficulty of opposing those who identify reason and faith and denounce opponents of revelation as opponents of common sense. Elsewhere he writes of the 'new-fashioned' theology which has torn down the dividing wall between religion and philosophy:

> Man reisst diese Scheidewand nieder, und macht uns unter dem Vorwande, uns zu vernünftigen Christen zu machen, zu höchst unvernünftigen Philosophen.[28]

John Buncle's religious views belong clearly to the category of this new theology, this 'Mistjauche', as Lessing called it.

If Lessing really did reject Buncle's religious standpoint, why was he critical of Wieland's scathing condemnation of Amory's novel? There are two reasons for Lessing's attitude. Firstly, *John Buncle* had been proscribed by the Imperial Book Commission.[29] Lessing, whose own writings had been censored in 1778, probably realized, as Franz Mehring[30] has pointed out, that Wieland's criticism could be construed by the authorities as a confirmation of and justification for their action. Lessing believed that if clarity was to be attained in religious matters, then freedom of speech was an essential prerequisite. The official suppression of such books as *John Buncle*, however hostile to orthodox Christianity they might be, was an obstacle in the path towards this clarity. Furthermore, the proscribing of the novel proved that the intolerance towards Arians and Socinians, and all reasonable worshippers of God, to which Reimarus had drawn attention, and which Lessing believed no longer existed, was being rekindled. Secondly, however justified Wieland's denunciation was, Lessing argued that it could still exercise a detrimental effect on some people. Amory's arguments might not possess any absolute validity, and yet, for certain people they could represent a necessary stage in the process of enlightenment. In denouncing the novel, Wieland may have deprived such people of an essential rung in the ladder of enlightenment. . . .

It was merely coincidental that Lessing began to take an interest in the work of Ferguson and Amory at the same time. *An Essay on the History of Civil Society* (1767) and *John Buncle* have nothing in common; nor can they be compared in terms of the influence they exerted on Lessing's thought. To the former he owed an important stimulus for his final treatise on religion, to the latter nothing more than the dubious pleasure of making the acquaintance of a fanatic eccentric. Yet, in Lessing's attitude to *John Buncle* can be seen a concrete example of that profound tolerance which he advocated so strongly in *Die Erziehung des Menschengeschlechts.*

Notes

[1] Lessing, *Gesammelte Werke,* Herausgegeben von Paul Rilla (Aufbau-Verlag, Berlin, 1954-58) vol. IX, p. 387.

[2] *Dictionary of National Biography* (London, 1885) vol. 1, p. 365.

[3] Amory, *The Life of John Buncle, Esq.* (vol. 1, London, 1756; vol. 2, London, 1766), vol. 1, p. 1.

[4] Ibid., vol. 1, p. 2.

[5] Hazlitt, *The Round Table* (no. 14, Sept. 17th, 1815); *Collected Works,* edited by Waller and Glover (London, 1902), vol. 1, p. 52.

[6] Amory, op. cit., Preface, p. ix.

[7] Ibid., vol. 2, p. 527.

[8] Ibid., vol. 2, p. 144.

[9] Ibid., vol. 2, p. 171.

[10] Ibid., vol. 2, p. 335.

[11] Ibid., vol. 2, p. 46.

[12] Ibid., vol. 2, p. 48.

[13] Ibid., vol. 2, pp. 57-8.

[14] Ibid., vol. 2, p. 366.

[15] Ibid., vol. 2, p. 372.

[16] Ibid., vol. 2, p. 484.

[17] Ibid., vol. 2, p. 203.

[18] Ibid., vol. 2, p. 137.

[19] Lessing, Brief an Mendelssohn, 9 Jan., 1771, *Werke,* vol. IX, p. 409.

[20] Lessing, Brief an Nicolai, 16 Febr., 1771, ibid., p. 417.

[21] Lessing, Brief an Nicolai, 30 März, 1779, ibid., p. 827.

[22] Amory, op. cit., vol. 1, p. 376.

[23] Ibid., vol. 1, p. 376.

[24] Ibid., vol. 1, pp. 377-8.

[25] Ibid., vol. 1, p. 379.

[26] Ibid. vol., 2, p. 510 n. 24.

[27] Ibid., vol. 1, p. 451.

[28] Lessing, Brief an Karl Lessing, 2 Febr., 1774, *Werke*, vol. IX, p. 597.

[29] Lessing, Brief an Nicolai, 30 März, 1779, ibid., p. 828.

[30] Franz Mehring, *Die Lessing-Legende* (Stuttgart, 1909), p. 386.

Ian Campbell Ross (essay date 1983)

SOURCE: "Thomas Amory, *John Buncle,* and the Origins of Irish Fiction," *Éire-Ireland: A Journal of Irish Studies,* Vol. XVIII, No. 3, 1983, pp. 71-85.

[*In the following essay, Ross suggests that* The Life of John Buncle, Esq. *derives from traditional Irish oral storytelling, noting particularly the work's reliance on anecdote, elements of fantasy, and its distinctive, eccentric narrator.*]

At the centre of Irish fiction is the anecdote.[1]

Thomas Amory's **The Life of John Buncle, Esq.,** published in two parts in 1756 and 1766, has for two centuries held an uneasy position on the fringes of the English literary tradition. Never widely read after its initial success, it has never lacked admirers either. Early reviewers responded uneasily, at once amused and bemused. Even the novel's subtitle, promising "Various Observations and Reflections, Made in several Parts of the World, and many extraordinary relations," does little to prepare readers for the story to follow. **John Buncle** is the tale, told by himself, of an Irish Unitarian, eight times married, who leaves Ireland to travel the north country of England and who, during the two decades of exploring and celebrating the sublime landscape he discovers there, meets with a bewildering array of Irish friends—many living in Utopian communities—to whom he discourses with equal eloquence and engagement on topics as varied as fluxions and the Spanish fly, monogamy and microscopes, together with a vast range of matters, both antiquarian and modern, of particularly Irish interest.

In 1756, both the *Monthly Review* and the *Critical Review* acknowledged the general interest of **John Buncle** by devoting exceptionally long notices to it—sixteen and nine pages respectively. Amory's book was successful enough to warrant the publication of the second part ten years later and a complete edition in four volumes appeared in 1770.[2] In the 19th century it was prized as a curiosity by, among others, Leigh Hunt and William Hazlitt, who termed Amory "our English Rabelais."[3] Republished in the early years of this century, it has more recently been called a "riotous compendium" by a critic who suggested that if anything like it were to appear nowadays "it would be judged a characteristic product of some *avant-garde* American novelist not yet middle-aged and living west of the Rockies."[4]

If **John Buncle** has always seemed peripheral to the tradition of the English novel, however, it is neither because Amory's book is, as George Saintsbury argued,—entirely *sui generis* nor because, as Saintsbury and most other 19th-century critics comfortably opined, its author was mad. **The Life of John Buncle, Esq.** has, quite simply, little to do with the English tradition in its narrow sense. It is, rather, an early attempt at a novel in English by an Irish writer: a novel founded on anecdote, one which exploits a rich and rewarding seam of fantasy and which, in addition, throws some light on the origins of Irish fiction.

John Buncle is one of the first Irish novels to insist on the importance of Ireland itself to the fiction:

> As to some strange things you will find in the following journal; and a life, in various particulars, quite contrary to the common course of action, I can assure you, gentlemen, in respect of the strange things, that however wonderful they may appear to you, yet they are, exclusive of a few decorations and figures, (necessary in all works), strictly true: and as to the difference of my life, from that of the generality of men, let it only be considered, that I was born in London, and carried an infant into Ireland, where I learned the Irish language, and became intimately acquainted with its original inhabitants. . . . [5]

For its time, the passage is startling but problematic also. Who, precisely, is speaking in this preface? Thomas Amory or John Buncle? Confusion between the two has been apparent since Amory's own lifetime. The author's son, Robert Amory, spoke in 1788 of "my father (John Buncle) Thomas Amory, esq."[6] In his *The Round Table* essay, Hazlitt wrote simply and symptomatically of "John Amory." More than a century later, Katharine A. Esdaile, in the optimistically entitled "The Real Thomas Amory" did much the same at greater length.[7]

What little biographical material concerning Thomas Amory we have comes from two principal sources: an article in the *St. James's Chronicle* of November 6,

1788, partly reprinted in *The Gentleman's Magazine* that same year, and a brief, though acerbic, correspondence, also in *The Gentleman's Magazine,* between Amory's son and one Louis Renas. This exchange, which strangely took place while the author was still alive—though in his ninety-seventh year—does little to answer with certainty even the most basic questions about Amory. It seems probable, though, that he was born in 1691 into a family which had settled in Ireland in the 17th century and which owned extensive lands in County Clare.[8] It is likely, also, that Amory spent most of his childhood, youth, and early adulthood in Ireland, principally in Clare and Dublin. Trinity College, Dublin, figures prominently enough in *John Buncle* to suggest that Amory knew it well and had perhaps, like Buncle, studied there, but there is no record that he did so. At some unknown date, Amory left Ireland to settle in London where, in 1755, he published the earlier of his two major works, **Memoirs of Several Ladies of Great Britain,** a fiction which gives first evidence of his interest in Gaelic culture. He died on November 25, 1788.[9]

Whatever the precise extent of Amory's experience of Ireland, his knowledge of the Irish language, and his acquaintance with the island's "original inhabitants," the importance of all these to **John Buncle** is both clear and considerable. Not merely in what is said, however, but in how it is said does Amory's novel reveal its Irish origins. A brief passage will serve as an example:

> As I travelled once in the county of *Kerry* in *Ireland,* with the *White Knight,* and the *Knight of the Glin* (22), we called at *Terelah O Crohanes,* an old Irish gentleman, our common friend, who kept up the hospitality of his ancestors, and shewed how they lived, when *Cormac Mac Cuillenan,* the *Generous,* (from whose house he descended) was king of *Munster,* and *Archbishop* of *Cashel,* in the year 913 (23). There was no end of eating and drinking there, and the famous *Downe Falvey* played on the harp. For a day and a night we sat to it by candlelight, without shirts or cloaths on; naked, excepting that we had our breeches and shoes and stockings on; and I drank so much burgundy in that time, that the sweat ran of a red colour down my body; and my senses were so disordered, that when we agreed to ride out for a couple of hours to take a little air, I leaped my horse into a dreadful quarry, and in the descent was thrown into a large deep water that was in a part of the frightful bottom, and by that means saved my life. When I came above water, I swam very easily out of the pit, and walked up the low side of the quarry as sober as if I had not drank a glass. This is a fact, whatever the critics may say of the thing. All I can say to it is, my hour was not come.
>
> (I, 288-92)

The first remarkable fact in this passage for the modern reader is that we find an Anglo-Irish view of the Gaelic aristocracy in the first half of the 18th century.

There are glimpses of peasant society elsewhere in mid-18th-century Irish fiction[10] but perhaps no earlier view of the other end of the social spectrum in an Irish novel. Certainly the self-portrait of a fictional hero travelling and living on equal terms with members of the Gaelic aristocracy has no obvious fictional precedent and anticipates both Maria Edgeworth and Lady Morgan by almost half a century.

The easy comparison with these writers, though, suggests a more striking feature of the passage: its unambivalent celebration of the scene it portrays. Here, as elsewhere, Amory's book has little in common with the dewy-eyed sentiment of Sydney Morgan's *The Wild Irish Girl* or the prim disapproval of Maria Edgeworth's account of King Corny and the Black Islands in *Ormond.* Indeed, it has much more in common with contemporary descriptions in Irish of life in the big houses, whether Gaelic or Planter in Gaelic areas, in the work of such 18th-century poets as Aodhagán Ó Rathaille or Seán Clárach Mac Domhnaill.[11] The reader will also notice the brief antiquarian aside as Buncle establishes the genealogy of his host's family and provides some general information concerning Cormac Mac Cuillenan.[12]

Quite apart from its content, however, the passage is remarkable for being pure anecdote. The opening formula—"As I travelled once in the county of *Kerry* in *Ireland*"—has numerous counterparts in **John Buncle:** "When I was a little boy in *Dublin*" (II, 3), "As I travelled once in the county of *Kildare* in *Ireland*" (II, 156), "when I was a young fellow" (II, 186), and so on. In these cases, as elsewhere, what follows is a self-contained and frequently fantastic tale avowedly based on personal experience. Such tales, moreover, invariably suggest the storyteller's acute sense of a present audience. The result is a book quite different from the typical 18th-century novel in the guise of fictional autobiography.[13]

What was unusual in the contemporary English novel, though, would soon be familiar enough in the Irish fictional tradition. In **John Buncle,** as in many subsequent Irish novels, we note the "imitation of a speaking voice engaged in the telling of a tale."[14] Given the particular emphasis the hero places in his preface on his Irish upbringing—on his knowledge of Irish and of Ireland's "original inhabitants"—it may not be unreasonable to suggest that Amory's debt to Irish oral narrative is a specific one.

The particular form of tale on which Amory repeatedly draws is *seanchas.* Whereas the *scéal* is acknowledged by teller and audience to be fiction—its events far removed from those of everyday life—the events related in *seanchas* are alleged by the storyteller to be true and his audience accepts that they are so. The *seanchaí* insists on the truth of his tale by personally guaranteeing its events: *"Ní scéal scéil atá agam air, nó bhí mé i láthair"* ("My account is no mere hearsay, for I was present"). It is not to be understood for this reason that *seanchas* was actually true; frequently, it owed almost as much to fantasy as did the *scéal*. The conventions under which it operated, however, insisted otherwise. If we understand *seanchas* in this way, we can understand also the nature of many of the anecdotes John Buncle tells us. Like that already quoted—though frequently even more so—these anecdotes are fantastic but the storyteller insists that they are true. It may be difficult to believe, Buncle admits, that in the course of his travels he has buried his bride-to-be, Agnes Dunk, only to meet her again some months later respectably married to a body-snatching doctor who has fortuitously rescued her from an evidently premature grave: "This is a hard account sure. But nevertheless, it is a fact" (II, 422). Such sentiments recur throughout **John Buncle**, the briefest formulation of them occurring towards the end of the first volume: "It is very strange, I confess. It is very true, however" (I, 219).

Through Amory's novel we find what Professor Kilroy has perceived in Irish fiction more generally: "a taste for anecdote, an unshakeable belief in the value of human actions, a belief that life may be adequately uncapsulated into stories that require no reference, no qualification, beyond their own selves."[15] Thus, we have the story of "*Mun. Hawley* of *Loch-Gur* in the county of Tipperary" who is able to "keep at the top of the outwheel of a water-mill, by jumping there, as it goes with the greatest rapidity round":

> He was a charming fellow in body and mind, and fell unfortunately in the 22d year of his age. In a plain field, by a trip of his horse, he came down, and fractured his skull. He did not think he was hurt: but at night as soon as he began to eat, it came up. A surgeon was sent for to look at his head. It was cracked in several places, and he died the next day. He and I were near friends.
>
> (II, 189)

Of John Buncle we might say—*mutatis mutandis*—as of Thady Quirk: "He tells the history of the Rackrent family . . . in the full confidence that Sir Patrick, Sir Murtagh, Sir Kit, and Sir Condy Rackrent's affairs, will be as interesting to all the world as they were to himself."[16]

The affairs of friends and acquaintances, casually related, constitute an important part of John Buncle's tale. Almost to a man or woman such friends and acquaintances are Irish—and not only in Ireland. Like many an Irish writer after him, Buncle discovers that to leave Ireland is not to be free of its influence. What is generally a mental or emotional link, however, is for Buncle more physical. As the hero travels through the

north of England, it frequently seems as though colonization has taken place in reverse. To knock on a door at random is to find it opened by a lady who addresses Buncle in Irish, asks him how he does, and reveals herself to be "*Imoinda*, of the county of *Gallway* in *Ireland;* who was your partner in country dances, when you passed the Christmas of the year 1715, at her father's house" (II, 183). To visit a London *bagnio* is to run into

> . . . an *Irish* gentleman of large fortune, with whom I was well acquainted. He was ever engaged in amours, and was some years after this hanged at *Cork*, for ravishing *Sally Squib*, the quaker.
>
> (II, 389)

For all the very real interest attendant on the accounts of Gaelic society, it is in such anecdotal descriptions, often very extended, of the Anglo-Irish, both at home and in England, that **John Buncle** is strongest. The tale of the "Conniving-house," a public house at Ringsend, for instance, is a vivid evocation of the hero's student days.[17] A chance encounter at Harrogate spa with no fewer than six companions of his youth gives Buncle a further opportunity to recall such times. The opening paragraph gives the general flavor of the much longer episode:

> Among the company I found at this agreeable place, were six *Irish* gentlemen, who had been my contemporaries in Trinity-College, *Dublin*, and were right glad to see me, as we had been Sociorums (a word of *Swift*'s) at the conniving-house at *Ringsend*, for many a summer's evening, and their regard for me was great. . . : These gentlemen were Mr. *Gollogher*, Mr. *Gallaspy*, Mr. *Dunkley*, Mr. *Makins*, Mr. *Monaghan*, and Mr. *O'Keefe*, descended from the *Irish* kings, and first cousin to the great *O'Keefe*, who was buried not long ago in *Westminster* Abby. They were all men of large fortunes, and, Mr. *Makins* excepted, were as handsome, fine fellows as could be picked out in all the world. *Makins* was a very low, thin man, not four feet high, and had but one eye, with which he squinted most shockingly. He wore his own hair, which was short and bad, and only drest by his combing it himself in the morning, without oyl or powder. But as he was matchless on the fiddle, sung well, and chatted agreeably, he was a favourite with the ladies. They preferred ugly *Makins* (as he was called) to many very handsome men. I will here give the public the character of these *Irish* gentlemen, for the honour of *Ireland*, and as they were curiosities of the human kind.
>
> (II, 146-7)

Given the nature of the particular individual Buncle has just described, it might be thought that his avowed motive for writing "for the honour of *Ireland*" makes him a not too distant forebear of Thady Quirk who tells his story *"'for the honor of the family'."*[18]

The irony lurking in Maria Edgeworth's italics and inverted commas, however, has no role in Amory's narrative. If Thady Quirk's tale of the Rackrents finally becomes a celebration in spite of the conscious attitudes of his creator, John Buncle and his creator are at one in their admiration of Ireland and its inhabitants.

This lack of irony has more general importance. Both *Castle Rackrent* and **John Buncle** are founded on the told tale; but, whereas the former demands the reader's perception of the authorial presence behind the narrating voice, no significant distance opens up between the narrator and author of the latter. The respective prefaces of the two fictions indicate perfectly the difference. *Castle Rackrent*'s is an editor's preface and one of the functions of the editor, perhaps the most important, is to place the narrator—"an illiterate old steward"—in relation to the urbane attitudes of the author. The preface to **John Buncle** is avowedly an author's preface, yet the voice which speaks from it is, apparently, identical in every respect to that which narrates the story which follows.[19] Thomas Amory, though, is not as naïve a writer as this apparently total identification with his principal character may make him appear. As much as Maria Edgeworth, Amory was aware that the spoken tale and the embodiment of the tale in a work of prose fiction are by no means one and the same thing. The kind of *novel* that depends on the told tale began as it had to, with a crisis of confidence in the continuance of the oral tradition.

The Life of John Buncle, Esq. could only have been written by a writer brought up in Ireland, and perhaps only by someone who had, indeed, "learned the Irish language, and become intimately acquainted with *(Ireland's)* original inhabitants." Equally certainly, however, **John Buncle** is the product of the century of Berkeley and Locke. In emphasizing the essential points of similarity between Irish oral narrative and the anecdotal narrative of **John Buncle** I have so far ignored certain features of both which may help us better to understand Amory's work and the origins of the Irish novel tradition in English.

The first such feature is the anonymity or otherwise of the storyteller; the second is the implicit claim made by oral culture to complete communication. In the *scéal,* the anonymity of the storyteller is complete. A traditional formula used by the teller of the *sean-scéal* is described by J. H. Delargy: *"Sin é mo sgéal-sa! Má tá bréag ann bíodh! Ní mise a chúm ná a cheap é"* ("That is my story! If there be a lie in it, be it so! It was not I who made or invented it.").[20] *Seanchas,* as we have seen, renounces this anonymity as the *seanchaí* guarantees to his audience the truth of events to which he claims to have been an eyewitness.[21] In the preface to **John Buncle,** Amory goes further and makes explicit the tension between the anonymous narrator of *scéal* and a named individual narrator:

> . . . were it within my power to choose, sure I am, that I would be for ever unknown. But that was impossible. In justice to myself, as before observed, and that tradition might not hand me down, when I am gone, in that variety of bad and foolish characters, which a malice, that knows nothing of me, whispers while I am living; it was necessary I should tell my own story
>
> (I, v-vi)

Throughout the whole of **John Buncle**, there is a greatly increased emphasis on the individuality of the story-teller. It is a commonplace to observe that, of all literary genres, the novel has laid greatest stress on individuality and that, at least initially, it played down its links with traditional imaginative literature. It thus became, in the early 18th century, the distinctive literary embodiment of the philosophical tendency towards individualism which begins with Descrates; is central to Locke's *Essay Concerning Human Understanding;* and which, by 1713, had found expression in Berkeley's confident assertion: "it is an universally received maxim, that *every thing which exists, is particular.*"[22] The emerging novel made individual experience the test of truth; partly for that very reason it adopted, as one of its most favored models, the autobiography. As the title indicates, *The Life of John Buncle, Esq.* is just such a book—a fictional autobiography. Precisely by considering it in this context, however, we can see how unlike contemporary English novels of this kind Amory's work really is. Whereas the more usual 18th-century fictional autobiography takes us from the birth of the narrator to the moment when he or she is writing, **John Buncle**'s narrative is based on the much shorter time-span allowed for by the anecdote. Specific dates are mentioned in the novel—Buncle leaves his father's home for England on May 5, 1725, and England for South America on July 5, 1736, for instance—but these have little importance for our experience as readers. Precisely because he believes that "life may be adequately encapsulated into stories that require no reference, no qualification, beyond their own selves"—precisely, that is, because he believes in the value of the anecdote—Buncle can disregard to a large extent the conventions of contemporary fictional autobiography.

In the opening pages of his **Life,** for instance, Buncle solves the very problem which defeats an exactly contemporary literary hero throughout nine volumes. Tristram Shandy may initially appear a most eccentric narrator, but his quest for a narrative which is at once truthful and linear is soon revealed as exemplary. In Sterne's novel, digressions followed in pursuit of truthfulness disrupt the linear narrative to such an extent that Tristram never succeeds in advancing his story beyond his fifth year. For Buncle, however, the problem which defeats Tristram throughout nine volumes does not exist: "The things of my Childhood are not worth setting down, and therefore I commence my Life from the first month of the seventeenth year of my Age" (I, 3-4). His children Buncle can dispatch with as much ease as his childhood:

> N. B. As I mention nothing of any children by so many wives, some readers may perhaps wonder at this, and therefore, to give a general answer, once for all, I think it sufficient to observe, that I had a great many, to carry on the *succession;* but as they never were concerned in any extraordinary affairs, nor ever did any remarkable things, that I heard of;—only rise and breakfast, read and saunter, drink and eat, it would not be fair, in my opinion, to make any one pay for their history.

> (II, 137)

Yet, for all the ease with which Buncle "solves" these particular narrative problems, the very existence of the qualifications and asides suggests an awareness of the conventional autobiography as much as of the anecdote. The opening words of the novel proper suggest the pressure to commit Buncle's tales to print:

> That the Transactions of my Life, and the observations and reflections I have made on men and things, by sea and land, in various parts of the world, might not be buried in oblivion, and by length of time, blotted out of the Memory of Men, it has been my wont, from the days of my youth to this time, to write down *Memorandums* of every thing I thought worth noticing, as men and matters, books and circumstances, came in my way; and in hopes they may be of some service to my fellow-mortals I publish them.

> (I, i)

We need not dismiss the moralist of the final clause to suggest that the desire for permanency is the principal motive here. Writing preserves experience, says Buncle; print validates that experience, we may add. However much the narrative organization of **John Buncle** reveals Amory's experience of an oral culture, the book itself is self-consciously the product of a typographic culture. The prose fiction of Thomas Amory, like that of other early Irish writers in English who draw on the tradition of the told tale—Edgeworth or Carleton, for instance—implies the imminent demise of that tradition. Thady Quirk may conclude his tale by declaring that "there's nothing but truth in it from beginning to end, that you may depend upon, for where's the use of telling lies about the things which every body knows as well as I do?" but he is nonetheless persuaded to have that tale "committed to writing."[23]

In the *Phaedrus,* Socrates attacks writing, the invention of the Egyptian god Thoth, which, he alleges, "will create forgetfulness in the learners' souls, because they will not use their memories."[24] An oral culture, though, depends not merely on the absence of a written or typographic culture but on the shared belief of those within the culture in its future. The fallibility of such cultures was an 18th-century commonplace. In *Tristram Shandy,* a novel which attaches great importance to the typographic culture to which it belongs, Sterne speaks of the "fatality of things committed to oral tradition."[25] By insisting that print alone guarantees experience, however, Amory not merely reflects the values of his own English-language, typographic culture, but he also anticipates those Gaelic storytellers attracted to the folk-tale collectors of the early 20th century by "the desire to have preserved in writing what had so long lived precariously by memory alone."[26]

John Buncle reveals itself as caught between two cultures in other ways also. Eighteenth-century philosophy emphasized individualism at the expense of a shared tradition of past wisdom and knowledge. In the work of Locke, it questioned also the limits of language and, hence, the possibility of absolute communication. In describing his undergraduate course of study at Trinity College, Dublin, Buncle mentions his admiration for Locke's *Essay Concerning Human Understanding.*[27] The praise is conventional enough for the mid-18th century, but the particular aspect of Locke that Buncle singles out has a peculiar relevance to the book as a whole. Locke, says the hero, "shewed me how greatly true knowledge depended on a right meaning of words and a just significancy of expression" (I, 6). By alluding to Locke in this way, however, Buncle raises doubts in the reader's mind as to the possibility of achieving or communicating "true knowledge." "Well might *Locke* write a chapter upon the imperfections of words," as another fictional autobiographer declared, thereby emphasizing the negative side of Locke's position.[28] Throughout Book II of the *Essay,* Locke does insist on the limitations inherent in language: "From what has been said in the foregoing Chapters, it is easy to perceive, what imperfection there is in Language, and how the very nature of Words, make it almost unavoidable, for many of them to be doubtful and uncertain in their significations."[29] He argues that, although all things that exist are particulars, "*It is impossible, that every particular Thing should have a distinct peculiar Name. . .* [as] it is beyond the Power of humane Capacity to frame and retain distinct Ideas of all the particular Things we meet with. . . ."[30]

Buncle insists on the particularity of his experience throughout his **Life.** Unlike Sterne who, in *Tristram Shandy,* uses Locke to raise themes of the individual's isolation and man's inability to communicate, Amory looks to a tradition which implies that absolute communication is indeed possible. By alluding to Locke as he does in the opening pages of his book, though, Amory invites the reader to question the principle on which that book is apparently based. *John Buncle,* in other words, is founded on the told tale but undermines the tradition on which it rests in three ways. First, it sets Locke against an older and more comforting view of language. Secondly, by its status as autobiography, it questions a tradition which gave value to accumulated and shared experience, and implies, instead, that access to truth is through individual experience alone. Thirdly, by embodying the anecdotal in a printed form, *John Buncle* raises doubts as to the future of the oral tradition on which it draws.

The tension between the rival attractions and claims of two cultures—one oral, the other typographic—is evident throughout Amory's book. The anecdote concerning the hero's visit to Terelah O Crohanes (I, 288-92), extends across five pages because it is heavily footnoted. The footnoted material itself is historical and antiquarian in nature, describing various features of Gaelic society: the aristocracy, the Psalters of Tara and Cashel, the provincial kings of Ireland, the historical importance of Tara as a legislative center, and the written sources of Irish history. Amory was clearly a sympathetic student of Gaelic society, and he introduces, if not always very accurately, a culture of which few English-speaking novel readers can have been more than remotely aware. And Amory is writing, it must be remembered, four years before James Macpherson began to publish *Ossian* and more than forty before the appearance of *The Wild Irish Girl.*

All this information is footnoted, though, and what Hugh Kenner has written of the footnote is relevant here: "The footnote's relation to the passage from which it depends is established wholly by visual and typographic means, and will typically defeat all efforts of the speaking voice to clarify it without visual aid."[31] In reading this section—and this section must stand for the very many similar ones throughout the entire novel—the reader is made simultaneously aware of the temporal and spatial dimensions of *John Buncle,* in the tale and its dependent footnotes respectively. The Gaelic past and the oral culture associated with it are controlled visibly on the page by a culture at once English and typographic.[32]

Yet, throughout John Buncle's narration the storytelling tradition remains stubbornly and very much alive. The fantasy associated with Irish oral narrative, for example, is everywhere present. "I have conversed with nations who live many degrees beyond the poor frozen Laplander. I have travelled among the barbarians who scorch beneath the burning zone" (II, 214), the hero declares, elsewhere assuring us that he has traversed the world from Astrakhan to Peru. In his

extensive travels in the English Lake District, Buncle explores with equal gusto the highest mountains and deepest caves. There, too, he encounters those Utopian communities—most often of beautiful and learned women—whose activities he recounts at length. The coincidence of meeting up with Irish friends in the most desolate of surroundings evokes less surprise than their varied and extraordinary talents. The abilities of one O'Regan, "an Irishman, and dancing master" who could jump repeatedly upon the shoulders of dancers moving in one direction while himself moving in the other, are typically described as "wonderful." Wonderful, too, for the reader, is the succession of beautiful, erudite, and devout Unitarian women Buncle marries. To single out the admirable Irishwoman, Harriet Noel, who first charms the hero with a learned and lengthy discourse on the identity of the language spoken before Babel, or Miss Melmoth, always a good conversationalist, even when the subject is "as it was one evening, the paulo post futurum of a Greek verb" (I, 97-8), is not to deny the exemplary attractions of the composite Miss Spence, who "had the head of *Aristotle,* the *heart* of a *primitive christian,* and the *form* of *Venus de medicis*" (II, 162). Of Buncle's tales and speculations we might say, as Vivian Mercier has remarked of the human, animal, and vegetable decorations of the Book of Kells: "their very multiplicity and the infinitely fertile invention which intertwined them can hardly fail to suggest, at both the conscious and unconscious levels, the infinite fertility and multiplicity of Nature."[33]

The Life of John Buncle, Esq. is an early example of an Irish novel founded on anecdote. It is also, as Kilroy has argued much Irish fiction to be, permeated by fantasy. Above all, it is a novel impossible to understand—as its author insisted in his preface—outside of an Irish context. If Thomas Amory, the contemporary of Locke and Berkeley, questions and seems finally to undermine the oral tradition on which he draws, his book nevertheless remains indebted to that tradition both for narrative organization and for its unambivalent celebration of a world of wonder. The fantasy of *John Buncle* eventually proved too much for some English readers. Of the second part, the *Critical Review* laconically said, in 1766: "This is an unreviewable performance because the nonsense we encounter in perusing it, is unsufferable."[34] The *Monthly Review,* meanwhile, unconsciously paid tribute as much to the Gaelic tradition on which Amory drew as to the book itself: "wild and wonderful as are the stories told by this strange adventurer, and monstrous, and even ridiculous as some of his narrations are, they are *splendidè mendaces.*"[35]

Notes

[1] Thomas Kilroy, "Tellers of Tales," *The Times Literary Supplement,* March 17, 1972, p. 301. At the outset

I wish to acknowledge my debt to Professor Cathal Ó Háinle, of Trinity College, Dublin, who has greatly helped my understanding of Irish oral narrative. The opinions in this essay, however, are my own.

[2] Amory's work was also translated into German as *Leben, Bemerkungen und Meinungen Johann Bunkels* (1778) by F. Nicolai. Thomas Cogan imitated Amory in his *John Buncle, Junior, Gentleman* (1776), which in turn prompted A. Stein's *Geschicte einiger Esel oder Fortsetzung des Lebens und der Meynungen des welt-berühmten J. Bunkels* (1782).

[3] William Hazlitt, "On John Buncle" in *The Round Table* (1817); Leigh Hunt, *A Book for a Corner* (1849). An abridgement of Amory's book, entitled *The Spirit of Buncle,* appeared in 1823, and a new edition, edited by J. H. Burn, in 1825.

[4] *The Life of John Buncle, Esq.,* ed. Ernest A. Baker (London: Routledge, 1904); George Watson, *The Story of the Novel* (London: Macmillan, 1979), p. 7.

[5] Thomas Amory, *The Life of John Buncle, Esq.* (London, 1756, 1766), I, vi-vii. All further references to this edition are given parenthetically in the text, thus: (I, vi-vii).

[6] Robert Amory, in a letter to *The Gentleman's Magazine,* LVIII (1788), 1062.

[7] Katharine A. Esdaile, "The Real Thomas Amory," *Essays and Studies,* XXVI (1940), collected by Arundell Esdaile (Oxford: Clarendon Press, 1941), pp. 45-72. Esdaile was unfortunately unable to discover any new information about her subject, and the "real" Thomas Amory is simply John Buncle shorn of the most outrageously implausible experiences attributed to him. It is necessary to insist on the valuelessness of this essay only because no more reliable account has been attempted in the meanwhile.

[8] The name "Thomas Amory" appears in "Names of Persons in the Grants Under the Acts of Settlement and Explanation [1661-1665] passed in the Reign of Charles II," and "Grants of Estates forfeited in Ireland Under the Williamite Confiscations [1688]"; see John O'Hart, *The Irish and Anglo-Irish Landed Gentry* (1884; rpt. Shannon: Irish University Press, 1969), pp. 452, 514.

[9] The only record of a Thomas Amory at Trinity College, Dublin is the following: "AMORY, THOMAS, Pen. (Mr. John Woodcock), July 12, 1677, aged 15; s. of Thomas; b. Dublin. B. A. Vern. 1681," in George Dames Burtchaell and Thomas Ulick Sadleir, *Alumni Dublienses* (Dublin: Alex. Thom, 1935), p. 12. All additional information and anecdote about Amory derives from *The Gentleman's Magazine* LVIII (1788), 1062 and LIX (1789), 107, 322, 372.

[10] For example, in William Chaigneau's *The History of Jack Connor* (1752); see Ian Campbell Ross, "An Irish Picaresque Novel: William Chaigneau's *The History of Jack Connor,*" *Studies,* LXXI (Autumn, 1982), 270-79.

[11] See, for example, Séan Ó Tuama and Thomas Kinsella, *An Duanaire 1600-1900* (Portlaoise: Dolmen Press, 1981), and Daniel Corkery, *The Hidden Ireland* (1924; rpt. Dublin: Gill and Macmillan, 1967), esp. pp. 50-56.

[12] See below, pp. 18-19.

[13] It may be doubted whether there is a "typical" 18th-century novel in the form of fictional autobiography, but *John Buncle* is markedly different from even such varied examples as Tobias Smollett's *Roderick Random* (1748), Robert Paltock's *Peter Wilkins* (1750), or Laurence Sterne's *Tristram Shandy* (1759-67), to take three roughly contemporary works.

[14] Kilroy, p. 301.

[15] *Ibid.,* p. 301.

[16] Maria Edgeworth, *Castle Rackrent,* ed. George Watson (London: Oxford University Press, 1964), p. 4.

[17] *John Buncle,* I, 87-88.

[18] *Castle Rackrent,* p. 4.

[19] As noted above, p. 3.

[20] J. H. Delargy, *The Gaelic Story-Teller,* Proceedings of the British Academy, XXXI (n.d.), p. 20.

[21] *Ibid.,* p. 20.

[22] George Berkeley, "First Dialogue between Hylas and Philonous," in *Works,* ed. A. A. Luce and T. E. Jessop (London and Edinburgh: Thomas Nelson and Sons, 1949), II, 192.

[23] *Castle Rackrent,* pp. 96 and 4.

[24] *Phaedrus,* trans. B. Jowett, *The Dialogues of Plato,* 4th ed. (Oxford: Clarendon Press, 1953).

[25] Laurence Sterne, *The Life and Opinions of Tristram Shandy, Gentleman,* ed. Ian Campbell Ross (Oxford and New York: Oxford University Press, 1983), III, xii, 145.

[26] Delargy, p. 23.

[27] Trinity College, Dublin, was the first educational establishment at which Locke's *Essay* is known to have been studied (at least as early as 1703); see R. B. McDowell and D. A. Webb, *Trinity College, Dublin 1592-1952* (Cambridge: Cambridge University Press, 1982).

[28] *Tristram Shandy,* V, vii, p. 288.

[29] John Locke, *An Essay Concerning Human Understanding,* ed. Peter H. Nidditch (Oxford: Clarendon, 1975), III, ix, 475-6.

[30] *Ibid.,* III, iii, 409.

[31] Hugh Kenner, *Flaubert, Joyce and Beckett: The Stoic Comedians* (London: W. H. Allen, 1964), p. 39.

[32] The very notion of the published anecdote is etymologically absurd.

[33] Vivien Mercier, *The Irish Comic Tradition* (1962; rpt. London: Oxford University Press, 1965), p. 48.

[34] *The Critical Review,* XXI (1766), 470.

[35] *The Monthly Review,* XXXV (1766), 34.

FURTHER READING

Criticism

Auty, Susan. "Perpetual Mirth." In *The Comic Spirit of Eighteenth-Century Novels,* pp. 180-83. Port Washington, N.Y.: Kennikat Press, 1975.

> Comments on the reasons for the popularity of *The Life of John Buncle* during the Romantic period in nineteenth-century literature.

Mulvihill, James. "Amory's *John Buncle* and Wordsworth's *Excursion.*" *Notes and Queries,* Vol. 235, No. 1, n.s. vol 37, March, 1990, pp. 25-6.

> Suggests that the character of the recluse Dorick Watson encountered by Buncle in his travels may have served as the literary source for "the figure of the Solitary" in Wordsworth's poem.

Additional coverage of Amory's life and career is contained in the following source published by The Gale Group: *Dictionary of Literary Biography*, Vol. 39.

Frances Brooke

1724-1789

(Also wrote under the pseudonym of Mary Singleton) English novelist, playwright, librettist, translator, and essayist.

INTRODUCTION

Known during her lifetime as a translator, novelist, essayist, and playwright, Brooke is chiefly remembered as the author of the first Canadian novel, *The History of Emily Montague* (1769). In both her fiction and nonfiction works, Brooke addressed social issues, particularly women's right to education and choice in marriage partners. She is also credited with helping to shape the epistolary novel into a vehicle for social criticism.

Biographical Information

Brooke was born in 1724 to Reverend Thomas Moore and his wife, Mary (Knowles) Moore, in Claypole, Lincolnshire. After the death of her father in 1727 and her mother in 1737, she was raised by relatives. At about age twenty-four, she was drawn to the theatrical and literary life of London, where she supported herself through translations and journalism while writing novels and dramas. In 1756, she married a clergyman, John Brooke. They had a son in 1757. In that year her husband was sent to British North America as an army chaplain, first at Louisbourg and then at Quebec. In 1763, Brooke joined him. While there she wrote *The History of Emily Montague*. This novel, published a year after the Brookes returned to England in 1768, is believed to be the first extended work of fiction with a Canadian setting.

In 1773 Brooke and the actress Mary Ann Yates become joint managers of King's Theatre in the London theater district. Unable to abtain a patent to produce plays, they staged ballets and operas for the next four years. In 1777 she published *The Excursion*. This novel attracted attention for its insider view of the theater scene and its criticism of the renowned actor-manager David Garrick. Late in life, Brooke achieved theatrical success with her historical tragedy *The Siege of Sinope* (1781). *Rosina*, a comic opera, was a popular and critical success when it was finally performed in 1782, some ten years after it was written. *Marian* (1788), another copmic opera, also did well. A year after Brooke's death in 1789, *The History of Charles Mandeville*, a sequel to *The History of Lady Julia Mandeville*, was published.

Major Works

Brooke published thirty-seven issues of a periodical called *The Old Maid* (1755-56), writing most of the content herself. Modeled after the popular magazine *The Spectator*, *The Old Maid* featured a mixture of fictional dialogues and critical reviews in which Brooke addressed contemporary social topics, including marriage, female education, and the morals and manners of the theater. Brooke wrote several plays that she was unable to have produced before she began writing novels. Her first, *The History of Lady Julia Mandeville* (1863) established Brooke as an author and showed the influence of the French epistolary romance novels, some examples of which she had translated into English. *The History of Lady Julia Mandeville* was widely popular in England and translated into French, earning the praise of Voltaire, who called it the best English novel since Samuel Richardon's *Clarissa* (1747-48) and *Sir Charles Grandison* (1753-54). In *Emily Montague*, Brooke turned her familiarity with the Canadian landscape to advantage. Her description of Niagara Falls in winter, for example, was much admired. *Emily Montague* infused the epistolary novel with the growing vogue of travel literature: the narrative consists of letters between English immigrants living in Quebec and their correspondents in England, and addresses such issues as the most effective way to colonize Quebec, perceived racial differences between the English, the French Canadians, and the native North Americans, the Church of England and Catholicism, the nature of a happy marriage, and the differences between men and women. The book was a critical and popular success, running to at least six editions in Brooke's lifetime and receiving favorable reviews in both English and French journals. *The Excursion* received some good reviews, but was never as popular as the previous works It departs from the epistolary format to introduce an ironic, detached narrator, who relates the trials of the novel's heroine with sympathy tempered by worldly wisdom. The novel is a satirical examination of what happens to a bold young woman who dreams of becoming a writer in London. It is thought to contain autobiographical elements. *The History of Charles Mandeville*, published posthumously, provided a happy resolution to the tragedy of her first novel. It features a character from *The History of Lady Julia Mandeville* and ends with his marriage to the best friend of the earlier novel's deceased heroine. The fact that Brooke did not attempt to publish the novel during her life may indicates that she was not satisfied with it. It received little critical or popular notice.

Critical Reception

Neglected for much of the nineteenth and twentieth centuries, Brooke has been reclaimed by feminist critics seeking women's literary traditions, and by Canadian critics tracing the origins of their national literature. Although the accuracy of the Canadian content of *Emily Montague* is open to debate, critics have noted its status as a New World novel, particularly in its stress on the disjunction between English and British North American landscape and social conventions. Recent criticism informed by post-colonial theory tends to be overtly political, examining this novel's treatment of imperialism, racial issues, and the exploitation of natural resources. Feminist critics have stressed Brooke's use of the sentimental novel to explore the limited scope of women's personal and professional lives during her era.

PRINCIPAL WORKS

The Old Maid [editor; as Mary Singleton] (essays, fictional letters, and criticism) 1755-56

Virginia: A Tragedy, with Odes, Pastorals, and Translations (drama) [first publication] 1756

The History of Lady Julia Mandeville (novel) 1763

The History of Emily Montague (novel) 1769

The Excursion (novel) 1777

The Siege of Sinope: A Tragedy (drama) 1781

Rosina; or, Love in a Cottage: A Comic Opera, in Two Acts (libretto) 1782

Marian: A Comic Opera, in Two Acts (libretto) 1788

The History of Charles Mandeville (novel) 1790

CRITICISM

Lorraine McMullen (essay date 1977-78)

SOURCE: "*All's Right at Last:* An Eighteenth-Century Canadian Novel," in *Journal of Canadian Fiction,* Vol. 21, 1977-78, pp. 95-104.

[*In the following essay, McMullen outlines the authorship controversy concerning* All's Right at Last, *and argues for the text's significance as the second*

Canadian novel; in theme and setting, the novel suggests Brooke's hand, though the work is of inferior quality to her earlier novels.]

> Could you believe that this divine girl should make me prefer the cold frost and snow of Canada to the mild winter of my native country; and that I would rather gaze on her bright eyes than partake of your most brilliant amusements?[1]

In 1774, five years after the publication of *The History of Emily Montague,* the circulating library of Frances and John Noble in London published *All's Right At Last; or, The History of Frances West.* The style is epistolary, the setting for the most part Canada, the plot improbable. Although published anonymously (no reputable writer would admit to an association with circulating libraries and their flimsy formula novels),[2] there is reason to believe that Frances Brooke is the author of this work. Whoever the author, *All's Right At Last* can lay claim to being Canada's second novel. As such, it merits our attention.

Unlike *The History of Emily Montague,* early events of this novel take place in England. An exchange of letters between the heroine, Fanny West, in London and Mrs. Darnley, her friend and mentor, in the country reveal Fanny's predicament. Her mother has unwisely brought Fanny to London where she is attempting to introduce her into society, with the hope that her beauty and accomplishments might allow her to marry above her station. Although filial obedience requires that Fanny concur with her mother's plans, she is dismayed at the situation in which she finds herself, and Mrs. Darnley warns her of the dire consequences which may ensue. The fears of Fanny and Mrs. Darnley are soon realized. The aristocratic and wealthy Lord Walton seeks out Fanny with intentions no one but Fanny's naive mother can conceive as honorable. However, Fanny is not without spirit. When Walton in a melodramatic scene attempts to rape her, Fanny reverses the situation and stabs him with his own sword. Not seriously injured, Walton turns the incident to his own advantage by circulating a report that Fanny has wounded him in a lovers' quarrel. She and her mother are placed under house arrest guarded by Walton's servants. Mrs. West dies, of shock and dismay it seems, whereupon Walton conceives a *Clarissa*-like plot to spirit Fanny away to his own estate and force her to become his mistress. At the last moment Fanny escapes to a friend through whom she then obtains a position as companion to a young bride. This woman, Mrs. Manwaring, is about to join her husband, the newly appointed Governor of Trois-Rivières. Thus the stage is set for Fanny's journey to Canada. The melodramatic incidents involved in the above situation comprise the first third of this novel and the remainder, with the exception of the resolution in England, takes place in Canada. This is the reverse of *The History of Emily*

Montague in which the first two-thirds of the action takes place in Canada and the last third in England.

On Fanny's arrival at Trois-Rivières, the romantic plot is immediately initiated. Her mistress's husband, Governor Manwaring, is revealed to be Henry Parker, the son of a family friend who had made a fortune in the British colony. Parker had followed his father's dying request to seek the hand of his old friend's daughter, Fanny, in England. When he met Fanny, Parker was led to believe that she was Walton's mistress and disappointedly arranged to return to Canada. Prior to departure he married Caroline Manwaring and took her surname to fulfill a requirement of his bride's inheritance; hence Fanny's astonishment at meeting him in Canada. Now both realize, too late, that they are in love. Canada was expected to provide a new start for Fanny, but Manwaring's love for her and hers for him complicate her situation, for the excessive sensibility of both makes it impossible to hide. To ameliorate the situation Fanny agrees to spend the winter in Montreal with a newly married friend, Bel Roachley, and accepts the advice of her acquaintances that she resolve her dilemma by marrying. She accepts Colonel Bellamy, the most eligible man in Canada, who is as attractive to the ladies as Fanny is to the men. Ironically, on the day of their marriage Fanny learns of the death of Caroline Manwaring, thus freeing the man she loves. Soon after, Bellamy is conveniently killed in a duel by a jealous husband who erroneously suspects him of an affair with his young bride. Manwaring has sailed to England and Fanny, now free, returns there for the happy resolution: "All's Right at Last."

Was this novel written by Frances Brooke? The listings in the *National Union Catalogue*,[3] in the *British Museum General Catalogue of Printed Books*,[4] and in Andrew Block, *The English Novel 1740-1850*,[5] suggest that Frances Brooke is probably the author. The title page of the novel indicates that it was published anonymously and that it was "Printed for F. and J. Noble at their respective Circulating Libraries, near Middle Row, Holborn, and Saint Martin's Court, near Leicester Square."[6] The reason usually given for ascribing the novel to Frances Brooke is its Canadian setting. However, added credence may be given to this claim by the existence in the British Museum of a French translation of the novel. The title page of the first volume of this translation reads: "Histoire/De Miss West/Ou L'Heureux/Denouement/Par Madame***,/ Auteur de l'Histoire d'Emilie Montague,/Traduite de l'anglais/ Premiere Partie A Rotterdam / Chez Bennet & Hake/MDCCLXXVII."[7]

There are also several internal reasons for considering that Mrs. Brooke may be the author, although this novel is not as successful as *The History of Emily Montague* or *The History of Julia Mandeville* (1763). The main interest of the novel resides in its portrayal of life in Canada and its commentary on marriage and society. Structurally, the novel lacks the unity which characterized Frances Brooke's earlier two novels or the later *Excursion* (1777). Fanny's desperate adventures in London provide a tale in themselves thinly linked with the Canadian events which follow. They do provide a reason for the penniless young woman to wish to leave England and they introduce, however briefly, the young man destined to provide the romantic interest and complicating factor in her Canadian experience. In this first part of the novel the author strongly criticizes the London social scene. Urban life is contrasted with rural in a manner reminiscent of *The History of Julia Mandeville*, which idealized country life and condemned the city. In that novel most of the action took place on the Belmont country estate and Julia's father described his reactions when required to leave his idyllic estate to spend a few days in London:

> You can have no idea, my dear Mr. Mandeville, how weary I am of being these few days only in town: that any one who is happy enough to have a house, a cottage in the country, should continue here at this season, is to me inconceivable; but that gentlemen of large property, that noblemen, should imprison themselves in this smoking furnace, when the whole land is a blooming garden, a wilderness of sweets; when pleasure courts them in her fairest form; nay, when the sordid god of modern days, when Interest joins his potent voice; when power, the best power, that of doing good, solicits their presence; can only be accounted for by supposing them under the domination of fascination, spell-caught by some malicious demon, an enemy to human happiness.[8]

In *All's Right at Last*, Bellamy writes of the London *beau monde*: "I almost tremble at the thought of returning with her [Fanny] to your world of dissipation and intrigue, where the fair married dames are so little tenacious either of their own honor, or that of their husbands: . . ." (II, 53-4, Letter XXXIV).

The corrupt life of London society, shallowness of its members, superficiality of its pleasures, and foolishness of involving oneself in its activities provide a major theme of Mrs. Brooke's later novel, *The Excursion*. In that novel Mrs. Brooke moves from the epistolary style of her earlier works to employ the voice of an acute and witty omniscient observer. *The Excursion* concerns the adventures of a young woman from a rural background who journeys alone to London to experience the excitement of the London *beau monde* and to attempt to publish her novel and play. Like Fanny West this young woman, Maria Villiers, very nearly comes to grief in a world which assumes that a single, unprotected young woman seeking to enter society is an adventuress, or at least fair prey. Just as Fanny's mother assumes that Lord Walton's intentions are honourable, so Maria in *The Excursion* assumes that Lord Melvile in his approaches to her is honourable. Both are proved wrong. *All's Right at Last* is more melodramatic with its attempted rape, stabbing, interception of letters, imprisonment, and attempted kidnapping. The later *Excursion* expands with more wit upon the theme of the naive young woman from a rural, therefore simple and innocent background, caught up in the corrupt London social world.

The tone of *All's Right at Last* alters when the scene shifts to Canada and the decadence of the old world is left behind. Fanny's letters to her friend Mrs. Darnley continue, and now provide the reader with her reactions to the new land and an ongoing report of her activities there. Her first response to Canada is ecstatic delight at the beauty of nature, somewhat mitigated by a nostalgia for England:

> We are at last arrived at this most delightful country, where nature has dealt her bounties with a lavish hand. How unclouded is the sky! How bright the sunshine! How beautiful is the earth enamelled with flowery sweets! Everything here is gay and smiling; yet, dear England, often do I breathe a sigh to the memory of thee.

> (I, 161, Letter XIX)

Other correspondents write from Trois-Rivières, Quebec, and Montreal, the three centres of activity and social life in Canada. As with the earlier part of the novel, the great majority of the Canadian letters are written by women. Various members of the colony comment on Fanny's impact on the new world: of course her beauty, charm, and sensibility—which capture the hearts of all eligible males—cause some resentment among the females.

The most lively writers are Lucy Santemore in Trois-Rivières; her sister, Belinda Roachley; and Lucy's friend in Quebec, Charlotte Bladon. The names Lucy and Bel will be familiar to readers of *The History of Emily Montague* who will recall Emily's confidante, Arabella "Bell" Fermor and Bell's friend, Lucy Rivers. Lucy Santemore is a mixture of French, English and possibly Indian blood as she indicates in a letter to Charlotte Bladon:

> Everlasting dancers are we Canadians. No wonder, with all the wildness of Indians, and all the vivacity of the Parisiens so blended in our compositions. My family, in particular have a mixture of both, with very little of the English gravity to moderate either. I have been told that my great, great grandmother was a Squaw. Heavens! no wonder I am a brunette.—How I ramble!

> (II, 29, Letter XXVII)

The tone and phrasing of this letter recall Bell Fermor.

Colonel Bellamy confirms Lucy's description of the liveliness of French Canadian women:

> The French ladies are no prudes and I adapted my behaviour to their taste. At Quebec, in particular, a lively young widow endeavoured to draw me into her snares. I followed her lead, while it amused me. Nothing in the least leading to a serious attachment appeared in my manner; I did not mean that there should. She had some wit, a great deal of levity, and was the prettiest woman in town. We flirted till a new face pleased me better. Madame de St. Savoir had more sense, and a more sentimental turn. I preferred her conversation to that of a mere giddy trifler.

> (II, 30-31 Letter XXXI)

Bellamy's attitude to French Canadian women is very like that of Colonel Ed Rivers before him:

> They are gay, coquet, and sprightly; more gallant than sensible; more flatter'd by the vanity of inspiring passion than capable of feeling themselves; and, like their European countrymen, prefer the outward attentions of unmeaning admiration to the real devotion of the heart. There is not perhaps on earth a race of females who talk so much, or feel so little, of love as the French.[9]

As with *The History of Emily Montague*, the Canadian winter and attempts to cope with it provide a main topic of discussion. Fanny writes to Mrs. Darnley:

> It is at present severely cold, in my opinion; but nothing, as the inhabitants tell me, to what I may expect a month hence; when it sets in for frost. Ah! I shiver at the bare description of a Canadian winter.

> Nature, however, gives us conveniences suitable to its inconveniences; for here are plenty of warm and beautiful furs. I have made up some dresses for the winter, which are both comfortable and becoming; something in the Turkish style, buttoned at the wrists, and close up to my chin. They are made of thick satin, and lined through, skirts and all, with squirrel skins. The men tell me I look better in them than in any other dress they ever saw me wear.

> (II, 21, Letter XXX)

Lucy Santemore's comment on Fanny's winter dress again reminds the reader of Bell Fermor:

> Already we are beginning to put on our furs. Fanny West yesterday, for the first time, appeared in a kind of polonese of crimson satin, buttoned at the wrist, and trimmed with beautiful ermin. The girl became it, and the men admired her more than ever. Our misses, silly souls! are all busy in getting dresses made in the same style, Such a mind to set fashions! I have no patience. Positively, though I shiver with cold, I will not (lest I be ranked among the number

of her imitators) put on a scrap of fur for a month to come.

(II, 199, Letter XXIV)

The enamoured Bellamy converts the rigours of the weather to good use to demonstrate the intensity of his love: "Could you believe that this divine girl should make me prefer the cold frost and snow of Canada to the mild winter of my native country; . . ." (II, 29, Letter XXXI). In a later letter he employs the wintry weather in a simile to describe the beauty of his beloved, in the process remarking somewhat ungallantly on the less fortunate effects of the climate on other ladies of Montreal:

> . . . love and furs keep me, between them, tolerably warm.
>
> This weather is a great enemy to the Ladies complexions. I never beheld such a set of livid, red-handed d—. There are but two exceptions; my Fanny, and her friend Roachley, who is a very pretty, smart, little creature. The new-fallen snow cannot put Fanny's transparent skin out of countenance. It has all its properties: as cold, and full as dazzling-white; with such a glow of health, her pure and eloquent blood speaks in her cheeks.

(II, 53, Letter XXXIV)

We are told that a variety of recreational activites are required to mitigate the effects of the extreme climate. Like *The History of Emily Montague* much attention is given to balls and social activities. Fanny writes to Mrs. Darnley:

> We live a life of constant gaiety and dissipation; too much for my taste. And yet we may justly be allowed to soften, as much as possible, the severity of the climate, by innocent and social recreations. We should freeze, were we not to keep ourselves warm, by associating together in dancing, to make our blood circulate. There is no giving you an idea of the intense cold at this season. The earth is now covered four feet deep with snow.

(II, 84-5, Letter XXXVIII)

Besides dances and balls, Fanny and her friends while away the winter with games, singing, and shuttle-cock. To these activities the gentlemen add bear hunting "accompanied by a party of savages" (II, 144, Letter XXXIV). In the summers, parties travel by carriole on sightseeing expeditions. A trip to Niagara Falls elicits from Miss West the stock eighteenth-century response to the sublime:

> How tremendously beautiful, how astonishing, how wonderful are the works of nature, and how various! Every thing I behold in this delightful country is new and surprizing. How much should I be amused and charmed were my mind at ease! Indeed while I gazed with a sort of pleasing horror on the foaming cataract, I was lost in wonder.

II, 2, Letter XXVIII)

Lucy describes in detail an outing on the Richelieu River shortly after Fanny's arrival. The party, with the ladies dressed *"en bergère,"* travels by barge, accompanied by musicians, and an elegant repast is spread on a cloth on an island bank. The scene is idyllic. Then, with apt wit, Lucy describes the fall into the river of one of Fanny's beaux in a gallant attempt to assist in disentangling her fishing line. "Do you know," writes Lucy, "that Franklin, yesterday, took the lover's leap? Not gracefully, indeed, after hanging his harp upon the willows; it was rather a slip than a jump" (II, 86, Letter XXII). The concerted efforts of two other chivalrous gentlemen, Manwaring and Hamilton, save Fanny from joining Franklin in the river.

Because Trois-Rivières is a business centre it is said to be much less exciting than Quebec or Montreal which are enhanced by the presence of British officers. Bel urges her sister in Trois-Rivières to visit her in Montreal, the liveliest of the three centres in Canada:

> Our assortment of beaux here are a thousand times smarter than any you can boast. Besides the divine Bellamy, we have half a hundred other red-coats, dear elegant obliging creatures, who have no one thing to do but to amuse the ladies. Your men are all immersed over head and ears in business: that, and this season, render their hearts as freezingly cold as our climate, invulnerable to all the darts of Cupid. Idleness is the nurse of love. Our gallant heroes would not know what to do with their time, were it not for that bewitching passion. Mars and Venus, you know, are sworn friends. But perhaps you are afraid of being metamorphosed into a pillar of ice, during your journey. Never fear, child; *amenez avec vous, votre amant,* and let his soft sighs keep you warm and melt your frozen heart.

(II, 66-7, Letter XXXVI)

Franklin of the Richelieu incident is doubly unfortunate. Not only is he rebuffed by Fanny but he then marries frivolous young Kitty Renton of Quebec. As our letter writers inform us, Kitty had left the stringent protection of a maiden aunt to enter into the social whirl where, only too susceptible to male charm, she found herself the talk of Quebec. Colonel Bellamy viewed Kitty as a young woman who was innocent from ignorance rather than from principle, and as a man of experience attempted to guide her in the ways of the world. A friendship on such terms was quite naturally misconstrued, and a major reason for Bellamy's departure from Quebec for Montreal was his wish to stem the gossip linking his name with

Miss Renton. At the time of Franklin's courtship and marriage to Kitty some months later, Charlotte Bladon made a point of commenting on Kitty's pallor and fainting spells. It is thus not the shock to the reader that it is to her husband to learn later that she has given birth to a son four months after their wedding. Kitty follows eighteenth-century novel tradition by dying properly remorseful, and Mrs. Bladon gives voice to the stock eighteenth-century response to the event: "May she be a warning to her sex! may it teach them to shun the flowery paths of vice, which sooner or later, will lead them to destruction!" (II, 167, Letter XLVIII). However, an earlier statement by Mrs. Bladon that it is only cowardice, in other words fear of pregnancy, that keeps most women chaste, seems truer to Mrs. Brooke's own more realistic view of the world. Kitty's situation calls to mind A.S.H.'s *Belinda* (1843)[10] which parodies the sentimental novel by reversing male-female roles, presenting Belinda as the seducer. But even Belinda bows to convention, and dies repentant after presenting her surprised husband with a son six weeks after their wedding.

Kitty's fall from grace operates as a parallel to Fanny's near loss of chastity in London. Although Fanny had escaped with her virtue intact, the accusation of guilt was sufficiently shameful to drive her from England. Fanny's mother, responsible for her situation, paid for her foolishness and lack of good sense by languishing and dying in London, in the midst of her daughter's woes. Thus Mrs. West, Fanny, and Kitty all pay for their transgressions. For Fanny, however, who has only the appearance of guilt, happiness is ultimately attained, but only after much travail.

An unusual aspect of this novel is its treatment of the marriage of Fanny and Bellamy. Bellamy is attractive, wealthy, honorable, and the most eligible young man in Canada. When Fanny learns on their wedding day of Caroline Manwaring's death and of her dying request that her husband marry Fanny, she collapses. This is hardly an auspicious beginning for a marriage. Bellamy confesses to a friend a short time later that their marriage is a disaster. Angry and frustrated by her coldness he accuses Fanny of contacting Manwaring. Bellamy's anger achieves what his gentleness could not, and jolts Fanny out of her depression. They resolve their differences and their union becomes a loving if not, for Fanny at least, a passionate one. Her acceptance of her role as loving wife is one further step in the series of trials Fanny must successfully undergo before attaining the grail, marriage to the one she truly loves. Eighteenth-century novels may include a reference to a brief unhappy previous marriage of convenience to an older man. But the exploration of a situation in which an admirable and loving husband attempts to cope with a virtuous but, for psychological reasons, unresponsive wife is unusual.

Ten different correspondents contribute to the fifty-two epistles which make up this novel. The early London incident is told in straightforward fashion primarily through an exchange of letters between Fanny and Mrs. Darnley, with two letters of Lord Walton revealing his plot to an accomplice and thus to the reader. But in Canada, the situation of the heroine is developed more complexly. Fanny moves from Trois-Rivières to Montreal, and letter writers must keep the reader informed not only of the progress of her courtship and marriage in Montreal, but also of the situations in the Manwaring residence at Trois-Rivières and of Kitty Renton in Quebec society. Letters to and from these three centres are skilfully interwoven to achieve these objectives. Most of the letters are written by women. Variety of tone is achieved through the variety of personality and attitude of the correspondents. The wit of Lucy Santemore and Bel Roachley provides relief from the earnestness of Fanny West.

Fanny's last comment on Canada, contrasting Montreal with London, extends beyond the opposition of the clear Montreal sky to smoky London air and suggests opposing moral climates:

> But I awoke from my delightful reverie, and instead of dear Montreal, where you are blessed with a clear, unclouded sky, found myself half stifled with London's thick smokey air, and choked with its dust: nay, even the heat incommodes me. The summers here, though far less warm, yet render me more languid than those of Canada.
>
> (II, 182-3, Letter LI)

In an earlier letter, Bellamy had underlined the same theme, referring to "your world of dissipation and intrigue [London] where fair married dames are so little tenacious either of their own honour, or that of their husbands" (II, 53, Letter XXXIV). In fact, Manwaring had been described in the first pages of the novel as a product of Canada who stands in marked contrast to the London gentlemen:

> His dress, his manner, his whole carriage speaks the man of worth and good sense, but I doubt not, you will find him greatly deficient in those superficial accomplishments which distinguish your fine gentlemen; nay, I am convinced he will give himself no sort of trouble to acquire what people of reason must despise: his person wants none of those tawdry ornaments which constitute the whole merit of that empty thing you call a Macaroni. He is handsome, manly, and well-bred; though his politeness is rather of a benevolent and amiable disposition, than from having been taught insipid and trifling forms of ceremony. He may be a little awkward in going through the ridiculous etiquette of your fashionable coteries, but he will, in conversation, display more understanding in half an hour, than your whole insipid circle of coxcombs

and belles, all put together, ever did, or will do, in their whole lives.

> (I, 33-4, Letter III)

Canada, then, like rural England is set in opposition to the superficiality and intrigue of London society.

A number of parallels with **The History of Emily Montague** have been observed. In terms of Canadian content this novel like the earlier one portrays the social life of upper class society, which is primarily English but includes a French Canadian element. It is worth noting that three Canadian correspondents are French Canadian: Lucy Santemore, Charlotte Bladon, and Bel Roachley. Social convention nevertheless remains that of England. Once more the attractiveness of the French Canadian woman to the British male is noted. In terms of characterization, the unfortunate Colonel Bellamy is very much like Colonel Rivers—generous, honorable, not above affairs of gallantry with experienced, mature women. Lucy Santemore and Bel Roachley are aggressive, lively women like Arabella Fermor. Bel is the first woman to befriend Fanny and like Lucy's friend Bell remains her support and confidante. Fanny approximates Emily Montague as a conventional eighteenth-century heroine of sensibility, virtue, and decorum. Like Emily she comments on her own sensibility:

> Oh! if the ladies here knew how little satisfaction I receive from the admiration of the men, they would cease to envy me. How much happier are they with hearts at ease, void of that painful and dangerous sensibility which is and ever will be the source of such calamity to/Your/Frances West.

> (II, 5-16, Letter XXVIII)

Fanny is correct. Sensibility does not always prove to be an asset to her. For example, it causes her to unwittingly display her love for Manwaring, thus bringing unhappiness to his wife and complicating her own situation. Manwaring shares this sensibility, an indication of their suitability to one another. On the death of his wife, for example, he says "Adieu to pomp and grandeur. I will fly to retirement, and there, unmolestedly enjoy my grief" (II, 42, Letter XLIII). Fanny notes a similar "melancholy delight" in grief after the death of her husband: "Time will soften the most deepseated sorrow. I feel this truth, and almost regret it; for I was beginning, by being long habituated to grief, to take a melancholy delight in indulging it" (II, 206, Letter LII). Like **The History of Emily Montague** the happy denouement takes place in England and includes an appropriately comfortable future, although throughout both novels marriage solely for title or material benefit has been frowned upon. **All's Right at Last** lacks the detailed nature description of **The History of Emily Montague**. The letters comprising the novel are fewer but generally longer although, like the earlier novel,

almost totally devoid of dialogue. There is no equivalent to William Fermor's essay-type reporting of social and political conditions in Canada. The tone is more feverish and emotional, the plot more involved and melodramatic. Yet this novel does provide another record of what it meant to experience Canada in the eighteenth century. Skilful interweaving of plot lines and the liveliness of the Canadian correspondents are the main contributing factors to its interest.

Notes

[1] Anon., *All's Right At Last, or, The History of Miss West* (London: F. and J. Noble, 1774), vol. II, p. 29, Letter XXI. Subsequent quotations from this work are indicated by volume, page, and letter number in parentheses immediately following the quotation.

[2] J.M.S. Tompkins, *The Popular Novel in England 1770-1800* (London: Methuen, 1932), p. 3, comments that "writers of standing dissociated themselves ostentatiously from the libraries." For a discussion of eighteenth-century libraries and their novels see Tompkins and Hilda M. Hamlyn, "Eighteenth-Century Circulating Libraries in England." *The Library* (London: Oxford University Press, 1947), 5th ser. I, 197-222.

[3] *The National Union Catalogue Pre-1956 Imprints* (London: Mansell, 1970), vol. 77, p. 641, includes this novel under Frances Brooke and notes "Attributed by Block to Frances Brooke."

[4] Only in the British Museum copy of the *British Museum General Catalogue of Printed Books*. This catalogue contains additions to the British Library holdings not yet included in the *General Catalogue* available to other libraries.

[5] Andrew Block, *The English Novel 1740-1850,* rev. ed. (London: Dawson, 1961), p. 165.

[6] *Op. cit.,* title page.

[7] *Histoire de Miss West ou L'Heureux Denouement* (Rotterdam: Bennett and Hake, 1777). In the British Museum.

[8] Frances Brooke, *The History of Julia Mandeville,* 7th ed. (London: J. Dodsley, 1782), vol. I, p. 85.

[9] Frances Brooke, *The History of Emily Montague* (Toronto: McClelland and Stewart, 1961), p. 24.

[10] A.S.H., *Belinda* (Toronto: House of Anansi Press, 1975). First published in 1843 by Bagg and Harmon, Detroit.

Lorraine McMullen (essay date 1980)

SOURCE: "Frances Brooke's Early Fiction," in *Canadian Literature,* Vol. 86, Autumn, 1980, pp. 31-40.

[*In the following essay, McMullen stresses the importance of Brooke's early writing, noting that her translations of French epistolary novels helped her develop her own novel-writing techniques. McMullen demonstrates that* The History of Lady Julia Mandeville *anticipates many of the themes and formal techniques employed in* Emily Montague.]

Finding herself at Quebec in 1763, Frances Brooke (1723-1789) made the most of the opportunity to transmute some of her experiences and observations into fiction. The result, *The History of Emily Montague* (1769), is well known in Canada. Yet criticism of this work has rarely, and then only briefly, alluded to Brooke's earlier writing which prepared her to make such effective use of her Canadian experiences.[1] Her earlier novel, *The History of Lady Julia Mandeville* (1763) was, in fact, more popular in its day than *Emily Montague* and deserves consideration in its own right.[2] Also ignored has been a consideration of influences on Mrs. Brooke's writing, with the one exception of Samuel Richardson, father of all eighteenth-century epistolary novelists. A study of Mrs. Brooke's translation of Madame Marie Jeanne Riccoboni's *Lettres de Milady Juliette Catesby à Milady Henriette Campley, son Amie* (1759) provides us with an indication of another influence at least as important as that of Richardson, that of Madame Riccoboni and the French novel of sensibility. *Emily Montague* then can be seen as a natural development in style, attitude, tone, and characterization, from Frances Brooke's earlier work, her own novel, and her translation from the French.

Sensibility was not English in origin. The main stream of sensibility novelists who influenced writers throughout Europe were French. As Maurice Lévy has noted, "France before England devoted itself to the problems of the heart and the passions."[3] Madame de la Fayette's *La Princesse de Clèves* (1678), with its portrayal of love as an overwhelming passion which brings suffering and joy, despair and ecstasy, had provided the early impetus, and Pierre Marivaux with *La Vie de Marianne* (1731-1736) is considered the founder of the French school of sensibility. Abbé Prévost's *Mémoires et aventures d'un homme de qualité qui s'est retiré du monde* (1728-1733), especially the last volume, *Manon Lescaut* (1733), which appeared in many editions in both French and English, influenced writers of both countries. E. A. Baker quotes from *Manon Lescaut:* "If tears and sighs are not to be described as pleasures, it is true nevertheless that they have infinite sweetness for a person in mortal affliction. The moments that I devoted to my grief were so dear to me that to prolong them I abstained from sleep."[4] These

lines could have appeared in any one of a number of subsequent eighteenth-century novels of sensibility, English or French.

At the time of Mrs. Brooke's translation of her novels, Madame Marie Jeanne Riccoboni (1714-1792) was becoming well known in both France and England for her novels of sensibility. Appearing only one year after the original French novel, with a second edition the same year and six editions by 1780, Mrs. Brooke's translation furthered Madame Riccoboni's popularity and was an impetus to the developing cult of sensibility in England. Madame Riccoboni explored especially the intense feelings evoked by love. Sorrow was always a necessary element, and her plots were constructed around heroines either betrayed or believing themselves betrayed. Although the way of life she described was generally realistic she tended to avoid reference to the mundane aspects of reality, and to unhappiness and tragedy except for that "sweet melancholy," in which the sentimental reader took pleasure and which demonstrated the excessive sensibility of her hero and heroine. As Francis Wright remarks, "In constructing a plot to develop sorrow, either transient or permanent, she sketched the prototype of the sentimental love story."[5]

When Frances Brooke translated Madame Riccoboni's *Lettres de Milady Juliette Catesby à Milady Henriette Campley, son Amie* in 1760, she selected one of the best novels[6] of a woman already widely known, and presumably a novel which she, herself, found congenial. The *Letters of Juliet Lady Catesby to her Friend, Lady Henrietta Campley*[7] is typical of Madame Riccoboni's works. The tone of the novel is highly emotional, voicing the increasingly distraught state of mind of the central character, Juliet Catesby, and her lover, Lord Ossory. As is usual with Madame Riccoboni, the plot revolves around the various complications which must be resolved before the two lovers are finally united. The novel is composed of thirty-nine letters from Juliet Catesby to her friend, Henrietta. At the onset the reader learns of Lady Catesby's hasty departure from the house she had been visiting to avoid encountering her former lover, Lord Ossory. She gives a lengthy and highly emotional account of her meeting several years earlier with Ossory, their love and decision to marry, his abrupt departure after a highly emotional but inexplicable scene, and his hasty marriage to another. His wife has died and now he is besieging Juliet with letters. After much emotional wavering, she finally consents to read Ossory's lengthy explanation of his earlier conduct. He confesses that, in a state of drunkenness following a party, he had seduced the young sister of a close friend and, learning later of her pregnancy and threatened suicide, felt obliged to marry her. Now, two years later, she is dead and he is free to reveal the story to Juliet. Satisfied with Ossory's explanation Juliet agrees to marry him.

From this novel Mrs. Brooke learned how to construct a tightly knit novel of sensibility. Her *History of Lady Julia Mandeville*,[8] which appeared three years after this translation, is composed of seventy-seven letters, the great majority of which are written by two central characters: Harry Mandeville, the lover of Julia, and Lady Anne Wilmot, a spritely, coquettish young widow, friend of the two lovers. Anne's letters to her own lover Colonel Bellville recount activities on the country estate of Julia Mandeville's father, Lord Belmont, where she and Harry are guests. Harry's letter to a friend, George Mordaunt, are occupied primarily with his description of his growing love for Julia. When he realizes the intensity of his love, Harry resolves to leave the Belmont estate in the hope of increasing his fortune sufficiently to marry her. Before he leaves, Harry and Julia vow to remain true to their love, but they acquaint neither Julia's parents nor Harry's father with the situation. Not long after, through a complicated set of circumstances, Harry is led to believe that Julia will marry Lord Melvin, son of a wealthy aristocratic friend of her family. He rushes to Belmont where he is critically injured by Melvin whom he has forced into a duel. Harry lives long enough to learn that the wedding plans of which he heard were intended for his own marriage to Julia and that he was to inherit the Belmont title and estate. Through chance Harry had never received the letter acquainting him with this happy resolution. Shortly after his death Julia dies of a broken heart.

The theme of noble and sentimental lovers exhibiting the utmost sensibility as they seek to resolve their difficulties is common to both novels and given full expression in both. Madame Riccoboni's lovers are finally happily united, although this is not the case in all of her novels.[9] Mrs. Brooke's Julia and Harry Mandeville die for love; however, there are two central pairs or lovers whose situations are happily resolved after various impediments are overcome: Anne Wilmot and Bellville; Anne's niece, Bell Hastings, and Lord Melvin. Bell's dilemma resembles that of Juliet Catesby; it is the result of an apparent betrayal, but as with Lady Catesby all is eventually explained satisfactorily.

In both novels the sensibility of the lovers is frequently demonstrated and as frequently referred to. Juliet Catesby gives an indication of the acute sensibility of herself and her lover as she recounts the moment when she and Ossory first revealed their love to each other: "One day, reading an affective Story of two tender Lovers who had been cruelly torn from each other, the Book fell from our Hands, our Tears began to flow . . ." (Letter XV). This scene not only demonstrates their tenderness in weeping for fictional lovers, but also foreshadows their own separation and provides an indication of the intensity of their emotions when such would occur. The emotional stress resulting from leaving Juliet to marry the woman he seduced does, in fact, cause Ossory to become seriously ill. Juliet Catesby's present suitor, Lord Harry, also shows his sensibility by collapsing when rejected. This in turn leads Juliet to exclaim, despite her dislike for him, that her heart is "too full of sensibility not to compassionate his Love, though too much prepossessed to return it" (Letter XXIII). In Mrs. Brooke's novel, Harry Mandeville, too, is beseiged by an unwanted suitor, a Miss Westbrook, daughter of a *nouveau riche* neighbour, and as he journeys forth to inform her that he cannot respond to her overtures his reaction to the situation is much like that of Juliet: "These trials are too great for a heart like mine, tender, sympathetic, compassionate, and softened by the sense of its own sufferings; I shall expire with regret and confusion at her sight." Harry's excessive sensibility is the major theme of his letters. He is the male counterpart of Riccoboni's Juliet Catesby. It is Harry who writes of the ennobling quality of love: "Why do closeted moralists, strangers to the human heart, rail indiscriminately at love? When inspired by a worthy object, it leads to everything that is great and noble; warmed by the desire of being approved by her, there is nothing I would not attempt"; and later, "The love of such a woman is the love of virtue itself: it raises, it refines, it ennobles every sentiment of the heart." Julia, too, in the Brooke novel, writes to her friend Emily Howard of her own sensibility, "Born with a too tender heart, which never before found an object worthy of its attachment, the excess of my affection is unspeakable. Delicate in my choice, even in friends, it was not easy to find a lover equal to that idea of perfection my imagination had formed."

Throughout Madame Riccoboni's novel we are immersed in the sufferings, the "exquisite pangs," of the separated lovers. It is only in the last section of Mrs. Brooke's novel, however, that we are plunged into the grief of the dying lovers and the anguish of their afflicted parents and friends. After the death of the two young lovers, Anne Wilmot writes: "Pleased with the tender sorrow which possessed my soul, I determined to indulge it to the utmost," words reminiscent of those of Prévost's *Man of Quality* quoted earlier: "If tears and sighs are not to be described as pleasures, it is true nevertheless that they have sweetness for a person in mortal affliction. The moments that I devoted to my grief were so dear to me that to prolong them I abstained from sleep." There is a genuine pleasure in sorrow for the individual of sensibility. The previously Edenic setting of the Belmont garden takes on gothic overtones as Anne writes:

> Pleased with the tender sorrow which possessed all my soul, I determined to indulge it to the utmost; and, revolving in my imagination the happy hours of chearful friendship to which that smiling scene had been witness, prolonged my walk till evening had, almost unperceived, spread its gloomy horrors round; till the varied tints of the flowers were lost in the deepening shades of night.

Awaking at once from the reverie in which I had been plunged, I found myself at a distance from the house, just entering the little wood so loved by my charming friend; the every moment increasing darkness gave an awful gloom to the trees; I stopped, I looked round, not a human form was in sight; I listened, and heard not a sound but the trembling of some poplars in the wood; I called, but the echo of my own voice was the only answer I received; a dreary silence reigned around; a terror I never felt before seized me; my heart panted with timid apprehension; I breathed short, I started at every leaf that moved; my limbs were covered with a cold dew; I fancied I saw a thousand airy forms flit around me; I seemed to hear the shrieks of the dead and dying; there is no describing my horrors.

It is worth noting that Horace Walpole's *The Castle of Otranto* was published the same year as *The History of Lady Julia Mandeville*, 1763. The melodramatic climax, the sudden violence, and the overtones of the final pages of Mrs. Brooke's novel differentiate her from Madame Riccoboni and indicate her awareness of the trend of the novel of sensibility toward the gothic.

Eighteenth-century readers apparently objected to the disastrous ending of Mrs. Brooke's novel. According to one report, "It has been often, however, wished that the catastrophe had been less melancholy; and of the propriety of this opinion the Authoress herself is said to have been satisfied, but did not choose to make the alteration."[10] Mrs. Brooke was living in the age that preferred Nahum Tate's *King Lear* (in which the ending had been altered to suit the tender sensibilities of the audience) to Shakespeare's tragedy. Having criticized the influential David Garrick in *The Old Maid* for preferring the "adulterated cup of Tate [Nahum Tate's *Lear*] to the pure genuine draught offered him by the master he avows to serve with such fervency of devotion,"[11] Mrs. Brooke is not the writer to alter the unhappy ending of her novel to placate her readers.[12]

Although the catastrophe has come about abruptly, for the reader a brief reference to *Romeo and Juliet* foreshadows the tragedy. Writing of this play Anne says:

We have seen them enact Romeo and Juliet.

Lady Julia seemed to sympathize with the heroine:

I'll not wed Paris; Romeo is my husband.

Indeed the similarity to *Romeo and Juliet* is not to be overlooked. At nineteen Julia is as innocent and naive a heroine as Juliet. She remains true to her lover from whom she is separated because of anticipated, rather than actual, parental opposition to their marriage. Harry rushes back because of a supposed plan of her father to marry her to another suitor. Like Romeo he dies

because he fails to receive the letter which would clarify the situation. The parents who failed to explain their plans to their children ultimately must bear a large share of the responsibility for the tragedy. As in *Romeo and Juliet* each has lost an only child, and, as the novel ends, each plans to erect a memorial monument.

Although a duel provides the climax to the novel, duelling is only one of the aspects of society on which Mrs. Brooke is commenting. It is not intended to have the prominence which Mrs. Laetitia Barbauld in 1810 ascribes to it when she speaks of *The History of Lady Julia Mandeville* as "a forcible appeal to the feelings against the savage practice of duelling."[13] Duelling also appears in Mme. Riccoboni's novel as an aspect of life which contributes to both Juliet's anguish and Ossory's dilemma. Juliet learns of the death of her only brother in a duel at the moment when she is most distressed by her apparent betrayal, and Ossory's unhappy situation is increased when he realizes that, were he not to marry the woman he seduced, her brother must surely challenge him to a duel; in all likelihood he would then add his friend's death to the woman's disgrace in the list of his culpabilities.

Didacticism and sentimentality characteristic of the novel of sensibility are very much in evidence in both of these novels. Yet the wit and humour which provide much of the attractiveness of the later *History of Emily Montague* are equally a part of Mrs. Brooke's first novel. In this respect she runs counter to the traditional novel of sensibility in which the excessively sentimental characters dominated by their emotions are more prone to tears than to laughter, and to emotional outbursts than to wit. Here certainly she differs radically from Madame Riccoboni, with whose heroine we are inclined to agree when she says about two-thirds through the novel:

A Reflexion strikes me, my Dear; it is that I certainly must weary you. I tell you my Thoughts as they rise, and Heaven knows they contain nothing amusing—.

(Letter XV)

Yet Lady Juliet Catesby, who never oversteps the bounds of propriety but remains a conventional heroine in outward behavior, makes a number of remarks which indicate her antipathy to the restrictions on women at the time and to the double standard governing the conduct of men and women. When her friend Henrietta's fiancé suggests that she should forgive Ossory since he is now repentant, Juliet seizes the opportunity to express her indignation at this male attitude:

My Lord Castle-Cary pretends, that all Resentment ought to yield to a sincere Repentance. With my Inferiors, I will govern myself by this Maxim; but never with my Friends. But, my Dear, it will not be useless to make a little Remark here. It is, that Man only establish this Principle, in Hopes to take Advantage of it; Accustom yourself to think, with my Lord Castle-Cary, that Repentance effaces all Faults, and depend on it, he will provide himself of sufficient Occasions to repent.—His Letter displeases me, I confess: I renounce his Approbation: It would cost me too dear, if I must buy it by a Weakness, which would degrade me in my own Eyes.

(Letter VII)

Later she writes:

O my dear *Henrietta*, the Men regard us merely as Beings placed in the Universe for their Amusement; to trifle with, in that Species of Infancy, to which they are reduced by those impetuous Passions, which they reserve to themselves the infamous Liberty of arousing with Confidence, and submitting to with Shame. They have left to that Sex they presume to typify as weak and irresolute, the difficult Task of resisting the softer Impulses of the Heart, of conquering Nature herself. Slaves to their Senses alone, when they appear to be so to our Charms; it is for themselves they pursue, for themselves they address us: They consider only the Pleasures we are capable of bestowing: They withhold their Esteem from the object of their pretended Adorations; and if they find in us Strength of Mind, and Dignity of Sentiments, we are *inhuman Creatures:* We pass the Limits their Tyranny has prescribed to us, and become unjust without knowing it.

(Letter XXII)

Possibly such feminist comments made the novel more congenial to Mrs. Brooke to translate; certainly they would reinforce her own feminist stance.

In Mrs. Brooke's novel, Julia Mandeville is, like Juliet Catesby, the conventional eighteenth-century heroine, but she plays a minor role in the novel which bears her name. The more prominent Anne Wilmot is the Brooke spokesman. While Riccoboni's Juliet Catesby rails against the injustices of the woman's situation in society, Brooke's Anne has learned to cope with the situation in which she finds herself in the eighteenth-century battle of the sexes, as these words suggest:

I am too good a politician in love matters ever to put a man out of doubt till half an hour before the ceremony. The moment a woman is weak enough to promise, she sets the heart of her lover at rest; the chace, and of consequence the pleasure, is at an end; and he has nothing to do but to seek a new object; and begin the pursuit over again.

The feminism which is evident in *The History of Emily Montague* is evident in the earlier Brooke novel through the persona of Anne who provides the humour as well as adding an air of realism to *The History of Lady Julia Mandeville*. One would expect such a lively character as Anne from the pen of Frances Brooke, whose highly successful *Old Maid* was the first periodical initiated by a woman,[14] and who was not afraid to cross swords with the powerful David Garrick, criticizing him in *The Old Maid* and later satirizing him in her novel *The Excursion* (1777).[15] Anne enjoys the new-found freedom of widowhood and, as almost half the letters of the novel are written by her, considerably livens up proceedings, providing an effective contrast to the emotional outpourings of Harry Mandeville. She is both of her age and outside of it. More than anyone else she is guided by right reason as well as elegant manners. As a friend of the young lovers whose own romance remains for the most part in the background she is in role and personality the forerunner of Emily Montague's young friend, Arabella Fermor. Anne is not a sentimentalist to the extent that Harry and Julia are, but rather practical and realistic. At one point, for example, she suggests that Harry should seriously consider marrying Miss Westbrook solely for her money. It is she who realizes the impracticality of Harry's plan to increase his fortune sufficiently in a year to marry Julia. Aware of the world she lives in, she assumes that Belmont would never consider the relatively fortuneless Harry for Julia despite his aristocratic name, elegant manners and excessive sensibility. In this assumption, however, she is wrong; benevolence wins over practicality with Belmont.

Anne is adroit at manipulating people and situations, a talent charmingly evinced when seemingly chance events at a ball produce happy results for Julia and Harry and unhappy for Miss Westbrook. We learn later that Anne has carefully plotted the whole incident, making full use of her understanding of human nature and her skills as a coquette.[16] Her practical nature is demonstrated by the solution she works out to evade the clause in her husband's will whereby the entire estate passes immediately to his niece, Bell Hastings, if she marries. She wins Bell's agreement to return half the estate to her on her marriage, for if Bell did not agree to this Anne would not marry and the young woman would receive no share of the estate. As Anne points out, the half she herself will receive is in fact the sum of her dowry which, once passed to her husband, is lost to her completely— another comment on woman's status in eighteenth-century society. Perhaps the best example of Anne's flouting of eighteenth-century convention, when it cannot be manipulated or avoided, is her admission to Lady Belmont, after some witty and elusive repartee, that she does, in fact, love Bellville and that, since marriage appears impossible for them, she intends to continue enjoying his company, despite the impropriety of such a relationship in the eyes of society.

Similarities between *The History of Lady Julia Mandeville* and the better known *History of Emily Montague* are immediately evident. Both are epistolary novels structured about three sets of lovers. In both, the majority of letters are written by the man involved in the central romance, a conventional eighteenth-century lover (Harry Mandeville and Ed Rivers) and by the woman participant in a secondary romance (Anne Wilmot and Arabella Fermor). In both novels the woman is the astute observer and commentator on the affairs of the other lovers. In both, this woman spokesman provides the more realistic, perceptive and witty attitude, and through her independent spirit reflects the feminism of the author. The disparity between temperament and outlook of the two central viewpoints, that of the conventional, rather prosaic male and that of the perceptive, articulate female, contributes to the tension of the novels and provides variety of tone and pace, an asset lacking in Riccoboni's novel with its single correspondent. Thematically both of Brooke's novels are concerned with courtship and its complexities, employing the sentimental romantic plot to which Madame Riccoboni had made such a signal contribution. In both novels Mrs. Brooke questions social conventions, arranged marriages, and materialistic values in general. In both, sensibility is the overriding virtue of hero and heroine.

Today we direct our attention more to the Canadian novel with its interpretation of eighteenth-century Canadian setting and its view of life in Quebec immediately after the conquest. Yet a return to the earlier and more popular novel adds to our understanding of Frances Brooke, of her craftsmanship and her thematic concerns, and helps us to see her in the context of her times. She learned from the French novel of sensibility and especially from Madame Riccoboni whom she translated: and there is no doubt that she took the overall structure and handling of narrative from her own first successful novel and adapted them to her new subject and new setting in *The History of Emily Montague*. Mrs. Brooke's popular translation of *Lady Catesby* and her own first novel contributed to the development of the English novel of sensibility. But Mrs. Brooke is also one of the earliest novelists to attempt a more realistic account of everyday events rather than a focussing on melodramatic incidents. This concern is evident in her portrayal of life on the Belmont estate with its outings, balls, and rural festivities, and later, in *Emily Montague*, of day-to-day events in Quebec, in which regional setting is incorporated more fully into the narrative. Thus she contributed to the newer movement toward realism as well as to the more currently popular cult of sensibility. A stylistic blending of the two modes is achieved largely through the voices of the two dissimilar correspondents in each novel, one a creature of extreme sensibility and the other an ironic observer. The contrasting images of women, the traditional eighteenth-century woman of feeling and

the witty, astute commentator, also contribute to the tension between the sensible and the realistic, the romantic and the ironic. Indeed, not the least of Mrs. Brooke's concerns is the role of women in eighteenth-century society; and a major attraction of both novels, one which differentiates her fiction from that of her mentor Madame Riccoboni and others of her time, is her creation of an intelligent and lively spokesman for women.

Notes

[1] There is one exception. W. H. New's excellent article "*The Old Maid:* Frances Brooke's Apprentice Feminism," *Journal of Canadian Fiction,* 2, No. 3 (Summer 1973), 9-12, shows the significance of Mrs. Brooke's periodical in her thematic and stylistic development.

[2] Three editions were published the first year, 1763, a fourth in 1765, and later editions in 1769, 1773, Dublin 1775, 1782. Also, reference to Mrs. Brooke usually identified her by describing her as the author of *The History of Lady Julia Mandeville.* Fanny Burney, when taken by her mother to meet her, spoke of Mrs. Brooke as "the celebrated authoress of 'Lady Julia Mandeville'" (*The Early Diary of Fanny Burney,* ed. A. R. Ellis, I, 283).

[3] Maurice Lévy, *Le Roman "Gothique" Anglais 1764-1824* (Toulouse: Université de Toulouse, 1968), p. 179.

[4] E. A. Baker, *The History of the English Novel* (New York: Barnes and Noble, 1929), V, 126.

[5] Francis Wright, *Sensibility in English Prose Fiction 1760-1814: A Reinterpretation* (New York: Russell and Russell, 1937), 21.

[6] George Saintsbury says that "*Milady Catesby* is well worth comparing with [Fanny Burney's] *Evelina,* which is some twenty years its junior, and the sentimental parts of which are quite in the same tone with it." *A History of the French Novel,* 2 vols. (New York: Russell and Russell, 1917, rpt. 1964), I, 435.

[7] All quotations from *The Letters of Juliet Lady Catesby to her Friend, Lady Henrietta Campley* are from the fourth edition (London: R. and J. Dodsley, 1764).

[8] All quotations from *The History of Lady Julia Mandeville* are from the seventh edition (London: J. Dodsley, 1782, 2 volumes). In volume 2 of this edition pages 193 to 240 do not exist. Signatures indicate that there are no leaves missing, but rather that pages have been incorrectly numbered. This fact has been confirmed by comparison with the 1763 edition.

[9] In her *Histoire du Marquis de Cressy* (1758), for

more advantageous marriage enters the convent.

[10] John Nichols, *Literary Anecdotes of the Eighteenth Century; comprising biographical memoirs of William Bowyer . . .* (London: Nichols, Son and Bentley, 1812-15), II, 346-47.

[11] Mary Singleton (pseud.), *The Old Maid,* A New Edition revised and corrected by the Editor (London: A. Millar, 1764), No. 18, p. 149.

[12] It is worth noting, however, that much later Mrs. Brooke wrote a sequel to *Julia Mandeville, The History of Charles Mandeville* (1790), in which she provides a happier ending. Charles, the supposedly long dead brother of Harry, returns to England a wealthy man and marries Emily Howard, Julia's confidante and her equal in sensibility. Since Emily has become a surrogate daughter to Julia's parents, the marriage provides a happy resolution for the families of both Harry and Julia.

[13] Laetitia Barbauld, ed., *The British Novelists* (London: Rivington, 1810), XXVII, p. i.

[14] As the title of his article indicates, W. H. New looks at the feminism in Brooke's *Old Maid* in his article "*The Old Maid:* Frances Brooke's Apprentice Feminism."

[15] See John Nichols' *Literary Anecdotes* re Mrs. Brooke's reference to Garrick in *The Old Maid.* Mrs. Brooke was criticized severely for this satire by the reviewer of *The Excursion* in *The Monthly Review,* LVII (1777), pp. 141-45, who devotes more space to praise of Mr. Garrick than to criticism of the novel. Garrick's own indignation is noted in the following letter:

> I hope you have seen how much I am abus'd in yr. Friend Mrs. Brooke's new Novel?—she is pleased to insinuate that [I am] an excellent Actor, a so so author, and Execrable Manager and a Worse Man—Thank you good Madame Brookes—If my heart was not better than my head, I would not give a farthing for the Carcass, but let it dangle, as it would deserve with It's brethren at ye End of Oxford Road—She has invented a Tale about a Tragedy, which is all a Lie, from beginning to ye End—she Even says, that I should reject a Play, if it should be a woman's—there's brutal Malignity for You—have not ye Ladies Mesdames *Griffith, Cowley & Cilesia* spoke of me before their Plays with an Over-Enthusiastic Econium?—

[Letter 1109, To Frances Cadogan, in *The Letters of David Garrick,* ed. G. Little and G. M. Kahrl (London: Oxford Univ. Press, 1963), III, 1172.]

[16] See volume I, pp. 126-29.

Mary Jane Edwards (essay date 1981)

SOURCE: "Frances Brooke's *The History of Emily Montague:* A Biographical Context," in *English Studies in Canada,* Vol. 7, No. 2, Summer, 1981, pp. 171-82.

[*In the following essay, Edwards discusses the religious references in* Emily Montague, *noting that Brooke's father, maternal grandfather, and husband were Church of England clergymen and that Brooke herself had a keen interest in promoting the tenets of the church.*]

Since its first publication by James Dodsley, the London bookseller, in April 1769, Frances Brooke's **The History of Emily Montague** has been considered in a variety of contexts.[1] In English literature it has been discussed as an epistolary novel in the tradition of Richardson; as a novel of sensibility; as a popular novel of the late eighteenth century; as a pre-romantic novel; and as an early feminine—and feminist—novel.[2] The influence of such French writers as Riccoboni and Rousseau on **The History of Emily Montague**, its position as one of the first English novels to deal with America, and its claim to be the first Canadian novel have also been debated.[3] If, as well as the editions of the novel in English, one discusses its translations into Dutch and French, then its contexts become even more international.[4] In this paper I propose to consider Frances Brooke's second novel in another context—that of her own life—by discussing yet another aspect of **The History of Emily Montague**—its religious references.

Frances Brooke introduces references to religion in the first letter sent from Quebec, the second letter of **The History of Emily Montague.** On 27 June 1766, Edward Rivers, the chief male character of this epistolary novel, reports to his sister Lucy that he has arrived in the colony. Then he adds: "you really, Lucy, ask me such a million of questions, 'tis impossible to know which to answer first; the country, the convents, the balls, the ladies, the beaux—'tis a history, not a letter, you demand." He does, however, comment briefly on such topics as the "religious veneration" he felt "approaching the coast of America" and "the view of Quebec": "it stands on the summit of a boldly-rising hill, at the confluence of two very beautiful rivers, the St. Lawrence and St. Charles, and, as the convents and other public buildings first meet the eye, appears to great advantage from the port."[5] With these references, Mrs. Brooke begins her consideration of religion, particularly as it pertains to the recently-acquired French colony of Canada.

References to religion recur throughout the novel. In letters written in the summer and fall of 1766, Rivers continues to report on various aspects of religion at

Quebec. On 4 July, for example, he begins the "particular account of the convents" at Quebec which Lucy has requested with the question, "Have you an inclination, my dear, to turn nun?" Although Rivers tosses other witty asides into his "account," it is basically a long, serious analysis of the "three religious houses at Quebec . . . the Ursulines, the Hotel Dieu, and the General Hospital"; a ceremony in which a nun took the veil; and Madame de la Peltrie, the builder of the Ursuline convent.

Rivers is factual in much of the analysis. The Ursulines wear a "black habit"; the nuns of the Hotel Dieu, a white habit "with a black gauze veil"; the sisters of the General Hospital, that of the Hotel Dieu, "except that to the habit is added the cross . . . a distinction procur'd for them by their founder, St. Vallier, the second bishop of Quebec." The "superior" of the Ursulines "is an English-woman of good family, who was taken prisoner by the savages when a child."[6]

As well as providing facts about the convents, Rivers describes his feelings towards them. These are often positive. The Ursulines' "superior" is "one of the most amiable women [he] ever knew, with a benevolence in her countenance which inspires all who see her with affection: I am very fond of her conversation, tho sixty and a nun." The Hotel Dieu's habit is "extremely becoming." The General Hospital nuns are "the most agreeable women"; they "are all of the noblesse, are many of them handsome, and all genteel, lively, and well bred; they have an air of the world, their conversation is easy, spirited and polite: with them you almost forget the recluse in the woman of condition."

On the whole, however, Rivers's feelings about the convents are more negative than positive. All the nuns, he decides, "have an air of chagrin, which they in vain endeavour to conceal; and the general eagerness with which they tell you unask'd they are happy, is a strong proof of the contrary." His "indignation" is awakened

> from having seen a few days since at the Ursulines, an extreme lovely young girl, whose countenance spoke a soul form'd for the most lively, yet delicate, ties of love and friendship, led by a momentary enthusiasm, or perhaps by a childish vanity artfully excited, to the foot of those altars, which she will probably too soon bathe with the bitter tears of repentance and remorse.

Admiration, yet pity, in fact, best summarize Rivers's view of both Madame de la Peltrie and the conventual system:

> Who can help admiring, whilst they pity, the foundress of the Ursuline convent, Madame de la Peltrie, to whom the colony in some measure owes its existence? young, rich and lovely; a widow in

the bloom of life, mistress of her own actions, the world was gay before her, yet she left all the pleasures that world could give, to devote her days to the severities of a religion she thought the only true one: she dar'd the dangers of the sea, and the greater dangers of a savage people; she landed on an unknown shore, submitted to the extremities of cold and heat, of thirst and hunger, to perform a service she thought acceptable to the Deity. To an action like this, however mistaken the motive, bigotry will alone deny praise: the man of candor will only lament that minds capable of such heroic virtue are not directed to views more conducive to their own and the general happiness. (1, 26-34)

Later these references to religion are picked up by other letter-writers. On 12 October 1766, the same day that Rivers tells Lucy how, haunted by the "idea" of Emily Montague, he "wander[s] about like the first man when driven out of paradise" (I, 170), Arabella Fermor writes:

> I have been making the tour of the three religions this morning, and, as I am the most constant creature breathing; am come back only a thousand times more pleased with my own. I have been at mass, at church, and at the presbyterian meeting: an idea struck me at the last, in regard to the drapery of them all; that the Romish religion is like an over-dressed, tawdry, rich citizen's wife; the presbyterian like a rude aukward country girl; the church of England like an elegant well-dressed woman of quality, "plain in her neatness" (to quote Horace, who is my favourite author). There is a noble, graceful simplicity both in the worship and the ceremonies of the church of England, which, even if I were a stranger to her doctrines, would prejudice me strongly in her favour. (I, 168)

Although Arabella makes one of the final references to religion when, back in England, she notes that "the two happiest people [she] ever knew were a country clergyman and his wife" (IV, 151), it is her father who discusses most thoroughly the "religious state of Canada" (II, 101) in his series of letters written to the "Earl of . . ." before he and his daughter and all their friends return home. One of Fermor's most complete analyses of the "religious state" of the colony occurs in a letter to the Earl dated 8 April 1767. Discussing the "poverty" and "indolence" of the Canadians, Fermor says one cause of both, as well as of a small population, is "their religion." He expresses surprise that "the French, who generally make their religion subservient to the purposes of policy, do not discourage convents, and lessen the number of festivals, in the colonies, where both are so peculiarly pernicious." Finally, he states: "It is to this circumstance one may in great measure attribute the superior increase of the British American settlements compared to those of France: a religion which encourages idleness, and makes a virtue of celibacy, is particularly unfavourable to colonization."

Having weighed the Canadians, Roman Catholicism, and French colonial policy and found all wanting, he turns to the present situation in the British North American province of Quebec. He premises his remarks on the certainty that the Canadians will eventually be converted to the Church of England and therefore that religion as a "cause of the poverty of Canada will by degrees be removed":

> . . . these people, slaves at present to ignorance and superstition, will in time be enlightened by a more liberal education, and gently led by reason to a religion which is not only preferable, as being that of the country to which they are now annexed, but which is so much more calculated to make them happy and prosperous as a people.

In the meantime, he argues that the Canadians should be granted "the free right of worshipping the Deity in the manner which they have been early taught to believe the best," and that they should not be deprived "of the rights of citizens on account of religion," especially "in America, where every other sect of dissenters are equally capable of employ with those of the established church; nay where, from whatever cause, the church of England is on a footing in many colonies little better than a toleration."

In the concluding paragraphs of the letter, Fermor takes up the question of a "national," "established" religion. A "national religion," he states, should be "the strongest tie to unity and obedience"; and he adds:

> . . . had all prudent means been used to lessen the number of dissenters in our colonies, I cannot avoid believing, from what I observe and hear, that we should have found in them a spirit of rational loyalty, and true freedom, instead of that factious one from which so much is to be apprehended.

The religion best adapted to the "civil constitution" and the "limited monarchy" of England is the Church of England; "the Romish religion is best adapted to a despotic government, the presbyterian to a republican." Since "the civil government of America is on the same plan with that of the mother country," the "religious establishment" should also be "the same, especially in those colonies where the people are generally of the national church; though with the fullest liberty of conscience to dissenters of all denominations." Finally, to help the "establishment" of the "national religion," he advocates the appointment of Anglican bishops:

> I would be clearly understood, my Lord; from all I have observed here, I am convinced, nothing would so much contribute to diffuse a spirit of order, and rational obedience, in the colonies, as the appointment, under proper restrictions, of bishops: I am equally convinced that nothing would so much

strengthen the hands of government, or give such pleasure to the well-affected in the colonies, who are by much the most numerous, as such an appointment, however clamored against by a few abettors of sedition.

> (II, 201-08)

These religious references serve various functions in *The History of Emily Montague.* They help unify the over two hundred letters written from many addresses in Canada and England by ten different characters. The details about religion in Canada add richness of texture to the novel and help Mrs. Brooke develop her political themes about the colony. The variety of tone and attitude to similar aspects of religion exhibited by the correspondents is one method she uses to characterize them. Rivers's description of the habits of the nuns is, for example, a much less witty and sprightly use of clothing imagery than Arabella's similes about her "three religions"; the style of her father's comparison of Anglicanism with Roman Catholicism and Presbyterianism is, in contrast to Arabella's, quite flat and abstract. Finally, the allusions to Adam and Eden provide the novel with an archetypal frame. In addition to their literary functions, however, these references have a biographical significance.

There are several reasons why Mrs. Brooke should display such a keen interest in religion, particularly that of the Church of England. The first have to do with her family background and early upbringing. Her father, Thomas Moore, was an Anglican clergyman; her mother, Mary Knowles Moore, was the daughter of an Anglican clergyman. Her paternal grandfather was also an Anglican clergyman. After Williamson Moore died in 1724, her father left Claypole, Lincolnshire, where he had been curate and where he had baptized Frances on 24 January 1723 O.S., and moved to his father's former parish of Carlton Scroop, Lincolnshire. After he died there in 1727, Mrs. Moore took her three young daughters to live with her mother, now the widow of the Reverend Richard Knowles, in Peterborough. Mrs. Knowles died in 1736, Mrs. Moore shortly after. The three Moore girls then went to live with Mrs. Moore's sister, Sarah, who had recently married Roger Steevens, an Anglican clergyman who was the curate at Tydd St. Mary, Lincolnshire. One sister, Katharine (b. 1725), died in 1738; Frances and Sarah (b. 1727) lived at Tydd until they were adults, although they frequently visited at Tinwell, Rutland, where Richard Knowles, an Anglican clergyman who was their mother's brother, was rector.

By late 1748, "Fan" had "gone to London" to make her way as a writer.[7] She never forgot, however, that she was the daughter, granddaughter, and niece of rural Anglican clergymen, and she never wandered from the paths of their mostly "rational," slightly "Tory," religious piety. In *The Old Maid* (1755-1756), the weekly periodical which was her first publication, "Mary Singleton, Spinster," its pseudonymous editor, compares "the childish follies" of "the church of Rome" and "the parallel phrenzy of our homebred enthusiasts" with "the truly sober and rational piety, which animates . . . the whole liturgy and ritual of the church of England."[8] Variations of these comparisons appear in several of her later works. One of the most memorable is Arabella's "drapery" passage in *The History of Emily Montague*.

By the time "Mary Singleton, Spinster," had prepared her remarks on the "piety" of the Church of England, her creator had become Frances Brooke, the wife of John Brooke, an Anglican clergyman who held livings in the diocese of Norfolk and Suffolk, including that of Rector of St. Andrew's, Colney. When Frances married John, however, he was living mostly in London. And in the spring of 1757, possibly even before the birth of his son John Moore on 10 June, John Brooke sailed in the fleet commanded by Admiral Holburne for Halifax and a planned expedition against the French fortress of Louisbourg. It was John Brooke's North American adventures that finally brought Frances Brooke, John Moore Brooke, who was to become an Anglican clergyman, and Sarah Moore, who was to marry an Anglican clergyman, to Canada. And it was his activities as an Anglican clergyman in Quebec that eventually led Frances to campaign on behalf of the Church of England there.

When Frances, John Moore, and Sarah arrived in Quebec in the fall of 1763, they were met by John, who from 1760 to 1768 was the only Anglican clergyman residing more or less permanently in Quebec. Brooke's official position was that of "Chaplain to the Town of Quebec and . . . parish priest to all his Majesty's Regiments."[9] Thus, he held regular services, married soldiers, and accepted the surrender of at least one deserter. Some of these activities were reported in the Quebec *Gazette*. On 21 March 1765, for example, it reported:

> Sunday last, being the Feast of St. Patrick, the Tutelar of Ireland, the Chief Justice of the Province, with other Civil and Military Officers, Gentlemen, and Merchants, of that Ancient and Loyal Kingdom, attended Divine Service at the Recolets Church; a Sermon suitable to the Day, on the Duty of Praise and Thanksgiving for national Benefits and Blessings, was preached by the Revd. Doctor Brooke, Chaplain of the Garrison, from Isaiah xlii. 12. "Let them give Glory unto the Lord, and declare his praise in the Islands."

In addition to carrying out the duties associated with this military appointment, Brooke often acted as chaplain to regiments stationed in Quebec whose commissioned chaplain was absent. In the same letter to Bishop Terrick of London in which he outlined his official position in Quebec, he also mentioned that he was Deputy Chaplain to the 15th, 47th, and 58th regiments during their respective stays in the town. And, as the only ordained Anglican clergyman in Quebec, he functioned—again unofficially—as parish priest for its civilian population. Thus, on 18 August 1766, the Quebec *Gazette* published a "certificate" signed by "J. Brooke, Chaplain to the Garrison," witnessing to the good character of "Philip Payn, of this City Merchant . . . a Man of Honesty and Integrity."

In carrying out both his official and unofficial duties, John Brooke was obviously caring as best he could for the Anglicans in Quebec. But these activities can be put in two other contexts. The first is the general context of the political situation of Canada in the 1760s: the military rule under General James Murray between 1759 and 1764; the proclamation of Canada as a British colony in 1764; and the establishment of a civil government in the colony, with its attendant complications and decisions in regard to such matters as law and religion, in the years following 1764, first under Murray, then after 1766, under Guy Carleton. The second is the specific context of three petitions with which Brooke was involved during these years. For if John's—and Frances's—activities are put in these two contexts, then it becomes clear that they also wished to get John appointed the official Anglican missionary—perhaps even the first Anglican bishop—in Quebec, to establish the Church of England as the "national" church in Canada, and to set up the means by which the work of the conversion of the Canadians to Anglicanism could begin.

The first of the three petitions with which Brooke was involved was sent in 1761 by the "Civil Officers, Merchants, Traders in Quebec"[10] to the Society for the Propagation of the Gospel in London. It was accompanied by two letters, one from General James Murray, the military governor of Quebec, and the other from John Brooke. Together they requested that the SPG appoint Brooke as Missionary at Quebec, that it support a schoolmaster and a schoolmistress there, and that it send Bibles and Books of Common Prayer in English and in French. The reasons for these requests were also made clear: an Anglican clergyman appointed by the SPG would have an official, civil status in the colony; the clergyman, the teachers, and the books would prevent Protestants from becoming Roman Catholics; their presence would also enable the work of converting Roman Catholics to Anglicanism to begin.

Although these documents were discussed by the SPG in January 1762, they were not answered until after Canada had been officially proclaimed a British colony. On 17 February 1764, the SPG agreed to inform Murray that it would not "fail to consider his request of having a Missionary appointed at Quebec as soon as the Government have taken that matter under their consideration." In the meantime, it would send John Brooke "30 French Bibles, 30 French Testaments, 50 small French and 50 small English Common Prayer Books."[11]

Brooke was also involved in the second petition sent to the Society for the Propagation of the Gospel by the merchants and civil officers of Quebec in November 1764. This time they requested that two Missionaries be appointed: Brooke and another who was fluent in French. Although Brooke sent two letters with this petition, neither he nor the Anglicans in Quebec were granted their request. On the advice of James Murray, who had quarrelled with the Brookes on various matters, the SPG decided not to appoint John Brooke as its Missionary at Quebec. On the advice of many, including Murray and his successor Guy Carleton, the British government eventually adopted a policy of "Lenity & Moderation . . . to the Roman Catholics,"[12] which allowed them to keep their own religion and clergy partly through failing to establish the Church of England as the "national" church in Canada.

When, for example, David de Montmollin, a French-speaking Huguenot, was appointed by the SPG as its Missionary at Quebec in 1768, Carleton changed his *mandamus.* In July 1768, he explained his reasons to the Secretary of State, the Earl of Hillsborough:

> On my Return from Montreal a Mandamus was presented by a Mr. Montmolin . . . directing me to admit and collate [him] to the Church and Parish of Quebec . . . to enjoy the same during life, *with all Rights dues, profits and Privileges as thereunto belonging in as full and ample Manner as the Ministers of Churches in any of our Colonies in America have usually held and enjoyed, or of Right ought to hold and enjoy the same.*
>
> As I find these words in every Mandamus, I look upon it as a Stile of Office, that has been adopted for many years for the other Provinces, and under that sanction, unnoticed, has slipped into those for this Province, tho' under very different Circumstances.
>
> These general and extensive Expressions have occasioned no small Difficulty already in Civil Matters, and been the cause of many Complaints, giving Authority to claim Fees of Office, etc. that are Burthensome, but if they are to be extended to ecclesiastical Property, to dispossess the People of their Parish Churches, and their clergy of their Tithes and all Parochial Dues, for our lawyers are clear these words import no less, the Evils must be much worse.
>
> As I judge it impossible this could have been designed, and that your Lordship could not have failed to communicate to me, if a Measure of such

Consequence had been resolved upon, I have in the mean while, and till I am certain of the King's Pleasure therein, granted [him a] Commission which leave[s] the Power to do all the good [he] can, or chuse[s] to do, without authorising [him] to do Mischief.[13]

The letter Carleton wrote to Bishop Terrick in August 1768, about the "few Protestants"[14] in Quebec was, ironically, carried across the Atlantic by John Brooke.

Two years before, Brooke had made a final effort to establish the Church of England in Canada. On 11 June 1766, he had petitioned "The Honourable James Murray" and "his Majesty's Honourable Council" of the Province of Quebec to grant him the buildings and lands of the Roman Catholic "Bishop's Palace" in Quebec until "such time as a Bishop of the Church of England shall be appointed to the See of Quebec." One reason he advanced for granting this petition was the need

> . . . to preserve the Seat of residence and its Demeans, hitherto belonging to the [Roman Catholic] Bishops of Quebec, for one of [the Church of England]; which besides its being the Establishment by Law, appears to his clearest judgment and conscience; for the promotion of true Piety to God, unsully'd by the follies of superstition, or the rage of enthusiasm; and of Honesty, Truth and Charity amongst Mankind; with reverence to the authority and loyalty to the persons of Princes, and upholding the respects and obligations of the several ranks and subordinations essential to civil Society; to be better and more happily constituted, than any Christian Establishment that he hath known or read of, to be subsisting now or ever to have taken place in the World.[15]

This petition was tabled by the Legislative Council on 17 June 1766, just before Murray left for England and the "interregnum" period Rivers describes in his first letter from Quebec began.

In his endeavour to promote Anglicanism in Canada, John Brooke was actively and ingeniously supported by his wife. Even before she left London in 1763, she had inserted in her first novel, ***The History of Lady Julia Mandeville***, a passage on Canada as "an acquisition beyond our most sanguine hopes," if, among other conditions, the Canadians "are allured to our religious worship, by seeing it in its genuine beauty, equally remote from their load of trifling ceremonies, and the unornamented forms of the dissenters."[16] But her campaign on behalf of her husband and her church became even more intense after she had been to Quebec. In fact, in January 1765, Mrs. Brooke, who had gone home for a few months, not only presented the 1764 petition to the Bishop of London, but she also added a letter of her own in which, making frequent references to her husband, she analysed the "religious state of Canada."

The letter itself does not appear to have survived. "Extracts" from it, however, are preserved in the SPG papers in the Lambeth Palace Library. The following are some of the most relevant:

> Mr. Brooke hath been very civil to the papists at Quebec.... Several parish priests think favourably of Protestantism, & one expressed his willingness to conform to the Religion of the Government.

> The Governor always saith the Romish Religion is a good one, & makes good Subjects. He gives every Discouragement to Protestants, is indifferent to all Religions, an excellent Officer, but cannot govern his passions.

> By the Capitulation the parish priests alone are left out of the protection of the Laws, & the people are not bound to pay them their tithes: the religious orders, native French, are supported in all their rights, & even the Corpus Christi procession, which inspires them with Fury against us. . . .

> The Seminary priests are a Branch of those of St. Sulpice at Paris, to whom part of their Revenues are remitted, all French, very rich & bigotted & active in making Converts. One of them lately went to a Fr. Protestant merchant on his Death Bed & threatened him with Damnation. Mr. Brooke & Capt. Holland, Surveyor Genl went to tell the Governor this, but he wd not hear them.

> The Jesuits also are native French, more learned & less violent than the Seminarians, perhaps less attached to France since their Expulsion.

> The Recollects are inoffensive, have no property but their House, church & Gardens, live on the alms of the English & French, lend us their church when they can spare it: they & the parish priests almost all Canadians.

> M. Reches, Curé of Quebec, the most bigoted priest in Canada, let the part of the Cath. Ch. yard on which alone the English are buried to build houses on; & suffered their Bodies, 25 at a time, to be dug up, & exposed. . . . Before the English came, the dead Protestants were thrown into the River.

> The discharged soldiers every day turn papists: else the priests will not marry them. Some will be married by Mr. Brooke, who marries & buries in French.

> Three convents of women in Quebec: two very poor . . . The Canadians are more attached to their Convents, than any other part of their Religion, as they educate & provide for their Daughters cheaply. Three, all young, one but 17, professed this Summer. The Superior of the Ursulines, an English woman,

> 60, very moderate. Some of the nuns say, that hereticks could not naturally be so good to the people as the English are, but that God hath miraculously turned their Hearts.

> The Canadians dislike our Church principally for want of music & shew. If we had a church the English people would buy an organ & maintain an organist.

> The Indians at Lorette have a good but bigoted missionary & a chapel, & mass in their own language, & like our religion as friendly to Liberty & some dislike Confession & Celibacy of priests, & the women sing in the service.

> For want of Schools our Boys go to the Jesuits or Seminarians, & our Girls to the Nunneries: where the Vicar General (& there is one still) will not let an English woman above 20 be taken for a Boarder. They attend continually to making Converts.[17]

If, then, one considers the religious references in *The History of Emily Montague* in the light of these historical documents, especially Mrs. Brooke's deposition to Bishop Terrick, the biographical significance of these references becomes clear. For in having her characters in *The History of Emily Montague* express doubts about the religions of dissent, including Roman Catholicism, as suitable complements to the English form of government, criticize even mildly the conventual system, praise the Church of England for its moderation, and support an Anglican episcopacy, Mrs. Brooke was not just being true to her family background and early upbringing. She was also entering the lists to champion her husband and her church in Canada.

There are several reasons why this joust was important to her. In England the Brookes were relatively poor; in Canada with preferment they could live more comfortably. In Norfolk John Brooke was one of many clergymen; in Quebec he had been, and might continue to be, the only English clergyman. Therefore, both he and his family would enjoy more social prestige and a more varied social atmosphere in this British North American garrison town, centre of trade, and provincial capital. But, as well as these selfish reasons, there was another, more altruistic one. Both John and Frances thought that the happiness and well-being of the Canadians depended on their becoming Anglicans. Thus, in campaigning for themselves, they were also fighting for what they believed was the best colonial policy for the future prosperity of the British North American province of Quebec.

By the time this "first Canadian novel" appeared, however, the Brookes had returned permanently, as it turned out, to their genteel poverty in England. The Anglicans in Quebec had not only failed to establish the Church of England as the "national church," but they were also without a missionary who spoke English well. By 1769, in fact, it was becoming clear that the real victors in the attempt to Anglicanize—and anglicize—the British province of Quebec were the Canadians, who by the Quebec Act of 1774 had most of their religious—and many of their other pre-conquest—rights formally restored. The dedication of *The History of Emily Montague*, then, to Guy Carleton, the governor perhaps most responsible for guaranteeing the cultural survival of the Canadians, adds a further irony to Mrs. Brooke's efforts on behalf of her husband and her church. That there is a biographical context for the religious references in *The History of Emily Montague*, however, not only allows for the kind of critical approach to the novel which this paper has attempted, but also illuminates Mrs. Brooke's significance as a contemporary commentator on Canada in the 1760s.

Notes

[1] A shortened version of this paper was delivered at the Annual Meeting of ACUTE at Saskatoon, Saskatchewan, 23 May 1979.

[2] See, for example, Ernest A. Baker, *The History of the English Novel,* V (1929; rpt. New York: Barnes & Noble, 1950); James R. Foster, *History of the Pre-Romantic Novel in England* (New York: MLA, 1949); and Philippe Séjourné, *Aspects généraux du roman féminin en Angleterre de 1740 à 1800* (Aix-en-Provence: Editions Ophrys, 1966).

[3] See, for example, Robert Bechtold Heilman, *America in English Fiction 1760:1800* (1937; rpt. New York: Octagon Books, 1968); Desmond Pacey, "The First Canadian Novel," *Dalhousie Review,* 26 (1946), 143-50; Henri Roddier, *J-J Rousseau en Angleterre au xviiie siècle, l'oeuvre et l'homme* (Paris: Boivin, [1950]).

[4] See, for example, *Historie d'Emilie Montague* (Amsterdam: Changuion, 1770), and *Histoire van Emelia Montague* (Amsterdam: Elwe, 1783).

[5] *The History of Emily Montague,* Four Volumes Reprinted in Two (London: J. Dodsley, 1769; rpt. New York & London: Garland, 1974), I, 6-9. Further references to this work are included in the text of the essay, by page and/or date.

[6] This superior, elected in 1760, was Esther Wheelwright (1696-1780), an "American," who was captured by Indians in 1703 and eventually brought to Quebec. She became "Mère de l'Enfant-Jésus" when she took her final vows as an Ursuline nun in 1714. (Pierre-Georges Roy, *A Travers l'histoire des Ursulines de Québec* [Lévis, 1939], pp. 143-44.)

[7] ALS, Roger Steevens to Sarah Moore, 23 December 1748, in Edmund Royds, *Stubton Strong Room-Stray Notes,* 2nd Series (Lincoln: Lincolnshire Chronicle, 1928), p. 7.

[8] *The Old Maid,* No. 22 (10 April 1756), pp. 127-32.

[9] Lambeth Palace Library, Fulham Papers, Volume 1, Numbers 110-11, ALS, John Brooke to Bishop Terrick, n.d.

[10] SPG, ALS, Civil Officers, Merchants, Traders in Quebec to SPG, 29 August 1761.

[11] SPG, "Journal," 16, 90.

[12] PAC Microfilm C-2225, ALS, Gideon Murray to James Murray, 20 March 1764.

[13] PAC MG 11, Volume 5, Part 2, 726-29, ALS, Guy Carleton to the Earl of Hillsborough, 21 July 1768.

[14] Lambeth Palace Library, Fulham Papers, Volume 1, Numbers 163-66, ALS, Guy Carleton to Bishop Terrick, 13 August 1768.

[15] AAQ, Série C, Diocèse de Québec, II, 183, TS.

[16] *The History of Lady Julia Mandeville* (London: R. & J. Dodsley, 1763), II, 47-49.

[17] Lambeth Palace Library, SPG, Volume 11, Numbers 25-26, Extracts from Mrs. Brooke's Letter to Bishop Terrick, 24 January 1765.

Mary Jane Edwards (essay date 1985)

SOURCE: Editor's Introduction, in *The History of Emily Montague,* edited by Mary Jane Edwards, CEECT edition, Carleton University Press, 1985, pp. xvii-lxxi.

[*In the following excerpt, Edwards examines the literary, biographical, and historical contexts of* The History of Emily Montague.]

[*The History of Emily Montague*] was typical of much eighteenth-century English literature. Its references to classical literature and mythology, and to the Chinese, Tartars, Turks, sultans, seraglios, and nabobs, and its quotations from the Bible, Shakespeare, Milton, and more recent English and French writers placed it squarely in the context of the eighteenth-century literary tradition. Its title linked it to the eighteenth-century vogue for both history and biography, genres in which Mrs. Brooke herself also worked during the course of her career; its journey motifs, to much popular travel literature. Its pairing of such character opposites as the coquette and the woman of sensibility, the rake and the man of feeling, gave it a dramatic structure reminiscent of the comedy of manners that Mrs. Brooke with her love of the theatre had often seen on the London stage. Finally, the exploration of such themes as the advantages of country life over city living and the dangers of travel in France for young men connected it with a broad range of eighteenth-century writing.

The History of Emily Montague is linked more specifically with other works of contemporary eighteenth-century fiction. The novels of Samuel Richardson, whom Mrs. Brooke may have known and whose "divine writings"[65] she most certainly admired, and those of his followers, including Mme Riccoboni, were particularly influential. They provided a model for Mrs. Brooke's use of the epistolary form, a form she had already practised successfully in *The History of Lady Julia Mandeville,* the fifth edition of which James Dodsley published in 1769. They gave precedents for her contemporary setting with its references to fashionable English county towns like Bath, such haunts of the beau monde in London as Vauxhall and Hyde Park, and respectable London addresses like Pall Mall and Clarges Street. They set patterns for her writing about an ordinary, recognizable, albeit upper-middle-class and aristocratic world, peopled with army officers, gentlemen farmers, and successful merchants, especially those who had gained wealth in the East Indies and similarly exotic places. They showed her how to develop complicated fables about the reforming and reshaping of both male and female characters and their preparation for marriages based on love, friendship, and mutual respect. Women writers especially encouraged the exploration of themes relating to women's feelings, their education, and their freedom to choose whom they married. Finally, since Richardson and his followers used their novels for "the noble purpose of alluring the heart to virtue, and deterring it from vice,"[66] they promoted the seriousness of the genre and thus its appropriateness as a vehicle to teach both moral maxims and political wisdom.

In *The History of Emily Montague,* then, Frances Brooke reflected much that was typical in eighteenth-century life and literature. She also revealed, however, a talent for using fiction to describe and interpret with accuracy and acumen the new subject of contemporary life in the British province of Quebec. Although the epistolary novel seems today a very artificial type of fiction, actual letters—some of which are still extant—form a kind of subtext to *Emily Montague*. One group comprises the occasional topical letters written by both John and Frances Brooke to various people in authority in London. The letter that Mrs. Brooke wrote to the Bishop of London in January 1765 is probably the most pertinent of these as it illuminates the treatment of religion in the novel.

Some personal correspondence is likewise relevant. There is a particularly interesting group of letters exchanged by Frances Brooke, Jane Collier and Sarah Moore in 1763-64. On 15 Oct. 1763, a few days after her first arrival in Quebec, Frances Brooke wrote a note to Jane Collier to thank her for the drawings Dr. Brooke had requested. From then on, the three women regularly wrote letters to each other; of the 119 known to be extant, Frances penned 16, Jane 30, and Sarah 73. Because Frances and Sarah lived at Sillery, and Jane on Palace Street in the town of Quebec, their letters were delivered back and forth by servants and friends. The shortness of some of these notes, the speed and the frequency with which they were exchanged, and their conversational tone resemble the letters between the fictional Emily and Arabella, especially those that occur toward the middle of the novel when Emily admits her love for Colonel Rivers (Letters 74-79).[67] Certain aspects of their content, too, including arrangements about carrioles, preparations for assemblies and trips to such places as Beauport, analyses of character, exchanges of books—Shenstone is recorded as Sarah Moore's favourite author—discussions of sentiment, sensibility, and friendship, and debates about Sarah's feelings for George Allsopp, all suggest parallels between the facts of Mrs. Brooke's life in Quebec and her rendering of the town and its society in fiction.[68] Unfortunately, no personal letters sent by the Brookes between Quebec and England appear to have survived, but the novel's account of sending and receiving mail via Quebec and New York is authentic.

Mrs. Brooke is equally accurate in her presentation of geographical and topographical detail. The itinerary of her first trip to Quebec in 1763 by way of the Island of Cowes is reflected in Rivers' voyage to Canada in the novel; that of her sister's and Mrs. Collier's return from Quebec to Dover in 1765, in Emily's journey home. Although neither Frances nor John Brooke seems to have sailed between New York and England, this was a common alternate route; from Quebec the traveller would get to New York by way of the St. Lawrence and then the Richelieu River, Lake Champlain, and Lake George south to the Hudson River, a route used in the novel by both Sir George Clayton and *"Monsieur le General"* (Letter 16). References in the novel to places between Quebec and Montreal suggest that Mrs. Brooke was acquainted with the area, if not from personal visits then through those of others. On her journeys to and from England, Mrs. Brooke sailed by such places on the Lower St. Lawrence as Cape Rosier and Kamouraska, and the islands of Barnaby, Bic, and Coudre. In the novel she relates a story about Toussaint Cartier, the hermit of Barnaby Island, that may have been one of the many circulating about this mysterious figure when she was living in Quebec. Mrs. Brooke knew best Quebec and its immediate environs. From her home in Sillery she went frequently to the town of Quebec; and when she could, she visited the surrounding area. Her familiarity with this region is reflected in the novel: Sillery is "four miles" from the place in the town where "the general's assembly" is held (Letter 50); Montmorency "is almost nine miles distant, across the great bason of Quebec" (Letter 80).

Familiar with this area, she was excited and inspired by its scenery. In 1771, she explained to Richard Gifford: "There is no description [in *The History of Emily Montague*] above nature. The lovely luxuriance the wild magnificence of Canada, woud do honor to the finest genius on earth either in landscape poetry or painting: I never think of the scenes there without feeling my imagination inflamd. . . . All I have seen of England is mean to it, except the views from the terraces of Nottingham & Windsor. And for a river, the Thames & Trent are spoonfuls of water to the St. Lawrence."[69] The following anecdote about Frances Brooke and Samuel Johnson, recorded by Hester Thrale in her diary in December 1777, reveals another aspect of Mrs. Brooke's enthusiasm for the river: "When Mrs Brooke upon her Return to England from Quebec told Mr Johnson that the Prospect *up* the River Saint Lawrence was the finest in the World—but Madam says he, the Prospect *down* the River St. Lawrence is I have a Notion the finest you ever saw."[70] Accounts of the topography and topology of Quebec permeate the novel. Arabella's descriptions of Montmorency Falls are particularly enthusiastic, as Mrs. Brooke attempts to convey "the wild magnificence" of the scene through her "Montmorenci-mad" coquette (Letter 81).

Reflected in characters in *The History of Emily Montague* is a wide range of local people. The Indians at the nearby Huron village of Lorette, which Mrs. Brooke often visited, are carefully described. There are quotations from Roman Catholic priests, several of whom both Brookes knew, and stories about nuns at the convents of Quebec; although she is not named in the novel, specific references are made to Esther Wheelwright, the English nun who was Mrs. Brooke's particular friend at the Ursulines. In addition to Madame Des Roches, who plays a key role in the plot of the novel, Mrs. Brooke portrays several Canadian women as being at the same social events as Arabella and Emily. She provides a good deal of information about the Canadians and their language, religion, seigneurial system, and other cultural institutions.

Several of her chief characters have been identified with people whom Mrs. Brooke knew in Quebec. Arabella Fermor is said to be modelled on Anna Marie Bondfield, the daughter of the Brookes' landlord and later the wife of their friend George Allsopp; Edward Rivers, on Henry Caldwell, an army officer in Quebec in the 1760s; and William Fermor, on John Brooke himself, whose view he shared. These identifications should probably not be taken too literally, however. Arabella has also been identified with Mrs. Brooke's friend, Mary Woffington Cholmondeley, the wife of Robert Cholmondeley, and with Alexander Pope's Belinda in *The Rape of the Lock* (1712), who was modelled on a real Arabella Fermor, and she could equally be a composite of Sarah Moore, Jane Collier, and Mrs. Brooke herself. Similarly Edward Rivers could just as easily be based on George Allsopp or Mrs. Collier's merchant brothers. Still, that these identifications were and still are being made suggests the verisimilitude of these and the other protagonists in the novel.

The events used by Mrs. Brooke to shape her plot are likewise authentic. Some have to do with changes in weather and seasons typical of the Canadian climate. Arabella records, for example, that in the last week of November the port of Quebec closed for the winter and the first snow came; her father, that in late April "the vast body of ice" which covered the St. Lawrence broke up at Quebec and thus the river reopened for shipping (Letter 131). Many of the social gatherings in the novel are similar to those Mrs. Brooke and her sister attended. Some of these are seasonal, but others, such as the numerous Thursday assemblies held by "the general," are tied to the actual political developments that the novel traces.

Political events, in fact, help control the chronology of *The History of Emily Montague*. The first letter written from Quebec is dated within a day of James Murray's departure for London on 28 June 1766, and Rivers, referring to the governor's leaving, notes that there is a "kind of interregnum of government" (Letter 2). When he arrived in September 1766, Murray's successor, Guy Carleton, travelled to Quebec from Montreal; in the novel both Rivers and Clayton travel with "the general" as he progresses down the St. Lawrence. Carleton's presence in Quebec was greeted with relief by many people, including the Brookes and the merchants; Rivers says that "a new golden age" is expected from "a successor" (Letter 2). For a while at least, Carleton was generally more popular with the various warring factions than Murray had been, although the latter still had supporters; in a letter dated 23 Nov. 1766, Arabella remarks on the "squabbling at Quebec" over "some dregs of old disputes" (Letter 45), but on 10 July 1767, her father laments that he will "leave Canada at the very time when one would wish to come to it," and states, "It is astonishing, in a small community like this, how much depends on the personal character of him who governs" (Letter 159). Mrs. Brooke's flattering remarks about Carleton in the dedication of her novel are thus reinforced.

Both the private and public themes of the novel, which are linked through images such as those of the Edenic myth and gardens, end on relatively happy notes. Although Rivers expresses "fears for Lucy's happiness" (Letter 200), in the end he is reconciled to her marriage to Temple. Fitzgerald's marriage to Arabella and Rivers' to Emily are each described as a sensible and loving union between two friends and equal partners. The difficulties in this latter match that might have been caused by Emily's jealousy of Rivers' friendship for Madame Des Roches are removed when Emily and Edward return to England. The appearance of Emily's father alleviates the financial problems that have beset the chief characters throughout the novel, while the discovery of Sir William Verville allows even the Sophia subplot to end propitiously. The society created through these marriages, unexpected appearances, and reconciliations is a pleasing blend of the country and the city; agriculture and commerce; aristocrats, merchants, officers, and servants; and educated, enlightened, and independent ladies and gentlemen.

The public themes, especially those concerned with North America, are left more open. The religious, educational, legal, and commercial problems of all the colonies of British North America receive attention, and to those relating to Quebec resolutions are offered: William Fermor, for example, advocates the need for schools to teach the Canadians English and for churches and an Anglican establishment to convert the Roman Catholics to the Church of England, both subjects dear to the Brookes. The novel is silent on any action in connection with these difficulties, however, and the role of Madame Des Roches as a source of tension between Emily and Edward, her name ("rocks"), and even the gifts she sends to Rivers and his bride imply Mrs. Brooke's awareness of the dangers inherent in these Canadian problems and their resolution. Nevertheless, the novel's opening with the old governor's departure, and its later emphasis on the new general's benevolence, underline an optimism about the future. And even though the novel ends with the chief characters cultivating their paradisaical gardens in rural England, the natural images that dominate the descriptions of Quebec suggest that a similarly sacramental society could be created in the "wild magnificence" of the new world. Mrs. Brooke presents, therefore, an essentially positive view of the potential of the new British colony. And even as she dedicated **The History of Emily Montague** to Guy Carleton in March 1769, six months after her husband's return from Quebec, she still may have hoped that their dream of preferment and settlement there could be realized.

Notes

⁶⁵ Frances Brooke, *The Excursion, A Novel. The Second Edition* (London: T. Cadell, 1785), Vol. 1, p. viii.

⁶⁶ Ibid.

⁶⁷ Throughout this introduction, the Arabic letter num-

bers are cited as they appear in the CEECT [Centre for Editing Early Canadian Texts] edition.

⁶⁸ Northamptonshire Record Office, "Correspondence between Dr. & Mrs Brooke, Miss Moore and Mrs Collier while living at Quebec," TS YZ4008, passim. I am preparing an edition of these letters and their two companion pieces, the journal of 1763 and that of 1765.

⁶⁹ Harvard, Houghton Library, fMS Eng 1310 (9), ALS, [Autograph Letter Signed], Frances Brooke to Richard Gifford, 21 May [1771].

⁷⁰ *Thraliana. The Diary of Mrs. Hester Lynch Thrale (Later Mrs Piozzi) 1776-1809*, ed. Katherine C. Balderston, Vol. 1 1776-1784, Second Edition (Oxford: Clarendon, 1951), p. 196. This anecdote is similar to that recorded about Johnson's view of Scotland by James Boswell in his diary of 6 July 1763: "'Sir,' said Johnson, 'I believe you have a great many noble wild prospects. . . . But, Sir, I believe the noblest prospect that a Scotsman ever sees is the road which leads him to England!'" See *Boswell's London Journal 1762-1763*, ed. Frederick A. Pottle (New York, London, Toronto: McGraw-Hill, 1950), p. 294. . . .

Ann Edwards Boutelle (essay date 1986)

SOURCE: "Frances Brooke's *Emily Montague* (1769): Canada and Woman's Rights," in *Women's Studies*, Vol. 12, No. 1, 1986, pp. 7-16.

[*In the following essay, Boutelle argues that Brooke's aim in* The History of Emily Montague *went beyond providing a colorful novel of Canadian frontier life, suggesting that she intended it to serve in part as a document in favor of women's rights and on the current unequal state of relations between men and women. Boutelle maintains that with this intent Brooke's novel* foreshadows the overtly feminist work of Margaret Fuller and Mary Wollstonecraft.*]

Today we remember Frances Brooke, if we remember her at all, as the first Canadian novelist. As a result of her husband's 1763 appointment to the chaplaincy of the garrison at Quebec, Brooke spent several years in the newly British colony of Canada, and she used this experience as background in her second novel, **The History of Emily Montague** (published by Dodsley in 1769).¹ Packed with lively details about the social life, agricultural practices, and cultural characteristics of the resident populations (British, Canadian, and Indian), the novel has long been hailed as the first Canadian novel. While Brooke herself would never have considered herself a Canadian, temporary residence in Canada has always provided good grounds for acceptance into the body of Canadian literature (witness Malcolm

Lowry). In Brooke's case, the specifically Canadian content of the work makes the case solider than most. It has even been argued that *Emily Montague* may be the first "American" novel.[2] At any rate, there *Emily Montague* stands, the grandmother of Canadian fiction (if not "American"), introduced in tiny excerpts at the beginning of the Canadian literature anthologies.

The novel is usually read for its historical and geographical significance first, and for its literary significance second. Brooke had been a friend of Richardson; and *Emily Montague*, like her first novel (*Lady Julia Mandeville*, 1763), is in the epistolary mode she had learned from him: letters flying back and forth, in this case, between three couples whose finally blissful connubial fates are intertwined.

However, unlike *Lady Julia Mandeville*, Brooke's Canadian novel disavows violence or the threat of violence. Very little actually happens in the novel: no one is seduced, murdered, or kidnapped: three couples marry—that is all—after the lengthy disentangling of the heroine from a previous engagement, the flirtatious delaying of a proposal and its answer, and the reform of a lively rake. Early in the novel, Brooke explicitly debunks the man-is-monster expectation which the Richardsonian novel had created: "We [men] are not half such terrible animals as mammas, nurses, and novels represent us" (p. 22). In its quiet emphasis on courtship and on the realities (including the economic realities) of the choices to be made, *Emily Montague* is a major step in the direction of Austen (while retaining the epistolary form and the veneration of sensibility).

Tension, meanwhile, is supplied—for want of plot—by the interplay of the various voices, some touches of dramatic irony, and the flashing play of revolutionary ideas (under the guise of a decorous and mannered surface). For every ounce of languishing sensibility, Brooke provides a balancing ounce of adventurous intelligence. There is enough of a pattern to these ideas to merit a new reading of the novel for its *theme*—and to support a belated recognition of the work as one of the earliest of feminist statements.

Supported by the emerging Romantic and democratic ideals of the time, Brooke argues forcefully for a marriage-ideal, a partnership based on balance, spontaneity, and equality. As background, she sketches in the disastrous consequences of forced or arranged marriages (infidelity, the sacrifice of youth to "age, disease, ill-nature, and a coronet" p. 219). In contrast to such unhappiness and corruption, Brooke presents her examples of the three couples finding each other *without* the assistance of family or friends, overcoming with glorious success all the minor obstacles in their paths: the soulful and lovely Emily Montague and her soulful and lovely Ed Rivers; the pert, flirtatious, and witty

Bell Fermour (named after Pope's Belinda-original) and her Irish-officer Fitzgerald; the lovely and soulful Lucy Rivers (sister of Ed) and her rakish and attractive Jack Temple. Despite the many complications, each couple finds its way to wedded bliss, and the novel ends with the confident line: "On Thursday I hope to see our dear groupe of friends re-united, and to have nothing to wish, but a continuance of our present happiness" (p. 316).

Brooke is careful, however, to establish that the basis of this happiness is more than the result of following the natural (and good) impulses of the heart. At the very core of the novel—exactly halfway through—she unfolds her radically daring theme: the ideal of equality within marriage. (The supposed author of these thoughts is Ed Rivers, in a letter to his sister Lucy, and this is one of the letters that serves to tie the three couples together, as well as to connect England and Canada.)

Brooke begins by quoting Madame de Maintenon's Griselda-like advice to the Duchess of Burgundy: "*They* [husbands] *are naturally tyrannical . . . they are masters, we have only to suffer and to obey with a good grace*" (p. 164). Ed, however, makes a quick turnaround: "That we are generally tyrannical, I am obliged to own; but such of us as know how to be happy, willingly give up the harsh title of Master, for the more tender and endearing one of Friend" (p. 164). He launches, climactically, into a panegyric to the married union of mind as well as heart, with equality as the *sine qua non*: "Equality is the soul of friendship: marriage, to give delight, must join two minds, not devote a slave to the will of an imperious lord; whatever conveys the idea of subjection necessarily destroys that of love, of which I am so convinced, that I have always wished the word OBEY expunged from the marriage ceremony" (p. 164). That a male character should be advocating the omission of "obey" from the marriage vows in 1769 is indicative of the sweeping radicalism of Brooke's position. It also reveals her political acumen: the argument is stronger when put in the mouth of a male character; and the argument is less easily traced to Brooke herself.

The ramifications of this ideal are quickly spelled out. In place of Madame de Maintenon's rules, Ed gives Lucy a different set: " . . . study the taste of your husband, and endeavour to acquire a relish for those pleasures which appear most to affect him . . . have separate apartments . . . be always elegant, but not too expensive, in your dress . . . spare no pains to improve your understanding, which is an excellent one" (p. 165). He concludes with an all-inclusive guideline: " . . . do not lose the mistress in the wife . . . have always the idea of pleasing before you, and you cannot fail to please" (p. 165). Then, with blithe impartiality and compelling logic, Ed turns to the responsibilities of the husband: " . . . observe every rule I have given to her, if you would be happy" (p. 165).

The free entering of such a union, without parental pressure and with full knowledge of the equal partnership implicit in the endeavour, is the ideal that Brooke proposes. The idea, for its time, is revolutionary enough to supply all the tension which the plot lacks. It is backed, moreover, by a recurrent and spirited sense of what it means to be a free woman: Emily insisting on her own right to decide, "with the genuine spirit of an independent Englishwoman, who is so happy to be her own mistress, and who is therefore determined to think for herself" (p. 99); Lucy pertly announcing her intent to marry Temple, despite her brother's warnings, but with her mother's support; and—the chief spokeswoman—Bell, whose father credits her with "the free spirit of woman" (p. 132), and who uses the same phrase in reference to herself (p. 148). While the other characters tend to languish and agonize, Bell zips and swirls her merry way through the pages of the novel ("I hate discreet young ladies that marry and settle; give me an agreeable fellow and a knapsack," p. 98). Many readers must mourn her final settling with the equally flirtatious Fitz.

Brooke's interest in the status of women and the possibilities open to them was in evidence long before her stay in Canada. Her first literary endeavor was the singlehanded publication of a weekly journal called *The Old Maid* (1755-56), written under the pseudonym of Mary Singleton, Spinster. While Brooke used this journal to question and to challenge the *status quo,* the stance is erratic and the philosophy as yet not clearly formulated. Meanwhile, in her other works written before and after *Emily Montague* (tragedies, light operas, novels, translations—all with non-Canadian backgrounds), the feminism is so muted as to be almost invisible. It is in *Emily Montague* alone that Brooke establishes herself as one of the most daring and avant-garde writers of her age.

What was there in the Canadian experience to open this woman's eyes (Bell describes both herself and Emily as "awakened," p. 189)?

To Brooke, a woman who had never before left England, Canada offered a new land, a testing ground, a place of possibility. Her survival of the three-month voyage (the Governor of Canada, Sir James Murray, had been unable to persuade his wife to make the trip) was in itself promise that the daring are rewarded. Once arrived, she found herself in an exceptional and interesting position: one of the few English-women in Quebec, at the center of the colony's social and political life, attached to the garrison and yet not of it, equipped with a good working knowledge of French. As Bell reveals, "What particularly pleases me is, there is no place where women are of such importance . . ." (p. 122). While Bell is commenting here on the social importance of women in the garrison culture, it is clear that the experience helped Brooke to reassess the differences in education between men and women: ". . . there is nothing so insipid as women who have conversed with women only; let me add, nor so brutal as men who have lived only amongst men" (p. 272).

Hence, officers' daughters are proposed by Brooke as the new prototype: women educated in and through the company of men, with Bell as the model of the new woman ("I am, thanks to papa, amazingly learned, and all that, for a young lady of twenty-two: but you will allow I am not the worse," p. 199). A Shavian life-force seems to surround Bell, signalling that she is the woman to be watched. And it is Bell herself who, finally and eloquently, is allowed to speak, as a woman, to a woman, for women: "'Tis a mighty wrong thing, after all, Lucy, that parents will educate creatures so differently who are to live with and for each other. Every possible means is used, even from infancy, to soften the minds of women, and to harden those of men; the contrary endeavour might be of use . . ." (p. 159). All of this leads to the new man and the new woman that Brooke proposes and illustrates: the man with a stronger dose of feeling, and the woman with a stronger dose of intellect.

Ed Rivers, somewhat awkwardly, is squeezed into the former role. In the first paragraph of the novel, we find him dropping "a tender tear" (p. 17); and he himself acknowledges that his "heart has all the sensibility of woman" (p. 111). Bell herself confirms his unique position: "Your brother is almost the only one of his sex I know, who has the tenderness of woman with the spirit and firmness of man" (p. 159). However, despite his potent name and his occasional boasting of affairs with older women, Ed Rivers appears comically over-burdened with sensibility—especially so in his efforts to deter Madame Des Roches' affections. His spirit, meanwhile, does not come close to matching Bell's flamboyant and irresistible energy.

Bell is a far more convincing ideal: "spirit and firm-ness" are there in abundance. While Ed Rivers has described both Lucy and Emily as joining "the strength of mind so often confined to our sex, to the softness, delicacy, and vivacity of her own" (p. 106), it is Bell Fermor who more accurately fits that role. As her name indicates, beauty and firmness come together in her person—another reason to lament the transition to Bell Fitzgerald.

While the garrison culture helped Brooke rethink the differences in education between men and women, the surrounding cultures also provided useful material. Her exposure to a solidly Roman Catholic environment (there were three convents in Quebec: the Ursulines, the Hotel Dieu, and the General Hospital) shocked her and angered her: "I cannot help being fir'd with a degree of zeal against an institution equally incompatible with public good, and private happiness; an institution which cruelly devotes beauty and innocence to slavery, regret, and wretchedness; to a more irksome imprisonment than the severest laws inflict on the worst of criminals" (p. 26). Brooke was quick to draw a parallel between life in the convent and life in an arranged marriage: "The cruelty therefore of some parents here, who sacrifice their children to avarice, in forcing or seducing them into convents, would appear more striking, if we did not see too many in England guilty of the same inhumanity, though in a different manner, by marrying them against their inclinations" (p. 188).

In contrast to the prison of marriage and the convent, the Indian culture at first promises the possibility of freedom. In the early pages of **Emily Montague**, Brooke's Indians could have walked out of the pages of Rousseau, so close are they to his description of the noble savage: ". . . other nations talk of liberty, they possess it . . . they assert and they maintain that inde-pendence with a spirit truly noble" (p. 38). Their govern-ment, meanwhile, suggests new political possibilities for women: "The sex we have so unjustly excluded from power in Europe have a great share in the Huron government; the chief is chose by the matrons from the nearest male relations, by the female line, of him he is to succeed" (p. 39). On the basis of the Indian model government and with a quick glance to the south, Brooke—through Rivers—pushes for enfranchisement and suggests the legitimacy of rebellion: ". . . *we* [men] are the savages, who so impolitely deprive you of the common rights of citizenship . . . I don't think you are obliged in conscience to obey laws you have had no share in making; your plea would be at least as good as the Americans, about which we every day hear so much" (p. 40).

Rivers's position here is backed by Bell, who also looks to the Indians as models of freedom for women: "I will marry a savage, and turn squaw . . . never was any thing as delightful as their lives; they talk of French husbands, but commend me to an Indian one, who lets his wife ramble five hundred miles, without asking where she is going" (p. 50). Bell, however, quickly reverses her stance: " . . . in the most essential point, they are slaves: the mothers marry their children without ever consulting their inclinations, and they are obliged to submit to this foolish tyranny. Dear England! where liberty appears, not as here among these odious savages, wild and ferocious like themselves, but lovely, smiling, led by the hand of the Graces" (p. 55).

The movement of Bell's thought here—from the initial hope of freedom, to an awed recognition of the attendant ferocity, and finally to a renewed appreciation of what England offers—is a movement that is echoed elsewhere in the novel. Presumably, a similar pattern of thought was experienced by Brooke herself.

Canada opened Brooke's eyes to new cultures, new approaches. It gave her the space, the distance, and the courage to experiment. It must also, however, have scared her.

In her novel, the land plays a key role in revealing her ambivalence. At first, vast and "sublime" (the adjective is used frequently), it promises a new Eden: "America is in infancy, Europe in old age" (p. 32). The abundance of possibility is emphasized over and over again: "This colony is a rich mine yet unopen'd; I do not mean of gold and silver, but of what are of much more real value, corn and cattle. Nothing is wanting but encouragement and cultivation . . . nature is here a bounteous mother, pours forth her gifts almost unsolicited" (p. 33). Brooke catalogues with obvious relish the fruits that spill forth from Canada's cornucopia: cranberries, strawberries, raspberries, currants, plums, apples, pears, cherries, grapes, musk melons (p. 60). Even the Canadians' native indolence (perhaps—she hints—a result of the climate) is not enough to prevent the profusion of fruits.

Later, the ferocity of the winter (when even the ink freezes), the isolation (as the last boat leaves), and the "sudden, instant, violent" changes of the seasons lead Brooke's characters to a new appreciation of England: "We have . . . none of these magnificent scenes on which the Canadians have a right to pride themselves; but we excel them in the lovely, the smiling; in the enamelled meadows, in waving cornfields, in gardens the boast of Europe; in every elegant art which adorns and softens human life; in all the riches and beauty which cultivation can give" (p. 235).

Brooke ends by taking the challenge of the new world back to England. As "cultivation" becomes her recommendation, the characters return to "Bellfield"—not to a dying Europe, but to a place of renewed civilization, renewing growth. The role of the new woman in the cultivation of head and heart, of harmony between the sexes, is reinforced by Bell's name. As W.H. New has noted, her name also suggests "farmer" (following eighteenth-century pronunciation)[3]; Bell herself jokes about becoming "an excellent farmeress" (p. 61). All this gives reinforcement to the farthest ramifications of Brooke's ideal. In the final sections of her novel, she surrounds her three couples with garden imagery. The new Adams and the new Eves are left to cultivate their affections and their virtues in the paradise of the English Bellfield: "The affections are the true sources of enjoyment: love, friendship, and, if you will allow me to anticipate, paternal tenderness, all the domestic attachments are sweet beyond words . . . 'Cela est bien dit, mon cher Rivers; mais il faut cultiver notre jardin.'" (p. 315).

Brooke, meanwhile, has quietly suggested that this role (the role of cultivator or of creator) is the truly heroic role on earth, the role closest to God's: " . . . the man who conveys, and causes to grow, in any country, a grain, a fruit, or even a flower, deserves more praise than a thousand heroes: he is a benefactor, he is in some degree a creator" (p. 178). Despite the masculine pronouns attending the farmer here, Bell Fermor's role in Bellfield can be seen as equally heroic.

The absence of violence in *Emily Montague* now appears in a new light—as Brooke's own disavowal of a heroism that destroys rather than creates. It is, of course, *her* voice (a voice that includes Bell's as well as Rivers's) which sounds throughout the work: intelligent, witty, passionate. Her easy moving between the male and female voices, her keen eye, her dashing forays into new territory, and her obvious familiarity with current thought,[4] all provide eloquent testimony to *her* "strength of mind," to *her* "softness, delicacy, and vivacity," to *her* "spirit and firmness." "Rivers" shrink before this "Brooke."

As an author, as a "creator," she wanted her work to reach women—that we know. In a letter to Dodsley in August of 1769, she wrote, " . . . one of the best judges of Literature I know . . . told me soon after it was publish'd that it would be lik'd by literary people, but that it wou'd not be so popular a book by much as *Julia Man[deville]*. That it wou'd be better liked by men than women; it has prov'd so I am afraid. Now a novel to sell shou'd please women because women are the chief readers of novels & perhaps the best judges."[5] Her acknowledgement of the superiority of women's judgement, here delicately qualified with "perhaps," is an insistent thread throughout the novel itself. Bell makes the point: "We are a thousand times wiser, Lucy, than these important beings, these mighty lords" (p. 126). Rivers confirms her claim: " . . . women are, beyond all doubt, the best judges of the merit of men" (p. 39).

While the American colonies gather for revolution, Brooke calmly suggests the rationale for a farther-reaching one: the freeing of woman. Her call for franchise, backed by her plea for a decent education for women, and accompanied by her insistence on what men and women can teach each other, is an early and dangerous expedition into territory later entered by Wollstonecraft, Fuller, and the feminist thinkers of the nineteenth and twentieth centuries. (It is both ironical and sadly typical that this most daring aspect of the novel has been invisible to those who praise it for its local color or historical detail.)

Brooke wanted her work to reach women. She wanted to show that the political corollary to her ideal marriage is a society which eschews violence, a society based on a balance between the sexes, a society where women (as well as men) are enfranchised and educated, and where men (as well as women) are taught to listen to their feelings and to cultivate virtue. With such an ideal, it was surely important to her that the book do more than sell: it should also persuade.

As Rivers acknowledges, the ladies "love writing much better than we do; and I should perhaps be only just if I said they writer better" (p. 43). In this work based on her experience in the new world, Brooke's own attempt to "write better" suggests the possibility of a world yet to be realised. The voice that may have failed to persuade in her own time reaches us now across the centuries. It is a voice that we can now—at last—clearly hear.

Notes

[1] *Emily Montague* was published in four volumes by T. Dodsley of London in 1769. A later edition (1734) forms the basis of the currently available New Canadian Library edition, introduced by Carl F. Klinck, edited by Malcolm Ross, and published by McClelland and Stewart of Toronto in 1961. Page numbers in my text refer to this edition.

[2] See Klinck's argument in his introduction to *Emily Montague,* pp. v-vii.

[3] William H. New, "Frances Brooke's Chequered Gardens," *Canadian Literature,* 52 (Spring 1972), p. 35.

[4] Brooke's familiarity with Rousseau's work is much in evidence in *Emily Montague.* Her inclusion of the *Candide* (1759) quotation is additional evidence that she is *au courant.*

[5] See Klinck's introduction, p. xii.

Robert Merrett (essay date 1992)

SOURCE: "The Politics of Romance in *The History of Emily Montague,*" in *Canadian Literature,* Vol. 133, Summer, 1992, pp. 92-108.

[*In the following essay, Merrett suggests that in* The History of Emily Montague *Brooke presented a negative view of British colonization of Canada.*]

The most interesting, because most problematic, claim that Mary Jane Edwards makes in her fine edition of *The History of Emily Montague* is that Frances Brooke expresses in her novel an "essentially positive view of the potential of the new British colony."[1] This claim is problematic for many contextual and textual reasons.

In the first place, although on March 22, 1769 Brooke dedicated her book to Guy Carleton, the recently appointed governor of Canada, and spoke glowingly of the country's prospects under his governance, her optimism is rendered questionable by her personal experience of the new province and by the frustration of her political wish to affirm the Conquest of Quebec. While the dedication praises Carleton's "enlightened attention" for bringing about a "spirit of loyalty and attachment to our excellent Sovereign" and a "chearful obedience" to British law (1), the text of her epistolary novel, in the course of plotting a retreat from Canada to England, necessarily embodies a much less positive attitude than announced by the dedication.

When Mr. Brooke returned to his wife and England in the autumn of 1768, he did so because his petition for a land grant had met with no more success than their joint campaign to establish the Anglican Church in Quebec.[2] Like many of their middle-class contemporaries, the Brookes opposed historical, social and political forces that they understood only partly and could resist hardly at all. Still, in the two years following Carleton's arrival in Quebec and before Mr. Brooke rejoined his wife, the couple must have had an inkling that the new governor would continue to implement the policies of John Murray, the former governor, who, if initially a benefactor to the Brookes, regarded them finally as opponents of his governorship and of his strategic and aristocratic sympathies for the habitants. Indeed, the novel's allusions to Carleton's political stance less celebrate his enlightenment than warn him against continuing Murray's appeasement of Quebec's French populace. Having written her book in Canada during the last months of Murray's term and revised it in England throughout the summer of 1768, Mrs. Brooke had time to grasp why the British government was abandoning the Royal Proclamation of 1763 and was ceasing to trumpet the Conquest of Quebec.[3]

However, *The History of Emily Montague* upholds the Proclamation without predicting the 1774 Quebec Act: while mirroring the facts behind the reversal of British policy, it fails to grasp this policy. Instead it aggravates this political contrariness in ways that question claims for Mrs. Brooke's optimism about Canada. She more eagerly resists political and economic change at home than she promotes Canada's future. She defends the Crown and attacks the Court by favouring military, Anglican and rural over commercial, dissenting and urban values in simple-minded, conventionally middle-class ways.[4] Her bourgeois reaction to aristocracy's growing political and economic power is salient in her emphasis on the freedom of choice for marriage partners: her stress on the right of lovers to choose mates without parental interference constitutes a rearguard attack on Lord Hardwicke's Bill of 1753, which forbade clandestine marriages and stipulated the fulfilment of ecclesiastical, legal, and familial conditions.

This Bill, originating in the House of Lords, was interpreted as a sign of the increasing power of the upper chamber over the House of Commons and as an attack on the social mobility and individual liberties of the middle class. Mrs. Brooke's insistent yet questionable attacks on arranged marriages signal the important because ultimately contradictory relation between politics and romance in *The History of Emily Montague*. Rather than looking ahead to 1774, she takes her bearings from the Royal Proclamation, hoping thereby to belittle the aristocracy's power in church, army, and society, a power epitomized to her by arranged marriages in the English upper classes.[5]

Narrative logic requires Mrs. Brooke to confront as well as to recognize the complexity of Canadian politics, but she writes of them with a vague, even self-exposing, sense of propaganda. Colonel Edward Rivers, her hero, hopes a "new golden age" will follow the "interregnum of government" after Carleton officially becomes governor (7). But hopes for the institution of British rule are beyond realization. When William Fermor, the military patriarch who is Mrs. Brooke's most serious commentator, leaves the colony, he testifies to the governor's "personal character" diffusing the "spirit of urbanity" through this "small community" (285). But he will not judge the governor's political conduct since Mrs. Brooke wishes to eulogize Carleton's personality by way of evading his adoption of French cultural values. Evasiveness leads her to both bury conquest motifs in her text and subsume politics to romance. When Indian women announce to Arabella Fermor, the patriarch's coquettish daughter, that the English conquerors of Quebec are their "brethren" (50), the theme that the aboriginal people are eager to have the British military system of land grants in full operation is somewhat implausibly reinforced. Fermor truly finds the "politics of Canada" to be "complex" and "difficult," but Mrs. Brooke derides this complexity by fancifully turning political evasiveness into female social power. Arabella thinks her preeminence at the governor's balls and assemblies vitally important since "we new comers have nothing to do with" the "dregs of old disputes." Her amusingly egotistic diversion of politics to the "little commonwealth of woman" (98) alerts readers to some of the social and cultural contradictions underlying Mrs. Brooke's propaganda.[6]

When Arabella declares that "[o]ur little coterie is the object of great envy; we live just as we like, without thinking of other people" (101), her sentiments indicate the typically self-exposing contradictoriness of the tiny community which Mrs. Brooke celebrates. This community sees itself as exiled from England yet able to exploit English patronage. It also feels superior to the *habitants* while appropriating French diction and *bons mots* to its speech. Pretending aloofness to Quebec politics, the community imposes its culture on the conquered. Claiming to live in isolation from the larger community, Mrs. Brooke's English characters seek to dominate it, with the result that they depend on it unconsciously. Thus, when Arabella's courtship of Captain Fitzgerald is interrupted by the failure of the French women at the governor's assembly to obey English dancing codes, her protest that the "whole province" knows of her courtship is profoundly inconsistent (188). This inconsistency is more than a matter of unintegrated geographical and cultural concepts; it stems from Mrs. Brooke's political evasiveness. Arabella first compares Quebec to a "third or fourth rate country town in England" (98); yet, on leaving, she prefers to live there rather than in "any town in England, except London" (281). Despite this shift of perspective, the theme of colonial progress stands up to neither contextual nor textual scrutiny. The aloofness to colonial politics analyzed in the context of the suppressed views of the *habitants* and governors shows how Mrs. Brooke encodes political ideas in ways neither historically accurate nor narratively compelling.

Historians of the years between 1763 and 1774 clarify what William Fermor admits to have been a politically complex era and help to assess Mrs. Brooke's ideological exploitation of romance. The necessarily dialectical stance of historians is instrumental to understanding the propaganda in *The History of Emily Montague*. For Kenneth McNaught, the Treaty of Paris was "an unqualified British victory" over French imperialism, but the Royal Proclamation effected the "most perilous conditions imaginable" for British control of North America by defining a "substantial minority nation" on the continent which exacerbated mercantile and military tensions in the empire.[7] Although the Proclamation counted on an influx of colonial Protestants, the mere six hundred merchants who came to live among the sixty-five thousand Canadians served to strengthen rather than weaken the religious and cultural identity of the habitants. If the merchants wanted the Proclamation enacted through a legislative assembly, the establishment of English common law, and the exclusion of Catholics from public office, Quebec's demography meant that "assimilation was soon replaced by a quite exceptional tolerance" of the Canadians.[8] Their compelling sense, moreover, that the Crown needed to find in Quebec a military resource against the turbulent New England colonies led governors Murray and Carleton to oppose both the merchants and the Proclamation by tolerating the seigneurial system and Catholic institutions. When the Quebec Act allowed the Canadian church to collect tithes, enabled Catholics to hold public office and endorsed French civil law, the assimilation promulgated by the Proclamation was officially suspended. However, as W. L. Morton says, the church's power remained strong on account of the "sheer inapplicability, in reason and humanity" of the Proclamation to the "circumstances of Quebec."[9] Thus, shortly after 1763 Catholics served

on juries and pleaded cases before the Court of Common Pleas. Five years, then, after the appearance of *The History of Emily Montague*, the British government decided Quebec's future was to be more French than English, a reversal Mrs. Brooke might have foreseen as she composed her novel. Yet she discounted political trends in Quebec in ways that expose the flaws of British colonialism and undermine her narrative authority. While she and her husband sided with mercantile interests in support of the Proclamation, her book does not uphold these interests. Besides wanting Catholic institutions taken over by Anglicans and reserved for the seigneurs, she wishes her military, genteel class both to dismantle and appropriate the seigneurial system of landholding. While Morton argues that the displacement of the seigneurial class was the Proclamation's most irreparable effect (154), Brooke holds that the French noblesse can be preserved and assimilated by a new aristocratic order modelled on the English hierarchical recognition of military and noble values (250).

Doubtless, national prejudice dulled Mrs. Brooke's contemporaries to the clash of political systems in the colony. But enthusiastic imperialism seems to have blinded her profoundly to this clash. Her contempt for the seigneurs (26) and for the French landholding system (140) together with her indulgent stance toward Rivers' political fantasies about purchasing a seigneury show that the novel's opposing wishes to demean and to appropriate French cultural forms prevent it from openly exploring the conflicts arising from the interaction of the European legal and political systems. Her hero's dreams of being "lord of a principality" (3) and acting *"en prince"* (85) by way of building a "rustic palace" for Emily (154) so that he can regard themselves as "the first pair in paradise" and his spouse as "the mother of mankind" (260) agglomerate sexual, religious and royalist fantasies, thereby concealing his wish to treble the value of his land in a country which, without these fantasies, he feels to be a "place of exile." Economic imperialism underlies Mrs. Brooke's refusal to describe the *habitants'* well-known complaints about the crudity of the British legal system.[10] Their sense of outrage at imprisonment for debt and for jail fees, their anger at the expense and infrequency of court hearings, and their humiliation at trial-by-jury in the face of huge numbers of capital offences are neither presented nor allowed to generate implications. The discrepancy between constitutional theory and political fact, manifest by the abandonment of the Test Act in the selection of Catholics to jury service as soon as 1764, is also suppressed by Mrs. Brooke's imperial and colonial mentality. Unable to admit the implausibility of the 1763 Proclamation, she chose to ignore that Carleton "utilisa au maximum l'élasticité des textes officiels pour redéfinir la politique anglaise."[11]

Mrs. Brooke's political views are yet more equivocal because her colonial and imperial ideas are interfused with notions of class and social hierarchy. Her evasion of the complex alliance between the governors and the *habitants* is inseparable from contradictory reactions to the long-time residents of Quebec and the newly arrived merchants. While her ambivalence toward the *habitants* and merchants promotes Augustan gentility, her novel contains a wider range of unacknowledged ideological conflicts which imply that her narrative heedlessly allows political, social, and cultural contradictions to coexist.

If Mrs. Brooke's commitment to the Royal Proclamation and the Conquest of Quebec appears to entail the degradation of French culture and appreciation of the merchant class, this is not the case simply. While she advanced the cause of Anglicanism in Quebec by siding with mercantile interests, her presentation of Sir George Clayton, the newly knighted baronet with close ties to the city, is negative. Moreover, although Fermor criticizes the economic and political restraints placed on the American colonies, his sense that they are "naturally inferior" (241) is one indication among many that Mrs. Brooke despised those who were supposed to swamp the *habitants* and embody the Proclamation. Since her stance toward the *habitants* is erratically authoritarian and sympathetic, it recoils on British policy as enshrined in the Proclamation. Thus, if Rivers mocks the noblesse's consciousness of rank (22) and laughs at the deference to titles in the French community (42), Fermor's propagandistic claim that the noblesse should be assimilated by a new system of titular honours binding this class to English military officers is not self-evident (250). Fermor's views of French culture often undermine British policy. If his claim that French officers have been assimilated by barbarous Indians stresses the hollowness of French culture (271) and defies its enlightenment (141), he weakens his claim by arguing that the convents in Quebec should be limited to children of the noblesse so as to preserve the old French hierarchy (274). His inconsistency is clear in light of the novel's repeated criticism of the convents as agents of celibacy and depopulation. His inconsistency is made more striking by his attacks on English economic and agricultural policies which, he fears, will so depopulate the countryside that it will become an "uncultivated desart" (221). His admiration of Rousseau and rejection of this philosopher's major idea of primitive virtue (271-72), shows that, while Fermor stresses English political dullness, he holds that his nation's culture is more enlightened than that of France. But the novel's action unravels this pretension. Despite the running debate about the worth of French manners, the characters always proclaim their refinement in terms of French gallantry. Arabella may dramatize herself by rejecting French gallantry (49), but she employs the phrase "British belles" earnestly (147). An ultimate sign of the appropriation of French modes is the closing masquerade at which Emily appears as a "French *paisanne*" (377).

Before analyzing Mrs. Brooke's ambivalence towards the merchant class and mercantile wealth, we should recognize how she translates Augustan sensibility into a mode of enlightenment that appropriates and bests French culture. For Mrs. Brooke, classical allusion, Horatian ideas of retirement, and religious Latitudinarianism coalesce into a myth of Anglican gentility. Although her characters are displaced from England by economic and political change, their familiarity with Greek and Roman letters betokens true Englishness. Rivers' knowledge of Virgil's *Georgics* (24) and Sophocles (38) confirms his gentility, and, if Arabella claims that Canadian scenery renews her appreciation of Greek and Roman myths (30), her mythical references pretend to a sensibility which exquisitely invalidates ideologies other than her own. Thus, she cites Horace to establish an image of female grace applicable to the Church of England but not to Presbyterianism or Catholicism (80). Far from steadily implying that the Canadian setting upholds classical mythology, Mrs. Brooke shows that her characters transport mythology with them as an aesthetic system for disguising and validating their distinctly Augustan notion of patriotism: her strategic mythology helps to uncover the political ideology motivating her romance. If deities reside in Canada, they do so mainly because of Emily. In her presence Canada is the habitation of the Graces (139), for she is Venus who is always attended by the Graces (23): in England Rivers sees her as led by them (355). But this romantic hyperbole is not restricted to Canada or Emily; Temple in England pictures his wife Lucy as Venus attended by the Graces (373), and, since England is supposedly alone among nations in permitting marital choice to women, the country is personified as Venus tended by the Graces (56). So, if Arabella projects nereids (30), naiads (301) and other "tutelary deities" (303) onto the Canadian scene, her refined posture with mythic sense is based on a nexus of political, class, and patriotic codes. In expressing a desire to address a poem to his "household Gods" (379) and in esteeming his "native Dryads" more highly than an "imperial palace" (407), Rivers shows that this nexus of codes implicitly affects or lays claims to a universal enlightenment in the name of a beleaguered rural, Anglican gentry.

To the degree Mrs. Brooke's gentrified heroes and heroines both disparage and appropriate French culture, so they are ambivalent about merchants and mercantile wealth. Vulnerability to inflation rates of twenty-five per cent in the 1760s partly explains their affected differentiation between the wealth of India and North America, between the wealth of imperial trade and colonial expansion. Although Canada holds out to Rivers and the others the prospect of new forms of landed wealth, the resolution of the plot depends far more on the riches of the Orient. Throughout, the characters contradict themselves about Indian wealth because they wish to associate it with city business interests. While Rivers spurns the wealth of nabobs (5), he wishes his sister to spend her portion of two thousand pounds on jewels when she marries Temple so that she will "be on a footing" with a "nabobess" (179). Despite the insistence that love and friendship are richer than an oriental monarch (330) and Lucy's claim that the return of Emily and Rivers from Canada is worth more than an argosy's treasure (311), Colonel Willmott, the patriarch who confirms Emily's marriage and endows her with his wealth, is a nabob (388). Although Rivers' house, Bellfield, is contrasted with an "imperial palace," Willmott's oriental wealth pays for the new wing and completes the original design (407). As final evidence of the questionable displacement of imperial wealth, consider Arabella's contention that "no nabobess" could be as happy as Emily and herself in marrying such poor men as Rivers and Fitzgerald (348): Arabella deliberately underrates their wealth which, if not ample enough for English peers, is far more considerable at the end than earlier in the novel.

Mrs. Brooke's ambivalence about mercantile wealth is clear in the way her characters belittle Clayton: they scorn him to uphold their social superiority but they are no less mercenary. Rivers looks down on Clayton as a "gentleman usher" whose unromantic sensibility fits him to marry a "rich, sober, sedate, presbyterian citizen's daughter" (51-52). Clayton's "splendid income" (74) leads Emily to reject his "parade of affluence" (58), "false glitter of life" (95) and "romantic parade of fidelity" (320). Arabella is completely dismissive about Clayton's prospect of marrying a rich citizen's daughter whose dowry is fifty thousand pounds and who brings with her the promise of an Irish peerage (121). Arabella's contempt arises from her avowed hatred of the "spirit of enterprise" that drives men to keep on acquiring money and land (347). But, if she derides the peerage by claiming that she would not give up the man she loves to the "first dutchess in Christendom" (124), her lover not only is the son of an Irish baronet but also has five hundred pounds a year plus a military salary (284-85), which he advances by exploiting the patronage system to become *"Monsieur le Majeur"* (404). The discrepancy between renunciation of wealth and mercenary calculation is sharper in Emily and Rivers since they articulate most forcefully the myth of rural independence. Emily has "the genuine spirit of an independent Englishwoman" since she resists patriarchal hierarchy (116), and Rivers believes that "we country gentlemen, whilst we have the spirit to keep ourselves independent, are the best citizens, as well as subjects, in the world" (342). The romance between Emily and Rivers, far from simply a matter of companionate individualism, entails an ironically ideological debasement of mercantile and aristocratic interests, as can be shown by an analysis of the lovers' financial attitudes and circumstances.

Rivers declares that love is "more essential, more real" than riches (266) and, if he admits that a "narrow fortune" is inconvenient, he sees mutual love as a "treasure" cancelling fortune's power over Emily and himself (264). Yet, familiarity with the "finest company in England" always reminds him there is a gap between his "birth" and "fortune" (297). Far from endorsing the heroines' view that "our whole felicity depends on our choice in marriage" (381) and far from consistently treating money metaphorically, Rivers is very concerned with money and profit. His acquisitiveness seems to be based on his sister's trust that "the future will pay us for the past" (311). His desire for affluence is evident in his wish to treble the value of his lands in Quebec by clearing and settling them (154). His attitude to his English estate is no less mercenary, despite his claims to the contrary. His redefinition of country gentlemen as the "best citizens" stresses the reciprocity of private and national profit: when he counts on "raising oaks, which may hereafter bear the British thunder to distant lands" (342), he focusses on the systematic integration of personal and public gain that will stem from country gentlemen supplying the materials for imperial ventures. Rivers' profoundly conformist ties to the crown and the constitution are reflected by his constant references to his investment in the funds. While he pretends that he wants a larger income only to entertain friends and to be philanthropical (341), the masquerade's costly elaborateness indicates his unacknowledged wish to imitate London fashion and urban luxury. The underlying acquisitiveness of Mrs. Brooke's characters is elicited by the changing references to Rivers' income and by Emily's dowry and other financial prospects. With his four thousand pounds in the funds, probably yielding five per cent (58), and his military half-pay, Rivers is said to have an income of four hundred pounds per annum at one time (301) and five hundred at another (312). The wish-fulfillment behind these erratic figures also motivates Mrs. Brooke's endowment of Emily with a settlement of twenty thousand pounds which, setting aside her prospects and Colonel Willmott's improvements to the estate, trebles Rivers' income (323). Doubtless, an income of fifteen hundred pounds per annum does not lift Rivers up to the "finest company in England," but it does move him from the merely land-based gentry to the class which gained from the financial revolution based on London capitalism. Certainly, his ultimate income depends far less on Canada than on imperial wealth from India.[12]

The conflicting renunciation of and dependence on monetary wealth confirms that Mrs. Brooke's characterization says less about Canada's immediate future than about the economic plight of Britain's gentry. For the oblique reliance on finance and on mercenary calculation draws out the submerged themes of the middle class's sense of displacement and its compensatory dreams of living in a more highly differentiated hierarchy responsive to its ideology of romance and sensibility. But, if cultural flexibility is an illusion that reveals her characters' loss of social and economic power, the same is true of their apparently progressive attitudes to gender, love, and marriage. As their myth of adaptation to Canada subsides, their fantasy of progressive romance merges into a social reaction that strengthens the forces they have been supposedly combatting throughout the novel. Their romantic strategies, far from being a compensation for relative poverty, in the end merely disguise their wealth and its imperial sources. The novel's closure so completely resolves the conflict between romance and money, individualism and patriarchy, that, in addition to undoing the motivation of the plot, it emphasizes that Canada in the 1760s was neither a fiscal nor a social haven for English gentry. Her merely formulaic reliance on parental and filial conflicts about love and marriage recoils then on Mrs. Brooke's concealment of the economic motives spurring herself and her characters to return from Quebec.

The commercial boom foretold by the Proclamation did not occur. Instead, a decade of recession followed, with many business failures and much fiscal muddle caused by the colony's three currencies.[13] Paper money was overvalued since coins were scarce, and the resulting speculation in French bills led the French émigrés to export huge sums of specie and the British traders to absorb such losses that the colony's capital growth was stunted. The Quebec economy did badly too because of falling agricultural prices as a result of over-production and international barriers to foreign markets. While Mrs. Brooke links Quebec to other cultures and to the international scene, she prefers to see its place in the world through utopian or nationalistic eyes. The result is that Quebec's economic problems manifest themselves in transferred and covert ways: if her characters pretend that romance transcends economic power, their sexual and cultural codes prove otherwise. Their letters, far from conveying epistolary pluralism, are uniformly nationalistic and imperialistic. The illusion of plural viewpoints and of radical stances to gender mask economic and political values that are reactionary and unsympathetic to Quebec's colonial burdens.

The elements of economic and political reaction in Mrs. Brooke's concept of romantic sensibility clarify the way she uses cultural and sexual codes. Rivers perhaps best exemplifies the reactionary impulses of what could be seen as progressive and experimental attitudes. The "tender tear" he lets drop at Carisbrook Castle in memory of the "unfortunate Charles the First" (3) and his oblique lament for General Wolfe, for the "amiable hero" who "expir'd in the arms of victory" (5), show that Rivers joins Stuart nostalgia to the pathos of military heroism. His sensibility is self-dramatizing and backward-looking in a manner that renders his pretensions to gentility questionable. He wishes to be "lord

of a principality" in Canada to "put our large-acred men in England out of countenance" (3). His ambition to be the "best *gentleman* farmer in the province" (24) and his concern for "dominion" (26) indicate that his fantasies about property and power divide him from indigenous cultural codes. In fact he trusts quite blindly to the political hierarchy that guarantees his estate in England and his freedom to traverse Quebec with a *valet de chambre* to look for land to develop (71). The foreign cultures he encounters only confirm his nationalism and aggrandize his already superior sensibility. He praises the Indians' hardy lifestyle mostly to denigrate "effeminate Europeans" (11). He also celebrates the Huron's matriarchal government to attack Europe's denial to women of the rights of citizenship (34). If he says that women may disobey laws not made by them (35), his feminism is not radical. He wishes English women to have the franchise so that canvassing for a parliamentary seat will be more enjoyable for men like himself who believe that women's real power is sexual and who refuse to be a "rebel to their empire" (158). The limits of his radicalism are evident when he concludes that European women have just as much right as the American colonies to complain about political disadvantage: in the context of Mrs. Brooke's consistent refusal to appreciate the American colonies, Rivers' comparison is gratuitous. The partial, prejudiced aspects of Rivers' sensibility are highlighted by his claim that Indian women will be civilized only if they arc feminized (119) and by his avowal, after decrying French manners, that Emily embodies the best cultural features of France and England (57). Like Arabella who sees the promenade at Quebec as a "little Mall" (49), he imposes English cultural signs on life in Canada confusedly. When hc talks of driving out "*en caleche* to our Canadian Hyde Park" (13), his histrionic English sensibility relies on French technology and manners. As with Arabella, Rivers' cultural volatility testifies to a vital personality but it reveals, too, the contradictions arising from a shallow, unthinking complacency. His indifference to Canadian politics is, like Arabella's, a mask for political power. Despite decrying the English parliamentary system, he unhesitatingly exploits it when he asks friends at Westminster to secure Mme. Des Roches's agricultural settlement (90, 277). Rivers' sensibility is romantic only in a very qualified way. When he offers Emily his Acadians as her "new subjects," since he pictures her in Edenic terms as the "mother of mankind" (260), his patriarchalism, royalist absolutism, and pseudo-worship of Emily cumulatively suggest that his sensibility is whimsically regressive.

William Fermor, the most explicit upholder of Mrs. Brooke's propagandistic interests, gives commentaries on Quebec marked by contradictions that testify, like Rivers', to erratic sensibility. If he tolerates Quebec's institutions, he also wants them redefined by the English constitution. Moreover, while he defends the

Proclamation by insisting Anglican bishops must supervise Catholic rites, he opposes it by spurning the assimilation of *habitants* by an influx of British subjects (220). Fear of depopulation at home weighs on him more than prescriptions for Quebec: preoccupied with the harmful effects of the Agrarian Revolution in England, he satirizes its alliance of economic and aristocratic power for displacing rural workers and shrinking the birth-rate. Despite this satire, despite his view of the superiority of the French agricultural system because of its intense use of labour (222), and despite his criticism of the British government's unjust taxation of the American colonies (242), he still idealizes church-state relations in England, asserting that God blesses its constitution before all others (233). The contradictions between his satire and his idealization of England, particularly the gap between his views that Quebec's population is a great asset to England and that it must be defined by English political values, show Fermor remote from the spirit of accommodation promoted by Murray and Carleton. Fermor's parting eulogy of Carleton's urbane character rather than of his political stance is unintentionally ironic since Fermor hardly appreciates the complex processes Carleton was ably managing: in his patriarchal condescension to Quebec, Fermor stresses the Conquest and the colony's need for British institutions with a dogmatism opposite to Carleton's flexibility. Fermor's conventional, if confused, application of gender terms to England manifests the easiness of his sensibility together with his actual political rigidity. His view of the "mother country" as the centre of trade and the colonists as bees that must return to enrich the "paternal hive" (241) vaguely conflates sexual images in the name of national sentiment. His claim that the French leaders of Quebec, by adopting a new order of English honours, would spur the *habitants* to commercial efforts for England's benefit reveals a similar sort of utopian vagueness. His view that the *habitants* will not gain from the "change of masters" (250) until reformed by Anglican priests and his rejection of Rousseau's primitivism show extreme rigidity. By claiming that the most virtuous Indians are the most civilized and that they demand English priests (285), Fermor, far from tolerating Carleton's political and cultural pluralism, equates civilization with England and its national church.

To a degree, however, Mrs. Brooke exposes the contradictory propaganda of patriarchy, in the process apparently giving critical force to the sensibility of women. She even has her heroes criticize themselves according to what they take to be feminist sensibility. Rivers, Fitzgerald, and Temple seem to begin to understand the social construction of gender, and as a result their sense of romance leads them to attempt to reform social and sexual convention. But, if Mrs. Brooke's use of romance appears to offer radical insights into society's constraints upon women, ultimately her novel reinforces what it criticizes.[14]

Emily cultivates a theory of emotional refinement which displaces courtly politics: for her, "tenderness" always outweighs being "empress of the world" (295). Likewise, Arabella scorns male acquisitiveness and naval imperialism: she debases the "lord high admiral of the British fleet" (310). By claiming to accept the women's criticism of political and military aims, Mrs. Brooke's male characters, especially Rivers, imply that relations between women and men must change, as must the institutions governing their relations. Since he feels most at home in a "feminized little circle" (326), Rivers pretends to a womanly sensibility and affects radical change. Although seeing himself as a rural gentleman, and therefore as a true citizen and loyal defender of church and state (343), he urges that the Anglican liturgy be revised by the removal of the word 'obey' from the wife's response in the marriage service (205) and he accuses the government of establishing "domestic tyranny" with its marriage law (371). He speaks on behalf of women because he is, he claims, one of the "few of [his] sex" to possess the "lively sensibility" of a woman (42). This androgyny is confirmed by Lucy and Arabella who see in him "an almost feminine sensibility" balancing his masculine "firmness of mind and spirit" (133, 198, 277). If, however, Rivers and his friends have the capacity to be "melted" to "the softness of a woman" by mothers, sisters, and wives (400), their feminism is condescending. Far from endorsing a distinctive female political outlook, it heightens sexual differences. Rivers' view that "Indian ladies . . . do not excel in female softness" (13) matches his instruction to his sister that she cultivate "feminine softness and delicate sensibility" (93). If he allows "a little pride in love" to women while holding that the man's role is "to submit on these occasions" (187), he also differentiates between the sexes by telling Lucy that "your sex" is to "avoid all affectation of knowledge" (206). His linking of companionate marriage with civic obedience shows that Mrs. Brooke's males do not take women's concerns as seriously as they claim. Despite their feminist pretensions, her heroes are no more averse than society in general to imposing constrictive roles upon women.

Mrs. Brooke's unsteady feminism is manifest in the way her women themselves differentiate between the sexes, allow matriarchal concepts to give way before conventional ideas of rank and nationalism, and promote romantic dependence on men. While calling Lucy "an exquisite politician" for keeping Temple at home by working hard to renew his domestic pleasures, Arabella insists that a woman always finds male more pleasing than female friends (378). When Emily affirms that she has acquired a "new existence" from Rivers' "tenderness" (340) she subsumes female claims of romantic transcendence to social and psychological truisms about sexual difference and marital roles. Mrs. Brooke's women embody an ideology that makes them secondary to men. If she associates England with Rivers' mother when insisting that he return to the world for which he was formed, Emily hails England as the "dear land of arts and arms" (212), thereby defending nationalistic and imperialistic values. Her social solidarity with Rivers is tacitly revealed by her sharing his judgment of Sir George Clayton.

The political limits of Mrs. Brooke's feminism are exposed by her dubious association of England with women's supposed free choice of marriage partners. Arabella's observation of foreign marital modes is superficial: having praised aboriginal matriarchy, she spurns it on learning that Indian mothers arrange their daughters' marriages (56). Emily and Arabella defend their native right to free choice in marriage by adopting romantic slogans. But they do not so much invent definitions of transcendent love as adopt the rules of love made up by Rivers. If the women feminize married love by pretending that it transcends money and social circumstance, he introduces slogans such as "souls in unison," "harmony of mind," and "delirium of the soul" (59). He promotes the transcendent concepts that Emily and he "were formed for each other" (185) and that they were friends in "some pre-existent state" (138). Having induced the "spirit of romance" in Emily (324), Rivers has strategically to offset the way it makes her unpredictable. The interpolated story that depicts Sophia as "romantic to excess" (360) confirms that Mrs. Brooke believes that women are made vulnerable by their "romantic generosity" (358). The political illusions arising from romance diminish women's intelligence. In likening the Church of England to "an elegant well-dressed woman of quality" (80) and claiming that women, unlike men, cannot be infidels because of their natural softness (107), Arabella unthinkingly links feminist romance to an institution whose theology opposes her feminism. Her application of "petticoat politics" to the creation of a "code of laws for the government of husbands" in the context of her tenet that England alone is enlightened about marriage manifests an inconsistency which reveals that Mrs. Brooke's feminist stance is not radically critical but complacently nationalistic (230-31).

While it may seem that the author uses the language of romance to denote the transcendent feelings shared by ideal couples and to validate the male's subordination to the female systematically, such is not the case. For Mrs. Brooke, romantic vocabulary does not apply exclusively to companionate marriage: it also elevates the male over the female as well as honouring the extended family and the gentry as a class. That is to say, the androgyny attributed to Rivers, seemingly on behalf of radical sexual experimentation, ultimately shows such experimentation to be redundant. While Rivers dismisses the liturgical vow of female obedience, making equality the basis of marriage (205), Emily from the first gives over her "whole soul" to him (189). To her, Rivers is "a god" (190) and the "most angelic

of mankind" (192). His tender image excludes all other ideas from her soul (226). Not only does she find his "mental beauty . . . the express image of the Deity" (247) but also she effaces herself before him, letting her every emotion be ruled by him (249). If she transforms his benevolence by the romantic claim that their souls conform, her romantic self-assertion does not displace theological ideas of self-effacement. Further, Emily's idolization of Rivers is not unique: his mother loves Rivers "to idolatry" too (254), proving that the words of romance are not systematic in companionate terms, a point accented by Emily's wish to secure the permission of Mrs. Rivers and of her father before she marries.

Far from constituting a private, intimate code between the heroine and the hero, the language of romance tightens society's patriarchal bonds. If Rivers idolizes his sister as well as Emily (177), Emily idolizes Mme. Des Roches as well as Rivers (219). If Rivers' eyes see no one lovely but Emily (165), she being the only object in his universe (224), so the whole creation contains no other woman for Temple than Lucy (226). Perhaps the strongest illustration of the conservative function of romantic codes is Arabella's pride in rebelling against patriarchal authority even as her father, unknown to her, controls her marital choice. The insubstantiality of radical, romantic action in the novel is evident from the predictable ways in which Mrs. Brooke solves the conflicts by contingency. Conflicts such as Emily's jealousy of Mme. Des Roches and her dispute with Rivers about delaying their wedding seem generated only to train the characters to offset languid marital moments by posturing with romance as distinct from developing radical visions through its means. If Arabella, on leaving Canada, mocks this "terrestrial paradise" and "divine country" (287), debasing thereby the terms of romantic idealization, her deliberate irony is indistinguishable in effect from accidental ironies. When Emily recalls her unwillingness to parade a romantic fidelity to Sir George (74, 320), it is impossible not to see that she so parades for Rivers. The masquerade closing the novel shows that the self-objectification by which Emily mediates honour to Rivers relies far more on social convention than on romantic transcendence.

The illusion of free romantic plays always reinforces patriarchal structure in *The History of Emily Montague*. If Rivers creates private domestic spaces for Emily, he is bent on engrossing and absorbing "every faculty" of her mind (331). He succeeds because she agrees to have "no will" but his, submitting to him as "arbiter" of her fate (332). The lovers' romantic gestures do not reduce their desire to be recognized by their class. Their pleasure in the "little circle" and "little empire" of rural retreat is ironic: their boasted indifference to the "parade of life" (341) heightens their wish to make their estate a social and political centre. The interpolated story of Miss Williams and the orphan allows the lovers to parade their benevolence, their contempt for aristocrats, and their influence in the "great world" (336). The tensions between their romantic self-containment and political program for marriage are never sustained by narrative dialectic however, as attested by the arbitrarily complete closure. When Emily wins her father's permission to wed Rivers, the threat of forced marriage dissolves, as in Arabella's case. It is not enough for Mrs. Brooke to reveal Colonel Willmott to be Emily's long-lost father; she must arrange that the patriarch chooses the same husband for his daughter as she chooses for herself. The closure's reliance on coincidences that displace plot-conflicts wholly, demonstrates that romantic resistance to patriarchy is a charade. By also having the lovers blessed providentially with wealth, Mrs. Brooke heightens her dependence on the sentimental dramatic formulae of plays such as Steele's *The Conscious Lovers*. In addition to remotivating money in a way the narrative resists, the closure elides married love, imperial wealth and patriarchal authority. That the ending rewards the rural gentry with financial wealth and social prestige is the ultimate devaluation of romance.

The closure, in epitomizing Mrs. Brooke's use of romance to champion the rural gentry and Anglicanism, debases narrative and political process. In its excessive symmetry, the closure does not present the author's discontent with politics in Quebec and England. The reduction of merchants and aristocrats to marital villains and the idealization of gentry as true citizens avoid rather than address political reality. The ending confirms the gentry's francophobia and Augustan nostalgia: they are patriots with an exaggerated sense of social exclusivity and their style of romance cultivates a likemindedness dismissive of cultural diversity. In seeming to reconcile ideological conflicts, the closure aggravates them: if matriarchy is admired, patriarchy is reinforced; if the liturgy is attacked, the Church is defended; if marriage is an agent of reform, it signals exclusive social contentment. No doubt, Mrs. Brooke shapes political facts with romance, and her novel does contain progressive ideas, as in the case of the motif of androgyny. But conformity seizes her innovations: old political ideas govern the new. Romance is static, not dialectical; the psychological thrills by which it offsets marriage's languid moments give way to a complacency aptly summed up by Rivers' phrases "peaceable possession" and "voluptuous tranquillity" (314). Far from allaying ideological conflict, the closure provokes unresolvable questions. If wealth and power are decried throughout the novel but appropriated to the ending and if prudence, maligned in the duration, finally outweighs transcendence, the final universalizing of themes debases their mediation.

This being so, the novel predicts little positive about Canada's colonial future. Its characters, far from considering the gap between political theory and fact,

merely widen that gap; adamant about the Conquest, they think to confirm France's defeat through their cultivation of French sensibility. But, by insisting that French romantic sensibility is best realized by refined English people, they define patriotism in French terms. Their assumption that England can and must assimilate Quebec not only fails to foresee the day when French will replace English law but also blinds them to the political action implied by their romantic illusions. *The History of Emily Montague* is less about Canada than about an overextended colonial empire and the strains of a mother country which supposedly most afflict the lesser, Anglican rural gentry whose refinement of English social hierarchy through romantic propaganda is their sole means of healing their own political displacement.

Notes

[1] Frances Brooke, *The History of Emily Montague,* ed. Mary Jane Edwards (Ottawa: Carleton Univ. Press, 1985): xliii. All references are to this edition.

[2] Despite Mr. Brooke's fruitless association with merchants in Quebec, he was paid as its chaplain until his death. See Lorraine McMullen, *An Odd Attempt in a Woman: The Literary Life of Frances Brooke* (Vancouver: Univ. of British Columbia Press, 1983): 79-83.

[3] On the Brookes' Anglicanism and "genteel poverty," see Mary Jane Edwards, "Frances Brooke's *The History of Emily Montague:* A Biographical Context," *English Studies in Canada,* 7:2 (Summer 1981): 171-82.

[4] While the novel tries to "deal honestly" with the "Canadian scene," it is "dominated by a bourgeois moral system" that values "prudence, caution, and respectability" highly: Desmond Pacey, "The First Canadian Novel," *Dalhousie Review,* 26 (1946-47): 147-50. The present essay develops William H. New's claim that Mrs. Brooke's novel is "indicative of the tension of the times": "Frances Brooke's Chequered Gardens," *Canadian Literature* 52 (Spring 1972): 37. Mrs. Brooke's hostility to aristocrats is best seen through the eyes of such historians as Derek Jarrett, *The Begetters of Revolution: England's Involvement with France, 1759-1789* (London: Longman, 1973), and John Cannon, *Aristocratic Century: The peerage of eighteenth-century England* (Cambridge: Cambridge Univ. Press, 1984), who emphasize the increasing economic and political power wielded by the aristocracy.

[5] On the Marriage Act, see Dorothy Marshall, *Eighteenth Century England* (London: Longmans, 1962): 225-27. Cannon, *Aristocratic Century,* describes the growing intermarriage among aristocrats and the relative immobility of the middle class in marriage (74-

92). McMullen, *An Odd Attempt in a Woman,* gives biographical reasons why the Brookes objected to the Marriage Act (9). Rivers definitely connects the Marriage Bill to the constitution (371).

[6] Ann Messenger, *His and Hers: Essays in Restoration and Eighteenth-Century Literature* (Lexington: Univ. of Kentucky Press, 1986), upholds Arabella's "complexity of self-awareness" (162) against Pope's diminution of the central character of *The Rape of the Lock.* Messenger assigns an "all-pervasive" irony to Arabella and an acute awareness of "irreconcilable contradictions" (164): Arabella is a self-conscious, not frivolous, coquette (165, 170). The present essay argues that Mrs. Brooke was fully in command neither of her epistolary medium nor of the strategic requirements of narrative dialectic.

[7] Kenneth McNaught, *The Pelican History of Canada* (Harmondsworth: Penguin, 1969): 45.

[8] *The Pelican History of Canada,* 47-48.

[9] W. L. Morton, *The Kingdom of Canada: A General History from Earliest Times* (Toronto: McClelland & Stewart, 1963): 153.

[10] W. J. Eccles, *France in America* (Vancouver: Fitzhenry & Whiteside, 1972): 223-24.

[11] André Garon, "La Britannisation" in *Histoire du Québec,* ed. Jean Hamelin (Montréal: France-Amérique, 1976): 260.

[12] Samuel L. Macey, *Money and the Novel: Mercenary Motivation in Defoe and His Immediate Successors* (Victoria: Sono Nis Press, 1983): 89-93, provides an interesting account of the growth of dowries and the relation of this growth to the 'financial revolution' and to the development of the national debt in the eighteenth century. Cannon, *Aristocratic Century,* "Marriage," 71-92, gives statistics about the tightening bonds between class, wealth and marriage in the period. He shows that, despite talk about companionate love, arranged marriages increased in number and increasingly fortified social hierarchy.

[13] Fernand Ouellet, *Economic and Social History of Quebec, 1760-1850* (Toronto: Macmillan, 1980): 53-102, explains how economic rivalry between aristocratic and bourgeois values eroded nationalistic concepts. He discusses also the growing power of aristocrats in government. His account clarifies why Mrs. Brooke both admires the governors' gentility and rejects their aristocratic sympathy for the displaced seigneurs and noblesse.

[14] Readers wishing to explore the issues raised by the present article are advised to consult Joseph Allen

Boone, *Tradition Counter Tradition: Love and the Form of Fiction* (Chicago: Univ. of Chicago Press, 1987) and Leslie W. Rabine, *Reading the Romantic Heroine: Text, History, Ideology* (Ann Arbor: Univ. of Michigan Press, 1985). Boone compellingly describes the ways in which conceptions of marriage and narrative techniques, whether traditional or progressive, are corollaries of one another while Rabine, through an analysis of the recoil of radical ideology upon itself in a series of romances, elaborates convincingly why progressive concepts in romance tend to be self-defeating.

Barbara M. Benedict (essay date 1992)

SOURCE: "The Margins of Sentiment: Nature, Letter, and Law in Frances Brooke's Epistolary Novels," in *Ariel,* Vol. 23, No. 3, July, 1992, pp. 7-25.

[*In the following essay, Benedict examines Brooke's use of the epistolary novel form to challenge the prevailing sentimental ideology of that genre.*]

The most popular form of literary sentimentalism in the eighteenth century was the epistolary novel.[1] The epistolary method aims to present human nature released from social convention, meditating on the faculty which sentimentalists saw as the spring of virtue: feeling. Through intimate letters describing characters' responses to emotions and events, these novels show sentiment even as it is being experienced, both to stir the reader's moral response and to demonstrate the sentimental thesis that moral virtue is natural instinct, not learned behaviour.[2] In these novels, romantic love most often provides the plot to prove this thesis. The popular sentimental novelist Frances Brooke, however, challenges the assumptions of sentimental ideology even while exploiting its conventions. Indicting social hierarchy and political oppression, Brooke defends sentiment against the tyranny of custom, law, privilege, and patriarchy, but she also warns the reader against sentiment undisciplined by sense or unlicensed by society.[3] By structuring her epistolary novels dialectically to oppose "natural" feeling with aesthetic and social conventions, Brooke explores the limitations of both sentimental and social values. At the same time, she locates the moral touchstone of her novels in the marginalized character of the female spectator who connects experience to culture, and undercuts the simplistic opposition of art and nature which seemed to legitimize revolutionary extremes even before the French Revolution. Brooke thus explores the proximity of social and sentimental ideals at their margins.

Known to Charles and Fanny Burney, Samuel Johnson, and David Garrick, Frances Brooke, *née* Moore (1724-1789), was a recognized, if also marginal, figure in London literary society both before and after her sojourn in Canada.[4] Apart from four, possibly five, novels, she wrote drama, started a periodical journal, translated French works, and composed poetry. her popular periodical, *The Old Maid*, reprinted at least twice in bound editions, exploits the power that marginality offers women. Published weekly from late 1755 until July 1756 under the pseudonym Mary Singleton, *The Old Maid* defines taste, comments on the social world, politics, theatre, and current events, and discusses the "female" questions of love and marriage in the manner of *The Spectator* and *The Female Spectator*.[5] The apologetic, teetotalling Old Maid, rather than experiencing love, recounts tales of her niece Julia, infatuated with the impoverished but well-born officer Belville, and their friends.

In her first number, like her "brother" Mr. Spectator, Mary Singleton credits her qualifications to her marginality, arguing that her distance from the bustle of politics and love guarantees her disinterest and so legitimizes her commentary. Whereas Mr. Spectator has travelled and learned, however, Mary Singleton has been merely left out. Many issues bear epigraphs ironically apologizing for the deficiencies of a virgin or spinster, and the Old Maid herself labels old women as, "except an old batchelor, the most useless and insignificant of all God's creatures," who must "service" the "public" to compensate for their selfishness presumably in not bearing children. Brooke challenges social prejudice, however, by political language: "every body knows an English woman has a natural right to expose herself as much as she pleases; . . . I should think it giving up the privileges of the sex to desist from my purpose" (Num. 1, 2-3). While this hyperbole parodies female expression, it also identifies female liberty with patriotic "natural rights." By calling on English law and "privileges" to sanction Mary Singleton's endeavour, Brooke suggests that women, precisely because their self-exposure is ridiculed, guarantee the English value of free speech.

Despite this threat, the Old Maid models disinterested observation. Her decorous diction, topical breadth, and rational tone proclaim her ability to organize social experience into moral commentary. The headpiece of the periodical illustrates the power and precariousness of her position: a Roman matron sits at a writing table listening to a warrior and a bard recite their tales, with the city's turrets looming in the background. A version of the common illustration of travelogues in which the Muse transcribes tales of adventure, this picture shows the writer as both translator of culture and recorder of others' heroic deeds.[6] By portraying the audience's own culture as remote, the periodical centralizes the marginality of its "author," the Old Maid: a Roman, that is, selfless patriot, she values hearing about, rather than experiencing, sensation, and like the reader understands experience by means of·language. Paradoxically, it is by their marginality that the Old Maid, and the reader,

serve as centres of sentimental value.[7]

Brooke, however, uses this marginal stance as listener, reader, or spectator to advocate a social role for women which turns their exclusion into social power: the role of connoisseur of the arts. Even while she laughingly advises old maids to write to her periodical instead of criticizing giddy girls, Mary Singleton implies that social exclusion frustrates women. She suggests a solution to this problem by observing that traditionally women have encouraged artistic merit, and hinting that, since art demonstrates the female value of love over the male value of war, women might improve society and their own positions by controlling artistic standards, and rewarding true artists, instead of flighty singers whose tantrums men applaud. Brooke adds that this role of artistic judge is fashionable, since a "French woman of distinction would be more ashamed of wanting a taste for the Belles Lettres, than of being ill dressed; and it is owing to the neglect of adorning their minds, that our travelling English ladies are at Paris the objects of unspeakable contempt, and are honored with the appellation of handsome savages" (Num. 3, Sat., Nov. 29, 1755). Brooke maintains that cultivated minds will improve behaviour: when a reader signing himself "Spectator" complains that by laughing a lady in the audience disconcerted an actress, Brooke apologizes for her sex and bids women act more cautiously in public (Num. 15, Sat. Feb 21, 1756). She thus implies that by self-observation women may turn from spectacles into spectators, a role which empowers them to purify culture.

Although it typically defines female heroism as romantic emotion rather than judgement, sentimental fiction allows spectators the power to judge society. Brooke honed this sentimental feature in her translations of Madame Riccoboni's epistolary novels of sensibility.[8] In the popular *Letters from Juliet Lady Catesby, To Her Friend Lady Henrietta Campley* (1760), for example, Brooke renders Riccoboni's idealized sensibility as a blend of reflection and observation, as Juliet learns her own nature from gazing on physical nature:

> I write to you, from the most agreeable Place, perhaps, in Nature: From my Window I have a View of Woods, Waters, Meadows, the most beautiful Landscape imaginable: Every thing expresses Calmness and Tranquillity: This smiling Abode is an Image of the soft Peace, which reigns in the Soul of the Sage who inhabits it. This amiable Dwelling carries one insensibly to reflect; to retire into one's self; but one cannot at all Times relish this Kind of Retreat; one may find in the Recesses of the Heart, more importunate Pursuers than those from whom Solitude delivers us.
>
> (Letter 3)

Written from the estate of a benevolent patriarch whose wisdom the ordered landscape reflects, this letter records

Juliet's desire to make her inside mirror the outside and render her self as tranquil as the scenery. Unlike the sublime which coopts reflection with emotion, as Brooke depicts in Canada, this "soft" beauty "carries" Juliet out of time and sensation "insensibly to reflect," and so discloses the parallel between internal and external nature. Just as the world contains hunters, so her heart holds "Pursuers," desires which have not been tailored to fit social forms. The story of her heroism is the story of regulating these desires by natural and social law, of conquest of her own nature. This epistolary heroine thus models the correspondence between the conquest of the wild and of the self.

In her first novel, however, Brooke depicts the tragic consequences of failing this conquest, a tragedy John Mullan locates in the very concept of sociability by sympathy (134). *The History of Lady Julia Mandeville* (1763) imitates *Romeo and Juliet* by portraying innocent lovers doomed by the tyranny of traditional prejudice and paternal power. Brooke, however, emphasizes the hero's flaw over society's. Whereas Shakespeare's lovers are caught in a feud which forbids their marriage, Lady Julia and her cousin Harry belong to the same family: it is Harry's own fear, rather than his father's prohibition, which pricks him to despair.[9] Ignoring his Rousseauan education in the true values of love, literature, and art, on which his father has spent his fortune, Harry does not ask openly for Julia's hand, as both fathers hope he will, but instead adopts the very prejudice he despises: convinced that his poverty disqualifies him from marriage, he plunges into a duel in which he dies, and kills Julia with grief. Thus, it is not so much paternal society as the hero himself who causes the tragedy.[10]

This novel edits sentiment with art not only in plot but also in form. By substituting letters for dramatic actions, Brooke centres the novel on the activities of observing, recording, and reflecting, exemplified not by the heroes but by the marginal character Lady Anne Wilmot. Lady Anne may well have been named after Queen Anne, whom Brooke praises in *The Old Maid* for her patronage of the arts. Her letters are juxtaposed with the sentimental epistles of the hero, Harry Mandeville. Preserving the pleasure of drama which David Hume had identified as a combination of sympathy and distance, Lady Anne describes strong emotions, but controls the reader's imaginative sympathy by contextualizing these feelings within the traditions of literature and society, evoked through irony, allusion, and quotation.

This language contrasts with Harry's sentimental diction. While interweaving aesthetic and sentimental language, Brooke creates a tension between the sentimental value for transparency and for spectatorial appreciation.[11] Harry describes Julia as a painting, even bedecked with the baroque conceit of "loves":

Lady Julia then . . . is exactly what a *poet* or *painter* would wish to *copy*, who intended to *personify the idea* of female softness; her whole *form* is delicate and feminine to the utmost *degree:* her complexion is fair, enlivened by the bloom of youth, and often *diversified* by blushes more beautiful than those of the morning. . . . Her countenance, *the beauteous abode of the loves and the smiles,* has a *mixture* of sweetness and spirit which gives *life and expression* to her charms.

(1.15; emphasis added)

These pictorial metaphors present love as courtly convention and spectacle, but Harry purifies these clichés by tracing Julia's beauty to her unspoiled nature: "As her mind has been adorned, not warped, by education, it is just what her appearance promises; artless, gentle, timid, soft, sincere, compassionate; awake to all the finer impressions of tenderness, and melting with pity for every human woe" (1.6). Harry detects these social virtues, this ideal female complacency, through the physical evidence of Julia's loveliness; his sentimental rhetoric equates appearance and behaviour, and so prohibits irony or social consciousness, both of which result from the disparity between appearance and behaviour. Julia is transparent; she is what she looks to be, and this is the condition for sentimental heroism.

Brooke challenges this ideal, however, because it invalidates the complexity of women's internal experience in a world where men rule. True perspective, the perspective which moralizes experience, derives from distance and the power of contrast which Lady Anne models. Lady Anne has suffered such abuse from her violent, brutish husband that she hesitates to marry her exemplary lover Bellville; moreover, she reiterates an ideal of mutual respect and friendship as the basis for marriage which the youthful Harry and Julia do not experience. With characteristic irony, moreover, she questions the practical morality of sentimental feeling. After Julia's death, she recounts to Bellville: "I am now convinced Emily Howard deserves that preference Lady Julia gave her over me in her heart, of which I once so unjustly complained; I lament, I regret, but am enough my self to reason, to reflect; Emily Howard can only weep . . . she seems incapable of tasting any good in life without her" (2. 176-77). Lady Anne finds happiness, or at least contentment, within her "self" through reason and reflection; the alternative, immersion in feeling and dependence on others, leads to misery.

Brooke reiterates this warning against immersion in feeling by a method later employed by Ann Radcliffe: the emblematic episode. After describing Emily's beautiful, even admirable, grief, Lady Anne recounts her own deviance from reason as, lost in feeling, she transgresses the boundaries of the estate, of day, of cultivated nature, and of reason.[12]

Awaking at once from the reveries in which I had plunged, I found myself at a distance from the house, just entering the little wood . . . a dread silence reigned around me, a terror I never felt before seized me, my heart panted with timid apprehension; I breathed short, I started at every leaf . . . my limbs were covered with a cold dew; I fancied I saw a thousand airy forms flit around me, I seemed to hear the shrieks of the dead and dying; there is no describing my horrors.

(2. 179-81)

By abandoning control of her fancy, Lady Anne becomes as vulnerable as a sentimental heroine. This is an example of the wrong way to "feel," yet it is also an evocative passage of stylistic virtuosity which challenges the hold of "reason" on the imagination. By treading on the borders of sanity, Lady Anne reasserts the importance of margins. Harry, whose passionate letters lack logic, order, and balance, similarly experiences sentiment beyond the bounds of reason; his excess costs him his life.

Lady Anne, however, shakes off this temporary indulgence to model for the reader the right way to feel: by evoking contrast and deriving a moral from detached comparisons. After remarking the sad difference between what is and what was, she herself comments on the aesthetic pleasures of tragedy:

Whether it be that the mind abhors nothing like a state of inaction, or from whatever cause I know not, but grief itself is more agreeable to us than indifference; nay, if not too exquisite, is in the highest degree delightful; of which the pleasure we take in tragedy, or in talking of our dead friends, is a striking proof; we wish not to be cured of what we feel on these occasions; the tears we shed are charming, we even indulge in them; Belville [sic], does not the very word *indulge* shew the sensation to be pleasurable?

Lady Anne moralizes the general effects of the aesthetic representation of sorrow; with the theoretical language of Addison and Hume, indeed, she comments on the reader's own experience of the very novel in which she appears. Representing herself as a spectator of experience, like the reader, Lady Anne thus cautions against indulgence even in the pleasures of fiction.

Brooke's second novel, *The History of Emily Montague* (1769), portrays sentiment on the margin of civilization in Canada. By juxtaposing letters from sympathetic characters with different perspectives, Brooke creates a dialogue on the nature of sexual relations, marriage, and liberty. Two central correspondences contrast social and sentimental discourse. The titular heroine, Emily, describes her feelings as she rejects her fiancé and falls in love with Colonel Ed Rivers. In contrast, her friend Arabella Fermor describes physical and social scenes with an allusive wit which fences feeling with irony. The sentimental Colonel Ed Rivers moralizes colonization and love to his crony John Temple in London. A few letters from Arabella's father Captain William Fermor contextualize the tale within "realistic" history.[13] It is Arabella, however, who tests the margins of sentiment by cultural observation.

Brooke structures the novel with a comic plot which banishes the central characters to the "wild" New World, where they recognize true nature and pair off before returning to cultivate their "gardens" in England (132; 408). While Emily must face social disapproval for breaking her engagement with the wealthy, handsome, but insensitive Sir George Clayton, she is rewarded for her fidelity to her feelings by marrying the laudable Colonel Ed Rivers and receiving a rich inheritance from a newly-discovered father. As in *The History of Lady Julia Mandeville*, however, social prejudice forms only part of the drama and suspense; the rest arises from internal doubts, realizations, and misunderstandings. Inset sentimental vignettes warn against this emphasis on emotion. In Canada, a "Hermit" forever distraught from the loss of his love demonstrates that feeling can make the world a wilderness, while in England the virtuous Fanny, impoverished foster mother to the love-child of her sentimental friend, recounts the fatal costs of loving not wisely but too well.

The most cogent critique of both sentimentalism and society, however, comes from the persistent comparison between the native Canadian Indians, the Canadian French, and the newly arrived English colonials. Generally, the English balance raw nature, represented by the Indians, and corruption, represented by the French, opposite extremes linked by their use of marriage as a political rather than a sentimental contract. Despite his sympathy for the notion of the noble savage, Ed illustrates that sentiment is a civilized luxury when he criticizes the behaviour of unmarried Huron women (34). Perhaps unaware that they wed on their parents' order, Ed observes that they are "liberal to profusion of their charms before marriage," albeit "chastity itself after."[14] In reverse fashion, French virgins wed for convenience and play the libertine afterwards: "Marriages in France being made by the parents, and therefore generally without inclination on either side, gallantry seems to be a tacit condition, though not absolutely expressed in the contract" (84). In both cases, women dissociate sexual pleasure from marriage. Both Ed and Arabella record that the sentimental relationship between the sexes results from English manners, not from nature. These examples suggest, moreover, that the "English liberty" of a woman's right to marry whom she pleases is not merely a sentimental but a sensible principle to preserve social morality.

The issues of marriage and sexual relations allow Brooke to explore ideas of "natural" and political behaviour.[15] Whereas Arabella admires the Huron women's freedom, Ed condemns their manners, vowing to Temple, "You are right, Jack, as to the savages; the only way to civilize them is to *feminize* their women . . . at present their manners differ in nothing from those of the men" (118-19). By "feminizing" women, that is, by teaching them to love their children more than their tribe, Ed hopes to civilize them. Despite her different perspective on this process of domestication, when Arabella learns of their system of marriage, she recants her praise of Huron freedom:

> I declare off at once; I will not be a squaw; I admire their talking of the liberty of savages; in the most essential point, they are slaves: the mothers marry their children without ever consulting their inclinations, and they are obliged to submit to this foolish tyranny. Dear England! where liberty appears, not as here among these odious savages, wild and ferocious like themselves, but lovely, smiling, led by the hand of the Graces. There is no true freedom any where else. They may talk of the privilege of chusing [sic] a chief; but what is that to the dear English privilege of chusing a husband? (56)

By mingling the jargon of marital engagement— "declare off"—with that of politics—"tyranny," "true freedom"—Arabella demonstrates the overlap between politics, manifested by law, and domestic relations or sentiment. She suggests that sentiment, "English liberty," and civilized refinement are interconnected: sentiment is not produced by such sublime nature as the Huron display; albeit nourished by female instinct, it is the fruit of culture.

Brooke further explores the limitations both of nature and of civilization by comparing Indian and English politics. The Huron political system represents a version of Rousseau's natural law with "no positive laws"—no written statutes—and, as one Indian avers, "we are subjects to no prince; a savage is free all over the world." Ed confirms that "they are not only free as a people, but every individual is perfectly so. Lord of himself, at once subject and master, a savage knows no superior . . ." (33). Living in the state of nature, practicing the epic virtues of hospitality, courtesy, and bellicosity, the Hurons escape European hierarchies of class and gender: Ed notes that the chief's power is limited and reasonable, while the "sex we have so unjustly excluded from power in Europe have a great share in the Huron government," choosing both the chief and his council. Just as he praises sexual equality in marriage, Ed condemns English politics as uncivilized tyranny: "in the true sense of the word, *we* are the savages, who so impolitely deprive [women] of the common rights of citizenship" (34-35). Thus, sentiment, sexual equality, and politeness result from culture.

Brooke contrasts sentimental and traditional politics by juxtaposing the letters of the other characters with the letters of Arabella's father, Captain William Fermor. In judging how suitable Canada is for settlement, William Fermor contextualizes the lovers' sentimental accounts of Indian freedom and personal relationships within the parameters of conventional social values. After Fermor records that, since they always long for home, the English will not settle well, Emily and Rivers discuss whether they can afford to leave the "exile" of Canada (224). Condemning the "[s]loth and superstition" of Canadians, Fermor advocates universal religion and rational labour in place of the religious plurality and native freedom his daughter admires (208-09). While deploring the softness of the English who cannot "bear the hardships" of settlement, he recommends winning the Canadians "by the gentle arts of persuasion, and the gradual progress of knowledge, to adopt so much of our manners as tends to make them happier in themselves, and more useful members of the society to which they belong," a perspective which satirizes the lovers' praise of Canadian liberty (220-21). He also traces the "striking resemblance between the manners of the Canadians and the savages" to infection of the French by "savage" "manners," although, in condemning Indian drunkenness, Fermor protests that it is "unjust to say that we [Europeans] corrupted them" since "both French and English are in general sober." This argument rationalizes Arabella's tale of taking wine to the Indian women and watching them get drunk while she asked them questions (272). Indeed, Fermor's perspective resembles his daughter's in its faith in cultivation: "From all that I have observed, and heard of these people, it appears to me an undoubted fact, that the most civilized Indian nations are the most virtuous; a fact which makes directly against Rousseau's ideal system" (272). Ed, on the other hand, admires the independence of the Indians in resisting European influence, even while he also condemns their indolence.

While editing Ed's sentiment, Brooke also demonstrates that the conventional perspective Fermor adopts, with its firm definition of "virtue," does not penetrate nature. When he describes scenery, he uses technical rather than picturesque language, finally admitting, "I am afraid I have conveyed a very inadequate idea of the scene . . . it however struck me so strongly, that it was impossible for me not to attempt it" (236). An enlightened father, he advocates conversation between the sexes to educate women to be "the most pleasing companions," and recommends moralists "expand, not . . . contract, the heart"; yet he claims possession over Arabella's affections. Fermor reiterates the conventional tenet that although English women may refuse their parents' choice of husband they may not marry where they will, yet Arabella's letters suggest that she embraces complete freedom of choice in marriage. Brooke emphasizes this contrast by juxtaposing Arabella's teasingly hyperbolic declaration of passion and secret marriage to Fitzgerald with Fermor's account of Fitzgerald's birth and fortune, the very standards of value all other characters, including Arabella, condemn as English corruption.

If Fermor, albeit enlightened, exemplifies the patriarchal values opposed to sentimentalism, Ed also reveals the effects of "male" education. Despite his sympathy for their "natural law," Ed does not reflect Indian morality. To women, he attempts to act with an internal delicacy which the stoic Indians do not share, yet his function in Canada is colonization. He opens the novel by quoting Milton and declaring himself ruler of the wilderness. Although Brooke repeatedly identifies his behaviour with "female" softness—"my heart has all the sensibility of woman," confesses Ed (133); "You . . . really have something of the sensibility and generosity of women," declares Arabella (347)—she also points out the link between his attitude towards sexual opportunity and his exploitation of land. Ed judges woman as a sentimental connoisseur:

> I hate a woman of whom every man coldly says, *she is handsome;* I adore beauty, but it is not meer features or complexion to which I give that name; 'tis life, 'tis spirit, 'tis imagination, 'tis—in one word, 'tis Emily Montague—without being regularly beautiful, she charms every sensible heart . . . she seems made to feel to a trembling excess the passion she cannot fail of inspiring: her elegant form has an air of softness and languor . . . her eyes, the most intelligent I ever saw, hold you enchain'd by their bewitching sensibility. (21)

Ed proves that his picture of her indeed describes her nature by remarking her "attentive politeness" in conversation and her "desire of pleasing." His cultural power of observation, moreover, makes him a "philosopher" not merely of physical scenery, but of human scenery too: "As I am a philosopher in these matters, and have made the heart my study, I want extremely to see her with her lover, and to observe the general increase of her charms in his presence" (21).

Brooke corrects Ed's idea that he can observe beauty unmoved by making him fall in love with Emily, but his very detachment does hurt another sentimental character, Madame des Roches. Madame des Roches enters the story when she asks Ed for legal help in adjudicating a property claim, a request Ed passes on to John Temple. This first encounter outlines the nature of their relationship: he is master of the rules which define territory, be this wild land or natural feeling. In a letter to Temple, Ed adopts the jargon of connoisseurship to describe sexual relations in society:

> Widows were, I thought, fair prey, as being sufficiently experienced to take care of themselves. . . . A woman in the first bloom of youth resembles a tree in blossom; when mature, in fruit; but a woman who retains the charms of her person till her understanding is in its full perfection, is like those trees in happier climes, which produce blossoms and fruit together.
>
> You will scarce believe, Jack, that I have lived a week *tête à tête,* in the midst of a wood, with just the woman I have been describing: a widow extremely my taste, *mature,* five or six years more so than you say I require, lively, sensible, handsome, without saying one civil thing to her. (84-85)

Although Ed contrasts this cultivated appreciation of women as products of nature to his feelings for Emily, he fails to recognize that he affects Madame des Roches: believing he loves her, she loves him. When he learns this, however, his response employs the language of imperialism: "I was at first extremely embarrassed: but when I had reflected a moment, I considered that the ladies, though another may be the object, always regard with a kind of complacency a man who *loves,* as one who acknowledges the power of the sex, whereas an indifferent man is a kind of rebel to their empire" (158). His sexual language mirrors his political behaviour.[16] Brooke again reminds the reader that men confuse sex and power when Ed's friend Temple, now married to Ed's sister Lucy, after praising his wife in a rapturous letter, hastily concludes: "Lucy is here. Adieu! I must not let her know her power" (373). This echoes Ed's misogynistic clichés: when he begins to love Emily, he calls her a "little tyrant" who wishes to add him "to the list of her slaves" (24).

Brooke links colonial attitudes to language also by silencing Madame des Roches. Like the Indians, she possesses no first name, exhibits sublime nature in her obdurate passion, and is heard only by translation in the letters of the English. Arabella alone, as a disinterested spectator, passes on her words when Madame des Roches congratulates Emily and vows eternal fidelity to Rivers, and even Arabella paraphrases them: "I thought of sending her letter to [Emily and Ed], but there is a certain fire in her style, mixed with tenderness . . . which would have given them both regret, by making them see the excess of her affection for him; her expressions are much stronger than those in which I have given you the sense of them" (282). When a jealous Emily offends Ed and Madame des Roches, Arabella undercuts Emily's complacent self-criticism with a parenthetical comment which adumbrates the implicit "colonization" of Ed: Emily "was peevish with me, angry with herself" and said "that *her* Rivers (and why not Madame des Roches's Rivers?) was incapable of acting otherwise than as became the best and most tender of mankind" (163-64). Arabella underscores Emily's desire to possess, or contain, Rivers, while Madame des Roches, the embodiment of wild nature, is banished to a solitary life in Canada, and even to madness pricked by poring over Ed's picture (283).

Brooke stresses her point that sentiment, like Burke's "beautiful," relies on art as well as nature by linking it with not only language but law and literature. The Indians have no "positive laws" because they "have no idea of letters, no alphabet, nor is their language reducible to rules": like Madame des Roches, "'tis by painting they preserve . . . memory" (85-86). Ed notes that they sing only on the subjects of war and male friendship, except for this single, "short and simple, tho' perhaps not inexpressive" lyric: "I love you / I love you dearly, / I love you all day long" (11). This emotional efficiency contrasts with both the ritualized language of complimentary courtship borrowed from the French, which Temple and occasionally Ed himself use, and with the stylized literature of sentiment which Arabella quotes and imitates. Indeed, Indian illiteracy demonstrates the degree to which sentiment, women's "power," relies on language, especially epistolary language. Both Indian women and men without sensibility lack the language of the heart. "Adieu! I never write long letters in London," asserts Jack Temple as he plays the roué at London assemblies (83). William Fermor apologizes for discussing his personal matters by blaming the nature of letters: "Your good-natured philosophy will tell you, much fewer people talk or write to amuse or inform their friends, than to give way to the feelings of their own hearts" (162). Similarly, Ed entrusts communication to women with a characteristically professional metaphor: "I shall quit my post of historian to . . . Miss Fermor; the ladies love writing much better than we do; and I should perhaps be only just, if I said they write better" (39). By chronicling the progress of love and self-realization through letters by women or feminine men, Brooke suggests that women regulate their reality, sensibility, through letters, as men regulate theirs, property, through law. Epistolary language connects experience and reflection, thus constructing the very morality the Indians lack: private memory and public history.[17]

Arabella exemplifies epistolary power. She articulates the balance between French artifice and Indian instinct, between masculine judgement and feminine sympathy, between literary and spontaneous language. While "Rivers" and "des Roches" evoke nature, the respective ideals of the beautiful and of the sublime, Arabella is named after Pope's model for Belinda in *The Rape of the Lock*. Like her namesake, she loves cards, masquerades, and coquetry; like Pope, she "wrote pastorals at seven years old" (387). As Ann Messenger has noted, she is thus both her own artist and artwork: her creation is herself, where Ed aims to create a kingdom (80). She herself observes that "[Emily] loves like a foolish woman, I like a sensible man" (198). While acknowledging Emily's love for Rivers, she warns her not to "fall into the common error of sensible and delicate minds, that of refining away your happiness" (45), and, admitting to "a certain excess of romance . . . in [her] temper" (280), teases herself for vanity in

the midst of a letter adjudicating the claims of physical and moral beauty (227-30). Arabella is the only character to describe the physical nature of Canada; moreover, she does so in picturesque language which contrasts the wild sublime and the pleasing beautiful:

> There are two very noble falls of water near Quebec, la Chaudiere and Montmorenci: the former is a prodigious sheet of water, rushing over the wildest rocks, and forming a scene grotesque, irregular, astonishing: the latter, less wild, less irregular, but more pleasing and more majestic. (29)

Arabella, however, like Rivers, ultimately values English beauty, "the lovely, the smiling," over "the savage luxuriance of America" (300).

Arabella's admirable perspective on nature and art mirrors her style, which, brimming with literary allusions and philosophical argument, permits her to retain her "independence" of judgement. This style contrasts with Emily's descriptions of emotional vacillation. In one letter enclosing a missive from Emily confessing dislike of her fiancé, Arabella concludes not only that Emily should be released, but that "long engagements . . . [are] extremely unfavorable to happiness" and that she will refuse one (131). Her ability to "read" others' feelings allows her to decide her own course; she judges from observation and education, not just sentiment. She also extrapolates from her own feeling and from literary authority to determine the nature of social concepts. Quoting a passage from Nicholas Rowe's *Tamerlane* and arguing that all people worship that same God despite their differences, Arabella paradoxically raises a distinction of gender:

> Women are religious as they are virtuous, less from principles founded on reasoning and argument, than from elegance of mind, delicacy of moral taste, and a certain quick perception of the beautiful and becoming in every thing.
>
> This instinct, however, for such it is, is worth all the tedious reasonings of the men . . . (107)

In correlating the "natural taste" for virtue and religion with gender, Arabella articulates a tenet of literary sentimentalism; at the same time, her argument that women act from instinct cultivated by good breeding locates religion in civilized sensibility rather than in wild nature. Her own reflections thus modify the literary authority she cites. Indeed, throughout the novel, Arabella exemplifies Locke's ideal of judgement as the result of reflection on the data of empirical observation and of sensation.

By the dialectic exploration of sentimental ideals in her epistolary novels, Frances Brooke delineates the uses and dangers of sentiment. Her epistolary structure juxtaposes the contemplative letters of marginal spectators with lovers' passionate epistles to demonstrate that it is on the edges of sentiment that moral perspective lies, not in the heart of feeling. In **The History of Lady Julia Mandeville**, Brooke locates sentiment in moral spectatorship rather than heroic action; in **The History of Emily Montague**, she shows that female softness is the luxury of a "civilized" society, and therefore must also be its responsibility. Brooke thus suggests that sentiment is neither a natural nor an entirely good quality, for, although it supplies an internal moral system parallelling the regulations of society, it weakens women in a world ruled by the laws of men. While she approves the ideals of independence, sexual equality, and sympathy, Brooke believes that both civilization and right sentiment ultimately balance out feeling and reflection, and that it is the spectator who can exercise this internal command. Hence, watching women, both liberated from conventional society and exiled from conventional feelings or roles as heroines, may and must internalize the social value of conquest to rule their own natures. By letters contextualizing sentiment through allusion and pictorial diction, these characters serve to criticize the failures of literary and social conventions which identify virtue with spontaneous emotion. Brooke shows that by tracing the margins of language, letters, and law, women may translate the values of sentimentalism into the values of society.

Notes

[1] See Tompkins, who distinguishes between Fanny Burney's and Brooke's "reasonable" plots and the crowd of unreasonable novels in *The Popular Novel in England, 1700-1800* (60); for an introduction to the forms and idea of sentimental fiction, see Todd. For good analyses of literary sentimentalism, see Brissenden and Sheriff: both emphasize the expressive and individualistic element of sentimentalism at the expense of recognizing the pleas for social responsibility and restraint in sentimental fiction.

[2] The first English epistolary novels of sensibility, Samuel Richardson's *Pamela or, Virtue Rewarded* (1740) and *Clarissa* (1747), depict heroines "writing to the minute," transcribing their reactions as they happen.

[3] Both Mullan and Dwyer identify restraint as a pervasive discourse within sentimental fiction.

[4] For a thorough account of Brooke and her works which notes the figure of the female spectator, see McMullen. Pointing to the reviews of her novels in the contemporary *Monthly Review* and *Critical Review,* as well as to Bonnell Thornton and George Colman's acid

remarks in *The Connoisseur,* McMullen demonstrates Brooke's popularity and her experience in the literary world of the mid-century. McMullen argues that Brooke probably wrote *All's Right at Last; or, The History of Miss West,* published in 1774 and set in Canada (141). Edwards concisely documents Brooke's social life in her "Introduction" to the Carleton edition of *Emily Montague* (xvii-liv).

[5] Shevelow explains that Brooke imitated Eliza Haywood's *The Female Spectator* but moved away from "the centrality of the essay-periodical" in its diversity of offerings (151, 175). McMullen argues that Brooke's periodical, lighter than both Haywood's *The Female Spectator* and Samuel Johnson's *Rambler,* imitated the "wit, irony, and didacticism" of *The Spectator* (15-16).

[6] Clifford describes a similar frontispiece to Father Lafitau's *Moeurs de sauvages ameriquains* showing "a young woman sitting at a writing table amid artifacts from the New World," Greece, and Egypt, with her pen identified as the source of truth, and Time and religious allegorical vistas behind her (21). Such frontispieces represent the control of foreign culture by the writer's translation; see Benedict, "The 'Curious Attitude'" (61-77, 96n. 28).

[7] Mullan locates the failure of sentimental fiction in its fantasy of locating social value in private experience (119-20).

[8] In 1770, Brooke translated *Memoirs of the Marquis de St. Forlaix* by Nicholas Etienne Framery (1745-1810); in 1771, she translated the Abbé C. F. X. Millot's *Elements of the History of England, from the invasion of the Romans to the reign of George the Second,* but she was undoubtedly most famous for her translations of Mme. Riccoboni's *Letters of Juliet MiLady Catesby.*

[9] Brooke's first love was the theatre; in her final novel, *The Excursion* (1777), she chronicles the attempts of a young heroine, Maria, to get her plays published by a hostile Garrick. For an examination of Brooke's theatrical career, see Berland.

[10] Markley argues that sentimental fiction naturalizes class inequality by portraying bourgeois benevolists as instinctively charitable, that is, aristocratic, and thus finessing the problem of class versus wealth. Brooke avoids the issue by confining her fiction to gentle or noble characters and retaining the nostalgic "paternal" system, which Brissenden identifies as the dream of sentimentalism, and which Mullan opposes to the new exchange economy (132).

[11] Brooke opposes the categories of the "authentic" and the conventional on the level of language, but most sentimental fictions also play with this opposition on

the level of structure. Braudy notes the pretence of sentimental fiction to authenticity by means of its transparent method, the recovered manuscript or the reprinted correspondence.

[12] MacCarthy perceives the "Gothic terrors" in this passage (71). Foucault discusses the eighteenth-century association of forgetfulness with madness; for an analysis of Radcliffe's similar use of pictorial descriptions of young women losing their sense of moral boundaries by wandering or wondering in nature, see Benedict, "Pictures of Conformity" (370).

[13] In her "Introduction" to *Emily Montague,* Edwards suggests that Brooke may have used some of her personal correspondence in the book (xxxviii-xxxix).

[14] While noting that women choose their chiefs and applauding the practice since "women are, beyond all doubt, the best judges of the merit of men," Ed nevertheless notes that since this chief is, in fact, the closest relative to the old chief by the female line, this power undermines women's chastity in marriage (34).

[15] Klinck avers that Brooke approves imperialism and entertains "conventional intolerance," but in fact her careful parallels and oppositions between different cultures suggest that she is using the conventions of imperialism and cultural intolerance to argue for women's freedom and protection, not for imperialism per se (x).

[16] Barash explores the overlaps between sexual and colonial exploitation in slave narratives which use the sentimental devices of dreaming and the possessive language of dominance.

[17] Clifford observes that dominant cultures view colonized or "primitive" cultures as without history (32); Frye, on the other hand, identifies *The History of Emily Montague* as a chronicle of the "primitivism" of the New World which is almost historical in empirical detail (170).

Works Cited

Barash, Carol. "The Character of Difference: The Creole Narrator as Cultural Mediator in Narratives about Jamaica." *Eighteenth-Century Studies* 23 (1990): 406-24.

Benedict, Barbara M. "The 'Curious Attitude' In Eighteenth-Century Britain: Observing and Owning." *Eighteenth-Century Life* 14.3 (1990): 59-98.

———. "Pictures of Conformity: Sentiment and Structure in Ann Radcliffe's Style." *Philological Quarterly* 68.3 (1989): 363-377.

Berland, K. J. H. "Frances Brooke and David Garrick." *Studies in Eighteenth-Century Culture* 20 (1990): 217-30.

Brissenden, R. F. *Virtue in Distress: Studies in the Novel of Sentiment from Richardson to Sade.* New York: Macmillan, 1974.

Brooke, Frances. *The History of Emily Montague.* Ed. Mary Jane Edwards. Ottawa: Carleton UP, 1985.

———. *The History of Lady Julia Mandeville.* London: R. Dodsley, 1763.

———. *The Old Maid.* London: A. Millar, 1755-56.

Braudy, Leo. "The Form of the Sentimental Novel." *Novel* 7.1 (1973): 5-13.

Clifford, James. *The Predicament of Culture: Twentieth-Century Ethnography, Literature and Art.* Boston: Harvard UP, 1988.

Dwyer. John. *Virtuous Discourse: Sensibility and Community in Late Eighteenth-Century Scotland.* Edinburgh: Edinburgh UP, 1987.

Foucault, Michel. *Madness and Civilization: A History of Insanity in the Age of Reason.* Trans. Richard Howard. New York: Random House, 1965.

Frye, Northrop. "Eighteenth-Century Sensibility." *Varieties of Eighteenth-Century Studies* 24.2 (1990-91): 157-72.

Klinck, Carl F. Introduction. *The History of Emily Montague.* By Frances Brooke. Toronto: McClelland and Stewart, 1961. v-xiv.

MacCarthy, B. G. *The Later Women Novelists, 1744-1818* 1938. Oxford: Blackwell, 1946.

Markley, Robert. "Sentimentality as Performance: Shaftesbury, Sterne and the Theatrics of Virtue." *The New Eighteenth Century: Theory, Politics, English Literature.* Ed. Felicity Nussbaum and Laura Brown. New York: Methuen, 1987. 210-30.

McMullen, Lorraine. *An Odd Attempt in a Woman: The Literary Life of Frances Brooke.* Vancouver: U of British Columbia P, 1983.

Messenger, Ann. *His and Hers: Essays in Restoration and Eighteenth-Century Literature.* Kentucky: U of Kentucky P, 1986.

Mullan, John. *Sentiment and Sociability: The Language of Feeling in the Eighteenth Century.* Oxford: Clarendon Press, 1988.

Riccoboni, Marie-Jeanne. *Letters from Juliet Lady Catesby, To Her Friend Lady Henrietta Campley.* Trans. Frances Brooke. London: Dodsley, 1760.

Sheriff, John K. *The Good-Natured Man: The Evolution of a Moral Ideal, 1660-1800.* Tuscaloosa: U of Alabama P, 1982.

Shevelow, Kathryn. *Women and Print Culture: The Construction of Femininity in the Early Periodical.* London: Routledge, 1989.

Todd, Janet. *Sensibility: An Introduction.* London: Methuen, 1986.

Tompkins, J. M. S. *The Popular Novel in England, 1700-1800.* Lincoln: U of Nebraska P, 1961.

Robin Howells (essay date 1993)

SOURCE: "Dialogism in Canada's First Novel: *The History of Emily Montague*," in *Canadian Review of Comparative Literature,* Vol. 20, Nos. 3-4, September-December, 1993, pp. 437-50.

[*In the following essay, Howells argues for the literary as well as the historical and documentary value of* The History of Emily Montague *as the first Canadian novel.*]

All utterance, says Bakhtin, is dialogic. Any given utterance occurs in relation to context: time, place, interlocutionary situation. It is implicitly engaged with all other utterance—reworking, replying, anticipating—and with the reality that it seeks to attain. Insofar as it incorporates multiple discourses, it is a dialogue with itself. The condition of all language is that of interaction and change: open, dynamic, ever-renewed. As such, it mimes the condition of the world. ("Monologic" utterance is the authoritarian attempt to close the dialogue, to have the final and self-consistent word, to fix the world.) Literature organises and structures the multi-voiced character of language. It orchestrates, as Bakhtin would say, the polyphony. Thus he has a special interest in quotation, direct or indirect, as speech engaged with and framed by speech. He places particular value on the introduction of orality, and popular or paraliterary genres, within the received literary orders. (The dialogic overlaps with the carnivalesque and implies a politics.) He rejoices in comic disruption and rewriting. Parody, doubling and multiplying are means of breaking down the solemn and the unique, relativizing the absolute and putting discourses into unresolved play.[1]

Prima facie there are various ways in which ***The History of Emily Montague*** might fit this bill. It is an epistolary novel. At the time of its publication—1769—the novel was low on the hierarchy of genres. It dealt with the everyday. The epistolary mode in particular offered informality and immediacy. With its customary plurality of correspondents, the letter-novel might be said to be innately dialogic. Certainly it mirrors, in Britain and France, the highly sociable culture of the period. ***Emily Montague*** combines the concrete and relatively "popular" freedom of English literary models with the greater decorum and stylisation of the French. Its author, Frances Brooke, had already negotiated this relation as a translator from the French. A woman of letters, she raised in her writings various public issues, including gender. A "wife," she had spent the mid-1760s with her husband, who was chaplain to the British garrison, in the just-conquered colony of Québec. ***Emily Montague*** sets the novel's love stories principally in that new and renewed world. It deals in social and ideological as well as personal interactions.

The work is entirely neglected in Britain, the place of its original publication. It has owed its modest fame in Canada mainly to its "documentary" qualities, and to its primacy in literary history. More recently, however, Canadian criticism has drawn attention to its aesthetic qualities and saluted its feminism.[2] Here, I want to argue for the exceptional intelligence and wit of this novel, chiefly at the level of the interdiscursivity: the dialogic reading highlights this aspect. After an initial overview I shall look at patterning and play in the following domains: collective confrontations and debates; epistolarity; intratextual and intertextual quotation; sociability, and the quest for Eden; final closure and the refusal of closure.

In this epistolary novel, there are two principal letter-writers. Ed. Rivers is a young half-pay officer who comes to Canada shortly after the cession of the colony to take up his right to a land-grant; Arabella Fermor is the daughter of a British captain stationed in Québec. Rivers is soon smitten by Emily Montague, a ward engaged to a vain baronet whom she eventually repudiates in favour of Rivers. Bell Fermor assists and teases them, while favouring a Captain Fitzgerald among her own admirers. Love, friendship, and marriage are discussed extensively in the letters. The accounts of Canada that they send home are complemented by those produced by Bell's father for their noble patron in England. When Ed.'s sister Lucy writes that their mother is pining for him, Ed. and Emily readily put off their own projects and hurry back home. There money is inherited and Emily's long-lost father is found. Lucy's marriage to Ed.'s friend Temple is complemented by the marriages of Bell with her Fitz in Canada, whence they return to England, and of Emily with her Ed.

From this summary it is already evident that the work, at least in its conclusion, is strongly stylised. Neat and providential endings are fairly typical of eighteenth- and nineteenth-century fiction. The three marriages occur at different times and places, appropriate to the more "realist" genre conventions of the novel. But their parallelism suggests theatrical comedy. The effect is to relativize each individual romance, taking it back into a general pattern. The couples are clearly differentiated. The principal duo, Rivers and Emily, are characterized by intense feeling. Bell and Fitz on the other hand are roguish. Temple and Lucy offer another permutation in that initially their characters differ. Rivers and Emily are clearly the most important couple. But their story would be wearisome without Bell and Fitz alongside. Bell and Fitz play at being lovers. Their roguish romance gently parodies the high-minded romance of the principal couple. The unique affair is, in Baxtin's framework, second-voiced.[3] Thus the affair is drawn back into the general play of love stories.

Sexual love is only one of the principles of pairing. There are also male, and female, couples. The opening letter, from Rivers to his friend Temple, invokes their "early sympathy, which united us almost from infancy" (1, 18).[4] Rivers and Temple are, however, initially opposed in their attitude to women. Temple is a rake, Rivers is not; Temple prefers young girls, Rivers values the mature mind. We have something very similar from the female side. Bell says "I have loved Emily almost from childhood" (157, 220). Their temperaments are however opposed: "the fire, the spirit, the vivacity, the awakened manner, of Miss Fermor" are contrasted by Ed. with "that bewitching languor, that seducing softness, that melting sensibility, in the air of my sweet Emily" (179, 248). The dispositions of Emily and Bell towards men are likewise opposed. *Mutatis mutandis,* the opposition parallels that between the two men. Emily writes of her feeling for Rivers: "I cannot love him more . . . from the first moment I saw him my whole soul was his." Bell replies drily, "I love, at least I think so; but, thanks to my stars, not in the manner you do. I prefer Fitzgerald to all the rest of his sex; but I . . . contrive sometimes to pass [the hours] pleasantly enough, if any other agreeable man is in the way" (106-107, 153-4).

Thus couples are variously cross-cut, with the parallels and oppositions thematized. Ed. on his feelings for two women defines a contrast. Emily in love declares an absolute. But Bell embraces the positions and holds them at an ironic distance. In the utterance just quoted, she does this on the level of register, by using heterogeneous discourses. "Thanks to my stars," implicating the universe in an individual fate, is heroic language. "Pass [the hours] pleasantly enough" is the language of the ordinary. The first overrates and the second underrates love. Mock-heroic and litotes both function to ironise the romance. We have seen how it is relativized from "below" by comic imitation, and cross-cut by other pairings. Here it is gently mocked from

"above." Through Bell's writing, as through the plot structure, the work ironically foregrounds its own romance conventions.

The work also deals in more general or collective confrontations. Frances Brooke has located her story at an extraordinarily rich historical and cultural intersection—the (re-)founding of a colony. She brings out fully the complex interrelations, and sets them in play. The most obvious is the comparison between England and Canada. Rivers and Bell are part of the first wave of British settlement in Québec. Just arrived, in their letters home they "naturally" offer repeated parallels and contrasts. Within the description of Canada, oppositions are also complementarities. Ed. writes that "The island of Montreal . . . is . . . highly cultivated, and tho' less wild and magnificent, more smiling than the country round Quebec" (6, 28). Bell assigns opposed qualities to "two very noble falls of water near Quebec, la Chaudiere and Montmorenci" (10, 36).

Social groups provide more complex matter. Ed. and Temple are both interested first in the opposite sex. Ed.'s initial affirmation is that the "Canadian ladies have the vivacity of the French, with a superior share of beauty" (2, 19). Temple demands *Comment trouvez vous les dames sauvages?* all pure and genuine nature, I suppose; none of the affected coyness of Europe" (3, 21). Further comparisons are already implied. The "Canadians" means the French Canadians. They will be compared, in the course of the novel, with various other peoples: the French, the British, and the Natives. French-Canadian women Ed. relates here to French women. The situation of the Native women—Hurons (11, 38)—will be compared in due course with that of Native men, and with the situation of women in England. In turn, as we shall see, the status of women will be put in parallel with that of colonials in America. Ed. and Bell will make their differing contributions; Fermor will offer more systematic versions. Many of these comparisons are valorised, but not always in a predictable direction.

Temple's question also heralds a philosophical debate arising from the fictional situation. His friend has gone from Europe to North America. Old World and New World at this time are the synecdoches of culture and nature. How do they compare? This too is developed in the narrative. But the question is first posed jokingly, in terms of a difference in sexual mores. This mocking debasement frames the more sober discussions which follow. Better, it is posed ironically by the confrontation of heterogeneous discourses within the utterance itself. Temple's writing operates here like Bell's. The high cultural *dames* juxtaposed with the natural *sauvages*. The standard opposition of culture and nature is ironised by overemphasis: "all pure and genuine" versus "affected coyness." Thus it is shown forth as discourse and taken back into play.

As story, and as debate, the oppositions are not static. We have just seen how one general comparison branches into another. We also have reversals. The grave Ed. expends much ink warning Temple that his libertine life will dull his emotions and his morals (Letters 14, 21, 36, 57). Ed. advises his sister Lucy not to associate with him, telling her that she is "young and inexperienced" (38, 79). But when Lucy at last replies, it is to turn the tables. Her first letter to Ed. observes that he himself, in his fascination with the betrothed Emily, is "acting a little like a foolish girl" (67, 112). Her second letter accompanies one from Temple: out of the blue they announce to Ed.—and to us—their marriage (Letters 96, 97). Bell is at first struck by the freedom given to Native women, which she considers superior to that of Englishwomen. "Absolutely, Lucy, I will marry a savage, and turn squaw" (16, 50). Soon, however, she discovers that "the mothers marry their children without ever consulting their inclinations," and she contrasts "this foolish tyranny" with "the dear English privilege of chusing a husband" (20, 55).

It is Bell who is concerned to assert, in a notable phrase, "the free spirit of woman" (101, 148). It is she who notes that the Protestant commonplace of "exclaiming violently against convents" can be turned against another kind of forced female vocation—the arranged marriage (Letter 132). Along with the witty comparison, we find the direct denunciation. Men and money are jointly responsible for tyrannising Emily: "this sweet girl has been two years wretched under the bondage [of] her uncle's avarice" (65, 109-10). Bell's position, however, is moderate: "Parents should chuse our company, but never even pretend to direct our [marital] choice" (65, 110). She concedes a good deal to authority. Ed. draws a more radical lesson, not from the Catholics but the Natives: "The sex we have so unjustly excluded from power in Europe have a great share in the Huron government." Then comes the witty reversal: "In the true sense of the word, we are the savages, who so impolitely deprive you of the common rights of citizenship." Women, arguably, are a colonised people with a legitimate juridical grievance. "I don't think you are obliged in conscience to obey laws you have had no share in making; your plea would certainly be at least as good as that of the Americans, about which every day we hear so much" (11, 40).

Feminist critics have recognised the interest of what Ed., as well as Bell, is given to say. But they are curiously deaf to Emily. Yet it is Emily who repeatedly refuses the demand of her guardians to accept the baronet. To them she declares her love for Rivers, and this despite that fact that he has made no proposal to her, even appearing to address his affections elsewhere. "I am compelled to say, that, without an idea of ever being united to Colonel Rivers, I will never marry any other man" (92, 137). Later she will be as scandalously open to Rivers himself. "My tenderness for you fills my whole soul, and leaves no room for any other idea" (125, 180). Fermor seems to be at the other extreme, a prudent man who disapproves of her break with the baronet. Yet he too urges women's equality (Letter 135). He—not Bell—first refers to "the free spirit of woman." But he ironises it by showing how it requires him to operate through counter-suggestion (Letter 87). Lucy's remarks partially confirm his point (Letter 97). Thus when we attempt to identify an authorial voice, in this case on "the woman question," we find a complexity of voices. We find not a static position but a dynamic and complex debate. That the men are more radical perhaps reflects the limitations on what a female in the period might respectably say. To put it in our terms, it shows that the internal dialogue functions too as a dialogue with the norms of the readership.

Formally, the narrative is constituted of letters. This in itself means there is no overall narrator, or single and authorised point of view. The authorial role in effect is limited to the title, the numbering of the letters, and implicitly to their selection and sequence. There are 228 letters in the novel, most short. Their length varies from several pages to a few lines.[5] This purely formal concentration and variety is reflected in the fictional correspondents. There are in all ten correspondents, and all who write letters also receive them. The two most prominent letter-writers are Ed. and Bell. They write exactly the same number of letters, 77 each. Third comes Emily, the titular protagonist, with 36 letters written. Fermor, Bell's father, sends twelve. Temple, Lucy and Fitzgerald write about half-a-dozen each. Mrs. Melmoth, the wife of Emily's guardian, sends four. Sir George Clayton, Emily's fiancé, writes one; the Earl in England writes one. The fact that all ten senders are also receivers is quite remarkable. This complexity of epistolary exchange, on the purely formal level, is emblematic of the dialogic relation. To the real reader, it is pleasing that letters by Bell and letters by Ed. should balance. It is delightful, however, that we actually have one more letter from Bell, which is contained within Ed.'s Letter 102; and one more letter from Ed., which is contained within Bell's Letter 111. This witty and doubled *abyme*—the entity mirrored within itself—occurs near the middle of the total correspondence.

Among the lower-ranked writers there are some interesting patterns of distribution. Lucy in London writes twice to her brother Ed., then twice to her friend Bell, then once to Emily. She *receives* by far the largest number of letters, sent from Canada. her five letters are quite neatly distributed through the text (Letters 67, 97, 141, 176, 180). Temple as a writer surfaces with a wider spread but similar distribution (Letters 3, 35, 96, 126, 143, 165, 210). Fermor's twelve are confined to approximately the middle third of the work (Letters 72, 87, 100, 117, 123, 130, 131, 133, 135, 138, 152, 159). Mrs. Melmoth's letters feature only in the early part; all four are reprimands to Emily. Fitzgerald—this is, exceptionally, a weakness—is not featured as a writer until near the end, and all his letters are to Ed. The two who each send just a single letter are perfectly balanced.

The Earl and Sir George Clayton are the only two titled writers. The former, the aged patron of Rivers and the Fermors, is a kind of patriarch. The latter is a booby. He writes to Emily once, as Emily writes to him just once. Thus the multiplicity of writers are held together formally by complex patterning in the work.

As we encounter a variety of writers, styles and topics from one letter to another, so we may have variety and openness *within* the individual letter. For variety of content, as one might expect, the palm goes to Bell. Her Letter 50 begins with two past anecdotes about Ed., then reports a discussion she and Emily have just had on religion. Next one hears about a carriole race in the snow, and finally of a ball at which "we danced till this minute." The letter is also divided, formally, into four segments. They are headed separately, and in this case heterogeneously. The superscriptions are "Silleri, Jan. 4," "Two o'clock," "Monday, Jan. 5," and "Silleri, Thursday, Jan. 8, midnight" (92-94). Such a range of topics, headings and time is exceptional even for Bell. But it is by no means uncommon for narrative letters to be chronologically segmented within themselves. Ed.'s letter 6 sets the record with seven segments. Thus the single writing instance or utterance is formally broken down. These narrative segments usually constitute a "writing to the moment" or as Bell puts it in the case cited above, "till this minute." The device of instantaneity also takes the form of interruption, pointing again to circumstantiality. The ending of the letters seems to be left open, to be continued. Even some of the more philosophical letters end with such formulae as "I must hurry to the post-office" (Letter 66), "I am interrupted" (Letters 100, 181), and "the coach is at the door" (Letter 161).

The letters "answer" each other. The textual sequence is usually determined by the date of writing, but not always. Some of the letters pass between persons in the same house (e.g., Bell's game in Letter 65). Here the rapid exchange resembles conversation. Others must travel various distances within the colony, or between Britain and Canada. Liaisons over different distances are superimposed, again holding together the writers and the world. Representation of the real time-gap for transatlantic letters (perhaps two months for the voyage; lengthened during the winter freeze-up of the St. Lawrence, which necessitated a land-journey to ports in New England) poses a problem for the textual sequence. Frances Brooke's basic solution, of a piece with the centre of interest, is to minimize the letters *from* England. Those we have are integrated into the Canadian sequence—placed not by date of composition but of Canadian reception, juxtaposed with the response. In general, Brooke manages her plurality of writers and of distances with great skill to produce an effect of interlocution.

Interlocution occurs not merely in the sense of a shared correspondence. It is represented textually as shared discourse. Language is cited, re-written, placed in new contexts. The paradigm here is quotation: this links the letters to each other, and the work to the total discursive system. The principal practitioner of all forms of quotation is Bell. We look first at internal quotation: Bell's Letter 15 replies to Emily's Letter 13 in which the ward muses about her feelings for Clayton and Rivers. Bell refers to Clayton as "an extreme pretty fellow, who is fond of you, whom *you see with pleasure, and prefer to all his sex*" (47-48). The italicised portion is taken from Emily's letter ("I prefer him to all his sex. . . . I see him with pleasure" [13, 45-46]). Bell presents Emily with her own language in order to reason with her. But thereby she foregrounds that language itself. Further, she gently fragments Emily's language. And by putting the fragments in an inappropriate frame—the flippant register of "extreme pretty fellow"—she most clearly ironises it. The pattern appears again later. Emily, now rejoicing in her passion for Rivers, demands rhetorically "Is there on earth a man who can please where he appears?" Bell replies "Yes, my dear, *there is a man on earth,* and even in the little town of Quebec, *who can please where he appears*" (Letters 75, 76, 119-20). Again we have Emily's language, quoted back to her, fragmented in its new context. The inserted portion—"even in the little town of Quebec"—ironises it by literalisation and diminution. The universal is brought down to the here and now. The rhetorical question—imposing its answer—is re-opened. It is drawn back into dialogism, as the unique Rivers is drawn back into the plurality of male possibilities.

Bell's Letter 15 also includes other kinds of quotation. Anticipating that Emily's appearance will challenge her own established reign over the men, she writes "I foresee strange revolutions *in the state of Denmark.*" The phrase from Shakespearian tragedy is brought down to earth by its burlesque application. Later she says *Mon cher pere* desires a thousand compliments." Here the other discourse is literally another language. It ironises, ever so gently, the name of the father. Somewhere between formal literary quotation and the use of a foreign phrase we might put the instances we cited earlier from the first letter by Temple. "All pure and genuine nature" is in effect a quotation from an ideological discourse—or from the parody of that discourse. *"Comment trouvez vous les dames sauvages?,"* preceding it, perhaps points towards Rousseau by being in French. But Temple's letter is larded with French: *"prenez garde, mes cheres dames"* and "the charms of the *beau sexe*" likewise appear within the linear sequence of English. *"O Venus! O Mere de l'Amour!"*

appears on a separate line as a verse quotation. Temple's statement that he has just arrived from Paris, and his rather heavily rakish allusions, offer realist or stereotypical motivations for his French phrases.[6] But he also quotes English verse: *"The bloom of opening flowers."* He quotes from classical wisdom: "Remember that *to know one's self* the oracle of Apollo had pronounced to be the perfection of human wisdom." He also quotes "Our fair friend Mrs. H.——[who] says ' . . . '." When Temple writes "'twas cruel to leave her, but who can account for the caprices of the heart?," perhaps we are invited to read this too as quotation. The elevated register and the commonplace sentiment suggest that we could put this line between inverted commas. More subtly, it too would be language shown forth, double-voiced, his but borrowed.

The bravura display of different kinds of quotation is not maintained in Temple's subsequent letters. Placed so early, it may however function to establish in the mind of the real reader—ourselves—an ironic intertextual framework for all that follows. We are also given near the start a meta-textual frame for the love story. Ed. affirms that women should not fear men. As he puts it: "We are not half such terrible animals as mammas, nurses, and novels represent us; and, if my opinion is of any weight, I am inclin'd to believe those tremendous men, who have designs on the whole sex, are, and ever were, characters as fabulous as the giants of romance" (4, 22). His formula contrasts reality and received fictions. But of course the "reality" that we are reading is also a fiction. Especially in the contexts set out above, the formula becomes reflexively ironic. This novel deprecates novels; this fiction is not fabulous; this love story is not a romance. In either case, the formula invites us to perceive that this narrative's meaning resides in its difference from and relation to the system of narratives. The story to follow will indeed entirely eschew seductions and combats, in favour of civilised social intercourse.

Formal literary quotation, in this work, is a manifestation of both social and textual intercourse which we may call high cultural interlocution. In the early letters we noted several examples of literary quotation. Subsequently, there will be instances in letters by Lucy, Emily, and Fermor (one each). There are half-a-dozen such in the letters of Ed., but these together are far outnumbered in the letters of Bell. By my count, formal literary quotation appears in twenty-two of her letters. Pope is the favourite (five instances), then Shakespeare (three) and Milton (three, of which one is his translation from Horace). She also calls upon Rowe, Cowley, Shenstone, Aphra Behn, Mary Wortley Montagu and *The Spectator*. Rarely—in anyone's letters—is the source identified.[7] These quotations are part of the common discursive currency of the correspondents. Implicitly, the real readers are assumed to share that currency.

Cultural interlocution, in turn, is a manifestation of sociability. Sociability is the principal value proposed by **Emily Montague** and it is clearly thematized. Ed. becomes aware of "all the force of . . . that social love to which we owe all our happiness here" (32, 71). Fermor flatly asserts "there are no real virtues but the social ones" (135, 194). Fermor is not just a reporter, but a philosopher and he urges the aged Earl against retreat from the world: "Why should any man retire from society whilst he is capable of contributing to the pleasures of it?" The qualities he lauds are "wit, vivacity, good-nature, and politeness" (87, 132). These are of course very much the qualities of this novel, along with virtuous example. It is the duty of virtue to be sociable, to maintain "that mutual confidence so necessary to keep the bonds of society from loosening." "Virtue is too lovely to be hid in cells, the world is her scene of action" (100, 146-47).

Sociability underlies the feminism of Fermor. "The two sexes are equal gainers, by conversing with each other: there is a mutual desire of pleasing, in a mixed conversation" (135, 193). Rivers urges women's freedom and education in almost identical terms. One of his earliest letters invokes "the pleasure of mix'd society, the only society for which I have any relish" (4, 22). For the love-match between the sexes, Bell considers individual difference to be both natural and providential. She says: "I am thinking, my dear, how happy it is, since most human beings differ so extremely from one another, that heaven has given us the same variety in our tastes" (139, 200). The Enlightenment philosophy of Fermor affirms that collective relations too are providentially established on the principle of difference. Here it is excess, rather than lack, that prompts interaction:

> Heaven intended a social intercourse between the most distant nations, by giving them productions of the earth so very different each from the other, and each more than sufficient for itself, that the exchange might be the means of spreading the bond of society and brotherhood over the whole globe. (123, 178)

Free trade, sociability, free intercourse between the sexes, and love itself are all presented in terms of variety and exchange. Variety and change is repeatedly declared by the protagonists to be that which attaches their desires. In geographical description, the St. Lawrence is presented as "interspers'd with islands which give it a variety infinitely pleasing" (2, 19). Its shores exhibit "the lovely confusion of woods, mountains, meadows, cornfields, rivers . . . intermixed" (24, 64). Even in the Canadian winter "the variety of objects new to an European, keep the spirits in a continual agreable hurry" (52, 95). Ed. affirms a universal rule: "a state of rest is ungraceful: all nature is most beautiful in motion." The appeal of Emily is not that she is "regularly beautiful": "'tis life,' 'tis spirit, 'tis animation'" (6, 30-31). For Bell, Ed. "looks like an angel this morning . . . his hair a little *degagée*, blown about by the wind, and agreeably disordered" (23, 62). This rococo aesthetic of mobility is also a rococo morality for marriage. Temple's character is "particularly formed to keep a woman's mind in that kind of play, that gentle agitation, which will forever ensure her affection" (101, 147). Bell on Fitz: "I wonder I don't grow tired of him; but somehow he has the art of varying himself beyond any man I ever knew" (156, 220). Underlying it is what one might call a rococo psychology. It is excellently if more soberly summarised by Fermor: "There is nothing the mind of man abhors so much as a state of rest: the great secret of happiness is to keep the soul in continual action, without those violent exertions, which wear out its powers, and dull its capacity of enjoyment; it should have exercise, not labor" (133, 190).

Restlessness however is not so easily assuaged. Augustan moderation in this novel is tempered by the quest for Eden.[8] Here is how Ed. explains, in the very first letter of the book, his departure for Canada:

> Love of variety, and the natural restlessness of man, would give me a relish for this voyage, even if I did not expect, what I really do, to become lord of a principality which will put our large-acred men in England out of countenance. My subjects indeed at present will be only bears and elks, but in time I hope to see the *human face divine* multiplying around me; and, in thus cultivating what is in the rudest state of nature, I shall taste one of the greatest of all pleasures, that of creation, and see order and beauty gradually rise from chaos. (1, 17)[9]

The discourses of patriarchy, sovereignty, colonization, transformation, improvement, and utopia are all evident here. So is the discourse of Eden. The New World offers a new beginning.[10] Juxtaposed with petty vanity and with elks, the grand discourses are gently ironised. They are placed within quotation marks, double-voiced, not dismissed but put into play. The other principal letter-writer and new arrival in Canada is Bell. Her first missive is Letter 10: "I am at present at an extreme pretty farm on the banks of the river St. Lawrence; the house stands at the foot of a steep mountain covered with a variety of trees, forming a verdant sloping wall, which rises in a kind of regular confusion, *'Shade above shade, a woody theatre'*" (10, 37).[11]

Bell's letter is superscribed "Silleri, August 24." She will live at Sillery with her father the captain for nearly a year. That winter Emily comes to stay, and Rivers and Fitzgerald are frequent visitors. The situation is presented as idyllic. In January Rivers writes, "I have passed the last two months in the most agreeable manner possible, in a little society of persons I extremely love. . . . I extremely dread our party's being dissolved, and wish the winter to last for ever, for I am afraid the spring will divide us" (51, 95). Bell, independently, echoes him. Any outsider "will derange our little coterie; and we have been so happy, I can't bear it" (53, 97). Projects for a more permanent idyll follow. Rivers seeks land for the ideal settlement. He writes from "Kamaraskas" (Kamouraska): "I have fixed on the loveliest spot on earth, on which to build a house" which he intends for his mother and Emily (85, 131). Later this becomes a project described as "a little Eden on Lake Champlain . . . our new little world of friendship" (146, 206). Rivers imagines "my own settlement advancing . . . I paint to myself my Emily . . . like the mother of mankind, admiring a new creation which smiles around her: we appear, to my idea, like the first pair in paradise" (145, 205).

But Lucy has already signalled the return to the Old World. She proposes a more civilised project: "It would be a better plan to turn farmer in Rutland . . . and . . . live very superbly all together in the country" (67, 112). Then, Rivers returns, to his mother and the estate of his childhood (169, 234). Bell too returns, quite cheerfully: Sillery is "a terrestrial paradise, but we have lived in it almost a year, and one grows tired of everything in time, you know" (160, 225). Though regretting "dear little Silleri," it is Ed.'s estate she now qualifies as "paradise" (202, 269). She, Fitzgerald and Rivers all now deplore the search for "very extensive prospects," hail "this sweet little retreat" and claim to be "content at home" (183, 253; 202, 269; 186, 255). The last quarter of the work, which is set in the home counties of England, includes much moralising. And not only do we have two marriages, but Emily is reunited with her long-lost father. Bell herself ruefully observes on "our romantic adventures being at an end, my dear; and we being all degenerated into sober people" (227, 312).

Yet closure is avoided, through various kinds of play. Bell refuses to grow up, or to allow Ed., to do so: "You are a boy, Rivers, I am a girl; and I hope we shall remain so as long as we live" (218, 300). What Rivers in Letter 1 called "the gay mistakes [a marvellously Baxtinian phrase] of the just-expanding heart" in "the spring of life," can continue. Fermor urged the aged Earl against "retiring into a small circle," declaring that he possessed "eternal youth" (87, 132). The patriarch's single letter is a celebration of youth (184, 253-54); in parallel, Ed. saw North America as "coeval with the world itself" (2, 19), but affirmed that "America is in infancy, Europe in old age" (7, 32).

Secondly, we note that Emily encounters her father at a masquerade. Rivers tells us that she is dressed as "a French *paisanne*: Lucy is . . . a sultana, blazing with diamonds: my mother a Roman matron" (213, 292). This heterogeneous assemblage perhaps offers a *mise-en-abyme* of the story: the Canadian experience, Temple's wealth, the imperial mother country. Emily's long-lost father is referred to as a "nabob" and an "oriental colonel" (304), and bestows wealth on her. He also reveals her story in Letters 219, 225, 226. We may observe that this belated revelation constitutes, with-in the novel, a new "history of Emily Montague." The other narrative within the last segment is the morally-improving story of the forsaken mother in Letter 207. The female protagonists of this tale are named Fanny and Sophia. These are the names of the heroines of Fielding's two comic novels (*Joseph Andrews* and *Tom Jones*) and this intertextual gaming reminds us that Arabella Fermor is named after the model for the heroine of Pope's mock-heroic *The Rape of the Lock.*

The best stroke however occurs, appropriately, in the last letter. In Ed.'s letter to Bell his utterances become increasingly abstract and sententious, until he abruptly punctuates them:

> Upon the whole. . . .
>
> The affections. . . .
>
> The beneficent Author of nature, who gave us these affections for the wisest purposes
>
> —
>
> "Cela est bien dit, mon cher Rivers; mais il faut cultiver notre jardin."
>
> You are right, my dear Bell, and I am a prating coxcomb. (228, 315)

The quotation, of course, is a re-writing of the last line of *Candide.* Its functions in Voltaire's narrative and in the letter are similar. It deflates the discourses of history and philosophy, insisting on the present and the practical. A lesson from Bell about cultivating the garden is surely to be linked with the fact that Ed.'s estate is called Bellfield. But is the garden merely one's private plot, or the whole world?[12] The ambiguity remains, in *Candide* and here. This non-closure of meaning is reflected in the re-opening of the quest, and of textuality. In *Candide* the last line is not only immediately preceded by a reference to the garden of Eden. It, or the two together, clearly refer back to the beginning of the work in which Candide is "expulsé du paradis terrestre" (beginning of chapter 2). We noted that in Brooke's novel the first letter by Ed. and the first letter by Bell each quotes from *Paradise Lost.* The final letter has Ed. pretending to quote Bell really (mis)quoting Voltaire on the garden. Intratextually and intertextually this is a smiling celebration of dialogism.

Notes

[1] On dialogism, see Bahktin 1981; on the carnivalesque, 1968; on quotation, Bahktin/Vološinov. The theorist's failure to provide or maintain a consistent definition of dialogism might itself be seen as an illustration of the principle.

[2] For the most authoritative account of Frances Brooke's life and works, see McMullen (1983a, 1983b). For a critical edition of *The History of Emily Montague,* with a substantial Introduction and Notes, see Edwards. For a judicious account of feminist elements in *Emily Montague* and *The Excursion,* see Rogers. Very perceptive on *Emily Montague,* if sometimes wayward, is New (1972, 1989).

[3] "Para-odia" means, literally, "alongside voicing" (Genette 17).

[4] Parenthetical references, in the form (Letter number, page number), refer to the pagination of the New Canadian Library edition. Quotations have been checked using Edwards, and corrected where necessary.

[5] In the NCL edition the whole text runs to just 300 pages. Thus the average letter (allowing for spacing between letters) is about one-and-a-quarter pages in length. The longest is five-and-a-half pages (Letter 11), the shortest three lines (Letters 29, 78).

[6] It is pleasing—at whatever level we read—to note that Ed. in his reply to Temple's gallic gallantries quotes the translation of a *native Indian* love lyric (4, 23). Items from the language of the New World appear in his first set piece on native customs: Letter 11.

[7] For most references see the Notes in Edwards.

[8] The topos of Eden in the novel is given attention in McMullen (1983a, 96-99). My reading however is concerned less with referentiality (the perception of Canada or England) and more with the discursive system (Eden as the figure of open possibility, the Quest ever-rewritten).

[9] The italicised phrase is from *Paradise Lost* (cf. note 11).

[10] Ed.'s arrival in Canada is presented in his second letter. It may be read in more specifically Bahktinian terms. He arrives during "a kind of interregnum of government" and "We are in expectation of a successor from whom we hope a new golden age" (2, 19-20). This is clearly intended by Brooke as a homage to the new governor, Carleton (as the date on the fictional letter and the Dedication of the novel both indicate). But it also suggests the wider change from the French to the British order, with

its new hopes. It hints at a new Kingdom. Emblematically it is any moment, with its infinite openness, its possibility of plenitude never come but always coming.

[11] Here too a quotation from *Paradise Lost*. Ed.'s quotation is from line 44 of Book III. The context in Milton is the poet's literal blindness and spiritual vision. (Ed. writes as his ship departs for the land he imagines but has not yet seen.) Bell's quotation is line 141 of Book IV. The context in Milton is the first description of Eden.

[12] The link between the quotation and "Bellfield" is made by New. He asserts that, placed at the end of the work, the quotation suggests most widely "the need both to recognize women's independence and to re-examine views of the colonies . . . [as] it reconfirms the book's structure of artifice" (New 1989, 59). This is very good. It is less important that New is wrong factually in claiming that Bell "refuses to go" to the masquerade (on the contrary, "your masquerade . . . is my passion" [214, 293]) and wrong again critically in asserting that "she will not confuse it with reality," when she above all in this novel represents the principle of play.

Works Cited

Brooke, Frances. *The History of Emily Montague* [1769]. Mary Jane Edwards, ed. Ottawa: Carleton University, Centre for Editing Early Canadian Texts, 1985.

———. *The History of Emily Montague* [1769]. New Canadian Library Edition. Toronto: McClelland and Stewart, 1961. Rpt. 1991.

Bakhtin, M.M. *Rabelais and His World.* Cambridge, Mass.: M.I.T. Press, 1968.

———. "Discourse in the Novel," Michael Holquist and Caryl Emerson, trans. *The Dialogic Imagination: Four Essays.* Austin: U of Texas P, 1981. 259-422.

Bakhtin, M. M. and V. N. Vološinov, *Marxism and the Philosophy of Language.* New York: Seminar Press, 1973.

Genette, Gérard. *Palimpsestes: La Littérature au second degré.* Paris: Seuil, 1982.

McMullen, Lorraine. *An Odd Attempt in a Woman: The Literary Life of Frances Brooke.* Vancouver: U of British Columbia P, 1983a.

———. "Frances Brooke (1724-1789)," *Canadian Writers and Their Works.* Downsview: ECW Press,

1983b. Vol. I. 25-60.

New, W.H. "Frances Brooke's Chequered Gardens," *Canadian Literature* 52 (Spring 1972): 24-38.
———. *A History of Canadian Literature.* Houndmills and London: Macmillan, 1989. 57-60.

Rogers, Katherine M. "Sensibility and Feminism: The Novels of Frances Brooke," *Genre* 11 (1978): 159-71.

Dermot McCarthy (essay date 1993/94)

SOURCE: "Sisters Under the Mink: The Correspondent Fear in *The History of Emily Montague,*" in *Essays on Canadian Writing,* Vols. 51-52, Winter 1993-Spring 1994, pp. 340-57.

[*In the following essay, McCarthy characterizes* The History of Emily Montague *as an essentially racist and bigoted narrative with a pro-colonialist point of view.*]

According to Frances Brooke's biographer, Lorraine McMullen, **The History of Emily Montague** (1769) was "required reading for early British travellers to Canada" (115), and the novel's most recent editor, Mary Jane Edwards, writes that it served as "a kind of guidebook" for tourists and emigrants (Introduction li). But what sort of "guidebook" is Brooke's novel two centuries later, and should it still be "required reading"? I think so, but not for the reasons offered by the historical, thematic, formalist, and, most recently, feminist critics who have kept it, in Carl F. Klinck's words, "long . . . in the canon of Canadian literature" (v).

Literary historians and critics have converged on Brooke's novel from four directions, seeing it as an originary object in Canadian literary history; as a discussion of European themes that employs the epistolary form and capitalizes on the exotic vehicle of a North American setting; as a sociocultural document and "celebration" of the unique Canadian space; and, finally, as a significant proto-feminist work in a revisionist-feminist literary history. Desmond Pacey sketched the main lines of this tradition in 1946. He identifies **Emily Montague** as "the first Canadian novel," yet he admits that its "Canadianism" is arguable (143). Since Pacey, only offshore critics seem to have noticed this issue (see Fitz 364; an exception is Berland 290, 298). In a doubly unfortunate turn of phrase, Pacey argues that, while "not a distinguished novel" (143), **Emily Montague** is nevertheless "a not unworthy progenitor of the Canadian novel" (145). Pacey's combination of qualitative and quantitative criteria develops the hybrid sociocultural/literary perspective to which Northrop

Frye gave canonic imprimatur in his conclusion to the *Literary History of Canada* in 1965; Pacey notes that

> Its artistic shortcomings are obvious: the plot is thin, conventional, repetitive, and poorly integrated with the informative sections of the book; the style is generally stilted and monotonous; the characters, with one or two exceptions, are traditional in conception and deficient in life; the whole performance is heavily didactic and sentimental. In spite of these manifest weaknesses, the novel remains of interest and value to us as a social, and to a lesser extent as a literary, document. (143)

Subsequent discussion has not dealt with the problem of the novel as originary object—with its selection by the tradition to begin the tradition that selects it—but has developed the other three approaches, with recent discussion particularly developing the feminist approach.

The second approach discusses the novel as "an embodiment of the literary forces at work in the second half of the eighteenth century," in particular, the "cult of sensibility" (Pacey 145). Berland's is the most sophisticated, Dahlie's the most dismissive, in this approach. Although it is "the first fictional treatment of the exile theme as it applies to Canada" (23), Dahlie judges it an inconsequential novel for the Canadian tradition because "exile seems to serve merely a decorative function" in it (30). The third approach, usually combined with the second, praises Brooke for being a "celebrant" who "seized upon what is the essence of the Canadian landscape, as contrasted with that of Europe: its magnitude of scale" (Pacey 146, 147). The Talmans, in the *Literary History of Canada,* put a different spin on Pacey's "weak-but-strong" argument by praising Brooke's divergence from generic norms: "no violence—none of the abductions, seductions, duels, highwaymen, or ghosts that we find in other such romances" (99). Edwards, in *The Oxford Companion to Canadian Literature,* adds a new theme in drawing attention to the book's "political content" (87), and the most bizarre discussion of the novel is Wayne Fraser's politico-feminist reading in *The Dominion of Women.*

Fraser offers a thoroughly incomprehensible view of Brooke's characterization. He disagrees with McMullen's view that Brooke was of "the English party" (2), that is, pro-traders and anti-French Canadian, and that William Fermor expresses her husband's and her own views, and he argues that "Closer examination of the novel reveals . . . that Brooke was sharply critical of the prevalent attitudes of the day" (3). Not only does Fraser reject the views that see Arabella as expressive of Brooke's opinion of the "commonwealth of women" (3), he also discusses Riv-

ers and Emily as if they were not Brooke's hero and heroine, the man and woman of sensibility. In fact, he discusses the novel as if it had nothing to do with that concept and ethos. His discussion of Arabella ignores her role and identity as a coquette and her function and effect in terms of variety and contrast, a narrative technique that Brooke continues from her earlier fiction (see McMullen 66, 84). But most incredible is the way in which Fraser's political reading of the novel ignores or denies the obvious in terms of plot and characterization, as well as the facts of Brooke's identity, position, and circumstances as presented in McMullen's research. To say that "The attitude of domination seen in Rivers and the response of total submission made by Emily are not positive bases for marriage, or for the British takeover of New France" (8) requires a disregard for what the novel plainly expresses: Rivers's and Emily's marriage is the ideal marriage of a man and woman of sensibility, and the achievement of this symbolic-emblematic union is the polemical goal of the sentimental project. As Berland shows, "In Emily and Rivers together, Brooke offers a visible example of the new order" (298).

Fraser's conclusion—that "Although historical evidence seems to suggest that Brooke supported the anglicization of Canada along with her husband, the evidence of the novel implies that perhaps, like [Arabella], Brooke was less than convinced by conventional opinions" (8)—is as stable as a two-legged stool. Brooke was the wife of the Anglican chaplain to the army of occupation, and McMullen shows convincingly that she was indefatigable in working for the success of her husband and, ipso facto, the Anglican Church in the newly acquired colony. Edwards, too, has shown that the religious views in *Emily Montague* reflect Brooke's "campaign on behalf of her husband and her Church" during her time in the colony ("Frances Brooke's *The History of Emily Montague*" 179) and, furthermore, that for Brooke, "the ultimate aim of Canadian politics must be to create a new England in Canada," not through emigration but by the Anglicization of Canadians (*"History of Emily Montague"* 22). To these ends, she was allied with the merchant faction against Murray and a supporter of his replacement, Carleton. She was obviously and thoroughly a colonizer, and Fraser's attempt to develop her as the voice of the *colonized* is nothing short of weird. The only time in the novel that we hear the voice of the colonized is when we hear Madame Des Roches; but, significantly, her words are always reported or contained by someone else's. In Brooke's novel, the colonized never speak; they are always spoken.

Pacey recognized Brooke as "obviously a determined feminist" (147), and W. H. New reads *Emily Montague* as emerging from her feminist writing in her satirical periodical, *The Old Maid*. But in New's judgement, "whatever social rebellion Frances Brooke can be said to espouse, she is not a thoroughgoing rebel. . . . [D]ecorum is the final arbiter of behaviour" (*"Old Maid"* 10). Katherine Rogers sees no compromise, however, in Brooke's attempt to combine her feminism and her belief in sensibility. Feminist approaches have resulted in some of the most exaggerated claims for Brooke's achievement in *Emily Montague,* as in Bennett and Brown's claim that Brooke "sees North American society as calling up new questions about the roles of women" ([1]), the "underdog feminist revisionism" of McMullen's biography (Carr 64), and Edwards's attempt to read it as a political novel (see *"History of Emily Montague"* 22). Unimpressed by Brooke as a feminist, however, Linda Shohet judges her to be, at best, "an early, intellectual Emily Post" (32).

Klinck, in his introduction to the 1961 New Canadian Library edition of the novel, added little to the discussion, but his ideologically naïve and evasive view that *"Emily Montague* is a *tour de force* in describing, not in defining, Canadian life" (x) is an approach that leads ultimately to the cotton-candy criticism of Clara Thomas, who praises the novel's "descriptive and domesticated charm" (659), as well as to the disturbing complacency in John Moss's description of the political setting in the novel as "the military presence of a petulant occupation" (*Patterns of Isolation* 25).

The History of Emily Montague should still be read because it is, in Edwards's surprisingly patriarchal metaphor, "a source of seminal archetypes for Canada itself" (Introduction liv). But the "seminal archetypes" that need to be recognized have to do with the racism and bigotry of the novel's collective voice and the problem of the mother-country/colony relations that it introduces. These archetypes, furthermore, need to be considered as figures of what Homi Bhabha calls "the spectacle of otherness" (195), as expressions of what Tzvetan Todorov terms "the problematics of alterity" (185), or what might be described as both the general and specific pathologies of alterity that characterize so much early Canadian writing. The bulk of the novel is a series of letters between correspondents in England and Quebec, as well as within the colony itself; the actual communication is, of course, between the author and the reader, and for a late-twentieth-century Canadian reader, corresponding with this novel can be both informative and unsettling because of what it reveals about traditions of cultural bias and imaginative myopia inherent in our cultural discourse.

For the purposes of my discussion, the source of authority of any one view in the novel is not the issue; rather, I am interested in the book as a canonic narrative that introduces and establishes certain perspectives, values, and binaries—what Edward Said describes as "the set of cultural forms and structures of feeling" produced by imperialism (10)—that became foundational in Canadian cultural discourse during the colonial period. The issue of who speaks for Brooke is not the point; the point is that the book contains and expresses a structure of ideas, values, and perspectives. Various critics, however, identify various characters as Brooke's vehicles. Most see the hero, Rivers, and Arabella Fermor, the heroine's friend, as expressing Brooke's feminist ideas and attitudes (see McMullen 104-05; Rogers 162; Dahlie 26; Berland 292; New, "Chequered Gardens" 25; Fitz 364; Messenger 170), though Rogers considers Arabella "too frivolous" (165) and therefore "not . . . a dedicated feminist" (164). McMullen believes that William Fermor, Arabella's father, represents Brooke's husband's views (which she shared) on the Catholic Church, the nuns and conventual system, and the French Canadians and Indians (68; see also 76-78, 91-93), and Dahlie argues as well that "the novel's ethical centre . . . [is William Fermor's view that] 'there are no real virtues but the social ones'" (23), though this view is also expressed by Rivers and Arabella.

In *Culture and Imperialism,* Said argues that from the late eighteenth century onward "imperialism and the novel fortified each other to such a degree that it is impossible . . . to read one without in some way dealing with the other" (71); specifically, he argues for a connection "between the patterns of narrative authority constitutive of the novel . . . and . . . : a complex ideological configuration underlying the tendency to imperialism" (70). The traditional approaches to Brooke's novel, including recent feminist readings, do not deal sufficiently with its ideological function in relation to the imperial-colonial values that it supports (though MacLulich does emphasize Brooke's sense of belonging to, representing, and expressing the power, authority, and prestige of "an occupying garrison" [22]). By considering the various forms of alterity and how they are presented in the novel, and by attempting to read it against its ideological grain in terms of its depiction of otherness—or, as Heather Murray has proposed, borrowing from Dennis Lee, reading to hear the "obstructions to cadence" as themselves expressive or performative of a work's relation to a "problematic public space" (78)—it may be possible to see precisely how *The History of Emily Montague* is a significant originary work in the canon of colonial writing in Canada.

The forms of alterity that organize *The History of Emily Montague* are the landscape, the French Canadians, and the Indians. As well, the novel's epistolary conventions foreground divisions of spatial and temporal otherness that complicate the novel's "domesticated charm" (Thomas 659). In what follows, however, I will only consider the figure of Madame Des Roches, the French-Canadian woman who, for a time, seems to rival the novel's English heroine as a possible wife for the hero, but who is, ultimately, rejected by him.

Madame Des Roches is important because she incorporates all the modes of alterity—race, sex, religion, and landscape—that represent the Other in Brooke's novel. As the most important embodiment of French Canada in the novel, Madame Des Roches is as powerful a presence in the Canadian portion of the narrative as the landscape itself, and her rejection should be understood in terms of the rejection of a future life in the colony by Brooke's principals. As attractive as she is, she embodies an Other that both repulses and attracts Brooke. She is a complex figure because, while the aspect of her identity that derives from her race places her among the conquered and inferior, the French Canadians and the Indians (both of whom Brooke presents in a version of what Syed Alatas has described as the "myth of the lazy native"), her sexual identity as woman and widow (for which Brooke, presumably, feels some sympathy) empowers her with a subversive energy that Brooke barely manages to control. With Madame Des Roches, as with other treatments of racial, sexual, and religious alterity involving women (for example, the French-Canadian nuns and Native women), Brooke's feminist agenda seems to clash at times with the imperial-colonial ideology that otherwise disciplines it.

On the surface, Madame Des Roches seems to be everything that the would-be emigrant hero is looking for: "she is very amiable; a widow about thirty, with an agreable person, great vivacity, an excellent understanding, improved by reading, to which the absolute solitude of her situation has obliged her; she has an open pleasing countenance, with a candor and sincerity in her conversation" (76). Yet this letter, which introduces her, also has embedded within it the reason for her ultimate rejection. In the anecdote about the hermit, which reads as a parable for Rivers, he hears the story of someone who marries against parental wishes and attempts to settle in the New World, only to meet with death and disaster. The hermit's isolation reflects Madame Des Roches's "absolute solitude," but his situation is a symbolic warning to Rivers—and to Brooke's reader—that, in marrying Madame Des Roches and settling in Kamouraska, he would be dooming himself, marrying death, in effect. The combination of isolation and pioneer achievement represented by Madame Des Roches leads D.M.R. Bentley to categorize her as the first example of "the *topos* of the female Crusoe in Canadian writing" (120), but I find Brooke's treatment of her more complex and ultimately too sinister for this. And while Bentley's point that "the writing of women about being women in the colonies is twice marginalized—once by being distant from the centre and once again by being of 'the second sex'— gives it, for many contemporary readers, a double interest" (119) is as generally apt as it is politically correct, in Brooke's case it seems particularly inept and insensitive: *The History of Emily Montague* presents its colonial subject for the entertainment and education of a metropolitan reader, and, as a "second[-]sex" writer, Brooke should present considerable difficulties to feminist readers with her racist, patriarchal, and patronizing treatment of French-Canadian and Indian women.

Rivers's letters make it clear that he is impressed with Madame Des Roches's many charms (see Letters 36, 85), but he has difficulty describing the exact nature of his feelings for her: "It is not love; for I love, I idolize another: but it is softer and more pleasing, as well as more animated, than friendship" (158). In the same letter, Rivers expresses his intention not only to have Madame Des Roches and Emily become friends but also to have his mother join them on the land that he hopes to purchase from this more-than-friend (159). That neither of these plans is possible soon becomes clear, and the reasons are as symbolic as they are obvious.

Madame Des Roches takes on symbolic significance as soon as she is introduced. Rivers discovers her in "the wildest country on earth; I mean of those which are inhabited at all" (76), and she is linked not only to the New World landscape but also, as a presence, to Emily as absence. The relation between the two women is based on a network of complementary oppositions: virgin/widow, English/French-Canadian, younger/older, one associated with the garrison world of Quebec/the other with the wilds of Kamouraska. Opposite versions of each other, their identities in difference become increasingly explicit as Brooke develops their rivalry for Rivers.

Because of the not-quite-false impression of Rivers's attraction to Madame Des Roches formed by Emily and her friend Arabella, when Madame Des Roches arrives at Quebec, Emily's immediate reaction is jealousy. The problem is that, as Brooke develops this altogether formulaic impediment to true love, her heroine is diminished in stature compared to Madame Des Roches, the rival whom Rivers has already rejected. In a sequence of letters in which she considers Madame Des Roches to be either "artful" or affected (see Letters 110, 112), then admits the possibility that "She is either the most artful, or the most noble of women" (197), Emily does not come off well. The turning point in her attitude comes in Letter 122, in which she confesses to her failings with Madame Des Roches. But the interesting point here is how the epistolary form itself mediates the heroine's admission of inferiority to her rival.

Letter 122 clearly presents Madame Des Roches as a woman of superior character, but her words are reported by Emily, and the form thus allows the inferior character to contain the superior, so that Emily's comparative weakness of character emerges as stronger than Madame Des Roches's superiority. Brooke's technique itself is expressive: she opens quotation marks in

Emily's letter when Emily begins to "quote" Madame Des Roches, but Emily continues to speak *for* the other woman as she "quotes" her in the third person—that is, there is no literal quotation, only reportage, even though the typographical code of first-person speech activates the expectation/impression of the former in the reader. Todorov argues that "the touchstone of alterity is not the present and immediate second person singular but the absent or distant third person singular" (157). Here the weaker character has the greater power of speech as she overwrites the voice of the other/ Other. It is an instance that illustrates how, in Brooke's novel, the colonized are *spoken for* rather than allowed to speak for themselves. Emile Benveniste posits that "The 'third person' is not a 'person'; it is really the verbal form whose function is to express the *non-person*" (qtd. in Fabian 85), and Fabian, discussing the way that anthropological discourse constructs the Other, builds on Benveniste's thesis: *"pronouns and verb forms in the third person mark an Other outside the dialogue*. He (or she or it) is not spoken to but posited (predicated) as that which contrasts with the personness of the participants in the dialogue" (85). This is precisely how third-person reference functions in Brooke's novel when the referents are French-Canadians and Indians. In this instance, we can see how Brooke's use of the epistolary form controls the Other, embodied in the figure of Madame Des Roches, by circumscribing, silencing, and, in effect, disembodying it.

Emily actually admits her inferiority to Madame Des Roches—"How superior . . . is her character to mine! I blush for myself on the comparison; I am shocked to see how much she soars above me: how is it possible Rivers should not have preferred her to me?" (218)— and while we share her mystification, we sense that this admission/submission insidiously gives her the upper hand and stronger presence. Emily's sudden generosity of spirit is not all that it seems, however; she ends this letter by suggesting that Madame Des Roches could not have loved Rivers as much as she herself does, otherwise she would not have given up the fight so easily (219)—though Madame Des Roches has confided to her that the loss of Rivers has "wounded her to the soul" (217). Emily's equivocation here points to the chasm at the centre of the novel's imaginative world. There is an unbridgeable gap between Emily and Madame Des Roches not only as characters in the romance plot but also as symbols in the novel. Emily remarks: "I wish my heart felt [Madame Des Roches's] merit as strongly as my reason. . . . I adore, I idolize her character; but I cannot sincerely wish to cultivate her friendship" (219). The rivalry for Rivers between Emily and Madame Des Roches is symbolically a struggle for the deepest loyalties of the British settler. Emily is England; Madame Des Roches, Canada. For Brooke, it is unimaginable that Rivers could prefer the latter: to do so would be not to choose the

New World so much as to reject the Old, the mother country.

But the abyss separating Emily and Madame Des Roches is also an illusion required by ideological praxis. The strange love/fear that Emily has for the other woman expresses the self/Other binary that they configure in symbolic terms. Brooke's characterization of these figures—like that of Emily and Rivers's sister, Lucy, earlier in the novel—is strangely narcissistic and laden with problematic metaphors of resemblance. Rivers tells Lucy that he would marry her if she were not his sister (21-22) and says that he loves Emily because she reminds him of Lucy. Emily says that she loves Rivers because he possesses "a sensibility similar to my own" (247). Their love is a form of self-love.

Madame De Roches is mysteriously incapable of breaking into this narcissistic circle, and yet she is uncannily close to being the face of the beloved reflected in the pool. Emily sees both herself and her beloved reflected in her rival. Her language in Letter 122—"I idolize her character"—echoes Rivers's (158) while it reverses his referents, suggesting the complex mirroring that occurs between self and Other in the novel. In a later letter, she asks: "Why should I dislike her for seeing you with my eyes, for having a soul whose feelings resemble my own?", and she proclaims: "if I was not Emily Montague, I would be Madame Des Roches" (248). This instability of the self/Other binary continues to the end. When Arabella leaves Madame Des Roches, even the racial denominators fundamental to characterization in the novel begin to blur: "She is less like a sprightly French widow, than a foolish English girl. . . . [Y]our little Bell seems, in point of love, to have changed countries with Madame Des Roches" (306).

Madame Des Roches's presence is only recognized in her absence. When she has left Quebec, Emily mourns her departure:

> We have lost Madame Des Roches; we were both in tears at parting; we embraced, I pressed her to my bosom: I love her, my dear Rivers; I have an affection for her which I scarce know how to describe. I saw her every day, I found infinite pleasure in being with her; she talked of you . . . ; I however found it impossible to mention your name to her; a reserve for which I cannot account; I found pleasure in looking at her from the idea that she was dear to you . . . : do you know I think she has some resemblance of you? there is something in her smile, which gives me an idea of you. (247)

That "lost" sounds more like Madame Des Roches has died than simply returned to Kamouraska, though for Brooke and her English characters dying or returning to Kamouraska are the same.

Emily can only love the woman in absentia, and, as the language in her letter suggests, it is her powerful "disciplinary gaze"—to use Bhabha's phrase—masked in sentiment though it is, that displaces Madame Des Roches to the domain of absence. Emily's professed sister-love for her erstwhile rival is "a disciplinary gaze upon difference that disavows the castrating and negating return of the look of the Other" (Bhabha 195). Brooke's "rhetoric of vision" (see Fabian [105]-41) has Emily turning back the threatening "look of the Other"—Madame Des Roches is so powerful a figure that simply speaking Rivers's name in her presence will make him vulnerable to her charms—by seeing the other as resembling her beloved. And as she loves Rivers because he is a reflection of her own soul (247), the mirroring illustrates what Todorov describes as the submission of the other to the self through a process that denies the other her own identity (185). He discusses the equality/inequality and identity/difference binaries as "the two great figures of the relation to the other that delimit the other's inevitable space" (146). Emily's relation to Madame Des Roches illustrates both his argument that equality becomes identity—overwhelming the other by making it reflect herself or her beloved, who, in this narcissistic instance, are the same—and that difference becomes superiority—when Emily's defeat of her rival "delimit[s] the other's inevitable space" by sending her back to the extreme, peripheral world of Kamouraska.

Emily might wish to be Madame Des Roches—an expression of the inversion that the pathology of alterity in Brooke's novel constructs—but Madame Des Roches could never be Emily Montague. The irony of making the Old World heroine the younger, virginal woman is significant. Madame Des Roches's fate is to be forever the widow, always *already* married to the spirit of the land, and to be forever yearning for the suitor who conquered her (and symbolically made her a widow in the first place) but did not stay to take full possession of her. We are told that Madame Des Roches chooses her fate, but she herself does not tell us this. When Arabella reports Madame Des Roches's final words to her, in Letter 157, once more we have the colonized character *spoken for* rather than speaking. Brooke again uses quotation marks and the third person, but this time she has the reporter explicitly contradict the sense of the typographical code when Arabella admits that Madame Des Roches's "expressions are much stronger than those in which I have given you the sense of them" (282). It seems that just as Emily is afraid to utter Rivers's name to Madame Des Roches, so Arabella is afraid even to write Madame Des Roches's words to anyone who might repeat them to Rivers or Emily.

Madame Des Roches leaves the novel as much a figure of enigmatic power and mysterious identity as she enters it. Like some tutelary goddess of the woods from which she came, and in which Rivers discovered her, she returns to the land that, both on the level of plot (as landowner) and on the level of symbol (as the spirit of the land), she openly and generously offered to Rivers, the representative of the conquering British. The ambiguity of her presence continues even in Arabella's final, joking suggestion that she kidnap her and take her to England:

> it is pity such a woman should be hid all her life in the woods of Canada: besides, one might convert her you know; and, on a religious principle, a little deviation from rules is allowable. . . . [Rivers] is an admirable missionary amongst the unbelieving ladies: I really think I shall carry her off; if it is only for the good of her soul.

She decides not to, she says, because her husband might "take a fancy" to her: "there is something very seducing in her eyes, I assure you" (304). In the threatening otherness of her religion and her sexual power, Madame Des Roches's attributes as an embodiment of the Other linger even as she disappears. For all their protestations of love and regret, it seems best for those concerned that Madame Des Roches and all that she represents remain "hid . . . in the woods" of the New World.

Madame Des Roches is such a powerful figure in Brooke's novel because she links race, sex, and religion, central definers of the Other, with landscape. In his discussion of the traditional metaphoric meanings of literary landscape, Leonard Lutwack identifies the forest with "an unruly sexuality that threatens tragedy for those who become involved with it." The forest, moreover, functions in terms of a garden/forest binary: "The garden is the body of a woman in a passive condition, waiting to be enjoyed, while the dense vegetation of the forest may portend the active entrapment of the male in the unseen, mysterious reproductive process that leads to revelation or to death" (99). From her first appearance in the novel, Madame Des Roches is identified with the forest wilderness that is her home. This identification contrasts with the explicit linking of Emily to the garden of Rivers's family estate, Bellfield, at the end of the novel. The descriptions of Madame Des Roches's appearance and sexual attractiveness also establish her as a figure of sexual power. Her identity as a widow associates her with death; or, more precisely, it is a symbolic warning to any man who might consider marrying her (see Edwards, *"History of Emily Montague"* 24-25).

Canada promises nothing but ruin and invisibility for Brooke's English characters. Emily's conviction that she will not "suffer [Rivers] to hide [his] shining merit in the uncultivated wilds of Canada, the seat of barbarism and ignorance" (212), and Arabella's pity for

Madame Des Roches, whose fate is to remain "hid all her life in the woods of Canada" (304), express another form of the pathology of alterity in the novel, the binary of visibility/invisibility. What these tourists see in the New World disturbs them because the Other is as attractive as it is fearful, and so their "disciplinary gaze upon difference" repositions the visible in the realm of the invisible. For Brooke's English characters, to remain in Canada would be to disappear, in effect, to suffer a living entombment. Emily wants Rivers to "leave Canada to those whose duty *confines* them here, or *whose interest it is* to remain unseen" (212; emphasis added). But it is Brooke, the metropolitan author, who dooms the colonized to invisibility, who confines them in her imperial discourse, and in whose interest it is to control the Other, as in the figure of Madame Des Roches, by silencing it—or speaking for and hiding it—making it invisible.

When the novel concludes with Rivers's explicit contrasting of the New World and the Old in terms of wild and cultivated nature, the forest and the garden, the symbolic relations between landscape and character are evoked. Emily is the tutelary goddess of Bellfield; Madame Des Roches is her antitype in the counterworld of Canada. Rivers announces to William Fermor that, "with all my passion for the savage luxuriance of America, I begin to find my taste return for the more mild and regular charms of my native country" (300), and he thus articulates the novel's ultimate disposition toward the Other in all its forms—sexual, racial, religious, and geographical. His list of differences inverts as it enumerates the New World deficit in terms of Old World surfeit:

> We have no Chaudieres, no Montmorencis, none of those magnificent scenes on which the Canadians have a right to pride themselves; but we excel them in the lovely, the smiling; in enameled meadows, in waving corn-fields, in gardens the boast of Europe; in every elegant art which adorns and softens human life; in all the riches and beauty which cultivation can give. (300)

Here Brooke employs the binary conventions of the picturesque and sublime in order to approve a sensibility that is sensitive to both, yet most fulfilled in the presence of the former. The New World is deficient because it is sublimely excessive.

Brooke makes clear the interrelations between the aesthetic and moral attributes of sensibility when she has Rivers lecture his friend, Temple, on the value of moderate emotion: "The tumult of desire is the fever of the soul; its health, that delicious tranquillity where the heart is gently moved, not violently agitated" (344). In the moral scheme of her novel, Brooke's representation of the New World places it on the other/Other side of these binaries: it is passion rather than charm, violent movement rather than orderly progression, magnificence rather than elegance, the place of the extravagant and irrational rather than of the decorous and rational, the condition of "fever" rather than of "health." "There is a moral principle involved in the choice a character makes between alternative places . . ." (Lutwack 70), and Rivers's rejection of Canada is a moral choice that Brooke shows, ultimately, to be the proper one. His choice confirms him as a man of sensibility, but it also shows us how Brooke's novel and its ideological program belong to that "consistency of concern" in British culture that "fixes socially desirable, empowered space in metropolitan England or Europe and connects it by design, motive, and development to distant or peripheral worlds . . . conceived of as desirable but subordinate" (Said 52). When Brooke has Rivers contrasts England with Canada so systematically, she shows us how the metropolitan culture maintains its cultural power partly through the "devaluation as well as the exploitation of the outlying colonial possession" (Said 59).

Rivers's desire for "*a woman* . . . who has a soul" (9), whose beauty is a manifestation of "life, . . . spirit" (21), is belied by his rejection of Madame Des Roches, who seems to fit the bill in every respect. But she is simply too much woman for Rivers, who may be an eighteenth-century man of sensibility but a wimp of imperial proportions for all that. Brooke's obsession with order and stability is a fundamental feature of her imperial colonial mentality. As Arabella's father, William Fermor, points out (140, 271), the French Canadians, as a race that has mixed with the savage and inhabited the wild, embody a threat to this order and stability. Progress will only come if this people can be transformed, brought within the pale of English and Anglican institutions. For Brooke, the Other must become "us," so to speak, if the New World is to become a successful extension of the Old. If not, the danger is that "we" become the Other.

The landscape, Natives, and French Canadians of Quebec compose "the spectacle of otherness" in Brooke's novel. As "spectacle," these various forms of alterity embody what the colonial power, by right of its civilizing mission, must conquer and convert, and, by embodying it so vividly, they further legitimize the colonial project by configuring the magnitude of otherness that threatens it. Brooke's depiction of Indians and French Canadians, particularly the Indian women, the nuns, and Madame Des Roches, is an instance of how, in colonial discourse, "the epithets racial or sexual come to be seen as modes of differentiation" (Bhabha 194) for establishing the domain of the Other. I believe that she uses the convention of the sublime to locate Canadian landscape in that realm as well.

"Living with the other, . . ." Julia Kristeva writes, "confronts us with the possibility or not of *being an other.* It is not simply—humanistically—a matter of our being able to accept the other, but of *being in his place,* and this means to imagine and make oneself other for oneself" (13). Brooke's fascination with the Other in her novel remains, in Joseph Conrad's phrase, "The fascination of the abomination" (9). If, as Bhabha argues, "The place of otherness is fixed in the West as a subversion of Western metaphysics and is finally appropriated by the West as its limit-text, the Anti-West" (195), then Brooke's "disciplinary gaze" upon the Canadian landscape, the French Canadians, and the Indians paradoxically acknowledges the power of their return look as it disempowers it. Françoise Meltzer, interpreting Jacques Lacan, has written that "the Other marks the place where the Subject refuses to recognize [her]self" (158). It is this refusal or failed recognition that *The History of Emily Montague* represents for the English-Canadian literary tradition, a misrecognition expressed most tellingly and ironically in her passionately contrived outburst: "*we* are the savages" (34).

The ambivalence in its representation of alterity provides *The History of Emily Montague* with whatever narrative energy it has, but it is, ultimately, a narrative of rejection, and so its energy is negative. It is the same kind of energy that we encounter in Susanna Moodie. Edwards's judgement that "Mrs. Brooke presents . . . an essentially positive view of the potential of the new British colony" (Introduction xliii) does not recognize the subordinate, if strikingly disproportionate, role that the Canadian portion plays in the plot, characterization, and overall form of the novel. The Canadian setting, which dominates the novel, is ultimately rejected and made subordinate by the main characters when, in the final movement, their rejection/departure displaces/replaces it in the margins of empire. Moreover, their rejection is not the sign of any failing on their part but quite the contrary. Canada may have "potential," but for Brooke, as for Moodie later, someone other than British men and women of sensibility will have to realize it.

I do not see how this novel, in Thomas's view, "constitutes an optimistic beginning for our fiction" (659-60). Brooke's inability to imagine her ambivalence into a polyvalent worldview is understandable given her time and background and the agenda that they imposed on her. However, her failure should not be endorsed by her critics, for to do so maintains not only that pathology of alterity but also the tragic continuity between the images that Brooke manufactures from her encounter with embodiments of the Other in the eighteenth-century colony and racial and religious stereotypes that continue to function, powerfully, in late-twentieth-century Canadian cultural discourse.

Works Cited

Alatas, Syed Hussein. *The Myth of the Lazy Native: A Study of the Image of the Malays, Filipinos and Javanese from the 16th to the 20th Century and Its Function in the Ideology of Colonial Capitalism.* London: Cass, 1977.

Bennett, Donna, and Russell Brown. "Frances Brooke." *An Anthology of Canadian Literature in English.* Ed. Bennett and Brown. Vol. 1. Toronto: Oxford UP, 1982, 1.2 vols. 1982-83.

Bentley, D. M. R. "Breaking the 'Cake of Custom': The Atlantic Crossing as a Rubicon for Female Emigrants to Canada." *Re(Dis)covering Our Foremothers: Nineteenth-Century Canadian Women Writers.* Ed. Lorraine McMullen. Ottawa: U of Ottawa P, 1989. 91-122.

Berland, K.J.H. "The True Pleasurable Philosopher: Some Influences on Frances Brooke's *History of Emily Montague.*" *Dalhousie Review* 66.3 (1986): 286-300.

Bhabha, Homi K. "Difference, Discrimination and the Discourse of Colonialism." *The Politics of Theory.* Ed. Francis Barker et al. Proc. of the Essex Conference on the Sociology of Literature. July 1982. Colchester: U of Essex, 1983. 194-211.

Brooke, Frances. *The History of Emily Montague.* Ed. Mary Jane Edwards. The Centre for Editing Early Canadian Texts Series 1. 1769. Ottawa: Carleton UP, 1985.

Carr, Graham. "Dated Lives: English-Canadian Literary Biography." *Essays on Canadian Writing* 35 (1987): 57-73.

Conrad, Joseph. *Heart of Darkness.* 1902. Harmondsworth, Eng.: Penguin, 1977.

Dahlie, Hallvard. *Varieties of Exile: The Canadian Experience.* Vancouver: U of British Columbia P, 1986.

Edwards, Mary Jane. "Brooke, Frances." *The Oxford Companion to Canadian Literature.* Ed. William Toye. Toronto: Oxford UP, 1983. 87-88.

——. "Frances Brooke's *The History of Emily Montague:* A Biographical Context." *English Studies in Canada* 7.2 (1981): 171-82.

——. "*The History of Emily Montague:* A Political Novel." *Beginnings: A Critical Anthology.* Ed. John Moss. Toronto: NC, 1980. 19-27. Vol. 2 of *The Canadian Novel.* 4 vols. 1978-85.

——. Introduction. *The History of Emily Montague.*

By Frances Brooke. Ed. Edwards. The Centre for Editing Early Canadian Texts Series 1. 1769. Ottawa: Carleton UP, 1985. xvii-lxxi.

Fabian, Johannes. *Time and the Other: How Anthropology Makes Its Object.* New York: Columbia UP, 1983.

Fitz, Earl E. "The First Inter-American Novels: Some Choices and Some Comments." *Comparative Literature Studies* 22 (1985): 362-76.

Fraser, Wayne. *The Dominion of Women: The Personal and the Political in Canadian Women's Literature.* Contributions in Women's Studies 116. New York: Greenwood, 1991.

Frye, Northrop. "Conclusion to a *Literary History of Canada.*" *The Bush Garden: Essays on the Canadian Imagination.* By Frye. Toronto: Anansi, 1971. 213-51.

Klinck, Carl F. "*The History of Emily Montague:* An Early Novel." Introduction. *The History of Emily Montague.* By Frances Brooke. 1769. Toronto: McClelland, 1961. v-xiv.

Kristeva, Julia. *Strangers to Ourselves.* Trans. Leon S. Roudiez. New York: Columbia UP, 1991.

Lutwack, Leonard. *The Role of Place in Literature.* Syracuse: Syracuse UP, 1984.

MacLulich, T.D. *Between Europe and America: The Canadian Tradition in Fiction.* Toronto: ECW, 1988.

McMullen, Lorraine. *An Odd Attempt in a Woman: The Literary Life of Frances Brooke.* Vancouver: U of British Columbia P, 1983.

Meltzer, Françoise. "Unconscious." *Critical Terms for Literary Study.* Ed. Frank Lentricchia and Thomas McLaughlin. Chicago: U of Chicago P, 1990. 147-62.

Messenger, Ann. *His and Hers: Essays in Restoration and Eighteenth-Century Literature.* Lexington: Kentucky UP, 1986.

Moss, John. *Patterns of Isolation in English Canadian Fiction.* Toronto: McClelland, 1974.

———. *A Reader's Guide to the Canadian Novel.* Toronto: McClelland, 1981.

Murray, Heather. "Reading for Contradiction in the Literature of Colonial Space." *Future Indicative: Literary Theory and Canadian Literature.* Ed. John Moss. Ottawa: U of Ottawa P, 1987. 71-84.

New, William H. "Frances Brooke's Chequered Gardens." *Canadian Literature* 52 (1972): 24-38.

———. "*The Old Maid:* Frances Brooke's Apprentice Feminism." *Journal of Canadian Fiction* 2.3 (1973): 9-12.

Pacey, Desmond. "The First Canadian Novel." *Dalhousie Review* 26 (1946-47): 143-50.

Rogers, Katherine. "Sensibility and Feminism: The Novels of Frances Brooke." *Genre* 11.2 (1978): 159-72.

Said, Edward W. *Culture and Imperialism.* New York: Knopf, 1993.

Shohet, Linda. "An Essay on *The History of Emily Montague.*" *Beginnings: A Critical Anthology.* Ed. John Moss. Toronto: NC, 1980. 28-34. Vol. 2 of *The Canadian Novel.* 4 vols. 1978-85.

Talman, James J., and Ruth Talman. "The Canadas (1763-1812)." *Literary History of Canada: Canadian Literature in English.* Ed. Carl F. Klinck. 2nd ed. Vol. 1. Toronto: U of Toronto P, 1976. 97-105. 4 vols. 1976-90. [Vol. 4 ed. W.H. New.]

Thomas, Clara. Rev. of *The History of Emily Montague,* ed. Mary Jane Edwards; and *Susanna Moodie: Letters of a Lifetime,* ed. Carl Ballstadt, Elisabeth Hopkins, and Michael Peterman. [Part of subsec., entitled "Canadian Literature," of sec. entitled "The New Books."] *Queen's Quarterly* 93.3 (1986): 659-61.

Todorov, Tzvetan. *The Conquest of America: The Question of the Other.* Trans. Richard Howard. New York: Harper, 1984.

Robert James Merrett (essay date 1994)

SOURCE: "Signs of Nationalism in *The History of Emily Montague; Canadians of the Old* and *The Imperialist*: Cultural Displacement and the Semiotics of Wine," in *Recherches Semiotiques-Semiotic Inquiry,* Vol. 14, Nos. 1-2, 1994, pp. 235-50.

[*In the following excerpt, Merrett discusses the cultural and symbolic meanings associated with wine in* Emily Montague.]

Wine—the fermented juice of the grape—may be a natural phenomenon yet it is also the product of complex vinification processes involving traditional but disputed histories: its origin and production have always been subject to legal rules and political restrictions. Its consumption has served society in many but contentious ways: as water-purifier, as beverage, as pain-killer, as palliative drug as well as in a wide range of customary and ritual functions illustrated in the body of this article. In society, wine constitutes sets of signifiers and signifieds. Encoded in writing, these sets inform and motivate textual signification by operating in systematic tension. By treating wine as sets of signifiers and analyzing its diverse political referents, this article shows how literary texts necessarily embody plural and even contrary codes and maintains that tensions between signifiers and signifieds mark and verify the interrelations of cultural and literary history.[2]

By the turn of the nineteenth century, wine in Britain had become a site of complex ideological tensions, because in the previous century it was at the centre of economic debate and had developed a typology based on political and cultural conflicts. Parliament's use of excise duties to block and to foster trade with European nations meant, for one thing, that Claret and Port were signs tending to divide Tories from Whigs, Jacobites from Hanoverians, and country squires from city merchants (Merrett 1991). Differentiations between French and non-French wines served as metonyms for factions holding divergent views on relations with France and on colonial and imperial expansion. That Britain was not a major producer partly explains the political energy and the cultural imagination directed by that nation to the systematic consumption of wine. British texts inscribe various systems of consumption since, in its rise to empire, internal disputes about foreign policy, about the economy, and about life-styles, together with Britain's financial and technical investments in the vineyards of France and Portugal, caused all wines—especially French wines which had long served the rituals of Crown, Court and military life—to become the focus of social debate (Merrett 1988b).

Not surprisingly, British literature imposed its wine codes on Canada as one way of celebrating the Cession of New France in 1763. One example is *The History of Emily Montague* (1769), a novel which, by incorporating the matrices of British wine codes, delimits the comparative basis of cultural and literary history vital to an appreciation of early Canadian texts. Its author, Frances Brooke, in stressing the Conquest, the need to have the habitants assimilated, and a program for establishing Anglicanism, sought to confirm the association of wine with aristocratic, military and imperial values, only to be resisted by the very signs she hoped to subject to her narrow-minded propaganda.[3]

Her military heroes, Captain Fitzgerald and Colonel Rivers, gain textual status by translating the consumption of wine into a system of refined, hierarchical values despite their supposedly limited economic means. When he changes quarters, Fitzgerald leaves "three months wine in the cellars" for a fellow officer (Brooke 1985 [1769]: 87). This comradeship gives him a "princely spirit" in the author's eyes (87). When he treats the master of a fast ship to a "bottle of very fine

madeira" (309) so that Arabella, his new wife, may be sure of having a letter reach England quickly, Fitzgerald's hospitality signals gentility and sensibility. In addition, his use of wine manifests strategic capacities which show that his economic means and social station are not as restrictive as the text pretends. Likewise, the supper hosted by Rivers at Québec is "admirable" for its "excellent wine" (111). Although the Colonel laments England's "luxury" (297), military and social status requires him to keep a "decent table" for friends (313). The hierarchical, imperial code that Fitzgerald and Rivers uphold is epitomized by the Earl with whom William Fermor, the patriarch, corresponds. The Earl glories in the power and refinement which owning the "best claret in the universe" indicates (326). If possession of great Bordeaux wines lets the Earl boast a supreme hospitality, it signals his habituation to conjoining aesthetic, political and nationalist referents which, if not wholly complacent, is uncritically formulaic.

For the Earl's society, consuming wine signifies enjoying economic and social privileges, cultivating a masculine camaraderie which prides itself on sensitivity to women, and supporting policies that further imperial rivalry with France and appropriation of that nation's culture. However, the meanings that wine has for Brooke's fictional society reveal themselves to be exclusive and arbitrary: her characters give significations to wine which show that, as a signifier, it has plural functions that they neither comprehend nor control. In making wine reinforce British culture, they also use it to demean Indians, habitants and the French. The result is that negative, erratic significations recoil on their political and social pretensions. When Rivers declares that Indians are "brutal slaves to their appetites" (Brooke 1985 [1769]: 222) and that, since the English and French are sober, they did not introduce drunkenness to the natives, he voices a European stance determined by propaganda and dismissive of history. The simple impulse to homogenize European societies shows itself to be self-defeating: the refusal to differentiate cultural systems is not just arbitrary; it undoes itself. When Fermor scorns the seigneurial system in which lords and retainers take brandy together, he rejects strange concepts of hierarchy and productivity (208). Yet this displacement manifests fear of French economic power. In promoting British colonialism, he calls for Québec to be assimilated by Anglo-Americans, not Britons. Not only does anxiety over depopulation at home lead Fermor to speak of New Englanders—often disparaged in the novel—as allies, but fear that colonies erode national economies drives him to call for domestic policies to offset France's larger population which, like economists of the day, he assigns to the intensive "cultivation of vineyards" (222). In Brooke's text, consuming French wine does and does not signify Britain's power over France: for, cultural appropriation is jostled by political diffidence; colonial power is informed by imperial vulnerability; and European solidarity is displaced by national competitiveness.

The urge in Brooke's characters to displace French culture from North America—even as they define themselves in its terms—reveals how much textual and national ideologies thrive on unacknowledged conflict between codes, this theme deriving from the irreconcilable functions which her characters give to wine and spirits. When the usually temperate Fermor is enraged by habitants' claims to be the "flower of the French nation" (Brooke 1985 [1769]: 141) and by their view that France is "the only civilized nation in the world" (141), he attacks their national affiliation for denying the Conquest: he asserts that France's military has been assimilated by "savage tribes" (271). But this retaliation clashes with Rivers' view that European mores transcend those of the indigenous peoples. Such a discrepancy exemplifies how the interdependencies between Canada, France and Britain subordinate characters and their prejudices to the steadier relations of social and textual signifiers.

When Arabella declares that French gallantry is depraved while English gallantry creates the "peace of families" (Brooke 1985 [1769]: 381), she is not in agreement with Rivers who holds that French gallantry "debases the mind less than ours" (26), even as he groundlessly declares all seigneurs to be illiterate. Arbitrary generalizations on behalf of Englishness are manifest in Arabella's attitudes to alcohol. Holding that Canada lacks "elegant arts" and "Genius" because the severe cold freezes the strongest wines and thickens brandy (103), she yet exploits wine and spirits remarkably. For one thing, she gives wine to Indian women who revere the English conquest of Québec, a gesture belying her alleged political indifference and undoing Rivers's claim that Europe has not debased natives with drink. Finding the company of the Indian women "ridiculous" (50), she treats them as "gypsies" (51) and spurns their festive spirit. The textual subversion of her stance becomes clearer when she utters a truism typical of rakes in eighteenth-century plays: brandy, she claims, makes her speak "like an angel" (105). Arabella's playfulness is offered as a comic relief to the political themes, but her wit exposes gaps in those themes, gaps pointing out incoherencies in the conquerors' cultural systems.

The transferred meanings given by Brooke's characters to drinking and wine take place in lexical fields that are both more diffuse and more involved than they know.[4] When Arabella announces that politics in Québec are "dregs of old disputes" towards which she adopts a "strict neutrality" (Brooke 1985 [1769]: 98), she utters a transcendent claim rendered untenable by her words. Dregs belong to wine: separating them out is not a matter of neutrality but of discrimination. Her analogy is reversible: as dregs are organic to wine,

so political disputes touch everyone in Québec. Dividing sumptuary and political signs, Arabella never realizes that systematic signification rejoins them. Similar semiotic irony is found in the gap between Emily's trust that she can use Rivers's "inebriation of tenderness' for her to induce him to return to his mother in England (212) and his belief that "inebriation" of passion is not "tenderness" (314). This conflict in the metonymy of drunkenness indicates that Brooke's characters do not share assumptions about romatic sentiments despite their high-flown amatory professions to do so.

Notes

[2] It is important to realize that all "five senses, smell, touch, taste, hearing, sight, can function in the process of *semiosis:* that is, as sign-producers or sign-receivers. The uses of perfume, of the texture of a fabric in clothing, the ways in which the tastes produced by cooking signal status, location, 'identity', 'foreigness' are manifold. Moreover, each of these senses responds in concert with the others to sign-systems designed to exploit them in differing hierarchies" (Hawkes 1977: 134-35). I have applied the semiotics of wine to cultural and literary history (see Merrett 1988a).

[3] Since an "author is not a perfect ego but a mixture of public and private, conscious and unconscious elements, insufficiently unified for use as an interpretive base," the present essay focuses on irony which, "of all figures, is the one that must always take us out of the text and into codes, contexts, and situations" (Scholes 1982: 14, 76). For a historical analysis of the political ironies in Brooke's novel, see Merrett (1992).

[4] According to Jacques Lacan, language, "like the unconscious, is an impersonal system outside the subject's control—a system from which the subject is irrevocably alienated" (Stout 1993: 189) . . .

Works Cited

Brooke, Frances (1985 [1769]) *The History of Emily Montague*. Ed. Mary Jane Edwards. Ottawa: Carleton University Press. . . .

Hawkes, Terence (1977) *Structuralism and Semiotics*. Berkeley: University of California Press. . . .

Merrett, Robert James (1988a) "Bacchus in Restoration and Eighteenth-Century Comedy: Wine as an Index of Generic Decline." *Man and Nature / L'homme et la nature* 7: 179-93. . . .

Scholes, Robert (1982) *Semiotics And Interpretation*. New Haven: Yale University Press.

Stout, John (1993) "Semiotics." In *Encyclopedia of Contemporary Literary Theory: Approaches, Scholars, Terms.* Ed. Irena R. Makaryk. Toronto: University of Toronto Press: 183-189. . . .

Paula R. Backscheider and Hope D. Cotton (essay date 1997)

SOURCE: Introduction in, *The Excursion,* edited by Paula R. Backscheider and Hope D. Cotton, University Press of Kentucky, 1997, pp. ix-xxxviii.

[*In the following excerpt, Backscheider and Cotton discus the literary context and form of* The Excursion, *including its critical reception and Brooke's later career; they argue for the novel's significance in the movement towards critical realism.*]

The Excursion *and Its Significance*

Thomas Cadell . . . the publisher of David Hume's *History of England,* Hannah More's *Percy* and *Fatal Falsehood,* and Samuel Foote's last four plays brought out Brooke's *The Excursion* in early summer 1777. Her earlier novels had featured a witty, strong-minded heroine and a sentimental, romantic one. Anne Wilmot in *Lady Julia Mandeville* had been called "the true woman of fashion" by *The Edinburgh Weekly Magazine* (13 November 1783), and the heroine of *The Excursion* is a woman of fashion wanna-be. Maria Villiers, lively, spontaneous, restless, and naive, schemes and cajoles until she is allowed to take a £200 inheritance to London, where she intends to marry a "ducal coronet"—that is, to marry into the nobility. Her guardian, Colonel Dormer, the uncle who loves his country retirement and nurtures his gardens with more discernment than his nieces, warns her against "worthless acquaintance, unmerited calumny, and ruinous expense." Ann Messenger notes that in the earlier novels "we see only the fringe" of the "heartlessness— the triviality and narcissism—of the fashionable world";[51] in *The Excursion,* Brooke makes it her subject.

The admonition from Maria's uncle locates Brooke's novel in a rapidly growing type. As in her earlier works, she draws heavily on the English courtship novel, which was by then a highly moral form, closely linked with the beginning of the female *bildungsroman.*[52] Unlike the heroines of English novels between 1680 and 1750, including Richardson's, these heroines are not threatened by rape, seduction, or being "swept away" by their own passions. Rather they are introduced into the way of the world and face loss of reputation because of social mistakes. Eliza Haywood's *The History of Miss Betsy Thoughtless* and Henry Fielding's *Amelia* (both 1751) are landmarks in this tradition.[53] Confront-

ed not only by schemers, cheats, and rakes but also by scenes of misery, misfortune, and need, the heroine must learn to protect her reputation while acting benevolently as well as when under active siege. As critics since the 1930s have pointed out, the topics and admired virtues in these novels are those of contemporary "conduct books," books that prescribed behavior in relationships between husbands and wives, parents and children, and employers and servants.[54] Katharine Rogers, has found *The Excursion* a "convincing education of a young woman—more convincing even than that of Fanny Burney's *Evelina.*"[55]

In *The History of Lady Julia,* Anne Wilmot often comments upon the simplicity and innocence of Julia and other characters. In *The Excursion,* that perspective is supplied by the narrator, whose tone combined with the London setting creates a "realistic" story of a young girl's initiation into society. Like Burney's *Evelina,* which was published the following year, *The Excursion* uses its heroine to depict an endangered, attractive adolescent in a fallen, glittering world. In a typical moment, Maria pauses to reflect on her uncle's categories of danger, and her naiveté is underscored in lines at which any worldling would smile—or sigh sadly: "As to calumny, such was her knowledge of the world, that she thought herself secure from its attacks, only by resolving not to merit them" (1:1:8). While Maria is struggling in the city and falling in love with a libertine, her stay-at-home sister Louisa has a nearly uneventful courtship with an exemplary young man. The novel includes most of the conventional characters and many of the familiar plots and episodes of the English courtship novel as written by Jane Barker, Eliza Haywood, Henry Fielding, and Oliver Goldsmith.

Brooke's literary and historical significance rests in part on her experimentation and development of the form of the English novel, and nothing Brooke does with traditional elements is conventional. Although many women novelists depict their heroines in the variety and sprawl of London, Brooke captures women's confinement even within the great, impersonal city. Tied to the few people she believes respectable, Maria must wait for introductions and invitations. She must be concerned about securing a companion for trips to the theatre and opera. As her money dwindles and her acquaintances drop her, she is imprisoned in Mrs. Merrick's house, and Brooke depicts her pacing and discomfited. Conventionally, rakes in novels tend to be heartless seducers and, as the narrator notes, even kidnappers. Brooke's Lord Melvile is an original, intriguing, individual character and another break with the expected. Attractive, polished, and skeptical to the last degree, he still has the "traces" of his "virtues" on his face. He makes the rounds of theatre, garden, cards, and mistress each night, but he can still blush and leave the sight of his mistress sitting at the head of his dead mother's table and beneath her portrait. His desires are elemental, yet streaked with romantic, domestic ones. He appears the dissolute, predatory social animal and also the apathetic worldling who expects little of life and, therefore, obeys his father without effort or resistance. Yet he can suddenly reveal conflicting impulses, including dreaming of an "affair of the heart" (1:4:10).

Brooke is one of the first novelists to create a wise, admirable older woman character who combines the roles of model, friend, and confidante: Lady Sophia, the foil to Mrs. Merrick and Lady Hardy. Here we see Brooke's observant eye and class consciousness. Mrs. Merrick is genteel, good-natured and well-intentioned, but she is unaware of the social forms and pastimes Maria needs to understand and is unable to cope with situations arising in London society. Lady Hardy, in contrast, has mastered these forms and pastimes but lacks the moral principles and "sensibility" that novelists of the period use to distinguish true aristocrats and persons of worth. Lady Sophia has some resemblances to Brooke's friend, Lady Elizabeth Cecil, who lived at the Manor House, Tinwell, and who in the mid-1750s had given her "a general invitation to while away an irksome hour with them; when I feel myself too much alone" (quoted in McMullen, 33).

Brooke's fictions have been called, not quite accurately, novels of sensibility, and the concept is central to the understanding of her novel. "Sensibility" is a difficult idea for the modern mind to comprehend.[56] Related to sense perceptions, it captured the connection and rapid transmission of feelings, such as sympathy or moral outrage, to physical feelings and signs of those feelings, such as tears or even violence. Sometimes simply defined as "fine feeling," it was not something the eighteenth-century thinker believed all people possessed in the same measure or even had at all. "Fine," then, took on implications for "taste" and "cultured" and, in turn, had links to both class and education. Unlike "mere" sentimentality, sensibility was the union of judgment with a conscious openness to feelings. By the 1770s and with increasing strength through the Romantic period, sensibility came to be associated with the qualities of mind that produce aesthetic objects, values, and judgments.

The possession and expression of sensibility was a test of human worth, and a hierarchy of characters within literary works could be established by their degree of true sensibility. The most discerning and virtuous displayed ideal sensibility, while some characters were callous and brutish and others mawkish and sentimental. Practices of conduct, such as scheming for social advantage, were condemned because they violated principles of sensibility. Elements of this system of making judgments can be found in *The Excursion.* Maria consistently displays sensibility, especially in her letters to her sister and in scenes composed to expose her heart.

Louisa's idealized suitor, Mr. Montague, has some natural sensibility, while Lord Melvile's is undeveloped and surprises him when it dictates his responses. It is described as a "warm susceptibility of soul," which his corrupted reason often suppresses. Colonel Herbert, perhaps the most admirable man in the book, has both natural and cultivated sensibility, combining feeling and reason. Brooke emphasizes that shared sensibility is the foundation for the happiest marriages. She illustrates the working of the quality in different kinds of people with different temperaments and educations. Mr. Hammond, for instance, combines sensibility with the wit and literary acumen associated with the London gentleman intellectual. True to the form, characters expound extensively upon such matters as the relationship between happiness and various life choices, as in the discussion between the senior Mr. Montague and Colonel Dormer in volume 2, book 8, chapter 3.

The novel also continues and adapts a much older strain of fiction and draws upon several identifiable kinds of novels. Seventeenth- and eighteenth-century English readers were raised almost as much on French novels as on English, and more on French before at least 1740. Within this French tradition was the very popular *histoire galante,* probably the major kind of fiction written by English women writers and a form perhaps written primarily for women readers.[57] This fiction explored and analyzed the emotions of love, what Du Plaisir called the "anatomy of the amorous heart."[58] It sought to identify and make fine discriminations among all the "tones" of love—each of the feelings of awakening love, of maturing affection, of rejection, and so on. The tradition that began with Madeleine de Scudéry, Marie-Catherine d'Aulnoy, Louise-Marie de Conti, Marie-Madeleine de Lafayette, and other "romance" writers was transferred to England and continued by writers such as Manley, Haywood, and Mary Collyer. This tradition, one that English women joined, has been obscured and nearly lost in the modern his-story of the English novel. So familiar was it that Brooke felt free to invoke it; in *The History of Lady Julia,* for example, she makes an unglossed reference to Celadon and Urania, major characters in Honoré D'Urfé's early seventeenth-century *L'Astrée* (164-65). Correspondence among women of the time shows continued careful reading of these and other French romances.[59] Twentieth-century critics have demonstrated, as Ellen Moers wrote in 1963, that "to be a woman writer long meant, may still mean, belonging to a literary movement apart from but hardly subordinate to the mainstream."[60] Indeed, many men belonged to alternate traditions as well, but women writers outweighed them exponentially in creativity and numbers.

Another characteristic of this French tradition was the commitment to the inseparability of what have come to be seen as "public" and "private" spheres. This idea was worked out through the lineage of the lovers, in the roles and information obtained in one sphere and used in the other, and in illustrations of how private conduct reveals the temperament, moral character, and opinions that determine public actions. In such novels the representations of individual characters often become critiques of whole classes as their education, ideology, and sense of privilege and responsibility construct them. Rightly or wrongly, critics have identified Lord Claremont, Melvile's father, with Lord Chesterfield. Reviews of Brooke's novel made strongly negative judgments of him and his book, *Letters Written by the Late Right Honourable Philip Dormer Stanhope, Earl of Chesterfield, to His Son, Philip Stanhope, Esq.,* which had been published three years earlier, in 1774, by Chesterfield's daughter-in-law. The *Gentleman's Magazine* said that the reader "will easily see" that Claremont is "formed on the detestable plan of Lord Chesterfield" (47 {August 1777}: 387), and *Town and Country* objected: "Mrs. Brooke seems to have had in her eye the precepts given by lord Chesterfield to his son upon gallantry, we can never suppose that nobleman, or any other man . . . would be the pimp and pander of his son" (9 {August 1777}: 433).

The Excursion *and the Fashionable World*

In context and content Brooke's novel is part of the fashionable world of the late 1770s. By that time, owning and reading certain kinds of novels was part of the social scene. Some novels, probably including this one, were marketed as fashionable commodities and touted as offering cultured entertainment as well as instruction in worldly behavior and timeless morality. Brooke's publisher, Cadell, made considerable profit from this kind of book and eventually published the six-volume *Historical Pocket Library,* which he advertised as "useful, moral, elegant."[61] Such books represent the *ton,* but they help readers distinguish between cultured conduct and decadence. The "right" people read Brooke's book, and they discussed it in polite gatherings. In addition to gendered virtues, such books taught manners. As Mary Granville wrote, "There is nothing I wish to much for Mary, *next* to right religious principles, as proper *knowledge* of the polite world. It is *the only means* of keeping her safe from an immoderate love of its vanities and follies, and of giving her that sensible kind of reserve" (3:227). *The Excursion* delivered these kinds of instruction, and readers and reviewers acknowledged it.

In some ways, the novel reflects Brooke's participation in fashionable society. It carefully follows the theatrical season of 1774-75 and exhibits firsthand knowledge of distinctive social behavior, popular opinions, and affectations in language. The *au courant* narrator uses both Italian and French to comment on events and people; the characters who are aspiring social climbers reveal themselves in part through their affected use of foreign terms and fashionable phrases. Brooke's languages contribute richly to the elevated, wryly ironic tone of the novel.

The moral judgments the novel makes were also fashionable. Even the creation and condemnation of a Chesterfield character was a fad, for he had come to signify "all that was most cynical and depraved in an outmoded concept of gentility."[62] In addition to being a good, modest "psychological" initiation and courtship novel, *The Excursion* is a sustained critique of the *ton* and fashionable London. Novels, plays, books, and sermons were all expressing concern about the pursuits, the idleness, and especially the gambling of the upper and even middle classes. Seen by many as threats to domestic harmony and the most important values of the society, the scenes and pastimes portrayed in Brooke's novel offer an intriguing representation of fashionable London and an idle, rather dissolute part of society, as well as insight into some widely held anxieties and opinions. Many believed that their era was one of unprecedented and dangerous idleness, luxury, hedonism, and extravagance. Londoners saw social gatherings and especially such public places as Ranelagh, Vauxhall, and the theatres becoming marriage markets where social climbing, attempts to repair fortunes, and seductions seemed common. In his mid-century poem *The Demi-Rep,* Edward Thompson captured the common opinion: "Have ye not Wives and Mistress[es]?—yet still / Go we to Ranelagh, or where we will / We find you there; for ye like jackalls prowl / About for prey, and smell at ev'ry hole" (33-34).

They—and Brooke's novel—were particularly concerned about gambling. Newspapers and periodicals repeated and made up scandalous gossip about those in society, and reports of gambling debts in the tens of thousands of pounds were common.[63] In the year before the publication of *The Excursion,* John Damer, son of a lord, committed suicide over his £70,000 debt, and the renowned Theresa Cornelys tried to reopen Carlisle House, a site for cards, balls, masquerades, and private concerts. Lady Hardy's house resembles Cornelys's in many ways. That women played cards and gambled seemed especially pernicious. Objections to this behavior ranged from a recognition that it was an addiction and, therefore, took women away from home and domestic duties, to fears that women in debt would be tempted or urged to pay off their creditors with sexual favors. Such fears had been expressed consistently and prominently at least since the time of Vanbrugh's *Provoked Husband* (1728). Even private correspondence reinforces this point. Mary Granville, for instance, wrote that she had read and wept over Edward Moore's *The Gamester* and commented that "it is a very proper play at this time to be represented." Speaking of her own gambling, she wrote in 1771 to a friend: "gaming, a vice of such a deep dye at present, that nothing within my memory comes up to it! The bite is more malignant than that of a mad dog, and has all the effects of it" (*The Autobiography,* 3:214, 4:335).

Brooke's novel might thus be seen as part of the "outburst of hostility to feminine extravagance."[64] It should be placed, however, with such witty attacks on fashionable behavior as Richard B. Sheridan's play *School for Scandal,* produced almost simultaneously with the publication of *The Excursion,* rather than with the host of pamphlets, sermons, and conduct books aimed primarily at women.[65] It is, in fact, entertaining to read this play in conjunction with Brooke's novel, since they share many satirical targets.

Brooke's narrative point of view—a "Bel Esprit," wise, worldly, wry, judgmental, and witty—is one of the most notable elements of this novel and bridges the fashionable context and content. Brooke saw this pose as offering women freedom. Anne Wilmot in *Lady Julia* says, "I early in life discovered, by the mere force of genius, that there were two characters only in which one might take a thousand little innocent freedoms, without being censured—those of a *Bel Esprit* and a *Methodist*" (74). Strong elements of the freedom, power, and wit of the "Bel Esprit" characterize the narrator in *The Excursion.* "Wit" in the eighteenth century was considered one of the higher kinds of intelligence and signified quick perceptiveness, particularly the ability to associate ideas and express them brilliantly. All the arts and especially the theatre relied on wit as John Locke explicated it: "For Wit lying most in the assemblage of Ideas, and putting those together with quickness and variety, wherein can be found any resemblance . . . , thereby to make up pleasant Pictures, and agreeable Visions in the Fancy."[66]

Distanced from the heroine, the narrator is both sympathetic and ironic, a difficult balance to achieve and maintain. Later Jane Austen would manage it more famously in *Pride and Prejudice* and *Emma. The Excursion* opens with the sisters watching a sunset and the passing of Lady H——'s "superb carriage, with a numerous train of attendants." The narrator comments that at that moment Maria felt "the poison of ambition." The juxtaposition of a glorious sunset and beautiful rural scene with the display of wealth introduces a value system, which is immediately juxtaposed with the thought of ordinary human beings. Not only Maria is self-absorbed; soon the reader finds out that Louisa, who turns quickly back to the sunset, is not concentrating on its beauty either.

The narrator judges behavior quickly and categorizes it bluntly; Maria at one point, for instance, looks like a crass "adventurer" (1:3:9) and at another behaves "like a miss educated in shades" (2:8:6), a pastoral Never-Never land. Of the girls' father, the narrator

observes that he was a squire, "a race happily almost extinct," who died young, "happily for his daughters" (1:1:2). The reader, as in many eighteenth-century novels, is told what to expect and led to study how it comes about and, when engaged with the character, to dread and then regret it. As early as the ninth chapter, when Maria is leaving her uncle's estate, we are told that she almost changes her mind about going to London, but "the fond Deceiver, Hope, painted to her lively imagination the gaudy scene which had originally misled her. . . . [E]very whisper of discretion . . . the pictures drawn by Truth and Nature, faded away before the dazzling blaze of a coronet" (1:1:9).

The narrator maintains a relationship with the reader, often sharing worldly smiles, regrets over the evil in humankind, and nods of agreement over commonplace opinions. Some sections slant into lectures: "Let their own experience, for they will never grow wise from yours, break the gay bubble" (1:2:1). The narrator may even, in the light of the reader's imagined desires, lament the responsibility for truth and candor (1:2:9). The influence of Henry Fielding's *Tom Jones* is evident in this novel, as it is in Haywood's *Miss Betsy Thoughtless.* Everywhere the awareness of the reader and of language contributes to the tone and the reader's enjoyment. Brooke juxtaposes classical and conventional poetic language with mundane situations: "How give wings to the lazy-footed time? How pass the tedious hours of Lord Melvile's absence?" (1:4:1) Sometimes the language unmasks social hypocrisy, as when the narrator says that Lady Hardy is what "every body knew to be what nobody chose to call her" (1:2:6). Brooke uses the same kinds of suspenseful, delayed gratification strategies that Fielding uses as she moves from one character to another, one location to another. The narrator assumes firm control of the story and the reader's interpretation by, for instance, stating motives in unequivocal terms. Of Mrs. Herbert it is said, "nothing but [Maria's] being fifty times handsomer than herself, could have prevented her giving her an invitation to her house in town" (1:1:6). Romantic illusions that Melvile would change because of Maria are brushed aside: he "forgot, before he reached Grosvenor Street, that there existed such a being as Miss Villiers" (1:2:9).

The narrator also provides thematic unity. Opposing the "bonds that hold society together"—community values—to the "individual"—of which the cardplayer is the most extreme example—Brooke takes a stand on a major intellectual issue in the period.[67] Also opposed are England and English education to the Grand Tour and French principles. Surprisingly strong in a novel of this date is sustained attention to good taste and the pleasures and benefits of the arts. The narrator sounds this theme first in a discussion of how the uncorrupted young will naturally prefer the theatre and good music to routs and card parties. The pleasures of tragedy are compared to those of comedy, and, in another place, the function of the theatre as a treasury of "national virtue" as well as of taste is asserted.

Reviews and Revision

The Excursion was reviewed in all the best periodicals, but one episode became news. The *London Review* began by titillating its readers: "with a masterly pencil, the author has pourtrayed the features of some distinguished personages." It then professed that it would "not refuse our readers . . . the opportunity of perusing the seventh chapter of the fifth book" (6 {August 1777}: 113). In the first edition, Brooke had chosen to introduce David Garrick into a major episode in the novel. She has the stage-struck Maria, through the intercession of Mr. Hammond, offer a play written as a vehicle for Garrick as actor-manager of Drury Lane. Garrick turns Maria's play down without reading it, and he cannot even recall whether it is a tragedy or comedy. Brooke satirizes Garrick, one of the two or three greatest theatrical geniuses of the century, as surrounded by servile petitioners and glorying pretentiously in his power to select among the hundreds of manuscripts offered him. She has him brag to Hammond about the "six-and twenty new tragedies on my promise-list" and the seven-year wait for production even after acceptance. Brooke captures his well-known stammer and identifies him in other unmistakable ways. In 1777 Garrick was retired and in ill health. The 1775-76 season had been his last; as he played one famous, signature role after another that year, the public sought tickets with frenzied urgency. These facts made Brooke's attack especially unwise.

Because of this episode, all but a few of the reviews were thinly disguised editorials with partisan literary comments. *Town and Country* called the attack on Garrick in **The Excursion** "the most scandalous chronicle we ever met with" and said that Mrs. Brooke was filled with "malignancy" (9 {August 1777}: 434). This hostile review also criticized her "incessantly boring" scraps of Italian and French. The *London Review* printed the Garrick scene, calling it an "admirable likeness" and "just" (6 {August 1777}: 113-17), and the *Critical Review* described it as "a humorous representation of the illiberal maxims of government, adopted by his theatrical majesty" (44 {July 1777}: 63). Even those who found the depiction accurate complained that it was not original and traced such satires back to James Quin and, more recently, to Tobias Smollett.[68] The perennial complaint was, in Oliver Goldsmith's words, that the stage, "instead of serving the people, is made subservient to the interests of an avaricious few."[69] Nearly all the reviews were mixed at best, but most acknowledged Brooke's characteristic "liveliness," solid creation of characters, and pleasant, clear style; they found the novel "instructive" and recommended it for such lessons as deterring "young ladies from launching out into the world, and affecting the *ton,* without discretion" (*Critical Review,* 44 {July 1777}: 63).

The longest, most severe review was in the *Monthly Review,* and it was an artful, anonymous attack by David Garrick himself.[70] Aimed at discrediting the novel and its author, the four-page review denied **The Excursion** the status of a novel by calling it "an heterogeneous mass" and levied charges of "venal" hypocrisy against Brooke. Garrick quotes from her own attack on the press in the novel ("Among the evils of the present hour . . .") and observes self-righteously: "How will the reader be startled to find that this very rigid censor exhibits . . . the most flagrant and unjustifiable instance of the licentiousness she . . . condemns!"[71] He ridicules the plot as "lame" and improbable and observes, "It happens a little unluckily for Mrs. Brooke's credit" that he can oppose "public and uncontrovertible facts" to her "imaginary" ones. He then quotes grateful letters to himself from Richard Cumberland, Elizabeth Griffith, and Hannah Cowley. Artfully including two women, he says that "instances are endless" of his discerning, supportive conduct toward aspiring playwrights.

Garrick then makes a bitterly sarcastic, frontal assault on the episode involving himself. He raises the issue that must have occurred to others: "Mrs. Brooke cannot surely have kept this stock of malice by her above twenty years." The reviewer continues, "Nothing can be more ungenerous than to attack a man, after he has quitted the field, and has retired, not only crowned with the laurel of genius, as Mrs. Brooke herself allows, but with the palm of virtue also, and . . . with the good wishes, and warm esteem of an admiring public" (144). Garrick, however, does not mention his part in thwarting Brooke far more recently than in the **Virginia** and Riccoboni incidents. She had tried to persuade him to read and stage a musical play of hers, perhaps **Rosina,** probably in the summer of 1776. Indicative of her distrust of him, she asked that he give her a prompt refusal if he could not stage it (McMullen, 133).

During this time, Brooke had become associated with another theatre. By 1771 she and the great actress Mary Ann Yates were intimate friends. When Yates and her husband Richard bought the King's Theatre in the Haymarket in May 1773 with James Brooke, Frances's brother-in-law, Frances became co-manager. The plan seems to have been to mount operas, musical performances, and plays there, but the Lord Chamberlain refused to license the theatre. King's, commonly known as the Opera House, then had to depend on music. In the first season the company mounted nine operas for a total of sixty-five performances and the next year added ballet with a star, Baccelli, from Italy. Brooke used her knowledge of languages to handle all of the foreign correspondence necessary to identify and engage talent from abroad. What Garrick had to do, if anything, with their inability to obtain a license can only be suspected.

In the spring of 1777, when the Yateses tried to get a license for a theatre in Birmingham, Garrick apparently tried to help. When Edmund Burke withdrew his support in late April, however, Garrick wrote, "God forbid that all the Patents in the World should injure Your Interest."[72] Brooke, so much a part of theatrical and literary London, could hardly have been unaware of Garrick's potential for mischievous, behind-the-scenes influence. In turn, Garrick suspected Brooke of delaying publication of her novel until after the vote on the license.[73]

Garrick's *Monthly Review* essay continued in its design to discredit by challenging the veracity of the incident. He demanded aggressively that Brooke produce "the *subline genius* who carried the play, the title of the *excellent tragedy,* and the name of the great *beauty* who wrote it" and ridiculed the "story of the *genius,* the *beauty,* the *tragedy,* the *manager,* and the *levee*" (144). As many feminist critics have demonstrated, women writers' bodies are almost always on the minds of reviewers. In a veiled *ad hominem* attack, Garrick notes that *The Excursion* presents "a great beauty" as the author of the play and demands she be named. What makes this such a mean-spirited thrust is that Brooke was a physically unattractive woman, and Garrick knew it. In 1774 Frances Burney, who became a good friend of Brooke, described her as "very short & fat, & squints, but has the art of shewing Agreeable Ugliness."[74]

In fact, Brooke might have chosen to generalize the experience or produce a composite. By the time she wrote *The Excursion,* she had also tried to persuade John Rich to produce *Virginia* and George Colman the Elder and Samuel Foote to produce *Rosina.* In a letter to her friend Richard Gifford in 1772, she wrote, "There is nothing to me so astonishing as that Colman should be another Garrick." In another letter, she observed that her only hope was that either Drury Lane or Covent Garden would have a play fail so that "one of them will have a vacancy & take it for their own sakes. I know neither will for mine."[75]

Brooke published a revision of *The Excursion* in 1785. Her alterations fall into two categories: (1) modifications aimed at changing the tone and the relationship between the narrator and the protagonist and (2) substantive rethinking of some incidents. Generally, the narrative point of view is sharpened. The narrator becomes slightly acerbic, faintly more judgmental, and a little more superior to Maria. Mrs. Merrick, for example, is established more firmly as a figure of doting naiveté, by, among other things, predicting acceptance of Maria's tragedy and calling it "a *sweet pretty* tragedy." In the new ending for volume 1, book 4, chapter 7, Maria congratulates herself on having "a perfect knowledge" of the world, and the narrator observes that hers is an error "into which people are very apt to fall at the age of eighteen." Many of the changes are simple additions of words; "sanguine as she naturally was," for instance, becomes "sanguine and romantic as she naturally was" (2:5:9).

The Garrick section is the part of the novel that Brooke revised most extensively. In the first edition, she had used a Fielding-style introduction for emphasis: "But [Mr. Hammond's] narrative, which we recommend to the perusal of all young votaries of the Dramatic Muse, will appear to most advantage in a separate Chapter." The second edition prefigures disappointment from the entrance of Hammond, which is blended into the chapter smoothly and emphasizes theatrical protocol: "There is, it seems, an etiquette in respect to the reception of theatrical pieces . . . which, however plausible . . ." With words such as "etiquette" and "plausible," Brooke makes Garrick's behavior seem standard and even fair. "From friendship to me," Hammond says, Garrick offered to read the play "before its due course"; even that would be a wait of twenty months. This version places Maria's youthful, ignorant imaginings at odds with both "etiquette" and practicality: "She had expected, with the impetuosity of her time of life, and perfect inexperience of the world, to hear it was going into immediate rehearsal . . . and had even regarded the profits as a bank on which she might have depended in . . . a few revolving weeks." Her thoughts are those of an impatient child, and her new fantasies—giving the profits to a charity as opposed to making the play a gift to the company—those of, in the narrator's words, "a romantic girl." She concludes, "the manager . . . had only pursued a regular system of business."

The narration of the play's reception shrinks from nine dramatic pages to three told in the third person in the revised version; the scene concludes with Mr. Hammond's essay-speech on the importance of the theatre to national culture and the unsuitability of women for theatrical pursuits. Originally it had included several paragraphs lamenting that "a man . . . of the most distinguished talents, the idol of the public" could behave in such a manner and imagining what an honest Garrick would say—he would confess the theatre's reluctance to expand or experiment and the public's unwillingness to support theatre. As Garrick brought Brooke's appearance into play in his review, she had brought his manhood under scrutiny. Had Garrick been honest, Brooke wrote in the first version, he would have used "the language of a man" with "sufficient courage to avow his principles of action." Though many lines are preserved in the second edition and theatrical practice criticized, the condemnation is general. Hammond's reflections are made idealistic, and his maxims described as not yet "known to exist" anywhere.

This revised section is important for another reason: Brooke strengthens Maria's aspirations as a playwright. A remarkable new passage portrays Maria listening to a speech intended "to dissuade her from a pursuit in which her whole soul was irresistibly engaged." This pursuit is one of the novel's groundbreaking aspects; alterations to such passages, then, have heightened significance. *The Excursion* develops themes of perpetual interest to Brooke: women's self-fashioning and the forces that construct personality. For all her self-confidence, Maria is experimenting with identities and finding them tested and obstructed. Confident of her charms and the basic benevolence of the world and the people in it, she believes that she can attract a man like Lord Melvile and that he will marry her. She imagines herself as his wife with the accompanying power and pleasure of that role. The conclusion of the story of her romances is as much the story of coming to terms with identity as it is a plot resolution.

To an even greater extent, Maria believes in herself as a writer. With a satisfaction that is both amusing and ominous, she values her epic poem at £100, her novel at £200, and her tragedy at £500. Perhaps only a few of her readers would have known how wildly inflated these prices were, but they would have recognized her naiveté and the fact that these were large sums of money. A middle-class family could live in London for £125 a year. *Paradise Lost* had been sold for £20, of which Milton received only £5, and Alexander Pope, the greatest poet of his generation, received £15 for *The Rape of the Lock,* his mock-epic. In Brooke's generation, Frances Burney was paid £20 for *Evelina* and John Cleland the same for *Fanny Hill.* To make anything approximating £500 from a play, there would have to be a long run and successful publication. *School for Scandal,* for instance, earned Sheridan £1,430.61.4 in the 1776-77 season and *She Stoops to Conquer* earned £501.38.6 for Goldsmith in seventeen (not all consecutive) performances during the 1772-73 season. Some extraordinarily successful playwrights sold publication rights to plays for £150. In *The Old Maid,* among numerous comments about the life and work of writers, Brooke wrote that "as to profit, [the writer] must be very successful indeed, if after neglecting every other means of raising a fortune, and devoting his days to the most painful of all labour, that of the mind, he gets a support equal to that which recompenses the toil of the meanest artisan" (14). *The Excursion* puts Maria in contact with the literary marketplace at most of its key moments; we see its petitioners, its "hurries," its network, and its prejudices.

Maria's satisfaction, however, lies in far more than her works' cash value, and her art has special interest for that reason. In one of the few representations of a woman writer by an early woman writer,[76] *The Excursion* captures an author's psychological relationship to her manuscripts. They are physical objects—objects to be touched, packed, stored with pride, touched again as possessions that combine memories of happy hours spent writing them and as finished works of art. We have access to an author's intimate as well as her economic thoughts and aspirations. Her manuscripts are to be reread, shared with those willing to read them, and with confidence and trepidation submitted to the commercial arena. Maria is proud of them; although she finds her judgment of her play confirmed by her friends, her high opinion of her work does not depend on others' evaluations. Brooke makes her a writer, not a person posturing as a writer.

In both editions of *The Excursion,* after her disappointments with her manuscript and with Melvile, Maria decides to save for her next novel the letter that she had so carefully composed for Melvile but had not sent. Preserving one of her well-written texts takes precedence with Maria over disappointment in love or any attempts to rescue the relationship. Although saving the letter for later use is funny, it also captures the necessarily opportunistic way writers draw upon experiences. In both editions, the reader as the narrator's interlocutor asks, "Is she not then cured of the disease of writing?" The narrator answers, "Alas! my friend, it is plain you have never been an author" (2:8:6).

In harmony with these sections on the experiences of a woman writer and the novel's brief discussions of "genius" and the "household gods" as women's "guardians," the preface to the second edition begins with a demand to be evaluated in the public, political sphere. "'I APPEAL TO THE PEOPLE' was the celebrated form in which a citizen of ancient Rome refused his acquiescence in any sentence of which he felt the injustice. On giving a new edition . . . I find myself irresistibly impelled to use the same form of appeal." Confronting her own bad health and the resultant scaling down of her writing plans, Brooke writes in a deeply reflective and yet combative tone, moving rather uneasily between the public sphere, the arena in which she worked, and the private, which she now claims as that most suitable for women, even women in whom the "animating fire" of genius glows. Her desire seems to be to reconcile the two spheres, for she argues that women should be allowed "public" approval and the right to "intermix such studies" as are appropriate to their abilities but will not "interrupt" their domestic duties.

Keying "appropriate" to level of ability, which in her case she implies is high, she asserts what eighteenth-century writers of both sexes often explained: the combination of ability, irresistible inclination, and duty demands publication.[77] From her early publication in *The Old Maid,* she had recognized her fertile brain; at one point she wrote that she felt "distress" over having to choose among a "superfluity" of subjects (85). Maria is given these traits. Hammond, who throughout both editions is held up to be thoroughly admirable and discerning, describes Maria as having a "muse of fire," and the essay-like discussions of the high purposes of the theatre and Maria's art imply her duty to persevere as a writer. Like so many women writers, Brooke shows considerable ambivalence toward "genius" and the urge to write.[78] In *The Excursion*, she describes Maria as having genius, "that emanation of the Divinity, that fatal gift of heaven, pleasing to others, *ruinous to its possessor*" (italics mine, 1:1:14). Brooke's preface outlines the "task," the duty of women of genius; among the responsibilities is to "impress the gentler, social, duties, on the hearts of the rising generation." Her novel, with its concern for the conduct and opinions that hold society together and form community, is to a considerable degree the practice of this theory.

Theatrical Success and Retirement from London

From 1779 until her death in January 1789, Brooke was never entirely healthy. In these years, however, she enjoyed the success as a playwright she had sought since her young womanhood. She also wrote a novel and worked on a brief, commissioned life of Samuel Richardson.[79] Her tragedy, *The Siege of Sinope*, was performed ten times in January and February 1781, enough to make it a moderate success. Thomas Harris, manager of Covent Garden, did what he could to contribute to the play's success. As the *Universal Magazine* noted, the scenes and props were elaborate and the costumes "new and elegant,"[80] both of which entailed more than customary expense. Loosely based on an Italian opera, the tragedy featured an excellent part for Mary Ann Yates. The reactions to it reveal the pettiness and carping of the competitive world in which Brooke worked. She was accused of expanding the part of Thamyris for her friend Yates, and the defense (that hers was true to the Italian, not the more familiar English version of the operatic story from Roman history) was ignored or greeted with skepticism. George Colman belittled the play in the *Monthly Review*, the periodical that consistently picked Brooke's work apart and characterized her achievements as mediocre. "From the acknowledged talents of the Writer of this tragedy," Colman wrote snidely, "we expected something of more importance than a meagre imitation of an Italian opera" (64 {February 1781}: 153).

Acknowledging the partisan nature of literary loyalties and reviewing, the *Critical Review*, which was consistently favorable toward Brooke, noted that "fastidious or splenetic readers" were taking "malignant pleasure" in "placing [the tragedy] in a gloomy and disadvantageous view" (51 {January 1781}: 158). She and Yates were attacked for allegedly parodying the mannerisms of the M.P. Charles James Fox and for inappropriately exposing his love of gambling in Arthur Murphy's epilogue.[81] A tribute published in the *European Magazine and London Review* at the time of her death notes that Brooke paid a price repeatedly for her theatrical efforts: "She certainly had some share of the libellous abuse which the management of that theatre . . . gave birth to" (15 {February 1789}: 100).

Brooke's revised *Excursion* (1785) appeared at a peak in the public's awareness of her literary achievement. *Rosina*, the comic opera she had tried so hard to get produced in the early 1770s, was finally mounted at Covent Garden on 31 December 1782. After *Rosina*, Brooke's reputation was as high as it had been after the publication of *Lady Julia;* the press regularly mentioned her and the *British Magazine and Review* published a short biography (February 1783). The influence of Brooke's years with the Opera House seems to have strengthened the play, and from the opening night it was a solid hit; it was performed more than two hundred times before 1800.[82] *Rosina* was admirably designed for the taste of the time. Drawn somewhat from the Book of Ruth, it took a familiar, lovely episode from James Thomson's "Autumn" in *The Seasons* and borrowed from a popular opera, *Les Moissonneurs,* by Charles Favart. The beautiful opening trio, "When the Rosy Morn Appearing," became a favorite in concert programs into the twentieth century.[83] William Shield's music contributed significantly to its popularity. In addition to his own compositions, he included popular French and Scottish tunes and carefully imitated the Highland bagpipe tunes as a way of contributing to the poignant moments. *Marian*, Brooke's second comic opera, which is similar to *Rosina*, was produced at Covent Garden on 22 May 1788. The lovely music, gentle sentimentality, and pastoral scenes and story appealed again to the London audience. Though expectations for it were extremely high, it was something of a disappointment. *Town and Country Magazine* called it "so long wished for, as being the production of Mrs. Brooke," but "very barren of incident" (20 {May 1788}: 235). It had four performances in the 1787-88 season and fourteen in 1788-89.

In the last five years of her life, Brooke was also at work on *The History of Charles Mandeville*, a sequel to *Lady Julia,* which continues the life of Anne Wilmot and narrates the life of Charles, older brother of the dead Harry. Charles has been shipwrecked on a utopian island, Youngland. This novel shows Brooke's continued engagement with English values, ethics, religion, and politics and with theories of government and education. In one episode, she emphasizes that the feather the Younglanders award for a virtuous action is of greater value than the load of jewels they give Charles upon his departure. Although Defoe had Robinson Crusoe reflect similarly upon the relative value of money and wealth when marooned on his island, Brooke is far more emphatic on this point. As in a number of utopias by women writers of Brooke's time, of which the best known is Sarah Scott's *Millenium Hall* (1762), human relationships, status determinants, and local government come in for detailed critique. Hayden White writes in "The Value of Narrativity in the Representation of Reality" that "the social system . . . creates the possibility of conceiving the kinds of tensions, conflicts, struggles, and their various kinds of resolutions that we are accustomed to find in novels and some kinds of histories."[84] These utopian novels by women and indeed all of Brooke's novels hold up the possibility of relationships governed by a sense of community and of values and resolutions outside the social system.

In 1785 Brooke left London for Sleaford, Lincolnshire, within six miles of her son's two livings in Folkingham and Helpringham, where he was respectively rector and vicar. Her husband continued to work in his parish in Colney, Norfolk. He died there 21 January 1789. Brooke survived her husband by only two days, and the two are buried in the parishes in which they died. Their son was Brooke's executor, saw her last novel through the press (published by W. Lane in 1790), and was buried in 1798 next to her in St. Denys Church, Sleaford. Her memorial plaque reads in part, "The union of superior literary talents with goodness of heart, rendered her works serviceable to the cause of those virtues of which her life was shining example" (quoted in McMullen, 212).

Brooke's was a life of adventure, achievement, and, indeed, virtue. Her struggle to remain a part of theatrical London during one of its most competitive times, her trip to Canada, and her varied, often pioneering, literary output offer a fascinating glimpse of an unusual woman's life. Her contribution to the development of the English novel deserves special attention. When she wrote, "formal realism," as Ian Watt called it, was not yet the dominant mode for the novel. Writers, among them a strong corps of women writers, were actively exploring the kinds of "truth" novels could tell, the ways novels could be made relevant and important to the larger culture, the kinds of authority they might have, and the forms and structures they might take. Brooke indicates her share in this endeavor in **The Excursion**, which has several short passages that comment on or ridicule forms of fiction then popular. At the time her novels were published, she was one of the many women who contributed to the new respectability of the form and established the novel as a chief "moral access to the public." By the time of her death, the novel was a major site for the testing and contesting of the great ideas of the era, including those of Rousseau, Paine, Burke, and Adam Smith. Her novels participate in these movements.

Notes

[51] Ann Messenger, *His and Hers* (Lexington: Univ. Press of Kentucky, 1986), 169.

[52] The term is from Sandra Gilbert and Susan Gubar's *Madwoman in the Attic* (1979; New Haven, Conn.: Yale Univ. Press, 1984); they distinguish the female coming-of-age novel from those that follow the shape of a male hero's life and define it as "a story of enclosure and escape," movement toward "an almost unthinkable goal of mature freedom [through] symptomatic difficulties Everywoman in a patriarchal society must meet and overcome" (339). Gilbert and Gubar identify the female *bildungsroman* with *Jane Eyre,* which I see not as a pattern-setting novel but a brilliant example of a kind of novel already well established. Margaret Doody reminds us that a *bildungsroman* about a woman at this early date is still rare in her *Frances Burney: The Life in the Works* (New Brunswick, N.J.: Rutgers Univ. Press, 1988), 45-46.

[53] I would argue that, by using a married woman, Fielding can create a female *bildungsroman* in which the heroine can have experiences not possible for the usual unmarried protagonist of the form.

[54] Nancy Armstrong relates the conduct books, the novel, and these social demands well in her *Desire and Domestic Fiction* [Oxford: Oxford Univ. Press, 1987], see especially chapters 2-4; see also Katherine Hornbeak, *Richardson's Familiar Letters and the Domestic Conduct Books* (Northampton, Mass.: Smith College Studies in Modern Languages 19, 1938); Joyce Hemlow, "Fanny Burney and the Courtesy Books," *PMLA* 65 (1950), 732-61; and Sylvia Marks, *Sir Charles Grandison: The Compleat Conduct Book* (Lewisburg, Penn.: Bucknell Univ. Press, 1986), 35-40.

[55] [Katharine M.] Rogers, "Sensibility and Feminism," [*Genre* II (1978),] 167, and see her useful discussion, 165-70.

[56] Chris Jones, for instance, writes that the concept of sensibility "poses an intriguing problem for the historian of ideas" ("Radical Sensibility in the 1790s," in *Reflections of Revolution,* ed. Allison Yarrington and Kelvin Everest {London: Routledge, 1993}, 68), and William Empson devotes sixty pages to it in *The Structure of Complex Words* (London: Chatto & Windus, 1951), 250-310. For further discussions of this term see Jones, "Radical Sensibility," 68-82; R.S. Crane, "Suggestions toward a Genealogy of the 'Man of Feeling,'" *ELH* 1 (1934), 205-30; Jean Hagstrum, *Sex and Sensibility* (Chicago: Univ. of Chicago Press, 1980); John Mullan, *Sentiment and Sociability* (Oxford: Clarendon, 1988); and Syndy Conger, ed., *Sensibility in Transformation* (London: Associated Univ. Presses, 1990).

[57] It is a common modern misconception that novels such as Frances Burney's were written for women. Men and women alike read romances and courtship novels, discussed them with each other, and did not fall into

the kinds of reader categories we have today. On English familiarity with French novels and early English writers, see Ros Ballaster, *Seductive Forms*[*:Women's Amatory Fiction from 1684 to 1740.* (Oxford: Clarendon, 1992)]

[58] Du Plaisir, *Sentiments sur les lettres et sur l'histoire avec des scrupules sur le style* (Paris, 1683), 52.

[59] See, for example, *The Autobiography and Correspondence of Mary Granville,* ed. Lady Llanover, 3 vols. (London, 1861) and its three-volume "second series" (London, 1862), for Granville's comments on *Clelia,* which the ladies read aloud "for the amusement of the society at the Bishop of Killala's" (1:363), *Cleopatra* and *Pharamond* (1:472), and *Zaide* (1:356). Granville also read *Lady Julia* (4:23-24) and Brooke's translated *Letters from Lady Catesby* (3:604).

[60] Ellen Moers, *Literary Women* (New York: Oxford Univ. Press, 1985), 42. The publication history of this book is interesting; copyrighted in 1963, it was not published until 1976.

[61] James Raven, *Judging New Wealth: Popular Publishing and Responses to Commerce in England, 1750-1800* (Oxford: Clarendon, 1992), 51-52; John Feather, *A History of British Publishing* [(London: Croom Helm, 1988),] 93.

[62] See Paul Langford, *A Polite and Commercial People* (Oxford: Clarendon, 1989), 565, and 586-87.

[63] Newspapers and periodicals also reported alleged debauchery and sexual scandals, purported bigamies, and even a wager over which sex a prominent person really was. See Paul Langford, *A Polite and Commercial People,* 571-72 and 582-87.

[64] The phrase is Langford's, 602; see his discussion of the growing anxieties about women's public conduct, 602-6.

[65] Among a number of plays that took the fashionable world for their subject, David Garrick's *Bon Ton: or, High Life above Stairs* (1775) was certainly known to Brooke and most of her readers.

[66] Locke, *An Essay Concerning Human Understanding,* ed. Peter Nidditch (1975; Oxford: Clarendon, 1987), 2:11:2, p. 156.

[67] Brooke describes gamesters as having "no age, no country, no party, no religion," 1:2:5.

[68] Women writers, too, had produced these satires. Charlotte Charke's' *The Art of Management; or, Tragedy Expell'd* (1735) shows Charles Fleetwood, then manager of Drury Lane, producing a comedy called *The Union of the Bear and Monkey* and offering to pay Merry Andrews £3 per week and the greatest tragic actress of the time 20 shillings a week, in other words one-third of his salary. Over a year, 20 shillings per week would be half a middle-class living wage.

[69] Goldsmith, *An Enquiry into the Present State of Polite Learning in Europe* (London, 1759). The second edition of this essay appeared in 1774, and it is not surprising that Brooke read it. *The Works of Oliver Goldsmith,* ed. Peter Cunningham, 10 vols. (New York: Putnam, 1908), 6:88.

[70] The authorship of this review is verified by Benjamin C. Naugle, *The Monthly Review* (Oxford: Clarendon, 1934), 16-17, and 67; and by Antonia Forster, correspondence, 6 May 1995.

[71] *Monthly Review* 57 (August 1777), 145.

[72] Quoted in [Lorraine] McMullen, [*An Odd Attempt in a Woman: The Literary Life of Frances Brooke.* (Vancouver: Univ. of British Columbia Press, 1983)] 165. Here and throughout, she transcribes "y" with a superscript "e," the period's abbreviation for "the," as "ye"; I have corrected this error. The entire letter is in Little and Kahrl, *Letters of Garrick,* 3:1163.

[73] Little and Kahrl, *Letters of Garrick,* 3:1172, in which he calls Brooke and Yates "wretches" and "Devils." McMullen lists other instances of bad feeling between Garrick and Brooke, 176-77.

[74] *The Early Journals and Letters of Fanny Burney,* 3 vols., ed. Lars E. Troide (Montreal and Kingston: McGill-Queen's Univ. Press, 1988), 2:4. Later Burney would express pleasure about her home's proximity to Brooke's (2:94), and in 1783 Brooke would propose that they collaborate on a new periodical. Burney refused, giving as her reason that she was "at present so little disposed for writing." Quoted in Margaret Doody, *Frances Burney: The Life in the Works,* 158-59. Burney may have in mind Sarah Scott's translation of *La Laideur amiable by Pierre-Antoine de La Place* (*Agreeable Ugliness,* 1754).

[75] Quoted in McMullen, 197 and 196 respectively.

[76] Jane Barker's Galesia novels represent the experiences of women writers and invite comparison. In Barker's time, the character of women writers was undergoing change and reevaluation, and identity as a writer is a more absorbing, difficult issue for her characters. See *Love Intrigues* (1713), *A Patch-work Screen for the Ladies* (1723), and *The Lining of the Patchwork Screen* (1726); these novels are being edited by Carol S. Wilson for Oxford and the Brown Women Writers Project series.

[77] Paula McDowell makes a persuasive argument for the empowering effect on women of seeing themselves as part of a "social, collective" "Member of the Body of the Nation," a sense of identity that was both older than and above the conception of the autonomous, unique individual. *The Women of Grub Street: Press, Politics and Gender in the London Literary Marketplace,* forthcoming.

[78] I have discussed women, genius, and creativity in my *Spectacular Politics* (Baltimore: Johns Hopkins Univ. Press, 1993), 101-2; women often refer to the urge to write as a "disease" or a "fever."

[79] Apparently intended to preface *Charles Grandison* if not an edition of [Samuel] Richardson's collected works, the biography became a piece in the *Universal Magazine of Knowledge and Pleasure* (January 1786), McMullen has speculated (187-89). There is no evidence that such an edition appeared near this time with Brooke's or anyone else's biographical introduction.

[80] *Universal Magazine of Knowledge and Pleasure* 68 (February 1781), 63.

[81] Whether the accusations against them were factitious or Harris as director or Arthur Murphy, the writer of the epilogue, set up Brooke and Yates cannot be known.

[82] McMullen, 202; she also records performances in Jamaica, the United States, and a 1966 recording by the London Symphony Orchestra, 202-3. Among many interesting testimonials to its popularity is the *Overture to Rosina. Adapted as a Lesson for the Harpsichord or Piano Forte* (1805).

[83] Alison Adburgham, *Women in Print,* [(London: George Allen and Unwin, 1972),] 116; McMullen says that it is "a direct translation" of Favart's second song, 200.

[84] Hayden White, *The Content of the Form* (Baltimore: Johns Hopkins Univ. Press, 1987), 14.

FURTHER READING

Biography

McMullen, Lorraine. *An Odd Attempt in a Woman: The Literary Life of Frances Brooke.* Vancouver: University of British Columbia Press, 1983, 237.

A detailed history of Brooke's life and writing, including summaries of works and their critical reception.

Criticism

Foster, James R. "From *Sidney Bidulph* to the *Placid Man.*" In *History of the Pre-Romantic Novel in England,* pp. 145-50. New York: Modern Language Association of America, 1949.

Discusses the literary influences on Brooke's major novels.

Green, Katherine Sobba. "Frances Moore Brooke: Emily Montague's *Sanctum Sanctorum.*" In *The Courtship Novel, 1740-1820: A Feminized Genre,* pp. 62-66. Lexington: University Press of Kentucky, 1991.

Examines the arguments for social reform that occur in *The History of Emily Montague.* The critic notes especially the effect that Brooke created by attributing feminist statements to male characters.

New, William H. "Frances Brooke's Chequered Gardens." *Canadian Literature* 52 (Spring 1972): 24-38.

Explores Brooke's imagery.

Rogers, Katharine M. "Sensibility and Feminism: The Novels of Frances Brooke." *Genre* II (Summer 1978): 159-71.

Addresses the balance of sentiment and realism in *The History of Emily Montague* and *The Excursion.*

Sellwood, Jane. "'A little acid is absolutely necessary': Narrative as Coquette in Frances Brooke's *The History of Emily Montague.*" *Canadian Literature* 136 (Spring 1993): 60-79.

Explores the idea that the character of Arabella Fermor serves a subversive function.

Teague, Frances. "Frances Brooke's Imagined Epistles." In *Transactions of the Eighth International Congress on the Enlightenment,* edited by H. T. Mason, pp. 711-12. Oxford: Voltaire Foundation, 1992.

Contrasts the letters of Ed Rivers and William Fermor with their reputed real-life counterparts, Henry Caldwell and Brooke's husband John Brooke.

Todd, Janet. "The Fantasy of Sensibility: Frances Brooke and Susannah Gunning." In *The Sign of Angelica: Women, Writing, and Fiction 1660-1800,* pp. 176-91. London: Virago, 1989.

Discusses *The History of Lady Julia Mandeville* as a fantasy of passive feminine power.

Additional coverage of Brooke's life and career is contained in the following sources published by The Gale Group: *Literature Criticism from 1400-1800,* Vol. 6, and *Dictionary of Literary Biography,* Vols. 39 and 99.

John Cleland

1709-1789

English novelist, dramatist, journalist, translator, and critic.

INTRODUCTION

Cleland is best known as the author of *Memoirs of a Woman of Pleasure,* popularly known as *Fanny Hill.* Written in epistolary form, the novel details the life of a naïve country girl who becomes a worldly-wise prostitute. Censored and suppressed since the time of its publication, Cleland's principal novel has become a minor classic of eighteenth-century prose. The *Memoirs* is one of a very few books from the eighteenth century that has been widely reprinted and read from the time of its first appearance. In the twentieth century, it has been seriously studied as well.

Biographical Information

Cleland was born in Surrey, England, to a prosperous middle-class family. In 1721 he enrolled in the prestigious Westminster School, where he was an outstanding student. His education ended suddenly after two years for unknown reasons. In 1728 Cleland joined the mercantile East India Company in Bombay, India. He advanced rapidly and eventually became the company's factor—a job that required management, negotiating, and diplomatic skills. Cleland was called home in 1740 to be with his ailing father. When his father died the next year, Cleland gave up his position in the East India Company and stayed in England. However, he received no inheritance on his father's death, and he fell into debt. He was prosecuted for nonpayment of bills around 1747 and jailed for over a year. While in jail Cleland wrote *Memoirs of a Woman of Pleasure.* He offered the manuscript to Fenton Griffiths, a printer, and to his brother Ralph Griffiths, a publisher and editor of the popular journal *Monthly Review.* Realizing the potential of Cleland's novel, Ralph Griffiths paid off Cleland's debts and bought the copyright to the *Memoirs* for twenty pounds. Griffiths also contracted with Cleland to provide an abridged edition of the *Memoirs,* entitled *Memoirs of Fanny Hill* (1750), perhaps in anticipation of the uproar that would greet the sexual content of the novel. Both books were extremely successful, and commentators guess that Griffiths made a fortune on his investment. Cleland, on the other hand, received no royalties from either work. Shortly after *Memoirs of a Woman of Pleasure* was published, a warrant was issued for Cleland's arrest, this time for writing a lewd book. It is unclear what legal actions, if any, were taken against Cleland. According to some sources, he was given a government grant to prevent him from writing another work like the *Memoirs.* Cleland did write another novel, *Memoirs of a Coxcomb* (1751), as well as several plays and books of linguistic theory. He also contributed political, social, and literary criticism to the *Monthly Review.* He died in 1789.

Major Works

In addition to being witty and erotically entertaining, *Memoirs of a Woman of Pleasure* provides a satiric attack on the morality of eighteenth-century society. Cleland ironically indicated that his protagonist's use of sexual commerce as a path to success closely resembled the financially motivated husband-hunting of the upper classes. Many readers found this sardonic social commentary as objectionable as the work's passages of erotic description. For these, Cleland did not rely on profanity, vernacular, or even realistic description. Instead, he used euphemism, simile, and metaphor to described male and female genitalia and a variety of sexual acts. The verbal richness of his prose has been compared to that of the metaphysical poets, and Cleland's prose style has been called one of the lushest, wittiest, and most interesting of the eighteenth century. It inspired a host of imitations. The sensual, uninhibited heroine of Cleland's novel has appealed to both male and female readers. She becomes and remains in control of her own life and sexuality; growing wealthy while unabashedly fulfilling her own desires, and the novel ends with her marriage to the man she loves.

Critical Reception

Memoirs of a Woman of Pleasure was virtually ignored by literary commentators until the twentieth century. Commonly referred to as "obscene" or "pornographic," the novel was not published legally in Great Britain or the United States until 1963. Before then it was dismissed as having no literary merit, existing solely to appeal to the "prurient interests" of readers. However, commentators have come to assess the *Memoirs* as one of the greatest examples of the subgenre "whore biography" that proliferated during the eighteenth century, exemplified by Daniel Defoe's *Moll Flanders* (1722). In his novel, Cleland neatly reversed the basic plot of Samuel Richardson's popular moralistic novel *Pamela,* in which a young woman repeatedly fights off the sexual advances of her employer and is rewarded by his proposal of marriage. Cleland subverts the formula that chastity will be rewarded and licentiousness punished: far from being destroyed by premarital sexual adventures: Fanny profits from them and marries after she has had a multitude of lovers and a range of sexual experiencess.

PRINCIPAL WORKS

Memoirs of a Woman of Pleasure. 2 vols. (novel) 1748-49; also published as *Memoirs of Fanny Hill* [abridged edition] (novel) 1750

Memoirs of a Coxcomb (novel) 1751

Titus Vespasian: A Tragedy (drama) 1755

The Ladies Subscription: A Dramatic Performance Designed for an Introduction to a Dance (drama) 1755

The Surprises of Love (novel) 1764

Genuine Memoirs of the Celebrated Miss Maria Brown, Exhibiting the Life of a Courtesan in the Most Fashionable Scenes of Dissipation. 2 vols. (novels) 1766

Specimen of an Etimological Vocabulary; or, Essay, by Means of the Analitic Method, to Retrieve the Antient Celtic (essay) 1768

The Woman of Honor. 3 vols. (novel) 1768

Additional Articles to the Specimen of an Etimological Vocabulary (essay) 1769

CRITICISM

John Hollander (essay date 1963)

SOURCE: "The Old Last Act: Some Observations on *Fanny Hill,*" in *Encounter,* Vol. XXI, No. 4, October 1963, pp. 69-77.

[*In the following essay, Hollander asserts that* Memoirs of a Woman of Pleasure *or* Fanny Hill *observes the conventions necessary to a successful pornographic work and presents an appealing, literary evocation of its central character.*]

Literary realism ends with pornography. Far from being the limiting border towards which the realistic novel has always moved, pornography, the true pornography which seeks to excite and succeeds in so doing, is closer to poetry than it is to prose fiction. It is, willy-nilly, hopelessly caught up in conventions, for example. Rather than being pragmatic and original, it depends upon an iconography of detail, conventionalisations of erotic elements, and a limited world of concern—pornography can never stray too far from its moorings, nor can it seek in a philosophical way for ultimate constituents of reality. In short, it can never actually be, in the euphemism of the semi-prudish, "clinical." Stylistically, too, it is hopelessly traditionalistic in spirit; in every age it tends to rely upon diction familiar enough not to alarm, and hence to distract, the sensibilities of its audience. While the various narrative devices that the novel has developed in the past two hundred years aim at description, at building a model of the world, the descriptions in pornography are always a means to the completion of the sorts of verbal act—arousing, inspiring, suggesting—to which poetry has traditionally directed itself. Probably the only Orphean music we ever hear, the only literature we ever read which realises the classical myth of the poetry that could make trees dance, is the first piece of pornography we are ever taken by. And finally, pornography is composed of encounters that are heroic, hyperbolic, hieratic and thoroughly unlikely. Such scenes need not convince, they need only work.

Nevertheless, confusions between the two *genres* of the novel and the pornographic work have multiplied during the past half century. In the first place, fiction grew more explicit about sex and in addition began to observe the convention that the editing-out of taboo words, from even Dickensian fidelities to popular speech, was a kind of betrayal of artistic purpose. Just as the twentieth-century novel has seen the inroads of lyric, drama, homiletic and encyclopedia, so, too, encapsulated sequences of pornography have found their way into recent fiction since (but not including) *Ulysses.*[1] The bed-scene has had its own literary history, too, and the fact that in the post-war American novel, for example, a detailed narration of a sexual initiation has become a kind of literary ritual, more a warrant of the author's novelistic *bona fides* than anything else, has increased the confusion. Such scenes often work pornographically, when they are well written, and though it is often the publisher's intention that they do so, the novelist has usually put them there for another reason. Finally, it has recently been necessary for responsible writers and readers to pretend in court (and to themselves as well—there has been no perjury, really) that sexual stimulation of the reader is a base effect and a baser motive, far below the transcendent moral plane of something called Literature. Mindless and evil-breeding laws have produced the civilised desperation-measure of the doctrine that the whole work, rather than a part of it, should be considered in prosecutions of books. This has led to critical denials, admittedly for humane purposes, that, in this case at least, one literary *genre* can be influenced by or contained in another; and literary critics who might want to discuss the influence of drama on Henry James' late novels, or the role of lyric in Hemingway's short stories, might rightly rage if legal expediency prevented them from doing so, at least in public.

It remains clear, however, that good novels can have pornographic interludes, just as it must always be remembered that for the right constellation of reader, background, book and scene, much writing in various genres can be read pornographically. Or, rather, misread, much in the way that texts can be misread as being allegorical or subversive or forgery (when they are not). The limits of the pornographic *genre* are the intentions of the work to arouse, and while the author's motive in so intending may be financial, satirical, comical, narcissistic or any combination of these, the test of its success, in a given literary milieu, is invariably in a physiological reaction.

The new burst of critical, moral and jurisprudential talk that may be produced by the publication of John Cleland's classic[2] in America may, I am afraid, compound the confusions even more. Originally published in 1748-9 with the clear purpose of being a "dirty book," *Fanny Hill* was unfortunately present at the birth of both conventions. While it is certainly the model for much of the pornography in English for the two hundred years following, the paucity of memorable English fiction in the mid-eighteenth century cannot help but focus our attention on its novelistic virtues. Its heroine shares an England with Pamela, Clarissa and Sophia Western (indeed, to a degree with Fielding's Shamela too) and she may certainly be said to inhabit a major novel in that her undeniable greatness lies not in what she does but in who she is. What sets out to be a success in one literary *genre* often becomes most interesting to later epochs because of its affinities with another, and certainly if the book had been written, *mutatis mutandis,* a century later, its claim to a significant place in the history of the English novel would have been negligible. But there it is to perplex us, a good book, important fictionally because of the way in which its protagonist talks about sexual bouts and other things as well, a success and an originator pornographically precisely because Cleland had the resources of a real talent and the background of Defoe and Richardson.

The particular talent was for euphemism. Many people who have never read *Fanny Hill* know that it triumphs in avoiding all the taboo words. While this was probably done to avoid prosecution, the barrier of the unprintable presented no more of a problem to Cleland than the very structure of English vocabulary itself. It is a truism by now that our language lacks those words, like the French "sexe," developed by societies that have come to terms less obliquely with Eros, which name sexual equipment and functioning without giggles,

medical escapes into Latinity, or descents into the good old forbidden terminology. But Cleland's success was in evolving, like a poet "a style from a despair." Fanny is a great creature because of the language in which Cleland has her talk, and the book's language and its protagonist's character are its greatest virtues. A diction full of turns and conceits was, by the middle of the eighteenth century, no longer acceptable in serious poetry. Augustan balance and antithesis, the devices of a style rivalling prose in its precision and controlled ornateness, had become the dominant convention, and since the time of Dryden, conceits in verse had been emblematic of frivolity, rather than of the tension and dialectic of Metaphysical wit. But it is just such a conceited and almost euphuistic diction to which Cleland turned in his descriptions of members and acts, in all the more highly operatic scenes for which the book's plot is the excuse.

Even in the "recitative" parts, however, his prose is tense and controlled. At the opening of the book, which consists of two long letters written to a lady of presumed quality by one of her acquaintance, Fanny announces her intention to recount truthfully her life as a prostitute:

> . . . I will not so much as take the pains to bestow the strip of a gauze wrapper on it, but paint situations such as they actually rose to me in nature, careless of violating those laws of decency that were never made for such unreserved intimacies as ours; and you have too much sense, too much knowledge of the ORIGINALS themselves, to sniff prudishly and out of character at the PICTURES of them.

"Such unreserved intimacies as ours"—they are those that govern the relation of book and reader as well. The growing notion of private experience and its value surrounds, as Ian Watt has pointed out, the early development of the English novel and its readership, and the overall rhetorical strategy of the book traps the reader in the woman-to-woman confidential relationship. After this opening remark, Fanny's apologies for the detail and elaborate sentiment of her descriptions are never aimed at rearranging ruffled modesty, but at the sympathetic objections of common sense. "I know you know all about this, dear, but just thinking about it now makes me want to tell you how super it was when he . . ." This, transcribed into modern shorthand, is the tactical move of her apology. Her only other disclaimers are about her motives. From the very beginning of her narration, economic necessity, even desperation, gives way only to nature, to sexual impulse itself, in determining her choice of action and response. She grows up in a village near Liverpool and, on the death of her artisan-class parents, comes innocently up to London to seek her fortune, arrives penniless and is discovered at an employment agency by a bawd who undertakes, with the help of her girls, the sale of Fanny's maiden-head to an ageing rake. This is all formulaic: we think of Polly Peachum's first song in *The Beggar's Opera* (to the tune of an inconsequentially gallant Purcell song) which likens virgins to flowers raised in the country and brought, like girls (indeed, like the very actress singing the song) to Covent Garden to "rot, stink and die." But Fanny's articulateness is so unusual that she herself must take note of it: she mentions her understanding, "naturally not a despicable one . . . which had, even amidst the whirl of loose pleasures I had been tost in, exerted more observation on the characters and manners of the world than what is common to those of my unhappy profession, who looking on all thought or reflection as their capital enemy, keep it at as great a distance as they can, or destroy it without mercy." These are, after all, the concerns of the novelist, rather than of the pornographer, and Fanny's moral and social insights throughout the book, her shrewd assessments of character and, as Peter Quennell reminds us in his introduction to the New York edition, of the relation between physical appearance and sexual preference, are, in a sense, bootlegged into the pornography. Thus, at an early stage of her sexual initiation, she observes Mrs. Brown, the old bawd, with a young Horse-grenadier; from behind yellow damask curtains in a closet, she watches their doings, at first rather repulsed by the exposed ugliness of the old woman, then herself excited by splendours of the young man. But she makes it clear that her reactions have been conditioned to a degree by the instructive caresses of one of the whores with whom she has, from the beginning, been bedded down. At the end of her description of the scene, conflicting feelings and her own physical release give her a sense of the great inevitability of nature in a magnificent sentence that ends with an almost Jamesian period:

> But, as the main affair was now at the point the industrious dame had brought it to, she was not in the humour to put off the payment of her pains, but laying herself down, drew him gently upon her, and thus they finish'd, in the same manner as before, the old last act.

But her philosophy, it must be remembered, is determined by the pornographic *genre* itself, for each substantive episode in the book must culminate in a mechanical or social variant of "the old last act." Her innocence is gradually lost through encounters with another girl, two scenes of observed activity, a failure of the horrid brute for whom she was being groomed to penetrate her and, finally, the loss of her virginity to Charles, a young man with whom she has fortuitously fallen in love at first sight. It is here that Cleland moves into the province of sentimental fiction. It is true love that, in the end, leads her to marriage and redemption, but only after she has been separated from him by the guiles of his avaricious father with designs on some money. Charles abducts her from her bordello to an

inn in Chelsea where he depucellates her, thinking her to be an experienced whore, with more than the usual gore and pain. Ten days later, she is established as his mistress in a flat in St. James', where for nearly a year she lives a high life. But one day he conveniently disappears, sent off on a wild-goose chase to the South Seas, and Fanny must resume her apprenticeship. She is taken up by a rich man, swallows her distaste for loveless liaisons, goes through all the shock of bourgeois married outrage when she espies him in the act with her own maid, plays him false in return with a rather improbably well-endowed young rustic and is eventually discovered and relieved of her post.

The second part of the novel opens with Fanny resuming, in a subsequent letter to her friend, the interrupted narrative:

> I imagined, indeed, that you would have been cloy'd and tired with a uniformity of adventures and expressions, inseparable from a subject of this sort, whose bottom, or groundwork being, in the nature of things, eternally one and the same . . . there is no escaping a repetition of the same images, the same figures, the same expressions, with this further inconvenience added to the disgust it creates, that the words JOYS, ARDOURS, TRANSPORTS, ECSTASIES, and the rest of those pathetic terms so con-genial to, so received in the PRACTICE OF PLEASURE, flatten and lose much of their due spirit and energy by the frequency they indispensably recur with, in a narrative of which that PRACTICE professedly composes the whole basis.

The irony here cuts several ways, because the reader is undoubtedly expecting more elaborate and varied sexual displays than he has seen in Part I, and because Fanny is undoubtedly proud, for Cleland and herself, of her literary success. She knows that she has conquered "the extreme difficulty of continuing so long in one strain, in a mean temper'd with taste, between the revoltingness of gross, rank and vulgar expressions and the ridicule of mincing metaphors and affected circumlocutions." With more gusto than ever, she proceeds to complete her narrative, telling of how she comes to inhabit the "safest, politest and, at the same time, the most thorough house of accommodation in town," run by the benevolent and industrious Mrs. Cole, where the girls and their customers "would, in the height of their humour, style themselves the restorers of the golden age and its simplicity of pleasures." The other girls narrate the histories of their sexual initiations, we are given several communal scenes, encounters with a flagellant and a fetichist, and a spied-upon homosexual doing.[3] During Fanny's stay at Mrs. Cole's, she amasses a good bit of money. The final episodes in her career concern the necessary last phases of her education by an old man, "a rational pleasurist" who, as she says, "much too wise to be ashamed of the pleasures of humanity, loved me indeed, but loved me with dignity." Unlike Mrs. Cole, who is a *déclassé* aristocrat, he is a self-made merchant with a large fortune, which, at his death eight months later, he providentially leaves to Fanny. But during her life with him she has learned, she says,

> . . . that the pleasures of the mind were superior to those of the body; at the same time, that they were so far from obnoxious to, or incompatible with each other, that, besides the sweetness in the variety and transition, the one serv'd to exalt and perfect the taste of the other, to the degree that the senses alone can never arrive at.

Thus it is that now, a child of the enlightenment, well tutored in town life and in self-respect by two wise, commercial protectors, she is in a position to welcome back her strayed true-love, Charles, after two and a half years of separation. They marry, live happily ever after, and the story concludes with a little paean to sexual virtue founded on experience, which Fanny goes to great lengths to insist is not hypocritical. Perhaps she is right, for if the book has any superficial moral at all, it is that innocence cannot flower in a climate where commerce blasts the blossom and instinct suffuses the root. True love and virtue are, for Fanny, the reward of vice.

Like other early novels, *Fanny Hill*'s resources are somewhat limited. There is very little dialogue, and even the long narrations by the other whores at Mrs. Cole's come from a previously established convention in pornography. Unlike Richardson, Cleland does not really make use of the epistolary form with its dramatic tensions of episode, event and letter all moving in and out of phase with each other. Unlike Fielding, he cannot set up a deliberate alternation of narrative and digression; indeed, the one device of controlling pace at his disposal is the adjustment of the "cooling off" periods between the erotic episodes, the passages where the art of fiction intrudes upon that of pornography. If Fanny lives the life of the body ("for me," she says "natural philosophy all resided in the favourite centre of sense, and who was rul'd by its powerful instinct in taking pleasure by its right handle"), she has been partially claimed by the life of the mind. Thus it is that few of her descriptions of people or acts are entirely free of psychologising. She can be brisk enough with, say, Phoebe, the girl at Mrs. Brown's who undertakes her initiation: "She was about five and twenty, by her most suspicious account, in which, according to all appearances, she must have sunk at least ten good years: allowance, too, being made for the havoc which a long course of hackneyship and hot waters must have made of her constitution." But she writes with an understanding amounting almost to tenderness, of how she "found, it seems, in this exercise of her art to break young girls, the gratification of one of those arbitrary

tastes, for which there is no accounting. Not that she hated men, or did not even prefer them to her own sex; but when she met with such occasions as this was, a satiety of enjoyments in the common road, perhaps too, a secret bias, inclined her to make the most of pleasure, wherever she could find it, without distinction of sexes." Fanny's rhetoric about sexual variation is surprisingly aristocratic (it is a taste or eccentricity, as opposed to bourgeois-rational "deviant" and petit-bourgeois "unthinkable").

She has the same intensity of insight about her own feelings, however. When she is taken by Mr. H——— for the first time after being separated from her Charles, she says of his embraces "not that they, as yet, gave me any pleasure, or prevail'd over the aversion of my soul, to give myself up to any sensation of that sort; what I suffer'd, I suffer'd out of a kind of gratitude, and as a matter of course after what had pass'd." But as always, physiology will win out with her; although the last one in the world to deny modesty and reticence their part in nature, she is ever aware of their terrible fragility. Her mistrust of innocence (which merely exposes one to the machinations of others) leads her to wage a kind of one-woman war on the green-sickness.

To this blend of sense and sensuality in her character, Fanny's experience has added literary cultivation, of which she is by no means self-conscious. Her language is full of warmed-over tags from Caroline poets, and an occasional hyperbole smacks of a diction even older—thus, of what pleased her so in the well-hung country bumpkin: "its dimensions, mocking either grasp or span, almost renew'd my terrors." A typical set-piece is part of her description of Phoebe's grand tour of her anatomy, with "two rising hillocks that just begin to shew themselves . . . down lower, over a smooth track, she could just feel the soft silky down, that had but a few months before put forth and garnish'd the mount-pleasant of those parts, and promised to spread a grateful shelter over the seat of the most exquisite sensation, and which had been, till that instant, the seat of the most insensible innocence." This is almost standard Renaissance erotic topography; there is even some of it in Spenser. Usually, though, her conceits are more wry, as when in a similar scene she talks of Phoebe's using her (Fanny's) hand "to procure herself rather the shadow than the substance of any pleasure."

Fanny has an unabashed capacity for making do financially, once she is firmly committed to the profession of courtesan. She praises Mrs. Cole for never really cheating her clients, but she can relate with relishing detail her own involvement, with that lady's help, in the well-known con-game of passing herself off as a virgin, with the aid of "method" acting and fake blood, for the costly benefit of a rake with particular preferences. In her entrepreneurial energy she seems a daughter of Moll Flanders. But in her exuberance and curiosity, her undeviating devotion to nature, she is an ancestor of Molly Bloom.

Her own fictional descendants have proliferated into anonymous multitudes, the first-person female narrators of standard Western pornography. Cleland virtually invented the formula of the sustained and unbroken story with all the sex described from the girl's point of view. It is the optimum strategic device of pornography, for it can excite any reader (masculine or feminine, active or passive), and it reminds us of the disposition of attributes in pastoral literature in any of its guises, where the simple and the articulate confront each other and where only the articulate is interested in brooding about the meeting. The simple element (country, natural, primitive) is potent and active, and the other (city, civilised, literary) passive, but capable of more complex reactions, and I think that the Romantic poets understood this very well. In any event, this is the pornographic tradition, and it is because of the conjunction of novel and erotic book in *Fanny Hill* that it seems to have got started. From what is known of the work's predecessors in English, it can be seen that Cleland depended upon previously established conventions to a certain degree. For example, there was the widely-translated *l'Académie des Dames* (itself a French translation, ca. 1680 from a Latin original twenty years earlier), which was first Englished around 1682. *L'Académie des Dames* keeps to the dialogue form that provided the structure for Renaissance treatises on everything from musical theory to carpentry. The spirit of the neo-classic stage has begun to infuse it, how-ever, for the two women of the dialogue, Octavie and Tullie (one experienced, one innocent) first describe, then act out some sex, and are later joined by two men. The conventions of pornographic dialogue (the cries from the girl of "No, no . . . yes, yes, do it some more . . . oh, oh," etc.) are very much in evidence here, and Cleland is no originator in this respect. But the questions of pacing such a narration, the treatment of many and various scenes and the interludes that are themselves necessary for the novelistic prop, and the problem, almost cinematic or musical, of arranging the relative length of scene and interlude is one first faced by Cleland and perhaps never managed better.

It is significant too that Cleland avoids the whole problem of pain and domination and their erotic role. With the exception of the flagellation episode, at which Fanny is rather piqued and amused than outraged, the world of the book lies outside the tradition of French political eroticism which, towards the end of the eighteenth century, was to be inaugurated by Laclos and Sade. Fanny's attitude to one of the latter's favourite tastes is made clear in only one incident. One night, after a (for her) unsatisfactory evening with Mr. Norbert, the jaded rake, she allows herself to be picked up by a sailor, and at the end of some rather boisterous and drunken preliminaries there is a misdirected effort on the sailor's part ("I feeling pretty sensibly that it was not going by the right door, and knocking desperately at the wrong one, I told him of it:—'Pooh!' says he, 'my dear, any port in a storm'.") But she soon puts it to rights. The whole affair is merely a matter for her eternal good humour, and emphasises again the blandly rational tolerance of her outlook. Projected into Sade's world, Fanny would show up rather as Graham Greene's Ida Arnold does in the twisted but purportedly authentic moral realm of Pinky's Brighton. (I cannot help but feel that Mr. Greene would not approve of her.) Her domain of sexual nature is as yet unaffected by the involvement of sexuality with the problems of will, freedom and the conflict of instinct and society which eventually are to become central to the concerns of modern fiction. For a modern reader, it is almost unbelievable that Fanny's innocent and Whiggish libido can be *interesting;* Cleland's triumph is that it is.[4]

It is enlightening to compare *Fanny Hill* with a book that in a sense is its mirror-image, blending novelistic and pornographic elements after over two hundred years of their divergent development. *Histoire d'O.* by the pseudonymous Pauline Réage emerges from a recent Parisian milieu of the *anti-roman* and the intellectual anguish over Sade, just as Fanny's story does from the ferment of early eighteenth-century London and an expanding reading public. A story of cruelty and humiliation, fitted out with such traditional trappings as abductions to a *château* and a sinister English aristocrat, it is an astonishing *tour-de-force* in which one feels that the assimilation of the traditional pornographic elements are there as a means towards an aesthetic, even a stylistic end. The brilliant and classical French prose is the result of this; in the case of *Fanny Hill,* the style is merely a means to an end, although some present-day readers will undoubtedly be misled into thinking of it as the book's one redeeming feature.

One is entitled to do this, of course; but it would perhaps be far more commendable to detest the whole book, as D. H. Lawrence would probably have done. His own sad failure to write convincingly about physical sex was accompanied by his almost shrill hatred of pornography, and nothing could contrast more with the gloomy and misleading rhetoric of "darknesses" in *Women in Love,* or the apocalyptic transfiguration of four-letter words in *Lady Chatterley,* than the clarity, ingenuity and apparent spontaneity of Fanny's language. Cleland's motives were primarily commercial. At the time of writing the book he was a penniless hack who had drifted back to England after losing a minor job with the East India Company. Following the book's commercial success and his eventual escape from actual penal conviction,[5] he reverted to trivia; his later novels and plays seem to come from a different hand. This one book was an accidental masterpiece. But to read it as a novel masquerading as erotica is to do it a disservice. It would be to give it just as much of a mistaken reading as Dante's Paola and Francesca gave, in the reverse direction, of that undoubtedly sententious French romance when, blaming it all on the book, they whined to the pilgrim-narrator that they "read no more that day."

Notes

[1] Not in Molly's soliloquy, certainly. The Gertie McDowell-Nausicaa episode is a *parody* of a kind of mild, sentimentalised pornography for ladies, neither explicit nor concise. In *Stephen Hero* romantic poetry is called "pornographic or impure" because it does not aim at catharsis. For a recent brilliant parody of *c.* 1920's pornography, see Edward Gorey's pseudonymous *The Curious Sofa* (by Ogdred Weary, New York 1962).

[2] *Memoirs of a Woman of Pleasure.* By JOHN CLELAND, Intro. by Peter Quennell. New York, G. B. Putnam's Sons, 1963. $6.00. I shall use the short title, *Fanny Hill,* throughout, for the book is usually called that by all but bibliographers. Cleland cut the book himself for a 1750 bowdlerisation called *Memoirs of Fanny Hill,* but I shall always refer to the original edition.

[3] This is mostly cut out of the New York edition, although all interior and exterior evidence indicates that it is Cleland's own writing. It is in what is probably without question the first edition, a copy of which is in the British Museum. Despite the publisher's claim on the jacket that this is an authentic text, this unfortunate deletion (which occurs between the first and second paragraphs on p. 256) seriously distorts the consistency of Fanny's methods of narration. The Olympia Press edition, while based on a nineteenth-century version, is substantially complete, however, although marred by misprints.

[4] Subsequent high-minded attempts to recapture this spirit have usually failed. Thus Restif de la Bretonne's anti-Sade pornography is tedious and, to me, hateful, although programmatically lighthearted. And even here, the obsessive incestuous motif is another matter entirely.

[5] The second volume of *Memoirs of a Woman of Pleasure* appeared in February, 1749. Nine months later, a warrant was issued for the author, printed and publisher. Cleland was bound over to appear at the King's bench, but no subsequent punitive action was taken. Cleland's letter to a Mr. Stanhope, perhaps an underling of the Under-Secretary of State, acknowledges authorship and repents of it, but argues that to prosecute the book is to give it publicity. He wonders that "it could so long escape the vigilance of the Guardians of the Public Manners, since nothing is truer, than that

more Clergymen bought it, in proportion, than any other distinction of men." The expurgated version, a year later, was again prosecuted after only two weeks, but again, there was no sentence. This letter was kindly shown to me by Mr. David Foxon of the British Museum.

B. Slepian and L. J. Morrissey (essay date 1964)

SOURCE: "What Is *Fanny Hill?*" in *Essays in Criticism,* Vol. XIV, No. 1, January 1964, pp. 65-75.

[*In the following essay, Slepian and Morrissey defend* Memoirs of a Woman of Pleasure *as a work of literature, arguing that as such, it is a novel of education and intentionally comic.*]

It is not surprising that the open publication in the United States of John Cleland's notorious **Memoirs of a Woman of Pleasure**—or **Fanny Hill,** as it is more commonly known—has resulted in a legal battle to suppress the book. What is strange is that although enlightened opinion uniformly held that *Lady Chatterley's Lover* and *Tropic of Cancer* were works of considerable literary value, there has been no such agreement as to the purpose or worth of the **Memoirs.** Even Mr. John Ciardi, poet, editor of the *Saturday Review,* and long time defender of banned books has announced that Cleland's novel is simple pornography. Although **Memoirs of a Woman of Pleasure** was first published so long ago as 1749 and although it has been continuously—if clandestinely—popular, it has never been subjected to serious critical scrutiny. We think that by a study of the novel's structure, themes, and especially its rhetoric, it can be proven that the **Memoirs** is not just pornography, but that it has real literary worth.

According to Eberhard and Phyllis Kronhausen in *Pornography and the Law: the Psychology or Erotic Realism and Pornography:* 'The characteristic feature in the structure of "obscene" books is the *build up of erotic excitement* in the course of the text. An "obscene" book may start out with a scene which is only mildly erotic and not highly stimulating. In progression, it will then become "hotter" and "hotter" until the story culminates in the description of the most sensual scenes, which are highly conducive to the arousal of erotic desires.' By this definition, **Memoirs of a Woman of Pleasure** is not hard-core pornography. Cleland does not begin with the simple and progress to the perverted and orgiastic.

Memoirs of a Woman of Pleasure consists of two 'letters' in which Fanny Hill tells of her life as a kept woman and prostitute. The first letter begins with the innocent Fanny falling into the hands of a madam and her jaded assistant, Phoebe, who arouses her homosexually as a preparation for heterosexual experience. While in the house of prostitution, Fanny peeps on two couples in the act of coition. Then, just as the madam is about to market her maidenhead, she falls in love, runs off, and is willingly seduced. After several blissful months, however, her lover, Charles, is forced by his cruel father to leave England; and Fanny, at the mercy of her unscrupulous landlady, must receive the addresses of another man, Mr. H. At first she refuses him, but after he has raped her, she accepts him as a keeper. Upon discovering his infidelity with her maid, a few months later, she seduces his naïve, young serving-man, Will, and pays him for her pleasure. She in turn is discovered by Mr. H., who sends her away. At this point the letter ends. Without a doubt the most sexually stimulating episodes in this letter are those at the very beginning when Fanny is in the house of prostitution. There she experiences and witnesses the kind of sexual variety and perversion that the hard-core pornographer would save for later. The episodes with Charles, Mr. H., and even Will are anticlimatic by comparison.

At the beginning of the second letter, Fanny goes to work at Mrs. Cole's genteel house of prostitution, where Emily, Harriet, and Louisa, the three other members of the 'sisterhood', treat her to tales of their loss of maidenhead. Then Cleland describes a variety of sexual and emotional experiences. First, the four girls and four young men have an orgy. Then, Fanny, by now an experienced prostitute, feigns a second maidenhead and gulls a dissipated customer. Next, she enjoys being treated like a common tavern whore by a drunken sailor. She is involved in flagellation and fetishism. She is told about and later witnesses male homosexuality. She helps Louisa seduce an idiot boy, 'good natured Dick'. After all this perversion, Fanny returns to more normal activity at a sexual picnic on the banks of the Thames. When Mrs. Cole closes her establishment, Fanny moves to the suburbs, where she meets a wealthy, elderly gentleman, who soon dies and leaves her his fortune. She travels into the country and is reunited with Charles; they return to the city and marry. The book ends. Once again it is apparent that *Memoirs of a Woman of Pleasure* has not the structure of hard-core pornography. The pornographer would put much earlier the tales of lost innocence with which the second letter opens. And the orgy, which follows immediately, he would put at the very end. The description of fetishism and homosexuality is not at all salacious. And the last three episodes, with their return to normality, moderation, and marriage, certainly suggest that the book is not just pornography. On the contrary, this is the conventional ending of the eighteenth century novel.

The real purpose of the structure of *Memoirs of a Woman of Pleasure* is what it is in any novel: to develop and reinforce theme. This novel has three important recurring themes. Cleland argues for the value of

experience, the value of reason and self-control, and the value of love. Because these themes are interrelated, they cannot be discussed entirely separately.

Memoirs of a Woman of Pleasure is a novel about the loss of innocence and the gaining of knowledge through experience. Descriptions of the loss of sexual innocence are frequent: Fanny, Will, Emily, Harriet, Louisa, and Dick all lose theirs. Because Cleland keeps returning to the subject, he gives it symbolic value: it seems to stand for loss of nonsexual innocence as well. At the beginning of the novel Fanny is a virgin in more ways than one. She does not know the value of money: eight guineas and seventeen shillings is an inexhaustible fortune. She cannot distinguish the tawdry from the elegant and so cannot recognize the face of vice: she mistakes the procuress and madam, Mrs. Brown, for a fine lady. As she tells us early in the book, she is easily corrupted because her 'native purity . . . had taken no root in education' (p 61).

In the course of the first letter, because she remains naïve, her character degenerates. At the beginning she is just an innocent country girl. Although she and Charles are in love, their relationship is illicit. Her alliance with Mr. H. is just a matter of sexual appetite. (Fanny considers this episode her 'first launch into vice'—p. 123.) Her seduction of the innocent Will is the act of an abandoned woman. And her paying him makes her no better than the bawd she had seen paying a young horse-grenadier earlier. Fanny's trouble up to this point is that although she has lost her sexual innocence she has not lost her non-sexual naïveté. Only when she comes to Mrs. Cole's at the beginning of the second letter does her character begin to regenerate. The division of the book into two parts is thus functional. The first shows the loss of sexual innocence and the decay of character; the second the loss of naïveté and the restoration of character. Fanny learns through experience that both kinds of innocence are dangerous, and so at the very end of the novel we learn that she has had her son initiated into the ways of the world in a most unusual manner:

> You know Mr. C*** O***, you know his estate, his worth, and good sense: can you, will you pronounce it ill meant, at least of him, when anxious for his son's morals, with a view to form him to virtue, and inspire him with a fix'd, a rational contempt for vice, he condescended to be his master of the ceremonies, and led him by the hand throu' the most noted bawdy-houses in town, where he took care he should be familiarized with all those scenes of debauchery, so fit to nauseate a good taste? The experiment, you will cry, is dangerous. True on a fool: but are fools worth so much attention?

The main thing that Fanny herself learns from experience is the value of reason and self-control. The young girl who 'set all consequences at defiance for the sake of following' her true love, Charles, is far different from the woman 'with self-denial to spare, and not overstrain him' (pp. 81, 294). Fanny becomes a rational pleasurist, one who uses reason to make pleasure more exquisite and more lasting.

Fanny's principal teacher is Mrs. Cole, who 'considered pleasure, of one sort or other, as the universal port of destination, and every wind that blew thither a good one, provided it blew nobody any harm' (p. 236). She taught her girls the 'rare alliance . . . of a necessary outward decency with unbounded secret liberty', and the art of 'reconciling even all the refinements of taste and delicacy with the most gross and determinate gratifications of sensuality' (pp. 162, 164). Mrs. Cole represents the reason that keeps the passions of her girls in check. When Emily 'los[es] sight of Mrs. Cole's cautions', she finds herself in the arms of a male homosexual (p. 251). When Mrs. Cole goes out for the day and leaves Louisa and Fanny in charge, Louisa seduces 'good-natured Dick', the idiot (p. 257). After Fanny's episode with the drunken sailor, Mrs. Cole 'represented so strongly . . . the nature and dangerous consequences . . . that [she] took resolutions never to venture so rashly again' (p. 233).

Eventually, Fanny learns to make her own judgements. She goes beyond her teacher and rejects some of the adventures Mrs. Cole offers her in the underworld of sex. Although she finds flagellation pleasurable, she resolves never to 'resort again to the violent expedient of lashing nature into more haste than good speed' (p. 248). She submits passively to the fetishist, but considers his desires the 'fooleries of a sickly appetite' (p. 249). When she witnesses an act of male homosexuality, she 'burn[s] . . . with rage and indignation' (p. 256). Finally, she says of Louisa's seduction of Dick, 'When women get once out of compass, there are no lengths of licentiousness that they are not capable of running' (p. 257). Fanny has found 'a secret satisfaction . . . in the sacrifice of a few momentary impulses' (p. 250).

With the dissipated Mr. Norbert, Fanny acts as a teacher herself:

> The love I had inspir'd him with bred a deference to me that was of great service to his health: for having by degrees, and with most pathetic representations, brought him to some husbandry of it, and to insure the duration of his pleasures by moderating their use, and correcting those excesses in them he was so addicted to, and which had shatter'd his constitution and destroyed his powers of life in the very point' for which he seemed chiefly desirous, to live, he was grown more delicate, more temperate, and in course more healthy. (pp. 233-234)

When Mr. Norbert leaves Fanny's tutelage for a Bath holiday, he returns to his life of dissipation and dies.

By the time Mrs. Cole closes her establishment, Fanny is ready to move to the suburbs, 'neatly and modestly' furnish a house, and live 'under the new character of a young gentlewoman . . . bounded . . . strictly within the rules of decency and discretion: a disposition in which you cannot escape observing a true pupil of Mrs. Cole' (p. 276). She is fit to be the mistress of the eldely gentleman, whom she calls a 'rational pleasurist'. He is her second and last teacher:

> From him it was I first learn't, to any purpose, and not without infinite pleasure, that I had such a portion of me worth bestowing some regard on; from him I received my first essential encouragement, and instructions how to put it in that train of cultivation, which I have since pushed to the little degree of improvement you see it at; he it was, who first taught me to be sensible that the pleasures of the mind were superior to those of the body; at the same time, that they were so far from obnoxious to, or incompatible with each other, that, besides the sweetness in the variety and transition, the one serv'd to exalt and perfect the taste of the other to a degree that the senses alone can never arrive at. (pp. 278-279)

One symbol of Fanny's coming of age as a rational pleasurist is her attire. The innocent Fanny dresses for her first morning in London 'as clean and as neat as my rustic wardrobe would permit' (p. 36). Mrs. Brown, the inept Madam, clothes her in the 'second-hand finery' of a London prostitute, and her 'little coquette heart flutter'd with joy' (p. 47). When Charles takes her out of the hands of Mrs. Brown, he dresses her in a 'less tawdry flaunting style' (p. 102). Mr. H., her first keeper, lavishes silks and laces upon her (p. 124). Finally, Mrs. Cole, the shrewd madam, teaches her the value of restraint. The dress of Mrs. Cole's girls 'had the more design in it, the less it appeared to have, being in a taste of uniform correct neatness, and elegant simplicity' (p. 162). By the end of her stay at Mrs. Cole's, Fanny can once again pass for an innocent: 'Now most certainly I was not at all out of figure to pass for a modest girl. I had neither the feathers nor *fumet* of a taudry town-miss: a straw hat, a white gown, clean linen, and above all, a certain natural and easy air of modesty' (p. 212). Now, fully experienced, she assumes the guise of innocence, but without rusticity and awkwardness.

A second symbol is her attitude toward money. The innocent who thinks eight guineas an inexhaustible fortune soon learns that lack of money is the root of evil: twice, she must offer herself up physically to avoid debtors' prison. Mrs. Cole teaches her to manage money prudently, so that she leaves with 'eight hundred pounds, . . . exclusive of cloaths, some jewels, some plate' (p. 276). By this time her education is so complete that her last teacher 'trusted' her with an independent settlement and later appointed her 'sole heiress and executrix' (p. 280). At the end of the novel, Fanny is rich. She and Charles and the children live a life of ease and gentility on the fruits of her labours. Fanny has learned the value of reason and self-control.

The other important thing that Fanny learns from her 'whirl of loose pleasures' is the difference between love and lust. She is initiated by a man she loves; at the end she finds and marries him. Her other experiences serve to teach her love's value. For Fanny—and for her creator—love means an immediate and powerful emotional response to the love object, a 'lightning-like impression' (p. 78). When Charles is forced to abandon her, Fanny has fits and miscarries his child. Love also means an enduring response. Frequently, Fanny compares her reaction to Charles with her reactions to her next two lovers, and just before Charles returns, she claims to have kept her heart inviolate. (It must be admitted that Cleland ineptly prepares for Fanny's declaration that 'forgotten him I never had'—p. 281—for up to this point, there is no reference to Charles in the second letter.) True, she has not kept her body inviolate, but for Cleland, mere physical fidelity is comparatively unimportant, just a matter of fate. 'Our virtues and our vices depend too much on our circumstances' (p. 116). Charles, who himself understands the power of circumstances, willingly marries Fanny, knowing all that she has done.

For each of the other men with whom she has a continuing relationship, Fanny comes to feel something akin to love. For Mr. H., who begins by raping her, she eventually has 'a kind of grateful fondness something like love' (p. 124). For Will, whom she seduces, she finally has a 'liking . . . so extreme, that it was distinguishing very nicely to deny that [she] loved him' (p. 151). The rational pleasurist 'touch [es her] heart, by an application to the understanding' (p. 278). But Charles inspires the immediate, enduring, and unmistakable emotion of love. When the naïve, young Fanny first sees Charles, asleep in a cold room with his chest bare, she instinctively wants to protect him. 'But on seeing his shirt-collar unbutton'd, and a bosom whiter than a drift of snow, the pleasure of considering it could not bribe me to lengthen it, at the hazard of a health that began to be my life's concern. Love, that made me timid, taught me to be tender too' (p. 79). The older, worldly-wise Fanny fully comprehends the value of love. She speaks of 'that delicate and voluptuous emotion which Charles alone had the secret to excite, and which constitutes the very life, the essence of pleasure' (p. 289).

The themes of *Memoirs of a Woman of Pleasure* and the structure give the book aesthetic value. So does the rhetoric. Indeed, the rhetorical effects are so striking that it is hard to understand how any attentive reader

can fail to see what Cleland was up to. Cleland had a problem—which he was conscious of—in writing the *Memoirs:* he had to keep the reader from being 'cloy'd and tired with uniformity of adventures and expressions, inseparable from a subject of this sort, whose bottom, or groundwork being, in the nature of things, eternally one and the same, whatever variety of forms and modes the situations are susceptible of, there is no escaping a repetition of near the same images, the same figures, the same expressions' (p. 159). Cleland's solution to this problem was one which causes his book to operate on two levels at once. On one level, Fanny is describing the sexual experiences from which she learns. On another, Cleland, by the wonderful variety in his terminology and metaphor, steps back for a comic look at sex. If the reader is merely titillated by *Memoirs of a Woman of Pleasure,* he is missing Cleland's point.

The most obvious variety is in the synonyms for the male and female organs. Here, Cleland is certainly being comic. The further one progresses in the book, the more one wonders what new variations can remain. The following is a partial list of synonyms for the male organ: 'machine', 'instrument', 'affair', 'capital part', 'weapon', 'grand movement', 'red-headed champion', 'sinew', 'weapon of pleasure', 'engine', 'gristle', 'body', 'member', 'treasure', 'pride of nature', 'masterpiece', 'column', 'truncheon', 'flesh brush', 'nail', 'object', 'play-thing', 'maypole', 'animated ivory', 'manhood', 'the sweet cause of my complaint', 'picklock', 'stretcher', 'rogue', 'battering ram', 'conduit pipe', 'piece of funiture', 'the proud distinction of his sex from mine', 'round, softish, limber, white something', 'king member', 'dear morsel', 'beloved guest', 'forces', 'plenipotentiary instrument', 'materials of enjoyment', 'master member of the revels', 'wedge', 'affairs', 'whitestaff', 'enemy', 'pleasure pivot', 'splitter', 'blind and furious guide', 'master-movement', 'round fillet of the whitest veal', 'steed', 'plant', 'standard of distinction', 'organ', 'handle', 'master-tool', 'battering-piece', 'brute-machine', 'label of manhood', 'piece of machinery', 'staff of love', 'stake', 'favourite piece of manhood', 'scepter-member', 'great seal of love', 'love's true arrow', 'sweet tenant', 'nipple of love'. The list for the female organ is just as long and just as comic.

The almost endless variety in Cleland's other figures of speech is equally amusing. Many of his metaphors for the different aspects of the relationship between the sexes are conventional: hunting, warfare, fire, and eating. But when he works changes on the conventions, they become comic. Within one scene, for example, he elaborates on three of them in new ways: 'Keen on the burning scent of his game, but unbroken to the sport: and, to carry on the figure, who could better THREAD THE WOOD than he, or stand fairer for the HEART OF THE HUNT? . . . This was just asking a person, dying with hunger, to feast upon the dish on earth the most to his palate. . . . Feeling that part of me I might call a furnace-mouth, from the prodigious intense heat his fiery touches had rekindled there, . . . the gleamy warmth that shot from it made him feel that he was at the mouth of the indraught. . . . This bred a pause of action, a pleasure stop, whilst that delicate glutton, my nether mouth, as full as it could hold, kept palating, with exquisite relish, the morsel that so deliciously ingorged it' (pp. 146-148).

Just as frequent, but somewhat less conventional, are the metaphors drawn from business, riding, and the theater. Words like 'tragedize', 'act', 'play', 'scene', 'actor', 'curtain', 'parts', 'benefit', 'cue', and 'promptership', used in such a context, would have amused Cleland's audience. If the modern reader sometimes misses the joke, it is perhaps because the playhouse is now further from the bawdyhouse. The business metaphors are of course particularly appropriate to the kind of sexual activity that Fanny engages in. She is not advised to gather her rosebuds while she may but 'to make your market while you may' (p. 113). Mrs. Cole, like a good Whig, 'delighted . . . in encouraging a brisk circulation of trade for the sake of the trade itself' (p. 157). The riding metaphors are equally appropriate. Talk abounds of steeds and bridles, of mounting, giving the spur, and keeping the saddle, and even of 'leaning forward and turning the crupper' (p. 247).

There are many other less frequently used metaphors. Part of Cleland's success in achieving comic variety stems from his ability to describe sex figuratively by drawing on such disparate things as music, religion, colleges, cockpits, nunneries, oceans, hermits, and the barnyard.

With one of his metaphors, Cleland is up to two tricks at once. Much of his landscape imagery is parody of the contemporary poetic and pictorial interest in the sublimity of nature. When a writer described the body of a prostitute with such phrases as 'luxuriant tracts of animated snow', 'white cliffs', 'narrow vale', 'embowered bottom-cavity', and 'delightful vista' (p. 199), a mid-eighteenth century reader, thinking of Thomson and Young, must have smiled.

Another especially clever kind of rhetorical trickery is Cleland's suiting of his metaphors to the occupations or backgrounds of some of Fanny's sex partners. When Fanny is attempted by a businessman, Cleland uses the jargon of business: 'bargain', 'sale', 'contract', 'premises', and 'possession' (pp. 48-53). When she makes love with a sailor, the imagery is nautical: 'seiz'd me as a prize', 'towed along as it were by this man-of-war', 'fell directly on board me', 'system of battery', 'any port in a storm', 'altering . . . his course', 'perfectly floated those parts, and drown'd in a deluge', and 'warm broadside' (pp. 230-232). Cleland uses the same kind of device in describing the horse-grenadier, Mr. H., and Will (pp. 63-65, 119-129, 130-133).

If one is still unconvinced that Cleland's intentions are comic, the proliferation of puns should dispel any doubts. From the beginning, when Fanny promises 'Truth! stark, naked truth', to the end, when she tacks on a 'tail-piece of morality', double meanings abound. Only the obtuse can read in context 'taking pleasure by its right handle', 'examining the bottom of things', 'shallow expedient', 'snug into port', 'pregnant circumstances' and the like without laughing.

The rhetoric, theme, and structure of the **Memoirs** give it some genuine literary merit. Any book that can be read in as many ways as this one can is not just pornography. Judges and reviewers can be wrong: those who were merely titillated would do well to look again. **Memoirs of a Woman of Pleasure** deserves to be read as carefully as John Cleland wrote it.

Leonie Kramer (essay date 1964)

SOURCE: "Matters of Sex," in *Quadrant,* Vol. VIII, No. 1, April-May 1964, pp. 49-52

[*In the following essay, Kramer argues that, contrary to the view of its supporters,* Memoirs of a Woman of Pleasure *(*Fanny Hill*) does not meet literary criteria but is instead mere pornography born of Cleland's financial troubles.*]

'If you do me then justice, you will esteem me perfectly consistent in the incense I burn to Virtue. If I have painted Vice in all its gayest colours, if I have deck'd it with flowers, it has been solely in order to make the worthier, the solemner sacrifice of it to Virtue.' So speaks Fanny Hill in her final peroration to the virtuous reader, who (with a reviewer's conscience) has pursued her through all the mazes of Vice in order to arrive at this edifying revelation. So speaks too, it would appear, Mr Peter Quennell, who in his evidence before the Bow Street Court, declared that 'as far as the book has a moral, it is that love is the justification and the crown of sexual activity'. What a strange, hesitant and Puritanical plea for a book which I hope no self-respecting critic would even consider reviewing, were it not for the fact that it raises certain general questions upon which even those people most decisive in other spheres hesitate to express themselves with conviction.

But to return to Mr Quennell. He found, too, that Fanny Hill (virtuous maiden) would have been horrified by Lady Chatterley. Perhaps it is worth remarking at this point that in the introduction to the American edition of the book Fanny Hill is invited to meet Christine Keeler—an association which seems altogether more appropriate and plausible than the one suggested by Mr Quennell [British Member of Parliament.] But there is some comfort to be derived from his evidence. He goes on record as agreeing that *Fanny Hill* deals explicitly with 'matters of sex'. To that opinion at least one can attach a resounding amen.

So much, at the moment, for Bow Street. It is even more instructive to turn to Judge Klein, Justice of the New York State Supreme Court, and to attend to his summary of the tests applied to *Fanny Hill.* There is, of course, the moral test (lightly touched upon by Mr Quennell); there is the literary test, and there is the 'social value' test. Louis Untermeyer, writer, poet, critic (and editor of an anthology of erotic poetry), testified that *Fanny Hill* contains the three great attributes of a good novel. To quote from the case, these are '(1) treatment of the subject matter with grace and beauty; (2) skilful and eloquent charm of writing; and (3) characters coming to life'. Mr Untermeyer characterized the book as a 'work of art'. It is recorded that 'plaintiffs did not produce a single literary expert to rebut the foregoing testimony'. It would be gratifying to think that at the time all literary experts were engaged upon their legitimate business—the examination of works of literary merit—and that they were able to spare no time for the 'memoirs of a lady of pleasure'.

Then there is the 'social value' test. The Court found that 'the book herein sought to be suppressed is an historical novel of literary value'. Here, to judge by the summary of proceedings, logic deserted the case. Mr Eliot Fremont-Smith, an editor of the review section of the New York Sunday *Times,* testified that 'with respect to the depiction of the act of sex, the book involved in this action does not exceed the limits of candour which have been established by the publication and acceptance of books sold through reputable bookstores and reviewed through reputable publications during the past several years'. What this has to do with the 'social value' test, and in what sense it may be supposed to support a view of *Fanny Hill* as 'an historical novel of literary value', is certainly beyond my powers to discover.

There is a final test, the 'prurient interest' test, in examination of which one is referred, with coincidental irony, to a case dignified by the title. 'Manual Enterprises v. Day, 370 U.S., 478'. Under this test, we are told, *Fanny Hill* cannot be regarded as offensive 'in the light of CURRENT community standards'. We are reminded that the novel has been in surreptitious circulation since its publication, and has been translated into every major European language. It is to be found in the British Museum and the Library of Congress. Benjamin Franklin is said to have owned a copy; in the New York Public Library is a copy which once belonged to Governor Samuel J. Tilden. *Fanny Hill* certainly does not lack referees. Then comes the extraordinary statement that were this book merely 'hard core

pornography', 'dirt for dirt's sake' or 'dirt for money's sake', 'it is extremely doubtful that it would have existed these many years under the aforementioned circumstances'.

In the last resort, of course, one can turn to facts. For John Cleland *Fanny Hill* was without doubt dirt for money's sake. Little is known about him, but what is known suggests that his career was both erratic and suspect. He had a diplomatic post in Smyrna, then went to Bombay, which he left after some kind of dispute with the residents. He wandered the continent and returned in poverty to England in 1749. In that year he wrote *Fanny Hill,* which is alleged to have brought him in £10,000—a remarkable sum for those days. For publishing it he was summoned before the Privy Council. A nineteenth century biographer suggests that he might more appropriately have been made to stand in the pillory. A pension was conferred upon him, perhaps to discourage him from bringing out a sequel to *Fanny Hill;* he wrote a few plays and philological work distinguished by its bad spelling. Mr Quennell was right on at least one point. Cleland, he announced, was a 'minor writer'.

The arguments from the New York case set out the three main lines which have been, and perhaps must be followed in a dispute of this kind. One can attempt to justify a doubtful book on moral, literary or sociological grounds. In the case of *Fanny Hill,* let me say at once, all these arguments seem to me untenable. It is true that on page 247 Fanny declares herself somewhat tardily for Virtue. But listen to her own inimitable accent, and judge its sincerity, not to mention its literary quality: 'The paths of Vice are sometimes strew'd with roses, but then they are for ever infamous for many a thorn, for many a canker-worm: those of Virtue are strew'd with roses purely, and those eternally unfading ones.' I find it impossible to see how any attentive reader of *Fanny Hill* could accept this pious conclusion at its face value, still less describe the moral of the book in Mr Quennell's generous terms. For the facts of the book are plainly at variance with the interpretation placed upon them.

The story of *Fanny Hill* is admirably summed up in the words of the music-hall song 'She was poor but she was honest'. Fanny, born in a little village near Liverpool, comes to London at the age of fifteen in the company of a young woman of that city who offers her protection. On arrival in London Fanny finds herself deserted, and the result of her appeal to a stranger to help her find board and lodging is her installation in a brothel. Here she is without much delay introduced to the art (and craft) of 'love'.

From this point in the narrative onwards, any notion that we are to sympathise with Fanny for arriving in a cruel, immoral world, or that we are to regard her as the innocent victim of men's brutality, simply cannot be entertained. She embarks on the loss of her innocence with eagerness and alacrity. At first she is merely a spectator; she witnesses and describes in ruthless detail the performances of others. (This is a characteristic Fanny never loses. Even when she has accumulated a vast fund of experience she is still given to peeping and staring at the embraces of her colleagues.) Then she is seduced by the young man, who, we are invited to believe, supplies the supposed moral of the book. Charles is Fanny's first, and she insists, only true lover. For eleven months she leads, we are told, a blissful existence with him. Then he vanishes completely, having been conveniently sent abroad on a voyage. Fanny goes through agonies of grief, but it is not long before she is engaged on the busy life of 'a woman of pleasure'. For the rest of the novel (and this is by far the greater part of it) consists of a recital of Fanny's own experiences with a variety of clients, and of her observation of the performances of her friends. Every single episode is described with the utmost particularity; not a detail is spared.

Cleland resorts to some obvious tricks in order to spin out the story and multiply the incidents. One whole section, for example, consists of a conversation between Fanny and several other young women of her 'house', in the course of which each in turn tells the story of her defloration. But most significant is the fact that every episode is related by Fanny with the greatest zest. She swoons, sighs and enthuses over the delights of 'love'; she apostrophizes in the most absurd and extravagant terms the physical attributes of her partners; and with mock-modesty she draws attention to her own charms. And after all this, after an extensive hymn of praise to lust, perversion and plain nastiness, we are invited to believe that, when Charles unexpectedly returns, and Fanny shares *his* bed for a change, she rediscovers 'true love'. *Their* transports we are not to confuse with those of Fanny's successful career; though in fact there is nothing to distinguish Charles's performance (except perhaps its virility), nor Fanny's enjoyment of it, from any of her other engagements in the book. It would take more than Fanny's summing up to convince any rational person of the validity of her moral. In describing her fortunate reunion with Charles she announces, 'Thus, at length, I got snug into port, where, in the bosom of virtue, I gather'd the only uncorrupt sweets: where, looking back on the course of vice I had run, and comparing its infamous blandishments with the infinitely superior joys of innocence, I could not help pitying, even in point of taste, those who, immers'd in gross sensuality, are insensible to the so delicate charms of VIRTUE, than which even PLEASURE has not a greater friend, nor than VICE a greater enemy'. Innocence, indeed! And the 'delicate charms of VIRTUE'. Passages such as these, together with Fanny's performances throughout the novel, add up to only one word—hypocrisy. Like those of her predecessor

Moll Flanders, Fanny's morals are dictated by expediency; her words and deeds are totally unrelated to each other.

The literary argument for *Fanny Hill* has no more to recommend it than the moral one. The statement quoted earlier that if the book were mere pornography it would not have existed for so long under circumstances of surreptitious publication is of course ridiculous. It is precisely in these circumstances that a book such as this is likely to survive; and *Fanny Hill* is not the only example of a work which has gone on quietly circulating, though officially it does not exist. But of more concern is Mr Untermeyer's testimony concerning 'the three great attributes of a good novel'. Firstly, he demands treatment of the subject matter with grace and beauty. It is difficult without quotation to show just how untenable this argument is; and I must content myself with stating categorically that the treatment of the subject matter in this novel is, in my opinion, designed only to stimulate a morbid interest in more-or-less normal sexual activities and in perversions. Grace and beauty are irrelevant considerations for the reader, as they were, I have no doubt, for the writer.

Mr Untermeyer's claim for the 'skilful and eloquent charm of writing' is easier to illustrate. In fact, *Fanny Hill* is written in a particularly heavy and turgid prose, which no competent stylist of the period could possibly have approved. It is a kind of eighteenth-century journalese, full of clichés and extravagant but essentially hackneyed images. When Charles and Fanny are reunited, Charles lays 'the broad treasures of his manly chest close to my bosom, both bleating with the tenderest alarms'. What would Swift, with his passion for the right words in the right order, have said to this sentence: 'Thus happy, then, by the heart, happy by the senses, it was beyond all power, even of thought, to form the conception of a greater delight that what I was now consummating the fruition of'? Even Dr Johnson at his most rhetorical would have laughed Cleland's efforts to scorn.

Finally, Mr Untermeyer testified to the characters coming to life. But, of course, there are no characters. The book is crammed with bodies with labels—Charles, Fanny, Phoebe, Harriet, and so on. They are suitably paired off and set to work for the reader's titillation; but as characters properly understood they simply do not exist. They might as well be animals on a stud farm. Nor, of course, are they intended to exist. Cleland is concerned with actions, not with the people who perform them; all his inconsiderable talents are devoted to the purpose of pornographic detail.

The 'social value' argument, it seems to me, can be dismissed briefly. I cannot imagine what any student of eighteenth century life would hope to learn from

Fanny Hill, except, admittedly, a good deal of repetitive information about female underclothes. Again a useful point of comparison is *Moll Flanders.* In Defoe's novel the account of the abundant life of petty criminals in London is as important and certainly as interesting as Moll's career. The book has the same kind of environmental life as do the novels of Dickens. The world of houses, streets, and crowds is real and accurately observed. But social background and *mis en scène* is no more important in *Fanny Hill* than it is in the *Decameron.* Nothing could be less appropriate to the text than the illustrations from Hogarth's *The Harlot's Progress* which adorn the American edition. Hogarth has precisely what Cleland lacks—acute observation of social conditions and a point of view.

So my final judgment on *Fanny Hill* is that it is without doubt in intention and design a pornographic book. I do not accept the view that pornography can be literature and vice versa. The impulse and intention of a pornographic work is, I believe, not only to shock by crudity, but actually to stimulate feelings of a prurient kind. When Cleland describes Fanny Hill's mounting sexual excitement as she watches the engagement of two 'lovers' he hopes to produce in his reader the effect that he is describing in his heroine. This kind of aim has nothing to do with literature. A good story from the *Canterbury Tales* or *Decameron* can be frank, or even coarse and vulgar; but its direction is entirely different. One is invited by Chaucer and Boccaccio to look at the absurdities and anomalies and hypocrisies of human beings, not to stare with concentrated attention at a restricted area of the human anatomy.

For these reasons, all the arguments which have been advanced in defence of *Fanny Hill* seem to me specious. I can find little virtue in the system of censorship which at present operates in this country; at the same time I think the opponents of all forms of censorship have not faced the issues which are raised by the publication of a book such as this. It is produced in enormous editions and sold cheaply; its appearance is accompanied by a positive storm of publicity. Apparently responsible people lose their heads over a deservedly neglected work which falsely lays claim to historical interest, and which would certainly not be published by a reputable firm if it were written today. Less responsible people—such as the publishers of the American edition—assert that Fanny Hill's experiences 'contain little more than what the community has already encountered on the front pages of many of its newspapers' in the reporting of the Profumo affair—an assertion which in itself is entirely false, and which would be no defence of *Fanny Hill* if it were true.

How John Cleland would laugh if he could witness the uproar that his book has caused yet again! He would, no doubt, fully appreciate the conclusion of his American publishers: 'And so, after being an outcast for more than 200 years, Fanny Hill has finally been made an honest woman, or at least as honest as Christine Keeler'. There could be no more substantial proof that the reason why Cleland wrote the book in 1749 is the reason why it has been published again in 1963, and is being so strenuously fought for. It is an ironical reversal of Fanny's fictional role. She may have been a kept woman, but she also has the satisfaction and distinction of keeping her publishers on her immoral earnings.

Myron Taube (essay date 1968)

SOURCE: "*Moll Flanders* and *Fanny Hill:* A Comparison," in *Ball State University Forum,* Vol. 9, No. 2, Spring 1968, pp. 76-80.

[*In the following essay, Taube compares Cleland's whore biography with Daniel Defoe's* Moll Flanders, *considering Cleland's novel more successful as pornography because it is less engaged with the realities of eighteenth-century life and presents scenes of idealized sexual fantasy.*]

Lionel Stevenson has pointed out that one ancestor of *Fanny Hill* is Richardson's *Pamela,* and that the pornography of *Fanny Hill* derives from what Coleridge called the "so oozy, so hypocritical, praise-mad, canting, envious, concupiscent" parts of Richardson's mind.[1] But *Fanny Hill* has even closer relations to the criminal literature of the early eighteenth century, particularly Defoe's *Moll Flanders.* Fanny and Moll are both orphaned young—Moll in childhood, Fanny in adolescence; both come to London to make their fortunes; both are seduced early; both are prostitutes who aspire to gentility; both are united with an earlier favorite; both find financial security as a result of an earlier sexual escapade—Fanny because of her affair with the "rational pleasurist," Moll as a result of her marriage to her brother. True, the epistolary form and the sleazy morality may have come from Richardson, but the pattern of Fanny's life came from Defoe, and the treatment of the material was a revolt against what Defoe stood for.

Fanny, like Moll, is in the picaresque tradition. But while Moll is a picaro engaged in the rough and tumble business of living, Fanny is a sexual picaro who, like Defoe's Roxane, stays in the upper middle class and moves from one sexual experience to another. Yet Moll and Roxane seem rounder, fuller, more alive than Fanny. They have more interests, more activities, even more emotions. Moll has doubts, fears, worries; Fanny has only orgasms and transports. Fanny is much more consistent and of a piece than Moll, but less complex. Moll is engaged in the serious business of life; Fanny is playing a game of musical beds.

Indeed, the most obvious difference between *Fanny Hill* and *Moll Flanders* is a quality that marks all hardcore pornography: the element of unreality, of exaggeration, of illusion. Defoe is so immersed in the real world that the real world is part of his style. He writes of facts and figures, of pounds and shillings. He gives three different itemized bills for three different grades of confinement;[2] a stolen item

> "was a peice [sic] of fine black lustring silk, and a peice of velvet; the latter was but part of a peice of about 11 yards; the former was a whole peice of near 50 yards; it seems it was a mercer's shop that they had rifl'd; I say, rifled, because the goods were so considerable that they had lost; for the goods that they recover'd were pretty many, and I believe came to about six or seven several peices of silk."
> (P. 170)

Never far beneath the surface is harshness and brutality. The world of *Moll Flanders* is the real world of Newgate and transportation. *Fanny Hill* is an attempt to escape this brutality. The world of *Fanny Hill* is a never-never land of well-bred gentlemen and elegant whores; it is a fairytale world of golden lads and rose-lipped maidens presided over by good fairies who are madams. The four-couple orgy at Mrs. Cole's brothel, with its formal setting, its introductory autobiographies, its delicate obscenities, has all the artificial elegance of a minuet.[3] The two-couple romp in the country comes out of the highly artificial pastoral convention (pp. 190-95). Indeed, almost all the descriptions of the characters—their delicate "blushes and confusions" (p. 135), nipples that are "sweetest buds of beauty" (p. 133), their "smooth polish'd snow-white skin" and "ruby-nippled globes" (p. 193)—have a certain China doll quality. We accept Peter Quennell's remark that *Fanny Hill* "is the product of a luxurious and licentious, but not a commercially degraded, era" (p. xiv), but we see that it is really an attempt to avoid the age, to escape the restrictions of the age by fleeing to a wonderworld of sexual permissiveness. Mr. Norbert leaves Fanny "a sum far above the state of his fortune" (p. 164); her "rational pleasurist" leaves her with "a genteel, independent settlement." (P. 200) How much was she left? We don't know. Moll would have told us, so also would have Roxane. But *Fanny Hill* is an attempt to flee from the commercial world in which Moll and Roxane—and Defoe—were immersed.

While both Moll and Fanny are picaresque prostitutes, their attitudes toward sex and life differ greatly. Moll is *homo economicus;* Fanny is *homo sexualis.* Fanny measures success or failure by the quality of her sexual experiences: the intensity and number of her orgasms. And since Cleland is interested only in sexual excitation, measurement by genitalia and orgasm are central to the success of the novel. For Fanny, sex is an end in itself; her measure of man is the amount of pleasure he gives, usually in proportion to the size of his phallus. Indeed, there is something democratic in her disregard of class or rank:

> at my age, and with my taste for pleasure, a taste strongly constitutional to me, the talent of pleasing, with which nature has endowed a handsome person, form'd to me the greatest of all merits; compared to which, the vulgar prejudices in favour of titles, dignities, honours, and the like, held a very low rank indeed. (P. 94)

The only significance of love for Fanny is that it heightens pleasure. Love is "the Attic salt of enjoyment; and indeed, without it, the joy, great as it is, is still a vulgar one, whether in a king or a beggar; for it is, undoubtedly, love alone that refines, ennobles and exalts it." (P. 210)

For *Moll Flanders,* love and sex play a very secondary role to her primary aim: financial security. For an eighteenth-century woman, the surest way to achieve security was through marriage. But Moll soon finds out that "marriages were here the consequences of politick schemes for forming interests, carrying on business, and that love had no share, or but very little in the matter." (Pp. 59-60)

And here, we believe, is the major difference between the treatment of sex in *Fanny Hill* and *Moll Flanders:* for Fanny the sexual experience is central; it alone exists, and any intrusion from the outside world, the ugly world, is rejected. After Fanny has her contact with the sailor, Mrs. Cole rebukes her for being so careless about risks to her health, as though inside the brothel is security and peace, while outside is pregnancy and disease. Cleland's descriptions of the physical are florid, pseudo-poetic, unreal. He is very careful, for example, to emphasize the sexual aspects of Fanny's first seduction: it begins with an introduction to manual stimulation, then voyeurism, and finally intercourse. So heightened is Fanny's sensitivity to the physical that she is aware of her own vaginal secretions and of how much semen is ejaculated into her. Moll has no such awareness. Moll is so immersed in the world of social and economic conflicts that she has little awareness of her own sexuality. Since she is interested only in financial, not sexual, success, the sex is an intrusion. She spawns children with as little concern as a guppy. Her first seduction is not sexual but social: it is part of Moll's attempt to rise in the world, a world whose rigid class distinctions were part of the brutality of eighteenth-century life. Defoe avoids any description of the physical act itself. Indeed, Moll has almost no awareness of what happens to her. Her first seduction, the equivalent of which leaves Fanny panting and sighing and groaning in ecstasies, occurs with no heightening of emotion: "I made no more resistance to him, but let him do just what he pleas'd, and as often as he pleas'd." (P. 27) Later, when she is an accomplished whore, Moll goes upstairs with a man to whom she "by little and little yielded to every thing, so that, in a word, he did what he pleas'd with me; I need say no more." (P. 196)

It is precisely here that Fanny would say more. And it is precisely here—in the treatment of sex—that Moll's character is split: for Moll's sexual experiences are not an integral part of her life, but something apart. She can slough off the sex act as something being done to her, rather than something in which she is taking part. And yet, despite the fact that she does not see herself as taking part in an action, Moll continues to moralize about it. Psychologically there are two Molls: one to whom the sex act is done, and one who stands aside and moralizes over it.

The reason for the split in Moll's personality, it seems to me, was the split that existed in Defoe himself. A member of the commercial middle class, a class that measured morality by financial success, Defoe as an artist found himself the spokesman for traditional values that were antithetical to those of a commercial society. Defoe himself could not clearly perceive what was God's and what was Caesar's. As a result, his characters often did things of which he approved as a commercial agent, but of which he disapproved as a moralist. The result was characters who often acted normally but who moralized abnormally; or, characters in whom the actions and the moralizing are not fused, not of a piece. For example, when he finds the bag of gold in the captain's cabin, Robinson Crusoe moralizes over it; he waxes Elizabethan in his *contemptu mundi* sermonizing, but he makes sure to put the gold on the raft to take to the desert island. The same kind of artificial moralizing occurs in *The Fortunate Mistress* when Roxane scruples about letting her "ill-got wealth, the product of prosperous lust and of a vile and vicious life of whoredom and adultery, be intermingled with the honest well-gotten estate of this innocent gentleman."[4] Defoe is not trying to show hypersensitive consciences in action; neither is he trying to show hypocrites in action. Rather, he is unconsciously revealing the split in his own sensibility: the artist in him wanted to go one way; the commercial entrepreneur went another way. Money—either the bag of gold or the wealth accumulated by a life of sin—has no moral value: it is neither good or bad. But Defoe the moralist, the product of the commercial class, must impose the morality from without.

Moll's major concern, like that of the commercial entrepreneur, is financial success. Her fear, like that of the rest of the middle class, was what Carlyle called, "The terror of 'Not succeeding'; of not making money."[5] And this motivation is why sex has nothing to do with Moll: she is concerned with money, and the means of achieving it are irrelevant. When Moll is seduced

for the first time, she moralizes that her vanity has led her astray. But led her astray from what? When she says that her loss of virtue is her "ruin," Moll really means that she did not get a high enough price: "if I had known his thoughts, and how hard he supposed I would be to be gain'd, I might have made my own terms, and if I had not capitulated for an immediate marriage, I might for a maintainance till marriage, and might have had what I would; for he was rich to excess, besides what he had in expectation. But I had wholly abandoned all such thoughts, and was taken up only with the pride of my beauty. . . . " (Pp. 24-25)

Because of the split in Defoe, because of his inability to reconcile the disparate demands of art and of middle-class commercialism, we rarely see Moll as a rounded woman, a woman in whom sexual nature and psychology are integrated. We do see her clearly when she is torn by her triangular relationship with the two brothers, culminating in the remarkable insight, "I never was in bed with my husband but I wished my self in the arms of his brother. . . . In short, I committed adultery and incest with him every day in my desires, which without doubt was as effectually criminal." (P. 53) There are similar moments, but Defoe cannot maintain this depth of perception and sensitivity. In most cases, he inserts between Moll and her sensuality the commercial sensitivity of the merchant-prostitute. For the morality of Moll is a commercial morality: Moll uses her sex as a product and measures her success or failure by the amount she receives. When she is picked up at Bartholomew Fair and is taken to a room, Moll comments. "[A]t first I seem'd to be unwilling to go up, but after a few words, I yielded to that too, being indeed willing to see the end of it, and in hopes to make something of it at last; as for the bed &c, I was not much concerned about that part." (P. 196) Moll's interest here, like Defoe's, is in profit, and had Defoe the artist left her alone, all would have been well. But Moll had to commence moralizing. And the moralizing came not from her, for sex meant nothing to her, but from Defoe. The *real* Moll does not moralize about her sexual nature; she uses it as a commercial product. And this is why Moll is so disturbed when she becomes a thief: being a prostitute, she is part of the great commercial tradition of middle-class England. Sex is part of a commercial transaction: there is a quid pro quo; one buys, one sells. The only immorality is a bad price or damaged goods. But when Moll becomes a thief, the great crisis in her life, she abandons the market place of supply and demand; she sinks to the lowest level a merchant can sink to: the taking of goods without payment.

Attempting to flee this commercial world, Cleland creates a unified and consistent fantasy. In his treatment of sex, Cleland is far more uniformly successful than Defoe. Desiring only to titillate, he produced an eighteenth-century Arcadian fantasy in which the only occupation and only concern is sex—not love, for that would mean involvement. On the other hand, in his attempt to give us the full-length picture of Moll, Defoe failed. Of course he aimed higher; of course he was a more serious artist; but his own inability to reconcile the split in himself between artist and puritan businessman led to a marred portrait of Moll. Yet how much a child of the commercial revolution Defoe is: his is much the same kind of split sensibility that D. H. Lawrence was to make a major theme in his novels.

Notes

1 *The English Novel: A Panorama* (Cambridge, Mass., 1960), p. 99.

2 Daniel Defoe, *Moll Flanders,* ed. James Sutherland (Riverside Edition, 1959), pp. 142-43. All further references are to this edition.

3 John Cleland, *Memoirs of a Woman of Pleasure,* ed. Peter Quennell (New York, 1963), pp. 105-45. All references are to this edition.

4 Daniel Defoe, *Roxana* (New York, n. d.), p. 248.

5 *Past and Present,* Bk. III, Ch. 2.

Leo Braudy (essay date 1970)

SOURCE: "*Fanny Hill* and Materialism," in *Eighteenth-Century Studies,* Vol. 4, No. 1, Fall 1970, pp. 21-40.

[*In the following essay, Braudy suggests that Cleland's* Fanny Hill *was influenced by the materialism that was part of the most advanced philosophic thought of Cleland's time.*]

> . . . I felt every vessel in my frame dilate—The arteries beat all chearily together, and every power which sustained life performed it with so little friction, that 'twould have confounded the most *physical precieuse* in France: with all her materialism, she could scarce have called me a machine—
>
> Laurence Sterne —*Sentimental Journey*

Fanny Hill presents an uncomfortable problem to both the theorist of pornography and the historian of literature; it has too broad a sense of social milieu and literary tradition for the writer interested in describing the "pure" elements of pornography as a literary genre, and it has too much erotic content for the literary historian to treat it with much seriousness. Its world is not so completely "hard core" as are the worlds of those nineteenth-century works that so obviously spring from

it. The atmosphere of *Fanny Hill* is too exuberant and Fanny's character too vital for either to be part of that gray, repetitive world that Steven Marcus has named "pornotopia."

Now that *Fanny Hill* has been generally available for a few years and the first furor of its republication has died down, Cleland's work seems far more central to "above ground" trends in eighteenth-century literature and philosophy than could be previously appreciated. The particular aspect of *Fanny Hill* I would like to explore in this essay is the relation of the novel to the materialism that was part of the most advanced philosophical thought of Cleland's time—the philosophic naturalism more familiarly advocated by Helvétius, d'Holbach, and especially Julien Offray de la Mettrie in his *l'Homme machine.* I would like to entertain the hypothesis that there is some relation between the view of sexuality presented fictionally in *Fanny Hill* and the view of human nature presented in more discursive philosophical form by La Mettrie in *l'Homme machine.* *Fanny Hill* might then be interpreted not only as a polemical attack against Richardsonian ideals of moral and sexual nature, but also as a defense of the materialist view of human nature popularized by the publication of *l'Homme machine* only a little over a year before.[1]

L'Homme machine was published in Leyden late in 1747 and was quickly seized by the authorities. Although it was not immediately known that La Mettrie was the author, the secret came out rapidly and La Mettrie fled Holland in January of 1748, taking advantage of an invitation from Frederick the Great to come to Berlin. Meanwhile, his publisher, Elie Luzac, despite a promise to the authorities to deliver all copies for destruction, succeeded in clandestinely putting out two more editions in 1748. In Europe the book's success was rapid and lasting. It reached England soon after its first appearance. A first translation appeared in 1749 and two more in 1750; the first erroneously ascribed *l'Homme machine* to the Marquis d'Argens, the second and third to La Mettrie.[2]

One difficulty in appreciating the importance of La Mettrie's work is our own lack of sympathy with the idea (or even the hypothesis) that man is essentially a machine. La Mettrie had no such problems. He believed the man-machine hypothesis could be humanistic, liberating, and a support for the uniqueness of the individual; and he says so in *l'Homme machine.* But between us and La Mettrie rises a barrier of interchangeable parts and assembly lines. Our natural response to the word "machine" or "mechanical" is negative. Our mind's eye is clouded with images ultimately derived from Karel Capek's *R.U.R.,* the endlessly identical marching soldiers in totalitarian war machines, or the image originating in eighteenth-century georgic of the machine despoiling the garden. The machine is the robot, and both are inhuman; they neither feel, nor procreate, nor err, nor change. Each is the same as every other machine.[3]

If the word "machine" summons up ideas contrary to our general beliefs about human nature, it is even more inimical to our ideas of the erotic, either in life or literature. Bad sexuality is "mechanical" or "clinical," that is, devoid of life and feeling and emotion. Pornography is bad because it stimulates "mechanistic" responses, that is, responses without the alloy of either mind or will. Many recent theorists of the erotic argue that if, in a post-Freudian world, we recognize the role of sexuality in defining the self, we must also recognize that the erotic impulse is directly opposed to a scientific and materialistic society that stifles and destroys the self.[4]

Such responses will not do for a proper understanding of either La Mettrie or Cleland. The machines La Mettrie invokes are not the repetitive machines of industrialism, but the machines of wonder, like the duck and flute-player of Jacques Vaucanson, or the young writer and organ player of Pierre Jacquet-Droz.[5] In order to appreciate how **Fanny Hill** may have emerged from a philosophical context in which the emphasis on the physiological and mechanical view of human nature was both liberating and individualizing, let us look for a moment at some of the topics discussed by La Mettrie in *l'Homme machine*.

La Mettrie begins his polemic by asserting that neither the Lockeans, nor the Leibnizians, nor the Cartesians have presented a compelling account of the nature of the soul. The true answers, he asserts, are to be found only in those writers who build their knowledge of man on a basis of physical fact; those who proceed from the metaphysical to the physical have caused all the trouble and confusion. The mind and the body, argues La Mettrie, are only different forms of the same substance. Their interconnections prove this. La Mettrie cites example after example of the dependence of the mental on the physical and the control that bodily events can have over the mind. He does not believe that the mental is reducible to the physical; but they are intimately interrelated and always proceed together: "Les divers Etats de l'âme sont donc toujours corrélatifs à ceux du corps" (p. 158). Despite the usually anti-psychological implications of the assertion that man is a machine, the great majority of La Mettrie's observations are directed toward psychological explanation. He argues, for example, that an understanding of normal fear and confusion or abnormal hypochondria and hysteria is impossible if one holds to the Cartesian belief in two separate substances for mind and body, but more feasible if one believes that mind is a more highly organized form of body.[6] Even the ability to innovate in speech, which Descartes reserved for man, must in La Mettrie's hypothesis be an ability that at least in principle can be taught to apes. Language, which La Mettrie defines as the ability to manipulate symbols, is all that separates man from apes, and even that barrier is not insurmountable: "Qu'étoit l'homme, avant l'invention des Mots & la connoissance des Langues? qui avec beaucoup moins d'instinct naturel, que les autres" (p. 162).[7]

How, then, is La Mettrie using a word like "soul"? Writers since Descartes had tended to concentrate on the separate realms of extension and spirit, rather than on that which connected the realms, the soul, situated according to Descartes, in the pineal gland. For this reason, there could be a double tradition of Cartesianism, in which both atheistic and orthodox natural scientists could equally proclaim their discipleship. But La Mettrie is not interested in defining the soul as a spiritual faculty that rules the lower being, or in assigning it to a specific place in the body. Instead, he considers the soul to be the principle of organization that unites body and mind. In *Historie naturelle de l'âme* (1745), he had elaborated the meaning of soul along a more spiritual line. Within *l'Homme machine,* in accordance with his general argument, the concept has become more physicalized. Soul frequently seems coextensive with words like *"organisation," "ressort," "matrice,"* and *"imagination." "Organisation,"* of course, is a general word of connection. Along with *"ressort"* it invokes the Cartesian image of the body as a clock, with La Mettrie's special twist to the basic metaphor: "Le corps humain est une Machine qui monte elle-même ses ressorts; vivante image du mouvement perpetuel" (p. 154). God is not required either as watchmaker or winder:

> . . . l'Ame n'est qu'un principe de mouvement, ou une Partie matérielle sensible du Cerveau, qu'on peut, sans craindre l'erreur, regarder comme un ressort principal de toute la Machine . . . (p. 186).[8]

Imagination and *matrice* are more interesting synonyms for soul. La Mettrie frequently writes as if soul and mind were similar: "L'Ame n'est donc qu'un vain terme dont on n'a point d'idée, & dont un bon Esprit ne doit se servir que pour nommer la partie qui pense en nous" (p. 180). In what Aram Vartanian calls "the first radical rehabilitation of the imaginative faculty in his epoch," La Mettrie then associates thought with imagination. Imagination makes connections, and these connections define man's true knowledge:

> Je me sers toujours du mot *imaginer,* parce que je crois que tout s'imagine, & que toutes les parties de l'Ame peuvent être justement réduites à la seule imagination, que les forme toutes . . . (p. 165).

But La Mettrie's originality does not stop here, for the most fascinating aspect of his use of imagination is its association with *matrice*. Previous metaphors of scientific discovery might invoke images of divine illumination or logical conclusion. La Mettrie's metaphors are most often sexual. Vartanian remarks on the fact that " . . . scientific and erotic curiosity seem for him to function together in a sort of alliance, each serving to strengthen and stimulate the other" (p. 32). And La Mettrie's metaphoric language is allied with his basic theme of the strong interconnection between imagination and sexuality. His metaphor for scientific insight is sexual penetration; his metaphor for the development of ideas is human generation and birth. The imagination is the womb (*matrice*) of ideas, and he calls the mind "cette matrice de l'esprit." *Matrice* as womb and *matrice* as matrix (of ideas) is a double meaning that La Mettrie plays upon throughout *l'Homme machine*. In one section, for example, he argues that organization is the first merit of man, and then must come education:

> Il est aussi impossible de donner une seule idée à un Homme, privé de tous les sens, que de faire un Enfant à une Femme, à laquelle la Nature auroit poussé la distraction jusqu'à oublier de faire une Vulve, comme je l'ai vu dans une, qui n'avoit ni Fente, ni Vagin, ni Matrice, & qui pour cette raison fut démariée après dix ans de mariage (p. 167).[9]

The association La Mettrie makes between sexuality and imagination, between sexual penetration and scientific insight, calls into question the traditional role to which sexuality had been assigned by philosophers. The earlier attitude emphasized the opposition between the cognitive operations of the mind and the distracting and trivial operations of the body. In more extreme though still familiar terms, sexual motives impelled the search for forbidden knowledge, the realm of evil and the devil. The body in general and sexuality in particular worked against man's effort to achieve wisdom and transcendence.[10]

La Mettrie uses sexual examples as well as sexual metaphors. Sexuality is so important in his language because it is central to his philosophy. If man has achieved so much more than animals because of his larger brain, he has concomitantly lost in instinct what he has gained in organization and understanding. Man must relearn his instincts in order to live fully and most humanly. And the instincts that need the most relearning are the sexual instincts, because they are so closely allied to the force of imaginative coherence and the exuberance of both physical and mental creativity:

> . . . c'est [l'imagination] encore qui ajoute à la tendresse d'un coeur amoureux, le piquant attrait de la volupté. Elle la fait germer dans le Cabinet du Philosophe, & du Pédant poudreux; elle forme

> enfin les Savans, comme les Orateurs & les Poetes (pp. 165-166).

> Mais si le cerveau est à la fois bien organisé & bien instruit, c'est une terre féconde parfaitement ensemencée, qui produit le centuple de ce qu'elle a reçu (p. 167).

La Mettrie's emphasis on sexuality and the idea of the body as machine is for him, as for many who followed his ideas, a liberation from theories of the inferiority of body to mind and from the neo-Cartesian orthodoxy that accepted the mechanical nature of the physical world but reserved final respect and adoration for the realm of spirit and soul. The true view of man, asserts La Mettrie, emphasizes both his physical and mental nature. Each man-machine is for him unique. Once the machine hypothesis has restored to man his human nature, political or social tyranny based on man's "divine part" will vanish.

Cartesian dualism furnished a philosophical foundation for physiological research. But the postulate of the two separate substances of body and spirit allowed the same metaphysical distrust of the body that had always existed. La Mettrie's machine hypothesis allows the body a dignity to equal the mind's. Instead of man being a Hamlet crawling between heaven and earth or a Gulliver whose disgust with his "lower" self finally leads him to reject the human race, La Mettrie's man, his mind and body part of the same being, could now rise even higher. "Pourquoi faire double ce qui n'est evidemment qu'un?" Like human beings in sexual intercourse the body and mind "se reunissent toutes suivant leur nature." "L'âme et le corps s'endorment ensemble," La Mettrie writes in another place. What more appropriate transition to *Fanny Hill?*

. . . . .

Much more factual information must be discovered about Cleland's life before any question of the direct influence of *l'Homme machine* on *Fanny Hill* can be resolved. Cleland's activities before the publication of *Fanny Hill* are vague at best. He was appointed a writer for the East India Company at Bombay on 10 February 1731 and took up official service there on 19 July 1731. He rose steadily in salary and rank, becoming Secretary for Portuguese Affairs, and later Secretary to the Bombay Council in January of 1739. He left Bombay sometime about 20 September 1740 and arrived back in England shortly before 26 March 1741, when he appeared before the East India Company Board of Directors. Why he left Bombay seems more obscure, although perhaps it was due to reports of the troubles of his father, William, who was a friend of Pope and died 21 September 1741. Cleland's activities until the publication of *Fanny Hill* are less certain. David Foxon reports that the first advertisements for

Fanny Hill he has been able to find are in the *General Advertiser* for 21 November 1748 (volume one) and in the *London Evening Post* for 14-16 February 1749 (volume two). But according to the records of the Beggar's Benison Society of Anstruther, Scotland, a work called *Fanny Hill* was read at a gathering in 1737.[11]

The special relation I would argue between *Fanny Hill* and the views of La Mettrie (including the actual use of the phrase "man-machine") is strong proof against a fully conceived Fanny Hill in 1737.[12] At best, the earlier date, if not spurious, might mark the appearance of a primitive version of the novel's earlier parts. If I might speculate further, perhaps this early version was then laid aside until the appearance of *l'Homme machine* furnished a polemical framework for Cleland's earlier and fragmentary *jeu d'esprit*. The perfunctory structure of the work supports this contention. The novel is divided into two letters, both directed to a female correspondent, to whom Fanny is describing and explaining her life.[13] In the second letter most of what might be called direct references to La Mettrie's ideas appear, although there is not an abrupt shift in attitude from the first to the second parts of the novel. The change, in fact, could be interpreted as part of Fanny's increased awareness.

Perhaps the most striking indication of Cleland's possible assimilation of the principles of philosophic naturalism is Fanny's constant use of the word "machine" to refer to the penis. As far as the OED and Eric Partridge can enlighten us, this usage seems to begin in English with Cleland, and he may also have been a precursor of its usage in French. One could argue that Cleland is only adapting a common military usage ("apparatus, appliance, instrument," reports the OED with a 1650 first reference) to his eighteenth-century version of the Renaissance topos of the siege of love.[14] But Cleland's image derives more directly from Descartes's characterization of the *bête-machine,* to cite the OED again, a being "without life, consciousness, or will." Cleland's usage again seems to be individual and unique, the two references cited in the OED being Robert Boyle's description of beasts (1692) and Alexander Hamilton's of soldiers (1770).[15]

Obviously then Cleland is implying something with his use of "machine" beyond Fanny's practice of elaborate euphemism and elegant variation. Fanny may actually be expressing a genuine wonder at the physiological reality of the human body and the philosophic statement of this reality contained in mechanistic language.[16] In incidents reminiscent of La Mettrie's examples, Fanny realizes that the body can make demands on the mind that the mind cannot resist. When Charles, her first lover (with whom she will be reunited and married at the end of the novel), begins to caress her, "My fears, however, made me mechanically close my thighs;

but the very touch of his hand insinuated between them, disclosed them and opened a way for the main attack" (p. 41). Sexual relations can be the perfect human instance of Cartesian *choc,* the direct collision between entities that defines the causal relations of the universe. But Cleland, like La Mettrie and unlike Descartes, continually emphasizes that, at least in sexual experience, human beings have as little consciousness or will as the *"bête-machine."* Mr. H—, one of Fanny's later lovers, is not so personally appealing as Charles. Yet the effect of intercourse is the same:

> . . . he soon gave nature such a powerful summons down to her favourite quarters that she could not longer refuse repairing thither; all my animal spirits then rush'd mechanically to that center of attraction, and presently, inly warmed, and stirred as I was beyond bearing, I lost all restraint . . . (p. 75).

In her narration, Fanny has an abundance of life and an acute sense of the world around her. She can make satiric comments about London society, briefly and effectively sketching someone she meets. But when sexual excitement begins, she seems to lose both will and self. Is Cleland therefore arguing against La Mettrie and asserting that sexuality is a threat to mind and personality?

In descriptive terms, Cleland does recognize that sexual indulgence invites a loss of self-consciousness and self-control. The body itself, defined in the sexual moment only by its physiological makeup, responds mechanically, like a mere machine. In an important scene in the second letter, Fanny goes along with her friend Louisa, who wants to lure "Good-natured Dick" into their rooms, to see if the half-witted delivery boy had been sexually oversupplied by nature for his mental shortchanging. Fanny, as she does so frequently, will only watch. But Louisa indulges fully, and the effect is more than she anticipated:

> . . . she went wholly out of her mind into that favourite part of her body, the whole intenseness of which was so fervously fill'd and employ'd; there she alone existed, all lost in those delirious transports, those extasies of the senses . . . In short, she was now as mere a machine as much wrought on, and had her emotions as little at her own command as the natural himself . . . (pp. 188-189).

If we take passages like this in purely descriptive terms, Cleland's view of sexuality is close to Richardson's. Both believe that the sexual instinct can be a threat to the control of the mind. For Pamela and Clarissa the loss of chastity threatens the loss of all morality and self-integrity. In this way, Cleland is much closer to Richardson than he is to Fielding, for whom sexuality is neither so momentous nor so problematic.

Cleland therefore proceeds from the same assumption about the importance of sexuality as Richardson. But his conclusions are quite different. Richardson seems to assert that sexuality is a threat from outside the "real" self. Cleland, on the other hand, uses the metaphor of military contest to express the engagement between man and woman rather than the despair of a riven self. Richardson further implies that sexuality is a looming horror from the primitive self that the needs of society and morality should have succeeded in repressing. Like La Mettrie, Cleland presents a more integrative view: instead of being a threat to the mind, the body, when its nature is properly understood, joins with the mind in the total human character. Fanny is fascinated by the physiology of sexual reactions not merely because Cleland wants to stimulate his readers but also because, in the development of her own character, she wants to know. Sexuality is a possible and much neglected way into knowledge of the self. Cleland emphasizes that it is not the only way: Fanny often loses her self-consciousness in the sexual act, but she uses the experience as part of a search for more consciousness. Louisa's transformation into a mere machine seems closely related to her previously expressed belief that her human nature may be thoroughly searched through masturbation:

> Here I gave myself up to the old insipid privy shifts of my self-viewing, self-touching, self-enjoying, *in fine,* to all the means of *self-knowledge* I could devise, in search of the pleasure that fled before me, and tantalized with that unknown something that was out of my reach . . . (p. 125).

Louisa's exclusive preoccupation with her sexuality therefore acts as a foil to Fanny's more comprehensive view.

Perhaps a whimsical answer to the questions "Why pornography in the eighteenth century?" and "Why Fanny Hill?" might involve the relation of the materialist viewpoint to the nature of pornography itself. Cleland may see pornography as another didactic form to stand beside both satire and the novel in the first half of the eighteenth century. Pornography is in fact a surer method. The stimulus of reading a scene in *Fanny Hill* makes in the reader's own nature the point made in the text. The reader may be moved to reconsider the merits of stoicism, reevaluate the powers of the mind to control the body, reread his Descartes, and think again of the dividing line between man and the *bête-machine.* By a species of imitative form, pornography enforces and answers the hypothetical question of La Mettrie:

> N'est-ce pas machinalement qu'agissent tous les Sphincters de la Vessie, du *Rectum* &c.? que le Coeur a une contraction plus forte que tout autre muscle? que les muscles erecteurs font dresser La Verge dans l'Homme, comme dans les Animaux qui s'en battent le ventre; & meme dans l'enfant, capable d'erection, pour peu que cette partie soit irritee? (p. 183).

Despite the loss of self and mental control that Cleland describes, he, again like La Mettrie, does not consider the emphasis on the sexual side of human nature to be reductive. Both Cleland and La Mettrie seem to deny the moral and theological implications in Descartes's association of body and beast: the beast is a machine because it lacks a soul; man without a soul would be a mere beast. Instead they consider their emphasis on the body to be positive and humanizing. In order to understand human nature more fully, one must first understand the sexual and physiological side of it. In her own way Fanny is presenting a program of action to supplement the polemic of La Mettrie's first paragraphs: trust the writers who begin with the body and then move to metaphysics, not those who go the other way. Yet sexuality is only a beginning. Body without mind, in another favorite image from *Fanny Hill,* is like food without savor. In mind lust is transmuted into love, and, as Fanny says, love is "the Attic salt of enjoyment."

Nowhere in *Fanny Hill* is Cleland's commitment to both the man-machine view of human nature and to the dignity that it can restore to the individual more apparent than in the scene in which Fanny and Louisa experiment on "Good-natured Dick." Dick is "withal, pretty featur'd," although his clothes and general appearance are in "so ragged a plight, that he might have disputed points of shew with e'er a heathen philosopher of them all" (p. 184). Dick is "good-natured" and a "natural" in the sense of those words that most interested both La Mettrie and Cleland. Louisa invites him upstairs for his payment and he responds with confusion. Fanny flirts with him, and watches his cheeks begin to glow: "The emotion in short of animal pleasure glar'd distinctly in the simpleton's countenance" (p. 185). When Fanny leads him further, her language emphasizes the natural level at which she aims (and may even allude to La Mettrie's next work *l'Homme plante,* published at Potsdam in 1748):

> My fingers too had now got within reach of the true, the genuine sensitive plant, which instead of shrinking from the touch, joys to meet it, and swells and vegetates under it . . . (p. 185).[17]

Dick's "plant" is no disappointment: "Nature, in short had done so much for him in those parts, that she perhaps held herself acquitted in doing so little for his head" (p. 186). When Louisa initiates further stages of the experiment, both the language and the themes are once again strikingly reminiscent of La Mettrie in *l'Homme machine:*

. . . she presently determined to risk a trial of parts with the idiot, who was by this time nobly inflam'd for her purpose, by all the irritations we had used to put the principles of pleasure effectually in motion, and to wind up the springs of its organ to their supreme pitch; and it stood accordingly stiff and straining, ready to burst with the blood and spirits that swelled it . . . to a bulk! (p. 186).

The "irritations" that Fanny speaks of are not those we commonly call irritations. They are, however, very close to the scientific definition of the principle of irritability that Vartanian asserts is "one of the most original and impressive features of *l'Homme machine*" (p. 20). As Vartanian explains, La Mettrie brilliantly proposed that irritability was "a general property of living substance," even though his examples dealt only with muscular contraction. "Contractility was, in his time, the only experimentally known phase of the irritable process." But La Mettrie's frequent use of erection as an example of mechanism does not seem wasted on Cleland.

A further reflection of La Mettrie's language in this short passage is the phrase, "to wind up the springs of its organ," which implies the metaphor of the body as a clock, held together by *"ressorts."* The final phrase (the ellipsis is Cleland's own) is so close to some lines of La Mettrie, that I am almost willing to drop my tentativeness and assert direct influence. La Mettrie is speaking of the interplay of the muscles and the imagination when the body reacts to the image of beauty,

qui en excite un autre, lequel étoit fort assoupi, quand l'imagination l'a éveillé: & comment cela, si ce n'est par le desordre & le tumulte du sang & des esprits, qui galopent avec une promptitude extraordinaire, & vont gonfler les corps caverneux? (p. 183)[18]

The importance of this scene is not exhausted by the possible parallels I have already mentioned. Louisa leads Dick to bed, "which he joyfully gave way to, under the incitations of instinct and palpably deliver'd up to the goad of desire" (p. 187). The two come together, and the great size of the "master-tool" of the "natural" causes Louisa to cry out in pain.

But it was too late: the storm was up and force was on her to give way to it; for now the man-machine, strongly work'd upon by the sensual passion, felt so manfully his advantages and superiority, felt withal the sting of pleasure so intolerable, that maddening with it, his joys began to assume a character of furiousness which made me tremble for the too tender Louisa (p. 187).

As she has before, Fanny thinks for a moment that the man might be too much for the woman, but Fanny also observes how the awakening of sexual feeling can be ennobling, even for one perhaps too deficient in mind to take advantage of it:

He seemed, at this juncture, greater than himself; his countenance, before so void of meaning, or expression, now grew big with the importance of the act he was upon. In short, it was not now that he was to be play'd the fool with. But, what is pleasant enough, I myself was aw'd into a sort of respect for him, by the comely terrors his motions dressed him in: his eyes shooting sparks of fire; his face glowing with ardours that gave another life to it; his teeth churning, his whole frame agitated with a raging ungovernable impetuosity: all sensibly betraying the formidable fierceness with which the genial instinct acted upon him (p. 187).[19]

In this passage and the descriptions that follow, Cleland adroitly keeps in solution two views of human nature that more frequently separate. Like La Mettrie, he is calling a truce between mechanism and vitalism, almost before the battle has really begun. Dick is the creature solely of his body, "instinct-ridden as he was" (p. 188), and Louisa too under the second onslaught of the "brute-machine" becomes "as mere a machine." The reference to brute-machine seemingly reinforces the reductive aspect of the sexuality. But Fanny has observed also the transfiguration of the half-wit in the grip of sexual passion; he is discovering an essential part of his human nature. There is a vitality and warmth in true sexuality that can liberate human nature, even when neither mind nor reason, soul nor spirit, is sufficient.

Both Fanny and Cleland believe that in the ideal sexual relationship the mind and body have equal share. Fanny's last lover before she is reunited with Charles, her first, is a "rational pleasurist";

. . . he it was, who first taught me to be sensible that the pleasures of the mind were superior to those of the body; at the same time, that they were so far from obnoxious to, or incompatible with each other, that besides the sweetness in the variety and transition, the one serv'd to exalt and perfect the taste of the other to a degree that the sense alone can never arrive at. (pp. 199-200)

Fanny has viewed her own adventures retrospectively through this union of body and mind that allows each its full role. She enjoys sex for its own sake, but her most pleasurable encounters mix body with mind:

. . . what an immense difference did I feel between this impression of a pleasure merely animal, and struck out of the collision of the sexes by a passive bodily effect from that sweet fury, that rage of active delights which crowns the enjoyments of a mutual love-passion, where two hearts, tenderly and truly united, club to exalt the joy, and give it spirit and soul that bids defiance to that end which mere momentary desires generally terminate in, when they die of a surfeit of satisfaction (p. 75).

Such speculations are common for Fanny, "whose natural philosophy all resided in the favourite center of sense," although not for her lover, Mr. H—, "whom no distinctions of that sort seemed to disturb." The "active delights" raise the "passive bodily effect" to full realization in the same way that Fanny's meditation and explanation make sense of her sexual adventures. And, as experience alone is nothing for her without an interpretation of that experience, so it is only in love that the physical and the mental are truly combined. Fanny's love for Charles is "a passion in which soul and body were concentre'd, and left me no room for any other relish of life but love" (p. 62). Her ability to experience as well as to meditate gives a vitality and exuberance to her character that affirms the rehumanizing program behind Cleland's sexual emphasis.

Fanny Hill is therefore much more than a piece of pornography whose only intent is mercenary.[20] In many ways it appears to be a detailed polemic in support of some of the most advanced philosophic doctrines of its time. If one test of a major novel is the extent to which it experiments with and changes the received assumptions of novelistic form, *Fanny Hill* surely qualifies for consideration. Cleland recognizes the unique relationship possible in erotic literature between the reader and the work. In *Fanny Hill* he raises this relationship to the level of artistic consciousness by making it not only a criticism of the Richardsonian epistolary method, but also an exploration of the forces of mind and body in human character. The erotic scenes in *Fanny Hill,* instead of being only stimulating, are both stimulating and an essential part of "the soft laboratory of love" in which Fanny herself mingles the correlative impulses of body and mind. Our view of what Cleland has achieved has become unfortunately clouded, less by the censorship of *Fanny Hill* than by the way in which Cleland has become the victim of his imitators, who repeat scene, motif, and style with no understanding that, when Cleland used them, they were something more than a cabinet of stylized gestures.

Fanny's world is larger than the merely sexual, as she herself is the first to point out. The natural freedom of sexuality also implies a natural world of social relations, which is behind Fanny's jibes at upper-class London life. Cleland here again resembles Richardson in his emphasis on the egalitarian possibilities of sexuality. But, as before, Richardson and Cleland come to opposite conclusions. Egalitarian sexuality is a threat in *Pamela* because it threatens the class lines of society and the social order itself. Like the medieval anti-feminists, Richardson considers the sexual impulse to be primarily reductive, with its origin in the devil. In Richardson's terms, however, the devil is an aristocrat,

and the licentious aristocracy is forfeiting its natural right to rule by allowing a lust that cuts across the barriers of class and upsets the rules of morality. Pamela's marriage to Mr. B. breaks the class divisions in the name of morality, although with the socially subversive implication that morally all human beings are equal.

In Cleland's world of class, it is sexuality that makes all men and women equal. The naked body implies the naked heart. Fanny comments derisively on "the false, ridiculous, refinements of the great," so inferior to the natural and unalloyed joys that can be found with people of lesser rank. Here are the first articulated beginnings of the sexual and moral primitivism that is so much more elaborately developed later in the century. Mr. H—'s servant Will gives Fanny more real pleasure (physical and mental) than Mr. H—'s "loftier qualifications of birth, fortune and sense" (p. 94). La Mettrie may retain his masculine point of view even while praising the exuberant sexual nature that had previously been associated primarily with women. But Cleland through Fanny is transmuted into the first feminist. Fanny may bear a love for Charles so great that she yearns for him in what seems to be a fairly submissive way. But when she discovers him bereft of status and fortune, she likes him even better, "broken down to his naked personal merit" (p. 206).

Since sexuality in Cleland is so invariably part of the natural, one might entertain the idea that a major figure behind the growth of eighteenth-century erotic literature both in England and France is John Locke. In addition to the mechanical metaphor, the most frequent descriptive image in *Fanny Hill* is the *paysage erotisé* or, perhaps more accurately, the *corps paysager*. The natural world of the body is an unspoiled Eden. The girls whom Fanny admires have healthy country looks. Sexuality at Mrs. Cole's establishment is edenic and countrified. Her clients "would at any time leave a sallow, washy-painted duchess on her hands, for a ruddy, healthy, firm flesh'd country maid" (p. 110).

> The authors and supporters of this secret institution would, in the height of their humours, style themselves the restorers of the golden age and its simplicity of pleasures, before their innocence became so injustly branded with the names of guilt and shame (p. 108).

The language of mechanism and the invocation of nature are therefore total complements in *Fanny Hill,* although later pornographic works, in which great machines penetrate mossy grots, have undoubtedly lost this kind of understanding. In line with his attack against the Cartesian assumption that the *bête-machine* was without feeling and his support of La Mettrie's belief in the soul of the man-machine, Cleland seems to reflect Lockean ideas about the purity of natural impulses in the state of nature, and his egalitarian motif also may have Lockean roots. Bolingbroke argued against the Lockean state of nature because natural equality undercut the idea of a hierarchical society. Cleland's natural world of sexuality obviously has similarities to the "pornotopia" that Steven Marcus discovered in nineteenth-century pornography. But Cleland's sexuality is related to a vital social and cultural context, however ideal it may be, whereas "pornotopia" remains hermetic and self-justifying. "Pornotopia" may be defined, in fact, as the innovations of *Fanny Hill* forced by censorship and by familiarity into dull repetition, the unique machine now turned out by assembly-lines.

Cleland invokes the natural body and the natural landscape in a deliberately natural use of language. Fanny is conscious of language as a problem, excuses herself "for having, perhaps, too much affected the figurative style," and apologizes to her correspondent:

> I imagined, indeed, that you would have been cloy'd and tired with uniformity of adventures and expressions, inseparable from a subject of this sort, whose bottom, or groundwork being, in the nature of things, eternally one and the same, whatever variety of forms and modes the situations are susceptible of, there is no escaping a repetition of near the same images, the same figures, the same expressions . . . (p. 105).

To remedy this cloying, Fanny calls upon the "imagination and sensibility" of her correspondent to supplement her work, in a manner very similar to Fielding's demands in *Tom Jones* that the reader fill in his own idea of feminine beauty when Fielding mentions Sophia Western. The inability of words to express the sexual experience either fully or adequately is most apparent when the subject is closest to nature:

> No! Nothing in nature could be of a beautifuller cut; then, the dark umbrage of the downy spring-moss that over-arched it bestowed, on the luxury of the landscape, a touching warmth, a tender finishing, beyond the expression of words, or even the paint of thought (p. 133).

Cleland contrasts the vitality of nature with the corrupt sophistications of society and the spurious niceties of art. Phoebe's labia, Fanny remarks, "vermilioning inwards exprest a small rubid line in sweet miniature, such as *Guido's* touch of colouring could never attain to the life or delicacy of" (p. 37). In the same way Charles's parts are

> surely superior to those nudities furnish'd by the painters, statuaries, or any art, which are purchas'd at immense prices; whilst the sight of them in actual

life is scarce sovereignly tasted by any but the few whom nature has endowed with a fire of imagination, warmly pointed by a truth of judgement to the springhead, the originals of beauty, of nature's unequall'd composition, above all imitation of art, or the reach of wealth to pay their price (p. 54).

Penises are compared to ivory columns and breasts to marble so that their actual superiority to these things of art may be clear: " . . . a well-formed fulness of bosom, that had such an effect on the eye as to seem flesh hardening into marble, of which it emulated the polished gloss, and far surpassed even the whitest, in the life and lustre of its colours, white veined with blue" (p. 136). Once again, a phrase of La Mettrie's in *l'Homme machine* seems apposite, another of La Mettrie's paeans to the imagination:

> Par elle, par son pinceau flatteur, le froid squélette de la Raison prend des chairs vives & vermeilles; par elle les Sciences fleurissent, les Arts s'embellissent, les Bois parlent, les Echos soupirent, les Rochers pleurent, le Marbre respire, tout prend vie parmi les corps inanimés (p. 165).

Many of the themes that I have found in *Fanny Hill* sound much like those usually associated with sentimentalism: the truth of feelings and instincts, the natural as the basic part of human nature, the superiority of nature to art, the inadequacy of language, and social egalitarianism. This is no error. *Fanny Hill* is a storehouse of sentimental themes that achieve full expression and circulation only in the 1760s and 1770s. Cleland looks forward to Sterne, the Smollett of *Humphry Clinker,* and the Diderot of *Le Rêve de d'Alembert* much more than he looks back to Defoe, Richardson, and Fielding. But unlike the self-conscious sentimentality of Sterne or the less self-aware sentimentality of Henry Mackenzie, sentiment in Cleland's *Fanny Hill* moves comfortably in complement to sexuality. La Mettrie's integration of sexuality and imagination and Cleland's of sexuality and sentiment are beautifully articulated accounts of previously inarticulate forces in the human personality. But the balance, at least in English literature, does not seem to last very long. Part of the melancholy in *Tristram Shandy* and the fun in *Sentimental Journey* is the association of Toby's sentiment with his impotence and Yorick's sentiment with his prurience.

As true first-generation philosophers, Cleland and La Mettrie share an optimism about man's ability to deal with his sexual nature once he has recognized it. Sterne deals with the same themes of imagination, sexuality, and sentiment. But for him they have become much more problematic. Toby retreats from his own body and feelings into the artifice of history, the reconstructed Battle of Namur, while Yorick refuses to acknowledge the frequently salacious impulse beneath his sentimental sightseeing. Yorick constantly digs at the materialists. He has emotions that "could not be accounted for from any combination of matter and motion." He is positive that he has a soul despite what the materialists say. But all his philosophy, like that of the misanthropic Matthew Bramble in the first parts of *Humphry Clinker,* seems the projection of his inability to understand the nature of his own body and how it affects his mind and feelings. Mackenzie's *The Man of Feeling* (1771) carries this divorce of "feeling" from physicality even further. Sterne makes the difficult relation between emotions and bodily feeling part of his theme. But Mackenzie indicates that the highest form of feeling has no physical dimension whatsoever. The purity of the emotional relationship between Harley, his hero, and Miss Walton, is ratified by their lack of physical contact, and Harley's death occurs at just the moment when they might finally be married.[21] Somewhere between the exuberant blend of sensation and sentiment celebrated by La Mettrie and Cleland has fallen the shadow of this eighteenth-century version of Petrarchan love. Sexuality has once again become a force that reduces human nature. In the late 1740s, *l'Homme machine* and ***Fanny Hill*** detailed a liberating combination of human imagination and bodily feeling that turned its face against centuries of philosophical subordination of body to mind. By the 1770s this potentially revolutionary force had become a secular religion of mere gesture, in which the only approved response of the body to a situation that involved human feeling was an interminable downpouring of tears.

Notes

[1] The difficult problem of the seventeenth- and eighteenth-century origins of pornography, as distinguished from bawdy or erotic literature in general, has been broached by David Foxon in *Libertine Literature in England, 1660-1745* (New Hyde Park, New York, 1965). Foxon's book also includes a detailed account of the publication and prosecution of *Fanny Hill.*

[2] Aram Vartanian, *La Mettrie's l'Homme machine: A Study in the Origins of an Idea* (Princeton, 1960), pp. 6-8, 137-138. My debt to Vartanian's thorough and subtle work will be apparent in the following pages. Further references to it will be included in the text.

[3] In *Culture and Society, 1780-1950* (New York, 1960), Raymond Williams comments frequently on the changing meaning of words as an index to the quality of change between eras. See especially "A Note on 'Organic'," pp. 281-282, in which Williams dates the distinction between "organic" and "mechanical" from Burke and Coleridge.

[4] Susan Sontag in "The Pornographic Imagination," *Partisan Review,* 2 (1967), 195-196, follows French

theorists in tracing the connection between machinery and pornographic eroticism to Sade:

> Sade's ideas—of the person as a "thing" or an "object," of the body as a machine and of the orgy as an inventory of the hopefully indefinite possibilities of several machines in collaboration with each other—seems mainly designed to make possible an endless, non-culminating kind of ultimately affectless activity.

Georges Bataille, whom Miss Sontag frequently cites, images the contrast in the picture of a naked girl on a bicycle: "le spectacle irritant, théoriquement sale, d'un corps nu et chaussé sur la machine" *Histoire de l'oeil* (Paris, 1967), p. 37.

[5] For photographs of these "automata" and a history of machines that concentrates more on wonder than on uniformity, see K. G. Pontus Hultén, *The Machine as seen at the End of the Mechanical Age* (New York, 1968), pp. 20-21.

[6] It is intriguing that a century usually characterized by its desire to reduce mystery to intelligibility could contain among its greatest empiricists men so interested in the diseases of mind and the vagaries of imagination. One example of this fascination may be the growing importance of doctors in the English novel, not as satiric butts for their use of jargon (as in Fielding), but as abettors of a pervasive hypochondria (as in Sterne and Smollett). Within a more clinical context, Michel Foucault in *Madness and Civilization* (New York, 1965) argues that madness in the eighteenth century served to identify the outsider (and by implication the "normal" society) in much the same way that leprosy had done in the Middle Ages. For his discussion of hysteria and hypochondria, two subjects frequently referred to by La Mettrie, see chapters IV and V, "Aspects of Madness" and "Doctors and Patients." See also *Minds and Machines,* ed. Alan Ross Anderson (Englewood Cliffs, N.J., 1964).

[7] Another parallel between the materialist and the pornographic perspectives is their common preoccupation with the problem of language. La Mettrie's views are discussed by Keith Gunderson in "Descartes, La Mettrie, Language, and Machines," *Philosophy,* 39 (1964), 193-222. See also Noam Chomsky, *Cartesian Linguistics, A Chapter in the History of Rationalist Thought* (New York, 1966). Cleland was also interested in the origins of language, first publishing a pamphlet entitled *The Way to Things by Words, and to Words by Things* (1766) and in 1768, *Specimen of an Etimological Vocabulary, or, Essay By Means of the Analitic Method, to Retrieve the Antient Celtic.*

[8] Compare the language used by Louis Racine, one of the last defenders of Cartesian animal automatism, in

a poem written prior to 1719: "Je ne puis rapporter cet étonnant savoir/Qu'à de secrets ressorts que le sang fait mouvoir." Cited by Leonora Cohen Rosenfield, *From Beast-Machine to Man-Machine* (New York, 1940), p. 58.

[9] It is difficult for the English or American reader to appreciate this aspect of La Mettrie's thought, since the only available translation of La Mettrie into English since 1750 (according to Vartanian's bibliography) has been that of Gertrude C. Bussey, published by Open Court and reprinted several times since 1912. The Preface remarks that the translation is based on Miss Bussey's Wellesley dissertation, corrected by M. W. Calkins with the help of M. Carret and George Santayana. But there is no way for the reader to find out, except by comparing the French and English texts, that a total of almost five pages—in words, phrases, and entire paragraphs—have been omitted from the English translation, their departure marked only by dots. I should say "bowdlerized" rather than "omitted," for the passages removed almost without exception refer to matters sexual. I have compared the Open Court edition with Miss Bussey's original, and her "correctors" have been even more scrupulous than she was, omitting passages that seem to contain sexual reference, although one or two actually do not. (Miss Bussey is at least consistent and also ellipsizes the corresponding French passages.) Stylistically, the Open Court translation also leaves much to be desired. *Matrice* for example, is almost invariably rendered as matrix, even when womb is the primary meaning.

[10] Although La Mettrie's argument serves to enhance the stature of sexuality in general, his own prejudices are still male-oriented. In the great controversy between the ovists and the spermatists over the origins of generation, La Mettrie leans to the spermatist position: "Il me paroît que c'est le Mâle qui fait tout, dans une femme qui dort, comme dans la plus lubrique" (p. 194). One intriguing indication of the way in which later pornography becomes fixated in eighteenth-century beliefs about physiology is the prevalence of the idea that both men and women ejaculate with orgasm. This belief, sanctioned by Hippocrates and Galen, was also supported by Descartes, who based his theory of generation on a "mélange des deux liqueurs." Maupertuis had revived the idea in *Venus Physique* (1745) and Buffon later held similar beliefs. La Mettrie takes a measured view: "Il est si rare que les deux semences se recontrent dans le Congrès, que je serois tenté de croire que la semence de la femme est inutile à la génération" (p. 194). See the discussion by Vartanian, footnotes 114 and 119, pp. 247-249.

[11] The DNB account of Cleland's foreign activities seems retrospectively colored by the notoriety of *Fanny Hill*. The statement that he was consul in Smyrna seems primarily based on a long footnote in John Nichols' *Literary Anecdotes of the Eighteenth Century* (6 vols., London, 1812) that calls Smyrna the place "where, perhaps, he first imbibed those loose principles which, in a subsequent publication, too infamous to be particularized, tarnished his reputation as an author" (II, 458). A search of the relevant Public Record Office documents shows no reference to Cleland at Smyrna in 1734, the date cited by the DNB. His honorable and successful career in Bombay was documented at the India Office Library, where I was helped very much by all the staff, especially Mr. Ian A. Baxter. The fact that Cleland was in India from 1731 to 1740 makes the so-called earlier performance of *Fanny Hill* at the Beggar's Benison even more suspect. The Beggar's Benison is described by Louis Clark Jones in *The Clubs of the Georgian Rakes* (New York, 1942), p. 230. G. Legman refers to the possible performance in *The Horn Book: Studies in Erotic Folklore and Bibliography* (New Hyde Park, N.Y., 1964), pp. 76-77, 250. It is supposed that the work was read by a relative of Cleland's named Robert Cleland, a charter member of the Beggar's Benison. The notes themselves were published privately in 1892, although the years 1733-1738 are represented by a resumé based on fuller notes that were destroyed. The exact reference is to 30 November 1737; "Fanny Hill was read." Another possibility, of course, is that the work in question has been lost, and Cleland has whimsically named his own work after it.

[12] What seems to be an early allusion to *Pamela* also makes the 1737 date difficult to support:

> . . . she told me, after her manner and style, "as how several maids out of the country had made themselves and all their kin for ever: that by preserving their VIRTUE, some had taken so with their masters, that they had married them, and kept them coaches, and lived vastly grand and happy; and some, may-hap, came to be Duchesses; luck was all, and why not I, as well as another?"; with other almanacs to this purpose. *Fanny Hill* (New York, 1963), pp. 5-6.

[13] Cleland's concept of the epistolary method can certainly bear comparison to Richardson's. In place of Richardson's effort to preserve immediacy and present the epistolary form as a virtually transparent medium for experience and emotion, Cleland explores its confessional and meditative possibilities.

[14] One immediately calls to mind the changes worked on this image by Corporal Trim and Uncle Toby, who, Tristram remarks, wanted to see his bowling-green battlefield with a desire like that of a lover for his mistress (*Tristram Shandy*, II, v).

[15] For an account of *bête-machine* references in English literature that does not, however, include

Cleland, see Wallace Shugg, "The Cartesian Beast-Machine in English Literature (1663-1750)," *JHI,* 29 (1968), 279-292.

[16] Cleland, of course, may be trying to express a subjective element in Fanny's perceptions by these exaggerations. Pamela's dislike for snakes and fear of the bull (that turns out to be a cow) may come to mind. Compare also the account in La Mettrie's philosophical pastoral *l'Art de jouir* (1751) of the *"berger"* and the *"bergère"* examining each other's parts for the first time, and the young girl's upset at her first sight of an erection. *l'Homme machine suivi l'Art de jouir,* intro. Maurice Solovine (Paris, 1921), p. 155.

[17] Who knows whether Shelley was aware of this earlier "sensitive plant"? In any case, Cleland seems to be the primary reference for anyone who wishes to trace an eroticized nature from Spenser and Milton to the Romantics. The natural and the sexual unite in *Fanny Hill* in a way that Thomson and other eighteenth-century poets of nature never explore so thoroughly. Similarly, conceptions of an idyllic and edenic sexuality appear in Cleland to presage Keats.

[18] There are other elements in *Fanny Hill* of what might be called a "scientific" language. Here is a particularly notable example: "Chiming then to me, with exquisite consent, his oily balsamic injection, mixing deliciously with the sluices in flow from me, sheath'd and blunted all the stings of pleasure, it flung us into an ecstacy that extended us fainting, breathless, entranced" (p. 97). "Chiming" may refer to "harmonizing like two bells." A more suggestive possibility in this context may be that Cleland is referring to "chyme" or "chyle," the milky, fluid mass in which food moves from the stomach to the intestine:

> Le corps n'est qu'une horloge, dont le nouveau chyle est l'horloger. Le premier soin de la Nature, quand il entre dans le sang, c'est d'y exciter une sorte de fièvre, que les Chymistes qui ne rêvent que fourneaux, ont dû prendre pour une fermentation (p. 186).

[19] Compare the effect on Harriet:

> In the mean time, we could plainly mark the prodigious effect the progressions of this delightful energy wrought in this delicious girl, gradually heightening her beauty as they heightened her pleasure. Her countenance and whole frame grew more animated; the faint blush of her cheeks, gaining ground on the white, deepened into a florid vivid vermilion glow, her naturally brilliant eyes now sparkled with ten-fold lustre; her languor was vanish'd, and she appeared, quick spirited, and alive all over (p. 134).

[20] Cleland actually received only £20 for *Fanny Hill*

(Foxon, *Libertine Literature,* p. viii).

[21] This motif has already been presaged in *Memoirs of an Oxford Scholar* (1756), ascribed without warrant to Cleland in a recent paperback edition. (This ascription may have occurred because the copy used by the publisher was that in the Beinecke Library at Yale, a copy that has "Cleland's Oxford Scholar" on the spine. I have seen two other copies, neither marked in this way.) In the *Oxford Scholar* the narrator alternates between erotic adventures and periods of extreme sentiment in which he laments his inability to marry the girl of his dreams, Chloe, because of family and financial reasons. At the end of the novel, when the obstacles have been cleared away in appropriate romance fashion, he and Chloe indulge sexually, whereupon, in about two pages, she dies. The epigraph is from Pope's *Eloisa to Abelard.*

Malcolm Bradbury (essay date 1971)

SOURCE: "*Fanny Hill* and the Comic Novel," in *The Critical Quarterly,* Vol. 13, No. 3, Autumn 1971, pp. 263-75.

[*In the following essay, Bradbury argues that as an example of the era's experimentation in novelistic form, Cleland's* Memoirs of a Woman of Pleasure *may not be exceptionally good, but it does demonstrate the attempts of eighteenth-century novelists to combine powerful individual episodes into a unified lengthy narrative.*]

Though a few years back it had the status of a *cause celebre* and an outrage, John Cleland's **The Memoirs of a Woman of Pleasure,** better known as **Fanny Hill,** can only seem in today's climate a modestly pornographic book. Indeed the very category of pornography is a receding one; and students of generic classification who set some store by the category and see it as a useful way of defining an aesthetic procedure had better be on their mettle. As it happens, **The Memoirs of a Woman of Pleasure** seems to me a pretty pure historical example of the species, a conscious exercise in the production of a certain sort of effect. But the problem with the term 'pornography' is that, in the very changeable climate of our times, it does have uncertain status. Contemporary critics have found themselves very baffled by the anti-humanist character of a lot of works which interest them. We have developed, after all, a large modern art of dehumanization, and resuscitated a whole tradition of it from the past; and from Swift to Nathanael West, from De Sade to Burroughs, from Voltaire to Genet, we can find the significant lines running and leading us further into that universe of fantasy (if fantasy is the right word for a process also recognizable in history) in which the human self is dwarfed and perhaps destroyed, in which physiological functions dominate, in which man (or woman) is put into object- or thing-status in a universe often apocalyptically surreal in character, and in which both social protest and emotional perversity can occur and some times coincide. Such works cannot really be taken as part of the humanist canon of literature; and yet, by a transitional fiction of our times, we can recognize in them qualities of artistic merit and literary achievement. So we often postulate that once a certain level of literary excellence has been reached the pornographic elements somehow, like the state after the revolution, wither away. This piety has been transferred into law and has proved unsatisfactory—indeed has shown our contemporary uncertainty about what constitutes both literary and moral virtue. For it is hard to postulate that literary virtue is redemptive, offering *another* value which subsumes or improves upon the pornographic elements of a work. Frequently it is the case that the literary endeavour is devoted to the best achievement of the pornographic element—to producing erotic stimulus and the sexual sublime. When criticism loses its moral and generic hierarchies, its belief that certain forms and procedures are higher than others, then technical success in any given sphere constitutes merit. We may still have some sense that certain kinds of literary proceeding—like the detective story and pornography—are inherently inferior; but we are not sure of the sense. And where the novel is concerned the very proliferation of types and species within it—from realism to romance, from facticity of types and species within it—from realism to romance, from facticity to fabulation—helps us not to be sure.

One of the interesting features of *Fanny Hill* is that the novel seems made up of just such a situation of generic uncertainty. The novel-form in England developed in a climate—a neo-classical climate—in which generic norms were being adduced and also sceptically questioned by the writers in the new form. It is fairly typical of the eighteenth-century novelist that he immerses himself freely in the contingencies of contemporary experience, ranging 'epically' through the classes and using multiple 'levels' of diction, while at the same time promising some overall effect or single moral end in the traditional classical way. Criticism has tended, in fact, somewhat to over-emphasize the empiricism, realism and verisimilitude of early fiction; but all the same a dissonance between general ends and particular means is familiar to us in eighteenth century novels, full as they are of prefatorial promises not lived up to in the actual working out of the narrative. As cultural sophisticates, we naturally discount the ends and explore the means, postulating either a conscious or even (as with Defoe in one critic's version[1]) an 'unconscious' irony at work in authorial creation. The dissonance has a traditional place in pornographic writing of a certain sort, and it is there in *Fanny Hill.* The explicit moral end is based on Fanny's discovery that normal marital love is richer than any other mode of pleasure; but of course on the way to that discovery we have been entranced by a sequence of 'episodes' that are developed—to use an appropriate metaphor—up to the hilt. We have this in a good deal of other fiction of the age as well; but of course the dissonance becomes the more marked when these are sexual episodes—and when, as I want to argue, Cleland creates these according to another aesthetic principle he gets from the neo-classical climate of the age: that of kinetically engaging the reader in various forms of pastoral and sexual sublime. Cleland may have been—or better certainly was—in part parodying the literary and aesthetic principles of his day; but in fact his book is a sophisticated and formally complex work, and he is obviously engaged in the aesthetic fascination of his enterprise. And as a result the book—while no-one would want to argue that it is startlingly good—has its distinctive merits. Indeed it opens up a number of quite striking possibilities in the working of that new form, the novel.

Part of Cleland's effort in the book is clearly that of a polite covering up of what he was doing: in short, he parodies literary seriousness in order to serve the erotic and pornographic possibilities of his story. He promises to anatomize the life of pleasure, and show its dangers—a theme familiar enough in the literature of the time—but at the same time he busily explores the erotic resources of literature, particularly as these had developed in the romance-tradition from which the novel partly derives and partly diverges. As a result, he shares with other novelists of his time a strong comic dimension that comes from relating new matter and new tones to old literary strategies. What one gets in many eighteenth century novels is what Fielding would call a comic 'diction', a mock-heroic element derived from breaking up traditional hierarchies and using low language for high events or the reverse. Cleland engages in a variety of tactics in this area; he works in a tone of sceptical realism, noting details of persons, places and society, attempting specific touches of verisimilitude, varying his language and attack from scene to scene. Of course there are two main reasons for not taking this quite as seriously as we would in an author like Fielding or Sterne. The first is that his first-person narrator, Fanny, is an *ingenue,* an instrument of the real narrator in several senses. And the second is that element of jest that tends to pervade any pornographic novel, which tends to resolve itself out into a mixture of crucial, titillating scenes and enabling material that allows the character or participants, emotions and postures in each sexual act to change and produce erotic variety.

When Brigid Brophy reviewed *Fanny Hill* in the *New Statesman* on the event of its reissue, she called it 'art of an artless kind'. One knows at once what she means; there is a familiar sense of manipulation, of avoiding the general human requirements of any given moment

('I skip over the natural grief and affliction I felt on this melancholy occasion', says Fanny of the death of her parents), that is a familiar aspect of cheap literature—though it is a not uncommon feature of episodic technique in fiction; Defoe does it all the time. But there is a distinction to be made between that artlessness which is incapable of being interested in such matters, and a deliberate artfulness which makes such elisions as a condition of gaining the effects the writer needs. *Fanny Hill* is in fact rather artlessness of an enormously artful kind, as one only has to see by comparing it with Defoe's *Moll Flanders*. Defoe has a similar type of heroine, has similar kinds of narrative device, and yet pursues really the opposite effect to that sought by Cleland—he seeks, though again by simplifying the available materials, to create a certain moral elevation derived from *limiting* the suggestiveness of a narrative evidently susceptible of much more erotic treatment. Both books use the familiar eighteenth-century structure of a largely episodic narrative line, in which set scenes are heavily worked and the connective materials between appear flimsy and no more than functional. Both have heroines who move from poor births to wealthy penitance, but where in *Moll Flanders* the main action starts with Moll's reaching the age of class- and monetary-awareness, in *Fanny Hill* it starts with Fanny's arrival at sexual awareness. Both are at first simple, ingenuous, and easily tempted toward depravity, initially drawn into the lives they live less by intention than influence from people and circumstances; and both books follow out those lives through one field of experience (as *Fanny Hill* is a pornography of sex, *Moll Flanders* is a pornography of money). And both heroines tell their own stories as retrospective first-person narrators from a standpoint of penitance, but mixing in a realistic telling with interspersed moral reflection applied post facto to the events. However, though, ironic readings of *Moll Flanders* have (as I've said) been offered us by critics, there is something recognizable about Mark Schorer's complaint that Defoe's 'technique' does not allow him to separate himself far enough from his material to explore it. But then Defoe was committed to sustaining an elaborate verisimilitude; his preface asserts a factual source for the book (Moll's 'own memorandum') and he claims that his own skill as novelist lies in creating a moral effect by redesigning the nature of his promisingly titillating narrative. 'There is in this story abundance of delightful incidents,' he says, 'and all of them usefully applied. There is an agreeable turn artfully given them in the narrating, that naturally instructs the reader, either one way or another.' The most self-conscious element of his art is in fact, by his own view, the capacity to create incidents which appear true and at the same time 'delightful' and 'instructive.' He picks his incidents for their variety and illustrates them very circumstantially; the element of the sensational in a theft or an incestuous relationship is always muted by a plain style and a careful detailing. It is Cleland and

not Defoe who is the ironic practitioner in this area. Cleland, too, claims realism and verisimilitude, but in a figure that is typical of the book as a whole: 'I will not so much as take pains to bestow the strip of a gauze wrapper on it [Truth],' writes Fanny, 'but paint situations as they actually rose to me in nature, careless of violating those laws of decency that were never made for such unreserved intimacies as ours . . . ' This is a familiar tactic, and here is no more *than* a tactic. Truth is truth to a particular locale; and even though Cleland is actually interested in detail and in creating social and environmental verisimilitude, he is primarily concerned with exploiting the possibilities available in the basic kind of incident, a sexual incident, he is limited to. Moll's story is the story of a human life, Fanny's the stylized tale of an ever-elaborating set of experiences in a single universe not only narrower than but at times outside human probability. And where Defoe undoubtedly shared some of Moll's ingenuousness, and does not make her experience or her judgments absurd, Cleland exploits his heroine both as regards the incidents he puts her in and his own relation to her opinions and judgments. But Cleland's urbanity is, in his book, a genuine presence: it derives both from a sense of literary style and competence and a sense of command over the values of his society. Like many of his contemporaries, Cleland tends to see the norms of sexual behaviour as deriving from an urban, aristocratic milieu. Fielding took the comic view, seeing that behaviour as an aspect of the world of follies and vices; Richardson tended toward a sentimental treatment, but, imaginatively granting place to the perspectives and values of the world of pleasure and sophistication, he put it into productive tension with the perspective of his lower-middle-class heroines. Both writers fully *include* that socio-moral world we associate with Restoration drama; they enter the world of pleasure, fops and wits, urban sexuality and experimentation, to consider if finally to distance and discard it. This is one difference between them and Defoe; and Cleland is closer finally to their climate than Defoe's. There are chronological reasons for this. **The Memoirs of a Woman of Pleasure** was putatively published in 1749 (Peter Quennell's preface to the Putnam edition goes into the difficulties of establishing date of publication of undercover writing); *The Fortunes and Misfortunes of the Famous Moll Flanders,* often called the first English novel, appeared only 27 years before, in 1722; but by 1749 *Pamela* (1740) and *Clarissa* (1748) had appeared, and *Tom Jones* came out that year. It would seem likely that Cleland was influenced by *Clarissa;* the one real difference between him and Richardson and Fielding is that he is interested neither in social nor in moral *tensions*. His book is without those variations between the classes, and the related moral hierarchies, which are the normal sources of tension in eighteenth century fiction. In this respect it approximates rather to the condition of romance or urbane pastoral.

Cleland's urbanity is, in fact, a certain sort of social and moral inclusiveness; Fanny moves through a social world that is classless in the sense that the world of sexuality is a genial democracy. She is a pleasure-advocate, a member of a stylised world of rakishness by which she is not really corrupted but matured. She explores, albeit at first passively, her own propensities, and she actually values them; in certain respects she becomes a sophisticated heroine, making interesting judgments about her experience. (Of course she is never as sophisticated as her author, who commands the action.) 'The inflammable principle of pleasure so easily fired at my age' is her only principle; she becomes a scientist of, an expert in, a moralist about, pleasure. Because of all this there is an absence of concern about those socio-moral matters so recurrent in eighteenth-century writing though, admittedly, Cleland has more pressing interests to attend to. The book is thus relatively static, bearing considerable resemblance to the earlier form of romance, likewise little concerned with the collision of values. Of course it states what much earlier romance coyly implies, and intrudes a species of realism. But my point is that it is very much part of the general climate of the new novel form, and offers an interesting redistribution of prevailing constituents. And Cleland's real problem in the book is to work out these constituents effectively.

How, in fact, does he do it? Cleland presents the book by making it a first-person narration in the form of two letters, written to a female correspondent who has asked Fanny to recount the story of her life of pleasure. The first letter deals with the innocent Fanny's rapid involvement with sexual emotion, the pleasures of enjoyment, and the chief erotic rewards, taking her to the point where she is compelled to submit to prostitution. The second deals with her life in a brothel, her rise to wealth, and her marriage to her first lover, to whom she presents the riches she has acquired. She starts her story by claiming the value of her wide experience; but she also says that by leaving the life of pleasure she is the better enabled to think and reflect about it. The result is that she is put in the narrative position both of reporting the episodes, all essentially sexual, and offering some sort of judgment on and organization of them. Fanny is thus put in the position of pseudo-author as well as heroine, and in this role she comments on the narrative problems as such. One particularly striking example occurs at the beginning of her second letter, where she writes to 'Madam':

> I imagined, indeed, that you would have been cloy'd and tired with uniformity of adventure and expressions, inseparable from a subject of this sort, whose bottom, or groundwork being, in the nature of things, eternally one and the same, whatever variety of forms and modes the situations are susceptible of, there is no escaping a repetition of the same images, the same figures, the same expressions, with this further inconvenience added to the disgust it creates, that the words JOYS, ARDOURS, TRANSPORTS, ECSTACIES, and the rest of those pathetic terms so congenial to, so received in the PRACTICE OF PLEASURE, flatten and lose much of their due spirit and energy by the frequency they indisputably recur with, in a narrative of which that practice professedly composes the whole bias. I must therefore trust to the candour of your judgment, for your allowing me the disadvantages I am necessarily under in that respect, and to your imagination and sensibility, the pleasing task of repairing it, by their supplements, where my descriptions flag or fail; the one will readily place the pictures I present before your eyes; the other give life to the colours where they are dull, or worn with frequent handlings.

> What you say besides, by way of encouragement, concerning the extreme difficulty of continuing so long in one strain, in a mean tempered with taste, between the revoltingness of gross, rank, and vulgar expressions and the ridicule of mincing metaphors and affected circumlocutions, is so sensible, as well as good-natur'd, that you greatly justify me to myself for my compliance with a curiosity that is to be satisfied so extremely at my expense.

Nothing, of course, could be franker about the difficulties of the species, though it is an odd inruption into a more or less realistic narrative. Still, it does draw attention to the artful skills of the book. Limited, as it is, in subject-matter, it can vary 'form and mode'—which in fact it does, treating the different sexual episodes with a variety that derives not only from the kind of congress involved or the kind of people participating, but also from the sentiments and literary treatment employed. One can see what is meant here near the opening of the book, where Fanny, still a virgin but living in a brothel, witnesses two sexual encounters. The treatment of the first, between a fat old lady and a Horse-Grenadier, is brisk, comic, spoofing: 'Droll was it to see that clumsy fat figure of hers drop down on the foot of the bed, opposite the closet-door, so that I had a full-front view of all her charms.' The second scene, between an attractive girl and a young Genoese merchant, dusky and handsome is attentive to features of physical charm and high attractiveness, and is presented in a heightened, romantic and sentimental tone. Limited in language, the writer can employ his skill in varying images and expressions in order to gain requisite variety and hence sustain continuing interest. According to this modest aesthetics of pornography we can work out the appropriate Aristotelian permutations: the plot is episodic and repetitious; the diction falls in the mean, tempered by taste, between 'vulgar expressions' and 'mincing metaphors'; 'the forms and modes the situations are susceptible of' afford the basic area of variation; and the area of effect on the reader, the kinesis, depends on imagination (to realize the scenes) and sensibility (to invigorate the language).

The book in fact works very close to this fairly literary prescription, with its emphasis on variation of form and mode. Despite its realism, it is notably figurative, especially in the second letter where Fanny becomes a devotee of the pleasurable life. Indeed she becomes the celebrant in a poetic exercise she herself is offered as describing. She lives in an idyllic brothel, to which she is initiated by elaborate, formal sexual rite, and passes 'from a private devotee of pleasure into a public one, to become a more general good.' The brothel is a 'secret institution' and those in it describe themselves humorously as 'the restorers of the golden age and its simplicity of pleasures, before their innocence became so unjustly branded with the names of guilt and shame.' Throughout this section, from the elegant artifice of the initiation rites onward, the style is elevated and courtly, celebrating 'the liberty of nature.' After various episodes involving sharp variations of tone and modes of description, there is a further ceremonial scene, a pastoral bathing scene, suddenly cut short:

> Accordingly we took to a bench, while Emily and her spark, who belonged it seems to the sea, stood at the sideboard, drinking to our good voyage; for, as the last observed, we were well under weigh, with a fair wind up channel, and full-freighted; nor indeed were we long before we finished our trip to Cythera, and unloaded in the old haven; but, as the circumstances did not admit of much variation, I shall spare you the description.

> At the same time, allow me to place you here an excuse I am conscious of owing you, for having, perhaps, too much affected the figurative style; though surely, it can pass nowhere more allowably than in a subject which is so properly the province of poetry, nay, is poetry itself, pregnant with every flower of imagination and loving metaphors, even if the natural expressions, for respect of fashions and sound, necessarily forbid it.

The reader might well sense a touch of desperation here, but Cleland is, I think, quite serious about his association between his subject and poetry. If the book is unusually without social and moral tensions, is static as romance is static, progressing rather through elaboration of mood than through event, then Cleland's pursuit of lyricism—the flowers of imagination and loving metaphors—seems conscious and purposeful. 'Fanny's' vocabulary is dense, energetic, evocative; and if she is in some of her adventures an innocent heroine she is quite a learned one—indeed, the language of the book is a fascinating mixture of realistic vernacular and the heightened and witty tone of the lightly learned. In fact it is finally in the maximization of the possibilities of language, in creating the variations with which the book progresses, that Cleland shows his powers. Of course he employs graphic physiological detail,

exploiting the kinetic effect of imitating sexual characteristics, sexual sensations, and the various dispositions of the sexual act, including both the abnormal and the fanciful. But he also has an elaborate vocabulary of response and of neo-scientific observation, of kinesis and emotion, by which erotic sensation and perception can be linked with intellectual, aesthetic and to a point moral experience. And then there is the figurative structure he derives from classical learning, scientific speculation, and philosophical discussion, especially in such areas of contemporary debate as about the sublime and the pleasurable. (Hence the courtroom point that the book offers many interesting first usages of words.) In short, Cleland does consciously and complicatedly exploit, in accordance with various assumptions and theories about the means by which art can affect readers, the variations between appropriate involvement and appropriate distance that can make his fable most effective. This, indeed, is the basis of his pornographic utopia, his sex-and-poetry pastoral.

In fact, *The Memoirs of a Woman of Pleasure* is about aesthetics as well as about sex, and this is the basis of its remarkable quality of literary vigour. What we might say is that the book is about the synaesthetic process in Fanny, her growing sense of the poetry of sexuality, of the value of vigour and transports; and that it is also a conscious effort at creating a like sense of intensity, aphrodisiacally conceived, in the reader. For Cleland assumes that poetry and lovemaking are essentially analogous—imaginative variation on a theme, invention allied to energy, and processes of intense sensation. Both are regarded as essences or universals in nature, and are part of a universe seen in terms of its springs of energy and forces of passion. The result is a vigorous energy in the writing, but it is also the case that Cleland's view is an abstract, sophisticated and witty one. The book is not, after all, a Lawrentian hymn to energy and force; there always remains something of the convention about it, a reserve of wit which may derive partly from Cleland's sense of the limitations of his enterprise but which has also to do with a sceptical temper running through the telling. A growing element of qualification runs through the book, and it is finally this that gives the book its pornographic as opposed to romance texture; the lyrical-erotic is qualified with a comic self-consciousness. In many scenes Cleland's forceful use of the tradition of amorous and erotic writing is clear. For instance, Fanny's first love-making is with a youth who is described with romantic attentiveness. There is a long listing of bodily characteristics, highly dependent on romance-writing:

> . . . besides all the perfections of manly beauty which were assembled in his form, he had an air of neatness and gentility, a certain smartness in the carriage and port of his head, that yet more distinguish'd him; his eyes were sprightly and full of meaning; his looks had in them something at once sweet and commanding. His complexion

outbloom'd the lovely-colour'd rose, whilst its inimitable tender vivid glow clearly sav'd it from the
reproach of wanting life, of [being] raw and dough-
like, which is commonly made to those so extremely
fair as he was.

This is a detailed, vigorous treatment in the romance
tradition, and the sensations aroused in the characters
are appropriate: 'to find myself in the arms of that
beautious youth was a rapture that my little heart swam
in. Past or future was equally out of the question with
me. The present was as much as all my powers of life
were sufficient to bear the transport of, without fainting.' The emotions of love, which are eventually the
refiner of lust and the culmination of pleasure, are not
only piously desired but supported with stylistic energy. When Fanny is taught late in the book by an elderly philosophical lover that the pleasures of mind are
superior to those of body—'at the same time, that they
were so far obnoxious to, or incompatible with each
other, that, besides the sweetness in the variety and
transition, the one served to exalt and perfect the taste
of the other, to a degree that the senses alone can
never arrive at'—this is something more than pretentious decor. The romantic first lover returns, and this
is the culmination of the action. Yet the very fact that
this is a kind of philosophical achievement creates an
odd modulation in the romantic sensibility.

For the book is not only about Fanny's efforts to achieve
the pleasurable sublime, but also to define it. Capable
of romantic feeling, she is also presented as an analyst
of the way in which feeling is promoted. Fanny is in
fact the whore as philosopher. This is hardly calculated to make her believable as a character; it means that
the author's hand is everywhere apparent. The book is
structured on a sophisticated proceeding whereby Fanny is granted a working mind to speculate about her
impulses; Fanny speaks of herself as one 'whose natural philosophy all resided in the favourite centre of
sense.' She sees herself as analogous to the musician,
the painter, the statuary, because she is concerned not
just with imitating nature but finding its force and fire,
the spirit of its being. She possesses, in fact, a sophisticated version of eighteenth-century pre-romanticism.
At one point she describes the male organ as 'the most
interesting moving picture in all nature,' appreciated
only by those who have the real fire of the imagination, the sexual correspondent breeze within. It is pref-
erable to art in being 'nature's unrivalled composition,' a sort of sensualist's Aeolian harp. She makes a
similar kind of point, about sexuality being nature's
art, when she speaks of her general philosophy: she
prefers the real pleasures offered by nature to oblique
ones, and complains of philosophies which overlook
the significance of pleasure and so 'for ever mistake
things the most foreign of the nature of pleasure itself.' Fanny's empirical enterprises into the kinetic joys
and transports of the sexual act are a 'study' as well;

her final aim is both a satisfactory sexual relationship
uniting mind and body and a satisfying general theory
of pleasure. Hence it is possible for Cleland to make
his novel a pornographic idyll in which realistic appreciation of erotic sensation is linked with a romantic
dream of the good life of superaesthesia. The sexual
organs being 'the seats of pleasure', the universe of
pleasure can be explored not only with titillating variation but according to a principle of development, as
Fanny moves through partners who afford considerable social, sexual and psychological range towards
the sexual utopia. But of course her observation, her
often highly scientific language, her wide range of
metaphorical reference, are touched with an obvious
absurdity. The absurdity lies, of course, in the improbable assimilation of the author's mind as speculator
into that of his character as agent, and it results in a
Boswellian dimension, a kind of comic self-consciousness familiar in an age in which paradox and dichotomy thrive and in which man is both animal and rational being, lecher and philosopher. Some critics have
read the book as a piece of mock-science, mock-learn-
ing and mock-romance created really to fill out the
spaces between the sexual episodes, an elaborate piece
of fakery with a marked discontinuity between the
sexual sections which are the book's *real* purport and
the other parts which are there to allow these sexual
episodes maximum effectiveness. The book is more
rounded than that, however; it has behind it the force
of a particular cultural style, the style of the rational
ideal under pressure, which creates a distinctive comedy of mind throughout the entire work.

Nonetheless, it is founded on a dissonance. To make
the book into a unity, Cleland would need to sustain
the integrity of Fanny's personality, sustain a continuing psychological as well as sexual interest in the characters, and set the episodes in a significant order of
development. To a large extent he does do this. The
sexual episodes are related to Fanny's personality, and
they characterize quite carefully her sexual partners.
They tend towards a significant pattern of development; and they anatomize pleasure misused as well as
used, show 'barrenness' and 'self-loathing'. There is a
steady gradation of erotic content, exploring first the
extent of the pleasures, and then the limits. The limits
are trespassed, but Fanny regrets this; of course Cleland still depicts such scenes. Hence though the progression serves the obvious purpose of opening up new
kinds of sexual situation, it also sustains a thematic
development; and because of this sense of design, there
is a certain rhetorical convincingness about the conclusion, where Vice is sacrificed to Virtue. For Fanny's
final love-making with Charles, her original lover, is
in more than one sense the consummation of all that
has happened:

> . . . as our joys grew too great for utterance, the
> organs of our voices, voluptuously intermixing,

became organs of the touch . . . and oh what touch! how delicious! . . . how poignantly luscious! . . . And now! now I felt to the heart of me! I felt the prodigious keen edge with which love, presiding over this act, points the pleasure: love, that may be styled as the Attic salt of enjoyment; and indeed, without it, the joy, great as it is, is still a vulgar one, whether in a king or a beggar; for it is, undoubtedly, love alone that refines, enobles and exalts it.

The passage—with its witty metaphysical intensity, its mixture of the vernacular-exclamatory and the literary—represents the end of a systematic quest. Admittedly there is a characteristic gap between the aptness of the sexual metaphor applied to speech and the final moral phrases, which is a recurrent problem in the book. Cleland hardly finds the language for *moral* intensity as readily as he does that for sexual intensity. Still, he tries hard, and the final passages are welldone: 'Thus, at length,' says Fanny, now married, 'I got snug into port,

> where, in the bosom of virtue, I gather'd the only uncorrupt sweets: where, looking back on the course of vice I had run, and comparing its infamous blandishments with the infinitely superior joys of innocence, I could not help pitying, even in point of taste, those who, immers'd in gross sensuality, are insensible to the so delicate charms of VIRTUE, than which PLEASURE has not a greater friend, nor VICE a greater enemy. Thus temperance makes men lords over those pleasures that intemperance enslaves them to: the one, parent of health, vigour, fertility, cheerfulnesss, and every other desirable good of life; the other of diseases, debility, barrenness, self-loathing, with only every evil incident to human nature.

It all has a certain ring of truth, and precisely because virtue is transposed into a species of pleasure—not a limitation of it, but the most delicate form in which it can appear. It is what the sexual aristocrats, the persons of taste, prefer, on aesthetic and synaesthetic grounds; it is the fulfilment of the aristocratic stance towards which Fanny has been developing. Yet of course it can't be entirely convincing.

For the problems are two. However consistently Fanny is drawn, we cannot but be aware of her unlikely status vis-à-vis the author. Her pretensions, when set against what she is and what she does, are somewhat ironic. It is not so much that Cleland is being whimsical; he seems perfectly interested in questions about how life might be led according to a pleasure-principle and he puts a lot of creative and linguistic energy into the effort. But he falls into the inevitable difficulty of the 'serious' pornographic novel, which is that the sexual scenes tend to have an interest—for the writer as well as the reader—in excess of any other element. And by

the very plurality of his tones, his way of exploiting the 'comic'—lower-class, vernacular, a-heroic—areas of literary art that lie outside and beyond romance, and his proliferation of varied sexual detail, he throws the quest into doubt. Not only is Fanny an unlikely philosopher, but the philosophy itself is creatively inconsistent. It is, of course, a point he doesn't miss, and on which Fanny goes on at the end to comment:

> You laugh, perhaps, at this tail-piece of morality, extracted from me by the force of truth, resulting from compar'd experiences: you think it, no doubt, out of place, out of character; probably too you may look on it as the paltry finesse of one who seeks to mask a devotee to Vice under a rag of a veil, impudently smuggled from the shrine of Virtue: just as if one was to fancy one's self compleatly disguised at a masquerade, with no other change of dress than turning one's shoes into slippers; or, as if a writer should think to shield a treasonable libel, by concluding with a formal prayer to the King. But, independent of my flattering myself that you have a juster opinion of my sense and sincerity, give me leave to represent to you, that such a supposition is more injurious to Virtue than to me: since, consistently with candour and good-nature, it can have no foundation but in the falsest of fears, that its passages cannot stand in comparison with those of Vice; but let truth dare to hold it up in its most alluring light: then mark, how spurious, how low of taste, how comparatively inferior its joys are to those which Virtue gives sanction to, and whose sentiments are not above making a sauce for the senses, but a sauce of the highest relish . . .

This is in its own way quite a rhetorical triumph, an effective and witty conclusion to the persuasive dimension of the novel, that dimension which organizes and theorizes about the significance of what has been given it and the reasons why it has been given. But of course it won't quite do. It won't do because it can be only an intellectual delight, a witty resolution, like some of Donne's. It won't do, then, because of the ends-and-means split which invests the whole tactic of the book; experience is instant and local, and interpretation structural and general, and given what experience *is* in this book the mind cannot place and shape it with the kind of relationship that exists between the author and his narrator-agent, a relationship in which she is both immersed performer and emotional philosopher, Cleland's own kinetic success as author comes over most strongly in passages quite different from the ones where Fanny asserts *her* own emotional success to come. In his preromantic and pre-Paterian day, Cleland has no language of the romantic senses that would allow him to give an immersed, psychologically convincing status to Fanny's final position, even if he wanted to. Inevitably, then, it is the sexual *episodes* that dominate the book; it is in the nature of things for Cleland that he cannot give the same kinetic force to the representations of the 'tasteful' and selective aspects of sexual pleasure as he can to the more inflammatory passages where the descriptions of sexual organs, sexual acts, and observed sexual ecstacies come out powerfully off the page. What in fact he does is to offer us a pretty pure case of a recurrent and well-recognised crux in eighteenth-century fiction, that of relating the power that resides in individual episodes to the generic and emotional unity of the work as a whole.

Of course what Cleland does do—and it is this that makes the book a modest *tour-de-force*—is to *recognize* the dissonance, and write a comic sexual romance in which it is wittily alive. The organic, kinetic dream of the book, which Cleland seeks in language and Fanny in the ultimate marital fornication, is made artificial and mechanical; it fulfils, in effect, the recipe of Bergsonian comedy. Cleland's treatment of the book is derived from a steady and consecutive fascination with emotional and imaginative intensity, from a lyric impulse. But he puts that activity into the context of a sophisticated eighteenth-century aesthetic debate about the way which both art and nature can move us. The mixture of lyrical and intellectual becomes a complex rhetorical strategy; and it produces an imbalance with profitable comic dividends. A vigorous book both intellectually and emotionally, it plays happily along the boderline where the worlds of mind and body meet. It is in fact a very Cartesian comedy; and today, when the species has returned with some force in the work of a novelist like Samuel Beckett, we can see something staple about it. It sets up possibilities in the new form of the novel, an area of relationship between romance and comedy, which later writers were to come back to. The result is as lively a disposition of those aspects of aesthetics and creative feeling which produce the pornographic mode as one could wish to find. 'Artless' is the last thing one can call it. It lives vigorously among the forms and mental and aesthetic sets that compose the eighteenth-century novel, and creates its own distinct possibilities; and for that, minor *tour-de-force* as it is, it surely deserves a solid place in fictional history.

Notes

[1] Dorothy Van Ghent, *The English Novel: Form and Function* (New York, Harper Torchbooks, 1961).

Edward W. Copeland (essay date 1972)

SOURCE: "*Clarissa* and *Fanny Hill:* Sisters in Distress," in *Studies in the Novel,* Vol. IV, No. 3, Fall 1972, pp. 343-52.

[*In the following essay, Copeland identifies and discusses the similarities between the metaphors used for descriptions of vice in* Fanny Hill *and for virtue in* Clarissa.]

A comparison of John Cleland's *Memoirs of a Woman of Pleasure* (1748-1749)[1] and Samuel Richardson's *Clarissa* (1747-1748)[2] demonstrates that these two improbably paired works have surprisingly much in common. Both heroines, for example, have similar suitors, similar unpleasant experiences in London, shared interests in problems of "delicacy," outstanding beauty, not to mention noteworthy cleanliness and neatness, and, most of all, heightened capacities for "feeling" with the greatest intensity. Peter Quennell, the editor of the 1963 New York edition of the *Memoirs,* even suggests that "*Clarissa* must certainly have influenced Cleland, and its predecessor, *Pamela; or, Virtue Rewarded,* published in 1740, may also have affected him."[3] I think Mr. Quennell is essentially right,[4] but John Richetti's recent study has made us aware of the large body of popular literature with conventions and "ideologies" not very different from Cleland's and Richardson's.[5] The question of "influence" is not the concern of this brief study. I am primarily interested in the nature of the conventions shared by *Fanny Hill* and Richardson's works. I have dwelt at some length upon a comparison of Cleland's novel and *Clarissa* because I think it will provide significant revelations about *Clarissa,* Richardson, and, most importantly, the nature of sentimental fiction.

There is no doubt of course that Cleland must be enrolled in the ranks of the anti-Pamelists. Fanny's townswoman Esther Davis, who has returned to the country from London with the badges of her success, "scowered satin gowns, caps border'd with an inch of lace, taudry ribbons, and shoes belaced with silver" (p. 5) encourages Fanny to make the experiment with an inspiring version of Pamela's story: "she told me, after her manner and style, 'as how several maids out of the country had made themselves and all their kin for ever: that by preserving their VIRTUE, some had taken so with their masters, that they had married them, and kept them coaches, and lived vastly grand and happy . . .'" (pp. 5-6). Pamela's pious cant serves to embellish Esther's cool abandonment of Fanny to the chances of London life: she said, Fanny reports, "that she wish'd me good luck, and hoped that I should always have the grace to keep myself honest, and not bring a disgrace on my parentage" (p. 8). This certainly has the appearance of a fleer at Pamela's own "good name, let who will be the tempter" (I, 4). Finally, there is Mr. H . . .'s memorable "seduction" of Fanny's maid Hannah in a scene that could be a direct parody of any one of Pamela's "trials":

> The first sight that struck me was Mr. H . . . pulling and hauling this coarse country strammel towards a couch that stood in a corner of the dining room; to which the girl made only a sort of aukward hoidening resistance, crying out so loud, that I, who listened at the door, could scarce hear her: "Pray sir, don't . . . , let me alone . . . I am not for your turn . . . You cannot, sure, demean yourself with

such a poor body as I . . . Lord! Sir, my mistress may come home . . . I must not indeed . . . I will cry out . . ." All of which did not hinder her from insensibly suffering herself to be brought to the foot of the couch, upon which a push of no mighty violence serv'd to give her a very easy fall, and my gentleman having got his hands to the stronghold of her VIRTUE, she, no doubt, thought it was time to give up the argument . . . (pp. 79-80).

The fumblings of Mr. B——in the "summer house," Mr. B——in Mrs. Jervis's closet, and Mr. B——as the "false Nan" could all be in the focus of Cleland's parody, but mainly there is the voice of Pamela herself, humbly, and weakly, protesting, "you have taught me to forget myself, and what belongs to me, and have lessened the distance that fortune has made between us, by demeaning yourself, to be so free to a poor servant . . ." (*Pamela* I, 12).

Although Cleland parodies *Pamela,* the important point here, I think, is that he also uses and exploits the potential eroticism of her "trials"; the similarity of the near pornography of *Pamela* and the frank pronography of the **Memoirs** is more striking than the parody itself. The latent eroticism of *Clarissa* also moves into sharper focus in the comparison. Clarissa's "odious" Mr. Solmes and the "monstrous" Mr. Crofts, Fanny's first suitor, lack many of the same charms. Both have disgusting persons; both "stare" rudely at their ladies, "affright" them, "squat" too near them, and definitely press their claims beyond all endurance. Clarissa and Fanny at first tolerate the presence of these unwelcome suitors for the sake of their "families": as Fanny says, "my gratitude for my benefactress made me extend my respect to all her cousin-head" (p. 21). When Crofts's intentions are made known, Fanny immediately lapses into that peculiarly Richardsonian state of inaction that afflicts Clarissa in moments of extreme distress: "I sat on the settee, by the fire-side, motionless, and petrified, without life or spirit, not knowing how to look or to stir" (p. 23). The "families" of both girls abandon their merchandizable charges to their respective suitors at teatime, and, the field clear, both men take sexual advantages. With her family present, the odious Solmes had moved a chair near Clarissa's, "and drew it so near mine, squatting in it with his ugly weight, that he pressed upon my hoop. I was so offended . . . that I removed to another chair" (I, 68); but later, seizing advantage of the Harlowes' absence, "he even snatched my trembling, my struggling hand," Clarissa writes, "and ravished it to his odious mouth" (I, 400). Fanny's trials with Mr. Crofts are different only in degree, comic in comparison, but just as distressing to Fanny: "The monster squatted down by me on the settee, and without farther ceremony or preamble, flings his arms about my neck, and drawing me pretty forcibly towards him, oblig'd me to receive, in spite of my struggles to disengage from him, his pestilential kisses. . . . I felt his

hand on the lower part of my naked thighs . . ." (p. 23). The protestations that follow are strongly reminiscent of the famous "fire-scene" in *Clarissa* where the heroine pleads with Lovelace to leave her: Fanny reports, "[I] threw myself at his feet, and begg'd him in the most moving tone, not to be rude, and that he would not hurt me. . . . 'I cannot love you, indeed I cannot! . . . pray let me alone . . . yes! I will love you dearly if you will let me alone, and go away . . .'" (p. 23). Fanny closes the scene in the same way that Clarissa ends one of her encounters with Solmes, by ringing the servant's bell with "such violence and effect as brought up the maid to know what was the matter. . . . " The maid finds Fanny "stretch'd on the floor, my hair all dishevell'd, my nose gushing out blood, which did not a little tragedize the scene, and my odious persecutor still intent of pushing his brutal point, unmoved by all my cries and distress . . ." (p. 25). Clarissa also falls on her nose in her trials, twice, once producing copious blood of which Lovelace reports, "Never was mortal man in such terror and agitation as I; for I instantly concluded that she had stabbed herself with some concealed instrument" (III, 240).

Fanny's "memoirs" written in tranquil old age admittedly keep these events in comic perspective, but she does not neglect to add that her fears were so great that when Crofts had taken his leave she "at first positively refused" to be put to bed "in the fear that the monster might return and take me at that advantage" (p. 26)—a strategy familiar to both Clarissa and Pamela. Significantly, when Fanny actually is raped later by Mr. H . . . , she is "insensible" like Clarissa and upon understanding what has happened is, of course, like her Richardsonian counterpart, "in transports of remorse" (p. 71).[6]

The ease with which Cleland can run Richardsonian scenes into pornography suggests that there are more basic similarities in methods and assumptions than these shared conventions or random borrowings might indicate. Paradoxically, the similarities are rooted more in philosophical and rhetorical *confusions* than in conscious comparison or emulation. The oft-repeated message in *Pamela* and *Clarissa* is that the virtuous life is the happy life; Fanny Hill's version might be interpolated, "the happy life is the virtuous life"—not an insignificant variation. The philosophical problem, which is discussed by Louis I. Bredvold,[7] is that of defining the moral life without including the conscience or giving a place to the moral judgment. "Constraint," Diderot writes, "destroys the grandeur and energy of nature. . . . But if hope is balanced by fear, sense of honor by love of life, inclination to pleasure by concern for health, you would see neither libertines, nor dare-devils nor cowards."[8] This is the lesson Fanny Hill learns from Mrs. Cole and from her elderly lover the "rational pleasurist"; it also provides her with the bridge to her "tailpiece of morality": "VIRTUE" is recommended as a "friend" of "PLEASURE" since "temperance makes men lords over those pleasures that intemperance enslaves them to: the one, parent of health, vigour, fertility, cheerfulness, and every other desirable good of life; the other, of diseases, debility, barrenness, self-loathing . . ." (p. 213). Sir Charles Grandison uses a similar argument to advance the cause of virtue: "What is it not, that, in this single article [intemperance], men sacrifice to false shame and false glory! Reason, health, fortune, personal elegance, the peace and order of their families; and all the comfort and honour of their after years. How peevish, how wretched, is the decline of a man worn out with intemperance!"[9] This is certainly the lesson to be drawn in *Clarissa* from the death of Belford's friend Belton. It is interesting that both Richardson and Cleland appear to be unaware of the implications of their defense of virtue—that moral values become no more than "statements of the needs or desires of the organism" (Bredvold, p. 44). Since the rhetoric of both versions of the happiness-virtue, virtue-happiness formulas is the same, casuistry is presented a fertile field for moral flights, shams, and dodges.

Richardson and Cleland create more confusion by consciously using the rhetoric of romantic passion to describe the "passion" of virtue. Answering Dr. George Cheyne's objection to the "warm" scenes in *Pamela*, Richardson insists on the fictional and moral utility of this rhetorical interchange: "I am endeavoring to write a Story which shall catch young and airy Minds, and when Passions run high in them, to shew how they may be directed to laudable Meanings and Purposes, in order to decry such Novels and Romances as have a Tendency to inflame and corrupt."[10] Ronald Crane quotes Richard Kidder's *Charity Directed* (1676) in which an even more radical version of the sentiment is advanced: "There is a Delight and Joy that Accompanies doing good, there is a kind of sensuality in it."[11] Finally, an ecstatic explanation of the operation of virtue in human nature offered by Madame de Staël suggests an even greater orgasmic potential of such virtuous rhetoric: "virtue thus becomes a spontaneous impulsion, a motive which passes into the blood, and which carries you along irresistibly like the most imperious passions."[12] In her reconsummation of love with the long-lost Charles, Fanny Hill experiences such a "spontaneous impulsion" in the ensuing mixture of physical and virtuous passion: "I was even sick with desire, and unequal to support the combination of two distinct ideas. . . . Ideas that, mingling streams, pour'd such an ocean of intoxicating bliss on a weak vessel, all too narrow to contain it, that I lay overwhelm'd, absorbed, lost in a abyss of joy, and dying of nothing but immoderate delight" (p. 209). Although Pamela disparages the "flighty vein" of such a "romantic" style, she too calls it into use to explain the virtuous principle: "While the *banks* of *discretion* keep the *proud* water of *passion* within their natural channel, all calm and serene glides along the silver current, enlivening the adjacent meadows, as it passes, with a brighter and more flowery verdure. But if the *torrents* of sensual love are permitted to descend from the *hills* of credulous hope, they may so swell the gentle stream, as to make it difficult, if not impossible, to be retained betwixt its usual bounds" (*Pamela* II, 456).[13] The pornographic landscape of **Fanny Hill** is not quite present, but the assumption is the same, that "passion," once it is unleashed, is uncontrollable and irresistible. Both Lovelace and Clarissa subscribe to this belief: it might well be said that Clarissa's death, ecstatic and almost embarrassingly sensual, is the consequence of the spontaneous, irresistible passion for virtue that Madame de Staël describes.

The "physiology of sensibility," if the awkward phrase is not too near tautology, was of real concern to Diderot and an unending source for the emotional iconography of Richardson and Cleland. The carefully recorded physical symptoms experienced by Diderot at the sight of a virtuous man are remarkably like Fanny Hill's in the presence of a not-so-virtuous one:

> Such a sight fills me with sweetness or kindness, kindles in me a heat and an enthusiasm in which life itself, if I had to lose it, would mean nothing to me; then it seems as if my heart were distended even beyond my body, as if it were swimming; a delicious and sudden sensation of I know not what passes over my whole body; I can hardly breathe; it quickens over the whole surface of my body like a shudder; I feel it most of all at the top of my brow, at the roots of my hair; and after that the indications of admiration and pleasure appear in my face mingled with those of joy, and my eyes fill with tears.[14]

The physical symptoms of virtue are described at what must certainly be their most extreme limits in Clarissa's death-scene. She has dressed herself in her "wedding garments," her shroud, to meet her "bridegroom"; her last moments are marked with romantic ecstasy:

> she spoke faltering and inwardly: Bless—bless—bless—you all—and now—and now [holding up her almost lifeless hands for the last time]—come—O come—blessed Lord—JESUS!

> And with these words, the last but half-pronounced, expired: such a smile, such a charming serenity overspreading her sweet face at the instant, as seemed to manifest her eternal happiness already begun (IV, 347).

Of the next morning, Belford writes, "We could not help taking a view of the lovely corpse, and admiring the charming serenity of her noble aspect. The women declared they never saw death so lovely before; and that she looked as if in an easy slumber, the colour having not quite left her cheeks and lips" (IV, 353). The body is transferred from London to Harlowe Place, and the signs of ecstasy do not disappear: "The corpse was very little altered, notwithstanding the journey. The sweet smile remained" (IV, 398). In *Fanny Hill* the physiology of *vice* produces almost identical symptoms, the major difference being that they are not so permanent as Clarissa's and must be repeatedly induced. Fanny describes such an "agony of bliss":

> a general soft shudder ran through all her limbs, which she gave a stretch-out of, and lay motionless, breathless, dying with dear delight; and in the height of its expression, shewing, through the nearly closed lids of her eyes, just the edges of their black, the rest being rolled strongly upwards in their extasy; then her sweet mouth appear'd languishingly open, with the tip of her tongue leaning negligently towards the lower range of her white teeth, whilst the natural ruby colour of her lips glowed with heightened life. Was not this a subject to dwell upon? (p. 135).

Although the role of objective observer is assumed in each of these passages from Diderot, Richardson, and Cleland, the rhetorical flourishes, the well-worn ornamental prose, the clichés, and the stylized gestures make it obvious that each of the authors is "working up" an emotion. Diderot's image of the heart distended beyond the body "as if it were swimming" suggests the common nature of the fantasies in the Cleland and Richardson passages: emotional states that are essentially solitary, unsharable, and incommunicable. The traditional definition of metaphor, "this is that," is taken at its most primitive value: there is no recognition of a distinction between the emotion and the image of it. "Half-ecstatic," oracular, and uncritically identified with the states described, here are the "process writers" described by Northrop Frye.[15] In both *Fanny Hill* and *Clarissa* there is the expectation that the fantasy worlds of heaven or of pornotopia represented by the "sweet smiles" will be accepted without reservation and with sympathetic participation. It is rhetoric at the most naive level of emotional propaganda.

Although it is generally recognized that works of literature are for the most part self-sufficient worlds fenced with the walls of their own fictions, it is also expected that the fictions have some relation to the other world of real experience as well. The task of these sentimental fantasists quoted above is precisely at the opposite pole from this: the real world of experience must be rigorously excluded. As handsome as Diderot's sentiments may be, we cannot verify or even believe in the actuality of his symptoms except as some sort of pathological eccentricity; our reaction nowadays is likely to be ironic amusement. Impossibly trapped by words in an attempt to present essentially nonverbal experiences, the writers of sentiment fall easy prey to Sheridan or Jane Austen. The Richardson passage, although it

succeeds in an important sense to be discussed later, fails to work or convince in the way the author intended because the reader not only feels that he is being unmercifully twisted by the arm to accept Belford's sympathetic participation in the scene, but because the "metaphor" of a well-staged death-scene does not, and cannot, represent what it purports to, heaven. The *Fanny Hill* passage does succeed as it was intended to do, I think, first of all, because Fanny, who is the representative of the nonerotic world as well as a participant in the erotic fantasies, gulls us into accepting them; and second, the world of erotic fantasy is peculiarly adapted to the "metaphor" of physical detail. As Steven Marcus sharply observes, "Keats's hope for literature in general has been ironically fulfilled: pornography proves itself upon our pulses, and elsewhere."[16]

In a last comparison of the *Memoirs* and *Clarissa,* I would like to call attention to the sealed-off hermetic qualities of the settings and rhetoric of the two novels. "The prose of a typical pornographic novel," Marcus writes, "consists almost entirely of clichés, dead and dying phrases, and stereotypical formulas; it is also heavily adjectival" (p. 279). The long-frozen diction of Fanny's "Joyous fires," "genial juices," "gleamy warmth," "luxuriant tracts of animated snow," and "interposing hillocks" does not interfere with the emotional complicity demanded by the ecstatic narrator because, in fact, the figures are indeed defunct as metaphors and cannot detract from the erotic fantasy in which, as Cleland confesses, all description is of that act "whose bottom, or ground work . . . [is] in the nature of things, eternally one and the same . . ." (p. 105). In short, the erotic fantasies of *Fanny Hill* are absolutely hermetic; even the detailed descriptions of the settings have meaning only as they offer convenient space for copulation; as for figurative language, the "sluices" and "conduits" of passion act as talismans for "the old last act," not metaphors.

It is surprising and disconcerting to have to admit that the rhetoric of *Clarissa* is also heavily adjectival, filled with clichés, stereotypical formulas, and exhortations to feeling; moreover, that the ornate rhetoric of this novel effects the same end of creating a world as fantastic and hermetic as that of Fanny Hill's incredible sexual "sensibility." This is the fictional world that Coleridge singles out in his famous comparison of Fielding and Richardson: "To take him [Fielding] after Richardson, is like emerging from a sick room heated by stoves, into an open lawn, on a breezy day in May."[17] The two styles that dominate the novel, Clarissa's overheated devotional style and Lovelace's "frothy" "Roman style," are each highly ornate, artificial, often oracular and usually more than "half-ecstatic." In this division of rhetoric, Lovelace's style is literally pitted against Clarissa's; the respective styles are recognized as immoral or moral in the same way that black and white hats in cowboy movies serve as talismans of good and evil. Within these two closed systems of reference the figurative language, the "metaphors" and the numerous "allusions" to dramatic literature, poetry, or the Bible do not serve their usual function of expanding the meaning of a situation outwards, but have reference only to the internal pattern of good and evil. Often in fact they are italicized by the correspondents to direct the application. Harlowe Place, London, the bedroom, the closet, the dining room, Hampstead, all these settings have meaning only insofar as they represent places of danger or safety for Clarissa—the same undeviating, single-minded descriptive orientation of *Fanny Hill.*

Finally, it must be noted that Lovelace's fantasies of sexual aggrandizement and Clarissa's horrific dreams, fears, and final vision of her heavenly "bridegroom" are generated by the central dramatic act, the rape. In a very real sense, the sex act is far more ever-present in *Clarissa* than it is in the Cleland novel where the erotic fantasies are modulated by Fanny's own breezy good sense. The closed circuit fantasies of Lovelace, Clarissa, and of the secondary figures as well receive no such wholesome, effective correction. The interpretation of the letters as artifacts falls to the reader. In the now much-mentioned death-scene of Clarissa, we must assume that Richardson expected us to participate warmly in the unyielding demands of the rhetoric, a leap of faith that only the most pious or naive reader would attempt today. Our sharpest reaction comes from the enormous sense of loss generated in the irony of her preparations for her heavenly "bridegroom." Facts of the world outside the fictional world of *Clarissa* do enter the novel, but the reader must bring them himself.

In conclusion, the confusion of terms used to describe sensual passion and virtuous passion is exploited by Cleland for the purposes of eroticism; in *Clarissa* I believe that these same confusions furnish a large part of the sexual energy that animates the rhetorical fantasies of both Lovelace and the heroine. But even more significant, I think, is the essentially hermetic nature of sentimental fiction that this brief comparison of *Fanny Hill* and Richardson's works makes so pointedly clear. The imbalance of perception, the near insanity of the obsessive attention demanded by the erotic illusion of the pornographic work, suggests a number of intriguing problems of method and effect in more *chaste* novels of sentiment—not the least, that longstanding and ironic family quarrel in sentimental literature between general "benevolence" and the individual gratification of "the man of feeling."

Notes

[1] The edition cited in this paper is that edited by Peter Quennell (New York: G. P. Putnam's Sons, 1963).

Fanny Hill, the popular title of the novel, will be used as well as the official title.

[2] 4 vols. (New York: E. P. Dutton, 1932). All page references to *Clarissa* will be to this edition.

[3] "Introduction," xi.

[4] The parallels to *Pamela* seem more frequent and obvious to me than those to *Clarissa.* It may or may not be deliberate, for example, that Fanny's adventures begin at the same age as Pamela's, at fifteen; that Fanny takes the same delight in details of clothing that Pamela does (*F. H.,* p. 19); that both girls are distinguished by their employers by being put in charge of personal linen (*F. H.,* p. 11; *Pamela* I, 1). Both girls also experience lesbian advances: Pamela, from Mrs. Jewkes (*Pamela* I, 91), and Fanny from Phoebe Ayres (*F. H.,* pp. 14-17). Both enjoy repeating the praises of others (*F. H.,* p. 19). Both recognize the superior charm of rustic garb (*F. H.,* p. 19), and both several times declare the superior joys of the simple life over aristocratic vice. Both spy from closets (*F. H.,* pp. 29, 35); both anticipate "dreadful trials" (*F. H.,* p. 22), and both gain reprieve with the aid of a violent "fever" (*Pamela* I, 155; *F. H.,* p. 27). Both of them consider "instruction" the true and unfailing sign of true love (*F. H.,* pp. 63, 199). Cleland states outright the major unexpressed premise of Richardson's *Pamela,* that a maidenhead is "a perishable commodity" (p. 18). Finally, in Mr. Norbert's attack on Fanny's simulated maidenhead (pp. 153-58), Fanny acts out Pamela's "natural" reactions—"silly infantile moods of repulse and complaint" (*F. H.,* p. 154). The edition of Richardson's *Pamela* cited in this paper is that edited by George Saintsbury, 2 vols. (New York: E. P. Dutton, 1957). I am indebted to Professor H. K. Miller for a number of the parallels suggested above.

[5] *Popular Fiction Before Richardson: Narrative Patterns, 1700-1739* (Oxford: Clarendon Press, 1969). Professor Richetti discusses a number of the narrative conventions of popular fiction that were available to both Cleland and Richardson. Chapter IV, "'As Long as Atalantis Shall Be Read': the Scandal Chronicles of Mrs. Manley and Mrs. Haywood," pp. 119-67, contains a provocative discussion of the emotional convention of the "erotic-pathetic cliché," that of "helpless and virtuous females destroyed by a malign and masculine ethos" (p. 124). Chapter V, "Mrs. Haywood and the Novella—the Erotic and the Pathetic," pp. 168-210, analyzes in detail Mrs. Haywood's *Love in Excess; or The Fatal Enquiry* (1719). Professor Richetti's description of the techniques and conventions of genteel eroticism and his analysis of "erotic shorthand" (pp. 200-201) have been particularly helpful in confirming my own ideas about similarities in the fiction of Cleland and Richardson.

[6] Professor Richetti observes that in Mrs. Manley's *New Atalantis* the Duke's rape of Charlot (his ward and a paragon of innocence), "The Rape is absolutely necessary to preserve Charlot's innocence. In terms of the implicit moral of the story, she has been taken unawares, and the love which follows is merely the irresistible result of that rape. Her desires have been triggered, as it were by the assault, and she is no more to blame for them than the rape itself" (p. 146). Clarissa's virtue is made even more extraordinary by her absolute refusal to succumb to the conventional effects of such a "happy fall."

[7] *The Natural History of Sensibility* (Detroit: Wayne State Univ. Press, 1962), pp. 29-49.

[8] Cited (and translated) by Bredvold, p. 45.

[9] *Sir Charles Grandison,* 7 vols. (London: Chapman and Hall, 1902), IV, 56.

[10] John Carroll, ed., *Selected Letters* (Oxford: Clarendon Press, 1964), pp. 46-47.

[11] "Suggestions Toward a Genealogy of the 'Man of Feeling,'" *The Idea of the Humanities* (Chicago: The Univ. of Chicago Press, 1967), I, 188-213.

[12] *De la littérature* (1800). Cited (and translated) by Bredvold, p. 25.

[13] Katherine Gee Hornbeak in *The Complete Letter Writer in English: 1568-1800* (*Smith College Studies in English,* 15, Nos. 3-4, 1934) suggests that this rhetorical fashion comes directly from the line of *préciosité* in letter writing that began with Jean-Louis Guez de Balzac and Jean Puget de la Serre and found its way into English in *The Academy of Compliments* (1640). From *The Beau's Academy* (1699), she quotes a passage similar in technique to Pamela's: *"I must confess I have cast Anchor in the Harbour of thy Love, do not cut the Cable of my Affections, lest I am adrift in a Sea of Misery . . ."* p. 66).

[14] Cited (and translated) by Bredvold, p. 32.

[15] "Towards Defining an Age of Sensibility," in *Eighteenth Century Literature,* ed. James L. Clifford (New York: Oxford Univ. Press, 1949), pp. 311-18.

[16] *The Other Victorians* (New York: Basic Books, 1964), p. 278.

[17] Thomas Ashe, ed., *Table Talk and Omniana of Samuel Taylor Coleridge* (London: G. Bell and Sons, 1923), p. 295.

William H. Epstein (essay date 1974)

SOURCE: "Fanny Hill," in *John Cleland: Images of a Life,* Columbia University Press, 1974, pp. 84-107.

[*In the following excerpt, Epstein discusses the possible sources for the* Memoirs of a Woman of Pleasure, *including both classical and contemporary texts as well as Cleland's own experience with the social and ethical standards of mid-eighteenth-century England.*]

We return now to the **Memoirs** and its historical context, to a consideration of how Cleland's novel both retained and departed from the thematic, structural, and stylistic characteristics of the works of pornography which preceded it. Although the works of various classical and medieval authors—such as Juvenal, Ovid, Catullus, Petronius, Boccaccio—contain what might be called pornographic elements, books which seem to devote most of their energy to sexual arousal did not appear regularly in Europe until the middle of the seventeenth century, perhaps as part of what David Foxon terms a general European revolt against the restrictive authority of church and state.[6] Before 1660 only the work of the Italian Pietro Aretino is noteworthy. The sonnets Aretino wrote to accompany Marcantonio Raimondi's engravings of Giulio Romano's depictions of the various positions of sexual intercourse were printed originally in 1527 and reprinted frequently, usually in altered form, during the next several hundred years. Besides the *Sonetti sui Sedici modi . . .' di Giulio Romano,* Aretino also produced a series of prose dialogues, published in 1534 and 1536, which featured most prominently two Roman whores discussing, "realistically but not obscenely,"[7] contemporary personalities and morals. These dialogues, called the *Ragionamenti,* also were frequently reprinted and translated, often as excerpts.

The pornographic works which began to appear regularly about 1660 borrowed and expanded the *Ragionamenti*'s basic format of a prose dialogue between two women. The first of these works is usually styled *La Puttana Errante* ("The Wandering Whore") and was probably published in Italy around 1660. Like the earlier combined effort of Aretino and Romano, it concentrates on sexual 'postures.' The possibilities of the dialogue are largely ignored. Nevertheless, it probably is, as Foxon claims, "the first imaginative prose work which deals directly and exclusively with physical sexual satisfaction."[8] Another of the mid-seventeenth-century's significant pornographic works was *L'Ecole des filles,* first published in France in 1655. Its authorship is uncertain. To the basic "Aretinesque form of a dialogue between an experienced woman and a virgin,"[9] *L'Ecole des filles* adds a simple domestic plot and an attack on social conventions. Its English translation, entitled *The School of Venus or the Ladies delight reduced into rules of practice,* was the object of government prosecutions in 1688 and 1745. A third of these early works, *Vénus dans le cloître, ou la religieuse en chemise,* was published in France in 1683. Attributed to Jean Barrin, it transforms the by-now standard dialogue format into a series of discussions between two nuns. "There is no obscene detail": the book concerns itself mainly with "nunnery intrigues" and attacks upon the authority of the church.[10] A translation of it is the book upon which Curll's 1728 obscenity conviction focused.[11]

The last—and most significant—of the pornographic works preceding the *Memoirs* is Nicolas Chorier's *Aloisiae Sigeae Toletanae Satyra Sotadica de arcanis Amoris et Veneris.* Known familiarly as *The Dialogues* or *Satyra Sotadica,* it was the work of an Italian, written in Latin, and probably published in France about 1660. Foxon identifies it, appropriately, as the first work in which "all the themes of later pornography are present."[12] Its wealth of detail, its exploration of various sexual practices and combinations, its occasional concern with libertine domestic and religious philosophy, and its frequently elegant and euphemistic language prefigure some of the dominant features of the *Memoirs.* Like the works previously discussed, it was reprinted and translated periodically during the next century. An English translation of the French version appeared in 1745, just three years before the *Memoirs.*

In the original version, Chorier's *Dialogues* consists of six conversations of varying lengths. The first five dialogues are between two women, Ottavia and Tullia, and cover roughly two-thirds of the book. In the sixth dialogue they are joined by two men, Lampridio and Rangoni, with whom they continue their conversation and with whom they also engage in the "Frolics and Sports" mentioned in the dialogue's heading. In fact, each of the dialogues is headed by a word or phrase which cleverly and metaphorically describes its primary topic. In the first dialogue, Ottavia, to be married the next day, discloses to her older cousin, Tullia, that her husband-to-be has already inflamed her with his advances; Tullia, in turn, informs her young friend that Ottavia's mother wishes Tullia to bed with her daughter to teach her the "hidden secrets of the bridal bed"; the dialogue is headed "The Skirmish." The second dialogue, during which Tullia, in bed now with Ottavia, professes her love and begins her instruction, is headed "Tribadicon," after a Greek synonym for Lesbians. The third dialogue, concerned with a detailed explanation of the uses of the male and female sex organs, is titled "Fabric," apparently referring to a metaphorical rendering of the word 'sperm.' The fourth dialogue, "The Duel," contains Tullia's detailed description of the pain and ecstasy of her own wedding night. "Pleasures," the fifth dialogue, focuses on the sexual intrigues beneath society's surface: Ottavia, now an experienced married woman, and Tullia trade stories and advice about how supposedly faithful and chaste wives, children, priests, and mothers—including themselves, their families, and retainers—enjoy a varied and secret sensuality.

The *Dialogues'* classical flavor is evident throughout the six dialogues. Nearly every sexual act is dedicated to Venus or Priapus; Greek and Latin authors are quoted frequently, both in serious and ironic contexts; catalogues of Greek and Roman synonyms and metaphors for the sexual organs, for intercourse, and for various other practices (most notably, anal intercourse, which is depicted but condemned) are included. The *Dialogues* serves also as an instruction booklet, designed not only to acquaint Ottavia (and its readers) with the mysteries of sensuality but also to argue for a double standard of public virtue and private lust. Tullia advises Ottavia about the two rules of conjugal prudence: do what you will but avoid public scandal, and always show due respect for "public rites and common customs." Later, in the context of a discussion of the hypocrisy of public officials, Tullia restates the first rule and links it to the general observation, "the whole world exercises the art of stage-playing." Hence, beneath society's facade Ottavia and Tullia indulge their sensuality to the fullest, luxuriating as they do in euphemistic and metaphorical descriptions of their actions. The female sex organ is invariably a "conch" or "garden" unlocked by a well-equipped lover's "key"; oft-repeated acts of sexual intercourse are battles involving "bold riders" brandishing "spears" and breaching entrenched battlements.[13]

Of the major pornographic works preceding the *Memoirs,* Chorier's *Dialogues* comes closest to matching its remarkable stylistic and thematic vitality. The other principal predecessors seem to pass on little more than the older woman-younger woman dialogue format— barely preserved in the *Memoirs'* external structure as two letters from Fanny Hill to an elderly acquaintance— and a general tendency to move from simpler to more complicated sexual discoveries and adventures. But from the *Dialogues* the *Memoirs* inherits, directly or indirectly, an elegant euphemistic style, a complex plotline which enables variety to overcome repetition, a self-conscious ironic sense of what is being done and how it is being described, and a penchant for exploring the philosophical bases of sexual freedom. That the *Dialogues* directly influenced the *Memoirs* is unlikely—the former owes too much to its Latin origins, its dialogue format, and its own time to have served as a model for such a representative, mid-eighteenth-century, English novel. Nevertheless, the similarities between the two books, and the less striking resemblances between the *Memoirs* and other early works of pornography, reveal part of the context within which the *Memoirs* appeared and indicate that some of its readers probably were able to recognize where and how the *Memoirs* subscribed to and deviated from established practices.

Within the context of a pornographic work which looked both backward and forward for stylistic, structural, and thematic impetus Cleland sought to incorporate his sense of some of the salient cultural and philosophical movements of his day. These movements, which cut across social and occasionally national boundaries, form the background of the **Memoirs'** perceptions of the world and suggest the kinds of special knowledge its author drew upon in fashioning the imaginative narrative of Fanny Hill. The **Memoirs** reveals, for instance, that Cleland probably was familiar with the realistic cultural and subcultural depiction of London "low life" which typified the works of such accomplished artists as Defoe and Hogarth and of such crude hacks as the anonymous authors of whore biography. The **Memoirs** indicates also that he must have been equally well acquainted with the middle-class ethical and structural concerns of Richardson's *Pamela* and of the groups of reactionary novels which it spawned, the anti-pamelas. Moreover, the **Memoirs** suggests that Cleland was keenly sensitive to the life style of the rarefied social circle which his parents cultivated, and that he may have been aware of certain trends in English and French philosophy which sought to counteract elitism's essential superficiality with a world-view based upon varying conceptions of natural morality. That this cultural and philosophical background informs and not merely adorns the **Memoirs** is a major reason for the book's vitality and durability. For the **Memoirs** manages to stimulate, often simultaneously, the physical and intellectual senses; and although ultimately the physical must dominate, the constant tension between the two preserves the book's essential vigor long after the details of other pornographic works have faded back into the subliminal realm of the purely instinctual. "In fact [writes Malcolm Bradbury) *The Memoirs of a Woman of Pleasure* is about aesthetics as well as about sex . . . ," and "it plays happily along the borderline where the worlds of mind and body meet."[14] To explore that borderline is to approach the boundaries of Cleland's intellect.

Cleland's presentation in the **Memoirs** of the situational hazards of a young, penniless girl cast adrift in the turbulence of London indicates that he relied upon much of the same background and structural phenomena as Defoe, Hogarth, and the writers of whore biography.[15] In one sense, the rampant prostitution of the early and middle eighteenth century was a result of England's relatively closed class structure, a structure which deprived a married woman of most of her legal rights and economic freedom and which denied both men and women the reasonable opportunity to improve their lot in life. Indeed, the scandalous nature of the horrifying options which confronted the young, unmarried woman was an acknowledged fact throughout the century. That the situation was not improving was also universally recognized, and hence a writer wishing to give a realistic biographical background to the story of a prostitute in the London of the 1740's would be drawing on essentially the same sociological factors as a writer concerned with the same topic in the 1720's and 1730's. Not surprisingly, then, the **Memoirs** shares some of the same concerns as Defoe's *Moll Flanders,* Hogarth's *Harlot's Progress* and other prints, and various anonymous authors' whore biographies.

The similarities between the **Memoirs** and *Moll Flanders* involve both the coincidental details and larger career patterns which Fanny and Moll—both atypical because unusually fortunate prostitutes—present in their narratives. For example, as L. J. Morrisey and B. Slepian point out, "Fanny's mother and Moll's foster mother both keep day schools . . . ; both are impressed by good clothes; . . . each mistakes a prostitute for a gentlewoman because of her good clothes; . . . each is described as neat and clean." Moreover, both Fanny and Moll are conscious of the economic and ethical structures of their lives and of the paradoxical opportunities their profession offers them to control and even to improve both their purse and their soul. Although throughout most of their careers both women "move promiscuously from man to man [,] each decides early on a favourite man, to whom she returns at the end, morally reformed, and, as a result of her promiscuity, rich."[16] Indeed, tabulation and accumulation of material possessions are characteristic of both Moll and Fanny. Moll's preoccupation with money and the security and freedom it can allow her is proverbial; we have long recognized that "her life is led almost exclusively among commodities."[17] Fanny too has the habit of settling her accounts at each stage of her career, of balancing, as does Moll, her financial gain against her spiritual loss. For example, she remembers exactly the bill she owed her landlady when Charles left her (23/ 17/6), the inadequate sum she had with which to pay it (7 gg.), and the obligation she felt to Mr. H—— when he settled the bill for her. She remembers too that when she left Mr. H— and went to Mrs. Cole's as a professional prostitute her "cloaths and moveables" were worth at least two hundred pounds.[18]

Of course, none of these parallels shows that Cleland had *Moll Flanders* in mind when he wrote the **Memoirs** or even that he had read the book; but, taken together, these similarities do indicate the kinds of basic thematic concerns and incidental details which Cleland was drawing on and which he shared, consciously or not, with one of the most popular and most influential works of the time. As Bradbury notes, "*Fanny Hill* is a pornography of sex, *Moll Flanders* is a pornography of money."[19] The implication is that even if Cleland was not familiar with Defoe's work, he was at home in his world.

On the other hand, a popular and influential cultural figure with whose work Cleland surely was familiar is Hogarth. To quote Peter Quennell: "*Memoirs of a*

Woman of Pleasure has a decidedly Hogarthian background; and its heroine and the painter's famous Moll Hackabout—also a country girl ensnared by a clever London bawd—are personages of much the same stamp. They belong to a similar world, the world of masquerades and Covent Garden *bagnios* and the fashionable bawdy houses of the West End."[20] Moll or Mary[21] Hackabout is Hogarth's center of artistic interest in a series of prints published in April 1732 entitled *Harlot's Progress.*[22] In graphic and sometimes frightening detail the series illustrates what was happening every day on the streets of London. The six prints follow this young country girl with the descriptive name from the moment she arrives in London and comes into the hands of "Mother" Needham, a pious bawd, and of her assistant Colonel Francis Charteris, whose "method of seduction was to post agents in innyards to spot newly-arrived girls from the country, and . . . to employ the girl as a servant in his house."[23] Fanny too arrives at a London inn a young country girl unaccustomed to the ways of the town. The next day she visits an "intelligence-office," where she finds "sitting in a corner of the room" a "squabfat, red faced" woman of "at least fifty" who, Fanny notes, "look'd as if she would devour me with her eyes."[24] The woman, Mrs. Brown, takes Fanny home and, under the guise of employing her as a servant, introduces her to a house of prostitution.

The other prints in *Harlot's Progress* depict Moll Hackabout's employment as a mistress to a proverbially rich Jew, her subsequent dismissal from his service for her attentions to a younger lover, her imprisonment, her death throes from the ravages of venereal disease, and finally her funeral and the ludicrous mourning which accompanies it.[25] Fanny's story corresponds only partially to this account—she too loses a wealthy keeper, Mr. H—, when she instigates an affair with Will, his young and well-endowed servant—and contains none of the dire consequences which distress Moll Hackabout. Yet both stories have a common starting point and rely upon much of the same background material.

Some of Hogarth's other prints indicate that Cleland also shared with the artist a few of the more specific details of this general setting. For instance, both Hogarth and Cleland make similar use of a well-known West End character of the 1740's, "Mother" Douglas, a prostitute notorious for her spiritual piety and her addiction to alcohol. "A resident of the Piazza, northeast corner of Covent Garden,"[26] she was a frequent object of artistic ridicule because of her notoriety and of her unusual combination of traits. Of the three times Hogarth depicted her, one was in a print published before the *Memoirs,* on 30 September 1747, entitled *Industry and Idleness,* where she is "the fat woman in the second cart, with a gin glass to her lips."[27] The two other prints, published in 1750 and 1761, concentrate on her extreme and incongruous piety.[28]

"Mother" Douglas, or a character based on her, also appeared in several literary products of the times, all of which were published after the *Memoirs.* She is called Mrs. Cole in one of these works, *The Minor* (1760), a farce by Samuel Foote, who was friendly with Cleland.[29] The use of the name Cole links her, as a real person and as an artistic character, to the prostitute of the same name who appeared some twelve years earlier in the *Memoirs.* Although Cleland did not emphasize those paradoxical qualities of extreme piety and alcoholism which typified "Mother" Douglas' character in Hogarth's prints and in Foote's farce, nevertheless he did draw on her reputation as London's wealthiest and most eccentric procuress. Fanny's initial impression of Mrs. Cole is evidence of whom Cleland had in mind:

> And as it happen'd, I could not have put myself into worse, or into better hands in all *London;* into worse, because keeping a house of conveniency, there were no lengths in lewdness she would not advise me to go in compliance with her customers, no schemes of pleasure, or even unbounded debauchery, she did not take even a delight in promoting: into better, because no body having had more experience of the wicked part of the town than she had, was fitter to advise and guard one against the worst dangers of our profession. . . . [30]

As London's most notorious woman of pleasure, "Mother" Douglas certainly would seem to fit this description. Moreover, that she "died wealthy, in June 1761, leaving costly furniture and pictures,"[31] indicates a lifelong concern with financial stability which may have been the stimulus for the same economic awareness in the *Memoirs'* Mrs. Cole. Although Fanny depicts Mrs. Cole as content to live on a modest income with which she eventually retires to a quiet life in the country, Fanny also reports that her mistress is forever conscious of the basic insecurity of a prostitute's life. Indeed, only through "the fruit of [her] deference to Mrs. Cole's counsels" is Fanny herself able to leave her employ with a sizable cash "reserve" totaling eight hundred pounds.[32]

Not only Fanny, then, but at least two of the *Memoirs'* other characters share a common cultural milieu with the characters of eighteenth-century England's most popular artist. Of course, this correspondence should not suggest that Cleland and Hogarth shared more than a cultural perspective, that, for example, Cleland must have been thinking of Moll Hackabout, "Mother" Needham, and "Mother" Douglas when he created Fanny, Mrs. Brown, and Mrs. Cole. Rather, those general and specific ways in which the *Memoirs* parallels Hogarth's prints suggest that Cleland was not working in a void, that certain basic approaches to the same material already had been tried and tested, and that Cleland seems to have been aware of those earlier efforts and of the uses to which he could put them.

Cleland may also have found artistic stimulus from other, less respectable sources. He seems to have been equally aware of the essential themes and approaches of certain subcultural phenomena, especially those of the so-called whore biographies, in which, according to John Richetti, "the explicitly erotic," as in the *Memoirs,* "was comic and sinful in that order." In these books, which enjoyed a popular vogue throughout the first part of the century, the whore usually is "the opportunist *par excellence,* the entrepeneur . . . who deliberately makes her spiritual ruin her material enrichment." Moreover, "she achieves power, pleasure . . . . , and independence impossible to eighteenth-century un-emancipated woman." The incompatibility of the closed class-structure which spawned her and her own apolitical brand of "radical social aggression" is recognized and treated comically. Hence, in whore biography, "all men are reduced to the level of potential clients, helpless pawns in an erotic game controlled by the whore."

Richetti describes "a good example of this comic emphasis," the 1723 *Authentick Memoirs of the Life Intrigues and Adventures of the Celebrated Sally Salisbury,* which consists for the most part of "a mock-heroic account" of "a series of scabrous and frequently brutal stories." Sally services "well-known aristocrats and politicians"; the descriptions of her adventures partake frequently of the kind of "anatomical survey," "leering comedy," and ironic moralizing which dominate Fanny's own narration. Other whore biographies present similar parallels to the *Memoirs;* like the *Memoirs,* they "tend naturally toward the simple social satire of traditional folk-tales and rogue stories" and, like Fanny, their heroines tend to conceive of the moral framework of their world as divided only between Virtue and Vice, as between chastity and impurity.[33] Indeed, Fanny's concluding "tail-piece of morality," with its implicit pun and sermonizing tone, is a recapitulation of the essential moral conflict of most whore biography:

> Thus, at length, I got snug into port, where, in the bosom of virtue, I gather'd the only uncorrupt sweets: where, looking back on the course of vice, I had run, and comparing its infamous blandishments with the infinitely superior joys of innocence, I could not help pitying, even in point of taste, those who, immers'd in a gross sensuality, are insensible to the so delicate charms of VIRTUE, than which even PLEASURE has not a greater friend, nor than VICE a greater enemy. Thus temperance makes men lords over those pleasures that intemperance enslaves them to. . . . [34]

Fanny too recognizes the potential hypocrisy and incongruity of this sermonette: that it appears "no doubt, out of place, out of character" and that (as in whore biography) it seems to be "the paltry finesse of one who seeks to mask a devotee to Vice under a rag of a veil, impudently smuggled from the shrine of Virtue."[35] Of course, Fanny's keener awareness of the paradox of her intellectual position distinguishes her from most of the heroines of whore biography. Nevertheless, the need she feels to justify her actions by placing them in the context of a moral framework of Virtue and Vice puts her squarely in their world. This correspondence suggests yet another approach to his material with which Cleland may have been familiar and which he may have found useful.

Whether, before he wrote the *Memoirs,* Cleland was thoroughly conversant with the influential cultural and subcultural themes and approaches of Defoe, Hogarth, and the writers of whore biography is not known. But surely he must have been aware of the basic social situations they depicted and even of some of the customary ways in which they handled their material. For the *Memoirs* contains itself, as do *Moll Flanders, Harlot's Progress,* and *The Authentick Memoirs . . . of Sally Salisbury,* with an essential problem which most eighteenth-century women were unable or unwilling to confront: how, in a man's world, were they to find peace and freedom? In fact, in a letter to Ralph Griffiths[36] written sometime in 1749—not long after the complete first edition of the *Memoirs* was available—Cleland examined this very question. Griffiths had lent him the two volumes of *Memoirs of Mrs. Laetitia Pilkington: wife to the Rev. Matthew Pilkington,* which Griffiths had published separately in 1748 and 1749 and which he later had advertised along with the revised edition of *Memoirs of Fanny Hill.*[37] Mrs. Pilkington's "Memoirs," printed together with her "Poems" and "Anecdotes of several eminent Persons, Living and Dead," give an especially horrifying account of some of the problems facing an eighteenth-century woman, an account to which Cleland reacted sympathetically. In her book Mrs. Pilkington reveals how her husband, a poor Irish preacher with literary pretensions, abandoned her at least twice, unsuccessfully tried to act as her procurer either to advance his projects or to prove her adulterous, and finally divorced her and left her penniless. With three children and "no other Fortune than my Pen," she had lived alone in London, arousing the wonder and, of course, the skepticism of the town. Only the intervention of Colley Cibber, the poet laureate, had rescued her from debtors' prison and enabled her to find a means—her *Memoirs*—of telling her story.[38]

That story was the one Cleland had read in "the 2 Volume of Letitia Pilkington" which he returned to Griffiths one day in 1749. In the note which accompanied the books he reported to their publisher that he had found in her story "a great deal of nature, which is enough to recommend it: but one reflexion and a very Just and favourable one to the sex in general has occurred to me on the perusal," he continued, obviously interested in the broader implications of Mrs. Pilkington's distress, to wit, that this woman would have, in all probability, made an irreproachable wife, had she not been married to such a villain, as her whole history shows her husband to have been: and indeed to do that sex Justice, most of their errors are originally owing to our treatment of them: they would be [to us?] what they ought to be, if we [would be?] to them what we ought to be.[39]

Of course, Mrs. Pilkington's story may have been discomforting enough to elicit the sympathy of most of her male readers: after all, she had depicted herself as a quintessential female victim, the dutiful and long-suffering wife of a brutal and contemptible man. Yet the legal and social environment which permitted Matthew Pilkington to mistreat his wife with little fear of penalty did not begin to change until well into the nineteenth century. The first Matrimonial Causes Act was passed in 1857; the first Married Woman's Property Act was enacted in 1870. Moreover, the eighteenth century witnessed little social agitation to improve women's rights. Hence, in the context of its times, Cleland's response to Laetitia Pilkington's story is reasonably liberal; it suggests that he was conscious of the basic ethical conflict which lurks beneath the surface not only of Laetitia Pilkington's *Memoirs,* but also of *Moll Flanders, Harlot's Progress, The Authentick Memoirs . . . of Sally Salisbury,* and *Memoirs of a Woman of Pleasure.* Indeed, that he was as concerned with "what we ought to be" as he was with "what they ought to be" is an indication that he was cognizant of one way in which that conflict could be resolved.

Of course, the *Memoirs* is not really "about" the problems facing eighteenth-century women, any more than it is "about," as Fanny claims at the end, the glorification of vice "in order to make the worthier, the solemner sacrifice of it, to virtue."[40] The complex rhetorical interplay between the essential details of Fanny's sexual life and the constantly shifting emotions and attitudes with which she views those details prohibit any simple conclusions about the book's final effect. Yet the evidence in the *Memoirs* and in Cleland's letter to Griffiths of a concern with such matters as the problems confronting women suggests that Cleland was aware of, and in some ways responsive to, certain social and cultural dilemmas. And he seems to have shared this awareness with such influential artists as Defoe, Hogarth, and the writers of whore biography.

The *Memoirs* also suggests that Cleland was familiar with another literary approach to the problems confronting women: the so-called anti-pamela movement—books which borrowed and parodied the epistolary form, the main plot, and, frequently, the characters and events of Richardson's *Pamela; or Virtue Rewarded* (1740). Essentially, the anti-pamelas attacked Richardson's

moral perspective;[41] they considered Pamela's unromantic social predicament unworthy of attention and the treatment of her stalwart chastity and unlikely social mobility sentimental and unrealistic. Spearheaded by Fielding in *Shamela* (1741) and later, to a lesser degree, in *Joseph Andrews* (1742), this literary counterattack involved the critical attention of a large segment of the cultural community and lasted throughout most of the decade of the forties.

In many of its implicit assumptions, the anti-pamela movement shared with Defoe, Hogarth, and the writer of whore biography a similar hard-headed view of the 'woman problem': that the artistic product which depicted the dilemma confronting contemporary women should offer an unsentimentalized perspective, a perspective in which the prime "virtue" should be experience and not innocence.[42] Consequently, the anti-pamelas—as had those earlier works—made extravagant appeals to the value of truth, especially "natural truth." Richardson, of course, had done the same, even having maintained that he was but the editor of an actual series of letters between a young servant girl and her parents. Indeed, Richardson's reliance on this convention forced many of his imitators and parodists to claim to be in possession of the true account of Pamela's life. Where the anti-pamela writers differed from Richardson was in the philosophical application of "the correspondence between words and reality";[43] they felt that *Pamela's* realistic evocation of everyday people and events had been used to evolve a sentimental resolution to a pragmatic problem.

The *Memoirs* shares the cultural perspective of the anti-pamela movement and suggests that Cleland was quite probably familiar with *Pamela* and its parodies. Fanny too feels the need to assure her readers that her story mirrors absolute truth and that that truth, though it may violate the "laws of decency," will not "snuff prudishly" through "the strip of a gauze wrapper" at "situations such as they actually rose to me in nature." At the very onset, Fanny promises that "Truth! stark naked truth, is the word."[44] Her metaphor of reality as nature in its naked state echoes the tone and substance of the introductory sections of the first anti-pamela, Fielding's *Shamela.* "'The author hath reconciled the *pleasing* to the *proper,*'" Fielding has *Shamela's* Parson Tickletext say of *Pamela,* "'the thought is everywhere exactly clothed by the expression; and becomes its dress as *roundly* and as close as Pamela her country habit; or *as she doth her no habit,* when modest beauty seeks to hide itself, by casting off the pride of ornament, and displaying itself without any covering. . . .'" Not only here but elsewhere Parson Tickletext makes ironic use—as does Fanny—of the metaphor of seeing nature unclothed. "'—Oh!'" he exclaims, "'I feel an emotion even while I am relating this: methinks I see Pamela at this instant, with all the pride of ornament cast off.'"[45]

The *Memoirs* also echoes *Pamela* more directly. Aside from certain general plot similarities—both novels have as a narrator and central character a young country girl forced out of her familiar surroundings by poverty and placed at the mercy of the upper classes—the *Memoirs* and *Pamela* share several incidental details of structural technique. For example, Fanny's encomium to "the solemner sacrifice . . . to virtue," which concludes her "tail-piece of morality" and which found its way onto the title page of the revised *Memoirs of Fanny Hill*, corresponds in tone and substance with the moral parables which appear in *Pamela*'s appendix and title page. "Now first Published In order to cultivate the Principles of virtue and Religion in the Minds of the Youth of Both Sexes," *Pamela*'s title page reads in part; the appendix, reinforcing pointedly the significance of the story's moral lessons, delineates the moral "applications" to which the "YOUTH OF BOTH SEXES" can put the book's "most material incidents."[46] Fanny's "tail-piece of morality" burlesques this technique, borrowing its ideas and placement in the text, but not its seriousness of purpose and tone. In so doing the "tail-piece" does not offer—as, for example, *Joseph Andrews* does—a viable and even attractive alternative to *Pamela*'s rigid moral posturing. Fanny merely makes statements; she never translates her words into action. She never goes through—as does Joseph Andrews—a learning process which can be accepted as resembling reality. Perhaps she too would like to be believed, but she makes no attempt to reinforce belief. Here is where she turns away from the effective anti-pamelas; unable to forge the medium of parody into an active instrument of realistic and constructive commentary, she must settle for something less.

Yet whatever Fanny settles for, her awareness of the structural and thematic concerns of *Pamela* and of such anti-pamelas as *Shamela* and *Joseph Andrews* indicates that the kind of interest in the 'woman question' which Cleland displayed in his letter to Griffiths may have been one of the more significant components of his developing artistic consciousness. Focused on an unsentimentalized concept of realism, this interest linked together a significant segment of the cultural and subcultural artistic community. Indeed, so intricately bound up in this concept is Fanny's narrative that it is difficult to avoid the conclusion that Cleland's awareness of this community and of its more noteworthy artistic products predated the publication of the *Memoirs*.[47]

The *Memoirs* also indicates that Cleland was keenly sensitive to the life style of the great and near-great, and to the manner in which the rarefied social circle to which his parents aspired comported itself. Fanny speaks often of "the great," whom she finds superficial and unnatural, unable to appreciate what she terms "the art of living." Indeed, throughout her narrative, as she describes the stages of her development from a poor country girl into a well-to-do woman of the town, Fanny

is forever conscious of that other world of quality. Men and women of quality have the freedom and the resources to seek and enjoy beauty, a process which she considers "the nature of pleasure itself." Yet they seldom find real pleasure, for, as she observes, they are "so grossly cheated by their pride." To Fanny this facade of pride creates and protects an insipid and trifling "system of life"; behind it are hidden "all the miseries, the follies, and impertinences of the women of quality." From almost the very beginning of her career Fanny is unwilling to sacrifice the freedom which she finds in seeking pleasure to "the vulgar prejudices in favour of titles, dignities, honours, and the like." Charles, her first lover, has neither position nor wealth (his father, like William Cleland, has had "a small post in the revenue" and "rather overliv'd his income") and has received "a very slender education." "Without those great or shining qualities that constitute a genius, or are fit to make a noise in the world," Charles, nevertheless, has something better—"the softer social merit: plain common sense, set off with every grace of modesty and good nature." Fanny, of course, is attracted at first to "nothing, but the beauties of his person," but later she has "full occasion" to discern and appreciate his "internal merit" as well.[48]

After Charles leaves her and she becomes a kept mistress, Fanny has another opportunity to discover that what makes a man truly noble is not "loftier qualifications of birth, fortune, and sense." Finding that her keeper is unfaithful, she decides to repay him in his own "coin" and instigates an affair with his servant Will. Will is a natural beauty, "as pretty a piece of woman's meat as you should see," whom "nature seem'd to have design'd for the highest diet of pleasure." After describing how she seduced Will, Fanny explains why she became involved with "a young fellow in too low a rank of life." First, she reasons, "my condition, strictly consider'd," was not "one jot more exalted." Yet, she asks, had she been above him, "did not his capacity of giving such exquisite pleasure sufficiently raise and enoble him, to *me* at least?" She recalls that, at this time, "the talent of pleasing, with which nature has endow'd a handsome person, form'd to me the greatest of all merits." What counts in her hierarchy of values is not "loftier qualifications of birth, fortune, and sense," which her keeper has and which have placed her "under a sort of subjection and constraint," but the ability to give sensual pleasure. Her "natural philosophy," she remembers, "all resided in the favourite center of sense."[49]

Later, Fanny defends her "minute detail" of her adventures with Will as an "exalted . . . pleasure" which "ought not to be ungratefully forgotten or suppress'd," even though she "found it in a character in low life." For pleasure, she explains, is often "purer" in a person of Will's station than "amongst the false ridiculous refinements" of the great. The low, unhindered by the artificial facade of pride, are "unsophisticate," "purer," closer to nature: unlike the great, they do not "for ever mistake things the most foreign to the nature of pleasure itself." In fact, as Fanny recognizes, her involvement with Will "bred one great revolution in my life"; discovered with Will by her keeper, she is cast "once more a-drift" and forced to find her own way. Left with more than two hundred pounds, she finds her way to Mrs. Cole's and sets out to become not merely a kept mistress but a professional woman of pleasure. She was now, she offers, "abandon'd to my own conduct, and turn'd loose upon the town, to sink or swim."[50]

Free at last to practice what she has preached, to seek pleasure and profit in an atmosphere of "freedom and intimacy" uncontaminated by the facade of pride, Fanny becomes a willing partner of "the authors and supporters" of a libertine society which gathers at Mrs. Cole's. The "veteran voluptuaries" who are "the founders, and patrons of this little Seraglio" have developed a philosophy which rejects the falseness of the privileged classes and which seeks to invert or subvert the traditional value system. They prefer "the pure native charms"; a "ruddy, healthy, firm-flesh'd country-maid" is prized more highly than "a sallow, washy, painted dutchess." They consider modesty, the emblem of the middle class, "their mortal enemy," "the poison of joy." They find "all force, or constraint," the weapon of the upper class, unnatural and unnecessary. Fanny, who sees in this libertine society a concrete working-out of her own "natural philosophy," is anxious to join "these profound adepts in the great art and science of pleasure." "Take notice, that I thought as I spoke," she reminds her correspondent as she describes how, of her own free will and for her own pleasure, she agreed to become an initiate of the society.[51]

Recent explorations of the *Memoirs'* similarities to contemporary French works, such as La Mettrie's *L'Homme machine* (1747) and D'Argens' *Thérèse philosophe* (1748), suggest that, in one way or another, Fanny fashions her "natural philosophy" from a matrix of philosophical systems that include the by-then traditional Lockean "pattern of spontaneous responses" and the more radical materialist notion of the body as machine.[52] Yet underlying Fanny's use of any formal system of philosophy is her quite pedestrian preoccupation with the superficiality of the world of quality. Behind all her attempts to develop a philosophy and a life style based on natural beauty is her recognition that a life of aristocratic luxury, the ultimate wishful-fillment of most men and women, is finally corrupt and debilitating. Indeed, "the miseries, the follies, and impertinences of the women [and men] of quality" is the dominant theme in most of Cleland's work. It emerges in his plays and other novels as the greatest threat to the harmony of the social fabric. Encumbered somewhat by Fanny's complex rhetorical and intellectual relationship to her past, this notion of the artifici-

ality of the nobility plays much the same role in the *Memoirs.*

Fanny's preoccupation with the foibles of the aristocracy may reflect Cleland's own sensitivity to that mode of living. One possible source of that sensitivity was the life style his parents so judiciously and energetically cultivated. His father's playing cards with Lady Marlborough at Tunbridge, his mother's keenly soliciting Chesterfield for a letter of introduction to Madame de Tencin were typical scenes from lives passed in the pursuit of the acceptance and favor of the aristocracy. Indeed, William and Lucy Cleland valued most highly what Fanny assigned "a very low rank indeed": the very stuff of a world based on external appearances only, "the vulgar prejudices in favour of titles, dignities, honours, and the like."[53] That Fanny's jaundiced view of the aristocracy rises directly from Cleland's own animus against his parents' life style seems likely, yet we should hesitate before imposing on him Fanny's entire value system. She is, after all, a character in a novel—a rather complex character, who assumes an existence of her own and who must resolve her own unique problems. Certainly, her awareness of and reaction to the "unnatural" world of the upper classes indicates that Cleland too was sensitive to his parents' life style and cognizant of one way in which its imposing facade could be scrutinized and, ultimately, rejected. Yet, despite his concern with this topic in his other works and even occasionally in his correspondence, Cleland may never have done more with the notion of 'natural morality' than construct a theoretical model for it in his writing.

Nevertheless, attacks on the nobility are among Cleland's favorite novelistic devices. In fact, the *Memoirs* suggests yet another way in which Fanny—and possibly Cleland—attempted to undermine the traditional values of the aristocracy. In the beginning of her second letter Fanny speaks of her narrative style, which she characterizes as "a mean temper'd with taste, between the revoltingness of gross, rank, and vulgar expressions, and the ridicule of mincing metaphors and affected circumlocutions." Fanny's appraisal of her style as a mean between the gross and the refined is strikingly similar to her description soon after of why Mrs. Cole's establishment "was the safest, politest, and at the same time, the most thorough house of accommodation": Mrs. Cole, Fanny reasons, "had found the secret so rare and difficult, of reconciling even all the refinements of taste and delicacy, with the most gross and determinate gratifications of sensuality." Fanny's style, then, is like the ideal bawdy house: it strikes a delicate balance between "the refinements of taste and delicacy" and "the most gross and determinate gratifications of sensuality." And, like that "most thorough house of accommodation," it disdains pretense, modesty, and constraint, and prizes natural truth, natural beauty, and freedom. Hence, like her "natural philosophy," Fanny's narrative style strives to break down the facade behind which society hides reality. For words, like clothes, are ornaments of pride: beneath their elegant surface is often concealed the "stark naked truth" which Fanny claims she is trying to reveal.[54]

Fanny's characteristic method of revealing truth is burlesque.[55] She borrows, and then exaggerates outrageously, the euphemistic diction and metaphorical construction of the most refined and cultivated contemporary prose styles. Like the most pretentious writers of the time, she luxuriates in the seemingly infinite depths of the periodic sentence, stretching its intricate phrasing and internal balances and antitheses to almost unbearable limits, creating out of the complexity of her sentence structure a parody of her own style. Onto this remarkably convoluted sentence structure she grafts the extended metaphors and buoyant euphemisms which set her style in motion and propel its ironic, often comic tone. Indeed, the extent to which Fanny will go to carry out a metaphor or avoid an obscene word is constantly surprising: her only limit seems to be, as John Hollander suggests, "the very structure of English vocabulary itself."[56] For instance, she displays her "talent . . . for euphemism"[57]—a talent which is euphuistic in its decorative elegance and seems to be her favorite stylistic device—nearly every time she describes the male or female sex organ or the various methods of sexual intercourse. Below are listed only a few of her "synonyms for the male organ"; but, as Morrissey and Slepian intimate, they indicate well the variety and richness of her euphemistic and metaphorial style: "red-headed champion," "weapon of pleasure," "gristle," "column," "truncheon," "flesh brush," "maypole," "animated ivory," "picklock," "battering ram," "conduit pipe," "plenipotentiary instrument," "whitestaff," "pleasure pivot," "splitter," "round fillet of the whitest veal," "scepter-member," "love's true arrow."[58]

Here, as well as in her metaphorical punning in describing the sexual act itself (when Fanny is made love to by a sailor, for example, she is not merely entered, but quite literally boarded) and in her overly complex sentence structure, Fanny is entering the self-conscious, undercutting realm of the burlesque. Once having entered this realm, she is able to externalize, to turn her style into a fine cutting edge with which she can slice through the veil of words behind which civilized society conceals itself. Hence, she avoids that sense of self-importance which gives to the world of quality its confining and sterile character.

Certainly, Cleland seems to have shared Fanny's intricate and convoluted manner of expression; it is the style he used to defend Soncurr, to describe the series of miniature portraits which he sent to Pope, to explain his role in creating the ***Memoirs*** to Stanhope and to

Stone. He seems also to have shared her ironic perspective; surely, for example, he was aware of the bishops' role in suppressing the ***Memoirs*** when he drily informed Stanhope "that more Clergymen bought it, in proportion, than any other distinction of men."[59] Yet to claim that in the ***Memoirs*** Cleland was expressing his own disapproval of the artificiality of the aristocracy or to assert that Fanny's rejection of the traditional values of the world of quality was a reflection of Cleland's repudiation of his parents' life style is to force Cleland's relationship to Fanny's narrative to the breaking point. Although he seems to have found neither peace nor security in the four haphazard decades he spent under his parents' influence, Cleland was not necessarily disenchanted with it. Indeed, his upbringing may have inured him to the vicissitudes of a career dependent upon patronage, and he may have accepted such disruptive events as his father's dismissal or his own forced departure from the East India Company as the inescapable consequences of ambition.

Yet whether or not Cleland shared Fanny's ironic perspective, the ***Memoirs'*** recognition of the artificiality of the upper-class and of the means by which that noble facade could be subverted indicates yet another way in which Cleland was cognizant of the many social levels through which he had passed and of the literary resources upon which he could rely to depict those levels. For the book itself reveals some of the ways in which Cleland was prepared to write the ***Memoirs*** and suggests how he was able to piece together a few of the fragments of his disordered life. The ***Memoirs'*** awareness of some of the more significant works and ideas of its time—*Moll Flanders, Harlot's Progress,* whore biography, *Pamela,* the anti-pamelas, the "woman question," "natural philosophy," burlesque, the artificiality of the great—brings into focus its author's artistic consciousness and explains why Cleland was ready to put words on paper. For the ***Memoirs*** is the transition point; it represents a moment of change and discovery in Cleland's life, a moment when the world seemed in perfect harmony with nature, when the past became knowable and the future possible. From this moment on Cleland's life would never undergo another drastic change. In the middle of his journey he had found himself, and what he had found he would choose to retain. Now, he was a writer.

Notes

[6] Foxon, *Libertine Lit.,* p. 51. In this and the following paragraphs I base my conclusions about the growth of European pornography and my selection of key seventeenth-century pornographic works upon Foxon's pioneering research, esp. pp. 19-45.

[7] Foxon, *Libertine Lit.,* p. 26.

[8] Foxon, p. 27.

[9] Foxon, p. 30.

[10] Foxon, p. 43.

[11] Foxon, p. 14.

[12] Foxon, p. 48.

[13] The summary of and quotations from Chorier's *Dialogues* in the preceding two paragraphs are based upon an English translation published by Brandon House in 1965. See, esp., pp. 12, 25, 39, 54, 83, 102, 135-36, 210, 263.

[14] "*Fanny Hill* and the Comic Novel," pp. 270, 275.

[15] Whore biography, as a term and as a "distinct type of popular criminal narrative," is discussed in Richetti, *Popular Fiction Before Richardson*, pp. 35-41.

[16] Morrissey and Slepian, "Fanny and Moll," p. 61.

[17] Rexroth, "Afterword," in Defoe, *Moll Flanders*, p. 307. Associations between *Moll Flanders* and the *Memoirs* are discussed also in McMaster, "The Equation of Love and Money in *Moll Flanders*," p. 137. But McMaster insists she is emphasizing "the nature of the difference" between the two books (p. 143, n. 15), and cites Donovan, "The Two Heroines of *Moll Flanders*" in *The Shaping Vision*, p. 23: "'though *Moll Flanders* and *Fanny Hill* both offer accounts of a long series of sexual encounters, they have virtually nothing else in common.'" Obviously I disagree, as do Morrissey and Slepian, Plumb in *Memoirs of Fanny Hill*, introd. p. xi, and Bradbury in "*Fanny Hill* and the Comic Novel," pp. 265-66.

[18] Cleland, *Memoirs*, pp. 67, 70, 104 [I, 149, 156, 226].

[19] Bradbury, "*Fanny Hill* and the Comic Novel," p. 266.

[20] Cleland, *Memoirs*, p. xii.

[21] There is disagreement as to whether her name is Moll or Mary. In Hogarth's advertisement for the publication of *Harlot's Progress* she is mentioned simply as M. Hackabout. See Paulson, *Hogarth's Graphic Works*, I, 141-49. For more information on *Harlot's Progress* see Paulson's *Hogarth: His Life, Art, and Times*, I, 229-98.

[22] Paulson, *Hogarth's Graphic Works*, I, 141.

[23] Paulson, *Hogarth's Graphic Works*, I, 144.

[24] Cleland, *Memoirs*, p. 9 [I, 16-18].

[25] Paulson, *Hogarth's Graphic Works*, I, 145-49, and II, 121-26.

[26] Paulson, *Hogarth's Graphic Works*, I, 246. See also Bleackley, *Ladies Fair and Frail*, p. 11.

[27] Paulson, *Hogarth's Graphic Works*, I, 201.

[28] Paulson, *Hogarth's Graphic Works*, I, 280, 246. These prints were *The March to Finchley* and *Enthusiasm Delineated*.

[29] Bleackley, *Ladies Fair and Frail*, p. 11, and Paulson, *Hogarth's Graphic Works*, I, 247, note the "Mother" Douglas-Mrs. Cole connection in Foote's play. Paulson also notes her role in the *Memoirs*. See also Trefman, *Sam. Foote*, pp. 110, 113.

[30] *Memoirs*, p. 103 [I, 224].

[31] Paulson, *Hogarth's Graphic Works*, I, 247.

[32] *Memoirs*, p. 197 [II, 216].

[33] Information about the essential themes and approaches of "whore biography" and about *Sally Salisbury* is from Richetti, *Popular Fiction Before Richardson*, pp. 35-38, 40-41, who suggests the relationship between "whore biography" and the *Memoirs*.

[34] *Memoirs*, p. 213 [II, 251-52].

[35] *Memoirs*, p. 213 [II, 252].

[36] "John Cleland to Ralph Griffiths," in Letters to R. Griffiths Ed. *Monthly Review*, MS. Add. c. 89. f. 29, in the Bodleian Library. Griffiths himself noted at the bottom that "The above was received from Mr. Cleland, in 1749." As far as I know, this letter has never been published.

[37] A copy of the first edition of Mrs. Pilkington's *Memoirs* is preserved in the British Museum. It was printed in three volumes in 1748, 1749, and 1754. The title-page of the first volume reveals that it was printed originally in Dublin, then reprinted in London and sold by Ralph Griffiths. The advertisement in the *General Advertiser* of 8 March 1750 for *Memoirs of Fanny Hill* reads, at the bottom under Griffiths' name, "*Of whom may be had, in Two Volumes, Price 6s.* Memoirs of the celebrated Mrs. *Laetitia Pilkington.*"

[38] See *Memoirs of Mrs. Laetitia Pilkington*, I-II, passim, and *DNB* s.v. "Pilkington, Laetitia (1712-1750)."

[39] Bodl. MS. Add. c. 89. f. 29. The letter has faded considerably and hence the text is partially corrupt.

[40] *Memoirs*, p. 214 [II, 254].

[41] A standard critical observation: for example, see Kreissman, *Pamela-Shamela,* p. 1, where the anti-pamelists are said to have attacked Richardson's "ethical outlook."

[42] The use of the words "innocence" and "experience" is suggested by Morrissey and Slepian, "What Is *Fanny Hill?*", p. 67, where the *Memoirs* is described as "a novel about the loss of innocence and the gaining of knowledge through experience," an oversimplification to which I do not subscribe. The distinction between "innocence" and "experience" in the early novel is suggested also by the distinction between "private experience" and "public attitude" in Watt's *Rise of the Novel,* pp. 166, 168.

[43] Watt, *Rise of the Novel,* p. 12.

[44] *Memoirs,* p. 3 [I, 4-5].

[45] Fielding, *Joseph Andrews and Shamela,* ed. Battestin, pp. 304-05. There are other parallels between the *Memoirs* and various anti-pamelas. Fielding's justification for his use of "vices" in the introduction to *Joseph Andrews* (p. 12) is similar to Fanny's "tail-piece of morality" and Griffiths' defense of the "fair quarter allowed" vice' in his review for the *Monthly Review,* 2 (March 1750), 432. Also Fanny's insistence that she "but paints situations such as they actually rose to me in nature" employs the metaphor of the writer as an artist painting nature, a metaphor which is used in *Shamela* by Conney Keyber ("Madam, . . . you have tickled up and brightened many strokes in this work by your pencil"—p. 301) and in *Memoirs of the Life of Lady H—, the celebrated Pamela, from her Birth to the present Time* (London, 1741?), where "The author . . . tells us at the outset that in this instance of 'virtue rewarded' the facts 'are related in their natural Colours . . . '" (as described and quoted by Sale, *Samuel Richardson: A Bibliographical Record of His Literary Career with Historical Notes,* pp. 126-27).

[46] Richardson, *Pamela,* I, 450. The *Memoirs* seems to parallel *Pamela* in other ways as well. For example, both novels claim to speak of reality, yet both fashion from their realistic depiction of the world a dreamland, a fantasy world of wish-fulfillment. For Pamela this fantasy involves religious and social reward for chastity and steadfastness; for Fanny the dream concerns material and even spiritual gain from sexual pleasure. Of course, the recognition of this parallel is of a purely critical nature: it describes a coincidental correspondence between the two novels which seems to be more nearly a result of similarities in the books' method than in their authors' artistic consciousness.

For the *Memoirs* as an imitation of *Pamela's* "epistolary plan" see Frank G. black, *The Epistolary Novel in the late Eighteenth Century,* p. 1 and n. 2, where he calls the *Memoirs* the "most notorious" of the "impudent prostitutions of the form" of *Pamela.* Black does not seem to be aware of the pun implicit in his statement.

[47] The *Memoirs'* relationship to *Pamela* or to the anti-pamela movement is noted also in Braudy, "*Fanny Hill* and Materialism"; *Memoirs,* ed. Quennell, p. xi; and Hollander, "The Old Last Act." Hollander and Quennell, as well as Brigid Brophy, "Mersey Sound, 1750," and Bradbury, "*Fanny Hill* and the Comic Novel," p. 267, also relate the book to Richardson's *Clarissa.* But the last three volumes of *Clarissa* were not published until Dec. 1748, a month after the first volume of the *Memoirs* was published; moreover, Volumes III and IV of *Clarissa* appeared in April 1748, a month or so after Cleland was committed to the Fleet and may already have begun composing the *Memoirs.* Hence, the *Memoirs* could not have owed anything to the completed *Clarissa,* although Cleland could have borrowed his epistolary technique and other technical features from the earlier volumes. Yet the *Memoirs* makes only the briefest pretense at epistolary technique (each volume is one complete letter) and it seems much closer in tone and substance to *Pamela.*

There is no evidence that Richardson was familiar with Cleland or his work. Neither Cleland nor the *Memoirs* is mentioned in Eaves and Kimpel, *Samuel Richardson: A Biography.* In a letter dated 11 April 1967, Elizabeth Brophy, who has read all of Richardson's unpublished correspondence in the British Museum, informs me that the has "come upon no reference to Cleland or to *Fanny Hill* in Richardson's correspondence." Mrs. Brophy notes, however, that Richardson "does comment unfavorably" on the *Memoirs of Laetitia Pilkington* and "condemned this vein of 'frank' memoir." Cleland, we remember, found Laetitia Pilkington's *Memoirs* enjoyable and instructive.

[48] *Memoirs,* pp. 56-57, 78-79, 94, 98 [I, 124, 126-27, 174, 207, 215].

[49] *Memoirs,* pp. 82, 94 [I, 181, 206-07].

[50] *Memoirs,* pp. 98, 101, 104 [I, 214-15, 221, 226-27].

[51] *Memoirs,* pp. 108, 110, 129-30, 139 [II, 11, 15-16, 58, 60, 80-81].

[52] Barry Ivker, "John Cleland and the Marquis d'Argens: Eroticism and Natural Morality in Mid-Eighteenth-Century English and French Fiction," American Society for Eighteenth-Century Studies, McMaster University, Hamilton, Canada, 8 May 1973; Braudy, "*Fanny Hill* and Materialism."

In an article printed in the August 1749 issue of the *Monthly Review* (which appeared six months after Volume II of the first edition of the *Memoirs* was published) Cleland indicated an awareness of La Mettrie's work. He described *The Logic of Probabilities* as "a short, but conclusive argument in favour of the Christian religion . . . [which is] levelled at the disbelievers in that faith, especially the authors of Man a Machine, and of the Philosophical Thoughts: Pieces wrote in the infidel strain" (I, 290).

[53] *Memoirs,* p. 94 [I, 207].

[54] *Memoirs,* pp. 105-06, 109 [II, 5, 12].

[55] Burlesque, of course, was not an uncommon eighteenth-century novelistic technique. Shepperson, *The Novel in Motley,* pp. 3-4, observes that the early novel received "only the most fitful and grudging attention. . . . In the absence of formal criticism, it is not surprising to find that parody and burlesque should have proved powerful agents in controlling the excesses of this youthful literary form. . . . Thus the burlesque novel was created as a necessary balance wheel to the serious novel. . . . " See also pp. 80-83, where Shepperson discusses "antidotes to sentimentality" and where he notes that *The Memoirs of Fanny Hill* was included "among the more lurid titles" in the circulating library catalogue prefaced to the published version of George Colman's *Polly Honeycomb.* See the Preface, pp. ix-xiii, and esp. xii, where both *Memoirs of Fanny Hill* and *Memoirs of a Coxcomb,* Cleland's second novel, are included. The circulating libraries were considered a major source of both sentimental and burlesque novels: the *Memoirs* could have been included in Colman's list as an example of the latter.

[56] Hollander, "The Old Last Act," p. 70.

[57] Hollander, p. 70.

[58] Morrissey and Slepian, "What Is *Fanny Hill?*", pp. 72-73. Morrissey and Slepian provide a longer list; I have chosen some of their examples.

[59] PRO, SP 36/111/157[r].

Nancy K. Miller (essay date 1980)

SOURCE: "A Harlot's Progress: II—*Fanny Hill,*" in her *The Heroine's Text: Readings in the French and English Novel, 1722-1782,* Columbia University Press, 1980, pp. 51-66.

[*In the following excerpt, Miller argues that* Memoirs of a Woman of Pleasure (Fanny Hill) *can be interpreted as a female* Bildungsroman *in the tradition of other apprenticeship or coming-of-age novels popular in the eighteenth century.*]

Unlike *La Vie de Marianne* and *Moll Flanders,* where prefatory material provides a summary of the story to come and the key to its *mode d'emploi,* **Fanny Hill** offers the reader no more than a name and a suggestive subtitle: **Memoirs of a Woman of Pleasure.**[1] Consequently, as narrator, Fanny herself must account for the authenticity of her text. And so she begins with what one might call the standard operating procedures of the fictional memoir. Just as Marianne writes to a female friend "dont le nom est en blanc" as an obligation ("Mais enfin, puisque vous voulez que j'écrive mon histoire, et que c'est une chose que vous demandez à mon amitié, soyez satisfaite: j'aime encore mieux vous ennuyer que de vous refuser"), and with some reluctance, fearful that to transcribe her story will undercut its impact ("Il est vrai que l'histoire en est particulière, mais je la gâterai, si je l'écris; car où voulez-vous que je prenne un style?"), Fanny writes to an anonymous "Madam" to fulfill a request— "I sit down to give you an undeniable proof of my considering your desires as indispensable orders"[2] —promising to adopt a style that reproduces her life *mimetically:* "I shall . . . use no farther apology, than to prepare you for seeing the loose part of my life, wrote with the same liberty that I led it" (15). But where Marianne, like Moll, withholds her own name ("N'oubliez pas que vous m'avez promis de ne jamais dire qui je suis; je ne veux être connue que de vous"), Fanny announces hers: "My maiden name was FRANCES HILL. I was born at a small village near Liverpool in Lancashire, of parents extremely poor, and, I piously believe, extremely honest" (16).

Honesty would seem to run in the family. Fanny's attachment to the truth requires the revelation of all pertinent details: "I will not so much as take the pains to bestow the strip of a gauze wrapper on it, but paint situations such as they actually rose to me in nature, careless of violating those laws of decency that were never made for such unreserved intimacies as ours" (15). Fanny justifies the relation of "the scandalous stages" of her life· because she is privileged in having "emerged, at length, to the enjoyment of every blessing in the power of love, health, and fortune to bestow" and this "whilst yet in the flower of youth" (15).[3]

Fanny's story begins as that of many a poor-but-honest maiden:

> My education, till past fourteen, was no better than very vulgar; reading, or rather spelling an illegible scrawl, and a little ordinary plain-work composed the whole system of it: and then all my foundation in virtue was no other than a total ignorance of vice, and the shy timidity general to our sex, in the tender stage of life when objects alarm or frighten more by their novelty than anything else: but then this is a fear too often cured at the expense of

innocence, when Miss, by degrees, begins no longer to look on a man as a creature of prey that will eat her (16).

Like Moll, Fanny's education in matters or morals is a non-education; innocence is only a function of ignorance. And like Moll again, Fanny codes the vicissitudes of her own experience within the text of the feminine condition in general.

The moral vacuum might not have been disastrous if Fanny had not lost her natural protectors, but: "I was now entering my fifteenth year, when the worst of ills befell me in the loss of my fond tender parents, who were both carried off by the smallpox, within a few days of each other; my father dying first, and thereby hastening the death of my mother, so that I was now left an unhappy friendless orphan . . ." (16). One misfortune engenders another: thus, when Fanny goes to London to "SEEK MY FORTUNE" (17) in the company of a more experienced friend, she is soon betrayed: "left thus alone, absolutely destitute and friendless" (19).

Though twice abandoned, Fanny is spurred on by the story of Pamela's success[4] as reported by the worldly-wise Esther Davis:

> As how several maids out of the country had made themselves and all their kin forever, that by preserving their VIRTUE, some had taken so with their masters that they had married them, and kept them coaches, and lived vastly grand, and happy, and some, mayhap, came to be duchesses: Luck was all, and why not I as well as another (17).

Needless to say, although poor and honest like Pamela to begin with, this is not the text of Fanny's success. A penniless orphan, her adventures begin with a search for employment. As we saw with Marianne, not only are the opportunities for work extremely restricted, but the job search itself is an obstacle course to the preservation of virtue. Fanny, for her part, less proud than the "virtuous orphan," looks for a place as a maid, and in her naiveté is hired by the madam of a brothel. With these givens, and the anticipatory information of the title of her memoirs, the advent of her sexual initiation is highly predictable. But where Moll draws the curtains of modesty, restricting the reader's view of her sexuality to its *consequences,* Fanny exposes the *process* of her sexualization. In fact, the text itself is precisely a text of exposure: it reveals what is covert in the more polite fiction of the period.[5]

Like Marianne and Pamela, Fanny is given a set of clothing appropriate to her new role, provided by her prospective protector and seducer: the man who is to take possession of that "perishable commodity . . . a maidenhead" (29). When the "rigging . . . out" (29)

process is completed Fanny contemplates her new self: "When it was over, and I viewed myself in the glass, I was, no doubt, too natural, too artless, to hide my childish joy at the change; a change, in the real truth, for much the worse, since I must have much better become the neat easy simplicity of my rustic dress than the awkward, untoward, tawdry finery that I could not conceal my strangeness to" (29). Fanny, like Marianne, with the ironic distance of retrospection, can perceive the superimposition of the two selves: the rustic innocent dressed as sophisticated woman of the world.[6] But at this moment of the narrative, young Fanny is not in a position to revel in the pleasures of the sophisticated narrator: "Well then, dressed I was, and little did it then enter into my head that all this gay attire was no more than decking the victim out for sacrifice whilst I innocently attributed all to mere friendship and kindness in the sweet good Mrs. Brown" (30). For, despite her initial exposure to sexuality at the hands of Phoebe (Mrs. Brown's assistant), Fanny is still operating as an innocent.

Mrs. Brown encourages Fanny to accept her new provider: "That he would make my fortune if I would be a good girl and not stand in my own light . . . that I should trust his honour . . . that I should be made forever" (33). These are exactly the terms and the language of Mr. B.'s proposition to Pamela; and again the verbal cliché announces the narrative cliché. Fanny fights off the first attack on her virginity, but as she explains: "Neither virtue nor principles had the least share in the defence I had made, but only the particular aversion I had conceived against the first brutal and frightful invader of my virgin innocence" (37). Fanny, like Moll, in the mimesis of truthful narration, is careful to separate the motives of her behavior; distinguishing, as it were, unflattering fact from flattering fiction. As an innocent, however, Fanny casts her seducer in the canonically negative terms of his role; and as if to justify her fragility, falls ill: "into a kind of delirious doze, out of which I waked late in the morning, in a violent fever: a circumstance which was extremely critical to relieve me, at least for a time, from the attacks of a wretch, infinitely more terrible to me than death itself" (38). Still a virgin, Fanny is entitled to the privileges of literary virtue: the brain fever of the pathetic, oppressed heroine. And she can articulate the vision of sexual aggression as a fate worse than death that sustains Pamela in her struggle.

Fanny makes a rapid recovery, however, and soon comes to desire "the ceremony of initiation" (39). As she explains, her attitude changed: "Conversation, example, all, in short, contributed, in that house, to corrupt my native purity, which had taken no root in education; whilst now the inflammable principle of pleasure, so easily fired at my age, made strange work within me, and all the modesty I was brought up in the habit (not the instruction) of, began to melt away like dew before the sun's heat; not to mention that I made a vice of necessity, from the constant fears I had of being turned out to starve" (39). Now faced with examples of immodest behavior, her mind cannot refute the evidence of her body; and her temperament further undermines her flimsy moral preparation. Fanny's use of metaphor here as elsewhere functions in direct counterpoint to the banality of the event at hand, dramatizing (and sentimentalizing) her maidenhood. Finally, however, and almost as an afterthought, Fanny adds to the euphemic tableau of innocence the logic of poverty: like Moll's "but that by the way." But the benefit of hindsight undercuts an overly self-righteous stance as she confesses: "Nothing . . . was wanting to . . . prevent my going out anywhere to get better advice. Alas! I dreamed of no such thing" (40). Fanny, by now, is hooked; and like Moll, she rushes to her ruin.

Her first complete experience of heterosexual intercourse is vicarious: she watches with her initiatrix through a crevice in a panel:

> For my part, I will not pretend to describe what I felt all over me during this scene; but from that instant, adieu all fears of what man could do unto me; they were now changed into such ardent desires, such ungovernable longings, that I would have pulled the first of that sex that should present himself, by the sleeve, and offered him the bauble, which I now imagined the loss of would be a gain I could not too soon procure myself" (49).

This voyeuristic prelude marks the beginning of Fanny's career as a woman of pleasure. Although Fanny will continue to account for her experience in the rhetoric of both sentimental and preromantic fiction, the valorization of the underlying premises of those fictions undergoes a radical transformation. Here, for example, her precious jewel, her maidenhood, is now a trinket she would gladly give up. Loss is transformed into gain, however, since her jewel can buy other treasures and pleasures which, like Mme de Merteuil in her youth, Fanny is burning to *know*. The sight of passion has turned her into an insatiable flame. Phoebe tries to relieve her but as Fanny puts it: "For my part, I now pined for more solid food, and promised tacitly to myself that I would not be put off much longer with the foolery of woman to woman" (51). Fanny's instinctive penchant for pleasure reads as a euphoric text of *libertinage;* her sexuality is not *bound* to an antisocial *system* of eroticism. As a result, throughout the novel a tension between two competing poles—sentimental (Richardsonian) teleology and fantasmatic (Sadian) repetition—is maintained.

Fanny, therefore, is saved from receiving the "essential specific" from just any male: "Love itself took charge of the disposal of me, in spite of interest, or gross lust" (51). She comes upon her man at dawn where he is sleeping off the effects of a night of reveling and it is love at first sight: "No! no term of years, no turn of fortune could ever erase the lightning-like impression his form made on me. . . . Yes! dearest object of my earliest passion, I command forever the remembrance of thy first appearance to my ravished eyes . . . it calls thee up, present; and I see thee now!" (52). Like Psyche fascinated by the beauty of sleeping Cupid's form, Fanny is compelled by the enchanting beauty of her Adonis (as she calls him).

Until the actual moment of her defloration, then, Fanny speaks the language of love's victim: "Past or future were equally out of the question with me. The present was as much as all my powers of life were sufficient to bear the transport of without fainting. . . . I was drove to it by a passion too impetuous for me to resist, and I did what I did because I could not help it" (56). Love as *fatum* prepares the inevitable end, which Fanny alternately fears and yearns for: "I wished, I doted, I could have died for him; and yet, I know not how or why, I dreaded the point which had been the object of my fiercest wishes; my pulses beat fears, amidst a flush of the warmest desires. This struggle of the passions, however, this conflict betwixt modesty and lovesick longings, made me burst again into tears" (57). As we saw with marianne, the sentimental heroine struggles with the double bind of fear and desire. For Fanny, although the dilemma is manifested in physiological terms, the conflict between opposing forces is nonetheless resolved by tears. In most eighteenth-century novels, the act of defloration, while the event toward or away from which the narrative moves, is euphemized, often to the point of silence. In *Fanny Hill,* on the contrary, the act is uncovered and indeed exploited.

Although readers like Leo Braudy describe the erotic topography of *Fanny Hill* as an "unspoiled Eden," and thus as "part of the natural,"[7] the parallels between Cleland's text and Sade's deliberately unnatural (or at least supernatural) universe are difficult to ignore. To the extent that both Cleland and Sade make explicit what is implicit in the sentimental inscription of the war between the sexes, it seems appropriate to zero in briefly on a moment in its unveiling. Below are juxtaposed Fanny's account of her defloration, and Justine's.[8]

> And, drawing out the engine of love assaults, drove it currently, as at a ready-made breach. Then! then! for the first time, did I feel that stiff horn-hard gristle, battering against the tender part. . . . Applying then the point of his machine to the slit, . . . then driving on with fury, its prodigious stiffness, thus impacted, wedgelike, breaks the union of those parts. . . . He improved his advantage, and . . . forcibly deepens his penetration; but put me to such intolerable pain, from the separation of the sides of that soft passage by a hard thick body, I could have

screamed out. . . . At length, the tender texture of that tract giving way to such fierce tearing and rending, he pierced somewhat further into me: and now, outrageous and no longer his own master, but borne headlong away by the fury and over-mettle of that member, now exerting itself with a kind of native rage, he breaks in . . . and one violent merciless lunge sent it, imbrued, and reeking with virgin blood, up to the very hilt in me. . . . I screamed out, and fainted away with the sharpness of the pain (58-59).

In his fury the monster lashes out against the altar at which he cannot speak his prayers. . . . [T]he chastened flesh yields, the gate cedes, the ram bursts through; terrible screams rise from my throat; the entire mass is swiftly engulfed, and darting its venom . . . the snake gives ground. . . . Never in my life have I suffered so much. . . . His weapon is raised and trained upon me . . . in a fury, he rattles the temple's porticos, he is soon at the sanctuary. . . . Not content to be master of the place, he wishes to reduce it to a shambles. Such terrible attacks, so new to me, cause me to succumb; but unconcerned for my pain, the cruel victor thinks of nothing but increasing his pleasure. . . . I fall back upon the throne which has just been the scene of my immolation, no longer conscious of my existence save through my pain and my tears . . . my despair and my remorse.[9]

In both accounts, the description of penetration is coded—no one is surprised—by martial metaphors. In a series of cruel assaults, the aggressor wreaks destruction upon his female adversary by deploying a weapon of propulsion. The feminine response, symmetrically, is coded as a military topography: the vulnerable territory under attack gives way to the invader. But if Cleland's epic favors the glory of the battlefield—once more unto the breach—by superposing the language of sacrilege on the language of military violence, Sade underscores the symbolic stakes of the intervention: his gates are not only the gates of war, but the entrance to the *temple,* which contains the altar and the sanctuary. Defloration becomes desecration. Justine never recovers from her immolation, but Fanny is saved by profane love. Unlike Justine, who remains the passive object of a masculine will to domination by the powers of the phallus, Fanny becomes a desiring subject animated by the "longitudinal fallacy."[10] For Charles, despite the violence he has done Fanny, is not a Sadian libertine: "When I recovered my senses, I found myself undressed and in bed, in the arms of the sweet relenting murderer of my virginity, who hung mourning tenderly over me, holding in his hand a cordial, which, coming from the still dear author of so much pain, I could not refuse" (59-60). Fanny has been mutilated and murdered, but the metaphor is converted from negativity to positivity since the murderer is antonymically sweet and penitent. The death of virginity, moreover, soon is viewed as rite of passage to another

realm: " . . . after a few enjoyments had numbed and blunted the sense of the smart . . . I arrived at excess of pleasure through excess of pain. But, when successive engagements had broke and inured me, I began to enter into the true unallayed relish of that pleasure of pleasures" (61).

If, however, in the effusion of first love, Fanny seizes the day with sublime confidence—"Or, what were all fears of the consequence, put in the scale of one night's enjoyment, of anything so transcendently the taste of my eyes and heart, as that delicious, fond, matchless youth?" (62)—in time she becomes subject to the literary laws of feminine anxiety: "I could not dispel the gloom of impatience and tender fears which gathered upon me, and which our timid sex are apt to feel in proportion to their love" (69). Fanny gives herself over completely to the love of her life: "He was the universe to me, and all that was not him was nothing to me" (72). And Charles demonstrates his acceptance of such a role by molding Fanny to his taste: he instructs her not only in the ways of love, but "in a great many points of life that I was, in consequence of my no-education, perfectly ignorant of" (73). In her eagerness to please her man, Fanny is the perfect pupil. Under Charles's tutelage, she loses her country ways. True to the economy of romance, Fanny is ready to sacrifice all in gratitude for her lover's affections: "I could have made a pleasure of the greatest toil, and worked my fingers to the bone, with joy, to have supported him" (73). Illicit love, however, must be punished. At the height of the idyll, "the barbarity of . . . fate" deals the "mortal, the unexpected blow of separation" (74). Charles's family removes him from Fanny's presence so that he might pursue a more appropriate path of fortune.[11] Fanny, again in her role as sentimental heroine, "fainted away, and after several successive fits, all the while wild and senseless, I miscaried of the dear pledge of my Charles's love: but the wretched never die when it is fittest they should die, and women are hard-lived to a proverb" (76). True to another proverb of the feminine text, a long illness ensues. But Fanny (to her regret) recovers: "My health returned to me, though I still retained an air of grief, dejection, and languour, which, taking off the ruddiness of my country complexion, rendered it rather more delicate and affecting" (76-77).

Fanny, now looking the victim's part as a result of her double loss, enters the cycle of retribution that follows wrongdoing in eighteenth-century novels of vice and virtue. The motherly landlady, who nursed Fanny back to health, insists on payment, threatening Fanny with prison and providing her with the means (a man) to discharge her debt. Fanny accepts him with a sense of fatality—"lifeless and indifferent to everything" (80). After he makes love to her for the first time, she is seized with remorse "for having suffered, on that bed, the embraces of an utter stranger. I tore my hair, wrung my hands, and beat my breast like a madwoman" (81). Fanny, however, survives this bereavement too; for as she comments: "Violent passions seldom last long, and those of women least of any" (81). Like Moll, Fanny often seeks to explain and justify behavior which she herself recognizes as reprehensible in a woman: "But our virtues and our vices depend too much on our circumstances; unexpectedly beset as I was, betrayed by a mind weakened by a long and severe affliction, and stunned with the horrors of a jail, my defeat will appear the more excusable, since I certainly was not present at, or a party in any sense, to it" (81).

The second time, however, having taken an aphrodisiac, Fanny has a more sophisticated dilemma to resolve:

> All my animal spirits then rushed mechanically to that centre of attraction, and presently, inly warmed, and stirred as I was beyond bearing, I lost all restraint, and yielding to the force of the emotion, gave down, *as mere woman,* those effusions of pleasure, which, in the strictness of still faithful love, I could have wished to have kept in. Yet oh! what an immense difference did I feel between this impression of a pleasure merely animal, and struck out of the collision of the sexes by a passive bodily effect, from that sweet fury, that rage of active delight which crowns the enjoyments of a mutual love passion . . . (84-85; italics mine).

Fanny distinguishes carefully between the biological urge experienced as *mere woman,* the uncontrollable part of herself, and the true passion of *love.* (Similarly, though in a loftier register, Marianne compared the instinctual coquetterie of all women to please, with her specific desire to please Valville. In both cases, however, the natural impulses of women as a sex are negatively coded.) Fanny castigates herself for her failure to be more than mere woman. And having betrayed the bonds of fidelity by base pleasure, she accepts the implications of an inferior destiny: "As soon as he was gone, I felt the usual consequence of the first launch into vice (for my love attachment to Charles never appeared to me in that light). I was instantly borne away down the stream, without making back to the shore" (86). "The first launch into vice" produces an inevitable trajectory.

Fanny becomes a kept woman: "And by this means I got into a circle of acquaintance that soon stripped me of all the remains of bashfulness and modesty which might be yet left of my country education, and were, to a just taste, perhaps, the greatest of my charms" (88). In her new incarnation, Fanny remains faithful to her protector until she is betrayed; then takes revenge by indulging herself with a local messenger boy. But "imprudent neglect" (108) leads to discovery. Her contract is revoked and she is, for the first time, on her own "turned loose upon the town, to sink or swim, as I

could manage with the current of it" (113). Fanny prepares to embark on a "new profession" and with this ends the first letter.

For the first half of the novel, Fanny is primarily characterized as a sentimental heroine whose experience of sexuality by ever increasing degrees makes her typologically different from her counterparts. Nevertheless, her sexual appetite and capacity for pleasure are maintained formally within the thematic structure of the sentimental education in which a young girl from the provinces is initiated into society. Until this point Fanny has been in protected situations (kept by men). The division of the novel into two parts, two installments of a long letter, underscores the change to come. The second letter, as in *La Vie de Marianne,* begins by a *re*motivation. The narrator separates herself from the object of the narration and comments on the problems of describing her sort of life "whose bottom, or groundwork being, in the nature of things, eternally one and the same . . . there is no escaping a repetition of near the same images, the same figures, the same expressions" (115). But if the courtesan's text inevitably becomes redundant, it is redundant in a particular way. The reader is invited to perceive difference within the sameness because Fanny registers a sense of progress before each adventure. Although the educative component of sexual exploration is a *topos* in the novel of erotic *Bildung,* in Fanny's case the impulse to self-knowledge seems more than rhetorical strategy. Braudy writes: "Fanny is fascinated by the physiology of sexual reactions not merely because Cleland wants to stimulate his readers but also because, in the development of her own character, she wants to know. Sexuality is a possible and much neglected way into knowledge of the self."[12]

Fanny must *learn* about "this new stage of my profession . . . passing thus from a private devotee to pleasure into a public one" (116). This phase of her education takes place under the auspices of Mrs. Cole, her "gouvernante" (113) and "faithful preceptress" (203), from whom Fanny discovers that it is the tradition of the trade to enter as a "virgin," that, "in the loss of a fictitious maidenhead, I should reap all the advantages of a native one" (116). On the evening during which Fanny is to be introduced to the habitués of the house, the program consists of each woman's relating to the audience the manner in which "she first exchanged the maiden state for womanhood" (121). (Fanny is exempt by virtue of her "titular maidenhead" and Mrs. Cole by her age.) Each girl tells her story, after which she and her partner of the evening make love in front of the audience. By the time it is Fanny's turn to be introduced to her companion, she has, like the first time, been stimulated by voyeurism. When she stands undressed, on display, she explains: "I had not, however, so thoroughly renounced all innate shame as not to suffer great confusion at the state I saw myself in"

(149). The enthusiastic response,[13] however, restores her composure: "I might flatter myself with having passed my examination with the approbation of the learned" (149). Again initiation is cast as education; the brothel becomes an institution of higher learning. Having completed the entrance requirements, she is admitted in good standing: "for that time, or indeed any other, unless I pleased, I was to go through no further trials, and that I was now consummately initiated, and one of them" (152).

Fanny's gallant of the night wants to take care of her but, in a replay of the first situation, his father sends him away. Although Mrs. Cole looks out for Fanny in her "widowhood," Fanny feels "fated to be my own caterer in this, as I had been in my first trial of the market" (154). Thus the structure of Part II self-consciously replicates that of Part I. This time, however, while waiting to be supplied with a provider, Fanny goes out on the street and attracts one. Still it is the landlady who arranges the counterfeit defloration. When her lover awakes, he finds the bedsheets stained: "The illusion was complete, no other conception entered his head but that of his having been at work upon an unopened mine; which idea . . . redoubled at once his tenderness for me, and his ardour for breaking it wholly up" (165). This lover, then, reenacts the behavior of Charles, the true initiator; and the recurrence of the same expression (the mine to be destroyed) reiterates the original polarization. The male is "like a cock clapping his wings over his downtrod mistress;"[14] the female, "the deep wounded, breathless, frightened, undone, no longer maid" (166). Fanny admits to a "faintish sense" of pleasure but maintains professional detachment: "I had no taste for the person I was suffering the embraces of, on a pure mercenary account; and then, I was not entirely delighted with myself for the jade's part I was playing, whatever excuses I might plead for my being brought into it; but then this insensibility kept me so much the mistress of my mind and motions, that I could the better manage so close a counterfeit, through the whole scene of deception" (166). Fanny, by now, can make many distinctions in her experience of sexuality: the passion of true love which is reserved for Charles; the exercise of animality, sheer pleasure when she has chosen her companion; and then her professional responsibilities which make sex a mere physical performance for which she has little enthusiasm and some guilt.

With time, however, Fanny accepts (indeed embraces) the vicissitudes of her destiny: "no condition of life is more subject to revolutions than that of a woman of pleasure" (172). Nevertheless, she establishes a hierarchy among her companions in vice and would separate herself in spirit from the literal truth of the stereotype. If, for example, her companions indulge in "criminal" acts, Fanny—with hindsight—indulges in self-serving moral commentary: "It will add, too, one more example of thousands, in confirmation of the maxim, that when women get out of compass, there are no lengths of licentiousness that they are not capable of running" (190). Fanny thus reinscribes the ideology of the text: the first step leads directly to the path of insatiable vice. But Fanny's attention to self-preservation—"I found a secret satisfaction in respecting myself, as well as preserving the life and freshness of my complexion" (184)—is an attempt to defy the maxim, to control her destiny despite the rigors of the scenario.

Indeed, Fanny's final incarnation as a woman of pleasure does not take place under Mrs. Cole's (that "severe enemy to the seduction of innocence" [203]) protection; she retires to the country. With money put aside, Fanny sets herself up with a "new character of a young gentlewoman, whose husband was gone to sea," and waits "without impatience for what the chapter of accidents might produce in my favour" (204). Fanny, like Moll, establishes the potential for a scene, but then waits for it to happen. However resourceful and experienced as adventuresses, they both claim to need a man in order to attain independence. Inevitably, moreover, the status of (autonomous) subject proves to be a doubly mediated one: Fanny and Moll cease to circulate as objects only when they are integrated within the family; neutralized by the bourgeois and Protestant morality that officially underwrites the English memorial novel as genre: the "spiritual" autobiography.

For Fanny, integration begins when in the face of prosperity loneliness leads to a reordering of values, a change of heart which terminates in marital bliss and familial harmony. Fanny's last adventure as a woman of pleasure occurs with an older gentleman. (He resembles Moll's gentleman from Bath, with the difference that Fanny, consistently luckier than Moll, obtains from him the financial security she had been seeking.) This relationship, as was the initial one with Charles, is doubled by an educative process: "From him it was I first learned, to any purpose, and not without infinite pleasure, *that I had such a portion of me worth bestowing some regard on;* from him I received my first essential encouragement and instructions, how to put it in that train of cultivation, which I have since pushed to the little degree of improvement you see it at" (206; italics mine). When the "rational pleasurist" (206) dies, and leaves Fanny at the head of a large fortune,[15] when she seems to have everything she ever wanted personal happiness becomes her concern: "My regret was a mighty and just one, since it had my only truly beloved Charles for its object" (207). Fanny here returns to her original vision of Charles and maintains, as does Manon to Des Grieux, that despite "all my personal infidelities, not one had made a pin's point impression on a heart impenetrable to the true love-passion, but for him" (207). Dismissing the contingencies of the flesh, Fanny celebrates the integrity of the spirit. In this Fanny, like Manon, demonstrates the time-worn paradox of the prostitute: the gold digger has a heart of gold.

Fanny's last adventure takes her to the country, where she hopes to fulfill two goals—to show off her success and to be a benefactress to distant relations—thus confirming her new socialization. But the journey is never completed. It is interrupted by a surprise meeting with Charles.[16] Beyond the satisfaction of love renewed, Fanny is particularly pleased at Charles's distress: "Charles reduced, and broken down to his naked personal merit, was such a circumstance, in favour of the sentiments I had for him, as exceeded my utmost desires" (212). Fanny can enjoy her love without any concern for money, that is to say, she can enjoy a heroine's destiny.[17] But despite the return of the "true refining passion" (213), Fanny and Charles are still joined in a posture of illicit desire. Charles, however, insists that Fanny allow him to *raise* her: "to receive his hand, by which means I was in pass, among other innumerable blessings, to bestow a legal parentage on those fine children you have seen by this happiest of matches" (219). Whereas in the initiatory sequence of illicit love, Fanny miscarries of Charles's child, the legal sanction of marriage results in healthy reproduction. The clichés of bourgeois happiness overcode the message of "happily ever after."

The tale of Fanny's exploits ends here, but in addition to this tribute to local morality, Fanny concludes her memoirs as a universal allegory: "Thus, at length, I got snug into port, where in the bosom of virtue, I gathered the only uncorrupt sweets" (219). Aware that some might find "this tail-piece of morality" (219) implausible, Fanny nonetheless pursues her literary prerogatives: "If I have painted Vice in all its gayest colours, if I have decked it with flowers, it has been solely in order to make the worthier, the solemner sacrifice of it to Virtue" (220). Thus the end of the narrative, by celebrating the victory of virtue over vice, officially delimits Fanny's destiny within the confines of the genre, the obvious violations it has incurred in the course of narration notwithstanding.

Although it can be argued that the content and recurrence of the violations are so extreme as to throw into question the pertinence of formal solidarity, if my reading of **Fanny Hill** has any validity at all, it will have shown the power of the eighteenth-century intertext to overdetermine the *shape* of a given fiction. For if books like Cleland's **Memoirs** "live . . . because they touch the dream life of men,"[18] nonetheless, when one reads **Fanny Hill** with two hands, so to speak, one cannot but recognize its very local color. At the very least as a linear *mapping*, **Fanny Hill** conforms to the pattern of a certain eighteenth-century narrative, of female *Bildung.*

Looking back, Fanny, no less than Marianne or Moll, can assess the road traveled: her progress and her mastery of self in the world. In the end, she can play with the metaphors of theatricality which, in eighteenth-century rhetoric, are the measure of mastered experience. Anticipating (and bypassing) her interlocutor's doubts as to the genuineness of her conversion from Vice to Virtue: "just as if one was to fancy one's self completely disguised at a masquerade, with no other change of dress than turning one's shoes into slippers," (220) Fanny would prove her case by reinstituting the principle of education. Her last words tell of her husband's initiation of his son, the better to "form him to virtue, and inspire him with a fixed, a rational contempt for vice." She thus marks her own distance from the very "scenes of debauchery" she once knew so well.

The disastrous downward curve of the harlot's progress is, in the final analysis, averted, indeed reversed, in favor of the "happy end" of virtue rewarded. As she had wished in the beginning, Fanny reaps Pamela's recompense: she moves from rags to riches, the bottom of the social ladder to the top. Such is the telic power of the structure of ascent in the English novel. . . .

Notes

[1] For an account of the publication (dates, titles, etc.) of Cleland's novel, see David Foxon's *Libertine Literature in England;* especially his appendix, pp. 52-63.

[2] I follow the Signet edition (New York, 1965); here, p. 15.

[3] Thus Fanny's memoirs, like Marianne's "life," are essentially truncated autobiography: narratives whose point of arrival is delimited by the end of adolescence.

[4] Leo Braudy notes the apparent literary allusion to *Pamela* in his "rehabilitation" of *Fanny Hill,* "*Fanny Hill* and Materialism," p. 29. In *Pamela-Shamela,* Bernard Kreissman suggests that the names Fanny and Pamela become interchangeable after 1740. He cites *Fanni, ou la Nouvelle Paméla* of Baculard d'Arnaud (1767) (p. 39), and John Piper's 1760 novel, *The Life of Miss Fanny Brown; or, Pamela the Second* (*A Clergyman's Daughter*) (p. 6). Curiously, however, he does not cite *Fanny Hill.*

[5] This relationship is both obvious and problematic. As Braudy points out, the novel "has too broad a sense of social milieu and literary tradition for the writer interested in describing the 'pure' elements of pornography as a literary genre, and . . . too much erotic content for the literary historian to treat it with much seriousness." "*Fanny Hill* and Materialism," p. 21. Braudy's case is based largely on the novel's ideological relations to materialism and sentimentalism. I argue for an eigh-

teenth-century *literariness* based on intertextuality and what Michael Riffaterre calls the renewal of cliché: "These . . . substitutions share a common feature: they force the reader to become aware of both the renewing element and the renewed element. This phenomenon of a double reading is therefore not different (except for the transformation) from what happens when the reader decodes a cliché: the cliché is simultaneously seen [for the first time] and already seen ["déjà vu"], perceived in the text and in the recollected metatext." *Essais de Stylistique structurale,* p. 170.

[6] In Pamela's "mirror" scene, however, and necessarily because she is writing "to the moment," specular pleasure is mitigated only by the possibility of a return to the old and "ordinary." At the time, the new self is perceived as entirely satisfactory: "And when I was equipped, I took my straw hat in my hand, with its two blue strings, and looked about me in the glass, as proud as anything—To say truth, I never liked myself so well in my life." The *topos,* in other words, is not so much about "then/now" as the vicissitudes of class, femininity . . . and representation.

[7] Braudy, "*Fanny Hill* and Materialism," p. 37.

[8] To read an episode of female sexualization as locus of violence in *Fanny Hill* with *Justine* requires a certain "violence" to Sade's text: a comparable scene not only involves several participants and more than one mode of penetration, but manifestations of sexual behavior characterized by the heroine as cruel and unnatural. For the sake of clarity I do not include them here. Nevertheless, since Justine rates the episode cited below as marking the destruction of her virtue—she was unconscious the very first time—the juxtaposition seems pertinent.

[9] To bring out the purely lexical relations between the two texts, I have cited Sade in translation (New York: Grove Press, 1966), pp. 569-72. The corresponding pages in French are pp. 134-36 (Paris: 10/18, 1969).

[10] The formulation is Peter Quennell's, quoted by J. H. Plumb in his introduction to the novel, pp. xiii-xiv. We might just as well speak of the longitudinal *phallacy.* Thus, for example, when Fanny decides to have an affair with Will, the messenger boy, she overcomes her initial fear in the face of his "oversized machine" (95), "a maypole of so enormous a standard . . . it must have belonged to a young giant" (94). Always an egalitarian, Fanny appreciates Will for "his outward form, and especially in that *superb piece of furniture* [nature] had so liberally enriched him with" (107; italics mine). Positive metaphor for Fanny, however, is negative metonymy for Justine. She fears perforation by a literal, concrete substitute: "one of those *articles of furniture* usually found in nunneries, which decency forbids me from naming and which was of an *exorbitant thick-*

ness" (p. 619; italics mine; in the French, p. 187). Fanny becomes enamored of size, Justine persists in fearing it. In both cases, whatever the modalities of reception, it is the (fantasmatic) phallus that is prized.

[11] Similarly, in *Manon Lescaut,* Des Grieux's father intervenes, though less successfully, to put an end to a *ménage* that disrupts the family order. In this sense, we are in the presence of a predictable sequence: when illicit love is grounded in a disparity of social condition, a member of the "wronged" family intercedes, in the name of higher and hierarchical values, to disunite the couple. Thus, Valville's relatives in *La Vie de Marianne,* Mr. B.'s sister in *Pamela,* Julie's father in *la Nouvelle Héloïse,* all perform in the same sequence. Rousseau "renews" the cliché by assigning inferiority to the male.

[12] Braudy, "*Fanny Hill* and Materialism," p. 31.

[13] The cries of admiration on the part of the spectators belong to the paradigm of preliminaries in the Sadian orgy. But where Fanny derives pleasure from her status as attractive commodity, Justine is appalled. (Again one might note that every act marked with a positive sign for Fanny is negativized for Justine.)

[14] This performance parodies the social and literary overvaluation of virginity as founding innocence and reinscribes the cliché: "The frank negation of the taboo occurs especially in the licentious novel, which takes pleasure in denouncing the fiduciary nature of this essence. The novice heroines are promptly lectured by their often eloquent 'protectresses' . . . Mrs. B., for example, who sells Fanny Hill's young beauty to a lord." Pierre Fauchery, *La Destinée féminine,* p. 312.

[15] Interestingly, it was Fanny's ability to manage money, which she attributes to Mrs. Cole's tutelage, that inspired her benefactor's confidence. In this respect, at least, her past paid off—as does, ultimately, Moll's. In both cases, however, financial success brings neither contentment, nor, more to the point, closure.

[16] The chance encounter between prospective lovers (Marianne and Valville outside the church, Manon and Des Grieux at the coach) or separated lovers (Moll and Jemmy at Newgate) functions as a literary checkpoint, a sign and reminder to the reader that "destiny" is at work and romance in the works. Surprise is furthermore the occasion for proof of unprepared hence authentic emotion. Here, Fanny swoons at her discovery of Charles. All of this as opposed, for example, to the resolutely unsentimental calculations of the *Liaisons.*

[17] Or, as Balzac writes of Eugénie's response to her Charles's misfortune: "Depuis la veille, elle s'attachait à Charles par tous les liens de bonheur qui unissent les

âmes; désormais la souffrance allait donc le corrobo-ret. N'est-il pas dans la noble destinée de la femme *d'être plus touchée des pompes de la misère* que des splendeurs de la fortune?" *Eugénie Grandet,* p. 69; italics mine. What price nobility?

[18] J. H. Plumb, in his introduction, p. xiii. He goes on to say: "In quality of writing, in delineation of char-acter, these *Memoirs* can hold their own with the gen-eral run of eighteenth-century literature. But these are not, of course, the reasons for its long and continuing success" (p. xiv). Plumb's tact is remarkable through-out.

FURTHER READING

Criticism

Boucé, Paul Gabriel, ed. *Sexuality in Eighteenth-Century Britain.* Totowa, NJ: Barnes & Noble Books, 1982, 262 p.

    Collection of essays dealing with social, cultural, and intellectual attitudes toward sex and virginity in eighteenth-century Britain, with some reference to Cleland and his works.

Brophy, Brigid. "Mersey Sound 1750." In her *Don't Never Forget: Collected Views and Reviews,* pp. 76-80. New York: Holt, Rinehart and Winston, 1967.

    Review of the 1963 edition of *Fanny Hill* in which Brophy describes the work as "a highly engaging little erotic tale" possessing true literary qualities.

Charney, Maurice. "Two Sexual Lives, Entrepreneurial and Compulsive: *Fanny Hill* and *My Secret Life.*" In his *Sexual Fiction,* pp. 71-92. London: Methuen & Co. Ltd., 1981.

    Compares the buoyant and colorful eighteenth-century *Memoirs of a Woman of Pleasure* with the somber and neurotic nineteenth-century *My Secret Life.*

Ikver, Barry. "John Cleland and the Marquis d'Argens: Eroticism and Natural Morality in Mid-Eighteenth Century English and French Fiction." *Mosaic* VIII, No. 2 (Winter 1975): 141-48.

    Finds *Memoirs of a Woman of Pleasure* almost unique in that is uses erotic writing to express philosophical ideas.

Rembar, Charles. *The End of Obscenity: The Trials of "Lady Chatterley," "Tropic of Cancer," and "Fanny Hill."* New York: Random House, 1968, 529 p.

    Includes chapters devoted to three obscenity/censorship trials of Cleland's novel.

Shinagel, Michael. "*Memoirs of a Woman of Pleasure:* Pornography and the Mid-Eighteenth-Century English Novel." In *Studies in Change and Revolution: Aspects of English Intellectual History, 1640-1800,* edited by Paul J. Korshin, pp. 211-36. Menston, Yorkshire, UK: Scolar Press Ltd., 1972.

    Considers Cleland "a major innovator in the develop-ment of libertine literature in England."

Solomon, Stanley J. "Subverting Propriety as a Pattern of Irony in Three Eighteenth-Century Novels: *The Castle of Otranto, Vathek,* and *Fanny Hill.*" *The Erasmus Review* 1, No. 2 (November 1971): 107-16.

    Asserts that *Fanny Hill* subverts literary propriety yet achieves a comic effect superior to mere pornography through its use of puns, euphemisms, and parody.

Additional coverage of Cleland's life and career is contained in the following sources published by The Gale Group: *Literature Criticism from 1400-1800,* **Vol. 3, and** *Dictionary of Literary Biography,* **Vol. 39.**

Oliver Goldsmith

1728(?)-1774

(Anglo-Irish novelist, dramatist, poet, essayist, journalist, critic, biographer, and translator.

INTRODUCTION

The Vicar of Wakefield (1766) is of the best-known novels of the eighteenth century. The story of the varying fortunes of a count y pastor and his family has entertained readers for over two centuries. Modern scholars have questioned Goldsmith's intent in *The Vicar*: most commentators interpret the story as a satire on the kind of sentimental novel that was popular at the time. However, Goldsmith's satiric touches are so subtle that the novel has also been read as a sentimental, pastoral novel.

Bibliographical Information

The son of an Anglo-Irish minister, Goldsmith graduated from Trinity University in 1750. Unable to settle on a profession, Goldsmith traveled across Europe and returned to London penniless and without employment. He found critical success as a magazine writer and proofreader, but not financial security. When he was arrested in 1762 for failing to pay his rent, he showed the manuscript of *The Vicar of Wakefield* to his friend Samuel Johnson. Johnson sold the book for £60, enough to pay Goldsmith's debts. The novel was not published until 1766. In the intervening years Goldsmith wrote and published two books of essays and one of poetry, *The Traveller* (1764). His later works include the play *She Stoops to Conquer* (1773), and additional collections of poetry and essays.

Plot

Set in rural eighteenth-century England, *The Vicar of Wakefield* chronicles the life of Vicar Charles Primrose, his wife Deborah, and their children. Narrated by the protagonist, the novel recounts the reversal of the Vicar's modest fortunes and a series of blows to the family's unity. Daughter Olivia marries a scoundrel who subsequently deserts her. The family looses all their money, and son George must end his engagement. The family is forced to move to a smaller house, which catches fire. Primrose is injured saving his family. Although destitute, Primrose finds the inner strength to rise above circumstances and to comfort those around him. The novel ends with a series of improbable resolutions that restore the Vicar and his family to their previous happiness and good fortune.

Main Themes

The Vicar of Wakefield presents an almost unique callenge to readers and critics: it can and has been read as an entertaining, sentimental account of pastoral England with a strong moral. Alternately, some commentators assert that the novel is a satire of this genre and that Primrose is not meant to evoke sympathy but ridicule. Goldsmith does focus on moral matters and on the relationship between people and their religion. The plot is similar to the biblical story of Job from the Old Testament: Primrose suffers misfortunes but does not despair. He holds fast to his faith and in the end regains all that he has lost. In addition, Goldsmith addresses various social concerns, most notably penal reform, as well as manners, behavior, and the hypocrisy and snobbery of a rigidly stratified class system.

Critical Reception

The Vicar of Wakefield was published in two volumes by Francis Newbery. The novel met with unexpected success and in its first year three London editions, one Dublin edition, and one unofficial Corke edition were published. In 1767 it was translated into French and German, and in 1768, it was translated into Dutch. The book continued to sell well, achieving even greater popularity after Goldsmith's death in 1774, and by 1800 another twenty-three London editions had appeared. An average of two editions were published per year throughout the nineteenth century, and the novel remained in print through the twentieth century. The popularity of *The Vicar of Wakefiel* puzzles critics, who generally agree that the novel is overly sentimental, the plot is hackneyed, the ending and the characters are unbelievable, and the work lacks unity. Much commentary on the novel attempts to identify its obvious appeal despite these flaws. Contemporary reviewers considered the novel an example of the current sentimental novel, noting that it shared with this didactic literary form a tendency to demonstrate the superiority of the simple Christian virtues of the middle class over the sophistication and worldliness of the wealthy. Most modern critics, however, maintain that the novel's seemingly sentimental touches are actually meant to be satiric thrusts at the conventions of sentimental literature. Much critical discussion focuses on the protagonist. By employing Primrose as both the main character and the narrator, Goldsmith allowed the reader to know only as much as Primrose knows himself. Primrose's own lack of insight, evident to the reader but not to him, supplies the narrative with irony and humor. Even those critics who agree that *The Vicar of Wakefield* is a satire often disagree about the extent to which Goldsmith was using the Vicar as a satiric figure. Richard J. Jaarsma contends that Goldsmith created the Vicar as one of literature's "most savage indictments of bourgeois values." Although many other critics agree that Primrose is presented somewhat ironically, the most common critical opinion is that Goldsmith intended the Vicar as an instrument, but not as the object, of satire.

CRITICISM

James R. Foster (essay date 1949)

SOURCE: "Sensibility among the Great and Near Great" in *History of the Pre-Romantic Novel in England,* Modern Language Association of America, 1949, pp. 104-38.

[*In the following excerpt, Foster discusses Goldsmith's views on morality and sentimentality as expressed in* The Vicar of Wakefield.]

Oliver Goldsmith (1730-74) was not such a strait-laced classicist that he could not see good in Richardson's brand of sentimentality. In fact, he approved of it:

however, not without some reservations and the thought that a dash of whimsey and humor might improve it. As for those perfervid souls who yearned for something more intense and drastic in the way of sentiment, he would have none of them. One of the objectives of the *Vicar of Wakefield*[1] was to act as a sedative and febrifuge, and at the same time to set an example of feeling properly controlled.

As a classicist Goldsmith could not believe in the natural goodness of man in theory, but his heart was tender and he sympathized with the unfortunate and refused to believe that any man was irredeemably depraved. Although not exactly a primitivist, he thought certain traits of the natural or uncivilized man superior to those of some Europeans. The savage, directed by natural law, seldom sheds blood except in revenge. But as society grows older and richer, it becomes morose and erects gibbets around its property. Severe and indiscriminate penal laws and the licentiousness of the people make more convicts in England than in half of Europe. The enormous number of laws produces new vices, and these in turn call for new laws, and thus law becomes the tyrant, not the protector, of the people. In **"The Deserted Village"** he warned against the danger of luxury, and with the fall of Rome in mind, feared that disorders in England caused by luxurious and wasteful living might destroy the nation.

In his opinion the sentimentalist who uses his pretended virtue, his good heart, as a blind for selfish indulgence is a base hypocrite. Goldsmith censured certain playwrights for giving in their sentimental pieces a one-sided picture of domestic life, omitting its faults and presenting only its virtues, and teaching the spectators to pardon, or even applaud the foibles of sentimental characters in consideration of the goodness of their hearts, with the result that folly, instead of being castigated, was approved. Doubtless he expected the good novelist to avoid these faults. One should look squarely at life, refuse to apologize for the sentimentalist who seeks to escape from a moral-ity which galls his kibe, and avoid viewing things through the false lens of romance. Goldsmith believed in love and did not think that it should be put in chains by the Marriage Act, but as for romantic matches and ecstatic raptures, they were found only in novels.

The Narcissus who parades his benevolence before as many as he can get to look at him is a pretender. Better far than such ostentation is the mask of misanthropy worn by the Man in Black,[2] who hides his tender heart behind a forbidding exterior and gives whenever an appeal is made to his sympathy. But impulsive benevolence is bad. Even Sir Charles Grandison was careful not to give alms to professional beggars. Sir William Thornhill is a man of feeling who has learned his lesson. As a youth his "passions were . . . strong, and as they were all on the side of virtue, they led it [i.e., benevolence] up to a romantic extreme." He had a sympathy for all mankind and a high opinion of men because the people who surrounded him took care to show him only the good side of their character. As he saw only the suppliant faces, he felt exquisitely the suffering of all, and "his soul laboured under a sickly sensibility of the miseries of others." So he gave until his money was all gone and he could give nothing but promises. Then the almsmen were dissatisfied and left him with reproaches and contemptuous remarks. Without their praise he felt very despicable, but their ingratitude brought him to his senses. Now he is careful to bestow his bounties upon more worthy people. He masquerades as Burchell in hopes of finding a woman who, disregarding rank and wealth, will marry him because of his merits as a man.

Goldsmith's kind of sentimentality is purged of affectation and excesses, and it is solidly based on a normal and healthy development of the sympathetic imagination. In it there is no cult of melancholy, although there is a touch of it in the scene where Olivia sings "When lovely woman stoops to folly," and the Primroses breakfast together on the honeysuckle bank where she had first met Squire Ned Thornhill, her seducer. Every object recalled her sadness. "But that melancholy," writes the author, "which is excited by objects of pleasure, or inspired by sounds of harmony, soothes the heart instead of corroding it." On this occasion Livy's mother too felt a "pleasing distress" and wept and loved her daughter as never before.

Goldsmith put not a little of himself in the *Vicar of Wakefield,* for through Sir William Thornhill (alias Burchell) he expresses his opinions, through George Primrose he gives a sketch of his own past, and he steeped the whole novel in the wistful memories of the tired London author dreaming of the pastoral simplicity and delicious serenity of his boyhood days. The book conforms to the sentimental pattern of a variety of trying scenes, yet it is uncommon because of its idyllic quality and because there is much more to it than just the stories of the two heroines. It is concerned with the whole Primrose family, and Parson Primrose as the *pater familias* is the most important figure. Sir William, the guardian angel of the family (a little like Sir Charles Lisdale in Sarah Fielding's *Ophelia*), is a younger Dr. Harrison and belongs to the Grandison type. The Vicar himself is a variant of the same type with traits from Abraham Adams. But he lacks the burly stoutness and grotesqueness of Fielding's parson. Although somewhat proud of his erudition and slightly mad on the subject of monogamy, at bottom the Vicar is sound and an enemy of false social ambition, pretense, affectation, and the tawdry finery of Vanity Fair, as is shown by his reproving of his wife and daughters when they tried to cut a fine figure before the parishioners. As with Adams, his honesty and good-heartedness blind him to the duplicity of scheming knaves. Besides he is prone to judge a man by his appearance and badly needs the lesson taught to Adams when that worthy was taken in by the fellow with the sweet face of a primitive Christian.

The author himself would have been the first to admit that as the world goes, things do not commonly turn out so well as they do in the novel, for he believed wordly prosperity depended more often on prudence than on virtue. Yet it is fitting that the ending should have a bit of the fairy tale about it, for wish fulfillment is not out of place in such a wistful sentimental story. Few of the readers of the hundred and more editions of the *Vicar of Wakefield* have expressed dissatisfaction with the happy outcome of events, and all have thought the novel, in spite of the fact that there is little absolutely new either in character or plot, one of the world's most delightful narratives.

Notes

[1] Written in 1762 and published in 1766.

[2] *Citizen of the World,* Letter XXVI.

Michael E. Adelstein (essay date 1961)

SOURCE: "Duality of Theme in the *Vicar of Wakefield*" in *College English,* Vol. 22, No. 5, 1961, pp. 315-21.

[*In the essay below, Adelstein argues that the key to understanding* The Vicar of Wakefield *is recognizing the transformation of Primrose.*]

The overwhelming and continuous popularity of *The Vicar of Wakefield* has caused critics in recent years to reason that such success must be attributed to more unity and coherence in the novel than had formerly been recognized.[1] Casting traditional evaluations aside, the latest appraisers of Goldsmith's novel have found harmony, contrapuntal balance, consistency, unity, careful planning, and elaborate pattern. The comments about *The Vicar* have run full cycle since Macaulay's frequently quoted statement that the plot was "one of the worst that ever were constructed."[2]

My contention is that truth in this instance is to be found somewhere between the polar extremes. I should like to suggest that Goldsmith did have the general outlines of his plot in mind but that he switched from the theme of prudence to that of fortitude. In this process, the central character was transformed from an innocent simpleton to a courageous, resolute hero. Much of the confusion about the novel has resulted from the failure to realize that Dr. Primrose, Part I, is not the same individual as Dr. Primrose, Part II.

I

Goldsmith concludes the first chapter of his novel with the summary statement that all the members of the Primrose family "had but one character—that of being equally generous, credulous, simple, and inoffensive" (p. 5). Such a description aptly applies to the narrator, the Vicar, who promptly in the following pages loses his fortune by carelessly entrusting it to a merchant, alienates Mr. Wilmot by indiscreetly advocating monogamy to the thrice-married gentleman and, consequently, brings about the dissolution of the George-Arabella marriage. All the ensuing misfortunes of the Primroses excepting the burning of their house result from the Vicar's blindness to the guile and unscrupulousness of others, especially Squire Thornhill. The very first words about this character ("scarce a farmer's daughter within ten miles round but what had found him successful and faithless") undoubtedly alerted the eighteenth-century reader and should have warned the Vicar about the true nature of this rake. Although apprehensive at first, Dr. Primrose gradually comes to accept him and his friends, Lady Blarney and Miss Carolina Wilelmina Amelia Skeggs.

In other respects the Vicar also demonstrates that he neither understands mankind nor the ways of the world. Believing that Moses is a shrewd trader, he sends his son to the fair to sell the family colt and to purchase a younger, more attractive horse. After Moses has been swindled into buying some worthless green spectacles, the Vicar decides to sell the remaining horse, Blackberry. Neither his son's experience nor Mrs. Primrose's advice serves as ample warning once the ingenuous clergyman has been referred to as "the great Primrose, that courageous monogamist, who had been the bulwark of the Church" (p. 73).

Following his folly at the fair, the Vicar continues in his own simple, credulous fashion. First, Burchell's letter is misinterpreted, then transparent snares are set to entice the rake into marriage, and finally Olivia is forced into a situation which causes her to run away with the Squire. At this point, through his own simplicity, the Vicar has lost his fortune, his daughter, his intended daughter-in-law, and nearly all of his material possessions. The wheels have also been set in motion for the final jail scene where the Vicar is confronted with even more overwhelming disasters.

The reason for reviewing the action in the first half of the novel is to show how the sequence of events lends itself to the interpretation that Goldsmith was planning to write a satire on idealism. The "generous, credulous, simple, and inoffensive" Dr. Primrose is clearly no match for the world. As such, he took his place among numerous other eighteenth-century characters who eventually discover that "no man can be good enough to enable him to neglect the rules of prudence."[3]

This viewpoint—that virtue by itself was not sufficient to withstand the temptations of life and the malice of people—was anti-sentimental in its ridicule of the supremacy of righteousness and the complacent trust in the inherent goodness of mankind. The eighteenth-century term "prudence" suggested the practical or worldly wisdom needed to live securely and happily in the real world.

The first half of *The Vicar,* therefore, implies by its sequence of episodes that Goldsmith was concerned with the prudence theme. The protagonist finds himself involved in a series of mishaps, nearly all of which are complicated and compounded by his own innocence, benevolence, and credulity. The basic handling of the plot is realistic rather than sentimental. Quite clearly, readers are to laugh at the honest, virtuous simpleton who suffers because he lacks worldly wisdom. Goldsmith's interest in this theme is further evident in his treatment of other characters and in several explicit statements.

The model figure in the novel is Sir William Thornhill, who has solved his own personal problems and eventually resolves those of the Primrose family. Formerly he had labored under "a sickly sensibility," he had carried "benevolence to an excess," he had innocently "loved all mankind," and although he had "talked like a man of sense, his actions were those of a fool" (p. 16). As a result of his experiences and his travels, Sir William learns the lessons of prudence.

Another who flounders before he is indoctrinated into the ways of the world is the Vicar's eldest son, George. Armed with his father's sentimental advice *("never saw I the righteous man forsaken, or his seed begging their bread"),* George, like the Vicar and Sir William, stumbles through a series of mishaps. After failing as a writer because he is unwilling to turn out pieces of "fruitful mediocrity," he discovers that his inability to flatter makes him ill-suited to be a companion, and that his simplicity results in his almost being shipped to an American plantation. Unable to teach English to the Dutch, and Greek to the Italians, George finally learns about life through his experiences as a cognoscento, a tutor, a traveling musician, a debater, and an actor.

Other members of the Primrose family, though to a lesser extent, belong to the pattern of the prudence theme. Olivia, "the child of simplicity," foolishly elopes with the Squire; Mrs. Primrose, ironically "extolled [for] her prudence," shares with her husband the responsibility for misjudging Burchell and others; Moses, "a discreet boy," loses in argumentation to the sophistic statements of the Squire and in the marketplace to the duplicity of Jenkinson; and although Sophia is probably named for the inherent wisdom she displays in perceiving Burchell's merit, she too is hoodwinked by "the ladies" and their tales of glamorous London.

The primary quality lacking in the Primroses is mentioned like a motif throughout the early part of the novel. The Vicar ironically praises his wife for "her prudence" and criticizes Mr. Wilmot for having only one virtue left, "which was prudence." The relative, who informs the Vicar of his lost fortune, suggests "that your prudence will enforce the necessity of dissembling, at least till your son has the lady's fortune secure" (p. 9). Shortly afterwards, the Vicar prefaces his remarks to his family on their moving to a new community by stating, "No prudence of ours could have prevented our late misfortune but prudence may do much in disappointing its effects" (p. 11). In all, the term is used in some fifteen instances in the first half of the novel and but twice in the second.

Linked with the emphasis on the importance of prudence is the corollary concept that virtue by itself is not sufficient to withstand the evils of the world. The general ineffectiveness and insignificance of virtue is dominant early in the novel. "No virtue was able to resist [the] arts and assiduity" of Squire Thornhill (p. 13); Sir William Thornhill's passions were unfortunately "all on the side of virtue . . . [leading] to a romantic extreme" (p. 16); and the news about Olivia's elopement reaches the Vicar just as he is extolling his "good and virtuous" children (p. 97). The chapter headings reiterate the ineffectiveness of virtue: "Scarcely any Virtue found to resist the Power of long and pleasing Temptation" (XVII) and "Happiness and Misery rather the result of Prudence than of Virtue in this life" (XXVIII).

The most complete rejection of the importance of simple virtue appears in a conversation between Burchell and Dr. Primrose. The latter asserts that "The ignorant peasant without fault is greater than the philosopher with many; for what is genius or courage without an heart? 'An honest man's the noblest work of God.'" Goldsmith's model character scorns this reasoning by deprecating Pope for the "hackneyed maxim" and by pointing out that scholars, statesmen, and "champions" with their faults should not be preferred to "the low mechanic, who laboriously plods on through life without censure or applause" (p. 81).

From the opening summary statement about the Vicar and his family to the point when he learns of Olivia's elopement, Goldsmith is concerned with the prudence theme. The gullibility of the Vicar, the experiences of Sir William Thornhill, the helplessness of George in his travels, the folly of Mrs. Primrose, the duplicity of Moses, and the deception of Olivia all combine with the repetition of the term "prudence" and the disparagement of simple virtue to suggest from an internal examination that Goldsmith was once again concerned

with the necessity and importance of prudence, a theme that recurs throughout so much of his work.[4]

II

At almost the moment that the Vicar learns about Olivia's absence, the nature of his character changes. The sententious simpleton grows in stature even as he sinks deeper into calamity. With the exception of a single aside (p. 119) and a single incidence (pp. 173-174), he loses all of his comic qualities. No longer does he probe gently into the petty vanities of life. His dual role—that of ironic narrator commenting upon his own ingénu indiscretions—terminates. Although the novel continues to be told from the same point of view, the character describing his experiences has changed. From Olivia's absence, his follies are minimized; his wisdom and humanity are emphasized. He has been transformed into an authority on monarchy, commerce, drama, penology, and the criminal code. The quixotic simpleton, formerly armed with the sword of idealism, now becomes almost a tragic hero who attacks life with the bare knuckles of reality. Goldsmith is no longer interested in prudence. The focus of the novel has changed from a consideration of how man can achieve happiness and success to the more realistic concern about how man can accept and learn to tolerate the suffering and misery of his plight. As Professor Sherburn states, "Submission, intrepidity, fortitude, these are the lessons Goldsmith wishes us to learn. . . ."[5]

Goldsmith's interest in this second theme is reflected in his treatment of the Vicar. Besides the external conflict already set in motion between Squire Thornhill and Dr. Primrose, an internal conflict, characteristic of tragedy, is established. Commencing with the news about Olivia, the Vicar passes through a series of spiritual crises. In each of these, he reacts violently, is consoled and comforted by others, and finally regains control of himself.

The first situation finds him lamenting the loss of Olivia in these words: "My children, go and be miserable; for we shall never enjoy one hour more. And oh, may Heaven's everlasting fury light upon him and his! thus to rob me of my child! . . . Go, my children, go and be miserable and infamous; for my heart is broken within me!" (pp. 97-98).

Moses calls upon his father to display "fortitude" and Mrs. Primrose urges her husband to consult the Bible. The Vicar finally manages to control himself after Moses tells him, "Your rage is too violent" and "It ill suited you and your reverend character thus to curse your greatest enemy" (p. 98).

The same pattern is repeated later in the story when the Vicar learns that his other daughter, Sophia, has been abducted. Once again he shouts his hatred at the wrong-doer, bemoans his abject state, and is unable to restrain himself. For the second time he is pacified and solaced by his wife and Moses.

The third episode is precipitated by the appearance of George in chains, wounded, and condemned to die. Losing all control of himself, the Vicar cries out, "Oh that this sight could break my heart at once and let me die" (p. 187).

George rebukes his father with the same words that Moses had employed previously, "Where, Sir, is your fortitude?" (p. 187).

But the Vicar cannot compose himself; his grief and anguish provoke a violent, wrathful outcry, "May all the curses that ever sunk a soul fall heavy upon the murderer of my children! May he live, like me, to see——" (p. 188).

George interrupts, reminds his father of "your age, your holy calling," and points out that "you have often charmed me with your lessons of fortitude; let me now, Sir, find them in your example" (p. 189).

These three situations exemplify the novel's internal conflict generated by Goldsmith's concern with the fortitude theme in the second part of the work. The climax follows swiftly with its moment of illumination signalled by the immediacy of the Vicar's chang-ed outlook: "I am *now* raised above this world. . . . From *this* moment. . . . I *now* see and am convinc-ed. . . ." (p. 189; the italics are mine).

The Vicar's lengthy thematic speech in the following chapter (XXIX) is significant in the light of the previous discussion because it resolves the problem created in the three episodes. It is important to the Vicar's personal spiritual crisis because it brings about the new realization that life is to be endured and that man must resign himself to probable discomfort and distress. It is, however, irrelevant to the external conflict, the Primrose-Squire Thornhill struggle, because it serves no function on this plot level. Artistically it is a blemish but from the standpoint of Goldsmith's changing conception of his central character and of his theme, the sermon is essential, vital, and important.

This fortitude theme developed from the altered nature of the Vicar. He is no longer the mild, calm, gentle, ironic individual who quietly and dispassionately lost his fortune and accepted deceit and chicanery. The protagonist of the second half of the novel is a disturbed, provoked, wrathful figure who curses his enemies and lacks the inner resources necessary to face his trials. The conflict, therefore, grows out of the Vicar's spiritual crisis and is resolved by the prison sermon. Theoretically, the Vicar, believing his own pronouncements about fortitude, submissions, and trust in the Eternal, will be able to withstand any new vicis-

situde. Because Goldsmith did not subject his character to another test, the contrivance of the happy ending has usually obscured the character transformation.

III

What has already been indicated about the change in the central character and in the theme of *The Vicar* should not be interpreted as applying to the outline of the plot. The structure of the action as distinct from the actors and from the meaning of the work remained intact. Commencing with the loss of the Vicar's fortune and the dissolution of George's marriage, the outline of the action is sketched. By chapter V, the Primroses have moved, George has departed, Burchell and Squire Thornhill have been introduced, and the ending has been foreshadowed. To readers of eighteenth-century novels, the plot is clear: Burchell, the prudent individual, will eventually rescue the "generous, credulous, simple, and inoffensive" Primroses from the snares of the rake, Squire Thornhill. In this process, the Vicar will exchange his naive belief in the goodness of mankind for a more mature and sophisticated conception of humanity. Olivia will realize the importance of discretion, which Sophia has seemingly innately acquired. George's experiences abroad will substantiate the lessons learned by his family at home. All of these developments are related to and unified by the theme of prudence which Goldsmith was interested in at the beginning of his novel.

Succeeding chapters contribute to the original plot scheme. Sophia and Olivia have their fortunes told by a gypsy, who predicts that the former will marry a baronet and the latter a squire. The Vicar protests too much at this foolishness for readers to ignore the device of the mocked prophecy clearly foreshadowing the novel's end.

Other evidence of Goldsmith's control over the plot scheme is apparent in his later use of insignificant incidents. Moses' folly at the fair is not only linked with the prudence theme but serves on the plot level to involve Mr. Flamborough in the swindle. The importance of this episode is revealed in the jail scene when Jenkinson, imprisoned on Flamborough's charges, befriends the Vicar and later exposes Squire Thornhill. Another trivial incident which plays a functional part later in the novel occurs in the seemingly irrelevant episode in which Sir William Thornhill reprimands the traveling George Primrose for dueling. Later in the jail scene the purpose of the meeting is apparent when George serves to identify Burchell. Goldsmith also employs the incident to provide one final twist to the plot as the Vicar's son, previously rebuked for dueling, now faces capital punishment for his reckless action in killing a servant.

Besides the careful use of minor incidents, there is a

cleverly conceived neoclassical balance and harmony in the novel. The plot runs full circle with the Vicar surrounded by his happy family at both beginning and end. Scenes and episodes are often matched with one another: Burchell's experiences parallel those of George; Squire Thornhill's affected pedantry is similar to that of Jenkinson; Burchell's early rescue of Sophia from the stream is repeated in his later liberation of her from Timothy Baxter; the Vicar establishes a routine for his family in jail as he had after their move from Wakefield; and Mrs. Primrose is as intent on carving at the wedding banquet as she had been originally at her "elegant" home in Wakefield.

Other evidence showing that Goldsmith had carefully planned his novel is ably presented by Hilles and Dahl. Indeed there no longer appears to be much validity to the numerous statements about the unplanned and unprepared ending of the novel.[6]

IV

The preceding discussion has indicated that although Goldsmith followed his original plot outline, he changed the theme of *The Vicar* and transformed the central character. Despite these inconsistencies, the novel is entertaining, interesting, and absorbing as a result of Goldsmith's ability to write dramatic scenes, to portray character vividly, and to expose mankind's foibles in a sympathetic, gently ironic, forgiving fashion.

The Vicar may be popular to countless readers through the centuries because of rather than in spite of its faults. It offers some of the detachment of the comic and some of the high seriousness of the tragic. It presents situations which are unbelievable to people who are believable. It mixes the idyllic atmosphere of a rural setting with the suggestive sordidness of city life and the bleakness of prison existence. It contains all the melodramatic trappings: disguises, villains, innocent heroines, seductions, swindles, abductions, surprises, and last minute rescue. It counterbalances these by sober reflections on commerce, monarchy, dueling, drama, poetry, penal law, and prison reform. There is indeed God's abundance in Goldsmith's slim volume. The novel, therefore, may mean different things to different critics. But to all it should stand as a representation of life which views the real and the ideal, recognizes the good and does not deny the evil, and laughs at humanity but yet sympathizes with it. Goldsmith urges us to accept the way of the world and the nature of man; he believes that man's lot is to endure, to work, and to hope. *The Vicar of Wakefield* despite its inconsistencies has lived through the years to help humanity do just that.

Notes

[1] I refer here primarily to Curtis Dahl, "Patterns in Disguise in 'The Vicar of Wakefield,'" *ELH*, XXV

(1958), 90-104. The seminal study of the novel's unified structure was Frederick W. Hilles' introduction to the Everyman's Library American Edition (New York, 1951). All page references are to Hilles' edition.

[2] Thomas Babington Macaulay, *Miscellanies* (Boston, 1900), III, 48.

[3] Henry Fielding, *The History of Tom Jones* (New York, 1903), I, 132. Others who learn the lessons of prudence include Peregrine Pickle, Roderick Random, Betsy Thoughtless, and David Simple.

[4] W. F. Gallaway, "The Sentimentalism of Goldsmith," *PMLA*, 48 (1933), 1167-1181.

[5] George Sherburn, "The Restoration and Eighteenth Century," *A Literary History of England,* ed. Albert C. Baugh (New York, 1948), p. 1061.

[6] See Walter Raleigh, *The English Novel* (London, 1922), p. 208; Charles H. Huffman, *The Eighteenth Century Novel in Theory and Practice* (Dayton, Va., 1924), p. 63; Harold Williams, *Two Centuries of the English Novel* (London, 1911), p. 109; and other studies.

Ronald Paulson (essay date 1967)

SOURCE: "The Novel of Manners" in *Modern Critical Views: Oliver Goldsmith,* edited by Harold Bloom, Chelsea House, 1987, pp. 7-14.

[*In the following essay, first published in 1967 and reprinted in 1987, Paulson argues that Goldsmith creates a new style of novel of manners in the first seventeen chapters of* The Vicar of Wakefield.]

The scene of the novel of manners . . . draws on both the satiric touchstone scene in which guilt is diffused and the satiro-sentimental scene of sexual threat and tears. Both the ironic observer of the Fielding novel and the Smollettian observer of delicate sensibility—one a controlling intelligence, the other a character—contribute to the heroine of the novel of manners. Those assistant satirists who surround the dumb man of feeling are as important as the spectra of different points of view in the Spectator Club and *Humphrey Clinker*. The essential elements, however, are the controlling and analytic intelligence of the Fielding novel and the Richardsonian concern with conscious-ness; but the latter, before it could influence the novel of manners, had to pass through satiric inter
mediaries.
It is possible to trace a line from the anti-romance of Cervantes, Sorel, and Furetière through the novels of Fielding, Smollett, and Burney to the novel of manners written by Jane Austen. The anti-romance contributes

the basic structure for a study of manners not concerned exclusively with conduct book problems (what to do when two equally stringent rules apply at once) or with a reportorial description of different manners (the various "spy" and travel narratives). The basic situation simply involves the juxtaposition of two sets of values or manners (ideal-real, aristocratic-bourgeois, natural-unnatural, free-confined, individualist-conformist) and a protagonist who touches both. The protagonist is between the two areas; not completely committed to either, he is insecure, an unknown quantity seeking to discover his true position in relation to them, or else he is solidly on the lower level but trying to pass himself off as the higher, or perhaps even trying to become the higher. The spectrum of possibility runs from the bastard or foundling who seeks self-identity to the fop who apes the externals of his betters.

The Richardsonian novel is a novel of manners in the sense that it is concerned with the relationship between the manners of the rising middle class and those of the declining aristocracy. If an analogy is possible between *Don Quixote* and *Pamela* or *Clarissa*, its usefulness lies in Richardson's employment of the romantically alluring image of the aristocratic rake to draw Pamela and Clarissa, with much talk of reforming him, to their respective fates. Richardson's aim is not criticism or analysis, however, but conflict, ending happily for Pamela, tragically for Clarissa. Neither heroine is presented primarily as aspiring to the aristocracy, but rather as pursued and persecuted by it. Clarissa in particular is ground to death between the wheels of the two classes. In both cases, Richardson expresses the feelings of the emergent bourgeoisie—a servant may marry her master, and a middle-class girl should be married, not raped, by an aristocrat (a view at variance with the Restoration comedy of manners); in short, the individual's integrity is paramount and depends on freedom of choice.

It was left for Fielding to turn from the dramatization of a conflict to an analysis of the relationship involved. Fielding, however, was not concerned with the relationship between the classes, but with the anti-romance subject of the relationship between the instincts of the individual and the code of manners that does not at every point fit them—either painfully distorting them or serving as a convenient mask for the hypocrite. Thus in *Joseph Andrews,* his anti-romance on *Pamela,* he opposes the real human behavior of Adams and Joseph to the middle-class manners of the Pamelas and Cibbers, which conceal or justify self-seeking. Quixotism is interpreted by Fielding as the ability to see through (or be unaffected by) the manners of one's society. In *Tom Jones* he uses the man motivated by natural feeling to criticize the conventions and customs of his society, including the aristocratic manners of the Bellasons and Fellamars. In a sense all of Fielding's work is constructed on the anti-romance situation; in his early

works he shows the foppish imitators of fashion, which in this case is the false ideal of "greatness." But he treats Jones as Cervantes did Quixote, putting him and the Fellamars side by side, as feeling and form, and letting them comment on each other. To the extent that the virtues and vices of feeling and form are balanced—some virtue on both sides—*Tom Jones* becomes a novel of manners.

Fielding's novel also enormously broadens the scope of satiric irony in order to express a point of view that is judicious, understanding, and sympathetic and can encompass both form and feeling. However, it still leaves a broad gap between *Tom Jones* and *Pride and Prejudice.* One of the important breaks is the relationship between persuasion and dramatization, between reader and protagonist. Fielding's technical equipment permitted the reader's growing awareness, but it worked less well when he wished to dramatize the growing awareness of a character. In *Tom Jones* he attempted to make Tom's self-recognition correspond to the reader's. As early as book 8 Tom speaks out to correct the Old Man of the Hill, whose experience, like Tom's, has been colored by betrayal but whose generalization is that all men are evil. Tom has discovered, somewhere along the line, about the same time as the reader, that this is an oversimplification. He shows this even more strikingly with the puppet-master who, unwilling to acknowledge man's mixed nature, presents only paragons to instruct his audience. Jones tells him that he should have included Punch: "so far from improving, I think, by leaving him out and his merry wife Joan, you have spoiled your puppet-show" (bk. 12, chap. 5). When the puppet-master's wife discovers her maid making love with the Merry Andrew on the stage, the truth of Tom's view becomes apparent, and the gypsy episode confirms Tom's and the reader's realization that mercy is better than strict justice, that evil is in many cases a spot that darkens a character but does not destroy it. Tom later appears to see Black George's failure (stealing the £500) as an objectification of his own at Upton and elsewhere, when he pleads for him: "you must suffer me to call it weakness rather than ingratitude; for I am convinced the poor fellow loves me" (bk. 18, chap. 11).

One wonders, however, if the knowledge of mixed character is connected with Tom's more important disasters. It shows understanding in his relations with Black George and Molly but has no effect when applied as self-knowledge to his own case; indeed one goes from his talk with the Old Man to his escapade with Mrs. Waters, after which his views about mixed character sound like special pleading. The knowledge administered helps the reader but not Tom. It is the reader who needs to know about the complexity of actions in order to understand Tom; Tom only needs to learn prudence and to know himself. Therefore in terms of the main action of the novel—the need to complement Tom's feeling with form—the enlightened party remains the reader, and the character seems unaware of his problem. Knowledge that all people are fallible is hardly a help toward self-knowledge or self-discipline. The truth, I suspect, is that Fielding is still primarily interested in Tom as a corrective and as an example of character vs. conduct; he is not really interested in Tom's perception—the sine qua non of the novel of manners.

An ingénu cannot serve as the protagonist of a novel of manners. Joseph Andrews' innocence (and to a lesser degree Tom's) forces the reader to focus on the evil glaringly exposed, not on the hero's problems that may have caused him to become entangled with knaves. Joseph is never embarrassed: to be embarrassed one must see as well as be seen. Tom's embarrassment (for example, when he learns that Sophia knows of his behavior at Upton) points in a direction that Fielding never fully explores. Among the satirists, Smollett is responsible for this strain. The novel of manners's protagonist and many secondary characters descend from the satiric observer as a character, whose gradual transformation we have followed from a public figure (whose motives and concerns are external and moral) to a private one (whose concerns are strictly internal and personal). Roderick Random acted as a satirist of society out of both desire for revenge (private) and moral conviction (public); by the time one reaches Captain Mirvan in *Evelina* personal considerations are the sole motive. However, only when an author can balance an interest in what happened per se with how it appeared to X, Y, and Z, can a novel like *Pride and Prejudice* be produced.

Dr. Primrose: The Ironic Hero

One of the missing links, the step beyond Fielding in the exploitation of irony as a fictional device, is supplied by Oliver Goldsmith's ***The Vicar of Wakefield*** (1766). This novel, so brilliant for at least half its length, is strangely underestimated, remaining a memory from childhood which, unlike *Gulliver* or *Crusoe*, cannot shake off the childish reading. There is perhaps no level the child has missed, and the pleasure of the adult is almost the same as that of the child. The *Vicar*'s great popularity and its influence on continental literature were due to Goldsmith's building his story on fairy-tale motifs and archetypal patterns that touched a sensitive chord in all readers and showed a way toward introducing romance into the realistic novel form. (Similar patterns in *Clarissa* were submerged under the close texture of observed experience—though they played their part in Richardson's popularity too.) As Smollett builds his novels around a structure of satiric exposition (with some romantic or sentimental plot elements), so Goldsmith builds his novel around the myths of the god who descends among humans as a traveler in search of hospitality, the ruler who passes among his people in disguise, and Jack and the Beanstalk. The most striking and central of the myths is the story of Job—his fortune lost, his house burnt down, both his daughters abducted, one (supposed) dead, his son about to be hanged, etc. The *Vicar* is a typical product of mixed genres, with many theatrical elements thrown in at the end.

In part, however, it is a close eighteenth-century precursor of *Pride and Prejudice,* and it still shows the scaffolding that has been shed or more thoroughly disguised by Austen. To begin, we must go back to a slightly earlier work. The first **"Chinese Letters"** were published early in 1760; they were reworked as much as possible and published as ***The Citizen of the World*** in May 1762. Goldsmith wrote the *Vicar* at this time or shortly after, although it was not published until 1766. In other words, Dr. Primrose follows chronologically hard on Lien Chi Altangi. Goldsmith's Chinese observer carries the associations of a country very unlike the Persia of Montesquieu's *Lettres Persanes,* with its seraglio, passion, and adventure; China recalls wisdom, tradition, conservatism, and the like. Unlike the noble savage (Voltaire's Huron), Lien Chi Altangi brings something more with him than simplicity; his comments are often sharpened by irony, particularly as he becomes accustomed to the new country and can analyze both it and China with some detachment, juxtaposing their different manners. But this is not to suggest that he is only an ironic observer. Often he sees the truth through a child's eyes or through the haze of conflicting conventions, and often at the beginning and occasionally at the end his divergent point of view exposes him to satire. In a memorable scene he is charmed by a young lady he meets on the street, from whom he generalizes about the kindness of English ladies; he never suspects that she is a prostitute until she fails to return the watch she has volunteered to have repaired for him. His true criticisms of the fantastic fashions of London women are followed by his adverse comments on their white teeth and unconstricted feet. He is, after all, Goldsmith points out, from a country with as many foolish customs of its own. The effect in general is of two sets of manners—some good, some bad—juxtaposed, rather than one set (bad) criticized by the other (good).

There is nothing new about this figure. The satirist tries to invent a central figure who can convey as much varied satire as possible. When Goldsmith came to write the *Vicar,* however, he must have begun with two ideas—to present a Parson Adams character and to have a Fieldingesque commentator as his supposed "author." The *Vicar,* it should be remembered, comes from the pen of an essayist; it represents Goldsmith's first step toward dramatic form. It is the first of the early novels to use an ironic narrator who is a central character of the action as well—both an ironist and the object of dramatic irony.

Dr. Primrose sees more than the people around him and lets the reader, and sometimes the people themselves, know about it. But the reader sees still more than Primrose does. In short, Goldsmith goes one step beyond Fielding, at the same time shedding some of the creaking machinery involved in the omniscient "historian" of Fielding's novels (but stopping far short of the irrational order of *Tristram Shandy*). He has made the irony part of his speaker's temperament, creating a more complex as well as a wittier person while at the same time adding a dramatic irony that was impossible in Fielding's kind of narrative. The situation is still basically a satiric one, focusing on the pretensions to gentility of Mrs. Primrose and her daughters. They are ridiculous; she is unpleasant. The family of a poor parson (he has come down in the world), they try to emulate the gentry with dress, carriage, even a family portrait, and they become prey to the aristocratic wolf who appears in the shape of Squire Thornhill.

Goldsmith duplicates the *Clarissa* situation of seduction, but he treats it in a different way from either Richardson or his satiric equivalent, Smollett. His focus is on the manners of the sheep rather than on the wolf, and it is not a sentimental focus; he studies their aspirations and the Quixotic effects in absurd behavior and in a blindness to the real situation in which a wolf is ap-proaching ever nearer. This emphasis is achieved by placing at the center of the narrative the clever man, the ironist who though he sees through his wife and daughters yet bows to their wishes. He may surreptitiously throw away their face washes, but he allows himself to be guided by them in the posing of the family por-trait, the dispatching of the good Burchell, and the encouraging of the evil Squire Thornhill. In fact, although he sees through his wife's values, he unconsciously shares some of them; his contempt of Burchell, the "man of broken fortune," emerges in his fear that his daughter Sophia may in fact fall in love with him:

> But I had too good an opinion of Sophia's understanding, and was too well convinced of her ambition, to be under any uneasiness from a man of broken fortune.
>
> Nor could I conceive how so sensible a girl as my youngest [Sophia], could thus prefer a man of broken fortune to one whose expectations were much greater.

To appreciate the originality of Goldsmith's conception one must look back on the *Vicar* from the vantage point of *Pride and Prejudice*. There the first-person protagonist has been replaced by a guiding intelligence resembling Fielding's ironic "historian," but the central character, Elizabeth Bennet, is an ironist like Dr. Primrose. While observing accurately the pretensions of those around her, she cannot see with complete clarity and is deceived by the manners of both Wickham

and Darcy (as Primrose is by Squire Thornhill and Burchell). The theme that emerges from this kind of a central character, however elemental in Dr. Primrose, is self-knowledge and the growth to self-realization. When he recognizes his mistake about the two Thornhills, Dr. Primrose also recognizes something—however rudimentary the treatment as compared with Austen's—about himself.

Dr. Primrose is in the position later taken over by Elizabeth Bennet, and he is rather like her in his self-assurance, wit, and limited insight. But he is the head of a family, and his equivalent (if not direct descendant) is Mr. Bennet, a more intelligent version who like Primrose regards his hideous wife and foolish daughters with weary irony but is easygoing; Mr. Bennet has given up the fight and merely observes amusedly. As a result he offers a contrast to his daughter Elizabeth, whose limitation is not withdrawal. Mr. Bennet is ultimately responsible for the fate of Lydia and realizes it, just as Dr. Primrose shares responsibility for the fate of Olivia and at length recognizes his mistake. The whole Primrose family is, in fact, lifted bodily into *Pride and Prejudice:* the ignorant, pretentious, social-climbing mother, the duped Olivia, and the one sensible daughter, Sophia, have their equivalents in Mrs. Bennet, her daughters, and the two sensible sisters, Elizabeth and Jane. The two suitors in the *Vicar* are like Wickham and Darcy—one with surface charm who is actually a Lovelace seducer (Squire Thornhill), the other less prepossessing, in fact somewhat cynical and misanthropic (Burchell). (Burchell bears the same relation to Primrose as Drybone [the Man in Black] to Lien Chi Altangi, telling his life story, serving as a guide, and allowing him to see beyond appearances. But Primrose dismisses his guide, and this is the beginning of his troubles.) The main question and plot stimulus of the *Vicar*—and of all Austen novels—is how to marry off the daughters. The first thought Dr. Primrose has when he learns that he has lost his fortune is how he will make suitable marriages for his daughters, and this concern drives him (against his better nature) into his wife's camp in his opinion of Burchell. By putting the father in the center, Goldsmith makes marriage the important matter of the novel—but of course from the father's point of view; Austen puts one of the marriageable daughters in the center but gives her some of the detachment of the father in relation to the mating rite.

The first difference between the two novels, as I have noted, is in the protagonist's role. From Fanny Burney's *Evelina* Austen no doubt learned the usefulness and flexibility of the bright young girl's point of view. Her very youth makes the theme more convincingly one of growth and self-knowledge. At the same time, however, by keeping a narrator who more clearly and unambiguously sees through Elizabeth—though is often parallel to Elizabeth—Austen avoids immersing the reader in Elizabeth's emotions. In this sense Goldsmith is braver than Austen, and like Swift he trusts to his own ability to keep the proper distance between Primrose and the reader without benefit of the omniscient narrator.

All that has been said about the *Vicar* applies only to the first seventeen chapters. Goldsmith may have run out of ideas at that point, or he may have picked up his real interest, the myth of Job. Suddenly he has Primrose embark on a journey (talking predictably about life as a journey), and he reverts to an older genre, the picaresque; he loses the wonderfully tight, controlled, and effective microcosm of the family and slips back into the world of the **"Chinese Letters"** with satiric essays on punishment, liberty, and contemporary drama. While a great part of the originality of the first part comes from its tightness of structure, Goldsmith now accepts Smollett's permissive definition of a novel and gives digressions such as George's account of his life. The romantic and mythic elements emerge to full prominence. Goldsmith makes Primrose a true Job, relies on coincidences (the meetings with Miss Wilmot, George, and Olivia), and builds the disguise imagery that was subordinated to the plot in the first half into a pseudo-unifying force. (Disguise is a common ground for the two conflicting aspects of the *Vicar*. As a romance motif, it helps to define Burchell's role as the disguised prince and the villainous abductors' role. As a device of the novel of manners, however, disguise runs from the posing of the Primroses above their proper class, to the whores who pose as Lady Blarney and Miss Carolina Wilelmina Amelia Skeggs, to Jenkinson who wears actual disguises as part of his confidence racket.) The ballads and interpolated tales become more frequent. As Frederick A. Hilles has pointed·out [in his introduction to the Everyman edition], these are necessary to make the narrative seem more real by contrast and, with the preposterous reversals and recognitions of the stories, to prepare the reader for thc cnd. But thc only blatant romance occurrence in the first half is the fall of Primrose's youngest into a raging stream, from which Burchell rescues her, and I am inclined to suspect that this, as well as the ballad of *Edwin and Angelina,* are interpolations in the light of the second half. The problem of the second half is not, however, germane to my argument, which is only that in the first seventeen chapters of the *Vicar* Goldsmith, starting with an anglicized Lien Chi Altangi, a family setting, and the problem of marriage, produced a new and original form which augmented the picaresque form of Fielding and contributed another stage in the transition from satire to Austen's novel of manners.

R. F. Brissenden (essay date 1974)

SOURCE: "The Sentimentality of *The Vicar of Wakefield*" in *Modern Critical Views: Oliver Goldsmith,* edited by Harold Bloom, Chelsea House, 1987, pp. 15-19.

[*In the essay below, first published in 1974 and reprinted in 1987, Brissenden considers the role of sentimentality in* The Vicar of Wakefield.]

The Reverend Dr. Primrose, Goldsmith's Vicar of Wakefield, is, like Parson Adams and Parson Yorick, a Christian hero. He "unites in himself," says the author in the advertisement to his tale, "the three greatest characters upon earth; he is a priest, an husbandman, and the father of a family." He is moreover the embodiment of some of the principal sentimental virtues. He is charitable, humane, optimistic and in general readier to think well rather than ill of his fellow men. All his family, he tells us, "had but one character, that of being all equally generous, credulous, simple, and inoffensive." Since his moral assessments of the situations in which he finds himself are spontaneous and unselfish, he could be described as a man of feeling, but feelings in his case are always grounded in a coherent set of Christian principles, and they are always vigorously implemented in positive action. He is a man of sentiment, of sense rather than sensibility; and his determination to govern his behaviour according to principle often gets him into comic trouble with the world. When his son George is about to marry Miss Arabella Wilmot, Primrose endangers the whole scheme by refusing to compromise his beliefs on the subject of monogamy which he discovers to be diametrically opposed to those held by Miss Wilmot's father. Principle again carries the day a short while later when, learning that he has suddenly lost his fortune, Primrose refuses to let the marriage proceed under false pretences.

The purpose of the action in the novel is to display the Vicar of Wakefield in a number of testing situations. "He is drawn," Goldsmith tells us, "as ready to teach, and ready to obey, as simple in affluence, and majestic in adversity." Like Job, he loses his fortune and practically loses his family. At the nadir of his adventures he is presented to us ill, injured, penniless and in prison. His house has been burned down, one of his daughters appears to have been ruined by the local nobleman, Squire Thornhill, and his eldest son George is also in prison, chained and under sentence of death for having sent a challenge to the man who has wronged his sister.

But Primrose never loses his faith nor his moral energy. He preaches to the other prisoners, and once he has got them to listen to him persuades them to spend their time in useful work—i.e, in making small articles which they can sell. "Thus in less than a fortnight I had formed them into something social and humane, and had . . . brought [them] from their native ferocity into friendship and obedience." At the same time he consoles his fellow sufferers with the promise that although the rich man may be happy on earth the poor and the wretched who believe in God will be rewarded with an eternity of bliss—a reward which they are much more likely to attain since poverty and imprisonment cut them off from so many dangerous temptations.

But Primrose's virtue is rewarded in a much more immediate and tangible manner. A good fairy arrives in the shape of the cheerful vagabond Mr Burchell, whom Primrose has befriended earlier on in the story. "Former benevolence [is] now repaid with unexpected interest," as the heading to chapter 12, volume 2 puts it. Mr Burchell turns out to be Sir William Thornhill in disguise, the philanthropic uncle of the wicked young Squire Thornhill. Sir William marries one of Primose's daughters, he provides a dowry for the other (who turns out to be genuinely married to his nephew), George's fetters are struck off, Primrose's fortunes are restored, and all's well that ends well. When Primrose, at the beginning of the novel, sends his son out into the world to seek his fortune he urges him to make the following text his consolation: *"I have been young, and now am old; yet never saw I the righteous man forsaken, or his seed begging their bread."* The happy dénouement would seem to be meant to demonstrate the validity of this hopeful statement.

But the whole process of the action of the story has been to negate it. The more virtuously Primrose and his family behave the more cruelly they are made to suffer at the hands of fortune and their fellow men. A synopsis of the plot up to, but not including, the happy reversal with which it is rounded off would make *The Vicar of Wakefield* sound like an episode in Sade's *Justine*—it seems to demonstrate not only that the practice of virtue is not rewarded in this world but also that it is likely to attract the most outrageously bad luck. The burning down of Primrose's house is like the final destruction and violation of Justine by a bolt of lightning—a gratuitous kick in the teeth delivered by the malevolent universe in which we have to live. The structure of *The Vicar of Wakefield,* regarded as a whole, is thus profoundly sentimental, in the modern sense of the term.

Its sentimentality for the most part, however, is not disturbing, and it is interesting to speculate as to why this should be so (the one distasteful element in the fortunate conclusion is the transformation of Squire Thornhill into a suitable husband for Olivia—he is a much nastier character in fact than Richardson's Mr B.). *The Vicar of Wakefield* remains a genuinely charming and delightful book. One of the main reasons for this is that the classically comic plot is so obviously artificial. It has the happy air of a deliberately contrived, almost magical ritual—a charm enacted against wicked men and evil days in which we are cordially invited to take part. Moreover Goldsmith's picture of

life in the country is at once realistic and idyllic: the framework may be artificial, but the domestic rural world of the Primroses which it encompasses is rendered with remarkable fidelity, liveliness and good humour. The catastrophes which overtake the family are kept in perspective by the gentle comedy—Primrose slyly tipping the face-wash in the fire, or Mr Burchell, with his chorus of "Fudge!," undercutting the high-flown sophisticated chatter of the London whores. It is easy to understand how the young Goethe, embarked on his own idyllic holiday with the family at Sesenheim, could feel, as he tells us in *Dichtung und Wahrheit,* that he had walked into the Primrose household itself.

Nonetheless in the final assessment there is something worrying about the novel, a discordant note which all Goldsmith's charm cannot completely disguise. And the source of the discord can be located not so much in the Vicar of Wakefield himself as in his guardian angel, the man who saves him and his family from destruction, Mr Burchell, or Sir William Thornhill in disguise. Sir William Thornhill, as he presents himself through the mask of Burchell to the Primroses, is a melancholy man of feeling. The conversation between him and the Vicar is of unusual interest, and deserves to be quoted at length:

> "What!" cried I, "is my young landlord then the nephew of a man whose virtues, generosity, and singularities are so universally known? I have heard of Sir William Thornhill represented as one of the most generous, yet whimsical, men in the kingdom; a man of consummate benevolence"—"Something, perhaps, too much so," replied Mr. Burchell, "at least he carried benevolence to an excess when young; for his passions were then strong, and as they were all upon the side of virtue, they led it up to a romantic extreme. . . . He loved all mankind; for fortune prevented him from knowing that there were rascals. Physicians tell us of a disorder in which the whole body is so exquisitely sensible, that the slightest touch gives pain: what some have thus suffered in their persons, this gentleman felt in his mind. The slightest distress, whether real or fictitious, touched him to the quick, and his soul laboured under a sickly sensibility of the miseries of others. Thus disposed to relieve, it will be easily conjectured, he found numbers disposed to solicit; his profusions began to impair his fortune, but not his good-nature; that, indeed, was seen to encrease as the other seemed to decay: he grew improvident as he grew poor; and though he talked like a man of sense, his actions were those of a fool."

In short he began to dissipate his fortune, and also to lose confidence in his ability to assess the characters and motives of his fellow men. In order to repair the damage both to himself and his finances "he travelled through Europe on foot." This left him (for some inexplicable reason) "more affluent than ever." And now, therefore, "his bounties are more rational and moderate than before; but still he preserves the character of an humourist, and finds most pleasure in eccentric virtues." Since Sir William Thornhill is so important in the moral scheme of Goldsmith's fable it is interesting to note the terms in which he describes himself. He has a "sickly sensibility," he has behaved more like a fool than a man of sense, "he preserves the character of an humourist," i.e., an oddity, and he "finds most pleasure in eccentric virtues." "Eccentric" is perhaps the key word: Thornhill is able to preserve his integrity and also to operate effectively if erratically as a moral agent only by functioning *outside* the society to which he belongs. He does not live on his estates, he moves amongst his tenants in disguise, he is utterly incapable *because of his exquisite sensibility* of playing a normal part in the community. Yet he represents in their most highly developed form the moral ideals of this society from which he is in a sense excluded. Primrose, the "normal" man, occupies a central place in this same society—husbandman, priest, and father—but it destroys him. Burchell / Thornhill is thus not merely a Harounel-Rashid figure, the romantic "someone in disguise" who turns up in the nick of time to set things right. He is a symbol of alienation, the dispossessed conscience of a sick society. And although like George Primrose (and presumably like Goldsmith in his happier moments) he recalls his travels on the Continent cheerfully enough, his motive for undertaking them was despair. Against the carefree image of the happy wanderer playing his flute to the simple peasants one should set the opening lines of *The Traveller,* which Goldsmith published in 1765 (a year before the appearance of *The Vicar of Wakefield*) and which bears the subtitle, *A Prospect of Society:*

> Remote, unfriended, melancholy, slow,
> Or by the lazy Scheld, or wandering Po;
> Or onward, where the rude Carinthian boor
> Against the houseless stranger shuts the door;
> Or where Campania's plain forsaken lies,
> A weary waste expanded to the skies,
> Where'er I roam, whatever realms to see,
> My heart untravell'd fondly turns to thee;
> Still to my brother turns, with ceaseless pain,
> And drags at each remove a lengthening
>   chain.

The implications of *The Vicar of Wakefield,* ostensibly a sentimental comedy, are thus at bottom as pessimistic and as elegiac as those of *The Deserted Village* and *The Traveller.* One feels that for Goldsmith society appears to be so irrational, so cruel, and so economically inefficient and inequitable, that it is extremely difficult if not impossible for the ordinary, well-intentioned, morally responsible man to live the good life. For Dr Primrose to survive he needs the magical assistance of Sir William Thornhill. It could be said that Tom Jones similarly needs the magical assistance of

Squire Allworthy—but he does not need it nearly so desperately. Allworthy in the end merely represents the good luck which Tom in a sense deserves: it is easy to believe that he would have had more than a fighting chance of winning through somehow on his own resources. But one cannot feel this about the Primrose family. The structure of *The Vicar of Wakefield,* and in particular the division of moral responsibility between the Vicar himself and Sir William Thornhill, reflects a radical disquiet with the nature of man and society, a disquiet which forces Goldsmith into sentimentality.

James H. Lehmann (essay date 1979)

SOURCE: *"The Vicar of Wakefield:* Goldsmith's Sublime Oriental Job" in *ELH,* Vol. 46, No. 1, Spring, 1979, pp. 97-121.

[*In the following excerpt, Lehmann explores Goldsmith's use of "Orientalized" interpretations of Job in* The Vicar of Wakefield. *The editors have included only those footnotes that pertain to the excerpted portion of the text reprinted below.*]

II

Lowth on Job is of paramount interest when we consider the possibility of understanding the Vicar as a Job-figure in any "doctrinal" sense. The most sophisticated such view is that of Martin C. Battestin's *The Providence of Wit.*[38] In the chapter entitled "Goldsmith: The Comedy of Job," Battestin confronts a problem that has vexed critics of this novel for some time, namely, the abrupt shift of tone and action that occurs midway through the book.[39] Once Charles Primrose leaves his family to retrieve the abducted Olivia, we move from the story of a family to the pilgrimage of an individual, from a controlled comedy of manners with controlled narrator to a rambling tale, often interrupted by other tales, in which sentiment and pathos dominate. One approach to this structural problem has been to treat the first half of the book as novelistic success, while viewing the second half as a sort of failure in its succumbing to the use of romance motifs.[40] Another approach to this problem has been to join the two halves thematically, and Battestin's essay attempts such a solution.[41] He seeks to show that the story of Dr. Primrose in both halves of the novel is the story of the Biblical Job. The analogy itself, Battestin admits, is not new.[42] What is new in his treatment is the way he specifies the theological meaning of the Job-analogy. In this reading, the hero of the novel follows the path of the Biblical Job in the sense that he learns the lesson, which, according to Battestin, was the common reading of Job in the period of *The Vicar's* composition. This lesson is the doctrine of equal providence, the belief "that, although the dealings of

Providence are unequal in this life, the sufferings of good men will be abundantly recompensed in the hereafter."[43] According to Battestin, Primrose learns this Christian "doctrine of futurity" in Chapter 28 and shows his new wisdom in Chapter 29 by preaching to his fellow prisoners on just this subject. In fact, the title of the latter chapter makes reference to the "equal dealings of Providence" (17).[44]

Primrose's doctrinal revelation marks his attainment of true knowledge. The theological term for Job's new knowledge, Battestin tells us, is "prudence." Whereas one might have knowledge (and Job had knowledge)[45] he might still lack *prudence,* the insight that God's justice persists despite its apparent abrogation in this world. Battestin supports his reading by citing a large number of contemporary theologians who wrote on Job, and by citing, too, a particular controversy which raged around Warburton and Bishop Thomas Sherlock during the middle decades of the century. He suggests that Goldsmith sided with the anti-Warburtonians, who maintained that a message of divine reward in resurrection ("equal providence") could be derived from the Book of Job (and hence from a work written before the Christian dispensation).[46]

Battestin's reading is an explicit rejection of recent attempts to read Goldsmith as ironic in his presentation of the hero. Because these readings do not take the theological context into account, he argues, they are anachronistic sophistications imposed on the text by modern critics.[47]

Now Battestin is certainly right in drawing attention to the exegetical tradition in his analysis of *The Vicar of Wakefield.* But it is not at all clear that the Job-analogy in the novel is meant to be taken in the spirit he suggests. In fact, Goldsmith plays a good deal with the Biblical story; the Biblical paradigm is often invoked only to be toyed with. This is so, as my survey of Lowth might have suggested, precisely because the exegetical tradition was itself undergoing a significant change during this period.

As a preliminary but significant example of the ways Goldsmith plays with his Biblical model, consider the term "prudence." Battestin wants this term to bear a great weight because it is the technical name of Job's insight; moreover, it is the term which for Battestin ties together the unifying motifs of disguise and blindness (noted earlier by Curtis Dahl)[48] and the theological understanding of divine providence. The trouble here is that prudence is an ambiguous term in *The Vicar.* Although Battestin refers to prudence only as a term of theological art, its other uses cannot be overlooked in attempting to discern the total meaning of the word in the text.[49] Thus, in the opening chapter, Mr. Wilmot is said to have only prudence left at the age of seventy-two (25). There is nothing theological

about this jesting use of the word. Nor is the term used doctrinally when Primrose tells his family that no prudence could have prevented their misfortune. Actually, prudence would have consisted in Primrose's silence about his Whistonian beliefs on strict clerical monogamy until *after* his family had been joined to the wealthy Wilmots (exactly what the messenger bearing news of the vicar's loss suggests). Prudence may well have theological connotations, but that would only make its use ironic, and irony is finally what Battestin cannot permit.[50]

There are other reversals of the Biblical types as well. Job's wife has become the Biblical Deborah, the female judge, ruling Israel and ruling, too, her passive nominal leader Barak (Judges 4, 5). And as in Judges, this Deborah is always described in military terms; she is the one who conducts sieges and plans battles.[51] Moses, the son, is something of a lawgiver: he always cites the ancients and argues weakly with Thornhill on matters of doctrine. His sententiousness, in short, is a parody of his Biblical namesake and type. And then there are the crucial changes in the order of the Biblical narrative, as when Deborah Primrose reprimands her husband for cursing his oppressor whereas Job's wife was the one who begged him to curse God and die. Like Parson Adams of *Joseph Andrews* (the *locus classicus* for Battestin's method), our Vicar often acts at variance with his prototype, deviating subtly but surely from his presumed prefiguration.[52]

There are many such deviations in *The Vicar of Wakefield,* but my purpose is not so much to list them as to indicate where Battestin has gone wrong in his general approach. Battestin's fundamental error arises from his assumption that the *analogical* structure persists in Goldsmith's fiction. Battestin has totally ignored the fact that from the 1740s onward new ways of reading the Bible were gaining ground in England and that such changes in reading would have suggested a number of possible alternatives for the application of a Scriptural text to a literary work. He does not consider that the way (a reader of) Pope would have read his Bible might differ from the way (a reader of) Goldsmith would have read the Bible. For example, Pope in his use of Balaam and Job in the *Epistle to Bathurst* (1733) assumes a definite series of theological connotations attached to those figures that can be read as constituting their *meaning;* Earl Wasserman's analysis of the *Epistle* was based on just this premise.[53] But a quarter century later the Bible was being read differently; it was seen not only as the vehicle for theological meanings, but also as a repository of sublime poetry in the Oriental mode. Battestin must be aware of this new Orientalized Bible, yet he pays no attention to it. The results of his exhaustive researches into the theological literature are thus prejudiced by his implicit decision to consider only the homiletic aspects of these writings and to ignore the grammatical and literary-critical work on the Bible that was flourishing at just this time.

Battestin's homiletic bias in this regard forces him also to assume that it was the Warburtonian controversy on "equal providence" that stimulated interest in the Book of Job. Thus, after listing the commentators ranged on each side, he writes, "in the same period appeared several other, more or less neutral, treatises reflecting the widespread interest in the subject which the controversy had generated. These include a variety of studies by Daniel Bellamy, William Worthington, Walter Hodge, Leonard Chappelow, Thomas Heath and Bishop Lowth."[54] The unexamined assumption that these "neutral" studies merely reflect the theological controversy leads Battestin to ignore the new Orientalizing of the Bible undertaken by just these "more or less neutral studies." It also leads him to ignore the fictional possibilities which a newly Orientalized Bible might present to writers such as Goldsmith.[55]

Battestin's evidence of Goldsmith's purportedly sincere interest in the controversy also deserves scrutiny. This consists of a review of Hawkins' contribution to the debate that appeared in the *Critical Review* of August, 1759. Its authorship by Goldsmith is uncertain, but in any case the following hardly reveals real interest in the affair:

> Mr. Hawkins seems to be pretty confident in the advantage of his cause; and this we may venture to say, that he seems to be on the safe side, for he is on the bishop's; and though he loses his cause he may gain a vicarage. As for the controversy, so much has been said on both sides, that we must really acknowledge ourselves sceptic in the debate . . . We can know enough and believe enough without being acquainted with a syllable of the matter: we could wish our divines would therefore rather turn their arms against the common enemy; and while infidelity is at the gate, not waste their time in civil altercation.[56]

This passage is clearly not the strongest basis upon which to found Goldsmith's interest in the Providential controversies surrounding the Book of Job. Rather, in Goldsmith as in other Job studies, the general indifference to the theological issues that Battestin holds most important suggests that he has ignored a crucial development in the mid-century reading of Job. Far from there being a consensus with regard to the specific theology of the work, there was not even unanimity as to whether the book was to be taken as *primarily* theological.

The new Orientalizing Bible readings, as exemplified by Lowth, are important therefore because they force us to reconsider the historical plausibility of a strictly theological reading of Job in *The Vicar of Wakefield*. What we have instead is a *secular* Job. Ronald Paul-

son has elaborated the distinction between *emblem* and *expression* in the art and literature of the eighteenth century.[57] We might apply this notion by noting that in the Orientalist tradition represented by Bishop Lowth, the emblematic quality of Scripture is confronted with the expressive potentialities of Hebrew poetry. For a new tradition of Biblical Orientalism, the emblematic readability of the Bible (the old typological framework in which the Old Testament is emblematic of the New) has been transformed into its sublime expressiveness. Scripture no longer *means* the way it once did. This "secular conversion" is never more manifest than in the Orientalizing of the Book of Job.[58]

III

I would suggest that there is a moral development in *The Vicar* that is closely related to a movement toward the attainment of the sublime. This movement takes our Job-figure from an essentially ironic condition to one that sublimely transcends irony through love and humility. Primrose *becomes* a Job-figure in the course of the novel, not because he acquires specific theological knowledge, but because he moves beyond an artificially self-conscious situation into the condition of genuine passion. He attains the sublime when he is motivated not by concern for appearances and social status, but by the natural and passionate love of his family and his fellow man.

This moral movement in the novel towards humility and the sublime can best be seen in the progress of the work's pictorial imagery. In Goldsmith's time sublime painting, like sublime Hebrew poetry, had to be uniquely expressive, not emblematic. As Reynolds put it, painting must strike its viewer in a single blow.[59]

Both halves of our novel contain many scenes with a strongly pictorial quality, but Goldsmith depicts these scenes differently in the two halves. In the "pre-exilic" first portion of the work Primrose's presentation of these pictorial scenes is intensely ironic. This is because his concern in representing his family is to curry favor with his social betters. This concern is morally flawed; in terms of the sublime work of art, Primrose's act of representation is mere parody. Once the vicar sets off on his journey, however, he becomes the object of forces beyond his control. Primrose no longer *creates* scenes; these are discovered or reveal themselves to him. It is just this powerlessness, and the recognition of powerlessness, that allows the narrator to transcend the irony that marks his earlier artifice. The frozen order of the earlier depictions gives way to a series of passionate events. Our hero recognizes moral truth just when these events convey not the ironic fiction-making of their author, but rather his perception of the overpowering significance of human love. As he loses control over his surroundings, he gains his ultimate redemption as a simple and sublime Job (and simplicity is an integral element of the Biblical and artistic sublime).[60] Especially in the pictorial culmination of each half of the book—the portrait scene in Chapter 16 and the prison scene in Chapter 29—we can contrast the irony of artifice with the simplicity of the sublime.

I am suggesting, then, that the identification of Job with the sublime in contemporary Biblical discourse allows us to re-evaluate the evident break in the style of the novel. While we seem to be moving (unhappily) from a delicate novelistic depiction of life as a social environment, to life as a journey, we are in fact advancing from an artificial and unnatural mode of self-realization to a wiser vision of human existence.[61] I would suggest, too, that a useful general notion for dealing with this transformation of pictorial imagery is that of the *frame*. This notion subsumes, in the first place, the general symbolism of spatial enclosure: frames, enclosures of all sorts, are a fundamental structure in the novel. In addition, we can talk of the *activity* of framing as it pertains to our hero-narrator. In this second sense, framing denotes a selection, delimitation, and depiction of reality by means of the imagery of enclosure. To the extent that scenes in our novel are fictionally enclosed and distanced, successive framings can be seen as the vehicles of Goldsmith's moral statement: if the activity of framing by the hero-narrator consists in the self-conscious wrenching of reality from its human context in order to re-present it (as it does, I believe, in the first half of the novel), then it is a fundamentally ironic activity. When, however, frames disclose a dominant concern for the human and the passionate, then they partake of the sublime. To return to the terminology of contemporary art criticism we might say that the sublime draws us away from the external accentuation of circumstances into the passionate center. Thus the sublime is attained only when the frame encloses that which strikes at a single blow, when the frame yields its own independent significance to the expressive force of its content. In the case of *The Vicar* ironic frames are those created by Primrose as narrator out of concern for external circumstances, social vanity, and acceptance by his social betters. Sublime frames, on the other hand, are those images of enclosure that reveal the passion of true human relationships based on love. Primrose does not create *these* scenes; they effectively create *him* and reshape his character as a sublime Job-figure. As we follow the transformation of frames in *The Vicar of Wakefield,* we follow the progress of a Job-figure transcending irony by assuming the role of sublime character.

The first half of *The Vicar* is replete with examples of framing, but none partakes of the characteristics of the Biblical sublime. The women spend their time watching themselves in mirrors. When they move to a new apartment, the narrator describes the new dwelling as if he were showing us a painting ("The eye was agreeably relieved" [32]). We are shown, through the many descriptions of the family's neat little enclosures, the pictorial and fundamentally external quality of their existence. The vicar himself is strongly implicated in this arranging process, and this despite his early assertion that "mere outside is so very trifling a circumstance with me" (20). He speaks of his family as a republic to which he gives laws, but these laws, as he tells us, are entirely ceremonial. This needless form of social creation, which is obviously no more than ornament, is thematically set against a similar scene in a different setting, the prison, in which Primrose does indeed establish a form of useful republic among the prisoners. At the Thornhill estate, however, frames are concerned with external circumstances and, hence, are ultimately ironic.

We have a sense in the novel, also, of the fragility of these self-conscious frames that reflects the precarious social situation of the family. This is emphasized at the beginning of Chapter 5 when the pastoral setting in which the Primroses are framed by the narrator is suddenly intruded upon by the hunting squire. The sense of violent intrusion into an enclosed family circle is equally apparent when the Misses Skeggs and Blarney enter in Chapter 11. One detects in these scenes the vulnerability of the family circle to the reality that surrounds it, but also the ironic vulnerability of the narrator (the creator of the circle) in his eagerness to appease those powers that surround him. The vicar's language in the course of Chapter 11 conveys perfectly the moral ambiguities of concern for the "mere outside"; the concern for the external sets in motion the need to accommodate oneself to the outside. That is what Primrose is doing in this chapter and that is what he does—as hero and as narrator—throughout the first half of the book.

The multiplying ironies in the first half at *The Vicar* should bring us back to the matter of Job. Powerlessness, after all, is the fundamental characteristic of Job in the Bible, and it is Primrose's lack of power that is being pointed out here. Given the general paradigm of Job, there is a pervasive irony underlying the early happy chapters. For Job has already fallen (i.e., lost his wealth) but life goes on. The anguished debate that followed immediately upon the Biblical Job's fall has been transformed into the hour and a half set aside daily by the vicar "for innocent mirth between my wife and daughter in philosophical arguments between my son and me" (33), or into the facetious debates between Thornhill and Moses on religious doctrine, or into Olivia's great skill in debating which, according to her proud mother, she has attained from reading the debates of Square and Thwackum, and of Robinson Crusoe and Friday (45). Clearly, the Job pattern is being parodied precisely to highlight the artificiality of the Primroses' existence.

It is during another framed scene that a simpler, more natural, and more sublime taste is first expressed by the virtuous Burchell. Our narrator describes his discussion of the virtues of the various poetic forms with Moses and the humble Burchell. "Two blackbirds answered each other from opposite hedges . . . every sound seemed but the echo of tranquility" (45). Within this verbally painted enclosure, the disguised lord sings the ballad of Edwin and Angelina. A moment earlier he had attacked the artificiality of the modern classicizing taste in poetry (a taste that had been defended by Moses, who always defends the ancients). The simple and the sublime, of course, were closely identified by contemporary theorists (and especially by apologists for the Bible's style).[62] Burchell's choice of the ballad form and his pronouncements on art introduce an important theme in the novel, and are a key to the new and different structure of its second half.

The artifice of framing and the irony of posturing are most clearly opposed to Goldsmith's ideal of the natural, the simple, and the sublime in Chapters 15 and 16. At the end of Chapter 15, after the vicar has misconstrued Burchell's letter, he and Deborah confront the disguised Sir William. Primrose cites Pope's line in praise of the honest man. To "the hackney'd maxim of Pope," Burchell responds, "we might as well prefer the tame correct paintings of the Flemish school to the erroneous but sublime animation of the Roman pencil" (79). Burchell rejects the correct in favor of the sublime (this dichotomy had often been applied to the Bible).[63] In a 1760 review of Kedington's *Critical Dissertations upon the Iliad of Homer,* Goldsmith had written:

> The merit of every work is determined not from the number of its faults but of its beauties . . . The great beauties of every work make it inestimable; its defects are only arguments of humanity, not weakness.[64]

For this reason, Goldsmith expresses a preference for the beauties of Italian painting over the more correct French style. Goldsmith on painting and Burchell on Pope should be considered in light of the Advertisement introducing *The Vicar of Wakefield:*

> There are a hundred faults in this thing, and a hundred things might be said to prove them beauties. But it is needless. A book may be amusing with numerous errors, or it may be very dull without a single absurdity.
>
> (13)

Opposed to this stands the ridiculous Primrose family portrait, in whose execution the vicar plays no small part. "The family use art which is opposed with still Greater" (81) is the punning title of Chapter 16. Literally, it refers to Deborah's schemes to ensnare the young Thornhill, which the narrator knows to be hopeless. But it also echoes the portrait scene in which, to outdo the Flamboroughs, as the vicar approvingly tells us, the family has been artistically represented in a single large frame. The artificiality of this framing is emphasized by the absurdity of the poses: Deborah is Venus surrounded by cupids, and Charles Primrose is depicted handing his sermons on clerical monogamy to his Venus-wife. The painter is asked to fill in "as many sheep as he could for nothing" (83), merely to populate this contrived, unnatural space. The resulting picture, a monstrous caricature of life, won't fit in the house (another, more natural, frame) and we are told that it remained in the kitchen, a monument, it would seem, to the folly and impossibility of the whole enterprise. Coming as it does immediately after the break with Burchell and the latter's discourse on art, and just when Thornhill, junior, successfully invades the family circle (he is to be Alexander the Great at the bottom of the painting), this scene highlights the falsely emblematic activity that betrays and exemplifies the moral flaw of our Job. Just before Olivia is taken, the vicar judges the relative value of the ballad and ode, condemning those odes that "petrify us in a single stanza" (90). The line applies all too well to Primrose's ironic situation as expressed in the grand family portrait.

The transition from scene to sentiment, from emblem to expression, begins with the news of Olivia's abduction. When Primrose learns that his daughter has been taken, a Job scene is played out with a significant reversal. His nature gets the better of him and he immediately curses his oppressor, only to be brought back to his paradigmatic role by his wife and son. (This bears comparison to Parson Adams' reaction to news of his boy's "drowning" in *Joseph Andrews*.)[65] The passionate outburst by our hero, however, marks a definite progress in Primrose's move toward the sublime, although the description of the family's grief reminds us that the Primroses are still described in *scenic* terms (to use another of Kenneth Burke's useful concepts).[66] Thus we are told:

> In this manner that night the first of our real misfortunes was spent in the bitterness of com-plaint . . . The next morning we missed our wretch-ed child at breakfast where she used to give life and cheerfulness to us all.
>
> (92)

Olivia is perceived as part of a breakfast picture; the scenic and the passionate coexist here. Only gradually will the latter come to dominate.

In the following chapter our narrator-hero recognizes that he may have been deceived as to the identity of the true villain. This is a crucial advance for Primrose, as he begins to recognize the fallibility of his constructions.[67] In his meeting with the company of actors he is shown to appreciate the matter of false imitation as he discourses on the theater. False imitation, too, is the theme of the political harangue that Primrose delivers (tyranny masquerades as liberty, according to the agitated vicar), as well as of the disguise of Arnold's butler. Passion dominates scene when George, the vicar's son, emerges from the company. The pattern of discovery, of emergence from a scene, is repeated in the discovery of Olivia at the inn. Whatever the literary success of Goldsmith's chain of events, we should bear in mind the contrast of the active, ironic creator of scenes, which our narrator is in the book's first half, and the suffering, passionate figure of the book's second half. The inns and rooms, the *frames* of the latter half, are utterly beyond the vicar's control.

The burning of Primrose's house underscores this devel-opment. It can be seen as the continuation of the Job motif (in the Bible, Satan is given dominion first over Job's property, then over his family, and finally over Job himself), but it is clearly much more than that. The Biblical Job bears no real human relationship to his surroundings, but it is just this relationship that is the subject of Goldsmith's fiction. Crucially, the destruction of the Primrose house is not the beginning of punishment (as it was for Job) so much as the confirmation of a process of salvation that involves a new awareness of the meaning of human and social frames. The burn on the arm, another Job-parallel, is similarly reversed. The sen-timental outburst by the vicar following the fire provides an interesting reversal of the Biblical *complaint* and a demonstration of a new, passionate perception:

> Observe this bed of straw and unsheltering roof; those mouldering walls and humid floor; my wretched body thus disabled by fire, and my children weeping round me for bread: you have come home, my child, to all this; yet here, even here, you see a man that would not for a thousand worlds exchange situations. Oh, my children, if you could but learn to commune with your hearts, and know what noble company you can make them, you would little regard the elegance and splendour of the worthless.

(135)

The culminating revaluation of frames comes in the jail scene. Goldsmith emphasizes the frame aspect of the prison: we see two cells, the general cell, "strongly grated and paved with stone" (141), and the individual cell. It is here, outside of society and away from the false self-dramatization of social framing, that the vicar is most sublime and most passionate. He establishes his society on faith and natural law, not on ceremony. He rejects the idea that property is founded in natural law, and argues that laws should reward as well as punish (143).[68] The family visiting the vicar, says Primrose, "can make a dungeon seem a palace" (140). Their

intrinsic *humanity* now defines them, rather than their self-conscious existence in society.

Finally, after resigning himself to his death and the death of his son, Primrose becomes the center of a culminating transformation of the social frame. At the end of Chapter 28 a pathetic scene is presented; Primrose rises to deliver his sermon:

> Thus saying, I made an effort to rise from my straw, but wanted strength, and was able only to recline against the wall. The prisoners assembled themselves according to my directions, for they loved to hear my counsel: my son and his mother supported me on either side; I looked and saw that none were wanting, and then addressed them with the following exhortation.

(160)

This is certainly a frame, but it takes us not to the false emblems of the first half of the *The Vicar,* but to its Biblical analogue in Exodus 17:12, where Moses' hands are held up by Aaron and Hur. As Meyer Schapiro has shown, this scene has a rich iconographic history: Moses' outstretched arms were taken to figure the sign of the Cross.[69] Thus the artificial self-framing of which our hero was guilty has now reached an opposite extreme. Helped by others, he transcends his scene and delivers his moving sermon. Scene and passion now define one another, and the frame is wholly natural, based entirely on the love of his family and his fellow prisoners. The message of his sermon is therefore doubly appropriate for our transformed (and transfigured) hero:

> No vain efforts of a refined imagination can soothe the wants of nature, can give elastic sweetness to the dank vapours of a dungeon or ease to the throbbings of a broken heart.

(162)

Primrose's closing sermon preaches a doctrine of love. Indeed, *The Vicar of Wakefield* is Goldsmith's artistic elaboration of the sublime of love. That Goldsmith considered love and the sublime inseparable can be seen in his review of Burke's *A Philosophical Inquiry into the Origin of our Ideas of the Sublime and Beautiful* in the *Monthly Review* for May, 1757. In an otherwise favorable notice, Goldsmith suggested that the author had not sufficiently considered love as an element of the sublime:

> Our Author by assigning terror for the only source of the sublime excludes love, admiration &c. But to make the sublime an idea incompatible with those affections is what the general sense of mankind will be apt to contradict . . . Our astonishment at the sublime as often proceeds from an increased love as from an increased fear.[70]

It is precisely the sublime of love that is attained by the end of the novel.

IV

There is a change, then, that corresponds to the break in the book after Chapter 17. That the change relates to Job is undeniable, but that it follows Battestin's theological reconstruction is less likely. Even after the sublime climax in Chapter 29, Goldsmith plays with the Biblical paradigm:

> The greatest object in the universe, says a certain philosopher, is a good man struggling with adversity, yet there is still a greater which is the good man that comes to relieve it.
>
> (167)

This sentiment is as close to romance motifs as it is distant from the point of the Book of Job. And the title of Chapter 30, we recall ("Let us be inflexible and fortune will at last change in our favour"), seems to have forgotten the lesson of the earlier chapter.[71]

Goldsmith's use of a Biblical type is thus complex in **The Vicar.** Overall, we can say that his free use of the Book of Job, and his emphasis upon a contrast between scene and sentiment, parallels in important ways new Biblical-critical notions of the sublimity of the Hebrew poetry and the particular, detheologized sublimity of Job in the works of Lowth and contemporary Semiticists. England's reception of biblical criticism was very halting: Lowth's primary influence on later work in England comes indirectly by way of Michaelis, Herder, and the German Romantics.[72] But that the Bible was sublime and was a species of Oriental literature was widely accepted. We don't know Goldsmith's precise acquaintance with the work of Lowth, but an Orientalizer like Goldsmith would certainly have been receptive to his very popular ideas. Our author's use of Job, then, is to give us a *human* rather than a *divine* message, and that message has much less to do with how we will fare in the next world than it has to do with how we ought to act and to know ourselves in this one.

Notes

[38] Martin C. Battestin, *The Providence of Wit: Aspects of Form in Augustan Literature and the Arts* (Oxford, 1974), pp. 193-214.

[39] Ronald Paulson, *Satire and the Novel in Eighteenth-Century England* (New Haven, 1967), p. 270. Compare also Sven Bäckman, *This Singular Tale: A Study of "The Vicar of Wakefield" and Its Literary Background,* Lund Studies in English No. 40 (Lund, 1971), p. 40: "In the very middle with Chapter XVII, comes the reversal or climax, and with it a marked change of mood, from light comedy to pathetic melodrama, with a considerable addition of more overt didacticism."

[40] Paulson, p. 274.

[41] The motif of disguise unifies the book according to Curtis Dahl, "Patterns of Disguise in 'The Vicar of Wakefield,' *ELH,* 25 (1958), 90-104.

[42] Battestin, p. 304, n. 11.

[43] *Ibid.,* p. 198.

[44] Arthur Friedman, ed., *Collected Works of Oliver Goldsmith* (Oxford, 1966), IV, 17. All references to *The Vicar of Wakefield* are to Volume IV of this edition.

[45] The notion that Job had knowledge but was blind to some higher widsom is very old. See, for example, Moses Maimonides, *The Guide of the Perplexed,* trans. Shlomo Pines (Chicago, 1963), pp. 486-97.

[46] Battestin, p. 200.

[47] Battestin's remark seems addressed primarily to Robert H. Hopkins, *The True Genius of Oliver Goldsmith* (Baltimore, 1969), especially the chapter entitled "Fortune and the Heavenly Bank: 'The Vicar of Wakefield' as Sustained Satire," pp. 165-230.

[48] See note 41.

[49] Battestin, pp. 204 ff. Prudence is defined as "distinguishing between goods real and only apparent" and closely related to the Providential reading of *The Vicar.* The *OED* gives as an obsolete meaning of prudence "foresight, providence." The last reference for this meaning is 1685. The strong possibility of a semantic change at the time of our novel adds another problematic element to Battestin's interpretation.

[50] Battestin denies that he is "denying an important element of irony in the work directed at Dr. Primrose, an element to which he himself calls attention by reflecting as narrator upon his own vanities and foibles" (p. 194). Yet the irony he allows is strictly limited by his commitment to a theological (hence, ultimately, unironic) reading of the book.

[51] She holds a "council on the conduct of the day" (37), she "shares the glory of the day" (44), she "conducts the siege of the squire" (55), and she takes shelter "from a defeat in clamour" (70). See Bäckman, pp. 96-97.

[52] Paulson has suggested ("Models and Paradigms: *Joseph Andrews.* Hogarth's *Good Samaritan,* and Fénelon's *Télémaque," MLN,* 91 [1976], 1186-1207) that Fielding often has the behavior of Joseph and

Parson Adams deviate from their Biblical types. Thus in Book 4, Chapter 8 of *Joseph Andrews,* Adams has been arguing that "no Christian ought to set his heart on any person or thing in this world but that, whenever it shall be required, or taken from him in any manner by divine Providence he may be able, peaceably, quietly, and contentedly to resign it" (ed. Maynard Mack [San Francisco, 1948], p. 308). Immediately thereafter, he learns of the "loss" of his son and promptly disobeys his own preaching. Battestin's thesis that Joseph Andrews is based on contemporary theological readings of Joseph and Abraham (a thesis he refers to as a model for his analysis of Goldsmith's novel, p. 197) is elaborated in *The Moral Basis of Fielding's Art* (Middletown, Conn., 1959).

[53] Earl R. Wasserman, *Pope's "Epistle to Bathurst": A Critical Reading with an Edition of the Manuscripts* (Baltimore, 1960), pp. 45-55.

[54] Battestin, p. 200.

[55] Goldsmith asserts that the matter (if it be of real importance) would have to be solved by linguistic analysis of the original Hebrew. This shows some acquaintance with those "neutral" studies Battestin refers to. Another passage indicating Goldsmith's impatience with doctrinal controversy ("speculative trifles") is in *Lady's Magazine* for December, 1760 (III, 154).

[56] Ed. Friedman, I, 200-01.

[57] Ronald Paulson, *Emblem and Expression: Meaning in English Art of the Eighteenth Century* (Cambridge, Mass., 1975), p. 82: "The most obvious change is from precise, verbalizable meaning to general impressions—from what Whately called emblematic to expressive form. Emblems of course remain, but Reynolds reduces the emblematic detail to a single, unambiguous gestalt."
[58] Lowth's treatment of a sublime, Oriental Job is the foundation for an entire tradition of European Orientalism. His influence, perhaps through Herder's work, persists in such writers as Carlyle and Ernest Renan. Writing of Job in his biography of Mohammed, Carlyle stresses Job's sublime and un-Jewish character (*On Heroes, Hero Worship and the Heroic in History* [1841; rpt. New York, 1897], p. 49). Renan considered Job the most ancient example of a "Semitic rhetoric" whose culmination is the Qur' n: *Le Livre de Job Traduit de l'hébreu . . . Etude sur l'age et le Caractère du Poème* (1859; rpt. Paris, 1865). Compare p. lxv and *SP,* I, 74.

[59] No truly great work can ever be mere "accentuation of many minute circumstances" (Paulson, *Emblem and Expression,* p. 82). For Herder, inspired by Lowth, in the Hebrew "everything is clear and strikes the eye at once" ([Vincent Freimarck, "The Bible in Eighteenth Century English Criticism," Diss. Cornell, 1950], p.

74; Renan, p. lxv).

[60] Herder [*Vom Geist der ebräischen Poesie,* 1782], p. 1; *SP* [*Studies in Philology*], I, 300; II, 85, 250.

[61] The vicar notes that life is a journey in Chapter 23 (135). See also Paulson, *Satire and the Novel,* p. 274.

[62] [David B. Morris, *The Religious Sublims: Christian Poetry and Critical Tradition in 18th Century England* (Lexington, Ky., 1972)], p. 92.

[63] Something in the Oriental character militates for the language of the sublime and against more correct forms, as in *SP,* I, 330: "The Orientals look upon the language of poetry as wholly distinct from that of common life, as calculated immediately for expressing the passions. If, therefore, it were to be reduced to the plain rule and order of reason . . . as if calculated for perspicuity alone, it would no longer be what they intended it and to call it the language of passion would be the grossest of solecisms." See also II, 89; I, 155; II, 85; I, 228; II, 95, 191, 225, 227.

[64] Friedman, I, 214-15.

[65] See note 52.

[66] Kenneth Burke, *A Grammar of Motives* (1945; rpt., Berkeley, 1969), pp. 127-70.

[67] "Being driven to that state of mind in which we are more ready to act precipitately than to reason right, I never debated with myself, whether these accounts might not have been given by persons purposely placed in my way, to mislead me . . ." (93-94).
[68] Friedman's note contains a sentence translated from Voltaire in Goldsmith's *Citizen of the World,* Letter LXXII: "The *English* laws punish vice, the *Chinese* laws do more, they reward virtue." We might again consider this advice in light of Burchell on Pope and painting, and in light of the theories of the Biblical sublime. See Morris, pp. 87 ff. The sublime always emphasizes the positive.

[69] Meyer Schapiro, *Words and Pictures: On the Literal and the Symbolic in the Illustration of a Text,* Approaches to Semiotics, no. 11, ed. Thomas A. Sebeok (The Hague, 1973), p. 17: "This episode was an important antetype of salvation. It was by assuming the posture of Christ on the cross and making of himself the sign of the cross that Moses overcame Amalek."

[70] Friedman, I, 29.

[71] There is also the matter of Burchell's healing Primrose's arm with the medicine in the bag he carries around (physic is his hobby). This is a Christ-image of sorts, though not a very serious one. Battestin was wise

to consign to a footnote his suggestion that Burchell is Christ since some typological interpretations read Elihu (son of *Barachel*) as a figure of Christ (p. 308, n. 54).

72 [Elinor S. Shaffer, *"Kubla Khan" and "The Fall of Jerusalem": The Mythological School in Biblical Criticism and Secular Literature, 1770-1880* (Cambridge, 1975)], pp. 17-144, and the informative notes. The thrust of Shaffer's argument is that the influence of the higher criticism in England appeared earlier than is generally acknowledged, with Coleridge, in other words, and not with George Eliot's translation of D. F. Strauss's *Leben Jesu.*

Raymond F. Hilliard (essay date 1983)

SOURCE: "The Redemption of Fatherhood in *The Vicar of Wakefield*" in *Studies in English Literature, 1500-1900,* Vol. 23, No. 3, Summer, 1983, pp. 465-80.

[*In the essay below, Hilliard argues that* The Vicar of Wakefield *is a realistic account of fatherhood and an allegory about sin and redemption.*]

The Vicar's many sanguine remarks on matrimony—"I wrote several sermons to prove its happiness,"[1] he says—are contradicted by his narrative, from beginning to end an account of the troubles which beset a man who has undertaken to marry and bring up a large family. Though Dr. Primrose is given to celebrating domestic life as a "concert," his story can be read as a succession of marital disputes (over such parental concerns as the treatment accorded the suitor of a daughter) which he generally loses to Deborah, his domineering wife. As spiritual "instructor" to a family whose members are "refractory and ungovernable" (p. 182), he proves ineffectual, his wife and children paying little heed to his "lectures"; as "guardian" of his children, he is equally inept, as we see, for example, when his daughter Sophia has to be saved from drowning by Sir William Thornhill-Burchell because her father, characteristically, is overpowered by his emotions at a moment of family crisis ("My sensations were even too violent to permit my attempting a rescue"). He fails also in the two primary responsibilities of eighteenth-century parents: situating sons in an occupation and supervising the selection of a marriage partner for each child. His eldest son, George, for instance, intended for one of the professions, spends three years as a desperate vagabond, deprived of both a "patrimony" and the girl he wished to marry. As for the Vicar's girls, his desire to see Olivia prosperously married contributes to that most dire of eighteenth-century family "calamities," the "ruin" of a daughter, and this by a philanderer whose actions mock her father's attachment both to the principle of "monogamy" and to the idea that "the days of courtship are the most

happy of our lives" (p. 23). Such ironies defeat the Vicar's every aspiration as paterfamilias. A man who worries about securing means to "support" his family, and who counts on his children for "support" and "comfort" in old age, he becomes an "uneasy" looker-on as his wife's "schemes" result in a rapid loss of the family's "provisions." Near the end, we find him "disabled" and imprisoned, the "father of a family" overcome by a feeling of helplessness: "my children all untimely falling about me, while I continue a wretched survivor in the midst of ruin!" (p. 159).

In eighteenth-century fiction, the paterfamilias, always partially emblematic as a figure of social and spiritual authority, is often vexed by his responsibilities or thwarted by a rebellious family. He is almost invariably to be found presiding over some version of an "earthly paradise" (the phrase is Fielding's in *Amelia*), an Edenic setting which, as the Vicar says of his two homes, serves as a "retreat" where harmonious family life can be protected against an outside "world" characterized by the instabilities of urban life. Typically associated with such qualities as "tranquillity," "harmony," "provision," and "order" ("utmost neatness" in Goldsmith's domestic novel), this setting is one where potentially egoistic energies can be controlled or sublimated, and the curbing of them is, at least in principle, a function of the father, real or surrogate. Two clergymen, Dr. Harrison in *Amelia* and Dr. Bartlett in *Sir Charles Grandison,* are probably the most emblematic, least "realistic" instances of the father-figure, but more interesting versions include Robinson Crusoe's strict father, who virtually provokes disobedience, and Richardson's Mr. Harlowe, whose authority is usurped by a son. As such examples suggest, the exercise—often the abuse or abdication—of paternal authority is of significant interest to eighteenth-century novelists, though usually insofar as it affects the life of a son or daughter. The early 1760s saw the seriocomic depiction of two fictional fathers—Sterne's Walter Shandy and Goldsmith's Dr. Primrose—whose role is more than secondary. Both look to the home as a haven in a heartless world, yet both are frustrated in the pursuit of domestic felicity, in part by an inability to govern the behavior of a wife and offspring. In this regard, the greater originality of Goldsmith's "singular tale" lies in his use of the hapless father as narrator-hero. In a more typical eighteenth-century story, a young protagonist, more or less explicitly repeat-ing the sin of Adam, is propelled by a predominant passion to break free of the restraints symbolized by the father-figure and the earthly paradise, undergoes a chastening experience of the "world," and in a comic ending, is "restored" to both the earthly paradise and the father, who also functions, ideally, as an analogue to the Providence that is said or implied to be responsible for a final distribution of rewards and punishments: in sum, a recapitulation of the biblical account of the Fall and Redemption of man. By contrast, *The Vicar* focuses on the trials of a father who allows his wife and children to invite the "world," in the person of Squire Thornhill, into their retreat. Of the other harried or delinquent fathers in eighteenth-century fiction, none, to my knowledge, is presented as a main character, and only one other, Smollett's Matthew Bramble, is allowed to tell his own, potentially incriminating story.

My aim here is to argue that in the emphasis on the Vicar's frustrations is betrayed a central intention of Goldsmith's, namely, to depict his protagonist as an inadequate, often delinquent husband and father who eventually redeems himself through the power of a self-sacrificing paternal love. More specifically, as a partially "realistic" novel about the anxieties of fatherhood, *The Vicar* portrays a paterfamilias whose inconsistent behavior reflects various tensions: between an inveterate timidity and the necessity to exert authority, for example, or between love for his children and a readiness to use them in the pursuit of money and status. At the same time, as an unlikely didactic tale which attempts to demonstrate a coherent solution to domestic perplexities like the Vicar's, the novel embodies an ideology shared by the popular domestic conduct books of the period, and in so doing relies on a network of biblical allusions that invite us not only to imagine the Vicar's career as exemplifying the scriptural drama of fall and redemption, but to see his words and actions in the controversial second half of the novel as paralleling those of Christ in his New Testament role as redeemer and exemplar. While supporting the view that *The Vicar* is not thorough-going satire, this reading of the novel will, I hope, shed further light on a long-standing aesthetic crux, the apparent break in the story at the end of chapter 17.

I

Although Goldsmith's satirical treatment of the Vicar's failings as a worldly clergyman has been exhaustively analyzed by "revisionist" and other critics of the novel, his interest in the protagonist's violations of widely-accepted eighteenth-century standards of paternal conduct, standards formulated in such perennially popular didactic works as Richard Allestree's *The Whole Duty of Man* (1663), William Fleetwood's *The Relative Duties of Parents and Children, Husbands and Wives, Masters and Servants* (1705), and Defoe's *The Family Instructor* (1712) and *Religious Courtship* (1722), has gone unexamined. As I shall suggest, particular passages in these and other conduct books might be used to gloss specific incidents in *The Vicar,* and crucial passages in the novel echo the language of the didactic writers; but without making an unnecessary claim for specific influence, I wish primarily to argue that between such writers and Goldsmith there is a significant confluence of opinion, that the novelist's concern with the Vicar's failures as paterfamilias might

be best understood against the background of contemporary efforts to define the "relative duties" of husbands and wives and of parents and children. Doubtless reflecting the anxieties of their audience, the didactic writers have in common a preoccupation with two related areas of domestic life: family governance, or the problem of "authority" in the family; and the threat of disruption in the family posed by the centrifugal ("worldly") tendencies of its members. As attempts to sustain patriarchal family patterns which, owing to a steady rise of what Lawrence Stone has called "affective individualism," were giving way to the so-called "companionate" marriage and to a relatively "affectionate" mode of child-rearing,[2] the conduct books espouse the conservative view that the principle of "subordination," regulating relations in what they see as a Providentially ordained familial and social hierarchy, is the basis of all order and morality;[3] in particular, they seek to harmonize relations within the family, and to safeguard the religious character of "holy matrimony," by laying down precepts derived from Scripture and by portraying the on-going drama of family life as one in which spouse, parent, and child enact the quest for Christian salvation.[4]

In the scheme of family subordination, a father is to "govern" by precept and example, the source of his authority being God, who "calls himself through-out the Holy Scriptures our *Father,* and from that Title and Relation calls for our Obedience."[5] As the chief guarantor of Christian morality in the family, a father is obliged, as the fictional one in *The Family Instructor* puts it, "to make all that are under my command, do their duty," an obligation which includes instructing his family in "the principles of the Christian religion"[6] and guarding them from the "Importunity of Temptations."[7] A source of "advice" and "approbation" in his family, he must treat a recalcitrant wife or child with "severity," for they owe him obedience and "reverence." He is cautioned against educating his children "about the Provision he designs to make for them,"[8] against encouraging them in an "idleness" unsuited to their likely station in life. In guiding them toward matrimony, he must resist any "eagerness of bestowing them wealthily," lest he "force them to marry utterly against their own inclinations"; for the appropriate basis of marriage is "the mutual kindness and liking of the parties," and in a truly religious courtship, "the virtue of the person chosen is more conducing, than all the wealth in the world."[9] In the execution of such duties, a father is to be assisted by a wife who, chosen because of her capacity for "virtuous and prudent Management," has a "Mind . . . influenc'd by the Laws of Christianity" rather than the "Ways of the World."[10] Like other writers, Fleetwood cites 1 Pet. 3:1 for validation of the precept that "because it is impossible, where there are two Persons and two Wills, but there will be Dispute in Matters of Debate and Doubt, which shall be uppermost and superiour, God hath decided it, as well by natural Indications, as by positive Commands, that Man shall reign and govern, and therefore Women are to be obedient and submissive."[11] Expatiating on the same biblical chapter, he mentions as the first of the "considerable" spiritual qualities wives should possess, a "*meek and quiet* good and gentle Temper . . . a silent, quiet and contented Mind under their Condition." He warns that wifely insubordination is likely to be motivated by "Pride" (proud women can "neither be good Wives, nor good Christians"), and to be expressed either as a desire to wear "splendid" clothes, especially when a woman appears in church, or as worldly ambition for the family ("'tis a wrong Course that People take, to be always thinking of their Family, or Fortune, and forget their Husbands Quality and Estate, by which alone they are to govern themselves").

That the general and specific concerns of the conduct manuals are reflected in the mistakes made by the Primrose family seems obvious enough. Though Dr. Primrose complains that his daughters' "breeding" is "already superiour to their fortune" (p. 55), he allows them to become increasingly "idle," and acquiesces in his wife's plan to get them situated in the London marriage "market" (p. 90). His better knowledge notwithstanding, he fails, as "governor," to prevent Olivia from acting the coquette with a pretended suitor of dubious reputation who is also a "free-thinker,"[12] an "invading enemy" (p. 44) whose "power" is that of a "long and pleasing temptation" (p. 86). For these defaults and others, eighteenth-century readers of the domestic treatises could point to the Vicar's failure to enforce his "authority," which he surrenders instead to a spouse who, like his daughters, has "entirely disregarded" (p. 56) his admonitions. As Defoe would describe it, this domestic arrangement is one in which "authority" is "quite turned upside down."[13] The often clamorous Deborah, demanding to sit at the head of the table and often calling the family into "council," imposes her will in such crucial decisions as the ones to sell the family horses, assumes effective control of her daughters' education (p. 43), and initiates the disastrous scheme to entrap Thornhill as a husband for Olivia.

But though the didactic writers shape and codify assumptions about the proper conduct of family life, and thereby enable us to appreciate how deeply a novel like *The Vicar* participates in a significant ethos of its time, it would be a serious distortion to imply that Goldsmith's portrayal of Dr. Primrose as paterfamilias can be fully elucidated by a schematic application of the ideals in the conduct books. On one level, as we are reminded by a sly joke of the Vicar himself, Goldsmith's rendering of Deborah as the dominant spouse is part of a comedy of manners about English wives who "manage their husbands" (p. 91). We are clearly meant to laugh, for instance, at the epitaph Dr. Prim-

rose has composed for her, because it typifies his generally oblique, feckless way of reminding her "of her duty to me" (p. 22). On this level, the novel reflects not a naive adherence to the always humorless prescriptions of the conduct manuals, but Goldsmith's awareness of a comic incongruity between the models delineated in such books and the reality of a marriage involving two people temperamentally disinclined to behave according to theory. The didactic writers, asserting that a father must govern because he is "superiour to the Mother, both in Natural Strength, in Wisdom,"[14] simply do not take into account the sort of man who, having been gulled out of a horse at a fair, writes that "No truant was ever more afraid of returning to school, there to behold the master's visage, than I was of going home" (p. 76).

Moreover, insofar as *The Vicar* is a "realistic" novel that rises above its own didactic aims, it depends on the relative complexity of Goldsmith's insights into the motivation of a paterfamilias like Dr. Primrose, a complexity foreign to the generally unsophisticated psychology of the didactic tracts. For the novel shows the Vicar as a father actuated by conflicting impulses—a "dread" of opposing his wife, a partial desire to see her schemes succeed, a need to believe that he is doing what is best for his children, and so on. His timidity, though but one ingredient of his character, explains much of his behavior: his longing to locate himself at the center of a "tranquil" domestic "circle"; his tendency to remain a passive "spectator" to his family's doings, and to rely on surrogates—on his "agent in town," on his sons, on Deborah—in his dealings (money, suitors, "places" for his children) with the outside world; his fear of aging or of becoming physically incapacitated, and the attendant worry about how to provide for his dependents ("my wretched body disabled by fire, and my children weeping round me for bread"); and on several occasions, his failure to enforce his authority, as when, trying to signal to his daughters to retire indoors after Thornhill's ominous first appearance, he has a wink of his own "counteracted by one from their mother" (p. 36). Small wonder that such a man is tempted on occasion to withdraw not only from the "world," but from the strenuous demands of his role: when his daughters ask for money so that they can consult a fortune-telling gipsy, he yields, remarking that "To say the truth, I was tired of being always wise, and could not help gratifying their request, because I loved to see them happy" (p. 57).

But timorousness or a distaste for exertion does not exclude, in the first half of the story, a considerable degree of complicity in his wife's ambitions. Much more than a relinquishment of authority is reflected, for instance, in such incidents as the one where the Vicar exacts a "positive promise" (p. 87) from Olivia to marry Farmer Williams in the event that Thornhill does not seek her hand, though even here the emphasis is on contradictory motives. After entering half-heartedly ("though I did not strenuously oppose, I did not entirely approve") into the plan to use Williams to catch Thornhill, he allows Olivia to lead on the unsuspecting Williams, forestalling any blame for himself by telling her that "every scheme . . . has been proposed and planned by yourself, nor can you in the least say that I have constrained you"; unlike his wife, however, he experiences much "uneasiness" as he observes his daughter agonizing in a "struggle between prudence and passion" (pp. 86-87). Elsewhere, in situations which might make him "uneasy" or force him to take responsibility for his family's undertakings, he protects himself by sermonizing disingenuously (pp. 68-70), by being non-committal (p. 65), or by assuming the pose of uninvolved, sometimes ironic spectator. When Burchell argues with Deborah about the plan to send the girls to town, for example, the Vicar "stood neuter" (p. 70), a negligent stance for a man who is duty-bound to wield authority as priest and paterfamilias. Similarly, his habit of describing his family's schemes as amusing follies ("harmless delusions") tends to disguise, as he may unconsciously hope it will, his failure to fill his role, and may account at least partially for the benign interpretations of his character that prevailed until recent years. The Vicar might be most aptly characterized as one of those "heads of families" mentioned by Defoe, "orthodox in opinion, but heterodox in practice," largely unconscious hypocrites who are adept at "throwing the guilt off from themselves."[15]

While Dr. Primrose himself is susceptible to the occasional promptings of a conscience, his single-minded wife, by contrast, can be ranked among the most uninhibitedly selfish and manipulative parents in eighteenth-century fiction. More than a humorous allusion to her warlike biblical namesake,[16] the battle metaphors Goldsmith uses in descriptions of Deborah point to her basic affinity with the "world," with "human nature on the wrong side" (p. 141), for the "world" in Goldsmith's novel is a place where "no man is so fond of liberty as not to be desirous of subjecting the will of some individuals to his own" (p. 121), and where "virtue" is always under "siege" by the likes of Thornhill, a villain motivated less by lust than, like Deborah, by an impulse toward "tyranny . . . and revenge" (p. 173). An ironic instance of the conduct-book stereotype whose duty is to safeguard her own and her family's "good fame," Deborah uses Olivia as a weapon in the competition for status, as a source of vicarious "triumph." So strong is the mother's competitiveness, in fact, that there is even a suggestion of suppressed rivalry between her and her daughters: watching Olivia dance in front of admiring neighbors, Deborah "could not avoid discovering the pride of her heart, by assuring [the Vicar], that though the little chit did it so cleverly, all the steps were stolen from herself" (pp. 53-54). In such a family situation, Sophia has learned

the value of "represt excellence from her fears to offend" (p. 21), while Olivia has adopted the conduct-book precept that a child's duty is to "please" ("all her care was to make us happy," says the Vicar after her elopement) as a way of getting along that leads eventually to her undoing by Thornhill (p. 127). Deborah pushes Olivia toward an irreparable loss of reputation ("infamy abroad, and shame at home"), and the inconsolable girl lapses into "decline" (p. 153) that feeds on "anxiety" (p. 234) and "over-wrought resentment" (page 135): it may be no accident that the least parodic, most poignant interpolated verses in the novel (chapter 24) concern this tragedy.

At another extreme, Goldsmith underlines the Vicar's failure to protect Olivia by introducing Burchell-Thornhill into the story as the exemplary father-figure Dr. Primrose is not: carrying a "big stick" and representing the "law" and "authority" (p. 169), Burchell tries hard to shield the daughters from Thornhill, stands up to Deborah when she rejects his "advice" (to George Primrose he is also an object of filial "reverence," p. 167), and treats the guilty with a "severity" they deserve. It is perversely fitting that Dr. Primrose should allow Deborah to take responsibility for expelling Burchell from their home (through one of her "harangues"), a symbolic "breach" of one of the "Christian duties" (p. 39) that leaves Thornhill entirely free to tempt Olivia. Burchell is variously associated with (on one level) the Christ who was rejected by a world he came to save (p. 39) and with the "conscience" (p. 71) Dr. Primrose ignores.

II

According to the conduct books, a person becomes truly Christian—Christ-like—by fulfilling the duties associated with his station in life; Defoe, for example, insisting on the obligation of parents "to do their duties more effectively in their families," stresses its relation to Christ's "great purpose of redemption," and associates "family reformation" with a re-establishment of paternal authority, with the setting up of "a family-government entirely new."[17] If I have emphasized the Vicar's transgressions as paterfamilias in the first half of the story, it is because the turning point in his career combines a decision to assert patriarchal authority for the first time with the first of several allusions to the words and deeds of Christ in the New Testament. In the first seventeen chapters of the novel we witness the repeated "mortifications" of the Primroses, the invariable failure of their worldly schemes; if we try to explain this pattern as part of a "realistic" story, we are forced to conclude that it is very improbable or entirely parodic. But if we consider it as part of a deliberate biblical allegory, it suggests instead that the Primroses are guilty, like the Hebrews of the Old Testament, of falling repeatedly, and that they are therefore punished repeatedly, as the Vicar ultimately recognizes, by "him that directs all things" (p. 157). The evidence for such a reading lies not only in early hints given us about a threat of evil to come from outside the Wakefield paradise and from within it (the orchard is robbed; the family shows undue concern with the behavior of the Squire and his wife at church), in references to Thornhill as a serpent, in the emphasis on "ingratitude," in the possibly ironic use of the name Deborah (she appears in the Book of Judges, which chronicles the repeated lapses of God's people, and their repeated defeats as punishment by a superintending God), and so on, but as I have suggested, in the general movement of the plot from exile to restoration. Yet *The Vicar* is distinguished from other eighteenth-century stories not by an unusual number of allu-sions to the Fall, but by its demonstration that only through a somewhat literal *imitatio Christi* can its flawed protagonist win redemption. What initiates and sustains the process of redemption is a paternal love that proves far stronger than the Vicar's worldly ambition or his temperamental weakness.[18]

The beginning of change in Dr. Primrose coincides with Olivia's elopement, "the first of our real misfortunes" (p. 92), as her father calls it, misfortunes which serve gradually to bring about his development as family redeemer. Not surprisingly, the Vicar's initial reaction to the loss involves a characteristic failure of patriarchal "fortitude," Moses having to reproach him for not being "my mother's comforter" (p. 92). But the Vicar's comic discomposure turns quickly into resolution when he hears his wife renouncing Olivia ("I will never call her daughter more") as a "vile strumpet" (p. 92). Occurring at the very end of chapter 17, this is the first of three significant occasions—each involving a successful effort by the Vicar to protect a child from Deborah—when he asserts his spiritual authority: "Wife . . . do not talk thus hardly: my detestation of her guilt is as great as yours; but ever shall this house and this heart be open to a poor returning repentant sinner" (p. 93). There follows immediately a decision to pick up his Bible and staff—a decision which, I suggest, marks the beginning of his conversion from the Old Adam to the New—in order to set out in search of Olivia; it is in sharp counterpoint to his self-serving histrionics on an earlier occasion when, initiating the "dispersion" of his family, he is forced to send George, similarly equipped, out "naked into the amphitheatre of life" (p. 27). During the Vicar's absence, which includes a prolonged illness owing to the "agitations" (p. 94) of his mind,[19] he makes a start toward abjuring his pride (p. 95), and when he finds his lost daughter, welcomes her home as a repentant sinner, promising to be "a guardian and an instructor" to her, and to shield her from both her "offended mother" and "the censure of the world" (p. 129). In the astonished Olivia's words, he takes "the miseries of my guilt upon yourself" (p. 126). The continuing allusion to the parable of the

Prodigal Son brings together several major motifs when the Vicar, at the end of chapter 22, insists that his vindictive spouse act the Christian mother: as Deborah berates Olivia,

> the unhappy victim stood pale and trembling, unable to weep or to reply; but I could not continue a silent spectator of her distress, where-fore assuming a degree of severity in my voice and manner, which was ever followed with instant submission, "I entreat, woman, that my words may be now marked once for all: I have here brought you back a poor deluded wanderer; her return to duty demands the revival of our tender-ness. The real hardships of life are now coming fast upon us, let us not therefore encrease them by dissention among each other. If we live har-moniously together, we may yet be contended, as there are enough of us to shut out the censuring world. . . . The kindness of heaven is promised to the penitent, and let ours be directed by the example. Heaven, we are assured, is much more pleased to view a repentant sinner, than ninety nine persons who have supported a course of undeviating rectitude. And this is right; for that single effort by which we stop short in the down-hill path to perdition, is itself a greater exertion of virtue, than an hundred acts of justice."
>
> (p. 132)

"Severity," "submission," the old-fashioned (by the 1760s) mode of address—such is the language associated with dutiful fathers in the conduct manuals. Never again will the Vicar be a culpably "silent" or ironic spectator; nor will he ever again be "obliged to comply" (p. 59) with his wife's wishes, as we see in his later refusal to desist from trying to reform his fellow prisoners.

But the Vicar's actions as, yes, a kind of Christ-figure—all performed in the face of increasing family calamities—include more than his forgiving a wayward daughter, for he undergoes his own version of the trials and death of Christ. The allusions which suggest that Goldsmith intends such a reading are less obvious than the Vicar's reference to the parable of the Prodigal Son, for the novelist has to avoid the risk of having his protagonist, a man once guilty of spiritual pride (chapter 2), seem to present *himself* as like Christ; I believe that the Vicar is completely unaware of them, and that they are made by an "implied author" whose point of view is a dominant one in the second half of the novel.[20] When Thornhill, having ruined Olivia, tempts Dr. Primrose with terms that would redeem his family in the eyes of the world (chapter 24), the Vicar chooses instead to go to jail, even though his family, now showing less fortitude than he, urge upon him the easier route of submission. The situation and the Vicar's words to the Squire ("Avoid my sight, thou reptile!") seem intended to recall Christ's comment to Peter when the apostle tempted him not to submit to punishment (crucifixion) at the hands of the chief priests and scribes (Mark 8:30-37): "Get thee behind me, Satan." Then, like Christ with Peter and his other followers at Gethsemane (Matt. 26:50-54), the Vicar rebukes his poorest parishioners when they try to rescue him from the officers who come to escort him to jail ("What! my friends . . . and is this the way you love me!") In prison he converts Mr. Jenkinson by his good example as a man unjustly persecuted, promising, like Christ in the New Testament (Luke 23:32-43), to seek leniency for the good thief from the man who has, quite justly, sent him to prison: "Well, sir . . . your kindness . . . shall be repaid with my endeavours to soften or totally suppress Mr. Flamborough's evidence, and I will send my son to him for that purpose" (p. 142). Later, in incidents probably meant to recall the scorn and ridicule heaped on Christ during his own imprisonment, the Vicar eventually wins over the more obdurate thieves (the jail is the "world" writ small) who mock him and reject his ministry (p. 144). And when Jenkinson suggests that Dr. Primrose purge himself of any vestige of pride by submitting to Thornhill, and thus provide for "the welfare of those who depended on me for support" (p. 154), the Vicar turns the other cheek completely:

> "Heaven be praised . . . there is no pride left me now. . . . On the contrary, as my oppressor has been once my parishoner, I hope one day to present him up an unpolluted soul at the eternal tribunal. No . . . I have no resentment now, and though he has taken from me what I held dearer than all his treasures, though he has wrung my heart . . . yet that shall never inspire me with vengeance. I am now willing to approve his marriage."

(p. 154)

He makes this submission only after hearing that Olivia is dead, having refused earlier out of fear that such a gesture would "send my child to the grave" (p. 153). His further act of Christian forgiveness is one of several that make up the comic reconciliation at the end of the story. When Sir William Thornhill later dispenses strict justice, for instance, the Vicar asks him to be merciful toward the Squire, and toward George Primrose, who, "in obedience to a deluded mother" (p. 168), has sought revenge on Thornhill. As *The Whole Duty of Man* tells us, the forgiving of enemies is the highest form of charity, "the most compleat way of imitating Christ's example."[21]

On a realistic, potentially tragic level, the Vicar's ordeal in prison represents his absolute helplessness as a merely human, fallen father to save himself and his family from the consequences of their mistakes; for though he keeps control of the family even while there ("I allotted to each of the family what they were to do"), he has to acknowledge an "utter inability to get free" (p. 147), experiencing his greatest frustration over the impossibility of comforting the dying Olivia ("my soul was bursting from its prison to be near the pillow of my child"), and over the prospect of leaving behind him "an helpless family of orphans" (p. 155). But without speculating on what may be, in some area of Goldsmith's imagination, the curious identification of the experience of fatherhood with a Christ-like suffering, we can say that on the level of deliberate allegory the Vicar's imprisonment is a ritual death, an equivalent to Christ's crucifixion and vicarious atonement. In this light, the improbable ending, which includes a "resurrection" of both the Vicar and Olivia, and the restoration of George and Sophia to their parents, can be seen to bring into conjunction the idea of the miraculous redemptive power of a self-sacrificing parental love and the biblical notion, implicit everywhere in the story, that happiness can be found not in self-reliance, not in schemes of self-advancement, but in a willingness to rely unreservedly on God's Providence. This notion is of course a central one in such representative eighteenth-century novels as *Robinson Crusoe* and *Pamela,* and is sometimes implied in a tension between a feeling that one should remain at home (in the earthly paradise) and an overwhelming urge to "pursue" happiness through a journey into the world. In other words, the biblical paradigm as used by eighteenth-century writers mirrors a tension characteristic of the literary genre that is usually said to be a product of the rise of individualism in the period, a tension between, on the one hand, a traditional Christian view of human existence based on such ideals as self-restraint, temperance, and quiescence, and on the other, a modern, secular view based on the principles of individualistic self-assertion and an active, restless "pursuit" of happiness.[22] In *The Vicar*—in the bosom of the protagonist himself—this tension inheres in the coexistence of competing ideals of marriage: domestic life supported on "a competence sufficient to give content" (p. 176), versus marriage as a means to fortune and status. But if novels such as *Robinson Crusoe* and *Pamela* strike us as deliberately ambiguous in their dramatization of such a tension, *The Vicar,* it seems to me, is characterized by its conservatism, by its absolute condemnation of tendencies toward self-sufficiency or self-aggrandizement, by its insistence that such tendencies, in the Providential scheme of things, are "vain." Again and again in the story, "schemes for the future" are "blown up" (p. 116) by "some unforeseen disaster" (p. 68), attempts to move "forward" prove futile.[23] In Jenkinson's traffic with the world he has learned that only "the honest man went forward" (p. 156), while his own cunning has left him (like the Vicar, whose family gets in trouble by putting its children "forward in the world") without "skill to avoid gaol" (p. 147). Time after time during his journey in search of "distinction" and "reward" (p. 107), George Primrose sets "boldly forward" (p. 147), but finds himself inevitably, like his father and sister, "unrewarded and abandoned to the world," "without one friend . . . to apply to" (p. 128). In the Vicar's words, "the good are joyful and serene, like travellers that are going towards home; the wicked but by intervals happy, like travellers that are going into exile" (p. 135).

The reconstitution of the Vicar's "home," the restoration of his family, does not occur even when he renounces his pride, for there follow two further trials—the abduction of Sophia and the imprisonment of George—which leave him finally and truly "stript of every comfort" (p. 157), not only of his home and fortune but of the grown children he was to provide for and from whom he has come to hope for "support." Remarkably enough, his words, "stript of every comfort," are the very ones used by Pamela Andrews when, imprisoned at Mr. B's Lincolnshire estate and deprived of her money and the assistance of Parson Williams, she must choose between the temptation to commit suicide (imagined as a form of self-reliance) and a religious duty to depend on Providence for her deliverance; like Richardson, Goldsmith is giving us, at the climax of his story, his version of a pervasive eighteenth-century fictional concern with the behavior of the self in extreme or "reduced" (the word is a favorite of Defoe's) circumstances. But if Richardson's portrayal of Pamela seems as ambiguous as Defoe's of Crusoe—we suspect that by stressing the sinfulness of suicide Pamela may be rationalizing her reluctance to plunge into a cold pond at night, and that she will continue to rely on her own "strategems" in the conflict with B—Goldsmith's protagonist makes an unequivocal decision to be an exemplary Christian father. Upbraided by George ("you have often charmed me with your lessons of fortitude; let me now, Sir, find them in your example") for another moment of fatherly weakness ("Oh, my boy, my heart weeps to behold thee thus, and I cannot, cannot help it"), the Vicar at last commits himself entirely to the care of Providence, the only recourse of "the naked, the houseless, the heavy-laden, and the prisoner" (p. 161), of the reduced self, in the world of this Christian story:

> "I am now raised above this world, and all the pleasures it can produce. From this moment I break from my heart all the ties that held it down to earth, and will prepare to fit us both for eternity. Yes, my son, I will point out the way, and my soul shall guide yours in the ascent."
>
> (p. 159)

I suspect that there is an allusion here to Col. 3:1-2 ("If ye then be risen with Christ, seek those things which are above. . . . Set your affection on things above, not on things on the earth"). In any event, physically supported by "my son and his mother" (an allusion to the description of the crucifixion in John 19:25-28?),[24] the Vicar completes the recovery of his ministry by preaching his sermon on Providence, an authentic confession of faith and hope that is in contrast to "the great sin of Presumption"[25] of which he was guilty

before his real suffering began. It is followed (p. 174) by what I take to be an allusion to the most complete New Testament rendering of the idea of Providential governance, Christ's comments in Luke 12 on the ravens and lilies.

Immediately after the sermon occurs the comic denouement, Providence manifesting itself at last in the "majestic" person of Sir William Thornhill, who was himself powerless (p. 165) to deliver the Primrose family before the Vicar's final profession of faith. Goldsmith emphasizes his protagonist's reform as a father not only by having him offer Sir William Sophia's hand in marriage, but by using three other characters as foils: Deborah is reluctant to see Sophia marry Burchell until it becomes clear that he is really Sir William; Mr. Wilmot remains mercenary in disposing of Arabella in marriage; and in a deliberate burlesque of the Vicar's earlier treatment of his daughters, Sir William pretends to make a match for Sophia with Jenkinson. With the Vicar's failures as a father—as governor, guardian, instructor, adviser, provider, comforter, and exemplar—no longer standing between his children and the accomplishment of their "warmest wishes" (p. 177), we are ready to celebrate the marriages that climax the comic ending, an ending that is only as unrealistic as the biblical promise it adumbrates.

Notes

[1] *Collected Works of Oliver Goldsmith,* ed. Arthur Friedman, 5 vols. (Oxford; Clarendon Press, 1966), 4:22. All quotations from *The Vicar* are from this edition; subsequent references will be cited in the text.

[2] Lawrence Stone, *The Family, Sex and Marriage in England 1500-1800* (New York: Harper and Row, 1977), pp. 221-480. Taking the Vicar's comments at face value, this historian more than once refers to the Primrose union as a "model of the ideal companionate marriage" (p. 361) in the period.

[3] Dr. Primrose of course mentions the principle of subordination in his sermon on Providence in chapter 29.

[4] "By discharging everyone his Duty," writes Fleetwood, *The Relative Duties,* 2nd edn. (London: Printed for John Hacke, 1716), pp. 234-35, 268, "the World in general would be happy, and each particular be easy in their Station and Relation"; "we shall, one Day, give a strict Account to God, and shall receive Reward or Punishment, according to our Diligence, or our Neglect . . . of those Duties."

[5] Fleetwood, p. 22.

[6] Daniel Defoe, *The Family Instructor,* 1st American edn. (Baltimore: Richards and Mallory, 1814), pp. 121 and 1.

[7] Fleetwood, p. 107.

[8] Fleetwood, p. 100.

[9] Richard Allestree, *The Whole Duty of Man* (London: Printed by John Bassett, 1727), pp. 315-16, 330.

[10] Fleetwood, p. 152.

[11] Fleetwood, pp. 248, 195, 185, 184. Throughout the period "the authority of the husband" (*Certain Sermons or Homilies Appointed to be Read in Churches,* Oxford: Univ. Press, 1840, p. 450) was reinforced by both the Anglican "Homily of the State of Matrimony" and *The Book of Common Prayer* ("The Form of Solemnization of Matrimony").

[12] The family debate over Thornhill as an irreligious suitor (pp. 44-45) occasions Goldsmith's deft allusion to *Religious Courtship.*

[13] *The Family Instructor,* p. 276.

[14] Fleetwood, p. 47.

[15] *The Family Instructor,* pp. 3, 71. The problem of judging the Vicar is compounded by Goldsmith's use of him as narrator. In recounting his story Dr. Primrose shows a father's need to convince himself that, even in the course of the egregious Williams scheme, "I only studied my child's real happiness" (p. 86).

[16] The suggestion is made by Sven Bäckman, *This Singular Tale: A Study of "The Vicar of Wakefield" and Its Literary Background,* Lund Studies in English, no. 40 (Lund: Gleerup, 1971), pp. 95-96.

[17] *The Family Instructor,* pp. 42 ff., 103.

[18] Frederick W. Hilles, "Introduction" to the Everyman's Library American Edition of *The Vicar* (New York: E. P. Dutton, 1951), p. x, makes passing mention of Goldsmith's use of the Fall motif. For a discussion of the Fall in relation to the structure of various eighteenth-century novels, see Ronald Paulson, "The Pilgrimage and the Family: Structure in the Novels of Fielding and Smollett," in *Tobias Smollett: Bicentennial Essays Presented to Lewis M. Knapp,* ed. G. S. Rousseau and P.-G. Boucé (New York: Oxford Univ. Press, 1971), pp. 57-58. In citing biblical paradigms, critics have more frequently emphasized Goldsmith's use of an analogy with the Book of Job. The most cogent development of this view is by Martin C. Battestin, *The Providence of Wit* (Oxford: Clarendon Press, 1974), pp. 193-214. James H. Lehmann, "*The Vicar of Wakefield:* Goldsmith's Sublime, Oriental Job," *ELH* 46 (Spring 1979):97-121, sees Goldsmith as using the Job-analogy to portray the Vicar as an avatar of "sublime humility," a condition the protagonist achieves when he is at last motivated by "the natural and passionate love of his family" (p. 106). With the notion that Goldsmith deliberately develops a Job-analogy I have no quarrel; rather, I believe that in depicting a movement toward redemption, he means to evoke two analogies, that the second half of the novel embodies an *imitatio Jobi Christique.* As I shall suggest, a Christ-analogy is consistent with the emphasis in the second half on such "New Testament" values as mercy and forgiveness.

[19] In the didactic literature of the period such illnesses are often said to coincide with the process of repentance or conversion—in the story of a rebellious wife in *The Family Instructor* (p. 340), for instance.

[20] Paulson, "Models and Paradigms: *Joseph Andrews,* Hogarth's *Good Samaritan,* and Fenelon's *Télémaque,*" *MLN* 91 (December 1976):1204, makes a valuable distinction in pointing out that the narrator of an eighteenth-century novel such as *Robinson Crusoe* often "imposes value-centered models of his own, separate from the self-images or ego-ideals of his characters" (p. 1204). I would argue that while the Vicar himself applies the story of Job to his own situation (see Battestin, p. 197), he is not conscious of the allusions to Christ's suffering and death.

[21] *The Whole Duty of Man,* pp. 392-93. In the second half of the story, the Vicar, atoning for an earlier willingness to participate in his wife's schemes of "vengeance" against Burchell, makes numerous intercessions in the name of "mercy."

[22] The traditional view is expounded in such a work as Thomas à Kempis's oft-reprinted *Of the Imitation of Christ,* Boswell's favorite book and one much admired by Dr. Johnson.

[23] Not even the Vicar's "pursuit . . . to reclaim" (p. 93) the lost Olivia is successful until he ends up, as he puts it, "despairing of ever finding my daughter more, but sending a sigh to heaven to spare and to forgive her" (p. 124).

[24] In these verses Christ commends his mother to the care of the disciple John, just as the Vicar has done in committing Deborah to the care first of George, and then of Moses. Lehmann, p. 113, refers to iconographic tradition in associating the passage in *The Vicar* with Exod. 17:12, perhaps a more likely source. A description of Moses having his hands held up by Aaron and Hur, the image was said to "figure the sign of the cross." Committed to the Job-analogy, Lehmann sees the Vicar as "transformed" and "transfigured" but apparently not as a Christ-figure.

[25] Thus described in *The Whole Duty of Man,* p. 11. In

the Vicar's sermon, he also demonstrates a readiness to look for his "truest comfort" and "support" in the promise of heavenly "bliss" (pp. 161, 163), a vision of which subsumes his earlier commitment to a mere domestic happiness ("all I held dearest upon earth").

D. W. Jefferson (essay date 1984)

SOURCE: *"The Vicar of Wakefield* and Other Prose Writings: A Reconsideration" in *The Art of Oliver Goldsmith,* edited by Andrew Swarbrick, Vision Press, 1984, pp. 17-32.

[*In the essay below, Jefferson argues that in* The Vicar of Wakefield, *Goldsmith created a form which transformed his writing weaknesses into strengths.*]

In the reassessment of authors that has taken place during the last half century, a process that has enhanced so many reputations, Goldsmith is not among those who have benefited, and the reason is not difficult to discover. His gifts were of the lighter kind. The aspects of eighteenth-century literature that he represents are akin to those associated with Addison, another Augustan who has not gained ground. Both writers had ease, grace, a pleasant humour. The present age attaches more importance to the deeper and weightier qualities of Samuel Johnson, whose work was scandalously underrated by critics in the nineteenth and earlier twentieth centuries, the supreme greatness of his finest prose going virtually unrecognized by generations of literary scholars and presumably of readers. That Johnson should now be receiving some of the praise so long withheld is very much as it should be, and it is not a matter for serious complaint if lighter talents should have suffered a degree of eclipse. But Goldsmith was greatly admired in Johnson's circle and he has been a much loved author for too long to be excluded from the kind of serious critical attention that others have received. Lightness is not the only issue. Sterne might be described as light by Johnsonian standards: Johnson himself could have put it more crushingly, but Sterne's reputation has enjoyed enormous enhancement in recent decades. There is something elusive about the nature of Goldsmith's achievement, and about the merits of *The Vicar of Wakefield,* with which we shall be mainly concerned.

His characteristic qualities, of mind and style, probably need to be seen as limitations before their positive aspects can be appreciated, and a brief glance at some minor works may be of use here. In *The Vicar of Wakefield* he found a medium in which the limitations do not count as such. They become virtues because the effect lies so much in what is not attempted as well as in what is. A limited writer with artistic tact and a sense of the felicitous cannot only produce a masterpiece; he can throw light on the character of other

masterpieces which attempt bigger things. The *Enquiry into the Present State of Polite Learning in Europe* (1759) is his earliest work of any importance, and while it provides some examples of his merits as a prose writer it also reveals characteristic weaknesses. The first impression it gives, as the question of cultural decline is broached in the opening pages, is of neatness and ease: 'The publick has been often excited by a false alarm, so that at present the nearer we approach the threatned period of decay, the more our fatal security increases' (I, 257).[1] His habit generally is to introduce topics with pleasantly turned phrases. His enterprise here involves the reduction of an enormously large area of material to a small compass; the course of ancient and modern learning, with reference in the modern period to several countries, is surveyed in about eighty pages. Goldsmith's light touch could have been entirely effective had it been combined with another quality: authority, evidence of solid knowledge, however little detail was to be used. The brief essay on the big subject can be an impressive literary vehicle, and of this there is no better example than Johnson's 'Introduction to the Political State of Great Britain', published three years before in the *Literary Magazine:* a masterly account of two centuries of history in about twenty pages, clear in outline, cool in manner, though with a few strokes of overwhelming moral condemnation of his country's policies. Goldsmith has no such strength. The prevailing attitude in the early chapters of the essay is of a facile Augustanism, an often embarrassing air of confidence in the value of a 'politeness' that can dismiss whole ages of bookishness and scholarly effort. 'Libraries were crammed, but not enriched with . . . works [which] effectually encreased our application, by professing to remove it.' '. . . if Terence could not raise [the reader] to a smile, Evantius was at hand, with a long-winded scholium to encrease his titillation' (I, 265, 266). Of the philosopher in the time of Lucian he says that 'he was chiefly remarkable for his avarice, his impudence, and his beard' (I, 268), one of several sallies that do no more for urbanity than for learning. He makes too frequent use of phrases like 'specious triflers' and 'speculative idlers'. The passage about men who 'carried on a petty traffic in some little creek . . . but never ventured out into the great ocean of knowlege' (I, 268) fails of its effect because Goldsmith himself gives so little evidence of important experience of the great writers or great issues of those ages. Occasionally there is a critical comment that makes eighteenth-century taste look absurdly provincial: '[Dante] addressed a barbarous people in a method suited to their apprehensions; united purgatory and the river Styx, St. Peter and Virgil . . . and shews a strange mixture of good sense and absurdity' (I, 274). But one passage at least may be quoted in which Augustan elegance and agility in phrasing are wedded to acute social observation. He is commenting on the conditions of authorship in France and England:

The French nobility have certainly a most pleasing way of satisfying the vanity of an author, without indulging his avarice. A man of literary merit, is sure of being caressed by the Great, though seldom enriched. His pension from the crown just supplies half a competence, and the sale of his labours, makes some small addition to his circumstances; thus the author leads a life of splendid poverty, and seldom becomes wealthy or indolent enough, to discontinue an exertion of those abilities, by which he rose. With the English, it is different; our writers of rising merit are generally neglected; while the few of an established reputation, are over paid by a luxurious affluence. The first encounter every hardship which generally attends upon aspiring indigence; the latter, enjoy the vulgar, and, perhaps, the more prudent satisfaction of putting riches in competition with fame. Those are often seen to spend their youth in want and obscurity; these are sometimes found to lead an old age of indolence and avarice. (I, 298-99)

He is at his best in places where his subject can be treated largely as one of social manners. Another example may be found in his rather refreshing comments on the poetic taste of the time. He objects to the current vogue of blank verse, and in general to a 'disgusting solemnity' in poetry. In both verse and prose he prefers the 'agreeable trifling which . . . often deceives us into instruction' (I, 319). In keeping with all this is his review of Gray's Odes (1757), where he laments that 'talents so capable of giving pleasure to all'—presumably in the *Elegy*—are 'exerted in efforts that, at best, can amuse only the few' (I, 112). In general he shows a preference for the literature of the early part of the century, which addressed itself to society and cultivated the virtue of ease, avoiding what he saw as heaviness and pedantry. But on the subject of blank verse one would have liked to know whether he responded to Thomson at his best. With no discussion of examples his comments here, as in most of the **Enquiry,** are somewhat superficial.

His limitations as well as his strengths are evident in his short biographical studies. Characteristically he begins his life of Bolingbroke on a promising note:

There are some characters that seem formed by nature to take delight in struggling with opposition, and whose most agreeable hours are passed in storms of their own creating. The subject of the present sketch was perhaps of all others the most indefatigable in raising himself enemies, to shew his power in subduing them; and was not less employed in improving his superior talents, than in finding objects on which to exercise their activity. (III, 437)

A 'sketch' of these aspects of Bolingbroke would have

been very acceptable; but as Friedman has shown, 'fully four-fifths' of the life were borrowed from the *Biographia Britannica,* and this was not material for the animated and personal account which the reader has been led to expect. Perhaps Goldsmith should not be judged on such obvious hackwork, but the discrepancy here gives an impression of irresponsibility. His life of Richard Nash is a different matter, and Donald A. Stauffer couples it with Johnson's life of Savage as an example of biography that aims at a close study of the human truth with an attempt to weigh moral strengths and weaknesses. Quoting the preface in which he claims to have described 'the man as he was . . . , a weak man, governing weaker subjects', Stauffer writes that Goldsmith 'deserves the praise accorded to a pioneer'.[2] The formidable comparison with Johnson, which inevitably haunts the study of Goldsmith, was suggested by a contemporary writer in the *Monthly Review:* 'A trivial subject, treated for the most part in a lively, ingenious, and entertaining manner. Mr. Samuel Johnson's admirable Life of Savage seems to have been chosen as the model of this performance' (quoted by Friedman, III, 282-83). The contrast between the two could hardly be steeper. Johnson's theme is tragedy and inordinate failure, relieved by flashes of goodness, with scenes of an underworld of desolation which he himself had experienced. As an exercise of moral realism, magnanimity and compassion, it stands by itself. Goldsmith took as his subject a man whose career is a monument to values or vanities that belong to society at its most artificial. The choice, if it was made with Johnson's work in mind, might almost be an act of self-recognition, showing Goldsmith's awareness of his fitness for surfaces rather than depths. But it shows also his gift, not exhibited everywhere, for cultivating with fine judgement the possibilities of a limited theme. Limited it is, but Nash touched many lives and attracted notice in a great variety of ways; so what might be called his experiment at Bath had consequences which, to a modern reader, is of very considerable sociological and documentary significance. It was a happy instinct that caused Goldsmith to illustrate his biography with such a wealth of anecdotes, letters, public notices and, finally, obituary compositions, items which in other biographies of this time a reader might be tempted to pass over. We can be grateful that a writer of Goldsmith's quality saw it as a task worth performing, and that he made so much of it. An element of paradox is present from the outset in his reference to 'the pains he took in pursuing pleasure, and the solemnity he assumed in adjusting trifles' (III, 288), and in the early part of the life the emphasis is on the more trivial part of his character. After his first successes at Bath, the level of praise is modest: 'But to talk more simply, when we talk at best of trifles. None could possibly conceive a person more fit to fill this employment than *Nash*' (III, 301), and here the reference is to his easy manner with fashionable people and his general vivacity. But gradually the evidence accumulates of his practical ability, the initiative that led to the improvement of accommodation and amenities, and the laws governing behaviour which he put up in the Pump-room. Two of these, one concerning manners, the other morals, may be quoted: '3. That gentlemen of fashion never appearing in a morning before the ladies in gowns and caps, shew breeding and respect. . . . 10. That all whisperers of lies and scandal, be taken for their authors' (III, 303). There were strict hours at which dancing should begin and end, rules relating to the orderly departure of ladies, and he conducted skilful propaganda against the wearing of boots in the rooms. He also introduced measures to prevent duels. In all this, and in many other matters, Nash grows in our estimation as a genuine reformer, shaping the community in accordance with new styles of living, and making his contribution to the development of outlook that we associate with the names of Addison and Steele, though he fell so far short of them in seriousness. As the ups and downs of his character are traced, his lavish generosity along with his vanity and irresponsibility, his substantial share in the establishing of a hospital juxtaposed with his more whimsical acts of charity, his genuine efforts to protect female virtue and save gamesters from ruin against a background of his own wasteful folly and habitual ostentation, we may admire Goldsmith's control of the effect. Extreme old age, relative poverty, failure to change his ways when nature and fortune no longer supplied the means: with these sobering themes the record concludes. On its own level it is as balanced a study as the life of Savage, though of course it lacks the momentous heights and depths and the sombre eloquence.

Goldsmith's style is ideal for the depiction of Bath's social life. Writing of the primitive pleasures of this and other resorts he describes them as

> merely rural, the company splenetic, rustic, and vulgar. . . . People of fashion . . . usually spent that season amidst a solitude of country squires, parsons wives, and visiting tenants. . . . To a person, who does not thus calmly trace things to their source, nothing will appear more strange, than how the healthy could ever consent to follow the sick to those places of spleen, and live with those, whose disorders are ever apt to excite a gloom in the spectator. The truth is, the gaming table was properly the salutary font, to which such numbers flocked. (III, 299)

'A solitude of country squires', 'the salutary font' are characteristic turns of phrase. The passages where Nash's character is summed up are full of well-shaped formulations; for example:

> He was naturally endued with good sense; but by having been long accustomed to pursue trifles, his mind shrunk to the size of the little objects on which it was employed. His generosity was boundless,

because his tenderness and his vanity were in equal proportion; the one impelling him to relieve misery, and the other to make his benefactions known. (III, 378)

What we learn from these works provides some approach to the question of where Goldsmith's gifts lie, and is relevant to our discussion of *The Vicar of Wakefield;* but the latter contains another element. It is a specifically Christian work, it exhibits values and beliefs the treatment of which must raise questions concerning the author's own central attitude to life. Goldsmith seems to have been a man of slender human capacity, and we can welcome the adjustment of his art whereby he succeeded in conveying these convictions without falsity. He chose a form which, as it were, reduces them to an appropriate scale. But there can be no doubt that he intends us to take them seriously. 'The hero of this piece', he writes in his Advertisement, 'unites in himself the three greatest characters upon earth; he is a priest, an husbandman, and the father of a family.' He dissociates himself from those who 'have been taught to deride religion', and who will therefore 'laugh at one whose chief stores of comfort are drawn from futurity'.

In an essay published over thirty years ago I discussed the process whereby the emotional effect of the calamities suffered by the vicar is reduced.[3] The episode of Olivia's abduction was described as 'between the serious and the comic', the account of the fire 'full of words which ought to suggest emotional intensity . . . but quite without emotiveness', the events having all the marks of 'story-book contrivance'. Some components—the autobiographical digressions, for example—were categorized as miniature versions of familiar traditions, while the narrative as a whole was a much modified and attenuated Book of Job. This view still seems to me to be valid in many respects, but my statement of it was over-simplified and I now welcome the opportunity to reconsider it. The passage in which the vicar, who has endured so much pain and affliction but has succeeded in winning the support of his fellow-prisoners, preaches an eloquent sermon to them, now seems to me moving and beautiful. The refined Augustan idiom of the sermon, so unsuitable to the occasion if we imagine the scene realistically, is both elevated and discreet. The use of this convention in the eighteenth century could be regarded as a distancing of religion in the interests of good manners, but Johnson could use this kind of language with breath-taking effect, and Goldsmith's sermon, if rather lightweight compared with the great *Ramblers,* has genuine purity of feeling. No harm results from the fact that in some of the phrases ('To fly through regions unconfined as air, to bask in the sunshine of eternal bliss, to carroll over endless hymns of praise . . .') the vicar loses himself a little in his dreams (such standardized dreams too) of heavenly happiness. There is room for some amusement, but as an Augustan set-piece the episode has nobility.

All students of *The Vicar of Wakefield* should be aware of Robert H. Hopkins's lengthy discussion of the book and its critics.[4] Hopkins argues that the author's intention is satirical at the expense of the vicar, and this view, although I disagree with it, may be regarded as a helpful background against which to develop an alternative one. My belief is that Goldsmith offers us the vicar in the same spirit of commendation as the Advertisement would suggest, and that the modifying elements in the portrait which a satirical theory would make use of are not in fact to be interpreted so negatively. The style of character portrayal has kinship with conventions we are familiar with in earlier writers. They are more boldly exploited by Fielding, whose techniques are relevant here. Parson Adams on most occasions uses the challenging and dignified idiom of a man of God to which he is abundantly entitled, though his misjudgement of circumstances often renders his performances comic; but in Chapter 8 of the second book something very surprising happens. It is as if he had been caught with his cassock off. In his very plebeian tale concerning the more mundane side of his existence, his style changes: it rambles, he has become ordinary. Of Sir Thomas he says: 'I have always found his kitchen, and his cellar too, open to me: many a time, after service . . . have I recruited my spirits with a glass of his ale.' And later he speaks of the occasions, 'such as the approach of an election', when he has thrown 'a dash or two' into his sermons, for which Sir Thomas has been grateful. We have no reason to conclude that he has done anything very base, and this remarkable chapter does Adams no harm. But we are reminded that there may be a commonplace side to gospel Christians, and that a poor parson's life had exigencies, which is not surprising. What is more relevant here is that eighteenth-century characters in the comic tradition are creations of artifice and rhetoric, sometimes shifting from one idiom to another, revealing not only a different side of character but also a change of persona. Goldsmith's method is not the same as Fielding's, but the vicar must be seen in terms of the style with which he is endowed as narrator, and this style has a generally formalizing effect. We may begin with an example that raises only very mildly the controversial issues relating to the suggestion of satirical intention. In Chapter VI, after an evening of simple entertainment (with gooseberry wine and old songs), the vicar's family realize that it is too late to send their guest Mr. Burchell to an ale-house; so the younger children vie with each other in offering a share of their beds:

> 'Well done, my good children,' cried I, 'hospitality is one of the first Christian duties. The beast retires to its shelter, and the bird flies to its nest; but helpless man can only find refuge from his fellow

creature. The greatest stranger in this world, was he that came to save it. He never had an house, as if willing to see what hospitality was left remaining amongst us. Deborah, my dear,' cried I, to my wife, 'give those boys a lump of sugar each, and let Dick's be the largest, because he spoke first.'

Gooseberry wine and lumps of sugar belong to the same level, but it is the mark of Goldsmith's style that the Christian eloquence can be so easily accommodated. The amiable mood of the episode forestalls any suggestion that the vicar is too ready with his moral lesson or that the humble system of rewards is a ridiculous anti-climax. The amiability operates through the style. It is a matter of easy assimilation of one kind of discourse to another.

The easy manner in which the vicar can refer to his more peculiar eccentricities expresses sublime unawareness, and in some kinds of literature such a style could be used satirically; but the easy manner is also Goldsmith's and it invites us to be amused rather than critical. One of the vicar's most egregious peculiarities is his obsession with strict monogamy, which causes him to compose an epitaph for his 'only' wife

> . . . in which I extolled her prudence, œconomy, and obedience till death; and having got it copied fair, with an elegant frame, it was placed over the chimney-piece, where it answered several very useful purposes. It admonished my wife of her duty to me, and my fidelity to her; it inspired her with a passion for fame, and constantly put her in mind of her end. (Ch. II)

We enjoy the neatness of Goldsmith's wit too much to complain of the perverse neatness of the vicar's logic. We do not accept the vicar at his own valuation, obviously; but we accept him, and this means that we accept Goldsmith and the tone of the narration generally. It might be said that both the vicar and his creator appeal to and are in need of our good humour, though for different reasons. The reader soon realizes that acceptance of Goldsmith as a novelist entails tolerance of many devices (such as the rôle of Mr. Burchell) which are inept by normal standards. But in the Advertisement he pleaded that 'a book may be amusing with numerous errors', and readers have found part of their amusement in the exercise of the tolerance he solicits. Goldsmith's tone is such as to induce tolerance of the many episodes in this story of contemporary life which are reduced to a fairy tale primitiveness.

One of the characteristics of this kind of artifice in eighteenth-century fiction is that it does not invite us to translate it into 'reality'. When Joseph Andrews writes very much in the style of a servant to his sister, a fellow servant, and in a later chapter cries out in the exalted rhetoric of the romances in his sickroom delirium, we are not invited to ask questions about his actual range of verbal expression. There is no actuality. But we can trust Fielding to keep his novels so alive that such specifications are unnecessary. A character can be created by these comic means and yet give a sufficient impression of human solidity. A similar principle holds good for the vicar. Such questions as 'How naïve is the vicar?' are not invited.[5] The story demands that in some matters he should appear to be totally lacking in powers of observation and reflection, but partly because it *is* a necessity required by the story (just as Elizabethan dramatic plots may require special credulity in the characters who are to be deceived) we are never in a position to say quite what sort of person he 'really' is. It is not the intention of this kind of fiction that we should ask such questions.

Sometimes the play between the vicar's excellent literary manners and competence as a reporter, and his apparently imperfect recognition of what he is reporting, produces considerable piquancy. For example, he fails to identify Squire Thornhill's dubious guests in the fact of very plain evidence of their true character, which he presents as sharply as we could wish:

> The ladies of the town strove hard to be equally easy [i.e. compared with Olivia], but without success. They swam, sprawled, languished, and frisked; but all would not do: the gazers indeed owned that it was fine; but neighbour Flamborough observed, that Miss Livy's feet seemed as pat to the music as its echo. . . . One of them, I thought, expressed her sentiments upon this occasion in a very coarse manner, when she observed, that by the *living jingo,* she was all of a muck of sweat. Upon our return to the house, we found a very elegant cold supper. . . .

In conversation with the vicar's wife and daughters

> . . . they once or twice mortified us sensibly by slipping out an oath; but that appeared to me as the surest symptom of their distinction, (tho' I am since informed that swearing is perfectly unfashionable.) Their finery, however, threw a veil over any grossness in their conversation. (Ch. IX)

Goldsmith endows the vicar here with a shifting and slightly ambiguous persona, such as humorous writers have adopted to portray absurdities without immediately exploding them. We are accustomed to a shifting persona in *Gulliver's Travels,* though misguided readers in recent times have tried to establish consistency. Two chapters later the proposal is made to find jobs in London for Olivia and Sophia through these ladies' good offices, and the vicar registers not the slightest suspicion. There is no way of accounting for this except by recognizing that here we have a literary joke, which consists in stretching the credulity of a character beyond intelligibility. But *The Vicar of Wakefield*

would not be the masterpiece it is if Goldsmith's strategies were not also a vehicle of meaning; though by its very nature the meaning is not to be precisely defined. Eighteenth-century fiction may be an issue of artifices, but ultimately we judge it as an imaginative statement about life. In exploring further the treatment of the vicar's relations with Mr. Thornhill we must try to understand what this highly artificial work is achieving.

In the passage where the vicar and his family receive from the landlord of an inn their first information about Mr. Thornhill the vicar's narrative gives Augustan neatness and polish and a flavour of comedy of manners, as well as moral correctness, to his statement:

> This gentleman he described as one who desired to know little more of the world than its pleasures, being particularly remarkable for his attachment to the fair sex. He observed that no virtue was able to resist his arts and assiduity, and that scarce a farmer's daughter within ten miles round but what had found him successful and faithless. Though this account gave me some pain, it had a very different effect upon my daughters, whose features seemed to brighten with the expectation of an approaching triumph, nor was my wife less pleased and confident of their allurements and virtue. (Ch. III)

The sexual response of the female members of the family rather modifies the image of ideal domestic, social and Christian order which, in an equally composed style, he describes in the next chapter:

> The little republic to which I gave laws, was regulated in the following manner: by sun-rise we all assembled in our common appartment; the fire being previously kindled by the servant. After we had saluted each other with proper ceremony, for I always thought fit to keep up some mech-anical forms of good breeding, without which freedom ever destroys friendship, we all bent in gratitude to that Being who gave us another day. (Ch. IV)

The order so felicitously depicted by the vicar is continually subverted by the elementary follies and vanities of wife and daughters in ways that could only occur in literature. Only in literature could the harmony and its disruption co-exist on such easy terms. Contradictions in real life could be much more complex and disturbing.

Sociability between the squire and the vicar's family immediately develops. When Mr. Thornhill makes an offer which amounts to a proposal to take Olivia into 'keeping', the vicar's resentment is on the grounds of honour, of which his family has the nicest sense: 'Honour, sir, is our only possession at present, and of that last treasure we must be particularly careful', as if family honour were the only issue at stake. We must ask ourselves whether the vicar's urbanity as a host, his reluctance to mention sin and damnation on a social occasion, accounts for this response, or whether some Augustan principle of moderation prompts him to withhold the more solemn sanctions when principles drawn from social custom are adequate for the occasion. He goes as far as urbanity could go when he apologizes for speaking so warmly, and Mr. Thornhill goes as far as moral unawareness (or is it insolence?) could go when he says:

> 'I protest nothing was farther from my heart than such a thought. No, by all that's tempting, the virtue that will stand a regular siege was never to my taste; for all my amours are carried by a coup de main.' (Ch. IX)

These words offend the two whores, who then

> began a very discreet and serious dialogue upon virtue: in this my wife, the chaplain, and I, soon joined; and the 'Squire himself was at last brought to confess a sense of sorrow for his former excesses. We talked of the pleasures of temperance, and of the sunshine in the mind unpolluted with guilt. . . . Mr. Thornhill even went beyond me, and demanded if I had any objection to giving prayers. (Ch. IX)

What are we to make of this; that is, if explanations need to be attempted? One view might be that the vicar's complaisance, respectable in this situation, is exploited by the cynical Thornhill, who then fools him with his assumed piety. But Goldsmith's game is surely more interesting than this. In a society where such mixtures of moral types might occur in company, rôles could change in unexpected ways. It is almost as surprising to find the vicar's wife discoursing on virtue as the London ladies. Can we be sure that the rake, if not genuine in his wish for prayers, is not at least desirous of making a conventionally harmonious gesture? But it must again be stressed that Goldsmith is not depicting his world realistically. His story demands distortions of attitudes and rôles. Yet such passages may tell us more about the eighteenth century, and the chaotic pressures and confusions within a society that liked to see itself in orderly terms, than straight social history. They are not translatable into social history, but they provide us with images of the comic imagination which raise questions about the reality.

These are not the images for which the book is best known, and most of those who have loved it have associated it with less problematic issues. **The Vicar of Wakefield** may be numbered among those late eighteenth-century texts, along with Cowper's *The Task* of nearly two decades later, in which the love of nature and the love of domesticity are pleasantly combined: an unpretentious expression of the English spirit which has become permanent. As in *The Task,* the drinking of tea gives completion to the Englishness:

> At a small distance from the house my predecessor had made a seat, overshaded by an hedge of hawthorn and honeysuckle. Here, when the weather was fine, and our labour soon finished, we usually sate together, to enjoy an extensive landscape, in the calm of the evening. Here too we drank tea. . . . (Ch. V)

Older features of the English popular tradition are also represented with an agreeable explicitness and fullness that remind one of Washington Irving's *Sketch Book,* another work which was endlessly reprinted in the nineteenth century. And, of course, Goldsmith, like Irving, has the viewpoint of a non-English connoisseur of the scene. The Virgilian *O fortunatos . . . agricolas,* another eighteenth-century theme, is in the background of the following passage:

> Remote from the polite, they still retained the primaeval simplicity of manners, and frugal by habit, they scarce knew that temperance was a virtue. They wrought with chearfulness on days of labour; but observed festivals as intervals of idleness and pleasure. They kept up the Christmas carol, sent true love-knots on Valentine morning, eat pancakes on Shrove-tide, shewed their wit on the first of April, and religiously cracked nuts on Michaelmas eve. (Ch. IV)

The style is such that it does not matter in the least whether any such rural perfection still existed, or had ever existed. The truth about any rural community would in any case include more than is suggested here. And there is the most obvious and elementary favourite: the episode of the green spectacles. It may not be a great example of wit, but it has no doubt been the sole representative of the coney-catching *genre* for countless readers. The gullibility of the innocent is one of the most familiar of themes and in this story the combination of the amusing with the innocuous was to be an infallible recommendation in the coming century. But there is more than this. With his genius for simplicity Goldsmith creates something like a fairy tale.

The twentieth century, which looks closely into texts and can even find a satirical intention in this one, may not easily appreciate Goldsmith's success in creating a work which became a legend. One understands only too well why Thackeray, after recoiling from Sterne, should have taken such pleasure in the thought of Goldsmith's 'sweet story'. With a few passages taken out it meets Victorian requirements for domestic literature, but this does not help its reputation today. This aspect of the legend is relevant historically because when the nineteenth century, so concerned with improvement, looked at the past, it was glad to have figures like Addison, Goldsmith and Cowper to represent a century in which other figures were in some respects alien or disquieting. But Goldsmith's more lasting achievement was the creation of a work which conveys quintessentially and with wonderful freshness certain parts of the English scene in an age when the scene was about to change. His instinctive sense of history, his artist's recognition of his rôle in relation to the changing world, is exquisitely manifest in his choice of subject for *The Deserted Village.* This was a poem that had to be written, and his authorship of this very special epitaph would be enough to place Goldsmith among the immortals, if he had done nothing else. *The Vicar of Wakefield* has none of its poignant feeling for worlds lost or about to be lost. And yet it too is a monument. Goldsmith could not have realized in what sense it was to be a monument, because he could not have foreseen the impossibility in the fiction of later periods of the peculiarly Augustan combination of elements present here. As a recapitulation in miniature of so many old fictional *motifs* it is an appropriate product of the decade before the old tradition ceased with the death of Smollett. As a personal achievement, a work of art within the limits of a genius that is at ease with its limits, it stands as a monument to virtues which greater writers of later periods have not always shown.

Notes

[1] All quotations from Goldsmith are given from the text of the *Collected Works of Oliver Goldsmith,* ed. Arthur Friedman, 5 vols. (Oxford, 1966). Volume and page numbers of this edition are cited except for quotations from *The Vicar of Wakefield* which have only chapter numbers.

[2] Donald A. Stauffer, *The Art of Biography in Eighteenth-century England* (Princeton and Oxford, 1941), p. 383.

[3] D. W. Jefferson, 'Observations on *The Vicar of Wakefield*', *The Cambridge Journal,* 3, No. 10 (1950), pp. 621-28.

[4] Robert H. Hopkins, *The True Genius of Oliver Goldsmith* (Baltimore, 1969), pp. 166-230. Sven Bäckman's *This Singular Tale. A Study of 'The Vicar of Wakefield' and its Literary Background* (Lund, 1971), which contributes valuable information and insights on points relating to the vicar and other characters, follows Stuart Tave, with some reservations, in placing the vicar among the 'amiable humorists'.

[5] This principle applies to the question 'How witty is he?' Ronald Paulson attributes wit to him, but if he is credited with all of Goldsmith's wit his naïvety becomes difficult to place. See *Satire and the Novel in Eighteenth Century England* (New Haven and London, 1967), p. 271.

Richard C. Taylor (essay date 1990)

SOURCE: "Goldsmith's First Vicar" in *Review of English Studies,* N.s., Vol. XLI, No. 162, May, 1990, pp. 191-9.

[*In the essay below, Taylor discusses the relation of Goldsmith's earlier work "The History of Miss Stanton" with* The Vicar of Wakefield.]

Recent studies of Oliver Goldsmith's *The Vicar of Wakefield* have focused on a question still unanswered, despite the efforts of W. O. S. Sutherland, Robert Hopkins, David Durant, and others: how do we account for the apparent sentimentality and implausibility of a novel written by an impassioned critic of 'romance' fiction? One obvious solution is that Goldsmith's novel is a satiric undermining of romance conventions. Sutherland sees *The Vicar* as a 'kindly satire' on the sentimental novel,[1] and Hopkins finds it a sustained, sophisticated burlesque of sentimentalist and trite fiction.[2] David Durant argues that the novel's sub-text demonstrates the impotency of didactic fiction.[3] Attempting to revive flagging interest in Goldsmith, these scholars have contributed to a critical appreciation for the subtlety of Goldsmith's craft.

The problem with many of these studies, however, is that they have treated *The Vicar* as an isolated text rather than as the culmination of years of critical analysis and experimentation. By the time Goldsmith completed his novel, presumably in 1762, he had worked for more than five years as a reviewer, editor, and essayist; and he had commented frequently—and perhaps inconsistently—on sentimentalism, didacticism, and satire in fiction. He had also developed a fruitful association with John Newbery, publisher of *The Vicar* (1766). Immortalized as the 'philanthropic bookseller' in Goldsmith's novel,[4] Newbery specialized in conduct books and didactic fiction for polite young 'ladies' and 'gentlemen'. With Goldsmith and Tobias Smollett he also helped establish the *British Magazine* in 1760.

In its first year the *British* was primarily a vehicle for Smollett's *Sir Launcelot Greaves,* a poorly received romance of knight-errantry. But it also published a series of exempla designed to edify parents and their children on the hazards of romantic love and the need for matrimonial prudence. The theme of these tales was consistent with Newbery's often-repeated solution to the 'depravity' of his age:

> It has been said, and said wisely, that the only way to remedy these Evils is to begin with the rising Generation, and to take the Mind in its infant State, when it is uncorrupted and susceptible of any Impression; To represent their Duties and future Interest in a Manner that shall seem rather intended

to amuse than instruct, to excite their Attention with Images and Pictures that are familiar and pleasing; To warm their Affections with such little Histories as are capable of giving them Delight, and of impressing on their tender Minds proper Sentiments of Religion, Justice, Honour, and Virtue.[5]

One of these exempla was Goldsmith's first experiment with romance: a letter **'To the Authors of the British Magazine'** with the running title **'The History of Miss Stanton'** (iii. 128-32). In narrative strategy and basic plot Goldsmith's first attempt at romance-writing clearly anticipated his later approach to the novel. Yet, for a tale that was 'something like the first rude germ' of *The Vicar,* as James Prior noticed first in 1837, **'Miss Stanton'** has received remarkably little attention.[6] Understood in its periodical context and in conjunction with Goldsmith's early critical commentary, this story provides important and largely neglected evidence that should be included in discussions of satiric intention and didacticism in *The Vicar.*

Framing the narrative, an anonymous writer **'To the Authors'** identifies himself as one 'unused to correspond with 'Magazines', but who believes that his 'true but artless tale' offers a sensible alternative to the 'fictitious stories of distress' crowding the journals. Hopkins, one of the few to consider the story seriously, sees in this introduction a clue to Goldsmith's 'antisentimentalism' and finds internal evidence in the narrative to suggest that the piece is an ironic attack on popular romance.[7] However, the narrator's complaint is not a general attack on a vicious genre: he finds many examples that have 'real merit in the design, as they promote that tenderness and benevolent love'— qualities which moralize good fiction. What he attacks, specifically, are those stories that 'vainly attempt by maxim, or reproof' to instruct: fictions with a concluding 'moral' that fails to undo the damage done by the plots' sensationalism.

The narrator introduces Mr Stanton, 'a clergyman with a small fortune . . . esteemed by the rich, and beloved by the poor', who lives in bucolic bliss with his beloved daughter Fanny. Shattering their tranquillity, the rake Mr Dawson, a dissimulating 'man of the world', wins the trust of father and daughter and elopes with the 'deluded' Fanny. The grief-stricken Stanton vows revenge, pursues and discovers Dawson, and challenges him to a duel. After the first volley Stan-ton falls, apparently dead. Seeing Fanny collapse upon the 'lifeless' figure of her father, Dawson repents of his infamous ways and immediately offers marriage to Fanny. Upon hearing the offer, Stanton rises up and admits to having 'pretended to be dead', and the two young people are 'immediately conducted to church'. After this 'instant' wedding they proceed to live as 'exemplary instances of conjugal love and felicity'.

Similarities between this 'farrago of foolery and anti-climax', as Austin Dobson calls it,[8] and *The Vicar* are readily apparent. Both begin with an admission of obvious narrative flaws—**'Miss Stanton'**'s artlessness and *The Vicar*'s occasional 'absurdities'. The cor-respondent to the *British Magazine* and Goldsmith himself in his Advertisement to the novel express their faith that these flaws will be outweighed by the virtues of sincerity, morality, and beauty. Both Parson Stanton and Vicar Primrose find the sanctity of their firesides disrupted by rakish seducers of their daughters, and they must reassert their parental authority to guarantee the 'proper' marriages of their offspring. Both narratives rely on the romantic staples of betrayal and elopement, imagined death, and ultimate reconciliation.

Several critics follow Prior in acknowledging **'Miss Stanton'** as an antecedent to *The Vicar,* yet they have been surprisingly cursory in their treatment of the tale. Hopkins uses **'Miss Stanton'** as further evidence of the pervasiveness of Goldsmith's ironic stance. Because of the utter implausibility of this 'true though artless' tale, he finds it 'a sly joke upon magazine readers'.[9] 'Artlessness', however, is part of the author's rhetorical strategy—probably not to launch an ironic assault on romantic conventions, as Hopkins argues, but to engage most effectively in the type of moral instruction the *British Magazine,* a 'Monthly Repository for Gentlemen & Ladies', featured throughout its pages. Ricardo Quintana dismisses **'Miss Stanton'** as 'another story with a far-fetched peripeteia at the close' and concludes with an unanswered question: 'What . . . did the reader of the *British Magazine* make of this? For that matter, what do we make of it today?'[10]

Part of the answer to this question lies in the early development of Goldsmith's views on the romance. In his first journalistic assignment as a reviewer for Ralph Griffiths's *Monthly Review* (1757), he was almost relentlessly hostile towards the genre. His treatment of a 'happily-ever-after' novel entitled *True Merit True Happiness* typifies the captious mood of these reviews and summarizes his complaint against the genre:

> Reader, if thou hast ever known such perfect happiness, as these romance-writers can so liberally dispense, thou hast enjoyed greater pleasure than has ever fallen to our lot . . . the young and the ignorant lose their taste of present enjoyment, by opposing it to those delusive daubings of consummate bliss they meet with in novels; and, by expecting more happiness than life can give, feel but the more poignancy in all its disappointments. (i. 17)

The author brings this same concern to *The Vicar;* he foreshadows the dangers into which the clergyman's daughters will fall: Mrs Primrose, who had been reading romances during her pregnancy, insisted on 'Olivia' and 'Sophia', two romantic names to which their father futilely objected (iv. 20). This act of naming illustrates the mother's frivolity and the father's failure to assert his authority. These parental failures engender their daughters' unrealistic expectations and eventual romantic distress.

A letter to his brother Henry in January 1759 seems, again, to damn the genre on the same grounds. Prescribing the proper upbringing for his nephew, Goldsmith wrote: 'Above all things let him never touch a romance, or novel, those paint beauty in colours more charming than nature, and describe happiness that man never tastes.'[11] But later in 1759, when he compiled his *Bee* series, he began to qualify his complaints and reconciled himself, at least in part, to the literary form he had ridiculed so often as a reviewer. In a dream narrative titled **'A Reverie'** but better known as **'The Fame Machine'**, the coachman, final arbiter of literary immortality, denies passage to Smollett for his work as a historian, but asks the author if he has any other literary claim: ' "None", replied the author, "except a romance; but this is a work of too trifling a nature to claim future attention." "You mistake (says the inquisitor) a well-written romance is no such easy task as is generally imagined" ' (i. 449).

Another partial concession to the form may have been a discrete justification of Goldsmith's experimentation with the genre. In Goldsmith's Chinese Letter LXXXI-II for the *Public Ledger* (15 October 1760) his fictional narrator Lien Chi Altangi warns that romances 'are no better than instruments of debauchery. They are dangerous fictions, where love is the ruling passion' (ii. 340). The narrator then qualifies his injunction: 'To be able to inculcate virtue by so leaky a vehicle, the author must be a philosopher of the first rank' (ii. 341). Significantly, Goldsmith's headnote to the letter attributes it to a 'modern philosopher of China'. Such a philosopher may indeed be capable of using the genre constructively: Letter LX, **'The History of the Beautiful Captive'**, is just such an example. In attempting his own romances Goldsmith tried to reform a genre he found both corrupt and appealing.

Throughout his early career Goldsmith maintained, as Newbery did, the importance of simple didacticism in fiction, especially in portrayals of parental responsibility and filial duty. His review of an anonymous burlesque on the romance, *A New Battledore for Miss in her Teens,* implicitly warns of the inappropriateness of satire in any treatment of such weighty matters:

> The author ironically recommends mercenary motives, as the properest inducements to matrimony; and, in the same strain, advises all young Ladies to place their affections on the fortunes, not the persons, of their admirers; but his irony is not

plausible enough to be truly humourous; and his satyr is too injudiciously applied to be useful; as the tender age and sex, to whom his piece is addressed, requires rather to be instructed, than ridiculed into a becoming conduct. (i. 19)

Satire might properly be directed at parents, even those basically decent fathers in **'Miss Stanton'** and *The Vicar* who fail to supervise adequately the amorous adventures of their offspring; it might also be aimed indirectly at the quick plot reversals common in romance fiction; but it should not interfere with a novel's moral obligation. An excessively tender father must suffer; so must his daughter, deluded by the false promises of romantic love. The rake, vehicle for this suffering, must himself be punished, reformed, and married off to the daughter. The result of this formula is not the 'happily-ever-after' bliss to which Goldsmith objected but a sort of uneasy truce and new-found humility.

In his Preface to Charles Wiseman's *A Complete English Grammar* (1764) Goldsmith links simplicity of style with virtue; his 'puff' for Newbery, in this passage, also further suggests his philosophical indebtedness to his bookseller:

> Were I to advise beginners, especially children, they should read only such Books as are easily understood, and written in the most plain and natural style, upon subjects capable of interesting the virtuous part of their passions, or subduing those which lead to vice. Nor can I here avoid recommending several of this nature, published by Mr. *Newbery,* which seem happily adapted to delight and rectify the growing mind, and lead it up to truth, through the flowery paths of pleasure. (v. 311)

For authors appealing to an audience of young people, directness and simplicity of style, subject, and method were essential. And to be most effective that message should be delivered with humour and delight, rather than unadorned platitudes.

While the narrator of **'Miss Stanton'** is hardly a 'philosopher of the first rank', he does not sensationalize his tale. Love is not its 'ruling passion', and Miss Stanton's happiness is assured only after her abductor's lust is exposed and punished. If the story were not told so plainly, if it exhibited the sort of 'debauchery' of which Lien Chi complains, if its morality failed to overshadow the excesses of its characters, then an ironic interpretation of the tale might be plausible. In fact, it exhibits none of the 'romantic' traits of which Goldsmith specifically complained, whether as magazine correspondent or as 'Citizen of the World'.

'The History of Miss Stanton' conforms reasonably well to Goldsmith's conception of the well-executed romance. It is designedly 'artless', told with a simple humour that makes its important didactic message palatable. Its laughably implausible ending—a 'fault' that may have justified its exclusion from the 1765 *Essays by Goldsmith*—obscures some virtues typical of Goldsmith's more successful prose. With his small fortune, his filial affection for his only daughter Fanny, and his ignorance of the 'artfulness' of society, Stanton clearly resembles Dr Primrose of *The Vicar*. Goldsmith develops the fireside tenderness of father and daughter sensitively and renders the contemptuous rake Dawson convincingly. In his account of the 'wily traveller's' elopement and false marriage with the naïve Fanny, the narrator justifies the self-confessed 'artlessness' of the tale: 'she [Fanny] had hitherto known only squires and neighbouring parsons, men really ignorant, or without sufficient art to conceal the art they use. But the insidious Mr. Dawson had learned in courts the whole art of pleasing' (iii. 130). Artfulness, here, is deception. The narrator's persona is that of a simple man, one unused to the complexities of 'the art that conceals art' in fiction. He presents his story unornamented and without the excess of platitude and moral reproof about which he complains in his introduction.

The ending of **'Miss Stanton'**—the absurd duel between the rake and the clergyman, the feigned death of Stanton, the conversion of Dawson, and the ultimate marriage—is appropriate to the obvious limitations of Goldsmith's persona and his stated intention. The conclusion is both absurd and abrupt, but the suddenness of its ending reminds the reader that the narrator has omitted the kind of awkward and extrinsic moralizing typical in these tales. The story's sentiment, however offensive to some readers, speaks for itself. While the conclusion may be poking gentle fun at the unsophisticated narrator, it is consistent with his aims; neither the avowed purpose of the tale nor its structure anticipates a satirical attack on closure in romance.

The verbal complexity and sly humour that typify Goldsmith's satiric prose are largely missing in this simple narrative. If the author's real intention is not ironic, what then is the point of the story? Prior's conclusion that **'Miss Stanton'** was 'obviously hurried to a conclusion and written probably when the press required an immediate supply of matter' is possible, but not particularly helpful given the importance of the tale to Goldsmith's *Vicar*.[12] Nor is there sufficient evidence to see the tale as con-sistently satirical. The tale's immediate context in the *British Magazine* provides further evidence of its probable impact on its readers and may help answer Quintana's query.

In the same issue Goldsmith contributed **'A True History for the Ladies',** an explicit attempt to moralize the romance:

> In the flowery paths of novel and romance, we are taught to consider love as a blessing that will last for life: it is exalted above its merits; and by teaching the young and unexperienced to expect more from it than it can give, by being disappointed of their expectations, they do not receive from it even those advantages it has to bestow. (iii. 120-3)

In a much more light-hearted tone than **'Miss Stanton'**, **'A True History'** tells of two brothers: the elder married above his station despite parental objection and the younger married 'from that rank of life immediately beneath his own' (iii. 122). The romantic passion of the older brother and his wife turned sour, while the other couple 'rubbed thro' life with much content, and now and then some sparring; entertained their friends comfortably enough, and provided very prettily for a numerous family, which for many years continued increasing' (iii. 123). The narrator of this tale, quite unlike that of **'Miss Stanton',** must allow for 'some sparring'—a note of comic realism making his tale more plausible. The twists of fate and the slyly disguised commentary in the story make it more characteristic of the narrator in *The Vicar*. In both stories and in both narrative veins, Goldsmith refuses to eschew improbability, yet maintains the didactic force of his story—though not through the artificially imposed 'moral' at the conclusion.

In his best fiction, Goldsmith complicates genuine didactic intention with satire. Ralph Wardle does not mention **'Miss Stanton'** in his biography of Goldsmith, but offers an explanation for the flatness of the story in comparison with the poignancy of *The Vicar* and much of the author's periodical work: 'And when he abandoned all pretensions to instruction and indulged in his innate desire to entertain . . . he had shown that he could outdo any writer in London.'[13] While almost all of Goldsmith's fiction is to some extent didactic, those pieces like **'Miss Stanton'** that are intended primarily to instruct are probably less successful than those in which the author allows himself the full range of his ironic wit. Conscious of his persona, the letter-writer to the *British Magazine,* the author refrains from his typical ironic undercutting.

The tale is not, however, devoid of charm and gentle wit, and it provides an early display of Goldsmith's talent for developing the narrative persona and the tale appropriate to that voice. The duping of the villain Dawson might be seen as a comic climax, humorous partly because of its implausibility. Readers might applaud the parson's triumph, while smiling at the earnestness of the letter-writer in his attempt to write his moral tale; and they might enjoy the quaintness of the rustic relationships that resemble those in *The Vicar*'s familial drama. Critics who have found the story an utter failure have missed one of the essential yet elusive traits of Goldsmith in much of his periodical fiction: the author's talent for creating a diversity of narrative voices, each dictating not only tone but structure and technique. In 'Miss Stanton', the narrator is decidedly not the sly satirist lambasting sentimentality. Nor is he a skilful pedant instructing through flawless exemplum. He is, rather, a man of feeling, frowning from outside the world of magazine fiction on the feeble attempts of 'didactic writers', and he tries his best to improve on the genre. His style is simple and direct and his conclusion consonant with his inexperience as a writer. One might deduce that Goldsmith felt the same sort of ambivalence towards the parson, who fails to exercise proper parental authority, as he later exhibits towards Primrose. And he recognizes the improbable twists and apparent unsophistication that would characterize such a narrator's attempts at fiction.

'The History of Miss Stanton' is not as artless and humourless as some critics have claimed, nor does it exemplify much of the subtle wit largely responsible for winning the author his fame. Though scholars might be tempted to find in the tale the early working out of complex levels of irony demonstrable in *The Vicar,* or perhaps to discover in the story a satiric assault on the romance, neither text nor context adequately supports such claims. Its resemblance to Goldsmith's novel, however, makes 'Miss Stanton' at least a useful companion piece in considering approaches to the novel, and its early display of the author's talent for fully assuming a variety of narrative stances makes it an important example of one of the most appealing and vexing aspects of Goldsmith's periodical fiction. This tale, considered in the context of Goldsmith's early prose and the periodical in which the story was published, shows that while the author deplored the use many of his contemporaries made of the romance, he saw in the form the possibility for serious didactic purpose. Despite the wildly implausible endings and sentimentality, even such rustic narrators as the correspondent and the Vicar might use the form for the instruction of their readers.

Notes

1 Sutherland, *The Art of the Satirist: Essays on the Satire of Augustan England* (Austin, 1965), 84-91.

2 Hopkins, *The True Genius of Oliver Goldsmith* (Baltimore, 1969), 166-230.

3 Durant, '*The Vicar of Wakefield* and the Sentimental Novel', *Studies in English Literature,* 17 (1977), 477-91.

4 *Collected Works of Oliver Goldsmith,* iv, *The Vicar of Wakefield,* ed. Arthur Friedman (Oxford, 1966), 94-5. Further references to Goldsmith's writing will be to Friedman's edition and will be cited in the text by volume and page numbers.

5 Newbery, An Address 'To the Parents, Guardians, and Governesses of Great Britain and Ireland' (London, 1761).

6 Prior, *The Life of Oliver Goldsmith, M.B. from a Variety of Original Sources* (London, 1837), i. 350.

7 Hopkins, *True Genius,* pp. 97-8.

8 Dobson, *Life of Oliver Goldsmith* (London, 1888), 77.

9 Hopkins, *True Genius,* pp. 97-8.

10 Quintana, *Oliver Goldsmith: A Georgian Study* (New York and London, 1967), 58, 107.

11 *The Collected Letters of Oliver Goldsmith,* ed. Katharine C. Balderston (Cambridge, 1928), 60.

12 Prior, *Life of Goldsmith,* i. 350.

13 Wardle, *Oliver Goldsmith* (Lawrence, Kansas, 1957), 108.

Peter Dixon (essay date 1991)

SOURCE: *"The Vicar of Wakefield"* in *Oliver Goldsmith Revisited,* Twayne, 1991, pp. 75-96.

[*In the following excerpt, Dixon examines the literary devices Goldsmith employs in* The Vicar of Wakefield.]

As a book reviewer Goldsmith was necessarily a student of title pages. In one of his earliest reviews he thus rebukes the author of *Memoirs of Sir Thomas Hughson, and Mr. Joseph Williams; with the Remarkable History, Travels, and Distresses of Telemachus Lovet:* "Fair promises! Yet like a Smithfield [i.e., Bartholomew Fair] conjuror, who, to draw company, exhibits at the door his best show for nothing, this author exhausts all his scanty funds on the title page." Another work may tempt us with hints of arcane thrills: *The History of Cleanthes, an Englishman of the Highest Quality.* From its title page "some readers may be induced to search into this performance for hidden satire, or political allegory," only to find an improbable and tepidly written romance.[1] A book's title is a contract between author and reader that the former is bound to honor. Goldsmith was acknowledging the responsibility of the writer to his public, at a time when that public was rapidly displacing the patron and the subscriber as the writer's paymaster.

A title can be honest and yet characterful. In a later review Goldsmith approvingly cited Samuel Butler's maxim: "There is a kind of physiognomy in the titles of books, no less than in the faces of men, by which a skillful observer will as well know what to expect from the one as the other" (1:212). What the title page of *The Vicar of Wakefield* presents is a teasing countenance, not unlike its author's in mingling seriousness and humor. Wakefield was proverbially a "merry" town. Its vicar may turn out to be as merry as his parishioners, or conversely may be found to stand in pious contrast to them; we are kept guessing. A mild surprise follows in the elucidatory phrase "A tale; supposed to be written by himself," for eighteenth-century readers would have expected a fictional autobiography to have been labeled "Memoir," or "History," or "Life and Adventures." There is, too, an arch contradiction in the phrase. A "tale" concerning Wakefield arouses expectations of the simple and the artless, whereas "supposed to be written . . ." is an admission that the autobiographical pretense is just that; a pretence, an artifice. Our suspicion of a twinkle in the eye of this title page is checked, however, by the severity of the epigraph, from Burton's *Anatomy of Melancholy: "Sperate miseri, cavete faelices"* (Be hopeful, you who are wretched; beware, you who enjoy happiness). We infer that we are about to read something moral, even morally didactic, an exemplification of rising and falling fortunes. The title page promises a curious compound, which may prove on analysis to be somewhat unstable. The book has certainly proved difficult to describe and assess. A contemporary reviewer called it "this very singular Tale." Later readers have judged it a charming idyll, or a romance in miniature. Others regard it as a satire on facile Christian optimism, clerical complacency, and simple-minded faith in man's innocence. Johnson declared it a "mere fanciful performance," containing "nothing of real life . . . and very little of nature." Ricardo Quintana believes that "the real theme of this seemingly innocent book is discovery about life."[2] The elements of the tale that have provoked such critical diversity and bewilderment may be analogous to the aspects of Goldsmith's tone and expression that caused his conversational sallies to be so variously interpreted: a deadpan look can be misread as solemnity; a twinkle in the eye may be dismissed as a trick of the light.

The book's anatomy is less controversial than its expressive features. Many critics have remarked on the formal symmetries: 32 chapters divided into two equal parts, matching (though in reverse order) the two halves of the Latin epigraph. Though the first misfortune—the absconding of the Vicar's banker—is a severe blow and immediately leads to the breaking off of his eldest son George's engagement to Arabella Wilmot, the Vicar's decision to move from Wakefield to a smaller country parish, and to cultivate a farm as well as his clerical duties, permits him to keep his family above the level of poverty. They do indeed suffer various embarrassing and irritating "mortifications," blows to their foolish pride. But it is only with Olivia's rash elopement with the villainous Squire Thornhill that, as the Vicar tells us, their "real misfortunes" begin. News of the elopement is brought in chapter 17, almost exactly halfway through the narrative. The Primrose family now experiences a series of "calamities" and feels true wretchedness. Their home is destroyed in a fire, and the Vicar loses both health and liberty as he is imprisoned for debt by the vindictive Thornhill. He is informed that his younger daughter has been abducted, and that his elder daughter is dead, and he believes that he and his son George, who now shares the same prison on a charge of manslaughter, will soon follow her. In terms of the epigraph, the family has not been sufficiently cautious and prudent while in the state of pastoral happiness; in misery they may hope for the good fortune that begins to shower upon them in chapter 30: "Happier prospects begin to appear."

As Geoffrey Carnall has noted, the turning point of the elopement is preceded by one of the three poems that the novel contains, the "Elegy on the Death of a Mad Dog." The other two poems also signal important though less momentous developments, each of which occurs at the midpoint of the two main divisions of the plot. The ballad of Edwin and Angelina (chapter 8) is followed by Thornhill's opening shots in the campaign to seduce Olivia, while Olivia's melancholy song "When lovely woman stoops to folly" (in chapter 24, ominously entitled "Fresh calamities") is no sooner concluded than Thornhill, defied by the Vicar, has him put in jail.[3]

Symmetries, contrasts, and parallels abound. The beginning and end of the novel display, but in very different lights, the Vicar's obstinacy over matrimonial matters.[4] He stubbornly and tactlessly maintains the doctrine that members of the clergy should never remarry, only to discover that Arabella Wilmot's father, the archdeacon of the diocese, is courting a fourth wife. At the end the Vicar's inflexibility over the sanctity of marriage is seen not as eccentricity but as courageous principle. He refuses to consent to Thornhill's marriage to the same Arabella because "it would be giving a sanction to adultery. While my daughter lives, no other marriage of his shall ever be legal in my eye" (4:153). The refusal of consent is actually a futile gesture, for Thornhill does not legally require his Vicar's agreement, but it is morally right. As the Vicar sees it, the marriage would be adulterous, and would certainly be a deathblow to his daughter.

Adversity has refined and strengthened the Vicar's moral character, as it also tempers his family's attitude to catastrophe. Again, a sequence of parallels and contrasts brings out the point. Life at Wakefield is not without its "little rubs": the Vicar's orchard is plundered by schoolboys, and his wife's custards are despoiled by cats and children. "But we soon got over the uneasiness caused by such accidents, and usually in three or four days began to wonder how they vexed us" (4:19). In chapter 3 the unexpected financial disaster demands that "near a fortnight" should be given up to grief. The studied vagueness ("three or four days," "near a fortnight") indicates the Vicar's slightly amused detachment from his family's excessive lamentations. When, however, the family home and almost all their worldly goods are destroyed by fire, a week suffices to restore cheerfulness, thanks to the support of neighbors and the Primroses' own efforts to withstand adversity.

The Vicar of Wakefield reveals, then, that schematic bent of Goldsmith's mind that is evident also in *The Traveller* and the *History of the Earth.* Yet the novel has frequently been criticized as something of a literary ragbag. Besides three poems, it contains the complete text of a sermon, a political harangue, the interpolated story of Matilda and her long-lost son, and a collection of satirical anecdotes in George Primrose's story of his adventures as a "philosophic vagabond." For good measure Goldsmith adds discussions of the language of poetry (chapter 8), contemporary taste in drama (chapter 18), and the shortcomings of the penal system (chapter 27).

The charge of miscellaneousness would appear to have some substance. The brief dialogue between the Vicar and the strolling player, which allows Goldsmith to denounce unthinking veneration for Shakespeare and Jonson, and to praise nature and simplicity, seems simply digressive, the author riding a hobbyhorse. The Vicar's political arguments in chapter 19, concerning equality, power, wealth, and the importance of the monarchy, also seem at first glance to have only a slender relation with the novel's development. His long speech is at least amusingly framed: the Vicar's hosts, masquerading as a member of parliament and his ladies, are in fact a butler and his fellow servants, part of the novel's large cast of impostors. More important, the kind of local tyrant that the Vicar begins by declaiming against is represented by Squire Thornhill. The reader is already aware of Thornhill's selfish cunning. The Vicar will soon feel his oppressive power. When he is taken to prison at Thornhill's instigation, he learns that in the very cell he occupies a debtor of the squire's, "no later than last year, died for want" (4:153). Thornhill is a powerful and unmerciful tyrant, and we infer that it is he, as landed proprietor, who has failed to check the decay of the county town where the Vicar is imprisoned. The town now consists "but of a few mean houses, having lost all its former opulence, and retaining no marks of its ancient superiority but the jail." Goldsmith adds, significantly, that this prison "had formerly been built for the purposes of war" (4:141); it had been the feudal stronghold of one of the warrior barons whose political descendant is Squire Thornhill. Having been the instrument of military oppression, the belligerent fortress has now become the instrument of legal oppression.

The Vicar's harangue is introduced by references to political journals; eight names are dropped by the butler in rapid succession. And the single paragraph of theatrical discussion in chapter 18 mentions eight dramatists. In each case a context of literary production and activity is quickly sketched. For the most part the digressions either concern literature itself (poetic language, contemporary drama) or exemplify a variety of literary and rhetorical forms: ballad, song, mock-elegy, sermon, political speech, brief romance. Their cumulative effect is to enforce a sense of literariness, to develop that hint about the novel's artifice that was let fall at the outset: "supposed to be written by himself." We are unmistakably reading a work of art, and the digressions, which might seem to run counter to the formal tightness and symmetry, in fact complement those highly artful features by their displays of poetical and rhetorical artistry. The effect, in D. W. Jefferson's words, is to "emphasise the story as story, to call attention to the differences between it and life, and to place it at a certain distance from life."[5]

Perhaps the clearest manifestation of authorial control is the repeated use of a single narrative device, the reversal-of-expectation of which Goldsmith was so fond. As the epigraph implies, optimism may be suddenly clouded, and pessimism unexpectedly cheered, and the novel's subsequent insistence on patterns of reversal begins to shape it into a demonstration of a single thesis: the vanity of human expectations. *The Vicar of Wakefield* has something in common with *Rasselas* and *Candide,* those excellent and recently published types of what Sheldon Sacks has called the "apologue," a work "organised as a fictional example of the truth of a formulable statement or set of statements."[6] Many of the insets or digressions share this pattern. Matilda's anguish is turned to joy, Angelina's despair to happiness. The mad dog, which dies while its victim recovers, baffles medical prognostication. George Primrose's narrative chalks up one defeated hope after another. His encounter with aristocratic grandeur is representative. Furnished (by none other than Squire Thornhill) with a letter of introduction to a "nobleman of great distinction, who enjoyed a post under the government," and having bribed his way into the great man's house, George contemplates the splendor around him: "the paintings, the furniture, the gildings, petrified me with awe, and raised my idea of the owner. Ah, thought I to myself, how very great must the possessor of all these things be, who carries in his head the business of the state, and whose house displays half the wealth of a kingdom; sure his genius must be unfathomable!" When the grandee enters, so does disillusionment: "'Are you,' cried he, 'the bearer of this here letter?'" Ungrammatical, vulgar, and rude, the nobleman makes a hasty departure on a pretext of business, and George is left gaping.

The reversals in George's narrative, as in the principal episodes of the first half of the novel, work toward a comic deflating of vanity, a disappointing of foolish ambitions, a disabusing of credulity. Mrs. Primrose's plan of arriving at church in a more genteel way than by walking over the fields—she wishes to impress the squire's fashionable lady friends—is thwarted by the recalcitrance of the farm horses (chapter 10). Moses' return from the fair, where Jenkinson has tricked him into parting with a colt for a gross of green spectacles, is preceded by his mother's foolish euphoria: "'Never mind our son,' cried my wife. 'Depend upon it, he knows what he is about. . . . I have seen him buy such bargains as would amaze one. I'll tell you a good story about that, that will make you split your sides with laughing—'" (4:67). We too experience the defeat of expectations (as we shared Altangi's frustration at the visitation dinner), for at that moment Moses returns, and the good story remains untold.

The other major episode of this kind is the family portrait (chapter 16). Not to be outdone by their neighbors, who have their likenesses taken by an itinerant painter, the Primroses, obsessed with gentility, commission a "large historical family piece." Their pride is dashed when they come to realize that the painting is indeed large, for it cannot be got through the door or accommodated on any wall. It becomes a local jest, so that their vanity is made ridiculous. Worse still, it raises the envy and malice of the locality, for Squire Thornhill has insisted on being in the picture, an honor not to be refused. So now "scandalous whispers began to circulate at our expense, and our tranquillity was continually disturbed by persons who came as friends, to tell us what was said of us by enemies." The Vicar's family, which ought to be a source of harmony and good relations in the community, is the source of discord. The disastrous group portrait is itself the image of disharmony, since the individuals are presented not with an eye to the whole composition, but as "independent historical figures." Mrs. Primrose is depicted as Venus, besprinkled with jewels; with absurd inappropriateness the Vicar, in his clerical habit, is offering his Venus a tract in favor of monogamy. Olivia, who believes that her beauty gives her power, chooses to appear as an Amazon, but dressed in coachman's gear. Her seducing conqueror, Squire Thornhill, is Alexander the Great, now lying at her feet but soon to hold the whip hand, for in the next chapter the "coachman" will herself be driven off in Thornhill's coach.[7]

Although this episode introduces some ominous notes, our response, as in the other cases of purely comic reversal, is uncomplicated. When fairer promises, of innocent peace or quiet happiness, are overturned, our reactions are less straightforward. Take the scene in which the Primroses enjoy the delights of rural relaxation. "At a small distance from the house my predecessor had made a seat, overshaded by an hedge of hawthorn and honeysuckle. Here when the weather was fine, and our labor soon finished, we usually sat together, to enjoy an extensive landscape, in the calm of the evening. Here too we drank tea, which now was become an occasional banquet, and, as we had it but seldom, it diffused a new joy, the preparations for it being made with no small share of bustle and ceremony" (4:35). Tea drinking is now something of a luxury, a small but significant pleasure that more affluent people take for granted. The admission that "it diffused a new joy" is realistic and unequivocal, with the understated "no small share of bustle" adding a note of mild amusement, the Vicar's habitual condescension to the females of the family. He proceeds: "On these occasions our two little ones [Dick and Bill] always read for us, and they were regularly served after we had done. Sometimes, to give a variety to our amusements, the girls sung to the guitar, and while they thus formed a little concert, my wife and I would stroll down the sloping field, that was embellished with bluebells and centaury, talk of our children with rapture, and enjoy the breeze that wafted both health and harmony." T. S. Eliot's words on "The Deserted Village" apply here perfectly: the melting sentiment is just saved by the precision of Goldsmith's language.[8] The fond cosiness of "little ones" and "little concert" is countered by the matter-of-factness of "they were regularly served," and by the slightly pedantic exactness of "they *thus* formed." Centaury is no conventional adornment of a meadow, while "harmony" is no vague metaphor, but the actual sounds of the music. Goldsmith's careful accuracy encourages us to believe that the parents are really, and justifiably, talking of their children "with rapture."

To suppose that this sort of idyllic contentment could last forever would be foolish. This pastoral scene, like others later, exists to be shattered: the calm and sanctity of this "usual place of amusement" is rudely demolished one autumn day by the intrusion of hunters pursuing a hard-pressed stag. Squire Thornhill, seen here for the first time, brings up the rear: "At last, a young gentleman, of a more genteel appearance than the rest, came forward, and for a while regarding us, instead of pursuing the chase, stopped short, and giving his horse to a servant who attended, approached us with a careless superior air." Thornhill has perceived a more enticing quarry and begins a different pursuit. This disruptive pattern is twice repeated. When the family, together with Burchell, are having an al fresco meal in their hayfield, their peace is again destroyed by a sportsman: the squire's chaplain wantonly shoots one of the blackbirds whose song has contributed to the rural enchantment (4:52). The third scene set in this same spot echoes the first: Olivia sings to Sophia's guitar, and Thornhill once more arrives, to mark down two new victims. The deep-dyed villain now plans to abduct Sophia and to oppress and ruin the Vicar. The ruin appropriately begins with Thornhill's steward driving away Primrose's cattle. The pastoral and peaceable world of hay and cider and cattle rearing is torn apart by the predators. Stags and blackbirds, fathers and tuneful daughters are fair game to this kind of landed gentleman and his dependents. It is a nice piece of ironic justice that at the novel's end we leave Squire Thornhill acquiring new skills. He is "learning to blow the French horn"; the hunting horn is replaced by the softer-toned instrument that often provided an accompaniment to the sort of *fête champêtre* that Thornhill and his crew have repeatedly contrived to spoil.

These recurrences of the "ravaged idyll" motif reveal the hand of art. To go further, as Robert Hopkins does, and suggest that Goldsmith is artfully burlesquing the conventions of pastoral, laughing at literary clichés, is to go too far.[9] Goldsmith is perfectly willing to mock the pastoral, as in *The Citizen of the World,* but to see burlesque in these scenes is to weaken the force of the aggression that disrupts them. The rural contentment, complete with warbling blackbirds and "familiar red-breast" (4:45), is accepted, in all its conventionality, because it is about to be destroyed. Pastoral felicity is short-lived, but it shows up the callousness of Thornhill, and the crassness of the chaplain, who gallantly offers his morning's bag to the alarmed Sophia.

The novel has other conventional aspects. Eighteenth-century fiction, short and long, contains a good many seduced daughters of clergymen. When, in the second half of the novel, Goldsmith presents his Fallen Woman, we note again the accuracy of detail. Into the more orthodox symptoms of Olivia's anguish and decline— "Her temples were sunk . . . and a fatal paleness sat upon her cheek"—Goldsmith inserts something more particular: "her forehead was tense" (4:152). As for the big scene, the Vicar's discovery of his abandoned daughter, Goldsmith both heightens the pathos and gently places it by controlling our attitude toward the narrator. The language of father and daughter is intensified by exclamation and repetition, and by a shift into the second person singular: "'Welcome, any way welcome, my dearest lost one, my treasure, to your poor old father's bosom. Though the vicious forsake thee, there is yet one in the world that will never forsake thee. . . .' 'O my own dear—' for minutes she could no more—'my own dearest good papa! Could angels be kinder? . . . But alas! papa, you look much paler than you used to do. Could such a thing as I am give you so much uneasiness? Sure you have too much wisdom to take the miseries of my guilt upon yourself'" (4:126). At this point, as the feeling threatens to become mawkish, Goldsmith moves into another key. The word "wisdom" triggers a reflex in the Vicar, and the responsible churchman takes over from the tender parent: "'Our wisdom, young woman?' replied I. 'Ah, why so cold a name, papa?' cried she. 'This is the first time you ever called me by so cold a name!'" This is well managed. Goldsmith at once deepens Olivia's distress and makes us smile at her father's tactlessness

as he mounts his high moral horse; his reaction is an example of the rigidity, the mechanical and automatic response that Bergson identified as the great source of laughter. The curious blend of sympathy and amusement is preserved in the Vicar's reply: "I ask pardon, my darling . . . but I was going to observe, that wisdom makes but a slow defence against trouble, though at last a sure one." In introducing his maxim ("I was going to observe . . .") the Vicar sounds exactly like a man of sentiment, an utterer of admirable aphorisms and fine platitudes. A habit of sermonizing is not easily sloughed off.

As the Vicar's troubles increase, as Thornhill becomes more vindictive, the melodramatic language ("Avoid my sight, thou reptile"), and the melodramatic timing ("Just as I spoke, my wife . . . appeared with looks of terror") become more evident. There is no denying that some of the reversals, engineered for pathetic contrast, are unduly prolonged. The climactic appearance of George, wounded and in chains, is heralded by whole paragraphs of misplaced hope and premature rejoicings at his safety. There is also no denying that Goldsmith shamelessly exploits the appeal of the youngest Primroses, Dick and Bill. The two boys remain obstinately outside the time scheme of the novel, perennial toddlers and prattlers, "chubby rogues," less often referred to by their names than by the sentimental appellation "little ones." We leave them seated on their father's knees, as a little earlier they have charmingly attempted to seat themselves on the knees of their old friend Burchell. One suspects that Goldsmith created two boys so that both a gentleman's knees may be picturesquely occupied; or both arms, as when their father bravely rescues them from their burning bedroom.

In the fire scene (chapter 22) Goldsmith appears to be recalling the similar disaster that deprives the hero of his home and belongings in Sarah Fielding's *Adventures of David Simple.* David's house, like the Vicar's, is a small thatched cottage, to which a legal suit has forced him to move. But whereas the cause of that fire is carefully explained, Goldsmith's blaze is quite unaccounted for. The house bursts into flames in order to enact the recurrent pattern of expectations being overthrown. Having recovered his lost daughter, the Vicar returns home full of affectionate anticipations of domestic bliss. "It was now near midnight that I came to knock at my door. All was still and silent. My heart dilated with unutterable happiness, when, to my amazement, I saw the house bursting out in a blaze of fire, and every aperture red with conflagration!" The timing could not have been more precise. "All the rapture of expectation" is yet once more cruelly turned to sorrow. The two youngest children, now referred to as both "babes" and "little darlings," helplessly lying in their bed as the flames encircle them, are the center of attention and feeling. "'Where,' cried I, 'where are my little ones?' 'They are burnt to death in the flames,' says my wife calmly, 'and I will die with them!'" Mrs. Primrose is coarse-grained and tough—her maiden name was Grogram, the name of a hard-wearing, serviceable fabric. These qualities, that make her seem crude and insensitive elsewhere in the book, here give her a calm strength (her husband's first reaction is to collapse), and the fire unexpectedly brings out her self-sacrificing, maternal feelings, just as Mrs. Hardcastle more comically redeems herself before the supposed highwayman: "Take . . . my life, but . . . spare my child" (5:207). It is the Vicar, however, who braves the flames, snatching Dick and Bill to safety just as the roof sinks in: "'Now,' cried I, holding up my children, 'now let the flames burn on, and all my possessions perish. Here they are, I have saved my treasure. Here my dearest, here are our treasures, and we shall yet be happy.'" That final optimism is predictably doomed to be of short duration. In the meanwhile we need not grudge the Vicar his jubilation or his manner of expressing it. When the Book of Proverbs declares that "In the house of the righteous is much treasure" (15:6), it is not referring to heaps of gold. It is not unreasonable to claim that the offspring of the righteous man may be among his treasures. In this world, as opposed to the next, even a vicar may be allowed to talk of his children as "treasures" without being guilty of materialism.[10]

In effecting the rescue the Vicar is injured, his arm "scorched in a terrible manner." Its condition deteriorates until, when he is in prison, what with the noisome air and the confinement, his strength is sapped and he feels himself sinking into his grave. These dire consequences of the conflagration exclude the spirit of burlesque. Goldsmith is not mocking the wild improbabilities of romance. We have to take the emotionalism for what it is, to accept that the episode of the fire is full of appeals for pity and sympathy (there are seven "littles" in a passage of 500 words) that are open and explicit. These straightforward appeals do not anticipate the artful tear-jerking of Henry Mackenzie's *The Man of Feeling* (1771). Even by the side of Frances Sheridan's *Memoirs of Miss Sidney Bidulph* (1761) they look old-fashioned and naive. It is significant that Goldsmith refrained from following Mrs. Sheridan in her pathetic scenes, since he took other things from her: the names Burchell and Arnold (the butler's employer), and a strong hint for the aftermath of the fire, and the Vicar's injury. Late in *Sidney Bidulph* a clergyman is clapped in prison by the would-be violator of his daughter, and suffers a palsy that incapacitates his right hand. When his daughter and Miss Bidulph (the narrator) visit the prison, the moment is affecting:

> Upon his daughter's going into the room, he lifted up his eyes to see who it was: he had a fine countenance; candour and sincerity were painted on it.
>
> My dear, you made a long stay, said he, in a

melancholy voice, I was afraid something had happened to you. What has detained you?

> Oh, Sir, said she, looking towards the door, I believe I met with a good angel, who is come to visit you in prison.
>
> I entered at these words: the venerable man rose.— A good angel indeed, if her mind be like her face. He bowed respectfully.
>
> Pray, sir, keep your seat.

The suppression of speech markers ("he said," "I answered") at the emotional climax strips the dialogue of prosaic elements. That compression, and the terse sentences, make us feel that we are catching our breath between each new, calculated assault on our feelings—assaults led by the deliberately religious language: "lifted up his eyes," "good angel," "is come." J. M. S. Tompkins has labeled this kind of writing "sophisticated simplicity." It appears intermittently in *David Simple,* and pervades *The Man of Feeling.* But these characteristic devices of sentimental fiction Goldsmith declines to exploit.[11]

Both *Sidney Bidulph* and *David Simple* explicitly relate the patient suffering of their protagonists to the archetypal narrative of reversed fortunes, the Book of Job. David Simple is almost overwhelmed by an unmitigated series of "worldly Misfortunes and Afflictions," but, like Job, he "patiently submitted to the temporary Sufferings allotted him."[12] Sidney Bidulph is "persecuted by a variety of strange misfortunes," some of which are fierce reversals: her husband is killed just when domestic felicity has been regained. She acknowledges the justice of her friend's calling her a "child of affliction," and she cries out with Job: "Why hast thou set me as a mark against thee?"[13] But the endings of these two characters are not like Job's, for they are not returned to their initial prosperity and happiness. They are uncompromisingly refused a poetic justice that would have acknowledged their virtues. Integrity and sensibility must be their own reward. Dr. Primrose, however, finds, like Job, that his latter end is blessed even more than his beginning. Released from prison, he withdraws from the celebrations and pours out his heart "in gratitude to the giver of joy as well as of sorrow."

First proposed by William Black in 1878, the analogy between **The Vicar of Wakefield** and the Book of Job has been widely accepted. Its fullest elaboration is in Martin Battestin's essay "Goldsmith: The Comedy of Job."[14] Battestin notes that Job, like the Vicar, is vain, being complacent about his own righteousness. Minor structural parallels include the messenger figures who bring the first unwelcome news to both men. Moreover, Dr. Primrose, having been informed of Olivia's elopement, having cursed the name of Thornhill (unlike Job, who refrained from cursing the man who hated him), and having been reproved by his son for thus forsaking his clerical character, recalls both the example of Christ and the words of Job: "I see it was more than human benevolence that first taught us to bless our enemies! Blest be his holy name for all the good he hath given, and for all that he hath taken away" (4:12; Job 1:21). Battestin points out that Hugh Kelly, the dramatic rival and sometime friend of Goldsmith, praised *The Vicar of Wakefield* for a "masterly vindication" of the ways of providence in its apparently unequal dispensations of happiness and misery.[15] Kelly was presumably thinking especially of chapters 28 and 29, with their weighty didactic headings:

> Happiness and misery rather the result of prudence than of virtue in this life. Temporal evils or felicities being regarded by heaven as things merely in themselves trifling and unworthy its care in the distribution.

> The equal dealings of providence demonstrated with regard to the happy and the miserable here below. That from the nature of pleasure and pain, the wretched must be repaid the balance of their sufferings in the life hereafter.

What Kelly claimed for the novel was what was widely held to be the "message" of the Book of Job: the seemingly unequal dealings of providence will be redressed in the life to come; they cannot be explained by reference to the operations of this world, but only by reference to futurity. Novels of the pattern of *David Simple* and *Sidney Bidulph* allude to Job in the same spirit as St. James did in his epistle: "Behold we count those happy which endure. Ye have heard of the patience of Job." *The Vicar of Wakefield,* closer to the structural pattern of its analogue, moves beyond celebrating patient endurance of calamity, into a doctrinal vindication of providence. Job's "I know that my redeemer liveth" has its counterpart in the peroration of the Vicar's prison sermon: "the time will certainly and shortly come, when we shall cease from our toil; when the luxurious great ones of the world shall no more tread us to the earth; when we shall think with pleasure on our sufferings below; when we shall be surrounded with all our friends, or such as deserved our friendship; when our bliss shall be unutterable, and still, to crown all, unending." The sermon is given a chapter to itself, without room for comment or reaction, almost as though it were a separately published, self-sufficient sermon. This virtual sealing-off from the fiction gives it a special status. It is absolute and unqualified. Yet it is not entirely sealed off. It offers the consolation of religion to the sufferer, but the consolation comes from one who is himself suffering.

The parallels between the Vicar and Job cannot be pressed too hard. The former is not "perfect and upright," nor is he the subject of a satanic experiment. The mishaps of the first part of the novel result from moral weakness, imprudence, and naïveté. Though the family's departure from Wakefield is in part the consequence of their banker's absconding, another factor is what Goldsmith would have censured as the Vicar's "injustice." As Eric Rothstein and Howard Weinbrot have argued, when the Vicar "made over" the whole of his stipend to the orphans and widows of the diocesan clergy (4:21), the implication of the verb is that he put his income into the hands of trustees for that purpose; his charitable contract is binding and irreversible. He is content to live on the interest of his considerable personal fortune, but when that is snatched away he has literally no income—the contract cannot be annulled—and he must find a living (in both senses) elsewhere.[16] In assigning his stipend to the needy the Doctor has been warmhearted, but also a trifle vain and self-congratulatory: "I . . . felt a secret pleasure in doing my [clerical] duty without reward" (4:21-22). Goldsmith's point is that he is failing in his duty to maintain the financial security of his family. In being generous to one group, he has been unjust to another. It is only fitting that spontaneous benevolence and vanity together should be his undoing at the fair, where the cunning Jenkinson uses those qualities to bait his hook.

It is his vanity that makes the Vicar so comically unreliable a narrator. He reports the discourse that he holds with Mr. Burchell as they travel to the new parish: "We lightened the fatigues of the road with philosophical disputes, which he seemed to understand perfectly." "Seemed" neatly conveys the Vicar's condescension, and masks his dishonesty. For Mrs. Primrose has overheard these disputes, and shrewdly adverts to them when Burchell makes an unexpected visit: "'Bless me,' cried my wife, "here comes our good friend Mr. Burchell . . . that run you down fairly in the argument.' 'Confute me in argument, child!' cried I. 'You mistake there, my dear. I believe there are but few that can do that.'" By the warmth of his reply the Vicar betrays his earlier want of sincerity, together with his unyielding pride in his mental abilities, while with the exclamatory "child" and "my dear" he attempts to put his wife in her place by condescending to her too.

The Vicar's real weakness is less his pride in himself than his pride in his daughters. Here too he is unreliable: "Mere outside [his daughters' good looks] is so very trifling a circumstance with me, that I should scarce have remembered to mention it, had it not been a general topic of conversation in the country." The Vicar at once proceeds to distinguish the respective beauties of his daughters, specifically in terms of sexual attractiveness. He weakly connives in the various schemes to secure Thornhill for Olivia, including the shabby plan to terrify the squire with a rival, a plan "which though I did not strenuously oppose, I did not entirely approve" (4:84). In much the same way he has acquiesced in the commissioning of the family picture, and in the unworthy sneering at the rival portrait of their neighbors, the Flamboroughs: their picture has "no variety in life, no composition in the world" (4:82). Those criticisms are not attributed to an individual speaker, but are as it were uttered by the family in chorus. The chorus may be led by Mrs. Primrose and her daughters, but the Vicar sustains his part.

The lure of gentility and smartness, in the persons of Thornhill and his London lady friends (in reality prostitutes), induces the family to abandon innocence, represented by the merriment of a Michaelmas Eve's celebration at the Flamboroughs' (chapter 11). The Primroses are setting their sights higher than this sort of fun and games, but with forbearance they "suffer" themselves to be happy. As he describes the "primeval pastime" of hunt the slipper, the Vicar insensibly slides into an appropriately earthy language. He talks of catching "a shoe which the company shove about under their hams from one to another, something like a weaver's shuttle." That the Vicar should be drawn unawares into the fun is part of Goldsmith's ingenious construction of a comic scene in his best vein, one that typically hinges on embarrassment:

> It was in this manner that my eldest daughter was hemmed in, and thumped about, all blowsed, in spirits [i.e., in high spirits], and bawling for fair play, fair play with a voice that might deafen a ballad singer [Goldsmith skillfully introduces another "low" entertainment], when confusion on confusion, who should enter the room but our two great acquaintances from town, Lady Blarney and Miss Carolina Wilhelmina Amelia Skeggs! . . . Death! To be seen by ladies of such high breeding in such vulgar attitudes! Nothing better could ensue from such a vulgar play of Mr. Flamborough's proposing.

The hypocritical shifting of blame is only too realistic, as the Primrose chorus positively shrieks its mortification. Like the great politician whom George encounters, these "great" ladies proceed to expose their falseness by coarse and ungrammatical language. They, not the merrymakers, are the vulgarians. But the Primroses are too imperceptive, too attentive to the outside of gentility, to be other than foolishly impressed.

The Vicar stands "neuter" (as he describes himself) in the argument between his wife and Burchell as to the advisability of Olivia and Sophia being put under the protection of Thornhill's female agents. What being "neuter" means is that he evades his parental responsibility, failing to take a firm line, or a line of any kind, but priding himself on a silly equivocation (4:65). When he goes on to silence his conscience, "by two or three specious reasons," for the unmannerly banishing of Burchell, he is on a morally slippery path. With the discovery of Burchell's letter-case, and the Vicar's compliance with the inspection of its contents, he is well down that path. Completely misunderstanding what Burchell is about on their behalf, the family sit "ruminating upon schemes of vengeance"—"ruminating" suggests pastoral, bovine innocence, but "vengeance" shows that innocence has been forsaken. The following scene presents the family at its vindictive worst, savoring—and it is the narrator's phrase—"the pleasure of approaching vengeance," plotting to entrap Burchell with a show of welcome before falling upon him with their upbraidings, their bitter fury and crude jests. The Vicar, convinced of Burchell's "unparalleled effrontery," priggishly treats his children, after Burchell's dignified exit, to a moral allegory about the shamelessness of guilt. The guilt is the family's, and their shamelessness is soon fully displayed: first with the ostentation and immodesty of the portrait, then with the open pushing of Olivia into Thornhill's way, so as to force him to declare himself. Finally, on the very evening that Olivia runs off with the squire, the Vicar's household mirth, the sign and symbol of innocence, is revealed as sadly tainted. Partway through the first bottle of the famous home-brewed gooseberry wine (famous because potent), the Vicar begins to sound like a toper: "Put the glass to your brother, Moses." He sounds like a roué when he goes on to praise Ranelagh Gardens, notorious for assignations, as an excellent marriage market. Calling for a second bottle and another song, he begins to boast of his happiness and his children's virtue. Such hubristic folly is riding for a fall. By the now predictable device of reversal, he immediately learns of Olivia's fate.

There is about this scene, as Robert Hopkins observes, a definite coarseness.[17] Goldsmith has deftly suggested a polluted high spirits, an excitement that is slightly hysterical. With this episode the Vicar has reached his moral nadir, and the reader has got just halfway through the novel. So far the Vicar has believed that, despite temporary setbacks, things have been going well; the reader perceives that in moral terms he has been steadily declining. Goldsmith now reverses these trends; henceforward we shall see the Vicar plunged into calamities, material and physical, but climbing slowly upward in moral status.

The most delicate revelations of the Vicar's shortcomings, as I have suggested, are the Vicar's own. There is evidence elsewhere, in *The Citizen of the World* and some of the early essays, that Goldsmith enjoyed manipulating a narrative in which the storyteller gives himself away, inadvertently letting slip the truth. We scarcely need Jenkinson to make the point that the Vicar is unwordly after reading that "Matrimony was always one of my favorite topics, and I wrote several sermons to *prove* its happiness" (4:22; my italics). The Vicar adds, more tentatively but still quite seriously, that "it was thus, perhaps, from hearing marriage so often recommended, that my eldest son, just upon leaving college, fixed his affections upon the daughter of a neighboring clergyman." In the same early chapter the Vicar shows himself to be superstitious, and proud, for to repeat the common saying that Wakefield possessed a parson lacking in pride, may be construed as a form of pride. A self-deceiving narrator, morally fallible and naive, is not easy to handle. For all Goldsmith's skill, there are moments when the credulity and gullibility, so well conveyed in the fairground episode, become unreal because inadequately anchored in personality. The Vicar is made to report, but made also to ignore, the warnings about Squire Thornhill's reputation. Again, Goldsmith wishes the reader to know that the disguised Burchell is the real Sir William Thornhill; we need to be assured that this god will sooner or later descend from his machine. To give the assurance Goldsmith contrives that, in his account of Sir William, Burchell should in the emotional heat of the moment begin to confuse his pronouns: "he now found that a man's own heart must be ever given to gain that of another. I now found that—that—I forget what I was going to observe" (4:30). The self-confident patrician is momentarily as confused as the unconfident Marlow, who, in his stammering interview with Kate, uses exactly the same words (5:146); but the Vicar simply fails to see the crucial revelation, even as he notes it down.

Here the Vicar-as-character is implausibly imperceptive, while the Vicar-as-narrator is in abeyance. At other times the narrator is too much in evidence, speaking with a hindsight that is normally suppressed. So he intervenes to explain the character's deception by Thornhill. As he begins his search for Olivia the Vicar is fed false information about her seducer's physical appearance and the direction the couple have taken. As narrator he admits that in his anxious haste "I never debated with myself, whether these accounts might not have been given by persons purposely placed in my way, to mislead me" (4:94). Goldsmith has sacrificed consistency of technique for a local effect. He wishes to remind us of the Machiavellian duplicity of the Vicar's adversary, because he is anticipating their next meeting, at which Thornhill arranges a commission for George, involving a posting abroad, so as to get his rival for Miss Wilmot out of the way. We are invited to savor the dramatic ironies as the Vicar pours out his gratitude to George's "generous patron" in an uncharacteristically fulsome manner, while the villain coolly laughs in his sleeve. Individual scenes in the novel are pointed, revealing, intense, but their virtues are sometimes gained at the cost of overall coherence.

The major difficulty with all fictions dependent upon a dramatized narrator, a narrator fully participating in the action, is what Wayne Booth has pithily called "confusions of distance."[18] How close is the narrator figure to the norms of the work? Is the reader's response so fully and finely controlled by the real, as opposed to the fictitious author, that there is no room for misunderstanding? *The Vicar of Wakefield* seems perversely to create confusion of distance. In his preface Goldsmith announces that "The hero of this piece unites in himself the three greatest characters upon earth; he is a priest, an husbandman, and the father of a family. He is drawn as ready to teach, and ready to obey, as simple in affluence, and majestic in adversity." This prepares us to meet someone who adds the role of paterfamilias to the attributes of Chaucer's poor parson and his ploughman brother. What it does not prepare us for is the Dr. Primrose we first encounter, guilelessly revealing himself as vain, smug, something of a crank, bossy but also cowardly, a character all too human and far from ideal. The claims of the preface relate only to the second half of the novel, where presumably Goldsmith felt himself on less secure ground, and where the occasional staginess of the language and heavy-handedness of the ironies betray a lack of confidence. The preface admits that the clerical figure whom Goldsmith has drawn will not find a sympathetic response. "In this age of opulence and refinement, whom can such a character please? Such as are fond of high life will turn with disdain from the simplicity of his country fire-side . . . and such as have been taught to deride religion will laugh at one whose chief stores of comfort are drawn from futurity." Fearing such hostility Goldsmith might well react by defensively protesting the ideal nature of Dr. Primrose.

The Vicar considered as vicar is not without his amusing weaknesses. At the beginning of the novel he prides himself on his tracts against deuterogamy; at the end, after all his tribulations, he proudly tells us that he read out "two homilies and a thesis of my own composing" to the unduly mirthful couples he is about to join in matrimony. In case we should be too severe on him, Goldsmith has thoughtfully provided three other clergymen as yard-sticks. Archdeacon Wilmot is a "prudent"—that is, avaricious—materialist, with an "immoderate passion for wealth" (4:176). With scant sense of Christian charitableness he discourages his daughter from visiting the Primroses in prison, on the grounds of impropriety. When Sir William distributes 40 guineas of largesse to the prisoners, "Mr. Wilmot, induced by his example, gave half that sum." A clergyman who has to be prompted to benevolence is unworthy indeed. Squire Thornhill's chaplain is unworthy in a different way. Besides being a slayer of blackbirds, he goes along with Thornhill's smutty joking and does not challenge his assumption that the chaplain has his eye on promotion rather than the care of souls. His London counterpart is Dr. Burdock, whose fashionable doings are reported by Misses Blarney and Skeggs. His name is that of a coarse weed, something altogether different from the pretty primrose. He is a metropolitan chaplain and fashionable hanger-on, a writer of scandalous vers de société that will stick like burs to his victims.

The preface asserts that the Vicar is "ready to obey." He is certainly obedient to the law, submitting to be taken off to prison, and reproving the parishioners who wish to rescue him by force. Despite the scoffing and practical jokes of the prisoners, he is "ready to teach" and persistent with his sermons. For him to relate his own majesty in adversity, however, is a trickier undertaking, and more than one reader has found him smug and self-regarding, as in the episode where Jenkinson brings the (false) news that Olivia has died of a broken heart, and advises the Vicar that he should now "sacrifice any pride or resentment of [his] own" to the welfare of his dependents.

> "Heaven be praised," replied I, "there is no pride left me now. I should detest my own heart if I saw either pride or resentment lurking there. On the contrary, as my oppressor has been once my parishioner, I hope one day to present him up an unpolluted soul at the eternal tribunal. No, sir, I have no resentment now, and though he has taken from me what I held dearer than all his treasures, though he has wrung my heart, for I am sick almost to fainting, very sick, my fellow-prisoner, yet that shall never inspire me with vengeance. I am now willing to approve his marriage, and if this sub-mission can do him any pleasure, let him know that if I have done him any injury, I am sorry for it." (4:154)

MacDonald Emslie convicts the author of carelessness: the beginning of this passage "is one of the worst examples of Goldsmith's leaving his Vicar open to the charge of spiritual snobbery."[19] Robert Hopkins believes that Goldsmith is deliberately exposing the Vicar's "lack of humility," revealed "by his attitude that he is already one of the chosen," since he envisages himself presenting Thornhill's soul to his Maker.[20] As a clergyman, however imperfect, Dr. Primrose carries a responsibility for the purity of the souls of his parishioners. How God will regard the Vicar's soul is a different, and an unraised question. The claim to be free of pride and resentment (which is a response to Jenkinson's use of those terms, not an unprompted boast), is shown to be valid at the end of the Vicar's speech. Now that his daughter is dead, as he believes, he cannot oppose Thornhill's marriage. His willingness to apologize for any injury he has done his enemy shows a truly Christian dignity in humility. Yet he is no plaster saint. That his moral victories are but temporary triumphs is hinted at by his syntax; the overinsistent "though . . . though . . . yet" warns us to expect the backsliding that comes a few pages later. When George is revealed as the latest victim of Thornhill's malice, his father does indeed display resentment in his passionate grief, and attempts the only vengeance in his power, that of unchristian cursing.

Prefaces are not always true to the texts they precede.

If Goldsmith's novel had fulfilled the promise of his preface it would have been a more uniform, more monolithic, and much duller book. As with the character of Beau Nash, we have to lay side by side the Vicar's evident failings, which Goldsmith brings out again in the final chapter, and his real merits: his tender forgiveness of his daughter and his refusal to sacrifice her peace of mind to his own; his fidelity to his calling in seeking to minister to his fellow prisoners; his principled stand against Thornhill, together with his subsequent submission and asking of pardon; his resolution "*never* to do evil" (4:128; his italics). The Vicar is a man of Christian principles who often (though not always, for he is only human) practices what he preaches.

The rejoicing in the final chapter, being human too, is not unalloyed; Goldsmith shades it with little piques and contretemps. But harmony and good-nature prevail, and the novel's domestic values are reaffirmed: the family is "assembled once more by a cheerful fireside." This last fireside is that of an inn, which gives freer rein to conviviality. Elsewhere the hearth, the literal focus of affectionate feelings, is emphatically a private place, even a place of refuge from which the "censuring world" is shut out (4:132). The fireside was Goldsmith's customary synecdoche for domestic content, though he never worked it as hard as he does here. The preface speaks of the "simplicity" of the Vicar's "country fireside"; the second paragraph of his tale says of their Wakefield existence that "all our adventures were by the fireside." The only function of their nameless and otherwise unmentioned servant is to kindle the fire, that fire within a neat hearth that greets the Vicar and his son on their return from agricultural labor (4:33). That the Primrose home should be destroyed by fire is therefore particularly horrifying. Less momentously, it is a bad sign when social ambition supplants domestic content, and the fire is dreaded as a spoiler of the girls' complexions (4:56). Significantly, when in chapter 11 Burchell utters his sardonic refrain of "Fudge!" to puncture the pseudo-fashionable conversation, he does so while sitting "with his face turned to the fire"; his eyes are on the values of the hearth, which the family is in danger of forgetting. It is Burchell too, or rather Sir William Thornhill, who endorses those values, echoing the words of the preface: "I have at his [the Vicar's] little dwelling . . . received that happiness that courts could not give, from the amusing simplicity around his fireside" (4:168). We in turn endorse this endorsement. The words of a paragon must be respected.

That Sir William is a paragon, with a good deal of Richardson's Sir Charles Grandison in his composition, is not in doubt. Skilled in medicine, he knows how to cure the Vicar's injured arm. Skilled in law, he assists in drawing up his nephew's marriage articles. Setting Christian morality before the aristocratic code, he refuses, like Grandison before him, to countenance dueling. He is both generous and just as he presides over the "trial" of Squire Thornhill, and as he first rebukes the parishioners who had anarchically aimed to rescue their priest, then cheers them up by giving them money to drink his own health—two complementary tactics for keeping the humble in their places. The adjective "majestic," which the preface accords the Vicar, is given by the text to Sir William alone, when he assumes "all his native dignity," and summons George to stand before him: "Never before had I seen anything so truly majestic as the air he assumed upon this occasion. The greatest object in the universe, says a certain philosopher, is a good man struggling with adversity; yet there is still a greater, which is the good man that comes to relieve it" (4:167). Thornhill is the book's secular hero, and is endowed with secular powers to accomplish his good purposes. His word is bond enough for Jenkinson to be allowed out of prison, and his influence with his friend the magistrate will be used to clear George's name. He applies pressure on Wilmot to have the marriage approved, and on the military authorities to get George promoted. He is evidently an approved and powerful member of the establishment, with no inhibitions about using worldly power on behalf of the virtuous but unworldly.

There remains in Sir William a trace of the whimsicality that characterizes Burchell. He teases Sophia somewhat cruelly before confessing his love, and he carries gingerbread, as always, to treat the two little Primroses. Conversely, Burchell has shown dignity and a strong sense of his legal rights in the episode of the letter-book. In many respects, however, the transition from Burchell to the baronet seems less like a shedding of disguise than a transforming of personality. It is impossible to reconcile the boast that "none have ever taxed the injustice of Sir William Thornhill" (4:168) with what we first see of Mr. Burchell. In chapter 3 the latter is unable to discharge his bill at the inn. He is out of pocket, the landlord explains to the Vicar, because "no later than yesterday he paid three guineas to our beadle to spare an old broken soldier that was to be whipped through the town for dog-stealing." The action is humane, but like the Vicar's making over his stipend, it incurs the charge of being unjust, and doubly so. The beadle is being bribed to suspend the operation of the law: the soldier is presumably guilty of theft, however we may deplore the brutality of the punishment. Second, Burchell's debt for his accommodation at the inn cannot now be paid. When he accepts a loan from the Vicar, Burchell admits to an "oversight" in parting with his money: it was a rash action undeserving the name of true benevolence. Yet we are soon assured, in the autobiographical sketch that Burchell/Thornhill gives, that though when he was young Sir William was foolishly and mistakenly generous, "his bounties are now more rational and moderate" (4:30). It is as though Burchell, the irrational, immoderate ego, is allowed to perpetrate what Sir William, the id, has renounced. Burchell and Thornhill are two sides of that kind of "double character" that Goldsmith later examined in Cyrillo Padovano.

In the Man in Black and Sir William Abner (3:181-82) Goldsmith had already treated the psychological type represented by the young Sir William Thornhill; he would return to it in Mr. Honeywood. These are all men of "romantic" (that is, impulsive and imprudent) generosity whose benevolence, rooted in timidity and lack of self-confidence, may prove their downfall. Such a man seeks esteem by giving; he courts praise for his prodigality because he lacks self-respect. Abner's decline begins when he ceases "to set a proper value" on himself. Young William Thornhill "had never learnt to reverence" his own heart and its impulses. So he "began to lose a regard for private interest"—a proper concern for his own good—"in universal sympathy," that seductive slogan. He loses also any power to discriminate between the false objects of charity and the deserving: "The slightest distress, whether real or fictitious, touched him to the quick, and his soul labored under a sickly sensibility of the miseries of others." Goldsmith distrusts sensibility even when it is healthy, since it can give rise to a debilitating sorrow for the woes of others that does neither the sufferer nor the person of sensibility any good. Miss Wilmot has "too much sensibility," so the Vicar kindly forbears to grieve her with the tale of his family's misfortunes (4:104). A diseased sensibility is likely to produce the melancholy brooding and early death that Goldsmith accords to Abner. Sir William Thornhill, who appears to be headed in the same direction, miraculously pulls himself together: he resolves simultaneously "to respect himself" and to restore his financial position. "For this purpose, in his own whimsical manner he travelled through Europe on foot, and now, though he has scarce attained the age of thirty, his circumstances are more affluent than ever" (4:30). If wealth can be gained by walking about the Continent, who would be poor? Sir William's experience belongs in the realm of fairy tale. George Primrose's is more normal: "travelling after Fortune is not the way to secure her" (4:106).

Poor Mr. Burchell still goes everywhere on foot, carrying the large staff for which (as Sophia tactlessly admits) the Primroses have laughed at him. Being laughed at is something that Burchell shares with his creator, together with his enjoyment of boisterous mirth and his affinity with children. "In general he [Burchell] was fondest of the company of children, whom he used to call harmless little men. He was famous . . . for singing them ballads, and telling them stories" (4:39). To be "fondest" of their company, to emphasize their harmlessness, suggests another aspect of timidity of temper, a shrinking from the pressures of the adult world. No one laughs at the patrician Sir William, who is famous not for ballad singing, but for public spirit.

He is a man "to whom senates listened with applause, and whom party heard with conviction" (4:168). He and his virtues are "universally known" (4:29). The magisterial, upright, great, and famous Sir William Thornhill is also, the fiction would have us believe, the relaxed, slightly eccentric, hay-making, fireside-enjoying Burchell. As we know from Reynolds, in real life Goldsmith found that the role of distinguished poet was incompatible with that of the easygoing, informal companion. Our sense of the discrepancy between Thornhill and Burchell testifies to the strain that such an accommodation imposes even in fiction.

In its lack of integration the Burchell/Thornhill character is representative of the book as a whole. It is less a question of the diversity of material that the novel contains—poetry and politics, confidence tricks and little fables—than that there is no single, or even dominant, manner of discourse. *The Vicar of Wakefield* is, as Clive Probyn says, "a novel of mixed modes."[21] As we are shown, in the first half of the book, the Vicar's descent into unworthiness, we are in a precisely and often very amusingly observed world of moral realism. At the same time we feel that we are reading an apologue, a schematic and unremitting demonstration that human hopes and wishes will inevitably be overthrown, that it is in their nature to be so. We seem at times to be reading an allegory, with a touch of the fairy story about it, in which Innocence and Simplicity, aided by Wise Power, triumph over Base Cunning. But we are also reading a Christian parable of "suffering and redemption."[22] It is undoubtedly to the novel's advantage that it is not as straightforward and singleminded as its own preface, and some of its critics, would make it. On the other hand, it has to be admitted that *The Vicar of Wakefield* is too protean to be fully satisfying.

Notes

[1] *Works* [*Collected Works of Oliver Goldsmith,* edited by Arthur Friedman, 5 vols. (Oxford: Clarendon Press, 1966)] 1:17, 57; see also 1:5, 21, 23.

[2] The novel is described as "this very singular Tale" in the *Monthly Review,* May 1766 (cited in *Works* 4:9). Schlegel and Carlyle saw it as romance and idyll; see G. S. Rousseau, ed., *Goldsmith: The Critical Heritage* (London: Routledge and Kegan Paul, 1974), 62, 280. For *The Vicar of Wakefield* as satire, see W. O. S. Sutherland, *The Art of the Satirist* (Austin: University of Texas Press, 1965), 84-91; Richard J. Jaarsma, "Satiric Intent in *The Vicar of Wakefield,*" *Studies in Short Fiction* 5 (1968): 331-41; Hopkins, *True Genius,* [Robert H. Hopkins, *The True Genus of Oliver Goldsmith* (Baltimore: Johns Hopkins University Press, 1969], chap. 5. Johnson's verdict is recorded by Fanny Burney; see *The Diary and Letters of Madame D'Arblay,* ed. Charlotte Barrett, with additional notes by Austin Dobson (London: Macmillan, 1904-5), 1:77.

For Ricardo Quintana's judgment see his *Oliver Goldsmith, a Georgian Study* (New York: Macmillan, 1967), 115.

[3] John Butt, *The Mid-Eighteenth Century,* edited and completed by Geoffrey Carnall (Oxford: Clarendon Press, 1979), 475.

[4] This contrast is pointed out by Oliver W. Ferguson in "Dr. Primrose and Goldsmith's Clerical Ideal," *Philological Quarterly* 54 (1975): 327. Others are noted by MacDonald Emslie, *Goldsmith: "The Vicar of Wakefield"* (London: Edward Arnold, 1963), 56, and Sven Bäckman, *This Singular Tale: A Study of "The Vicar of Wakefield" and Its Literary Background* (Lund, Sweden: C. W. K. Gleerup, 1971), 40 ff.

[5] D. W. Jefferson, "Observations on *The Vicar of Wakefield,*" *Cambridge Journal* 3 (1949-50): 626. Jefferson is discussing the general effect of conventional elements in the eighteenth-century novel.

[6] Sheldon Sacks, *Fiction and the Shape of Belief: A Study of Henry Fielding* (Berkeley and Los Angeles: University of California Press, 1964), 8.

[7] A cruder version of the whipper whipped occurs in a late essay, "A Register of Scotch Marriages" (*Works* 3:219).

[8] T. S. Eliot, "Poetry in the Eighteenth Century," in Boris Ford, ed., *The Pelican Guide to English Literature,* vol. 4, *From Dryden To Johnson* (Harmondsworth: Penguin, 1957), 275.

[9] Hopkins, *True Genius,* 204-5.

[10] Robert Hopkins is very severe on the Vicar for his use of the word "treasure"; see *True Genius,* 185-86, 210-12, 220. His argument is countered by Irvin Ehrenpreis, *Literary Meaning and Augustan Values* (Charlottesville: University of Virginia Press, 1974), 31-33, and by Thomas R. Preston, "The Uses of Adversity: Worldly Detachment and Heavenly Treasure in *The Vicar of Wakefield,*" *Studies in Philology* 81 (1984): 232-36.

[11] Frances Sheridan, *The Memoirs of Miss Sidney Bidulph* 3 vols. (London, 1761), 2:321-22; J. M. S. Tompkins, *The Popular Novel in England, 1770-1800* (London: Constable, 1932), 109.

[12] Sarah Fielding, *The Adventures of David Simple,* ed. Malcolm Kelsall (London: Oxford University Press, 1969), 311; see also pp. 384, 414.

[13] Sheridan, *Sidney Bidulph* 1:5; 2:102, 413.

[14] William Black, *Oliver Goldsmith* (London, 1878),

87; Martin C. Battestin, *The Providence of Wit: Aspects of Form in Augustan Literature and the Arts* (Oxford: Clarendon Press, 1974), 193-214.

15 Battestin, *Providence of Wit,* 208.

16 Eric Rothstein and Howard D. Weinbrot, "The Vicar of Wakefield, Mr. Wilmot, and the 'Whistonean Controversy,'" *Philological Quarterly* 55 (1976): 226-27.

17 Hopkins, *True Genius,* 191.

18 Wayne C. Booth, *The Rhetoric of Fiction* (Chicago: University of Chicago Press, 1961), 311 ff.

19 Emslie, *Vicar of Wakefield,* 24.

20 Hopkins, *True Genius,* 216.

21 Clive T. Probyn, *English Fiction of the Eighteenth Century, 1700-1789* (Harlow, Essex, England: Longman, 1987), 157.

22 Battestin, *Providence of Wit,* 196.

David Aaron Murray (essay date 1997)

SOURCE: "From Patrimony to Paternity in *The Vicar of Wakefield*" in *Eighteenth-Century Fiction,* Vol. 9, No. 3, April, 1997, pp. 327-36.

[*In the following essay, Murray contends that ultimately* The Vicar of Wakefield *concerns the nature of authority and transformation.*]

In his Advertisement to **The Vicar of Wakefield,** Oliver Goldsmith declared that his hero, the Reverend Dr Primrose, "unites in himself the three greatest characters upon earth; he is a priest, an husbandman, and the father of a family."[1] He is also the narrator of a story, and in all four of these positions of authority, Primrose is quixotically ineffective. As a priest he pursues his "peculiar tenet" (p. 13) of strict monogamy to the point of alienating parishioners, even before the initial loss of fortune that precipitates the novel's action. As a husbandman he proves to be comically inept in managing his resources. Throughout the first half of the novel he is an unreliable narrator. But it is in his role of father that the greatest disparity appears between his own image of himself and his actual authority.

Throughout the book Primrose attempts to exercise fatherly authority in three ways: through control of resources, through direct commands, and through wise adages. In all three ways he largely fails. He is "careless of temporalities" (p. 13) in the disposal of material resources, and his entrusting of the family fortune to an unscrupulous merchant precipitates the first of the chain of catastrophes that the family undergoes. His direct commands are ignored. Though he describes their new dwelling as "the little republic to which I give laws," most of his "edicts" are ignored or flouted. The very first Sunday after their removal becomes "a day of finery, which all my sumptuary edicts could not restrain" (p. 25). He admits at the beginning of chapter 10 that "all my long and painful lectures upon temperance, simplicity, and contentment, were entirely disregarded" (p. 49). When his wife and daughters revive the idea of riding a coach to church, Primrose resists for a while; but in the end "All these objections . . . were over-ruled; so that I was obliged to comply" (p. 52). At the very first meeting of the family with Squire Thornhill, Primrose's attempts to discourage their acquaintance are ignored: "As I did not approve of such disproportioned acquaintances, I winked upon my daughters in order to prevent their compliance; but my hint was countermanded by one from their mother" (p. 28).

Primrose's adages and maxims are about as effective as his commands. He admires Whiston's epitaph for his wife so much that he engraves one for his own wife as well, "in which I extolled her prudence, economy, and obedience till death." Although the Vicar is quite capable of sly humour at his family's expense, he seems sincere here. The epitaph is no mere reproof to a woman who proves vain and silly and exhibits little prudence in urging Olivia's match with Squire Thornhill at all costs. Instead, Primrose insists that the epitaph "answered several very useful purposes. It admonished my wife of her duty to me, and my fidelity to her; it inspired her with a passion for fame, and constantly put her in mind of her end" (p. 13).

One way of dealing with the discrepancies between Primrose's imagined (and prescribed) role and his actual behaviour is to stress the primarily satiric nature of the book. Either Goldsmith is poking fun at the bourgeoisie (especially hypocritical clergymen), or he is indulging in harmless self-parody. One may conclude, as has one of Goldsmith's biographers, that the discrepancies are humorous lapses in what, after all, is supposed to be merely satiric fun; to read into the novel sustained social criticism, as Ricardo Quintana does, is "perhaps to attribute to Goldsmith too deadly an intention"; perhaps Goldsmith is finally "amusing himself from beginning to end."[2]
A more sophisticated approach is provided by critics who themselves either admired the novel or sought to explain its enduring popularity throughout the nineteenth century and its appeal to such figures as Goethe. They have sought to minimize its discrepancies of plot and character by anchoring the novel in a controlling moral or didactic scheme whose coherence has hitherto been unrecognized. Martin Battestin's well-known argument for the pervasive influence of the Job parable on the story's structure is the model here.[3]

Raymond Hilliard, for example, reads the *Vicar of Wakefield* in the context of the conduct-books, popular throughout the eighteenth century, which prescribed Christian family roles and duties. According to Hilliard, Goldsmith's complex and humorous portrait of Primrose is a comment on the limitations of the humourless conduct manuals, but it nevertheless agrees with their vision of paternal love as a redeeming force.[4]

But the changes undergone by the Vicar in his "redemption of fatherhood" (as Hilliard calls it) may reflect not merely his own personal transformation from an imprudent overreacher to a humble pastor and father whose Job-like sufferings have purified him. Hilliard's focus on the traditional qualities of Christian fatherhood as outlined in the conduct manuals is not exactly wrong, but it ignores, I think, the extent to which the Vicar's fatherly authority is established on a new footing, rather than simply restored, by the end of the book. Primrose does not become the kind of father he tried and failed to be in the first part of the novel. Instead he re-establishes his authority as pastor and father on the basis of a new and sentimental ethic of sincerity, forged out of his identification with the prisoners in the crucial jail scene.

The transformation of Primrose's fatherly authority may be made clear by contrast with the account presented by John Bender in his essay on prison reform and *The Vicar of Wakefield.*[5] While I agree with Bender that the novel may yield some insight into larger changes in how authority and fatherhood were perceived in the late eighteenth century, I disagree with him completely about what those changes were. I propose that Richard Sennett's earlier work on the "public man" of the eighteenth century offers a much more compelling account of the changes that Bender wants to discuss.[6]

Bender, relying heavily upon Michel Foucault's well-known work on the early nineteenth-century penitentiary, attempts to extend Foucault's notion of the "surveillance principle" in Bentham's Panopticon in order to explain larger changes in government and social practice. As Bender has it, government was moving from "personal" modes of governance relying on fictions of personal dependence between squire and tenant which obscured class relations to "impersonal" modes of governance utilizing the surveillance principle. The ruptures and discontinuities in *The Vicar of Wakefield* reveal a Goldsmith torn between his conscious politics as a country conservative who idealized George III and his narrative practice, which reveals a nascent nineteenth-century omniscient narrator struggling against still-lingering conventions derived from romance elements in the plot.

Bender is eager to see nineteenth-century mimetic techniques, especially the omniscient narrator, as a reflection of the structures of domination inherent in the

penitentiary. But his arguments about "emerging" social forms and narrative techniques mean that he allows himself to explain Goldsmith's narrative conventions not on their own terms, but as embryonic or imperfect anticipations of the nineteenth-century omniscient narrator. In his eagerness to get to his real target—nineteenth-century realism—Bender strains his reading of Goldsmith's narrative techniques: "*The Vicar of Wakefield,* though written in the first person and not self-evidently part of the pre-history of free indirect discourse, nonetheless reaches toward this technique. Primrose's private observations take on the perspective of impersonal narration, though hidden under the first-person."[7] This is simply a piece of mystification; one might as well say that black is hidden under white.

But Bender's primary disability, in my view, is an uncritical acceptance of certain post-Romantic conceptions of what "personal" and "impersonal" mean. Bender might have avoided this error had he been familiar with Richard Sennett's *The Fall of Public Man* (1974). In that earlier work, Sennett subjected the beliefs underlying the modern use of these terms to a searching analysis, employing a social history of the eighteenth century in which the terms are almost exactly the opposite of Bender's. In Sennett's account, mid-eighteenth-century London enjoyed a rich civic life in coffee houses, theatres, public parks, and private clubs, based on meaningfully *impersonal* codes that allowed strangers to interact without inquiring into each others' backgrounds.

Sennett's agenda is to attack the post-Romantic "intimate ethic," which, in his view, impairs political life by transforming practical questions of group interest into questions of personality. Far from viewing the post-Romantic era as one of increasing im-personality, Sennett instead sees a social landscape in which private personality has invaded the public realm, transforming questions of political interest into questions of belief in authoritative personalities based on their personal qualities. Sennett complains that

> The reigning belief today is that closeness between persons is a moral good. The reigning aspiration today is to develop individual personality through experience of closeness and warmth with others. The reigning myth today is that the evils of society can all be understood as evils of impersonality, alienation, and coldness.[8]

The mid-eighteenth century, for Sennett, was the great age of sociability precisely *because* its civic life rested on humane artifice and impersonality. "Wearing a mask is the essence of civility,"[9] and the eighteenth century was the great age of civility precisely because it was an age of masks and disguises.

The wearing of masks extended to relations based upon authority. What Bender calls "personal relations" between patriarchal landowners and dependents, which used archaic forms of address and ceremony, were constructs whose impersonality was evident. As E.P. Thompson remarks (on his way to conclusions different from mine), "the same man who touches his forelock to the squire by day—and who goes down in history as an example of deference—may kill his sheep, snare his pheasants or poison his dogs at night."[10] The dependent's daytime deference was not simply a lie. The role had its own validity. Paternalism, whether the king's or a landowner's, was a public fiction whose roles were fixed by convention and could be stepped into by any petitioner or benevolent squire. Bender calls these relations "personal," but they are products of an ethos far different from the intimate, authentic, and anti-theatrical one we appeal to today when we speak of "personal" relationships.

In *Authority,* Sennett provides a more detailed discussion of the changes in patriarchal authority during the end of the eighteenth century. What Thompson loosely calls the "paternalistic" society of the mid-eighteenth century should more properly, according to Sennett, be described as *patrimonial.* In a patrimonial system authority is based on the transmission of property from father to son. Not only large property owners but even guild tradesmen passed on their positions to their sons. Towards the end of the eighteenth century the patrimonial system began to break up under the impact of industrialism. A paternalistic society, in Sennett's more precise usage of the term, is one in which "the patrimony itself does not exist."[11] In the early nineteenth century:

> the material organization of life was in so much flux that a man was in danger who based his claims to power on his ability to pass on a fixed amount of property to someone else. . . . If a male were to legitimate his power, he would have to do so in terms of symbols and beliefs cut loose from such material tests. . . . In a paternalistic society no father can guarantee to his children a known place in the world; he can only act protectively.[12]

Sennett does not use *The Vicar of Wakefield* as an example here, but this passage is a good statement of the way in which the Vicar's authority changes by the end of the novel. Primrose "dies" as a patrimonial father who attempts to exercise authority based on control of resources, but is "resurrected" as a paternalistic one (in Sennett's usage) whose authority comes from his ability to "act protectively" towards the prisoners and, finally, his family.

The initial disconnection between the Vicar's public and private selves both mirrors and parodies the split between public and private that was accepted as normative at the time. The split is personified by his double—Burchell/Sir William. Burchell personifies the potency of action that Primrose lacks. The two men share many characteristics. They are both plagued by greedy relatives in the periods of their initial prosperity. Primrose's "cousins, too, even to the fortieth remove, all remembered their affinity, without any help from the Herald's office, and came very frequently to see us" (pp. 9-10). In describing his alter ego Sir William Thornhill, Burchell uses language that could easily apply to both men: "He loved all mankind; for fortune prevented him from knowing that there were rascals . . . his profusions began to impair his fortune . . . though he talked like a man of sense, his actions were those of a fool" (p. 21).

It is true that the failings of the two men are not entirely similar. Thornhill's main failing has been an excessive benevolence, while Primrose's has been lack of prudence. His protest to the children after the initial loss of fortune that "no prudence of ours could have prevented our late misfortune" does not square with his quite evident imprudence, and pride as well. His entrusting of the family fortune to an untrustworthy merchant is hardly the result of prudence, since during his later abortive trip to the fair, he will admit that "this was one of the first mercantile transactions of my life," yet he insists "I had no doubt about acquitting myself with reputation" (p. 66).

The Job-like trials which Primrose undergoes in descending degrees do not simply chastise him; they integrate his personality and transform him into an effective authority who, in the prison, is finally able to act as the paternal figure he has presented himself as being throughout the novel. His ability to act authoritatively increases in tandem with his increasing reliability as a narrator. Hints of his increasing effectiveness appear before his incarceration; he is able, for example, to save his two youngest children from their burning house, in contrast to his earlier paralysis and displacement by Burchell when Sophia was in danger of drowning. When he sets out to reform the prisoners, he is at first mocked and derided; but he persists, "perfectly sensible that what was ridiculous in my attempt, would excite mirth only the first or second time, while what was serious would be permanent" (p. 148). What Primrose here says about himself may be applied to the novel as a whole, for Goldsmith evidently does not intend his satire to apply to the principles that the Vicar articulates.

Bender is right when he says, "In his small nation, the prison, the vicar personally displaces—and then enacts laws to replace—the structures of authority that prevail elsewhere in the world of the novel and that have reduced him to his plight as a prisoner. He acts to retell the story by a different set of rules—those of the penitentiary."[13] But the new rules of the penitentiary turn out not to be "impersonal" at all in Bender's sense; quite the opposite. The Vicar's new authority as narrator and patriarch is sincere and sentimental, not impersonal. Sennett makes clear the distinction that Bender misses: "In the *ancien régime,* public experience was connected to the formation of social order; in the last century, public experience came to be connected with the *formation of personality*" (emphasis added).[14]

Dissociated from his patrimony and all temporal advantages, Primrose, *because sincere,* can now present himself to his fellow prisoners as an authoritative personality: "I previously observed, that no other motive but their welfare could induce me to this; that I was their fellow prisoner, and now got nothing by preaching" (p. 144). Since the Vicar likewise has nothing to hope for by misleading himself about events (such as Burchell's letter), so he has also become a more reliable narrator. For Bender, "the impersonal principle of inspection . . . is enacted as the story of a personal intervention by Dr. Primrose."[15] But it is precisely the ties of sympathy and sentiment that allow Primrose to assume an authoritative role among the prisoners. His authority, based as it is on his *own transformation,* affects the prisoners interiorly as the authority of the jailer and magistrate cannot.

The motif of disguise is crucially bound up with the novel's exploration of what constitutes a legitimate authority. For the first half of the novel, Primrose is, in a sense, disguised from himself. Sir William Thornhill is disguised as Burchell. Mrs Primrose and the two daughters attempt a kind of disguise by dressing above their station, and the Squire's two disguised prostitutes are comments on where such dressing may lead. The only legitimate authority who disguises himself is Burchell, and the purpose of his disguise is precisely to find an authentic relationship with a woman that is based on sentiment rather than appearances. To put it another way, Burchell's wealth and position actually function as a kind of disguise that he must lose before he can find his "true" self. Even then, it is only when rejoined with the Vicar that Sir William is able to recognize his nephew's conduct for what it is. His obtuseness has been implausible up to this point, but if he and the Vicar are regarded as two halves of a fractured authority figure, then their reunion contains a logic that depends on something deeper than plausibility.

The most intriguing episode involving disguise is the seeming digression in which Primrose, returning from a fruitless effort to track down his recently eloped daughter Olivia, is befriended by "a very well-drest gentleman" who invites him to his manor for dinner in order to continue a political debate begun in a tavern. As the debate becomes heated, Primrose is on the point of being ejected from the house when the real master and mistress return, revealing that Primrose's host was "all this while only the butler, who, in his master's absence, had a mind to cut a figure, and be for a while the gentleman himself" (p. 99). The butler's appearance is totally believable in its own terms; the Vicar is even forced to admit that "he talked politics as well as most country gentlemen do" (p. 99). Although the scene is comic, the Vicar cannot be accused of the same kind of imprudence he displays in being gulled by Jenkinson. The arrival of the Arnolds, the real master and mistress, prefigures the dénouement. In both cases, the Vicar's disinterested fortitude is rewarded by the marvellous intervention of authority figures who reveal the truth of a situation and vindicate the Vicar.

Jenkinson is an example of the kind of trickster who could flourish in an age when social appearances carried their own code of public belief. "I was thought cunning from my very childhood," he tells Primrose; "at twenty, though I was perfectly honest, yet every one thought me so cunning, that not one would trust me. Thus I was at last obliged to turn sharper in my own defence" (p. 146). The fact that his appearance is untrustworthy not only does not prevent him from making a living by deception, it forces him into it! Jenkinson must become what he seems to be, because social life depends so much on appearances.

Beneath the humorous paradox lies part of the truth of Primrose's assumption of his authority. Jenkinson is obviously able to inspire trust, but this trust is made up of appearances, of impersonal codes of dress and behaviour. When Moses confronts Jenkinson in prison, he asks, "'I can't help wondering at what you could see in my face, to think me a proper mark for deception.' . . . 'My dear sir,' returned the other, 'it was not your face, but your white stockings and the black ribband in your hair, which allured me'" (p. 145). Although Sennett praises the coffee-house era as a privileged moment of liberating "impersonality," it is clear that Goldsmith distrusts social interaction and authority that is based on appearances. An intimate ethic based on sincere self-disclosure must replace the old code of impersonal appearances, so hospitable to frauds and tricksters.

Prison proves to be the place in which the new sentimental ethic of intimacy and sincerity achieves its first realization. It is noteworthy that Goldsmith stages his "trial" scene within the prison, instead of removing it to a courtroom, as he could easily have done. Although Sir William is regularly—and not incorrectly—seen as the *deus ex machina* who is in charge of the dénouement, it is interesting that he also must learn the true situation about his nephew's conduct from the Vicar. In the first half of the novel it is Burchell who appears all-knowing and whose hints Primrose and his family ignore. In the second half, it is Sir William who seems implausibly ignorant for a *deus ex machina.* Though Primrose remarks at the moment of Sir William's uncovering that "Never before had I seen any thing so truly majestic as the air he assumed upon this occasion" (p. 169), it is Primrose himself who seems more majestic.

Sir William has been suffering from his own disconnection; the man "to whose virtues and singularities scarce any were strangers" (p. 170) has in fact been a stranger throughout the book. Sir William has been praised as a material benefactor, but it is the Vicar who effects the transformation of the prison from a place of external punishment to a place "of penitence and solitude, where the accused might be attended by such as could give them repentance if guilty"—and here appears a seeming lapse—*"or new motives to virtue if innocent"* (p. 149).

The Vicar's awkward generalization from his own experience inadvertently exposes the claims that an authority based on personality can make. Prison can improve the innocent as well as the guilty! With this statement we are well into a sentimental ethos. The restored Primrose embodies a new principle of authority, one that elicits a trust based on the authority's own sincere self-transformation. *The Vicar of Wakefield* initiates a search for new forms of legitimate authority, then provides a fantasy resolution in the union of Sir William and Primrose. This accounts for the sentimentality that proves deeper than comedy and explains the work's enduring popularity throughout the nineteenth century.

Notes

[1] Oliver Goldsmith, *The Vicar of Wakefield* (London: Oxford University Press, 1974). References are to this edition.

[2] A. Lytton Sells, *Oliver Goldsmith: His Life and Works* (London: George Allen and Unwin, 1974), p. 270.

[3] Martin Battestin, *The Providence of Wit: Aspects of Form in Augustan Literature and the Arts* (Oxford: Clarendon Press, 1974).

[4] Raymond Hilliard, "The Redemption of Fatherhood in *The Vicar of Wakefield*," *Studies in English Literature* 23 (1983), 465-80.

[5] John Bender, "Prison Reform and the Sentence of Narration in *The Vicar of Wakefield*," in *The New Eighteenth Century: Theory, Politics, English Literature*, ed. Felicity Nussbaum and Laura Brown (New York: Methuen, 1987).

[6] Richard Sennett, *The Fall of Public Man: On the Social Psychology of Capitalism* (New York: Knopf, 1974).

[7] Bender, pp. 184-85.

[8] Sennett, p. 259.

[9] Sennett, p. 264.

[10] E.P. Thompson, "Patrician Society, Plebeian Culture," *Journal of Social History* 7 (1974), 382-405.

[11] Richard Sennett, *Authority* (New York: Knopf, 1980), p. 53.

[12] Sennett, *Authority,* p. 54.

[13] Bender, p. 180.

[14] Sennett, *Fall,* p. 24.

[15] Bender, p. 181.

Raymond Adolph Prier (essay date 1997)

SOURCE: "Charlotte's 'Vicar' and Goethe's Eighteenth-Century Tale about Werther" in *Narrative Ironies,* edited by A. Prier and Gerald Gillespie, Rodopi, 1997, pp. 283-97.

[*In the essay below, Prier argues that Johann Wolfgang von Goethe's novel* Die Leiden des jungends Werther *was influenced by Goldsmith's* The Vicar of Wakefield.]

> "Indeed, pappa," replied Olivia, " . . . I have read a great deal of controversy. I have read the disputes between Thwackum and Square; the controversy between Robinson Crusoe and Friday the savage, and I am now employed in reading the controversy in Religious courtship."
>
> *The Vicar of Wakefield*[1]

Olivia reads books, and the Vicar, seemingly satisfied with his daughter's intellectual qualifications in this instance, sends her off to help his wife concoct a "gooseberry-pye" (45), an act perhaps a bit more culinary than Charlotte's cutting bread and butter, but just as ironically amusing if one takes the position of early nineteenth-century English wags. Goethe read books too, perhaps even the same books as Olivia. The one book, however, that probably exerted the greatest influence over his own novelistic art was one Olivia could not have read because she was part and parcel of its fiction: *The Vicar of Wakefield.*

The nature of this influence is revealed in an experience of his youth he relates in the last third of the tenth book of *Dichtung und Wahrheit (Poetic Fiction and Truth).*[2] There he examines an escapade orchestrated by a certain Weyland that validates the title of his autobiography as does no other: a disguised visit to the country vicar Brion's family in Sesenheim in which, with minor variation, the members become identified with the family characters of Goldsmith's ironic tale. The older daughter becomes Olivia. The younger daughter, Goethe's beloved Friedricke, becomes Sophia (a name well-worn in *Tom Jones* and in the German form "Sophie" also Charlotte's younger sister in *Werther*— one indication among many that Goethe never wanted to identify totally with his novel's main character). The son becomes Moses; Weyland, by his own design, a better-behaved Mr. Thornhill; and Goethe himself, as if for those of us interested in which character in the *Vicar of Wakefield* he realized was the author-narrator, Mr. Burchell. Primrose's son George in Goldsmith's novel shares his name with the son of an innkeeper, whose clothes Goethe-Burchell slips on to examine Weyland's merry prank. Thus living out Goldsmith's artful irony, disguised and fully reflecting on the events themselves, Goethe became other than what he was. Thus too did he experience life as what even Aristotle might have eventually construed as the supreme irony: a real fiction.

Wherein, however, lies the quick of this experience? Goethe answers in a way present critics might wish to ponder:

> Schreiben ist ein Missbrauch der Sprache, stille für sich lesen ein trauriges Surrogat der Rede. Writing is a misuse of speech; to read for oneself in silence, a dismal surrogate for conversation.

> (WA *Dichtung und Wahrheit 10* I.27.373)

In Sesenheim, he marvels at his "Sophia's" way with words. More specifically, he marvels at her *voice:*

> Es war mir sehr angenehm, stillschweigend der *Schilderung zuzuhören,* die sie von der kleinen *Welt* machte, in der sie sich bewegte, und von denen Menschen, die sie besonders schätzte. *Sie brachte mir dadurch einen klaren und zugleich so liebenswürdigen Begriff von ihrem Zustande bei,* der sehr *wunderlich* auf mich wirkte. . . . Sie wurde zuletzt immer redseliger und ich immer stiller. Es hörte sich ihr gar so gut zu, und da ich nur ihre *Stimme* vernahm . . . so war es mir, als ob ich in ihr Herz sähe. . . .

> (It was very pleasant for me to hear in silence the *descriptive representation* she made of the small *world* in which she moved and of those people she especially treasured. She imparted *to me thereby a clear and simultaneously very amiable notion of her condition* that worked in me in a exceedingly *wondrous* way. . . . She became in the end evermore talkative; I, always more silent. She was a delight to listen to, and since I heard her *voice* . . . thus it appeared to me as if I saw into her heart. . . .

> (WA *D & W 10* I. 27.355-56, emphasis mine)[3]

To stress even more strongly the centrality of the narrating voice as character in his fictive-made-real-made-

narrative prank on the German vicar's family, Goethe tells us that he told aloud *in his own voice* "The New Melusina," a tale he later introduced into *Wilhelm Meisters Wanderjahre,* and the name character of which he slips into *Werther* (AV 6a/b).[4] He does not, however, insert the tale into the text at hand, not because we could find it by turning to the *Wanderjahre, but for fear that he might destroy* "the rustic reality and simplicity, which pleasingly *surrounds* us here" ("den ländlichen Wirklichkeit und Einfalt, die uns hier gefällig *umgibt*") (WA *D & W 10* 1.27.372, emphasis mine). "Sophia's" voice has recreated a world, just as he recreates worlds in his own tales. In the telling of tales lie the human sympathies, the worlds shared between the author and his audience, between the narrator and his character, and between the characters themselves. These comprise the "uns" to which Goethe refers above: not only the readers of *Dichtung und Wahrheit,* but also the *readers as participants in the fictive, textually-induced reality of Goethe's German vicarage that surrounds them.* Goethe's ironic "vicarian disguise," his voice, and that of "Sophia" has drawn us into a world of narrative that, hence, must also be somehow "ironic." Through her and his "descriptive representation," *through their voices,* we enter into their conditions, see into their hearts, and know what tensions, contradictions, and differences lie about them.

Sesenheim, then, came to signify for Goethe much more than an ironic prank for his own and others' amusement, for from it also sprang the world of Werther's Waldheim, where was lodged the irony of fictive truth. Therein Goethe propelled a voice, incapable of any ironic perception itself, and forced us to look within its character's heart. For those inhabiting the eighteenth-century, ironically perceived world *about* him, Werther's world is veiled at best, at worst locked. Thus, in the relationships between Werther's voice and especially the voices of his beloved and of the narrator, Goethe develops a hybrid sense of irony in the novel. His irony is not constructed upon Quintilian's simple rhetorical notion of *dissimulatio,* nor upon Dr. Johnson's simple "mode of speech in which the meaning is contrary to the words." It does, however, involve *the relationship* of voices in the novel that are in conflict and exist there, at best, in a state of only partially mutual understanding. As the reader of Goethe's *Werther* understands these voices and their relationships and as that reader becomes aware of the place of the allusions to Goldsmith's *Vicar* and, for that matter, other extraneous texts, he too will become aware of that irony Goethe understood emitting from those fictively real voices in Sesenheim. He grasped an irony which he later averred, is "hazardous" indeed (WA *Farbenlehre* II.l.xii).[5]

There are several general resemblances between Goldsmith's *Vicar* and Goethe's *Werther:* Primrose's and Werther's pastoral notions of country life; the harsh injustice they suffer at the hands of a corrupt and corrupting society; "the chaotic pressures and confusions within a society that liked to see itself in orderly terms";[6] and the honored role as father of the family that both Primrose and Charlotte's father, Amtmann S., share. But a specific correspondence that, like Olivia's reading habits, has to do with books, yet like Goethe's experience in Sesenheim deals with voices and worlds, lies between Goldsmith's "A Ballad" (chapter 7) and Goethe's translation of Ossianic song, both voiced, at least in part, by wandering female narrators, separated from the world and suffering the loss of the beloved:

> "Turn, gentle hermit of the dale,
>   And guide my lonely way,
> To where yon taper cheers the vale,
>   With hospitable ray.
> "For here forlorn and lost I tread,
>   With fainting steps and slow;
> Where wilds immeasurably spread,
>   Seem lengthening as I go."
>
> (Goldsmith, 47)

Goethe and Macpherson eliminate any human presence on the order of the hermit and significantly isolate and internalize the narrating voice of the wandering female lover, disassociating it completely from the world of the other human beings:

> "Es ist Nacht!—ich bin allein, verlohren auf dem stürmischen Hügel. Der Wind saust im Gebirge, der Strom heult den Felsen hinab. Keine Hütte schützt mich vor dem Regen [,] mich Verlassne auf dem stürmischen Hügel."
>
> (AV 137a/b)

And Macpherson's "translation from the original," printed as a song, perhaps emitted from some Ossianic collective voice, is without Goldsmith's immediately personalizing and "envoicing" quotation marks or those of Goethe introduced in the revised version of *Werther* (compare AV 136a and b). Macpherson:

> It is night; I am alone, forlorn on the hill of storms. The wind is heard in the mountain. The torrent pours down the rock. No hut receives me from the rain; forlorn on the hill of the winds.[7]

Goethe's translation from the English raised a sticky narratological issue that would plague him for the rest of his life: the attitude of an author toward his text and the characters therein. Goldsmith's poem is his own. He indicates that such might be the case by introducing it into his novel through the narrating voice of Mr. Burcell, who, in learned disquisition, mouths what we may learn from another source was Goldsmith's own poetic taste.[8] Primrose, the gullible, naively perverse butt of Goldsmith's authorial stance, *does not voice the poem,* and chapter 8 of the novel closes with an ironic and characteristically eighteenth-century comment on the relationship of the sexes:

> But as men are most capable of distinguishing merit in women, so the ladies often form the truest judgments of us. The two sexes seem placed as spies upon each other, and are furnished with different abilities, adapted for mutual inspection. (52-53)

Goethe's authorial relationship to and treatment of his prose lyric and protagonist are strikingly different. By the very fact that he, as author, has translated a then-famous historical model and subsequently set it into the voice of his first-person narrator, he forces his audience to conclude that Werther and he are one in the explosively central issue at hand: the creation of the song. Goldsmith works to avoid any possible narrational confusion between the author and his protagonist. His poem is much more an integral part of his text because, in maintaining his distance from his primary narrator, he has guaranteed a consistency in his own voice and in those of his characters. No such sensible distance is exemplified in Goethe's translation of Ossian. In fact its force lies in what seems a confusion of the author and his protagonist. The result, one must admit, however, is riveting, for it opens us to Werther's world: after the long insertion of the Ossianic threnody, instead of a statement on the mutually judgmental relationship between men and women or the like, quite the opposite takes place: Goethe's Charlotte bursts into tears, and Werther rushes off forever departed from his beloved, intent on suicide:

> Lebe wohl, Lotte! auf ewig lebe wohl!
>
> (Farewell Lotte! Eternally farewell!)
>
> (AV 146a/b)

Goethe has here broken decisively with the eighteenth-century ironic tradition, and the reader can afford to be amused only at the expense of a lack of human understanding. No human being reading *Werther* can avoid the overwhelming seduction of the protagonist's voice and in that way ignore his world. But is Werther's lyric voice the only voice in the novel as a whole? No, for, although the narrating voice would seem to be internalized totally within the novel's title character, another narrator always stands behind it, one whose world is distinctly separated from Werther's: "der Herausgeber an den Leser" ("the editor to the reader"). Goethe amplified this view considerably in the revision of his original text.

Why did Goldsmith's simpler irony demand no such voice, no such narrational intrusions? Why does Goldsmith never break the illusion of his first-person protagonist-narrator, whereas Goethe aborts it so decisively?

Lilian Furst, in a perceptive reading of *Werther,* cut to

the heart of what must have been Goethe's complexly ironic intention when she characterized Werther as predominantly the man of sensibility and Charlotte as, for the most part, the woman of sense.[9] Thus, she suggests that in spite of what Werther in his own voice might feel or fantasize about his beloved, the author, in league with Charlotte and, by extension, other voices, endeavors to sketch distinctions the hero does not.

But let us return to Goethe's text. Part I, June 16th: Charlotte has been reading a novel she dislikes and hands it back to one of the ladies in the carriage on the way to the "Klopstock" ball. This novel has been one in a line of at least two unacceptable ones the ladies have supplied for her *amusement*. We are only *told* that she cites the others. Werther is astonished by what *he* takes to be her intelligence in the matter. *Charlotte* illuminates further her critical point of view:

> Wie ich jünger war, sagte sie, liebte ich nichts so sehr als Romane. Weiss Gott wie wohl mir's war, wenn ich mich Sonntags so in ein Eckchen setzen, und mit ganzem Herzen an dem Glück und Unstern einer Miss Jenny Theil nehmen konnte.

> ("When I was younger," she said, "I enjoyed nothing more than novels. God knows how content I was when on Sundays I could settle myself down in a little corner and partake wholeheartedly in the fortune and misfortune of a Miss Jenny.")

(AV 22a/b)

Charlotte describes herself here as a naive, perhaps even gullible reader of a text written on the order of Richardson's *Pamela. But that was in the past.* Charlotte is not finished with her discourse on the novel.

Claiming that she has no time to read in such a way *now,* she declares, in a manner both reflective and philosophical, that her favorite author is one in whom she finds her world reflected or taken up again ("in dem ich meine *Welt* wieder finde"—AV 231/b, emphasis mine), with whom things occur as they do *about* her ("bei dem es zugeht wie *um* mich"—AV 23a/b, emphasis mine), and, yet, whose history or story (*Geschichte*) becomes to her as interesting and heartfelt as her own domestic life, which is no Paradise ("kein Paradies"—AV 23a/b), but on the whole a source of unspeakable happiness. This time Werther cites her example: ***The Vicar of Wakefield.*** What does this woman of sense see in Goldsmith's ironic masterpiece? It is never completely revealed in the body of Goethe's text because, faced with the "truth" (*Wahrheit*) *for him* in what she says, Werther in an unreflective, epistolary voice intrudes in characteristic consternation: "Ich bemühte mich meine Bewegungen über diese Worte zu verbergen" ("I did everything I could to cover my agitation at these words"—AV 23a/b).

The voice of the editor-narrator, however, is not eclipsed, but returns at this point after two previous incursions into the text: at the inception of the novel when he admonishes that the book and not Werther be our friend (AV 2a/b) and when in a glossing footnote he advises that:

> Der Leser wird sich keine Mühe geben die hier genannten Orte zu suchen; man hat sich genöthigt gesehen, die im Originale befindlichen wahren Nahmen zu verändern.

> (The reader need not waste his time seeking the places named here; one has seen it necessary to alter the existing true names in [Werther's] original text.)

(AV 121/b)

In the present instance, before Lotte's disquisition on the novel and after Werther's enthusiastic abortion of her views, two more glosses in the form of footnotes adorn the text and are identical in both the original and second version: the first, in which the voice of an impersonal third-person narrator ("Man sieht sich genöthiget," "One sees that it is necessary"—AV 22a/b) deletes the names of the rejected novels with the ironic, clearly tongue-in-cheek excuse that no author would care about the judgement "of just one girl" ("eines einzelnen Mädchens") and "an unstable young person" ("eines jungen, unstäten Menschen") (AV 22a/b); and again impersonally, the second:

> Man hat auch hier die Nahmen einiger vaterländischen Autoren weggelassen. Wer Theil an Lottchens Beyfalle hat, wird es gewiss an seinem Herzen fühlen, wenn er diese Stelle lesen sollte, und sonst braucht es ja niemand zu wissen.

> (One has also omitted here the name of several native authors. He who shares in little Lotte's approval will certainly feel it in his heart if he should have read this passage [in the above text]—and otherwise no one surely needs to know.)

(AV 23a/b)

What is this collusion of cognoscenti? What do they share that others like Werther, do not? *An appreciation of an eighteenth-century, ironic point of view.* And to what end? The way a tale is told and the way, subsequently, the author construes the voices and lives of his characters. Charlotte is no naive girl snuggled in the corner reading a book. She tells openly that hers is an experience involving an ironic and complex relationship among a text, reality, and our text at hand. She is in league with the playfully ironic editor-narrator. He is of her world.

Thus Charlotte's voice in *Werther* promulgates the ironically constructed world that the author creates about her as both she and he read, a world that is not Werther's. The *process* of her and our experience lies lodged in her own discourse on the novel: Goethe allows her to "find again her own *Welt*" through an author, "with whom events occur as they do about me" ("bey dem es zugeht wie um mich"). The communication between the two worlds is open and mutually cultivating.

Werther does not and cannot inhabit Charlotte's world, for no similarly imaginative, ironic experience applies to his voice, to this man of sensibility. Further clues to a harsh difference in perspective between Werther and the life and world of his beloved lie in editorial intrusions throughout the original novel and the new matter Goethe added in the revision of 1787. Two major examples of "reconstruction" come immediately to the reader's eye: the incorporation of the *Bauernbursch* (peasant lad) throughout the revised novel and the telltale reworking of the long editorial interruption.

The naive reading-public, in the main no different from today's, had misread Charlotte's discourse on the novel and, for that matter, the novel itself in its 1774 version. It should surprise no one, therefore, that Goethe might rewrite his original text to stress even more carefully the tale about Werther's alien and disintegrating world (*Welt*) and the striking opposition of the ironic world surrounding his *Unwelt.*

The *Bauernbursch,* an absolute antithesis to the peasant George of Drusenheim, just outside Goethe's German vicarage in *Dichtung und Wahrheit,* is that naive chap in love with an older, wealthy woman. He appears first in the new letter of Part I, May 30th in the revised text (AV 16b). He reappears in the revised Part II within the letter of September 4th as the sorry figure now deprived of love through the manipulations of his unscrupulous mistress and her covetous brother (AV 93-96b). Werther's voice in this new text undergoes a self-analysis that is central not only to any desire on Goethe's part to dissociate himself from the folly of his main character, but especially to reemphasize the isolation of Werther's voice and world. While professing an expected identification with the *Bauernbursch,* Werther, nevertheless, exposes the "difficult" social position of the woman involved: the brother's professed claims to her estate. All this once again lodges Werther in consternation, but, from the reader's point of view, a very revealing one:

> Was ich dir erzähle, ist nicht ubertrieben, nichts verzärtelt, ja ich darf wohl sagen, schwach schwach hab' ich's *erzählt* und vergröbert hab ichs, indem ichs mit unsern hergebrachten sittlichen Worten *vorgetragen* habe.

(What I tell you is not exaggerated, in nothing

overindulged. Yes, I might indeed venture to say, "Weakly, weakly have I *narrated* my tale and have made it coarse in so far as I have *reported* it with the language of our conventional morality.")

(AV 95b, emphasis mine)

We discover that the *Bauernbursch* murders the new lover of his ex-mistress in the revised "Editor to the Reader" (AV 119-21b). Most of the telling takes place in the context of a confrontation between, on the one hand, Lotte's father, the novel's Primrose, and Albert, by now in the novel Charlotte's husband, and, on the other, Werther. The father and Albert succeed in maintaining that all concerned must heed the law. In short, *they maintain a moral and ethical world within and without the Bauernbursch that Werther cannot.* And, in a quotation out of the mouth of Werther and set off from the rest of the text, the editor-narrator makes this clear:

> "Du bist micht zu retten Unglücklicher! ich sehe wohl dass wir nicht zu retten sind."
>
> ("Unfortunate man, thou art not to be saved! I see clearly that we are not to be saved.")

(AV 121B)

The voices of the father, Albert, and the editor in the revision ultimately stress what in fictive reality must be the narrative context.

In the revised novel's second book, Goethe's additions or "narrative corrections" deal with the direct clarification in Werther's penned voice of his wretched isolation, his delusion as seen on the part of the narrator, the world of Charlotte and Albert, and the reader, and the now inherently alien and destructive presence of Nature (the new letters of Part II, February 8th, June 16th, September 4th, September 5th, October 27th, November 26th). Also added are a Catullan-charged, sexually obsessive description of Charlotte-Lesbia with her bird (Part II, September 12th); a pathetically rhetorical, but tellingly petrarchistic reduction of Werther's world to "a whole litany of antitheses" (Part II, November 22nd); and, most importantly, a rewritten and greatly extended intrusion by the editor-narrator.

The editorial intrusion of the original completes the novel and arises after all letters by date cease. The intrusion of the revision consists of both narrative comment and four dated or timed letters. Two of the dated letters, much crazed, appear outside the editor-narrator's purview in the original version (Part II, December 8th and December 17th, revised to December 12th and December 14th and hence more intense because of their temporal proximity). The first concerns Werther's suicidal bout with an equally encrazed Nature; the second, Werther's long-overdue realization of the suicidal lust he possesses for his beloved.

Why has the voice of an editorializing narrator co-opted these two letters? To prove that the editor's voice is really only Werther's (Blackall, 44-45) or to describe more strongly the distinction between a more conventional eighteenth-century *Unwelt* and Werther's "unworldly" isolation? Goethe's revisions of his text in this matter and in others suggest strongly the second reason. The revised editor-narrator also accomplishes Goethe's goal by voicing actions on the part of Charlotte and Albert that differ subtly from those in the original text. In general, the husband and wife are drawn more decisively into the context of an even happier, more "vicarian" and conversational eighteenth-century world than Goethe had originally constructed for them. Both versions illuminate this world in which

> . . . eine gute Freundinn . . . machte die Unterhaltung bey Tische erträglich; *man* zwang sich, *man* redete, *man* erzählte, *man* vergass sich.

> (. . . a good woman friend . . . made the conversation at table bearable: *one* forced oneself [to cope], *one* spoke, *one* narrated stories, *one* forgot oneself.)
>
> (AV 152a/b, emphasis mine)

The "new" editor-narrator, true to the now dangerously ironic separation or relationship of the characters' worlds, no longer voices Albert's antipathy (*Widerwillen)* and mistrust (*Mistrauen)* toward Werther (compare AV 116-117a and 116-117b), but only his "overt dislike of the act of suicide ("einen entschiedenen Widerwillen gegen die That"), "a strange circumstance" ("ein sonderbarer Umstand") that Goethe's revised text finds him "forced to add" (150b). There also appears in the narrative context a new set of voices in the form of "Albert's friends," who now offer a much more neutral interpretation of Charlotte's husband: "einen reinen, ruhigen Mann der nun eines langgewünschten Glückes teilhaftig geworden" ("a pure, quiet man, who had come to partake of a happiness for which he had long wished") (compare AV 117a and 117b). In the case of Charlotte, the "new" editor-narrator describes her in a decidedly more sympathetic light. Goethe adds two paragraphs in the editor-narrator's voice extolling the propriety of her character (AV 128-129b). No longer are we told directly of the internal struggle between her will and "the fire of Werther's embraces." Such a condition turns into merely a possibility and assumes the form of a question. The original text had extolled her pride in her own actions that caused her to reflect with antipathy (*Widerwillen)* upon the guilt (*Schuld)* of Werther and upon her hatred of him. Werther's *Schuld* is conspicuously absent in Goethe's revision (compare AV 149a and 149b). In short, both Albert and Charlotte react less to and, hence, become very much less a part of Werther's self-narrated world. In the novel's last pages, Albert's incapacity to follow the corpse and his wife's life-threatening crisis occur, not in a context

of guilt, but of human sympathy for a man whose world they knew not at all.

Thus in *Werther* Goethe has elevated the irony of the eighteenth-century novel into an irony of fictive truth, a dangerous world of voices whose tales are at best only partially understood by the characters and narrators within the novel, but felt with a troubled sense of resignation by the reader. Always Goethe validates his irony with texts extrinsic to his own. Always they aid the reader in his quest for the "real."

The most powerful text behind *Werther* is **The Vicar of Wakefield,** and I have already referred to Macpherson's *Ossian* in terms of Werther's isolated and isolating narrative voice. Three others come to any careful reader's mind: Klopstock's "Die Fruhlingsfeier" of 1759, Lessing's *Emilia Galloti* of 1772, appearing only two years before the original version of *Werther,* and Homer's *Odyssey* of mythical date.

No text intrudes more impulsively into the text of *Werther* than Klopstock's "Die Frühlingsfeier." No other, including Ossian's, creates greater "narrative difficulties." Charlotte's impulsive grasping of Werther's hand and *her* voicing of the poet's name elicit an identical appeal to experience within the novel's text and assume a similar experience on the part of the reader. In Goethe's German novel, there was no reason to cite, let alone translate, the famous model text. But like Macpherson's, it is lyric, pregnant with sensibility, in short Wertheresque. Yet, the narrative context into which Goethe set it is more complex than might be assumed on first reading, for it also stresses the difference between Charlotte and Werther. Her view of the approaching storm and her memory of the poem devolve from an ironic sense of the fictively real. It is an appreciation of a lyric glimpse into a world best comprehended by reflective and reflected narrative. As Goethe adds to Werther's voice in his revision of the text:

> [Ich] erinnerte mich sogleich der herrlichen Ode die ihr in *Gedanken* lag. . . .

> [I] remembered immediately the magnificent ode which lay in her *thoughts*. . . .
>
> (AV 28b, emphasis mine)

What Goethe expresses with these words is a very old, essentially rhetorical link among memory, recall, and art, one Charlotte might be said to entertain in Petrarch's echoing chamber of her mind, but one Werther recognizes only in terms of experience unmitigated by any sense of irony. His recognition shatters his world; her recognition creates hers. Thus again an extratextual allusion becomes a hazardous irony.

Similarly the intrusion of the then contemporary text

of *Emilia Galotti* tells us more of narrated worlds than of itself. Although the eighteenth-century viewer probably saw the play as reflecting an insight into life, just as Charlotte and Goethe had accepted Goldsmith's *Vicar,* neither Werther nor we can read Lessing's work in that way through the context of *Werther,* where it symbolizes a man's last expression of his world. The text supplies the reader with no comforting, knowable *Unwelt,* and it is for this reason, very probably, that its place in the novel has always been so highly problematic.

But who specifically has read the play in the novel? Werther, and Werther, to be blunt, cannot read right. In this Goethe has drawn the line between his main character and himself with a harsh and definitive stroke.

Werther's defect is part and parcel of his growing inability to create in any sphere of art, that is of ironic self-reflection, whatsoever. In the addition of the *Bauernbursch* in book one, Goethe reemphasizes exactly the choice of stunning experience over painting (*Mahlerei*) and poetry (*Dichtkunst*) in the revised text (AV 16b). As far as stories go, not only is Werther unable to narrate one in writing (Part I, June 16: "Ich bin vergnügt und glücklich, und so kein guter Historienschreiber," "I am delightfully diverted and happy, and therefore no good writer of story [or history]"—AV 18a/b), he is incapable of reading seriously one of the world's oldest tales: Homer's *Odyssey.* The reader first comes upon him as he skips through it in a self-indulgent, cavalier way with a cup of coffee at hand (AV Part I, May 26th a/b). Goethe himself, on the other hand, viewed Homer's text much more complexly from even as early as 1771 when he linked Sophocles to the Bard (WA *Zum Schäkespears Tag* 1.37.131, see 1.38.286). For him that epic would never have recalled merely a flaccid, pastoral genre. Moreover, unlike Werther, he would have understood the doubly dangerous irony inherent in the action of Penelope's suitors as they carved up her husband Odysseus' kine (AV Part I, June 21st a/b). How could Werther's thoughts not link Penelope to Charlotte and Albert to Odysseus? Because he was incapable of creating himself through reflected ironies. Goethe's and Charlotte's ability to read involves just this kind of irony and went on to create the appealing *Unwelt* in *Werther.* Werther has no ironic claim because reading has lost its human complexities. It provides him no *Unwelt,* no irony of the fictively real.

Goethe's sense of irony in the telling and experience of a story about and around his characters' voices, therefore, extends beyond merely establishing a trustworthy narrator with a steady perspective.[10] His juxtaposition of imploding and cultivating worlds creates narrative conflicts within the novel that continually cry in vain for resolution. The voicing of immediate experience, no matter how well defined by a strong voice

from a wider context, must always cause conflicting sympathies on the part of a reader. But, although it might be tempting to isolate such voices antithetically either in the realm of narrative sense or in that of lyric sensibility, it is more fruitful to speak of the textual interaction between the two that forms the structure and parameters of Goethe's first novel.

"Klopstock!," "Emilia Galotti," "Homer," and Goethe's and Werther's translation "einiger Gesänge Ossians" ("of several Ossianic songs") (AV 136a/b) are positively employed models in that they skew Goethe's ironic view of the world to fruitful ends. Such extratextual intrusions would continue to jell in the novels that were to follow. Yet, his own ironic sense of narration would not have arisen were it not for Goldsmith's ironic *The Vicar of Wakefield.* In a letter to Zelter in 1829, Goethe wrote of his then present identification with the Vicar Primrose and acknowledged fully his debt to eighteenth-century irony: "It would be impossible to reckon," he wrote, "what Goldsmith and Sterne have directly contributed to the chief characteristics of my development" (WA *Briefe* IV.46.193-94). This essay has made only preliminary attempts at a guess.

As for the reader of Goethe's *Werther,* the author's jest in answer to Christoph Friedrich Nicolai's contemporary satire *Die Freuden des jungen Werthers* might well be heeded:

Und wer mich nicht verstehen kann,
Der lerne besser lesen.

Loosely translated:
If you're too dumb to get my gist
Learn to read with better wit.
    (WA "Auf Nicolai" *D & W 13* 1.28.231)[11]

Notes

[1] Oliver Goldsmith, *Collected Works,* ed. Arthur Friedman, Vol. 4 (Oxford: Clarendon, 1966), 45. After initial citation, any further reference to a work will be indicated in abbreviated form within parentheses in my text.

[2] Johann Wolfgang von Goethe, *Werke,* ed. by commission of Grandduchess Sophie von Sachsen, 133 vols. (Weimar: Bohlau, 1887-1919). Cited as WA.

[3] All translations from the German are my own.

[4] Johann Wolfgang von Goethe, *Die Leiden des Jungen Werthers,* ed. Erna Merker, I. Text Erste und Zweite Fassung (Berlin: Akademie-Verlag, 1954). Cited as AV. Goethe's *Werther* appeared in an original version in 1774 and in a revised one in 1787. Setting aside some "cleansing" revision of orthography, punctuation, and dialectical pungency, the difference between the two lies in shorter altered or intensified descriptions of the

major characters' behavior and in longer major additions that ultimately attain the same end. For those parts of the text that have only been "cleansed" in the revision, I shall quote the revised version, but indicate the similarity between the two by "a/b"; texts only in the original, by "a"; and those only in the revision by "b." To Eric A. Blackall *Goethe and the Novel* (Ithaca, London: Cornell UP, 1976), 44-55, must be given the credit for first comparing the two versions extensively in narrative terms.

[5] See Lilian R. Furst's "The Metamorphosis of Irony," in *Fictions of Romantic Irony* (Cambridge, Mass.: Harvard UP, 1984), 23-48.

[6] D.W. Jefferson, "*The Vicar of Wakefield* and Other Prose Writings: A Reconsideration," in *The Art of Oliver Goldsmith,* ed. Andrew Swarbrick (London: Barnes and Noble, 1984), 30.

[7] James Macpherson ("Translator"), *The Poems of Ossian,* 2 vols. (London: Strahan & Cadell, 1784), I.207.

[8] See chapter eleven of Goldsmith's *An Enquiry into the Present State of Polite Learning.*

[9] Lilian R. Furst, "The Man of Sensibility and the Woman of Sense," *Jahrbuch für Internationale Germanistik* 14:1 (1983), 13-36.

[10] Victor Lange, "Goethe's Craft of Fiction," *Publications of the English Goethe Society* N.S. 22 (1952-1953), 31-63; on this point, see 40.

[11] I should like to thank Albrecht Strauss for his suggestions at the final stages of this essay.

FURTHER READING

Biography

Ginger, John. "Goose-Pie and Gooseberries." In *The Notable Man: The Life and Times of Oliver Goldsmith,* pp. 157-85. London: Hamish Hamilton, 1977.

   Discusses events in Goldsmith's life at the time he was writing of *The Vicar of Wakefield.*

Wardle, Ralph. *Oliver Goldsmith.* Lawrence: University of Kansas Press, 1957, 330 p.

   Comprehensive biography, utilizing contemporary sources and providing a less disparaging view of Goldsmith's personality than had previously appeared.

Wibberley, Leonard. *The Good-Natured Man: A Portrait of Oliver Goldsmith.* New York: William Morrow, 1979, 255 p.

   Warmly sympathetic biography that is based solely on contemporary accounts of Goldsmith's life.

Criticism

Battestin, Martin C. "Goldsmith: The Comedy of Job." In *The Providence of Wit: Aspects of Form in Augustan Literature and the Arts,* pp. 193-214. Oxford: Clarendon Press, 1974.

   Argues that Goldsmith used the Book of Job as a paradigm for "his own tale of Christian suffering and redemption."

Dykstal, Timothy. "The Story of O: Politics and Pleasure in *The Vicar of Wakefield.*" *ELH* 62, No. 2 (Summer 1995): 329-46.

   Considers the role of Olivia and suggests what her behavior reveals about the Vicar's political theories.

Ferguson, Oliver W. "Goldsmith as Ironist." *Studies in Philology* LXXXI, No. 2 (Spring 1984): 212-28.

   Argues for a more precise and moderate position on the role of irony in Goldsmith's works.

Grudis, Paul J. "The Narrator and *The Vicar of Wakefield.*" *Essays in Literature* I, No. 1 (January 1973): 51-64.

   Reconsiders the significance of satire and irony in *The Vicar of Wakefield* by reexamining the role of Dr. Primrose.

Jeffares, A. Norman. *"The Vicar of Wakefield."* In *Goldsmith: The Gentle Master,* edited by Sean Lucy, pp. 38-49. Cork, Ireland: Cork University Press, 1984.

   Examines the timeless appeal of *The Vicar of Wakefield.*

Paulson, Ronald. "Dr. Primrose: The Ironic Hero." In *Satire and the Novel in Eighteenth-Century England,* pp. 269-75. New Haven, CT: Yale University Press, 1967.

   Discusses *The Vicar of Wakefield* as a significant contribution to the evolution of the English novel. The critic in particular examines Goldsmith's use of a first-person narrator who comprehends less than the reader.

Laurence Sterne

1713-1768

English novelist, satirist, and essayist.

INTRODUCTION

Sterne's fame as an author rests largely on two works, the novel *Tristram Shandy, Gentleman* and the travel essay *A Sentimental Journey through France and Italy*. During his lifetime, he was subject to intense praise as well as bitter criticism, regarded by some readers and commentators as a satirist comparable with François Rabelais and Miguel de Cervantes, and condemned by others as utterly immoral. Increasingly, his work has been appreciated by modern critics tracing the gensesis of fictional experiments with realism, psychology, and metanarrative.

Biographical Information

Sterne was born in Ireland to poor parents. In 1723 he began attending a school in Halifax, Yorkshire; however, when his father died penniless in 1731, Sterne was forced to discontinue his education. Two years later a cousin arranged for him to enter Jesus College, Cambridge, as a sizar, which allowed Sterne to defray university expenses by working as a servant to other students. At Cambridge he met John Hall-Stevenson, a rich and reckless young man whose home—Skelton Castle, renamed "Crazy Castle"—figures prominently in accounts of Sterne's life as the site of drinking parties, a library of erotic literature, and episodes of debauchery. After receiving a bachelor's degree from Cambridge Sterne became a clergyman, He was ordained a deacon in 1736, a priest in 1738, and afterward received various appointments in Yorkshire. In 1741 Sterne married Elizabeth Lumley. The couple had a daughter and eventually separated. Until the publication of *Tristram Shandy,* Sterne's only written works were his sermon, periodical essays on politics, and *A Political Romance* (1759), a satirical allegory concerned with local church politics. This last work displays some of the humor and narrative flair of Sterne's major fiction. Sterne's masterwork, *Tristram Shandy, Gentleman,* received mixed reviews, but a wide contemporary readership elevated both the book and its author to celebrity status. A visit to Europe in 1765 provided Sterne with the material for *A Sentimental Journey through France and Italy* (1768), an essay on his travels in which heightened subjectivity, emotionalism, and narrative verve serves as a striking contrast to the conventional literary travelogue. A few weeks after the publication of *A Sentimental Journey,* Sterne died in London of tuberculosis.

Major Works

Sterne's *Tristram Shandy* is an unusual work by the literary standards of any period, but it stands out particularly in the century that saw the birth and early development of the realistic novel. While such novels as Daniel Defoe's *Moll Flanders,* Samuel Richardson's *Pamela,* and Henry Fielding's *Tom Jones* display their authors' attempts to make prose fiction a means for depicting contemporary life, *Tristram Shandy* demonstrated aspirations of an entirely different kind. Its characters, although profoundly human, are also profoundly odd and do not have the significant connections with their society held by characters in the great realistic novels of the time. *Tristram Shandy*'s style is one of cultivated spontaneity and unpredictability, a series of digressions rather than the progressive movement of events common in the works of Sterne's contemporaries. Perhaps most conspicuously, its narrator is concerned with relating his "Life and Opinions" instead of the more typical "Life and Adventures" of the eighteenth-century *Bildungsroman,* making the novel a largely plotless discourse on an encyclopedic array of subjects. The opinions expounded in the novel, aside from the manic commentary of Tristram himself, are those of the principal characters, especially the narrator's father, Walter Shandy. In the world of *Tristram Shandy,* human life is marked by the obsessive pursuit of some dominant preoccupation, which the narrator terms a "hobby horse." For Walter Shandy, his obsession in the constant weaving of elaborate and absurd theories, the random development of which reflect Sterne's interest in John Locke's writings on the association of ideas. For the narrator's uncle Toby, whom critics have often viewed as one of the most vivid and admirable characters in literature, the imaginary reliving of his battle experiences is his hobby horse. The narrator's own mania consists most obviously of the comic spirit that he introduces into his description of even the most depressing aspects of his world, such as the death of the character Le Fever. Sterne's other major work, *A Sentimental Journey,* is important as a nonfictional memoir that conveys much the same sensibility as the fictional *Tristram Shandy.* An account of Sterne's travels in France and Italy, this memoir has as its central concern the subjective side of the author's experiences rather than the traditional objective rendering of people and places. In fact, in *A Sentimental Journey,* Sterne pays minute and self-conscious attention to his own feelings, and frequently shows himself as a manipulator of situations purely for the sake of experiencing the resulting emotion. In one of the more famous instances of this behavior, Sterne resists his lust for a chambermaid and thereby discovers the pleasures of passion restrained. Another episode, "The Dead Ass," has frequently been singled out for the intensity of emotion Sterne exhibits for the death of an animal. Sterne's preoccupation with feelings, especially those of tender pathos, led to his establishing the word "sentiment" as it is understood today, imbuing the word with heightened, somewhat artificial emotion when it previously had denoted "thought" and "moral reflection."

Critical Reception

Eighteenth and nineteenth century commentary on Sterne tended to be biographical in nature: in particular, Sterne was assumed to share or at least approve the opinions and behavior of his character Tristram Shandy. Thus, an appraisal of Sterne's works became inseparable from an appraisal of his life, either to demonstrate a reprehensible similarity between the two or to discover a paradoxical contrast. By contrast, twentieth-century critics have emphasized the remarkable likeness between Sterne's narrative techniques and the formal experimentation of modern literature. These critics focus particularly on Sterne's unorthodox punctuation, his use of nonverbal devices like drawings, his disregard for sequence, and his self-conscious focus on his own method of composition. Despite the evidence presented by several scholars that *Tristram Shandy* borrows heavily and blatantly from a number of sources, including Robert Burton's *Anatomy of Melancholy* and Rabelais's *Gargantua* and *Pantagruel,* few twentieth-century critics have questioned the success with which Sterne adapted these borrowings to his own purposes, and transformed old material into an original work of literature.

Painstaking examination and description of his own inner feelings and reactions characterizes *A Sentimental Journey* as well as Stern's personal letters. This fact provoked a major controversy in nineteenth-century criticism with regard to the sincerity of everything Stern wrote. Modern critics, however, credit Sterne with an unusual facility for taking an ironic view of his most intense feelings. Alternatively, they find in his work a satirical mockery of sentiment. Perhaps the most important factor contributing to the ambiguities in Sterne's work as well as to the controversies surrounding it is his provocative humor. Some critics have seen this quality of Sterne's writing as an end in itself. Others, including the English Romantics, perceive more profound motives underlying these works. For example, a number of studies contend that Sterne's humor derives from an acute awareness of the ultimate evil and suffering of human existence and that each farcical antic is an allusion to grim truth. Whether or not it is justified to place Sterne in the philosophical company of modernists who blend comedy and despair in their works, late-twentieth-century commentators are largely in agreement that Sterne is an exceptional case of an eighteenth-century writer whose works are particularly sympathetic with the concerns and temperament of twentieth-century readers.

PRINCIPAL WORKS

The Case of Elijah and the Widow of Zerephath (sermon) 1747

The Abuses of Conscience (sermon) 1750

A Political Romance, Addressed to —Esq. Of York (satire) 1759

The Life and Opinions of Tristram Shandy, Gentleman. 9 vols. (novel) 1760-67

The Sermons of Mr. Yorick. 7 vols. (sermons) 1760-69

A Sentimental Journey through France and Italy, by Mr. Yorick 2 vols. (travel essay) 1768

Letters from Yorick to Eliza (letters) 1773

CRITICISM

A. A. Mendilow (essay date 1952)

SOURCE: "The Revolt of Sterne," in *Laurence Sterne: A Collection of Critical Essays,* edited by John Traugott, Prentice-Hall, Inc., 1968, pp. 90-107. Reprinted from A. A. Mendilow's *Time and the Novel,* Peter Nevill, Ltd., 1952. "Notes have been shortened or dropped without notice."

[*In the following essay, Mendilow asserts that with Tristram Shandy, Sterne modernized the novel format through his use of "time-shifts," or digressions, that more accurately approximate the way in which people think than does more usual linear narrative.*]

It was clearly high time to do again for the English novel what Furetière and the other realists had done so effectively for the French: to flout the conventions of plotting, with its special and arbitrary requirements of the beginning, middle, and end; of the chronological sequence of action which denied artistic form altogether, of the principle of causality, which involved rigid selection and economy of incident in the interests of an artificial patterning of the action. Sterne was very deeply interested in the problems these conventions raise, namely the relationship between reality and fictional illusion. Above all, he wished to arouse his readers to the realization that these *are* conventions, that they should not be taken for reality, not even for valid symbols, let alone transcripts of reality, that, as Thomas Warton wrote of the early romances, "reality is disguised by the misrepresentations of invention."[1] At the very outset he had determined not to confine himself "to any man's rules that ever lived," and more truly than Fielding he could claim the right to say:

> I shall not look on myself as accountable to any court of jurisdiction whatever; for as I am, in reality, the founder of a new province of writing, so I am at liberty to make what laws I please therein.[2]

The great aim of Sterne was to give as true a picture as possible of real human beings as they are in themselves, not as they imagine themselves to be, nor as others judge them to be by their actions and outward behavior alone. This meant the shifting of emphasis from the external to the internal event, from the patterned plot artificially conceived and imposed on the characters, to the free evocation of the fluid, ever-changing process of being. It also brought him face to face with the problem of the limitations of language to convey all this; he had to investigate the ways by which a sequential medium could be manipulated to express simultaneity and the flow of human consciousness.

Though the idea of trying to indicate the inner as distinct from the outer man reached the fullest expression in Sterne, it was of course far from new in fiction, as, in their way, the "romans de longue haleine" and the novels of Richardson had shown. The claims of the two diametrically opposed schools of writing were put very clearly and forcefully, both in practice and theory. The followers of the French anti-Romance realists sided with the view of Fielding that:

> The only ways by which we can come at any knowledge of what passes in the Minds of others, are their words and Actions; the latter of which hath by the wiser Part of Mankind been chiefly depended on, as the surer and more infallible Guide.[3]

His sister, on the other hand, discussing Virgil's use of plot, declared that

> when we stop at those outward Circumstances, and perceive not the further Intention, we read as children see Tragedies, who place their chief Delight in the Noise of the Kettle-drums and Trumpets;[4]

and again in another of her critical prefaces:

> The motives to actions, and the inward turns of the mind, seem in our opinion more necessary to be known than the actions themselves; and much rather would we chuse that our readers should clearly understand what our principal actors think, than what they do.[5]

Mary Mitford was even more explicit:

> With regard to novels, I should like to see one undertaken without any plot at all . . . without any preconceived design further than one or two incidents and dialogues, which would naturally suggest fresh matter, and so proceed in this way, throwing in incident and characters profusely, but avoiding all stage tricks and strong situations. . . . [6]

Sterne's awareness of the degree to which the accepted conventions limited the expression of this greater inwardness in fiction, and of the discrepancy between reality and fictional illusion is what makes him so strikingly akin to modern novelists.

> The excellencies of Sterne [said Coleridge] consist in bringing forward into distinct consciousness those minutiae of thought and feeling which appear trifles, yet have an importance for the moment, and which almost every man feels in one way or other.[7]

When an author is trying to give an impression of a character, not in terms of a melodic progression of actions or descriptions, but as "a system of harmonic vibrations," to use a phrase of Sterne himself;[8] when he becomes involved in those levels of the mind that lie below the rationalizing, conscious plane of being, he is drawn into many new linguistic and literary problems. He must try to devise novel techniques and conventions to convey the illusion of simultaneity in spite of a consecutive medium, and to find some way of equating the mind's flickerings backward and forward in time with the forward movement of language. He must somehow overcome the effect of discreteness made by words which chop up into separate units the indivisible flow of experience. He must consider whether he should not substitute a loose rhythm for the tight metre of the close plot which tries to force into a pattern that which is not amenable to any such conventions of structure and time.

> Life does not . . . present that combined plot, (the object of every skillful novelist), in which all the more interesting individuals of the *dramatis personae* have their appropriate share in the action and in bringing about the catastrophe. Here, even more than in its various and violent changes of fortune, rests the improbability of the novel.[9]

The innovations by virtue of which Sterne merits in a double sense the title of "first of the moderns" were not the outcome of mere chance; they were not struck out by the author in ignorance of what he was about. It is only on a cursory reading that *Tristram Shandy* gives the impression of being haphazardly constructed. In fact it is built to a very deliberate plan worked out in detail by a writer who was aware of the technical possibilities of the novel and was consciously experimenting in new principles and conventions. The validity of his approach is shown by the fact that the modern novel has followed the path he blazed rather than in the footsteps of his sedater contemporaries. Like Sterne, the writer of today is preoccupied with the problems of time in fiction; what the associationist psychology of Locke with its corollary of the "time-shift" technique was to the one, Bergson's *durée* and theory of intuition is to the other. Alike, they have been led to challenge the formal principles of narration based on the sequential relating of successive events. Alike, they have abandoned the close and closed pattern of the plot imposed on the novel by the principle of limited selection, a principle determined by tradition rather than by the desire to get closer to the truth of life. Alike, they have tried to develop a less arbitrary kind of selection on a qualitative rather than quantitative basis, chosen for its power to convey an illusion of reality, rather than for artistic shapeliness or adequacy to prove or illustrate some thesis. In particular, they are concerned with psychological time and duration rather than with chronological time and separated moments. They aim at conveying the effect of an all-pervading present of which past and future are part, in preference to an orderly progression in time of separated discontinuous events.

Although Sterne flouts the principle of chronological succession in fiction so flagrantly, he astonishes us by the accuracy with which the dates, scattered as they are in scores of so-called "digressions," are nevertheless made to cohere. In the usual single-thread and parallel plots moving forward in a straight line, this would not be remarkable. The adherence to the rule of sequential narration is sufficient to place events in their relative temporal positions, and any calendar dating that may be required is comparatively simple. Even where an expository passage is intercalated, the difficulties are not great, for such exposition is presented in a single block which is in direct temporal relation to the main forward-moving issue. Where however the principle of time-shift based on the free association of ideas is followed, the relative positions in time of events is not easy to determine; and where, as in *Tristram Shandy,* the "digressions" are so numerous and so short and are themselves so often broken up by yet further digressions, and furthermore where the fictional time of the novel covers so long a period (on the shortest reckoning three quarters of a century), and where the scope of action is so elastic and the characters and incidents so varied, to maintain and control the chronology consistently is a feat reminiscent of a juggler keeping a large number of balls in the air at the same time. Not the smallest incident but its date is given or can be deduced or, at the very least, can be fitted into its chronological order: Aunt Dinah's lapse with the coachman (1699), the imprisonment of Trim's brother by the Inquisition (1704), the death of Le Fever (1706), the cow breaking into my Uncle Toby's fortifications (1718), the marriage of Obadiah (1712) and the birth of his first child (1713), the death of Yorick (1749). There is scarcely an incident, no matter how slight, no matter where it occurs in the book, no matter how often it is interrupted and taken up again, but falls into its correct place in time in relation to every other incident. Slips in dating are very rare, one or two at most. Many of these incidents, especially those relating to Uncle Toby, can be checked against historical events. Every piece in the jigsaw puzzle is found to fit into its place. This is itself evidence against unplanned writing, demanding as it must have done an intricate system of cross-references. We know that Sterne was a careful and deliberate writer who constantly worked over his manuscripts time and again until they finally satisfied his fastidious taste and judgment.

Noteworthy, too, is the naturalness with which this chronological dating is worked into the substance of the novel. The times are not paraded but are slipped in quite casually in the course of other matters. They are often revealed, not by the specific mention of a date, but as taking place at some certain time before or after some other event the date of which can perhaps be deduced from a chance reference to some historical event. The remarkable thing is that all these times and dates fall in their correct places when checked against each other. They do so because, instead of being presented, as it were, outside the characters, as a background against which these characters are plotted, they form part of their consciousness and emotional experience, and are in consequence readily called to mind, naturally and without effort, through the working of association.

What interests Sterne much more than chronological dating however is the discrepancy between duration in terms of chronological and psychological time. His main interest lies in the states of mind and the character of the protagonists rather than in their actions, in what they are and think and feel, not so much in what they do. The true duration therefore is subjective, measured by values, not by the clock; it consequently varies in length with each individual, having regard to the circumstances and frame of mind in which he happens to be. The external, objective, unvarying duration as measured by the pendulum has little place in the novel, except as presenting a contrast to psychological duration, for it has in itself no validity in the sphere of feeling and thinking. This is the principle which Sterne owed as he told Suard,

> à l'étude de Locke, qu'il avait faite au sortir de l'enfance, et qu'il refit toute sa vie. . . . [10]

This principle he was the first to apply deliberately to fiction:

> It is about an hour and a half's tolerable good reading since my Uncle Toby rang the bell, when Obadiah was ordered to saddle a horse, and go for Dr. Slop, the man-midwife;—so that no one can say, with reason, that I have not allowed Obadiah time enough, poetically speaking, and considering the emergency too, both to go and come:—though, morally and truly speaking, the man perhaps has scarce had time to get on his boots. If the hypercritic will go upon this; and is resolved after all to take a pendulum, and measure the true distance betwixt the ringing of the bell, and the rap at the door;—and, after finding it to be no more than two minutes, thirteen seconds, and three fifths,—should take upon himself to insult over me for such a breach in the unity, or rather probability of time;—I would remind him, that the idea of duration, and of its simple modes, is got merely from the train and succession of our ideas,—and is the true scholastic pendulum,—and by which, as a scholar, I will be tried in this matter—abjuring and detesting the jurisdiction of all other pendulums whatever.

> I would therefore desire him to consider that it is but a poor eight miles from Shandy Hall to Dr. Slop, the man-midwife's house;—and that whilst Obadiah has been going those said miles and back,

I have brought my Uncle Toby from Namur, quite across all Flanders, into England:—That I have had him ill upon my hands near four years:—and have since travelled him and Corporal Trim in a chariot-and-four, a journey of near two hundred miles down into Yorkshire—all which put together, must have prepared the reader's imagination for the entrance of Dr. Slop upon the stage,—as much, at least (I hope) as a dance, a song, or a concerto between the acts. (II, 8)

In this passage, Sterne is, as elsewhere in *Tristram Shandy,* playing on the several different kinds of time that operate in the novel. Firstly, he jocularly correlates the time taken by the reader to read, with the time that the events related in the novel take to happen. This chronological measurement of the act of reading is furthermore effectively contrasted with the reader's sense of the passage of time; that is, his psychological time as judged by values as distinct from the other measured by scales outside him. These questions naturally involve the technique of narration which to be effective must reduce any sense of discrepancy between the different kinds of time and so give an illusion of reality and truth.

But Sterne is concerned with the distinction between chronological and psychological duration not only as it affects the reader. He is equally interested in the relationship between the two as experienced by the characters themselves, and as it affects *their* sense of the passage of time.

> It is two hours and ten minutes—and no more—cried my father looking at his watch, since Dr. Slop and Obadiah arrived,—and I know not how it happens, brother Toby—but to my imagination it seems almost an age. . . . Though my father said, "he knew not how it happened,"—yet he knew very well how it happened;—and at the instance he spoke it, was pre-determined in his mind to give my Uncle Toby a clear account of the matter by a metaphysical dissertation upon the subject of duration and its simple modes, in order to show my Uncle Toby by what mechanism and mensurations in the brain it came to pass, that the rapid succession of their ideas, and the eternal scampering of the discourse from one thing to another, since Dr. Slop had come into the room, had lengthened out so short a period to so inconceivable an extent.—"I know not how it happens—cried my father,—but it seems an age."—'Tis owing entirely, quoth my Uncle Toby, to the succession of our ideas. [Walter Shandy continues a little later]: To understand what time is aright, without which we never can comprehend infinity, insomuch as one is a portion of the other—we ought seriously to sit down and consider what idea it is we have of duration, so as to give a satisfactory account how we came by it.—What is that to anybody? quoth my Uncle Toby. For if you will turn your eyes inwards upon your mind, continued

my father, and observe attentively, you will perceive, brother, that whilst you and I are talking together, and thinking, and smoking our pipes, or whilst we receive successively ideas in our minds; we know that we do exist, and so estimate the existence, or the continuation of the existence of ourselves, or anything else, commensurate to the succession of any ideas in our minds, or any such other thing coexisting with our thinking—and so according to that preconceived—You puzzle me to death, cried my Uncle Toby.—'Tis owing to this, replied my father, that in our computations of time, we are so used to minutes, hours, weeks, and months—and of clocks (I wish there was not a clock in the kingdom) to measure out their several portions to us, and to those who belong to us—that 'twill be well, if in time to come, the succession of our ideas will be of any use or service to us at all. Now, whether we observe it or no, continued my father, in every sound man's head there is a regular succession of ideas of one sort or other, which follow each other in train. . . . (III, 18)

This exploitation of the principle of psychological duration allows Sterne to vary his tempo by expanding or telescoping the time by the clock to accord with the artistic effect he is concerned with producing. In an early fragment Sterne wrote

> Glasses can make an inch seem a mile. I leave it to future ages to invent a method for making a *minute* seem a *year.*

In *Tristram Shandy* he was to invent the method himself. By playing the different values of psychological and chronological time against each other, and by emphasizing the difference between them, he can at will convey a sense of urgency and hurry, or of relaxation, waiting and suspense.

Judged chronologically, **Tristram Shandy** has neither beginning, middle, nor end.

The novel starts in the year 1718 and ends in the year 1713, and in the interim goes as far forward as 1766 and backward to the time of Henry VIII. It is built up of a large number of interwoven and interrelated episodes, of "digressions" as critics commonly call them. The term is inapt. "Digression" implies a minor divagation from what is discernible in the novel as the strict line of forward moving narration. Where a book begins with some "constituted scene" or "discriminated occasion"[11] which forms the first of a consecutive series leading to some fixed timepoint, strictly speaking, any chronological departure from the series, such as retrospective or anticipatory flashes or inserted exposition, constitutes a digression. Such a novel is to be distinguished from that where more than one thread of action is followed; there the alternated transfer of interest from one to another of a parallel series is inevitable, and provides the chief means of arousing

suspense. In pattern-plots based on causality, any departure from the main issue by the introduction of episodes such as do not contribute to the catastrophe may likewise be held to be digressive. Richardson proudly claimed in his preface to *Sir Charles Grandison* that

> There is not one episode in the whole . . . but what tends to illustrate the principal design.

The ideal for this kind of plot had been concisely put by Addison who said of the epic:

> . . . nothing should go before it, be intermix'd with it, or follow after it, that is not related to it.[12]

In the thesis novel, elements irrelevant to the central idea or not contributing to the general view of life which it is the author's intention to expound, constitute digressions. In every case, digressions must digress—whether from some clearly defined pattern, purpose, or line of action. They could be dispensed with and leave no vital break or flaw in the main structure. A novel cannot consist of nothing but digressions. But in *Tristram Shandy* there is no forward-moving line or architechtonic plot from which to digress. There is no point of departure from which the line could start, for Sterne realizes that, as Mme. de Staël observed:

> Human life exhibits but a series of commencements, in which no precise line or limit is discernible.[13]

Like the school of writers hit off by Butler, Sterne can therefore

> Make former times shake hands with latter, And that which was before come after.

He moves at will backward and forward in time without regard for chronological logic, and whatever temporal point he deals with, he treats as a constituted scene in its own right, that is, as a dramatic present, and not as past or future relative to some major event in the story.

In his description of his method as working forward and backward along the line of his story,[14] Sterne is misled into using the word "line" by the common practice of limiting the narration to one or more main characters followed chronologically along single or parallel lines from one period to another. An apter description of his method might be to say that he worked in stipple on a broad canvas. Proust adopted what is essentially the same method, save that he expanded the episodes or "discriminated occasions" into large time-blocks to which he devoted—it might be a whole section or even an entire volume. His scenes, like those of Sterne, are presented in temporal sequence but are linked by the association of ideas and lengthened or shortened (usually lengthened) by being conceived in terms of psychological duration. Nor are any of his episodes digressive. In both, the picture grows, not part by part but as a whole, into an indivisible unity out of the multitude of scattered strokes of the brush distributed in no fixed order; these strokes finally are seen to cohere and blend into a single, wider whole. This whole can only be guessed at in *Tristram Shandy,* which is incomplete and therefore appears fragmentary; had Sterne lived to finish his book, and as he carefully proves to himself with the aid of mathematics it could never be finished (IV, 13), it might theoretically be possible at the end to piece out a full picture of the Shandy *ménage,* possibly even including the hero himself.

By breaking up the story and every little episode and scene in it into small disjointed fragments presented, chronologically speaking, in pell-mell disorder, Sterne has evolved a technique that allows of several different effects at once. He can trace the fleeting impressions and associations that float in the minds of characters, including Tristram himself as a quasi-autobiographer during the act of writing. He can bring an effect into high relief by artfully relating it to some other contrasting effect. He can build up a climax by an accumulation of several incidents, or create a single emotional impression by bringing together elements selected from many stages in the life-story of the various characters. He can give rein to his fancy for the ludicrous, or create suspense by breaking off at some crucial moment and switching over to some other incident. He can also give the equivalent of empty spaces, intervals of waiting and *longueurs* by his "digressions."

Sterne shows himself an adept at expanding the moment and contracting the years at his pleasure. Especially, he can create an impression of all the parts of the story proceeding simultaneously, each at its own pace and in its own direction.

> When a man is telling a story in the strange way I do mine, he is obliged continually to be going backwards and forwards to keep all tight together in the reader's fancy. (VI, 33)

Removal or transposition of the episodes in *Tristram Shandy* would leave gaps in the picture or snap the delicate links which bind part to part, for every episode has its right context from which it cannot be wrenched. Not only does he achieve effects of simultaneity when dealing with events that are going on at the same time, but he even telescopes together the two journeys Tristram made to Auxerre, one as a young man with his father and uncle, the other in search of health some twenty years later, bringing himself up with the rueful comment:

> I have been getting forward in two different journeys together, and with the same dash of the pen—for I have got entirely out of Auxerre in this journey which I am writing now, and am got halfway out of Auxerre in that which I shall write hereafter—There is but a certain degree of perfection in every thing; and by pushing at something beyond that, I have brought myself into such a situation, as no traveller ever stood before me; for I am this moment walking across the market-place of Auxerre with my father and my uncle Toby, in our way back to dinner— and I am this moment also entering Lyons with my post-chaise broke into a thousand pieces—and I am moreover this moment in a handsome pavilion built by Pringello, upon the banks of the Garonne, which Mons. Sligniac has lent me, and where I now sit rhapsodizing all these affairs. (VII, 28)

Sterne is, in this passage, hinting at the fundamental limitation of language as a symbolic medium for expressing experience; the inevitable conflict that must arise when a consecutive "horizontal" time-form is used to express simultaneity of impression and the "vertical" sense of the process of living. In this and similar passages, he can give cross-sections of life at one moment at different places and with different people, or open up long temporal perspectives of one character, or telescope the temporal perspectives of several characters into one overwhelming present in which all of them are, at the same time and for each of their individual times, whether past, present, or future, in relation to one another, simultaneously involved. Every part is a dramatic present. As he puts it, this technique saves him dramatically, even if it damns him biographically (II, 8).

Not only is the novel as a whole constructed without regard for chronological beginning, middle, and end. Even the digressions, or more truly, the episodes related by the device of the time-shift, share the same characteristic, and jump back and forth and interweave in the most surprising fashion. Thus Walter Shandy's prostration on learning of the mishap to the bridge of his newly born's nose is interrupted by the contretemps over the jointure between Tristram's great-grandfather and his wife. This in turn is broken into by Tristram's defeat of Eusebius's intention to define the word "crevice," and so goes back naturally to his grandparents and his father and their feelings in the matter of paying the same jointure to the long-lived great-grandmother, with a short discussion on heredity. Into all this enters the dispute between Tristram, Didius, and Tribonius on the question of proprietary rights in the opinions of others, and so by way of Slawkenbergius on noses back to Walter Shandy's prostration (III, 29 to IV, 2).

Sterne was fully conscious of what he was about. He goes out of his way to meet objections to the technique he has evolved, and insists that there is a method in his seeming madness, and that definite principles of composition underlie his apparent vagaries. He commends himself on "a master-stroke of digressive skill," namely that

> tho' my digressions are all fair, as you observe— and that I fly off from what I am about, as far, and as often too, as any writer in Great-Britain; yet I constantly take care to order affairs so that my main business does not stand still in my absence.

> I was just going, for example, to have given you the great outlines of my uncle Toby's most whimsical character;—when my aunt Dinah and the coachman came across us, and led us a vagary some millions of miles into the very heart of the planetary system: Notwithstanding all this, you perceive that the drawing of my uncle Toby's character went on gently all the time;—not the great contours of it,—that was impossible,—but some familiar strokes and faint designations of it, were here and there touched on, as we went along, so that you are much better acquainted with my uncle Toby now than you was before.

> By this contrivance, the machinery of my work is of a species by itself; the two contrary motions are introduced into it, and reconciled, which were thought to be at variance with each other. In a word, my work is digressive, and it is progressive too,— and at the same time. . . .

> Digressions, incontestably, are the sunshine;—they are the life, the soul of reading!—take them out of this book, for instance,—you might as well take the book along with them. . . .

> All the dexterity is in the good cookery and management of them, so as to be not only for advantage of the reader, but also of the author, whose distress, in the matter, is truly pitiable: For, if he begins a digression,—from that moment, I observe, his whole work stands stock still:—and if he goes on with his main work,—then there is an end of his digression.

> This is vile work.—For which reason, from the beginning of this, you see, I have constructed the main work and the adventitious parts of it with such intersections, and have so complicated and involved the digressive and progressive movements, one wheel within another, that the whole machine, in general, has been kept a-going. (I, 22)

The difficulty lies in understanding what Sterne means by his "main work." He is paying lip-service to his title: *The Life and Opinions of Tristram Shandy, Gentleman.* It has been pointed out that the life is largely that of Uncle Toby, and the opinions those of Walter Shandy; and Tristram is no gentleman in the modern sense of the word. Were his book what the title proclaims it to be, Uncle Toby's character would itself constitute a digression. Fortunately it is not a life of Tristram Shandy, and Uncle Toby and Aunt Dinah are not digressions, but take their place in the book in their own right. The greatness of Sterne lies precisely in this, that the different characters in it are not incidental to any hero. He gives roundness to every figure, implying that each one is, for himself the center of his own little world, and that each little world is relevant to the whole book. All these spheres, we feel, whether they are fully treated or no, exist. They intersect, forming segments of varying sizes common to each other. The main characters do not, as in many novels, live in a vacuum, isolated from everyone and everything that does not directly contribute to their progression toward some crucial point in their lives. Many apparently pointless digressions will be found to strengthen this effect of everyone living in himself at the same time and following his own path, irrespective of the part he may be playing in any major episode. Modern novelists aim at the same effect in their use of "breadthwise cutting"—temporal cross-sections of a group of people or even of a whole section of society. Sterne's method is the forerunner of the polyphonic technique, as contrasted with the melodic and harmonic techniques of his contemporaries, a system further elaborated in the contrapuntal experiments of de Quincey, Conrad, Joyce, Gide, Huxley, and others.

The episodes in *Tristram Shandy* fall into two main categories. Those linked to one another by the association of ideas in the minds of the characters, and those linked in the mind of the quasi-autobiographer himself. These so-called digressions contribute to the use by Sterne of the device of time-shift a century and a half before Conrad and Madox Ford adopted it as a principle of composition under the name of impressionism.

> We agree [writes Ford] that the general effect of a novel must be the general effect that life makes on mankind. A novel must therefore not be a narration, a report. Life does not say to you: In 1914, my next door neighbour, Mr. Slack, erected a greenhouse and painted it with Cox's green aluminum paint . . .

Here follows a short series of incidents in strict chronological sequence.

> If you think about the matter you will remember, in various unordered pictures, how one day Mr. Slack appeared in his garden and contemplated the wall of his house. You will then try to remember the year of that occurrence and you will fix it as August 1914 because having had the foresight to bear the municipal stock of the city of Liège you were able to afford a 1st class season ticket for the first time in your life. You will remember Mr. Slack—then much thinner because it was before he found out . . . etc.

He continues in this strain, bringing in a large part of his life in the process of describing Mr. Slack's greenhouse. He maintains therefore that the interrupted method of the time-shift is invaluable for giving a sense of the complexity that is life.

> In the pre-war period the English novel began at the beginning of a hero's life and went straight on to his marriage without pausing to look aside . . . such a story was too confined to its characters and too self-centeredly went on, *in vacuo*. If you are so set on the affair of your daughter Millicent with the young actor that you forget that there *are* flower shows and town halls with nude statuary your intellect will appear a thing much more circumscribed than it should be.[15]

He claims elsewhere that

> that technique is identical with that of all modern novelists, or of myself . . . or Proust.[16]

He might have added—or of Sterne.

One essential feature of the time-shift technique is that the author does not describe or summarize for the reader events occurring in the intervals between constituted scenes. Knowledge of the relative position in time of the scenes is pieced together from internal evidence within them. No matter how interrupted or broken up an episode may be by inserted or intervening events, between the breaks there must be no author's links such as summaries, temporal explanations, or expositions. This is the method used by Sterne in **Tristram Shandy.** With rare exceptions, every full action is presented directly as happening; nothing is reported as having happened. The impression is of direct as opposed to reported action and speech, and the extensive use of dialogue strengthens this effect of dramatic present. The book consists almost exclusively of constituted scenes and discriminated occasions, presented without introduction or reference to their calendar relation to preceding or succeeding scenes. This is the true time-shift, and it emphasizes the effect of every part as a present, not as relatively past or future.

The result is that there are no fixed time-points to which episodes bear reference, no beginning from which everything proceeds sequentially and to which events are relative in time. The nearest approach to such a time-point is the birth of Tristram, given as the fifth day of November, 1718 (I, 5).

> It is from this point [the death of my brother Bobby that occurred actually a few weeks later] properly that, the story of my Life and my Opinions sets out,

he says at the end of the fourth volume. But the bulk of the book deals with events that took place long before this date, events that are not presented in the

form of exposition but on their own merits as deserving a place equal to any others. On one other occasion, while dealing with Uncle Toby's amours, he writes that the armistice between Uncle Toby and the merry widow lasted till

> about six or seven weeks before the time I'm speaking of. (I, 32)

This refers likewise to Tristram's birth, the date of which was given about 180 pages earlier. On the next occasion when he mentions the date of the hero's birth, from which, in the regular novel, the fictional time of the action might be conceived to start, it is to mock at the whole convention of sequential narration:

> A cow broke in (tomorrow morning) to my uncle Toby's fortifications. . . . Trim insists on being tried by a court-martial. (III, 38)

Where every episode is presented as in a dramatic present, there can, strictly speaking, be no anticipatory passages or passages of exposition, for there is no fixed line from which to divagate. Such passages when they occur are retrospective or anticipatory only in relation to the time of one incident, and the events the author looks forward to may have been narrated already. Future and past are not future and past in time but before and after in order of narration, which is a very different matter. Thus, when in the course of recounting the circumstances surrounding the birth of the hero in 1718, Sterne promises an account of the love affairs of Uncle Toby, it is a promise to tell of something that occurred in 1713.

It is noteworthy that Sterne frequently gives the exact dates on which he is engaged in narrating various episodes, that is, his own real time or, if you will, the real time of the pseudo-autobiographer at the time of writing. Attendant details relating to that real time are added—Jenny's purchases, his cough, his surroundings, and so on. Sterne makes great play with the contrast between the real time and the fictional time of the events he is recording. The act of writing is chronologically consecutive, whereas the fictional time shifts constantly as he focuses his attention onto some or other point in the whole of his past spread out at once before him. This past grows as his real present moves forward, and this presents him with the following dilemma:

> I am this month one whole year older than I was this time twelve-month; and having got, as you perceive, almost into the middle of my fourth volume—and no farther than to my first day's life— 'tis demonstrative that I have three hundred and sixty-four days more life to write just now, than when I first set out; so that instead of advancing, as a common writer, in my work with what I have been doing at it—on the contrary, I am just thrown

so many volumes back—was every day of my life to be so busy a day as this—And why not?—and the transactions and opinions of it to take up as much description—And for what reason should they be cut short? as at this rate I should just live 364 times faster than I should write—It must follow, an' please your worships, that the more I write the more I shall have to write . . . was it not that my Opinions will be the death of me, I perceive I shall lead a fine life of it out of this selfsame life of mine; or, in other words, shall lead a couple of fine lives together. (IV, 13)

A similar quandary confronts Walter Shandy as he writes his system of education for his son:

This is the best account I am determined to give of the slow progress my father made in his *Trista-paedia;* at which (as I said) he was three years, and something more, indefatigably at work, and, at last, had scarce completed, by his own reckoning, one half of his undertaking: the misfortune was, that I was all the time totally neglected and abandoned to my mother; and what was almost as bad, the very delay, the first part of the work, upon which my father had spent the most of his pains, was rendered entirely useless,—every day a page or two became of no consequence. (V, 16)

Fictional and real time are continually brought into the closest relation, and the shifting points of reference in the narration are further complicated by the shifting points of reference in the real time of the narrator. The real and fictive presents are thus amusingly contrasted.

The frequent references in *Tristram Shandy* to the real time of the narrator are not evidence of the intrusive author such as leads to a division of interest between the author in his own person and his characters.

. . . perhaps there is not a better Criterion of the merit of a book, than our losing sight of the author.

Such references to the writer's present are justifiable in a first-person novel, for the autobiographer is himself within the framework. What is fully permissible in *Henry Esmond* constitutes a blemish in *Vanity Fair* where it jars the reader out of the fictional time in which he is immersed back into the real time in which he is engaged in the act of reading. In *Tristram Shandy* the interpretations of events and the analyses of the character of Walter Shandy, Uncle Toby, Trim, and the rest come, not as from outside the novel, but to illustrate the character and opinions of Tristram who, as autobiographer, is himself a character in the novel. *Tristram Shandy,* it is true, is more biography than autobiography, but that may in a large part be attributed to its being a fragment and not a complete whole. The observations of Tristram are as much in place as those of Captain Marlowe and the other observers in Conrad's novels, where the device of refraction through intervening minds forms the basis of a highly complex technique.

It must be admitted, however, that Sterne, unlike Conrad, does stretch the truth considerably in making Tristram describe what he did not witness and could not possibly have learned from other sources. In spite of his protests, it

render[s] my book from this very moment, a professed Romance, which, before, was a book apocryphal. (II, 8)

At first Sterne did try to give some degree of verisimilitude to his cognizance of such events as the contretemps between Walter Shandy and his wife at the begetting of Tristram

in the night, betwixt the first Sunday and the first Monday in the month of March, in the year of our Lord 1718. (I, 4)

In this case, he gives his source of information:

To my uncle Mr. Toby Shandy do I stand indebted for the preceding anecdote, to whom my father . . . had oft, and heavily complained of the injury. (I, 3)

Later, however, he abandons all pretence of coming by his information as limiting his powers too seriously, and with unclipped wings he soars into the convention of the omniscient author, a convention artificial in itself and accepted as compatible only with the third-person novel. Sterne might have learned from his predecessor Richardson how punctilious the autobiographical novel could and perhaps should be in such matters, but *Tristram Shandy* would have been fatally circumscribed and fettered by the lesson.

Just as the comments of Tristram are not extraneous to the book and are not therefore to be taken as from an intrusive author, the short stories inset into the novel are not of the excrescent kind such as mar, technically speaking, the form of so many earlier and later novels. The tale of Le Fever or Trim's unfinished story of the King of Bohemia are part of the fabric of the main narrative into which they are inserted. Their removal would leave an irreplaceable gap in the structure. They throw light, and are indeed the best comment on the character of Trim and Uncle Toby; even Slawkenbergius's tale of the noses has the effect of strengthening the impression of Walter Shandy's intellectual foibles, and confirming a central *double entendre.*

These tales offer interesting examples of the technique of "Chinese boxes." Sterne writes a book about Tristram Shandy writing his life in which he, in the year 1760, relates how Trim in 1723 tells the story of Le

Fever's death in 1706; or how Walter Shandy translated for the benefit of his brother the work of Slawkenbergius on noses in the course of which there is given the story of Julia and Diego. One is reminded of Gide writing a novel, *Les Faux-Monnayeurs,* about a novelist, Edouard, who is writing a novel called *Les Faux-Monnayeurs* about a novelist who is writing a novel the title of which, mercifully, we are not given, but which perhaps we can guess.

Sterne was one of the earliest writers to realize that literature is one of the time arts, and is therefore limited by the very nature of its medium, language. The writing of a novel involves, in consequence, a number of temporal factors and conventions which can be exploited in various ways. Little wonder that Diderot, whose article on "Composition" for the *Encyclopédie* furnished many of the ideas of Lessing's "Laocoön," was so deeply impressed and influenced by Sterne; little wonder that Lessing himself, the critic who first adequately analyzed the essential differences between the space and time arts, proclaimed that he would have given ten years of his own life to prolong Sterne's by one. Mrs. Montague wrote that Sterne "really believes his book to be the finest thing the age has produced." He was perhaps not so far out in his belief. Not till modern times do we find so intelligent an attempt to consider the aesthetic and philosophic implications of the novel. Not till Gide and Proust and James and Joyce and Virginia Woolf is there any comparable picture in fiction of the process of living, of life caught in the very act of being. Sterne, moreover, paralleled this with his picture of himself in the process of creating his book. There is in **Tristram Shandy** a threefold development: the characters as they evolve; the author as he works out his conception; and the reader whom Sterne is educating to understand fiction aright.

"A mighty maze! but not without a plan."

One of Coleridge's many unwritten masterpieces was to be an essay

> on one who lived not *in time* at all, past, present, or future,—but beside or collaterally.[17]

He forgot that Sterne had anticipated his idea in **Tristram Shandy.**

Notes

[1] *History of English Poetry, 1774-81,* Sect. III.

[2] *Tom Jones,* II, 1.

[3] *Champion,* December 11, 1739.

[4] Preface to *History of the Countess of Dellwyn,* 1759.

[5] Preface to *The Cry,* 1754, written in collaboration with Miss J. Collier.

[6] Letter to Sir William Elford, May 13, 1815. *Letters of Mary Russell Mitford,* ed. Brimley Johnson.

[7] Lecture on *The Nature and Constituents of Humour,* etc. *Literary Remains* (1836), I, 142.

[8] Letter to Mrs. Vesey, June 1761.

[9] Review of Jane Austen's *Emma,* published December 1815, in the *Quarterly Review,* October 1815.

[10] *Mémoires Historiques sur le XVIII siècle, et sur M. Suard,* par Dominique-Joseph Garat, 2nd ed. (1821), II, 149.

[11] Henry James's terms for a scene presented dramatically as "present."

[12] *Spectator,* January 5, 1712. The theory, deriving from Le Bossu, is expounded more fully by Blackmore: *Preface to Prince Arthur,* 1695.

[13] *Essay on Fictions,* prefaced to *Zulma,* English trans. 1813, Vol. I, p. 9.

[14] "Provided he keeps along the line of his story,—he may go backwards and forwards as he will,—'tis still held to be no digression" (V, 25).

[15] Ford Madox Ford, *Joseph Conrad, a Personal Remembrance* (1924), pp. 191-92.

[16] Ford Madox Ford, *It was the Nightingale* (1934), p. 194.

[17] *Table-Talk,* August 4, 1833.

Melvyn New (essay date 1969)

SOURCE: "Sterne and the Anglican Church," in his *Laurence Sterne as Satirist: A Reading of "Tristram Shandy,"* University of Florida Press, 1969, pp. 5-28.

[*In the following excerpt, New argues that Sterne's* Sermons *reveal his belief in "right reason," a rational morality which is possible only when supported by religion. New maintains that Sterne's religious beliefs can be seen in* Tristram Shandy, *a satire on human appetite and excesses.*]

That sterne was a clergyman of the Anglican church has proved, more often than not, a source of embarrassment to his critics. If the modern critic is not as apt as the Victorian critic to wax indignant over the imposture, he is, nonetheless, unwilling to give the forty-five sermons which survive a meaningful place in the Sterne canon.[1] John Traugott, for example, refuses to treat them as religious documents; they are rhetorical exercises. He concludes a cursory examination of them with a dismissal of their religious significance: "At any rate it is clear that while Sterne was not perfectly suited for the ministry he nevertheless owed the Church a great debt: it first permitted . . . him to express himself."[2] Traugott argues that the sermons are not to be taken seriously—either as religious doctrine or even as serious attempts at moral persuasion. They present instead, he says, "kittenish mocking of affections . . . ever on the verge of comedy," and his entire discussion is designed to show them in a Shandean light.[3]

Lansing V. D. H. Hammond's account of the sermons is basically a source study, but its findings have far-reaching consequences for a proper understanding of Sterne's Christianity. In the first place, if we accept his well-argued conjecture that most, perhaps all, of the sermons were written prior to 1750, indeed, "in rudimentary form" between 1737 and 1745, we are faced with the interesting proposition that the sermons belong, at least in date, to the Augustan period.[4] Even more significant is Hammond's belief that "with the single exception of Swift's *Sermons,* apparently first published in 1744, Sterne made no use in his own discourses of any writing which had not already appeared in print before 1733."[5] Without discounting the incentives of fame and fortune, it can be inferred that Sterne's willingness to publish his sermons in 1760, and again in 1766, indicates a continued commitment to the religious principles he had worked out twenty years before.[6]

The sources of Sterne's religion are Latitudinarian, Tillotson and Clarke being, according to Hammond, the major sources of the sermons.[7] For Hammond, Sterne's Latitudinarian tendencies suggest the unorthodox cast of his religion, but he is cautious in his final statement of Sterne's position. He is aware, in the first place, of the common rationalistic heritage of Latitudinarianism and deism, citing in evidence Robert Kilburn Root's comment that "except in the heat of controversy, it is not easy to distinguish between the religion of an orthodox divine such as Swift and the freethinking deists whom he despised."[8] Hammond is also aware, however, of the several attacks on deism in the sermons. Moreover, Sterne's attitudes toward miracles and mysteries "indicate an acceptance of certain fundamental Christian principles to which no advocate of a purely 'natural' religion would be willing to subscribe."[9]

Unfortunately, Hammond saves Sterne from heresy only to condemn him for superficiality. He notes the indifference to "doctrinal Christianity" and the concern with doctrines not necessarily "peculiar to or distinctive of the Christian religion; his precepts tend to make of Christianity a moral philosophy rather than a religion. . . . " Sterne's failure to marshal authorities and copious quotations and his amazing freedom from the "contemporary language of polemics" are also seen, by Hammond, as indications of Sterne's unorthodox and lukewarm Christian commitment.[10] Hammond, like Traugott, ultimately leaves us with a picture of Sterne as a nominal, Shandean Christian, much like the erstwhile projector of "An Argument Against Abolishing Christianity in England." It is, I believe, a false picture.

A true picture of Sterne's Christianity depends on an understanding of the Latitudinarianism at its roots. The label, it will be recalled, was originally a term of contempt for the Cambridge Platonists, pointing primarily at their advocacy of religious toleration. Insofar as Latitudinarianism implies tolerance, the label is apropos. When, however, it is used to suggest an indifferent sort of Christianity, one at an opposite end from Anglican orthodoxy, then it needs careful qualification. The purpose of the Cambridge Platonists and of their followers, the Latitudinarians, was not the repudiation of orthodoxy but rather its re-establishment after the Interregnum. It was a normalizing and moderating purpose, and its primary instrument was reason. Between the Calvinistic extremism of the Puritans and the politic extremism of Laud, the Cambridge Platonists sought a compromise in the reasonableness of Christianity and of Christian men, hoping to throttle forever the spirit of faction that had dominated seventeenth-century life in England. "The appeal to reason," writes G. R. Cragg, "is the most conspicuous characteristic of the Cambridge school."[11]

The reasonableness of the Cambridge Platonists sought to unite all Christians "on the common ground of the great essentials of religion," while, at the same time, it de-emphasized the finer points of dogma and doctrine which had so disturbed contemporary English Christianity. But it was not the facile reasonableness which would later produce *Christianity Not Mysterious,* not the rationalism which repudiates mysteries simply because they are mysteries.[12] Seeking the middle ground, the Cambridge Platonists worked out the compromise between reason, faith, and revelation that served throughout the eighteenth century to unite varying degrees of Christian orthodoxy within the Anglican church. Debates over doctrinal issues would continue and at times would grow vituperative; but the fierce, disruptive struggles of the seventeenth century yielded to the essential governance of one Church, catholic in nature and flexible in doctrine.

On the question of moral conduct, compromise was again the primary concern of the Cambridge Platonists. Moral laws were divinely revealed, but they were also reasonable; and right conduct was based neither on the inexorable authority of the Calvinistic God nor, as in Hobbes, on obedience to a civil ruler, but rather on one's personal response to the right reason within. Eventually this restoration of free will and moral responsibility became the foundation for religious toleration and, in fact, for both deist and Methodist dissent. The essential intent of the Cambridge Platonists, however, was the re-establishment of a Christian's moral responsibility in the face of Calvinist and Hobbist authorities—and the reaffirmation of right reason, hedged by the authority of revelation, as the cornerstone of morality.

In many ways the Latitudinarians are second-generation Cambridge Platonists, although they inherit far more of the rationalism than the mysticism of their teachers. Against the two enemies of the established Church, Catholicism and Puritanism, reason proved the more effective weapon. At times the emphasis on reason was bound to suggest deism, the religion that reason could discover for itself; but the Latitudinarians had a more orthodox view of man's rational capacity: " . . . reason, by recognizing the limitations latent in our knowledge, is the true corrective to dogmatism. So far from making us overconfident, reason encourages diffidence and humility. . . . We are surrounded by such unfathomable mysteries that any form of dogmatism is intolerable arrogance."[13] The continued respect for mystery and the desire to prove reason in accord with revealed Christianity place the Latitudinarians in the center of eighteenth-century Anglicanism.

The Latitudinarian emphasis on reason had far-reaching effects on sermon-writing throughout the eighteenth century. The rejection of "endless debate about theological niceties" freed the sermon from the interminable citation of authorities and extensive quotations of seventeenth-century discourses. The reaction against Calvinism and predestination put renewed emphasis on the Gospel and the Church as guides for moral conduct. The darkness and anger of the Calvinistic God was displaced by a God of light, a God of love and benevolence. This reaction against Calvinism made Latitudinarianism seem more unorthodox than it ever intended to be. Its true direction, however, is conservative: It aims for a reconciliation of reason and revelation, morality and religion. The sermons of the Latitudinarians are moral rather than polemical, temperate rather than fiery, simple rather than intricate. Their aim is not to "liberalize" Anglicanism, but to return it to the center of English religious life after a century of near disaster.[14]

It is of no slight significance to the study of Sterne's Christianity that Locke agrees with the Latitudinarian divines on many major issues. Locke's *The Reasonableness of Christianity* must be considered a document of the Latitudinarian movement, and his *Essay Concerning Human Understanding,* an explanation of the nature of the rationalism which made the movement possible. The rationalistic revolt against dogma, however, is carried further by Locke than by the Latitudinarians; they turned from authority only in reaction to the dogmatism of the seventeenth century, while Locke's revolt was part of his larger struggle against the entire scholastic method. In fact, Locke's revolt against authority and his insistence on an intellectual, almost mathematical, concept of God provide a good illustration of the distance between Latitudinarianism and deism, for Locke is able to find a comfortable middle ground between the two.[15] Similarly Locke's reduction of Christianity to a belief in Jesus as the Messiah is more simplistic than the Latitudinarians would have wished. However, when pressed on the issue, Locke explained that a belief in Christ included a belief in all the doctrines known to come from Christ, thus returning to a fundamentally orthodox position.[16]

Locke also reinforced the Latitudinarian claim that morality was the subject of Christianity, maintaining both theologically and epistemologically that moral conduct is the proper study of mankind. It is on this vital issue that Locke, like the Latitudinarians, shows the essentially orthodox position of his religious views. He had already demonstrated in the *Essay* that reason is a limited faculty; in *The Reasonableness of Christianity* he stresses the weakness of men and the need, except for the relatively few, of a system of rewards and punishments to ensure moral conduct. At times this system is one of calculating prudence; at times it is the promise of immortality; and at yet other times it is a return to the authority of the Bible and tradition. Locke's insistence on the incapacity of men to follow right reason is a view he shares with the Latitudinarians. It contrasts sharply with the deistic and moral-sense schools which brought morality within everyone's capacity.

One of the most significant studies of Swift in recent years, Phillip Harth, *Swift and Anglican Rationalism,* convincingly places the admittedly orthodox Swift within the Latitudinarian tradition. Harth attempts to dull the initial shock of this assertion by using the term "Anglican rationalists" to emphasize "the characteristic which distinguishes them as apologists of the Church of England."[17] Noting first that the older view of Swift as a skeptic in religion has now been replaced by Ricardo Quintana's illustration of his orthodoxy, Harth suggests that this orthodoxy needs a more accurate definition than the fideism now being associated with Swift.[18] The cause of this association is the false dichotomy we have seen in connection with Sterne between "orthodoxy" and "rationalism," which, Harth writes, "misinterprets the religious situation in Restoration England."

I have, to some extent, already indicated that situation. The crucial struggle of Anglicanism was against Puritan and Catholic dissent; deism or freethinking was also an enemy, of course, but the dangers were less immediate. In this struggle the most important single issue was the role of reason and revelation in religion; according to Harth's simplified but valid schematization, it became a question of mediating between "revelation, no reason" dissenters and "reason, no revelation" deists. The fideist position was, of course, common to many Orthodox Anglicans, but, as the century drew to its close, exclusive revelation became more and more associated with the Puritans. The identification of the Catholics as fideists is in part polemical, but the rationalism of the Latitudinarians could well insist that scholastic logic and transubstantiation were unreasonable. At any rate, the linking of dissenters with Catholics on the supposition that they are possessed by essentially the same "unreason" persists even to Sterne's sermons, for example, "On Enthusiasm."[19] The Cambridge Platonists, the Latitudinarians, and Locke all joined to maintain that, in Harth's words, "reason and revelation are not incompatible in religion. On the contrary, reason and revelation together provide the grounds for religion, so that each plays its proper role in the religious sphere and neither can be ignored." Swift, according to Harth, also maintained this position, "historically . . . the mainstream of tradition in the Catholic and Anglican churches."[20]

For Harth, Swift's place in the Latitudinarian tradition is of significance primarily because of the proof it offers that *A Tale of a Tub* makes use of a traditional set of polemical devices. Sterne, too, in his satire against Catholics may possibly be echoing rather faintly these Restoration polemics. My own primary concern, however, is with the set of norms an orthodox position in the Anglican church makes available to the satirist. Apart from its classical and traditional Christian (Catholic) sources, the moral outlook of Augustan satire (the normative values against which man was measured) was provided in large measure by the orthodox stance of Anglicanism on the nature of man and the possibilities and potentialities of his achieving a moral life. At the same time deviations from the orthodox norm provided many of the targets of Augustan satire. It is no accident, as Louis Landa points out in his introduction to Swift's sermons, that "however brief the treatment, his ideas are present extensively [in the sermons]; and we can assess the nature of his mind and define his position in the eighteenth century from the sermons as clearly as we can from his other works."[21]

The relationship between satire and orthodoxy can be seen in the sermon "On the Trinity," Swift's "most elaborate statement on Christian doctrine" and one which "exhibits clearly the orthodoxy and conventionality of his religious views."[22] The subject is the role of mystery in the Christian scheme; Swift explains why it has a rightful place:

> It would be well, if People would not lay so much Weight on their own Reason in Matters of Religion, as to think every thing impossible and absurd which they cannot conceive. How often do we contradict the right Rules of Reason in the whole Course of our Lives? *Reason* itself is true and just, but the *Reason* of every particular Man is weak and wavering, perpetually swayed and turned by his Interests, his Passions, and his Vices. Let any Man but consider . . . how blinded he is by the Love of himself, to believe that Right is Wrong, and Wrong is Right, when it maketh for his own Advantage. Where is then the right Use of his Reason, which he so much boasteth of, and which he would blasphemously set up to controul the Commands of the Almighty?[23]

That these beliefs in the limits of reason, the power of the passions and self-interest, and the inordinate pride of man operate at the core of Swift's satire is common knowledge. Moreover, Swift makes certain in this sermon on the Trinity that we understand the limits even of right reason: "But because I cannot conceive the Nature of this Union and Distinction in the Divine Nature, am I therefore to reject them as absurd and impossible; as I would, if any one told me that three Men are one, and one Man is three? . . . But the Apostle telleth us, *We see but in part, and we know but in part;* and yet we would comprehend all the secret Ways and Workings of God."[24] Significantly, Landa associates this skepticism with the limitations of reason demonstrated in the *Essay Concerning Human Understanding*. And just as Locke brings skepticism to bear on the systematizing of scholastic philosophers, so Swift uses it to free his sermons from the abstruse speculations of scholastic theologians and those Anglican clergymen who had allowed the spirit of contention to lead them into complex and futile controversies.

Swift's purpose in his sermons is rather bluntly stated at the opening of "On the Trinity": "This Day being set apart to acknowledge our Belief in the Eternal TRINITY, I thought it might be proper to employ my present Discourse entirely upon that Subject; and, I hope, to handle it in such a Manner, that the most Ignorant among you may return home better informed of your Duty in this great Point, than probably you are at present."[25] The refusal to enter into doctrinal disputes, evident in both Swift's and Sterne's sermons, has its roots in the insistence that the function of the clergy is to explain, as simply as possible, the Christian duties of their communicants. The interest in simplicity dominates the advice Swift gives in "A Letter to a Young Gentleman, Lately entered into Holy Orders";[26] the interest in duty is explained in "On the Trinity": "So, that the great Excellency of Faith, consisteth in the Consequence it hath upon our Actions. . . . Therefore, let no Man think that he can lead as good a moral Life without Faith, as with it; for this Reason, Because he who hath no Faith, cannot, by the Strength of his own Reason or Endeavours, so easily resist Temptations, as the other who depends upon God's Assistance in the overcoming his Frailties. . . . "[27] This fast union of morality and religion is one of the marks of Latitudinarian Anglicanism which distinguishes it from the deistic assumption of moral conduct as a possibility quite distinct from religion. Sterne, I shall demonstrate, also takes this orthodox approach.

Swift's sermon "Upon the Excellence of Christianity" is also of significance to the present discussion, for here Swift defends the Christian system of rewards and punishments against the moral systems of the Greek and Roman philosophers. His discourse returns him to the limits of man as a moral creature and to the necessity of the union between religion and morality: "Now, human nature is so constituted, that we can never pursue any thing heartily but upon hopes of a reward. . . . But some of the philosophers gave all this quite another turn, and pretended to refine so far, as to call virtue its own reward, and worthy to be followed only for itself: Whereas, if there be any thing in this more than the sound of the words, it is at least too abstracted to become an universal influencing principle in the world, and therefore could not be of general use."[28] Of this attack on the classical philosophers (and modern deists) Landa writes: "Swift follows the traditional line of argument in contending that for the generality of mankind, only Christianity has provided a really effective incentive to reject vice in favour of virtue—the doctrine of future rewards and punishments; effective because it is sensibly attuned to selfish human nature, its appeal being to man's higher self-interest—his eternal welfare."[29] In Augustan satire this union of morality and religion becomes the demand for a recognition of individual insufficiency and the need for acknowledging external controls as a curb to pride and folly. For the rational Christian as for the rational satirist, right reason informs him, above all, of the inadequacy of the very reason he seeks to re-establish.

A third sermon, "On the Testimony of Conscience," explores these problems further and is of particular interest because of Sterne's discourse on the same subject, "The Abuses of Conscience Considered."[30] Swift's sermon is an attack, once again, on a moral system independent of religion, and more particularly, according to Landa, on Shaftesbury's theory of the moral sense. The view that conscience functions independently of the laws of God, that man possesses a "natural sense of right and wrong which exists prior to and independently of the idea of God" was, for Swift, a false and dangerous heresy. Once again, Landa links Swift to Locke, citing Locke's statement from the *Essay* that "the true ground of morality . . . can only be the will and law of a God, who sees men in the dark, has in his hand rewards and punishments, and power enough to call to account the proudest offender."[31]

The position, Landa notes, is an orthodox one.

The crux of both Swift's and Sterne's sermons is that the testimony of conscience cannot be trusted; that the conscience is abused by our other interests. Swift writes: " . . . whenever our Conscience accuseth us, we are certainly guilty; but we are not always innocent when it doth not accuse us: For very often, through the Hardness of our Hearts, or the Fondness and Favour we bear to our selves, or through Ignorance, or Neglect, we do not suffer our Conscience to take any Cognizance of several Sins we commit."[32] Sterne's views clearly coincide:

> I own . . . whenever a man's Conscience does accuse him . . . that he is guilty. . . .
>
> But, the converse of the proposition will not hold true,—namely, That wherever there is guilt, the Conscience must accuse; and, if it does not, that a man is therefore innocent. . . . did no such thing ever happen, as that the conscience of a man, by long habits of sin, might . . . insensibly become hard . . . —Did this never happen:—or was it certain that self-love could never hang the least bias upon the judgment . . . could no such thing as favour and affection enter this sacred court . . . were we assured that INTEREST stood always unconcern'd . . . and that PASSION never got into the judgment seat, and pronounced sentence in the stead of reason, which is supposed always to preside and deter-mine upon the case . . . then, the religious and moral state of a man would be exactly what he himself esteemed it . . . (IV, 12[27]; ***Sermons***, II, 68-69).

It has long been noted that the comment in ***Tristram Shandy*** "when a man gives himself up to the government of a ruling passion,—or, in other words, when his HOBBY-HORSE grows headstrong,—farewell cool reason and fair discretion!" is an echo of Swift's famous remark in *A Tale of a Tub*: "But when a Man's Fancy gets *astride* on his Reason, when Imagination is at Cuffs with the Senses . . . the first Proselyte he makes, is Himself. . . . " That the same idea appears in the "Abuses of Conscience Considered," with its roots in Swift's "On the Testimony of Conscience," speaks to those critics who slight the echo of *Tale of a Tub*, insisting that Sterne's view of irrational behavior was far different from Swift's, indeed, far more "Christian" than Swift's. On the contrary, it seems evident that both men drew their views from the same source—the orthodox position of the Anglican church on the question of man's ability to find a moral life by himself. Of this morality without religion, Swift says: " . . . those Men who set up for Morality without regard to Religion, are generally but virtuous in part; they will be just in their Dealings between Man and Man; but if they find themselves disposed to Pride, Lust, Intemperance, or Avarice, they do not think their Morality concerned. . . . "[33] Sterne reaches the same conclusion:

[The duties of religion and morality] are so insep-
arably connected together, that you cannot divide
these two *Tables,* even in imagination (tho' the
attempt is often made in practice) without breaking
and mutually destroying them both.

I said the attempt is often made;——and so it is;—
—there being nothing more common than to see a
man, who has no sense at all of religion . . . who
would yet take it as the bitterest affront, should you
but hint at a suspicion of his moral character. . . .

Let him declaim as pompously as he can . . . it will
be found at last to rest upon . . . either his interest,
his pride, his ease . . . (*Sermons,* II, 75-76).

Herbert Read was the first critic to notice that this
view of the conscience is essentially a "classical doctrine"; his opinion has been further defended in Arthur
H. Cash's article "The Sermon in *Tristram Shandy.*"[34]
Working primarily from Lockean psychology, rather
than from Latitudinarian theology (whose influence he
slights), Cash's conclusions are nevertheless much the
same as my own: (1) Sterne's sermons consistently
suggest the inability or reluctance of men to judge their
own behavior because their passions interfere with their
reason; (2) the ethic which results from this view of
man is "at bottom . . . conservative," because it reaf-
firms the orthodox union of religion and morality; and
(3) "no one who ever looked into the sermons could
doubt Sterne's orthodox view of divine commands."
The only serious difference of opinion between Cash
and me arises from his distinction between the *parson*
who sees the failure of self-governance as "deplorable," and the *novelist* who sees it as "laughable."[35]
Cash raises the question of Sterne's apparent faith,
revealed here and there in the sermons, in what seems
to be a "moral sense," but he is unable to reconcile
such faith with a conservative ethic. Nevertheless, he
insists that the "soft view" of man is predominant in
the "novels" which are free from Swiftian satire and
written in "the liberal spirit"—thus questioning the
significance of his whole study.[36] I shall suggest below
that this "soft view" is part of Sterne's Latitudinarian
heritage, the survival of polemical arguments against
the Puritan view of man, but by no means unorthodox
itself.

Cash illustrates very effectively the importance of recognizing Sterne's ethics as conservative. Stressing first
Sterne's rationalism, he uses it as an argument against
those who regard Sterne as a sentimentalist. He demonstrates, for example, that the famous line from *Tristram Shandy,* "REASON is, half of it, SENSE," is in context not at all an affirmation of sensibility, but rather
"that rare instance when Tristram reveals his moral
values by telling us that he and his family have been
the dupes of their appetites and senses—the very point
Sterne makes in *The Abuses of Conscience Con-*

sidered. . . ."[37] At the same time, he emphasizes Sterne's
allegiance to religion, noting particularly his insistence
on the union of religion and morality: "By his admission that moral practice can be effected only through
a fear of God's retribution, Sterne acknowledges a
fundamental self-concern in man. The concession sets
him apart from the more sophisticated rationalists of
his own generation, who argued that true morality had
to be practiced *for its own sake.*"[38] In short, Sterne's
rationalism saves him from sensibility, while his religion saves him from "sophisticated" rationalism, that
is, from deism. The intimate relationship between deism and sensibility suggests that, polemically, Sterne's
position is an orthodox one, diametrically opposed to
the liberalizing tendencies in eighteenth-century
thought.

This orthodoxy is revealed again and again in the sermons of Sterne; there can be little doubt that Sterne in
his sermons not only shares with Swift an orthodox
Christianity, but that this conservative position is what
provides the moral background of Augustan satire. For
example, the very first sermon in Volume I, "Inquiry
after Happiness," is a "vanity of human wishes" discourse—a traditional meeting place of sermon and
satire.[39] It is surely not fortuitous that the first sermon
written under the *nom de plume,* Yorick, should take
man through the stages of life, proving at each stage
that all is vanity; Sterne could hardly have been unaware that the serious import of *Hamlet*'s Yorick was
precisely this. Nor is it fortuitous that this first sermon
should contain the following description of a young
man's quest for happiness:

The moment he is got loose from tutors and
governors, and is left to judge for himself, and
pursue this scheme his own way—his first thoughts
are generally full of the mighty happiness which he
is going to enter upon. . . .

In consequence of this—take notice, how his
imagination is caught by every glittering appearance
that flatters this expectation.—Observe what
impressions are made upon his senses, by diversions,
music, dress and beauty—and how his spirits are
upon the wing, flying in pursuit of them . . . (I, 1;
Sermons, I, 8).[40]

The uncontrolled and uncontrollable range of Tristram's
interests, which the modern critic praises as the desire
to capture the diversity of life, assumes in this sermon
the far different implications of vanity and naïveté.
Sterne's answer to hedonism in general is the traditional answer of Ecclesiastes: fear God and keep His
commandments.[41] The union of religion and morality,
so fundamental to the meaning of this first discourse,
is the most persistent message of Sterne's sermons.[42]

As with Swift, the source of this message is Sterne's

view of the limits of man. We have already seen the outlines of this view in the "Abuses of Conscience Considered"; it receives a similar statement in "Self-Knowledge," where Sterne tells us that "we are deceived in judging of ourselves, just as we are in judging of other things, when our passions and inclinations are called in as counsellors, and we suffer ourselves to see and reason just so far and no farther than they give us leave" (I, 4; *Sermons,* I, 38).[43] Most interesting in this sermon is Sterne's analysis of the possibilities of moral teaching in the face of self-interest; he suggests the moral fable: " . . . as they [moral instructors] had not strength to remove this flattering passion which stood in their way and blocked up all the passages to the heart, they endeavoured by stratagem to get beyond it, and by a skilful address, if possible, to deceive it. This gave rise to the early manner of conveying their instructions in parables, fables, and such sort of indirect applications, which, tho' they could not conquer this principle of self-love, yet often laid it asleep . . . till a just judgment could be procured" (*Sermons,* I, 40). Much has been made by Hammond and others of Sterne's tendency to dramatize his sermons, the implication being that Sterne was more interested in the story he told than in the doctrine he preached. Nothing could be further from the truth, for Sterne's addition of a narrative dimension to several of his sermons is a quite traditional practice in pulpit oratory. Sterne learned much about narrative in writing his sermons; but, above all else, he learned the value of a story as an agreeable vehicle for the often unpleasant task of telling men what they really are. Yorick's comment on preaching, "For my own part . . . I had rather direct five words point blank to the heart," has also been viewed as indicative of Sterne's religious laxity, his "happy-go-lucky disposition."[44] It is clear, however, that Yorick is opposing in this passage the heart to the head as respective seats of truth and hypocrisy. That the heart for Sterne is more closely connected with right reason than with moral sensibility is suggested by the phrase "till a just judgment could be procured" from "Self-Knowledge." When self-deceit is pierced by a story, the heart does not reveal the glory of the naturally moral man, but the truth of the limited man whose reason tells him he must fear God and keep the commandments.[45]

The strongest attacks on self-deception, however, occur in "Pharisee and Publican in the Temple" and "Pride."[46] In the first, Sterne analyzes the character of the Pharisee as an example of the "worst of human passions;—pride—spiritual pride, the worst of all pride—hypocrisy, self-love. . . . " His dramatization of the Pharisee's prayer in the temple is brilliantly ironic:

> GOD! I thank thee that thou hast formed me of different materials from the rest of my species, whom thou hast created frail and vain by nature, but by

choice and disposition utterly corrupt and wicked.

> Me, thou hast fashioned in a different mould. . . .
> I am raised above the temptations and desires to which flesh and blood are subject—I thank thee that thou hast made me thus—not a frail vessel of clay, like that of other men . . . (I, 6; *Sermons,* I, 73).

Apparent through the irony is Sterne's view of man, "frail and vain by nature." Those critics who expect from an eighteenth-century Anglican clergyman a Calvinistic commitment to unrelieved depravity will, of course, find Sterne quite liberal; but those who understand that eighteenth-century orthodoxy was molded during the Restoration, in reaction to Puritan theology, will see that Sterne's view of man is essentially conservative—man, not irrevocably corrupt, but yet "frail and vain by nature . . . by choice and disposition utterly corrupt and wicked." Sterne's several suggestions of the existence of the innate moral sense must be reconciled with this view and not simply accepted as a deistic glorification of man's moral capability.[47]

The sermon "Pride" offers a more systematic attack on this vice of "little and contracted souls." On the one hand, Sterne argues with those "satyrical pens" that write "all mankind at the bottom were proud alike," for, he says, there are thousands of men of the most unaffected humility (IV, 9 [24]; *Sermons,* II, 33-34). On the other hand, Sterne supports these same "satyrical pens" insofar as "Pride is a vice which grows up in society so insensibly . . . that upon the whole, there is no one weakness into which the heart of man is more easily betray'd,——or which requires greater helps of good sense and good principles to guard against" (*Sermons,* II, 34). Moreover, in explaining that the origin of pride is in meanness of heart, the vice of "little and contracted souls," Sterne can do no better than to quote "one of our poets . . . in that admirable stroke he has given of this affinity, in his description of a *Pride which licks the dust.*" Sterne's attack on satire in this sermon is often taken out of context as indicative of his negative attitude toward the genre; no recognition is shown that in the same paragraph he gives a qualified assent to the satirists, and in the next quotes Pope's *Epistle to Dr. Arbuthnot* to support his view.[48] The use of satire to attack pride is suggested again in "Job's Account of the Shortness and Troubles of Life Considered" (II, 10). Sterne raises the question at the end of this survey of human misery of what purpose it serves to expose the dark side of human life, and finds it of great importance, since "the holding up this glass to shew him his defects . . ." cures man's pride and gives him humility—"which is a dress that best becomes a short-lived and a wretched creature" (*Sermons,* I, 124). When Sterne criticizes satirists, as he does in "Vindication of Human Nature" (I, 7) where he takes exception to those satirists who have "desperately fallen foul upon the whole species" (*Sermons,* I, 83), he is not necessarily aligning himself with the general attack on satire prevalent in the middle of the century.[49] His obvious taste for the Augustans and our own understanding of them make it at least as possible that he was drawing a distinction between invective and satire; Dryden, Pope, and Swift would do no less.[50]

For Sterne, as for Locke, the Latitudinarians, and the Augustans, excessive pride is inextricably linked to enthusiasm and dissent. The sermon "Humility," for example, becomes strongly polemical, reminding us of the strength of Methodism among the lower classes during the 1740's.[51] Sterne again turns to irony:

> However backwards the world has been in former ages in the discovery of such points as GOD never meant us to know,——we have been more successful in our own days:——thousands can trace out now the impressions of this divine intercourse in themselves. . . .

> It must be owned, that the present age has not altogether the honour of this discovery;—there were too many grounds given to improve on in the religious cant of the last century; . . . when, as they do now, the most illiterate mechanicks, who as a witty divine said of them, were much fitter to *make* a pulpit, than get into one,—were yet able so to frame their nonsense to the nonsense of the times, as to beget an opinion in their followers . . . that the most common actions of their lives were set about in the Spirit of the LORD (IV, 10 [25]; *Sermons,* II, 49-50).

The witty divine is obviously Swift, and Sterne begins to sound more like him with every stroke: "When a poor disconsolated drooping creature is terrified from all enjoyment,—prays without ceasing 'till his imagination is heated,——fasts and mortifies and mopes, till his body is in as bad a plight as his mind; is it a wonder, that the mechanical disturbances and conflicts of an empty belly, interpreted by an empty head, should be mistook for workings of a different kind from what they are . . ." (*Sermons,* II, 51).

It is the sermon "On Enthusiasm," however, which most clearly reveals Sterne's use of Latitudinarian arguments to reject the pride of deism and dissent. Noting the deist's tendency to ignore revelation and the dissenter's contrary tendency to "destroy the reason of the gospel itself,—and render the christian religion, which consists of sober and consistent doctrines,—the most intoxicated,—the most wild and unintelligible institution that ever was . . . ," he defines his purpose to "reduce both the extremes . . . to reason [and] . . . to mark the safe and true doctrine of our church . . ." (VI, 11 [38]; *Sermons,* II, 187). Above all, his theme is to prove the wisdom of "our sufficiency being of God";

his text is John 15:5: *"For without me, ye can do nothing."* Sterne's arguments for the necessity of revelation are traditional; his arguments against enthusiasm are also traditional, including an interesting linking of enthusiasm with Catholicism: "Already it [enthusiasm] has taught us as much blasphemous language;—and . . . will fill us with as many legendary accounts of visions and revelations, as we have formerly had from the church of Rome. . . . When time shall serve, it may as effectually convert the professors of it, even into popery itself,—consistent with their own principles . . ." (*Sermons,* II, 197). Throughout his attack on the extremes, Sterne persists in arguing the rational middle way, ending with a benediction which defines, exactly and emphatically, his orthodox religious position: " . . . I have little left to add, but to beg of GOD by the assistance of his holy spirit, to preserve us equally from both extremes, and enable us to form such right and worthy apprehensions of our holy religion,—that it may never suffer, through the coolness of our conceptions of it, on one hand,—or the immoderate heat of them, on the other;—but that we may at all times see it, as it is . . . the most rational, sober and consistent institution that could have been given to the sons of men" (*Sermons,* II, 198).

Article IX of the Thirty-Nine Articles, "Of Original or Birth-Sin," reads in part: "Original Sin standeth not in the following of *Adam* (as the *Pelagians* do vainly talk), but it is the fault and corruption of the Nature of every man, that naturally is engendered of the offspring of *Adam;* whereby man is very far gone from original righteousness, and is of his own nature inclined to evil, so that the flesh lusteth always contrary to the spirit. . . . " As Anglicans, both Swift and Sterne accepted this view of man's nature; it molded their vision of the life they wrote about and the form that that vision took. Article IX, to be sure, rejects the Calvinistic extreme of total depravity, and we search in vain for this view in either Sterne or Swift. Article IX does, however, make absolutely clear that man is not only susceptible, but indeed inclined, to sin; that he possesses, as Ernest Tuveson comments, "a positive tendency to do evil, a mysterious dynamic spirit of perversity for which there is explanation in Genesis and remedy in the Gospel."[52] Such contrariness makes the teachings of the Christian church absolutely vital to man's ethical life; thus, for Sterne and Swift, morality is never to be separated from religion, wisdom never to be divorced from revelation. The faculty of reason is, of course, essential to man, but right reason is never contradictory to revelation. Reason is our most reliable faculty, but it too is rendered imperfect by the perverse tendency to evil which makes revelation our only certain means of salvation.

It is here in the Anglican view of willful and insistent perversity that the Augustan vision of man takes its literary foothold, for in the abuse of reason can be found the root of all religious, social, political, and literary aberrations, all the targets of Augustan satire. If in the religious life the doctrines of the Anglican church provided the norms against which deviations could be measured, the ordered universe suggested that in every other sphere of human endeavor, analogous deviations could be measured by analogous standards. Man's tendency to evil operated in literature as well as in religion, in polite society as well as in the state. It is not at all fortuitous that Swift uses a literary hack to satirize religious enthusiasm, or that the epic action of Pope's *Dunciad* should bring "The Smithfield Muses to the Ear of Kings."[53] For the Augustan satirist, bad writing is a natural symbol for the moral corruption that demands and supplies it, and thus he has, ready at hand, the metaphorical and symbolic patterns which contribute so greatly to the tensions and complexities of his writings. As Geoffrey Tillotson notes, "for Pope, a bad author was to literature what a fool or a knave was to life."[54]

Finally, the relation of the Augustan vision to the Anglican sense of man's perverse inclination to evil suggests the norm by which, ultimately at least, its satire operated. As in religion an acknowledgment of the limitations of man necessarily implies a dependence on the authority of the Church, so in all other realms of conduct authority of some kind is indicated. A rigid codification of that authority—whether it be ecclesiastical, critical, or political—is rarely attempted, the authority more often than not revealing itself by its expressed sensitivity to deviations from its spirit rather than by a crystalization of its law. This may, in fact, prove the ultimate virtue of Augustan authority, at its best—that it refuses to be categorical, that it resists the systematic fallacy, to which Puritans and projectors alike were so prone. Augustan authority rather tends to invite man to look for the operation of reason or common sense or nature; to look for generality, moderation, and compromise; and to acknowledge his inherent weakness, limitation, and need for discipline, tradition, and control. The authority or norm, in other words, is not so much abstractly defined as it is pragmatically revealed or exposed: In each sphere of human activity it emerges, characteristically, from the satiric consideration of deviations. In short, more important to an understanding of the moral world of Augustan satire than any precise measure of its norm is the simple fact of the norm itself. The ultimate field of that norm is Anglicanism; not, however, some specific doctrine of Anglicanism violated, say, by Puritan enthusiasm, but the acceptance by the satirist (and his audience) of an orthodox Christian position, catholic enough to include Pope, as normative.

Similarly, I would suggest that deviations from the norm, while as various as man's contrary imagination, all spring essentially from the same source: man's prideful rebellion against his own limited nature and the authority placed over him to discipline his waywardness. I have already shown how Swift and Sterne agree in finding excessive pride at the root of both deism and dissent. If we turn to *Gulliver's Travels,* we note that pride is still the central concern. Edward Rosenheim, for example, writes: "I do not think the crucial concepts in *Gulliver's Travels* are 'man' or 'animal' or 'rational,' for all the obvious importance of these terms. In the *Travels,* as in the *Tale,* Swift's most profound intellectual commitments hinge, I believe, upon his conception of knowledge and of pride. . . . "[55] Kathleen M. Williams recognizes the same problem: "Swift frequently comments on man's strange inability, shared with no other animal, to know his own capacities, and the form which this inability most often takes . . . is a refusal to realise how narrowly we are bounded by our bodies, by senses and passions and by all the accidents of our physical presence in a material world."[56] And we need not agree completely with Tuveson's reading of Book IV, to accept the validity of this view of Gulliver among the Houyhnhnms: "The dilemma and despair . . . [of Gulliver], in his inevitable failure to be able to emulate the patterns of perfection, in his failure to understand the whole situation, would be those of anyone who attempts to account for human nature without original sin."[57] The refusal to recognize, because of pride, one's own limited nature; the refusal to accept, because of pride, the authority of what has been: These are the essential vices of Augustan satire. And conversely, the use of the reason to control pride and acknowledge one's limitations; the use of the reason to argue against pride the necessity for authority: These are the essential virtues by which these vices are measured and condemned. In the tense interplay of authority, pride, and reason, the Augustans defined their satiric vision; it is as well, I believe, the vision Sterne accepted and upheld in his satire, *Tristram Shandy.*

Notes

[1] For the texts of the sermons I have used *The Sermon of Mr Yorick,* vols. I and II (Shakespeare Head ed., 1927), hereafter cited within the text as *Sermons.* I have also adopted Hammond's system of enumeration: Roman numerals indicate the volume; Arabic numerals, the number originally given to a sermon within that volume; and Arabic numerals within parentheses, the cumulative number of the sermon in the complete collection.

[2] *Tristram Shandy's World: Sterne's Philosophical Rhetoric* (Berkeley, 1954), p. 106.

[3] *Ibid.,* p. 101.

[4] *Laurence Sterne's* Sermons of Mr. Yorick (New Haven, 1948), pp. 56-57. For a criticism of this view, see M. R. B. Shaw, *Laurence Sterne: The Making of a Humorist, 1713-1762* (London, 1957), pp. 103-4.

[5] Hammond, p. 56.

[6] Cf. Arthur Hill Cash's similar defense for his use of the sermons in *Sterne's Comedy of Moral Sentiments: The Ethical Dimension of the* Journey (Pittsburgh, 1966), pp. 25-29.

[7] Hammond, pp. 78-81.

[8] *Ibid.,* p. 91; Hammond is quoting from Root, *The Poetical Career of Alexander Pope* (Princeton, 1938), p. 181. Cf. G. N. Clark, *The Later Stuarts: 1660-1714* (Oxford, 1934), pp. 30-31: "This insistence on reason was characteristic of English theology from the time of Locke to that of Joseph Butler . . . of the orthodox as well as of the deists, and it was developed by the . . . latitudinarians. . . . " That this is so only increases the importance of distinguishing between the orthodox position and the deistic heresy; cf. Sir Leslie Stephen, *History of English Thought in the Eighteenth Century,* 3rd ed. (New York, 1902), I, 74 ff.

[9] Hammond, p. 92. Cf. S. L. Bethell, *The Cultural Revolution of the Seventeenth Century* (London, 1951), p. 17. Bethell corrects Clark's view that the Latitudinarians rejected revelation for reason.

[10] Hammond, p. 92.

[11] *From Puritanism to the Age of Reason* (Cambridge, 1950), p. 42.

[12] *Ibid.,* pp. 42 ff. That the Cambridge Platonists had a strong mystical strain need not concern us here; as forerunners of the Latitudinarians their fundamental contribution was their belief that reason could not contradict faith; that faith would only support reason; and that reason and revelation were one.

[13] *Ibid.,* p. 67.

[14] Cf. Bethell, pp. 17-18. Bethell's essay convincingly demonstrates the orthodoxy of the Latitudinarian position on reason and revelation.

[15] See, especially, the discussion of revelation in *Essay Concerning Human Understanding,* IV, xviii-xix. Cf. Cragg, pp. 122-24.

[16] Cf. Stephen, pp. 95-97.

[17] Chicago, 1961, p. 20.

[18] *Ibid.,* pp. 20-21. See Quintana, *The Mind and Art of Jonathan Swift* (New York, 1936) and *Swift: An Introduction* (London, 1955). For Swift as a fideist see Kathleen Williams, *Jonathan Swift and the Age of Compromise* (Lawrence, Kan., 1958).

[19] Harth, pp. 21-23. Of course, in the heat of polemics, it was just as easy to link Catholicism to deism, as Swift does in "An Argument Against Abolishing Christianity in England."

[20] Harth, p. 23.

[21] *The Prose Works,* ed. Herbert Davis (Oxford, 1948), IX, 101.

[22] *Ibid.,* p. 107.

[23] *Ibid.,* p. 166.

[24] *Ibid.,* pp. 161-62.

[25] *Ibid.,* p. 159.

[26] *Ibid.,* pp. 63-81. See especially his remarks on the proper language for a sermon, pp. 65-66; on the quoting of learned authorities, pp. 75-76; on the need to explore the mysteries of the Church, p. 77. Nothing in this advice is significantly different from Latitudinarian reforms in sermon-writing.

[27] *Ibid.,* p. 164.

[28] *Ibid.,* p. 244.

[29] *Ibid.,* p. 113.

[30] Hammond lists the parallel passages (pp. 151-52), but considers them insignificant (p. 83). Another of Sterne's sermons, "Self-Knowledge" (I, 4), borrows extensively from "The Difficulty of Knowing One's Self," published with Swift's sermons in 1744 or 1745, although considered today of questionable authorship. See Swift, *The Prose Works,* IX, 103-6, 349-62.

[31] *The Prose Works,* IX, 115. Landa is quoting from *Essay Concerning Human Understanding,* I, ii, 6.

[32] *The Prose Works,* IX, 150.

[33] *Ibid.,* pp. 152-53.

[34] *The Sense of Glory* (Cambridge, 1929), pp. 144-45; *ELH,* XXXI (1964), 395-417.

[35] Cash, pp. 400-404.

[36] *Ibid.,* pp. 414-17.

[37] *Ibid.,* p. 410.

[38] *Ibid.,* p. 411.

[39] In searching for a metaphor for the vanities of dignity, honor, and title, Sterne suggests the "Satyrist's

comparison of the chariot wheels,—haste as they will, they must for ever keep the same distance" (I, 1; *Sermons,* I, 10). The satirist is Persius (V, 71-72).

⁴⁰ Cf. "Pride" (IV, 9[24]; *Sermons,* II, 36); Sterne, in discussing the effects of pride on a weak brain, seems again to describe Tristram: The weak mind filled with pride is sure "to become the very fool of the comedy."

⁴¹ Five of the fifteen sermons of Volumes I and II deal in a central way with the vanity of this world: in addition to I, 1, see I, 2; II, 8; II, 10; II, 15.

⁴² See, for example, the strong statements in III, 6 (21); IV, 11 (26); V, 2 (29); V, 3 (30); V, 5 (32); V, 6 (33); VI, 7 (34); VII, 16 (43). V, 5 (32) is of especial interest in that it is a "30th of January" sermon, long an index of political views. Sterne's attack on both "the guilt of our forefathers in staining their hands in blood," and the rebellion of 1745, suggests an essentially conservative position.

⁴³ Cf. "The Character of Herod" (II, 9), where Sterne suggests that although we are made in God's image, innocent and upright, we are creatures all too easily swayed by our passions, particularly our ruling passion (*Sermons,* I, 101-11).

⁴⁴ Hammond, pp. 99-101.

⁴⁵ Cf. "The Prodigal Son" (III, 5 [20]; *Sermons,* I, 227): "I know not whether the remark is to our honour or otherwise, that lessons of wisdom have never such power over us, as when they are wrought into the heart, through . . . a story which engages the passions. . . . Is the heart so in love with deceit, that where a true report will not reach it, we must cheat it with a fable, in order to come at truth?"

⁴⁶ I, 6, and IV, 9 (24). See also, "Self-Examination" (II, 14; *Sermons,* I, 160-68).

⁴⁷ Cf. "Vindication of Human Nature" (I, 7). This sermon, often cited as an example of Sterne's "soft view" of man, is no more than an orthodox argument against Hobbes' doctrine of universal selfishness. Sterne argues that although the brightness of God's image has been "sullied greatly" by the fall, and by our "own depraved appetites," yet it is a "laudable pride . . . to cherish a belief, that there is so much of that glorious image still left upon it, as shall restrain him from base and disgraceful actions . . ." (*Sermons,* I, 82-83). The orthodoxy of this "divine residue" and its distance from any sort of deistic or Shaftesburian moral sense should be apparent.

⁴⁸ "Beauty that shocks you, Parts that none will trust,/ Wit that can creep, and Pride that licks the dust." *An Epistle to Dr. Arbuthnot,* 11. 332-33; the lines describe Sporus.

⁴⁹ See Bertrand A. Goldgar, "Satires on Man and 'The Dignity of Human Nature,'" *PMLA,* LXXX (1965), 535-41.

⁵⁰ Cf. "Evil-Speaking" (II, 11), and "The Levite and his Concubine" (III, 3 [18]). In the latter the attack on satire is actually an attack on the *false* wits of the age who set up as libelers.

⁵¹ The satiric reaction to Methodism is surveyed in Albert M. Lyles, *Methodism Mocked* (London, 1960). The Jacobite scare in 1745 suggests one reason for the anti-Catholicism of the sermons; in short, Sterne's Anglicanism was facing essentially the same challenges Swift's faced a quarter century before.

⁵² "Swift: The Dean as Satirist," *UTQ* [*University of Toronto Quarterly*], XXII (1952-53), 370. See also, Donald Greene, "Augustinianism and Empiricism: A Note on Eighteenth-Century English Intellectual History," *ECS* [*Eighteenth Century Studies*], I (1967), 39-51.

⁵³ See Aubrey L. Williams, *Pope's* Dunciad: *A Study of Its Meaning* (Baton Rouge, 1955). Of this "analogy," Williams writes: "The inundation of England by purveyors of bad art, and the untutored or degenerate taste which hailed their literary efforts, was a 'conjuncture' of events suggesting a general slackening in the moral and social fibre of the nation." Artistic deterioration, he adds, is the "metaphor by which bigger deteriorations are revealed" (p. 14).

⁵⁴ *On the Poetry of Pope* (Oxford, 1938), p. 35.

⁵⁵ *Swift and the Satirist's Art* (Chicago, 1963), p. 220.

⁵⁶ "'Animal Rationis Capax.' A Study of Certain Aspects of Swift's Imagery," *ELH,* XXI (1954), 196.

⁵⁷ Tuveson, p. 369. See also Samuel H. Monk, "The Pride of Lemuel Gulliver," *Sewanee Review,* LXIII (1955), 48-71; Edward Wasiolek, "Relativity in *Gulliver's Travels,*" *PQ* [*Philological Quarterly*], XXXVII (1958), 110-16; James Brown, "Swift as Moralist," *PQ,* XXXIII (1954), 368-87. Brown comments at one point: " . . . the fault is that of pride, the condition ignored is Original Sin, the final result is vicious action—moral chaos" (p. 381).

Richard A. Lanham (essay date 1973)

SOURCE: "The Self-Serving Narrator," in his *Tristram Shandy: The Games of Pleasure,* University of California Press, 1973, pp. 93-130.

[In the following essay, Lanham contends that seemingly random interruptions of the main narrative by the protagonist/narrator of Tristram Shandy *derive from classical examples of digression.]*

I

Tristram's fondness for philosophically justified digression has bemused his admirers into overlooking the older narrative pattern from which the digressions depart. For all his joking about Locke's history-book, Tristram was writing one himself, an intellectual autobiography. His proceedings will be those of a classic chronicler, he declares early in Book I:

> He will have views and prospects to himself perpetually solliciting his eye, which he can no more help standing still to look at than he can fly; he will moreover have various
>
> Accounts to reconcile:
> Anecdotes to pick up:
> Inscriptions to make out:
> Stories to weave in:
> Traditions to sift:
> Personages to call upon:
> Panegyricks to paste up at this door . . .
>
> To sum up all; there are archives at every stage to be look'd into, and rolls, records, documents, and endless genealogies, which justice ever and anon calls him back to stay the reading of:—In short, there is no end of it;—for my own part, I declare I have been at it these six weeks, making all the speed I possibly could,—and am not yet born:—I have just been able, and that's all, to tell you *when* it happen'd, but not *how;*—so that you see the thing is yet far from being accomplished. [I, xv, 37]

However jocular this declaration of purpose, and however much he later departed from it, it shows Tristram looking back to [a] kind of Herodotean narrative. . . . The classical historians had shown him a very different kind of pattern, one where narrative gave way at regular intervals to rhetorical occasion. Whether fictionalized public debate, oracle, formal character, apostrophic moral reflection, or narrative digression in the high style, these interruptions all offered opportunity for indirect, ironical commentary on the chronicle they interrupted. Such an interruption—Thucydides' Pericles praising the Athenians, Livy's Hannibal rallying his troops, or Sallust's Cato exhibiting his antique yet sterile virtue—hardly digresses in the usual sense of the word. It stands as part of the narrative rather than ornament to it. Tristram puts this narrative lesson to two uses. He borrows the integral digression for himself; he borrows the narrative-digression-narrative-digression pattern for his Father and Uncle Toby. The chronicles of both proceed by narrative descriptions, comment plus generalization, alternating with the highly dramatic set pieces that make *Tristram Shandy* so easily excerptable. Tristram, introducing Toby, will tell us of his great modesty, then later show it in action, show it transmuting, for example, Le Fever's embarrassing manner of death into a tableau incapable of making a young person blush. Or he will let his father develop one of his "thousand little sceptical notions of the comick kind," in an apostrophe, then contrast notion and subsequent behavior. The reader, much as with Thucydides, Livy, or Sallust, must keep on his toes, continually compare telling and showing. The comparison often aims for irony. As with the historians (and with Shakespeare the historian) we become self-conscious about the rhetorical occasion, develop a feeling for the backstage. In this narrative tradition, context is crucial and excerpting the primal curse. So with *Tristram Shandy.* The sentimental bouquet-gatherer, like Gielgud reciting posies from Shakespeare, is bound to misunderstand and distort. Such bouquet-picking leads to curiously parallel misconceptions, too: Coleridge praising Shakespeare's language of natural description in *Venus and Adonis* but missing its bawdily comic context, and Bagehot praising Sterne's fidelity to plain scenery and plain feeling but repudiating its context. Watkins calls Sterne "the first real impressionist among English novelists," and others have pointed to a connection with Richardson's mastery of immediate detail which might make him the second. But all these estimations,[1] to be useful, ought never to lose sight of the narrative context in which such a Wordsworthian eye for the daisies of feeling recur. In *Tristram Shandy,* the public occasion always has a private frame.

Tristram makes his game from this classical method of narrative. Two changes signal a shift to the game sphere. He juggles two or three of these narrative-speech progressions at the same time. He digresses for pleasure, not from narrative need. If we were to try, impossibly, to disentangle the narrative threads of *Tristram Shandy,* we might find a narrative-speech-narrative-speech pattern for Walter Shandy, one for Toby, perhaps one for Yorick. Tristram's game, or part of it, is to juggle them, to let them fall finally into a meaningful superposition, one atop the other. Yorick must dive for a chestnut when we expect Walter to dive for the mysteries of name-giving; Tristram must kiss the critic's hand when the context leads us to expect him to kiss another part of the body; Toby, amidst the birth pangs that produce Tristram headfirst, must discourse on not hurting a hair on a fly's head. This alternation creates a Thucydidean pattern raised to the third power. Tristram controls the interweaving. He is no jocular Joyce, however, only pretending to trust God for the second sentence. Behind the pretense of chaos may lie careful chronology, but not always a master intelligence. Process literature this novel is, vaguely realizing itself toward a termination coincident with the author's conscious intention. Sterne's preconscious voice, Tristram, confesses throughout the novel both that he really is helter-skelter and that he only seems so, that the digressions interrupt the main story, are the main story. Confessions aside, he does not proceed at random. But his consistent principle in digression and juggled narrative hardly satisfies critical expectation. Tristram does as he pleases. Yet if, as is generally recognized, his game is the novel itself, should it surprise that his playing seeks play's characteristic reward? He is not a Shandy for nothing.

II

Tristram thinks literary genre a kind of game. Inventing a new type, the song of himself, he can invent the rules for it. None others apply: "In writing what I have set about, I shall confine myself neither to his rules, nor to any man's rules that ever lived" (I, v, 8). What more natural than his choosing the rules under which he would rest most easy? He thus stipulates at the outset a relationship with his hobby different from that his Father and Uncle use. Their responses are *mechanized* by their obsessions. He intends that his shall be liberated. Questions arise. Who is Tristram's opponent? In what kind of game does one player make up such rules as he pleases, and seemingly as he goes along? His opponents can be only two: Circumstance and Us. Tristram has trouble telling his story but the trouble forms part of the story he wants to tell. "One would think," he tells us himself, "I took pleasure in running into difficulties of this kind, merely to make fresh experiments of getting out of 'em—"(VIII, vii, 545). It is so. Circumstance proves an obstruction, more often than not, of his own contriving. He represents himself as involved in a Herculean effort to *comply* with standards, to preserve above all narrative and thematic continuity. A few lines before those just quoted:

> I declare, I do not recollect any one opinion or passage of my life, where my understanding was more at a loss to make ends meet, and torture the chapter I had been writing, to the service of the chapter following it, than in the present case.

But the struggle really dramatized is not his compliance with the regular rules of any one genre. He does not manfully wrestle with Art. Instead, he dramatizes Ease warping Art to its own particular purposes. Stedmond comes close to Tristram's real business.

> Tristram as clown-author draws attention to the very real obstacles which lie in the path of artistic accomplishment, emphasizes the human frailties of even the greatest authors, and creates a critical awareness in the reader of some of the goals which authors have sought; in the process of all this he is perhaps calling into question the attainability of these goals, or even the desirability of attaining them.[2]

But this makes *Tristram Shandy* into a more ambitious critical treatise than it is. Tristram deposes only that conventional artistic purpose is not his, that he lives not for Art but for Pleasure. In its pursuit he scorns his second possible opponent, Us, as much as the recalcitrant Circumstance so much supposed to intimidate him. Self-conscious as he is, poseur to his fingertips, still he makes us play his game. It is a new one. We try to figure out *what the rules are*. He remains to us cavalier. Follow me if you can. His particular pleasure lies elsewhere—in himself. In this sense the novel is *not* (*pace* Traugott) rhetorical at all. It turns in on itself. Tristram pleases himself. His game is an *ilinx,* a self-imposed dizziness. At this game one can play. No audience needed. The implication of this stands central to our interpretation of *Tristram Shandy.* Both Tristram and his novel are autoerotic not rhetorical. They aim not to persuade but to please themselves. We may admire their world, but we are not asked to join it. In a limited but very real sense neither novel nor narrator cares what we think.

When Tristram seems solicitous about his reader, he has more often than not his own designs in mind. He is a man of many morals. Part of his game with the reader is to offer a constant farrago of philosophic reflection and moralizing, challenging him to take his ironic or serious pick. We are told that mirth is at the center of the universe and mocked for our grave faces. At the same time, within the unprepossessing Silenus box of jesting lurks real philosophic wisdom. We seek it out. And are mocked for that. We are damned if we do and damned if we don't. This strategy denies us a single point of view in the novel, a philosophic control as it were, and then continually alerts us to the need for one. Thus we must constantly search for a key, a basis for interpretation, and feel silly for doing so. As Burckhardt prefaces his try, "To look for the 'law' of *Tristram Shandy* is one of the least promising enterprises in criticism."[3] The strategy tells the critical history of the novel. We accept one or the other of the various morals offered—sentimentality (the Victorians), stoical humor (Stedmond, Piper), the vanity of learning (Jefferson), the artificiality of literary convention (Lehman), the vanity of words and need for fellow-feeling (Traugott), the dependability of moral sentiment and orthodox religion (Cash)—and interpret the rest of the novel as supplementary if it agrees, ironic if it does not. The sentiment was for a long time seen as pure and unalloyed but that day, I take it, is now over. When Le Fever is killed off, we weep as self-conscious, ironical weepers should. Sentiment may still be, in Toby, the book's center, but Traugott's penetrating analysis of its rhetoric calls that and all—since it calls words—in doubt. A radical skepticism seems now the only general position and a dependence on the goodness of feeling the only path out of a vast perplexity.

The reader, then, is deliberately made uneasy, and his unease backlights Tristram's perfect ease. Tristram knows his way around in his own world perfectly. He should. He has made it to please himself. The reader's search for a key to the novel is really a search for a way to enjoy a pleasure—living in a world one *has* made, one has (Kenneth Burke's term) *earned* by a full understanding—similar to Tristram's. We may put this search into two frames of reference. We may say that the reader is offered a critical and rhetorical problem (understanding the novel) whose solution will lead to a moral awareness (the moral wisdom inside the Silenus box), a final point of view. Or we may say that the reader is offered a posture of puzzlement and discomfort. He does not know whether to laugh or cry. He must always analyze first. A point of view will make him again easy because he will once more be able to respond spontaneously. His naïveté will have been restored. If we think of Tristram's deliberate puzzlement of the reader (that is, think of *Tristram Shandy*) as Tristram's game, and of ourselves as invited to play it in order to gain the freedom and pleasure of the novel's world, do we not have an analogy with Toby's character, with the movement from absorption in game to a liberation of the feelings, a true spontaneity? We are, that is, invited to follow Toby's example. We too will be laughed at, but we will gain, in a hopefully more sophisticated way, what Toby has gained, a universe where our feelings are reliable, can be depended upon.

Thus it is a mistake, I think, to entertain the idea of fellow-feeling, social sympathy, as an external point of view brought into the novel—or even found there, internal—which will lead us out of the maze Sterne's radical discounting of language creates. It seems rather something you earn by finding your way out of the maze, penetrating the novel's rhetoric. We must understand before we can feel. What we must understand, as we see it in Yorick and the Shandy brothers, is that pleasure, satisfaction, is the necessary precondition to the kind of selfless feeling for others on which a true society—rather than merely a collection of individuals—must be based. Toby has undergone this training unaware. For us it will be self-conscious. Thus that the novel is sentimental, rather than full of sentiment, is to be expected. One of the lessons Tristram teaches us is that when we feel for others, we do so largely for the pleasure of the feeling. The Victorian objection that none of Sterne's sentiment is sincere must be very much to the point. It is in the nature of feeling, we are thus told, to be self-serving. When we are invited to observe ourselves feeling, and enjoying feeling, for other people, we are not to conclude that this is a satirical reflection on our hypocrisy. There is nothing hypocritical about taking pleasure. Furthermore, it is the necessary precondition to spontaneous feeling. Sentimentality must precede sentiment. We will feel for others only when we have felt enough for ourselves.

A great deal has been made of *Tristram Shandy* as a deliberate attempt to point out the inadequate narrative method Sterne saw in the eighteenth-century novel and to remedy it. Thus Fluchère argues:

> La digression est plus qu'une exaltante affirmation de liberté, elle devient le docile instrument de capture d'un réel malévole et fuyant, elle explore les domaines secrets de l'espace et du temps, de la connaissance et du mystère.[4]

Is it impertinent to ask what are these secrets of time and space? What are the victories of Sterne's narrative method? Apart from the penetralia of free association, how much do the digressions expand our ideas of time and space? Very little. To make Sterne a prophet of fictional technique seems equally uncalled for. If conventional form had a symbolic value for him it must have been a general one—the Censor, the Public Life's discipline. Plot equals Duty. The novel's response is Tristram's. Too coy, too concerned with dramatizing his breaking the rules, he avoids ceremoniously the discipline of form. He does it, we might add, not to philosophize about communication, though he invites us to do this, but because he enjoys it. Sir Walter Scott, we remember, had called *Tristram Shandy* "no narrative but a collection of scenes, dialogues, and portraits, humorous or affecting, intermixed with much wit, and with much learning, original or borrowed." And a modern historian of Sterne's commentators says flatly: "No one can argue sensibly that the novel is of a piece."[5] Are we not now at a point where we can admit the soundness of this view (lasting after all as it has almost from Sterne's day to this) and still see a single pattern, a unifying force and psyche, in Tristram and the kind of hobbyhorse he rides? Might we not see the struggle between philosophical self and rhetorical self *allegorized* by the struggle between conventional and "easy" narrative?

III

We might begin our discussion of Tristram's vertigo with the famous Shandean dash. It has come to represent Sterne's allegiance to a reality greater than ordinary chronological and syntactical narrative can provide. One of a graduated series of interruptions the novel offers, does it not incarnate the pleasure-principle much rather? The breakings-off, often on a scale larger than the Shandean dash comprehends, can, from Tristram's point of view, hardly be called a principle of interruption at all. They keep us off balance; this, positively stated, they do for him too. He, as he says himself, continually rushes about. Not to fetch a metaphor from too far, we might call him a juggler. Centered in his poise, in his search for it, stands a fondness for keeping several things going at once. We must know him as a literary borrower, see his sources as sources, so as to relish their orchestration into his theme.

(We recall Sterne's fondness for vertiginous sources, Rabelais for example.) Tristram does not make over a novel's regular components into a new vehicle for new space and time. He but juggles them. A misplaced preface, two chapters left empty to be filled later make a virtuoso point. Watch! Tristram pulls it off. He drops nothing. And a gamesman, too, we see him checking rein on the novel's other hobbies, insuring none runs away. So, too, with the vertinginous flight from Death which parades his bleeding lungs across Europe; how else does it fit the Yorkshire Epic of Shandy Hall than as part of Tristram's virtuoso display? So also Tristram's (probably we should say Sterne's) continual sensitivity to the *motions* of his own body—blood flowing, heart pounding. To the *ilinx* we can also refer his interest in gesture and in physical balance and (reaching for the left-hand pocket handkerchief with the right hand) imbalance. Finally might we not think the periodic-two-volume appearance of the novel as Tristram's attempts to regain inner balance, as an *act* (in both senses) which symbolized poise regained? From this viewpoint, all Tristram's obstacles make sense as self-induced. Such are the rules, the artificial barriers of any *ludus* with a single player. Tristram plays solitaire in a real sense, a game by himself with his life and what he thinks of it which, for his own purposes, he lets us share. We should not press Tristram's self-sufficient isolation too far. Yet, so generally received is his character as complacent stooge for his audience, the point should be made.

Tristram tells us that he will continue his regular installments until he dies. And, with perhaps an interruption,[6] it seems really to have been Sterne's design. He poses his fictional self a permanent challenge to continue, to keep up the improvising forever. Each will have his opinion on how well the later volumes answer the challenge, but the challenge itself galvanizes the book as hobby. Its failure to present a theme—for the Life and Opinions conception expands to gas before our eyes—challenges the improvisational power increasingly. Will he be able to go on? If you have no theme, no subject, you will end up like Lyly, like Nash, like Tristram, talking about yourself. Will your personality be adequate to sustain it? To control it? Again the game is an effort at balance, control. To intensify the game, Tristram not only puts the regular parts of the novel in confused motion,[7] he holds our attention on the verbal surface of the novel,[8] even on the physical components of the book, putting all these at odds to deny us a firm point of view.

Sterne's wit constituted, Traugott tells us, "a description of experience in terms of unlikely relations."[9] Surely as one such description, Tristram plays his wit on the interfaces between the prose styles he not only juggles but parodies. Without going out of bounds we might remark in passing the configuration into which Tristram's game here falls. At the center of his utterance ranges the *sermo cottidianus,* the colloquial style that is Sterne's great glory. It is, as Glaesener shrewdly observed in his 1927 *TLS* essay, a de-Latinized prose. One surrounded, we might add, by Latinized ones. It functions as stylistic control, the symbol of Tristram talking—and writing—as fast as he can—but always in imaginative control. His agility in moving from style to style, from curse to mock-heroic invocation to *Tristrapaedia,* to travelbook, to high pathos, always with his own style running through and informing the others, displays yet again his virtuoso, self-pleasing balance. In this effort to preserve its balance and complementarily destroy ours, **Tristram Shandy** much resembles some Elizabethan prose fictions, *Euphues* for example in one way, *The Unfortunate Traveller* in another.

According to Howes, Coleridge was "the first critic to recognize so clearly the sharp distinction between the humor to be found in Sterne's characters, who display a thorough knowledge of human nature, and the more questionable humor to be found in Sterne's style and manner."[10] This effort to split off Tristram from his novel came partly from misunderstanding the kind of game he plays with the reader, and more importantly with himself, but more from misapprehending Tristram the bawdy joker. To this much misunderstood role, our consideration of Tristram must now turn.

Part of the philosophizing that Sterne's comedy has undergone in recent years has been a conception of the bawdry as Shakespearean, reductive. It aims to puncture man's inflated sense of motive and self, remind him of his body. "In his use of the equivoque he is close kin to Shakespeare, most of whose jollier puns— lucky for him—are no longer understood."[11] So too, Fluchère: "Elle est donc un instrument docile entre les mains de l'auteur comique et du satiriste, qui en usent libéralement pour rabaisser par le rire l'orgueil de l'homme à des proportions raisonnables."[12] And when it is not pointing to the limitations of nature, its affair is a still more serious marking out the boundary conditions of language. "Puns and double meanings emphasize the unstable nature of language, its dynamic qualities which are so difficult to control. One can never really be sure of saying what one means."[13] (In a world so Jung and easily Freudened as that of **Tristram Shandy,** though, might it not be the other way around? You say what you really mean no matter what you say.) Instead of shocking for cheap effect, leering at the reader to make sure he gets the joke (Thackeray's old complaint), Sterne is cultivating with his reader the carefully controlled self-conscious relationship Traugott finds at the heart of **Tristram Shandy**'s rhetoric. The reader is made to expose his own false pudicity, and, moving it aside, to grasp Tristram's principal topic, his sexual misfortunes. Thus the social hypocrisy surrounding sexuality is exposed and a new, more healthy decorum opened out. The method by which this is done is a broad range of equivocation, from scholarly equivalents that sterilize what they describe (*os pubis, argumentum ad rem*) to general words (nose, hornworks) bearing a particular and well-known innuendo, to very general words (thing, it) which can bear any amount of innuendo.[14]

Persuasive as this argument is, and restorative of Sterne to his proper place in the first rank of comic writers, it may mistake if not Sterne's seriousness, his *kind* of seriousness. What seems to separate Sterne's bawdry from its Shakespearean counterpart is its fleshlessness, its manifest disinclination to arouse. As C.E. Vaughan remarks shrewdly of the bawdry in **Tristram Shandy:** "It works, as it were, in a void which he has created specially for the purpose and of which he alone, of all writers, holds the secret. In this dry handling of the matter, the affections of the reader are left unenlisted and unmoved."[15] By "void" I take him to mean context. Two of the bluest in the novel, Phutatorius with his chestnut and the Abbess of Andouillet with her novice, are also among the most revealing of Sterne's unique kind of bawdy joking.

The incident of the hot chestnut is, rather like the chestnut itself, dropped into a seemingly irrelevant parenthesis. (It begins in IV, xxiii, 302 ff.) At the beginning, Walter Shandy wonders to Yorick if Tristram's disastrously mistaken christening can be reversed; at the end, Kysarcius delivers his after-the-Visitation-Dinner paper on the subject. And in between Sterne does his best to obscure the relevance of his frame. The brothers Shandy go to the Visitation dinner in a chapter of ten pages (IV, xxiv) which Tristram has torn out of the book. Walter tells us that he hates great dinners (IV, xxiii, 302) before we know to which dinner he refers. Yorick tears up his Visitation Sermon to light pipes with before we know that he has preached it. We are in the midst of Didius's discussion of Tristram's naming blunder (IV, xxix, 326) without that previous managing of the conversation (IV, xxiii, 302) which Yorick desiderates. And when the dinner is over, Walter is "hugely tickled" with the subtleties of the disputation but, so far as we can see, no wiser than when he set out. We are invited to reassemble the scattered bones of the fruitless errand around the dramatic interlude that "Zounds!" introduces, the only part of the parenthesis narrated in ordinary chronological time.

The loose strands are manifestly there to reweave, of course. The indecorum in Phutatorius's breech breaches the social decorum of the whole company. Indecorum of another sort has been on Tristram's mind. It was why he left out Chapter XXIV:

> —But the painting of this journey, upon reviewing it, appears to be so much above the stile and manner of any thing else I have been able to paint in this

book, that it could not have remained in it, without depreciating every other scene; and destroying at the same time that necessary equipoise and balance, (whether of good or bad) betwixt chapter and chapter, from whence the just proportions and harmony of the whole work results. [IV, xxv, 315]

We are thus to add to our sense of the chestnut's social, a sense of its literary, indecorum. And, as is often the case with Sterne, his insistence on its being out of place invites us to redefine the scene until it has a place. To this theme of indecorum we are thus made aware of, we must add another, the uses of eloquence. Yorick puts his sermon to use by tearing it up into tapers. And after the interruption, Phutatorius is counseled to put a sheet or two of his own recently reprinted *de Concubinis retinendis* to use as a fomentive dressing for his scorched *membrum virile*. Sandwiched between these two illustrative incidents we have an example of true eloquence, one that does indeed mock both Yorick's eloquence which has preceded and Kysarcius's which is to follow. "Zounds!" It interrupts Yorick's depreciation of his own candied utterance:

> I have undergone such unspeakable torments, in bringing forth this sermon, quoth *Yorick,* upon this occasion,—that I declare, *Didius,* I would suffer martyrdom—and if it was possible my horse with me, a thousand times over, before I would sit down and make such another: I was delivered of it at the wrong end of me—it came from my head instead of my heart—and it is for the pain it gave me, both in the writing and preaching of it, that I revenge myself of it, in this manner.—To preach, to shew the extent of our reading, or the subtleties of our wit—to parade it in the eyes of the vulgar with the beggarly accounts of a little learning, tinseled over with a few words which glitter, but convey little light and less warmth—is a dishonest use of the poor single half hour in a week which is put into our hands—'Tis not preaching the gospel—but ourselves—For my own part, continued *Yorick,* I had rather direct five words point blank to the heart—. [IV, xxvi, 317]

It also deflates it. Not even five words are needed. When unspeakable torment really fathers eloquence, one will do. Tristram interrupts this interruption to quash Toby, brought to his feet by "point blank," and to alert us to still another kind of indecorum, this time religious.

> —when a single word, and no more, uttered from the opposite side of the table, drew every one's ears towards it—a word of all others in the dictionary the last in that place to be expected—a word I am ashamed to write—yet must be written—must be read;—illegal—uncanonical—guess ten thousand guesses, multiplied into themselves—rack—torture your invention for ever, you're where you was—In short, I'll tell it in the next chapter. [IV, xxvi, 317-318]

Tristram protests too much, of course. Zounds was not precisely God's Wounds, even on such an occasion. But the rhetorical climax is thus properly and fully built. Indecorum and Eloquence come together in a word. The explosion occurs on carefully prepared thematic ground.

Sterne has remforced this thematic structure with some resolute punning that yokes together decorous and indecorous scene, true and false eloquence. Amid the canonical transactions and the port, for example, Phutatorius's "whole thoughts and attention were taken up with a transaction which was going forwards at that very instant within the precincts of his own *Galligaskins,* and in a part of them, where of all others he stood most interested to watch accidents" (IV, xxvii, 319). Within the Cathedral precinct, then, we have another kind of precinct altogether, and in place of an accident of the logical sort (something inessential to the conception of an object—a good many float around this dinner table) quite another kind. When the deplorable accident happens, the metaphor chosen to describe it puns on the physical manner of the accident: "it so fell out, however, that one was actually sent rolling off the table" (IV, xxvii, 320). Tristram begins a pun on "door" when he describes what the chestnut fell into: "—let it suffice to say—it was that particular aperture, which in all good societies, the laws of decorum do strictly require, like the temple of *Janus* (in peace at least) to be universally shut up."

Whether or not it was, like the temple of Janus, far more open than shut, we are not told. It seems likely, however, that we are to extend the comparison in a bawdy way. Phutatorius's breeches, like the temple doors, are closed in peace but opened for war. "The neglect of this punctilio," a cliché we are invited to literalize tells us, "had opened a door to this accident." From accident as sudden misfortune, Tristram turns to philosophic accident, uncaused occurrence. It may have a meaning, after all, and one related to Phutatorius's treatise *de Concubinis retinendis.* We are meant to keep this in mind until, when Yorick owns to a sin he did not commit, the episode's discussion of accident becomes fully clear. Meanwhile, Tristram's use of the accidents of language continues. The gap in Phutatorius's breeches, to Tristram—as a historian determined not to dip *his* pen in the controversy—resembles a gap in a manuscript account, a "hiatus." A literally apt cliché once again tells us that "Phutatorius was not able to dive into the secret of what was going forwards below." And when Yorick picks up the chestnut Phutatorius has flung down, the injured party takes so irrevocable a conviction that he looks on his injurer "that *Euclid*'s demonstrations, could they be brought to batter it in breach [the exclamation, we should recall Tristram telling us, was definitely not canonical], should not all have power to overthrow it." And the soul of the jest is explained when we see the literal "chucking

the chestnut hot into *Phutatorius*'s   " become "a sarcastical fling at his book." A book, we are again reminded with a pun, which "had inflamed many an honest man in the same place." Thus the "master-stroke of arch-wit" becomes literally as well as figuratively a stroke. Yorick, however, was not guilty of it, we are almost-assuredly told. His sense of humor was too "tempered" to make it hot for an enemy in this way. But he will not stoop to explain why he stooped for the chestnut ("he could not stoop to tell his story to them"). He thus takes the rap for casting the chestnut into the aperture: "This heroic cast produced him inconveniences in many respects." Cast of mind and cast of hand become one. The mental and the physical thus wordplayfully conflated come together most heroically when Phutatorius's injury is treated by the sanative particles floating on a page from his own book, hot, or rather cool, off the press from round the corner. The scene reminds one of the Wife of Bath, tearing from Janekyn's book the leaves that describe her own literary ancestry, the leaves from which she has been created. Literal and imaginative reality are, for comic effect, brought to the same level. Just as Yorick's sermon fires his listeners by lighting their pipes, Phutatorius finds his book "best to take out the fire" of the chestnut.

The reader ought not fear, in such a universe of bawdy convertibility, that he will read *in sensu obscaeno* what was innocently meant. A calculated synergism of innuendo, in fact, invites him to look for—and find—bawdry everywhere. It is tempting to see in this surface pattern of wordplay a manifestation of that ineluctable human physicality that the chestnut's genial warmth asserts with more drama. Low and high come yoked together only, and Sterne can pivot on a pun from one to the other; the bawdry makes an essentially philosophical statement. Tempting but, I think, finally wrong. For the presiding deity of Sterne's wordplay is not Truth but Ease. The butt of the joke, after all, is Phutatorius. No one has accused him of neglecting the flesh. He needs no Mercutio in his garden. Nor does Walter Shandy, whose philosophy *includes* the Ass Kicking. Nor Tristram, who tells us in a pun (IV, xxv, 314) that the sinister turn of his own and all the Shandys' lives, has come from that bend sinister on the coach. Nor does any Petrarchan gush need ventilation. The pattern of punning, like the wordplay of other sorts, leads nowhere outside the context of the scene itself. It aims only to make us comfortable within it. It caters to a mind on vacation from philosophy, a mind at play. The innuendo doubtless must be classed as false wit, fancy rather than judgment, scheme rather than trope. Yet few can have wondered, with a *bawdy* pun, "by what perverseness of industry" *it* was ever found. The sense of endless connection may be a device of low wit but it is infinitely reassuring. Once used to it, we follow Sterne's transitions with ease, cease to worry over the narrative discontinuities. We are no longer in a world we never made and no longer, therefore, worry about that world's unfathomability. Rather than probing the infinite undependability of language from a philosophical point of view, Sterne is demonstrating how it can become a dependable, pleasure-giving thing to man—from an imaginative point of view. Sterne finds it, in fact, one of man's great weapons *against* chance as well as being expressive of it. Undependable, not to trust, language certainly is. But in this passage Tristram turns the proposition around. Language helps us get something back from the deceiving universe. It goes far, in this episode, toward creating a comic fitness that counterstates the social and literary indecorum. By this means, Sterne offers, not a grin-and-bear-it comic stoicism but an assertive, free-swinging comic world where justice works with joyful gusto. A new kind of eloquence (traditional, though, in its combining of word and gesture into convincing *ethos*) and a new kind of decorum emerge from the scene, from the careful structure leading up to, and surrounding, "Zounds!"

The principal actor in the scene is not Phutatorius but Yorick. He both creates the scene's comedy and defines it. In the epigram from *Encheiridion V* which stood on the title page of Volumes I and II,[16] Sterne gives fair warning of a concentration on attitude rather than event. And when the event stands out as really crucial, it tends to disappear altogether. So it is here. We are led to believe, but not all the way to belief, that Yorick did not drop the hot chestnut into Phutatorius's breeches. It seems that he did not, but it would have been very like him to do so. Why not let him father the joke? Would it be any the less funny if he had nudged the chestnut? It seems so. What Yorick does, finally, is capitalize on chance. If we follow Sterne's lead that the falling-in was accidental, we should not follow it that the picking-up was innocent. If Yorick does not pull the prank, at least he does not deny it. And by refusing to deny it, he really allows the joke to take place. The burn is false wit, Hazlitt's second level of the three levels of the laughable.[17] It is Freud's lower level, the harmless rather than the tendentious joke.[18] By taking credit for the event, lending chance a human (and aggressive) motive, connecting Phutatorius's sins with, and philosophizing about, the member receiving the injury, Yorick performs his role as jester. By stooping to pick up the chestnut, he gives sense to chance, domesticates it, makes use of it to restore an ethical balance, both for Phutatorius individually and for the whole company and its exalted speculations. He performs, that is, on the narrative level the role the wordplay performs on the literal—or imagistic—level. He takes a chance event (a hot chestnut falls where it ought to; two words share a same, comically appropriate—with, hence, its degree of "ought-to-"sense) and capitalizes on its accidental humor to make wit. Yorick, then, teaches us what to do with chance. Capitalize on it for purposes of jest. The incident through which he

does it thus becomes clearly related to this context. The brothers Shandy go to the dinner to find out what they can do about the terrible name chance has given Tristram. They are not the wiser for it, but Tristram clearly is. For his name stands for the peculiar fate life has given him and capitalizing on this fate for comic purposes is precisely what he is doing in this episode and throughout *Tristram Shandy.*[19] From a knight of sadness he must, through his book, become a knight of joy. He must renounce his name. Thus the narrative level of the episode becomes an allegory of the relation between true and false wit. Real accident causes the one; true wit is created when accident becomes, is made to become, expressive of man's purpose.

There is, then, a lesson of wit to be learned here as well as one in—as Sterne lets us know in plain words—"How finely we argue upon mistaken facts" (IV, xxvii, 319). This second has been often pointed out. Walter Shandy again philosophizes in excess of the stimulus. But, if we may for a moment play the simpleminded reader of satire, what would we have him reason? "Merciful Heavens! There goes another one of those hot chestnuts! Will Phutatorius never learn?" Walter is set up here to be put down so that we do not notice Tristram using essentially the same device, a high style for a low subject, an apparatus and nomenclature of learning to describe a scene for which, also, "there is no chaste word throughout all Johnson's dictionary." The tradition of learned wit has for a long time been recognized in Sterne,[20] but Walter's function as lightning rod for it seems less familiar. The juxtaposition is one between an unaware comic disproportion of style and subject (Walter Shandy's) and an aware one (Tristram's, and ours). Here, too, the structure of the bawdry seems to suggest a difference between true wit and false. Sterne does not seem to be saying that "Zounds" and the mistaken responses it provokes show, really, how finely we argue on mistaken facts. For we see the company arguing really finely on a mistaken fact when they hold Yorick guilty for tipping in the chestnut. Both judgments, so far as we know (alas, Poor Locke), are factually mistaken, but one is much truer than the other. One makes beautiful comic sense, the other poor serious sense. We are asked to choose to look at life comically and, so far as things have meaning for men, meaningfully, or to look at life seriously and mistakenly. Sterne aims to point, that is, a difference not only between true wit and false but between wit and judgment, between seeing differences and seeing resemblances.

Why, one might ask, this particular chance? Sterne seems to suggest an explanation when he makes Yorick's stooping for the chestnut echo Othello's familiar falling for the handkerchief.

It is curious to observe the triumph of slight incidents

over the mind:—What incredible weight they have in forming and governing our opinions, both of men and things,—that trifles light as air, shall waft a belief into the soul, and plant it so immoveably within it. [IV, xxvii, 322]

Iago says of his trap for Othello:

> I will in Cassio's lodging lose this napkin,
> And let him find it. Trifles light as air
> Are to the jealous confirmations strong
> As proofs of holy writ.
>
> [III, iii]

This is the particular chance which character has prepared for, which we can turn to our own purposes. No good at reasoning, we are better at opportunism. The contrast here (comedy makes sense of one accident—Zounds—while serious philosophy fails with another—Tristram instead of Trismegistus) looks very like that between the *Knight's Tale* and the *Miller's Tale*. The moral would seem to be the same. Sharp-eyed living will do more for you—Dr. Johnson kicking the stone to refute Berkeley—than formal ratiocination. Chance and character are likely to lend to a meaningless world a meaningful pattern. If we do not know what to ask for, still we get what we deserve. This trusting to chance fits nicely with Tristram's professed method of composition, which trusts to a higher but nearly as inscrutable power.[21]

The incident of the chestnut, then, itself provides the answer to the question of the narrative parenthesis that encloses it: What do you do if by chance you have been named, as it were, sadly? You establish a comic decorum, a comic justice. You make a joke because a joke makes sense of the world. Yet all this does not add up to a philosophical bawdry. For the bawdry is there, like the rest of the highly conceited rhetorical structure, to educate the reader only in how to get pleasure. If we must call it philosophical, it is Hedonistic, not comically Stoic. Sterne gets down in the bawdy ditch not to philosophize on what a piece of mixed work is man but because that is where the jokes are. It is Sterne's dirty joking that has kept alive his much discussed learned wit. If we come to the day when sexuality is as public as eating, **Tristram Shandy** will be as dead as *Euphues*. So will Rabelais, who pinned his learned comedy to the same star.

If, with the chestnut, Sterne dramatized the role of the jester, in the affair of the Abbess of Andouillets and her novice he illustrates the role of the jest. The narrative parenthesis is wedged into a context of swift coach travel. It begins with Tristram going on at a tearing rate toward Fontainebleau:

> Still—still I must away—the roads are paved—the posts are short—the days are long—'tis no more

than noon—I shall be at *Fontainbleau* before the king. [VII, xix, 502]

And when it ends shortly after, he is still on the way:

> What a tract of country have I run! [VII, xxvi, 510]

And, in the next sentence and chapter, he has arrived at Andouillets and is describing it. The episode thus sandwiched is appropriately enough about getting on. It is a blue one indeed. The Abbess comes on stage in a syntactical confusion that renders her part of the geography of Burgundy and Savoy as well as part of the history of European muscular therapy, all in a single sentence:

> The abbess of *Andouillets*, which if you look into the large set of provincial maps now publishing at *Paris*, you will find situated amongst the hills which divide *Burgundy* from *Savoy*, being in danger of an *Anchylosis* or stiff joint (the *sinovia* of her knee becoming hard by long matins) and having tried every remedy——first, prayers and thanksgiving; then invocations to all the saints in heaven promiscuously—then particularly to every saint who had ever had a stiff leg before her—then touching it with all the reliques of the convent, principally with the thigh-bone of the man of *Lystra*, who had been impotent from his youth—then wrapping it up in her veil when she went to bed—then cross-wise her rosary—then bringing in to her aid the secular arm, and anointing it with oils and hot fat of animals—then treating it with emollient and resolving fomentations——then with poultices of marsh-mallows, mallows, bonus Henricus, white lillies and fenugreek—then taking the woods, I mean the smoak of 'em, holding her scapulary across her lap—then decoctions of wild chicory, water cresses, chervil, sweet cecily and cochlearia—and nothing all this while answering, was prevailed on at last to try the hot baths of *Bourbon*—so having first obtain'd leave of the visitor-general to take care of her existence—she ordered all to be got ready for her journey: a novice of the convent of about seventeen, who had been troubled with a whitloe in her middle finger, by sticking it constantly into the abbess's cast poultices, &c.—had gained such an interest, that overlooking a sciatical old nun, who might have been set up for ever by the hot baths of *Bourbon, Margarita*, the little novice, was elected as the companion of the journey. [VII, xxi, 504-505]

Everything in the passage arouses our suspicion—stiff joints, hard knee, long matins, remedy, prayers, invocations, the thigh-bone of the man of *Lystra*, the secular arm, all the healing nostrums (Heaven knows the key to them), the poor novice's middle finger. And it may be that we get the general outline of the relationship involved. If so, it is hard to see how its bawdiness can be philosophized. Part of man's necessary awareness of his physical self? Not exactly. Part of a satire on the hypocrisy of society in insisting that such a natural relationship be hidden? This does not seem quite what Tristram has in mind. A satire on the Church? Again, nothing in the passage indicates it. To what end, then does the bawdry tend? Perhaps the very surplus of innuendo indicates what the narrator is about. For much of the innuendo really points in vain to a bawdy equivalent. It really makes no sense that the *Abbess* has the stiff leg, or has a name that puns on little sausages. And all the funny-enough treatments for this irrelevantly suggested male member lead nowhere. If a stiff joint represents what she wants, why is the whole elaborate catachresis organized around the *healing* of the stiff joint? Unless, very perhaps, the healing represents an act of intercourse, the particular cure for a stiff joint which the Abbess seems most to desire. But, one might reply, this is not a metaphysical poem. The innuendo was not meant to withstand this kind of analysis. This is precisely the point. It is infinitely, but very vaguely, suggestive. One cannot build upon it a philosophical justification of the life of the flesh. The language does not yoke spirit and flesh together in a resigned yet hopeful Stoic vision. It yokes them together merely for the fun of playing with words. Look, for example, at the opening three and a half lines, where, by a mistaken pronoun reference, the Abbess is confused with the territory in which she resides. Shakespeare does much the same thing in *Venus and Adonis* when Venus compares herself to a richly landscaped park and Adonis to a deer invited to sport therein.

> "Fondling," she saith, "since I have hemmed
>   thee here
> Within the circuit of this ivory pale,
> I'll be a park, and thou shalt be my deer:
> Feed where thou wilt, on mountain or in dale;
>   Graze on my lips; and if those hills be dry,
>   Stray lower, where the pleasant fountains lie.
> "Within this limit is relief enough,
> Sweet bottom-grass, and high delightful plain,
> Round rising hillocks, brakes obscure and
>   rough,
> To shelter thee from tempest and from rain.
>   Then be my deer, since I am such a park.
>   No dog shall rouse thee, though a thousand
>   bark."

[lines 229-240]

The same thing but not at all the same kind of thing. The wit, for Shakespeare, comes from the, as who should say, extensive firmness of his comparison. The earthy *effictio* is spelled out—and relevant—to the last detail. Sterne's comparison, so far as I can see, is relevant to nothing at all. Its basis is not intellectual correspondence but the ease of irrational comparison. If the pronoun reference is a plain mistake, so much the better. For the whole passage appeals to a deliberately unintellectual easiness of bawdy convertibility. Once one sets up an environment of bawdy equivalency like this, anything goes. Surely this is precisely why Tristram sets it up. Sexual word play is more pleasurable than any other kind because it releases the rational censor on the meaning of words more fully than any other kind. They are free, in this kind of context, truly to mean whatever we want them to mean. The sexuality is not so important as freedom from the censor. Thus we see, I think, the reason for the curious fleshlessness of Tristram's innuendo. His aim is not sexual titillation but primal, childlike verbal pleasure, and the first is primarily the means to the second. In the freedom that such an indefinitely encouraged punning engenders, we can see the peculiar nature of Tristram's context, of the void in which his bawdy joking takes place.

The passage aims initially then at giving us pleasure, not equipping us with a Stoic resignation. It is true that Tristram invites an indirect moral response by directing our attention to what Piper calls his trial by prudery: he must tell us what two words will make a French post-horse go and these two words are unmentionable in polite company. He makes a great fuss about this, telling us first that:

> Now as these words cost nothing, I long from my soul to tell the reader what they are; but here is the question—they must be told him plainly, and with the most distinct articulation, or it will answer no end—and yet to do it in that plain way—though their reverences may laugh at it in the bed-chamber—full well I wot, they will abuse it in the parlour: for which cause, I have been volving and revolving in my fancy some time, but to no purpose, by what clean device or facete contrivance, I might so modulate them, that whilst I satisfy *that ear* which the reader chuses to *lend* me—I might not dissatisfy the other which he keeps to himself. [VII, xx, 503]

His fingers burn to try, he tells us. And later, in the high style, just before the verbal consummation: "—and how to tell them—Ye, who can speak of every thing existing, with unpolluted lips—instruct me—guide me—" (VII, xxiv, 509). No one makes so much of contravening convention if he really wants to preserve it, and if he is making an ironic gain at the reader's expense in destroying it, I fail to see what that gain is. What he is really doing is setting up a series of artificial obstacles to the saying of the two words, so that our pleasure, when we hear them, will be that much the greater. Far from mocking the reader's false modesty (his two artificially separated ears) Tristram takes pains to *erect* precisely this false modesty where none stood before. And, again, his pleasure is not in decorum per se but in the pleasure to be gained from wittily destroying it.

The destruction comes in solving the Abbess's problem. Her mules will not get on. The prospect generates a brief passage of innuendo in which the wish fathers the thought.

> We are ruin'd and undone, my child, said the abbess to *Margarita*—we shall be here all night—we shall be plunder'd—we shall be ravish'd—
>
> —We shall be ravish'd, said *Margarita,* as sure as a gun.
>
> *Sancta Maria!* cried the abbess (forgetting the *O!*)—why was I govern'd by this wicked stiff joint? why did I leave the convent of *Andouillets?* and why didst thou not suffer thy servant to go unpolluted to her tomb?
>
> O my finger! my finger! cried the novice, catching fire at the word *servant*—why was I not content to put it here, or there, any where rather than be in this strait?
>
> —Strait! said the abbess.
>
> Strait—said the novice; for terrour had struck their understandings—the one knew not what she said—the other what she answer'd.
>
> O my virginity! virginity; cried the abbess.
>
> —inity!—inity! said the novice, sobbing. [VII, xxii, 508]

The intercourse thus promisingly begun is interrupted by the need to get the mules moving and then resumed in a verbal model for sexual intercourse which solves the nun's problems—how to say these two words politely, get going, and satisfy their sexual frustrations—and Tristram's as well:

> All sins whatever, quoth the abbess, turning casuist in the distress they were under, are held by the confessor of our convent to be either mortal or venial: there is no further division. Now a venial sin being the slightest and least of all sins,—being halved—by taking, either only the half of it, and leaving the rest—or, by taking it all, and amicably halving it betwixt yourself and another person—in course becomes diluted into no sin at all.
>
> Now I see no sin in saying, *bou, bou, bou, bou, bou,* a hundred times together; nor is there any turpitude in pronouncing the syllable *ger, ger, ger, ger, ger,* were it from our matins to our vespers: Therefore, my dear daughter, continued the abbess of *Andouillets*—I will say *bou,* and thou shalt say *ger;* and then alternately, as there is no more sin in *fou* than in *bou*—Thou shalt say *fou*—and I will come in (like fa, sol, la, re, mi, ut, at our complines) with *ter.* And accordingly the abbess,

giving the pitch note, set off thus:

> *Abbess,* Bou—bou—bou
>
> Margarita,—ger,—ger,—ger
>
> *Margarita,* Fou—fou—fou
>
> Abbess,—ter,—ter,—ter.

The two mules acknowledged the notes by a mutual lash of their tails; but it went no further.—'Twill answer by an' by, said the novice.

> *Abbess,* Bou-bou-bou-bou-bou-bou-
>
> *Margarita,*—ger, ger, ger, ger, ger, ger.
>
> Quicker still, cried *Margarita.*
>
> Fou, fou, fou, fou, fou, fou, fou, fou, fou.
>
> Quicker still, cried *Margarita.*
>
> Bou, bou, bou, bou, bou, bou, bou, bou, bou.
>
> Quicker still—God preserve me! said the abbess—They do not understand us, cried *Margarita*—But the Devil does, said the abbess of *Andouillets.*

The function of the jest here lies in its sudden and simultaneous solving of all these problems by a verbal device. The formula of verbal complementation devised can stand, I think, as a model for the function of the jest. It gets us out of uncomfortable and otherwise unsolvable situations in a pleasurable way. Embarrassment orchestrates into duet. That Tristram has *made up* most of the barriers over which the joke triumphs says no more than that he has authored the joke. That we cooperate in thus consenting to put on stage a false modesty few of us (it is part of the novelist's relation with the reader's private self) really possess, is simply to say that we are the willing audience all jokes require. Here again we should stress not the undependability of words but quite the reverse. They are infinitely serviceable, the indispensable buffer between man's insatiable desire and unyielding circumstance. They help us get on and enjoy getting on. It is no accident that the episode is preceded by a "chance" allusion to the word "gay" and "spleen" and is followed by puns on slow-rising (VII, xxvii, 514), Saint *Optat,* and finally the famous reference to what, garters in hand, he did *not* do with Jenny, and the rubric VEXATION upon VEXATION (VII, xxx, 518-519). Tristram is determined to preserve his gust for joy midst the anguish of his sexual frustrations, and his chief mechanism for so doing is precisely a joke like this, in which language, rather than sublimating, *substitutes for* sexual satisfaction.

It is a mistake, I think, to apply to a passage like this the canons of Augustan wit. It is false wit that reigns, no doubt, one made up of superficial schemes. Yet the intellectual criteria that Johnson applies to Cowley, for example, precisely misfit this occasion. Tristram is not trying to satisfy the standards of intellectual connection and consistency but to evade them. Logically, there is no solution to any of the problems. Tristram does not clarify a problem, as a metaphysical poet would do. He dodges it. Watkins compares Sterne to the metaphysicals: "Undoubtedly Sterne frequently indulges in equivocation for its own sake, like the metaphysicals in their conceits."[22] In their elaboration, Sterne's conceits may resemble those of the metaphysicals, but the force of his wit seems to move in an opposite direction. Sterne aims, or at least Tristram aims, not at coherence but at pleasure. "That wit is the most refined and effectual," Hazlitt tells us, "which is founded on the detection of unexpected likeness or distinction in things, rather than in words."[23] But what if, as here, words make the mules go better than corn? What if, as with Tristram, words are things? In a sense, then, the Victorians were right about Tristram's sexual innuendo. It *is* for its own sake. It *does* come more from the head than the heart. High seriousness cannot redeem it. Once again the Victorian objection isolates the central issue, Tristram's final loyalty to pleasure. The infinitely manipulatable world of punning exists not to teach us a lesson but to put Tristram, with all his deficiencies, at ease.

In the "Poetic Categories" chapter of *Attitudes Toward History,* Kenneth Burke draws a pertinent distinction between burlesque and satire.

> The writer of burlesque makes no attempt to get inside the psyche of his victim. Instead, he is content to select the externals of behavior, driving them to a "logical conclusion" that becomes their "reduction to absurdity." By program, he obliterates his victim's discriminations. He is "heartless." He converts every "perhaps" into a "positively." He deliberately suppresses any consideration of the "mitigating circumstances" that would put his subject in a better light. . . . Hilariously, he converts a manner into a mannerism. The method of burlesque (polemic, caricature) is partial not only in the sense of *partisan,* but also in the sense of *incompleteness.* As such, it does not contain a well-rounded frame within itself; we can use it for the ends of wisdom only insofar as we ourselves provide the ways of making allowances for it; we must not be merely *equal* to it, we must be enough *greater than* it to be able to "discount" what it says. [pp. 54-55]

Though often using the methods of burlesque, Sterne ranks in these terms a satirist. But, we frequently learn, his satire is peculiarly gentle. We can now see why. Tristram supplies a central frame of reference, the games of pleasure; we can see, if he takes a swipe at

Locke, just why he does it. But the satire, because of its game matrix, can never toughen: the *object* is not to attack the victim but to amuse Tristram. Tristram, if a satirist, is a self-serving one. To such an attacker, every victim is an additional source, not of rage and exasperation, but of pleasure. When someone lurks, immune to such use, just outside the game sphere, as with Mrs. Shandy (with, Tristram tells us, all the other Shandy women), no pleasure comes from the attack and it turns dull and flaccid. Such people, and only such, cannot bask in the novel's genial tolerance of private amusement. They seem scarcely alive. The standards for life, those that supply satiric point of view, are the standards of game. The only character who really meets them (alone in his self-consciousness about motive) acknowledges to himself that his motive is pleasure. We readers class ourselves as equals or victims, depending on our willingness to recognize this essential motive in him, the tale he tells, and ourselves.

We have perhaps ignored ourselves, ignored Tristram's audience. Of course he is an actor, harrows his resources of feeling to benefit the audience.[24] And he keeps his eye continually on it. But its demands, like all others, he just as continually tries to avoid, dramatizes his trying to avoid. His relation to us is like his relation to everything else. What fun can be gotten from us? Critics find Tristram's, and the novel's, relation to audience a pretty metaphysical matter. Fluchère, for example:

> C'est un aveu implicite que le livre n'existe pas en soi, dans l'impersonnalité indifférente de l'oeuvre d'art, mais qu'il recevra son sens et pourra remplir sa fonction d'après l'accueil qui lui sera fait.[25]

In this view, we function as audience by restoring to narrative and spiritual coherence Tristram's skillful chaos. He digs the hole; we fill it up. But this spoils the game! Misapprehends what Tristram is doing! He invites us to search for the center of the Silenus box but, as with Rabelais, from this center emerges, not the stern voice of coherence, but the Abbey of Thélème. *Fay ce que vouldras.* To try putting the pieces together, is to become audience for the **Sermons,** not **Tristram Shandy,** become one of the satirized. Surely our role points rather to admiring Tristram's performance than to weeping for a world where such desperate enactments need to take place. We should admire him not for his success in reenacting the blooming and buzzing confusion of an absurd world but for his success, as a precocious child in the garden of Western culture, in pleasing himself. The narrative structure of **Tristram Shandy** imitates his play: the pleasure-principle at work on the principles of narrative itself.

How shall we criticize, appraise such a structure? The standards of "process literature" Northrop Frye has pointed out[26] as very different from those for the finished, balanced, classical creation. How does this difference apply to Tristram Shandy?

> The question of structure in ***Tristram Shandy*** may be discussed, I think, without reference to the question of whether the novel is a finished whole, for what we need to know is not whether the book might have been continued, or even whether it reaches a stable point of rest, but what principle, if any, controls its seemingly erratic and aimless progression.[27]

If we can agree that Tristram's *ilinx,* his dizzying pursuit of pleasure, provides such a center, where do we stand? How can such an artifact be criticized? The easy answer simply asks, "Did you enjoy it?" In other words, ***Tristram Shandy's*** critical reputation answers our question. It worked. Tristram won. Sterne won. The book sold. No negligible reply this. Tristram's concern for sales is *in* the book. Sterne's concern for fame is *in* the **Letters,** in everything he ever wrote. ***Tristram Shandy*** is improvisational, one of those seminal books about nothing in particular, a rhetorical gesture for fame. The reader's central role in the novel is to buy it. The book's major function is to sell. These categories, crass and simpleminded, fit the novel well. There has been a great fuss about the genre of ***Tristram Shandy.***[28] Surely part of its *ludus* is farce, a great expandable skin stuffed (enfarced) with a mishmash that pleased Sterne and Sterne thought would please. The book is full of topical appeals.[29] "Of course the sentimental setpieces are there to be enjoyed," we might surprise the old joker in saying. "What else are they for, Pray?" No small part of the book's power—and critical reputation—comes from palming off these period-piece rehearsals so well. After all, we know what self-conscious sentiment, what sentimentality is because of Sterne.

But a document does not join the immortals by incidental appeal, however well honed. If, like the Victorians, we find little else, then let "historical interest" describe it. The modern view sees the novel philosophizing about communication, about language. Tristram is a loser, an antihero, doomed to failure but bracing up. Reading the novel as we have we must emphasize instead Tristram's success. He pleases us. He pleases himself. And he can do the first because he has done the second. His interest for us will lie precisely in the revelation his game makes about the nature of all games and, more largely, of all human motive. They return, finally, to pleasure. They cherish no theme beyond it. They are ends in themselves. "True play," as Huizinga says, "knows no propaganda; its aim is in itself, and its familiar spirit is happy inspiration."

One perennial perplexity remains to plague us. When do we say Tristram and when do we say Sterne? Laurence Sterne left tracks in his books as perhaps no other novelist ever has. Walter, Toby, Tristram, Yorick, may all be manifestations of their Creator,[30] but they are certainly manifestations of their creator, and he was a role-player to the last well-dramatized, long-foreseen breath. "The world has imagined," the man tells us, "because I wrote Tristram Shandy, that I was myself more Shandean than I really ever was."[31] But there is simply no telling how Shandean he *really was.* "Really was" simply slides off an old actor like Sterne whose *essence* remained *pure potential,* the power to be anyone. Even the context of the letter whence the just-cited passage discounts it. It is a formal letter, to a nobleman. Sterne is his polite self, the self of the last letters to the Jameses, very much on his p's and q's. As a working distinction, we talk of Tristram when we mean the narrator of ***Tristram Shandy*** or confine our discussion to the novel. Speaking of the novel as written in a certain time and place, we may use Sterne. And so too of what Tristram does *not see,* his character as satirized.

From among Sterne's perpetual roles, it is useful to precipitate out two at this point, jester and clergyman. Sterne, like Samuel Clemens, found the mask essential, essentially liberating. And it is tempting to see, in Tristram, a discrete mask. To analyze such a mask in Freudian terms, for example, comes so naturally we feel uneasy. The sublimated impotence, the castration complex on every page, now the theme of bastardy Professor Rader has suggested, which would allow Tristram to kill off his father in the story (if Yorick is his father), the importance of infancy and prenatal experience—all come to mind as naturally as breathing. I am not competent to pursue this line of investigation. But it is a miracle someone has not done it a bit better than de Froe. Such an analysis would tell us much of Sterne and perhaps even of the novel.[32] I wish to suggest a different train of reasoning, grouping Tristram with the other jester's mask, Yorick, to contrast it with the authentic clergyman's mask. Had we been Sterne's contemporary, we could have seen more clearly the nature of his dual statement about mankind. For the **Sermons** appeared along with ***Tristram Shandy*** and were, through the figure of Parson Yorick, confusingly tied to the novel. In the **Sermons** Parson Yorick allows his auditors a conventional moral identity. Whatever motive may be, none doubts, in that world, what it should be. Man has a discrete self for which he is totally responsible. The purpose there is frankly rhetorical, to move the will by playing upon the heart. This, precisely, the Tristram mask does not do. ***Tristram Shandy*** does not teach a conventional ethical lesson, or an absurdist one either. It explicitly denies us a conventional moral identity, makes actors of us all. It makes no statement finally about what we ought to do, but makes a final one about why we do it. It reduces motive to pleasure. It denies us the final moral responsibility high seriousness requires, denies us the tragic self. Tristram is the mask created to scoff at this self. It laughs at our perpetual need to clothe our pleasures with moralizing. It counterstates the **Sermons.** It constitutes Sterne's secular statement. It stands for the self and its needs as the **Sermons** stand for the other. The resemblances between the literary techniques of the two statements are incidental; the difference is fundamental. Sterne the man may well have denied that **Tristram Shandy** works this way. And the commentators seeking high seriousness of whatever kind will certainly do so. But the logic of the narrative structure Tristram creates seems inescapable. In a game world, the only thing you cannot deny is game, and its only yield and motive is pleasure.

Tristram-Sterne thus takes his place in a distinguished group of narrative masks: The Ovid of the *Ars Amatoria;* Chaucer the Canterbury Pilgrim and the narrator of *Troilus and Criseyde;* Rabelais; the Cervantes of *Don Quixote* if not of the *Novelas Ejemplares.* Like all these nonlovers he is a commentator and observer, a student of ritual, interested more in the physical structures built on feeling and ideas than in either by itself. And like all, he finally finds the dramatic metaphor for society to prevail, and the role metaphor for individual identity. Whether the attitude toward the play and the roles is loving or savage, whether the observer is amused or horrified, the same reductive attack on the nobility of our motives gets underway. We start shrinking. We begin to feel that particular paralysis creeping over us which perhaps Tristram's game of frenetic activity exists to combat, the paralysis of motive-seeking. Why, if we only play games, bother to play them? What is worth doing? And what framework creates worth? These are Hamlet's questions and Hamlet's paralysis. **Tristram Shandy's** close and yet puzzling relation to that character and that play suggest some answers.

Notes

1 They began early. Alan B. Howes cites a Mary Rerry's praise of Sterne's minute painting of detail—like a Dutch genre-painting—in 1789. (*Yorick and the Critics: Sterne's Reputation in England, 1760-1868* [New Haven, 1958], p. 108.

2 John M. Stedmond. *The Comic Art of Laurence Sterne* (Toronto, 1967), p. 68.

3 Sigurd Burckhardt, "*Tristram Shandy's* Law of Gravity," *ELH,* XXVIII (1961).

4 Henri Fluchère, *Laurence Sterne, de l'homme à l'oeuvre* (Paris, 1961), p. 248.

5 Sir Walter Scott, *Sir Walter Scott: On Novelists and Fiction,* ed. Ioan Williams (London, 1968), p. 74; Lodwick Hartley, *Laurence Sterne in the Twentieth Century* (Chapel Hill, N.C., 1966), p. 67.

6 Sterne wrote in 1766 (to Edward Stanley?) that he meant to stop *Tristram Shandy* after the ninth volume and "begin a new work of four volumes, which when finish'd, I shall continue Tristram with fresh spirit." (Laurence Sterne, *Letters of Laurence Sterne,* ed. Lewis P. Curtis [Oxford, 1935], p. 284.)

7 Look, for example, at the *motion* implied in Alan D. McKillop's description of Bobby's death: "Thus we have in the space of a few chapters concurrent actions which taken together give the impression of depth or extension, interruption and frustration, futile rhetoric, imperfect communication, surprising cause-effect sequences, unpredictable transitions and associations of ideas, trivial physical symbols for great things, and the basic idea of the machine." (*The Early Masters of English Fiction* [Lawrence, Kan., 1956], p. 200.)

8 See Robert A. Donovan, *The Shaping Vision: Imagination in the English Novel from Defoe to Dickens* (Ithaca, N.Y., 1966), p. 90.

9 John M. Traugott, *Tristram Shandy's World: Sterne's Philosophic Rhetoric* (Berkeley and Los Angeles, 1954), p. 28.

10 Howes, *Yorick and the Critics,* p. 116.

11 Ernest N. Dilworth, *The Unsentimental Journey of Laurence Sterne* (New York, 1948), p. 109.

12 Fluchère, *Laurence Sterne, de l'homme à l'oeuvre,* p. 433.

13 Stedmond, *Comic Art,* p. 44.

14 I am paraphrasing here William Bowman Piper's excellent discussion of "Tristram's Trial by Prudery," *Laurence Sterne* (New York, 1965), pp. 66 ff.

15 C. E. Vaughan, "Sterne and the Novel of His Times," *Cambridge History of English Literature,* X (Cambridge, 1913), 51-74.

16 "It is not actions, but opinions concerning actions, which disturb men."

17 "The essence of the laughable then is the incongruous, the disconnecting one idea from another, or the jostling of one feeling against another. . . . The accidental contradiction between our expectations and the event can hardly be said, however, to amount to the ludicrous: it is merely laughable. The ludicrous is where there is the same contradiction between the object and our expectations, heightened by some deformity or inconvenience, that is, by its being contrary to what is customary or desirable. . . . The third sort, or the ridiculous arising out of absurdity as

well as improbability, that is, where the defect or weakness is of a man's own seeking, is the most refined of all, but not always so pleasant as the last, because the same contempt and disapprobation which sharpens and subtilises our sense of the impropriety, adds a severity to it inconsistent with perfect ease and enjoyment. This last species is properly the province of satire." (William Hazlitt, *Lectures on the Comic Writers,* I—"On Wit and Humour," *The Collected Works of William Hazlitt,* ed. A. R. Waller and Arnold Glover [London, 1903], VIII, 7-8.)

[18] The whole passage, in a way, rehearses the development of the joke as Freud describes it in *Jokes and Their Relation to the Unconscious* (trans. James Strachey, 2d ed., [New York, 1960], pp. 137-138): "We are now able to state the formula for the mode of operation of tendentious jokes. They put themselves at the service of purposes in order that, by means of using the pleasure from jokes as a fore-pleasure, they may produce new pleasure by lifting suppressions and repressions. . . . The joke . . . from its beginning to its perfecting . . . remains true to its essential nature. It begins as play, in order to derive pleasure from the free use of words and thoughts. As soon as the strengthening of reasoning puts an end to this play with words as being senseless, and with thoughts as being nonsensical, it changes into a jest, in order that it may retain these sources of pleasure and be able to achieve fresh pleasure from the liberation of nonsense. Next, as a joke proper, but still a non-tendentious one, it gives its assistance to thoughts and strengthens them against the challenge of critical judgement, a process in which the 'principle of confusion of sources of pleasure' is of use to it. And finally it comes to the help of major purposes which are combating suppression, in order to lift their internal inhibitions by the 'principle of fore-pleasure.' Reason, critical judgement, suppression— these are the forces against which it fights in succession; it holds fast to the original sources of verbal pleasure and, from the stage of the jest onwards, opens new sources of pleasure for itself by lifting inhibitions. The pleasure that it produces, whether it is pleasure in play or pleasure in lifting inhibitions, can invariably be traced back to economy in psychical expenditure, provided that this view does not contradict the essential nature of pleasure and that it proves itself fruitful in other directions."

[19] See, in this connection, Piper's discussion of the role of chance in the novel, *Laurence Sterne,* pp. 49-51.

[20] D. W. Jefferson, "*Tristram Shandy* and the tradition of Learned Wit," *Essays in Criticism,* I (1951), 225-248.

[21] It fits, too, and nicely indeed the play whence Yorick fetches his name. For Hamlet has a plan no more than Tristram, plays a desperate opportunism (what else can he mean by "Let be?") and, like Yorick, gets credit for a revenge chance puts in his way.

[22] W. B. C. Watkins, *Perilous Balance* (Princeton, 1939), p. 124.

[23] Hazlitt, *Lectures on the Comic Writers:* I—"On Wit and Humour," p. 22.

[24] See Martin Price, *To the Palace of Wisdom* (New York, 1964), p. 337, for a fine statement of this case.

[25] Fluchère, *Laurence Sterne, de l'homme à l'oeuvre,* p. 235.

[26] Northrop Frye, "Toward Defining an Age of Sensibility," in *Eighteenth Century English Literature,* ed. James L. Clifford (New York, 1959).

[27] Donovan, *The Shaping Vision,* pp. 113-114.

[28] See Hartley's amusing collection of conjectures (*Laurence Sterne in the Twentieth Century,* p. 22).

[29] Not in the narrow sense. Sterne rightfully boasted to Dodsley that he had gotten all the local detail out of the book.

[30] Stedmond, *Comic Art,* p. 53.

[31] Sterne, *Letters,* pp. 402-403.

[32] *Tristram Shandy* seems, in fact, almost a book *about* sublimation and the whole Freudian theory of literature.

Works Cited

. . . Burke, Kenneth. *Attitudes Toward History.* Rev. ed. Boston: Beacon Press (Beacon Paperback), 1961.

———. *Counter-Statement.* 2d. ed. Chicago: University of Chicago Press (Phoenix Paperback), 1957. . . .

Cash, Arthur J. *Sterne's Comedy of Moral Sentiments: The Ethical Dimension of the "Journey."* Pittsburgh: Duquesne University Press, 1966.

———. "The Sermon in *Tristram Shandy.*" *ELH,* vol. XXXI (1964). . . .

Glaesner, H. "Laurence Sterne," *TLS* (1927) pp. 361-362. . . .

Lehman, B. H. "Of Time, Personality and the Author, A Study of *Tristram Shandy:* Comedy." *Studies in the Comic,* University of California Publications in English, vol. III, no. 2 (1941). . . .

Traugott, John, ed. *Laurence Sterne: A Collection of Critical Essays.* Englewood Cliffs, N.J.: Prentice-Hall (Spectrum Paperback), 1968.

————. *Tristram Shandy's World: Sterne's Philosophic Rhetoric.* Berkeley and Los Angeles: University of California Press, 1954. . . .

Susan G. Auty (essay date 1975)

SOURCE: "Smollett and Sterne and Animal Spirits: *Tristram Shandy,*" in her *The Comic Spirit of Eighteenth-Century Novels,* Kennikat Press Corp., 1975, pp. 119-47.

[*In the following essay, Auty observes that in* Tristram Shandy, *Sterne poked fun at the foolishness of human nature even as he acknowledged the pathos of the human condition.*]

The tenacious resistance of **The Life and Opinions of Tristram Shandy, Gent.,** to the stroke of Posterity's hatchet-man, Oblivion, is striking testimony to the special strength and resilience of this great comic work. Ever since Johnson made his famous pronouncement on its fate, "Nothing odd will do long. **Tristram Shandy** did not last," distrust and amazement have been voiced by critics who begrudge the presence of Sterne's work alongside the other great productions of the eighteenth century. Praise for the many handles that Sterne so obligingly offered the critics "to suit their passions, their ignorance or sensibility"—the satire, the sentiment, the wit—is tempered with astonishing frequency by a suggestion that the walking stick itself is rather slight, a frail object incapable of supporting the wonderful variety of shapes and styles that it has apparently been designed to do. That is, the comedy that informs the whole work has been duly recognized and noted in passing, and Sterne has been given credit as a humorist, but the comedy has rarely been appreciated as the source of its endurance and special character.

Until recently, much of **Tristram Shandy**'s uniqueness, and Sterne's comic freedom, has been mistaken for mere eccentricity and accordingly judged as trivial. The value of everything that Sterne found "Laugh-at-able" in his own way has been found wanting in exact proportion to the heartiness of Sterne's laugh. Even Ernest Dilworth, in attempting to counter Sterne's reputation as an eminent sentimentalist, comes to the unfortunate conclusion that he is a great, if typically shallow, jester: "It was part of the genius and limitation of Sterne that he saw best what was within a few feet of his nose; if he knew no dimensions in depth, he was master of the subtleties of the façade; his only interior was a hearthside one, and the firelight made a merry place, miles from the dark corners of the room. . . . The difference between Sterne and other shallow men is that he made comic art of what is called a disability."[10] If Mr. Dilworth did not aspire to being somewhat of a jester himself, one could only gasp incredulously at his final distinction. A comic genius simply may not, like the Tale Teller's "wise" man, be content with the "films and images that fly off one's senses from the superficies of things," one cannot be Swift's gullible fool and be alive to the irony of man's inherent absurdity and nobility, as the great jester is. Dilworth did not appreciate Sterne's comedy any more than did his predecessors.

The more recent critical trend, however, has been to disparage comedy that is not rooted in a satirical criticism of life. Thus, admirers of Sterne's novel have been defending his reputation with evidence of his corrective intentions and corrosive wit. John Stedmond was among the first to put forward the suggestion that Tristram's Life and Opinions might be a satiric appeal to the audience for discrimination and taste, similar to Swift's *Tale.* In such an assessment, the comic appeal for tolerance and amusement of Tristram's self-made mess is apparently judged to have insufficient significance. In a later work, however, Stedmond indicates his disapproval of "apologists for comic works [who] often cite their satiric elements, their 'thoughtful' laughter."[11] Yet the critical attitude that colored Stedmond's early views is no less in evidence today. A powerful temptation to see **Tristram Shandy** as a satire of the same order and potency as *Tale of a Tub* has led Melvyn New to misunderstand the essential comedy of the work, to reject Sterne's humorously oriented intellect. He sees **Tristram** as Sterne's attack "against human pride, which creates out of its own barrenness magnificient edifices to its own passions and follies and complex systems bearing no relationship to reason and reality."[12] By not allowing himself to feel the force of Sterne's delight in man's passions, follies, and systems, which are some of the ways open to man to fight against the natural shocks of life, New fails to see that Sterne's portrayal of the Shandy family is not at all bitter or corrective in intent. While mocking the hopeless attempts, either through reason or sentiment, to triumph over illness, impotence, death, and all the other hazards of life, Sterne is also positively admiring the perseverance of mankind in the face of all-too-certain failure. It is this admiration that New fails to set against his interpretation of Sterne's mockery. In **Tristram Shandy,** Sterne looks at the world critically and yet tenderly, and while making the nature of life's perplexities painfully clear, he is, above all, concerned with endorsing man's struggle with those perplexities: therein lies the richness of the comedy and the novel.

The strange mixture of satire and admiration that gives rise to comedy in **Tristram Shandy** is imaged in the character of Yorick, whose own outlook is partly satirical, partly sentimental, and who is described by Tristram with an indulgence that is both ironic and loving. In this attempt to describe him, Tristram repeats the self-mocking words of Yorick with affection:

> At different times he would give fifty humourous and opposite reasons for riding a meek-spirited jade of a broken-winded horse, preferably to one of mettle; . . . in all other exercitations, he could spend his time, as he rode along slowly,—to as much account as in his study;—that he could draw up an argument in his sermon,—or a hole in his breeches, as steadily on the one as in the other;—that brisk trotting and slow argumentation, like wit and judgment, were two incompatible movements.—But that upon his steed,—he could unite and reconcile every thing,—he could compose his sermon,—he could compose his cough,—and in case nature gave a call that way, he could likewise compose himself to sleep. (20)

Yorick's lighthearted yoking of the hole in his breeches with the argument in his sermon, or the composition of his sermon with the composure of his cough serves as verification of Tristram's earlier observation that the parson "loved a jest in his heart—and as he saw himself in the true point of ridicule, he would say, he could not be angry with others for seeing him in a light, in which he so strongly saw himself" (19). We are made to feel very kindly towards this country parson, and yet to see him as a ludicrous figure. Knowing that Yorick is meant to embody Sterne's account of himself, and that Tristram acts simply as Sterne's puppet in publishing the characterization, increases our sense of the self-mockery and self-adulation in Sterne's joke on himself. Also evident is Sterne's ability to see himself with the same comic eye out of which he sees the rest of the world and, in turn, his ability to regard the world with the same tenderness as he regards himself. His image of himself is the image he has of man in general; like Eliot's Prufrock, his Yorick is both an ironic self-portrait and a more universal composite of a pitiful, comic, helplessly self-conscious human being, whose irony is his greatest charm.

Sterne's Yorick is at all times the Fool, and was purposely and aptly named for him. As a Fool, both laughable and lovable, he lets himself get involved in such hopeless situations as the one concerning his horse. Yorick loved a fine horse; his neighbors loved riding his horse; Yorick loved his neighbors and therefore hardly ever rode his own horse, "the upshot of which was generally this, that his horse was either clapp'd, or spavin'd, or greaz'd;—or he was twitter bon'd, or broken-winded, or something, in short, or other had befallen him which would let him carry no flesh;—so that he had every nine or ten months a bad horse to get rid of,—and a good horse to purchase in his stead" (21). Yorick's solution to this problem is none other than the comic solution to life as a whole; rather than worrying about a new horse all the time, or fretting

about the worsening condition of the old, he was "content to ride the last poor devil, such as they had made him, with all his aches and infirmities, to the very end of the chapter" (21). If things are so bad that they cannot get worse, one may as well laugh at them and enjoy them. That Tristram confirms the value of this philosophy is apparent not only in his approval of Yorick's behavior, but in the very act of writing his own history, which is at once a hopeless task and very entertaining. Moreover, we may deduce that Sterne concurs with these views from our own affection for the two characters, an affection which is grounded equally in derision and delight.

Yorick's death scene is one of the most complex entanglements of jest and earnest, satire and sentiment, mockery and sympathy in the book. On the one hand, Yorick dies, and is a stark reminder of the moral borne by his namesake, that of inevitable mutability: "Where be your gibes now, your gambols, your songs, your flashes of merriment, that were wont to set the table on a roar." On the other, Sterne makes us do what Hamlet knows the Queen is unable to do, "Laugh at that."[13] Grief multiplied to proportions far more grand than its cause, as Sterne shows figuratively in the countless plaintive voices reciting "Alas, poor Yorick," is comic; the overwhelming blackness of the page inserted as a symbol for death, a giant sob caught within the pages of a book, is by its tangible presence comic as well. It is as if a clown walks across the stage at this moment with a placard that reads, "Weep." That the death is Yorick's, and that Yorick is a representation of Sterne, and that the page thus represents self-pity for an event which has not happened—as if the clown were mourning his own death as he walked across—is comically ironic: here is grief without any cause at all, the grief at one's own eventual death that is most comically and pitifully felt by all human beings.

Sterne's humor and eccentricity are deliberate and carry within their deliberateness a perception of the world which gives *Tristram Shandy* its meaning. The implications of this consciously comic vision have only rarely been considered, first by Nietzsche and more recently by critics who have begun to explore the nature of Sterne's comicality.[14] Nietzsche expanded Goethe's praise of Sterne's liberating effects in a paragraph subtitled, "The Freest Writer," and paid tribute to his remarkable nobility of spirit, his ability to "be right and wrong at the same time, to interweave profundity and farce":

> May he be satisfied with the honour of being called the freest writer of all times, in comparison with whom all others appear still, square-toed, intolerant and downright boorish! . . . He was—if language does not revolt from such a combination—of a hard-hearted kindness, and in the midst of the joys of a grotesque and even corrupt imagination he showed the bashful grace of innocence. Such a carnal and

spiritual hermaphroditism, such untrammelled wit penetrating into every vein and muscle, was perhaps never possessed by any other man.[15]

Nietzsche's extravagance is matched only by Sterne's own, and his language is only fitting to describe an author who playfully writes "SPLEEN" after mentioning the word "gay" in order "to keep up a good understanding amongst words . . . not knowing how near [one] may be under a necessity of placing them to each other" (502).

Fluchère considers the importance of accident in Sterne's style and explains his casual freedom in terms of his sense of the unfettered nature of the world: "The incoherent, the rhapsodic, the baroque—everything that is included in the word eccentricity and all that in traditional criticism calls forth the word disorder, arises in Sterne . . . from the recognition of the fact that the world is an immense field of experience, and man a being curiously determined by countless contingencies each of which exists in a very personal relation to him."[16] The structure of the book Fluchère traces to Sterne's desire "to translate the processes of the mind, operating on a given human situation, into a verbal representation that will completely render both its substance and its potentialities."[17]

These intricate and incomprehensible processes also account for much of the comedy of the work. The wit that is a by-product of the mind's strange activities joins forces with the pathos that arises from our sense of the helplessness of the mind to control its own process, its inability to make sense of the world with the material provided, and produces comedy: the wit and the pathos help us to accept and appreciate the puzzles that continually trouble the intellect by making the effort seem worthwhile in itself and the accomplishment, however incomplete in the face of the facts, splendid in the face of the obstacles. Sterne makes us see that the eccentric is really the normal, or as B.L. Reid incisively observes: "*Tristram Shandy* is the absurd made comically programmatic. The formalizing of the artifice conduces both to comedy and to philosophical statement. By so intricately manipulating the anarchy of experience, Sterne asserts a tyrannizing control that at once renders the absurd laughable and declares it representative, philosophically normative."[18] To bring alive his own comic vision of the real world, to show that the absurd is the normal—both comically and pathetically so—and to dramatize the need for tolerance and courage and lightheartedness in dealing with such absurdity, Sterne created the world of Tristram Shandy, a world in which evidence of grotesque incompatibility—of people with other people, of people with the world—is everywhere.

The curious inclusiveness of this world, which is really quite exclusive—consisting of a very limited number of characters who meet in an even more limited number of places—may be traced to the haphazard occurrence of events and thoughts which give, as Smollett required, a "large, diffus'd picture of life." Whereas writers of the "new species" usually designated certain events and then looked at the portion of life attached to those events, Sterne chose rather to designate Shandy Hall and look at the portion attached to that small enclosure, which becomes a microcosm in the process, not a microcosm of people but of life, with all its illogical, unexpected events and contingencies.

The comedy one senses in a world where the unexpected is the everyday occurrence is intertwined with a sense of tragedy as well, as both Reid and Rufus Putney have perceptively discussed.[19] There is a fatality in the absurdity that is inescapable and frightening, a fatality which is responsible for crushed noses, dissolved arguments, irrelevant digressions, and other misfortunes which are for the most part comic to the outsider and tragic to the human being involved. Sterne intimates the presence of terrors that lurk in the backgrounds of destiny, waiting to ambush us, but he does so not to frighten but to prepare and protect: the preparation and protection he offers is comedy, a comic vision strong enough not to ward off impending evils but to allow one to live with them when they turn up. Thus, the deliberate eccentricity, the deliberately anarchic view of a world in which individuals must manage, each in their own way, to overcome private adversities. Laurence Sterne offered the world his comic work avowedly in the hope that he could arm his readers with his own consciousness of the need for laughter: "I humbly beg, Sir [he wrote in his Dedication to Pitt] that you will honour this book by taking it . . . into the country with you; where, if I am ever told, it has made you smile, or can conceive it has beguiled you of one moment's pain—I shall think myself as happy as a minister of state" (3).

It would seem that Sterne "paints his face" and puts on "his ruff and motley clothes" to higher purpose than Thackeray was able to comprehend; beguilement is the business of the jester and underlying his display of merriment is the need for such beguilement and the need for the display to end in laughter. Sterne shows his genius in being able to plead the necessity and carry off the jest at the same time:

> But mark, madam, we live amongst riddles and mysteries—the most obvious things, which come in our way, have dark sides, which the quickest sight cannot penetrate into; and even the clearest and most exalted understandings amongst us find ourselves puzzled and at a loss in almost every cranny of nature's work; so that this, like a thousand other things, falls out for us in a way, which tho' we cannot reason upon it,—yet we find the good of it, may it please your reverences and your worships— and that's enough for us. (293)

Tristram's deference to "madam" and his formal address to the various dignitaries give this passage an ironic tone that leads one to assume at first that he means not one jot of what he says. Yet if one bears Tristram's history in mind, and remembers specifically that Tristram, not Sterne, is speaking, the source of the irony becomes clear; it is not that Tristram is saying a thing which is not, it is rather that he is acutely aware of the truth of his assertion—that life is an insoluble puzzle—having had so much occasion to escape from the riddles and mysteries of life; it is irony directed at himself for being in such an unfortunately excellent position to offer his opinion. We are not meant to reject Tristram's observations, but rather to see how ludicrously true they are, how pitiable a thing man would be if he did not escape our pity by the wonderfully irrational contrivance of finding the "good of it." The irony does not detract from the real cheerfulness with which Tristram notes that Nature, the "dear Goddess," provides us with the necessary impulses and gestures to overcome provoking shocks.

Sterne, too, in real life called upon irrational spirits to make his escape. In the later volumes of **Tristram Shandy** we may consider Sterne himself to be speaking when Tristram describes his encounters with Death:

> Now as for my spirits . . . I have much—much to thank 'em for: cheerily have ye made me tread the path of life with all the burdens of it (except its cares) upon my back; in no one moment of my existence, that I remember, have ye once deserted me, or tinged the objects which came in my way, either with sable, or with a sickly green; in dangers ye gilded my horizon with hope, and when DEATH himself knocked at my door—ye bad him come again; and in so gay a tone of careless indifference, did ye do it, that he doubted of his commission—
>
> "—There must certainly be some mistake in this matter," quoth he. (479)

This description is such a thinly disguised account of Sterne's own struggles to stay alive that one feels the pathos of it acutely. But Sterne's "careless indifference" or rather his determination to be carelessly indifferent does not allow us to pity him; we may admire his courage and laugh at his self-characterization, but we must recognize fully that he is alive to make fun and therefore not deserving of pity.

That Sterne places life over death, the present over the past, comes out especially in the supposedly sentimental passages, especially LeFever's death scene. Over the years he has infuriated readers with his inability to refrain from the last spoiling word (if one sees him as a helplessly shallow jester) or disturbed them with his demand that they not give in to the comfortable pathos he has aroused (if one sees him as a writer with a comic purpose). Sterne does not "go on," in reply to his own question, but chooses to start another chapter both for the stated reason that he is "impatient to return to [his] own story" (426), and for the more important reason that sorrow for the dead is too easy and satisfying a feeling, too much like self-pity, and the time could be better spent in actively living. Thus Tristram continues his rhapsodical work, having inserted the black page following Yorick's death as a symbol of his genuine grief and his determination to mock it. Take advantage of the moment, greet life with an open-house reception, such are the real lessons of his "sentimental" passages. Feed an ass for curiosity, measure Janatone right now:

> [H]e who measures thee, *Janatone,* must do it now—thou carriest the principles of change within thy frame; and considering the chances of a transitory life, I would not answer for thee a moment; e'er twice twelve months are pass'd and gone, thou mayst grow out like a pumkin, and lose thy shapes—or, thou mayst go off like a flower, and lose thy beauty—nay thou mayst go off like a hussy—and lose thyself. (490)

Despite the lighthearted references to "shapes" and to aunt Dinah who went off like a hussy, Sterne feels deeply the sad inevitable changes that occur to living things in the course of living. But his response is not to mourn but to appreciate what there is at the moment; his flippancy does not deny the essential pathos of mutability, it insists on it and consequently on the need to act while one has the opportunity.

Because Sterne sees an individual lifetime as a "fragment," spleen and anger, the bilious and saturnine passions, both of which clog up the channels of the blood that make "the wheel of life run long and chearfully round," are crimes against nature. Thus Sterne takes on the vital job of jester and shows, in the book that is his jest, the effectiveness of deliberate mirth in ridding the system of its wasteful passions. Tristram's personal fight against disillusionment with life is the impetus behind his writing; and in turn, his writing is his salvation, or as Fluchère sees it, Tristram's efforts are an answer to the challenge that the facts of his life present him with: "Autobiography thus becomes a sort of revenge for a wasted life, an absurd and farcical revenge it is true, but one which can restore the balance."[20] Tristram himself asserts the probable success of such a plan: "I will answer for it the book shall make its way in the world, much better than its master has done before it—Oh Tristram! Tristram! can this but be once brought about—the credit, which will attend thee as an author, shall counterbalance the many evils which have befallen thee as a man" (337).

The whole character of Tristram, the misdirected Homunculus grown into the image of a man, is dedicated to demonstrating the value of his battles against his unfortunate past, against despair or, on the petty every-day level, the spleen. The careless tone in which he informs us that he has been "the continual sport of what the world calls fortune" evinces the comic view of the world that lies behind it:

> [T]hough I will not wrong her by saying, She has ever made me feel the weight of any great or signal evil;—yet with all the good temper in the world, I affirm it of her, that in every stage of my life, and at every turn and corner where she could get fairly at me, the ungracious Duchess has pelted me with a set of as pitiful misadventures and cross accidents as ever small HERO sustained. (10)

Fortune is here transformed into a big bully, torment-ing the small figure of Tristram with the likes of peb-bles and a few stones; Tristram forgives her with the slight grudge that a helpless young boy bears towards his more powerful companion who has on the whole amused him but who has hurt him somewhat in doing so. The knowledge that he has lived through the expe-rience unscathed and has thus perhaps earned a bit of respect from the rough-playing Duchess helps him with his forgiveness and prepares him to accept the next attack with relative equanimity.

Critics, the everyday counterparts of the ungracious Duchess, get the same good-natured reaction from Tristram: "If any one of you should gnash his teeth, and storm and rage at me, as some of you did last MAY . . . don't be exasperated, if I pass it by again with good temper,—being determined as long as I live or write (which in my case means the same thing) never to give the honest gentleman a worse word or a worse wish, than my uncle *Toby* gave the fly" (162). Spleen might prevent Tristram from writing, which would be tantamount to dying, so he has his little joke in equat-ing the "honest" critics with Uncle Toby's fly and then continues merrily on his way.

Faith, not resolve, may provide the necessary defense against life's sudden shocks. Walter and Toby Shandy are Sterne's representatives of this equally effective means of bearing the burdens of existence as well as possible. A conversation between them, or rather a discourse by Walter on the occasion of his son's un-fortunate delivery, shows the differing nature of their faiths:

> Though man is of all others the most curious vehicle, said my father, yet at the same time 'tis of so slight a frame and so totteringly put together, that the sudden jerks and hard jostlings it unavoidably meets with in this rugged journey, would overset and tear it to pieces a dozen times a day—was it not, brother *Toby,* that there is a secret spring within us—Which spring, said my uncle *Toby,* I take to be Religion.—Will that set my child's nose on? cried my father . . . the spring I am speaking of, is that

great and elastic power within us of counterbalancing evil, which like a secret spring in a well-ordered machine, though it can't prevent the shock—at least imposes upon our sense of it. (277-78)

Walter's secret spring in this case turn out mirthfully to be the all-powerful name, Trismegistus, an unparal-leled product of his hobby-horse-dominated mind. The contrast between Walter's concept of a "great and elas-tic power" and the absurd generation of that power is comic, and the comedy in turn reinforces the notion of man's great resilience. Any little thing will do to coun-terbalance evil provided one believes in its power to do so. Uncle Toby's simple faith in Religion is not any more practical, as his brother is quick to point out, than choosing a high-sounding name. What is impor-tant, for the characters and the readers, is the convic-tion that all is not lost, that the family will survive this crisis and that one may laugh at the whole event.

One might fairly suppose that Sterne is advocating a world of fools in the happy state of being well de-ceived. Being in a perpetual state of deception howev-er is not to be confused with the conscious decision to disavow evil, misery and death. The one is based on the Panglossian error that this is the best of all possible worlds, the other is closer to the Spinozistic idea that it is best to "keep one's pecker up," no matter what is coming. If one refuses to grant recognition, to give cruelty and death their due, however much one knows they are a part of life, then one is in a stronger position to appreciate the kindness and goodness in life and get on with the business of living. Gulliver, most would agree, could have managed life much better without his voyage to the land of the Houyhnhnms and his sudden apprehension of human weakness. If Gulliver changes from a fool to a knave in the course of his travels, from an innocent and alert observer of human-ity to an embittered flayer of mankind, one can see that Swift clearly hopes that he will find his way to the sane and reasonable state that lies between them, the one in which observation leads to useful correction, not outrage. Though Sterne is not as concerned with the correction of society as is Swift, both would grant that the achievement of individual generosity and gen-tility, both dependent on personal happiness, is a con-tribution towards a corrected society that every person should be able to make. Because Swift's emphasis is more on the necessity for the contribution than on the personal achievement alone, his plea is the more im-passioned for having the more to accomplish, and at the same time the more embittered for the unlikelihood of its being heard. Sterne would be satisfied with a more fanciful result, a "kingdom of hearty laughing subjects," being convinced that "disorders in the blood and humours, have as bad an influence . . . upon the body politick as body natural" (338). The implication is that if each one takes care of his own spiritual health, that of the country will come naturally.

Not everyone is able to laugh, especially not, like Laurence Sterne, in the "same tender moment" as they cry. Hobby-horses may substitute for outright laughter; indeed, they are but different, personalized forms of the comic vision. A man is characterized as much by his hobby-horse as his head, Sterne asserted, for it delineates the special path along which he chooses to make his way in the world. Their value to the characters of *Tristram Shandy* is that of all comedy: they make the world navigable if not quite conquerable. Uncle Toby's allows him, as Stanley Eskin observes, to organize and understand the chaos at Namur and to make sense of the rest of life by connecting it with his military experience.[21] Walter is able to categorize and intellectualize all the troublesome stray bits of emotion or chance that might interfere with his previously laid-out plans.

The frustration and anguish felt by Toby as a result of his complete puzzlement by words, and in turn his inability to express the exact nature of his wound to other people or himself, is relieved to a great extent by Trim's happy suggestion of a tangible replacement for mere words—the bowling green. Not only do the models remove the ambiguity from his military vocabulary, they also scale the events which gave rise to the original confusion down to an unfrightening size. It is this combination of tangibility and smallness that makes the fortifications comic, or rather Uncle Toby comic, just as any gentleman who acclimatized himself to riding on trains by playing with electric models would be. The bowling green is essentially a giant playground, and Uncle Toby, guilty by association, is no more than an overgrown child. But the suggestion that Toby's guilt is forced upon him by the baffling nature of real life and the overwhelming size of the world outside the bowling green gives the comedy a serious heart and makes Uncle Toby as noble as he is comic. The bravery of his attempt to make sense of an apparently nonsensical situation—that is, life—redeems any failure in his attempt. There is a real need to bring life down to size and to clarify with objects the ideas that govern it; the fulfilment of this need is therefore natural and commendable, even though the fulfilment is only a substitution, a makeshift apparatus rather than an actual achievement. The achievement consists, of course, in accepting the substitution and going on with life.

Toby's brother Walter is not really very different from himself. Whereas the one uses models to understand the facts of reality, the other uses words, uses them indeed as if they were models, to make the facts of reality fit a neat and pleasant pattern, which they do not naturally do. Both Uncle Toby and Walter Shandy are rather dignified characters, and believe implicitly in the dignity of man; they both depend upon their hobby-horses to keep them neatly mounted and to keep the road they follow free from possible pitfalls. To Toby, no military maneuver is too complex for comprehension once it has been imitated exactly and no fact of life is too incomprehensible if it can be related to its military counterpart. Just so, to Walter, no fact is unbearable if one can express it in words, which are not themselves inimical, but rather reasonable and orderly. One can work with words as one cannot with emotions, which are apt to change suddenly or be illogical. Words serve as well as models for reducing events down to a manageable size, and have the advantage over Toby's toys of being reasonable, and even—if necessary—generously ambiguous. Walter uses his theories to uphold his view of the order of reality and the nobility of man, and need only reject as arrant nonsense any expressions that do not affirm his assumptions:

> As for that certain, very pale, subtle, and very fragrant juice [affirmed] to be the principal seat of the reasonable soul . . . my father could never subscribe to it by any means; the very idea of so noble, so refined, so immaterial, and so exalted a being as the *Anima,* or even the *Animus,* taking up her residence, and sitting dabbling, like a tad-pole, all day long, both summer and winter, in a puddle,— or in a liquid of any kind, how thick or thin soever, he would say, shock'd his imagination; he would scarce give the doctrine a hearing. (148-49)

His dismissal is as ridiculous and magnificent as Uncle Toby's bowling green activities are. His narrow-mindedness is absurd, especially in a philosopher, and yet his protection of man's dignity from unworthy explanations, from ignominious hypotheses, is touching and says more for the frailty but also the reality of that dignity than any noble explanation could. Man's determination to make the best of himself and of life takes the comical form of a hobby-horse, and Sterne in his dramatized dissertation on hobby-horses demonstrates both the comedy and the nobility of man, who is no more than a homunculus with props, but who manages nevertheless.

The value to Tristram of a hobby-horse is perhaps greatest of all, for his enables him to see comically on his own, to laugh outright; that is, the need in Tristram for a prop, a mount with which to overcome hurdles is replaced by a readiness to laugh that is derived from his rides on his hobby-horse. His sitting down to write represents a conscious search for an explanation, a justification for his life, and by mounting his hobby-horse, by attempting to order his life into the neat and logical pattern of My Life and Opinions, he succeeds in overcoming the need for justification and logic by laughing at it and himself, by stumbling on the road and enjoying it. Tristram becomes a true comic hero, whose heart is as "determined as the phoenix." The image is Christopher Fry's and rests on his notion of the unswerving concentration of the mythical bird to bring about his own rebirth: "What burns must also light and renew, not by a vulnerable optimism but by a hard-won maturity of delight, by the intuition of comedy, and active patience declaring the solvency of good."[22] That Tristram does not chase away his hobby-horse, but continues writing his book after the first few exhilaratingly muddled pages, is because he does not choose to, for the little filly turns out to be amusing for itself:

> What a rate have I gone on at, curvetting and frisking it away, two up and two down for four volumes together, without looking once behind, or even on one side of me, to see whom I trod upon!—I'll tread upon no one,—quoth I to myself when I mounted—I'll take a good rattling gallop; but I'll not hurt the poorest jack-ass upon the road. . . .

> Now ride at this rate with what good intention and resolution you may,—'tis a million to one you'll do some one a mischief, if not yourself—He's flung—he's off—he's lost his seat—he's down—he'll break his neck—see!—if he has not galloped full amongst the scaffolding of the undertaking critics! (298)

Tristram's frisky rides. are as exhilarating to us as to him. Our feeling of pleasure is similar to that aroused by Smollett's energetic sentences: in both cases the author's zest for experience is contained within the writing.

Norman Holland sees the hobby-horse as central to the comedy of the work, and explains its double-value: "On the one side of the paradox, Sterne pokes fun at his characters by making silly (but real) things suddenly pop onto this personal road and topple over both hobby-horse and rider. On the other side of the paradox, Sterne pokes fun at the serious obstacles of reality by having the characters jump his hobby-horse triumphantly over them."[23] One must see, though, that in writing *Tristram Shandy* Sterne surely concentrates on the latter virtue of the hobby-horse, for the silliness of the character almost always goes unnoticed in the light of his triumphs. What Holland refers to as a paradox is simply comedy's normal method of dealing with human beings: characters are created with such ludicrous proportions and shortcomings that one cannot be surprised if they fail to surmount an obstacle or two, and one laughs at their shame (while delighting in their energy); if however, they manage, in spite of their ludicrous make-up, to conquer a hurdle unexpectedly, one laughs all the more at their surprising dexterity. We may note that it is the characters who are not equipped with effective hobby-horses who are most often seen to get splashed by the mud in the road—most notably and literally, Dr. Slop. Because he lacks the ability to laugh at himself, and because he cannot fall and get up again without displaying his lack of resiliency—physical and mental—we laugh at his silliness and shame much more than if he did it for us

and we feel no sense of his having triumphed over his short, squat, human body. But comedy never entirely deprecates its subject, for he is invariably a member of the human race, which is comedy's true subject and darling. Our laughter is not entirely at the shame of Slop; a good deal of it may be attributed to our pleasure in the exaggeration, the vitality of the scene. Moreover, our laughter at the farcical elements of the incident makes us feel more kindly towards the foolish figure, for as Sydney Smith rightly pointed out after Sterne's time, but in a passage especially applicable to his kind of humor, "contempt accompanied by laughter, is always mitigated by laughter, which seems to diminish hatred, as perspiration diminishes heat."[24] Our laughter makes us remember his humanity, man's proneness to stumble, and we forgive his silliness as much as we delight in it.

Sterne has indicated in a more straightforward manner than the pages of his novel permit that affectionate comedy is the only acceptable kind. Setting up for a man of wit "on the broken stock of other people's failings" is, according to his sermon, what "has helped to give wit a bad name, as if the main essence of it was satire." He goes on in "The Levite and His Concubine" to distinguish between nasty and kindly humor:

> Certainly there is a difference between Bitterness and Saltness,—that is,—between the malignity and the festivity of wit,—the one is mere quickness of apprehension, void of humanity,—and is a talent of the devil; the other comes down from the Father of Spirits, so pure and abstracted from persons, that willingly it hurts no man; or if it touches upon an indecorum, 'tis with that dexterity of true genius, which enables him rather to give a new colour to the absurdity, and let it pass. (I, 214)

Sterne surely intended *Tristram Shandy* to be utterly without bitterness, and one may determine his success by using Dr. Slop as a touchstone. The supposedly vicious lampoon of Dr. Burton (apparently a relic of the "Yorkshire epic" that *Tristram Shandy* originally was) would have no life for us today if it were simply a splenetic creation. So many of the characters in *The Dunciad* are merely dead names to us because they are based so closely on people who died and were not worth remembering (except perhaps to explain some of the jokes in the poem). *The Dunciad* triumphs over the bulk of its ghostly subjects mainly because of the incomparably alive creation that Dulness herself is: had Pope written his epic and left out his goddess (an impossible assumption) our interest in it would surely be dulled in proportion to its subject. What saves the caricature of Dr. Burton from being bitter and gives it life today is that Sterne's abuse of the overstuffed doctor is, Work rightly notes, "as ludicrous as rancorous" (lxv). If we are to believe Sterne, his portrait is Cervantic rather than satiric, and Slop's fall was not meant maliciously but comically: the humor arises not from the image of the would-be Burton besmirched with mud and *"unwiped, unappointed, unanealed"* (107), but rather from "describing silly and Trifling Events, with the Circumstantial Pomp of great Ones."[25] Of course we laugh actually at a combination of Sterne's jest at the expense of the Roman Catholic doctor and at the enlargement of the trifling event, but it is well to note that other barbs aimed at the Church, such as those in the sermon scene, are not nearly so funny as this, which is supported by the humorous description of the fall. Sterne does not deal in lampoons, though he may incidentally lampoon—the test is whether or not the passage is comic even if we are unaware of an existing original. He is concerned rather with characters who are so uniquely absurd that they may be mistaken for representations of real people, but are more fittingly taken as general representatives of the human race, comic types of a comical species.

These representatives suggest the appropriateness of tolerance and openness in one's relationships with human beings. Sterne sees to it that the relationship with his characters is that of one person to others, not of a reader to fictitious creations. One feels quite certain after reading **Tristram Shandy** that one has never met anyone quite like either of the Shandy brothers. Yet just as certainly one feels that they serve very well as models of the human race; we would not be surprised if we met a Walter or a Toby in the street tomorrow. Like all great comic characters, especially Falstaff, they are made to seem outlandish and ordinary at once. Just as Falstaff, who manages to sum up every human characteristic ranging from sophistication to naiveté, roguery to honesty, churlishness to gentility, is still miraculously life-sized, not larger, so the Shandy brothers—one with an oversized sensibility, the other with an oversized mentality—are loved for their very grotesqueries, which prove them to be ordinary fallible human beings. By emphasizing that the ordinary is made up of separate pieces of the extraordinary, comedy fulfills one of its primary functions, which is paradoxically to make the ordinary seem not especially outlandish, to make us understand that incongruity must be reconciled with our prejudiced notions of the regular and the typical.

Sterne's ability to make his characters' oddities obvious without straining our sense of the possible distinguishes him as a comic artist. Only Walter Shandy would choose to define the right end of a woman—which only Toby Shandy would need to have defined for him—by comparing "all the parts which constitute the whole of that animal" not anatomically, but "analogically" (102). Yet in the context of the discussion, and of Uncle Toby's extreme modesty, Walter's approach is perfectly sensible, if nonetheless unusual and peculiar to himself. Uncle Toby more often than his brother surprises and delights us with his interpreta-

tions of the topic under discussion, but one can never faithfully say that his way of looking at things is illogical or unbelievable; on the contrary, his remarks are often remarkably to the point and no more absurd than what has passed for sense from the other speakers:

> But what are these, continued my father . . . to those prodigies of childhood in *Grotius, Scioppus, Heinsius* . . . and others—some of which left off their substantial forms at nine years old. . . . But you forget the great *Lipsius,* quoth Yorick, who composed a work the day he was born;—They should have wiped it up, said my uncle *Toby,* and said no more about it. (410-12)

All the naiveté and compassion that characterizes Uncle Toby is summed up in this one statement, which is delightfully laughable and yet eminently sensible. The conversation has been bordering on the incredible and Toby's down-to-earth observation is needed to offset the spur that Yorick has given to Walter's hobby-horse. The same is true of Toby's firm intervention in the argument concerning the duchess of Suffolk: "Let the learned say what they will, there must certainly, quoth my uncle *Toby,* have been some sort of consanguinity betwixt the duchess of Suffolk and her son—" (331). That Toby should need to state such an obvious point is not entirely his fault; the fact has been somewhat obscured by the findings of the learned. Nevertheless, Sterne teases him for his innocent acceptance of nonsense in the line that follows: "The yulgar are of the same opinion, quoth Yorick, to this hour." These little scenes may be admired for their wit, but should be valued for their comedy, for the understanding they show of the way in which sense and nonsense may cohabit happily in the human mind and the way in which odd individuals are indeed unique in their oddities but are typical in being odd.

Tristram's assessment of the wonderfully assorted members of his family accurately accounts for the loving reception bestowed upon them by readers of each successive generation: "I believe in my soul . . . the hand of the supreme Maker and first Designer of all things, never made or put a family together . . . where the characters of it were cast or contrasted with so dramatic a felicity as ours was" (236). We are not tempted to look for an ironical undertone, for the statement only confirms what we feel. Separately, but most delightfully together, the Shandy household entertains us with the miracles of oddity to be found among the human race, casually collected under one roof. A brief look at the famous kitchen scene shows the mastery with which Sterne sketches in whole characters with a few lines of dialogue. The gatherings in the kitchen are dramatically "parallel" we are told to the ones in the parlor of the family; the servants of Shandy Hall show the same kind of peculiarities, the same sort of individualities in their reactions to a piece of news as the members of the family do. If there is a sameness in this kitchen group not found in the other, it is the selfishness that seems to override all their other passions. All but Trim, who stands above the group with his oratorical authority, accept the news of Bobby's death according to the differences it will make to their lives. Susannah, with the vanity of a maid, instantly envisions the colored dresses of her mistress; she speeds the burial in her imagination so that the period of mourning will begin all the sooner and accordingly passes the news along with a small addition: "Master Bobby is dead and *buried*." The "fat foolish" scullion adopts a simple attitude toward the death; with a kind of animal sense of self-preservation, "So am not I," she responds to Obadiah's excited, "He is dead! he is certainly dead!" (360). Obadiah's own reaction consists of the thought that the household staff "shall have a terrible piece of work in it in stubbing the ox-moor," now that the alternative of Bobby's trip abroad is ruled out.

Their acute concern with themselves is in no way cause for satirical chastisement in Sterne's eyes. Rather than being corrosive in his wit, he seems to admire the poor dropsical scullion's forthrightness above all: Bobby is dead, as surely as she is alive, and the fact that she was not the one to die cannot help pleasing her, regardless of any affection she might have felt. What succeeds, however, in moving her as well as the rest of the group is Trim's timely reminder of human mortality: "Are we not here now, continued the corporal, (striking the end of his stick perpendicularly upon the floor so as to give an idea of health and stability)—and are we not—(dropping his hat upon the ground) gone! in a moment!" (361). As Tristram wisely notes, none of us are "stocks and stones." Even the fat foolish scullion melts at the thought of her own inevitable weakness. The selfishness does not disturb Sterne because he feels so poignantly the enormity of the knowledge of death that each human being must overcome. Much more than in the carefully set up apostrophe that follows may Sterne's true sentiment be felt at this moment, for the apostrophe turns out to be nothing more than a jest on Trim's old hat. But, in ending with a jest, he also reveals the depth of his own feeling and his need to laugh it away.

To all the strange creatures who people the world of *Tristram Shandy* Sterne extends honest feelings of affection and pathos; these feelings are deeply grounded in his comic vision, in his unflagging delight with life and his awareness that the delight may be tinged with pain. That he is most effective in conveying the honesty and depth of his feelings when he is most humorous may be verified by a comparison of the two Maria episodes in his novels. If Sterne truly meant us to feel his great sorrow for the hapless Maria in *A Sentimental Journey,* he does not succeed with such blatant appeals to our refined and elevated feelings: "I sat down close by her; and Maria let me wipe [the

tears] away as they fell, with my handkerchief. I then steep'd it in my own, and then in hers, and then in mine, and then I wip'd hers again, and as I did it, I felt such indescribable emotions within me, as I am sure could not be accounted for from any combinations of matter and emotion" (270). He describes the acuteness of Yorick's feelings, but we are left only to doubt the quality of such pathos which we cannot share because he has given us no more cause than a wet handkerchief. Even the self-parodying Shandean remark that follows—"I am positive I have a soul; nor can all the books with which materialists have pestered the world ever convince me to the contrary"—does not convince us of his soul's sympathy with humanity, for Sterne turns our attention to Yorick's soul not to rebuke his or our natural impulses towards too easily felt tenderness, but to celebrate his own such impulses.

Tears are conspicuously missing from the parallel account in *Tristram Shandy:*

> MARIA look'd wistfully for some time at me, and then at her goat—and then at me—and then at her goat again, and so on alternately.
>
> —Well, *Maria,* said I softly—What resemblance do you find? (631)

By directing the humor at himself, and continuing to do so for the rest of the incident even while protesting that he will refrain from mirth for the rest of his days to honor the "venerable presence of Misery" that Maria represents for him, Sterne reveals much more truly his genuine pity and makes the reader feel his emotion. Here he is not causelessly blubbering at the sight of tears, he is trying to follow the thoughts and feelings of a helpless young girl, he is trying to understand what she feels about life at that moment. All his sympathy is contained in his apparently thoughtless remark, for it shows his awareness at that moment of the absurdity of life and, in turn, his consciousness of the pain to which Maria is therefore exposed.

That his pathos is so unsatisfactory without his humor is not surprising when one traces the source of his refined feelings to his sense of absurdity. The sounds of human dissonance that are everywhere heard in a theoretically harmonious world impress Sterne with the need for a sensitive adjustment to reality, a comic adjustment that takes the discord into account while deriving pleasure from the whole composition. Nothing amuses Sterne more than the unlikely match between Walter Shandy and his wife, though his understanding of the submerged tragedy of their foolish relationship—Walter's consuming vexation, Mrs. Shandy's inconceivable placidity—shows clearly in his depiction of their marriage. There is no satire in his account of Walter's perpetually puzzled despair at having wound up with such an unphilosophical mate, one who is unable to distinguish between "a point of pleasure and a point of convenience." His situation becomes emblematic of the entire human experience: one may be perfectly well-equipped, so one thinks, to get on top of considerations of fate and forture, and still be floored by stray bits of irrationalism, in the form of emotion or chance, that constantly get in the way. One feels, along with Sterne, the terrible uncertainty of human relationships, and therefore the terrible uncertainty of each human being about his own life. Mrs. Shandy's ability to floor her husband to the point of making him doubt the soundness of his rational conclusions simply by mindlessly agreeing with him is perfectly shown in the comical "bed of justice" scene, in which the make-up of Tristram's breeches is being discussed:

> —They should be of leather, said my father, turning him about again.—
>
> They will last him, said my mother, the longest.
>
> But he can have no linings to 'em, replied my father.—
>
> He cannot, said my mother.
>
> 'Twere better to have them of fustian, quoth my father.
>
> Nothing can be better, quoth my mother.—
>
> —Except dimity—replied my father:—'Tis best of all,—replied my mother.
>
> (438)

Mrs. Shandy's compliance is matched only by her husband's increasing exasperation at that compliance. Sterne catches the placidity of the one and the annoyance of the other in the timing of their lines and the punctuation. Mrs. Shandy speeds up her replies in the same proportion as Mr. Shandy speeds up his suggestions. When he interrupts her with "—Except dimity," she replies in the same paragraph, and her remark is prefaced with a dash and appears as a clause following the colon that concludes his. Sterne's observation of speech here is no less perceptive than his attention to gestures, with the same intent: to reveal the struggle involved in carrying on a simple conversation. Mrs. Shandy's automatic responses are no different from Uncle Toby's automatic pipe-smoking or "Lillabullero" whistling. Both of them do not wish to be troubled by ideas or opinions that do not match their own or in any way threaten the serenity (or in Mrs. Shandy's case, vacuity) of their minds. The precisely recorded conversation reveals how dangerous it would be for Mrs. Shandy to consider the matter of the breeches seriously, which would mean having a genuine opinion in opposition to her dogmatic husband's. In the face of opposition, we know, Walter would not have faltered. The humor of the scene lies in the apparent stupidity of the one and the corresponding distress of the other, but the true comedy arises from our realization that neither can truly assert himself—Mrs. Shandy because it would be to no avail, Mr. Shandy because he is foiled by a lack of opposition and thus wavers, which is the true cause of his distress.

A hobby-horse may provide the courage required to meet a world that is too big or too puzzling, as the Shandy characters show, but it may have the unfortunate side-effect of aggravating the ordinary estrangement of people. An enormous amount of affection and bravery is required to overcome the normal jeopardy of misunderstanding that plagues the different forms of human communication, and hobby-horses, so necessary to making one's way in the world, increase the amount of effort that is needed to make one's way with people. If the hazards of human relationships are symptomatic of the world's jest-swollen belly, then Sterne suggests that wit and instruction may be found out from the admirable attempts of the Shandy family to understand each other and make themselves understood. The brothers have each developed their own methods of contending with the misfiring of the other's thoughts. Walter goes into a passion; Uncle Toby smokes his pipe or whistles. Precisely because they are armed against the possibility of spleen and rage in their meetings together, they are not afraid to try once again to communicate and thus they succeed on an emotional if not a literal level. Unlike Gulliver, who changes from a responsive human being into a bitter, reserved madman as a result of his disillusioning attempts to understand his position in relation to other people, the Shandy brothers offer an optimistic resolution to the problem.

The two brothers are endlessly comical and at the same time touchingly admirable because they do not avoid the risks of conversation, no matter how painful the attempt may prove at the time. Walter is decidedly anguished at the renewed proof Toby offers of his unalterable simplicity in their discussion of—or rather Walter's dissertation on—truth and the study of noses:

> 'Tis a pity, said my father, that truth can only be on one side, brother *Toby,*—considering what ingenuity these learned men have all shewn in their solutions of noses.—Can noses be dissolved? replied my uncle *Toby.*—
>
> —My father thrust back his chair,—rose up,—put on his hat,—thrust his head half way out,—shut the door again,—took no notice of the bad hinge,—returned to the table . . . (239)

Toby meets this performance with his usual good nature:

'Twas all one to my uncle *Toby,*—he smoaked his pipe on, with unvaried composure,—his heart never intended offence to his brother,—and as his head could seldom find out where the sting of it lay,—he always gave my father the credit of cooling by himself.—He was five minutes and thirty-five seconds about it in the present case. (240)

Superficially the comedy of this scene may be attributed to the ridiculous wit of Toby's answer and to the gestures so analytically and dramatically exposed by Sterne. But neither the wit nor Bergson's mechanistic explanations get at the heart of the scene, which lies in the failure and the ultimate success of the two brothers to share their lives with each other. The success is comic success, that of accepting the fact that they are intractably opposite and must begin again as best they can. The process of acceptance is seen both as disturbing and rewarding. That it is reanimating as well is attested by Walter's relaunching of his deep philosophy into the ever-shallow waters of his brother's mind, and by his brother's ever-patient admission of the vessel:

> —Why, by the *solutions* of noses, of which I was telling you, I meant as you might have known, had you favoured me with one grain of your attention, the various accounts which learned men of different kinds of knowledge have given the world, of the causes of short and long noses.—There is no cause but one, replied my uncle *Toby,*—why one man's nose is longer than another's, but because God pleases to have it so.—That is *Grangousier's* solution, said my father. (240)

Despite the apparent consensus, the two are clearly back to where they started in understanding one another verbally, yet the comic point has been made: the attempt is what counts in establishing human relationships.

Toby's ability to make himself understood by Trim is directly related to the absence of words in their most remarkable communications. The memory of shared activity leads to new action, while their common hobby-horse allows them to participate equally. The directness with which they are able to fall into step with one another stems from the essentially childlike faith that each understands the other. Indeed, the only time the possibility of mutual incomprehension arises is when Trim describes his adult passion for the fair Beguin, and tries to do so in adult terms. Toby refuses to admit the facts of Trim's experience, or to allow Trim to admit them in words, the effect of which he knows will not be erased by any amount of whistling. The division between them never really occurs, though, for Trim offers no contradiction to Toby's version of what happened when Trim seized the hand of the fair Beguin. Rather than permit a misunderstanding to arise

between them, they resort to their usual faith in the other to understand what is going on, just as Toby does whenever he begins to whistle. This faith is both comic in itself and basic to comedy: Toby and Trim, and Toby and Walter, are funny in their successful attempts to respect the oddities of the other; they are also reassuring in a world where less valiant attempts, less openness and tolerance, can result in coldness and permanent despair.

Tristram, too, it is apparent from his narrative, respects—even more, cherishes—the quirks of the people who are so much a part of his life, and one feels that he equally well loves the entire human race (as Sterne would have us believe of himself). To approach *Tristram Shandy* as satire is to be required to see the story that Tristram tells as "one great anatomy of the fools and knaves who affect him," and his recollections as "a long list of consequences to himself."[26] Yet his many apostrophes acclaiming the merits of various people may mock false sentiment, but they do not mock the characters themselves. Even when faced with the ludicrous picture of his uncle decked out in pursuit of the Widow Wadman, Tristram eschews the opportunity to raise a malicious laugh:

> Had SPLEEN given a look at [the wig], 'twould have cost her ladyship a smile . . . he could as soon have raised the dead.
>
> Such it was—or rather such would it have seem'd upon any other brow; but the sweet look of goodness which sat upon my uncle *Toby's,* assimilated every thing around it so sovereignly to itself, and Nature had moreover wrote GENTLEMAN with so fair a hand in every line of his countenance, that even his tarnish'd gold-laced hat and huge cockade of flimsy taffeta became him. (601)

Her ladyship still smiles at the extravagance of the outfit, but not mockingly at Uncle Toby's simple-mindedness. Nor is there any note of resentment mixed with the affection in Tristram's voice when he explains his father's peculiar penchant for theories: "In truth, there was not a stage in the life of man, from the very first act of his begetting,—down to the lean and slipper'd pantaloon of his second childishness, but he had some favourite notion to himself, springing out of it, as sceptical, and as far out of the high-way of thinking, as these two which have been explained" (145). Tristram's fondness is expressed in the Shakespearian description and in the note of admiration for his father's achievement at having ambled along such strange paths so consistently throughout his life.

His concern, for the most part identical with Sterne's own, for his imagined audience's happiness is more than a mere formality, or so we are made to believe by his attentiveness. His command that we laugh at him or do anything, only keep our tempers, shows a wish for our well-being that is related to his announced reason for writing his book—to drive away the spleen. The thing that strikes one above all is that he is trying to make the choicest experiences of his family come alive so that we may receive the same amount of delight from them as he still does. That he enjoys the absurdity of many of the events is obvious from his warm mockery at such great length of the marriage settlement, the visitation dinner, the great curse, and his own continuing efforts to make some order out of his haphazard family history. Indeed, Tristram's readiness to include himself among the odd creatures of his family serves not only to make him truly a part of that family and therefore more than simply an ironic narrator of a mixed-up tale, but also to soften any rough satirical edges.

He bears no grudges, makes no serious accusations, for he is one of them, and they are all members of the same comical human race. The ironic remarks that he makes at the expense of his father or his uncle are gentle and understanding of the anomalies imposed upon them by Nature, some of which have been accidentally passed on to himself. The extravagance of his father's *Tristrapoedia* is surely equal to that of his uncle's great wig, and Tristram in this case is affected directly by its profound uselessness (whereas the wig harmed no one who did not die from laughing at it). He does not deny the foolishness of his father's wisdom:

> [H]e was three years and something more, indefatigably at work, and at last, had scarce complcatcd, by his own rcckoning, onc half of his undertaking: the misfortune was, that I was all that time totally neglected and abandoned to my mother; and what was almost as bad, by the very delay, the first part of the work, upon which my father had spent the most of his pains, was rendered entirely uscless,—every day a page or two became of no consequence.—(375)

But rather than blaming his father for neglecting him, he generalizes his observation so that Walter seems merely the victim of a common human failing:

> —Certainly it was ordained as a scourge upon the pride of human wisdom, That the wisest of us all, should thus outwit ourselves, and eternally forego our purposes in the intemperate act of pursuing them. (375)

Tristram pities his father rather than himself and he pities mankind in general for being susceptible to the tricks of Time and other natural laws, as he is himself both directly and indirectly: his own inability to supply a minute of reading time for a minute of his life is a curiosity of Time that he must accept, and the cause of his having to order his life into reading matter is a result of his father's having been duped by Time into neglecting him.

The law of Chance exercises similar control over his life, so that he finds himself accidentally circumcised at the age of five, having directly encountered the chance effects of a loose window sash. Tristram identifies the culprits who were indirectly responsible for the accidental occurrence, his uncle having directed Trim to find some weights for the battlefield equipment—a request that is in turn related to the chance occurrence at Namur—but he focuses the reader's attention on the wonder of the coincidence, not on the foolishness of his uncle's hobby-horse. He dismisses the whole disaster with a "'Twas nothing."

Tristram's propensity to overlook or rationalize the shortcomings of the people around him has, not surprisingly, a comic effect on "his" work. Like Sterne's his comic vision makes a joke of the world and a miracle of the human race that somehow manages to make the world its home. A lament for man that Tristram makes at the beginning of Book Five is subverted by a jest at his own expense, an expense which Sterne himself shares, for the charge concerns the method by which **Tristram Shandy** is composed:

> Who made MAN, with powers which dart him from earth to heaven in a moment—that great, that most excellent, and most noble creature of the world— that *miracle* of nature, . . . the *image* of God . . . the *ray* of divinity . . . the *marvel* of *marvels* . . . to go on at this pitiful—pimping—pettifogging rate? (343)

If one takes the whole statement as ironic, then man is not "the most excellent, and most noble creature" and Tristram does not really go sneaking on at a pitiful rate, that is, one must conclude from previous references that his work is a brilliant and original work of art that will contribute to the "stock" as well as the "bulk" of man's learnings. If once accepts the assertion of man's nobility, then Tristram, and in effect Sterne, is indulging in a characteristic bit of conscious and comic self-pity in the hopes of winning our sympathies. Either way, the image of human species does not suffer, for an individual may triumph over his pitiful condition or else humanity is noble in spite of his apparently ignoble ways. One is left with the inevitable conclusion that on the one hand man is ludicrous and paltry, the inhabitant of a world that imposes pettiness upon him, and on the other, man's belief in his own nobility allows him to triumph over his birthright by acting with stature and becoming truly noble.

Unlike Swift, no matter how much Sterne reduces the scale of mankind in order to dramatize the difficulties man has in making his way through life, he maintains his capacity for admiration and amusement. Swift's whole purpose in Book Two of *Gulliver's Travels* is to demonstrate "how contemptible a thing [is] human grandeur" and he does so by dramatizing with terrifying minuteness the insults that Gulliver is forced to endure. Our admiration for Gulliver's efficiency in dealing with the flies, for instance, is offset by our sense of his false pride: he does not accept the ludicrousness of his position among giants any more than he rejects the value of the honor bestowed upon him by the Lilliputians, the title of "nardac" for his bravery and strength. For all his objectivity, Gulliver is blind to his own absurdity. The objective observer in *Tristram Shandy*, who like Gulliver is himself an object of observation, is as acutely aware of his own inadequacy to life as Sterne and the readers are. One certainly has the sense of man's physical and mental insufficiency in *Tristram Shandy*—the impotence of both mind and body apparently afflicting the Shandy men has often been noted—but one does not feel as if the magnitude of the soul is diminished by the body's failure to house it properly or the mind's to protect it from the shocks of the world. The bravery of all three—Walter, Toby, and Tristram—in attempting to cope with the demands of the world more than replaces the dignity lost by their homunculean drawbacks and their use of hobby-horsical props. Moreover, their bravery is admirable because, unlike Gulliver's, it is grounded in the knowledge of their own smallness and inefficiency and in a faith in the great and elastic power within them to counterbalance their own absurdity.

The faith, which is expressed in hobby-horsical activities or simply in a self-mocking jest, arms its possessor against the clashes of other absurdities and allows him to act with tolerance and courage. The faith itself becomes the means by which man triumphs over his characteristic puniness. Tristram's book, Fluchère rightly claims, is "a dazzling testimony to his victory over words and things, a proof of his vitality and vigilance."[27] Toby would have been basely betrayed into solitude and despair, first by his wound, were it not for his whole-hearted commitment to his bowling green war, and second, by the peace of Utrecht, were it not for the likeness between love and war that Mrs. Wadman happily encourages him to discover. He valiantly forges ahead with a siege at her doorstep, thus maintaining the dignity and orderliness that soldiering gives to his life and that he so painstakingly preserved on his green. Walter's fruitless mental voyages into the realm of auxiliary verbs in search of the North-west passage of the intellect is counterbalanced by the equanimity— that is, the real fruit of his mental voyages, with which he is then able to meet the irrationalities of other people. His puzzlement is no less than Toby's many times, and his idolatry of reason makes puzzlement a difficult thing to bear. Nevertheless, Walter triumphs consistently over his demands for rationality by rationally absolving his helplessly befuddled brother of any in-

tentional crime and acting tenderly and affectionately towards him. Each of the three manages his little stock of understanding and ability with husbandry, and turns the potential cause for ridicule—his life on earth—into a call for celebration.

Whereas Smollett, in *Peregrine Pickle*, urges the acceptability of Fortune, Chance, and Evil in life by making their dangers seem challenging and stimulating, Sterne offers the possibility of triumph over these dangers. Of all Smollett's characters, only Commodore Trunnion would find himself at home in *Tristram Shandy*, for he alone has a fully developed comic faith in man's ability to live happily and peacefully, which arms him with the necessary power to do so. Sterne demonstrates the necessity and value of the comic imagination by showing us that the public outrages of Nature are nothing to the private ravages of despair and the concomitant ills of spleen and aloofness, and by showing us that we may overcome these with determination and affection, with conscious mirth that protects the mirthful against the forces of despair and loneliness. . . .

Notes

[10] Dilworth, p. 108.

[11] Stedmond's suggestion was first made in "Satire and *Tristram Shandy*," *SEL* I (1961), 53. A revised version of this article appears in the later work, *The Comic Art of Laurence Sterne*. The quotation is from p. 6.

[12] New, p. 2.

[13] Norman Holland comments on these lines (*Hamlet* V.i.212-215) in his article, p. 422.

[14] See Richard Lanham, '*Tristram Shandy*': The Games of Pleasure (Berkeley: University of California Press, 1973), which appeared after the completion of this study. His chapter entitled "Games, Play, Seriousness" is of particular interest.

[15] Nietzsche, VII, 60-62.

[16] Fluchère, p. 268.

[17] Fluchère, p. 77.

[18] Reid, pp. 110-11.

[19] Reid, pp. 124-27; Putney, "Laurence Sterne," pp. 159-70.

[20] Fluchère, p. 73.

[21] Eskin, p. 274.

[22] Fry ["Comedy," in *Comedy: Meaning and Form*, ed. R. Corrigan], p. 17.

[23] Holland, p. 422.

[24] Quoted in Tave, p. 86.

[25] Sterne, *Letters*, p. 77; 1 January 1760.

[26] Paulson, p. 252.

[27] Fluchère, p. 72. . . .

Works Cited

Primary Sources

. . . Sterne, Laurence. *The Letters of Laurence Sterne*, edited by L. Curtis. Oxford: Clarendon Press, 1935.

————. *The Life and Opinions of Tristram Shandy, Gent.*, edited by J. Work. New York: Odyssey Press, 1940.

————. *A Sentimental Journey Through France and Italy by Mr. Yorick*, edited by G. Stout, Jr. Berkeley: University of California Press, 1967.

————. *The Sermons of Mr. Yorick*. 2 vols. Oxford: Basil Blackwell, 1927. . . .

Secondary Sources

Corrigan, R., ed., *Comedy: Meaning and Form*. San Francisco: Chandler Publishing, 1965.

Dilworth, Ernest Nevin. *The Unsentimental Journey of Laurence Sterne*. New York: King's Crown Press, 1948.

Eskin, Stanley. "*Tristram Shandy* and *Oedipus Rex*: Reflections on Comedy and Tragedy," *College English* XXIV (1963), 271-77.

Fluchère, Henri. *Laurence Sterne From Tristram to Yorick*, translated by B. Bray. London: Oxford University Press, 1965.

Holland, Norman. "The Laughter of Laurence Sterne," *Hudson Review* IX (1957), 422-30.

New, Melvyn. *Laurence Sterne as Satirist: A Reading of "Tristram Shandy."* Gainesville: University of Florida Press, 1969.

Nietzsche, Friedrich. *The Complete Works of Friedrich Nietzsche*. Translated by O. Levy. Edinburgh, 1911.

Paulson, Ronald, and Lockwood, Thomas, eds. *Henry Fielding: The Critical Heritage*. London: Routledge, 1969.

Putney, Rufus. "Laurence Sterne, Apostle of Laughter," in *The Age of Johnson: Essays Presented to C.B. Tinker*. New Haven: Yale University Press, 1949, pp. 159-70.

————. "The Plan of *Peregrine Pickle*," *PMLA* LX (1945), 1051-65. . . .

Reid, B.L. *The Long Boy and Others: Eighteenth-Century Studies*. Athens, Ga.: University of Georgia Press, 1969. . . .

Tave, Stuart, M. *The Amiable Humorist: A Study in the Comic Theory and Criticism of the Eighteenth and Early Nineteenth Centuries*. . . .

Helene Moglen (essay date 1975)

SOURCE: "The Irony of Character," in *The Philosophical Irony of Laurence Sterne*, University Presses of Florida, 1975, pp. 65-96.

[*Moglen examines the major characters of* Tristram Shandy *and concludes that, in addition to representing accurate portraits of the human condition, each is delineated via the same "diverse" and "eccentric" ways by which Sterne structured his novel.*]

Tristram Shandy is a novel of ideas. Its form is part of the idea, not a background for it, and the characters themselves are aspects of the intellectual quest, all constructed from some pivotal irony, subject to some central paradox, treated with sceptical insight as well as love. That is not to say that Sterne's people are two-dimensional representatives of specific positions, spokesmen for the successive stages of a dialectical formula, as Traugott would have it. They inhabit their personalities quite fully, although it is true that their personalities are limited by the uncompromising points of view from which they perceive the world. We watch them interpreting, acting, interacting, responding. Their realities meet, clash, and destroy one another, yet remain curiously intact, for each character has a basic integrity, a core of inflexible ego that keeps him unique and self-sufficient.

The odd way in which Sterne related the particular and the abstract (the irreducible human quality and far-reaching universal propensities) began in his pre-Shandean sermons, for it must be remembered that the man of letters had his birth in the man of God. Sterne's later sermons (the earlier sermons, published last, are primarily exercises in borrowing) reveal the author's persistent attempts to discover the motives of men's actions, the basic elements of personality and character. Lansing Van Der Heyden Hammond points this out in his book *Laurence Sterne's "Sermons of Mr. Yorick"*: "Time and again throughout the **Sermons** he reverts, obviously with the best of intentions, to the tenet that morality alone is insufficient as a motivating factor in human behavior—but invariably the naturalistic implications, not the teleological, are the ones he lingers over and illustrates" (p. 95). As a minister Sterne had surprisingly little interest in theological matters or traditional questions of doctrine. He was a moral philosopher who was concerned with the social effects of action rather than with their supernatural sanctions. As Hammond wrote, it was Sterne's desire to emphasize "the less striking, homelier virtues which count for so much in everyday living: toleration and kindliness, patience and understanding, thoughtfulness and sympathy, modesty and sincerity" (p. 96). These are also the saving virtues of the otherwise perverse characters of *Tristram Shandy.*

It is not surprising, therefore, although it is certainly unconventional, that Sterne would elaborate upon and even distort the texts upon which his sermons were based. When he could not find what he wanted in his text, he had no difficulty in composing a new one for his use. For example, when he deals with "The Character of Herod," he explains: "With this view, it may not be an unacceptable application of the remaining part of a discourse upon this day, to give you a sketch of the character of Herod, not as drawn from scripture,—for in general it furnishes us with few materials for such descriptions. . . . "[1] Similarly, in his sermon "The Levite and His Concubine," Sterne does not make use of the whole Biblical story which ends with the Levite's surrender and subsequent dismemberment of his concubine. He uses only the first half of his source, paradoxically demonstrating with it the importance of courtesy and mercy: "It serves no purpose to pursue the story further; the catastrophe is horrid: and would lead us beyond the particular purpose for which I have enlarged upon this much of it,—and that is, to discredit rash judgement, and illustrate from the manner of conducting this drama, the courtesy which the *dramatis personae* of every other piece, may have a right to."[2] In general, when we compare Sterne's sermons with the sources given us in Hammond's appendix, we find that Sterne tends to concretize the generalization by relating every point of view to a particular personality. Whenever possible, he adopts a dramatic form of narrative, changing his own voice and implicating his audience with an explicit address or direct quotation. As Traugott suggests, the result of his technique is the involvement of the reader in a dialectic which emphasizes the crucial role of interpretation in differentiating the hidden truth from the obvious illusion. This was to be used with great effect in the novel.

In "The Prodigal Son," which is typical of the mature sermons, Sterne muses upon the father's attempts to dissuade his son from undertaking his journey, describes sentimentally the emotional moment of departure, comments liberally upon the youth's impulsive foolishness, elaborates upon his repentant thoughts as he entreats Heaven to help him, and offers with great relish both a detailed account of the boy's lapses into sin and an ironic description of the falsity of the world. Rejecting more conventional discussions of the parable, Sterne concludes with some up-to-date comments of his own about the Grand Tour and its educational values. The sermon seems quite prophetic of *Tristram Shandy* in that it bears the strong imprint of Sterne's personality with his propensity for the dramatic and digressive, his sharp ear for dialogue, his desire to surprise through jarring eccentricities of style and deft portrayals of emotional states, his basically secular, practical orientation, and his marvelous sense of the absurd and incongruous.

Of course, the didactic purpose of the sermons demanded a relative simplicity of structure and characterization. The concept of a "ruling passion" was particularly useful since it enabled Sterne to draw his moral issues clearly, centering motive and consequence upon a single peculiarity of character to which a definite value could be assigned. Using the "obsessions" of his major figures as the focal points of his sermons, Sterne was able to satisfy simultaneously the dramatic and moral demands of his work. Thus, in analyzing Herod, who is driven by "ambition, an immoderate thirst, as well as jealousy of power," Sterne explains his method of illuminating the character of his hero: "The way to which is—in all judgments of this kind, to distinguish and carry in your eye, the principal and ruling passion which leads the character—and separate that, from the other parts of it,—and then take notice, how far his other qualities, good and bad, are brought to serve and support that."[3]

This view of character, which had its roots in Locke's associationism, required a more sophisticated application in the complex situations and ideas of *Tristram Shandy.* In the Shandean world Sterne no longer had defined signposts by which to steer. Although his moral, artistic, and intellectual values might have remained fundamentally the same, they now had to function and validate themselves in a universe of constantly changing perspectives. Given free rein in the disorderly world of secular activity, the hobbyhorse—a concrete expression of the ruling passion—became a more unruly and complexly defined beast than Tristram himself suggests. "For my hobby-horse, if you recollect a little, is no way a vicious beast; he has scarce one hair or lineament of the ass about him——'Tis the sporting little filly-folly which carries you out for the present hour——a maggot, a butterfly, a picture, a fiddle-stick——an uncle *Toby*'s siege, or an *any thing,* which a man makes a shift to get astride on, to canter it away from the cares and solicitudes of life . . ." (VIII.xxxi.584). The hobbyhorse is a serious matter—as serious, Sterne reveals with great insight, as a child's game. It is both a function and an implied criticism of the romantic impulse. It is an expression of the urge to create value and an expression of the urge to sublimate or escape the limiting conditions of the actual. It is the illusion that lends importance to life by interpreting and re-creating reality. It reflects both the strength and the weakness of its possessor, derived as it is from his abilities and directed toward his aspirations. Thus Tristram does not exaggerate when he says "'Tis as useful a beast as is in the whole creation—nor do I really see how the world could do without it" (VIII.xxxi.584). It is either with less insight or greater irony that he comments earlier that " . . . so long as a man rides his HOBBY-HORSE peaceably and quietly along the King's highway, and neither compels you or me to get up behind him,——pray, Sir, what have either you or I to do with it?" (I.vii.13). Indeed, one of *Tristram Shandy*'s primary themes has to do with the inevitable entanglement of hobbyhorses, with the rider's insistence that everyone should get up behind him. It is the thoroughness of the individual's involvement, the intensity of his commitment, that makes conflict unavoidable. And while the collision among riders disturbs the smoothness of the journey, it also prevents one from venturing too far from the common path.

In *Tristram Shandy,* then, the hobbyhorse becomes the focal point of the total personality. It connects the world of thought with the world of action and reveals the central irony of each character. The emergent ironic patterns, expressive of the disparity between aspiration and realization, are compared with one another to create a total picture of the perverse and abortive course followed by human relationships.

To consider these patterns in more detail, it is convenient to identify two distinct groups of characters: the first distinguished by its members' rationality, sophistication, and rhetorical finesse, the second by the individual's reliance upon intuition and sensibility. Walter, Tristram, and Yorick will, of course, be found in the first group; Toby, Trim, the Widow Wadman and Mrs. Shandy are in the second.

Walter Shandy.—Of all the Shandys, Walter's commitment to rationalism is the most extreme and explicit. He believes firmly in the mind's capacity for discovering, creating, and verbalizing truths which can lay claim to some objective validity. He is the scholar whose hobbyhorse (the creation of systems, the formalization of knowledge) is born from his attempts at reconciling the pure world of mind with a physical world that is volatile and full of contradiction. Walter's curiosity is endless. His love of the obscure and secret analogy, the unsuspected and surprising unity hidden in the physical object or the suggestive word, is insatiable and indiscriminate: "Then reach me my breeches off the chair, said my father to *Susannah*——There is not a moment's time to dress you, Sir, cried *Susannah*—— the child is as black in the face as my——As your, what? said my father, for like all orators, he was a dear searcher into comparisons . . ." (IV.xiv.287). Yorick's opinion of Walter's insights can be defended: " . . . there was a seasoning of wisdom unaccountably mixed up with his strangest whims, and he had sometimes such illuminations in the darkest of his eclipses, as almost attoned for them:——be wary, Sir, when you imitate him" (V.xlii.404). But Tristram's judgment is more generally applicable: "My father . . . [forced] every event in nature into an hypothesis, by which means never man crucified TRUTH at the rate he did . . ." (IX.xxxii.644). It is, of course, the irony of Walter's position that his confidence in reason's resources encourages the creation of imaginative illusions and leads him to formulations that are altogether at variance with precepts of commonsense.

Paralleling Walter's paradoxical faith in the absolute power of reason and the eccentric and amateurish way in which he exercises his faculty is the almost magical control he attributes to the word and the affective, rather than analytic, possibilities which he inevitably explores in his own rhetoric. He believed "That there was a strange kind of magick bias, which good or bad names, as he called them, irresistibly impress'd upon our characters and conduct" (I.xix. 50). Here we find one of those problems which Locke had encountered: with what validity can one hypothesize a fixed core of meaning that is somehow separable from the relativity of a word's contextual definition and implication? Walter's suspicion of the name "Tristram" arises partially from ignorance. He considers the name's proper derivation, but he recollects erroneously the nature of the men who had answered to it historically by overlooking the great medieval hero who bore it: " . . . he says there never was a great or heroic action performed since the world began by one called *Tristram*——nay he will have it, *Trim,* that a man can neither be learned, or wise, or brave . . ." (IV.xviii.295).

It is precisely because of Walter's attitude that Tristram's name comes to exert an influence upon the boy's conduct and character. Sterne knew what Locke felt but would not accept: that language, when considered in a psychological context, could assume a frightening life and power of its own. While it held great promise as the tool of social intercourse, the implementation and perhaps basis of man's ability to reason, its rich potentialities concealed many traps. Of these, Walter is frequently a victim. He is presented as a practitioner of language, a rhetorician, an orator: "He was certainly irresistible, both in his orations and disputations;—— he was born an orator;——Theodidaktos.——Persuasion hung upon his lips, and the elements of Logick and Rhetorick were so blended up in him,——and, withall, he had so shrewd a guess at the weaknesses and passions of his respondent,——that NATURE might have stood up and said,——"This man is eloquent" (I.xix.51-2). But Walter's skill is intuitive, not conscious or rational: " . . . it was a matter of just wonder . . . that a man who knew not so much as the names of his tools, should be able to work after that fashion with 'em" (I.xix.53). Thus we have the paradox of the scholar or academician whose oratory springs from an intuitive ability and has an emotional appeal, but is no more based upon reason than are his fanciful systems, the children of a fertile and eccentric imagination. For Walter, argument is a game in which substance is made subordinate to method. It involves the assumption and acting out of various roles, as in his disagreement with Mrs. Shandy about the attendance of a midwife at the birth of his second child, "when he had done arguing the matter with her as a Christian, and came to argue it over again with her as a philosopher . . ." (II.xix.146). Walter's love of language—indeed, his addiction to forms of expression—is carried to its extreme and paradoxical end with his theory of the auxiliary verb, a parody of Aristotle's ten categories. Walter rejects the metaphor, prize of wit and imagination, the *sine qua non* of his own technique. Instead he suggests: "Now the use of the *Auxiliaries* is, at once to set the soul a going by herself upon the materials as they are brought her; and by the versability of this great engine, round which they are twisted, to open new tracts of enquiry, and make every idea engender millions" (V.xlii.405). The word, therefore, becomes father to the idea and restricts and determines the form of reality.

This odd impracticality, the ironic result of an attempt to achieve accuracy of thought and expression, is only one example of the conflict between the theoretical and the practical that frustrates and typifies Walter's life. His concoction of grandiose, abstract theories is linked most frequently to an inability to understand and control his own motivations and actions. Thus, his concern for money and reputation, in addition to a more honorable interest in the well-being of his family, motivates his opposition to his wife's confinement in the city. It is not surprising that he would rationalize his motives, but his rationalization is resourceful beyond any reasonable expectation. He attributes his refusal to a fear that the state would eventually collapse as a result of the movement of men and money to the city. And even here his altruism is brought into question as he expresses his concern for the demise of the squirearchy (I.xviii.47). Any matter that piques his intellectual curiosity causes him to sacrifice the concrete requirements of his family to the more abstract delights of the mind. He gleefully plays a practical joke on Dr. Slop, revealing the fit forms of swearing by having Slop read a form of the excommunication of the Roman Church. Meanwhile his wife lies in bed,

awaiting the doctor's obstetrical services (III.xi.171-79). Similarly, Walter becomes immediately and passionately involved in the pedantic foolishness of the visitation dinner and forgets that he has come in order to change Tristram's name, the retention of which, he feels, invites certain doom (IV.xxix.326). He is a man with well-developed opinions about door hinges, but he has never bothered to oil that one which is an eternal problem to him, although " . . . three drops of oyl with a feather, and a smart stroke of a hammer, had saved his honour for ever" (III.xxi.203). How then can we or Mrs. Shandy be surprised when, hearing from Obadiah the news of his son's circumcision, he returns from a hurried trip upstairs, not with bandages and medicine, but with *Spencer de Legibus Hebræorum Ritualibus* and *Maimonides* (V.xxvii.384).

This unusual conflict between abstract interests and practical concerns frequently expresses itself in a dichotomy of emotion and reason—the most dehumanizing aspect of Walter's character. One is disquieted by Walter's blithe inquiry: "What is the character of a family to an hypothesis? . . . Nay, if you come to that——What is the life of a family . . ." (I.xxi.69). Involved as he is in the excitement of his own ideas, he is able to see his wife only as an object, a piece of personal property whose functions, abilities, interests, and life itself are defined as they relate to him. "It is very strange . . . that my wife should persist . . . in trusting the life of my child . . . to the ignorance of an old woman;——and not only the life of my child, brother,——but her own life, and with it the lives of all the children I might, peradventure, have begot out of her hereafter" (II.vi.99-100).

Walter's responses to incidents which would induce in most people a paroxysm of grief are the deformed offspring of a strangely incongruous and divided spirit. They indicate the extent to which Walter's hobbyhorse is a self-defeating attempt to construct for himself a meaningful reality that bridges isolation and frustration. The funeral oration "My Father's Lamentation" (a compendium of classical mourning literature) in response to Bobby's death, the rhetorical exercise presented on the occasion of Tristram's unexpected circumcision, and his expression of grief by the assumption of a stylized posture when he learns of the crushing of his younger son's nose—all convey Walter's attempts to counter the unexpected and impersonal thrusts of fate with the only controls at his disposal, those of gesture and language. The man seems frequently to disappear behind his contrivance, and it is only rarely that we are allowed to glimpse the emotion that defies formalization. One of these moments is given to us in the image of Walter beside his brother's grave, perceived, presumably, by a more mature Tristram and recalled, therefore, with a fuller degree of consciousness and understanding. "——Where——All my father's systems shall be baffled by his sorrows; and, in spight of his philosophy, I shall behold him, as he inspects the lackered plate, twice taking his spectacles from off his nose, to wipe away the dew which nature has shed upon them——When I see him cast in the rosemary with an air of disconsolation, which cries through my ears,——O *Toby!* In what corner of the world shall I seek thy fellow?" (VI.xxv.452). Less directly, we are left to detect the strains of emotionality that fairly scream through the intensity of Walter's intellectual attacks and belie the nature of his involvement:

> My father had such a skirmishing, cutting kind of a slashing way with him in his disputations, thrusting and ripping, and giving every one a stroke to remember him by in his turn——that if there were twenty people in company——in less than half an hour he was sure to have every one of 'em against him.

> What did not a little contribute to leave him thus without an ally, was, that if there was any one post more untenable than the rest, he would be sure to throw himself into it. . . . (VIII.xxxiv.588)

Walter is ruled by his fear of spontaneity—a fear that is ironic in a man whose richness of imagination and intensity of spirit do, in fact, militate against the coldness and formality of a purely rational approach. In moments of greatest crisis the numbed philosopher is able to summon expressive forms which give him an illusory sense of controlling the uncontrollable reality. It is before the more ordinary circumstances of his relationships that the defenses crumble and his humanity is exhibited in all of its glorious illogicality and inadequacy.

The consistency of Walter's characterization and the piteousness of his circumstances are most fully revealed through his sexual conflict. It is in the physical functioning of man that Walter finds the most frightening signs of his own vulnerability and the most unhappy possibilities of spontaneous response. Walter's attempts to formalize the spontaneous inevitably end in failure and the attempt changes not only his life, but also the lives of his descendants. Indeed, Tristram's unfortunate fate is largely linked to his father's attitude toward sexuality, which is, one feels, only partially determined by the incapacities of age: "As a small specimen of this extreme exactness of his, to which he was in truth a slave,——he had made it a rule for many years of his life,——on the first *Sunday night* of every month throughout the whole year,——as certain as ever the *Sunday night* came,——to wind up a large house-clock which we had standing upon the back-stairs head, with his own hands:——and being somewhere between fifty and sixty years of age . . . he had likewise gradually brought some other little family concernments to the same period, in order, as he would often say to my

uncle *Toby,* to get them all out of the way at one time, and be no more plagued and pester'd with them the rest of the month" (I.iv.8).

The repressive nature of the Shandys' sexual relationships is the ultimate expression of their inability to relate to one another: " . . . cursed luck! said he, biting his lip as he shut the door,——for a man to be master of one of the finest chains of reasoning in nature,—— and have a wife at the same time with such a head-piece, that he cannot hang up a single inference within side of it, to save his soul from destruction" (II.xix.147). But, more than this, Walter's final, bitter repudiation of the sexual act reveals its importance to him as an instance of the natural, spontaneous, and emotional elements in man which prove his animality and balance his spiritual and rational aspirations. "——That provision should be made for continuing the race of so great, so exalted and godlike a Being as man——I am far from denying——but philosophy speaks freely of every thing; and therefore I still think and do maintain it to be a pity, that it should be done by means of a passion which bends down the faculties, and turns all the wisdom, contemplations, and operations of the soul backwards——a passion, my dear, continued my father, addressing himself to my mother, which couples and equals wise men with fools, and makes us come out of caverns and hiding-places more like satyrs and four-footed beasts than men" (IX.xxxiii.644-45).

It is, then, his refusal to recognize the needs of his own nature, and his inability to reconcile the practical demands of a contradictory, obscure, and frequently illogical world with the strivings of his soul and mind, that make of Walter a tragi-comic figure. Tristram's plea is well-founded: "Will not the gentle reader pity my father from his soul?——to see an orderly and well-disposed gentleman, who tho' singular,——yet inoffensive in his notions,——so played upon in them by cross purposes;——to look down upon the stage, and see him baffled and overthrown in all his little systems and wishes; to behold a train of events perpetually falling out against him, and in so critical and cruel a way, as if they had purposely been plann'd and pointed against him, merely to insult his speculations" (I.xix.55-56). But still, while Walter seems doomed to suffer all the agonies of a cruelly impervious fate, his suffering is actually the absurd result of his absurdly limited vision. The unfortunate incidents which fill his life—as slight as the misnaming of one of his sons, as important as the death of the other—are all equally diminished by the nature of the consciousness which defines them. It is rather his isolation that achieves a tragic dimension: an isolation that grows from the disparity (we are reminded again of Locke) between the forms of his aspiration and the materials of the empirical world. The individuality of his experience alienates him both from himself—natural functions divided against vain strivings—and from others, who are also unique and also lonely.

Tristram.—In Tristram, Sterne gives us a new version of the paradox that plagues Walter. The father's fascination with processes of thought becomes in the son a preoccupation with the functioning of wit. Both would control and make meaningful the forms of reality with their particular methods of perception and expression. Both are defeated by the subjective limitations of imagination. On the level of action and communication they are rendered impotent.

Tristram makes it quite clear, at the well-known opening of his story, that his physical and intellectual endowments were thoughtlessly determined at the very moment of his conception: "I wish either my father or my mother, or indeed both of them, as they were in duty both equally bound to it, had minded what they were about when they begot me; had they duly consider'd how much depended upon what they were then doing;——that not only the production of a rational Being was concern'd in it, but that possibly the happy formation and temperature of his body, perhaps his genius and the very cast of his mind;——and, for aught they knew to the contrary, even the fortunes of his whole house might take their turn from the humours and dispositions which were then uppermost . . ." (I.i.4). As if the absurdity of his begetting were not a sufficiently negative force in the determination of his life, Tristram goes on to describe himself as a fool of Fortune, whose life has been filled not with great evils but with "pitiful misadventures and cross accidents" (I.v.10). It is with the descriptions of these misfortunes and accidents that the first six volumes are primarily concerned.

It must be noted, however, that Tristram's version of the catastrophic circumstances of his conception rests upon a favored theory of his father. Similarly, the effect on his life of the small misfortunes and accidents which are treated as critical milestones in his development can be largely attributed to passionate attitudes, communicated passionately to him. In short, it is in the subtly created relationship of the father to the son that we find the real roots of Tristram's own development.

Walter's beliefs and aspirations are determining factors, not because they have reference to a validating reality, but because they become in themselves versions of reality, positive causes of action. Nowhere is this clearer or more important than in the influence of Walter's name theory upon Tristram's life: its determination of the limits of Tristram's aspirations and the ironic forms of his failure. Trismegistus is the name that Walter carefully chooses for his son. Tristram is the name the child is mistakenly given. "But, of all the names in the universe, he had the most unconquerable aversion for TRISTRAM;——he had the lowest and most contemptible opinion of it of anything in the world—

—thinking it could possibly produce nothing in *rerum naturâ,* but what was extreamly mean and pitiful . . ." (I.xix.55). It is toward Trismegistus, the Egyptian god of fertility, inventor of writing, creator of language, reckoner of time, that the youngest of the Shandy males must eternally strive.[4] Like Sisyphus, he will come repeatedly within a hair's breadth of success, only to meet defeat—as Tristram: his life molded by the name chosen but not given, molded by Walter's prenatal expectations and postpartum disappointment. But, as with Sisyphus, the absurdity of his situation will contain within it the seeds of an ironic success that is part, not of the result, but of the effort.

Tristram does recognize, to some extent, the strength of Walter's influence upon him. For example, when he speaks of the muddle into which he has gotten both the reader and himself while trying to unify the diverse parts of his story, he explains: "——But 'tis my father's fault; and whenever my brains come to be dissected, you will perceive, without spectacles, that he has left a large uneven thread, as you sometimes see in an unsaleable piece of cambrick, running along the whole length of the web, and so untowardly, you cannot so much as cut out a ** . . . or a fillet, or a thumbstall, but it is seen or felt——(VI.xxxiii.462-63). Like Walter, Tristram is not attracted to an idea because of its relevance. The smallest association is sufficient to stimulate him and, once stimulated, he is engrossed by the possibilities for its development. Thus, after he presents Locke's explanation of the failure of the understanding to retain impressions and illustrates it in the little scene involving Dolly and the sealing wax, he acknowledges: "Now you must understand that not one of these was the true cause of the confusion in my uncle *Toby*'s discourse; and it is for that very reason I enlarge upon them so long, after the manner of great physiologists,——to shew the world what it did *not* arise from" (II.ii.86). Although Tristram is able to view his father's obsessive love of systematizing with some degree of objectivity and is clearly unwilling to go to the same extremes in his intellectual commitments, he is unable to resist the lure of an original hypothesis. Speaking of his father's views on swearing, he says: "The hypothesis is, like most of my father's, singular and ingenious too;——nor have I any objection to it, but that it overturns my own . . ." (III.xii.183). In the course of the book he does put forth many hypotheses of his own. They are concerned with such diverse matters as the inability of wit or judgment to develop in a northern climate (III.xx.196), the cyclical movements of history, with special emphasis on epistemological and cultural areas (I.xxi.64-65), and the advisability of using goat's whey as a cure for impotence and milk coffee to treat consumption (VII.xxx.518).

In general, there is a basic difference between the attitudes of father and son toward themselves, which determines the nature of their intellectual postures. The difference is one of perspective and imagination. While Tristram does share his father's eccentric interests, he is drawn always to the element of wit that is involved in the composition of an idea, rather than to the ramifications of the metaphysical exercise. "I am not such a bigot to *Slawkenbergius,* as my father;——there is a fund in him, no doubt; but in my opinion, the best, I don't say the most profitable, but the most amusing part of *Hafen Slawkenbergius,* is his tales,——and considering he was a *German,* many of them told not without fancy . . ." (III.xlii.241). Tristram's acute interest in the possibilities of wit grows from his recognition of relativity as a dominant principle in the subjective universe. This recognition prevents him from committing himself absolutely to any statement or judgment. Like Walter, he delights in setting up a proof that will support a particular hypothesis; but, unlike his father, he is able to discover afterward without difficulty or upset that his hypothesis is somehow irrelevant to the proof (I.xxi.65). Further, this recognition of relativity is closely linked to his poetic and sentimental awareness of the transitory nature of work, life, and love: "Time wastes too fast: every letter I trace tells me with what rapidity Life follows my pen; the days and hours of it, more precious, my dear *Jenny!* than the rubies about thy neck, are flying over our heads like light clouds of a windy day, never to return more——every thing presses on——whilst thou art twisting that lock,——see! it grows grey; and every time I kiss thy hand to bid adieu, and every absence which follows it, are preludes to that eternal separation which we are shortly to make" (IX.viii.610-11).

If Tristram cannot evade his imprisonment in a world without objective certainties, he is able to penetrate many of the mysteries which characterize the isolated positions of its inhabitants. It is part of Tristram's weakness that he is attracted to Walter's hypotheses at the same time that he is aware of their gratuitous nature. It is also an indication of his strength. His consciousness is more inclusive and critical. For him (here he differs from Locke) wit is the superior faculty. He delights in its exercise, in the discovery of paradox, in the revelation of irony. If he frequently cannot differentiate or order, he can (and always does) enjoy the spectacle of a kaleidoscope world whose component parts are endlessly shifting and recombining to present each individual observer with a uniquely formed totality.

Tristram's hobbyhorse is the book he is writing: "What a rate have I gone on at, curvetting and frisking it away, two up and two down for four volumes together, without looking once behind, or even on one side of me, to see whom I trod upon!——I'll tread upon no one,——quoth I to myself when I mounted——I'll take a good rattling gallop; but I'll not hurt the poorest jack-ass upon the road——So off I set——up one lane——down another, through this turn-pike——over

that, as if the arch-jockey of jockeys had got behind me" (IV.xx.298). To recount his story and offer his opinions is Tristram's way of communicating the nature of his experience. To present it with immediacy is to experience directly as he creates. The only formalism is the arbitrary order imposed by his mercurial wit. Attempting to translate his mode of perception and expression into the major work of his life. Tristram unknowingly reveals the central irony of his position. He would compensate for the externally imposed failures which he must suffer as a man with the self-generated success that he will achieve as an author. "Oh, *Tristram! Tristram!* . . . the credit, which will attend thee as an author, shall counterbalance the many evils which have befallen thee as a man——thou wilt feast upon the one——when thou hast lost all sense and remembrance of the other!" (IV.xxxii.337). He defeats his purpose, however, because his work is a truer reflection of his perverse vision than he is able to appreciate. In accordance with his view of the world as a half-mad system of arbitrary relationships, Tristram obligingly dons a fool's cap in which to face his audience,[5] although he does, on occasion, insist upon the real presence, the face behind the fool's grin: . . . if I should seem now and then to trifle upon the road,—— or should sometimes put on a fool's cap with a bell to it, for a moment or two as we pass along,——don't fly off,——but rather courteously give me credit for a little more wisdom than appears upon my outside . . ." (I.vi.11). He is so dominated by the cheerful, exaggerated inconsistency of his licentious wit that his art becomes merely another facet of his determination. The control, as we shall see, is Sterne's. The failure is Tristram's. His curious, confusing relationship with the reader, his exuberant enjoyment of baroque rhetoric, his love of paradox, and his indulgence in verbal practical jokes all combine to make a seeming mockery of artistic form.

In a curious way, then, the dichotomies which plague Walter are oddly transmuted in Tristram. Walter's delight in the functioning of mind becomes in the more aware Tristram an enjoyment of the possibilities of wit. Walter's adherence to rationality carries him into an abstract world that has no parallel in reality. Tristram's creation of paradox provides us with linguistic and intellectual patterns that comment upon reality while trapping us in the limitations of his subjective and eccentric awareness. As Walter's obsession with reason causes his denial of spontaneity, Tristram's love of the metaphorical defies the exertion of control and makes a great irony of his central purpose—to know and explain. Both escape into an area in which action and expression are deprived of their effectiveness.

Yorick.—Between Walter and Tristram stands Yorick, the third and most firmly grounded "man of reason," who suggests still another possibility for the functioning of the rational mind, and another ironic example of frustration and disappointment. Since Tristram, as the narrator, functions largely outside of the novel's action, and since the nature of his relationship with the reader prevents him from being completely reliable as a reporter, Yorick is useful in providing a norm against which the other characters can be measured. When Yorick meets the effete or unnatural, his response is pure practicality: "I wish, *Yorick,* said my father, you had read *Plato;* for there you would have learnt that there are two LOVES——I know there were two RELIGIONS, replied *Yorick,* amongst the ancients——one——for the vulgar, and another for the learned; but I think ONE LOVE might have served both of them very well" (VIII.xxxiii.587). He meets the abstract with a similar kind of parry: "I wish there was not a polemic divine, said *Yorick,* in the kingdom;——one ounce of practical divinity——is worth a painted ship load of all their reverences have imported these fifty years (V.xxviii.387). In short, Yorick's hatred of the hypocritical, his ability to penetrate and undermine affectation, his commonsense and uncompromised values, and his clearsightedness in a world that seems always to be viewed in distorting mirrors, are all attributes which make him an effective commentator able to introduce a note of reason, although he is unable to effect any change in events or personality.

It is through his identification of both Tristram and Yorick with the figure of the jester that Sterne draws the closest parallel between them. As jesters they share a love of laughter, a sense of the absurd, a verbal dexterity and lively wit, a dislike of all that is not honest, and a recognition of individual eccentricity and social affectation. Further, both are raised to a level of tragi-comic seriousness and given universal reference by their closeness to death: Tristram's omnipresent sense of a fatal illness and, therefore, of the transitory; the association of Yorick with Hamlet's fool, who is himself a symbol of the impermanence of human values. There is an important difference here, however, for Tristram and Yorick are both types of the wise fool whose mockery masks sense. Tristram alone is victimized by his own wit.

As with all the central characters of **Tristram Shandy,** Yorick's personality is organized around a basic irony, a tension between the abstract and practical levels of behavior. Those qualities which seem most admirable make him vulnerable to the senseless malice of the community: " . . . it was his misfortune all his life long to bear the imputation of saying and doing a thousand things of which (unless my esteem blinds me) his nature was incapable. All I blame him for——or rather, all I blame and alternately like him for, was that singularity of his temper, which would never suffer him to take pains to set a story right with the world, however in his power. . . . he ever looked upon the inventor, the propagator and believer of an illiberal report alike so injurious to him,——he could not stoop to tell

his story to them——and so trusted to time and truth to do it for him" (IV.xxvii.324). In his alienation from his congregation he becomes the very antithesis of the successful pastor: full of humanity and good will that cannot be communicated or implemented, the ineffectual and increasingly sceptical shepherd of a rebellious flock.

However, the bulk of responsibility lies not with Yorick himself but with the community, which can neither understand nor appreciate him. What they construe as Yorick's pride is revealed to be rare objectivity and modesty. Rather than disclose a flattering truth about himself, Yorick prefers to appear as a figure of low comedy: "His character was,——he loved a jest in his heart——and as he saw himself in the true point of ridicule, he would say, he could not be angry with others for seeing him in a light, in which he so strongly saw himself . . ." (I.x.19). Similarly, his "wild way of talking" is revealed to be little more than good commonsense, and his chief indiscretion is an honesty that will not be compromised: "In a word, tho' he never sought, yet, at the same time, as he seldom shun'd occasions of saying what came uppermost, and without much ceremony;——he had but too many temptations in life, of scattering his wit and his humour,——his gibes and his jests about him.——They were not lost for want of gathering" (I.xi.27).

Yorick shares Tristram's critical awareness, his perception of paradox, his psychological acumen. But he is not limited by Tristram's obsessive concern with ambiguity. His associations and his style are controlled and direct. Therefore, he cannot, like the brothers Shandy, be betrayed by the subjectivity within, by a disparity between his aspirations and his means of achieving them. It is for this reason that Yorick has no need of a hobbyhorse; his mount is real, if pathetic. Instead, he is betrayed by the subjectivity without—a victim of the relativity and fallibility of opinion and judgment. Although Yorick can meaningfully organize his own perceptions, these have no effect on the behavior of others. For the majority, appearance (variously perceived) is reality. It is Yorick's comprehension of the values that belie appearance that is the cause of his estrangement from the community which he would serve.

Toby.—Although none of the other characters is idealized in the way that Yorick is, there are others who, with Tristram, share Yorick's corrective function. For Sterne, a simple commonsense perspective is the *sine qua non* that can cut through illusion and hypocrisy. To the extent that they possess this kind of perspective, both Toby and Trim contain within themselves an antidote to their own eccentricities, a corrective of total obsession. Toby's intuitive responses ground him in the matter at hand. Because he is dominated by his emotions, which are in turn stimulated by the particular event, his attention, once fixed, is tenacious. His mind rejects the more tortuous paths of abstraction which delight the sophisticated intelligence. Thus, when he attends the visitation dinner with his brother, so that they may determine the possibility of changing Tristram's name, he and Yorick are alone in remembering their purpose. His naïve directness and modesty contrast sharply with the Scholastics' self-concerned quibbling over problems of legality, church history, and semantics. When Toby learns that the members of the court had ruled unanimously that the Duchess of Suffolk was not of kin to her own child, he asks a question that a concern for human values necessitates, a simple question that indicates with naïve curiosity the absurdity of applying abstract reasoning to fundamental human issues: "And what said the duchess of *Suffolk* to it? said my uncle *Toby*" (IV.xxix.330). It is essentially the same as his response to Walter's attempts at recounting the various reasons suggested by philosophers to explain short and long noses: "There is no cause but one . . . why one man's nose is longer than another's, but because that God pleases to have it so" (III.xli.240).

But for all of Toby's directness, he cannot keep himself from becoming involved in one of the most puzzling paradoxes of the Shandy's altogether puzzling universe. Expressed through his hobby-horsical love of military campaigns, this involvement is the most extreme sign of his inability to function in *any* but a subjective world. He is not tempted by the elaborate, abstract exercises of reason, and is not even able to use logical concepts to explain that kind of experience which does not directly impinge upon his own. For this reason he can only communicate on a limited, primarily intuitive level. The only kind of experience with which he is equipped to deal is that which refers to fundamental human emotions. Thus his wisdom is nurtured on simplicity and develops from an absolute inability to comprehend multiplicity. This differs substantially from the sophisticated, philosophical awareness that is Yorick's.

There is never any question about Toby's humanity. His possession of this quality is established early in the novel when we are allowed to hear him addressing an imprisoned fly: "I'll not hurt a hair of thy head:——Go, says he, lifting up the sash, and opening his hand as he spoke, to let it escape;——go poor devil, get thee gone, why should I hurt thee?——This world surely is wide enough to hold thee and me" (II.xii.113). The story of Le Fever provides us with indisputable proof of his benevolence, as it does of his loyalty, tenderness, optimism, and total susceptibility. Taken together they explain Hazlitt's observation that "uncle Toby is one of the finest compliments ever paid to human nature."[6] Taken together they also underscore the paradox of Toby's hobby: the obsession of a man of love with the forms and procedures of war. Like all

of the Shandy obsessions, his contains an element of the universal. Toby himself hints at this in his odd explanation of belief that the ox is a more suitable animal than the bull to stand symbolically with woman as the founder of society: "For when the ground was tilled, said my uncle *Toby,* and made worth inclosing, then they began to secure it by walls and ditches, which was the origin of fortification" (V.xxxi.391). Toby does recognize that war is a fundamental expression of some basic biological need: "If, when I was a school-boy, I could not hear a drum beat, but my heart beat with it——was it my fault?——Did I plant the propensity there?——did I sound the alarm within, or Nature?" (VI.xxxii.460). But his recognition is marvelously limited: marvelous in its human misunderstanding and in its self-deception, for Toby's justification of his obsession is a brilliant network of truth and falsity, of petty detail and grand concern. It is a sincere and flawed attempt to make intelligible the classically obscure relationship of ends and means. It is a testimony to the thoroughness of the paradox, the intensity of the conflict between the illusion and the reality. Questioned about the way in which man is shaped for the terrors of war, Toby responds: "——But why did you not add, *Yorick,*——if not by NATURE——that he is so by NECESSITY?——For what is war? what is it, *Yorick,* when fought as ours has been . . . upon principles of *honour*——what is it, but the getting together of quiet and harmless people, with their swords in their hands, to keep the ambitious and the turbulent within bounds'? And heaven is my witness, brother *Shandy,* that the pleasure I have taken in these things,——and that infinite delight, in particular, which has attended my sieges in my bowling green, has arose within me, and I hope in the corporal too, from that consciousness we both had, that in carrying them on, we were answering the great ends of our creation" (VI.xxxii.462).

The most striking part of Toby's defense lies in its conclusion: in the confusion of the game with its object. Indeed, it is the extent to which Toby is unable to differentiate between the two, the extent to which one becomes a complete substitute for the other, that makes Toby's obsession so fascinating and invests it with a psychological validity of its own. Toby's explanation of his motivations and his description of the development of his interest suggest that the grimmest aspects of war have been repressed in much the same way that he has escaped from an awareness of his wound. In a sense, the affliction of his wound represents the only infusion of the ideal with the real—in this case, a physical fact that cannot be denied.

Significantly, it is not Toby's instinct for life that restores his health. His wound, a scar from the contact of mind and body with the undeniable fact of war, is healed when the reality is made acceptable: when it is, in effect, sublimated. "The desire of life and health is implanted in man's nature;——the love of liberty and enlargement is a sister-passion to it: These my uncle *Toby* had in common with his species;——and either of them had been sufficient to account for his earnest desire to get well and out of doors;——but I have told you before that nothing wrought with our family after the common way;——and from the time and manner in which this eager desire shew'd itself in the present case, the penetrating reader will suspect that there was some other cause or crotchet for it in my uncle *Toby*'s head . . ." (II.iv.92). The cause is Trim's creation of a game that has all the fascinations of war, drawing its inspiration, progress, and form from actual campaigns, but sharing none of war's horrors. It is, in effect, a concretization of the meaning which war has always had for Toby. And the soldier's fidelity to (as well as Tristram's description of) the smallest details having to do with the accoutrements and techniques of battle gives the illusion its reality for both Toby and the reader. At the same time, the irony of the exquisite complications of warfare—the rational control of that which is a sign of man's irrationality—is underlined.

Of course, the irony is always reciprocal. If reality gives the lie to Toby's illusion, that illusion—harmless in the protected quiet of the bowling green—accentuates the questionable concomitants of his noble utterances: " . . . the knowledge of arms tends so apparently to the good and quiet of the world——and particularly that branch of it which we have practised together in our bowling-green, has no object but to shorten the strides of AMBITION, and intrench the lives and the fortunes of the *few* from the plunderings of the *many* . . ." (IX.viii.609-10). Although Toby's wholehearted, childish immersion in his hobby has its delightful side, there is a more menacing aspect to it in his dependence for the continuation of his play upon the continuation of actual combat and in his sorrow at the signing of the Peace of Utrecht.

It is further significant that when the regrettable peace forces Toby to turn from the delights of war, it is by the lures of love that he is tempted.[7]

> ——No more was he to dream, he had fixed the royal standard upon the tower of the *Bastile,* and awake with it streaming in his head.

> ——Softer visions,——gentler vibrations stole sweetly in upon his slumbers;——the trumpet of war fell out of his hands,——he took up the lute, sweet instrument! of all others the most delicate! the most difficult!——how wilt thou touch it, my dear uncle *Toby?* (VI.xxxv.466)

That his immersion in military affairs had been a substitute for romance is suggested by this comparison of Toby, about to embark on his bowling-green adventure, with an ardent lover: "Never did lover post down to a belov'd mistress with more heat and expectation, than my uncle *Toby* did, to enjoy this self-same thing in private" (II.v.98).

Toby's new excursion into romance with the Widow Wadman serves the same purpose as his experimentation with the war games. They represent different expressions of the same impulse and, just as the complications of the game offered an escape from the harsher realities of the wound, so too with the maneuvers of love. Unfortunately for Toby, it is not as easy with the Widow Wadman to cloak the reality in the illusion. In the first place, he is not as familiar with the rules and procedures of this contest: " . . . he knew not (as my father had reproach'd him), so much as the right end of a Woman from the wrong, and therefore was never altogether at his ease near any one of them——unless in sorrow or distress; then infinite was his pity . . ." (IX.iii.602-603). In the second place, the game cannot be played for an extended period of time. The campaign is brief and the victor is expected to claim his reward. Just as Toby does not want the rewards of war—he bemoans the signing of the treaty, for it means that the reality must deny the illusion—neither does he wish to claim the reward of this other combat, sexual fulfillment. His wound, the only reality with which Toby must cope although he will never fully comprehend it, hinders him and negates the possibility of sublimation. When the crisis arrives he can only sidestep the issue and withdraw. When asked his reasons for wishing to marry, he replies, "They are written . . . in the Common-Prayer Book" (IX.xxv.634). Finding himself put off by the Widow's indelicate concern, he trades the new hobby for the old pleasures and proceeds to read about the Siege of Jericho (IX.xxv.635). The frustrations, tragic as well as comic, are inherent in the paradox of his situation.

Toby and Walter.—As we have observed with regard to Walter and Tristram, the hobbyhorse can be seen as a result of the individual's method of perceiving and his mode of expression. In other words, it provides the bridge between the world of thought and the world of action. The confidence in the power of wit and reason which is shared by Tristram and his father extends also to their love of rhetoric, their fascination with forms of expression. Both interests are reflected in their "hobbyhorsical" preoccupations. Toby, on the other hand, is not a man of thought and expression. He is rather the man of feeling and action. With significant irony Sterne interrupts Toby, in his first dramatic scene, after Toby has repeated the words "I think . . . I think." He is left gesturing mutely with his pipe as Tristram begins a long digression (I.xxi.63), and is picked up later when the long pause is lamely concluded: "I think, replied he,——it would not be amiss, brother, if we rung the bell" (II.vi.99).

Toby's early love of the military reflects his adherence to simple, formularized values as well as his desire to express himself directly through action. Sustaining his wound, he is not only forced into contact with a harsh, irrefutable reality, but is also, in his attempt to describe clearly the place and circumstances of his mishap, forced to rely upon language and abstract reasoning: " . . . the many perplexities he was in, arose out of the almost insurmountable difficulties he found in telling his story intelligibly, and giving such clear ideas of the differences and distinctions between the scarp and the counterscarp,——the glacis and covered way,——the half-moon and ravelin,——as to make his company fully comprehend where and what he was about" (II.i.82). In a sense, it is his inability to master language that is responsible for the perpetuation of his sickness. As Tristram explains: "T'was not by ideas,——by heaven! his life was put in jeopardy by words" (II.ii.87). His hobby is born from his lack of verbal success, and with his new-found approximation of action comes also an approximation of health. Still, when he attempts to function anywhere beyond this play world of soldiers and campaigns, when he attempts to communicate with anyone whose interests and responses differ to any extent from his own, he faces the same acute problems. Because of the polar differences that exist in Toby's and Walter's perceptions of the world, their relationship emphasizes the propensities and weaknesses of each.

It is necessary to recognize the depth of feeling, the good will and common sympathy, that exists between the two brothers. Typical is Toby's immediate response to Trim's explanation of the Widow Wadman's repeated inquiries into the nature of his wound: "——Let us go to my brother *Shandy*'s, said he" (IX.xxxi.643). Nor is Walter's attachment to Toby any less strong. "He was, however, frank and generous in his nature;——at all times open to conviction; and in the little ebullitions of this subacid humour toward others, but particularly toward my uncle *Toby,* whom he truly loved;——he would feel more pain, ten times told (except in the affair of my aunt *Dinah,* or where an hypothesis was concerned) than what he ever gave" (II.xii.114). But Toby is as little able to overcome the pressure of Walter's rhetoric to discover his meaning as he is able to overcome the narrowness of his own associations. And the nature of Toby's customary response is a constant cause of disturbance to Walter: " . . . it is one of the most unaccountable problems that ever I met with in my observations of human nature, that nothing should prove my father's mettle so much, or make his passions go off so like gun-powder, as the unexpected strokes his science met with from the quaint simplicity of my uncle *Toby*'s questions" (III.xli.239). Even when Walter vows that he will never again tease his brother about his hobbyhorse, his own language—reflecting the irresistible attraction that the subject has for him—undercuts the force of his intention. "May my brains be knock'd out with a battering ram or a catapulta, I care not which, quoth my father to him-

self,——if ever I insult this worthy soul more" (III.xxiv.212). When the brothers do respond to one another's pronouncements, the cause can always be traced to a misinterpretation growing out of a private association. Thus Walter, at one point, becomes interested in Toby's discussion of fortification because he finds in it ripe ground for a dissertation upon trade (II.xiv.117-18). Or Toby wrongly defines a word when there is more than one possible meaning that could be assigned to it. "'Tis a pity, said my father, that truth can only be on one side, brother *Toby,*——considering what ingenuity these learned men have all shewn in their solutions of noses.——Can noses be dissolved? replied my uncle *Toby*" (III.xli.239). But more often than not Toby merely provides Walter with a convenient presence at which he can philosophize. Unhappily Walter is doomed to be a teacher who cannot teach since Toby is the student incapable of learning.

The irony of their relative positions is continually emphasized by the effect which each unconsciously achieves, an effect that seems frequently to stand in direct contradiction to the one intended or expected. It is with good reason that uncle Toby is compared to the Cynic philosopher Diogenes, who refuted the arguments of Zeno against motion: " . . . the Philosopher would use no other argument to the sceptic, who disputed with him against the reality of motion, save that of rising up upon his legs, and walking a-cross the room . . ." (I.xxiv.78). For the irrefutable simplicity of Toby's commonsense response seems often to contain more relevance, more meaning, more profound intuition, than all of Walter's elaborate theorizing.

> As the antients agree, brother *Toby,* said my father, that there are two different and distinct kinds of *love,* according to the different parts which are affected by it——the Brain or Liver——I think when a man is in love, it behoves him a little to consider which of the two he is fallen into.

> What signifies it, brother *Shandy,* replied my uncle *Toby,* which of the two it is, provided it will but make a man marry, and love his wife, and get a few children. (VIII.xxxiii.585-86)

Of course, there is another, deeper irony here that is inherent in the nature of their lives. Walter, despite his analytical and rational approach, has married and begotten children, while Toby, although not lacking in feelings proper to his sex, seems doomed to a childless bachelorhood. It is but another example of the illusory and deceptive effect of language in its tenuous relation to thought and its more tenuous relation to reality.

Similarly, Toby's gestures, his facial expressions, his habit of whistling Lillabullero "when anything shocked or surprised him;——but especially when any thing, which he deem'd very absurd, was offered" (I.xxi.69), all declare the impotence of language, its in feriority to a more delicate and subtle method of communication. Meaning shines through the intuitive response while it is hidden beneath the obliquity of the complex, carefully planned utterance.

Trim.—Trim and Toby's relationship offers the only example of communication on an explicitly verbal as well as a mute, intuitive level. The irony of their relationship consists of the domination of master by servant, for although Toby frequently acts as a kindly guardian to Trim, gently reprimanding his lapses of taste, it is Trim who draws the pattern for their lives and emerges as the stronger, more lucid of the two. Trim is more consistent than any of the Shandys. He is not ruled so much by an obsession as he is by a kindly understanding of his master's needs and a sincere concern for the practice of basic moral and humanitarian precepts.

Although it is true that Trim is willing to mount Toby's hobby-horse and share with him a total imaginative immersion in the minutiae of their play battles, one does not feel that he is as deeply committed. He delights in his own inventiveness in working out the details of their game, and he is not immune to the delights of play, but his real interest is in his master's well-being. His purpose is therapeutic; when one form of therapy becomes impractical, he throws himself without regret into the development of the next possibility, the romance with the Widow Wadman.

If Trim could be said to have a hobbyhorse of his own, it would be this: "The fellow lov'd to advise,—or rather to hear himself talk . . ." (II.v.95). Trim is an orator, and because he is a subtle mixture of the intuitively artful and the intuitively artless, he functions as a foil for both Toby and Walter. A central irony of his characterization grows out of the paradox developed between art and nature.[8] Trim is the natural orator whose instinct approximates art. Nevertheless, he is unable to differentiate art from nature and can only comprehend fiction when it is reduced to concrete terms. He resorts, as does Toby, to the use of gesture and posture in order to express himself; but while Toby's dependence is clearly the result of impotence before language, Trim's bears the force of intention. Asked for an opinion, he formally arranges himself in a particular attitude before replying: "Prithee *Trim,* said *Yorick,* without staying for my father's leave,—tell us honestly—what is thy opinion concerning this self same radical heat and radical moisture? . . . The corporal put his hat under his left arm, and with his stick hanging upon the wrist of it; by a black thong split into a tassel about the knot, he marched up to the ground where he had performed his catechism; then touching his under jaw with the thumb and fingers of his right hand before he

opened his mouth,——he delivered his notion thus" (V.xxxviii.400). But his knowledge of the gesture which can most effectively be employed, the posture which can most eloquently be assumed, is intuitive. It is prompted by his fine sense of the dramatic and facilitated by a matter-of-fact acceptance of his own body.

Trim's rhetoric—indeed his whole method of approaching and interpreting the objective world—is characterized by his commonsense perspective, literalness, and lack of imagination. Unlike Walter, he is never led astray by a richly fabricating wit or a playful fancy. Trim tends always to particularize the abstract and translates everything into experiential terms. He is unable to differentiate between imaginative materials and phenomenological occurrences, although he is himself, in his instinct for rhetoric, presented as an artist. He must submerge the work of art and the theoretical formulation in the chaotic mass of personal experience. His emotional rendering of Yorick's sermon "On Conscience" demonstrates this, just as the responses of Toby, Walter, and Dr. Slop to his reading comprise a statement about their epistemological and aesthetic orientations.

In Walter's and Trim's responses to Bobby's death we are given "two orators . . . contrasted by nature and education, haranguing over the same bier" (V.vi.359). Walter's route, which proceeds by way of metaphor, reference, and allusion, is a circuitous one, while Trim, we are told, goes "strait forwards as nature could lead him, to the heart" (V.vi.359). His speech is the more effective of the two, for it is not obscured by the oddments of learning. Trim is, in a sense, the ideal orator, for his rhetoric is an expression of the whole man. His eloquence is derived from his conviction of the correctness of his cause and reflects the generosity of his heart and the strength of his values. In this sense he satisfies the classical Platonic rules of oratory. While Walter's primary concerns are intellectual and aesthetic (this is true of his perceptions as well as his mode of expression), Trim's orientation is principally moral. He deals in clear absolutes, never recognizing that more than one meaning may be assigned to a value term. Thus, when Dr. Slop gives his permission for Trim to read the sermon on the grounds that they all take equal risks on which side of the church it is written, Trim replies: "'Tis wrote upon neither side . . . for 'tis only upon *Conscience,* an' please your Honours," (II.xvi.120). Trim's naïve simplicity does more here to undercut the doctor's position than would a direct attack. He produces a similar effect with similar means when he speaks of the misfortunes of people he has known, while Walter lies prostrated after learning that Tristram's nose has been crushed in the birth process:

> O!—these are misfortunes, cried *Trim,*—pulling out
> his handkerchief—these are misfortunes, may it

please your honour, worth lying down and crying over.

——My father could not help blushing. (IV.iv.275)

Trim emerges as a more balanced human being than most of Sterne's other characters. Through his morality and humanity, the world of thought and the world of action are united, and there is no disparity created between his aspiration and the reality against which it is measured. His judgments are not marred by Walter's eccentricities or Toby's unknowing optimism, and both perspective and deliberation mark his actions. That the functioning of his body is as normal as the functioning of his mind and conscience—typified by the same easy acceptance and righteous confidence—is made clear by his relationship with Bridget. Walter, Toby, and Tristram are unable, for a combination of physical and psychological reasons, to allow themselves the satisfactions of normal sexual pleasures. Walter and Toby find their escapes in games of the intellect and the imagination. Tristram finds his in art and in a harmless but frustrated sentimentality.

Thus, on one side we have Toby's unnatural modesty and the Widow Wadman's elaborate machinations as she attempts to discover the extent and significance of Toby's wound. In contrast, we are given Trim's and Bridget's direct acceptance of the real issue. What is illegitimate curiosity in the widow becomes justifiable concern in the maid. The cause, one infers, lies in the readiness of the suitors and the attitudes of the social groups to which they belong: " . . . and in this cursed trench, Mrs. *Bridget,* quoth the Corporal, taking her by the hand, did he receive the wound which crush'd him so miserably *here*——In pronouncing which he slightly press'd the back of her hand towards the part he felt for—and let it fall" (IX. xxviii.639). Throughout *Tristram Shandy,* Sterne demonstrates that sexual potency, as an alternative mode of communication, is a function of the whole man, reflecting his capacities and the balance of his faculties. Trim is the most normal of the people who inhabit Tristram's world. The directness of his approach and his firm grounding in the practical and realistic demand the sacrifice of his imagination but allow him to move with physical and intellectual freedom, unhampered by the irrational demands of obsession or the stringent controls of society.

Mrs. Shandy.—At the opposite end of the spectrum stands Mrs. Shandy, who is defined almost exclusively in negative terms: she is Locke's "white paper," unmarred by experience, passive in her perception of the world, seemingly unable to interpret meaningfully or express her impressions, performing her female functions more by accident than through intent. Totally lacking in imagination, she is also without curiosity: "—That she is not a woman of science, my father would say—is her misfortune—but she might ask a question"

(VI.xxxix.472). A woman who prefers to remain at home knitting a pair of worsted breeches for her husband rather than joining her family on their Grand Tour, Mrs. Shandy is without ideas or interests and is therefore possessed of few associations, depending upon habit and tradition for her responses. Because her ability to learn is so restricted, she is virtually unable to express herself: "Now she had a way . . . and that was never to refuse her assent and consent to any proposition my father laid before her, merely because she did not understand it, or had no ideas to the principal word or term of art, upon which the tenet or proposition rolled. She contented herself with doing all that her godfathers and godmothers promised for her—but no more; and so would go on using a hard word twenty years together—and replying to it too, if it was a verb, in all its moods and tenses, without giving herself any trouble to enquire about it" (IX.xi.613).

There are no scenes of greater comic frustration in *Tristram Shandy* than those which present the dialogues between Tristram's mother and father: " . . . a discourse seldom went on much further betwixt them, than a proposition,—a reply, and a rejoinder; at the end of which, it generally took breath for a few minutes, (as in the affair of the breeches) and then went on again" (VI.xxxix.472). The patterns of their conversations also contain an elementary paradox. Typically, in the "Bed of Justice" which is held to decide the advisability of putting Tristram into breeches (VI.xviii.437), Mrs. Shandy's continual agreement—intellectual as well as sexual—implies criticism through its passivity. Her extreme flexibility implies a basic, mindless inflexibility and her willingness is tantamount to refusal. In her neutrality, extremes meet and negate one another. Further, their lack of communication extends to sexual matters, and their physical and intellectual incompatibility are reciprocal metaphors. Although they approach their conjugal bed from opposite extremes of temperament and orientation, Walter's accusation of his wife might with justice be applied to him as well: "You never will distinguish, Mrs. *Shandy,* nor shall I ever teach you to do it, betwixt a point of pleasure and a point of convenience.—This was on the *Sunday* night;—and further this chapter sayeth not" (VI.xviii. 438-39). The relationship between Mr. and Mrs. Shandy is one of the novel's numerous instances of the difficulties that arise when one attempts to distinguish cause from effect. Their misfortune arises not so much from their own individual circumstances as from the impossibility of combining their two temperaments. Tristram makes it clear that they share—albeit unconsciously—the responsibility for the misfortune of his destiny. "A temperate current of blood ran orderly through her veins in all months of the year, and in all critical moments both of the day and night alike. . . . And as for my father's example! 'twas so far from being either aiding or abetting thereunto, that 'twas the whole business of his life to keep all fancies of that kind out of her head

. . . And here am I sitting, this 12th day of *August,* 1766, in a purple jerkin and yellow pair of slippers, without either wig or cap on, a most tragicomical completion of his prediction, "That I should neither think, nor act like any other man's child, upon that very account" (IX.i.600).

Occupying this negative position in terms of potentiality, achievement and aspiration, Mrs. Shandy plays a minor but curiously contemporary and parodic role. Northrop Frye has written in his *Anatomy of Criticism:* "To the extent that the encyclopaedic form concerns itself with the cycle of human life, an ambivalent female archetype appears in it, sometimes benevolent, sometimes sinister, but usually presiding over and confirming the cyclical movement" (p. 322). Indeed, there is in Mrs. Shandy's presence something of the universal principle of female endurance which persists amid the paradoxes of her position and her personality. She is the woman—the life-force—who remains remote and uninvolved. She is the mother who, in the earliest moments of procreation, flaws the very life she creates because she rejects her own sexuality. She is an absurd Penelope, a silent and frigid Molly Bloom. But within the peculiar, alien demands of her milieu, despite the extraordinary limitations which are imposed upon her from within and without, she does continue to function, and follows, however unenthusiastically, the patterns set down for her.

Sterne seems anxious to convey in his characterization of Mrs. Shandy a sense of an irreducible human quality—purged of all that is meaningful save an inarticulate demand for sympathy: sympathy for her personal situation and for the chaotic collection of circumstances that have created it. It seems important that we are not allowed to see her response to the news of Bobby's death. A strong response would make of her a completely different, more conventional character, and her usual passivity would in this case become intolerable. It is only by maintaining her in neutrality that Sterne can create the polar image that is more limited in its universality but not essentially different from that of all the Shandys.

Sterne follows the same basic technique with his other characters, immersing them in just enough complexity to give them depth while keeping his world sufficiently abstract. In a curious way, the qualities of characterization that are responsible for his realism are responsible also for the abstract universality. These qualities grow out of his awareness of the empiricist paradox and his desire to communicate it in specifically human terms. As we have seen, the hobbyhorse, which expresses the uniqueness of the individual, develops from the control of the external world by the internal economy peculiar to each man. The relation of rational, imaginative, and physical powers determines whether the individual will function principally in a

world of intellect, art, action, or instinct; this in turn determines which of the faculties and functions will remain undeveloped and even unused. In such a world, where uniqueness is confirmed by a lack of successful communication, eccentricity must be the rule.

By concentrating upon these basic functions Sterne does, of course, achieve a certain universality in his characterizations, and by keeping outside of the complexities and superficialities of a world that is defined by social values, he cannot avoid a measure of abstraction. Because of the intensely personal nature of each man's response, all gestures toward creating a meaningful, communicable concept are made invalid—all but the attempt itself: the repeated movement outside oneself, the continuation in the face of all frustration and negation.

In some fundamental way, then, Sterne defines his characters as he organizes his structure: through diversity and eccentricity. And his people—much as the form of his book—are subject to the whims and pressures of external forces. Just as they cannot control the world outside of themselves, so too are they unable to determine the course and manner of their own lives. The irony of them all, as we have seen, is the disparity between their aspirations and the reality, their distortions of the world and their delusions about themselves. They are important because they tell us about the nature of the human mind, the nature of the human predicament, the possibility of human salvation. Together their lives compose a pattern which represents universal—not individual—potentiality and limitation. The unity of *Tristram Shandy* is thematic. Just as the form and structure work to create an image of confusion, so do the characters achieve their definition in isolation and alienation. There are dramatic scenes (vignettes) and the drama of monologue, but there is no progressive dramatic movement. The characters are part of a universal paradox, subject to the ironies that besiege their lives, motivating and defeating them. These ironies are inevitable in a completely subjective world in which neither circumstance nor language can claim absolute reference. . . .

Notes

[1] "The Character of Herod," in *The Sermons of Mr. Yorick,* I:105.

[2] *Sermons,* I:211.

[3] "The Character of Herod," p. 107.

[4] M. K. Singleton, in his essay "Trismegistic Tenor and Vehicle in Sterne's *Tristram Shandy,*" relates (albeit not very persuasively) *Tristram Shandy* to Greek and Latin Trismegistic or Hermetic Literature.

[5] Martin Esslin, *The Theatre of the Absurd,* pp. 231-33, points out that the tradition of the clown derives from the mime plays of antiquity in which the clown's absurd behavior reflected his inability to understand simple logical relationships. The court jester who descended from the MIMUS was characterized by his inverted logic, his use of false syllogisms, free associations, and real or feigned madness.

[6] Quoted in Alan B. Howes, *Yorick and the Critics: Sterne's Reputation in England, 1760-1868,* p. 112.

[7] A. R. Towers, "Sterne's Cock and Bull Story," [in *ELH,* vol. xxiv (1957)] also discusses the role of displacement in Toby's hobby.

[8] See William S. Farrell, "Nature vs. Art as a Comic Pattern in *Tristram Shandy[,]*" [in *ELH,* vol. xxx (1963)]. Farrell discusses at length the expression of the art-nature paradox in the rhetorical patterns of the novel.

James E. Swearingen (essay date 1977)

SOURCE: "The Problem of Interpretation or Criticism under the Aspect of the Hobby-Horse: Hermeneutics and Hobby-Horses," in his *Reflexivity in* Tristram Shandy: *An Essay in Phenomenological Criticism,* Yale University Press, 1977, pp. 6-25.

[*In the following excerpt, Swearingen suggests that Sterne has created a narrator in* Tristram Shandy *whose intent is "self-interpretation" in order to sort out the perpetual "misinterpretation" that dogs his family and, consequently, his own life.*]

It will eventually be argued in this discussion that Tristram's whole enterprise is a hermeneutics, a process of self-interpretation which is required by his awareness of being part of a family and of a tradition in which there has been serious misinterpretation. It is not surprising that the parson whose sermons interpret biblical texts by imaginatively filling out the human setting of those texts should raise the problem of a general hermeneutics in a work that professes to give an account of the mind. Nothing is more obvious to the most casual reader of the novel than the fact that in Shandy Hall every mode of experience down to the simplest sense perception—of the crevice in the parlor wall, say—offers a problem of interpretation. Historically, hermeneutics may still have been an ancillary discipline of rules for interpreting biblical and legal texts, but in Sterne's novel it undergoes an intuitive expansion of application that was not to reach its full theoretical development until the twentieth century.[9]

A reasonable starting place is with the narrower question of interpreting the novel, and Tristram does not leave us without advice on that point:

> Writing, when properly managed, (as you may be sure I think mine is) is but a different name for conversation: As no one, who knows what he is about in good company, would venture to talk all;—so no author, who understands the just boundaries of decorum and good breeding, would presume to think all: The truest respect which you can pay to the reader's understanding, is to halve this matter amicably, and leave him something to imagine, in his turn, as well as yourself. [II.ii.108-09]

"Conversation" in Tristram's remark is more than metaphoric: it is an effort to preserve the original spontaneity of spoken language and to overcome the inherent recalcitrance of the written word in catching the movement of thinking. The intention acknowledged in this passage is to write in a way that will keep the reader's imagination "as busy as my own"; but that indication of how the writing is to be carried forward also implies how reading is done when it is rightly done, implicitly, a prescription about how the text is to be interpreted. In *Truth and Method,* Hans-Georg Gadamer makes extensive use of the analogy of conversation as a means of describing the event of interpretation which underlies even the most sophisticated epistemological methods. Tristram's similar concern with the event of understanding the spoken word is also concentrated in that term *conversation* which is the foundation of his reflections, and it invites one to consider what exactly constitutes authentic conversation and authentic interpretation. Three features in Gadamer's discussion (pp. 330 ff., 344 ff.) are especially revealing, though the analysis may appear to make illicitly free use of a casual analogy in the passage quoted above from the novel. I believe, however, that the point of view will be amply justified in the course of the ensuing discussion when interpretation is viewed ontologically, that is, as a way of being instead of merely a way to knowledge.

The first requirement for conversation is that the conversants engage in a give and take in which each tries to enter into what the other says rather than talking at cross-purposes. Such an openness to the other is the posture of one who, unlike the Shandys, is willing to risk the security of one's prior grasp of reality by listening to what another says. Authentic conversation presupposes such an attitude of true enquiry and such a will to understand. Since the implication of that openness for the reader is a requirement for considerably more than mere aesthetic appreciation of the form and technique of his book, it will be well to ask what exactly Tristram requires in this respect, what quality of openness he expects in the exchange with his text. The question is important enough to him that he teases and taunts the reader throughout the novel for inattention, misreading, and misinterpretation. Most conspicuous, however, is the vivid example of how Yorick's sermon on a good conscience, the most important self-contained text within the book because of its normative function, is abused by inattention to its inner significance on the part of the company assembled at its reading in the parlor. It attacks conscience as undependable, inconsistent, and deceptive, thereby accounting for its own poor reception as due to human resources for subverting it. The reading completed, Walter expresses an attitude of abstract aesthetic appreciation: "Thou hast read the sermon extremely well, *Trim,* quoth my father. . . . I like the sermon well . . . 'tis dramatic,——and there is something in that way of writing, when skilfully managed, which catches the attention" (II.xvii.140-41). The character in the novel most guilty of the self-deceptions which the sermon anatomizes listens only to the aesthetic surface, one might say "listens away from" the moral and religious meaning that informs the words and that he is called upon to appropriate. Thus well before Kant's *Critique of Judgment* completes the subjectivization of aesthetics, Sterne criticizes that aesthetic consciousness which ignores the existential roots in the context of the world from which and about which a text speaks and makes it accessible to an audience. Language for him is still preeminently a signifying milieu which demands that one understand what is said. Walter's response demonstrates how those connections between a text and its world may be dissolved by the preference for the pure immediacy of surface attractiveness, stripping it of its power to speak, judging it in abstraction from the context to which it belongs, and neutralizing its claim to truth.

How fully Sterne is in agreement with his conservative Augustan forebears, for whom art and nature were complementary and nature the framework and norm within which art functioned, may also be inferred from the passage. Aesthetic consciousness was destined to dissolve that old sovereignty of nature and to detach art from reality. In *Either/Or* Kierkegaard makes a moral analysis of the aesthetic as a way of life that demonstrates how it abstracts its object of interest from all ties with the life to which it belongs and attempts to hold it in the simultaneity of purely immediate experience. To do so is for the ego to assume a universal and sovereign authority over everything in a manner comparable to the spirit of technology. Inherent in that spirit is the impulse to dissolve the unity of being and to make the ego the measure of all things, treating the world as a collection of tools or, in the case of the aesthete, pleasures to be manipulated for the immediate gratification of the ego.[10] The subjective consequence which interests Kierkegaard is that the need for continuity and unity in life itself is frustrated by that self-destructive demand for immediacy. Tristram plainly discourages our dwelling on the aesthetic appearances

of his work by encouraging us to see the significance of the work in its relation to reality and to grasp what it attempts to say. His criterion of conversation, in contrast to autonomous aesthetic consciousness, demands that one become engaged with the extra-aesthetic content of his work, with the book's context of meaningfulness. Gadamer's description of the way in which a common world of reference underlies the comprehension of a text summarizes the point clearly:

> Inasmuch as we encounter the work of art in the world and a world in the individual work of art, this does not remain a strange universe into which we are magically transported for a time. Rather, we learn to understand ourselves in it, and that means that we preserve the discontinuity of the experience in the continuity of our existence. Therefore it is necessary to adopt an attitude to the beautiful and to art that does not lay claim to immediacy, but corresponds to the historical reality of man. The appeal to immediacy, to the genius of the moment, to the significance of the 'experience', cannot withstand the claim of human existence to continuity and unity of self-understanding. The experience of art must not be side-tracked into the uncommittedness of aesthetic awareness. . . . Art is knowledge and the experience of the work of art is a sharing of this knowledge. [Gadamer, pp. 86-87]

However, openness even to the world that speaks through the work does not exhaust the implications of Tristram's example of interpretation as conversation.

The second characteristic of conversation that is pertinent to Tristram's statement is a "fusion of horizons" that occurs when there is a meeting of minds. One who suspends his own point of view in order to understand the perspective of another, as when the physician interviews his patient or the attorney his client, is not conversing in the true sense of the term: no *con*versation can occur because the *with* is suspended and there can be no exchange of views and mutual expansion of the understanding of both parties. Likewise, in interpreting the text, if a reader tries to suspend his own point of view and to cultivate a detached appreciation of the perspective Tristram adopts toward his life, he thereby ignores the historical dimension of his own being and fails in his task, for all understanding is interpretation and requires assimilation of the new materials to the old structures of its preunderstanding. The aim is "not to get inside another person and relive his experiences"; reproduction, were it possible, would not be interpretation.[11] Detaching himself from his own orientation, attempting to suspend his own historical conditioning insures a reader's failure as conversationalist, for Tristram has laid down the prior condition that his reader engage in an exchange that presupposes the integrity of each person's horizon. And he never forgets that the reader is maintaining his own horizon as demonstrated by frequent interrogation about what he thinks, how he feels, how he is responding. Never in the annals of fiction is the awareness of the integrity of the reader more explicit and sensitive than here.

The third feature of conversation according to Gadamer's analysis is that when it is real it is an activity that guides the conversants rather than being guided by them. Its extraordinary value in this regard is that it leads one into new territory, revealing the unthought and even uncovering what heretofore lay concealed in one's own thinking. Thus when Tristram comments on his "most religious" manner of proceeding, writing "the first sentence——and trusting to Almighty God for the second" (VIII.ii.540), he is not being facetious; he is admitting that he is surrendering himself to the conversation rather than approaching his task with a preconceived method. His ideal requires that both he and his reader abandon themselves and their methods of procedure to the free play of the event in which new meanings unpredictably occur. This question of method is exceedingly important, for choosing a rational method establishes a ratio between reader and text. Questions imply answers and methods filter from experience what the methods have prejudged as important. The general problem of interpretation is not a matter of settling on a procedure for finding what one seeks as in those enquiries where the goal is established in advance; it is a more primitive experience and a more extensive concept than the scientific one of method. Whereas the question of method properly belongs to the domain of objective knowledge, the general problem of understanding is concerned with a mode of being rather than a mode of knowing. In fact, understanding is coextensive with "the total human experience of the world."[12] However, the example of conversation—and hence the denial of method—would appear to be limited by the stasis of Tristram's side of the exchange. How can the relationship be a dialogue when the printed word is a unilateral speaking, a kind of denial of reciprocity? The answer is that the text speaks in the reading and, by Tristram's having anticipated and in large measure controlled our responses, we participate, even more than in reading most books, in the advent of meaning that is not only a common ground of understanding, but also a literal fusing of horizons.[13] This is the real meaning of Tristram's confidence that our association with him in the reading will lead gradually from acquaintance to the kind of unique understanding and affection that exists between friends (I.vi.10-11).

According to contemporary hermeneutic theory a linguistic event does not consist merely of univocal statements about particular things or events; it puts into words in a less intense way than does poetry the manner in which one comports oneself toward the whole of being. In authentic conversation, then, one listens not only to what is said but to the unsaid, the horizon of meaningfulness, that wells up within it. In the compli-

cated act of reading this means that while holding on to one's own relation with being, one must catch, beyond the literal references of words spoken, another manner of comportment within the whole of things which is part of the meaning of what is said. It is in this sense that language is inherently speculative. In Gadamer's words, "the finite possibilities of the word are oriented towards the sense intended, as towards the infinite" (p. 426). Accordingly, it will be part of the purpose of this critical study to attempt to retrieve in all its original vitality the problem that occupies Tristram's attention. He insists that we respond to the question with which he is engaged and that we think it through with him. Our thinking is not a reiteration of his, but a reworking which is completely unlike abstract aesthetic appreciation. To retrieve Sterne's problem may even involve a certain violence in wresting the book free from the pattern of references that customarily surround it, and it is in this sense that the present study is speculative: to retrieve the problem of being that lies at the heart of the work and to explore new ways in which the meaning of the text deploys itself in the cultural horizon of the twentieth century. The tension between Tristram's thinking and our own parallels the dialectical relation between his thinking and the family tradition from which he springs and which occupies most of his reflections. The close relation between understanding an "other"—person, event, text, or tradition—and understanding oneself, Tristram's ultimate aim in his book and ours in the reading, occupies Paul Ricoeur in his essay "Existence and Hermeneutics." He remarks that "all interpretation is to conquer a remoteness, a distance between the past cultural epoch to which the text belongs and the interpreter himself. . . . It is thus the growth of his own understanding of himself that he [the exegete] pursues through his understanding of the other. Every hermeneutics is thus, explicitly or implicitly, self-understanding by means of understanding others" (pp. 16-17).

Tristram's enquiry is stimulated and shaped by a need to understand himself through discovering his relations to a tradition. He does not look back for positive historical fact, doubting, questioning the integrity of his tradition, for the old dichotomy between reality and appearance, events-in-themselves and events-as-they-appear, has been obviated by the ontological character of the events of understanding. His, like other histories, is no more discovered than invented. As readers often observe, there is no way that he could have a visually accurate picture of Trim's oratorical posture as he reads the sermon in the parlor or know his exact tone of voice as he discourses on death to the servants in the kitchen. He could not have positive knowledge of a thousand other details, many of which occurred before he was even born. What is important is why this lack of verification is at the least irrelevant, and perhaps even an advantage. Tristram's procedure leaves little doubt that his imaginative grasp of his heritage has, from the point of view of historical objectivism, altered the "facts"; but the ultimate result is a kind of preservation of the truth that he *is,* as a participant in that tradition, rather than positive knowledge of alien events with which he has no living tie. To the scientific mind such an apparently careless disregard for verification must remain fallacious until it recognizes that the empirical principle itself derives, laden with prejudgments, from just such a primitive and precritical engagement with the historical world. In an entirely different sense, Tristram is highly critical, not factually but morally. His reflections are critical of the aberrations in the life of Shandy Hall, and he comes gradually to a superior understanding which in effect is a purifying of the tradition as represented in a comically debased form by Walter, Toby, and Elizabeth Shandy. The form of that purification is the retrieval of a much older and wiser stratum of his tradition represented by Yorick. His problem is not one of historical knowledge; it is interpretive and, hence, necessarily historical in a more radical sense. While it may be assumed, then, that Tristram has not deliberately misrepresented his family history, on the ground that misrepresentation would hinder rather than serve his purposes, the issue of historical accuracy simply does not fall within the purview of his project. His concern is with the primitive events of understanding as a mode of being. Our own act of participation in his book, which on his model requires that we let the text become contemporaneous and address us in our present world, will, however, raise the issue of validity in an urgent form.

The implications of Tristram's analogy interpreted in this way are extensive for criticism and need to be made explicit since they demand an approach to the text substantially different from critical methods based on the model of scientific knowledge which assumes a false objectification. In fact, the implications weigh heavily against all procedures which stress either side of the subject-object schema that underlies most modern literary theory. On the one hand there is the realist assumption that a text is an objective thing-in-itself to be manipulated according to specified methods by an unconditioned reader, and, on the other, the idealist assumption that the reader projects his own meaning into the text, using it to launch into his own orbit. Both ignore the fact that the event of understanding is anterior to this epistemological model of a subject confronting an alien object and calls for a critique of positivity. That model is not simply given in primary experience as is so often assumed; it is an abstraction, derived from concrete experience, for the purpose of dealing with a world of objects. As such it is specifically unsuited to literary criticism. More appropriate for critical purposes is the analogy of human relationships such as Tristram's conversation. Gadamer uses the term *I-Thou* to distinguish three different qualities of relationships which parallel ways of addressing a

text and offer distinct critical alternatives.

The first is an "I," a subject, confronting a "Thou" who is not a thou at all but an it, an object with which the subject has nothing in common; the resulting relationship of "objectivity" consists in subsuming the object under various universal concepts by specific methods of procedure. Thus one may find that a person exemplifies one or another trait of "human nature," to use an eighteenth-century category, or, as in twentieth-century social science, he may predict how the person would behave under some specified circumstances. In such a "scientific" procedure everything about the person that does not exemplify some universal concept is submerged, including the uniqueness that is the person himself. The objective habit of mind approaches all reality with what Victor Shklovský calls an "'algebraic' method of thought" which facilitates one's dealing with a world of objects with great economy though the price of that abstract economy is the gradual evacuation of reality which, one might argue, it is a function of art to rehabilitate.[14] An objectivist posture toward a text strips it of its power to make a personal claim on the reader and effectively silences it. In the domain of natural science it is as true as in the study of literature that the event of understanding cannot itself be understood by constructing and retrospectively imposing such a pattern on the event of interpretation. Subjects and objects are possible only because of the rich texture of relationships that obtain in the world prior to reflection. A realist criticism that attempts to study the text objectively, as if it were an autonomous entity, is uninterested in the concealed processes by means of which the object is accessible and in the subjective conditions that influence the way it presents itself to consciousness. "To speak of the being of a thing as it 'actually is' is to indulge in metaphysical speculation: as it is for whom? There is no human perspective from which one can say what a being 'actually is.'"[15]

Underlying the objectivist position is a legitimate concern with the question of verification and an apprehension of the critical anarchy, not to say generally shabby thinking, that would be fostered by an unrestrained impressionism. Hermeneutical theorists, especially Gadamer, though the criticism applies better to Heidegger, have been blamed for an indifference to the possibility of valid interpretation.[16] All critics are convinced, of course, that there is a discernible difference between getting a point of interpretation right and getting it wrong, but that does not imply that only one way of interpreting a text is admissible. What needs to be examined carefully is the notion of objectively valid results. Just as the object "as it really is" is as problematic in physics as in historical criticism, so is the notion of objective validity. In the introduction to the *Cartesian Meditations,* Edmund Husserl observes that the phrase "objectively valid results . . . signifies nothing but results that have been refined by mutual criticism and that now withstand every criticism" (p. 5). Not even the positive sciences "attain actualization of a system of absolute truths"; they must settle for "an infinite horizon of approximations" (p. 12). As Aron Gurwitsch puts it, objectivity is "identifiableness, i.e. the possibility of reverting again and again to what, through the present experienced act, is offered to consciousness."[17] Hence, that claim may be said to have objective, empirical validity which withstands public criticism. In discussing the historian's effort to achieve objectivity, Ricoeur says that the meaning of such objectivity is an educated subjectivity, that is, "not just *any* subjectivity," not "a subjectivity adrift," but one shaped by history whose predispositions derive from the tradition of which it is part and "are dimensions of historical objectivity itself."[18]

The task of criticism is not to dissect a rationally structured object with the intellectual scalpel from a position of detached contemplation. There are dimensions of the critical enterprise that can be and should be reduced to method, regions that require empirical research and formal analysis; but those regions of enquiry presuppose a more primitive *living* relationship with the text which makes rational analysis worth the trouble and establishes the directions of interest which it will take. A pertinent example for the study of **Tristram Shandy** is the case of the historical text. Approached as an objective entity the historical text can be nothing more than an object of antiquarian interest which has lost the power to speak. Antiquarianism which attempts to reconstruct some original meaning or the response of the original audience fails utterly to understand the historical nature of either the text or the interpreter and thus misses the work entirely. As R. G. Collingwood correctly observes, the historian "is a part of the process he is studying, has his own place in that process, and can see it only from the point of view which at this present moment he occupies within it."[19] The proper aim is not the futile effort to restore the irretrievable life of the past or to return to some original meaning; it is to establish that reciprocity between historian and text that was described above as a fusion of horizons. When judiciously practiced, historicism escapes its absurdly deterministic implications by searching for formative influences rather than "causes" in the strict sense. Its excesses are frequent enough, however, to justify the observation that whatever antecedents might be recoverable, a writer is a self, a transcendence, that does not respond to ideas in books as billiard ball responds to cue.[20] In his relatedness to himself there is an open space of reflection that breaks the deterministic friction of causality, setting him at a distance from the self that is acted upon by causes and motives. The motives for thought and the influences giving it shape are as likely to be "a good dinner" or "a bad wife"[21] as the reading of Montaigne; but, in any case, there is an agency guiding from the front as causes push from behind.

The idealist who stresses the opposite pole of the subject-object relation in criticism chooses a relation to the text that corresponds to Gadamer's second "I-Thou" model in which the thou is a reflection of the I. In personal relationships the thou is thereby allowed a uniqueness of its own, but at the same time that uniqueness is subordinated to projective patterns of explanation by which one establishes supremacy over the other. There is reciprocity in this relationship, but it does not allow the other to speak for himself. As a model of interpretation it has one advantage over the objectivist position in that it closes the distance between reader and text and allows the intimacy of encounter that is the beginning of meaning. But the advantage is offset by the absence of any principle restraining the imposition of wanton subjective patterns that distort the objective outlines of the text. The threat posed by this subject-centered impressionism is qualified by one fact that is not always recognized: the projecting of patterns of meaning is not the completely private gesture of a *solus ipse* isolated within the walls of its own subjectivity. The fabric of prejudgments that are thus imposed on the text are part of the historical sedimentation of the tradition in which one lives with others and with the text itself. The issue is simply the difference between what Ricoeur calls a "bad" or uncultivated subjectivity and a "good" or educated one.[22]

Criticism based on the subject pole of the subject-object schema contains a practical truth which has often been overlooked to the detriment of literary studies. Classroom experience richly demonstrates the impossibility of engaging readers in abstract analysis of such features of a work as form until imaginative reading or imaginative teaching has enabled the text to establish its authority over the prestructured consciousness of the reader by means of the dialectic of participation. Once that interaction has taken place, analysis has its *raison d'etre*, namely, the extension of the understanding and the power of the work. To proceed in the opposite direction is to encourage the common, naive misunderstanding of criticism as stifling the life of the text. When all the formal problems have been explained, the life of the author written, the books in his library cataloged, sources and influences traced, and archetypes explicated, the central challenge of the text and the reason it is read will still be untouched unless the reader's separation from the work has been overcome by a bridging of the gulf that divides his values, experiences, and preconceptions from the horizon of the work. What is needed is close attention to the actual patterns of understanding in concrete experience which can show the way that interpretation occurs, as distinguished from the calculation of abstract methods with their lumber of philosophical presuppositions.

The third "I-Thou" relation illuminates the hermeneutic experience in precisely the way that is needed; the thou, whether person or text, is allowed to reveal itself in its own integrity in the manner of authentic conversation. It assumes neither a commitment to an underlying philosophical system nor a presuppositionless starting point; it leaves the act of interpretation in its inherent setting, what Heidegger has taught us to recognize as "the hermeneutical circle," and thereby makes full allowance for the historical and finite character of both reader and text. By means of the sedimentation of experience in his tradition, his standpoint in history, and his language, he brings a rich texture of prejudices to his reading which are the subjective conditions out of which his kinship with the text grows and which are to some extent objectively present in the work itself. Increase in understanding causes revisions and corrections in those prejudices, but without them there could be no understanding, the text would not even be identifiable as a work of art. It should also be observed that the understanding of the necessary role of bias encourages such corrections, whereas objectivism conceals them from itself by assuming the possibility of an ideal or at least a partial objectivity. This structure of preunderstanding completes the circle of believing in order to understand and understanding in order to believe. Such a basis of criticism combines the ideals of truth to the objective outlines of the work with authentic response on the part of the historically situated reader whose horizon of interests makes his kinship with the text possible. *Tristram Shandy,* for example, attracts our attention first because it says things that seem true and important in the context of modern life and of our own thinking. At the same time that we attend to the author's intent in what the novel says, insofar as that is knowable to him or to us, we also understand it in ways he could not have foreseen, in the light of modern ideas and historical events of which he could have no knowledge. When Melvyn New remarks that the "meaningful context" of the novel "is not the novels of Proust and Beckett, but rather the Augustan view of man," he corrects a frequent error in historical understanding, but he also uses the term "meaningful" in a highly uncritical way that excludes the necessary contemporaneity of all understanding.[23] It is important to note that this dialectic is not a mere theoretical compromise between realism and idealism. That would combine the philosophical disadvantages of each rather than going behind both to their origin in the "life-world" and thereby escaping the disadvantages of each.[24] It is a description of the process of interpretation, what, for better or worse, happens in the event of understanding, combined with the thesis that although the inherent process may be elaborated by rational and methodical enquiries, the relationship is and must remain hierarchical. Systematic enquiry can bring speculative processes to clarity in retrospect, but it can only make explicit what is already implicit in the exchange in which one has been caught up and transformed. It cannot control without destroying that rela-

tionship: "The question is," as Humpty Dumpty says, "which is to be master—that's all."

It has been remarked above that the act of reading is an effort to recover more than is actually said, more than the work considered as a series of discursive statements can say. A criticism that aspires to become engaged with the text in the manner of conversation may properly be called speculative. The shift in emphasis in the word *speculation* over the last two hundred years illustrates the problem well: the primary meaning of the term in Dr. Johnson's *Dictionary* is "contemplation" and only secondarily "conjecture," whereas the reverse is now the case, so influential has the ideal of exact knowledge become. But since literature belongs to the world in which we live rather than the world known to science, the old and venerable sense of the term may be employed to articulate that free play of mind which Tristram properly demands. To engage in such a venture is to accept the risk of doing criticism under the aspect of the hobby-horse. The restriction of the concept of validity to those derivative enquiries which admit of genuine scientific precision and objectivity frees the critical impulse to attend to all that happens in the interaction with a text but without thereby enabling it to claim immunity from rational examination and revision. It might be objected that such an unmethodical criticism, in seeking to stimulate imaginative explorations of new appropriations of meaning such as renew the vitality of a cultural tradition, also encourages idiosyncrasy and even nonsense. That is no doubt true, but little is risked. There has never been a noticeable shortage of nonsense in the world, whatever methods have been in the ascendency, and the fact has rendered a service to humanity in that it "opens the heart and lungs . . . and makes the wheel of life run long and chearfully round" (IV.xxxii.338). Besides, "so long as a man rides his HOBBY-HORSE peaceably and quietly along the King's highway, and neither compels you or me to get up behind him,——pray, Sir, what have either you or I to do with it?" (I.vii.13). What is compelling in criticism as in any other discipline, is the advent of understanding, the act of interpretation in which illumination occurs. The important difference is between the comic incrustation of Walter Shandy's rationalism (which entertains without convincing because it offers no direct enlightenment) and the experience of clarity in the understanding of our common mode of being which derives from Tristram's reflections. . . . Just as it is possible for conclusions to be valid which are of no interest to anyone, so it is possible, at the opposite extreme, for insights to be of the greatest moment to a whole culture and yet lie beyond the bounds of validity in any rigorous sense of the term. Something of the kind is evident in the cases of mystery and paradox. Or again, Heidegger's reflections on the poetry of Hölderlin and Rilke or his explorations of the etymologies of Heraclitean Greek are, on the one hand, a scandal to objective criticism and deserve severe examination for the liberties that they take with texts, and yet they may be seen, on the other hand, as of greater importance to the life of the culture in some cases than the texts that occasion them. It is surely an important dimension of the life of those German poems and those Greek fragments that they have fostered such radical thought and illumination. Moreover, it is a predictable consequence of critical finitude that among the hobby-horses of today is the orthodoxy of tomorrow and the dogma of the day after. . . .

Notes

⁹ The modern development of hermeneutics begins with Friedrich Schleiermacher who undertakes to interpret texts, specifically scripture, by means of understanding the individual personalities of the writers (*Hermeneutik,* trans. Heinz Kimmerle). Wilhelm Dilthey deepens the study of the writer by claiming that the individual can be understood only from the broad perspective of historical lived experience. Heidegger, in turn, overcomes the romantic illusion that reader and text, subject and object, interpenetrate in the interpretive encounter and avoids Dilthey's relativism of historical perspectives with its underlying psychological notion of lived experience by expanding the hermeneutic question to the nature of interpretation itself as the primary activity of man (*Dasein*), the being who seeks to interpret his own experience. Heidegger's own development of the question moves from interpreting the interpreting being in *Being and Time* to attempting to understand the hermeneutical experience in *Unterwegs zur Sprache,* the essence of which he locates in language and the role of Hermes, the bringer of tidings and the god of boundaries.

¹⁰ See pp. 184-92 [of James E. Swearingen, *Reflexivity in "Tristram Shandy"* (Yale University Press, 1977)] where this dimension of Walter's character as rhetor is explored.

¹¹ Gadamer, p. 345. This reconstruction of others' experience was the goal of the early hermeneutics of Schleiermacher.

¹² Schleiermacher, p. xi.

¹³ The phenomenological metaphor of horizon brings into view the whole spatial, temporal, and cultural context of meaningfulness of an object or phenomenon, the encircling sphere that constitutes the setting within which an object reveals itself as what it is. Thus Heidegger introduces the thesis of *Being and Time* with the statement, "Our provisional aim is the Interpretation of *time* as the possible horizon for any understanding whatsoever of Being" (trans. John Macquarrie and Edward Robinson, p. 21). Later Heidegger gives

up the concept of horizon as belonging to metaphysics and its concern with objects (*Siendes*) and their representation rather than with being (*Sein*).

¹⁴ "Art as Technique," in *Russian Formalist Criticism: Four Essays,* trans. Lee T. Lemon and Marian J. Reis, p. 11.

¹⁵ Richard Palmer, *Hermeneutics: Interpretation Theory in Schleiermacher, Dilthey, Heidegger, and Gadamer,* p. 229.

¹⁶ Emilio Betti in *Die Hermeneutik als allgemeine Methodik der Geisteswissenschaften* and E. D. Hirsch in *Validity in Interpretation* both argue this point against Gadamer. Hirsch is concerned with limiting hermeneutics to a philological method of establishing the "verbal meaning" of a text as opposed to its "significance" for the reader. But Gadamer is interested in a different question, and one that apparently does not interest Hirsch since he excludes it from hermeneutics, namely, the distinguishing features of all events of understanding. Based on Gadamer's response to Betti in Supplement I of *Truth and Method* where he insists, "I am *not proposing a method,* but I am describing *what is the case*" and thus going "beyond the concept of method . . . to envisage . . . what always happens" (Gadamer's italics, pp. 465-66), one suspects that his intention is to dissolve the question of validity in instances of premethodical understanding by confining it to its proper scientific sphere.

¹⁷ "On the Intentionality of Consciousness," in *Philosophical Essays in Memory of Edmund Husserl,* ed. Marvin Farber, p. 83.

¹⁸ "Objectivity and Subjectivity in History," in *History and Truth,* trans. Charles A. Kelbley, pp. 30-31.

¹⁹ *The Idea of History,* p. 248.

²⁰ See the discussion of the epistemology of sophism in chapter 4 [of James E. Swearingen, Reflexivity in "Tristram Shandy" (Yale University Press, 1977)].

²¹ Duke Maskell, "Locke and Sterne, or Can Philosophy Influence Literature?" *Essays in Criticism* 23 (1973), 25.

²² "Objectivity and Subjectivity in History," p. 30.

²³ "Sterne and Henry Baker's *The Microscope Made Easy,*" *Studies in English Literature* 10 (1970), 597.

²⁴ Husserl introduces the term *life-world* (*Lebenswelt*) to refer to the primordial world of immediate experience as opposed to the complexly conditioned, cultural world given by science.

Works Cited

. . . Betti, Emilio. *Die Hermeneutik als allgemeine Methodik der Geisteswissenschaften.* Tübingen: J.C.B. Mohr, 1962. . . .

Collingwood, R. W. *The Idea of History.* New York: Oxford University Press, 1956. . . .

Gurwitsch, Aron. "On the Intentionality of Consciousness." In *Philosophical Essays in Memory of Edmund Husserl,* edited by Marvin Farber. Cambridge: Harvard University Press, 1940. . . .

Heidegger, Martin. *Being and Time.* Translated by John Macquarrie and Edward Robinson. New York: Harper & Row, 1962. . . .

Hirsch, E. D. *Validity in Interpretation.* New Haven: Yale University Press, 1967. . . .

Husserl, Edmund. *Cartesian Meditations.* Translated by Dorian Cairns. The Hague: Martinus Nijhoff, 1973. . . .

Kant, Immanuel. *The Critique of Practical Reason.* Translated by Lewis White Beck. New York: Bobbs-Merrill, 1956.

———. *The Critique of Pure Reason.* Translated by Norman Kemp Smith. New York: Macmillan and Co., 1958.

Kierkegaard, Sören. *Fear and Trembling and the Sickness Unto Death.* Translated by Walter Lowrie. New York: Doubleday Anchor, 1954. . . .

Maskell, Duke. "Locke and Sterne, or Can Philosophy Influence Literature?" *Essays in Criticism* 23 (1973), 22-39. . . .

New, Melvyn. "Sterne and Henry Baker's *The Microscope Made Easy.*" *Studies in English Literature* 10 (1970), 591-604. . . .

Palmer, Richard. *Hermeneutics: Interpretation Theory in Schleiermacher, Dilthey, Heidegger, and Gadamer.* Evanston: Northwestern University Press, 1969. . . .

Ricoeur, Paul. "Existence and Hermeneutics." Translated by Kathleen McLaughlin. In *The Conflict of Interpretations: Essays in Hermeneutics,* edited by Don Ihde. Evanston: Northwestern University Press, 1974. . . .

[Ricoeur, Paul]. "Objectivity and Subjectivity in History." In *History and Truth,* translated by Charles A. Kelbley. Evanston: Northwestern University Press, 1965.

Schleiermacher, Friedrich Ernst Daniel. *Hermeneutik.* Translated by Heinz Kimmerle. Heidelberg: Carl C. Winter, 1959. . . .

Shklovský, Victor. "Art as Technique." In *Russian Formalist Criticism: Four Essays,* translated by Lee T. Lemon and Marion J. Ross. Lincoln: University of Nebraska Press, 1965. . . .

Martin C. Battestin (essay date 1978)

SOURCE: "*A Sentimental Journey* and the Syntax of Things," in *Augustan Worlds,* edited by J. C. Hilson, M. M. B. Jones, and J. R. Watson, Leicester University Press, 1978, pp. 223-39.

[*In the following essay, Battestin contrasts the emotional and sexuasl connection between characters in* A Sentimental Journey *with the solipsism that renders the characters in* Tristram Shandy *essentially isolated and unconnected to others.*]

Recently I made a case for the fundamental—it might be said, revolutionary—modernity of **Tristram Shandy** (1759-67), in which Sterne, repudiating the Augustan faith in symmetry and rational order, devised a form to mirror and to mitigate the disturbing subjectivist conception of reality he found implicit in Locke's *Essay concerning Human Understanding*—a form that defines the world in terms of the processes of the mind while implying, in its appeal to the senses and the imagination, the means of communication and relationship.[1] Enforced by the mechanism of the mind and the inefficacy of rational discourse to bridge the gulf that separates us, solipsism and frustration are the conditions of life at Shandy Hall, relieved only in those humanizing moments when, by means of the sympathetic or the sexual imagination, we are, in Walter's words, led out 'of our caverns and hiding-places' into communion with another.[2]

In **A Sentimental Journey through France and Italy** (1768) Sterne resumed these themes, but transmuted and softened them by asserting more confidently than before the possibility of relationship, achieved through the sensuous and imaginative apprehension of what I will call the syntax of things. The phrase is convenient because it would have carried for Sterne and his contemporaries a double reference, pointing not only to the logical process of grammatical predication, by which subject is coupled with object or acts upon it, but also to the universal grammar of Nature herself, the system of interrelationships that obtains in what Yorick prefers to call the 'great—great SENSORIUM of the world'.[3] The two senses of *syntax,* linguistic and metaphysical, will help to clarify the ways in which, even at the most elementary and essential level of his narrative, Sterne's form implies his meaning.[4] In carrying his reader along with him on this 'quiet journey of the heart in pursuit of NATURE, and those affections which rise out of her, which make us love each other—and the world, better than we do' (p. 219), Yorick means so to conduct his narrative that we participate in it, that, in the process of reading, we will ourselves become, in terms of the metaphoric classifications of the Preface, 'Sentimental Travellers' capable of responding to life and the vexatious circumstances of our mortality with compassion, and of course with laughter: his reader, he warns, must eventually 'determine his own place and rank in the catalogue' of travellers, whether 'Idle', 'Inquisitive', 'Lying', 'Proud', 'Vain', 'Splenetic', or 'Sentimental'—'it will be one step towards knowing himself . . . ' (pp. 82-3). Both these transactions—the journey of the heart in pursuit of Nature and the narrator's striving to achieve a closer, ameliorative relationship with his reader—may be seen to have a linguistic analogue in the paradigm of the sentence itself, in which the subject (and here especially the subjective *ego* of the first-person narrative) is linked through a copulative or transitive verb to an object beyond itself. Happily, in addition to being helpful in clarifying the interdependence of theme and form in *A Sentimental Journey,* this analogy has the advantage of having occurred to Sterne himself: for Tristram, at least, Yorick, the humorous, philandering parson who is our subject, is 'as heteroclite a creature in all his declensions' as any parsing student of the human comedy could wish for;[5] and, as Yorick himself assures us, his relationships with others are always predicated 'according to the mood I am in, and the case—and I may add the gender too, of the person I am to govern' (p. 124).

If the grammatical paradigm may thus imply the establishment of human relationships, however, the notorious syntactical eccentricities, ambiguities, and interruptions of *A Sentimental Journey* will remind us that, in art as in life, such relationships are seldom so neatly accomplished. Nor, perhaps, is it always desirable that they should be. Sterne's fiction in a sense anticipates E. E. Cummings's observation that 'life is not a paragraph',[6] rounded and coherent, its premises neatly fulfilled. For Tristram it was rather a fluid, open-ended, whimsical thing that would be conterminous with the narrative he was writing; for Yorick it is, however brief, 'a large volume' of sentimental adventures (p. 114). Like Cummings, too, Sterne understood that in this process Death, from whom Yorick flees toward the pleasant valleys of Italy, is no mere 'parenthesis',[7] but rather the final full stop, whose symbol in *Tristram Shandy* had been blackness filling the pages to the very margins. Understandably, therefore, Yorick inclines to a loose, unconventional punctuation, preferring dashes to periods, and in the narrative of his journey breaks off in mid-sentence as in mid-career, leaving us with the image of himself reaching out toward one kind of syntactical completion he covets, but grasp-

ing only the blank vacuity of the unprinted page. On 18 March 1768, with a poignant and appropriately shandean irony, Fortune decreed that Sterne should come to the end of his own volume of adventures, with half his book still to write.

Because Death at last won his race with Sterne, Yorick has remained in that final comical attitude ever since, prevented by impassable mountain roads from reaching his destination, his more immediate objective eluding his grasp. We will never know, then, what Sterne's final intention for his work may have been. Yet to judge from the part of the book he did complete, it would appear that *A Sentimental Journey* represents a modification of one of the conventional thematic motifs of journey literature, that it was in some sense designed, in Gardner Stout's phrase, as 'a comic "Pilgrim's Progress" for the man of feeling'.[8] The stages measuring the spiritual distance Yorick travels in the first two volumes are, on the one hand, the early chapters entitled 'The Monk' and 'The Desobligeant' and, on the other hand, the later episodes concerning Maria and the peasant family whose charity and simple piety are celebrated in 'The Supper' and 'The Grace': seen in this way, Yorick's true progress is from solipsism toward communion, from self-love toward a felt apprehension of the syntax of things. Just how much mental travelling this process will require is suggested upon Yorick's arrival at Calais by his inability to translate his fine-sounding sentiments into deeds. His spirits heightened by a good dinner and a bottle of burgundy, he is in an expansive, altruistic mood. Generalizing from his own generous sentiments, he imagines mankind almost literally as subjects in search of predication, looking round 'for an object to share' their money with; the benign motions of such a soul as his seem proof sufficient against those cynical French materialists who represent man as a mere machine actuated by self-interest (pp. 68-9). Far from oversetting their creed, however, he will instantly seem to confirm it when he refuses alms to the kindly Franciscan who intrudes upon this complacent reverie. The practical demand upon his charity summons up all his selfish impulses and brings reason rushing to their justification: 'The moment I cast my eyes on him, I was predetermined not to give him a single sous; and accordingly I put my purse into my pocket—button'd it up—set myself a little more upon my centre' (p. 70). The doctrine of *L'Homme machine* is thoroughly congenial to Yorick's present mood, who could wish to believe that, since 'the ebbs and flows of our humours' depend upon physical causes beyond our control, there is 'neither sin nor shame' in our actions (p. 70). His purse buttoned up in his pocket, his portmanteau securely locked against all solicitations, Yorick rationalizes his meanness by reminding the monk that he is presuming upon a fund which is the rightful property of the truly unfortunate, 'the lame, the blind, the aged and the infirm'— that charity, as Fielding's Mrs Tow-wouse declared in behalf of the niggardly everywhere, begins at home: 'but of all others, resumed I, the unfortunate of our own country, surely, have the first rights; and I have left thousands in distress upon our own shore' (p. 73).

Critics have found in such episodes evidence for Sterne's persistent mockery of his hero;[9] but it is Yorick, we must remember, who has the honesty to embarrass himself by telling us about them. And he knows better: 'I have behaved very ill; said I within myself; but I have only just set out upon my travels; and shall learn better manners as I get along' (p. 75). As a traveller requires a vehicle to make his progress, so, in the journey of life (the metaphor again is Yorick's own, p. 114), the vehicle must be our own sensibilities, the quality of which will determine our experience of the world. Reality for Sterne is subjective; we create the world in our own image. The Sentimental Traveller, which Yorick will become, can transform a waste land into a garden, for he goes sympathetically, seeking connexions and relationships that will improve and nourish his heart:

> I pity the man who can travel from *Dan* to *Beersheba,* and cry, 'Tis all barren—and so it is; and so is all the world to him who will not cultivate the fruits it offers. I declare, said I, clapping my hands chearily together that was I in a desart, I would find out wherewith in it to call forth my affections—If I could not do better, I would fasten them upon some sweet myrtle, or seek some melancholy cypress to connect myself to—
>
> (pp. 115-16)

The Splenetic Traveller, for whom Smollett is the archetype, will find at his journey's end that 'heaven itself' is a hell, its happiest mansion only a place to 'do penance . . . to all eternity'; for he has 'brought up no faculties' to appreciate felicity (p. 120).

At this first stage of his journey, however, Yorick's 'vehicle', as we have seen, is cramped and in need of repair. 'Discontented with himself' (p. 76), his spiritual condition after the initial encounter with the monk is symbolized by the ruined *desobligéante,* a single-seat chaise which, having made the tour of Europe and 'not profited much by its adventures' (p. 87), sits mouldering in the farthest corner of the innyard. Finding it 'in tolerable harmony with [his] feelings' (p. 77), Yorick enters this useless and unsociable conveyance, completes his isolation by drawing the curtain to shut out the figure of the monk, an object of charity, and proceeds to write his Preface; it would have been better, as he remarks to the English traveller who interrupts him, 'in a *Vis a Vis*' (p. 85). Later, when the process of his sentimentalizing has opened his heart, he will exclaim, '—Surely—surely man! it is not good for thee to sit alone—thou wast made for social inter-

course' (p. 167); now the *desobligéante* provides the emblem of his self-enclosure.

Yet the symbolism of Yorick's situation here is not entirely negative. It includes two further curious circumstances pointing to a distinctive feature of Sterne's conception of his craft: the notion that an important means of escaping the condition of solipsism is the act of authorship itself. Writing for Tristram, like the Hobby-horses of his uncle and father, is a device for ordering the confusing multiplicity of one's fugitive experience;[10] unlike most Hobby-horses, however, which tend to confirm us in our isolation, writing about one's private experience is the means of apprehending its latent significance and, therefore, of rendering it intelligible. It is thus the very activity of writing the Preface that sets Yorick's otherwise useless vehicle in motion, beginning, as it were, both the process of his mental travelling out of himself and the process of his developing relationship with us, his readers. By the time he finishes the Preface, Yorick declares, 'I had wrote myself pretty well out of conceit with the *Desobligeant*' (p. 87); his writing seems a kind of therapy, purging his mind of its discontents. What is more, the episode concludes with a dramatization of the fact that only as readers of his narrative may we become participants of the journey it recounts, which is ideally the mutual progress of both author and reader toward self-knowledge and benevolence. Sterne abruptly interjects into the scene a pair of English travellers who have been drawn to the *desobligéante* by the motion Yorick's writing has imparted to it. Though as characters in the narrative they cannot actually have heard the question which concludes his Preface—'Where then, my dear countrymen, are you going—' (p. 85)—they are nonetheless made to answer it: 'We are only looking at this chaise, said they.' Responding thus improbably to the written words, these English travellers seem surrogates for us, Sterne's English readers, who, as we will see, by such surprising strategies of his art will be made to answer that same crucial question.

That this curious parable of the *desobligéante* points to an ultimate concern of Sterne's narrative is confirmed by the subject itself of the Preface, the writing of which has set the machine in motion. Springing naturally from Yorick's mood and situation, the Preface sounds the dominant theme of the **Journey:** the difficulties of communication, of leaving our homes (and our selves) behind to seek new relationships abroad. That Sterne means us to regard Yorick's confinement in the *desobligéante* as a symbol of our fundamental solipsism seems clear from the phrasing of the opening sentence, which universalizes his discontent and isolation: 'nature', Yorick observes, 'has set up by her own unquestionable authority certain boundaries and fences to circumscribe the discontent of man . . . laying him under almost insuperable obligations to work out his ease, and to sustain his sufferings at home':

'Tis true we are endued with an imperfect power of spreading our happiness sometimes beyond *her* limits, but 'tis so ordered, that from the want of languages, connections, and dependencies, and from the difference in education, customs and habits, we lie under so many impediments in communicating our sensations out of our own sphere, as often amount to a total impossibility.

(p. 78)

In *A Sentimental Journey* the impediments to breaking 'out of our own sphere' are many, and they cannot be circumvented without much ingenuity and diligence. For one thing, and most essentially, there is the whole intractable mechanism of the self, with all its appetites and vanities—the mechanism described by the likes of Hobbes and the French *philosophes* and which Yorick symbolizes not only by the *desobligéante,* but by the caged starling, crying ' "I can't get out—I can't get out" '—whose prison is secure and permanent: the door of the cage, Yorick declares, 'was twisted and double twisted so fast with wire, there was no getting it open without pulling the cage to pieces—I took both hands to it' (p. 197). It is the 'poor starling', emblem of the confined and therefore tormented self, that Yorick, and his author, bear as the crest to their arms (p. 205). As Gardner Stout has argued, Sterne, while keeping his place within the Latitudinarian tradition of benevolism, felt in no inconsiderable degree the force of the Augustinian and Hobbesian doctrine that man is a creature of pride and the sport of his appetites. In a fit of selfishness Yorick first refuses the monk charity, and, when he finally offers the snuff-box to make amends, he is motivated as much by vanity and the desire to get on with his philandering as by the impulses of disinterested benevolence (p. 98). He is even disposed, in simile at least, 'to fight a duel' with the innkeeper over the price of a post-chaise: 'Base passion! said I . . . base, ungentle passion! thy hand is against every man, and every man's hand against thee—' (p. 89). No sooner does he feel the 'impulse' to share his coach with an attractive young woman whom he imagines to be in distress than 'Every dirty passion, and bad propensity in my nature, took the alarm': Avarice, Caution, Cowardice, Discretion, Hypocrisy, Meanness, Pride—all start up, like prudent counsellors, to secure the citadel of the ego (pp. 104-6). Even much later in Paris, Vanity will intrude upon the process of his sentimentalizing, which is then well along: he revels in his lionizing by a coterie of worldly 'children of Art' whose favours he has won by flattery—'a most vile prostitution of myself to half a dozen different people' (p. 266).

For Sterne, moreover, not only the selfish passions, but reason itself—the faculty that philosophers from Aristotle and the Stoics to Swift's Houyhnhnms had regarded as the primary agent of morality—works to ensure the condition of solipsism and self-delusion. As the example of Walter Shandy perpetually crucifying

Truth may suggest, no novelist of the period went as far as Sterne in disparaging what the humanist tradition took to be the noblest faculty of the soul. In passages such as Yorick's summoning up plausible arguments to justify his meanness to the monk, Sterne seems especially close, in fact, to the shocking author of *A Treatise of Human Nature* (1739), for whom reason was 'the slave of the passions, and can never pretend to any other office than to serve and obey them'.[11] Thus Yorick insists that the purifying of the soul and the calming of the heart's 'commotions' are not to be entrusted 'to reason only', but to the influence of the more benign social affections: 'I can safely say for myself, I was never able to conquer any one single bad sensation in my heart so decisively, as by beating up as fast as I could for some kindly and gentle sensation, to fight it upon its own ground' (p. 226). At other times he would seem to anticipate the Wordsworthian notion that we murder to dissect. As he stands before the remise door holding the hand of an attractive stranger in the first real moment of sentimental communion he has experienced on his journey, Yorick makes the mistake of trying to analyse the circumstances that account for his happiness: 'you thank Fortune', replies the lady, disengaging her hand, ' . . . you had reason— the heart knew it, and was satisfied; and who but an English philosopher would have sent notices of it to the brain to reverse the judgment?' (p. 96). As for the Stoic confidence that philosophy can render us invulnerable to misfortune, Sterne mocks it as a delusion; and, as a man of feeling, he condemns the inhumanity of the doctrine of self-sufficiency it implies. All Yorick's 'systematic reasonings' (p. 198) to persuade himself that there is no more inconvenience in imprisonment in the Bastille than in a confinement for the gout are overthrown in a moment by the cry of the caged starling, awakening his affections and bringing home vividly to his imagination 'the miseries of confinement' (p. 201). As a work of art and morality, Yorick's narrative of his journey, sentimental though it may be, owes everything of course to his author's thoughtful anatomy of the human comedy, and to the sister faculties of the mind, wit and judgment. Yet Yorick insists, 'this is not a work of reasoning' (p. 177), for in Sterne's view the senses and the sympathetic imagination can alone redeem us.

Cooperating with our rationality in the work of self-enclosure are language itself and the prescribed polite forms of social conversation, systems invented by men to facilitate intercourse but which, as they are normally applied, effectively reinforce our privacy. A 'hundred little delicacies' (p. 107) stand in Yorick's way as he tries to know his companions better, and the final chapter comprises a veritable 'Case' of their efficacy in preventing such connections. Our dialogues, furthermore, as those memorable ones between Walter Shandy and his brother attest, are at best only intersecting monologues, each man using words whose meaning eludes the other, hampered not only by the general curse of Babel, but by the impenetrable privacy of our individual experience and the decorums that conceal the heart beneath a fine brocade of formality.

To circumvent such formidable impediments to communication as these, Sterne looked to another, non-verbal kind of language, anticipating what certain twentieth-century psychologists have called 'body language'; and, as a novelist, he attempted to turn the very imprecision of words to his advantage. A useful illustration of both these strategies is the chapter called 'The Translation'. Words being the clumsy things they are, Tristram, we recall, had wished for a Momus's glass that he might see into the soul of man,[12] and Yorick protests that his ambition in pursuing women is 'to spy the *nakedness* of their hearts, and through the different disguises of customs, climates, and religion, find out what is good in them, to fashion my own by—' (pp. 217-18). The better to achieve this goal of an immediate, intuitive apprehension of another's self, he perfects his skill at rendering an unspoken language with its own rules of syntactical connexion. As Yorick enters the box at the Opera, the old French officer who occupies it puts down his book, removes his spectacles and places them in his pocket. Though no word has been spoken, the sense of this kindly action is instantly translatable, as is the bow Yorick makes in return, because it is expressed in the universal language of looks and gestures and attitudes, a kind of automatic writing of the heart by which the motions of the soul may be read in those of the body. So, earlier in *Tristram Shandy,* Walter's physical attitude as he lies sprawled on his bed grieving over the death of his son is more eloquent testimony of his feelings than any words could supply. The grammar and idioms of this language are immediately intelligible:

> There is not a secret so aiding to the progress of sociality [declares Yorick], as to get master of this *short hand,* and be quick in rendering the several turns of looks and limbs, with all their inflections and delineations, into plain words. For my own part, by long habitude, I do it so mechanically, that when I walk the streets of London, I go translating all the way; and have more than once stood behind in the circle, where not three words have been said, and have brought off twenty different dialogues with me, which I could have fairly wrote down and sworn to.
>
> (pp. 171-2)

For the purpose of communication and relationship, then, words are less useful than the body, reason than the sympathetic imagination. The most satisfactory moments of communion between characters in Sterne's fiction are accordingly those achieved in silence by touch and intuition. Though their spoken discourse fails to bring them together, Toby's hand placed on his brother's shoulder unites them instantly in mutual af-

fection. In *A Sentimental Journey,* indeed, hands are often the means of syntactical connexion, in both senses of the word *syntax.* The holding of hands, the feeling of another's pulse, becomes for Yorick not only (as, say, in *Paradise Lost*) a sign of harmony between man and woman, but the actual means by which their hearts are made intelligible, one to another. The first true moment of relationship he experiences on his journey, Yorick's sentimental intercourse with the lady at the remise door, continues over the course of many pages, while her hand remains in his, their 'communications'—which lead the English travellers to suppose they 'must be *man and wife* at least' (p. 104)—made possible chiefly by the silent rendering of the fingers' subtle pressures: 'The pulsations of the arteries along my fingers pressing across hers', Yorick observes, 'told her what was passing within me' (p. 97). Later, like a true sentimental physician, Yorick will reckon 'the temperature' of the beautiful *grisset* by counting the throbs of her pulse, since, he believes, 'it is the same blood which comes from the heart, which descends to the extremes' (p. 164). At such moments Sterne enacts the cordial part that Fortune played in Yorick's encounter with the lady in Calais, promoting Friendship's cause by taking 'two utter strangers by their hands—of different sexes, and perhaps from different corners of the globe' (p. 96), the physical union enabling a kind of *concordia discors* of the heart.

This, then, is the essential message of the chapter called 'The Translation': that for the Sentimental Traveller who seeks connexions and relationships, the body's 'short hand' may be more revealing than the spoken word, that our intuitions may compensate for the limitations of the intellect. But, as the chapter also makes clear, Sterne goes farther than this in circumventing the obstacles to communication he found so persuasively delineated in *An Essay concerning Human Understanding.* As man of feeling and as author, he continually exploits the very quirks of mind and language of which Locke complained. It is the mechanism of association that brings Yorick closer to the stranger at the Opera by connecting him in Yorick's mind, despite the separation of time and place, with the idea of Captain Tobias Shandy, 'the dearest of my flock and friends, whose philanthropy I never think of at this long distance from his death—but my eyes gush out with tears' (p. 170). Similarly, it is the ambiguity of words that enables Sterne to achieve a simultaneity of thematic, as well as comic, implications—the multiplicity of connotations comprising a sort of linguistic equivalent of the syntax of things in the 'great SENSORIUM of the world'. The word *translation* in the chapter we are considering can also denote the idea of movement from one place to another, specifically from a situation of isolation outside to a situation of communion within: thus Yorick enters the box and takes his place baside the old officer who reminds him of Toby, the type of philanthropy, as later the Marquesina invites him to enter her coach and carries him to her home—'the connection', Yorick assures us, 'which arose out of that translation, gave me more pleasure than any one I had the honour to make in Italy' (p. 173). Yet another sense of the word seems to lurk here in true shandean fashion, the sense of *translation* as sexual transport—though, of course, Yorick and the Marquesina are ostensibly recalling their awkward encounter in the passage to the concert hall:

> Upon my word, Madame, said I when I had handed her in, I made six different efforts to let you go out—And I made six efforts, replied she, to let you enter—I wish to heaven you would make a seventh, said I—With all my heart, said she, making room—
>
> (p. 173)[13]

Yorick's philandering and his irrepressible bawdry are not, I think, quite to be dismissed as a case of arrested adolescence. They seem rather to be manifestations of Sterne's belief that, given the inadequacies of those traditional instruments of communication, reason and language, the way out of the self must be through the senses and the imagination, and most especially through the recognition that it is our common sexuality that draws us together in spite of the conventional strictures of morality and the proscriptions of propriety. Though the Sentimental Traveller's ultimate goal is an awareness of the unity and interrelatedness of all beings in the great Sensorium of creation, his first approaches to that condition must be through the frank acceptance of his sexual nature; it is this specifically—source of so much awkwardness and laughter in Shandy Hall—that 'makes us come out of our caverns and hiding-places'. Yorick is nothing less than a 'connoisseur' of women (p. 219) because he believes that *Eros,* the longing of the self for union with another, is the instrument of charity and fellow-feeling. He travels with the picture of Eliza about his neck because, as he assures the innkeeper at Montreuil, he has

> been in love with one princess or another almost all my life, and I hope I shall go on so, till I die, being firmly persuaded, that if ever I do a mean action, it must be in some interval betwixt one passion and another: whilst this interregnum lasts, I always perceive my heart locked up—I can scarce find in it, to give Misery a sixpence; and therefore I always get out of it as fast as I can, and the moment I am rekindled, I am all generosity and good will again; and would do any thing in the world either for, or with any one, if they will but satisfy me there is no sin in it.
>
> (pp. 128-9)

The 'Fragment' that follows is meant as a kind of parable of this creed. In the reformation of Abdera, 'the vilest and most profligate town in all Thrace', it is the 'pathetic' apostrophe to Eros in Euripides'

Andromeda, not Democritus's more Augustan applications of 'irony and laughter', that cleanses the city of malice, transforming it at once into an image of the Golden Age: 'Every man almost spoke pure iambics the next day, and talk'd of nothing but Perseus his pathetic address—"O Cupid! prince of God and men"—in every street of Abdera, in every house—"O Cupid! Cupid!" . . . The fire caught—and the whole city, like the heart of one man, open'd itself to Love.' It is worth stressing that this miraculous transformation of a corrupt people is accomplished not through the intellectual appeals of philosophy or satire, but through the 'pathetic' mode of poetry that 'operated more upon their imaginations', the faculty of the mind most nearly allied to the senses, in which the images and motions of desire are vicariously experienced: ' 'Twas only in the power, says the Fragment, of the God whose empire extendeth from heaven to earth, and even to the depths of the sea, to have done this' (p. 131). As Yorick later explains to the Count, though he is travelling in pursuit of Nature and a universal benevolence, the journey is accomplished only through a process of refining the 'affection' he feels 'for the whole sex' (p. 216). The hearts of women, not the Palais Royal or the Louvre, are the temples he 'would rather enter in' (p. 218).

The pursuit of Nature, then, begins in the frank—which is not to say salacious—acceptance of our sexuality, and Sterne as an author means to involve us in this humanizing enterprise. He does so not only in such sentimental passages as the above, but in those bawdy jokes for which he is equally celebrated. These jokes, moreover, are almost invariably the effect of a distinctive rhetorical strategy calculated, no less than the pathos of Perseus's apostrophe to Eros, to operate upon our imaginations. As in the third sense of the word *translation* discussed above, this strategy is the *double entendre*—some object or action or word which at the level ostensibly intended by the author is perfectly straightforward, but which at another level which the reader's imagination, however reluctantly, is teased into supplying, carries a less 'innocent' meaning.[14] The classic instance of this technique in Sterne's fiction is Tristram's elaborate protestation that the word *nose* in his book always and invariably means a nose and nothing more (or less); as a consequence we never afterward encounter the word without supplying a phallic reference. In *A Sentimental Journey* numerous other examples come to mind, such as the 'proposal' Yorick wishes to make to the young woman at Calais (p. 113), or the gloves which the beautiful *grisset* holds open to receive his hand (p. 168). Better still is the titillating encounter between Yorick and the *fille de chambre* related in the chapters called 'The Temptation' and 'The Conquest'. As they sit side by side on the bed in his room, the essentially sexual nature of their interest in each other is obliquely symbolized by the purse she has made to hold his crown:

I'll just shew you, said the fair *fille de chambre,* the little purse I have been making to-day to hold your crown . . . it was of green taffeta, lined with a little bit of white quilted sattin, and just big enough to hold the crown—she put it into my hand—it was pretty; and I held it ten minutes with the back of my hand resting upon her lap—looking sometimes at the purse, sometimes on one side of it.

(p. 236)[15]

Having heightened our expectations with further descriptions of 'innocent' intimacies - the *fille de chambre* passing 'her hand in silence across and across [Yorick's] neck' as she mends his stock, Yorick returning the favour by fondling her feet as he fastens the buckle of her shoe—Sterne breaks off the chapter in mid-sentence with the image implanted firmly in the reader's mind of his hero and the temptress tumbling together on the bed: 'and putting in the strap—and lifting up the other foot with it, when I had done, to see both were right—in doing it too suddenly—it unavoidably threw the fair *fille de chambre* off her centre—and then—' (p. 236). In such a predicament even the chastest of Sterne's readers will be inclined to construe the title of the following chapter, 'The Conquest', in a sexual sense. But, as always in Sterne, *honi soit qui mal y pense.* What Yorick has conquered of course is not his companion's virtue, but the temptation she posed. What has ultimately been tested by Sterne's coy presentation of the episode is the quality of his prudish or 'stoical' reader's imagination. By implicating us in the joke, furthermore, he has, for all our vaunted rationality and decorous self-possession, made us face the fact that we are, as nature would have us be, essentially sexual creatures, and that, indeed, the communion of hearts begins in the inclinations of the body:

YES—and then—Ye whose clay-cold heads and luke-warm hearts can argue down or mask your passions—tell me, what trespass is it that man should have them? or how his spirit stands answerable, to the father of spirits, but for his conduct under them?

If nature has so wove her web of kindness, that some threads of love and desire are entangled with the piece—must the whole web be rent in drawing them out?—Whip me such stoics, great governor of nature! said I to myself—Wherever thy providence shall place me for the trials of my virtue—whatever is my danger—whatever is my situation—let me feel the movements which rise out of it, and which belong to me as a man—and if I govern them as a good one—I will trust the issues to thy justice, for thou hast made us—and not we ourselves.

(pp. 237-8)

But if, not unlike the progress of Plato's philosopher in the *Symposium,* that of the Sentimental Traveller must begin in sexual desire, its goal is something finer and more generous. At Calais, before he 'put [himself] into motion' (p. 114), Yorick's selfishness in the affair of the monk had belied his complacent opinion of his own altruism and served to confirm the cynical materialism of the *philosophes.* By the time he has reached the Bourbonnois, however, the instrument of his sensibilities has been more finely tuned, his sexual epicureanism transmuted into the higher delights of a general and disinterested benevolence. The episode of the *fille de chambre* has a counterpart in Yorick's quite different relationship with Maria of Moulines. Sitting close by her side, his feelings are those of compassion not desire, the purity of his affection, untainted by any baser motive, providing at last the refutation of the materialists he has been seeking:

I sat down close by her; and Maria let me wipe [her tears] away as they fell with my handkerchief.—I then steep'd it in my own—and then in hers—and then in mine—and then I wip'd hers again—and as I did it, I felt such undescribable emotions within me, as I am sure could not be accounted for from any combinations of matter and motion.

I am positive I have a soul; nor can all the books with which materialists have pester'd the world ever convince me of the contrary.

(p. 271)

The famous apostrophe to Sensibility which this episode inspires is the culmination of Yorick's sentimental education and of his passage, begun in discontent in the *desobligéante,* from solipsism to a more expansive realm 'beyond' himself: 'all comes from thee, great—great SENSORIUM of the world! which vibrates, if a hair of our heads but falls upon the ground, in the remotest desert of thy creation' (p. 278). This, the apprehension of the syntax of things, is the moment of grace in Sterne's religion of the feeling heart, his own peculiar refinement of the Latitudinarian tradition which, as R. S. Crane has shown,[16] already offered its own peculiarly optimistic reconstruction of Christian assumptions about human nature. The two chapters that follow clearly imply that the sentimental pursuit of Nature in which Yorick, priest and man of feeling, has been engaged is ultimately for Sterne a religious act, having even its own readily improvised sacraments and rituals.[17] 'The Supper', though merely a meal of bread and wine shared with a peasant family, becomes a type of eucharist—'a feast of love', as Yorick calls it (p. 281). 'The Grace', the dance of thanksgiving in which Yorick beholds '*Religions* mixing' (p. 284), is in a deeper sense an expression of that gift of the Holy Spirit without which there could be no '*Work of Redemption*'[18]—the capacity for love, for feeling those 'generous joys and generous cares beyond [ourselves]' (p. 278).

The trouble with this reading of *A Sentimental Jour-*

ney is, of course, that the work—or at least the part of it that Sterne completed—does not end with the celebration of communion, but with another, and the most notorious, of his bawdy jokes. If the book is a 'comic "Pilgrim's Progress" for the man of feeling' as I believe with Gardner Stout it was in some sense meant to be—it is certainly no conventional allegory, any more than it is 'a work of reasoning'. Perhaps the genre to which it is more nearly allied is that of spiritual autobiography, in which, typically, the narrator recounts his unsteady and (since there is always the possibility of a relapse) inconclusive progress from a condition of alienation and despair to a state of grace.[19] But Sterne rejoiced in what he has Yorick call the *'Novelty of my Vehicle'* (p. 82), and he has always been an embarrassment to genericists.

What interests me about the concluding chapter of *A Sentimental Journey* is that, even in its abrupt shift of the tone from one of an exuberant piety to a sort of arch and irreverent verbal pruriency, it comprises a fitting coda and recapitulation of the motifs Sterne has been sounding throughout the work. Serving as prelude to 'The Case of Delicacy' itself is Yorick's description of the terrain over which he passes on his way toward his destination. Between the safe and friendly valleys of France and those of Italy stand those 'mountains impracticable' which impede the passage of 'the way-worn traveller', confronting him with 'the sudden turns and dangers of your roads—your rocks—your precipices—the difficulties of getting up—the horrors of getting down' (p. 285). In this book of obstacles to translations of all kinds—closed doors and drawn curtains, buttoned pockets and locked portmanteaus, the wretch's prison and the starling's cage, not to mention the differences in languages, educations, customs and habits that obstruct us 'in communicating our sensations out of our own spheres'—one of the most noticeable is the great stone that halts Yorick's sentimental journey in mid-career. Greater still than this, however, is the obstacle of mutual embarrassment, thoughts 'too delicate to communicate' (p. 288), that separates Yorick and the attractive Piedmontese whom circumstances oblige to share the only room in the inn: 'There were difficulties every way [Yorick observes]—and the obstacle of the stone in the road, which brought us into the distress, great as it appeared whilst the peasants were removing it, was but a pebble to what lay in our ways now' (pp. 287-8).

In conducting his travellers out of this impasse and leading his readers to the end of the second volume, Sterne presents a sort of comic parable of the theme of estrangement and communion which he has already elaborated. Obliged to sleep side by side in two beds narrowly separated, Yorick and his companion, like two hostile nations, enter into a 'two hours negociation' leading to 'a treaty of peace' between them (p. 288). Dictated by the requirements of decorum, the articles of the treaty are calculated to multiply the 'barriers' separating them and to prevent communication: first, the opening of the lady's bedcurtains, which, besides being of 'a flimsy transparent cotton', are 'too scanty to draw close', is secured by corking pins; second, Yorick must lie all night in his breeches; and third, he is forbidden to 'speak one single word'—except, of course, that he may say his prayers. What the proprieties of social decorum have thus put asunder, however, the irrepressible operations of the sexual imagination—Yorick's, the lady's, and most especially the reader's—will join together. Before allowing the joke to continue, Sterne pauses to make his point inescapably clear: that the real author of his hero's titillating adventures with the opposite sex has been the reader all along. How the lady and the parson contrive to get to bed in such a situation, he will 'leave to the reader to devise; protesting as I do it, that if it is not the most delicate in nature, 'tis the fault of his own imagination—against which this is not my first complaint' (pp. 289-90). Possessing the same lively imagination as the reader, neither Yorick nor the lady can sleep for thinking of each other. 'O my God! said I'—an 'ejaculation' on Yorick's part that instantly elicits the chiding of the lady, so warm that 'she weakened her barrier by it' and the bed curtains part in a shower of corking pins:

> Upon my word and honour, Madame, said I—stretching my arm out of bed, by way of asseveration—
>
> (I was going to have added, that I would not have trespass'd against the remotest idea of decorum for the world)—
>
> —But the Fille de Chambre hearing there were words between us, and fearing that hostilities would ensue in course, had crept silently out of her closet, and it being totally dark, had stolen so close to our beds, that she had got herself into the narrow passage which separated them, and had advanc'd so far up as to be in a line betwixt her mistress and me—
>
> So that when I stretch'd out my hand, I caught hold of the Fille de Chambre's

So Sterne—twice breaking off the syntax of Yorick's narrative (at the beginning and most hilariously at the end of this famous passage)—leaves him frozen forever in a gesture that may serve as the dramatic correlative of the human desire for another sort of syntactical completion, the subjective ego set apart, yet reaching out to close the gap that separates us. The final broken sentence, however, its grammatical predication never closed on the page itself, is nevertheless most certainly completed in the imagination of Sterne's reader. For, as Yorick has been at some pains to make clear in relating his sentimental journey, the imagination is our means of apprehending the syntax of things. At such moments in his fiction Sterne in his relations with his reader almost literally enacts the linguistic metaphor he had playfully applied to his hero: that 'heteroclite . . . creature in all his declensions' whose predications are formed 'according to the mood I am in, and the case—and I may add the gender too, of the person I am to govern.'

Notes

[1] See *The Providence of Wit: Aspects of Form in Augustan Literature and the Arts* (1974), esp. pp. 241-69.

[2] *The Life and Opinions of Tristram Shandy, Gentleman,* ed. Ian Watt (Boston, Mass., 1965), 495.

[3] *A Sentimental Journey through France and Italy. By Mr. Yorick,* ed. Gardner D. Stout, Jr (Berkeley and Los Angeles, 1967), 278. Subsequent citations of *A Sentimental Journey* will be to this edition. The first meaning of *syntax* given in Johnson's *Dictionary* is 'A system; a number of things joined together', which he illustrates by Glanville's phrase, 'the whole *syntax* of beings'.

[4] For an excellent discussion of the relation of style and meaning in Sterne's masterpiece, see Ian Watt's essay, 'The Comic Syntax of *Tristram Shandy*', in H. Anderson and J. S. Shea (eds), *Studies in Criticism and Aesthetics, 1660-1800: Essays in Honor of Samuel Holt Monk* (Minneapolis, 1967), 315-31.

[5] *Tristram Shandy,* ed. Watt, p. 20.

[6] See Cummings's delightful poem beginning, 'since feeling is first / who pays any attention / to the syntax of things' from *is 5* (1926); in his *Complete Poems, Volume One 1913-1935* (1968), 290.

[7] *Loc. cit.*

[8] See Stout's excellent article in *English Literary History,* xxx (1963), 395-412, which served as the basis of Section IV of the Introduction to his edition.

[9] See, for example, Rufus Putney, 'The evolutions of *A Sentimental Journey*', *Philological Quarterly,* XIX (1940), 349-69, and 'Laurence Sterne, Apostle of Laughter', in *The Age of Johnson: Essays Presented to Chauncey Brewster Tinker* (New Haven, 1949), 159-70; and Ernest N. Dilworth, *The Unsentimental Journey of Laurence Sterne* (New York, 1948), ch. V. In a similar vein, though better balanced, is John M. Stedmond's discussion of 'The Faces of Yorick' in *The Comic Art of Laurence Sterne: Convention and Innovation in 'Tristram Shandy' and 'A Sentimental Journey'* (Toronto, 1967), ch. VI.

[10] On this aspect *of Tristram Shandy,* see *The Providence of Wit,* esp. pp. 261-2.

[11] David Hume, *A Treatise of Human Nature,* II.iii.3 ('Of the influencing motives of the will'); in L. A. Selby-Bigge (ed.) (1888), 413. Though Sterne of course regretted Hume's infidelity, he admired him personally; in *A Sentimental Journey* Yorick praises him as 'a man of an excellent heart' (p. 122 and nn. 28, 31). For an attempt to establish Hume's influence on Sterne, see the article by Francis Doherty, *Essays and Studies, 1969* (1969), pp. 71-87.

[12] Watt, ed, 55.

[13] At least one of his first readers found a sexual innuendo in Sterne's account of his relationship with the Marquesina. See Stout's edn, 344.

[14] For an excellent discussion of this strategy in *Tristram Shandy,* see Robert Alter, '*Tristram Shandy* and the game of love', *American Scholar,* XXXVII (1968), 316-23. Alter, indeed, sees the *double entendre* as 'the basic rhetorical device—almost the narrative method—of *Tristram Shandy*' (p. 317).

[15] As Stout's note on this passage makes clear, 'purse' was a common slang term for the female pudendum (p. 236n.). The passage also illustrates one of Sterne's favourite rhetorical methods for assuring that the 'innocent' and sexual references of an object are held together in the reader's mind. Yorick's gaze alternates between the purse and the *fille de chambre*'s lap, suggesting—but of course never explicitly stating—that he is himself aware of the sexual innuendo. Similarly, as Yorick and the *grisset,* whose husband has just left the shop, stand silently facing each other across the narrow counter, with the gloves between them, Sterne uses the same rhetorical alternation of reference to imply what is mutually on their minds:

> The beautiful Grisset look'd sometimes at the gloves, then sideways to the window, then at the gloves— and then at me. I was not disposed to break silence— I follow'd her example: so I look'd at the gloves, then to the window, then at the gloves, and then at her—and so on alternately
>
> (p. 168)

Again the *locus classicus* of the technique occurs in *Tristram Shandy,* as Maria appears to discern a certain ambivalence about Tristram's interest in her, a perception leading her companion to exclaim, 'What a *Beast* man is' (Watt, ed, 484):

> MARIA look'd wistfully for some time at me, and then at her goat—and then at me—and then at her

goat again, and so on, alternately—

—Well, Maria, said I softly—What resemblance do you find?

[16] See 'Suggestions toward a genealogy of the "Man of Feeling" ', *ELH: A Journal of Literary History,* I (1934), 205-30.

[17] In this context consider how Yorick regards the snuff-box given him by the kindly and forgiving Franciscan: 'I guard this box, as I would the instrumental parts of my religion, to help my mind on to something better; in truth, I seldom go abroad without it; and oft and many a time have I called up by it the courteous spirit of its owner to regulate my own, in the justlings of the world' (p. 101).

[18] Sterne's phrase for *A Sentimental Journey.* With Stout I am inclined to see in it something more than Sterne's facetious wish that his final work would redeem his literary and financial fortunes. (See Stout's edn, 18 and 40 n.43.)

[19] Critics have recently demonstrated Defoe's affiliation with this tradition: see G. A. Starr, *Defoe and Spiritual Autobiography* (Princeton, 1965), and J. P. Hunter, *The Reluctant Pilgrim: Defoe's Emblematic Method and Quest for Form in 'Robinson Crusoe'* (Baltimore, 1966).

Michael Rosenblum (essay date 1978)

SOURCE: "The Sermon, the King of Bohemia, and the Art of Interpolation in *Tristram Shandy,*" in *Studies in Philology,* Vol. LXXV, No. 4, October 1978, pp. 472-91.

[*In the following essay, Rosenblum argues that there are two types of interruptions in the narrative of* Tristram Shandy: *the "digressions," which stresses the interconnectedness of things, and the "interpolations," which stress discontinuities in the accounts of events.*]

I

Our age likes to define man as a maker of fictions which he uses, legitimately or not, to make himself at home in the world. Man wants to orient himself in time and space, to discover his "whenabouts and whereabouts," and since neither one o'clock nor the boundaries of the state of New Jersey exist in nature, he invents temporal and spatial markers, such fictions as hours and days, latitude and longitude. Thus are established chronology and geography, arts which Uncle Toby tells Trim are essential to soldiers—and, we would add, essential to everyone else as well. Another way men use fictions to make themselves at home in the

world is by the construction of narratives, another kind of orienting fiction. An obvious use of narrative is to make fictions of continuity, to show the relationships between separate events. Less obviously, but no less necessary, is the use of narrative for discontinuity, making related events intelligible by disentangling them. It's often been said that *Tristram Shandy* is a narrative about the nature of narrative. More specifically, I would say that it is an examination of the sloppy way in which less self-conscious narratives connect the discontinuous and disconnect the continuous.

Whether the world is ultimately continuous or discontinuous (or, as is more likely, those categories have meaning only in relation to the human intelligence which uses them), we are often frustrated by the appearance of continuity where we want discontinuity, and vice versa. The celebrated opening of *Tristram Shandy* examines the assumption that both life and narratives are discontinuous enough for us to be able to isolate a beginning. According to received opinion, both begin at birth; but Sterne shows us what we knew all along but chose to ignore in the interests of making any start at all: that birth is only an episode in a continuum of closely related events. Before the child there is the foetus, and before that the homunculus. And since the narrator's intention is to pursue the ultimate causes for his singular nature, the theme of the opening books being "How I became Tristram Shandy," he must go farther back to such remote but crucial events as his mother's marriage contract, his great-grandmother's jointure, and his uncle's would at the Siege of Namur.

What protects us from the alarming continuity of all phenomena, the "one-damn-thing-after-anotherness" of experience, are such demarcating fictions as "the beginning." Ordinarily we don't inquire into such protective fictions too closely lest we grow dizzy, but Tristram does not fear dizziness. The good doctors of the Sorbonne innocently welcome a technological breakthrough which will allow them to baptize an infant before it emerges from the womb. But Tristram points out that baptism can be carried even a few stages backward in the life of the embryo—"*par le moyen d'une petite canulle,* and *sans faire aucun tort au père.*"[1] Tristram is as usual being mischievous; but beyond the mischief lies a real question: at what point does mere germ plasm become an immortal soul capable of salvation or damnation? Puzzles about continuity lead to an analogous question: when does a series of words become deeds? The theologian Didius conjectures about the number and kinds of errors a priest could make in his recital of the baptismal formula before his words would cease to constitute a valid baptism. The abbess of Andoüillets and Margarita break "Bouger" into syllables in the hope that halving the venial sin will dilute it into no sin at all. Where we most need a fixed boundary, we are most plagued with continuity, the imperceptible and infinite degrees by which one thing or moment shades off into another. We wish to say this is the first moment of life, or this is the exact moment of death; or (to shift to another dimension where continuity also bedevils us) this is the exact place where the wound was got.

Sterne is equally skeptical about the ease with which narratives conveniently give us the continuity we want. When we read most narratives we feel that continuity is natural; one event leads us inevitably to another. Writing and reading a narrative are like travelling along a road, a road that, we hope, is smooth and straight. And maybe even downhill, so that the lucky reader and writer will pick up momentum as they advance. The basic metaphor (a book is a kind of a road) is a favorite with Sterne; but he has no use for easily travelled roads. Only fools would want to go the shortest distance between two points in the shortest possible time. His road, as he always reminds us, has twists and turns, with even a roadblock or two. But what most slows down the traveller along *Tristram Shandy* is the discontinuity of the road. Like the road which goes from two lanes to one, from blacktop to gravel, Sterne's road is always changing—typographically, linguistically, or temporally. Sometimes it is in plain type, sometimes in italics, gothic, or no type at all (the famous mottled, blank, or blackened pages). Usually the road is in English, but sometimes it is in Latin (or alternating Latin and English), or French, or even Italian or Greek. Sometimes we are travelling in 1718, or 1748, or 1695, or any combination of those times.

In the famous engravings of lines and loops which close Volume VI, Sterne has given his map of the road. For all their twists and turns the lines representing the digressions suggest continuity rather than discontinuity, because no matter how curled and looped the squiggles are, the line itself is unbroken. "This" leads to "that" because there is no boundary between "this" and "that." The account of the birth leads to the account of the midwife which leads to Yorick's horse which leads to Yorick's character which leads to Yorick's death. (*There's* an end, at any rate.) While the digression emphasizes the connectedness of events and of the narrative which relates them, what I will call the interpolation emphasizes the discontinuities in our accounts of events. Where the digression sneaks up on us (the narrator starts talking about one thing and by degrees finds himself talking about something else), the interpolation is sharply set off against what precedes it and what follows it. The interpolation shifts to another kind of language. The main road of *Tristram Shandy* is the language of the autobiographical narrative, but in the interpolation we switch to the language and conventions of the sermon (Volume II), the legal contract (the marriage articles of Volume I), the theological deliberation (the Doctors of the Sorbonne in Volume I), the curse (Volume III), the mock-

romance (The Tale of Slawkenbergius in Volume IV or The Fragment on Whiskers in Volume V), the educational handbook (the *Tristrapaedia* of Volume V), the personal history (Trim's tale of the Fair Beguine in Volume VIII), or the travel book (Volume VII): The road then is heterogeneous, composed of mixed rather than uniform materials.

Another way of putting it is to say that the road is not entirely a new one since it incorporates previous verbal structures. In order to set down the words of *Tristram Shandy* Tristram/Sterne consulted either genuine documents or actual literary texts, or pretended to consult mock-documents and pseudo-quotations. In the first category are the record of the deliberations of the Doctors of the Sorbonne on the tenth of April in 1738, or the curse of Bishop Ernulf (Sterne's footnote attests to the authenticity of both documents). The most important of the "real" documents is the sermon preached at the cathedral church at York in July of 1750. In the second category of actual literary texts are the famous "borrowings" from Rabelais, Burton, Locke, etc. In the third category of the pretended document there are Mrs. Shandy's marriage settlement, Walter's letter to Toby, and the *Tristrapaedia*. In the fourth category one could put the pretended literary quotation like the Tale of Slawkenbergius or the Fragment Upon Whiskers.

In all four categories Sterne is incorporating printed or written (or ostensibly printed and written) texts into the main narrative. An equally important class of speech which purports to be anterior to the narrative is the speech of the live voice: either the oral recitation of a memorized text, the telling of a tale or a "true" story, or the reading aloud of a written text. Where the written text is associated with Walter, Tristram, and Yorick, the star performer of the oral mode is Trim, who recites the Ten Commandments, who tells (almost) the Story of the King of Bohemia and his Seven Castles, who recounts his own true history in the story of the Fair Beguine, and his brother Tom's in the parallel history of the Sausage-Maker's Widow. For a while it appears that Trim is to be the chosen instrument for the recital of Le Fever's story, but at the crucial moment the narrator remembers that he has left Mrs. Shandy listening at the door. Since Trim likes to hear himself read aloud, he is chosen for the most extended oral performance of all, the reading of Yorick's sermon. Also in the class of reading a written text aloud is Slop's rendition of the curse of Ernulf. A variation of this class is Walter's performance ("half-reading, half-discoursing") of his *Tristrapaedia*.

The interpolation as I am defining it, then, is an extended and contrasting insertion into the main narrative which actually follows or pretends to follow a pre-existing verbal formulation. Of course the premise of any realistic narrative is that it follows pre-existing speech, dialogue being only the record of what "someone" has said. The difference is that in the interpolation "what someone has said" is shaped or controlled even before he has said it. The tale of the King of Bohemia or the story of Le Fever is presumably more or less in Trim's head before he gets the opportunity to begin it: if not the actual words, at least the order of events and the conventions for telling a story. His performance is not unique and spontaneous, but generic and artificial since it is being shaped by "rules"—in this case the rules of story-telling. On this basis any extended speech deliberately cast into a mold by the speaker could be considered an interpolation. Thus we might include Walter's speech on the death of Bobby since it is a deliberate imitation of a classical oration, or Toby's apologetical oration—though perhaps here the conventionality is to be attributed more to the narrator than to the intentions of the speaker.

The interpolation calls our attention to the element of "preformedness," the presence of an independent construction within the larger narrative. In *The Poetics of Quotation in the European Novel,* Hermann Meyer describes the quotation as "a bit of preformed linguistic property shaped by another"[2] in the works of such writers as Rabelais, Cervantes, and Sterne. What I'm calling the interpolation shows how much of language is "preformed" in a broader sense. The interpolation, unlike the quotation, doesn't necessarily imitate a specific speech act (these words in this order), but the *form* of a speech act: the sermon, oration, curse, etc. Thus it reminds us of some simple truths about how men speak. We use one master code, the English language, which contains all the rules for syntax and the possibilities of diction from which the individual speaker must choose. Between the total system of the language and the individual utterance, there is another level, what Jakobson calls a "system of interconnected sub-codes," or what Todorov calls "the rules of discourse."[3] Speech thus is cast into forms; everything is a manner-of-speaking. Telling a story is not a natural act, a mere automatic recital of what happened: telling and listening to a story mean knowing the rules for following a story.[4] Men don't just speak the English language—they tell jokes, anecdotes, made-up stories, and "true" stories; they give orations and they give sermons.

II

Tristram Shandy is a book full of many strange things, but perhaps nothing stranger than the appearance of "On the Abuses of Conscience" in Volume II. For one thing, although it is broken into repeatedly, the sermon is given in its entirety, and thus provides one of the few times that the word "FINIS" can appear unequivocally in ***Tristram Shandy.*** More surprising is the fact that Sterne should put a sermon into the secular, not to say profane, context of ***Tristram Shandy.*** Sermons were something to be delivered in church or to be published separately or as part of a homogeneous collection. They were not (until Sterne did so) to be published within a novel. Of course Sterne has a great fondness for theological and ecclesiastical material. But in such episodes as the deliberations of the Doctors of the Sorbonne, the curse of Ernulf, the tomb of St. Maxima, and the pilgrimage of the Abbess of Andoüillets, the lore is drawn from the Church of Rome, which for Sterne puts it within the realm of literature—satire. The sermon, however, comes from Sterne's own church and pulpit, making its inclusion a breach of decorum only to be matched by the publication of the collected sermons in the name of Yorick. Both Yorick and his creator are casual about their "used" sermons; one cuts them into strips to light his pipe and the other uses them to fill out the pages of his novel.

Why should Sterne want to include a sermon in Volume II? Why *this* sermon? The questions are inevitable and, as is usually the case with Sterne, lend themselves to a wide variety of answers. It is conventional for a group of characters in early fiction to read an accidentally discovered manuscript in order to pass the time (though it is typical of Sterne to insert a sermon into the "slot" where a reader of Cervantes or Fielding might expect to find a romance such as "The Curious Impertinent" or "The Unfortunate Jilt"). We can also relate the themes of the sermon to the themes of ***Tristram Shandy*** as a whole, or we can emphasize the kinds of responses that the sermon elicits from the characters.[5] All of these answers make sense, but I think the best answer is that Sterne put in the sermon because he chose to, and that choice is totally arbitrary. To use a fancy word from modern poetics (which already exists in Uncle Toby's critical vocabulary), the appearance of the sermon at this point is contingent. Perhaps habit and critical ingenuity have diminished our capacity to feel the full force of the contingent in Sterne. What is at first surprising and inexplicable may eventually come to seem necessary and even inevitable: How could there be a ***Tristram Shandy*** *without* a complete Anglican sermon somewhere within its first hundred pages? Yet one of Sterne's feats as a novelist (or Tristram's as an autobiographer) is his ability to show how any contingency can become part of a pattern, how the apparently discontinuous can be experienced as continuous. But we can't appreciate this feat unless we see fully how arbitrary the inclusion of the sermon is.

In order to emphasize the arbitrariness Sterne gives a precise account of the train of events leading up to the discovery and reading of the sermon. The immediate starting point is the thoughts that take place in Toby's head at the moment of Slop's appearance in the Shandy parlor. Toby assumes that Slop's rapid arrival is the effect of Obadiah's summons but one need not be a student of Hume to realize that this is a faulty inference of cause and effect. The un-Humean conclusion leads to a Lockean association of ideas: "Your sudden and unexpected arrival . . . instantly brought the great *Stevinus* into my head . . ." (II, 12; p. 84). We are led from Toby's head to Stevinus, to what the book of Stevinus which Trim has fetched might contain (in the way of chariots) to a sermon stuck between the pages. The sequence, like every other one in *Tristram Shandy,* is at once totally unpredictable and yet totally intelligible. There is an explanation for everything, though it may take a while to find it. We discover that the sermon is planted between the pages of Stevinus because the author of the sermon had borrowed the volume earlier. Chance has brought them a sermon. Chance has also made it difficult for Walter to make use of Dr. Slop's professional services, but Walter sees that something can be made of the convergence of the Protestant sermon and the Catholic Slop. Because a sermon has been stuck incongruously between the pages of a military treatise, we have the even greater incongruity by which an authentic, mid-century Anglican sermon of mildly Latitudinarian persuasion can find its way into the pages of a novel.

Sterne is, I think, less interested in the contents of "On the Abuses of Conscience" than he is in the fact that it belongs to so highly conventionalized a genre. Though Sterne wouldn't have put it in these terms and would have mocked anybody who did, the question that underlies the whole episode is "What are the formal properties of the sermon as a kind of discourse?" The very first thing noted about the sermon, the means by which Trim identifies it as a sermon rather than a chariot, is a formal feature: "'tis more like a sermon, for it begins with a text of scripture, and the chapter and verse; and then goes on, not as a chariot,—but like a sermon directly" (II, 15; p. 90). Quotation from scripture is a distinctive attribute of the genre, the sermon being that kind of composition which not only takes its point of departure, but also receives its ultimate authority, from the word of God. A sermon is always governed by rules; not only rules for how the text is to be written, but also rules for the circumstances of delivery of the text. In recent years Richard Ohmann has applied J. L. Austin's influential account of "speech acts" to the study of literature. The notion that each kind of speech act has its own rules helps us to see exactly why the sermon episode is so funny. According to Austin, any "illocutionary act" must meet the following criteria if it is to be considered "felicitous": "(1) the participants are qualified and appropriate, (2) the circumstances are right, (3) the verbal component is spoken accurately and completely, (4) the speaker's beliefs and feelings are those required for performance of the act in good faith, and (5) the participants conduct themselves appropriately afterwards."[6] It is easy to see that Trim's delivery of the sermon is a kind of Art of the Fugue of infelicity. The speaker is not an ordained clergyman, nor is he the author of the text which he is reading. The site is not a church where the participants are worshiping, but the Shandy downstairs parlor where they are killing time. The speaker breaks into tears before he can complete the text and is repeatedly interrupted by his auditors. The speaker undertakes the reading not because he wishes to reform his auditors, but because he likes to hear himself read aloud. The only effect of the sermon is that Slop falls asleep, which may or may not be in accord with the rules of sermons. These various "infelicities" are of course more striking when we realize that in July of 1750 the sermon was part of a felicitous speech act: given by a clergyman in consecrated space before a body of the (one hopes, appreciative) faithful.

To break the rules for sermons is to remind us what those rules ordinarily are. Sterne's formal bias, his concern with "the message for its own sake"[7] is evident, as it is evident throughout all of *Tristram Shandy.* Sterne contrasts what the sermon usually is with what the sermon can become. It is not one, but four different messages, or four ways of conceiving the relation of sender to receiver. First, there is the original sermon as preached and published by Laurence Sterne, whose auditors and readers would understand it as a serious Anglican sermon. The second kind of message takes place within the fictional world. There it is hard to decide whether the sender is Yorick who wrote the sermon, Trim who reads it, or (more likely) Walter who encourages Trim to read it. Walter's intention is to tease his auditors and thereby divert himself. The third way of analyzing the message takes us outside of the fictional world. At this level the sender is Laurence Sterne, novelist, one of whose resources as a novelist is access to the sermons of Laurence Sterne, clergyman. The addressee is the reader, who is intended to admire the way a sermon can be used in a novel, and the way in which Sterne can brilliantly anticipate the charges of plagiarism which were to be brought against him. Yes, he says, the preacher Sterne is as much a plagiarist as Sterne the novelist. *Both* steal from Parson Yorick.

If the first message was sermon as sermon, the second sermon as a way to pass the time, the third sermon as novelist's material, the fourth is sermon as come-on or "puff." Toby says "it does not appear that the sermon is printed, or ever likely to be" (II, 17; p. 95). Toby is wrong three times over as both the contemporary and modern reader cannot help noticing. The sermon was printed in August of 1750, and "is" in print at the very moment the reader scans the text of *Tristram Shandy.* Moreover, the footnote at this point announces Sterne's further intention of making the sermon part of the collected sermons of Yorick: "That in case the character of Parson Yorick and this sample of his sermons is liked,—that there are now in the possession of the Shandy family, as many as will make a handsome volume, at the world's service . . ." (II, 19; p. 108). To return momentarily to Austin's fourth rule, one would assume that the "good faith" of the speaker requires his disinterestedness. He should not have any ulterior designs upon his auditors other than his professed one (design enough) of their salvation. Sermons surely are not to be the means by which other sermons are sold. But the sender at the fourth level is the prospective publisher of four volumes of sermons, and the addressee is the original contemporary audience, with, the publisher hopes, a fondness for sermons and an extra guinea or two to spend. With this stroke we are moved from the realm of the sermon or the novel into the real outer world in which the reader lives, breathes, and spends his money.

I have been arguing that the comedy of the sermon episode depends upon Sterne's playing with the rules of discourse. To understand a sermon is to know its particular manner of speaking. This means knowing how its metaphors are to be taken and how it is related to other kinds of speaking such as historical narration. When the sermon evokes the "piteous groan" of a victim of the Inquisition and asks the congregation to "see the melancholy wretch who utter'd it," Trim thinks the wretch is his brother Tom. Trim, Slop, and Walter argue about the proper interpretation of the passage: "I tell thee, *Trim,* again, quoth my father, 'tis not an historical account,—'tis a description.—'Tis only a description, honest man, quoth *Slop,* there's not a word of truth in it.—That's another story, replied my father" (II, 17; p. 105). In taking the words literally as a historical account Trim reveals his ignorance of the way figurative language can operate in a sermon. As Walter tells him, the passage is a description, or more precisely, the figure *hypotyposis.*[8] It's not Tom but a construct of language, an allegorical abstraction whose cellmates are Mercy, Religion, and Justice.

Toby and Mrs. Shandy have the same kind of difficulty in recognizing a special manner-of-speaking when they listen to Walter's response to the news of Bobby's death. His speech is a neo-classical form of the speech of consolation. Just as the sermon is an intertwining of the words of the sermonizer with the pre-existing words of the prophets, apostles, and God, the neo-classical orator mingles his own situation and words with his classical source, producing a conventional double-speaking with which the classically educated gentleman of the eighteenth century would be familiar. Needless to say, this is a code that is unavailable to either Toby or Mrs. Shandy. "Returning out of *Asia,* when I sailed from *Aegina* towards *Megara, (when can this have been? thought my uncle Toby) . . .*" (V, 8; p. 267). The calendar established by Walter's mode of discourse points to the time when Servius Sulpicius took the trip to which the words refer, the time shortly thereafter when he wrote his letter of consolation to Cicero, the time when Cicero incorporated it into his *Epistolae ad Familiares,* the "present" time (1719) when Walter speaks those words, and 1761 when Tristram writes those words. But mostly "no year of our

Lord" as Walter tells the incredulous Toby. Mrs. Shandy has the same trouble with Walter-as-Socrates' enumeration of "three desolate children."

This same question—how are our coordinates for referring to time and space changed by different kinds of discourse[9]—is raised most explicitly by Trim's attempt to tell the tale of the King of Bohemia. If the events of a story can be said to happen (and that's just what a story seems to assert), then they must be "situatable" in time and in space. Trim and Toby assume that language works in the same way as it does elsewhere. Toby insists that Trim tell exactly when the story takes place, and Trim in his innocence chooses the year 1712. Toby's objection is sound: to have even one giant, as Trim modestly proposes, means that it must be set "some seven or eight hundred years out of harms way" where the teller is safe from the niggling demands of formal realism. But it's not so clear that Toby is right to assume that the date implies all of the historical events of the year. Does 1712 mean that, among other things, the narrative is alluding to the secret agreement by which the Duke of Ormand, commander of the British forces, was prevented from engaging in battle with the French?

And similarly, when Trim says Bohemia, does that automatically mean, whether or not he specifies it, that we are to infer "landlocked" as one of its properties?[10] The means by which Bohemia's geography becomes a part of Trim's tale and finally terminates it illustrates Sterne's formal interest in the rules that regulate telling and listening to a story. Trim is unable to get on with his tale because he and Toby get bogged down in the discussion of the importance of chronology and geography. On his fifth attempt to tell the tale Trim introduces the epithet "unfortunate" to describe the King of Bohemia. I assume that the king was not unfortunate in the original version of the story; he becomes so only the fifth time around, when the frustration of the teller of the tale is attributed to the subject of the tale. When Toby inquires "why unfortunate?" Trim is much too polite to tell the real reason, and so he must invent a reason. Given Bohemia, he makes the inference that the king lives in a landlocked country by the analogous process by which 1712 begets the Duke of Ormand's disgrace. From there it is only a small jump to invent the attribute which will explain "unfortunate": the king's love of navigation. What is "outside" the tale, the map of Bohemia and Trim's frustration as a storyteller, changes the tale—another illustration of the general rule in **Tristram Shandy** that no system or secondary world (whether it be sermon, tale, or fortification) is uncontaminated by what is outside it.

Toby and Trim are naive in their understanding of how stories work, just as they are naive in their response to the sermon. But at the same time their misunderstandings do reflect ambiguities in the codes themselves. In their own fashion Toby and Trim are puzzling over real questions. We can smile along with Walter over Trim's difficulties with the "naked wretch," or his intention of handing over the crown that Toby will give him to the women and children who are the victims of fanaticism. Although the fanatic and his victims are hypothetical, the sermon is also asserting that there are real people for whom they stand. Within the framework of the sermon real claims are being made about alleged Catholic cruelty in battle and the suffering caused by the Inquisition. In other words, Tom is not on an entirely different plane of reality than the naked wretch of the sermon. Trim has difficulty with the sermon because at this point it is speaking a complex combination of the figurative and literal, the hypothetical and the historical.

Toby and Trim also raise real questions about the construction of stories: To what extent are stories self-enclosed constructions creating their own time, space, and causality, and to what extent are they bound to the pre-existing chronology, geography, and the order of events of the "real" world? The writer can take the map, the almanac of facts, and the calendar of events that constitute history as his necessity, or else he can see them for what they are—contingent because they could be otherwise. And because they could be otherwise, as an artist he is free to imagine them otherwise. Toby objects when Trim confuses the area of his choice with the area in which he is constrained, when he tries to pass off what is necessary as his own free choice. Toby approves of Trim's saying that "the King of Bohemia with his queen might have walk'd out, or let it alone;—'twas a matter of contingency, which might happen, or not, just as chance ordered it" (VIII, 19; p. 437). But when Trim says that there "happening throughout the whole kingdom of Bohemia, to be no sea-port town whatever," Toby argues that Trim is confusing the contingent and the necessary. Bohemia's seacoast is not subject to the control of any narrator. For the pious Toby the primary world is not contingent but providential, the configuration of Europe being such that the inhabitants of Germany do not drown.

For the modern novelist the realm of the contingent is enlarged. It is unlikely to Toby that the seas could overflow into the lowlands of Europe, but Roquentin in *Nausea* can conceive of the seat of a tram car turning into a donkey's paw. For Roquentin the only necessity is that which he creates within his own narrative. A modern writer is likely to claim more for his sovereignty as a storyteller, insisting upon his right to "re-invent the world," as when the author of *Ada* bends and warps our spatial and temporal coordinates, grafts the twentieth century onto the nineteenth, and playfully crossbreeds the continents. Such wheeling and dealing with "reality" reflects a willingness to assert the autonomy of narratives.[11] A less extreme formulation, more in accord with the conservative spirit of Toby's

poetics, is that the novelist works within a dialectic of sovereignty and constraint. Narratives which are totally free or totally bound are uninteresting. Trim discovers that even with the fairy-tale-like King of Bohemia he is still obliged to follow rules.[12]

III

Telling a story or giving a sermon is a very special kind of speaking, and so is writing an extended narrative like *Tristram Shandy*. which is made up of many manners of speaking. In fashioning so piebald a work Sterne is demonstrating something of the actual linguistic discontinuity of real life in which we shift automatically from one code to another, making our continuities out of patched-together discontinuities. By reminding us of how we are always shifting our coordinates, the interpolation defamiliarizes something which we might otherwise take for granted. In this sense the interpolation is the instrument of Sterne's realism, realism being defined here (following the Russian Formalists' definition of art) as the means by which we are forced out of our customary orientation, those mental habits which familiarize and so cheat us out of the world.

I would assume that it is the goal of realism to enlarge our sense of what can be and therefore what ought to be put into novels: the background noise, the competing messages, the remote circumstances which a tidier narrative would reject as irrelevant. Chekhov showed that people do not speak as consecutively or as intelligibly as the conventions for representing speech on the stage suggest. In a similar way the interpolation enlarges our sense of how men use words. The real subject of *Tristram Shandy* (and perhaps of all novels—and to that extent Shlovsky's famous claim about its typicality is true) is how men use words. Certainly the main activity of the Shandy family is almost entirely verbal: they talk, read, write, and listen.[13] William Gass has argued that the true source of the storyteller's verisimilitude is not the imitation of nature, but the attempt to follow "as closely as he can our simplest, most direct and and unaffected forms of daily talk."[14] The mysterious "reality" of Walter and Toby is bound up with Sterne's representation of their speech, but precisely because Sterne is such a great realist he does not confine himself to the simplest and most direct forms of speech. Instead Sterne gives us the highly formalized speech, the full range of oral and written messages which Walter and Toby send and receive. Realism in the eighteenth-century novel means quite simply the representation of such contemporary forms as the sermon, the guide-book, and the neo-classical oration, in the same way that realism in the modern novel would mean representing such characteristic modern forms as the commercial or the telephone conversation. At the same time verbal reality in *Tristram Shandy* is made up of such unlikely performances as the recitation of the Ten Commandments, a paragraph from Rabelais, and a twelfth-century formula for ex-communication.

I would also assume that it is the goal of realism to demonstrate the multiplicity of possible viewpoints that may be taken towards the world.[15] A discontinuous narrative, a motley narrative stitched together out of different ways of speaking (and stitched together with black thread so that all the seams will show) acknowledges that each account has its own way of making sense of the world. Sterne knows that there are many ways of speaking, none of them privileged or uniquely authoritative. A single way of speaking, like a single hobby-horse, is reductive because we are confined to only one way of interpreting the world. But the contemplation of more than one hobby horse or the bringing together of many ways of speaking in successive interpolations is expansive and liberating. For Sterne the established ways of handling historical or autobiographic narrative are not the only ways. He is always aware of making choices, adopting one convention rather than another. To write is to obey certain rules, and if we are confined to one set of rules we may forget that there are others, or that we are working within a system which is neither natural nor inevitable. As the philosopher Nelson Goodman puts it, "the world is as many ways as it can be truly described, seen, pictured etc. and . . . there is no such thing as *the* way the world is."[16] Lest we forget, the interpolation forces us to shift, immersing us successively in the account of the world given by legal contracts, literary quotations, letters, mock-romances, sermons, travel-guides, educational handbooks, and imitations of oral narration.

Finally I would argue that the interpolation educates the reader in an attitude towards experience which can be described as Shandian. Things put themselves in our path and we must allow them to testify, to yield full measure of instruction, wit, and mystery. When the train of association in Toby's head leads to Stevinus, Walter is willing to allow the sailing chariot to become the new center of interest, and when the chariot leads to the sermon, he is willing to listen to that too. There is the great impending event, the birth of Tristram abovestairs, but Walter is downstairs, and he need not confine his interest to the birth any more than Tristram as narrator need focus on the "main" event. Neither Walter nor Tristram asks how the sermon is relevant, or asks it to justify itself in relation to something else. Events need not be subordinated to one another because each event is potentially its own center. Yorick has borrowed Stevinus in the first place because he is "inquisitive after all kinds of knowledge." Walter welcomes the reading of the sermon because he has such a "strong propensity . . . to look into things which cross my way, by such strange fatalities as these . . ." (II, 17; p. 91). Where the father likes to see where circumstances will lead, the son likes to trace events back

to their origins: "My way is ever to point to the curious, different tracts of investigation, to come at the first springs of the events I tell" (I, 21; p. 50). This kind of inquisitiveness is the first cause of everything in **Tristram Shandy,** just as everything in the *Iliad* follows from the wrath of Achilles. Walter, Yorick, and Tristram are admirers of the gratuitous act and connoisseurs of the contingent. Chance is for them and for the reader the opportunity to break out of the closed circle of experience. Chance offers one of the few pleasures that Walter and Tristram can consistently enjoy, the delight in seeing the way in which the purely contingent yields a pattern.

I have quoted the maxim that art gives us the world back again by making it strange. For somebody like Walter the world is already made strange: "The truth was, his road lay so very far one side, from that wherein most men travelled—that every object before him presented a face and section of itself to his eye, altogether different from the plan and elevation of it seen by the rest of mankind" (V, 26; p. 289). Sterne has made sure that we make our way along his "road" in the same way Walter makes his way along his, circumspectly, deliberately, and with surprise. To invoke the Formalists once more, we are made to feel the stones of the road. Our speed depends upon our familiarity with the road and the kinds of guesses which we think we can safely make as to what lies ahead. The interpolations, among other aspects of the book, make it difficult for us to feel confident about what lies ahead, since the road is always changing. Because the road is always new, we are convinced that it is worthy of our closest attention.

Notes

[1] I, 21; p. 48. All references are to Ian Watt's edition of *Tristram Shandy* (New York, 1965).

[2] Hermann Meyer, *The Poetics of Quotation in the European Novel* (Princeton, 1968), p. 6. See also Mixail Baxtin's observation that "to the prose writer the world is full of other people's speech acts; he orients himself among these, and he must have a keen ear for perceiving and identifying their peculiarities." "Discourse Typology in Prose," in *Readings in Russian Poetics: Formalist and Structuralist Views* (Cambridge, Mass., 1971), ed. Ladislav Matejka and Krystyna Pomorska, p. 194.

[3] See Roman Jakobson, "Linguistics and Poetics," in *Style in Language,* ed. Thomas Sebeok (Cambridge, Mass., 1966), and Tzvetan Todorov's "Structuralism and Literature," in *Approaches to Poetics,* ed. Seymour Chatman (New York, 1973).

[4] See W. B. Gallie, "What Is a Story," in *Philosophy and the Historical Understanding* (New York, 1964).

[5] In a fine and persuasive account of the sermon in the context of the work as a whole, J. Paul Hunter argues that Sterne's emphasis on the response to the sermon "demonstrates what will not, and what will, move the minds of men." See "Response as Reformation: *Tristram Shandy* and the Art of Interruption," *Novel,* IV (1971), 132-46. In *The Comic Art of Laurence Sterne* (Toronto, 1967), J. M. Stedmond suggests that the sermon "seems to represent the closest thing to a straightforward 'norm' against which to gauge the comedy of the first two volumes" (p. 84). For a treatment of the sermon as theology, see Arthur H. Cash, "The Sermon in *Tristram Shandy,*" *ELH,* XXI (1964), 395-417.

[6] Richard Ohmann, "Literature as Act," in Chatman, p. 83.

[7] Jakobson, p. 356.

[8] William J. Farrell, "Nature versus Art as a Comic Pattern in *Tristram Shandy,*" *ELH,* XXX (1963), 16-35.

[9] In their own unsophisticated way Trim and Toby have stumbled upon the theoretical issues pursued more systematically in Käte Hamburger's *Die Logik der Dichtung* (Stuttgart, 1957).

[10] I don't think we have to worry whether or not Trim had read *Winter's Tale,* but it would be interesting to know at what point the "seacoast in Bohemia" had become notorious as the spatial counterpart of what would be an anachronism in time.

[11] In an interview John Barth argues that "if you are a novelist of a certain type of temperament, then what you really want to do is re-invent the world. . . . a certain kind of sensibility can be made very uncomfortable by the recognition of the *arbitrariness* of physical facts and the inability to accept their *finality.* Take France, for example: France is shaped like a tea pot, and Italy is shaped like a boot. Well, okay. But the idea that that's the only way it's ever going to be, that they'll never be shaped like anything else—that can get to you after a while." See *The Contemporary Writer,* eds. L. S. Dembo and Cyrena N. Pondrom (Madison, 1972) p. 23.

[12] In fact the fairy tale, of which we require the least fidelity to the outside world, is conversely the most bound by its very distinctive conventions. Stories are always constrained, either by the demands of realism, by the conventions of particular genres, or by the fact that a story as it unfolds constitutes a system. Once certain choices have been made, other possibilities are excluded.

[13] Perhaps this is because the domain of language is safer. The "doing" which is an alternative to "saying" is always suspect. "And pray what was your father saying?" asks the stupid reader at the end of the first chapter (Walter is clearly "doing," not "saying"). Toby thinks that at the end of the tale of the Beguine Trim "made a speech." See also David Grossvogel's emphasis on the importance of live speech in Sterne in *Limits of the Novel* (New York, 1972), p. 32.

[14] William Gass, *Fiction and the Figures of Life* (New York, 1972), p. 32.

[15] The following pronouncements on realism are offered in the knowledge that no generalizations about the goal of realism are likely to win universal consent. For a recent, able defense of what seems to me a very traditional view of realism in the novel, see J. P. Stern, *On Realism* (London, 1973).

[16] Nelson Goodman, *Language of Art* (Indianapolis, 1968), p. 6.

Arnold Weinstein (essay date 1981)

SOURCE: "New Worlds and Old Worlds: *Tristram Shandy,*" in his *Fictions of the Self: 1550-1800,* Princeton University Press, 1981, pp. 214-32.

[*In the following excerpt, Weinstein demonstrates the originality of* Tristram Shandy *for its time, pointing out that the novel focuses on wordplay and innuendo rather than on plot and narrative coherence.*]

. . . I would submit that **Tristram Shandy,** in a manner that resembles Joyce's *Ulysses,* is built on and out of the fragments of crumbling traditions and institutions. In his fine essay on the tradition of learned wit in **Tristram,** D. W. Jefferson's essential conclusion is that "the theme of **Tristram Shandy** may be seen in terms of a comic clash between the world of learning and that of human affairs."[1] Comic though that clash is, I think that Sterne is depicting a cleavage, a gulf between the profuse materials of scholastic authority and learning which appear on every page of **Tristram,** and not only in the words of Walter Shandy, but in Toby and Tristram as well, the constant web of erudite allusion, on the one hand, and the already modern sense, on the other, that humans are adrift, unmoored, cut loose from these systems that used to give structure to life. The Past is ubiquitous in **Tristram;** Greek, Latin, Dutch, and French sources are cited, and often cited at considerable length, for virtually every event in the novel, but Sterne is having his pleasure with them, turning them into puns, exploding them into fantasy. Let us consider the following learned discussion:

> Gastripheres, for example, continued Kysarcius,
> baptizes a child of John Stradling's *in Gomine gatris*

&c. &c. instead of *in Nomine patris,* &c.—Is this a baptism? No,—say the ablest canonists; inasmuch as the radix of each word is hereby torn up, and the sense and meaning of them removed and changed quite to another object; for *Gomine* does not signify a name, nor *gatris* a father.—what do they signify? said my uncle Toby.—Nothing at all—quoth Yorick.—Ergo, such a baptism is null, said Kysarcius. (p. 247)[2]

Beyond the wordplay the thing itself, the ceremony and significance of baptism, does not remain intact, and that is because wordplay is inevitably corrosive. Corrosive but also extensive, projective: Sterne's narrative strategy is to make a revolutionary new purchase on language, discrediting old realms but spawning and then occupying new ones. I do not want to overstate my case: it is well known that the medieval Christian tradition was resilient enough to house and tolerate a considerable amount of parody and self-satire, but wordplay, in Sterne, is already on the way to becoming creative rather than satirical, and, as such, it will be an indispensable tool for Tristram in narrating his life and opinions; it will also be a tool for Laurence Sterne to employ in completing a book and in expressing a vision in a world where nothing can be completed and everything has already been said.

Yorick's sermon on conscience, happily inserted among the pages of Stevinus, nicely states the already modernist problems of authority, judgment, and orientation which beset Sterne. Conscience is defined as "the knowledge which the mind has within herself" (p. 95), and is therefore quite close to the notion of consciousness; but Sterne is aware that conscience is unreliable, that, in all too many cases, "this domestic God *was either talking, or pursuing, or was in a journey, or peradventure he slept and could not be awoke*" (p. 97). Conscience is not to be trusted alone; it needs to be abetted by a law, a firmer one than jurisprudence offers, one setting forth the principles of morality and religion. But those principles themselves, augustly quoted from the Bible, the Sorbonne, and other repositories of authority, are no longer sound, function primarily as touchstones to punning and satire. We need laws, but they are crumbling, we are reduced to conscience and consciousness, but they are fallible. This was Sterne's situation, much as it is our own; it was his precise literary situation as well, since he was clearly not to continue in the path of Defoe, Richardson, or Fielding, and his satire would be unlike that of Pope or Swift. His solution, spiritually and literarily, is to do his own thing: "to write a book is for all the world like humming a song—be but in tune with yourself, madam, 'tis no matter how high or how low you take it" (p. 238). This is no easy matter, for he must do battle with the critics constantly, those critics who judge all by rules and laws, and he must also find his own thing. For the novelist, the Old World is an aesthetic as well

as a cultural issue. We have seen the role that tradition and convention play in *Manon Lescaut, Werther* and *Clarissa;* yet, Prévost, Goethe, and Richardson were content to use traditional forms of mimesis in their quarrel with tradition. Sterne goes a quantum leap further: he revolutionizes the form of the novel, finding sustenance everywhere along the way: the innocuous givens of time, place, and sequence, comfortably relied on by mimetic fictioneers, are jostled and overturned by Sterne, yielding new vistas, adumbrating new realms. The hitherto transparent *conventions* of storytelling are brilliantly foregrounded by Sterne, energized and fictionalized in themselves: the words which used docilely to tell the novelist's story now tell their own. Sterne, beset by impotency at every turn, is to discover the potency of language: The crumbling Old World is to be, not overcome (as Des Grieux, Werther and Clarissa were to learn), but shaped anew.

How can a single writer reverse the Humpty Dumpty story and put the world back together again? Sterne's strategy is to stake out a new area where wholeness, authority and accomplishment will again be possible. It comes in the guise of a Gonopsychanthropologia, a depiction of the origin of the human soul. How does the self come to be what it is? Sterne gives us, comically but not altogether comically, four controlling factors: (1) the disposition of the animal spirits at conception, (2) the safety of the cerebellum at birth, (3) the wholeness and length of the nose, and if a male, of another organ as well, and (4) the name. And, on these fronts, as we all know, Tristram Shandy, hero of a genuine *Bildungsroman ab ovo,* is a cosmic loser: animal spirits dispersed, cerebellum smashed, nose crushed, other organ almost removed, and Tristram for a name. Nineteenth-century positivism produced fictions that would account for a person's character by his "background," his parents, his socio-economic conditions, heredity, and environment. Sterne is both funnier, and surely as close to the mark, in his insistence (rather, Walter Shandy's insistence) that the real formative stage of the self occurs between conception and birth. Whatever the scientific validity of Walter's position, Tristram emerges—unlike the richly endowed Des Grieux, Werther, and Clarissa—as a character cursed by Fortune and marked by the conditions of his birth. How can a success story be possible?

Most readers and critics assume that Sterne was not seriously concerned with Gonopsychanthropologia, but I would suggest that he is vitally interested in offsetting the rigorous determinism inherent in Walter Shandy's view, and that he is showing you, all the time, just how he and you can conquer such determinism. We are well into the fourth volume of ***Tristram Shandy*** before we even get to all the details of Tristram's birth: Sterne has manifestly been up to other things, in fact just about everything including the kitchen sink: anecdotes about Yorick, a Sorbonne document on baptizing foetuses before birth, Uncle Toby's wound and his subsequent hobbyhorse, Ernulphus' curse, the author's preface (midway in the 3rd volume), considerable lore about sieges and fortifications, the immortal tale of Hafen Slawkenbergius, even the story of Licetus "born a foetus, of no more than five inches and a half in length, yet he grew to that astonishing height in literature, as to write a book with a title as long as himself—the learned know I mean his Gonopsychanthropologia, upon the origin of the human soul" (p. 212). Tristram has taken a long time in coming out, but, once there and permanently disadvantaged, Walter is so struck down as to wish his child had been Licetus instead, the five and one-half-inch foetus. Five and one-half inches is not very big. Things are low as we close Chapter 19 of Vol. 4. Chapter 20 goes as follows:

> What a rate have I gone on at, curvetting and frisking it away, two up and two down for four volumes together, without looking once behind, or even on one side of me, to see whom I trod upon!—I'll tread upon no one,—quoth I to myself when I mounted—I'll take a good rattling gallop; but I'll not hurt the poorest jack-ass upon the road—So off I set—up one lane—down another, through this turnpike—over that, as if the arch-jockeys had got behind me.

> Now ride at this rate with what good intention and resolution you may,—'tis a million to one you'll do some one a mischief, if not yourself—He's flung—he's off—he's lost his seat—he's down—he'll break his neck—see!—if he has not galloped full amongst the scaffolding of the undertaking criticks!—he'll knock his brains out against some of their posts—he's bounced out!—look—he's now riding like a madcap full tilt through a whole crowd of painters, fiddlers, poets, biographers, physicians, lawyers, logicians, players, schoolmen, churchmen, statesmen, soldiers, casuists, connoisseurs, prelates, popes, and engineers—Don't fear, said I—I'll not hurt the poorest jack-ass upon the king's high-way—But your horse throws dirt; see you've splash'd a bishop—I hope in God, 'twas only *Ernulphus,* said I—But you have squirted full in the faces of Mess. *Le Moyne, De Romigny,* and *De Marcilly,* doctors of the *Sorbonne*—That was last year, replied I—But you have trod this moment upon a king.—Kings have bad times on't, said I, to be trod upon by such people as me.

> —You have done it, replied my accuser.

> I deny it, quoth I, and so have got off, and here am I standing with my bridle in one hand, and with my cap in the other, to tell my story—And what is it? You shall hear in the next chapter. (p. 223)

No five and one-half-inch foetus here, no problem with animal spirits, cerebellum, noses, and other organs, not even names. Instead we have a prancing, galloping

author, leaving Tristram's birth because he is free to, taking apart critics because they deserve it and he can do it, bearing no malice but nonetheless splashing Sorbonne bishops and trodding on the king. Here we witness a celebration of strength, of potency, of authority, of unbridled freedom; it is a peculiar sort of freedom, namely the kind that Sterne has been demonstrating and even celebrating since the outset: the freedom of imagination and language which is unshackled, unbound by the petty narrative business at hand of getting Tristram born, untrapped by the determinist prison that Walter thinks his son has been born into. Among the traditions which Tristram is free to transgress is the linear fiction of fiction, the notion that things must proceed 1, 2, 3 in a life or in a story: "Could a historiographer drive on his history, as a muleteer drives on his mule,—straight forward;—for instance, from Rome all the way to Loretto, without ever once turning his head aside either to the right hand or to the left,—he might venture to foretell you to an hour when he should get to his journey's end;—but the thing is, morally speaking, impossible" (p. 28). Our consciousness of life is multiple and simultaneous, and the power of writing can overcome event and sequence through digression and metaphor, for surely you have recognized that the man on the prancing horse, like Wallace Stevens' capable young rider, is a metaphor of the imagination. We are corporally limited and determined, but we can and do live in and through metaphoric extensions of reality. The mind is its own place, and the hazards of birth may form it, but they cannot control it.

The mind is its own place, and it—in keeping with the dominant metaphor of the novel—is under siege. Sterne's characters occupy their minds much like hermits, rarely going forth to see what it is like outside. Humans, according to Sterne, are without the advantages of some kind of Momus' glass:

> . . . had such a glass been there set up, nothing more would have been wanting, in order to have taken a man's character, but to have taken a chair and gone softly, as you would to a dioptrical beehive, and look'd in,—viewed the soul stark naked;—observed all her motions,—her machinations;—traced all her maggots from their first engendering to their crawling forth;—watched her loose in her frisks, her gambols, her capricios; and after some notice of her more solemn deportment, consequent on such frisks, &c.—then taken your pen and ink and set down nothing but what you had seen, and could have sworn to:—But this is an advantage not to be had by the biographer in this planet. . . . (pp. 55-56)

And he later adds, "Our minds shine not through the body, but are wrapt up here in a dark covering of uncrystalized flesh and blood; so that if we would come to the specifick characters of them, we must go some other way to work" (p. 56). The muleteer may take the body straight from Rome to Loretto, but Sterne is recording a different trip. The route that he chooses toward the inner life of characters is, of course, the *hobbyhorse,* the ruling passions and fantasies of individuals which establish their perceptual grid. Uncle Toby's is probably the most developed, and Sterne delights in exchanges such as the following, as Doctor Slop is holding forth on the advancement of medical technology: "Sir, it would astonish you to know what Improvements we have made on late years in all branches of obstetrical knowledge, but particularly in that one single point of the safe and expeditious extraction of the foetus,—which has received such lights, that, for my part, (holding up his hands) I declare I wonder how the world has—I wish, quoth my uncle Toby, you had seen what prodigious armies we had in Flanders" (pp. 108-109). This is more than a comic principle; it is also a recognition that the sounds and sights of the world are refracted, when human beings perceive them, into the preconceived frames inside of us.

"At best," as Benjamin Lehman says, Sterne's characters "understand one another only by fits and starts. A pervasive loneliness is at the core of each, as in life itself."[3] Blindness looms large in the novel of failed relationships, but there is nothing tragic in Sterne's book, not only because he renders the hobbyhorsical blinders as palpably laughable (especially in courtship between Toby and Widow Wadman), but also because the locked-up selves can still communicate through feeling. Sterne's cult of sensibility is the other side of this solipsism. Certain set pieces, such as the tearful death of Yorick at the outset, Uncle Toby's speech to the fly, the episode with the dying Le Fever—these scenes, dated as they may appear today, indicate that feeling and sentiment go where words cannot. This dimension of Sterne was prized by his contemporaries, but it is the very oddity of his text, an oddity which Doctor Johnson augured would not wear well, that constitutes its major appeal today. I would suggest that Sterne's narrative tricks are in collusion with his sentimentalism. Above all, as if to *enact* the bond of comradeship and tenderness depicted among characters, the book seeks a very special relationship with its reader. Early on, Sterne, much like Fielding in *Joseph Andrews,* addresses the reader as a fellow-traveller and expresses hope that their acquaintanceship will grow into familiarity and finally friendship. But, unlike in Fielding, to be Tristram's friend is to meet him at least halfway, to make a very different kind of voyage, to keep one's own imagination as active as the author's is, even to project that imagination.

The reader is expected to fill in the asterisks, pursue the innuendo, double the double-entendre. This, often enough, works: the reader does the sexual imagining at hand, can feel the hypnotic power of the Widow Wadman's eyes or the sympathy between Walter and Toby;

but, very often, this kind of response to one of the characters cannot be forthcoming, because Sterne is busy doing tricks, prancing or digressing, showing us his authorial sleight-of-hand tricks. Tristram's digressions are also, as he shrewdly says, progressive, and a certain amount of interruption and ellipsis is good for a man, whets his appetite and keeps him on his toes. Digressions are, we learn, "the sunshine—they are the life, the soul of reading" (p. 55). But black pages, graphs, left-out chapters, mind-boggling mix of chronology: the reader would have to be a kind of emotional plastic man to sentimentally move into all these items. Why all these pyrotechnics? Consider the following:

> I told the Christian reader—I say Christian—hoping he is one—and if he is not, I am sorry for it—and only beg he will consider the matter with himself, and not lay the blame entirely upon this book—

> I told him, Sir—or in good truth, when a man is telling a story in the strange way I do mine, he is obliged continually to be going backwards and forwards to keep all tight together in the reader's fancy—which, for my own part, if I did not take heed to do more than at first, there is so much unfixed and equivocal matter starting up, with so many breaks and gaps in it,—and so little service do the stars afford, which, nevertheless, I hang up in some of the darkest passages, knowing that the world is apt to lose its way, with all the lights the sun itself at noon day can give it—and now, you see, I am lost myself! (p. 351)

Going through *Tristram Shandy* is a strange voyage, a continuous search for that "northwest passage to the intellectual world." The reader must consent to lose himself in Sterne's world if he is to grasp Sterne's meaning. Now there is a new kind of vicious taste, we are told, "of reading straight forwards, more in quest of the adventures, than of deep erudition and knowledge which a book of this cast, if read over as it should be, would infallibly impart with them" (p. 43). Let us take Sterne seriously here, not just when he speaks of erudition and of knowledge, but especially when he admonishes us not to read straight forwards, but to read over. To read for adventures is to seek out a certain thread of plot, whether it be Tristram's birth or Toby's amours; what is *not* connected with the birth or the amours is digressive, perhaps distracting; it has almost a different ontological status, for it is the non-story extra-language. If a text has only a few asides or rhetorical chapter headings, we can accept such a story non-story duality: but *Tristram Shandy* rubs our noses into it, flaunts the unimportance of its stories, wraps any and all linear plots into bowknots, or better still, slipknots. In short, Sterne reminds us over and over that the reality of his text is the reality, *not* of any tidy particularized story, but of language itself. Sterne revels in mixing levels of plot and time, in leaving characters frozen at keyholes and on beds, because they are all, in the final analysis, red herrings, and the only discourse that counts is that of the narrating Tristram. Tristram tells us: "All my heroes are off my hands;— 'tis the first time I have had a moment to spare,—and I'll make use of it, and write my preface" (p. 142), because his heroes and his preface have equal rights in his project. There are no second-class words. As readers and critics, we underline what seems important and relegate the rest to some enormous murky room where "details" are stored. Sterne's belief in language is so democratic that it verges on anarchy. The words themselves are real and potent, capable of instant creation, even spontaneous combustion; a chapter closes with Toby and Walter shaking their heads together for different reasons: the next chapter sovereignly begins: "Holla!—you chairman—here's sixpence—do step into that bookseller's shop, and call me a day-tall critick. I am very willing to give any one of 'em a crown to help me with his tackling, to get my father and my uncle Toby off the stairs, and to put them to bed" (p. 214).

Language spawns meanings; regardless of the grammatical tenses, it creates presence; and it makes, in the mind of the reader, its own place. The prancing author who spattered bishops and trod upon the king happened only in language, and, of course, language is the New World of **Tristram Shandy.** This book generates new lands, magnificent places such as the Promontory of Noses. Where is the Promontory of Noses? When asked by Widow Wadman where he received his wound, Toby replied, "You shall see the very place, Madam" (p. 479). That place is neither Toby's groin, nor the particular trench near the citadel of Namur, but the realm of the mind. It is the culminating *double entendre* of the novel, indeed the culminating figure of my entire study: language creates a world, a place to live. The analogical, metaphorical, associational potency of language enables a vivid new lease on life, for it authorizes tangential realms and punning paths along which the hobbyhorsical mind can move. The syntagmatic course is not thereby halted; rather, it bifurcates, sets off in new directions, narrativizes vertically, along the axis of metaphor, rather than proceeding apace, like a muleteer. Sterne powerfully demonstrates the appeal of such new roads, showing them to be much more than the aberrant mistakes of lunatic characters, but more essentially a treasure-house of imaginative ventures. The Promontory of Noses points already to Rimbaud's "Promontoire," to dream-scapes and figural realms where exploration and activity may genuinely take place. Widow Wadman's *siege* on Uncle Toby, mirroring and imaging Toby's obsession with other kinds of sieges, brilliantly displays the potential of such an analogical, even a *comparative,* structure: Sterne marvelously inverts his amatory and his military discourses, creating high comedy and laying bare the essential sameness of love and war.

But that is not all. The comic framework and the stylistic foregrounding of Sterne's performance is untroubling: we laugh at the delightful mixture of languages and strategies, for the mimetic charge of Sterne's language, the strangely manipulable world of *signifiés,* is never dominant: war and love are *not* the same, but the links between them take priority in Sterne's text, and the endless digressions come to seem legitimate.

Let us, however, do some linking and associating and digressing on our own, by returning (mentally) to a vastly different kind of *siege,* notably Lovelace's siege of Clarissa in Richardson's novel. Richardson is dreadfully mimetic, and his book is one precisely of imprisonment, of lack of room: for Clarissa—and for Richardson—there can be no analogical reprieve, no metaphorical exit, no digression wherein the verbal medium might aggrandize and open up the material. We are talking about more than comedy and tragedy here; it is more specifically a matter of language's projective and dodging power and the kinds of stories that can be told. What Diderot does to Prévost, Sterne does to Richardson: the mimetic donnée of the fable—erotic pursuit and siege—is internalized and imploded, yielding a magnificent set of new departures, new worlds, breaking the tragic limits of the mimetic love story by transforming it all into verbal discourse. Cervantes and Fielding had written novels of the road, but the only journeys made in **Tristram Shandy** are made on hobbyhorses, not on horses. And, he is also saying, hobbyhorses are our truest and finest mode of transportation. When Thoreau said, "I have traveled a great deal in Concord," he was talking about the mobility of the mind, its ability to imagine and thereby add to the pitiful data of our lives. Sterne shows repeatedly that language can express that inner itinerary, that voyage which transforms the reader into fellow-traveller just by virtue of reading. Reading itself is emblematic of the Sterne paradox and breakthrough: the body is immobile, the fingers move slightly, the eyelids twitch, and nothing else shows whatsoever: imagine a photograph of someone reading; all the motion and life is internal. Sterne brings the inner mobility and freedom of the mind to language.

At the beginning of Vol. 5, Tristram asks the question which must haunt all writers:

> Tell me, ye learned, shall we for ever be adding so much to the *bulk*—so little to the *stock?*

> Shall we for ever make new books, as apothecaries make new mixtures, by pouring only out of one vessel into another?

> Are we for ever to be twisting, and untwisting the same rope? for ever in the same track—for ever at the same pace?

Shall we be destined to the days of eternity, on holy days, as well as working-days, to be shewing the *relicks of learning,* as monks do the relicks of their saints—without working one—one single miracle with them? (p. 259)

This quotation pointedly returns us to the old sources and traditions, the visible relics which clutter Sterne's book like a cathedral-junk shop, an Old World that can interest the writer only if he can transform it into a New World. ***Tristram Shandy*** does show things coming to life, but it is more than the child of Walter Shandy and his wife. Generation is everywhere. At one point Walter is trying to explain to Toby what an analogy is, and he is interrupted in the process: "Here a devil of a rap at the door snapp'd my father's definition (like his tobacco pipe) in two—and, at the same time, crushed the head of as notable and curious a dissertation as ever was engendered in the womb of speculation;—it was some months before my father could get an opportunity to be safely deliver'd of it" (p. 78). The metaphor, or more precisely the analogy, is one of childbirth, and what is being born is an idea. At another point, Tristram defines hypothesis: "It is the nature of an hypothesis, when once a man has conceived it, that it assimilates every thing to itself, as proper nourishment; and, from the first moment of your begetting it, it generally grows the stronger by every thing you· see, hear, read, or understand" (p. 114). Hypothesis and metaphor are the very soul of creativity, for they extend the real. Sterne's book is not about the birth of Tristram, but more substantially and compositely about the birth of ideas, the life of the mind, that old Gonopsychanthropologia, the origin of the soul. Ideas have distinct advantages over people: they cannot be castrated or have their noses flattened; they are not subject to physical dangers because they are not corporeal; time and space do not worry them, since they generate their own; they do not even need to be possible:

> Didst thou ever see a white bear? cried my father. . . .
>
> A white bear! Very well. Have I ever seen one? Might I ever have seen one? Am I ever to see one? Ought I ever to have seen one? Or can I ever see one? (for how can I imagine it?)
>
> If I should see a white bear, what should I say? If I should never see a white bear, what then?
>
> If I never have, can, must or shall see a white bear alive; have I ever seen the skin of one? Did I ever see one painted?—described? Have I ever dreamed of one?
>
> Did my father, mother, uncle, aunt, brothers or sisters, ever see a white bear? What would they give? How would they behave? How would the white bear have behaved? Is he wild? Tame? Terrible? Rough? Smooth?
>
> —Is the white bear worth seeing?
>
> —Is there no sin in it?
>
> —Is it better than a black one? (p. 307)

Here is the prolific, generative, mind at work, spewing forth hypotheses, making life beyond the niggardly categories of logic and truth. Here is the writer at the crossroads of the paradigmatic and syntagmatic resources of language, refusing to choose, having his cake and eating it. This is the life-making process that is celebrated throughout the book, that underlies all the digressions, that replaces the story of Tristram's birth with the graphic spectacle of its own. It is the life of Tristram's mind, and, committed to language, it is Tristram's book.

Sterne's novel works a miracle, because it gets onto paper and into words the private mechanisms and private topographies which, given there is no Momus' glass for our kind, we would never perceive otherwise. Not just our inner mind set, but the tangential world of connotation is given expression in Sterne. To understand ***Tristram Shandy*** is to read it *à demi mot,* to enter into connivance with Sterne, who is ever decorous in what he says but often bawdy in what he suggests. Sterne says noses, and we know better;[4] he describes the fair Bedouine rubbing Trim's knee and above, and we keenly follow the action; he threatens to do a chapter on buttonholes, and our mind starts a wondering:

> Button-holes!—there is something lively in the very idea of 'em—and trust me, when I get amongst 'em—you gentry with great beards—look as grave as you will—I'll make merry work with my buttonholes—I shall have 'em all to myself—'tis a maiden subject I shall run foul of no man's wisdom or fine sayings in it. (p. 217)

Sterne alerts us to the multivalence of our language, multivalent because of all the additional realms of discourse which may be brought in, especially the censored realm of sexual discourse. Whiskers and knots will never be the same after Sterne. In the chapter on whiskers, we see how the Lady Baussiere becomes so obsessed with whiskers that she sees them everywhere and sees nothing else. We are warned that the unsaid meanings, the connotations, can so gain the upper hand, that some words will be discredited forever: night caps, chamber pots, spigots, and faucets. These are all reputable words, Old World words, but, at Sterne's hands, they show their backsides. That is, they do so only if we give our connivance.

Toward the end of this narrative, the dense metaphorical clusters tend to become luminous with meaning. Toby's fortifications and sieges not only mirror warfare itself, but take on their full value in the love battle with Widow Wadman, and the sexual skirmishes in the sentry box actualize the metaphor. Sterne seems to be saying that a powerful enough obsession will eventually leave the realm of thought and of language and become flesh. One of the finest lessons of *Tristram Shandy* is that our hobbyhorses may lead us into rather than away from life. When Tristram's brother Bobby dies unexpectedly, out come the relics and Walter becomes a speaking dictionary:

> "Returning out of Asia, when I sailed from Aegina towards Megara," (when can this have been? thought my uncle Toby) "I began to view the country round about. Aegina was behind me, Megara was before, Pyraeius on the right hand, Corinth on the left.— What flourishing towns now prostrate upon the earth! Alas! Alas! said I to myself, that man should disturb his soul for the loss of a child, when so much as this lies awfully buried in his presence— Remember, said I to myself again—remember thou art a man."—
>
> Now my uncle Toby knew not that this last paragraph was an extract of Servius Sulpicius's consolatory letter to Tully.—He had as little skill, honest man, in the fragments, as he had in the whole pieces of antiquity.—And as my father, whilst he was concerned in the Turky trade, had been three or four different times in the Levant, in one of which he had staid a whole year and a half at Zant, my uncle Toby naturally concluded, that in some one of these periods he had taken a trip across the Archipelago into Asia; and that all this sailing affair with Aegina behind, and Megara before, and Pyraeius on the right hand, &c. &c. was nothing more than the true course of my father's voyage and reflections.—'Twas certainly in his manner, and many an undertaking critick would have built two stories higher upon worse foundations.—And pray, brother, quoth my uncle Toby, laying the end of his pipe upon my father's hand in a kindly way of interruption—but waiting until he finished the account—what year of our Lord was this?—'Twas no year of our Lord, replied my father.—That's impossible, cried my uncle Toby.—Simpleton! said my father,—'Twas forty years before Christ was born.
>
> My uncle Toby had but two things for it; either to suppose his brother to be the wandering Jew, or that his misfortunes had disordered his brain. (pp. 267-268)

Relics though they are, Walter's remembered fragments are being put to a humane use that is as serious as it is comic. It is legitimate and wise for the activities of the mind to offset the disasters of the flesh. Those old writers are proving their mettle and, much like Fielding's Parson Adams, Walter has travelled and seen a

great deal more than Toby or anyone can know. His ship voyage is a nautical version of the ubiquitous hobbyhorse. The games of *Tristram Shandy* are not unlike the quilts woven by shell-shocked soldiers; the play of the fingers and the play of the mind can offset the disasters visited upon the body and the soul. Sterne's view of language as natural resource, as saving grace, is the view of a therapist: "A blessing which tied up my father's tongue, and a misfortune which set it loose with good grace, were pretty equal" (p. 266). The parity implied by this vision is civilized and humane, for it measures human event in a wonderfully rich and elastic manner, allowing us to recoup, mentally, what we lose, materially.

But Tristram himself commands fully and finally our interest as the figure in whom life and mind merge. If the narratives of Toby, Walter, Trim, and others are discontinuous, the narrative of Tristram, i.e., his project of describing his life, subsumes them all and never falters. He has found potency and economy. Nothing can be extraneous to him, since he has only one project: to display, *through* a narrative, the quality of his mind. The play of that mind, its inner voyages and games— this is Sterne's new setting. At one point he claims that the fame of his book will counterbalance the evils that have befallen him as a man. Not so much the fame of the book as the very nature of the book will redress the misfortunes of his life. The determinist prison that the body is subject to can be exploded through thought and language alone. The impossible is only a ten-letter word; Tristram suavely proves that he is in three places at once as he writes from Lyon about two visits to Auxerre and simultaneously about his arrival in Lyon; the times of memory and writing time itself are interwoven in a rich tapestry, because the mind can enjoy just such liberty. The mind knows no limits, and Tristram goes on to add that "the measure of heaven itself is but the measure of our present appetites and concoctions" (p. 376). Heaven, the last bastion of the Old World, has been miraculously novelized, metamorphized, and internalized. Desire, perhaps even more than thought, is the animating force, the demiurge of Sterne's world, financing both the benevolence and the pornography, endlessly potent in its visions and fabrications. There is no life so poor or maimed, so truncated, that it cannot be converted into a rich and whole book. Tristram's misfortunes are transformed as they become merely the materials of his life, and literature—rather than England or France—becomes the field where he lives.

But no one has ever died in literature, since words do not know time. Consciousness, thought, desire, and language permit us to make a figure of our life and to splatter bishops and kings while doing it; they enable us to be in three places at once, to mix luxuriantly our levels of discourse. But the person behind the entire operation, the house for the generative mind, is rooted in time and space. Book 7 depicts Tristram's journey through France, his flight from Death, and it is an integral part of the novel. Our bodies are in time. Churches and books may remain fixed, but Janatone evolves: "But he who measures thee, Janatone, must do it now—thou carriest the principles of change within thy frame" (p. 373). Sterne's characters are frequently frozen in dramatic postures and left for whole chapters, but living people follow other laws:

> Time wastes too fast: every letter I trace tells me with what rapidity Life follows my pen; the days and hours of it, more precious, my dear Jenny! than the rubies about thy neck, are flying over our heads like light clouds of a windy day, never to return more—everything presses on—whilst thou art twisting that lock,—see! it grows grey; and every time I kiss thy hand to bid adieu, and every absence which follows it, are preludes to that eternal separation which we are shortly to make.—

—Heaven have mercy upon us both! (p. 469)

Here is a wisdom beyond comedy, a tragic sense of evanescence which accounts for the intermittent stasis *within* the novel. Time is too often dealt with as a literary problem, but it only appears in literature because it is a *human* problem, one that literature can miraculously resolve. Language and desire can spawn new worlds, and Toby's hobbyhorse moves him back and forth between England and Flanders quicker than the flash of an eye. But Tristram's vile cough punctuates every book of this prancing novel, and the spectre of impotency—not a man with an unloaded gun, but a man containing, as we all do, a time bomb—that spectre must eventually kill desire. *Tristram Shandy* indelibly traces the connections, the blood-line between Old Worlds and New Worlds, determinism and freedom, life and art. . . .

Notes

1 D. W. Jefferson, "*Tristram Shandy* and the Tradition of Learned Wit," reprinted in *Laurence Sterne: A Collection of Critical Essays,* ed. John Traugott (Englewood Cliffs: Prentice Hall, 1968), p. 162.

2 Laurence Sterne, *The Life and Opinions of Tristram Shandy, Gentleman,* ed. Ian Watt (Boston: Houghton Mifflin, 1965).

3 Benjamin H. Lehman, "Of Time, Personality, and the Author: A Study of *Tristram Shandy,*" reprinted in *A Collection of Critical Essays,* p. 28.

4 Surely, pornography must take honors in the category of fiction that enlists reader involvement. Pornography is a prototype of "generative" reading, for it counts on the reader to do the crucial extra imagining. This is especially true for the tongue-in-cheek variety that Sterne employs; the notorious description of the fair Bedouine rubbing Trim's "knee" has led Jean Jacques Mayoux to suggest that the reader is transformed into a voyeur of a masturbation scene; the reader-spectator is obliged to "compromise himself to the point of becoming a responsible actor" ("Laurence Sterne," in *A Collection of Critical Essays,* p. 110). There is, nowadays, much criticism devoted to "reader activity"; it would be interesting to investigate the role of sexual imagining in such activity.

Howard Anderson (essay date 1985)

SOURCE: "Structure, Language, Experience in the Novels of Laurence Sterne," in *The First English Novelists: Essays in Understanding,* Tennessee Studies in Literature Vol. 29, edited by J. M. Armistead, The University of Tennessee Press, 1985, pp. 185-223.

[*In the following essay, Anderson describes Sterne's novels as full of "surprises" and tries to show how a patient reader learns both to expect and be enlightened by these surprises (or unconventional narrative techniques) so that, ultimately, Sterne's novels "come to matter. . . . "*]

Tristram Shandy and *A Sentimental Journey*[1] are surprises waiting for readers. "I wish either my father or my mother, or indeed both of them, as they were in duty both equally bound to it, had minded what they were about when they begot me. . . . " Tristram's first words to us are urgent, without context, unintroduced. Here is Yorick: "They order, said I, this matter better in France." What the matter is, we have no present way of knowing; our route of discovery is to accompany him on his hasty journey across the Channel.

These initial surprises, anticipatory of greater ones, are Sterne's characteristic mode of approach, and not only in the novels. Consider the opening of the sermon which, though he had himself preached it ten years earlier, he ascribes to Parson Yorick when inserting it in the second volume of *Tristram Shandy:* "For we *trust* we have a good conscience" (II.xvii.88). Here Walter Shandy's response is a sort of surrogate for the reader's,[2] no doubt emulating that of many of those assembled to hear the sermon when the Reverend Mr. Sterne addressed the congregation at the cathedral church of York. Tristram's father is critical of the tone in which the text is read: "Certainly, *Trim,* quoth my father, interrupting him, you give that sentence a very improper accent; for you curl up your nose, man, as if the Parson was going to abuse the Apostle." Walter, the cathedral congregation, and perhaps the reader as well all have ideas about how a scriptural text should be read—preconceptions unlikely to jibe with the skeptical tone Trim gives it. To Walter's embarrassment, however, Trim turns out to have been more fully in touch with Yorick's use of the text than any of the listening company. The context provided by what follows invests the scriptural quotation with a new meaning, different from that furnished by the original passage in the Epistle to the Hebrews—not contradicting, but intensifying it.

Though Walter Shandy acknowledges the error of his assumption within a page or two, he does not usually find it so easy to admit when he is wrong. And for the reader beginning one of Sterne's novels, the narrator's opening gambit may be more alienating than inviting. Like Walter (who often serves as stand-in for our own overconfident intellects), we discover that they are intended to be both. Tristram and Yorick present themselves to us as zanies: Yorick only the more specifically as the kind of traveler who plunges into his life story regardless of the preparation, or wishes, of the person sitting beside him. Wherever we come from as we open these books, there is little chance that we will understand what is happening, and just as little that we will be able to avoid condescending to a speaker who approaches us with such a breathless lack of self-awareness. Our attitude is ensured as Tristram plunges on from that first sentence with a rambling speculation upon the animal spirits (apparently) until we lose sight of the initial subject altogether. Far from pausing to remind us what that was, he drops us into a fragment of a conversation: "*Pray, my dear,* quoth my mother, *have you not forgot to wind up the clock?*" And finally, again nonstop, he concludes this initial chapter with a terse exchange between a putative reader and himself: "Pray, what was your father saying?——Nothing." That Mr. Shandy was indeed *saying* nothing is the joke. But it is one that we are barely in a position to get the point of. As we move on, then, our initial condescension may be marked by defensiveness attendant on a dull realization that we do not quite understand what we had thought was so simple.

Many readers never recover from this uncomfortable sense of having been played with by Tristram Shandy, or from the comparable feeling that Yorick is forever one step ahead of us, always leaving us to wonder just where we are as he skips across France and Italy. Those who do recover—that is, those who come to like being played with, rather than resenting it—probably find the remedy partly in the self-recognition these narrators teach us to wrench out of our initial defensiveness and bafflement. Tristram, after evoking responses along the lines I have just sketched, startles us within a couple of pages by showing that he is perfectly aware of his unconventionality and has chosen this unorthodox point of departure self-consciously indeed. Ironically acknowledging his reader's right to be "let into the whole secret from first to last, of every thing which concerns you," he asserts that in beginning with his conception he is politely complying with contemporary

taste. The irony is enriched by the fact that we have not been ready to appreciate what he has been letting us into. Then his sophisticated self-awareness emerges, not without ambiguity, as he cites a most respected classical critic as authority for his choice of a starting point: "Right glad I am, that I have begun the history of myself in the way I have done; and that I am able to go on tracing every thing in it, as *Horace* says, *ab Ovo*" (I.iv.4).

Should we be inclined at this point once again to try a laugh at Tristram's expense—remembering that in the *Ars Poetica* Horace commended Homer for *not* starting the *Iliad* with Helen's emergence from the egg, but *in medias res* instead—Tristram catches us: "*Horace,* I know, does not recommend this fashion altogether: But that gentleman is speaking only of an epic poem or a tragedy;——(I forget which)——besides, if it was not so, I should beg Mr. *Horace*'s pardon;—— for in writing what I have set about, I shall confine myself neither to his rules, nor to any man's rules that ever lived." The reader by now senses that if anyone lacks self-awareness, it is not Tristram. This narrator's grip on the conventions of storytelling is more secure than our own; the assumptions about narrative procedure that we have gleaned (more or less consciously) from our reading of other books are not entirely adequate preparation for reading this one. Specifically, we are led to consider the limitations of conventional beginnings—how few there are, and how arbitrary—and to grant that Tristram's, which at first seemed merely random, is both *ab Ovo* and *in medias res*. More important, it may well be connected with what is to follow in ways we cannot anticipate. His concept of conception, while eccentric, begins to speak to us. In short, questioning Tristram's judgment leads us to question our own. Willingly or not, we start to see the need of accepting guidance from the teller in making out the tale. *Tristram Shandy* exemplifies the impulse and the necessity of unconventional narrative to teach us how to read it as we go along. In the process, we learn a good deal about reading in general and, at the same time, about our relation to experience outside of books.

The opening of *A Sentimental Journey* is equally sudden. Sterne's habit of immersing the reader in a conversation (indeed *in medias res*) has the effect it always has in *Tristram Shandy,* pushing us to flail about for a context, for other words to give meaning to the ones we are hearing. Who is speaking? Is he really saying that he sets off for France merely in order to put himself into a position of authority on what the French "order better"? And what *is* that? What is the purpose of this trip? Again it is hard to imagine a more arbitrary jumping-off point. By conventional narrative standards, this speaker does not exist for us at all; yet who can deny the impression of life and vigor—the presence—of whoever he is? Readers are challenged to resist, but again, whether altogether willingly or not, we are unlikely to escape being carried along by the persuasive power of Yorick's voice. Perhaps most important, it is nearly impossible to avoid the curiosity and questioning that *engage* us in conversation with Yorick as they do with Tristram. In this novel there is much less discussion of narrative method than in the earlier book; Sterne may in fact have depended to a considerable extent on Tristram to teach us how to listen to Yorick. But in both books the process and the purpose of the experience are similar. A reader's expectations (at whatever level of consciousness) are baffled by the lack of contexts usually taken for granted; the bafflement fuels a search for meaning; the search in turn leads to recognition of our dependence on the narrator—or better, our engagement with him—in a journey of discovery.

The desire for meaning, the recognition of context as the provider of meaning and of conversational intercourse as the means to context—this is the pattern of the experience Sterne engages us in and of what he has to teach us. Sterne can never force us to like the experience or the lesson, but his narrators do their best to win our participation by mocking challenges to our self-reliance and, on the other hand, insinuating appeals to our confidence. As early as the sixth chapter of his first volume, Tristram slips from the former to the latter mode in his first open acknowledgement that his aims require our cooperation:

> In the beginning of the last chapter, I inform'd you exactly *when* I was born;——but I did not inform you, *how*. No; that particular was reserved entirely for a chapter by itself;——besides Sir, as you and I are in a manner perfect strangers to each other, it would not have been proper to have let you into too many circumstances relating to myself all at once.——You must have a little patience. I have undertaken, you see, to write not only my life, but my opinions also; hoping and expecting that your knowledge of my character, and of what kind of a mortal I am, by the one, would give you a better relish for the other: As you proceed further with me, the slight acquaintance which is now beginning betwixt us, will terminate in friendship.——*O diem praeclarum!*——then nothing which has touched me will be thought trifling in its nature, or tedious in its telling. Therefore, my dear friend and companion, if you should think me somewhat sparing of my narrative on my first setting out,——bear with me,——and let me go on, and tell my story my own way:——or if I should seem now and then to trifle upon the road,——or should sometimes put on a fool's cap with a bell to it, for a moment or two as we pass along,——don't fly off,——but rather courteously give me credit for a little more wisdom than appears upon my outside;——and as we jogg on, either laugh with me, or at me, or in short do any thing,——only keep your temper. (I.vi.6-7)

Beginning with ironic modesty (he has already let us

into more details about his origins than a "proper" teller would do), the passage emerges from irony in its straightforward statement that the narrative depends on our tolerance and good nature. The development and exercise of those faculties, indeed, turn out to be a prime purpose shaping the experience. We undergo steady pressure to fly off from Tristram's annoyingly erratic narrative. Only "True *Shandeism*" can make us willing to keep reading, as it" opens the heart and lungs, and like all those affections which partake of its nature . . . forces the blood and other vital fluids of the body to run freely thro' its channels, and makes the wheel of life run long and chearfully round" (IV.xxxii.237).

"True Shandeism" is analogous to the "sentiment" through which Yorick appeals and which he attempts to communicate to his reader. Both are grounded in patience, good temper, tolerance, which in turn imply sympathy, consideration, fellow-feeling, capacities for love. In the preface that Yorick pauses to write while seated in a *desobligeant* at Calais, he establishes the premise that "the balance of sentimental commerce is always against the expatriated adventurer" (p. 78). The odds against the exercise of sentiment are not unlike those against Shandean good humor. The foreign world insists on levying inconvenience and petty hardship upon the traveler: "He must buy what he has little occasion for at their own price——his conversation will seldom be taken in exchange for theirs without a large discount——." As in **Tristram Shandy,** obstacles to communication stand at the center of the problem, with selfishness and intolerance the prime causes.

Yorick's attempt to overcome barriers to communication issues from his definition of himself as a "Sentimental Traveller," in contrast to a long list of alternatives, but particularly (and repeatedly), the Splenetic (pp. 81-82). "Spleen and jaundice" are the objects against which he most consistently aims his lance as he makes his quixotic way across the landscape. "Smelfungus" epitomizes the prejudiced and angry traveler whose only response to new experience is resentment that it is different from the old: "The learned SMELFUNGUS travelled from Boulogne to Paris——from Paris to Rome——and so on——but he set out with the spleen and jaundice, and every object he pass'd by was discoloured or distorted——He wrote an account of them, but 'twas nothing but the account of his miserable feelings" (p. 116). To nurture the conversation without which there is no communication, Yorick enlists sentiment as Tristram relied on Shandeism: variant forms of the good nature that can connect human beings.

I

We have begun to see that these narratives constitute tests for the examination and exercise of these capacities in the reader. In *A Sentimental Journey* as in *Tristram Shandy,* these tests of our patience and of our expansive potential appear most regularly in departures from straightforward narrative into digressions (Tristram) and flights of sentiment (Yorick).

The events upon which Tristram's "Life" is based are few and unhappy. His conception, we have observed, is scattered. When he finally emerges from the womb, it is with the dubious aid of a forceps that crushes his nose. His christening, where his father hopes to endow him with a lucky name, results in the opposite: the name he gets means "the sad one."[3] Still a little boy, he is the victim of a falling window sash that (at the very least) circumcises him as he aims to relieve himself one night. At the end of the book, his parents are still debating whether or not it is time to put the child into trousers. These barren facts might be neatly summed up by Hobbes's famous description of life in a state of nature—"nasty, brutish, and short." Tristram himself, just before the chapter begging the reader to "keep your temper," has described the world he was brought forth into as "scurvy and disasterous":

> I wish I had been born in the Moon, or in any of the planets . . . for it could not well have fared worse with me in any of them . . . than it has in this vile, dirty planet of ours,——which o'my conscience, with reverence be it spoken, I take to be made up of the shreds and clippings of the rest . . . for which cause I affirm it over again to be one of the vilest worlds that ever was made;——for I can truly say, that from the first hour I drew my breath in it, to this, that I can now scarce draw it at all, for an asthma I got scating against the wind in *Flanders;——*
> ——I have been the continual sport of what the world calls Fortune; and though I will not wrong her by saying, She has ever made me feel the weight of any great or signal evil;——yet with all the good temper in the world, I affirm it of her, That in every stage of my life, and at every turn and corner where she could get fairly at me, the ungracious Duchess has pelted me with a set of as pitiful misadventures and cross accidents as ever small HERO sustained. (I.v.5-6)

The dismal facts of Tristram's life are interspersed among rambling digressions that interrupt and disconcert the reader in quest of a story much as Mrs. Shandy's question jarred her husband's concentration at the book's (and Tristram's) outset. By the usual criterion of narrative connection—cause and effect—their relevance seems indecipherable. To speak just of the first volume, our expectation that Tristram's conception will lead to his birth is foiled by the story of Yorick and the midwife, by a facsimile of the Shandy's marriage settlement, by the insertion of a pronouncement by the Doctors of the Sorbonne concerning prenatal baptism, and by a long description of Uncle Toby's character as it is elucidated by his response to the story of Aunt

Dinah and the coachman. Yet as we look back (which is what Tristram is doing all along), we can see that the material of these digressions does indeed connect with Tristram's life. While all of it centers in other people, all of it affects the conditions of Tristram's birth. This narrator, then, pushes us to contemplate a scheme of cause and effect more esoterically complex than those we have been taught to look for in fiction or in life. When Tristram pauses near the end of Volume I to congratulate himself on what his method has accomplished, we must, perhaps grudgingly, concur that

> in this long digression which I was accidentally led into, as in all my digressions (one only excepted) there is a master-stroke of digressive skill, the merit of which has all along, I fear, been overlooked by my reader,——not for want of penetration in him,——but because 'tis an excellence seldom looked for, or expected indeed, in a digression;——and it is this: That tho' my digressions are all fair, as you observe,——and that I fly off from what I am about, as far and as often too as any writer in *Great Britain;* yet I constantly take care to order affairs so, that my main business does not stand still in my absence. (I.xxii.51)

What is to happen to Tristram Shandy has been decided in the lives of other people; to tell of *their* lives and opinions *is* to further the main business of Tristram's book.

At the same time, it is impossible to take Tristram's scheme of cause and effect quite seriously. For instance, we are never fully persuaded that Toby's embarrassed recoil from ideas associated with his aunt's elopement is a more decisive cause of Tristram's troubles than any of a thousand others—all of which remain undiscovered in his past and unrealized in his imagination. Tristram's search for the reasons why he is what he is persuades us instead that it is the search that matters, and what he makes of what he finds. In this way, *Tristram Shandy* comically subverts the solemn foundation of empiricism by disputing the hegemony of factual cause and effect in fiction and in life. First among the rules whose authority he disputes whenever the chance arises—"Is man to follow rules——or rules to follow him?"—mechanical causation draws Tristram's subversive energy. The epigraph from Epictetus with which the novel sets out points to the importance of this theme: "It is not things that disturb men, but their judgments about things."

But Tristram does not merely put in question the precedence of facts in the causal hierarchy by implying that one will serve as well as another and by burying the conventionally important one under a heap of the esoteric; the effect of such a process is to reduce the unhappy events to the merest framework for an expansive comic structure. Tristram's life in outline is the material of tragedy, at least of domestic tragedy; for if he has not (as he admits) suffered any "great or signal evil," what he has undergone nonetheless provides sufficient reason for bitterness. His "pitiful misadventures and cross accidents" are of a private nature, but to have his face disfigured by the loss of his nose—not to mention the diminution administered by the falling window—would in itself be enough to sour many men on life.

Instead, like a Shakespeare alternately bringing tragedy and comedy out of parallel material in *Romeo and Juliet* and *A Midsummer Night's Dream,* Tristram chooses to make his misadventures into comedy. He accomplishes the transformation by planting them in the nurturing context of the digressions:

> By this contrivance the machinery of my work is of a species by itself; two contrary motions are introduced into it, and reconciled, which were thought to be at variance with each other. In a word, my work is digressive, and it is progressive too,———and at the same time.
>
> This, Sir, is a very different story from that of the earth's moving round her axis, in her diurnal rotation . . . though I own it suggested the thought,———as I believe the greatest of our boasted improvements and discoveries have come from some such trifling hints.
>
> Digressions, incontestably, are the sunshine,———they are the life, the soul of reading;———take them out of this book for instance,———you might as well take the book along with them;———one cold eternal winter would reign in every page of it; restore them to the writer;———he steps forth like a bridegroom,———bids All hail; brings in variety, and forbids the appetite to fail. (I.xxii.52)

The grandeur of the images Tristram applies to his work is as self-mocking as it is heroic, but the images are appropriate nonetheless: a man's life may indeed be pictured by its parallels to a cosmic system that moves in several orbits at once (despite appearances to the contrary). The image of digressions as the life-giving sunshine is even more compelling: the cold facts of Tristram's life, as of every life, are simple, and heading deathward (with or without the aid of "an asthma got scating against the wind in *Flanders*"). So, Tristram shows, what matters is not the facts, but what he makes of them.

In Volume IV, Tristram denies that his book is intended as an attack on "predestination, or free will, or taxes," asserting instead that "if 'tis wrote against any thing,———'tis wrote, an' please your worships, against the spleen" (IV.xxii.218). I should say that in so directing his book, he does indeed distinguish the aspects of life where determinism applies from those in which we have choice. Tristram cannot choose to be undamaged by forceps or window sash; no act of will or imagination will free him from his asthma, or from the death that follows on its heels in Volume VII. But he can and does choose how he will see them—with patience, good temper, tolerance, and humor. Opting for a vision (and a principle of narrative selection) that fences against the spleen, he achieves a healthy and life-giving perspective:

> If 'tis wrote against any thing,———'tis wrote . . . against the spleen; in order, by a more frequent and a more convulsive elevation and depression of the diaphragm, and the succussations of the intercostal and abdominal muscles in laughter, to drive the *gall* and other *bitter juices* from the gall bladder, liver and sweetbread of his majesty's subjects, with all the inimicitious passions which belong to them, down into their duodenums. (IV.xxii.218)

So Tristram Shandy's "digressive artistry"[4] is by no means merely decorative. It is the blood nourishing a *self* created with his art. In this it parallels the integral function of sentiment in Yorick's *Sentimental Journey* and in his identity. Another way of putting it is to say that sentiment is to Yorick's journey what opinions are to Tristram's life. And just as that "life" frequently took perceptible shape against patterns established by fictional convention, so the "journey" reflects against conventional travel narratives and guidebooks, popular since before the eighteenth century. Such works concentrate on the local sights (*videnda*), often with excruciating circumstantiality—precisely how wide and long is the Piazza San Marco, how tall the Campanile, and so on. Their circumstantiality—feeding the modern passion for facts (compare what we have just seen in *Tristram Shandy*)—had often lent itself to parody and, by extension, to satire excoriating the reduction of the *real* to the brutally material. *Gulliver's Travels* is the preeminent example of this kind of parody and satire. While probably no reader in 1768 came to a work written by the celebrated Laurence Sterne anticipating a conventional travel book—Volume VII of *Tristram Shandy* had already parodied the form—Yorick's unique definition of sentiment exerts its demand in opposition to the simpler visual and muscular capacities required by conventional tours and encouraged by conventional tour books.

Sterne's own "asthma"—in reality the tuberculosis that would cause his death just after the publication of *A Sentimental Journey*—inspired his trips to southern France and Italy between 1762 and 1766. In Volume VII of *Tristram Shandy,* published in 1765, he had already written what he called "a laughing good temperd Satyr against Traveling (as puppies travel)."[5] As Gardner Stout has shown, Sterne's distinctively different treatment of some of the same materials in *A Sentimental Journey* (different in the ways he covers the same ground) was due in part to a shift in popular and critical taste (Introduction, p. 10). Ralph Griffiths, a spokesman for those who had grown "indifferent to the oddities and hostile to the indecencies of Vols. III-VIII," wrote in the *Monthly Review* of February 1765:

> One of our gentlemen once remarked, in *print* Mr. Shandy—that he thought your excellence lay in the PATHETIC. I think so too. . . . Give us none but amiable or worthy, or exemplary characters; or, if you will, to enliven the drama, throw in the *innocently humorous.* . . . Paint Nature in her loveliest dress—her native simplicity. Draw natural scenes, and interesting situations—In fine, Mr. Shandy, do, for surely you can, excite our passions to *laudable* purposes—awake our affections, engage our hearts—arouze, transport, refine, improve us. Let morality, let cultivation of virtue be your aim—let wit, humour, elegance and pathos be the means; and the grateful applause of mankind will be your reward.

The sentimental, blending pathos and elegance, is less often pierced by witty ambiguities in Yorick's travels than in Tristram's. And as Griffiths's recommendations indicate, Yorick's excursions into sentiment were unlikely to meet the bafflement, or downright resistance, that Tristram's digressions invited. Nevertheless, Sterne again gives the sentimental elements of the journey their shape by placing them in contrast to the results of more mundane journeys:

> By sending Tristram on a Shandean variation of the Grand Tour governed by the principles of laughter and good humor, rather than by the spleen, Sterne took an important step toward Yorick's **Journey.** And by diverting Tristram from the beaten track of his forerunners in order to demonstrate that such digressions can lead to delightful experiences . . . he indicated the route which Yorick, the Sentimental Traveller, was to take. (Stout, Introduction, p. 11)

Chief among the predecessors whom Sterne employs as a running foil to his moving scene is Tobias Smollett. Already established as a novelist and as editor of the *Critical Review,* Smollett had published in 1766 his own *Travels through France and Italy.* A physician before he was a writer, Smollett was even more aware than most travelers of the unsanitary conditions he encountered, the daily filth taken for granted by the people he traveled among. It is hardly saying too much to call him obsessed with these sordid facts of life in France and Italy (and *Humphry Clinker,* published in 1771, shows him equally appalled by comparable outrages in Great Britain). Smollett was in bad health when he went abroad, which gave him reason to be especially impatient of inconvenience—but again left him open to contrast with tubercular, humorous Sterne. Even the most universally admired *videnda* arouse only his grudging appreciation; in an infamous passage he reluctantly describes his partial admiration of the Venus de Medici at Florence:

> I believe I ought to be entirely silent, or at least conceal my real sentiments, which will otherwise appear equally absurd and presumptuous. It must be want of taste that prevents my feeling that enthusiastic admiration with which others are inspired at sight of this statue. . . . I cannot help thinking that there is no beauty in the features of Venus. . . . Without all doubt, the limbs . . . are elegantly formed, and accurately designed, according to the nicest rules of symmetry and proportion; and the back parts especially are executed so happily, as to excite the admiration of the most indifferent spectator.[6]

Such a target was too much for Sterne. This is the living figure who lurks behind the allegorical Smelfungus:

> I met Smelfungus in the grand portico of the Pantheon——he was just coming out of it——'Tis *nothing but a huge cock-pit,* said he——I wish you had said nothing worse of the Venus of Medicis, replied I——for in passing through Florence, I had heard one had fallen foul upon the goddess, and used her worse than a common strumpet, without the least provocation in nature. (pp. 117-18)

Set against such a foil, Yorick's sentimental response to feminine beauty and spirit is uniquely striking. While the Splenetic Traveller diminishes the established beauties of the places he visits, the Sentimental one occupies himself in seeking out those as yet undiscovered.

Unconcerned whether the backsides of statues are "accurately designed" or not, Yorick experiences his most memorable encounters with living human beings. Most of them are women, of course—Madame de R, Maria at Moulines, the Fille de Chambre, the Grisset whose pulse he feels:

> I am sure you must have one of the best pulses of any woman in the world——Feel it, said she, holding out her arm. So laying down my hat, I took hold of her fingers in one hand, and applied the two fore-fingers of my other to the artery—

> —Would to heaven! my dear Eugenius, thou hadst passed by, and beheld me sitting in my black coat, and in my lack-a-daysical manner, counting the throbs of it, one by one, with as much true devotion as if I had been watching the critical ebb or flow of her fever—How wouldst thou have laugh'd and moralized upon my new profession?—Trust me, my dear Eugenius, I should have said, "there are worse occupations in this world than feeling a woman's pulse." (pp. 164-65)

This sentimental foray off the beaten track might be

open to the charges of indecency that critics like Griffith had levied against the later volumes of **Tristram Shandy**—and the charges have been made. But by juxtaposing his physical-emotional intercourse with women like the Grisset against the bloodless perverseness of a Smelfungus, Sterne makes Yorick's digressions into the byways look attractively human.

Furthermore, just as Tristram's digressive artistry manages at the same time to be progressive, Yorick's sentimental experiences are ends in themselves *and* expand his consciousness toward further ends. The incident with the Grisset contributes to his discernment of qualities distinguishing the French from the English. When the young woman's husband enters and complacently observes Yorick's intimacy with his wife, the Sentimental Traveller takes the opportunity to reflect that, while "in London a shopkeeper and a shopkeeper's wife seem to be one bone and one flesh . . . in Paris, there are scarce two orders of beings more different: for the legislative and executive powers of the shop not resting in the husband, he seldom comes there——in some dark and dismal room behind, he sits commerceless in his thrum night-cap, the same rough son of Nature that Nature left him" (p. 166).

Yorick's inclination to promote tolerance of foreign mores might be construed here as a stance favorable to his own sexual interests. And in fact it does serve his interests to be uncritical of what might be considered lax or even corrupt by a tougher moralist. But his bemused acceptance, even enjoyment, of foreign ways extends also to behavior which might affront his delicate sensual enjoyment. In a passage that seems first to allude to Shandean hobbyhorses, he remarks:

> It is alike troublesome to both rider and his beast—
> —if the latter goes pricking up his ears, and starting all the way at every object which he never saw before——I have as little torment of this as any creature alive; and yet I honestly confess that many a thing gives me pain, and that I blush'd at many a word the first month——which I found inconsequent and perfectly innocent the second.

> Madame de Rambouliet, after an acquaintance of about six weeks with her, had done me the honour to take me in her coach about two leagues out of town——Of all women, Madame de Rambouliet is the most correct; and I never wish to see one of more virtues and purity of heart——In our return back, Madame de Rambouliet desired me to pull the cord——I ask'd her if she wanted any thing——
> —*Rien que pisser,* said Madame de Rambouliet—

> Grieve not, gentle traveller, to let Madame de Rambouliet p—ss on——And ye fair mystic nymphs! go each one *pluck your rose.* (pp. 181-83)

In this case, Yorick's digression is superficially *anti*-sentimental. Yet while it does not conform to the popular demand for the "elegant" and the "pathetic," Yorick's response embodies his steady insistence that true sentiment be grounded in acceptance and sympathy. And again, these qualities take on definition as characteristic of the Sentimental Traveller when placed against an early letter among those in Smollett's *Travels,* where he fumes (at much greater length than I will quote): "Will custom exempt from the imputation of gross indecency a French lady, who shifts her frowsy smock in presence of a male visitant, and talks to him of her *lavement,* her *medecine,* and her *bidet!*" (p. 35).

Finally, the passage provides another example of the general purpose motivating Yorick's journey: the comparison of foreign manners and customs. While Madame de Rambouliet's manner of expressing her physical need may not "order this matter better" than if she had called it plucking a rose, Yorick's point is that both expressions are equally a matter of linguistic custom. Neither way of speaking is morally superior—though we may suspect that he favors the more direct expression. Beyond that, we may sense that the willingness of a woman of Madame de Rambouliet's character to acknowledge her physicality without blushing circumlocution confirms Yorick in his deepest purpose: the integration of his physical, emotional, and spiritual being.

Smollett, as a model for the Splenetic Traveller, is only the most noted and frequent foil to Yorick. The characterization of the Sentimental Traveller takes shape also in contrast to the Vain or Proud Traveller (among the types listed in the preface written in the *desobligeant*). "Mundungus, with an immense fortune," is a notable example of such a traveler: he "made the whole tour . . . without one generous connection or pleasurable anecdote to tell of; but he had travell'd straight on looking neither to his right hand or his left, lest Love or Pity should seduce him out of his road" (p. 119). Such total insulation from his fellowmen would be hard for Yorick to accomplish even if he wanted to, as necessity requires that he bargain for vehicles and accommodations. But just as the contrast with Smelfungus stresses the moral benefits of tolerant good humor, so placing Yorick against Mundungus defines the value of sympathy and fellow feeling. Mundungus has the attributes of the selfish man whom Sterne had described in a sermon on the Good Samaritan, which he published as one of the **Sermons of Mr. Yorick** in 1760. This "sordid wretch," in contrast to the Samaritan himself,

> goes to the end of his days, in the same selfish track in which he first set out . . . as if afraid to look up, lest peradventure he should see aught which might turn him one moment out of that straight line where interest is carrying him——or if, by chance,

he stumbles upon a hapless object of distress . . .
unwilling to hazard the inconveniences which pity
might lead him into upon the occasion.[7]

Sterne chose in *A Sentimental Journey* to capitalize
upon the fashionable taste for sentiment that he had
himself been most instrumental in establishing. But
Yorick's essays in the sentimental do not confine themselves merely to the elegant and pathetic qualities which
for readers like Griffiths constituted the meaning of
the concept. Sympathy, grounded in the good temper
and tolerance that make it possible, is the soul of
Yorick's sentimental response to the figures he encounters as he crosses the landscapes of France and
Italy. The Sentimental Traveller's manners are striking, but it is generous spirit that finally distinguishes
him from Smelfungus and Mundungus, even as it allows him to grant them pitying acceptance:

> Peace be to them! if it is to be found; but heaven
> itself, was it possible to get there with such tempers,
> would want objects to give it——every gentle spirit
> would come flying upon the wings of Love to hail
> their arrival——Nothing would the souls of
> Smelfungus and Mundungus hear of, but fresh
> anthems of joy, fresh raptures of love, and fresh
> congratulations of their common felicity——I
> heartily pity them: they have brought up no faculties
> for this work; and was the happiest mansion in
> heaven to be allotted to Smelfungus and Mundungus,
> they would be so far from being happy, that the
> souls of Smelfungus and Mundungus would do
> penance there to all eternity. (p. 120)

II

For both Tristram and Yorick, then, "experience is the
force that mediates between the human character and
its hidden destiny"; Wolfgang Iser's potent description
of what happens in *Pilgrim's Progress* applies equally
to the relations between Sterne's storytellers and their
unique, but communicable, experience.[8] "Character" in
this sense constitutes inherited capacities—the modes
of seeing and feeling that Tristram receives from his
father and uncle and mother; Yorick's innate self-grat-
ifying inclination to spend two livres a bottle for wine
and his perverse reluctance to give much to charity.

"Destiny" remains elusive for Tristram and Yorick as
for everybody else. But it manifests itself in events like
the ones we have seen descend upon Tristram; it is
finally embodied in Death, which pursues him across
the Channel in Book VII and lies in wait for him and
Yorick somewhere beyond the last pages of their narratives. And "experience"? That is even harder to pin
down; but so far in this inquiry it has begun to emerge
from the narrators' efforts to get beyond their inherited
and innate limitations, both physical and spiritual. It
takes from as they resist and move beyond the impulse
to settle bitterly for the conditions they are born to—

an effort that the likes of Smelfungus in both books
decidedly do not make.

We have noticed that the abiding purpose of the digressions in the two books is connective. Tristram's
carry him toward the men (and occasionally women)
who inhabit his past, and simultaneously into conversation with the reader. Both these complementary
motions serve to establish and connect him with himself, as well. Yorick's sentimental impulses are similarly communicative and reflexive. I should like to
consider now the central part that Sterne's language—
more specifically, his conscious *view* of language—
plays in the integrative "experience" that Sterne embodies in the digressive progress of his two novels.

Sterne's verbal associationism is the most notorious
linguistic feature of *Tristram Shandy*. From Samuel
Richardson, who called it "too gross to be inflaming,"[9]
to F.R. Leavis, for whom Sterne's "irresponsible (and
nasty) trifling" was reason enough to leave him out of
The Great Tradition,[10] double-entendre has been the
chief target of hostile critics. "Give up your Long
Noses . . . your Andoüillets . . . try your strength
another way . . . Mr. Shandy," begged Ralph Griffiths
in the letter I quoted from earlier. But while to such
readers Sterne's irrepressible play on words seems only
a tasteless ornament, verbal associationism is in fact
vital to what Tristram aims to discover and reveal.

We should begin by recognizing that sexual double-
entendre is only one of the forms of associationism
that pervade the book; its function, as we shall see, is
to connect narrator and reader. Meanwhile, Tristram's
father and uncle are engaged in their private obsessions, or hobby-horses, based in associations of ideas
that give individual words radically contradictory meanings for each of them. The following exchange is exemplary:

> To understand what *time* is aright [begins Walter
> Shandy] . . . we ought seriously to sit down and
> consider what idea it is, we have of duration. . . .
> In our computations of *time*, we are so used to
> minutes, hours, weeks, and months,——and of
> clocks (I wish there was not a clock in the kingdom)
> to measure out their several portions to us . . . that
> 'twill be well, if in time to come, the *succession of
> our ideas* be of any use or service to us at all.
>
> Now, whether we observe it or no, continued my
> father, in every sound man's head, there is a regular
> succession of ideas of one sort or other, which
> follow each other in train just like——A train of
> artillery? said my uncle Toby.——A train of a fiddle
> stick!——quoth my father. (III.xviii. 138-39)

Uncle Toby, the old soldier entirely preoccupied with
warfare and fortification, seizes upon the first word

that makes sense to him in his brother's dissertation. Simultaneously, Walter, obsessed with categorizing phenomena and winning arguments, is furious that Toby invests "train" with a meaning dragged in from the language of war.

Sterne's play on the power of verbal association to block, rather than promote, communication early won him credit as a Lockean.[11] For Locke, "a natural correspondence and connexion" between ideas characterizes normal thought, as he describes its processes in *An Essay concerning Human Understanding,* the work that established the direction of modern epistemology. In a chapter added to the fourth edition, he distinguishes this "natural correspondence" from those misconceptions of "chance or custom" that give rise to mental aberration:

> Ideas that in themselves are not all of a kind, come to be so united in some men's minds, that it is very hard to separate them; they always keep in company, and the one no sooner at any time comes into the understanding, but its associate appears with it; and if they are more than two which are thus united the whole gang, always inseparable, show themselves together.[12]

Such aberration Locke calls "by so harsh a name as madness," for "opposition to reason deserves that name" (I:528). It is the intrusion of this madness that we have just observed in Toby. More specifically, Tristram tells us as he begins his account of Toby's hobbyhorse, it is not ideas as such, but *words* that cause Toby trouble—the fact that the same words convey different ideas to different people (II.ii.62).

Toby's hobbyhorsical associations, in collision with Walter's through most of the novel and with the Widow Wadman's in Volumes VIII and IX, provide much of the comedy of the book. This emphasis on Toby's hobbyhorse, with the fact that nearly all the other characters (Yorick and Trim excepted) have their own comparable obsessions, implies that such "madness" is more common than Locke seems to allow. With the good-natured tolerance characteristic of him, Tristram asserts from the start that so long as they do not harm other people, he has nothing against hobbyhorses:

> If you come to that, Sir, have not the wisest men in all ages, not excepting *Solomon* himself,——have they not had their HOBBY-HORSES——their running horses,——their coins and their cockle-shells, their drums and their trumpets, their fiddles, their pallets,——their maggots and their butterflies?——and so long as a man rides his HOBBY-HORSE peaceably and quietly along the King's highway, and neither compels you or me to get up behind him,——pray, Sir, what have either you or I to do with it? (I.vii.8)

Some of them, however, *do* harm others: Tristram's satire on the hobbyhorses of public figures and of professionals whose selfish preoccupations take precedence over their responsibilities is a cutting counterpoint to the generous warmth and humor we have looked at. But his dominating point about hobbyhorses seems to be that as no one is immune, we had better understand their etiology in order to avoid being trapped like the Shandys.

Tristram can be said to inherit the linguistic naiveté of his uncle and father and the solipsism it leads to as his fundamental problems. The verbal sophistication that liberates him emerges from close attention to his own responses and those of other men and women. His observations form experience useful in salvaging his damaged family heritage. The story of the fate of the word *whiskers* at the Court of Navarre is an instance of how Tristram learns, and transmits his experience with language to us:

> *La Guyol, La Maronette, La Sabatiere,* fell in love with the Sieur *de Croix* . . . —*La Rebours* and *La Fosseuse* knew better—*De Croix* had failed in an attempt to recommend himself to *La Rebours;* and *La Rebours* and *La Fosseuse* were inseparable.

> The queen of *Navarre* was sitting with her ladies . . . as *De Croix* passed. . . . He is handsome, said the Lady *Baussiere.*—He has a good mien, said *La Battarelle.*—He is finely shaped, said *La Guyol.*—I never saw an officer of the horse-guards in my life, said *La Maronette,* with two such legs——Or who stood so well upon them, said *La Sabatiere*—But he has no whiskers, cried *La Fosseuse*—Not a pile, said *La Rebours.* (V.i.241)

Such is the potency of the word *whiskers* that it is soon impossible for the handsome cavalier to hold up his head—he "found it high time to leave *Navarre* for want of whiskers"—and the word "in course became indecent" (V.i.243).

The lesson Tristram draws from his parable is one he reiterates, with variations, from the time the forceps crushes his nose. In every case, parallels with sexual shapes endow our response to the objects named with energy, ensuring attention: "There are some trains of certain ideas which leave prints of themselves about our eyes and eye-brows; and there is a consciousness of it, somewhere about the heart, which serves but to make these etchings the stronger—we see, spell, and put them together without a dictionary" (V.i.242). Because Sterne can count on his readers' participation in sexual interests, whether or not we will admit to it, words with sexual connotations provide his surest means of teaching us that language is radically connotative and symbolic.

Sterne wrote in a century that saw the publication of the first dictionaries, with their implication that the main function of language is the denotation, naming, of objects. Following Locke, even the inner processes by which objects are perceived are themselves objectified and, as it were, pinned down with a name. Tristram repeatedly attacks such a conception of language, insisting that words are defined in use by human beings who express themselves and communicate with one another. For the ladies at the Court of Navarre, as for Tristram and us, the connection between facial hair and more primary sexual characteristics invests first the hair and then its name with symbolic connotations. In the more famous instance of the word "nose," correspondences in physiological shape affect the sexual connection, so that the word carries meanings that can be summoned up merely by Tristram's insistent emphasis.

The chapter on noses (III.xxii) is a succinct exercise in the power of context and expressive tone to determine meaning. The more Tristram attempts to clarify his meaning, the greater the ambiguity:

> I define a nose, as follows [he concludes],——intreating only beforehand, and beseeching my readers, both male and female, of what age, complexion, and condition soever, for the love of God and their own souls, to guard against the temptations and suggestions of the devil, and suffer him by no art or wile to put any other ideas into their minds, than what I put into my definition.——For by the word *Nose,* throughout all this long chapter of noses, and in every part of my work, where the word *Nose* occurs,——I declare, by that word I mean a Nose, and nothing more, or less. (p. 159)

The last two words of the chapter are a supreme example of Tristram's skill in teaching us how our minds work through verbal play.[13] Because our perceptions are inclined to fuse things in our minds through parallels of some of their qualities, the power of language lies not in its denotative rigor but rather in connotative and symbolic expressiveness. Sterne's double-entendres constitute a short course in poetry, initiating the reader (accustomed to dictionaries) into the principles of symbolism, which is the mainstay of his effort to communicate with us in *Tristram Shandy.* We perceive, whether we want to or not, that the word *nose* speaks of more than one thing at once. Equally important, we engage with Tristram as he speaks the word to us, acknowledging (with amusement or impatience) that what it means is between us.

Sterne's "irresponsible (and nasty) trifling," then, amounts to a concentrated justification of wit, which Hobbes described as the capacity to notice similarities in things otherwise much unlike. Wit requires seeing together, urging recognition of shared perception. For Locke, its value was decisively inferior to that of judgment, which links things on the basis only of marked similarities and separates them by equally marked differences; judgment, then, is the basis of the scientific method. Locke attacks wit and fancy together as "abuses of words" that have no proper use but for trivial ornamentation:

> Since wit and fancy find easier entertainment in the world than dry truth and real knowledge, figurative speeches and allusion in language will hardly be admitted as an imperfection or abuse of it. I confess, in discourses where we seek rather pleasure and delight than information and improvement, such ornaments as are borrowed from them can scarce pass for faults. But yet *if we would speak of things as they are,* we must allow that all the art of rhetoric, besides order and clearness; all the artificial and figurative application of words eloquence hath invented, are for nothing else but to insinuate wrong ideas, move the passions, and thereby mislead the judgment; and so indeed are perfect cheats: and therefore, however laudable or allowable oratory may render them in harangues and popular addresses, they are certainly, in all discourses that pretend to inform or instruct, wholly to be avoided; and where truth and knowledge are concerned, cannot but be thought a great fault, either of the language or person that makes use of them. (II:46; emphasis added)

Tristram Shandy knows that to deny wit and fancy the capacity to transmit truth and knowledge is to deny literature the serious place it had traditionally occupied as an enricher and instructor of human experience. He gives his best energies to opposing such a move.

In challenging Locke's view, Sterne takes on what was becoming the dominant modern attitude toward literature. Early in the history of Western thought, Plato had attacked poetry as a seducer of the reason; the Sophists had subverted its prestige in developing a program to divorce rhetoric (the pleasing and persuasive elements of language) from logic (language's claims to truth). But Aristotle effectively countered these concepts by arguing that persuasive and true language can and must be fused, that poetry and rhetoric must be grounded in logic and ethics. Thus understood, poetry "holds up the miror to nature," providing an irreplaceable means of seeing ourselves—as mirrors reflect our own faces, invisible except by indirection. Aristotle's powerful image established and described poetry's power from his time through the Renaissance. It is cited in sixteenth-century defenses of poetry (like Sidney's) against the incursions of the Puritans. And its force is typically buttressed by support from Horace's description of poetry as *"dulce et utile."* The latter retained its influence into the eighteenth century, translated into French by Boileau, for instance (in his much-quoted *Art Poetique*), as *"plaire et instruire,"* and into English as to "instruct by pleasing."

But Locke, the Royal Society that adopted his view, and the whole tendency of empirical philosophy and modern science were all pushing out wit and establishing judgment as the only means to truth. As we have seen, *Tristram Shandy* implicitly opposes this usurpation from its opening page. Then in the "Author's Preface" that Tristram snatches time to write in the middle of Volume III, Sterne directs a full-scale attack against the conception of literature that would reduce his novel (and all others) to mere entertainment. His tone, as usual, is playful, but perhaps more than usually direct:

> All I know of the matter is,——when I sat down, my intent was to write a good book; and as far as the tenuity of my understanding would hold out,——a wise, aye, and a discreet,——taking care only, as I went along, to put into it all the wit and judgment (be it more or less) which the great author and bestower of them had thought fit originally to give me,——so that, as your worships see,——'tis just as God pleases. (III.xx.140)

The critics of his first two volumes agree, he says, that there may be some wit in them, "but no judgment at all . . . for that wit and judgment in this world never go together; inasmuch as they are two operations differing from each other as wide as east is from west." Tristram knows precisely where to lay the blame for this heresy and how to deal with it: "So, says *Locke*,——so are farting and hickuping, say I" (III.xx.141).

His means of retaliation is emblematic of the whole preface—and of the whole novel. The crude but effective figure of speech brilliantly makes his point that wit can reveal truth. Continuing, he argues that wit and judgment are inseparable, that to place one above the other is a modern error. Illustrations, he says, serve mainly to "clarify the understanding, previous to the application of the argument itself, in order to free it from any little motes, or specks of opacular matter, which if left swimming therein, might hinder a conception and spoil all" (III.xx.141). Wit makes it possible to appreciate the infinite connective parallels in creation; judgment distinguishes them, elucidating significant differences, deciding which similarities matter more and less.

Tristram's preface calls attention to itself as a parody of the usual novelistic preface. While it performs the function of such an essay, describing the purpose and method of the larger work, it does so without recourse to the discursive and logical language typical of prefatory essays. In his first two volumes, Sterne had exercised his reader in reasoning by analogy. In the preface he floods us with images that figure forth what the book is about. Tristram justifies his use of witty illustrations *with* an illustration: "wiping the looking glass clean." He defends the inseparability of wit and judg-

ment by leaping up and pointing to the knobs on the back of his chair:

> ——Here stands *wit,*——and there stands *judgment,* close beside it, just like the two knobbs I'm speaking of. . . . You see, they are the highest and most ornamental parts of its *frame,*——as wit and judgment are of *ours,* and like them, too, indubitably both made and fitted together, in order as we say in all such cases of duplicated embellishments,——to *answer one another.* (III.xx.146)

The reader who has been attentive to Tristram through the first two volumes will by this time hear several meanings even in the word "answer." The most obvious in the context of the paragraph—ornamental symmetry—is deepened by the larger context of our experience in the first two volumes. There, "answer" has proved to mean response, lively, irresistible engagement with what we hear from Tristram. To answer is to be in conversation, in communication, in connection.

He sustains the metaphor through two more long paragraphs, weaving an argument radically dependent on the figurative power of language: "It is by these observations, and a wary reasoning by analogy in that kind of argumentative process, which *Suidas* calls *dialectick induction,*——that I draw and set up this position as most true and veritable" (III.xx.144). Calling wit and judgment the "top ornaments of the mind of man, which crown the whole entablature," he asks "who does not wish . . . to be, or to be thought at least master of the one or the other, and indeed of both of them, if the thing seems any way feasible, or likely to be brought to pass" (III.xx.146-47). The reason that men of influence have so surprisingly forgone the effort to gain credit for both wit and judgment is not really hard to find. The "graver gentry," so grave indeed as to have no hope of gaining credit for wit, "raised a hew and cry against the lawful owners." Even "the great *Locke,* who was seldom outwitted by false sounds,——was nevertheless bubbled here" (III.xx.147).

Thus self-centered egoism, with the humorlessness it invariably breeds, is as always the enemy of true Shandeism. This combination, in its determination to eradicate wit, has established "the Magna Charta of stupidity." Tristram appears content that he has proved to us our capacity to learn through metaphor and symbol, aware that he has engaged us in a conversational quest for meaning. In the same tone with which he had expressed his tolerance of hobbyhorse riders at the outset of the book, he sidesteps the graver gentry whom he has just anatomized for us: "I have no abhorrence whatever, nor do I detest and abjure either great wigs or long beards,——any further than when I see they are bespoke and let grow on purpose to carry on . . . imposture——for any purpose,——peace be with them;——mark only [he stresses the moral with a pointing hand],——I write not for them" (III.xx.147).

The redemption of the vital human function of wit underwrites Sterne's double-entendre as a means of exploring with the reader the connections between mind and body. It instills purpose into the central structural metaphors of both *Tristram Shandy* and *A Sentimental Journey,* making words like "hobbyhorse" and "journey" into a kind of vigorous shorthand standing for a rich range of experience that the reader and narrator share. Finally, his redemption of verbal wit spills over to illuminate physical gesture as well: Walter Shandy awkwardly reaching across his coat to extricate a handkerchief from his pocket, Corporal Trim dropping a hat to indicate death's descent, or Tristram jumping up in frustration to hurl a blotted page into the fire all speak a body language inseparable from the metaphoric verbal one.

"A man and his HOBBY-HORSE," says Tristram as he launches into his description of Toby's,

> tho' I cannot say that they act and re-act exactly after the same manner in which the soul and body to upon each other: Yet doubtless there is a communication between them of some kind, and my opinion rather is, that there is something in it more of the manner of electrified bodies,——and that by means of the heated parts of the rider, which come immediately into contact with the back of the HOBBY-HORSE.——By long journies and much friction, it so happens that the body of the rider is at length fill'd as full of HOBBY-HORSICAL matter as it can hold;——so that if you are able to give but a clear description of the nature of the one, you may form a pretty exact notion of the genius and character of the other. (I.xxiv.55)

Tristram elsewhere repeats that the hobbyhorse does not constitute the entire character, remarking for example that Toby's moral behavior transcends his hobbyhorse. But as he sets about "drawing Toby's character from his HOBBY-HORSE," he emphasizes the physical connection suggested by the metaphor: a man's obsession is especially like horseback riding in the excitement it arouses, partaking of sexual stimulation. Later he speaks of Toby posting down to his bowling green—the site of his fortifications—like a lover eager to join his mistress.

Such descriptions have been read as reducing hobbyhorsical mankind to mechanisms, with sexual desire—simple or sublimated—as the key to the machine. That interpretation seems to be encouraged by Tristram's pronouncement upon Corporal Trim's story about falling in love with the Fair Beguine "quite suddenly" as she massaged the upper part of his leg: "Whether the corporal's amour terminated precisely in the way my uncle *Toby* described it, is not material; it is enough

that it contain'd in it the essence of all the love-romances which ever have been wrote since the beginning of the world" (VIII.xxii.406). But what we have seen of the transformation of the merely material into wit suggests that such a mechanical view of hobbyhorses (and of love) is inadequate. While Tristram steadily insists that "soul and body" interpenetrate one another (thus mocking hypocrites who deny their own sexual nature), his emphasis on the elaborate construction of Toby's hobbyhorse directs attention to its complexity. Its sources in Toby's physical (and probably sexual) wound are simple. But equally, the resultant structure—illustration, game, raison d'être—is richly multifarious. In the figure of the hobbyhorse, soul and body mesh in a child's game, with the wonder and subtlety of the connection presented for our contemplation as surely as its childishness.

A related image, that of the journey, is as important as the hobbyhorse to the structure of *Tristram Shandy*—even more so in *A Sentimental Journey*—and to Sterne's vision of the human situation. Neither image is new. The *Oxford English Dictionary* shows that "hobbyhorse" was in common use as a name for a child's toy or preoccupation long before Sterne expanded it; the journey is an ancient image figuring forth human life. Consistent with his larger intention of revealing the familiar to us in a new light, Sterne revivifies the metaphor—biblical, Homeric—in recounting Tristram's run from Death in Volume VII. Drawing on parallels he had begun to explore in his sermons,[14] Sterne invests the image with intensity by starting Tristram's journey as a race against Death, that "son of a whore [who] has found out my lodgings" (IX.i.336).

Tristram marks the image as his own, transforming it unforgettably, by his means of eluding Death. He is able to slip away because Death finds himself uniquely abashed by his victim's nonchalance and humor. Addressing his own high spirits, Tristram says: "In no one moment of my existence, that I remember, have ye once deserted me . . . when DEATH himself knocked at my door——ye bad him come again; and in so gay a tone of careless indifference, did ye do it, that he doubted of his commission——'There must certainly be some mistake in this matter,' quoth he" (IX.i.335).

Aware that Death's setback is certain to be temporary, Tristram resolves to fly while he can. The verbs he chooses to describe his plan are themselves images that only Shandean high spirits could apply to a travel cure:

> Then by heaven! I will lead him a dance he little thinks of——for I will gallop, quoth I, without looking once behind me to the banks of the *Garonne;* and if I hear him clattering at my heels——I'll scamper away to mount *Vesuvius*——from thence to *Joppa,* and from *Joppa* to the world's end, where,

if he follows me, I pray God he may break his neck———. . . .

Allons! said I; the post boy gave a crack with his whip———off I went like a cannon, and in half a dozen bounds got into *Dover*. (IX.i.436)

Starting like this, Tristram pulls the reader along through a volume that identifies witty agility as a life-saving power, with good humor (again) as *the* capacity necessary to stay alive.

In *A Sentimental Journey,* travel as an image figuring spiritual development is, if anything, more prominent than in Volume VII of *Tristram Shandy.* Gardner Stout has studied the ways in which Yorick's journey to health evokes seventeenth-century Puritan accounts of spiritual pilgrimage, notably John Bunyan's *Pilgrim's Progress* (Introduction, pp. 38-40). While this world is a very different kind of test for Bunyan's Christian than it is for Sterne's, their movement through its landscape provides both with chances to reveal their spiritual fiber. If Christian is struggling through on his way to heaven, Yorick too seeks a better world in "NATURE, and those affections which rise out of her, which make us love each other———and the world, better than we do" (p. 219). Stout concludes that Yorick's "travels may be said to combine the 'seventeenth-century ideal of *pélerinage de l'ame*' with the 'eighteenth-century ideal of cosmopolitanism and sociability,' for by traveling with him the reader can develop the faculties essential to participation in this joyful religion." As I remarked earlier, sentiment is to the *Journey* what Tristram's opinions are to his life: "incontestably the sunshine." To journey with Tristram and with Yorick is to invest travel with spirits, and high spirits with a spirituality they had never revealed before Sterne.

Finally, Sterne's success at bringing physical nature (man's included) to function as a sign of the spiritual allows the extension of metaphoric language beyond words—to gesture. "A man's body and his mind, with the utmost reverence to both I speak it, are exactly like a jerkin, and a jerkin's lining;———rumple the one———you rumple the other" (III.iv.114). From this principle it follows that attitudes, in the sense of posture and gesture, indicate attitudes of mind and spirit. In both novels Sterne calls for our close attention to them.

Corporal Trim and his hat will serve to represent jerkin's lining and jerkin. When word of the death of Tristram's brother Bobby reaches Shandy Hall, it sends their father into a paroxysm expressed through quotation of ancient authorities on the brevity of life and the transiency of things. In the kitchen the response differs. "My young master in *London* is dead! said Obadiah" (V.vii.252), and each of the servants thinks his or her own thoughts. Tristram remarks, "Well might

Locke write a chapter upon the imperfections of words"—for to Susannah, "dead" summons up only thoughts of the green satin dress she will get when her mistress goes into mourning. To Obadiah, Bobby's death means that the master will invest his money in "stubbing the ox-moor" instead of a grand tour for his son, and "we shall have a terrible piece of work of it." Their unanimous creatural self-concern is uttered with massive simplicity by the scullery maid as she scours a fish kettle: "He is dead! said *Obadiah*,———he is certainly dead!———So am not I, said the foolish scullion."

But for Tristram this self-concern constitutes as well a brute self-awareness; by now we may anticipate that even such material will serve as a base for expansion. While the word "dead" remained nearly dead for all of them, a metaphorical gesture stirs them to move out of themselves. Corporal Trim is again the effective rhetorician:

> Are we not here now, continued the corporal, (striking the end of his stick perpendicularly upon the floor, so as to give an idea of health and stability)———and are we not———(dropping his hat upon the ground) gone! in a moment!———'Twas infinitely striking! *Susannah* burst into a flood of tears.———We are not stocks and stones.———*Jonathan, Obadiah,* the cook-maid, all melted.———The foolish fat scullion herself . . . was rous'd with it. (V.vii.253).

Tristram comments, perhaps not just hyperbolically, that to understand and master persuasive rhetoric as Trim has done would enable a speaker to rally support for "the preservation of our constitution in church and state." Perhaps he means that properly to understand how people connect with things, and the mind with the body, would ensure both social and personal integration.

He concludes by again emphasizing that it is the inseparability of mind and body that involves us in a gesture like Trim's, moves us, and leads us out (the root meaning of *educare*). We are "but men cloathed with bodies, and governed by our imaginations." Given those facts, we cannot be unaffected by what stimulates the senses. Furthermore, "of all the senses, the eye . . . has the quickest commerce with the soul,———gives a smarter stroke, and leaves something more inexpressible upon the fancy, than words can either convey———or sometimes get rid of" (V.vii.253). As it is their common mortality that has encroached upon Trim's audience through their eyes, it seems that death, like sex, is another of those "certain ideas which leave prints of themselves about our eyes and eyebrows . . . a consciousness of it, somewhere about the heart" (V.i.242). Locke also considered vision preeminent among our sensory faculties. But Tristram parts company with him to show that what sight connects us with, and how it happens, radically contradicts Locke's assumptions about the connection between language, speaker, and listener. Like "hobbyhorse" and "journey"—to use them once more as representative of Sterne's purposes with language—Trim's hat comes to hold for his watchers and for the reader a lively experience even in the face of death.

III

Sterne's anticonventional narrative structures and his antiempirical mobilization of language may thus be said to constitute the chief means to the "experience" of narrator and reader in *Tristram Shandy* and *A Sentimental Journey.* Hans-Georg Gadamer distinguishes literary experience so conceived as corollary to *all* experience rather than an event discrete unto itself:

> Inasmuch as we encounter the work of art in the world and a world in the individual work of art, this does not remain a strange universe into which we are magically transported for a time.
>
> Rather, we learn to understand ourselves in it, and that means that we preserve the discontinuity of the experience in the continuity of our existence. Therefore it is necessary to adopt an attitude to . . . art that does not lay claim to immediacy, but corresponds to the historical reality of man. The appeal to immediacy, to the genius of the moment, to the significance of the "experience," cannot withstand the claim of human existence to continuity and unity of self-understanding. The experience of of art must not be side-tracked into the uncommittedness of aesthetic awareness. . . . Art is knowledge and the experience of the work of art is a sharing of this knowledge.[15]

While each event, each moment, in a text has its own identity, literary moments are not qualitatively different from others. Such a conception of art deprives it of the "magic" with which it is endowed by more Romantic theories, but it ratifies vital connections between art and the rest of life of the kind we have explored in discussing the preface in *Tristram Shandy.* In such a view, reading provides intense (and in that limited sense "immediate") experiences which take their shape against the background of the experience we bring to them, issuing in perspectives that in turn shape our further experience.

A.D. McKillop's description of Tristram Shandy as narrator suggests that the relationship I have just described between readers and what they read parallels that of the narrator and what he tells: Tristram Shandy is "both inside and outside the moment; he is not only the knower of English empirical philosophy, but the philosopher who writes with confidence about the knower."[16] Such conceptions of the relations between

reader, narrator, and work return us to the crucial function of conversation as a model for narrative in Sterne's novels. Here is Tristram's most direct pronouncement on the subject:

> Writing, when properly managed, (as you may be sure I think mine is) is but a different name for conversation: As no one, who knows what he is about in good company, would venture to talk all;— —so no author, who understands the just boundaries of decorum and good breeding, would presume to think all: The truest respect which you can pay to the reader's understanding, is to halve this matter amicably, and leave him something to imagine, in his turn, as well as yourself. (II.xi.77)

As we have seen, leaving the reader "something to imagine" is precisely the function of Sterne's witty language and digressive structure. His vision—and use—of a language rooted in physical human nature and of digressions (Tristram's opinions, Yorick's sentiment) that impede conventional narrative progress aim to persuade the reader to "think as well as read" (I.xx.42).[17] That is, they make it almost impossible for a reader to ignore Sterne's narrators as speakers with their own sometimes baffling but always definite points of view on any subject they introduce. Simultaneously, Sterne's language makes it hard for readers to avoid trying to locate and articulate their own relations to what they find themselves involved in. "Never in the annals of fiction," says James Swearingen, "is the awareness of the integrity of the reader more explicit and sensitive than here."[18]

Iser's theoretical analysis of the reading process and Swearingen's study of reflexivity, both phenomenological in their approaches, provide terms especially useful for appreciating the purposive nature of conversation in Sterne's novels. Iser begins by stressing that reading a literary text is conversational in that it involves text and reader in mutual creation of the literary work, which "must lie halfway between the two":

> The convergence of text and reader brings the literary work into existence, and this convergence can never be precisely pinpointed, but must always remain virtual, as it is not to be identified either with the reality of the text or with the individual disposition of the reader. . . .
>
> It is the virtuality of the work that gives rise to its dynamic nature, and this in turn is the precondition for the effects that the work calls forth. As the reader uses the various perspectives offered him by the text in order to relate the patterns . . . to one another, he sets the work in motion, and this very process results ultimately in the awakening of responses within himself. (*Implied Reader,* 274-75)

Swearingen uses a phenomenological term to describe

the points of view of the two parties to a conversation; he calls them "horizons" (*Reflexivity,* 10). While conversation fuses the horizons, such mingling takes place only to the degree that the differing points of view have first been defined and understood by the participants: "Detaching himself from his own orientation, attempting to suspend his own historical conditioning insures a reader's *failure* as a conversationalist" (p. 11; my emphasis).

Iser situates the origins of the dynamic nature of the process in "gaps" which—again as in conversation—we are invited to fill in from our own direction. Without these "elements of indeterminacy, the gaps in the text, we should not be able to use our imagination" (*Implied Reader,* 283).[19] Probably the best Sternean endorsement of this view of reading is found in a letter to one of his own readers who had sent him a double-handled walking stick, calling it "shandean statuary." Sterne responded:

> Your walking stick is in no sense more *shandaic* than in that of its having *more handles than one*——The parallel breaks only in this, that in using the stick, every one will take the handle which suits his convenience. In **Tristram Shandy,** the handle is taken which suits their passions, their ignorance or sensibility. There is so little true feeling in the *herd* of the *world,* that I wish I could have got an act of parliament, when the books first appear'd, "that none but wise men should look into them." It is too much to write books and find heads to understand them. . . . A true feeler always brings half the entertainment with him. His own ideas are only call'd forth by what he reads, and the vibrations within, so entirely correspond with those excited, 'tis like reading *himself* and not the *book.* (**Letters,** 411)

The distinction Sterne makes between the "herd" and the "true feeler" is of the greatest importance: the ignorant reader forces the text to fit his assumptions; the better response begins with *inward* movement ("vibrations") that issues in defining the self through the text.

The letter serves to introduce the fundamental purpose of narrative as conversation. In a relationship where to speak and to listen are also to interpret, what begins as a means of knowing results in "a mode of being" (*Reflexivity,* 12). Swearingen defines "Tristram's ultimate aim in his book and ours in reading" as articulating "the close relation between understanding an 'other'—person, event, text, or tradition—and understanding oneself" (p. 14). Similarly, for Iser, "the production of the meaning of literary texts . . . does not merely entail the discovery of the unformulated, which can then be taken over by the active imagination of the reader; it also entails the possibility that we may formulate ourselves and so discover what had previously seemed to elude our consciousness" (*Implied Reader,* 294).

Such analyses of conversation in its relation to the reading process reveal that when, as we found in our discussion of Tristram's preface, Sterne "holds up the mirror to nature," he does so through an art conceived as alive and moving. If Aristotle's formulation of the function of poetry was usually taken to mean that great literature is a kind of static warehouse of "truth," both Tristram and Yorick transform the concept, engaging the reading in a demonstrative experience of art *as* truth.

Sterne is extremely resourceful in engaging the reader's participation in his narrator's quest after his own nature. His most direct means involves Tristram in writing problems that turn out to have ontological implications for the reader as well. We have already encountered some of these in considering the way Tristram chooses to begin his "life and opinions." While he presented himself as assured in the manner of his setting forth, we have seen that in raising the issue of suitable starting places, he makes it a question with more than literary implications. Where does a life—my life?—really begin? Once underway, he reverts periodically to the question of what is suitable for inclusion, and in doing so pushes the "true feeler" to explore the boundaries of his own selfhood:

> O ye POWERS! (for powers ye are, and great ones too)——which enable mortal man to tell a story worth the hearing,——that kindly shew him, where he is to begin it,——and where he is to end it,——what he is to put into it,——and what he is to leave out,——how much of it he is to cast into shade,——and whereabouts he is to throw his light! . . .

> I beg and beseech you . . . that wherever, in any part of your dominions it so falls out, that three several roads meet in one point . . . that at least you set up a guide-post, in the center of them, in mere charity to direct an uncertain devil, which of the three he is to take. (III.xxiv.151)

Such a passage, putting into question what makes up the *story* of a life, simultaneously questions what makes up life itself. Telling and reading *are* interpreting.

This conjunction becomes more intense when telling is placed in an adversary relation against the time available to do it. If, once again, an adjunct of Sterne's program is to instill new life into time-worn cliché, then *ars longa, vita brevis* opens in an unexpected direction as Tristram complains how impossibly little time he has to get so much down on paper: "I am this month one whole year older than I was this time twelve-month; and having got . . . almost into the middle of my fourth volume——and no farther than to my first day's life——'tis demonstrative that I have three hundred and sixty-four days more life to write just now, than when I first set out" (IV.xiv.207).

Ars longa has always meant that art lasts a long time compared to a human life. Grumbling that it *takes* a long time (never mind whether it will last) provides a laugh for those who summon up the implied cliché, while at the same time the crazily formidable narrative goal lures us again to consider the relation between event and interpretation in our own lives. Later he turns from humorous concern about whether his book will "swim down the gutter of Time" toward Posterity (*ars longa* in the traditional sense) to carry us suddenly into poignant awareness of how brief life really is:

> I will not argue the matter: Time wastes too fast: every letter I trace tells me with what rapidity Life follows my pen; the days and hours of it, more precious, my dear *Jenny,* than the rubies about thy neck, are flying over our heads like light clouds of a windy day, never to return more——every thing presses on——whilst thou art twisting that lock,— —see! it grows grey; and every time I kiss thy hand to bid adieu, and every absence which follows it, are preludes to that eternal separation which we are shortly to make.——

> ——Heaven have mercy upon us both! (IX.xi.430)

Thus artistic problems of narrative inclusion (the resistance of the narrative medium to life) fuse with existential problems (the resistance of life's own medium—time—to life), forcing ontological thoughtfulness.

The "true feeler" will stand in need of all the good-humored acceptance of life that Tristram and Yorick have fostered. For Tristram and Yorick exist to make us laugh and make us willing to explore serious questions about ourselves. We have already noticed many of these questions in studying Sterne's purpose with language and structure. Overall, it is perhaps not too much to say that these questions and purposes are in the service of integration for both narrator and reader. Certainly the interdependence of body and mind that pervades both ***Tristram Shandy*** and ***A Sentimental Journey*** tests us as readers, with the aim in the long run of making us accept ourselves as we are and be the better for it. As Sterne says in one of his sermons, "'Tis one step towards acting well, to think worthily of our nature" (***Sermons,*** I:82). But such self-respect is, as we have seen, won (if at all) at the cost of almost steady embarrassment and frequent pain. Like Tristram, whose pitiful body has "been the continual sport of what the world calls Fortune" (I.v.6), the reader of Sterne's novels has the chance to come to terms with the body—or spend a lifetime complaining about it.

But reconciling mind with body is not the only reconciliation Sterne attempts in his two long conversations with the reader. In ***A Sentimental Journey*** even more explicitly than in ***Tristram Shandy,*** he implicates us with his narrator in confronting the obdurate problems that human society, as well as individual human na-ture, pose to the traveler through life's foreign landscapes. The problem of communication takes on further urgency where one's native tongue is itself alien. Yorick confronts the fact that he is without a passport in a country at war with his own; he glimpses the possibility of imprisonment. And of course he skirts all perils by his wit, his subtle empathy, and the privileged position that allows him to exercise them. Recognizing that he *is* so privileged, we should also acknowledge that anyone who reads his ***Journey*** enjoys (by definition?) some comparable resources. Again, the presence in Yorick's route of a "herd" of travelers with all the same privileges, who nonetheless cannot or will not summon his wit and sympathy, places his *choice* of them in strong relief. And the bitter refusal of Smelfungus and Mundungus to do anything but rail against the abundant beauty through which they pass makes Yorick's participation in the peasants' gesture of grace (in the next to last chapter of the book) a profound acknowledgment of life's value even in a world that has given him his share of troubles:

> It was not till the middle of the second dance, when, from some pauses in the movement wherein they all seemed to look up, I fancied I could distinguish an elevation of spirit different from that which is the cause or the effect of simple jollity.——In a word, I thought I beheld *Religion* mixing in the dance——but as I had never seen her so engaged, I should have look'd upon it now, as one of the illusions of an imagination which is eternally misleading me, had not the old man, as soon as the dance ended, said, that this was their constant way . . . after supper was over . . . to dance and rejoice; believing, he said, that a chearful and contented mind was the best sort of thanks to heaven that an illiterate peasant could pay——

> ——Or a learned prelate either, said I. (pp. 283-84)

Once again Sterne has so constructed his dialogue with the reader that it is impossible to deny the relevance of the alternatives offered—gratefulness vs. bitterness— regardless of what we think about heaven.

By their nature, the existential contradictions Sterne works and plays at reconciling are all linked with one another: the difficulty of comprehending our life story, compounded by the persistence of time in piling on more and more for us to interpret, results in the first place from conflicting impulses of mind and body—all of which make life seem as much damnation as blessing. The most inclusive and daunting contradiction of all is the presence of death in the midst of life—the most intimidating challenge to living fully. Sterne takes it on implicitly in the same early chapter of ***Tristram Shandy*** that tells us the date of his hero's birth: "I can truly say, that from the first hour I drew my breath . . . to this, that I can now scarce draw it at all, for an asthma I got in scating against the wind in *Flanders;*——

—I have been the continual sport of what the world calls Fortune" (I.v.6). That shadow is the darkest that Tristram confronts. He faces it with the same comic vision that encompasses such "pitiful misadventures and cross accidents" as his crushed nose and extreme circumcision. Introducing the threat of death, he refuses to exploit its tragic potential, opting instead for the mock-heroic. When much later he refers again to his illness, it is to comment that his most recent attack resulted from laughing too hard—as usual, at one of life's incongruities:

> To this hour art thou not tormented with the vile asthma thou gattest in skating against the wind in *Flanders?* and is it but two months ago, that in a fit of laughter, on seeing a cardinal make water like a quirister (with both hands) thou brakest a vessel in thy lungs, whereby, in two hours, thou lost as many quarts of blood; and hadst thou lost as much more, did not the faculty tell thee——it would have amounted to a gallon?——

(VIII.vi.384)

Sidestepping the ultimate danger with that final humorous prevarication is precisely the opposite of ignoring the threat's reality.

The extra-fictional connection of Tristram's illness with Sterne's own tuberculosis contributes to intensify that reality. As early as his Cambridge days, Sterne had been afflicted—he woke one morning to find he had "bled the bed full"—and his lungs never healed. Even a reader unacquainted with the facts of Sterne's life might start to sense an autobiographical reference in this ominous note as it is repeatedly inserted among the private and relatively small-scale trials of Tristram. Swearingen remarks that the voices of Sterne and Tristram "are neither equivalent nor clearly discriminated. One senses that the living voice must often be speaking from his own experience. . . . The problems encountered in the process of writing, for example, are not fictional problems, one is convinced, even if they are the ostensible concerns of Tristram" (*Reflexivity,* 4). Death, in the circumstantial guise of a "vile asthma," begins to stand out as a concern insinuating itself beyond the fiction toward the author and back again. Thus the reader also, more and more enmeshed in a web of conversation bonding him with the narrator, finds it impossible to distance the threat or extricate himself from the issues raised by its presence.

The fact that Yorick and Tristram, too, "are neither equivalent nor clearly discriminated" has the effect of emphasizing the role of death as threat and motivator. The story of Yorick's destruction by the solemn and vindictive targets of his humor is told within the first dozen chapters of **Tristram Shandy:** his descent from Hamlet's dead court jester, his generosity of spirit, his death with a joke on his lips, his grave marked "Alas, poor YORICK!"—and Tristram's two black pages. Then he is resurrected to play out at length the part his brief tragicomedy had prepared us for: Tristram's clearest exemplum of a life well lived. To say the least, Yorick's cheerful acceptance of life's blows, including the final one, fuses him with Tristram as both offer brilliant resistance to death's dominion.

And then consider some of the further autobiographical interweaving of Sterne, Tristram, and Yorick. Having begun Tristram's tale, including the short life and death of Yorick, in the first volumes of **Tristram Shandy,** and having published volumes of his sermons as those of "Mr. Yorick," Sterne (whose own life was steadily more well known) broke the retrospective patterns established in his novel to leap into Tristram's adult travels in Volume VII. Such a break calls attention to Sterne's direct experience by the urgency with which illness and danger of death suggest a motivation not only of Tristram's journey but of his author's decision to grasp it as subject for his work. And finally, in choosing to retell his own and Tristram's journey as Yorick's **Sentimental Journey,** Sterne infuses the sentimental with the dangerous, and Yorick's urgent pursuit of life partakes of Tristram's earlier escape from death.

By this time, readers of Sterne who have come through **Tristram Shandy** and gone on to **A Sentimental Journey** will be occupied with uncertainty about where they have arrived. Conception, asthma, humor, death, unexpected journeys—Sterne's aim is to submerge us in them and get us to swim in them, or transcend them. Learning to swim is a more modest conception than transcendence. Either will suffice to suggest the vision Sterne makes available through good-natured travel in the world and humorous reflection in art. The vision, transcendence, mode of motion in a foreign medium—all are epitomized in a passage from the midst of Tristram's travels:

> ——Now this is the most puzzled skein of all—— for in this last chapter, as far at least as it has helped me through *Auxerre,* I have been getting forwards in two different journies together, and with the same dash of the pen——for I have got entirely out of *Auxerre* in this journey which I am writing now, and I am got half way out of *Auxerre* in that which I shall write hereafter——There is but a certain degree of perfection in every thing; and by pushing at something beyond that, I have brought myself into such a situation, as no traveller ever stood before me; for I am this moment walking across the market-place of *Auxerre* with my father and my uncle *Toby,* in our way back to dinner——and I am this moment also entering *Lyons* with my post-chaise broke into a thousand pieces——and I am moreover this moment in a handsome pavillion built by *Pringello,* upon the banks of the *Garonne,* which Mons. *Sligniac* has lent me, and where I now sit rhapsodizing all these affairs.

——Let me collect myself, and pursue my journey.
(VII.xxviii.362)

And yet it must be admitted that there are readers for whom the experience Sterne offers remains uncompelling. For some, the invitations to good-humored participation in a joint search for self-definition may seem merely a mocking challenge. Appeals to our confidence may lead no further than the next embarrassing encounter with one of our own false assumptions or one of the narrator's dirty jokes. Responses to Sterne were from the start, and they remain, very strong and very mixed. A perceptive reader like Horace Walpole could find that the first volumes of **Tristram** "make one smile two or three times at the beginning, but in recompense make one yawn for two hours,"[20] and he goes on to comment on the "odd coupling" of the sermon in the first volume with a good deal of bawdy. A few laughs paid for with a great deal of boredom, an unlikable mixture of high sentiment and low talk—these are descriptions of how many readers still feel.

Coleridge, who loved Sterne's works, nevertheless describes (in appreciating them) some elements that may add up to a negative effect on many readers:

> A sort of *knowingness,* the wit of which depends, first on the modesty it gives pain to; or secondly, the innocence and innocent ignorance over which it triumphs; or thirdly, on a certain oscillation in the individual's mind between the remaining good and the encroaching evil of his nature, a sort of dallying with the devil, a fluxionary act of combining courage and cowardice . . . so that the mind has in its own white and black angel the same or similar amusements as might be supposed to take place between an old debauchee and a prude. . . . We have only to suppose society *innocent*—and [these effects are] equal to a stone that falls in snow; it makes no sound because it excites no resistance. [These effects account] for nine tenths [of our response]; the remainder rests on its being an offence against the good manners of human nature itself.[21]

I am not concerned here to show again the ways in which Sterne works to place these various affronts to the reader in the service of "experience"; rather, what Coleridge appreciates, simply (or complexly) puts off many readers.

Women readers may find Sterne's approach to them (especially in **Tristram Shandy**) as prudes and hypocrites hard to get beyond, regardless of how strong a case one makes for interpreting that treatment as aimed at the prudish in *all* of us, of both sexes. And the fact that both Tristram and Yorick sketch their female characters first as libidinous and mostly mindless may turn away female readers altogether. (On this score, Swearingen's appraisal of the role of Elizabeth Shandy in her son's story does more than anything else I know to reassess her much-maligned character.)

Along with what can easily be taken as misogynist in Sterne, a general air of masculine impotence—or at least disability—hangs over the novels, from Walter Shandy's premature ejaculation right to the last act of Yorick's journey: "So that when I stretch'd out my hand, I caught hold of the Fille de Chambre's" (p. 291). Toby Shandy—in Swearingen's words, "the man of feeling with the wound upon the groin" (*Reflexivity,* 215)—is in so many ways a model of sympathy that one may come to the conclusion that sentiment is achieved only at the cost of sexual potency and action. Some of Yorick's sexual contretemps encourage that equation, as does Tristram's acknowledgment of his own incapacity (at least temporarily) with his "dear *Jenny*" (VII.xxix.363). To distinguish Tristram the narrator, who sees such failures and discontinuities as the symptoms of a malaise his work exists to heal, may not be enough to redeem him—for many readers—as a character crippled by an infirmity that pervades his world.

Such reservations, or revulsions, may come between many readers and the kind of experience I have described, believing that it coheres in the manifold means by which Sterne seeks us out and engages our participation. My own purpose has been to show how Sterne's books come to *matter* for a reader. In other words, to corroborate one of Walter Shandy's many statements that mean more than he knows: "Every thing in this world, said my father, is big with jest,——and has wit in it, and instruction too,——if we can but find it out" (V.xxxii,276).

Notes

[1] References are to *Tristram Shandy,* ed. Howard Anderson (New York: Norton, 1980), and to *A Sentimental Journey,* ed. Gardner D. Stout, Jr. (Berkeley: Univ. of California Press, 1967), and to Stout's Introduction in the latter.

[2] J. Paul Hunter, "Response as Reformation: *Tristram Shandy* and the Art of Interruption," *Novel* 4 (1971), 133.

[3] Tristram Shandy's two names imply the dialectic between tragic fact and comic treatment in his "life and opinions."

[4] See William Bowman Piper, *Laurence Sterne* (New York: Twayne, 1966).

[5] *Letters of Laurence Sterne,* ed. Lewis P. Curtis (Oxford: Clarendon Press, 1935), 231.

[6] Tobias Smollett, *Travels through France and Italy,* ed. Thomas Seccombe (London: Oxford Univ. Press,

1935), 235-36.

7 *The Sermons of Mr. Yorick,* 2 vols. (Oxford: Basil Blackwell, 1927), I:29.

8 Wolfgang Iser, *The Implied Reader: Patterns of Communication in Prose Fiction from Bunyan to Beckett* (Baltimore: Johns Hopkins Univ. Press, 1974), 24.

9 *Selected Letters of Samuel Richardson,* ed. John Carroll (Oxford: Clarendon Press, 1964), 341.

10 F. R. Leavis, *The Great Tradition* (Garden City, N.Y.: Doubleday, 1954), 11.

11 See Kenneth MacLean, *John Locke and English Literature of the Eighteenth Century* (New Haven, Conn.: Yale Univ. Press, 1936).

12 John Locke, *An Essay concerning Human Understanding,* ed. Alexander Campbell Fraser, 2 vols. (Oxford: Clarenden Press, 1894), I:529.

13 Cf. Ian Watt, Introduction to *Tristram Shandy* (Boston: Houghton Mifflin, 1965), xxv; and Richard A. Lanham, *"Tristram Shandy": The Games of Pleasure* (Berkeley: Univ of California Press, 1973).

14 Cf. Stout, Introduction, p. 47, n. 64.

15 Hans-Georg Gadamer, *Truth and Method* (New York: Seabury Press, 1975), 86-87.

16 A. D. McKillop, *The Early Masters of English Fiction* (Lawrence: Univ. of Kansas Press, 1956), 210.

17 Earlier in the same chapter, Tristram has explained that his aim in sending "the lady" reader back to see if she can discover a clue to his mother's religion is "to rebuke a vicious taste which has crept into thousands besides herself,——of reading straight forwards, more in quest of the adventures, than of the deep erudition and knowledge which a book of this cast, if read over as it should be, would infallibly impart with them" (I.xx.41).

18 James Swearingen, *Reflexivity in "Tristram Shandy": An Essay in Phenomenological Criticism* (New Haven, Conn.: Yale Univ. Press, 1977), 11.

19 Iser remarks a few pages earlier that the "unwritten" in the text, which "stimulates the reader's creative participation," had been noticed by Virginia Woolf in her study of Jane Austen (pp. 275-76). In *The Common Reader,* 1st ser. (London: Hogarth Press, 1957), 174, Woolf wrote: "Jane Austen is thus a mistress of much deeper emotion than appears upon the surface. She stimulates us to supply what is not there. What she offers is, apparently, a trifle, yet is composed of some-thing that expands in the reader's mind and endows with the most enduring form of life scenes which are outwardly trivial."

20 *Horace Walpole's Correspondence with Sir David Dalrymple,* ed. W. S. Lewis, Charles H. Bennett, and Andrew G. Hoover (New Haven, Conn.: Yale Univ. Press, 1951), 66.

21 *Coleridge's Miscellaneous Criticism,* ed. Thomas M. Raysor (Cambridge, Mass.: Harvard Univ. Press, 1936), 121.

David McNeil (essay date 1990)

SOURCE: "Sterne: Military Veterans and 'Humours,'" in his *The Grotesque Depiction of War and the Military in Eighteenth-Century English Fiction,* University of Delaware Press, 1990, pp. 144-67.

[*In the following essay, McNeil asserts that Sterne's major works reveal his affection for war veterans even while* Tristram Shandy *in particular demonstrates that Sterne is well aware that any enjoyment of the trappings of war demonstrates the violent, irrational side of human nature.*]

The Charm of the Military Veteran

Laurence Sterne was charmed by the military character. This charm obviously had its roots in family history; Sterne's father served as an ensign in Chudleigh's Foot Regiment and saw action in the Spanish Succession War after which he was posted to Jamaica.[1] Although Sterne went to live with relatives in York who raised him, he never lost the soft heart that he had for the military veteran and that inspired the incomparable figure of uncle Toby. Sterne's love for the military character is explicitly stated in *A Sentimental Journey* when Yorick steps into a box at the Comic Opera and sees a "kindly old French officer" sitting there quietly by himself:

> I love the character, not only because I honour the man whose manners are softened by a profession which makes bad men worse; but that I once knew one—for he is no more . . . Captain Tobias Shandy, the dearest of my flock and friends, whose philanthropy I never think of at this long distance from his death—but my eyes gush out with tears. For his sake, I have a predilection for the whole corps of veterans . . .[2]

This passage suggests that the creation of uncle Toby was inspired by Sterne's acquaintance with a soldier he knew through his father, or by Roger Shandy himself whom Sterne described as an innocent. However Sterne came by his character, uncle Toby remains one of the most, if not the most, single quixotic figures in English literature by virtue of the complexity of his military "humour."

Yorick encounters several veterans in *A Sentimental Journey,* and their military stories tend to be colored by a somber sense of misfortune. First, there is the Calais monk who alludes to "some military services ill requited," which resulted in his abandoning "the sword" (*SJ*, 102). Then there is, of course, Yorick's valet who had been a regiment drummer: "La Fleur had set out early in life, as gallantly as most Frenchmen do, with *serving* for a few years; at the end of which, having satisfied the sentiment, and found moreover, That the honour of beating a drum was likely to be its own reward, as it open'd no further track of glory to him—he retired . . ." (*SJ,* 124-25). Yorick's hiring of La Fleur, who "could do nothing in the world but beat a drum and play a march or two upon the fife" (*SJ*, 124), is motivated solely by a sense of benevolence that is more than fairly recompensed by La Fleur's good nature and company. Finally, there is the "old soldier" beggar "who had been campaign'd and worn out to death in the service," to whom Yorick gives "a couple of sous" (*SJ*, 133), and the Chevalier de St. Louis who is selling *"patès"* at Versailles (*SJ*, 209-11). The latter is a victim of regimental disbandment, and when the king learns of his plight, which the old soldier suffers without a harsh word, "he broke up his little trade by a pension of fifteen hundred livres a year" (*SJ*, 211). All of these portraits are infused with that endearing sentimentality that few novelists other than Sterne can successfully manage.

The situation in England resembled that of France. Hence despite the services offered by institutions like the *L'Hôtel des Invalids* or Chelsea Hospital, it was generally thought that veterans were not well treated for their sacrifices. In Hogarth's "The Times, Plate II" (engraved 1762 or 1763, published 1790), the spray of water that symbolizes government assistance completely misses a group of maimed war veterans. John Collier's "The Pluralist and Old Soldier" (1763) is a dialogue between a begging veteran who lost a leg at Guadeloupe and has not received his pension and a "well-fed pluralist" who tells the veteran to be-gone.[3] For those invalids who, for whatever reason, were refused admission to Chelsea or who did not receive pensions, the government did nothing except give them the right to beg in public. The veteran and his family described in the poem "The Volunteer" (1791) endure all kinds of miseries that culminate in a most inglorious end: "Some merciful volley then shatters a leg, / And his crutches procure him permission to beg."[4]

Consequently, it is not surprising that sentimental portraits of military veterans are quite common in the eighteenth century.[5] There seem to be two extreme types: the loquacious soul who, like uncle Toby, is always anxious to verbalize his experience; and the rather silent or pithy stoic whose experience has a significance that lies beyond language. Examples of the first include Goldsmith's "broken soldier" from "The Deserted Village," who sits by the good preacher's fire "and talked the night away; / Wept o'er his wounds, or tales of sorrow done, / Shouldered his crutch, and shewed how fields were won."[6] "The Old General" (1740), by Sir Charles Hanbury Williams, contains a portrait that is very close to uncle Toby's "humour":

> If you name one of Marlbro's ten campaigns,
> He tells you its whole history for your pains:
> And Blenheim's field becomes by his reciting,
> As long in telling as it was in fighting.[7]

Another comic example is Goldsmith's Mr. Hardcastle who is all too eager to command attention with his stories of Marlborough and Prince Eugene. The same type can be seen in satiric prints such as Bunbury's "Fought His Battles All O'er Again." . . . One might also think of Defoe's Colonel Jack who "lov'd to talk to Seamen and Soldiers about the War" and from whom he imbibes an oral history, as Jack says,

> . . . those old Soldiers and Tars love to talk with me too, and to tell me all the Stories they could think of, and that not only of the Wars then going on, but also of the Wars in *Oliver's* time, the Death of King *Charles* the first, and the like.

> By this means, as young as I was, I was a kind of an Historian, and tho' I had read no Books . . . [8]

The soldier who has had to face life-or-death situations on a daily basis bears an experience that demands extraordinary attention and discourse.

Because language cannot adequately contain the meaning of the military experience, veterans are often portrayed as lapsing into cliché or being somewhat distant and silent. A veteran of the battle of Dettingen delights Boswell's curiosity for a moment with simple comments like, "Salvation is promised to those that die in the field."[9] Another example of this type is the old soldier whom Wordsworth describes in *The Prelude*.[10] The poet is walking home one summer evening when he encounters an "uncouth shape" (bk. 4, line 387); becoming curious, he looks more closely to see a "meagre man" standing alone "in military garb" and eventually presses the veteran with questions (bk. 4, lines 393, 398):

> His history, the veteran, in reply,
> Was neither slow nor eager; but, unmoved,
> And with a quiet uncomplaining voice,

A stately air of mild indifference
He told in a few plain words a soldier's
    tale—

(bk. 4, lines 417-21)

Wordsworth prompts the veteran to "speak of war, battle and pestilence" (bk. 4, line 437), and the old man's response gives the impression of a resigned stalwartness:

He all the while was in demeanour calm,
Concise in answer; solemn and sublime
He might have seemed, but that in all he said
There was a strange half-absence, as of one
Knowing too well the importance of his
    theme,
But feeling it no longer.

(bk. 4, lines 440-45)

The veteran's parting words, spoken with a "ghastly mildness in his look" (bk. 4, line 458), reflect the humble faith and strength that Wordsworth admired in many of his rustic figures: "My trust is in the God of Heaven, / And in the eye of him who passes me!" (bk. 4, lines 459-60). There is a heroic sense of resolution and strength that attaches itself to such figures who suffer hardship and often mutilation and yet who are not embittered. An excellent example is the begging veteran with the wooden leg who is described in *The Citizen of the World,* Letter 199. The "intrepidity and content" of the veteran despite his misfortune impress his beholders who subsequently acknowledge that "an habitual acquaintance with misery is the truest school of fortitude and philosophy."[11] Moving from the particular to the universal, one could claim that the pervasiveness of war in history immunizes us against its horrific barbarism and cruelty.

Several prototypes for Sterne's uncle Toby can be found, beginning with Shadwell's Captain Blunt, whose companions are forever reliving past battles (see *The Volunteers*). Yet Shadwell's veterans feature the hard celebrating and resolve that look ahead more to the "Sodger Laddie" and "doxy" of Burns's "The Jolly Beggars" than they do *Tristram Shandy.* In contrast to Sterne's meek Toby, Burns's "Sodger Laddie" is a rollicking ex-trooper:

And now tho' I must beg, with a wooden arm
    and leg,
    And many a tatter'd rag hanging over my
    bum,
I'm as happy with my wallet, my bottle and
    my Callet,
    As When I us'd in scarlet to follow a
    drum.[12]

The grotesque depiction of the veteran often includes references to lost limbs. Nelson recognizes the black

humor in Burns's "Jolly Beggars" and in an Irish song in which a woman facetiously comments on how "queer" her soldier-beau looks on his return:

You haven't an arm and you haven't a leg,
You're an eyeless, noseless, chickenless egg;
You'll have to be put with a bowl to beg:
    Och, Johnny, I hardly knew ye![13]

Goldsmith chose to mingle the sentimental with an abrupt style, and this combination makes him more like Sterne—as in the following picture in *Threnodia Augustalis:*

The hardy veteran after struck the sight,
Scarr'd, mangl'd, maim'd in every part,
Lopp'd of his limbs in many a gallant fight,
In nought entire—except his heart.[14]

Major Matchlock of *The Tatler* may also have figured into the genesis of Sterne's Captain Shandy. Matchlock "has all the Battles by Heart" and is held "in great Esteem" among his fellow tatlers.[15]

However, it is not until Steele's Captain Sentry— Matchlock's counterpart in *The Spectator*—a "Gentleman of great Courage, good Understanding, but invincible Modesty,"[16] that we discover a "humourous" military character who is modest and delicate rather than brash and boisterous. His military "humour" is, of course, animated whenever he has an occasion to indulge in military history. Like so many of Sterne's military veterans, Captain Sentry is noteworthy for how his lack of preferment has not left him embittered, as the Spectator himself remarks: " . . . I never heard him make a sower Expression, but frankly confess that he left the World because he was not fit for it."[17] Sentry, however, is an extremely sketchy figure (Matchlock, a ghost). Smollett's Commodore Trunnion seems to rate as the first fully realized military quixotic in the English novel. Yet Trunnion, actually falls into the category of the old sea dog, not known for modesty.[18] Seamen represent a separate subgroup insofar as their peculiar roughness and ignorance of social refinements were standard jokes.

This survey brings us back to Sterne. The especially intriguing feature of *Tristram Shandy* is how Sterne puts the reader in the awkward position of feeling sorry for uncle Toby because the Peace of Utrecht ends the War of the Spanish Succession, and the end of the war means the end of uncle Toby's miniature reenactments on the bowling green. Uncle Toby and Corporal Trim get their pleasure out of recreating Marlborough's campaigns and battles as accurately as they can; their harmless play depends upon, and is not merely tied to, the real war.[19] (In this sense the bowling green campaigns are different from Wemmick's castle.) After the peace is announced, Walter Shandy cannot resist executing a subtle "back-stroke" at his brother's hobbyhorse that expresses the paradox beautifully: "Never mind, brother *Toby* . . . by God's blessing we shall have another war break out again some of these days; and when it does,—the belligerent powers, if they would hang themselves, cannot keep us out of play."[20] As much as the reader may find uncle Toby (or Captain Shandy) endearing, and as much as his hobbyhorse is amusing, the notion of wanting "another war"—or of seeing the present one continued, which describes Toby's exact desire—is perfectly disturbing.

The grotesque best explains this paradoxical structure as well as the military theme that is an integral part of the Shandean dialectic. Not surprisingly, both Wolfgang Kayser and Mikhail Bakhtin single out Sterne as a writer of the grotesque. Kayser points to how the grotesque is more appropriate than a number of other descriptive generic terms, including satire, for identifying Sterne's art: "I emphatically subscribe to the classification of Sterne as a writer of the grotesque, for the categories of humor, satire, and irony . . . fail to do full justice to the form and content of *Tristram Shandy.*"[21] According to Bakhtin, Sterne stands out as an eighteenth-century writer who continues the carnival elements of the grotesque.[22] Laughter, which Bakhtin sees as the key carnival element, clearly dominated the corresponding element of fear in the medieval grotesque, reached a climax in the fiction of Rabelais, and then gradually became extinct when the romantic grotesque exorcised the "comic" and intensified the "terrifying world."[23] Sterne is the exception who writes neither condemnatory satire nor pure romantic sentimentality but rejuvenates a kind of saturnalia that is akin to Rabelais's world. Although a few critics have already linked *Tristram Shandy* to the grotesque, their comments tend to address Sterne's general tragicomic sentimentalism or his disjointed narrative form as opposed to the military subject.[24] In *Tristram Shandy,* the bowling green hobbyhorse represents war as a ludicrous game; conversely, the battle wound represents war as fearful destruction.

The modern theory of the grotesque as a ludicrous-fearful duality differs slightly from the primary meaning that the English word "grotesque" had during the eighteenth century. Johnson defined "Grotesque" as "Distorted of figure; unnatural; wildly formed"—a meaning that reflects the pejorative connotations that the word then had.[25] The adjectival sense of "grotesque" as unnatural is still current (OED #2) and remains somewhat pejorative in connotation.[26] Sterne himself seems to use "grotesque" in this way (but without a clearly pejorative connotation) when Tristram self-consciously introduces his portrait of Corporal Trim.[27] It is also interesting to note that after the second installment of *Tristram Shandy* appeared in 1761, a writer for the *Critical Review* associated Sterne's humor with the "grotesque" and raised the subject of laughter as

being worthy in and of itself:

> Every body had heard of the different species of humour; grave humour and gay humour, genteel humour and low humour, natural humour and extravagant humour, grotesque and buffoonery. Perhaps these two last may be more properly stiled the bastards of humour than the power itself, although they have been acknowledged and adopted by the two arch priests of laughter *Lucian* and *Rabelais.* They deserve to be held illegitimate, because they either desert nature altogether, in their exhibitions, or represent her in a state of distortion. Lucian and Rabelais, in some of their writings, seem to have no more purpose in view, unless the design of raising laughter may in some cases be thought a moral aim.[28]

For Sterne, raising laughter certainly was a moral aim, or at least laughter could serve a therapeutic function and partially redeem mankind.[29] The art of cultivating laughter is the art of recognizing the comic in life, in Walter Shandy's words, "Every thing in this world . . . is big with jest . . . if we can but find it out" (*TS,* 1:470). This is the point at which the two senses of "grotesque" meet; what is perceived as unnatural (according to an erroneous assumption about rational behavior as a norm) and fearful may also be seen as ludicrous. Shandeism, therefore, squares with Bakhtin's profound view of carnival laughter as a kind of instinctive folklore celebration of the more frightening aspects of our existence such as death and war—a celebration of the ludicrous, of inexorable birth-death cycles.

Sterne was sensitive to a double-edged effect, similar to that of the grotesque, in laughter itself, and this sensitivity is at the heart of why "satire," as it is usually defined, inadequately accounts for how the military theme is treated in *Tristram Shandy.* When two parties feel that they are *laughing together* they also feel like allies insofar as they accept a common ludicrous point even if they themselves are the object of it. On the other hand, if one of the two feels *laughed at,* then offense and animosity may result. Sterne is eager to enjoy true comedic laughter but aware that human nature, as sensitive as it is, is often fearful about being the victim of insolence. Tristram tells the reader that uncle Toby's bowling green campaigns could be a satire against the magnificent pomp and ceremony with which Louis XIV took the field, except that uncle Toby could not insult anyone: Ironically, the very denial of satiric intent only raises the subject of satiric possibility, which is as far as Sterne means to go. Military ostentation can be seen as ludicrous. Likewise, Tristram does not mean to characterize "the militiating spirits of [his] country" (*TS,* 1:360) in uncle Toby. And one must not forget that the novel is dedicated to William Pitt, the champion of the British cause in the Seven Years' War, which went on while Sterne was bringing out the first three installments of ***Tristram Shandy.*** The Dedication recommends that Pitt take the novel "into the country" where it may beguile him "of one moment's pain" for when a man laughs "it adds something to this Fragment of Life" (*TS,* 1:i). Despite these qualifications and the military background of his father, Sterne nevertheless ridicules the human propensity for fragmentation and conflict, but he does not do so with any vain desire to laugh man out of his folly. Uncle Toby's wish to continue the war strikes a fearful chord and no more. Sterne's belief is that redemption lies in laughter itself, and if Tristram is writing against anything, it is, as he says, "the spleen" (*TS,* 1:360).

Still, laughter is extremely volatile as Trim is well aware when he proposes it as a means of disarming the daunting gravity of courting Widow Wadman: "All womankind . . . love jokes; the difficulty is to know how they chuse to have them cut; and there is no knowing that, but by trying as we do with our artillery in the field, by raising or letting down their breeches, till we hit the mark" (*TS,* 2:753). The highest role one can hope to play in the fallen world is that of the self-sacrificing butt, which is what Yorick does in ***Tristram Shandy:*** " . . . he chose rather to join in the laugh against himself" (*TS,* 1:20).[30] Conflict arises, however, when others are not willing to join in the comic fun for most consider a joke directed at them to be a declaration of war:

> . . . it happens, that a person laugh'd at, considers himself in the light of a person injured, with all the rights of such a situation belonging to him; and when thou viewest him in that light too, and reckons up his friends, his family, his kindred, and allies,—and musters up with them the many recruits which will list under him from a sense of common danger;—'tis no extravagant arithmetic to say, that for every ten jokes,—thou hast got a hundred enemies.

> (*TS,* 1:31)

When it is considered inappropriate or made at somebody's expense, humor can create rather than alleviate tension. The idea of laughing at another—satirizing an individual for example—recalls Hobbes's view of laughter as being a "sudden glory" derived from a feeling of superiority.

Sensitivity is the key to uncle Toby's Cervantic attraction,[31] for his military affectation or "humour" constitutes a sharp Jonsonian ridicule. This parodox of being a man-at-arms and yet a man so harmless, innocent, and naive puts Toby at the center of Sterne's grotesque rendering of the military theme in ***Tristram Shandy.*** The military veteran who possesses a blind professional simplicity and kindness of heart emerges as a character type in eighteenth-century fiction, the very opposite of the *miles gloriosus.* Uncle Toby, however, may

be the most lovable of these characters; he literally cannot hurt a fly. On the other hand, he may be the most unnerving as well, insofar as his perverse wish to continue the war is concerned.

War Games and Wounds

Laughing at a serious subject like war seems callous and bound to offend, but it is here that Sterne's subtlety plays such an important role. Neither Tristram nor the reader ever laugh directly at war; we laugh at the hobbyhorse, and the hobbyhorse is both a mock-heroic of adult play and a travesty of the War of the Spanish Succession. As Rabelais's Picrocholine War is both a mock-allegory of a lawsuit in Rabelais's home village, according to Bakhtin, and a satire against the aggressiveness of Charles V, so Sterne's uncle Toby is both a man at play and a man at arms.[32] For those who, like uncle Toby, feel themselves to be emotionally caught up in the military spirit, to go to war is—grotesquely or unnaturally enough—an expression of love. Toby defends his wish to continue the war by arguing that it is based on his love of honor and liberty (see *TS,* 2:557, 753). Violence is sometimes necessary to curb greater violence. Sterne's madcap narrator may describe uncle Toby's "amours" as the "choicest morsel" of his story (*TS,* 1:401), but the bowling green reenactments clearly form another key episode that Sterne could have expanded if he had felt more hobbyhorsical. What the reader gets in the novel, according to Tristram, is only a "sketch" of uncle Toby's entire "campaigns" (*TS,* 2:536), which Tristram is considering to publish as a separate work and which he estimates will, by itself, consist of three books.

Uncle Toby's hobbyhorse is the epitome of war as play or game. The reality of war is symbolized by Toby's war wound, and it is important to see the connection between the two. Toby's hobbyhorse originates from his attempt to communicate the circumstances that led to his horrific wound at the siege of Namur. The wound is as horrific as Sterne could have made it—a piece of a parapet breaks off and hits Toby in the groin, crushing his hip bone and confining him to his room for four years. It is an unheroic and freak accident that can only be blamed on the conflict itself, since the parapet was presumably hit by British artillery. But it is the diction of technicalities that plagues poor Toby (and his audience) more than anything else, when he tries to explain his sacrifice both to himself and the world: the "distinctions between the scarp and counterscarp,—the glacis and covered way,—the half-moon and ravelin" (*TS,* 1:94) are too much to handle. Language fails. Toby confuses himself as much as his audience and is in danger of sliding into fatal despair when he suddenly gets the idea to consult a map.

Ichnography appeals to the demand of the mind for rational explanation, and here Peter Stevick's comments are relevant: "Uncle Toby's fortifications and battle diagrams are, among other things, his defense against the possibility that his function, as part of the 'prodigious armies in Flanders,' may have been meaningless or incomprehensible."[33] As an individual soldier, Toby plays less than a "miniature" role in the siege of Namur. But explaining how he was injured is crucial to him for in Tristram's words, "The history of a soldier's wound beguiles the pain of it" (*TS,* 1:88). One map leads to another, to the science of fortifications, and then to the hobbyhorse itself, which Toby rides with all his love away from death's door.[34] His play-fantasy constitutes the essence of how the grotesque mode is used to address the subject of war, because it effectively distances the reader (and Toby too for that matter) from the reality of battle. I have already discussed the board war game in *Ferdinand Count Fathom* essentially as a wish-fulfillment being played out by King Theodore—the occupation of Genoese territory. For uncle Toby, the bowling green imitation is his mission.

It has been suggested that uncle Toby's miniature re-enactments may have derived from Sterne's possible knowledge of "raree" or puppet shows.[35] Reenactments of military victories were popular parts of theatrical entertainments; for instance, the battle of Dettingen (in particular, George Darraugh's recapture of an English standard) was reproduced several times on the London stage in August 1743.[36] The main difference, however, between such shows and Toby's fun on the bowling-green is that the latter constitutes a private hobby that can produce great personal pleasure at the risk of public embarrassment. (Toby, however, is too far gone to be self-conscious about the puerility of his hobby.) The more important, albeit obvious, source for the bowling green reenactments is the military miniature, those wonderful toy soldiers and artillery pieces that were often given to monarchs-to-be to play with and were eventually mass-produced for the public about the time Sterne was writing **Tristram Shandy.**[37] These miniatures were constructed out of papier-mâché, cardboard, and wood carvings; tin eventually became the most common material. Some miniatures were elaborately mechanized. Louis XIII and his war-loving successor had mechanical soldiers designed by none other than Vauban himself, the famous French military engineer; they "moved, marched, fired, shot and retreated."[38] The wood carvers of southern Germany even produced a splendid "movable fortress," which reminds one of uncle Toby's changeable model town (*TS,* 2:539-40).

Although there is no direct evidence linking Sterne to military miniatures, it is clear that through his father he would have known many soldiers and people in the military coterie who could have collected them.[39] Miniature artillery pieces were often given to veterans. The significance of the miniature as a reproduction is its abstract nature, which it shares with military history

and tableaux. In his discussion of Charles LeBrun and battle painting, Norman Bryson claims that "one sees a marked tendency towards a signification that is highly abstract": "the model here is the war-room. . . . a simulacrum of the battlefield, the war-room is also its real theatre . . . nothing essential is lost."[40] For the military strategist, this "simulacrum" allows one to be indifferent to the materiality of armies: "the martial body is enciphered, made into a statistical entity, a vortex of abstract force."[41] As a veteran and soldier's soldier, Toby is certainly not indifferent to the flesh, but only when it appears as such, as in the case of LeFever; otherwise, the bowling green campaigns are nothing but abstract games.

Before proceeding any further, one should note that there are no miniature soldiers on uncle Toby's bowling green. Toby and Trim are in effect toy soldiers or play as such in wielding spade and shovel to cut the breaches in the walls or in arranging the artillery pieces to copy the steps of the actual siege carried on by their commander Marlborough. Their commitment to reproducing the actual events of the war forms the key to the novel's theme of automatism or *l'homme machine,* because uncle Toby's hobby-horsical joy is to play out a reproduction that is entirely under the control of a greater force. To match exactly the real campaign is Toby's order, and a military man to the core (which is to say a puppet on strings), he thrills in the carrying out of that order without question and as perfectly as he can. This mechanical aspect can also be linked to the grotesque, which according to Kayser often shows a world in the process of dissolution—a world in which the human body is reduced to a marionette or automaton.[42] A commitment to duty, not the intellect, makes a good soldier, as suggested by uncle Toby's remark about the "*Walloon* Officer at the battle of *Landen,* who had one part of his brain shot away by a musket-ball,—and another part of it taken out after by a *French* Surgeon; and, after all, recovered, and did his duty very well without it" (*TS,* 1:173). The mechanical feature of uncle Toby's hobbyhorse is Sterne's subtle way of identifying the comic in military discipline and behavior. Furthermore, Toby and Trim's obsession with sequential detail and precision also reflects the discursive emphasis of military history. One thinks of Marlborough himself, who personally directed de Vos's representations of troop deployments in the Blenheim tapestries so that they coincided as accurately as possible with the Duke's own memories.

Uncle Toby's habitual association of whatever might be uttered by others (e.g., moisture, lashings) with his own military experience is perhaps the more central part of his mechanical "humour," which has traditionally been explained by Sterne's adaptation of Lockean epistemology.[43] Northrop Frye aptly describes the comic quality of the mechanical in his comments on "blocking character" or the Jonsonian "humour": "The principle of the humour is the principle that unincremental repetition, the literary imitation of ritual bondage, is funny. . . . Repetition over-done or not going anywhere belongs to comedy, for laughter is partly a reflex, and like other reflexes it can be conditioned by a simple repeated pattern."[44] The mechanical aspect of uncle Toby's behavior can also be seen as the element that connects the ludicrous antics of the bowling green campaigners with Sterne's greater comic vision of human conflict. As we have seen, the tradition of learned wit includes a comic stoicism with regard to war and natural catastrophes (plagues, floods, famines, etc.) that arises from a sense that these phenomena are part of inevitable cycles (see *AM,* 2:127).[45] Tristram alludes to the cyclical theory of war that was part of the popular culture of the Renaissance: " . . . *war begets poverty, poverty peace*" (*TS,* 1:72) and continues thus—peace begets prosperity, prosperity envy, and envy leads back to war. Writing on the subject of Sterne and late eighteenth-century ideas of history, Stuart Peterfreund claims, "Cyclicality . . . was in general viewed with a sentiment . . . approaching comfort arising from familiarity."[46] Again as we saw with Swift, a cyclical or determined view lends itself to the comic; the certain swings of fortune might as well be accepted, even celebrated. Henri Bergson's identification of the "mechanical" in human behavior as being the source of the comic or ludicrous can easily be extended to this cyclical theory.[47] If it is inevitable that humankind will fall into conflict, then we have nothing to do but continue on our merry way, stay in motion, and make the best peace we can—as Tristram does in France during the Seven Years' War.

When Tristram is arrested in Volume 7 for not paying a post fee to French officials, Sterne seems to be mock-heroically representing the Seven Years' War, or France's attempt to confine British expansion. In spite of the dedications to Pitt, who opposed the peace treaty of 1763 because he considered it too generous towards France, Sterne suggests that everyone should be willing to sacrifice something to obtain peace: "AND SO THE PEACE WAS MADE;—And if it is a bad one—as Tristram Shandy laid the corner stone of it—nobody but Tristram Shandy ought to be hanged" (*TS,* 2:638). In *A Sentimental Journey,* Yorick is detained in Paris specifically on account of the war. When a passport is finally issued to him to allow him to continue, it is issued to "let Mr. Yorick, the king's jester, and his baggage, travel quietly along" (*SJ,* 228). Again, humor is, for Sterne, the best way to make peace with the world and go merrily forward.

In *An Essay on Man,* Pope alludes to the justification of human suffering that is based on the hypothesis that mortal afflictions are part of some greater divine plan. The Miltonic echo, "Laugh where we must, be candid where we can; / But vindicate the ways of God to man;" forms the rationale for Pope's later lines on war:

Who knows but he, whose hand the light'ning forms,
Who heaves old Ocean, and who wings the storms,
Pours fierce Ambition in a Caesar's mind,
Or turns young Ammon loose to scourge mankind?[48]

As pointed out in the introduction, the scourge theory of war, like the cyclical, was a popular Renaissance belief and derived from both classical and biblical sources. Satire has also been called a scourge,[49] and in this punitive function it may again be linked to war. If the cyclical or mechanical view of war possesses a ludicrous kind of inevitability, then the scourge theory conversely may be said to imply a kind of fearful expectation of punishment. Therefore, the combination of a sense of the inevitable and the idea of divine wrath, which can be located in Clarendon and Voltaire as well as Pope, incorporates the basic ludicrous-fearful dichotomy of the grotesque.

Lockean epistemology and a cultural sense of war memory run deep; furthermore, their relationship is given to sentimentalism. Cultural war memories are triggered by a variety of sensory phenomena that have historic properties (e.g., old battlefields, national music, roll calls). Thus Boswell contemplates the battle of Culloden on his trip to Scotland with Johnson:

> There is a certain association of ideas in my mind upon that subject [battle of Culloden], by which I am strongly affected. The very Highland names, or the sound of a bagpipe, will stir my blood and fill me with a mixture of melancholy, and respect for courage; and pity for the unfortunate, and superstitious regard for antiquity; and inclination for war without thought; and, in short with a crowd of sensations.[50]

Sterne keeps the reader well away from the possibility of such melancholy by emphasizing the "humourous" quality of Toby and Trim. Still, the reader is never allowed to forget the reality of battle as represented by the war wound, and this maintains the necessary fearful-ludicrous duality.

Like his master, Corporal Trim has been maimed by war. He was hit in the knee by a "musket-bullet" at the battle of Landen. Trim likes to see the positive side of his fate, and his remarks may actually be Sterne's way of subtly satirizing the inadequate pensions awarded to veterans, especially the disabled: "that the shot which disabled me at the battle of Landen, was pointed at my knee for no other purpose, but to take me out of his [King William's] service, and place me in your honour's [uncle Toby's], where I should be taken so much better care of in my old age" (*TS,* 2:693). Uncle Toby and Trim are so proud of their wounds that the only real dispute that arises between them is "Whether the pain of a wound in the knee is not greater than a wound in the groin" (*TS*, 2:696). For them the pain is emblematic of their love of country and freedom or of the highest principles of humanity. This paradoxical relationship between love and war is central to *Tristram Shandy*.[51]

Hence, however ludicrous the mechanical aspect of war can be, Sterne uses the war wound motif to remind his readers of what is fearful about war—the pain and injury suffered by so many. Besides Captain Shandy and the corporal, there are a number of other figures in the novel who have been victimized by battle: LeFever, his son, and even Cervantes—whose "wither'd stump" is referred to in Tristram's "Invocation" (*TS*, 2:780). (Cervantes's left hand was mangled at the battle of Lepanto—lucky for us it was not his right!). Their maimed bodies are living proof of the unnatural injury of war. When Tristram defends his purpose in the novel, he claims that uncle Toby's wound "is a wound to every comparison of that kind" (*TS*, 1:360), and one may interpret this ambiguous statement in two ways: it is either of the military kind or of the groin kind. One is probably safe in saying that Sterne wants the reader to associate the two within the greater symbolic structure of the novel; the threat of castration, which is what Toby's wound signifies, reflects the danger that war poses to the human species. Tristram's wound also represents the threat of castration; the curtain falls while he is relieving himself at the window. And Tristram's can also be called a war wound; for after all the curtain only falls because Trim has taken and melted down the weights on the sash-window pullies to add a few cannon to the bowling green artillery. As much as Sterne makes his readers laugh, he can also make them wince.

Adding to the bowling green miniatures becomes a subtle means for Sterne to express what seems to be a clear yet indirect indictment of the cost of war. As with all hobbies, the bowling green campaigns are sure to incur some expense. Trim wants to use a pair of "jack boots" to make "two mortar pieces for a siege next summer" and this arouses some objection from Walter Shandy. It turns out that the "jack boots" date back to the civil wars and were worn by Roger Shandy "at the battle of *Marston-Moor*" (*TS*, 1:241-42); this confers a sentimental value on the boots, and Walter does not want to part with them. When uncle Toby offers his brother ten pounds for the boots, his brother goes into a harangue about how much money has been spent outfitting the bowling green. But uncle Toby will not be easily denied in his campaign: " . . . 'tis for the good of the nation" (*TS*, 1:242). Walter Shandy relents at this good-natured, yet absolutely mad, response. Sterne dissolves the distance created by the hobbyhorse fantasy whenever it serves his purpose. Trim enthusiastically melts down a good part of uncle

Toby's rain gutters and spouts and even his pewter shaving basin, "going at last, like *Lewis* the fourteenth, on to the top of the church, for spare ends" (*TS*, 1:451).[52] Sterne does not want to upset his reader unduly. The sash-window incident throws a scare into the bowling green campaigners and suspends their fun but only temporarily. Likewise, one might say that on the surface Sterne's novel keeps us laughing, for the action certainly remains comic even if we laugh nervously at times.

Surely one of the most exquisite features of Sterne's art as a comic novelist is the yoking of the vulgar with the heroic. When the news of Tristram's misfortune at the window arrives in the parlor, uncle Toby is giving an account of the battle of Steenkirk to Yorick, who more than any other character enjoys seeing others in full gallop on their hobbyhorses. Yorick draws Toby into the full vigor of his spirit by allowing him to indulge himself in the particulars of "the strange conduct of count *Solmes* in ordering the foot to halt, and the horse to march where it could not act; which was directly contrary to the king's commands, and proved the loss of the day" (*TS*, 1:452). Enter Trim all in a panic about how he is responsible for Tristram's injury. Toby gallantly contests for the blame by insisting that Trim was only following orders, and this leads Yorick to draw an analogy between the historical account and the hobbyhorsical crisis: "Had count *Solmes, Trim*, done the same at the battle of *Steenkirk*, said *Yorick*, drolling a little upon the corporal, who had been run over by a dragoon in the retreat,—he had saved thee" (*TS*, 1:453). Yorick knows that such a remark will only give the pair a chance to escape, momentarily at least, from the immediate crisis back into their glorious rememberances. This they do and the climax comes when Trim blames Solmes for his wound for "had we drub'd them soundly at *Steenkirk*, they would not have fought us at *Landen*" (*TS*, 1:454). The subject of blame relates directly to the immediate crisis concerning Tristram's injury. Although Trim goes too far in accusing Solmes, both Trim and Toby feel responsible for the fall of the curtain. Sterne's point is clear enough: life is a confused muddle of intent and accident.

The History of Discord and the Discord of History

As mentioned, part of Toby's military "humour" is to indulge in the history of King William's wars at every opportunity. This fascination with battles and sieges is clearly understandable according to the "curiosity value of grotesque art," which Clayborough claims "is considerable."[53] The bizarre and monstrous attracts and fixes the human eye, a circumstance that is evident when the citizens of Strasbourg all follow the stranger with the huge nose and later find that their city has fallen into French hands (*TS*, 1:323-24). It may be remembered that much of the attractiveness of military art and the theater of war lies in their monstrous symmetry and conformity: uniforms, parades, and—of course—fortifications. Tristram, himself, is disappointed that he could not "take an exact survey of the fortifications" of Calais, which he calls "the strongest in the world" (*TS,* 2:583). But conversely the human imagination is also drawn in numerous ways to the monstrosity and spectacle of violence. For Toby, military history is resplendent with unnatural heroism and glory. And although his single-track enthusiasm strikes the reader as ludicrous, the eighteenth-century tactic, about which he and Trim get so worked up, of advancing right up to the opposing line and drawing the enemy fire before discharging one's own musket is itself fraught with the fearful: "some regiments . . . marched up boldly . . . and received the enemy's fire in their faces, before any one of their own platoons discharged a musket" (*TS,* 1:454). This standard procedure of withholding one's fire amounted to a battle of nerve to see which side could control the fear of its individual soldiers—sacrifice the few to achieve the greater objective (see "Introduction," pp. 23-24).

Moreover, to be enjoyed to the full, an enthusiasm must be shared; the *raconteur* must have an audience. Corporal Trim and Captain Shandy have each other, and their friendship forms one of the main sentimental lines of the novel. The delight with which they describe past battles reaches a climax when they are addressing Yorick on how to fight the French: "There is no way but to march cooly up to them,—receive their fire, and fall in upon them, pell-mell—Ding dong, added *Trim.*—Horse and foot, said . . . uncle *Toby.*—Helter skelter, said *Trim.*—Right and left, cried . . . uncle *Toby.*—Blood an' ounds, shouted the corporal;—the battle raged,—*Yorick* drew his chair a little to one side for safety . . ." (*TS,* 1:454-55). Because the soldier's profession involves such awesome performances of duty in the face of death, it is natural for the military to amuse themselves, and others, with stories of their trade. In Book 12 of *The Metamorphoses,* Nestor entertains the Greeks after a day of slaughter by relating the battle between the Lapithae and the Centaurs. Militarism feeds on its own history. When Yorick decides to entertain Toby by reading him Rabelais's account "of the battle fought single hands betwixt *Gymnast* and captain *Tripet,*" uncle Toby brims with anticipation and requests that Trim be called in since "the description of a battle, will do the poor fellow more good than his supper" (*TS,* 1:462-63). Yorick's Rabelaisian joke is lost on the pair because for them the story of a battle should be the story of heroic love and sacrifice. Moreover, it comes as no surprise that Toby's favorite biblical passage is the siege of Jericho. The history of a military event may, as Tristram believes, beguile a veteran's pain, and this notion offers some explanation for the profusion of military memoirs and accounts from all ages. It may also partially account for the military emphasis in what Bryson defines as the lowest level of historiography—a narrative that "consists almost exclusively in a listing of battles, and where the work of history as an interpretative discipline is at a minimum."[54] Literary parodies of such historiography include Gulliver's accounts of Europe to the Brobdingnagian king and later to his Houyhnhnm master, and Toby's campaign stories.

Toby answers the charge of cruelty against the soldier's profession when he justifies his reasons for wanting to continue the war. Based on the irreconcilable plurality of the world, his justification is irrefutable: "'Tis one thing, from public spirit and a thirst of glory, to enter the breach the first man . . . and 'tis another thing to reflect on the miseries of war: (*TS,* 2:556). One cannot debunk the ideals of soldiery by pointing to the horrible consequences of war. Those satirists who do exercise too much wit and not enough judgment. H. J. Jackson points out that uncle Toby's defense "was taken from an outright attack upon war in Burton's *Anatomy* and observes, "Sterne inverted the bias . . . when he transposed the passage into *Tristram Shandy.*"[55] This is true, but Jackson may dismiss Toby's defense too easily. For Sterne and Burton, war is a terribly complex and ambiguous issue. Burton certainly rages against the soldier's profession in his tirade, but later in the "Satyricall Preface" he actually says that the world is so fraught with madness that what it needs more than anything is "another Attila [or] Tamberlane" (*AM* 1:96). And Toby's idea of his military role involves nothing but benevolence: "what is it, but the getting together of quiet and harmless people, with their swords in their hands, to keep the ambitious and the turbulent within bounds?" (*TS,* 2:557). Shaftesbury makes one of the most lucid statements on how "most savage" war ironically brings out the most heroic affections:

> 'Tis strange to imagine that war, which of all things appears the most savage, should be the passion of the most honest heroic spirits. But 'tis in war that the knot of fellowship is closest drawn. 'Tis in war that mutual succour is most given, mutual danger run, and common affection most exerted and employed. For heroism and philanthropy are almost one and the same. Yet by a small misguidance of the affection, a lover of mankind becomes a ravager; a hero and deliverer becomes an oppressor and destroyer.[56]

As paradoxical as Toby's martial benevolence is, England under William of Orange did feel a responsibility to help curtail the aggression of Louis XIV.

The military theme in *Tristram Shandy* is characterized by this kind of contradiction. Sterne may satirize man's fallen nature but he also accepts and even celebrates the stubborn endurance of human folly. Although uncle Toby is a perfect simpleton, it is his very simplicity that puts him in touch with the naturalness of his role in the world. When his heart follows the beat of a drum, he believes that in sallying forth he is answering the great end of his creation. And so he is, at least in his own eyes. Uncle Toby is also a Carlylean man of action and duty; according to him, a benevolent deity will judge in the end: "God Almighty is so good and just a governor of the world, that if we have but done our duties in it,—it will never be enquired into, whether we have done them in a red coat or a black one" (*TS*, 2:506). The camaraderie of soldiers transcends conflict, and conflict remains an integral part of the world.

The Shandy brothers can be seen as representatives of an archetypal dialectic or discord that manifests itself in the Shandy parlor, a microcosm of the world theater. Walter will talk of philosophical matters, the Captain military, and other than a few tolerances on the part of the former never the twain shall meet. While Tristram is being born, uncle Toby mounts his hobbyhorse and begins a discourse on the relative merits of the ravelin and the demibastion. His brother cannot hold his irritation:

> By the mother who bore us!—brother *Toby* . . . here you have got us, I know not how, not only souse into the middle of the old subject again:—But so full is your head of these confounded works, that tho' my wife is this moment in the pains of labour,— and you hear her cry out,—yet nothing will serve you but to carry off the man-midwife [Dr. Slop] . . . I wish the whole science of fortification, with all its inventors, at the Devil;—it has been the death of thousands,—and it will be mine, in the end.

(*TS*, 1:129-30)

Images of birth and death mingle together. Uncle Toby may be his brother's worst provoker, but he also cannot hurt a fly, and when he sends his brother a tender and innocent glance, Walter Shandy melts with shame. Although a soldier by profession, Toby himself usually responds to provocation by smoking his pipe or whistling Lilliburlero. Whistling is a good way to reach a cease-fire in a hostile exchange of words, but the song Lilliburlero is ironically a mockery of Irish Catholics (the satirical content perhaps accounts for its popularity among the military; see *TS*, 3:113-15). In any case, Sterne's positive comic vision can be seen in the fact that while the Shandy brothers rarely communicate outside of a few sentimental moments, their differences never lead to a lasting or serious conflict. Uncle Toby may interrupt his brother's exposé on the radical moisture to recall the rain-drenched siege of Limerick, but his brother cannot stay angry. The larger characters on the world stage have the same propensity for inadvertent provocation but without the fraternal sentiment. Interrupting his own characters, Tristram gives the reader an anecdote about how Francis I sought to strengthen the understanding between France and Switzerland. Ironically misunderstanding results, and instead of achieving closer relations, the two countries find themselves in a state of war (*TS*, 1:357-59).

For Sterne as for many other comic writers, language miscarries. In fact, Tristram's "Well might *Locke* write a chapter upon the imperfections of words" (*TS*, 1:429—which of course Locke did, *Essay*, bk. 3, chap. 9) is the keynote of the novel and guides an analysis of its abundant war metaphors. Uncle Toby and Trim advance on the widow Wadman and Bridget from two flanks, but a breakdown in communications between the male pair leads to another hilarious misconception. Touched by the widow's inquisitiveness about the particulars of where he received his wound, Toby thinks about his map, "You shall lay your finger upon the place" (*TS*, 2:773). To him the widow's query is proof of her humanity, and so it is, but in more of a physical than idealistic context. In the end, uncle Toby's wound remains as bewitching and obscure to the reader as it does to the widow.

Tristram describes the courtship in the language of "Love militancy" (*TS*, 2:673) or in terms of war metaphors, a practice that goes back at least as far as Ovid and that reminds us of the love-war paradox. Like war, love or courtship often takes on the semblance of a game. Reminiscent of Mrs. Waters's "artillery of love" in that famous seduction scene of *Tom Jones* (bk. 9, chap. 5), widow Wadman uses her "eye" as a "cannon" and succeeds in blowing up uncle Toby, whose heart has been left vulnerable after the demolition of Dunkirk. Putting a hand on his breast, the gallant veteran turns to Trim and murmurs, "She has left a ball here" (*TS*, 2:712). The language of "Love militancy" is an accurate means of identifying the aggressive party—normally the male but not in this case. Despite his profession, uncle Toby is neither aggressive nor suspicious. It is Trim who devises a plan of attack and who recognizes the proximity between what he and his master have dedicated their lives to and what hits uncle Toby so unexpectedly: "Love . . . is exactly like war, in this; that a soldier, though he has escaped three weeks compleat o' Saturday-night,—may nevertheless be shot through his heart on Sunday morning" (*TS*, 2:700). Once inside her parlor, uncle Toby walks right up to the widow as he would to the French and blurts out that he is in love. As devotion to liberty and justice inspires Toby to fight under William of Orange, so he handles his courtship as if it were a military decree.

Furthermore, Sterne uses Trim to draw attention to the more physical connection between war and love when Trim relates the story of how love burst upon him "like a bomb" as a fair Beguine nurse rubbed "every part" of his frame (*TS*, 2:700, 703). However, Sterne does not just degrade the subject of physical love as uncontrollable passion; it is life, the life of us all and the life of Tristram's book. If war threatens the human species, love saves it, or in the words of Mrs. Shandy, "keeps peace in the world . . . [and] replenishes the earth" (*TS,* 2:721). (Mrs. Shandy, largely ignored by Tristram, represents the maternal figure of love and life.) But this kind of love can also cause war as Swift suggests in the "Digression of Madness" (*Tale of a Tub,* sec. 9). The Trojan War rates as the greatest mythic example of love-begetting-war in Western literature, and the only harsh word that uncle Toby ever speaks in his life regards Helen of Troy whom he calls a "bitch" (*TS,* 2:556) for her part in that conflict.

War metaphors pervade Sterne's novel and suggest that the Shandean universe is a dialectic, that reality is not a state of flux but a state of conflict. To Walter Shandy, the speculative philosopher, it is imperative "to investigate truth and fight for her on all sides," but truth is known "not to surrender herself sometimes up upon the closest siege" (*TS,* 1:271, 282). Bombarded with all kinds of connected thoughts whenever he continues his *Tristra-paedia,* Walter Shandy discovers that "the life of a writer . . . was not so much a state of *composition,* as a state of *warfare*" (*TS,* 1:447). To Tristram, whose book is an elaborate improvisation on Locke's philosophy, the world is about equal in its stock of wit and judgment; wit leads to satire and conflict, but judgment makes "up matters as fast as ever they went wrong" (*TS,* 1:229). When another communication miscarries at Tristram's christening, Walter Shandy wails that "heaven has thought fit to draw forth the heaviest of its artillery against me" (*TS,* 1:353-54). Siege and fortification, aggression and defense, are the rhythms of the world.

While recounting uncle Toby's bowling green campaigns, Tristram mentions that "the most memorable attack in the whole war" was fought during the siege of Lille, it being "the most gallant and obstinate on both sides,—and . . . the most bloody too, for it cost the allies themselves that morning above eleven hundred men" (*TS,* 2:543). The grotesque formula for how man views war partially lies in the implied apposition between memorable, gallant, obstinate, and bloody. The more blood, the more memorable; the more bizarre or irrational, the more curious. Sterne is only playing with the reader when he has Tristram say that he cannot resist giving the reader a fifty-page description of the "most memorable" (*TS,* 2:584) siege of Calais—a threat that he does not carry out. But there is a very serious side to Walter Shandy's last harangue, which begins as a lament on the grotesque side of physical love and turns into an attack on the glorification of war. Accordingly, the first part is addressed to Mrs. Shandy, the maternal figure of love, and the second to uncle Toby, the fraternal figure of fragmentation:

> That provision should be made for continuing the race of so great, so exalted and godlike a Being as man . . . I still think and do maintain it to be a pity,

> that it should be done by means of a passion which bends down the faculties . . . continued my father, addressing himself to my mother . . . and makes us come out of our caverns and hiding-places more like satyrs and four-footed beasts than men.
>
> . . . . .
>
> —The act of killing and destroying a man, continued my father raising his voice—and turning to my uncle Toby—you see, is glorious—and the weapons by which we do it are honourable—We march with them upon our shoulders—We strut with them by our sides—We gild them—We carve them—We inlay them—We enrich them—Nay, if it be but a *scoundril* cannon, we cast an ornament upon the breech of it.

(*TS,* 2:806-7)

Despite the serious side, the harangue reasserts the comicality of life and death and rates as the most memorable run in Walter Shandy's oration. Lila Graves cites the "satyrs" reference in her argument that there is a "coherent imagistic pattern" of "man/beast references" in the novel; she then relates this pattern to Locke's attack on the doctrine of distinct essences and belief that there are no perfect divisions between man/beast or rational/irrational beings.[57] As Tony Tanner suggests, humankind is in reality more grotesque and less rational than we think.[58] The indictment of the glorification of war is, of course, a universal theme, yet one that has a special significance in an age that saw the lavish decorative art of Marlborough's Blenheim Palace and the *Salon de la Guerre* at Versailles. Keeping with the Shandean dialectic, Sterne has both uncle Toby and Yorick ready "to batter the whole hypothesis to pieces" (*TS,* 2:807) before Obadiah interrupts with his Cock and Bull story, the finale.

Walter's last harangue remains unanswered, and the silence on the part of Toby and Yorick, while preserved only through Obadiah's timely interruption, has the effect of implicating the reader in the statement itself. It may be said, therefore, that Sterne's closing segment climactically recapitulates the ludicrous and fearful incongruity of human discord by moving beyond the Shandy parlor and involving the greater audience of the novel. And as much as most readers feel the tickle of Shandean laughter in **Tristram Shandy,** uncle Toby's naive idealism and wish to continue the war will never cease to give them a gentle shudder as well.

Abbreviations

AM Robert Burton. *The Anatomy of Melancholy.* Edited by Holbrook Jackson. 3 vols. 1932. Reprint. London: Everyman, 1968. . . .

SJ Laurence Sterne. *A Sentimental Journal Through France and Italy by Mr. Yorick.* Edited by Gardner D. Stout, Jr. Berkeley and Los Angeles: University of California Press, 1967. . . .

TS Laurence Sterne. *The Life and Opinions of Tristram Shandy, Gentleman.* Vols. 1-3 of *The Florida Edition of the Works of Laurence Sterne.* Edited by Melvyn New, Joan New, Richard A. Davies, and W. D. Day. Gainesville: University Presses of Florida, 1978-84.

Notes

[1] Roger Sterne fought under Marlborough and ended his military career as a lieutenant—the highest rank that a commoner without money could expect to attain. On the military environment of Sterne's childhood, see Arthur Cash, *Laurence Sterne: The Early and Middle Years* (London: Methuen, 1975), 1-23, 36-39.

[2] Laurence Sterne, *A Sentimental Journey Through France and Italy by Mr. Yorick,* ed. Gardner D. Stout, Jr. (Berkeley and Los Angeles: University of California Press, 1967), 170-71; all subsequent citations are made to this edition (hereafter cited as *SJ*).

[3] *New Oxford Book of Eighteenth-Century Verse,* 511. The poem was published with an accompanying print in 1773.

[4] Ibid., 786, lines 40-41.

[5] See J. Walter Nelson, "War and Peace and the British Poets of Sensibility," *Studies in Eighteenth-Century Culture,* vol. 7, ed., Rosann Runte (Madison: University of Wisconsin Press, 1978), 345-66.

[6] *Collected Works of Oliver Goldsmith* 4:293, lines 155-58.

[7] *Oxford Book of Eighteenth-Century Verse,* 295.

[8] Defoe, *Colonel Jack,* 11. Later, on his tobacco plantation, Jack does read much history, especially military, and he travels to Ghent just to see the fortified city and military preparations, to his "Delight"; see 157, 172, 183-84.

[9] *Boswell's London Journal: 1762-1763,* 22 December 1762, 100.

[10] William Wordsworth, *The Prelude,* in *Poetical Works,* ed. Thomas Hutchinson, rev. Ernest de Selincourt (1936; reprint, Oxford: Oxford University Press, 1975), 520-21; all subsequent citations are to this edition.

[11] *Collected Works of Oliver Goldsmith* 2:465.

[12] *Poems and Songs of Robert Burns* 1:197.

[13] Nelson, "War and Peace," 357. "Johnny, I Hardly Knew Ye," in *Eighteenth-Century English Literature,* ed. Geoffrey Tillotson, Paul Fussell, Jr., and Marshall Waingrow, with Brewster Rogerson (New York: Harcourt Brace Jovanovich, 1969), 1525.

[14] *Collected Works of Oliver Goldsmith* 4:338.

[15] *The Tatler,* No. 132, 3:99. On Steele and the military, see Richard H. Dammers, "Soldiers and Philosophers: Captain Steele and Captain Ayloffe," *Eighteenth-Century Life* 3, no. 2 (December 1976): 52-55.

[16] *The Spectator,* No. 2, 1:11.

[17] Ibid.

[18] See Ronald Paulson, *Satire and the English Novel* (New Haven: Yale University Press, 1967), 285.

[19] In *The Philosophical Irony of Laurence Sterne* (Gainesville: University Presses of Florida, 1975), 85, Helene Moglen observes, "Although Toby's wholehearted, childish immersion in his hobby has its delightful side, there is a more menacing aspect to it in his dependence for the continuation of his play upon the continuation of actual combat and in his sorrow at the signing of the Peace of Utrecht." This fact is not emphasized in the most extensive study of the "game" or "play" aspect of Toby's hobbyhorse; see Richard A. Lanham, *"Tristram Shandy": The Games of Pleasure* (Berkeley and Los Angeles: University of California Press, 1973), 37-51, 77-92. Lanham claims (85), "Sterne sees . . . Toby's war as a kind of applied pastorality, using the mechanism of pastoral to discharge quite unpastoral impulses."

[20] *The Florida Edition of the Works of Laurence Sterne* ed. Melvyn New, Joan New, Richard A. Davies, and W. D. Day (Gainesville: University Presses of Florida, 1978-84), 2:552; all subsequent citations are made to this edition (hereafter cited as *TS*).

[21] Kayser, *Grotesque,* 51.

[22] See Bakhtin, *Rabelais,* 36-37, 47; and Bakhtin, *The Dialogic Imagination,* 237, 308-10.

[23] Bakhtin, *Rabelais,* 38-9, 90; and Bakhtin, *The Dialogic Imagination,* 237.

[24] See Bosmajian, "The Nature of the Grotesque Image in Eighteenth-Century English Literature," which includes an insightful chapter on *Tristram Shandy:* and Lilian R. Furst, "The Dual Face of the Grotesque in Sterne's *Tristram Shandy* and Lenz's *Der Waldbruder,*" *Comparative Literature Studies* 13 (1976): 15-21,

which concentrates on the narrative disjointedness of the novel. See also Jean Claude Dupas, "*Tristram Shandy:* une rhapsodie grotesque," *Bulletin de la Société d'études anglo-américaines des XVIIe et XVIIIe Siècles* 6 (June 1978): 61-75. None of these critics is specifically concerned with the novel's military content.

[25] Samuel Johnson, "Grotesque," vol. 1 of *A Dictionary of the English Language,* 5th ed. (London: W. & A. Strachan, 1784).

[26] Barasch has made the most detailed study to date of how "grotesque" began to be used as an art, and then generic, term from the late seventeenth to the late eighteenth century; see his *The Grotesque: A Study in Meanings,* 56, 103, 144.

[27] *TS,* 2:544: "Let me stop and give you a picture of the corporal's apparatus; and of the corporal himself in the height of this attack just as it struck my uncle *Toby,* as he turned towards the sentry box, where the corporal was at work,—for in nature there is not such another,—nor can any combination of all that is grotesque and whimsical in her works produce its equal." Bosmajian refers to this use of "grotesque."

[28] Anonymous, *Critical Review* 11 (April 1761), quoted from *Sterne: The Critical Heritage,* ed. Alan B. Howes (London: Routledge & Kegan Paul, 1974), 125. I am indebted to Bosmajian for this source.

[29] Patricia Spacks's comments on comedy and point-of-view in *Tristram Shandy* are appropriate in this context; see *Imagining a Self* (Cambridge: Harvard University Press, 1976), 138: "Perhaps it can be argued that comedy distinguishes itself from tragedy entirely by its point-of-view. . . . One stamps his foot at the universe: how grotesque!"

[30] Yorick's philosophy of humor, of course, derives from the grotesque gravedigging scene in *Hamlet* 5.1.

[31] See Edward Niehus, "Quixotic Figures in the Novels of Sterne," *Essays in Literature* 12, no. 1 (1985): 49: "In sentimentality, as in most things human, Sterne saw elements of both the absurd and the noble, the comic and the serious." Alan B. Howes holds that Sterne combines Rabelaisian and Cervantic humour in his characterization; see "Laurence Sterne, Rabelais, and Cervantes: The Two Kinds of Laughter in *Tristram Shandy,*" *Laurence Sterne: Riddles and Mysteries,* ed. Valerie Grosvenor Myer (London: Vision and Barnes & Noble, 1984), 55.

[32] Lanham, *"Tristram Shandy,"* 88, draws upon Huizinga's *Homo Ludens* and the game theory of others; he ultimately sees Toby's hobbyhorse as a combination of pastoral and chivalrous play.

[33] Peter Stevick, "Miniaturization in Eighteenth-Century English Literature," *University of Toronto Quarterly* 38, no. 2. (1969): 173.

[34] Hobbies are supposed to be therapeutic, and Michael Deporte discusses uncle Toby's somewhat mad game on the bowling green in exactly this respect; see his *Nightmares and Hobbyhorses: Swift, Sterne, and Augustan Ideas of Madness* (San Marino, Calif.: Huntington Library, 1974), 114-19.

[35] See J. M. Stedmond, "Uncle Toby's 'Campaigns' and Raree-Shows," *Notes and Queries* 201, New Series, no. 3 (1956) 28; and George Speaight's "Reply" in the same issue, 133-34.

[36] *The London Stage, 1660-1800, Part 3: 1729-1747,* ed. Arthur H. Scouten (Carbondale: Southern Illinois University Press, 1961), 1059-60.

[37] On the history of military miniatures, see Max von Boehn, *Puppets and Automata,* trans. Josephine Nicoll (New York: Dover, 1972), 37-47; and Fraser, *A History of Toys,* 18, 61, 74, 86.

[38] Ibid., 86.

[39] In Arthur Cash's words, *Laurence Sterne,* 16, "It was indeed a family of soldiers that Laurence grew up in."

[40] Bryson, *Word and Image,* 36.

[41] Ibid.

[42] Kayser, *Grotesque,* 183: "The mechanical object is alienated by being brought to life, the human being by being deprived of it. Among the most persistent motifs of the grotesque we find human bodies reduced to puppets, marionettes, and automata." See also ibid., 198.

[43] Exactly how Sterne adapts Locke's philosophy has been the subject of much criticism on *Tristram Shandy.* See Peter Briggs, "Locke's Essay and the Tentativeness of *Tristram Shandy,*" *Studies in Philology* 82, no. 4 (1985): 502, 506, wherein Briggs argues, "Sterne quite consistently adopted Lockean notions of the mind's *mechanisms* for understanding, but with equal consistency he reserved for himself the right to interpret the *value* of those mechanisms"; as an example, he cites Locke's negative view of fantasies and concludes, "Sterne agreed with Locke as to what a fantasy was, but he saw in fantasy a real potential for human good; military fantasies cure Uncle Toby's wound when the reasonable measures urged by doctors fail, and imagined battles on the bowling-green add life and color to an otherwise drab and frustrated retirement."

[44] Frye, *Anatomy of Criticism,* 168.

[45] Deporte, *Nightmares,* 126, argues that the mechanical or "determined" quality about the Shandean world is "one reason why the novel contains so little true satire."

[46] Stuart Peterfreund, "Sterne and Late Eighteenth-Century Ideas of History," *Eighteenth-Century Life 7,* no. 1 (1981): 48.

[47] Henri Bergson, *Laughter,* trans. Cloudesley Brereton and Fred Rothwell (London: Macmillan, 1911), 69. In this context, it is interesting to note Northrop Frye's claim (*Anatomy of Criticism,* 62) that "cyclical theories of history [are] . . . a typical phenomenon of the ironic mode."

[48] *An Essay on Man,* ed. Maynard Mack (London: Methuen, 1950), 1: 14, 35; Epistle 1, lines 15-16, 157-60.

[49] Especially in the Renaissance; see Alvin Kernan, *The Cankered Muse* (New Haven: Yale University Press, 1959), 93.

[50] James Boswell, *A Tour to the Hebrides,* ed. Frederick A. Pottle and Charles H. Bennett (New York: Literary Guild, 1936), 106-7.

[51] Sterne probably inherited it from Robert Burton who in the Third Partition of *The Anatomy of Melancholy* argues persuasively that the extreme all-for-love attitude is responsible for more war and madness than anything else.

[52] James Aiken Work suggests that this is a reference to the fact that Louis XIV financed many of his "long and expensive campaigns" by obtaining "forced loans from the clergy," but the editors of the Florida edition believe that Sterne may have meant the statement to be literal since church bells were commonly confiscated for their valuable metal (see *TS,* 3:368).

[53] Clayborough, *Grotesque,* 72.

[54] Bryson, *Word and Image,* 36.

[55] H. J. Jackson, "Sterne, Burton, and Ferriar: Allusions to the *Anatomy of Melancholy* in Volumes Five to Nine of *Tristram Shandy,*" *Philological Quarterly* 54 (1975): 464.

[56] Right Honourable Anthony Earl of Shaftesbury, "An Essay on the Freedom of Wit and Humour," in *Characteristics of Men, Manners, Opinions, Times, etc.,* ed. John M. Robertson (London: Grant Richards, 1900), 1:75-76.

[57] See Lila V. Graves, "Locke's Changeling and the Shandy Bull," *Philological Quarterly* 60, no. 2 (1981): 260, 258. Graves believes that Sterne may have been influenced by Locke's views on the "changeling" and "monster."

[58] Tanner, "Reason and the Grotesque," 828-31. See "Introduction," p. 19.

Bibliography

. . . Bakhtin, Mikhail. *The Dialogic Imagination.* Translated by Caryl Emerson and Michael Holquist; edited by Michael Holquist. Austin: University of Texas Press, 1981.

———. *Rabelais and His World.* Translated by Helene Iswolsky. Cambridge: MIT Press, 1968.

Barasch, Frances K. *The Grotesque: A Study in Meanings.* The Hague: Mouton, 1971. . . .

Bergson, Henri. *Laughter.* Translated by Cloudesley Brereton and Fred Rothwell. London: Macmillan, 1911. . . .

Boehn, Max von. *Puppets and Automata.* Translated by Josephine Nicoll. New York: Dover, 1972.

Bosmajian, Hamida. "The Nature and Function of the Grotesque Image in Eighteenth-Century English Literature." Ph.D. diss., University of Connecticut, 1968. . . .

[Boswell, James]. *Boswell's London Journal: 1762-1763.* Edited by Frederick A. Pottle. New York: McGraw-Hill, 1950. . . .

Briggs, Peter. "Locke's Essay and the Tentativeness of *Tristram Shandy.*" *Studies in Philology* 82, no. 4 (1985): 493-520. . . .

Bryson, Norman. *Word and Image: French Painting of the Ancien Régime.* Cambridge: Cambridge University Press, 1981. . . .

Burns, Robert. *The Poems and Songs.* Edited by James Kinsley. 3 vols. Oxford: Clarendon Press, 1968. . . .

Cash, Arthur. *Laurence Sterne: The Early and Middle Years.* London: Methuen, 1975. . . .

Clayborough, Arthur. *The Grotesque in English Literature.* Oxford: Clarendon Press, 1965. . . .

[Defoe, Daniel]. *Colonel Jack.* Edited by Samuel Holt Monk. London: Oxford University Press, 1965. . . .

Deporte, Michael. *Nightmares and Hobbyhorses: Swift,*

Sterne, and Augustan Ideas of Madness. San Marino, Calif.: Huntington Library, 1974. . . .

Fraser, Antonia. *A History of Toys.* London: Spring Books, 1972. . . .

Frye, Northrop. *Anatomy of Criticism.* Princeton: University of Princeton Press, 1957. . . .

Goldsmith, Oliver. *Collected Works.* Edited by Arthur Friedman. 5 vols. Oxford: Clarendon Press, 1966.

Graves, Lila V. "Locke's Changeling and the Shandy Bull." *Philological Quarterly* 60, no. 2 (1981): 257-64. . . .

Howes, Alan B., Ed. *Sterne: The Critical Heritage.* London: Routledge & Kegan Paul, 1974. . . .

Jackson, H. J. "Sterne, Burton, and Ferriar: Allusions to the *Anatomy of Melancholy* in Volumes Five to Nine of *Tristram Shandy.*" *Philological Quarterly* 54 (1975): 457-70. . . .

Johnson, Samuel. *A Dictionary of the English Language.* 5th Ed. 2 vols. London: W. & A. Strachan, 1784. . . .

Kayser, Wolfgang. *The Grotesque in Art and Literature.* Translated by Ulrich Weisstein. Bloomington: Indiana University Press, 1963. . . .

Kernan, Alvin. *The Cankered Muse.* New Haven: Yale University Press, 1959. . . .

Lanham, Richard A. *"Tristram Shandy": The Games of Pleasure.* Berkeley and Los Angeles: University of California Press, 1973. . . .

Moglen, Helene. *The Philosophical Irony of Laurence Sterne.* Gainesville: University Presses of Florida, 1975. . . .

Niehus, Edward. "Quixotic Figures in the Novels of Sterne." *Essays in Literature* 12, no. 1 (1985): 41-60. . . .

Paulson, Ronald. *Hogarth: His Life, Art, and Times.* 2 vols. New Haven: Yale University Press, 1971. . . .

———. *Satire and the English Novel.* New Haven: Yale University Press, 1967. . . .

Peterfreund, Stuart. "Sterne and Late Eighteenth-Century Ideas of History." *Eighteenth-Century Life 7,* no. 1 (1981): 25-53. . . .

Shaftesbury, Right Honourable Anthony, earl of. "An Essay on the Freedom of Wit and Humour." In vol. 1 of *Characteristics of Men, Manners, Opinions, Times, etc.* Edited by John M. Robertson. London: Grant Richards, 1900. . . .

Smollett, Tobias. *The Adventures of Peregrine Pickle.* Edited by James L. Clifford. Revised Paul-Gabriel Boucé. Oxford: Oxford University Press, 1983.

———. *The Adventures of Roderick Random.* Edited by Paul-Gabriel Boucé. Oxford: Oxford University Press, 1979.

———. *The Complete Works.* Edited by Thomas Roscoe. London: George Bell, 1887.

———. *The Expedition of Humphry Clinker.* Edited by Lewis M. Knapp. London: Oxford University Press, 1966.

———. *Ferdinand Count Fathom.* Edited by Damian Grant London: Oxford University Press, 1971.

———. *The Life and Adventures of Sir Launcelot Greaves.* Edited by David Evans. London: Oxford University Press, 1973.

———. *The Reprisal: or, the Tars of Old England. Plays and Poems.* London: T. Evans and R. Baldwin, 1777.

———. *Travels Through France and Italy.* Ed. Frank Felsenstein. Oxford: Oxford University Press, 1981. . . .

Spacks, Patirica. *Imagining a Self.* Cambridge: Harvard University Press, 1976.

Speaight, George. "Reply to J. M. Stedmond [see below]." *Notes and Queries* 201, New Series, no. 3 (1956): 133-34.

Speck, W. A. "Swift and the Historian." In *Proceedings of the First Münster Symposium on Jonathan Swift,* edited by Hermann J. Real and Heinz J. Vienken, 257-68. Munich: Wilhelm Fink Verlag, 1985.

Stedmond, J. M. "Uncle Toby's 'Campaigns' and Raree-Shows." *Notes and Queries* 201, New Series, no. 3 (1956): 28. . . .

Steele, Sir Richard. *The Tatler.* Edited Donald E. Bond. 3 vols. Oxford: Clarendon Press, 1987. . . .

Sterne, Laurence. *The Florida Edition of the Works.* Vols. 1-3. Edited by Melvyn New, Joan New, Richard A. Davies, and W. D. Day. Gainesville: University Presses of Florida, 1978-84.

———. *The Life and Opinions of Tristram Shandy,*

Gentleman. Edited by James Aiken Work. New York: The Odyssey Press, 1940.

———. *A Sentimental Journey Through France and Italy by Mr. Yorick.* Edited by Gardner D. Stout, Jr. Berkeley and Los Angeles: University of California Press, 1967.

Stevick, Philip. "Miniaturization in Eighteenth-Century English Literature." *University of Toronto Quarterly* 38, no. 2 (1969): 159-73. . . .

Tanner, Tony. "Reason and the Grotesque: Pope's *Dunciad.*" In *Essential Articles for the Study of Alexander Pope,* edited by Maynard Mack, rev. ed., 825-44. Hamden, Conn.: Archon, 1968. . . .

Wordsworth, William. *The Prelude.* In *Poetical Works.* Edited by Thomas Hutchinson. Revised by Ernest de Selincourt. 1936. Reprint. Oxford: Oxford University Press, 1975. . . .

Elizabeth Kraft (essay date 1992)

SOURCE: "*Tristram Shandy* and the Parody of Consciousness," in her *Character and Consciousness in Eighteenth-Century Comic Fiction,* The University of Georgia Press, 1992, pp. 100-18.

[*In the following essay, Kraft argues that Sterne saw narrative form as imperfect because a story is understood differently by each narrator as well as by each reader, and that thus through the pointedly chaotic form of* Tristram Shandy, *Sterne hoped to show that narrating a life cannot possibly result in the quantification or identification of that life.*]

Henry Fielding and Charlotte Lennox both regard the structurings of consciousness with a skeptical eye. Even so, they seem to accept with few questions the propensity of consciousness to seek narrative form; at least, that seems to be the operation of the mind that interests them the most—the way the individual consciousness puts together its experiential gleanings, the conclusions it draws, the revisions it makes, the interpretation and reinterpretation of others and of self upon which thought and action are based. In its effort to give shape to human experience, narrative takes many forms. Lennox and Fielding admit that, though most of these narratives fall short of truth, the conscious mind recognizes in the very act of creating narrative a kind of truth: a recapitulation of the first fiat, a making of order out of chaos, which approximates, though it can never fully realize, the narrative of human existence in a divinely ordered world.

Laurence Sterne disagrees. Not with the inherent limitation of narrative—that he is more than willing to admit. Sterne, like Fielding and Lennox, clearly recognizes the self-interest—the hobbyhorsical self-justification—that precipitates and governs most narrative acts, and he recognizes it as a factor that deceives and misleads both teller and hearer or drives them completely asunder.[1] In *Tristram Shandy,* of course, narrative generally signals isolation in that it, like every act of communication in the novel, is spoken in one frame of reference and understood in another (as in the familiar example of the Widow Wadman's narrative-initiating query: "And whereabouts, dear Sir, . . . did you receive this sad blow?" [2: 793]). The lesson Tristram insists on teaching the world—"'To let people tell their stories their own way'" (2: 785)—has a corollary in his readers' insistence on *reading* his story *their* own way.[2] On every level, in other words, the novel demonstrates the fundamental chaos of human existence, an existence in which the narrative act is the single most poignant indication of our inability to order. More than Fielding or Lennox, Sterne sees narrative as a peculiarly human order, as fundamentally and quintessentially different from the divine order. As a consequence, he finds more abhorrent than they do the notion that identity should be equated with a consciousness that takes a narrative form.

For Sterne as for Swift, self-knowledge is simply a matter of recognizing our flawed natures, our basic incompleteness.[3] While Locke himself does not argue for human perfection, his notion of self as consciousness assumes that to record the individual's experiences is to establish individual identity.[4] Completion, if not perfection, is implied; and novels of identity, in their typical movement toward conclusion, in their silence about the process of selectivity, in their physical existences as book, page, and ink, both personify and embody the abstract notion of permanence. As such, Sterne perceives, the novel—particularly as it centers on human existence—personifies and embodies a lie based on sinful pride.

While Tristram's narrative seeks to repeat the lie, it is clearly unable to do so. Tristram does not move toward a conclusion; he is anything but silent about the process of selectivity; and, while his story does have a physical form, it is one that draws attention to its artificiality, with its dashes, astericks, and blank and marbled pages. In all of these characteristics, which, in Mikhail Bakhtin's words, throw over the construction of the narrative the "mantle of materiality" (374), *Tristram Shandy* points to its own parodic nature.[5] That it is a parody of the novel as form is, of course, widely accepted. In addition, however, the work Victor Shklovsky calls "the most typical novel in world literature" (57) also suggests that the genre itself is fundamentally parodic in its distortion of human life and consciousness, based as it is on an assumption of the mechanistic nature of identity—the causally determined, the "beginning, middle, and end."[6]

Before I discuss Sterne's parodic treatment of what he regards as the parody of identity represented by the novel, I want to situate this discussion in the corpus of Sterne criticism. Traditionally, there seem to have been two schools of thought about Sterne's authorial stance and the nature of *Tristram Shandy.* One position is that Sterne is a benign humorist primarily interested in the creation of character and the "realistic" reflection of life. Critics of this position tend to regard *Tristram Shandy* (and *A Sentimental Journey*) as an expression of the school of "feeling," a novel that teaches us tolerance for the shortcomings of ourselves and of others.[7] A logical corollary to this position is the identification of Sterne with both Tristram and Yorick, a practice certainly encouraged by Sterne himself. *Tristram Shandy* and *A Sentimental Journey* thus become, in a sense, apologia for Sterne's life, and our proper response to both Sterne and his characters is a sympathetic recognition, if not celebration, of a common human condition of fallibility, impotence, and disappointment. I myself once subscribed to this line of argument.[8]

The other way of reading Sterne also recognizes the presence of sentimentality and self-justification in his novels, but it sees them, the characters, and the narrative itself as objects of satire. These readings emphasize Sterne's Anglicanism and describe him as a kind of latter-day Swift, who speaks in the character of a hack in order to prompt our recognition, once more, of a common human condition of fallibility, impotence, and disappointment—a recognition that, this school maintains, should chasten pride rather than provoke embrasive sympathy.[9] In considering Sterne's treatment of the relationship between consciousness and narrative, I have come to find this line of argument the more persuasive. Given that the novel of feeling credits the emotional and psychological states of its characters through a narrative that traces the development and results of these conditions, *Tristram Shandy* cannot be thus defined: for, while Tristram's purpose is to explain his identity, his "figure in the world," by informing us of the "tracks and trains" into which his "animal spirits" have been put (1: 1-2), he does so by reducing the formula to absurdity. Interruption, incongruity, and frustration define his life from the moment of his conception just as they define his narrative, positing an incomplete and incoherent identity that seeks but is denied the complete and coherent form of narrative.[10] Tristram's efforts to find stable identity in temporal experience fail, as all such efforts, being human, will.

The parallels between the Scriblerian *Memoirs of Martinus Scriblerus* and Sterne's *Tristram Shandy* suggest a shared concern about modern materialist efforts to define identity in terms of experientiality.[11] Sterne's echoing of this work also implies both a shared attitude toward the subject and a further refinement on the Scriblerian argument. The history of Martin Scri-

blerus, like Tristram's own, begins before his conception and is dominated by his father's efforts to control as well as create his life. Like Walter Shandy, Cornelius Scriblerus subscribes to arcane and amusing superstitions that lead to a variety of absurd behaviors. For example, he performs his "conjugal duty" only when the wind is in the west, following the Aristotelian beliefs that "the grossness and moisture of the southerly winds occasion the procreation of females, and not of males," that the western wind had the opposite effect, and, more generally, "that the Semina out of which Animals are produced, are Animalcula ready formed, and received in with the Air" (96-97). During Mrs. Scriblerus's pregnancy, Cornelius has the embryonic child "entertained . . . with a Consort of Musick once in twenty four hours, according to the Custom of the Magi" (97). Cornelius also notes the *"Prodigies"* that attend Martinus's birth, among them Mrs. Scriblerus's dream of a "huge *Ink-horn*" and a swarm of wasps that invade the nursery (98). In the infant's appearance Cornelius finds the defects of Cicero, Alexander, Marius, and Agesilaus; and he hopes soon to note the stutter of Demosthenes (100).[12] In other words, common to both Cornelius and Walter is the belief that they can form or predict the identity of their sons.

Yet, like Walter, Cornelius finds himself continually thwarted. Planning to establish early on his son's relationship with ancient virtuosi, he has the child christened in a shield, an "invaluable piece of Antiquity," rusted with the "beautiful Varnish of Time" (103). Cornelius discovers to his horror and to his child's near injury that "the Maid . . . had scoured it as clean as her Andirons" (103). And if circumstances did not frustrate his designs, the ancients themselves often did by contradicting each other. Still, "his Reason was so pliant and ductile, that he was always of the opinion of the last he read." His most fundamental characteristic is that, like Walter Shandy, "he reckon'd it a point of honour never to be vanquish'd in a dispute" (125). He typically argues from ancient precedent and seems to proceed from the assumption that man exists as a part of universal forces to be reckoned only by prognostics and divination, as he reveals on the day of Martinus's christening: "'This day, my Friends, I purpose to exhibit my son before you; a Child not wholly unworthy of Inspection, as he is descended from a Race of Virtuosi. Let the Physiognomists examine his features; let the Chirographists behold his Palm; but above all let us consult for the calculation of his Nativity" (102).

However, also like Walter, Cornelius is a peculiar blend of a precious kind of antiquarianism, an outmoded sense of man's relationship to the universe, and modern notions about epistemology and human identity. He particularly reflects the Lockean theory of sensual acquisition of knowledge and thus materialistic identity. His insistence on certain foods for Martinus, even though he grounds this regimen in the thought of Horace and Lycurgus, also reflects a materialist sensibility, as does his stamping gingerbread with the "Letters of the Greek Alphabet" so that Martinus could ingest knowledge along with his favorite sweet. Cornelius's educational system has the predictable result of creating a complete materialist: "Martin's understanding was so totally immers'd in *sensible objects,* that he demanded examples from Material things of the abstracted Ideas of Logick" (119). Asked to give a definition of a lord mayor, Martinus immediately exposes the limitations of his grounding in the sensible, for, having seen only one lord mayor, he defines the general by the particular. Martinus believes in the intimate relationship between experience and identity, the physical and the spiritual. His notion of physiognomy, for example, shares none of the superstition that governs his father's belief in the same method of revealing character. Martin's is a thoroughly experiential understanding: "He observ'd that the Soul and Body mutually operate upon each other, and therefore, if you deprive the Mind of the outward Instruments whereby she usually expresseth, that Passion, you will in time abate the Passion itself; in like manner as Castration abates Lust." "All Muscles," he believed, "grow stronger and thicker by being *much us'd;* therefore the habitual Passions may be discerned in particular persons by the *strength* and *bigness* of the Muscles us'd in the expression of that Passion" (131). Tristram, the inheritor of *his* father's similar habits of mind, echoes the notion of material revelation of the soul in his famous metaphor of the jerkin: "A Man's body and his mind, with the utmost reverence to both I speak it, are exactly like a jerkin, and a jerkin's lining;—rumple the one—you rumple the other" (1: 189). He, too, is a materialist, a self-styled prisoner of his experiences and sensations.

Martin's prevailing interest is in the mind. This interest leads him to a quest for the body's "Seat of the Soul," which he seeks through anatomical dissection, focused particularly on the exploration of the pineal gland, and through applications to the society of freethinkers who inform him of their design to make a "Hydraulic Engine" of a man that can be wound up once a week to "reason as well as most of your Country Parsons" (141). He entertains, as well, a freethinker's argument that explains the relationship between consciousness and the individual through the analogy of John Cutler's "pair of black worsted stockings, which his maid darn'd so often with silk, that they became at last a pair of silk stockings": "Now supposing those stockings of Sir John's endued with some degree of Consciousness at every particular darning, they would have been sensible, that they were the same individual pair of stockings both before and after the darning; and this sensation would have continued in them through all the succession of darnings; and yet after the last of all, there was not perhaps one thread left of the first pair of stockings" (140).[13] Finally, Martin's equation of identity and mind leads to his ludicrous

marriage with a Siamese twin, whose separate consciousness cannot be denied anymore than her shared corporality can—a marriage annulled "upon a natural, as well as legal Absurdity" (163). As Christopher Fox notes, Martin's inquiries and experiences in large part serve to examine the ridiculous extremes to which the arguments (both materialist and antimaterialist) about human identity were wont to go (88-89). Yet, Fox also observes, the Scriblerian's antipathy for the scholastic arguments about identity also reveals a concern about "the theological and ethical questions that controversy raised" (95).

Tristram's own search for identity suggests the same sort of double-focus satire that Fox describes in the *Memoirs*—satire that proceeds from a theological conservatism all too aware of the implications of an experientially defined sense of self. As Martin's materialism leads him into an absurdity with regard to the identity of another individual, Tristram's leads him into an absurd effort at self-definition, a shift in perspective that speaks to the habit of conflating identity with consciousness expressed in narrative form.[14] Sterne perceives as yet another materialistic sophistry the confusion of self-conscious narrative with who one is. Tristram, too, rejects the mechanistic life story, preferring to travel his own route (at least in the beginning), a preference for psychological freedom made all the stronger by his fear of physical determinism, which he has inherited from his father.

James E. Swearingen has described Tristram's method as a "sifting, reflecting, deciphering, appropriating [of] his heritage, his intentions, and even, occasionally, his activities in the present" (50), which results in the "recording of a stratified consciousness" rather than in the writing of an experiential tale (51). It is true that Tristram rejects the notion of the empirical consciousness advanced by Locke in favor of what Swearingen calls the consciousness of intentionality. Tristram's is a deliberate search for self-definition "whereby he uncovers stratum after stratum of his own consciousness in order to find out what kind of 'thing' he is" (Swearingen 75). But try as he might to define new methods for discovering himself, he is continually confronted with the demands of narratology. His readers, for example, assume that, in expressing his life, he will render his experience in narrative form; and he finally comes to share the belief that he and his story are one, though, throughout, there is something in him that resists the narrative line. As we witness his difficulty in telling his story (a struggle that reaches its crisis in volume 7), we realize that the act of structuring is far from a natural response of the conscious mind to the events of life. In Tristram's dilemma resides Sterne's denial that the narrative of consciousness is an analogous recapitulation of the presence of the divine in the mind of man. Swearingen argues that, in *Tristram Shandy,* Sterne "carries out the analysis that Locke only suggests and that Husserl defines in the *Crisis of European Sciences*" by perceiving and demonstrating that the nature of consciousness is a "transcendental subjectivity" (36, 26-46). While I agree with Swearingen that Sterne, in having Tristram define consciousness thus, has anticipated many of the phenomenological "discoveries" of the twentieth century, I find Swearingen's celebratory attitude toward Tristram's modernity quite a contrast to Sterne's own satirical attitude toward his protagonist's secular, transient, and admittedly modern imagination.

Tristram's resistance to narrative manifests itself in his tendency to stray off the narrative track, to digress. He justifies his proclivity for wandering by styling his work his "Life *and* Opinions," suggesting that, like any good narratologist, he is modifying the form he is adopting, meeting his obligation to be *sui generis:* "My work is digressive, and it is progressive too,—and at the same time," Tristram says toward the end of volume 1, going on to praise especially that element not generally associated with the telling of a life: "Digressions . . . are the sun-shine;—they are the life, the soul of reading;—take them out of this book for instance,—you might as well take the book along with them" (1: 81).[15] This celebration of digression notwithstanding, it is immediately apparent that Tristram finds maintaining a balance between the two movements of his narrative quite difficult. Sometimes, he explains, the author of such a work as his is thrown into a "distress . . . truely pitiable" in his effort to control his text: "For, if he begins a digression,—from that moment, I observe, his whole work stands stock-still;—and if he goes on with his main work,—then there is an end of his digression" (1: 81). Still, Tristram sees himself as the skillful builder and operator of a narrative mechanism: "From the beginning, . . . you see, I have constructed the main work and the adventitious parts of it with such intersections, and have so complicated and involved the digressive and progressive movements, one wheel within another, that the whole machine, in general, has been kept a-going;—and, what's more, it shall be kept a-going these forty years, if it pleases the fountain of health to bless me so long with life and good spirits" (1: 81-82).

Although Tristram himself employs the metaphor of machinery to describe his narrative, he objects to any mechanistic tendencies his readers might evidence. He mocks their attention to form: "And what of this new book the whole world makes such a rout about?—Oh! 'tis out of all plumb, my Lord,—quite an irregular thing!—not one of the angles at the four corners was a right angle.—I had my rule and compasses, &c. my Lord, in my pocket.—Excellent critic!" (1: 213). The passage perhaps grows out of the actual response to the work, for a principal animadversion in early reviews of the novel has to do with the very quality on which Tristram prides himself. William Kenrick,

for example, observes that Tristram's "historical Readers . . . are not a little apprehensive he may, some time or other, give them the slip in good earnest, and leave the work before his story be finished" (471). Kenrick recommends that Tristram pay "a little more regard to going straight forward, lest the generality of his Readers, despairing of ever seeing the end of their journey, should tire, and leave him to jog on by himself" (471 n. 1).[16] Tristram makes it clear, however, that such forward movement is neither natural nor inevitable. In telling "a story worth the hearing," an author makes choices. There *are* no rules, Tristram suggests in his address to the "Powers" of storytelling. In constructing a tale, "mortal man" does not know "where he is to begin it,—and where he is to end it,—what he is to put into it,—and what he is to leave out,—how much of it he is to cast into shade,—and whereabouts he is to throw his light!" (1: 244). Such confusion is true of Tristram and all "biographical freebooters." Tristram exposes what the others disguise with their seamless constructions, that is, the arbitrariness of the narratives they write: "A sudden impulse comes across me—drop the curtain, *Shandy*—I drop it—Strike a line here across the paper, *Tristram*—I strike it—and hey for a new chapter!" (1: 336). In this sense, digression is akin to sudden insight, though the revelation concerns, not the order of the authoritative, but the chaos of the tentative.

In the beginning, Tristram's digressive imagination provides him a source of freedom, but by volume 5, the situation has changed. His digressions are no longer the result of the whimsy or curiosity of the present moment; rather, they are the result of the obligatory contracts he made with the reader in the whimsy or curiosity of the past.[17] They are, moreover, subjects about which he has become self-conscious since the time he first mentioned them. Now, he worries, whiskers, chambermaids, and buttonholes are inappropriate topics for the readership he has come to know: "I'm sorry I made it—'twas as inconsiderate a promise as ever entered a man's head—A chapter upon whiskers! alas! the world will not bear it—'tis a delicate world—but I knew not of what mettle it was made—nor had I ever seen the underwritten fragment; otherwise, as surely as noses are noses, and whiskers are whiskers still; (let the world say what it will to the contrary) so surely would I have steered clear of this dangerous chapter" (1: 409). Still, there is the matter of Tristram's "small account . . . with the reader," his promises, his "book-debts" (1: 433-34). Further, there is Sterne's need to complete his satire. It is thus that chapter 7 of book 5 comes to replace the promised digression on chambermaids and buttonholes. Though Tristram says it "is nothing, an't please your reverences, but a chapter of *chamber-maids, green-gowns, and old hats,*" it suggests much about the relationship between readers, misreaders, narrative convention, and identity (1: 434).[18]

The chapter begins with Obadiah's announcement to the Shandy servants that "my young master in *London* is dead!" (1: 429). Susannah's mind turns first to the thought of Mrs. Shandy's "green sattin nightgown," and then, as she imagines for her mistress a period of mourning followed by her own death from sorrow, to the thought of the rest of the wardrobe: "What a procession! her red damask,—her orange-tawny,—her white and yellow lutestrings,—her brown taffata,—her bone-laced caps, her bed-gowns, and comfortable under-petticoats.—Not a rag was left behind" (1: 430). The other characters are equally hobbyhorsical—Obadiah thinking of the ox-moor, the coachman of the last time he had driven poor Bobby.[19] The reactions prompted by the report are in fact simply variations on that of the "fat foolish scullion," who remarks, to Obadiah's reiterated "he is certainly dead," "So am not I" (1: 430). It is Trim who manages to focus the servants' attention on the universality of Bobby's fate. Imitating the posture in which he had read Yorick's sermon on the abuses of conscience, he drops his hat in physicalization of his response to Obadiah's news: "'Are we not here now; . . . and are we not . . . gone! in a moment?'" (1: 432). As Tristram observes, "Nothing could have expressed the sentiment of mortality, of which it was the type and fore-runner, like it,—his hand seemed to vanish from under it,—it fell dead," as bodies do (1: 432).

Sigurd Burckhardt's argument that "gravity" is "the law of the novel" recognizes that *Tristram Shandy* sets up a metaphoric equivalence between words, engines, narrative, self-consciousness—all the tools of human existence (70). Words, like "green gowns" and "old hats," have a tendency to turn into bawdy; engines, like bridges, forceps, window sashes, and squirts, are inclined to fail; narrative, especially Tristram's, tends to disintegrate; self-consciousness quickly becomes paralysis and shame. Gravity, in other words, characterizes mortal life, and even the devices created by human beings to raise themselves above the condition of mere physicality are, because human, subject to its laws. This characteristic of any human endeavor is precisely that of which Tristram speaks in his response to Bobby's death, Trim's emblem, and Susannah's tears: "We are not stocks and stones . . . nor are we angels . . . but men cloathed with bodies, and governed by our imaginations;—and what a junketting piece of work of it there is, betwixt these and our seven senses, especially some of them, for my own part, I own it, I am ashamed to confess" (1: 431-32).[20] Of the senses, Tristram, like Locke, privileges the eye, but as an engine of revelation that leads to spiritual insight rather than a tool of sensory perception. It has, he maintains, "quickest commerce with the soul," leaving "something more inexpressible upon the fancy, than words can either convey—or sometimes get rid of" (1: 432).

Tristram asserts that the proper understanding of Trim's "eloquence" is necessary to "the preservation of our constitution in church and state,—and possibly the preservation of the whole world" (1: 431); clearly he, or at least Sterne, means that recognition of human mortality, fallibility, and imperfection is requisite to spiritual survival.[21] But what Tristram also implies, I think, is the importance of the momentary as a suggestion of the ineffable, the inexpressible spark of divinity that resides in the corporeal form. His apostrophe at the end of the chapter is addressed to "ye who govern this mighty world . . . with the *engines* of eloquence, . . . ye who wind and turn the passions, . . . ye . . . who drive, . . . ye also who are driven"; and his charge is to "meditate . . . upon *Trim*'s hat"—not simply its physicality as emblem of mortality, but also its efficacy as purveyor of sudden spiritual insight (1: 433). Trim's hat is the revelation of the unexpected, not the flattering portrait of sequential narrative.

The purpose of human existence, Sterne holds, is to acknowledge, not to deny, mortality. As Trim explains to Obadiah, Susannah, Jonathan the coachman, and the fat scullion, the best way to deal with Death is to face him: "The man who flies, is in ten times more danger than the man who marches up into his jaws" (1: 436). While Trim seems to mean that death is more likely to attend the cowardly than the brave, Tristram's ensuing experiences suggest another level of meaning: the narrative structure itself—the straightforward, progressive story, in its semblance of sequence and of wholeness—is nothing more than a denial of Death.

In volume 4, Tristram notes the "strange state of affairs between the reader and myself" caused by his narrative procedure: "I am this month one whole year older than I was this time twelve-month; and having got, as you perceive, almost into the middle of my fourth volume—and no farther than to my first day's life—'tis demonstrative that I have three hundred and sixty-four days more life to write just now, than when I first set out; so that instead of advancing, as a common writer, in my work with what I have been doing at it—on the contrary, I am just thrown so many volumes back" (1: 341). "I shall never overtake myself," he continues, "whipp'd and driven to the last pinch, at the worst I shall have one day the start of my pen" (1: 342). As he becomes more and more preoccupied with the pursuit of the narrative line, he subordinates all to the need to tell his story. In volume 6, we find, he is driven still by the urge for unity—"When a man is telling a story in the strange way I do mine, he is obliged continually to be going backwards and forwards to keep all tight together in the reader's fancy" (2: 557-58)—and the end of the volume finds him resisting the impulse to digress. He refuses to preface his discussion of Toby's amours with a definition of love, for, he says, "I can go on with my story intelligibly, with the help of the word itself" (2: 564-65). There is something wistful in his continuing, "When I can get on no further,—and find myself entangled on all sides of this mystick labyrinth,—my Opinion will then come in, in course,—and lead me out" (2: 565); but he is so concentrating on the progressive narration of his life that he is simply unable to indulge the digressive fancy of his opinion, though he does leave a blank page on which, if he is so inclined, the reader can "paint to . . . [his] own mind" the picture of Uncle Toby's Widow Wadman (2: 566-67).

Following this discussion are the famous linear representations of the first five volumes of **Tristram Shandy.** They portray Tristram's celebration of the increasing flatness of his narrative line in a ludicrous physicalization by which we, as readers, are alerted to the dullness of narrative that follows a predictable course. Tristram exults: "From the end of *Le Fever*'s episode, to the beginning of my uncle *Toby*'s campaigns,—I have scarce stepped a yard out of my way," hoping that he may "go on with my uncle *Toby*'s story, and my own, in a tolerable straight line, . . . turning neither to the right hand or to the left," following the "pathway for Christians," the "emblem of moral rectitude" (2: 570-72). Tristram hopes, in other words, that he can reach the narrative perfection that stands for human perfection. That he—or, that is, Sterne—wants us to doubt the validity of this approach, however, is suggested by the observation that the straight line is also the best line for a row of cabbages.

In volume 7, Tristram does literally what Sterne has suggested the straightforward narrative does figuratively: he pursues his path in a straight line. As William V. Holtz notes, this volume contains "the most chronologically direct and rapidly paced portion of Tristram's story, in which his meandering narrative mule is replaced by a post chaise and horses, and digressive freedom by progressive urgency." "Were he to diagram this volume," Holtz continues, "the line would be the straightest of any, especially in the earlier chapters" (131). But this holds true for only the first half of the volume, during Tristram's preoccupation with his escape from death.[22] Motion, he says, disagreeing with Bishop Hall, is life, and the faster one goes, the more one is living and the less likely one is to encounter death. Movement, direct and swift, becomes everything to Tristram; he will stop for nothing: "I know no more of Calais, . . . than I do this moment of *Grand Cairo;* for it was dusky in the evening when I landed, and dark as pitch in the morning when I set out" (2: 580). Even a "rosy" young woman returning from her matins receives Tristram's rebuke for unwittingly catching his attention and tempting his delay: "How can you be so hard-hearted, MADAM, to arrest a poor traveller going along without molestation to any one" (2: 585). As the girl is out of earshot during the greater part of Tristram's speech, we can assume it is his own impulse to dally and digress that he is trying to fight here.

All of this urgency to move forward, however, results only in delay, for the post chaise breaks down repeatedly, and the feeling of delay even when it is moving, for "the precipitancy of a man's wishes hurries on his ideas ninety times faster than the vehicle he rides in" (2: 586). Now not just running from death, Tristram is also in pursuit of his ideas: they come tumbling out, one on top of another, without even the eccentric order of his usual reflection. As he moves "CRACK, crack—crack, crack—crack, crack" through Paris (2: 599), his mind jumps from the nasty streets, to the filthy wall, to the ship, to the lamps, soup, and salad; he will not pause to convey sustained thought of any sort:

> No;—I cannot stop a moment to give you the character of the people—their genius—their manners—their customs—their laws—their religion—their government—their manufactures—their commerce—their finances, with all the resources and hidden springs which sustain them: qualified as I may be, by spending three days and two nights amongst them, and during all that time, making these things the entire subject of my enquiries and reflections—

> Still—still I must away—the roads are paved—the posts are short—the days are long. (2: 604)

In effect, Tristram discovers, he has come a long way, but he does not know where he has been: "What a tract of country have I run! . . . There's FONTAINEBLEAU, and SENS, . . . and a score more upon the road to LYONS—and now I have run them over—I might as well talk to you of so many market-towns in the moon, as tell you one word about them" (2: 615). Finally, however, Tristram asks for his foolscap and attempts to reclaim his habit of digressive reflection. In Auxerre he is successful; about this city, he says, he could talk "forever," because he had been there once before with his father and Uncle Toby, and his father's reflections have furnished him "enough to say upon AUXERRE" (2: 617). This digression is a movement both away from the narrative line and away from self.

From this point on, volume 7 is as digressive as any of the preceding volumes. Tristram sells his post chaise and, inadvertently but significantly, sells his "remarks," too; he has a "conversation" with an ass who blocks his way, for "a minute is but a minute," after all, he says, "and if it saves a fellow creature a drubbing, it shall not be set down as ill-spent" (2: 630-31). He slows down, echoing Trim's sentiment in defiance of death: "Why," he asks, "should I fly him at this rate?" (2: 645).

As volume 7 concludes, we see Tristram crossing a plain in continuance of his journey, but here his movement is less frenzied, his spirit calmer; as in earlier volumes, he proceeds digressively. He stops and talks to those he meets, whomever they are, "beggars, pilgrims, fiddlers, fryars." He dances with a "sun-burnt daughter of Labour" (2: 648-49). But perhaps most significantly, he refuses to answer the question put to him by the commissary: "And who are you?" "Don't puzzle me," Tristram says before moving on. "In short," Tristram says, "by seizing every handle, of what size or shape soever, which chance held out to me in this journey—I turned my *plain* into a *city*" (2: 633, 648). Human life is not a straight line, Tristram finds. Although he ends volume 7 by vowing to "go on straight forwards, without digression or parenthesis, in my uncle Toby's amours" (2: 651), what he observes at the beginning of volume 8 is more to the point: "Notwithstanding all that has been said upon *straight lines* in sundry pages of my book—I defy the best cabbage planter that ever existed . . . to go on cooly, critically, and canonically, planting his cabbages one by one, in straight lines, and stoical distances, especially if slits in petticoats are unsew'd up—without ever and anon straddling out, or sidling into some bastardly digression" (2: 655). In *"Freeze-land"* or *"Fog-land,"* Tristram says, such a focus on progression might be feasible, but the names of these places suggest fixity and obscurity, not the "clear climate of fantasy and perspiration" that characterizes the imaginative corporeality that is the world of **Tristram Shandy** (2: 655).

The autobiographical narrative is, of course, a hobby-horse, a "sporting little filly-folly which carries you out for the present hour—a maggot, a butterfly, a picture, a fiddle-stick—an uncle Toby's siege—or an *any thing,* which a man makes a shift to get a stride on, to canter it away from the cares and solicitudes of life" (2: 716).[23] It is a story of self-justification, reflecting individual preoccupations; it is not to be taken for truth any more than Uncle Toby's reenactments of the Siege of Namur are to be taken for the battle itself. But narrative can serve truth. Sterne makes this point quite clearly by inserting his sermon "The Abuses of Conscience" in his novel.[24] He further supports this idea in "Self-Knowledge," another sermon on a related topic.

In fact, to compare Swift's "On the Testimony of Conscience" and Sterne's "Abuses of Conscience" is to reveal a shared emphasis on self-knowledge. The sermons are generally parallel. Both Swift and Sterne understand conscience as "an Accuser and a Judge," discourage accepting what the world calls "honesty" or "morality" or "honor" as evidence of conscience, and conclude that, "unless Men are guided by the Advice and Judgment of a Conscience founded on Religion, they can give no Security that they will be either good Subjects, faithful Servants of the Publick, or honest in their mutual Dealings; since there is no other Tie thro' which the Pride, or Lust, or Avarice, or Ambition of Mankind will not certainly break one Time or other" (Swift, "Conscience" 158).

Yet in spite of Sterne's fundamental agreement with Swift as to the role of conscience and the need for standards of judgment grounded in sound training in the principles of religion, and in spite of Sterne's belief, shared by all the Scriblerians, that man is by nature flawed and that his inquiry into himself *should* reveal limitations, he feels that the stumbling block to such knowledge is less the failure to reflect than the failure to recognize reflexivity. The only significant difference between Sterne's "Self-Knowledge" and Swift's "The Difficulty of Knowing One's Self" suggests as much. Swift tells the story of Hazael, who was sent to Elisha the prophet for news about the king of Syria's future health. While there, Hazael heard from the prophet another, more personal prediction: weeping, the prophet tells him, *"I know all the Evil that thou wilt do unto the Children of Israel; their strong Holds wilt thou set on fire, and their young Men wilt thou slay with the Sword, and wilt dash their Children, and rip up their Women with Child"* ("Difficulty" 349). Swift reports that "*Hazael* not knowing himself so well as the other did, was startled and amazed at the Relation, and would not believe it possible that a Man of his Temper could ever run out into such enormous Instances of Cruelty and Inhumanity" ("Difficulty" 349-50). Hazael's story illustrates, Swift says, the way "most Men . . . are wonderfully unacquainted with their own Temper and Disposition" ("Difficulty" 350).

Sterne mentions Hazael in his sermon, but only in passing. His biblical reference is to quite another story and is offered for a different end: to illustrate "the deceitfulness of the heart of man to itself" ("Self-Knowledge" 53)—its active deception, not simply its ignorance. The prophet Nathan was sent to David to "bring him to a conviction of . . . [his sins], and touch his heart with a sense of guilt for what he had done against the honour and life of Uriah" ("Self-Knowledge" 58). The "direct road" to pointing out such defects to one who has them, Sterne has already told us, is "guarded on all sides by self-love, and consequently [is] very difficult to open access," so Nathan takes the route of other "public instructors" before him:

> As they had not the strength to remove this flattering passion which stood in their way and blocked up all the passages to the heart, they endeavoured by stratagem to get beyond it, and by a skilful address, if possible, to deceive it. This gave rise to the early manner of conveying their instructions in parables, fables, and such sort of indirect applications, which, though they could not conquer this principle of self-love, yet often laid it asleep, or at least overreached it for a few moments, till a just judgment could be procured. ("Self-Knowledge" 57-58)

Nathan tells David a story, "not so parallel to David's as he supposed would awaken his suspicion, and prevent a patient and candid hearing, and yet not so void of resemblance in the main circumstances, as to fail of striking him when shown in a proper light" ("Self-

Knowledge" 58-59). Upon hearing the story, David felt his anger "kindled at the man," thus enabling Nathan's closing comment, "Thou art the man," to provoke both recognition and remorse ("Self-Knowledge" 60, 62).[25]

The narrator's role is that of an instructor who provides a standard of judgment that results in a momentary awareness, a reevaluation—not prediction, as in Swift's exemplum, but interpretation. Narrative as a tool of indirection is used to dislocate the subject self from the object self. It is not a moment of consciousness but it precipitates one through disjunction, which necessitates a reflexive self-knowledge.

The interplay of author/narrator/reader is complex. It involves, on one level, the story of God/Nathan/David and, on another, Sterne/Yorick/reader, behind which, of course, is Sterne and his congregation. For Sterne, this kind of interplay was endlessly fascinating, emphasizing, as it does, the relationship between artistry and enlightenment. The task of a sermon writer or a storyteller, as Sterne seems to have defined it, was to bring the listener/reader through revelation to self-knowledge. The moment of self-recognition is the significant moment of consciousness. The "Thou art the man!" moment occasions true self-knowledge. Opposed to that is the self-consciousness of self-justification, the overt attempt to interpret one's actions and thoughts to the advantage of self—the self-centered abuses of conscience, in other words. It is significant, I think, that in this sermon Sterne clearly delineates self-love as the primary impediment to true enlightenment, in contrast to Swift, who assigns equal status to sensual distractions, business, and unwillingness.

In *Tristram Shandy* Sterne depends on the reader's propensity to seek answers in the progression of narrative. Tristram explains: "My way is ever to point out to the curious, different tracks of investigation, to come at the first springs of the events I tell;—not with a pedantic *Fescue,*—or in the decisive Manner of *Tacitus,* who outwits himself and his reader;—but with the officious humility of a heart devoted to the assistance merely of the inquisitive;—to them I write,—and by them I shall be read" (1: 74). Through its very disconnection, Tristram's narrative teases readers into thought: they must piece together the chain of events for themselves, unjumbling Tristram's confusing chronology in search of a narrative line. The combination of complete disdain for the ordering of the tale and the scrupulousness apparent in the coherence of detail makes us aware that the narratives we write represent a learned response to the disorder of experience, a response learned, by and large, from novels, which have taught us to beg the question of spiritual identity in the search for narrative expression of the human life.[26] As Donald R. Wehrs has put it, in the end, Sterne believes "the stories we can know and the stories we can become remain incomplete and equivocal" precisely because

we are human and not divine (147).[27] Our moment of insight, our recognition of the cheat of narrative, should occur at the end of the novel, when Mrs. Shandy unwittingly voices the question that has kept us reading Tristram's tale to this point: "L——d! . . . What is all this story about?" In Yorick's response we have our answer and our enlightenment: "A COCK and a BULL, . . . and one of the best of its kind, I ever heard" (2: 809).

The jester is not so much a truth teller as one who points the way to truth. In the service of another (just as Yorick preaches by the authority of God), he is distinguished by an ability to perceive the disjunctions of his world and what they suggest about the enduring truth—the true narrative of man's fall and redemption through Christ—which is often ignored by the teller of coherent tales of self or of others. The jester's is no narratological consciousness formed by sensation and reflection. His is a moment's insight, impersonal and disconnected. For that reason, I think, Sterne found the persona both suitable and functional. The three lives of his sermon on the abuses of conscience witness his commitment to the truth it contained, his belief in the ability of that truth to transcend and even profit by the various contexts, and his desire to bring to the attention of his readers and followers the disjunction between himself, his various roles in life, and the truth he voiced by divine authority. He reveled in his celebrity, but in its comedy, its fundamental instability, not in anything it suggested about his importance or his ultimate identity. His adoption of both Yorick and Tristram as pseudonyms speak to the temporality of fame and the public mask, as does his lack of concern about the consistency of the personae.[28] He donned each, however, to point us toward what he saw as the fundamental truth of human existence—mortality—and the fundamental truth of spiritual existence—immortality. In spite of the implications of narrative and of Lockean psychology, Sterne maintains that identity is finally a matter, not of proof, but of faith.

Notes

[1] The relationship between putative author and reader in *Tristram Shandy* has been variously interpreted. Wayne C. Booth, for example, finds that the narrator's ambiguity and unreliability cast the burden of determining meaning onto the reader (*Rhetoric* 235-40). Howard Anderson, too, sees that the narrator is untrustworthy but feels that the novel nevertheless requires the reader's complete reliance on him. Helene Moglen finds that the subjectivity that isolates the novel's characters also ultimately separates the reader and Sterne (55-56). See also Hartley and Dowling.

[2] Sterne asks our patience and trust in the first volume as well as the last: see *Tristram Shandy* 1: 9.

3 See Swift's "Difficulty of Knowing One's Self," Sterne's "Self-Knowledge," and the discussion below.

4 On Sterne's response to and use of Locke's theory of perception in general, see Peter M. Briggs. Briggs argues that Sterne "had little argument with Locke as to how cognitive processes worked, but placed different values on those workings," reversing Locke's valuation of reason over imagination (505). W. G. Day also notes Sterne was no "committed disciple" of Locke (80). See also Maskell and Traugott 3-61.

5 Bakhtin refers specifically to Sterne's use of "lengthy and abstract discussions . . . [which have a] retarding function and interrupt the story at its most intense and tension-filled moment" (374). See also Dane's discussion of the antipoetics of *Tristram Shandy* (162-72).

6 See Shklovsky 57. On *Tristram Shandy*'s parody of causality, see Iser 24-30.

7 See, for example, Brissendon; Lanham 50-51; Olshin; Graves; and Anderson. In dividing the large and complex body of Sterne studies into two broad camps, I am admittedly oversimplifying the arguments of his critics. Many (Olshin, for example) see the novel as advancing both an awareness of shortcomings and a human sympathy: as Olshin says, quite rightly, "Life-affirmation and cynical satire" can and do coexist (371). Ultimately, however, most analyses of *Tristram Shandy* emphasize either the novel's celebration of pleasure or its awareness of a longing these pleasures will not serve, though most also acknowledge the fact that both ideas are central to Tristram and to Sterne.

8 In "Tristram Shandy and the Age That Begot Him," I made clear my support of this point of view.

9 The most persuasive of these critics are John Stedmond, Melvyn New, Sigurd Burckhardt, and, on *Sentimental Journey,* Kenneth MacLean. In discussing Sterne's attitude toward sympathy, MacLean invokes Adam Smith, who notes that sympathy is too often mere self-indulgence. As a side note, it is interesting that, while Swift ends his sermon "The Difficulty of Knowing One's Self" by recommending the Golden Rule, Sterne's sermon "Self-Knowledge" insists on daily self-examination in quiet and solitude, an examination that should yield awareness of "several irregularities and unsuspected passions" (67). Still, in Swift the focus is on neither a celebration of common weaknesses nor a patronizing regard for the unfortunate, but avoiding the censuring of others through the admission of one's own guilt.

10 In *Sterne's Fiction and the Double Principle,* his recent, provocative reading of *Tristram Shandy,* Jonathan Lamb recognizes the way the novel both exploits and explodes the notion of textual and individual completion; see especially chapter 4, "Narratives and Readings."

11 See Stedmond 49-54; New, *Sterne as Satirist* 53-69; and Cash, *Early and Middle Years* 278. For background on the intellectual milieu in which *Memoirs* was written, see Fox 96-117 and Kerby-Miller's note on the Scriblerians and the freethinkers (280-85).

12 As Kerby-Miller points out (197-98), these prognostics and analogies would be seen as evidence of pride and egoism.

13 Here Sterne parodies the Clarke-Collins controversy, which Christopher Fox discusses as confronting the notion of a transient self (108).

14 The most remarkable evidence of this principle I have yet encountered occurs in Sarah Fielding's novel *The Governess.* The novel concerns nine young girls, most of them under twelve years of age, each of whom is called upon to instruct and entertain the others by relating "the History of her Life."

15 On the digressive structure of *Tristram Shandy,* see, among others, Hunter, "Response as Reformation"; Piper 31-46; Rosenblum; and Iser 71-82.

16 Kenrick's review appeared anonymously in the *Monthly Review*'s 1759 appendix, and his sentiment was echoed privately by Horace Walpole in a 1760 letter to Sir David Dalrymple: "The great humour . . . consists in the whole narration always going backwards. I can conceive a man saying that it would be droll to write a book in that manner, but have no notion of his persevering in executing it" (473). Early readers and critics also objected to the novel's bawdy sense of humor and its specific satire: see Cash, *Later Years* 21-23, 32-37.

17 On the way the story grows "out of the reader's desire to know more," see Preston 153, 151-59.

18 And, of course, there are the salacious puns, as the Florida edition notes: "'To give a *green gown*' meant to 'tumble a woman on the grass,'" and "old hat" refers to the "'female pudend'" (*Tristram Shandy* 3: 358).

19 See Swearingen, who discusses this episode as revealing "the intentional arcs of different characters," their intersubjectivity (64).

20 The Florida edition notes in Tristram's speech an echo of Sterne's forty-third sermon (3: 356).

21 As the Florida edition notes, here Sterne echoes Thomas Sheridan (*A Discourse . . . Introductory to His Course of Lectures on Elocution*), who placed great emphasis on oratory for the survival of church and

state. Sterne's allusion in the context of a discussion of mortality has obviously a satirical intent (*Tristram Shandy* 3: 355-56).

[22] On book 7 and Tristram's reclamation, see Columbus; Brienza; and Lamb 105-57, esp. 140, 149, 157.

[23] This description is an echo of his early definition of the hobbyhorse (1: 12).

[24] Kenrick calls the insertion of the sermon a "masterly" stroke by which "it will probably be read by many who would peruse a sermon in no other form" (472). On the sermon itself and its relationship to matters of canon, textual corruptibility, and truth, see Zimmerman and Brown, "Tristram." On the relationship of the sermon to the more specific limitation of self-judgment, see New, *Sterne as Satirist* 16-21; Cash, *Sterne's Comedy* 25-29; and Reed 159-60. Sander L. Gilman points out the veiled inclusion of another of Sterne's sermons, "Trust in God," in Walter's speech to Toby in volume 4, chapters 7-8 (Gilman 77-79).

[25] See New, *Sterne as Satirist* 20-21.

[26] On Sterne's scrupulous attention to the chronology of his tale, see Baird.

[27] "Narrative," Wehrs maintains, "however artfully contrived, remains an all-too-human exertion," and he places Sterne within the skeptical tradition represented by Montaigne, Cervantes, Erasmus, and Rabelais (128, 130-42). For other studies that situate *Tristram Shandy* within the context of Sterne's religious belief, see New, "Exuberant Wit," and Harries.

[28] Lamb argues that Sterne's use of the Tristram/Yorick personae was in effect his own self-creation, evidence of his "illusion that he was inhabiting his own text," indeed, becoming his own text, as Tristram does (82-83, 104). Ultimately, however, Lamb suggests that, in spite of "Sterne's growing weakness for reading himself into his fiction" (104), he, like Tristram, recognizes the peril of a "single, self-sufficient reading" (105). For a similar suggestion, see Preston 189-95. See also James; and Dussinger, who describes Yorick as a posture who never reveals his "real self" (*Discourse* 176-77).

Ann Jessie Van Sant (essay date 1993)

SOURCE: "Locating Experience in the Body: The Man of Feeling," in her *Eighteenth-Century Sensibility and the Novel: The Senses in Social Context,* Cambridge University Press, 1993, pp. 98-115.

[*In the following excerpt, Van Sant discusses A Sentimental Journey to support her argument that Sterne uses emotional sensibility as well as physical sensitivity as satirical devices to focus the readers' attentions—and intellects—upon themselves.*]

The Abbé de Condillac's statue touches first itself and then the world and thus discovers the existence of each.[1] It is an epistemological rather than a psychological statue, and Condillac's real interest in his examination of touch lies in the recurring eighteenth-century epistemological problem of how to verify knowledge of what is *outside* the self. Self-discovery is a step toward discovery of the external. But Condillac's centralizing of touch in an epistemological context has a psychological parallel in Laurence Sterne's **A Sentimental Journey.** Yorick verifies himself by intensifying his experience in the structures of feeling. He situates himself so as to be touched by the world, and his story occurs in his own physiological landscape. In this chapter, I examine the body of the man of feeling and ask what happens when it becomes prominent in a report of experience. I argue that the body of sensibility, which leads to both sentimental and satiric reports on the world, is inherently parodic. Further, I suggest that despite definition by reference to a feminized standard of delicacy, this body is not a woman's body and could not become the sustained location of women's experience.

> 'Tis going, I own, like the Knight of the Woeful Countenance, in quest of melancholy adventures—but I know not how it is, but I am never so perfectly conscious of the existence of a soul within me, as when I am entangled in them.[2]

Though he travels in France, Yorick's "road," as Virginia Woolf says, is "often through his own mind, and his chief adventures . . . with the emotions of his own heart."[3] And though he is a contemporary continental traveler, he is also a parodic knight. As he places himself, so he belongs, in company with Don Quixote,[4] notwithstanding the latter's sublime incapacity to turn the mind's eye inward and Yorick's incapacity to do otherwise. Both isolate themselves from public reality by having adventures in their own created worlds.

But unlike Don Quixote, who exteriorizes a private vision and has no powers of internalization, Yorick often interiorizes external event. His tendency to subordinate the world to his own "interpreting sensibility"[5] looks back not only to Don Quixote's stylized encounters with a world continually interpreted into existence but also to spiritual autobiographers, for whom (as for Yorick) the external event is important not in itself, but as it figures in the internal landscape. As they looked inward to discover in their souls marks of sin and marks of grace, he discovers, to himself and to the reader, all his varied sensations: the workings of his heart, lungs, and nerves; his impoliteness, his dirty passions, and his tender sensibility. His extraordinary self-preoccupation is a mode of self-study.

Sterne uses traditional narrative forms associated with the journey (romance, contemporary travelogue, spiritual autobiography), but his development of discrete episodes allows him to feature the activation of Yorick's sensibility. As much of the narrative of *Clarissa* is shaped by an investigative provocation, the narrative of *A Sentimental Journey* is shaped by isolable episodes of delicate stimulation. "I declare," declares Yorick, "that was I in a desert, I would find out wherewith in it to call forth my affections" (115). The world, from Dan to Beersheba, is an instrument for stirring his sensations. He goes on the road not to rescue widows and virgins but to watch them—and record his experience.

In his journey to see Maria, Yorick involves himself in the distress of the "disordered maid," in order to create a psychological event in himself. After experiencing "undescribable emotions" during the encounter with her, he can exclaim: "I am positive I have a soul; nor can all the books with which the materialists have pester'd the world ever convince me of the contrary" (271). Moving from the sight of suffering to the internal motions it activates, he is able to locate the operations of his soul and confirm its existence by entangling himself in her melancholy story. His observation is doubled.[6] He looks at Maria in order to pity her, but the pitying response that he raises in himself becomes evidence in his own investigation. Sympathy for distress and an investigative approach to experience coincide in Sterne's pathetic scenes.

Further, for Yorick, *in quest of melancholy adventures* means *in search of exquisite sensations*. Though Sterne rather frequently separates his sentimentalism from concern with the body—"[M]y Journey," he writes, "shall make you cry as much as ever it made me laugh—or I'll give up the Business of sentimental writing—& write to the Body,"[7]—nevertheless, Yorick's adventures take place in a refined physiological interior. "I felt every vessel in my frame dilate" (68), he expansively reports as he experiences his imaginary benevolence just before colliding with the reality of Father Lorenzo, the mendicant monk. In *A Sentimental Journey,* not only is sensation the basic unit of experience; it replaces adventure as the basic unit of narrative.

By creating an interior landscape, Sterne limits the scale of Yorick's adventures but extends fictional territory. "—What a large volume of adventures may be grasped within this little span of life by him who interests his heart in every thing . . . the pleasure of the experiment has kept my senses, and the best part of my blood awake, and laid the gross to sleep" (114). The most minuscule occurrence gains the status of an event. Only a character whose vibrations are worth reporting could

have eighteen chapters of adventure in Calais, without even spending the night. And only in such a context could the varying pressure of a woman's hand provide material for a fully developed episode. So thoroughly reordered is the understanding of experience that an exchange of snuff boxes between strangers becomes an action in the largest sense.

With his adventures located in nerves, fibers, and blood vessels, Yorick has what we might call microsensation. The moment of friendship between the sentimental traveler and the monk achieves its importance as it causes reverberations in the nervous and circulatory systems of participants and readers. The resulting adjustment of attention to the events of physiology allows Sterne to give near-epic force to a sentimental exchange. Yorick and Father Lorenzo with their snuff boxes are, *mutatis mutandis,* Glaucus and Diomedes with their armor.

This miniaturization of experience is Sterne's chief means of sentimentalizing Yorick's world.[8] To see further the character of Sterne's miniaturized events, we can compare him with Robert Burns, who also arranges an unexpected and miniaturized point of view but does not depend on a sensationist psychology. Like Yorick, the poet's speaker notices ordinarily unremarkable objects and remarks. But the mountain daisy's significance rests on external reference: the daisy is analogous to, or an emblem of, the artless Maid, the simple Bard, and suffering worth. (Even the louse, whose tiny world briefly occupies full stage, gives way, in order for a moral to be drawn, to a reference point that belongs to our larger frame.) A temporary reordering of scale allows the featuring and reassertion of a value (a sentiment) already known and simply in need of revivification. Significance in Burns is derived from the comparison to which the miniaturizing strategy gives rise.

Though Sterne and Burns were both interested in delicate perception, Burns's speaker is a keen observer while Yorick is a sensitive one. Burns's perceptual shifts, and thus his emotional attitudes, are intellectually rather than organically defined. Sterne's are both: his reordering of scale rests not simply and often not at all on the creation of a point of view for an object that ordinarily does not have a perceptible one,[9] but on a redefinition of experience itself. The poet's speaker has a remarkable eye, Yorick a delicate set of nerves. The snuff box therefore achieves an absolute rather than a comparative significance.

Sensibility, as we can see in Yorick, translates the body into its own most delicate structures, producing for the man of feeling an intensified world. Though he probably would not have used Yorick as a confirming example, Hugh Blair, in a sermon on sensibility, delineates the condition of refined feeling:

Sensibility heightens, in general, the human powers, and is connected with acuteness in all our feelings . . . [The man of a virtuous sensibility] lives in a different sort of world from what the selfish man inhabits. He possesses a new sense,[10] which enables him to behold objects which the selfish man cannot see.[11]

Heightened powers, acuteness of feeling: these special blessings mark not only a refined but an expansive world, one available to the man of sensibility because of his specialized body.

The separation of the man of sensibility from the ordinary world is not, however, always a sentimentalizing gesture. John Locke speculates in his *Essay* about the isolation and inconvenience that heightened perception would cause. Concerning the eye, he says, "[I]f that most instructive of our Senses, Seeing, were in any Mar 1000, or 100000 times more acute than it is now by the best Microscope . . . he would come nearer to the Discovery of the Texture and Motion of the minute Parts of corporeal things . . . But then he would be in a quite different World from other People: Nothing would appear the same to him, and others."[12] Similarly, Samuel Johnson's illustrative quotation for *microscope* (from Richard Bentley's *A Confutation of Atheism from the Structure and Origin of Human Bodies*) shows that enhanced perceptual capacities would produce extreme discomfort: "If the eye were so acute as to rival the finest *microscopes,* and to discern the smallest hair upon the leg of a gnat, it would be a curse and not a blessing to us."[13] In his sermon on sensibility, Blair uses the figure of microscope to describe the magnifying powers of the kind of perception that he called a "false species of sensibility." People overly "refined in all their sensations . . . produce disquiet and uneasiness, to all with whom they are connected": "In consequence of examining their friends with a *microscopic eye,* what to an ordinary observer would not be unpleasing, to them is grating and disgusting" (emphasis added).[14] Microsensation can aggravate as well as enhance feeling. These writers use an image and deal with a theme that Pope made familiar in *The Essay on Man:*

> Why has not Man a microscopic eye?
> For this plain reason, Man is not a Fly.
> Say what the use, were finer optics giv'n
> T'inspect a mite, not comprehend the heav'n?
> Or touch, if tremblingly alive all o'er,
> To smart and agonize at ev'ry pore?
>
> Pope, *Essay on Man,* Epistle I, ll. 193-8.[15]

The cultural fascination with the figure of the microscope preceded and followed widespread use of the term *sensibility,* but it was especially suitable as a metaphor for conveying the genetal heightening of sensory powers attributed to a more than ordinarily delicate physical structure. And because it suggests not only acuteness but disorder, it allowed a number of writers to convey the isolation and distortion that would result from such extraordinary sensory powers.

Matthew Bramble, in Tobias Smollett's *Humphry Clinker,* embodies the condition of over-refinement. Created "to smart and agonize at ev'ry pore," he is forced to see what others can overlook and to analyze a "compound of villainous smells" into its sources ("putrid gums"; "imposthumated lungs").[16] He is what Frances Burney's Lady Louisa claims to be—"nerve all over."[17] In his character, Smollett brings together the man of feeling and the man of humor, defining excess by acuteness of sensation rather than humoral imbalance. Bramble is, in other words, a traditional physiological character type with a new physiology. And appropriately for a character in a medically defined literary tradition, he reports his experience to his doctor—as if Smollett had accepted as a challenge Yorick's advice to Smelfungus: "You had better tell it, said I, to your physician" (118).

With his "morbid excess of sensation" (18), Bramble is what we might call a "touchy" man of feeling. As his nephew describes him, "He is as tender as a man without a skin; who cannot bear the slightest touch without flinching" (48). Registering experience directly on the nerves, he, even more than Yorick, has not so much a physical as a physiological body—and it determines the nature of his experience. Sensuality, for example, is generally out of his range. A man without skin runs few risks of the flesh. With "nerves of uncommon sensibility" (63), Smollett's character necessarily perceives the world as painful or repugnant.[18] Bramble's experience, in fact, is rather like that caused by Gulliver's reduced size in Brobdingnag. For both Bramble and Gulliver, the fineness or delicacy of the sensory register magnifies all objects of sensation and renders them gross. What Swift accomplishes by physically relocating Gulliver in a land too large for his sensory receptors, Smollett achieves by making Bramble's sensory capacity too acute for London life. His body is created for satiric perception.

Delicacy of the nervous system does for all the senses what the microscope does for vision. And, thus, a refined sensibility can lead either to sentimental or to satiric report of experience. Pope treats heightened powers as a problem of disproportion and thus adopts a traditional satiric or moral stance, one that coincides with that expressed by Locke and Bentley. All three develop the disease, disorder, distortion range of possibilities for heightened sensory powers. In this view, over-refinement can be treated just as any other excess is treated. Smollett similarly exploits the image of disorder, but because he emphasizes touch, he creates a character who sometimes inhabits a sentimental world.

On account of the pain he experiences through being touched by the world, his body can become an object of sympathy. Nevertheless, on the whole, Matthew Bramble, like Gulliver, has a fantastical body, suited to be an index of the world's or his own disorder.

Sterne's explorations raise different issues. Though often parodic, he is not a traditional satirist or moralist pointing to a standard of the mean or of proportion. Instead, his use of the body of sensibility shows that it is naturally at odds with itself. The ambiguous nature of the idea of sensibility, both in medical literature and the general culture, has received critical attention. Sensibility combines debility with refinement, "privilege" with "affliction."[19] What I want to emphasize here is that the body itself is inherently contradictory; it is a parodic body.

It is, first, a physiological body. And, second, it is feminized. The physiological body both coincides with and runs counter to the feminized body. Women were, as a matter of medical observation, thought to have more delicate nervous systems than men.[20] But in addition, *delicacy* and other idealizing terms—*noble, ultimate, fine*—had at. this time a technical status in physiology. Hermann Boerhaave explains that "we call a nerve that vessel which is the *ultimate* and most *delicate.*"[21] Albrecht von Haller calls nerve fluid "the *noblest* humour of the body"[22] and uses the term "*finer* anatomy"[23] to describe what is made visible by injections in blood vessels. Alongside a clinical and specialized scientific vocabulary describing the nervous system, then, is a range of terms that seem to suggest that the physiological body is, itself, in many instances a feminized body.

The coincidence between the physical structures of sensibility and a feminine standard of refinement arises in part because these structures were accessible only through microanalysis, which paradoxically became the basis for an imagined immateriality of the body. In a note in his edition of *L'Homme Machine,* Aram Vartanian indicates the idealizing function of the microscope: "In laying bare for the first time the extremely complex structures of even the crudest organisms, the microscope had profoundly altered the scientific imagination of the period. As a result, matter seemed to lose much of its classic grossness and, in proportion to the anatomical perfections it displayed, became capable of functions which, owing to their apparent excellence, had traditionally been placed beyond the range of merely material factors."[24] The microscopic size of these structures, together with their complexity, gave rise then to an idealized body.

This imagined immateriality of physical structures is crucial to an understanding of Sterne's use of sensibility. It must, for example, be the basis for Yorick's conviction that his smoothly functioning arteries con-

stitute an argument against materialism. Though philosophically specious ("the *most physical précieuse* in France" could have used Yorick's evidence to support her own case),[25] his claim is imaginatively persuasive. It is this understanding of sensibility that underlies the commonplace declarations that it is opposed to the material and sensual. To appreciate the transformation of physical structures, we can contrast to these delicate nerves and fibers the brain, which, although obviously central to medical research on the nervous system, never became part of the ordinary vocabulary of sensibility. This exclusion occurred partly because the heart was regularly substituted for the brain (in popular thinking, sensibility is located anatomically in a quasi-metaphorical heart and literal nerves), but partly because as a physical structure, the brain cannot be sufficiently refined.

But nerves and fibers do not always coincide with the feminized standard used in the general culture and in medicine to characterize the nervous system. These minute internal structures often call their own physicality into view. They literalize as well as etherialize the idea of the inner being. In his essay of 1747, Jerome Gaub, obviously fascinated by interior complexity, describes "neural man," which, he says,

> is distributed throughout the entire body and so intermingled with each of its parts that if separated from these parts it could present a simulacrum or skeletal image of a man. Furthermore, this structure of nerves is no less animated from within by its motive power than it itself stirs up the rest of the body's inert mass throughout which it extends. In this sense it represents a kind of man within a man.[26]

This literal inner man—this clinical version of the man of sensibility—creates a tension with the idealized, feminized body that it underlies. This "embodied" tension defines a naturally parodic field.[27]

Sterne exploits the essential ambiguities of sensibility and thereby achieves the instability of tone that defines his fictional world. The parodic quality of Sterne's episodes often inheres in their delicacy. The miniaturization that arises from microsensation is not only refining but reductive. Minute perceptual capacities simultaneously heighten and trivialize experience. More importantly, however, sensibility is a source of Sterne's parody because the physiological body necessarily physicalizes experience. The nervous "simulacrum or skeletal image of a man" is continually present as Yorick reports his most delicate connections. The organic nature of experience accounts, then, not only for Sterne's delicate intensity but also for its undermining. Yorick is an imaginary knight with real nerves. ("I knew not that contention could be rendered so sweet and pleasurable a thing to the nerves as I then felt it" [100]. "The pulsations of the arteries along my fingers pressing across hers, told her what was passing within me" [97].) The refinement of experience is at odds with the structures of its creation. Sensibility is thus the basis not only for Sterne's delicate sentiment but also for the mock-heroic reductiveness that runs counter to it.[28] Sterne's imagination is fundamentally parodic. His parody of sensibility, however, derives not from some opposing idea but from sensibility itself, from its miniaturizing and physicalizing force.

The parodic tension inherent in the miniaturizing and physicalizing force of sensibility is made further complex by the sexual suggestiveness of refined contact. Delicate sexual impulse is part of sensibility's heightening of responses.[29] Though Yorick feels his way across France, this sexualized experience, too, is countered by the physiological body on which it depends. Physiologically pathetic scenes are matched by physiologically sexual scenes. Carnality is as little likely to be an issue for Yorick as for Matthew Bramble. Yorick is a traveling nervous system whose tender experiences collapse in clinical parody. With his feminized and physiological body defining two extremes for which there is only a parodic resolution, he is isolated from ordinary physicality.

The body of sensibility creates a context for the central parodic juxtaposition in *A Sentimental Journey:* that between benevolence and impotence. With some frequency, Sterne announced that he was not, except in a minimal way, a sexual being. He claims that he was early on refined out of all form for "connubial bliss" and declares in a letter that he has not, since age thirty nine, had any "commerce whatever with the sex, not even with [his] wife."[30] Modern readers generally assume that such statements contain as much truth as wit and that Sterne's carefully cultivated reputation for impotence was deserved. What contemporary readers call "lust in disguise," seems as likely to be a form of undisguise.[31] Sterne has Yorick raise the idea of a refined sensuality only to deny his own powers. The sexual suggestiveness of the benevolent encounter with the lady is a false suggestiveness: "In a word, I felt benevolence for her; and resolv'd some way or other to throw in my mite of courtesy—if not of service" (95). The tender feeling is animated and mildly contaminated by the possibility that this parodic knight is also a parodic man and cannot throw in a mite of service.

The fusion of benevolence with a confession of impotence is further developed when Yorick, after a struggle between various prudential considerations and a desire to follow the lady to Brussels, rapturously outlines the pleasure he seeks from listening to her story:

> [W]ith what a moral delight will it crown my journey, in sharing in the sickening incidents of a tale of misery told to me by such a sufferer? To see

her weep! and though I cannot dry up the fountain of her tears, what an exquisite sensation is there still left, in wiping them away from off the cheeks of the first and fairest of women, as I'm sitting with my handkerchief in my hand in silence the whole night beside her (145-6).

The language of moral life has frequently absorbed expressions of desire. Isaac Barrow, in one of the sermons that R. S. Crane sees as a source for the man of feeling, calls the spiritual pleasure associated with beneficence "virtuous voluptuousness."[32] But the term *exquisite sensation* cannot be altogether subordinated to the idea of *moral delight*. Yorick displays his own inactivity ("sitting with my handkerchief in my hand in silence the whole night beside her") in a way that makes his innocence less significant than his display of it. With actual physiology the usual territory of Yorick's experience, Sterne exploits the instability of the term *sensation* to create a collision of the moral, sexual, and physiological suggestiveness of sensibility. No resolution is possible, and readers remain at the juncture that creates parody and demands interpretation.

The same pattern is further developed in the scene with the grisset. Yorick uses here, alternately and in combination, emotional and organic ideas of the heart: the heart as center of passional and spiritual life, source of idealized love, on the one hand, and, on the other, the heart as the physical organ pumping blood through the body's envisioned physical structures. Extending the figurative value of the heart to include the physical function of its outerworks, Yorick implies that if one has a good heart, a good pulse will be the index of it: if you want to see the heart, feel the pulse. Sight has been thoroughly subordinated to touch, and the sentimental traveler has become a doctor, applying his forefingers to the woman's artery. Eugenius, the reader, and all the world look on—at an encounter that takes place between his nerves and her circulatory system. With experience transferred to interior physical structures and activity in the external world made secondary to the internal response it excites, stimulates, or provokes, it is the vibration that counts. Sexual activity located in the nervous system can occur only in an attenuated form. The two modes of interiorization—fantasy and monitoring of internal organs—are interdependent but jarring.

Through such a display of Yorick's internal operations, Sterne creates a complex relation with his readers, an analysis of which is implied in an aphorism by Goethe: Yorick "is a model in nothing and a guide and stimulator in everything."[33] He is provocative. Made comic by the collision between romantic and physiological uses of the heart, the episode with the grisset shifts into a coy confirmation that we are watching a scene of substituted sexual pleasure: "Trust me, my dear Eugenius, I should have said, 'there are worse occupations in this world *than feeling a woman's pulse.'*—But a Grisset's! thou wouldst have said—and in an open shop! Yorick—" The word *pulse* not only creates a comic confusion of literal and metaphorical meanings, but by the end of the scene carries a further heightened suggestiveness. Through his dislocating use of intimacy and clinical encounter, Sterne forces readers to be both observer and observed. His presentation of Yorick's search for sensations makes psychologically possible the interior scrutiny that philosophers require their readers to adopt as a rhetorical stance for proper reading. That is, he initiates—as an unavoidable psychological process—a turning of the mind's eye inward.[34] In Sterne's fiction, episodes that begin with observation take the attention to organic sensitivity, which, giving rise to parody, leads back to observation. As Locke wants his readers to locate the operations of the understanding, Sterne makes them locate the experiencing, *affectable* self—as a more persuasive object of attention than the mind's operations. Sterne's arrangement of Yorick's sensation seeking is, finally, intellectualized. . . .

Notes

[1] For a discussion of the significance of touch in Condillac's statue's exploration of itself and the world, see Chapter 5 [of Ann Jessie Van Sant, *Eighteenth-Century Sensibility and the Novel: The Senses in Social Context* (Cambridge: Cambridge University Press, 1993)].

[2] Laurence Sterne, *A Sentimental Journey Through France and Italy by Mr. Yorick,* ed. Gardner D. Stout, Jr. (Berkeley and Los Angeles: University of California Press, 1967), p. 270. All further references will be to this edition and will be included in the text. My reading of Sterne has been influenced, and my study aided, by the notes and discussion that appear in this edition.

[3] Virginia Woolf, "Introduction" to the World's Classics edition of *A Sentimental Journey* (London: Oxford University Press, 1928), pp. viii-ix.

[4] In his introduction, Stout refers to Yorick's "sentimental knight-errantry" and says, "Yorick's benevolent impulses are the counterpart, in an age of sensibility, to Don Quixote's chivalric ideals" (p. 44).

[5] In *Robert Burns and the Sentimental Era* (Athens, Ga.: University of Georgia Press, 1985), Carol McGuirk discusses the central position that men of feeling give to themselves as they participate in pathetic scenes: "Sentimental novels following Sterne, however, made the presence of an interpreting sensibility seem more important than the wretchedness described" (p. 5).

[6] See Jean Jacques Mayoux ("Laurence Sterne," in *Laurence Sterne, A Collection of Critical Essays,* ed. John Traugott [Englewood Cliffs, New Jersey: Prentice-Hall, 1968]) for an analysis of sentimental "witnessing": "The witness is necessary to the sentimental scene" and "For as sadness wants solitude, so sentimentalism wants this grouping and this reciprocal witnessing" (111-12). Sterne arranges pathetic scenes in a traditional way, but he also fragments vision, thus bringing attention to the observer/reader's responses.

[7] *Letters of Laurence Sterne,* p. 401 (letter no. 219; Nov. 15, 1767).

[8] That is, of investing common objects with momentary momentousness. See Alan Dugald McKillop's chapter on Sterne in *The Early Masters of English Fiction* (Lawrence: University of Kansas Press, 1956), rpt. in *Laurence Sterne, A Collection of Critical Essays,* pp. 34-65. McKillop discusses Sterne's love for miniatures and his use of "the principle of the tremendous trifle" (49).

[9] An exception is the *désobligeant,* "standing so many months unpitied in the corner of Mons. Dessein's coach-yard" (87-8).

[10] In declaring that the man of sensibility has a "new sense," Blair's models are the "moral sense" philosophers. His version of enhanced perception depends on an analogy to sense perception but is also related to organic sensitivity.

[11] Hugh Blair, *Sermons,* III, 127. Blair goes on to characterize the experience of the man of sensibility: "At the same time his enjoyments are not of that kind which remain merely on the surface of the mind. They penetrate the heart. They enlarge and elevate, they refine and ennoble it" (127-8).

[12] John Locke, *An Essay on Human Understanding,* p. 303 (II, xxiii, 12).

[13] Samuel Johnson, *A Dictionary of the English Language, microscope.* The section of Bentley's work from which this material is taken is quoted by Marjorie Hope Nicolson ("The Microscope and English Imagination," in *Science and Imagination* [Ithaca, NY: Cornell University Press, 1956], p. 208). Bentley's work is *A Confutation of Atheism from the Structure and Origin of Human Bodies,* a Boyle lecture delivered in 1692, reprinted in *Sermons Preached at Boyle's Lectures . . . By Richard Bentley,* ed. Alexander Dyce (London, 1738).

[14] Blair, *Sermons,* III, 127, 129.

[15] Alexander Pope, *Essay on Man. The Twickenham Edition of the Poems of Alexander Pope,* Vol. III-1,

ed. Maynard Mack (New Haven: Yale University Press, 1951), pp. 36-8. In the notes to lines 193-206, Mack refers to a number of works that emphasized the suitability of human perceptual powers for the world of perception. Magnification, though an enhancement of visual power, would amount to a disorder.

[16] Tobias Smollett, *Humphry Clinker,* ed. James L. Thorson (New York: W. W. Norton and Co., 1983), p. 62. All further references will be to this edition and will be included in the text.

[17] Frances Burney, *Evelina* (New York: W. W. Norton and Co., 1965), p. 267.

[18] Matthew Bramble calls another character in the novel "thin-skinned" and thereby provides the *OED* with its first example of this term.

[19] John Mullan, "Hypochondria and Hysteria: Sensibility and the Physicians," *Eighteenth-Century Studies,* vol. 25, no. 2 (1984), pp. 146, 148.

[20] "Women," according to Robert Whytt, "in whom the nervous system is generally more moveable than in men, are more subject to nervous complaints, and have them in a higher degree." Whytt's *Observations on the Nature, Causes, and Cure of those Disorders which are commonly called Nervous, Hypochondriac, or Hysteric, To which are prefixed some Remarks on the Sympathy of the Nerves,* p. 540.

[21] Lester S. King, Introduction to *First Lines of Physiology by the Celebrated Baron Albertus Haller,* trans. William Cullen. A reprint of the 1786 edition, *The Sources of Science,* No. 32 (New York and London: Johnson Reprint Corporation, 1966), p. xxvi.

[22] *First Lines of Physiology,* p. 223.

[23] *Ibid.,* Introduction, p. xxxv.

[24] Aram Vartanian, *La Mettrie's L'Homme Machine: A Study in the Origins of an Idea* (Princeton, NJ: Princeton University Press, 1960), p. 81. Karl Figlio ("Theories of Perception") quotes this section in a note. Figlio's argument runs the other way: that is, he is interested in the influence exerted on physiological investigation by non-medically-based ideas of the *integrity of the mind.* Vartanian, on the other hand, is interested in the fact that physiological micro-analysis influenced ordinary and philosophical ways of thinking about the body and mind.

Traces of the discussion of complexity can be found in various general essays. For example, the essayist who defined sensibility as a *"peculiar structure"* or "habitude of mind" (*Monthly Magazine,* 2 [1796], 706) refers to this issue, as does Frank Sayers (M.D.) in an essay

called "Perception": "[I]t will be granted, I believe," he writes "that the mind, *whether immaterial,* or *the result of organization,* has certainly a wholeness or unity belonging to it." *Disquisitions, Metaphysical and Literary* (London, 1793), p. 64 (emphasis added).

[25] In "The Sensorium in the World of 'A Sentimental Journey,'" John Dussinger also discusses this section of *A Sentimental Journey:* "Ironically, a *physical précieuse* in La Mettrie's camp could very well have called Yorick a machine and not at all be confounded by his vigorous emotionalism, which on the contrary reveals the very force of living matter from within" (pp. 9-10).

[26] Rather, *Mind and Body in Eighteenth Century Medicine,* p. 64.

[27] Spiritual autobiographers, too, imagined their experience in physiological terms and with a potentially comparable conflict between the anatomical details and the spiritual project. See Introduction for material quoted from Thomas Watson's *Christian Soldier.*

[28] See McGuirk, *Robert Burns and the Sentimental Era,* p. 3 ff. for a discussion of Burns's mock-heroic quality. The phrase, as McGuirk points out, was used by Burns's brother.

[29] See Brissenden, "The Sentimental Comedy: *A Sentimental Journey*" (in *Virtue in Distress,* p. 78) for a discussion of the correspondence between heightened moral and heightened sexual responsiveness.

[30] *Letters of Laurence Sterne,* p. 343 (letter no. 196, May [2]1, 1767).

[31] There is much critical commentary on Sterne's impotence and his literary use of it. I am here interested in its physiological context.

[32] "A man may be virtuously voluptuous, and a laudable epicure by doing much good; for to receive good, even in the judgment of Epicurus himself (the great patron of pleasure), is nowise so pleasant as to do it." *Theological Works,* 2. 225. Quoted by Crane in "Suggestions toward a Genealogy of the 'Man of Feeling,'" p. 228. Crane points out that Fielding approvingly quotes this passage.

[33] *Sterne, The Critical Heritage,* p. 434.

[34] This is the task of a philosophical rhetorician. My general view of Sterne is very much influenced by John Traugott, both by his *Tristram Shandy's World: Sterne's Philosophical Rhetoric* (Berkeley: University of California Press, 1954) and by discussions with him.

Bibliography

. . . Blair, Hugh. *Lectures on Rhetoric and Belles Lettres,* 2nd ed., 3 vols. London: Printed for W. Strahan; T. Cadell, in the Strand; and W. Creech, in Edinburgh, 1785.

————. *Sermons,* 3 vols. New York: Samuel Campbell, 1802. . . .

Brissenden, R. F. *Virtue in Distress: Studies in the Novel of Sentiment from Richardson to Sade.* New York: Barnes and Noble, 1974. . . .

Crane, R. S. "Suggestions toward a Genealogy of the 'Man of Feeling,'" *ELH,* 1 (1934), 205-30. . . .

Dussinger, John A. "The Sensorium in the World of 'A sentimental Journey,'" *Ariel,* 13 (1982), 3-16. . . .

Figlio, Karl. "Theories of Perception and the Physiology of Mind in the Late Eighteenth Century," *History of Science,* 12 (1975), 177-212. . . .

Haller, Albrecht von. "A Dissertation on the Sensible and Irritable Parts of Animals." Rpt. in *The Bulletin of the Institute of the History of Medicine,* 4 (1936), 651-99. . . .

Howes, Alan B., ed. *Sterne, The Critical Heritage.* London and Boston: Routledge & Kegan Paul, 1974.

————*Yorick and the Critics: Sterne's Reputation in England, 1760-1868.* New Haven: Yale University Press, 1958. . . .

Johnson, Samuel. *Dictionary of the English Language.* London, 1755. . . .

Locke, John. *An Essay Concerning Human Understanding,* ed. Peter H. Nidditch. Oxford: Clarendon Press, 1979. . . .

McGuirk, Carol. *Robert Burns and the Sentimental Era.* Athens, Ga.: University of Georgia Press, 1985. . . .

Rather, L. J. *Mind and Body in Eighteenth Century Medicine,* a study based on Jerome Gaub's *De regimine mentis.* London: The Wellcome Historical Medical Library, 1965. . . .

Sterne, Laurence. *Letters of Laurence Sterne,* ed. Lewis P. Curtis. Oxford: Clarendon Press, 1935, 1965.

————. *The Life and Opinions of Tristram Shandy, Gentleman,* ed. Melvyn New and Joan New, 3 vols. Gainesville, Fla.: University of Florida Press, 1978.

————. *The Life and Opinions of Tristram Shandy, Gentleman,* ed. James A. Work. Indianapolis and New York: Bobbs-Merrill Co., 1940.

————. *A Sentimental Journey Through France and Italy,* ed. Gardner Stout. Berkeley and Los Angeles: University of California Press, 1967.

————. *The Sermons of Mr. Yorick,* introd. and ed. Wilbur Cross, 2 vols. New York: J. F. Taylor & Co., 1904.

The Tatler, ed. Donald F. Bond, 3 vols. Oxford: Clarendon Press, 1987. . . .

Traugott, John. "*Clarissa*'s Richardson: An Essay to Find the Reader," in *English Literature in the Age of Disguise,* ed. Maximillian Novak (Berkeley, Los Angeles, and London: University of California Press, 1977), pp. 157-208.

————. *Laurence Sterne, A Collection of Critical Essays,* ed. John Traugott. Englewood Cliffs, NJ: Prentice-Hall, 1968.

————. *Tristram Shandy's World: Sterne's Philosophical Rhetoric.* Berkeley: University of California Press, 1954. . . .

FURTHER READING

Bibliography

Hartley, Lodwick. *Laurence Sterne in the Twentieth Century: An Essay and a Bibliography of Sternean Studies, 1900-1965.* Chapel Hill: The University of North Carolina Press, 1966, 189 p.

Annotated bibliography of biographical and critical works about Sterne and his writings that is aimed at students who are "not yet . . . thoroughly familiar" with Sterne's work.

—. *Laurence Sterne: An Annotated Bibliography, 1965-1977, with An Introductory Essay-Review of the Scholarship.* Boston: G. K. Hall and Co., 1978, 103 p.

Later version of Hartley's 1966 bibliography, updated to provide "an annotated list of Sternean studies for the most highly productive . . . period of this area of scholarship in the century."

Biography

Cash, Arthur H. *Laurence Sterne: The Later Years.* London: Methuen and Co., 1986, 390 p.

Covers the final eight years of Sterne's life, when

Sterne had become famous as the writer of the first volumes of *Tristram Shandy.*

Howes, Alan B., ed. *Sterne: The Critical Heritage.* London: Routledge and Kegan Paul, 1974, 488 p.

Literary biography of Sterne's works, focusing on early public and professional reactions to his writings.

Shaw, Margaret R. B. *Laurence Sterne: The Making of a Humorist, 1713-1762.* London: The Richards Press, 1957, 274 p.

Examines the circumstances and events in Sterne's life which led to his writing *Tristram Shandy.*

Criticism

Alter, Robert. "*Tristram Shandy* and the Game of Love." *American Scholar* 37, No. 2 (Spring 1968): 316-23.

Argues that Sterne "gave sexuality a large role in his fiction both because . . . it play[s] a large role in our lives" and because he found it an apt metaphor for other aspects of the human condition.

Anderson, Howard. "Answers to the Author of *Clarissa:* Theme and Narrative Technique in *Tom Jones* and *Tristram Shandy.*" *Philological Quarterly* 51, No. 4 (October 1972): 859-73.

Contrasts the isolated, misanthropic world of Richardson's *Clarissa* with the narrative-driven, social worlds of Fielding's *Tom Jones* and Sterne's *Tristram Shandy.*

Baker, Ernest A. "Sterne." In his *The History of the English Novel, Vol. IV Intellectual Realism: From Richardson to Sterne,* pp. 240-76. New York: Barnes and Noble, Inc., 1930.

Examines Sterne's work in light of his literary predecessors and with regard to his part in the sentimentalist of the eighteenth century.

Barnett, George L., ed. *Eighteenth-Century British Novelists on the Novel.* New York: Appleton-Century-Crofts, 1968, p.?

Provides eighteenth-century authors' assessments of their own works, including Sterne's humorous comments on the digressions in *Tristram Shandy.*

Battestin, Martin C. "Swift and Sterne: The Disturbance of Form." In his *The Providence of Wit: Aspects of Form in Augustan Literature and the Arts,* pp. 215-69. Oxford: The Clarendon Press, 1974.

Discusses the ways in which Swift and Sterne focused on and made use of "chaos" in their writing.

Booth, Wayne C. "The Self-Conscious Narrator in Comic Fiction before *Tristram Shandy.*" *PMLA* LXVII, No. 2 (March 1952): 163-85.

Argues that Sterne's innovations in *Tristram Shandy* are not experiments in chaos, but in creating unity out of the chaos already explored by earlier writers.

Brady, Frank. "*Tristram Shandy:* Sexuality, Morality, and Sensibility." *Eighteenth-Century Studies* 4, No. 1 (Fall 1970): 41-56

Discusses Sterne's preoccupation with sex in *Tristram Shandy,* and argues that it is interconnected with religion and with the author's efforts to write "honestly" about human nature.

Conrad, Peter. *Shandyism: The Character of Romantic Irony.* New York: Barnes and Noble, 1978, 190 p.

Ranks *Tristram Shandy* within the artistic milieu of its period, arguing that this novel is a genuinely original work that deserves an important place in any study of the history of Romanticism.

Drew, Elizabeth A. "Laurence Sterne: *Tristram Shandy.*" In her *The Novel: A Modern Guide to Fifteen English Masterpieces,* pp. 75-94. New York: Dell Publishing Co., Inc., 1963.

Describes Sterne as a "forerunner" of modern novelists whose intention is to entertain both himself and his readers.

Holtz, William V. *Image and Immortality: A Study of* Tristram Shandy. Providence: Brown University Press, 1970, 175 p.

Examines *Tristram Shandy* from three perspectives: the tradition of literary pictorialism, the novel as an emerging genre, and Sterne's own sensibility.

Howes, Alan B. *Yorick and the Critics: Sterne's Reputation in England, 1760-1868.* New Haven: Yale University Press, 1958, 186 p.

Traces the critical climate surrounding Sterne's work from the initial reviews of the first two volumes of *Tristram Shandy* in 1760 until the centenary of his death in 1868.

Jefferson, D. W. "*Tristram Shandy* and the Tradition of Learned Wit." *Essays in Criticism* 1, No. 3 (July 1951): 225-48.

Argues against the view that *Tristram Shandy* is merely chaotic and instead affirms that Sterne's novel possesses its own "artistic scheme" that adheres to some extent to "traditional form and thematic pattern."

Laird, John. "Shandean Philosophy." In his *Philosophical Incursions into English Literature,* pp. 74-91. Cambridge, England: Cambridge University Press, 1946.

Discusses Sterne's humanistic philosophy as it unfolds in *Tristram Shandy, A Sentimental Journey,* and the *Sermons.*

Loveridge, Mark. *Laurence Sterne and the Argument about Design.* Totowa, NJ: Barnes and Noble Books, 1982, 242 p.

Examines Sterne's interest in narrative pattern, design and form in his novels. The critic considers contemporary influences on *Tristram Shandy* and comments on the influential nature of Sterne's novel in turn.

McKillop, Alan Dugald. "Laurence Sterne." In his *The Early Masters of English Fiction,* pp. 182-219. Lawrence: University of Kansas Press, 1956.

Calls Sterne one of the great innovators of English literature. The chapter ofers an examination of the morality, humor, and narrative artistry of *Tristram Shandy.*

Muir, Edwin. "Laurence Sterne." In his *Essays on Literature and Society,* pp. 49-56. London: The Hogarth Press, 1949.

Praises Sterne's ability to probe his characters' minds while maintaining a sense of non-intrusive narration.

Paulson, Ronald. "Sterne: The Subversion of Satire." In his *Satire and the Novel in Eighteenth-Century England,* pp. 248-62. New Haven: Yale University Press, 1967.

Argues that *Tristram Shandy* is more of a satire of the novel form than a satiric novel.

Petrie, Graham. "Rhetoric as Fictional Technique in *Tristram Shandy.*" *Philological Quarterly* XL VIII, No. 4 (October 1969): 479-94.

Discusses Sterne's use of traditional rhetorical devices in *Tristram Shandy* to develop character and structure narrative.

Priestley, J. B. "The Brothers Shandy." In his *The English Comic Characters,* pp. 128-57. New York: Dodd, Mead and Company, 1931.

Character studies of Uncle Toby and Walter Shandy.

Reid, Ben. "The Sad Hilarity of Sterne." *The Virginia Quarterly Review* 32, No. 1 (Winter 1956): 107-30.

Argues that the comic nature of Sterne's novels is firmly grounded in tragedy, and that like Shakespeare's characters, Sterne's characters approach unfortunate fates with dignity.

Rothstein, Eric. *"Tristram Shandy."* In his *Systems of Order and Inquiry in Later Eighteenth-Century Fiction,* pp. 62-108. Berkeley: University of California Press, 1975.

Asserts that a "covert order," dependant on the value systems and feelings of human beings, accounts for the structure of *Tristram Shandy.*

Stevenson, John Allen. "Sterne: Comedian and Experimental Novelist." In *The Columbia History of the British Novel,* edited by John Richetti, pp. 154-80. New York: Columbia University Press, 1994.

Asserts that Sterne experimented with narrative form and novelistic convention in *Tristram Shandy* not "to revolutionize the novel . . . but to have fun with the conventions he saw hardening all around him."

Stout, Gardner D., Jr. "Yorick's *Sentimental Journey:* A Comic *Pilgrim's Progress* for the Man of Feeling." *ELH* 30, No. 4 (December 1963): 395-412.

Approaches *A Sentimental Journey* as an ostensibly paradoxical work which, when examined more closely, offers a unified vision of human existence through a fusion of sentimental and comic components.

Traugott, John. *Tristram Shandy's World: Sterne's Philosophical Rhetoric.* Berkeley: University of California Press, 1954, 167 p.

Sees *Tristram Shandy* as a work in which philosophical and rhetorical forms are used ironically to demonstrate that passion, not reason, is the basis of human behavior.

Woolf, Virginia. "The *Sentimental Journey.*" In her *The Common Reader, Second Series,* pp. 78-85. London: The Hogarth Press, 1932.

Reprints Woolf's 1928 introduction to the World's Classics edition of *A Sentimental Journey.* Woolf discusses the novel's emphasis on pleasure in all aspects of life and commends the novel's "brilliant ease and beauty."

Additional coverage of Sterne's life and career is contained in the following sources published by The Gale Group: *Literature Criticism from 1400-1800,* Vol. 2, *Contmporary Dictionary of British Literary Biography, 1660-1789, Dictionary of Literary Biogrpahy,* Vol. 39, and *DISCovering Authors.*

Literature Criticism from 1400 to 1800

Cumulative Indexes

How to Use This Index

The main references

Calvino, Italo
1923–1985 .... CLC 5, 8, 11, 22, 33, 39,
73; SSC 3

list all author entries in the following Gale Literary Criticism series:

BLC = *Black Literature Criticism*
CLC = *Contemporary Literary Criticism*
CLR = *Children's Literature Review*
CMLC = *Classical and Medieval Literature Criticism*
DA = *DISCovering Authors*
DAB = *DISCovering Authors: British*
DAC = *DISCovering Authors: Canadian*
DAM = *DISCovering Authors: Modules*
    DRAM: *Dramatists Module*; *MST*: *Most-Studied Authors Module*;
    MULT: *Multicultural Authors Module*; *NOV*: *Novelists Module*;
    POET: *Poets Module*; *POP*: *Popular Fiction and Genre Authors Module*
DC = *Drama Criticism*
HLC = *Hispanic Literature Criticism*
LC = *Literature Criticism from 1400 to 1800*
NCLC = *Nineteenth-Century Literature Criticism*
PC = *Poetry Criticism*
SSC = *Short Story Criticism*
TCLC = *Twentieth-Century Literary Criticism*
WLC = *World Literature Criticism, 1500 to the Present*

The cross-references

See also CANR 23; CA 85-88;
obituary CA116

list all author entries in the following Gale biographical and literary sources:

AAYA = *Authors & Artists for Young Adults*
AITN = *Authors in the News*
BEST = *Bestsellers*
BW = *Black Writers*
CA = *Contemporary Authors*
CAAS = *Contemporary Authors Autobiography Series*
CABS = *Contemporary Authors Bibliographical Series*
CANR = *Contemporary Authors New Revision Series*
CAP = *Contemporary Authors Permanent Series*
CDALB = *Concise Dictionary of American Literary Biography*
CDBLB = *Concise Dictionary of British Literary Biography*
DLB = *Dictionary of Literary Biography*
DLBD = *Dictionary of Literary Biography Documentary Series*
DLBY = *Dictionary of Literary Biography Yearbook*
HW = *Hispanic Writers*
JRDA = *Junior DISCovering Authors*
MAICYA = *Major Authors and Illustrators for Children and Young Adults*
MTCW = *Major 20th-Century Writers*
NNAL = *Native North American Literature*
SAAS = *Something about the Author Autobiography Series*
SATA = *Something about the Author*
YABC = *Yesterday's Authors of Books for Children*

20/1631
See Upward, Allen
A/C Cross
See Lawrence, T(homas) E(dward)
Abasiyanik, Sait Faik 1906-1954
See Sait Faik
See also CA 123
Abbey, Edward 1927-1989 **CLC 36, 59**
See also CA 45-48; 128; CANR 2, 41
Abbott, Lee K(ittredge) 1947- **CLC 48**
See also CA 124; CANR 51; DLB 130
Abe, Kobo 1924-1993**CLC 8, 22, 53, 81; DAM NOV**
See also CA 65-68; 140; CANR 24, 60; DLB 182; MTCW 1
Abelard, Peter c. 1079-c. 1142 **CMLC 11**
See also DLB 115, 208
Abell, Kjeld 1901-1961 **CLC 15**
See also CA 111
Abish, Walter 1931- **CLC 22**
See also CA 101; CANR 37; DLB 130
Abrahams, Peter (Henry) 1919- **CLC 4**
See also BW 1; CA 57-60; CANR 26; DLB 117; MTCW 1
Abrams, M(eyer) H(oward) 1912- **CLC 24**
See also CA 57-60; CANR 13, 33; DLB 67
Abse, Dannie 1923- **CLC 7, 29; DAB; DAM POET**
See also CA 53-56; CAAS 1; CANR 4, 46, 74; DLB 27
Achebe, (Albert) Chinua(lumogu) 1930-**C L C 1, 3, 5, 7, 11, 26, 51, 75; BLC 1; DA; DAB; DAC; DAM MST, MULT, NOV; WLC**
See also AAYA 15; BW 2; CA 1-4R; CANR 6, 26, 47, 73; CLR 20; DLB 117; MAICYA; MTCW 1; SATA 40; SATA-Brief 38
Acker, Kathy 1948-1997 **CLC 45, 111**
See also CA 117; 122; 162; CANR 55
Ackroyd, Peter 1949- **CLC 34, 52**
See also CA 123; 127; CANR 51, 74; DLB 155; INT 127
Acorn, Milton 1923- **CLC 15; DAC**
See also CA 103; DLB 53; INT 103
Adamov, Arthur 1908-1970 **CLC 4, 25; DAM DRAM**
See also CA 17-18; 25-28R; CAP 2; MTCW 1
Adams, Alice (Boyd) 1926-**CLC 6, 13, 46; SSC 24**
See also CA 81-84; CANR 26, 53, 75; DLBY 86; INT CANR-26; MTCW 1
Adams, Andy 1859-1935 **TCLC 56**
See also YABC 1
Adams, Brooks 1848-1927 **TCLC 80**
See also CA 123; DLB 47
Adams, Douglas (Noel) 1952- **CLC 27, 60; DAM POP**
See also AAYA 4; BEST 89:3; CA 106; CANR 34, 64; DLBY 83; JRDA
Adams, Francis 1862-1893 **NCLC 33**
Adams, Henry (Brooks) 1838-1918 **TCLC 4, 52; DA; DAB; DAC; DAM MST**
See also CA 104; 133; DLB 12, 47, 189

Adams, Richard (George) 1920-**CLC 4, 5, 18; DAM NOV**
See also AAYA 16; AITN 1, 2; CA 49-52; CANR 3, 35; CLR 20; JRDA; MAICYA; MTCW 1; SATA 7, 69
Adamson, Joy(-Friederike Victoria) 1910-1980 **CLC 17**
See also CA 69-72; 93-96; CANR 22; MTCW 1; SATA 11; SATA-Obit 22
Adcock, Fleur 1934- **CLC 41**
See also CA 25-28R; CAAS 23; CANR 11, 34, 69; DLB 40
Addams, Charles (Samuel) 1912-1988**CLC 30**
See also CA 61-64; 126; CANR 12
Addams, Jane 1860-1945 **TCLC 76**
Addison, Joseph 1672-1719 **LC 18**
See also CDBLB 1660-1789; DLB 101
Adler, Alfred (F.) 1870-1937 **TCLC 61**
See also CA 119; 159
Adler, C(arole) S(chwerdtfeger) 1932-**CLC 35**
See also AAYA 4; CA 89-92; CANR 19, 40; JRDA; MAICYA; SAAS 15; SATA 26, 63, 102
Adler, Renata 1938- **CLC 8, 31**
See also CA 49-52; CANR 5, 22, 52; MTCW 1
Ady, Endre 1877-1919 **TCLC 11**
See also CA 107
A.E. 1867-1935 **TCLC 3, 10**
See also Russell, George William
Aeschylus 525B.C.-456B.C. **CMLC 11; DA; DAB; DAC; DAM DRAM, MST; DC 8; WLCS**
See also DLB 176
Aesop 620(?)B.C.-564(?)B.C. **CMLC 24**
See also CLR 14; MAICYA; SATA 64
Affable Hawk
See MacCarthy, Sir(Charles Otto) Desmond
Africa, Ben
See Bosman, Herman Charles
Afton, Effie
See Harper, Frances Ellen Watkins
Agapida, Fray Antonio
See Irving, Washington
Agee, James (Rufus) 1909-1955 **TCLC 1, 19; DAM NOV**
See also AITN 1; CA 108; 148; CDALB 1941-1968; DLB 2, 26, 152
Aghill, Gordon
See Silverberg, Robert
Agnon, S(hmuel) Y(osef Halevi) 1888-1970 **CLC 4, 8, 14; SSC 30**
See also CA 17-18; 25-28R; CANR 60; CAP 2; MTCW 1
Agrippa von Nettesheim, Henry Cornelius 1486-1535 **LC 27**
Aherne, Owen
See Cassill, R(onald) V(erlin)
Ai 1947- **CLC 4, 14, 69**
See also CA 85-88; CAAS 13; CANR 70; DLB 120
Aickman, Robert (Fordyce) 1914-1981 **C L C 57**

See also CA 5-8R; CANR 3, 72
Aiken, Conrad (Potter) 1889-1973**CLC 1, 3, 5, 10, 52; DAM NOV, POET; SSC 9**
See also CA 5-8R; 45-48; CANR 4, 60; CDALB 1929-1941; DLB 9, 45, 102; MTCW 1; SATA 3, 30
Aiken, Joan (Delano) 1924- **CLC 35**
See also AAYA 1, 25; CA 9-12R; CANR 4, 23, 34, 64; CLR 1, 19; DLB 161; JRDA; MAICYA; MTCW 1; SAAS 1; SATA 2, 30, 73
Ainsworth, William Harrison 1805-1882 **NCLC 13**
See also DLB 21; SATA 24
Aitmatov, Chingiz (Torekulovich) 1928-**C L C 71**
See also CA 103; CANR 38; MTCW 1; SATA 56
Akers, Floyd
See Baum, L(yman) Frank
Akhmadulina, Bella Akhatovna 1937- **C L C 53; DAM POET**
See also CA 65-68
Akhmatova, Anna 1888-1966**CLC 11, 25, 64; DAM POET; PC 2**
See also CA 19-20; 25-28R; CANR 35; CAP 1; MTCW 1
Aksakov, Sergei Timofeyvich 1791-1859 **NCLC 2**
See also DLB 198
Aksenov, Vassily
See Aksyonov, Vassily (Pavlovich)
Akst, Daniel 1956- **CLC 109**
See also CA 161
Aksyonov, Vassily (Pavlovich) 1932-**CLC 22, 37, 101**
See also CA 53-56; CANR 12, 48
Akutagawa, Ryunosuke 1892-1927 **TCLC 16**
See also CA 117; 154
Alain 1868-1951 **TCLC 41**
See also CA 163
Alain-Fournier **TCLC 6**
See also Fournier, Henri Alban
See also DLB 65
Alarcon, Pedro Antonio de 1833-1891**NCLC 1**
Alas (y Urena), Leopoldo (Enrique Garcia) 1852-1901 **TCLC 29**
See also CA 113; 131; HW
Albee, Edward (Franklin III) 1928-**CLC 1, 2, 3, 5, 9, 11, 13, 25, 53, 86, 113; DA; DAB; DAC; DAM DRAM, MST; WLC**
See also AITN 1; CA 5-8R; CABS 3; CANR 8, 54, 74; CDALB 1941-1968; DLB 7; INT CANR-8; MTCW 1
Alberti, Rafael 1902- **CLC 7**
See also CA 85-88; DLB 108
Albert the Great 1200(?)-1280 **CMLC 16**
See also DLB 115
Alcala-Galiano, Juan Valera y
See Valera y Alcala-Galiano, Juan
Alcott, Amos Bronson 1799-1888 **NCLC 1**
See also DLB 1

See Sanders, Lawrence

Andrewes, Lancelot 1555-1626   **LC 5**
See also DLB 151, 172

Andrews, Cicily Fairfield
See West, Rebecca

Andrews, Elton V.
See Pohl, Frederik

Andreyev, Leonid (Nikolaevich) 1871-1919
          TCLC 3
See also CA 104

Andric, Ivo 1892-1975   **CLC 8**
See also CA 81-84; 57-60; CANR 43, 60; DLB
147; MTCW 1

Androvar
See Prado (Calvo), Pedro

Angelique, Pierre
See Bataille, Georges

Angell, Roger 1920-   **CLC 26**
See also CA 57-60; CANR 13, 44, 70; DLB 171,
185

Angelou, Maya 1928-**CLC 12, 35, 64, 77; BLC
1; DA; DAB; DAC; DAM MST, MULT,
POET, POP; WLCS**
See also AAYA 7, 20; BW 2; CA 65-68; CANR
19, 42, 65; CLR 53; DLB 38; MTCW 1;
SATA 49

Anna Comnena 1083-1153   **CMLC 25**

Annensky, Innokenty (Fyodorovich) 1856-1909
          TCLC 14
See also CA 110; 155

Annunzio, Gabriele d'
See D'Annunzio, Gabriele

Anodos
See Coleridge, Mary E(lizabeth)

Anon, Charles Robert
See Pessoa, Fernando (Antonio Nogueira)

Anouilh, Jean (Marie Lucien Pierre) 1910-1987
**CLC 1, 3, 8, 13, 40, 50; DAM DRAM; DC
8**
See also CA 17-20R; 123; CANR 32; MTCW 1

Anthony, Florence
See Ai

Anthony, John
See Ciardi, John (Anthony)

Anthony, Peter
See Shaffer, Anthony (Joshua); Shaffer, Peter
(Levin)

Anthony, Piers 1934-   **CLC 35; DAM POP**
See also AAYA 11; CA 21-24R; CANR 28, 56,
73; DLB 8; MTCW 1; SAAS 22; SATA 84

Anthony, Susan B(rownell) 1916-1991 **T C L C
84**
See also CA 89-92; 134

Antoine, Marc
See Proust, (Valentin-Louis-George-Eugene-)
Marcel

Antoninus, Brother
See Everson, William (Oliver)

Antonioni, Michelangelo 1912-   **CLC 20**
See also CA 73-76; CANR 45

Antschel, Paul 1920-1970
See Celan, Paul
See also CA 85-88; CANR 33, 61; MTCW 1

Anwar, Chairil 1922-1949   **TCLC 22**
See also CA 121

Apess, William 1798-1839(?)**NCLC 73; DAM
MULT**
See also DLB 175; NNAL

Apollinaire, Guillaume 1880-1918**TCLC 3, 8,
51; DAM POET; PC 7**
See also Kostrowitzki, Wilhelm Apollinaris de
See also CA 152

Appelfeld, Aharon 1932-   **CLC 23, 47**

See also CA 112; 133

Apple, Max (Isaac) 1941-   **CLC 9, 33**
See also CA 81-84; CANR 19, 54; DLB 130

Appleman, Philip (Dean) 1926-   **CLC 51**
See also CA 13-16R; CAAS 18; CANR 6, 29,
56

Appleton, Lawrence
See Lovecraft, H(oward) P(hillips)

Apteryx
See Eliot, T(homas) S(tearns)

Apuleius, (Lucius Madaurensis) 125(?)-175(?)
          CMLC 1

Aquin, Hubert 1929-1977   **CLC 15**
See also CA 105; DLB 53

Aragon, Louis 1897-1982   **CLC 3, 22; DAM
NOV, POET**
See also CA 69-72; 108; CANR 28, 71; DLB
72; MTCW 1

Arany, Janos 1817-1882   **NCLC 34**

Aranyos, Kakay
See Mikszath, Kalman

Arbuthnot, John 1667-1735   **LC 1**
See also DLB 101

Archer, Herbert Winslow
See Mencken, H(enry) L(ouis)

Archer, Jeffrey (Howard) 1940-   **CLC 28;
DAM POP**
See also AAYA 16; BEST 89:3; CA 77-80;
CANR 22, 52; INT CANR-22

Archer, Jules 1915-   **CLC 12**
See also CA 9-12R; CANR 6, 69; SAAS 5;
SATA 4, 85

Archer, Lee
See Ellison, Harlan (Jay)

Arden, John 1930-**CLC 6, 13, 15; DAM DRAM**
See also CA 13-16R; CAAS 4; CANR 31, 65,
67; DLB 13; MTCW 1

Arenas, Reinaldo 1943-1990   **CLC 41; DAM
MULT; HLC**
See also CA 124; 128; 133; CANR 73; DLB
145; HW

Arendt, Hannah 1906-1975   **CLC 66, 98**
See also CA 17-20R; 61-64; CANR 26, 60;
MTCW 1

Aretino, Pietro 1492-1556   **LC 12**

Arghezi, Tudor 1880-1967   **CLC 80**
See also Theodorescu, Ion N.
See also CA 167

Arguedas, Jose Maria 1911-1969 **CLC 10, 18**
See also CA 89-92; CANR 73; DLB 113; HW

Argueta, Manlio 1936-   **CLC 31**
See also CA 131; CANR 73; DLB 145; HW

Ariosto, Ludovico 1474-1533   **LC 6**

Aristides
See Epstein, Joseph

Aristophanes 450B.C.-385B.C.**CMLC 4; DA;
DAB; DAC; DAM DRAM, MST; DC 2;
WLCS**
See also DLB 176

Aristotle 384B.C.-322B.C.   **CMLC 31; DA;
DAB; DAC; DAM MST; WLCS**
See also DLB 176

Arlt, Roberto (Godofredo Christophersen)
1900-1942**TCLC 29; DAM MULT; HLC**
See also CA 123; 131; CANR 67; HW

Armah, Ayi Kwei 1939-   **CLC 5, 33; BLC 1;
DAM MULT, POET**
See also BW 1; CA 61-64; CANR 21, 64; DLB
117; MTCW 1

Armatrading, Joan 1950-   **CLC 17**
See also CA 114

Arnette, Robert
See Silverberg, Robert

**Arnim, Achim von (Ludwig Joachim von
Arnim)** 1781-1831   **NCLC 5; SSC 29**
See also DLB 90

Arnim, Bettina von 1785-1859   **NCLC 38**
See also DLB 90

Arnold, Matthew 1822-1888**NCLC 6, 29; DA;
DAB; DAC; DAM MST, POET; PC 5;
WLC**
See also CDBLB 1832-1890; DLB 32, 57

Arnold, Thomas 1795-1842   **NCLC 18**
See also DLB 55

Arnow, Harriette (Louisa) Simpson 1908-1986
          CLC 2, 7, 18
See also CA 9-12R; 118; CANR 14; DLB 6;
MTCW 1; SATA 42; SATA-Obit 47

Arouet, Francois-Marie
See Voltaire

Arp, Hans
See Arp, Jean

Arp, Jean 1887-1966   **CLC 5**
See also CA 81-84; 25-28R; CANR 42

Arrabal
See Arrabal, Fernando

Arrabal, Fernando 1932-   **CLC 2, 9, 18, 58**
See also CA 9-12R; CANR 15

Arrick, Fran   **CLC 30**
See also Gaberman, Judie Angell

Artaud, Antonin (Marie Joseph) 1896-1948
          TCLC 3, 36; DAM DRAM
See also CA 104; 149

Arthur, Ruth M(abel) 1905-1979   **CLC 12**
See also CA 9-12R; 85-88; CANR 4; SATA 7,
26

Artsybashev, Mikhail (Petrovich) 1878-1927
          TCLC 31
See also CA 170

Arundel, Honor (Morfydd) 1919-1973**CLC 17**
See also CA 21-22; 41-44R; CAP 2; CLR 35;
SATA 4; SATA-Obit 24

Arzner, Dorothy 1897-1979   **CLC 98**

Asch, Sholem 1880-1957   **TCLC 3**
See also CA 105

Ash, Shalom
See Asch, Sholem

Ashbery, John (Lawrence) 1927-**CLC 2, 3, 4,
6, 9, 13, 15, 25, 41, 77; DAM POET**
See also CA 5-8R; CANR 9, 37, 66; DLB 5,
165; DLBY 81; INT CANR-9; MTCW 1

Ashdown, Clifford
See Freeman, R(ichard) Austin

Ashe, Gordon
See Creasey, John

Ashton-Warner, Sylvia (Constance) 1908-1984
          CLC 19
See also CA 69-72; 112; CANR 29; MTCW 1

Asimov, Isaac 1920-1992 **CLC 1, 3, 9, 19, 26,
76, 92; DAM POP**
See also AAYA 13; BEST 90:2; CA 1-4R; 137;
CANR 2, 19, 36, 60; CLR 12; DLB 8; DLBY
92; INT CANR-19; JRDA; MAICYA;
MTCW 1; SATA 1, 26, 74

Assis, Joaquim Maria Machado de
See Machado de Assis, Joaquim Maria

Astley, Thea (Beatrice May) 1925-   **CLC 41**
See also CA 65-68; CANR 11, 43

Aston, James
See White, T(erence) H(anbury)

Asturias, Miguel Angel 1899-1974 **CLC 3, 8,
13; DAM MULT, NOV; HLC**
See also CA 25-28; 49-52; CANR 32; CAP 2;
DLB 113; HW; MTCW 1

Atares, Carlos Saura
See Saura (Atares), Carlos

See also CA 65-68; CAAS 15; CANR 19, 52,
73; DLB 130
Banville, John 1945-   **CLC 46**
See also CA 117; 128; DLB 14; INT 128
Banville, Theodore (Faullain) de 1832-1891
NCLC 9
Baraka, Amiri 1934-**CLC 1, 2, 3, 5, 10, 14, 33,
115; BLC 1; DA; DAC; DAM MST, MULT,
POET, POP; DC 6; PC 4; WLCS**
See also Jones, LeRoi
See also BW 2; CA 21-24R; CABS 3; CANR
27, 38, 61; CDALB 1941-1968; DLB 5, 7,
16, 38; DLBD 8; MTCW 1
Barbauld, Anna Laetitia 1743-1825**NCLC 50**
See also DLB 107, 109, 142, 158
Barbellion, W. N. P.   **TCLC 24**
See also Cummings, Bruce F(rederick)
Barbera, Jack (Vincent) 1945-   **CLC 44**
See also CA 110; CANR 45
Barbey d'Aurevilly, Jules Amedee 1808-1889
NCLC 1; SSC 17
See also DLB 119
Barbusse, Henri 1873-1935   **TCLC 5**
See also CA 105; 154; DLB 65
Barclay, Bill
See Moorcock, Michael (John)
Barclay, William Ewert
See Moorcock, Michael (John)
Barea, Arturo 1897-1957   **TCLC 14**
See also CA 111
Barfoot, Joan 1946-   **CLC 18**
See also CA 105
Baring, Maurice 1874-1945   **TCLC 8**
See also CA 105; 168; DLB 34
Baring-Gould, Sabine 1834-1924   **TCLC 88**
See also DLB 156, 190
Barker, Clive 1952-   **CLC 52; DAM POP**
See also AAYA 10; BEST 90:3; CA 121; 129;
CANR 71, INT 129, MTCW 1
Barker, George Granville 1913-1991   **CLC 8,
48; DAM POET**
See also CA 9-12R; 135; CANR 7, 38; DLB
20; MTCW 1
Barker, Harley Granville
See Granville-Barker, Harley
See also DLB 10
Barker, Howard 1946-   **CLC 37**
See also CA 102; DLB 13
Barker, Jane 1652-1732   **LC 42**
Barker, Pat(ricia) 1943-   **CLC 32, 94**
See also CA 117; 122; CANR 50; INT 122
Barlach, Ernst 1870-1938   **TCLC 84**
See also DLB 56, 118
Barlow, Joel 1754-1812   **NCLC 23**
See also DLB 37
Barnard, Mary (Ethel) 1909-   **CLC 48**
See also CA 21-22; CAP 2
Barnes, Djuna 1892-1982**CLC 3, 4, 8, 11, 29;
SSC 3**
See also CA 9-12R; 107; CANR 16, 55; DLB
4, 9, 45; MTCW 1
Barnes, Julian (Patrick) 1946- **CLC 42; DAB**
See also CA 102; CANR 19, 54; DLB 194;
DLBY 93
Barnes, Peter 1931-   **CLC 5, 56**
See also CA 65-68; CAAS 12; CANR 33, 34,
64; DLB 13; MTCW 1
Barnes, William 1801-1886   **NCLC 75**
See also DLB 32
Baroja (y Nessi), Pio 1872-1956**TCLC 8; HLC**
See also CA 104
Baron, David
See Pinter, Harold

Baron Corvo
See Rolfe, Frederick (William Serafino Austin
Lewis Mary)
Barondess, Sue K(aufman) 1926-1977 **CLC 8**
See also Kaufman, Sue
See also CA 1-4R; 69-72; CANR 1
Baron de Teive
See Pessoa, Fernando (Antonio Nogueira)
Baroness Von S.
See Zangwill, Israel
Barres, (Auguste-) Maurice 1862-1923**TCLC
47**
See also CA 164; DLB 123
Barreto, Afonso Henrique de Lima
See Lima Barreto, Afonso Henrique de
Barrett, (Roger) Syd 1946-   **CLC 35**
Barrett, William (Christopher) 1913-1992
CLC 27
See also CA 13-16R; 139; CANR 11, 67; INT
CANR-11
Barrie, J(ames) M(atthew) 1860-1937 **TCLC
2; DAB; DAM DRAM**
See also CA 104; 136; CDBLB 1890-1914;
CLR 16; DLB 10, 141, 156; MAICYA; SATA
100; YABC 1
Barrington, Michael
See Moorcock, Michael (John)
Barrol, Grady
See Bograd, Larry
Barry, Mike
See Malzberg, Barry N(athaniel)
Barry, Philip 1896-1949   **TCLC 11**
See also CA 109; DLB 7
Bart, Andre Schwarz
See Schwarz-Bart, Andre
Barth, John (Simmons) 1930-**CLC 1, 2, 3, 5, 7,
9, 10, 14, 27, 51, 89; DAM NOV; SSC 10**
See also AITN 1, 2; CA 1-4R; CABS 1; CANR
5, 23, 49, 64; DLB 2; MTCW 1
Barthelme, Donald 1931-1989**CLC 1, 2, 3, 5, 6,
8, 13, 23, 46, 59, 115; DAM NOV; SSC 2**
See also CA 21-24R; 129; CANR 20, 58; DLB
2; DLBY 80, 89; MTCW 1; SATA 7; SATA-
Obit 62
Barthelme, Frederick 1943-   **CLC 36, 117**
See also CA 114; 122; DLBY 85; INT 122
Barthes, Roland (Gerard) 1915-1980**CLC 24,
83**
See also CA 130; 97-100; CANR 66; MTCW 1
Barzun, Jacques (Martin) 1907-   **CLC 51**
See also CA 61-64; CANR 22
Bashevis, Isaac
See Singer, Isaac Bashevis
Bashkirtseff, Marie 1859-1884   **NCLC 27**
Basho
See Matsuo Basho
Bass, Kingsley B., Jr.
See Bullins, Ed
Bass, Rick 1958-   **CLC 79**
See also CA 126; CANR 53
Bassani, Giorgio 1916-   **CLC 9**
See also CA 65-68; CANR 33; DLB 128, 177;
MTCW 1
Bastos, Augusto (Antonio) Roa
See Roa Bastos, Augusto (Antonio)
Bataille, Georges 1897-1962   **CLC 29**
See also CA 101; 89-92
Bates, H(erbert) E(rnest) 1905-1974**CLC 46;
DAB; DAM POP; SSC 10**
See also CA 93-96; 45-48; CANR 34; DLB 162,
191; MTCW 1
Bauchart
See Camus, Albert

Baudelaire, Charles 1821-1867 **NCLC 6, 29,
55; DA; DAB; DAC; DAM MST, POET;
PC 1; SSC 18; WLC**
Baudrillard, Jean 1929-   **CLC 60**
Baum, L(yman) Frank 1856-1919   **TCLC 7**
See also CA 108; 133; CLR 15; DLB 22; JRDA;
MAICYA; MTCW 1; SATA 18, 100
Baum, Louis F.
See Baum, L(yman) Frank
Baumbach, Jonathan 1933-   **CLC 6, 23**
See also CA 13-16R; CAAS 5; CANR 12, 66;
DLB 80; INT CANR-12; MTCW 1
Bausch, Richard (Carl) 1945-   **CLC 51**
See also CA 101; CAAS 14; CANR 43, 61; DLB
130
Baxter, Charles (Morley) 1947- **CLC 45, 78;
DAM POP**
See also CA 57-60; CANR 40, 64; DLB 130
Baxter, George Owen
See Faust, Frederick (Schiller)
Baxter, James K(eir) 1926-1972   **CLC 14**
See also CA 77-80
Baxter, John
See Hunt, E(verette) Howard, (Jr.)
Bayer, Sylvia
See Glassco, John
Baynton, Barbara 1857-1929   **TCLC 57**
Beagle, Peter S(oyer) 1939-   **CLC 7, 104**
See also CA 9-12R; CANR 4, 51, 73; DLBY
80; INT CANR-4; SATA 60
Bean, Normal
See Burroughs, Edgar Rice
Beard, Charles A(ustin) 1874-1948 **TCLC 15**
See also CA 115; DLB 17; SATA 18
Beardsley, Aubrey 1872-1898   **NCLC 6**
Beattie, Ann 1947-**CLC 8, 13, 18, 40, 63; DAM
NOV, POP; SSC 11**
See also BEST 90:2; CA 81-84; CANR 53, 73;
DLBY 82; MTCW 1
Beattie, James 1735-1803   **NCLC 25**
See also DLB 109
Beauchamp, Kathleen Mansfield 1888-1923
See Mansfield, Katherine
See also CA 104; 134; DA; DAC; DAM MST
Beaumarchais, Pierre-Augustin Caron de 1732-
1799   **DC 4**
See also DAM DRAM
Beaumont, Francis 1584(?)-1616**LC 33; DC 6**
See also CDBLB Before 1660; DLB 58, 121
**Beauvoir, Simone (Lucie Ernestine Marie
Bertrand) de** 1908-1986**CLC 1, 2, 4, 8, 14,
31, 44, 50, 71; DA; DAB; DAC; DAM MST,
NOV; WLC**
See also CA 9-12R; 118; CANR 28, 61; DLB
72; DLBY 86; MTCW 1
Becker, Carl (Lotus) 1873-1945   **TCLC 63**
See also CA 157; DLB 17
Becker, Jurek 1937-1997   **CLC 7, 19**
See also CA 85-88; 157; CANR 60; DLB 75
Becker, Walter 1950-   **CLC 26**
Beckett, Samuel (Barclay) 1906-1989 **CLC 1,
2, 3, 4, 6, 9, 10, 11, 14, 18, 29, 57, 59, 83;
DA; DAB; DAC; DAM DRAM, MST,
NOV; SSC 16; WLC**
See also CA 5-8R; 130; CANR 33, 61; CDBLB
1945-1960; DLB 13, 15; DLBY 90; MTCW
1
Beckford, William 1760-1844   **NCLC 16**
See also DLB 39
Beckman, Gunnel 1910-   **CLC 26**
See also CA 33-36R; CANR 15; CLR 25;
MAICYA; SAAS 9; SATA 6
Becque, Henri 1837-1899   **NCLC 3**

See also DLB 192

Beddoes, Thomas Lovell 1803-1849 **NCLC 3**
See also DLB 96

Bede c. 673-735 **CMLC 20**
See also DLB 146

Bedford, Donald F.
See Fearing, Kenneth (Flexner)

Beecher, Catharine Esther 1800-1878 **NCLC 30**
See also DLB 1

Beecher, John 1904-1980 **CLC 6**
See also AITN 1; CA 5-8R; 105; CANR 8

Beer, Johann 1655-1700 **LC 5**
See also DLB 168

Beer, Patricia 1924- **CLC 58**
See also CA 61-64; CANR 13, 46; DLB 40

Beerbohm, Max
See Beerbohm, (Henry) Max(imilian)

Beerbohm, (Henry) Max(imilian) 1872-1956 **TCLC 1, 24**
See also CA 104; 154; DLB 34, 100

Beer-Hofmann, Richard 1866-1945 **TCLC 60**
See also CA 160; DLB 81

Begiebing, Robert J(ohn) 1946- **CLC 70**
See also CA 122; CANR 40

Behan, Brendan 1923-1964 **CLC 1, 8, 11, 15, 79; DAM DRAM**
See also CA 73-76; CANR 33; CDBLB 1945-1960; DLB 13; MTCW 1

Behn, Aphra 1640(?)-1689 **LC 1, 30, 42; DA; DAB; DAC; DAM DRAM, MST, NOV, POET; DC 4; PC 13; WLC**
See also DLB 39, 80, 131

Behrman, S(amuel) N(athaniel) 1893-1973 **CLC 40**
See also CA 13-16; 45-48; CAP 1; DLB 7, 44

Belasco, David 1853-1931 **TCLC 3**
See also CA 104; 168; DLB 7

Belcheva, Elisaveta 1893- **CLC 10**
See also Bagryana, Elisaveta

Beldone, Phil "Cheech"
See Ellison, Harlan (Jay)

Beleno
See Azuela, Mariano

Belinski, Vissarion Grigoryevich 1811-1848 **NCLC 5**
See also DLB 198

Belitt, Ben 1911- **CLC 22**
See also CA 13-16R; CAAS 4; CANR 7; DLB 5

Bell, Gertrude (Margaret Lowthian) 1868-1926 **TCLC 67**
See also CA 167; DLB 174

Bell, J. Freeman
See Zangwill, Israel

Bell, James Madison 1826-1902 **TCLC 43; BLC 1; DAM MULT**
See also BW 1; CA 122; 124; DLB 50

Bell, Madison Smartt 1957- **CLC 41, 102**
See also CA 111; CANR 28, 54, 73

Bell, Marvin (Hartley) 1937- **CLC 8, 31; DAM POET**
See also CA 21-24R; CAAS 14; CANR 59; DLB 5; MTCW 1

Bell, W. L. D.
See Mencken, H(enry) L(ouis)

Bellamy, Atwood C.
See Mencken, H(enry) L(ouis)

Bellamy, Edward 1850-1898 **NCLC 4**
See also DLB 12

Bellin, Edward J.
See Kuttner, Henry

Belloc, (Joseph) Hilaire (Pierre Sebastien Rene Swanton) 1870-1953 **TCLC 7, 18; DAM POET; PC 24**
See also CA 106; 152; DLB 19, 100, 141, 174; YABC 1

Belloc, Joseph Peter Rene Hilaire
See Belloc, (Joseph) Hilaire (Pierre Sebastien Rene Swanton)

Belloc, Joseph Pierre Hilaire
See Belloc, (Joseph) Hilaire (Pierre Sebastien Rene Swanton)

Belloc, M. A.
See Lowndes, Marie Adelaide (Belloc)

Bellow, Saul 1915- **CLC 1, 2, 3, 6, 8, 10, 13, 15, 25, 33, 34, 63, 79; DA; DAB; DAC; DAM MST, NOV, POP; SSC 14; WLC**
See also AITN 2; BEST 89:3; CA 5-8R; CABS 1; CANR 29, 53; CDALB 1941-1968; DLB 2, 28; DLBD 3; DLBY 82; MTCW 1

Belser, Reimond Karel Maria de 1929-
See Ruyslinck, Ward
See also CA 152

Bely, Andrey **TCLC 7; PC 11**
See also Bugayev, Boris Nikolayevich

Belyi, Andrei
See Bugayev, Boris Nikolayevich

Benary, Margot
See Benary-Isbert, Margot

Benary-Isbert, Margot 1889-1979 **CLC 12**
See also CA 5-8R; 89-92; CANR 4, 72; CLR 12; MAICYA; SATA 2; SATA-Obit 21

Benavente (y Martinez), Jacinto 1866-1954 **TCLC 3; DAM DRAM, MULT**
See also CA 106; 131; HW; MTCW 1

Benchley, Peter (Bradford) 1940- **CLC 4, 8; DAM NOV, POP**
See also AAYA 14; AITN 2; CA 17-20R; CANR 12, 35, 66; MTCW 1; SATA 3, 89

Benchley, Robert (Charles) 1889-1945 **TCLC 1, 55**
See also CA 105; 153; DLB 11

Benda, Julien 1867-1956 **TCLC 60**
See also CA 120; 154

Benedict, Ruth (Fulton) 1887-1948 **TCLC 60**
See also CA 158

Benedict, Saint c. 480-c. 547 **CMLC 29**

Benedikt, Michael 1935- **CLC 4, 14**
See also CA 13-16R; CANR 7; DLB 5

Benet, Juan 1927- **CLC 28**
See also CA 143

Benet, Stephen Vincent 1898-1943 **TCLC 7; DAM POET; SSC 10**
See also CA 104; 152; DLB 4, 48, 102; DLBY 97; YABC 1

Benet, William Rose 1886-1950 **TCLC 28; DAM POET**
See also CA 118; 152; DLB 45

Benford, Gregory (Albert) 1941- **CLC 52**
See also CA 69-72; CAAS 27; CANR 12, 24, 49; DLBY 82

Bengtsson, Frans (Gunnar) 1894-1954 **TCLC 48**
See also CA 170

Benjamin, David
See Slavitt, David R(ytman)

Benjamin, Lois
See Gould, Lois

Benjamin, Walter 1892-1940 **TCLC 39**
See also CA 164

Benn, Gottfried 1886-1956 **TCLC 3**
See also CA 106; 153; DLB 56

Bennett, Alan 1934- **CLC 45, 77; DAB; DAM MST**
See also CA 103; CANR 35, 55; MTCW 1

Bennett, (Enoch) Arnold 1867-1931 **TCLC 5, 20**
See also CA 106; 155; CDBLB 1890-1914; DLB 10, 34, 98, 135

Bennett, Elizabeth
See Mitchell, Margaret (Munnerlyn)

Bennett, George Harold 1930-
See Bennett, Hal
See also BW 1; CA 97-100

Bennett, Hal **CLC 5**
See also Bennett, George Harold
See also DLB 33

Bennett, Jay 1912- **CLC 35**
See also AAYA 10; CA 69-72; CANR 11, 42; JRDA; SAAS 4; SATA 41, 87; SATA-Brief 27

Bennett, Louise (Simone) 1919- **CLC 28; BLC 1; DAM MULT**
See also BW 2; CA 151; DLB 117

Benson, E(dward) F(rederic) 1867-1940 **TCLC 27**
See also CA 114; 157; DLB 135, 153

Benson, Jackson J. 1930- **CLC 34**
See also CA 25-28R; DLB 111

Benson, Sally 1900-1972 **CLC 17**
See also CA 19-20; 37-40R; CAP 1; SATA 1, 35; SATA-Obit 27

Benson, Stella 1892-1933 **TCLC 17**
See also CA 117; 155; DLB 36, 162

Bentham, Jeremy 1748-1832 **NCLC 38**
See also DLB 107, 158

Bentley, E(dmund) C(lerihew) 1875-1956 **TCLC 12**
See also CA 108; DLB 70

Bentley, Eric (Russell) 1916- **CLC 24**
See also CA 5-8R; CANR 6, 67; INT CANR-6

Beranger, Pierre Jean de 1780-1857 **NCLC 34**

Berdyaev, Nicolas
See Berdyaev, Nikolai (Aleksandrovich)

Berdyaev, Nikolai (Aleksandrovich) 1874-1948 **TCLC 67**
See also CA 120; 157

Berdyayev, Nikolai (Aleksandrovich)
See Berdyaev, Nikolai (Aleksandrovich)

Berendt, John (Lawrence) 1939- **CLC 86**
See also CA 146; CANR 75

Beresford, J(ohn) D(avys) 1873-1947 **TCLC 81**
See also CA 112; 155; DLB 162, 178, 197

Bergelson, David 1884-1952 **TCLC 81**

Berger, Colonel
See Malraux, (Georges-)Andre

Berger, John (Peter) 1926- **CLC 2, 19**
See also CA 81-84; CANR 51; DLB 14, 207

Berger, Melvin H. 1927- **CLC 12**
See also CA 5-8R; CANR 4; CLR 32; SAAS 2; SATA 5, 88

Berger, Thomas (Louis) 1924- **CLC 3, 5, 8, 11, 18, 38; DAM NOV**
See also CA 1-4R; CANR 5, 28, 51; DLB 2; DLBY 80; INT CANR-28; MTCW 1

Bergman, (Ernst) Ingmar 1918- **CLC 16, 72**
See also CA 81-84; CANR 33, 70

Bergson, Henri(-Louis) 1859-1941 **TCLC 32**
See also CA 164

Bergstein, Eleanor 1938- **CLC 4**
See also CA 53-56; CANR 5

Berkoff, Steven 1937- **CLC 56**
See also CA 104; CANR 72

Bermant, Chaim (Icyk) 1929- **CLC 40**
See also CA 57-60; CANR 6, 31, 57

Bern, Victoria
See Fisher, M(ary) F(rances) K(ennedy)

Bernanos, (Paul Louis) Georges 1888-1948
    TCLC 3
    See also CA 104; 130; DLB 72
Bernard, April 1956-   CLC 59
    See also CA 131
Berne, Victoria
    See Fisher, M(ary) F(rances) K(ennedy)
Bernhard, Thomas 1931-1989 CLC 3, 32, 61
    See also CA 85-88; 127; CANR 32, 57; DLB
    85, 124; MTCW 1
Bernhardt, Sarah (Henriette Rosine) 1844-1923
    TCLC 75
    See also CA 157
Berriault, Gina 1926- CLC 54, 109; SSC 30
    See also CA 116; 129; CANR 66; DLB 130
Berrigan, Daniel 1921-   CLC 4
    See also CA 33-36R; CAAS 1; CANR 11, 43;
    DLB 5
Berrigan, Edmund Joseph Michael, Jr. 1934-
    1983
    See Berrigan, Ted
    See also CA 61-64; 110; CANR 14
Berrigan, Ted   CLC 37
    See also Berrigan, Edmund Joseph Michael, Jr.
    See also DLB 5, 169
Berry, Charles Edward Anderson 1931-
    See Berry, Chuck
    See also CA 115
Berry, Chuck   CLC 17
    See also Berry, Charles Edward Anderson
Berry, Jonas
    See Ashbery, John (Lawrence)
Berry, Wendell (Erdman) 1934- CLC 4, 6, 8,
    27, 46; DAM POET
    See also AITN 1; CA 73-76; CANR 50, 73; DLB
    5, 6
Berryman, John 1914-1972CLC 1, 2, 3, 4, 6, 8,
    10, 13, 25, 62; DAM POET
    See also CA 13-16; 33-36R; CABS 2; CANR
    35; CAP 1; CDALB 1941-1968; DLB 48;
    MTCW 1
Bertolucci, Bernardo 1940-   CLC 16
    See also CA 106
Berton, Pierre (Francis Demarigny) 1920-
    CLC 104
    See also CA 1-4R; CANR 2, 56; DLB 68; SATA
    99
Bertrand, Aloysius 1807-1841   NCLC 31
Bertran de Born c. 1140-1215   CMLC 5
Besant, Annie (Wood) 1847-1933   TCLC 9
    See also CA 105
Bessie, Alvah 1904-1985   CLC 23
    See also CA 5-8R; 116; CANR 2; DLB 26
Bethlen, T. D.
    See Silverberg, Robert
Beti, Mongo   CLC 27; BLC 1; DAM MULT
    See also Biyidi, Alexandre
Betjeman, John 1906-1984 CLC 2, 6, 10, 34,
    43; DAB; DAM MST, POET
    See also CA 9-12R; 112; CANR 33, 56; CDBLB
    1945-1960; DLB 20; DLBY 84; MTCW 1
Bettelheim, Bruno 1903-1990   CLC 79
    See also CA 81-84; 131; CANR 23, 61; MTCW
    1
Betti, Ugo 1892-1953   TCLC 5
    See also CA 104; 155
Betts, Doris (Waugh) 1932-   CLC 3, 6, 28
    See also CA 13-16R; CANR 9, 66; DLBY 82;
    INT CANR-9
Bevan, Alistair
    See Roberts, Keith (John Kingston)
Bey, Pilaff
    See Douglas, (George) Norman

Bialik, Chaim Nachman 1873-1934 TCLC 25
    See also CA 170
Bickerstaff, Isaac
    See Swift, Jonathan
Bidart, Frank 1939-   CLC 33
    See also CA 140
Bienek, Horst 1930-   CLC 7, 11
    See also CA 73-76; DLB 75
Bierce, Ambrose (Gwinett) 1842-1914(?)
    TCLC 1, 7, 44; DA; DAC; DAM MST; SSC
    9; WLC
    See also CA 104; 139; CDALB 1865-1917;
    DLB 11, 12, 23, 71, 74, 186
Biggers, Earl Derr 1884-1933   TCLC 65
    See also CA 108; 153
Billings, Josh
    See Shaw, Henry Wheeler
Billington, (Lady) Rachel (Mary) 1942- C L C
    43
    See also AITN 2; CA 33-36R; CANR 44
Binyon, T(imothy) J(ohn) 1936-   CLC 34
    See also CA 111; CANR 28
Bioy Casares, Adolfo 1914-1984CLC 4, 8, 13,
    88; DAM MULT; HLC; SSC 17
    See also CA 29-32R; CANR 19, 43, 66; DLB
    113; HW; MTCW 1
Bird, Cordwainer
    See Ellison, Harlan (Jay)
Bird, Robert Montgomery 1806-1854NCLC 1
    See also DLB 202
Birkerts, Sven 1951-   CLC 116
    See also CA 128; 133; CAAS 29; INT 133
Birney, (Alfred) Earle 1904-1995CLC 1, 4, 6,
    11; DAC; DAM MST, POET
    See also CA 1-4R; CANR 5, 20; DLB 88;
    MTCW 1
Biruni, al 973-1048(?)   CMLC 28
Bishop, Elizabeth 1911-1979 CLC 1, 4, 9, 13,
    15, 32; DA; DAC; DAM MST, POET; PC
    3
    See also CA 5-8R; 89-92; CABS 2; CANR 26,
    61; CDALB 1968-1988; DLB 5, 169;
    MTCW 1; SATA-Obit 24
Bishop, John 1935-   CLC 10
    See also CA 105
Bissett, Bill 1939-   CLC 18; PC 14
    See also CA 69-72; CAAS 19; CANR 15; DLB
    53; MTCW 1
Bitov, Andrei (Georgievich) 1937-   CLC 57
    See also CA 142
Biyidi, Alexandre 1932-
    See Beti, Mongo
    See also BW 1; CA 114; 124; MTCW 1
Bjarme, Brynjolf
    See Ibsen, Henrik (Johan)
Bjoernson, Bjoernstjerne (Martinius) 1832-
    1910   TCLC 7, 37
    See also CA 104
Black, Robert
    See Holdstock, Robert P.
Blackburn, Paul 1926-1971   CLC 9, 43
    See also CA 81-84; 33-36R; CANR 34; DLB
    16; DLBY 81
Black Elk 1863-1950 TCLC 33; DAM MULT
    See also CA 144; NNAL
Black Hobart
    See Sanders, (James) Ed(ward)
Blacklin, Malcolm
    See Chambers, Aidan
Blackmore, R(ichard) D(oddridge) 1825-1900
    TCLC 27
    See also CA 120; DLB 18
Blackmur, R(ichard) P(almer) 1904-1965

CLC 2, 24
    See also CA 11-12; 25-28R; CANR 71; CAP 1;
    DLB 63
Black Tarantula
    See Acker, Kathy
Blackwood, Algernon (Henry) 1869-1951
    TCLC 5
    See also CA 105; 150; DLB 153, 156, 178
Blackwood, Caroline 1931-1996CLC 6, 9, 100
    See also CA 85-88; 151; CANR 32, 61, 65; DLB
    14, 207; MTCW 1
Blade, Alexander
    See Hamilton, Edmond; Silverberg, Robert
Blaga, Lucian 1895-1961   CLC 75
    See also CA 157
Blair, Eric (Arthur) 1903-1950
    See Orwell, George
    See also CA 104; 132; DA; DAB; DAC; DAM
    MST, NOV; MTCW 1; SATA 29
Blair, Hugh 1718-1800   NCLC 75
Blais, Marie-Claire 1939-CLC 2, 4, 6, 13, 22;
    DAC; DAM MST
    See also CA 21-24R; CAAS 4; CANR 38, 75;
    DLB 53; MTCW 1
Blaise, Clark 1940-   CLC 29
    See also AITN 2; CA 53-56; CAAS 3; CANR
    5, 66; DLB 53
Blake, Fairley
    See De Voto, Bernard (Augustine)
Blake, Nicholas
    See Day Lewis, C(ecil)
    See also DLB 77
Blake, William 1757-1827 NCLC 13, 37, 57;
    DA; DAB; DAC; DAM MST, POET; PC
    12; WLC
    See also CDBLB 1789-1832; CLR 52; DLB 93,
    163; MAICYA; SATA 30
Blasco Ibanez, Vicente 1867-1928 TCLC 12;
    DAM NOV
    See also CA 110; 131; HW, MTCW 1
Blatty, William Peter 1928-CLC 2; DAM POP
    See also CA 5-8R; CANR 9
Bleeck, Oliver
    See Thomas, Ross (Elmore)
Blessing, Lee 1949-   CLC 54
Blish, James (Benjamin) 1921-1975 CLC 14
    See also CA 1-4R; 57-60; CANR 3; DLB 8;
    MTCW 1; SATA 66
Bliss, Reginald
    See Wells, H(erbert) G(eorge)
Blixen, Karen (Christentze Dinesen) 1885-1962
    See Dinesen, Isak
    See also CA 25-28; CANR 22, 50; CAP 2;
    MTCW 1; SATA 44
Bloch, Robert (Albert) 1917-1994   CLC 33
    See also CA 5-8R; 146; CAAS 20; CANR 5;
    DLB 44; INT CANR-5; SATA 12; SATA-Obit
    82
Blok, Alexander (Alexandrovich) 1880-1921
    TCLC 5; PC 21
    See also CA 104
Blom, Jan
    See Breytenbach, Breyten
Bloom, Harold 1930-   CLC 24, 103
    See also CA 13-16R; CANR 39, 75; DLB 67
Bloomfield, Aurelius
    See Bourne, Randolph S(illiman)
Blount, Roy (Alton), Jr. 1941-   CLC 38
    See also CA 53-56; CANR 10, 28, 61; INT
    CANR-28; MTCW 1
Bloy, Leon 1846-1917   TCLC 22
    See also CA 121; DLB 123
Blume, Judy (Sussman) 1938-   CLC 12, 30;

DAM NOV, POP
See also AAYA 3, 26; CA 29-32R; CANR 13, 37, 66; CLR 2, 15; DLB 52; JRDA; MAICYA; MTCW 1; SATA 2, 31, 79

Blunden, Edmund (Charles) 1896-1974 **C L C 2, 56**
See also CA 17-18; 45-48; CANR 54; CAP 2; DLB 20, 100, 155; MTCW 1

Bly, Robert (Elwood) 1926-**CLC 1, 2, 5, 10, 15, 38; DAM POET**
See also CA 5-8R; CANR 41, 73; DLB 5; MTCW 1

Boas, Franz 1858-1942 **TCLC 56**
See also CA 115

Bobette
See Simenon, Georges (Jacques Christian)

Boccaccio, Giovanni 1313-1375 **CMLC 13; SSC 10**

Bochco, Steven 1943- **CLC 35**
See also AAYA 11; CA 124; 138

Bodel, Jean 1167(?)-1210 **CMLC 28**

Bodenheim, Maxwell 1892-1954 **TCLC 44**
See also CA 110; DLB 9, 45

Bodker, Cecil 1927- **CLC 21**
See also CA 73-76; CANR 13, 44; CLR 23; MAICYA; SATA 14

Boell, Heinrich (Theodor) 1917-1985 **CLC 2, 3, 6, 9, 11, 15, 27, 32, 72; DA; DAB; DAC; DAM MST, NOV; SSC 23; WLC**
See also CA 21-24R; 116; CANR 24; DLB 69; DLBY 85; MTCW 1

Boerne, Alfred
See Doeblin, Alfred

Boethius 480(?)-524(?) **CMLC 15**
See also DLB 115

Bogan, Louise 1897-1970 **CLC 4, 39, 46, 93; DAM POET; PC 12**
See also CA 73-76; 25-28R; CANR 33; DLB 45, 169; MTCW 1

Bogarde, Dirk **CLC 19**
See also Van Den Bogarde, Derek Jules Gaspard Ulric Niven
See also DLB 14

Bogosian, Eric 1953- **CLC 45**
See also CA 138

Bograd, Larry 1953- **CLC 35**
See also CA 93-96; CANR 57; SAAS 21; SATA 33, 89

Boiardo, Matteo Maria 1441-1494 **LC 6**

Boileau-Despreaux, Nicolas 1636-1711 **LC 3**

Bojer, Johan 1872-1959 **TCLC 64**

Boland, Eavan (Aisling) 1944- **CLC 40, 67, 113; DAM POET**
See also CA 143; CANR 61; DLB 40

Boll, Heinrich
See Boell, Heinrich (Theodor)

Bolt, Lee
See Faust, Frederick (Schiller)

Bolt, Robert (Oxton) 1924-1995**CLC 14; DAM DRAM**
See also CA 17-20R; 147; CANR 35, 67; DLB 13; MTCW 1

Bombet, Louis-Alexandre-Cesar
See Stendhal

Bomkauf
See Kaufman, Bob (Garnell)

Bonaventura **NCLC 35**
See also DLB 90

Bond, Edward 1934- **CLC 4, 6, 13, 23; DAM DRAM**
See also CA 25-28R; CANR 38, 67; DLB 13; MTCW 1

Bonham, Frank 1914-1989 **CLC 12**

See also AAYA 1; CA 9-12R; CANR 4, 36; JRDA; MAICYA; SAAS 3; SATA 1, 49; SATA-Obit 62

Bonnefoy, Yves 1923- **CLC 9, 15, 58; DAM MST, POET**
See also CA 85-88; CANR 33, 75; MTCW 1

Bontemps, Arna(ud Wendell) 1902-1973**C L C 1, 18; BLC 1; DAM MULT, NOV, POET**
See also BW 1; CA 1-4R; 41-44R; CANR 4, 35; CLR 6; DLB 48, 51; JRDA; MAICYA; MTCW 1; SATA 2, 44; SATA-Obit 24

Booth, Martin 1944- **CLC 13**
See also CA 93-96; CAAS 2

Booth, Philip 1925- **CLC 23**
See also CA 5-8R; CANR 5; DLBY 82

Booth, Wayne C(layson) 1921- **CLC 24**
See also CA 1-4R; CAAS 5; CANR 3, 43; DLB 67

Borchert, Wolfgang 1921-1947 **TCLC 5**
See also CA 104; DLB 69, 124

Borel, Petrus 1809-1859 **NCLC 41**

Borges, Jorge Luis 1899-1986**CLC 1, 2, 3, 4, 6, 8, 9, 10, 13, 19, 44, 48, 83; DA; DAB; DAC; DAM MST, MULT; HLC; PC 22; SSC 4; WLC**
See also AAYA 26; CA 21-24R; CANR 19, 33, 75; DLB 113; DLBY 86; HW; MTCW 1

Borowski, Tadeusz 1922-1951 **TCLC 9**
See also CA 106; 154

Borrow, George (Henry) 1803-1881 **NCLC 9**
See also DLB 21, 55, 166

Bosman, Herman Charles 1905-1951 **T C L C 49**
See also Malan, Herman
See also CA 160

Bosschere, Jean de 1878(?)-1953 **TCLC 19**
See also CA 115

Boswell, James 1740-1795 **LC 4; DA; DAB; DAC; DAM MST; WLC**
See also CDBLB 1660-1789; DLB 104, 142

Bottoms, David 1949- **CLC 53**
See also CA 105; CANR 22; DLB 120; DLBY 83

Boucicault, Dion 1820-1890 **NCLC 41**

Boucolon, Maryse 1937(?)-
See Conde, Maryse
See also CA 110; CANR 30, 53

Bourget, Paul (Charles Joseph) 1852-1935 **TCLC 12**
See also CA 107; DLB 123

Bourjaily, Vance (Nye) 1922- **CLC 8, 62**
See also CA 1-4R; CAAS 1; CANR 2, 72; DLB 2, 143

Bourne, Randolph S(illiman) 1886-1918 **TCLC 16**
See also CA 117; 155; DLB 63

Bova, Ben(jamin William) 1932- **CLC 45**
See also AAYA 16; CA 5-8R; CAAS 18; CANR 11, 56; CLR 3; DLBY 81; INT CANR-11; MAICYA; MTCW 1; SATA 6, 68

Bowen, Elizabeth (Dorothea Cole) 1899-1973 **CLC 1, 3, 6, 11, 15, 22; DAM NOV; SSC 3, 28**
See also CA 17-18; 41-44R; CANR 35; CAP 2; CDBLB 1945-1960; DLB 15, 162; MTCW 1

Bowering, George 1935- **CLC 15, 47**
See also CA 21-24R; CAAS 16; CANR 10; DLB 53

Bowering, Marilyn R(uthe) 1949- **CLC 32**
See also CA 101; CANR 49

Bowers, Edgar 1924- **CLC 9**
See also CA 5-8R; CANR 24; DLB 5

Bowie, David **CLC 17**
See also Jones, David Robert

Bowles, Jane (Sydney) 1917-1973 **CLC 3, 68**
See also CA 19-20; 41-44R; CAP 2

Bowles, Paul (Frederick) 1910- **CLC 1, 2, 19, 53; SSC 3**
See also CA 1-4R; CAAS 1; CANR 1, 19, 50, 75; DLB 5, 6; MTCW 1

Box, Edgar
See Vidal, Gore

Boyd, Nancy
See Millay, Edna St. Vincent

Boyd, William 1952- **CLC 28, 53, 70**
See also CA 114; 120; CANR 51, 71

Boyle, Kay 1902-1992**CLC 1, 5, 19, 58; SSC 5**
See also CA 13-16R; 140; CAAS 1; CANR 29, 61; DLB 4, 9, 48, 86; DLBY 93; MTCW 1

Boyle, Mark
See Kienzle, William X(avier)

Boyle, Patrick 1905-1982 **CLC 19**
See also CA 127

Boyle, T. C. 1948-
See Boyle, T(homas) Coraghessan

Boyle, T(homas) Coraghessan 1948-**CLC 36, 55, 90; DAM POP; SSC 16**
See also BEST 90:4; CA 120; CANR 44; DLBY 86

Boz
See Dickens, Charles (John Huffam)

Brackenridge, Hugh Henry 1748-1816**N C L C 7**
See also DLB 11, 37

Bradbury, Edward P.
See Moorcock, Michael (John)

Bradbury, Malcolm (Stanley) 1932- **CLC 32, 61; DAM NOV**
See also CA 1-4R; CANR 1, 33; DLB 14, 207; MTCW 1

Bradbury, Ray (Douglas) 1920-**CLC 1, 3, 10, 15, 42, 98; DA; DAB; DAC; DAM MST, NOV, POP; SSC 29; WLC**
See also AAYA 15; AITN 1, 2; CA 1-4R; CANR 2, 30, 75; CDALB 1968-1988; DLB 2, 8; MTCW 1; SATA 11, 64

Bradford, Gamaliel 1863-1932 **TCLC 36**
See also CA 160; DLB 17

Bradley, David (Henry, Jr.) 1950- **CLC 23; BLC 1; DAM MULT**
See also BW 1; CA 104; CANR 26; DLB 33

Bradley, John Ed(mund, Jr.) 1958- **CLC 55**
See also CA 139

Bradley, Marion Zimmer 1930-**CLC 30; DAM POP**
See also AAYA 9; CA 57-60; CAAS 10; CANR 7, 31, 51, 75; DLB 8; MTCW 1; SATA 90

Bradstreet, Anne 1612(?)-1672**LC 4, 30; DA; DAC; DAM MST, POET; PC 10**
See also CDALB 1640-1865; DLB 24

Brady, Joan 1939- **CLC 86**
See also CA 141

Bragg, Melvyn 1939- **CLC 10**
See also BEST 89:3; CA 57-60; CANR 10, 48; DLB 14

Brahe, Tycho 1546-1601 **LC 45**

Braine, John (Gerard) 1922-1986**CLC 1, 3, 41**
See also CA 1-4R; 120; CANR 1, 33; CDBLB 1945-1960; DLB 15; DLBY 86; MTCW 1

Bramah, Ernest 1868-1942 **TCLC 72**
See also CA 156; DLB 70

Brammer, William 1930(?)-1978 **CLC 31**
See also CA 77-80

Brancati, Vitaliano 1907-1954 **TCLC 12**
See also CA 109

Brancato, Robin F(idler) 1936-　　CLC 35
　See also AAYA 9; CA 69-72; CANR 11, 45;
　CLR 32; JRDA; SAAS 9; SATA 97
Brand, Max
　See Faust, Frederick (Schiller)
Brand, Millen 1906-1980　　CLC 7
　See also CA 21-24R; 97-100; CANR 72
Branden, Barbara　　CLC 44
　See also CA 148
Brandes, Georg (Morris Cohen) 1842-1927
　TCLC 10
　See also CA 105
Brandys, Kazimierz 1916-　　CLC 62
Branley, Franklyn M(ansfield) 1915-CLC 21
　See also CA 33-36R; CANR 14, 39; CLR 13;
　MAICYA; SAAS 16; SATA 4, 68
Brathwaite, Edward Kamau 1930-　CLC 11;
　BLCS; DAM POET
　See also BW 2; CA 25-28R; CANR 11, 26, 47;
　DLB 125
Brautigan, Richard (Gary) 1935-1984CLC 1,
　3, 5, 9, 12, 34, 42; DAM NOV
　See also CA 53-56; 113; CANR 34; DLB 2, 5,
　206; DLBY 80, 84; MTCW 1; SATA 56
Brave Bird, Mary 1953-
　See Crow Dog, Mary (Ellen)
　See also NNAL
Braverman, Kate 1950-　　CLC 67
　See also CA 89-92
Brecht, (Eugen) Bertolt (Friedrich) 1898-1956
　TCLC 1, 6, 13, 35; DA; DAB; DAC; DAM
　DRAM, MST; DC 3; WLC
　See also CA 104; 133; CANR 62; DLB 56, 124;
　MTCW 1
Brecht, Eugen Berthold Friedrich
　See Brecht, (Eugen) Bertolt (Friedrich)
Bremer, Fredrika 1801-1865　　NCLC 11
Brennan, Christopher John 1870-1932TCLC
　17
　See also CA 117
Brennan, Maeve 1917-1993　　CLC 5
　See also CA 81-84; CANR 72
Brent, Linda
　See Jacobs, Harriet A(nn)
Brentano, Clemens (Maria) 1778-1842NCLC
　1
　See also DLB 90
Brent of Bin Bin
　See Franklin, (Stella Maria Sarah) Miles
　(Lampe)
Brenton, Howard 1942-　　CLC 31
　See also CA 69-72; CANR 33, 67; DLB 13;
　MTCW 1
Breslin, James 1930-1996
　See Breslin, Jimmy
　See also CA 73-76; CANR 31, 75; DAM NOV;
　MTCW 1
Breslin, Jimmy　　CLC 4, 43
　See also Breslin, James
　See also AITN 1; DLB 185
Bresson, Robert 1901-　　CLC 16
　See also CA 110; CANR 49
Breton, Andre 1896-1966CLC 2, 9, 15, 54; PC
　15
　See also CA 19-20; 25-28R; CANR 40, 60; CAP
　2; DLB 65; MTCW 1
Breytenbach, Breyten 1939(?)-　CLC 23, 37;
　DAM POET
　See also CA 113; 129; CANR 61
Bridgers, Sue Ellen 1942-　　CLC 26
　See also AAYA 8; CA 65-68; CANR 11, 36;
　CLR 18; DLB 52; JRDA; MAICYA; SAAS
　1; SATA 22, 90

Bridges, Robert (Seymour) 1844-1930 TCLC
　1; DAM POET
　See also CA 104; 152; CDBLB 1890-1914;
　DLB 19, 98
Bridie, James　　TCLC 3
　See also Mavor, Osborne Henry
　See also DLB 10
Brin, David 1950-　　CLC 34
　See also AAYA 21; CA 102; CANR 24, 70; INT
　CANR-24; SATA 65
Brink, Andre (Philippus) 1935-　CLC 18, 36,
　106
　See also CA 104; CANR 39, 62; INT 103;
　MTCW 1
Brinsmead, H(esba) F(ay) 1922-　　CLC 21
　See also CA 21-24R; CANR 10; CLR 47;
　MAICYA; SAAS 5; SATA 18, 78
Brittain, Vera (Mary) 1893(?)-1970　CLC 23
　See also CA 13-16; 25-28R; CANR 58; CAP 1;
　DLB 191; MTCW 1
Broch, Hermann 1886-1951　　TCLC 20
　See also CA 117; DLB 85, 124
Brock, Rose
　See Hansen, Joseph
Brodkey, Harold (Roy) 1930-1996　　CLC 56
　See also CA 111; 151; CANR 71; DLB 130
Brodskii, Iosif
　See Brodsky, Joseph
Brodsky, Iosif Alexandrovich 1940-1996
　See Brodsky, Joseph
　See also AITN 1; CA 41-44R; 151; CANR 37;
　DAM POET; MTCW 1
Brodsky, Joseph 1940-1996 CLC 4, 6, 13, 36,
　100; PC 9
　See also Brodskii, Iosif; Brodsky, Iosif
　Alexandrovich
Brodsky, Michael (Mark) 1948-　　CLC 19
　See also CA 102; CANR 18, 41, 58
Bromell, Henry 1947-　　CLC 5
　See also CA 53-56; CANR 9
Bromfield, Louis (Brucker) 1896-1956TCLC
　11
　See also CA 107; 155; DLB 4, 9, 86
Broner, E(sther) M(asserman) 1930- CLC 19
　See also CA 17-20R; CANR 8, 25, 72; DLB 28
Bronk, William 1918-　　CLC 10
　See also CA 89-92; CANR 23; DLB 165
Bronstein, Lev Davidovich
　See Trotsky, Leon
Bronte, Anne 1820-1849　　NCLC 71
　See also DLB 21, 199
Bronte, Charlotte 1816-1855 NCLC 3, 8, 33,
　58; DA; DAB; DAC; DAM MST, NOV;
　WLC
　See also AAYA 17; CDBLB 1832-1890; DLB
　21, 159, 199
Bronte, Emily (Jane) 1818-1848NCLC 16, 35;
　DA; DAB; DAC; DAM MST, NOV, POET;
　PC 8; WLC
　See also AAYA 17; CDBLB 1832-1890; DLB
　21, 32, 199
Brooke, Frances 1724-1789　　LC 6, 48
　See also DLB 39, 99
Brooke, Henry 1703(?)-1783　　LC 1
　See also DLB 39
Brooke, Rupert (Chawner) 1887-1915 TCLC
　2, 7; DA; DAB; DAC; DAM MST, POET;
　PC 24; WLC
　See also CA 104; 132; CANR 61; CDBLB
　1914-1945; DLB 19; MTCW 1
Brooke-Haven, P.
　See Wodehouse, P(elham) G(renville)
Brooke-Rose, Christine 1926(?)-　　CLC 40

See also CA 13-16R; CANR 58; DLB 14
Brookner, Anita 1928- CLC 32, 34, 51; DAB;
　DAM POP
　See also CA 114; 120; CANR 37, 56; DLB 194;
　DLBY 87; MTCW 1
Brooks, Cleanth 1906-1994　　CLC 24, 86, 110
　See also CA 17-20R; 145; CANR 33, 35; DLB
　63; DLBY 94; INT CANR-35; MTCW 1
Brooks, George
　See Baum, L(yman) Frank
Brooks, Gwendolyn 1917- CLC 1, 2, 4, 5, 15,
　49; BLC 1; DA; DAC; DAM MST, MULT,
　POET; PC 7; WLC
　See also AAYA 20; AITN 1; BW 2; CA 1-4R;
　CANR 1, 27, 52, 75; CDALB 1941-1968;
　CLR 27; DLB 5, 76, 165; MTCW 1; SATA 6
Brooks, Mel　　CLC 12
　See also Kaminsky, Melvin
　See also AAYA 13; DLB 26
Brooks, Peter 1938-　　CLC 34
　See also CA 45-48; CANR 1
Brooks, Van Wyck 1886-1963　　CLC 29
　See also CA 1-4R; CANR 6; DLB 45, 63, 103
Brophy, Brigid (Antonia) 1929-1995 CLC 6,
　11, 29, 105
　See also CA 5-8R; 149; CAAS 4; CANR 25,
　53; DLB 14; MTCW 1
Brosman, Catharine Savage 1934-　　CLC 9
　See also CA 61-64; CANR 21, 46
Brossard, Nicole 1943-　　CLC 115
　See also CA 122; CAAS 16; DLB 53
Brother Antoninus
　See Everson, William (Oliver)
The Brothers Quay
　See Quay, Stephen; Quay, Timothy
Broughton, T(homas) Alan 1936-　　CLC 19
　See also CA 45-48; CANR 2, 23, 48
Broumas, Olga 1949-　　CLC 10, 73
　See also CA 85-88; CANR 20, 69
Brown, Alan 1950-　　CLC 99
　See also CA 156
Brown, Charles Brockden 1771-1810 NCLC
　22, 74
　See also CDALB 1640-1865; DLB 37, 59, 73
Brown, Christy 1932-1981　　CLC 63
　See also CA 105; 104; CANR 72; DLB 14
Brown, Claude 1937- CLC 30; BLC 1; DAM
　MULT
　See also AAYA 7; BW 1; CA 73-76
Brown, Dee (Alexander) 1908-　CLC 18, 47;
　DAM POP
　See also CA 13-16R; CAAS 6; CANR 11, 45,
　60; DLBY 80; MTCW 1; SATA 5
Brown, George
　See Wertmueller, Lina
Brown, George Douglas 1869-1902 TCLC 28
　See also CA 162
Brown, George Mackay 1921-1996CLC 5, 48,
　100
　See also CA 21-24R; 151; CAAS 6; CANR 12,
　37, 67; DLB 14, 27, 139; MTCW 1; SATA
　35
Brown, (William) Larry 1951-　　CLC 73
　See also CA 130; 134; INT 133
Brown, Moses
　See Barrett, William (Christopher)
Brown, Rita Mae 1944-CLC 18, 43, 79; DAM
　NOV, POP
　See also CA 45-48; CANR 2, 11, 35, 62; INT
　CANR-11; MTCW 1
Brown, Roderick (Langmere) Haig-
　See Haig-Brown, Roderick (Langmere)
Brown, Rosellen 1939-　　CLC 32

See also CA 77-80; CAAS 10; CANR 14, 44

Brown, Sterling Allen 1901-1989 **CLC 1, 23, 59; BLC 1; DAM MULT, POET**
See also BW 1; CA 85-88; 127; CANR 26, 74; DLB 48, 51, 63; MTCW 1

Brown, Will
See Ainsworth, William Harrison

Brown, William Wells 1813-1884 **NCLC 2; BLC 1; DAM MULT; DC 1**
See also DLB 3, 50

Browne, (Clyde) Jackson 1948(?)- **CLC 21**
See also CA 120

Browning, Elizabeth Barrett 1806-1861 **NCLC 1, 16, 61, 66; DA; DAB; DAC; DAM MST, POET; PC 6; WLC**
See also CDBLB 1832-1890; DLB 32, 199

Browning, Robert 1812-1889 **NCLC 19; DA; DAB; DAC; DAM MST, POET; PC 2; WLCS**
See also CDBLB 1832-1890; DLB 32, 163; YABC 1

Browning, Tod 1882-1962 **CLC 16**
See also CA 141; 117

Brownson, Orestes Augustus 1803-1876 **NCLC 50**
See also DLB 1, 59, 73

Bruccoli, Matthew J(oseph) 1931- **CLC 34**
See also CA 9-12R; CANR 7; DLB 103

Bruce, Lenny **CLC 21**
See also Schneider, Leonard Alfred

Bruin, John
See Brutus, Dennis

Brulard, Henri
See Stendhal

Brulls, Christian
See Simenon, Georges (Jacques Christian)

Brunner, John (Kilian Houston) 1934-1995 **CLC 8, 10; DAM POP**
See also CA 1-4R; 149; CAAS 8; CANR 2, 37; MTCW 1

Bruno, Giordano 1548-1600 **LC 27**

Brutus, Dennis 1924- **CLC 43; BLC 1; DAM MULT, POET; PC 24**
See also BW 2; CA 49-52; CAAS 14; CANR 2, 27, 42; DLB 117

Bryan, C(ourtlandt) D(ixon) B(arnes) 1936- **CLC 29**
See also CA 73-76; CANR 13, 68; DLB 185; INT CANR-13

Bryan, Michael
See Moore, Brian

Bryant, William Cullen 1794-1878 **NCLC 6, 46; DA; DAB; DAC; DAM MST, POET; PC 20**
See also CDALB 1640-1865; DLB 3, 43, 59, 189

Bryusov, Valery Yakovlevich 1873-1924 **TCLC 10**
See also CA 107; 155

Buchan, John 1875-1940 **TCLC 41; DAB; DAM POP**
See also CA 108; 145; DLB 34, 70, 156; YABC 2

Buchanan, George 1506-1582 **LC 4**
See also DLB 152

Buchheim, Lothar-Guenther 1918- **CLC 6**
See also CA 85-88

Buchner, (Karl) Georg 1813-1837 **NCLC 26**

Buchwald, Art(hur) 1925- **CLC 33**
See also AITN 1; CA 5-8R; CANR 21, 67; MTCW 1; SATA 10

Buck, Pearl S(ydenstricker) 1892-1973 **CLC 7, 11, 18; DA; DAB; DAC; DAM MST, NOV**

See also AITN 1; CA 1-4R; 41-44R; CANR 1, 34; DLB 9, 102; MTCW 1; SATA 1, 25

Buckler, Ernest 1908-1984 **CLC 13; DAC; DAM MST**
See also CA 11-12; 114; CAP 1; DLB 68; SATA 47

Buckley, Vincent (Thomas) 1925-1988 **CLC 57**
See also CA 101

Buckley, William F(rank), Jr. 1925- **CLC 7, 18, 37; DAM POP**
See also AITN 1; CA 1-4R; CANR 1, 24, 53; DLB 137; DLBY 80; INT CANR-24; MTCW 1

Buechner, (Carl) Frederick 1926- **CLC 2, 4, 6, 9; DAM NOV**
See also CA 13-16R; CANR 11, 39, 64; DLBY 80; INT CANR-11; MTCW 1

Buell, John (Edward) 1927- **CLC 10**
See also CA 1-4R; CANR 71; DLB 53

Buero Vallejo, Antonio 1916- **CLC 15, 46**
See also CA 106; CANR 24, 49, 75; HW; MTCW 1

Bufalino, Gesualdo 1920(?)- **CLC 74**
See also DLB 196

Bugayev, Boris Nikolayevich 1880-1934 **TCLC 7; PC 11**
See also Bely, Andrey
See also CA 104; 165

Bukowski, Charles 1920-1994 **CLC 2, 5, 9, 41, 82, 108; DAM NOV, POET; PC 18**
See also CA 17-20R; 144; CANR 40, 62; DLB 5, 130, 169; MTCW 1

Bulgakov, Mikhail (Afanas'evich) 1891-1940 **TCLC 2, 16; DAM DRAM, NOV; SSC 18**
See also CA 105; 152

Bulgya, Alexander Alexandrovich 1901-1956 **TCLC 53**
See also Fadeyev, Alexander
See also CA 117

Bullins, Ed 1935- **CLC 1, 5, 7; BLC 1; DAM DRAM, MULT; DC 1**
See also BW 2; CA 49-52; CAAS 16; CANR 24, 46, 73; DLB 7, 38; MTCW 1

Bulwer-Lytton, Edward (George Earle Lytton) 1803-1873 **NCLC 1, 45**
See also DLB 21

Bunin, Ivan Alexeyevich 1870-1953 **TCLC 6; SSC 5**
See also CA 104

Bunting, Basil 1900-1985 **CLC 10, 39, 47; DAM POET**
See also CA 53-56; 115; CANR 7; DLB 20

Bunuel, Luis 1900-1983 **CLC 16, 80; DAM MULT; HLC**
See also CA 101; 110; CANR 32; HW

Bunyan, John 1628-1688 **LC 4; DA; DAB; DAC; DAM MST; WLC**
See also CDBLB 1660-1789; DLB 39

Burckhardt, Jacob (Christoph) 1818-1897 **NCLC 49**

Burford, Eleanor
See Hibbert, Eleanor Alice Burford

Burgess, Anthony **CLC 1, 2, 4, 5, 8, 10, 13, 15, 22, 40, 62, 81, 94; DAB**
See also Wilson, John (Anthony) Burgess
See also AAYA 25; AITN 1; CDBLB 1960 to Present; DLB 14, 194

Burke, Edmund 1729(?)-1797 **LC 7, 36; DA; DAB; DAC; DAM MST; WLC**
See also DLB 104

Burke, Kenneth (Duva) 1897-1993 **CLC 2, 24**
See also CA 5-8R; 143; CANR 39, 74; DLB 45, 63; MTCW 1

Burke, Leda
See Garnett, David

Burke, Ralph
See Silverberg, Robert

Burke, Thomas 1886-1945 **TCLC 63**
See also CA 113; 155; DLB 197

Burney, Fanny 1752-1840 **NCLC 12, 54**
See also DLB 39

Burns, Robert 1759-1796 **LC 3, 29, 40; DA; DAB; DAC; DAM MST, POET; PC 6; WLC**
See also CDBLB 1789-1832; DLB 109

Burns, Tex
See L'Amour, Louis (Dearborn)

Burnshaw, Stanley 1906- **CLC 3, 13, 44**
See also CA 9-12R; DLB 48; DLBY 97

Burr, Anne 1937- **CLC 6**
See also CA 25-28R

Burroughs, Edgar Rice 1875-1950 **TCLC 2, 32; DAM NOV**
See also AAYA 11; CA 104; 132; DLB 8; MTCW 1; SATA 41

Burroughs, William S(eward) 1914-1997 **CLC 1, 2, 5, 15, 22, 42, 75, 109; DA; DAB; DAC; DAM MST, NOV, POP; WLC**
See also AITN 2; CA 9-12R; 160; CANR 20, 52; DLB 2, 8, 16, 152; DLBY 81, 97; MTCW 1

Burton, Richard F. 1821-1890 **NCLC 42**
See also DLB 55, 184

Busch, Frederick 1941- **CLC 7, 10, 18, 47**
See also CA 33-36R; CAAS 1; CANR 45, 73; DLB 6

Bush, Ronald 1946- **CLC 34**
See also CA 136

Bustos, F(rancisco)
See Borges, Jorge Luis

Bustos Domecq, H(onorio)
See Bioy Casares, Adolfo; Borges, Jorge Luis

Butler, Octavia E(stelle) 1947- **CLC 38; BLCS; DAM MULT, POP**
See also AAYA 18; BW 2; CA 73-76; CANR 12, 24, 38, 73; DLB 33; MTCW 1; SATA 84

Butler, Robert Olen (Jr.) 1945- **CLC 81; DAM POP**
See also CA 112; CANR 66; DLB 173; INT 112

Butler, Samuel 1612-1680 **LC 16, 43**
See also DLB 101, 126

Butler, Samuel 1835-1902 **TCLC 1, 33; DA; DAB; DAC; DAM MST, NOV; WLC**
See also CA 143; CDBLB 1890-1914; DLB 18, 57, 174

Butler, Walter C.
See Faust, Frederick (Schiller)

Butor, Michel (Marie Francois) 1926- **CLC 1, 3, 8, 11, 15**
See also CA 9-12R; CANR 33, 66; DLB 83; MTCW 1

Butts, Mary 1892(?)-1937 **TCLC 77**
See also CA 148

Buzo, Alexander (John) 1944- **CLC 61**
See also CA 97-100; CANR 17, 39, 69

Buzzati, Dino 1906-1972 **CLC 36**
See also CA 160; 33-36R; DLB 177

Byars, Betsy (Cromer) 1928- **CLC 35**
See also AAYA 19; CA 33-36R; CANR 18, 36, 57; CLR 1, 16; DLB 52; INT CANR-18; JRDA; MAICYA; MTCW 1; SAAS 1; SATA 4, 46, 80

Byatt, A(ntonia) S(usan Drabble) 1936- **CLC 19, 65; DAM NOV, POP**
See also CA 13-16R; CANR 13, 33, 50, 75; DLB 14, 194; MTCW 1

See also AAYA 17; CA 45-48; CANR 42

Carroll, Lewis NCLC 2, 53; PC 18; WLC
See also Dodgson, Charles Lutwidge
See also CDBLB 1832-1890; CLR 2, 18; DLB
18, 163, 178; JRDA

Carroll, Paul Vincent 1900-1968 **CLC 10**
See also CA 9-12R; 25-28R; DLB 10

Carruth, Hayden 1921- CLC 4, 7, 10, 18, 84;
PC 10
See also CA 9-12R; CANR 4, 38, 59; DLB 5,
165; INT CANR-4; MTCW 1; SATA 47

Carson, Rachel Louise 1907-1964 **CLC 71;**
DAM POP
See also CA 77-80; CANR 35; MTCW 1; SATA
23

Carter, Angela (Olive) 1940-1992 CLC 5, 41,
76; SSC 13
See also CA 53-56; 136; CANR 12, 36, 61; DLB
14, 207; MTCW 1; SATA 66; SATA-Obit 70

Carter, Nick
See Smith, Martin Cruz

Carver, Raymond 1938-1988 CLC 22, 36, 53,
55; DAM NOV; SSC 8
See also CA 33-36R; 126; CANR 17, 34, 61;
DLB 130; DLBY 84, 88; MTCW 1

Cary, Elizabeth, Lady Falkland 1585-1639
LC 30

Cary, (Arthur) Joyce (Lunel) 1888-1957
TCLC 1, 29
See also CA 104; 164; CDBLB 1914-1945;
DLB 15, 100

Casanova de Seingalt, Giovanni Jacopo 1725-
1798 **LC 13**

Casares, Adolfo Bioy
See Bioy Casares, Adolfo

Casely-Hayford, J(oseph) E(phraim) 1866-1930
TCLC 24; BLC 1; DAM MULT
See also BW 2; CA 123; 152

Casey, John (Dudley) 1939- **CLC 59**
See also BEST 90:2; CA 69-72; CANR 23

Casey, Michael 1947- **CLC 2**
See also CA 65-68; DLB 5

Casey, Patrick
See Thurman, Wallace (Henry)

Casey, Warren (Peter) 1935-1988 **CLC 12**
See also CA 101; 127; INT 101

Casona, Alejandro **CLC 49**
See also Alvarez, Alejandro Rodriguez

Cassavetes, John 1929-1989 **CLC 20**
See also CA 85-88; 127

Cassian, Nina 1924- **PC 17**

Cassill, R(onald) V(erlin) 1919- **CLC 4, 23**
See also CA 9-12R; CAAS 1; CANR 7, 45; DLB
6

Cassirer, Ernst 1874-1945 **TCLC 61**
See also CA 157

Cassity, (Allen) Turner 1929- **CLC 6, 42**
See also CA 17-20R; CAAS 8; CANR 11; DLB
105

Castaneda, Carlos 1931(?)- **CLC 12**
See also CA 25-28R; CANR 32, 66; HW;
MTCW 1

Castedo, Elena 1937- **CLC 65**
See also CA 132

Castedo-Ellerman, Elena
See Castedo, Elena

Castellanos, Rosario 1925-1974 CLC 66; DAM
MULT; HLC
See also CA 131; 53-56; CANR 58; DLB 113;
HW

Castelvetro, Lodovico 1505-1571 **LC 12**

Castiglione, Baldassare 1478-1529 **LC 12**

Castle, Robert

See Hamilton, Edmond

Castro, Guillen de 1569-1631 **LC 19**

Castro, Rosalia de 1837-1885 NCLC 3; DAM
MULT

Cather, Willa
See Cather, Willa Sibert

Cather, Willa Sibert 1873-1947 **TCLC 1, 11,**
31; DA; DAB; DAC; DAM MST, NOV;
SSC 2; WLC
See also AAYA 24; CA 104; 128; CDALB 1865-
1917; DLB 9, 54, 78; DLBD 1; MTCW 1;
SATA 30

Catherine, Saint 1347-1380 **CMLC 27**

Cato, Marcus Porcius 234B.C.-149B.C.
CMLC 21

Catton, (Charles) Bruce 1899-1978 **CLC 35**
See also AITN 1; CA 5-8R; 81-84; CANR 7,
74; DLB 17; SATA 2; SATA-Obit 24

Catullus c. 84B.C.-c. 54B.C. **CMLC 18**

Cauldwell, Frank
See King, Francis (Henry)

Caunitz, William J. 1933-1996 **CLC 34**
See also BEST 89:3; CA 125; 130; 152; CANR
73; INT 130

Causley, Charles (Stanley) 1917- **CLC 7**
See also CA 9-12R; CANR 5, 35; CLR 30; DLB
27; MTCW 1; SATA 3, 66

Caute, (John) David 1936- **CLC 29; DAM**
NOV
See also CA 1-4R; CAAS 4; CANR 1, 33, 64;
DLB 14

Cavafy, C(onstantine) P(eter) 1863-1933
TCLC 2, 7; DAM POET
See also Kavafis, Konstantinos Petrou
See also CA 148

Cavallo, Evelyn
See Spark, Muriel (Sarah)

Cavanna, Betty **CLC 12**
See also Harrison, Elizabeth Cavanna
See also JRDA; MAICYA; SAAS 4; SATA 1,
30

Cavendish, Margaret Lucas 1623-1673 LC 30
See also DLB 131

Caxton, William 1421(?)-1491(?) **LC 17**
See also DLB 170

Cayer, D. M.
See Duffy, Maureen

Cayrol, Jean 1911- **CLC 11**
See also CA 89-92; DLB 83

Cela, Camilo Jose 1916- CLC 4, 13, 59; DAM
MULT; HLC
See also BEST 90:2; CA 21-24R; CAAS 10;
CANR 21, 32; DLBY 89; HW; MTCW 1

Celan, Paul **CLC 10, 19, 53, 82; PC 10**
See also Antschel, Paul
See also DLB 69

Celine, Louis-Ferdinand CLC 1, 3, 4, 7, 9, 15,
47
See also Destouches, Louis-Ferdinand
See also DLB 72

Cellini, Benvenuto 1500-1571 **LC 7**

Cendrars, Blaise 1887-1961 **CLC 18, 106**
See also Sauser-Hall, Frederic

Cernuda (y Bidon), Luis 1902-1963 CLC 54;
DAM POET
See also CA 131; 89-92; DLB 134; HW

Cervantes (Saavedra), Miguel de 1547-1616
LC 6, 23; DA; DAB; DAC; DAM MST,
NOV; SSC 12; WLC

Cesaire, Aime (Fernand) 1913- CLC 19, 32,
112; BLC 1; DAM MULT, POET; PC 25
See also BW 2; CA 65-68; CANR 24, 43;
MTCW 1

Chabon, Michael 1963- **CLC 55**
See also CA 139; CANR 57

Chabrol, Claude 1930- **CLC 16**
See also CA 110

Challans, Mary 1905-1983
See Renault, Mary
See also CA 81-84; 111; CANR 74; SATA 23;
SATA-Obit 36

Challis, George
See Faust, Frederick (Schiller)

Chambers, Aidan 1934- **CLC 35**
See also AAYA 27; CA 25-28R; CANR 12, 31,
58; JRDA; MAICYA; SAAS 12; SATA 1, 69

Chambers, James 1948-
See Cliff, Jimmy
See also CA 124

Chambers, Jessie
See Lawrence, D(avid) H(erbert Richards)

Chambers, Robert W(illiam) 1865-1933
TCLC 41
See also CA 165; DLB 202

Chandler, Raymond (Thornton) 1888-1959
TCLC 1, 7; SSC 23
See also AAYA 25; CA 104; 129; CANR 60;
CDALB 1929-1941; DLBD 6; MTCW 1

Chang, Eileen 1920-1995 **SSC 28**
See also CA 166

Chang, Jung 1952- **CLC 71**
See also CA 142

Chang Ai-Ling
See Chang, Eileen

Channing, William Ellery 1780-1842 N C L C
17
See also DLB 1, 59

Chaplin, Charles Spencer 1889-1977 CLC 16
See also Chaplin, Charlie
See also CA 81-84; 73-76

Chaplin, Charlie
See Chaplin, Charles Spencer
See also DLB 44

Chapman, George 1559(?)-1634 LC 22; DAM
DRAM
See also DLB 62, 121

Chapman, Graham 1941-1989 **CLC 21**
See also Monty Python
See also CA 116; 129; CANR 35

Chapman, John Jay 1862-1933 **TCLC 7**
See also CA 104

Chapman, Lee
See Bradley, Marion Zimmer

Chapman, Walker
See Silverberg, Robert

Chappell, Fred (Davis) 1936- **CLC 40, 78**
See also CA 5-8R; CAAS 4; CANR 8, 33, 67;
DLB 6, 105

Char, Rene(-Emile) 1907-1988 CLC 9, 11, 14,
55; DAM POET
See also CA 13-16R; 124; CANR 32; MTCW 1

Charby, Jay
See Ellison, Harlan (Jay)

Chardin, Pierre Teilhard de
See Teilhard de Chardin, (Marie Joseph) Pierre

Charles I 1600-1649 **LC 13**

Charriere, Isabelle de 1740-1805 NCLC 66

Charyn, Jerome 1937- **CLC 5, 8, 18**
See also CA 5-8R; CAAS 1; CANR 7, 61;
DLBY 83; MTCW 1

Chase, Mary (Coyle) 1907-1981 **DC 1**
See also CA 77-80; 105; SATA 17; SATA-Obit
29

Chase, Mary Ellen 1887-1973 **CLC 2**
See also CA 13-16; 41-44R; CAP 1; SATA 10

Chase, Nicholas

See also CA 104; 165; DLB 192
Claudius, Matthias 1740-1815   **NCLC 75**
  See also DLB 97
Clavell, James (duMaresq) 1925-1994**CLC 6, 25, 87; DAM NOV, POP**
  See also CA 25-28R; 146; CANR 26, 48; MTCW 1
Cleaver, (Leroy) Eldridge 1935-1998**CLC 30; BLC 1; DAM MULT**
  See also BW 1; CA 21-24R; 167; CANR 16, 75
Cleese, John (Marwood) 1939-   **CLC 21**
  See also Monty Python
  See also CA 112; 116; CANR 35; MTCW 1
Cleishbotham, Jebediah
  See Scott, Walter
Cleland, John 1710-1789   **LC 2, 48**
  See also DLB 39
Clemens, Samuel Langhorne 1835-1910
  See Twain, Mark
  See also CA 104; 135; CDALB 1865-1917; DA; DAB; DAC; DAM MST, NOV; DLB 11, 12, 23, 64, 74, 186, 189; JRDA; MAICYA; SATA 100; YABC 2
Cleophil
  See Congreve, William
Clerihew, E.
  See Bentley, E(dmund) C(lerihew)
Clerk, N. W.
  See Lewis, C(live) S(taples)
Cliff, Jimmy   **CLC 21**
  See also Chambers, James
Clifton, (Thelma) Lucille 1936- **CLC 19, 66; BLC 1; DAM MULT, POET; PC 17**
  See also BW 2; CA 49-52; CANR 2, 24, 42; CLR 5; DLB 5, 41; MAICYA; MTCW 1; SATA 20, 69
Clinton, Dirk
  See Silverberg, Robert
Clough, Arthur Hugh 1819-1861   **NCLC 27**
  See also DLB 32
Clutha, Janet Paterson Frame 1924-
  See Frame, Janet
  See also CA 1-4R; CANR 2, 36; MTCW 1
Clyne, Terence
  See Blatty, William Peter
Cobalt, Martin
  See Mayne, William (James Carter)
Cobb, Irvin S. 1876-1944   **TCLC 77**
  See also DLB 11, 25, 86
Cobbett, William 1763-1835   **NCLC 49**
  See also DLB 43, 107, 158
Coburn, D(onald) L(ee) 1938-   **CLC 10**
  See also CA 89-92
Cocteau, Jean (Maurice Eugene Clement) 1889-1963**CLC 1, 8, 15, 16, 43; DA; DAB; DAC; DAM DRAM, MST, NOV; WLC**
  See also CA 25-28; CANR 40; CAP 2; DLB 65; MTCW 1
Codrescu, Andrei 1946-**CLC 46; DAM POET**
  See also CA 33-36R; CAAS 19; CANR 13, 34, 53
Coe, Max
  See Bourne, Randolph S(illiman)
Coe, Tucker
  See Westlake, Donald E(dwin)
Coen, Ethan 1958-   **CLC 108**
  See also CA 126
Coen, Joel 1955-   **CLC 108**
  See also CA 126
The Coen Brothers
  See Coen, Ethan; Coen, Joel
Coetzee, J(ohn) M(ichael) 1940- **CLC 23, 33, 66, 117; DAM NOV**

See also CA 77-80; CANR 41, 54, 74; MTCW 1
Coffey, Brian
  See Koontz, Dean R(ay)
Cohan, George M(ichael) 1878-1942**TCLC 60**
  See also CA 157
Cohen, Arthur A(llen) 1928-1986   **CLC 7, 31**
  See also CA 1-4R; 120; CANR 1, 17, 42; DLB 28
Cohen, Leonard (Norman) 1934- **CLC 3, 38; DAC; DAM MST**
  See also CA 21-24R; CANR 14, 69; DLB 53; MTCW 1
Cohen, Matt 1942-   **CLC 19; DAC**
  See also CA 61-64; CAAS 18; CANR 40; DLB 53
Cohen-Solal, Annie 19(?)-   **CLC 50**
Colegate, Isabel 1931-   **CLC 36**
  See also CA 17-20R; CANR 8, 22, 74; DLB 14; INT CANR-22; MTCW 1
Coleman, Emmett
  See Reed, Ishmael
Coleridge, M. E.
  See Coleridge, Mary E(lizabeth)
Coleridge, Mary E(lizabeth) 1861-1907**TCLC 73**
  See also CA 116; 166; DLB 19, 98
Coleridge, Samuel Taylor 1772-1834**NCLC 9, 54; DA; DAB; DAC; DAM MST, POET; PC 11; WLC**
  See also CDBLB 1789-1832; DLB 93, 107
Coleridge, Sara 1802-1852   **NCLC 31**
  See also DLB 199
Coles, Don 1928-   **CLC 46**
  See also CA 115; CANR 38
Coles, Robert (Martin) 1929-   **CLC 108**
  See also CA 45-48; CANR 3, 32, 66, 70; INT CANR-32; SATA 23
Colette, (Sidonie-Gabrielle) 1873-1954**TCLC 1, 5, 16; DAM NOV; SSC 10**
  See also CA 104; 131; DLB 65; MTCW 1
Collett, (Jacobine) Camilla (Wergeland) 1813-1895   **NCLC 22**
Collier, Christopher 1930-   **CLC 30**
  See also AAYA 13; CA 33-36R; CANR 13, 33; JRDA; MAICYA; SATA 16, 70
Collier, James L(incoln) 1928-**CLC 30; DAM POP**
  See also AAYA 13; CA 9-12R; CANR 4, 33, 60; CLR 3; JRDA; MAICYA; SAAS 21; SATA 8, 70
Collier, Jeremy 1650-1726   **LC 6**
Collier, John 1901-1980   **SSC 19**
  See also CA 65-68; 97-100; CANR 10; DLB 77
Collingwood, R(obin) G(eorge) 1889(?)-1943 **TCLC 67**
  See also CA 117; 155
Collins, Hunt
  See Hunter, Evan
Collins, Linda 1931-   **CLC 44**
  See also CA 125
Collins, (William) Wilkie 1824-1889**NCLC 1, 18**
  See also CDBLB 1832-1890; DLB 18, 70, 159
Collins, William 1721-1759 **LC 4, 40; DAM POET**
  See also DLB 109
Collodi, Carlo 1826-1890   **NCLC 54**
  See also Lorenzini, Carlo
  See also CLR 5
Colman, George 1732-1794
  See Glassco, John

Colt, Winchester Remington
  See Hubbard, L(afayette) Ron(ald)
Colter, Cyrus 1910-   **CLC 58**
  See also BW 1; CA 65-68; CANR 10, 66; DLB 33
Colton, James
  See Hansen, Joseph
Colum, Padraic 1881-1972   **CLC 28**
  See also CA 73-76; 33-36R; CANR 35; CLR 36; MAICYA; MTCW 1; SATA 15
Colvin, James
  See Moorcock, Michael (John)
Colwin, Laurie (E.) 1944-1992**CLC 5, 13, 23, 84**
  See also CA 89-92; 139; CANR 20, 46; DLBY 80; MTCW 1
Comfort, Alex(ander) 1920-**CLC 7; DAM POP**
  See also CA 1-4R; CANR 1, 45
Comfort, Montgomery
  See Campbell, (John) Ramsey
Compton-Burnett, I(vy) 1884(?)-1969**CLC 1, 3, 10, 15, 34; DAM NOV**
  See also CA 1-4R; 25-28R; CANR 4; DLB 36; MTCW 1
Comstock, Anthony 1844-1915   **TCLC 13**
  See also CA 110; 169
Comte, Auguste 1798-1857   **NCLC 54**
Conan Doyle, Arthur
  See Doyle, Arthur Conan
Conde, Maryse 1937-   **CLC 52, 92; BLCS; DAM MULT**
  See also Boucolon, Maryse
  See also BW 2
Condillac, Etienne Bonnot de 1714-1780 **LC 26**
Condon, Richard (Thomas) 1915-1996**CLC 4, 6, 8, 10, 45, 100; DAM NOV**
  See also BEST 90:3; CA 1-4R; 151; CAAS 1; CANR 2, 23; INT CANR-23; MTCW 1
Confucius 551B.C.-479B.C.   **CMLC 19; DA; DAB; DAC; DAM MST; WLCS**
Congreve, William 1670-1729 **LC 5, 21; DA; DAB; DAC; DAM DRAM, MST, POET; DC 2; WLC**
  See also CDBLB 1660-1789; DLB 39, 84
Connell, Evan S(helby), Jr. 1924-**CLC 4, 6, 45; DAM NOV**
  See also AAYA 7; CA 1-4R; CAAS 2; CANR 2, 39; DLB 2; DLBY 81; MTCW 1
Connelly, Marc(us Cook) 1890-1980   **CLC 7**
  See also CA 85-88; 102; CANR 30; DLB 7; DLBY 80; SATA-Obit 25
Connor, Ralph   **TCLC 31**
  See also Gordon, Charles William
  See also DLB 92
Conrad, Joseph 1857-1924**TCLC 1, 6, 13, 25, 43, 57; DA; DAB; DAC; DAM MST, NOV; SSC 9; WLC**
  See also AAYA 26; CA 104; 131; CANR 60; CDBLB 1890-1914; DLB 10, 34, 98, 156; MTCW 1; SATA 27
Conrad, Robert Arnold
  See Hart, Moss
Conroy, Pat
  See Conroy, (Donald) Pat(rick)
Conroy, (Donald) Pat(rick) 1945-**CLC 30, 74; DAM NOV, POP**
  See also AAYA 8; AITN 1; CA 85-88; CANR 24, 53; DLB 6; MTCW 1
Constant (de Rebecque), (Henri) Benjamin 1767-1830   **NCLC 6**
  See also DLB 119
Conybeare, Charles Augustus

See also CA 89-92; DLB 9, 206

Davis, Rebecca (Blaine) Harding 1831-1910
TCLC 6
See also CA 104; DLB 74

Davis, Richard Harding 1864-1916 **TCLC 24**
See also CA 114; DLB 12, 23, 78, 79, 189;
DLBD 13

Davison, Frank Dalby 1893-1970 **CLC 15**
See also CA 116

Davison, Lawrence H.
See Lawrence, D(avid) H(erbert Richards)

Davison, Peter (Hubert) 1928- **CLC 28**
See also CA 9-12R; CAAS 4; CANR 3, 43; DLB
5

Davys, Mary 1674-1732 **LC 1, 46**
See also DLB 39

Dawson, Fielding 1930- **CLC 6**
See also CA 85-88; DLB 130

Dawson, Peter
See Faust, Frederick (Schiller)

Day, Clarence (Shepard, Jr.) 1874-1935
TCLC 25
See also CA 108; DLB 11

Day, Thomas 1748-1789 **LC 1**
See also DLB 39; YABC 1

Day Lewis, C(ecil) 1904-1972 **CLC 1, 6, 10;**
DAM POET; PC 11
See also Blake, Nicholas
See also CA 13-16; 33-36R; CANR 34; CAP 1;
DLB 15, 20; MTCW 1

Dazai Osamu 1909-1948 **TCLC 11**
See also Tsushima, Shuji
See also CA 164; DLB 182

de Andrade, Carlos Drummond
See Drummond de Andrade, Carlos

Deane, Norman
See Creasey, John

de Beauvoir, Simone (Lucie Ernestine Marie
Bertrand)
See Beauvoir, Simone (Lucie Ernestine Marie
Bertrand) de

de Beer, P.
See Bosman, Herman Charles

de Brissac, Malcolm
See Dickinson, Peter (Malcolm)

de Chardin, Pierre Teilhard
See Teilhard de Chardin, (Marie Joseph) Pierre

Dee, John 1527-1608 **LC 20**

Deer, Sandra 1940- **CLC 45**

De Ferrari, Gabriella 1941- **CLC 65**
See also CA 146

Defoe, Daniel 1660(?)-1731 **LC 1, 42; DA;**
DAB; DAC; DAM MST, NOV; WLC
See also AAYA 27; CDBLB 1660-1789; DLB
39, 95, 101; JRDA; MAICYA; SATA 22

de Gourmont, Remy(-Marie-Charles)
See Gourmont, Remy (-Marie-Charles) de

de Hartog, Jan 1914- **CLC 19**
See also CA 1-4R; CANR 1

de Hostos, E. M.
See Hostos (y Bonilla), Eugenio Maria de

de Hostos, Eugenio M.
See Hostos (y Bonilla), Eugenio Maria de

Deighton, Len **CLC 4, 7, 22, 46**
See also Deighton, Leonard Cyril
See also AAYA 6; BEST 89:2; CDBLB 1960 to
Present; DLB 87

Deighton, Leonard Cyril 1929-
See Deighton, Len
See also CA 9-12R; CANR 19, 33, 68; DAM
NOV, POP; MTCW 1

Dekker, Thomas 1572(?)-1632 **LC 22; DAM**
DRAM

See also CDBLB Before 1660; DLB 62, 172

Delafield, E. M. 1890-1943 **TCLC 61**
See also Dashwood, Edmee Elizabeth Monica
de la Pasture
See also DLB 34

de la Mare, Walter (John) 1873-1956**TCLC 4,**
53; DAB; DAC; DAM MST, POET; SSC
14; WLC
See also CA 163; CDBLB 1914-1945; CLR 23;
DLB 162; SATA 16

Delaney, Franey
See O'Hara, John (Henry)

Delaney, Shelagh 1939-**CLC 29; DAM DRAM**
See also CA 17-20R; CANR 30, 67; CDBLB
1960 to Present; DLB 13; MTCW 1

Delany, Mary (Granville Pendarves) 1700-1788
LC 12

Delany, Samuel R(ay, Jr.) 1942-**CLC 8, 14, 38;**
BLC 1; DAM MULT
See also AAYA 24; BW 2; CA 81-84; CANR
27, 43; DLB 8, 33; MTCW 1

De La Ramee, (Marie) Louise 1839-1908
See Ouida
See also SATA 20

de la Roche, Mazo 1879-1961 **CLC 14**
See also CA 85-88; CANR 30; DLB 68; SATA
64

De La Salle, Innocent
See Hartmann, Sadakichi

Delbanco, Nicholas (Franklin) 1942- **CLC 6,**
13
See also CA 17-20R; CAAS 2; CANR 29, 55;
DLB 6

del Castillo, Michel 1933- **CLC 38**
See also CA 109

Deledda, Grazia (Cosima) 1875(?)-1936
TCLC 23
See also CA 123

Delibes, Miguel **CLC 8, 18**
See also Delibes Setien, Miguel

Delibes Setien, Miguel 1920-
See Delibes, Miguel
See also CA 45-48; CANR 1, 32; HW; MTCW
1

DeLillo, Don 1936- **CLC 8, 10, 13, 27, 39, 54,**
76; DAM NOV, POP
See also BEST 89:1; CA 81-84; CANR 21; DLB
6, 173; MTCW 1

de Lisser, H. G.
See De Lisser, H(erbert) G(eorge)
See also DLB 117

De Lisser, H(erbert) G(eorge) 1878-1944
TCLC 12
See also de Lisser, H. G.
See also BW 2; CA 109; 152

Deloney, Thomas 1560(?)-1600 **LC 41**
See also DLB 167

Deloria, Vine (Victor), Jr. 1933- **CLC 21;**
DAM MULT
See also CA 53-56; CANR 5, 20, 48; DLB 175;
MTCW 1; NNAL; SATA 21

Del Vecchio, John M(ichael) 1947- **CLC 29**
See also CA 110; DLBD 9

de Man, Paul (Adolph Michel) 1919-1983
CLC 55
See also CA 128; 111; CANR 61; DLB 67;
MTCW 1

De Marinis, Rick 1934- **CLC 54**
See also CA 57-60; CAAS 24; CANR 9, 25, 50

Dembry, R. Emmet
See Murfree, Mary Noailles

Demby, William 1922-**CLC 53; BLC 1; DAM**
MULT

See also BW 1; CA 81-84; DLB 33

de Menton, Francisco
See Chin, Frank (Chew, Jr.)

Demijohn, Thom
See Disch, Thomas M(ichael)

de Montherlant, Henry (Milon)
See Montherlant, Henry (Milon) de

Demosthenes 384B.C.-322B.C. **CMLC 13**
See also DLB 176

de Natale, Francine
See Malzberg, Barry N(athaniel)

Denby, Edwin (Orr) 1903-1983 **CLC 48**
See also CA 138; 110

Denis, Julio
See Cortazar, Julio

Denmark, Harrison
See Zelazny, Roger (Joseph)

Dennis, John 1658-1734 **LC 11**
See also DLB 101

Dennis, Nigel (Forbes) 1912-1989 **CLC 8**
See also CA 25-28R; 129; DLB 13, 15; MTCW
1

Dent, Lester 1904(?)-1959 **TCLC 72**
See also CA 112; 161

De Palma, Brian (Russell) 1940- **CLC 20**
See also CA 109

De Quincey, Thomas 1785-1859 **NCLC 4**
See also CDBLB 1789-1832; DLB 110; 144

Deren, Eleanora 1908(?)-1961
See Deren, Maya
See also CA 111

Deren, Maya 1917-1961 **CLC 16, 102**
See also Deren, Eleanora

Derleth, August (William) 1909-1971**CLC 31**
See also CA 1-4R; 29-32R; CANR 4; DLB 9;
DLBD 17; SATA 5

Der Nister 1884-1950 **TCLC 56**

de Routisie, Albert
See Aragon, Louis

Derrida, Jacques 1930- **CLC 24, 87**
See also CA 124; 127

Derry Down Derry
See Lear, Edward

Dersonnes, Jacques
See Simenon, Georges (Jacques Christian)

Desai, Anita 1937-**CLC 19, 37, 97; DAB; DAM**
NOV
See also CA 81-84; CANR 33, 53; MTCW 1;
SATA 63

de Saint-Luc, Jean
See Glassco, John

de Saint Roman, Arnaud
See Aragon, Louis

Descartes, Rene 1596-1650 **LC 20, 35**

De Sica, Vittorio 1901(?)-1974 **CLC 20**
See also CA 117

Desnos, Robert 1900-1945 **TCLC 22**
See also CA 121; 151

Destouches, Louis-Ferdinand 1894-1961**CLC**
9, 15
See also Celine, Louis-Ferdinand
See also CA 85-88; CANR 28; MTCW 1

de Tolignac, Gaston
See Griffith, D(avid Lewelyn) W(ark)

Deutsch, Babette 1895-1982 **CLC 18**
See also CA 1-4R; 108; CANR 4; DLB 45;
SATA 1; SATA-Obit 33

Devenant, William 1606-1649 **LC 13**

Devkota, Laxmiprasad 1909-1959 **TCLC 23**
See also CA 123

De Voto, Bernard (Augustine) 1897-1955
TCLC 29
See also CA 113; 160; DLB 9

BLC 1; DA; DAC; DAM MST, MULT;
WLC
See also CDALB 1640-1865; DLB 1, 43, 50,
79; SATA 29

Dourado, (Waldomiro Freitas) Autran 1926-
CLC 23, 60
See also CA 25-28R; CANR 34

Dourado, Waldomiro Autran
See Dourado, (Waldomiro Freitas) Autran

Dove, Rita (Frances) 1952-CLC **50, 81; BLCS;
DAM MULT, POET; PC 6**
See also BW 2; CA 109; CAAS 19; CANR 27,
42, 68; DLB 120

Doveglion
See Villa, Jose Garcia

Dowell, Coleman 1925-1985   **CLC 60**
See also CA 25-28R; 117; CANR 10; DLB 130

Dowson, Ernest (Christopher) 1867-1900
TCLC 4
See also CA 105; 150; DLB 19, 135

Doyle, A. Conan
See Doyle, Arthur Conan

Doyle, Arthur Conan 1859-1930TCLC **7; DA;
DAB; DAC; DAM MST, NOV; SSC 12;
WLC**
See also AAYA 14; CA 104; 122; CDBLB 1890-
1914; DLB 18, 70, 156, 178; MTCW 1;
SATA 24

Doyle, Conan
See Doyle, Arthur Conan

Doyle, John
See Graves, Robert (von Ranke)

Doyle, Roddy 1958(?)-   **CLC 81**
See also AAYA 14; CA 143; CANR 73; DLB
194

Doyle, Sir A. Conan
See Doyle, Arthur Conan

Doyle, Sir Arthur Conan
See Doyle, Arthur Conan

Dr. A
See Asimov, Isaac; Silverstein, Alvin

Drabble, Margaret 1939-CLC **2, 3, 5, 8, 10, 22,
53; DAB; DAC; DAM MST, NOV, POP**
See also CA 13-16R; CANR 18, 35, 63; CDBLB
1960 to Present; DLB 14, 155; MTCW 1;
SATA 48

Drapier, M. B.
See Swift, Jonathan

Drayham, James
See Mencken, H(enry) L(ouis)

Drayton, Michael 1563-1631   **LC 8; DAM
POET**
See also DLB 121

Dreadstone, Carl
See Campbell, (John) Ramsey

Dreiser, Theodore (Herman Albert) 1871-1945
**TCLC 10, 18, 35, 83; DA; DAC; DAM
MST, NOV; SSC 30; WLC**
See also CA 106; 132; CDALB 1865-1917;
DLB 9, 12, 102, 137; DLBD 1; MTCW 1

Drexler, Rosalyn 1926-   **CLC 2, 6**
See also CA 81-84; CANR 68

Dreyer, Carl Theodor 1889-1968   **CLC 16**
See also CA 116

Drieu la Rochelle, Pierre(-Eugene) 1893-1945
TCLC 21
See also CA 117; DLB 72

Drinkwater, John 1882-1937   **TCLC 57**
See also CA 109; 149; DLB 10, 19, 149

Drop Shot
See Cable, George Washington

Droste-Hulshoff, Annette Freiin von 1797-1848
NCLC 3

See also DLB 133

Drummond, Walter
See Silverberg, Robert

Drummond, William Henry 1854-1907TCLC
25
See also CA 160; DLB 92

Drummond de Andrade, Carlos 1902-1987
CLC 18
See also Andrade, Carlos Drummond de
See also CA 132; 123

Drury, Allen (Stuart) 1918-1998   **CLC 37**
See also CA 57-60; 170; CANR 18, 52; INT
CANR-18

Dryden, John 1631-1700LC **3, 21; DA; DAB;
DAC; DAM DRAM, MST, POET; DC 3;
PC 25; WLC**
See also CDBLB 1660-1789; DLB 80, 101, 131

Duberman, Martin (Bauml) 1930-   **CLC 8**
See also CA 1-4R; CANR 2, 63

Dubie, Norman (Evans) 1945-   **CLC 36**
See also CA 69-72; CANR 12; DLB 120

Du Bois, W(illiam) E(dward) B(urghardt) 1868-
1963   **CLC 1, 2, 13, 64, 96; BLC 1; DA;
DAC; DAM MST, MULT, NOV; WLC**
See also BW 1; CA 85-88; CANR 34; CDALB
1865-1917; DLB 47, 50, 91; MTCW 1; SATA
42

Dubus, Andre 1936- CLC **13, 36, 97; SSC 15**
See also CA 21-24R; CANR 17; DLB 130; INT
CANR-17

Duca Minimo
See D'Annunzio, Gabriele

Ducharme, Rejean 1941-   **CLC 74**
See also CA 165; DLB 60

Duclos, Charles Pinot 1704-1772   **LC 1**

Dudek, Louis 1918-   **CLC 11, 19**
See also CA 45-48; CAAS 14; CANR 1; DLB
88

Duerrenmatt, Friedrich 1921-1990CLC **1, 4,
8, 11, 15, 43, 102; DAM DRAM**
See also CA 17-20R; CANR 33; DLB 69, 124;
MTCW 1

Duffy, Bruce (?)-   **CLC 50**

Duffy, Maureen 1933-   **CLC 37**
See also CA 25-28R; CANR 33, 68; DLB 14;
MTCW 1

Dugan, Alan 1923-   **CLC 2, 6**
See also CA 81-84; DLB 5

du Gard, Roger Martin
See Martin du Gard, Roger

Duhamel, Georges 1884-1966   **CLC 8**
See also CA 81-84; 25-28R; CANR 35; DLB
65; MTCW 1

Dujardin, Edouard (Emile Louis) 1861-1949
TCLC 13
See also CA 109; DLB 123

Dulles, John Foster 1888-1959   **TCLC 72**
See also CA 115; 149

Dumas, Alexandre (pere)
See Dumas, Alexandre (Davy de la Pailleterie)

Dumas, Alexandre (Davy de la Pailleterie)
1802-1870   **NCLC 11; DA; DAB; DAC;
DAM MST, NOV; WLC**
See also DLB 119, 192; SATA 18

Dumas, Alexandre (fils) 1824-1895NCLC **71;
DC 1**
See also AAYA 22; DLB 192

Dumas, Claudine
See Malzberg, Barry N(athaniel)

Dumas, Henry L. 1934-1968   **CLC 6, 62**
See also BW 1; CA 85-88; DLB 41

du Maurier, Daphne 1907-1989CLC **6, 11, 59;
DAB; DAC; DAM MST, POP; SSC 18**

See also CA 5-8R; 128; CANR 6, 55; DLB 191;
MTCW 1; SATA 27; SATA-Obit 60

Dunbar, Paul Laurence 1872-1906   **TCLC 2,
12; BLC 1; DA; DAC; DAM MST, MULT,
POET; PC 5; SSC 8; WLC**
See also BW 1; CA 104; 124; CDALB 1865-
1917; DLB 50, 54, 78; SATA 34

Dunbar, William 1460(?)-1530(?)   **LC 20**
See also DLB 132, 146

Duncan, Dora Angela
See Duncan, Isadora

Duncan, Isadora 1877(?)-1927   **TCLC 68**
See also CA 118; 149

Duncan, Lois 1934-   **CLC 26**
See also AAYA 4; CA 1-4R; CANR 2, 23, 36;
CLR 29; JRDA; MAICYA; SAAS 2; SATA
1, 36, 75

Duncan, Robert (Edward) 1919-1988CLC **1,
2, 4, 7, 15, 41, 55; DAM POET; PC 2**
See also CA 9-12R; 124; CANR 28, 62; DLB
5, 16, 193; MTCW 1

Duncan, Sara Jeannette 1861-1922TCLC **60**
See also CA 157; DLB 92

Dunlap, William 1766-1839   **NCLC 2**
See also DLB 30, 37, 59

Dunn, Douglas (Eaglesham) 1942- CLC **6, 40**
See also CA 45-48; CANR 2, 33; DLB 40;
MTCW 1

Dunn, Katherine (Karen) 1945-   **CLC 71**
See also CA 33-36R; CANR 72

Dunn, Stephen 1939-   **CLC 36**
See also CA 33-36R; CANR 12, 48, 53; DLB
105

Dunne, Finley Peter 1867-1936   **TCLC 28**
See also CA 108; DLB 11, 23

Dunne, John Gregory 1932-   **CLC 28**
See also CA 25-28R; CANR 14, 50; DLBY 80

Dunsany, Edward John Moreton Drax Plunkett
1878-1957
See Dunsany, Lord
See also CA 104; 148; DLB 10

Dunsany, Lord   **TCLC 2, 59**
See also Dunsany, Edward John Moreton Drax
Plunkett
See also DLB 77, 153, 156

du Perry, Jean
See Simenon, Georges (Jacques Christian)

Durang, Christopher (Ferdinand) 1949-CLC
27, 38
See also CA 105; CANR 50

Duras, Marguerite 1914-1996CLC **3, 6, 11, 20,
34, 40, 68, 100**
See also CA 25-28R; 151; CANR 50; DLB 83;
MTCW 1

Durban, (Rosa) Pam 1947-   **CLC 39**
See also CA 123

Durcan, Paul 1944-CLC **43, 70; DAM POET**
See also CA 134

Durkheim, Emile 1858-1917   **TCLC 55**

Durrell, Lawrence (George) 1912-1990   **C L C
1, 4, 6, 8, 13, 27, 41; DAM NOV**
See also CA 9-12R; 132; CANR 40; CDBLB
1945-1960; DLB 15, 27, 204; DLBY 90;
MTCW 1

Durrenmatt, Friedrich
See Duerrenmatt, Friedrich

Dutt, Toru 1856-1877   **NCLC 29**

Dwight, Timothy 1752-1817   **NCLC 13**
See also DLB 37

Dworkin, Andrea 1946-   **CLC 43**
See also CA 77-80; CAAS 21; CANR 16, 39;
INT CANR-16; MTCW 1

Dwyer, Deanna

See Hubbard, L(afayette) Ron(ald)
Eluard, Paul   **TCLC 7, 41**
    See also Grindel, Eugene
Elyot, Sir Thomas 1490(?)-1546   **LC 11**
Elytis, Odysseus 1911-1996 **CLC 15, 49, 100;**
    DAM POET; PC 21
    See also CA 102; 151; MTCW 1
Emecheta, (Florence Onye) Buchi 1944-**C L C**
    14, 48; BLC 2; DAM MULT
    See also BW 2; CA 81-84; CANR 27; DLB 117;
    MTCW 1; SATA 66
Emerson, Mary Moody 1774-1863 **NCLC 66**
Emerson, Ralph Waldo 1803-1882 **NCLC 1,**
    38; DA; DAB; DAC; DAM MST, POET;
    PC 18; WLC
    See also CDALB 1640-1865; DLB 1, 59, 73
Eminescu, Mihail 1850-1889   **NCLC 33**
Empson, William 1906-1984**CLC 3, 8, 19, 33,**
    34
    See also CA 17-20R; 112; CANR 31, 61; DLB
    20; MTCW 1
Enchi, Fumiko (Ueda) 1905-1986   **CLC 31**
    See also CA 129; 121
Ende, Michael (Andreas Helmuth) 1929-1995
    CLC 31
    See also CA 118; 124; 149; CANR 36; CLR
    14; DLB 75; MAICYA; SATA 61; SATA-
    Brief 42; SATA-Obit 86
Endo, Shusaku 1923-1996 **CLC 7, 14, 19, 54,**
    99; DAM NOV
    See also CA 29-32R; 153; CANR 21, 54; DLB
    182; MTCW 1
Engel, Marian 1933-1985   **CLC 36**
    See also CA 25-28R; CANR 12; DLB 53; INT
    CANR-12
Engelhardt, Frederick
    See Hubbard, L(afayette) Ron(ald)
Enright, D(ennis) J(oseph) 1920-**CLC 4, 8, 31**
    See also CA 1-4R; CANR 1, 42; DLB 27; SATA
    25
Enzensberger, Hans Magnus 1929-   **CLC 43**
    See also CA 116; 119
Ephron, Nora 1941-   **CLC 17, 31**
    See also AITN 2; CA 65-68; CANR 12, 39
Epicurus 341B.C.-270B.C.   **CMLC 21**
    See also DLB 176
Epsilon
    See Betjeman, John
Epstein, Daniel Mark 1948-   **CLC 7**
    See also CA 49-52; CANR 2, 53
Epstein, Jacob 1956-   **CLC 19**
    See also CA 114
Epstein, Joseph 1937-   **CLC 39**
    See also CA 112; 119; CANR 50, 65
Epstein, Leslie 1938-   **CLC 27**
    See also CA 73-76; CAAS 12; CANR 23, 69
Equiano, Olaudah 1745(?)-1797 **LC 16; BLC**
    2; DAM MULT
    See also DLB 37, 50
ER   **TCLC 33**
    See also CA 160; DLB 85
Erasmus, Desiderius 1469(?)-1536   **LC 16**
Erdman, Paul E(mil) 1932-   **CLC 25**
    See also AITN 1; CA 61-64; CANR 13, 43
Erdrich, Louise 1954-   **CLC 39, 54; DAM**
    MULT, NOV, POP
    See also AAYA 10; BEST 89:1; CA 114; CANR
    41, 62; DLB 152, 175, 206; MTCW 1;
    NNAL; SATA 94
Erenburg, Ilya (Grigoryevich)
    See Ehrenburg, Ilya (Grigoryevich)
Erickson, Stephen Michael 1950-
    See Erickson, Steve

See also CA 129
Erickson, Steve 1950-   **CLC 64**
    See also Erickson, Stephen Michael
    See also CANR 60, 68
Ericson, Walter
    See Fast, Howard (Melvin)
Eriksson, Buntel
    See Bergman, (Ernst) Ingmar
Ernaux, Annie 1940-   **CLC 88**
    See also CA 147
Erskine, John 1879-1951   **TCLC 84**
    See also CA 112; 159; DLB 9, 102
Eschenbach, Wolfram von
    See Wolfram von Eschenbach
Eseki, Bruno
    See Mphahlele, Ezekiel
Esenin, Sergei (Alexandrovich) 1895-1925
    TCLC 4
    See also CA 104
Eshleman, Clayton 1935-   **CLC 7**
    See also CA 33-36R; CAAS 6; DLB 5
Espriella, Don Manuel Alvarez
    See Southey, Robert
Espriu, Salvador 1913-1985   **CLC 9**
    See also CA 154; 115; DLB 134
Espronceda, Jose de 1808-1842   **NCLC 39**
Esse, James
    See Stephens, James
Esterbrook, Tom
    See Hubbard, L(afayette) Ron(ald)
Estleman, Loren D. 1952-**CLC 48; DAM NOV,**
    POP
    See also AAYA 27; CA 85-88; CANR 27, 74;
    INT CANR-27; MTCW 1
Euclid 306B.C.-283B.C.   **CMLC 25**
Eugenides, Jeffrey 1960(?)-   **CLC 81**
    See also CA 144
Euripides c. 485B.C.-406B.C.**CMLC 23; DA;**
    DAB; DAC; DAM DRAM, MST; DC 4;
    WLCS
    See also DLB 176
Evan, Evin
    See Faust, Frederick (Schiller)
Evans, Caradoc 1878-1945   **TCLC 85**
Evans, Evan
    See Faust, Frederick (Schiller)
Evans, Marian
    See Eliot, George
Evans, Mary Ann
    See Eliot, George
Evarts, Esther
    See Benson, Sally
Everett, Percival L. 1956-   **CLC 57**
    See also BW 2; CA 129
Everson, R(onald) G(ilmour) 1903- **CLC 27**
    See also CA 17-20R; DLB 88
Everson, William (Oliver) 1912-1994 **CLC 1,**
    5, 14
    See also CA 9-12R; 145; CANR 20; DLB 5,
    16; MTCW 1
Evtushenko, Evgenii Aleksandrovich
    See Yevtushenko, Yevgeny (Alexandrovich)
Ewart, Gavin (Buchanan) 1916-1995**CLC 13,**
    46
    See also CA 89-92; 150; CANR 17, 46; DLB
    40; MTCW 1
Ewers, Hanns Heinz 1871-1943   **TCLC 12**
    See also CA 109; 149
Ewing, Frederick R.
    See Sturgeon, Theodore (Hamilton)
Exley, Frederick (Earl) 1929-1992 **CLC 6, 11**
    See also AITN 2; CA 81-84; 138; DLB 143;
    DLBY 81

Eynhardt, Guillermo
    See Quiroga, Horacio (Sylvestre)
Ezekiel, Nissim 1924-   **CLC 61**
    See also CA 61-64
Ezekiel, Tish O'Dowd 1943-   **CLC 34**
    See also CA 129
Fadeyev, A.
    See Bulgya, Alexander Alexandrovich
Fadeyev, Alexander   **TCLC 53**
    See also Bulgya, Alexander Alexandrovich
Fagen, Donald 1948-   **CLC 26**
Fainzilberg, Ilya Arnoldovich 1897-1937
    See Ilf, Ilya
    See also CA 120; 165
Fair, Ronald L. 1932-   **CLC 18**
    See also BW 1; CA 69-72; CANR 25; DLB 33
Fairbairn, Roger
    See Carr, John Dickson
Fairbairns, Zoe (Ann) 1948-   **CLC 32**
    See also CA 103; CANR 21
Falco, Gian
    See Papini, Giovanni
Falconer, James
    See Kirkup, James
Falconer, Kenneth
    See Kornbluth, C(yril) M.
Falkland, Samuel
    See Heijermans, Herman
Fallaci, Oriana 1930-   **CLC 11, 110**
    See also CA 77-80; CANR 15, 58; MTCW 1
Faludy, George 1913-   **CLC 42**
    See also CA 21-24R
Faludy, Gyoergy
    See Faludy, George
Fanon, Frantz 1925-1961   **CLC 74; BLC 2;**
    DAM MULT
    See also BW 1; CA 116; 89-92
Fanshawe, Ann 1625-1680   **LC 11**
Fante, John (Thomas) 1911-1983   **CLC 60**
    See also CA 69-72; 109; CANR 23; DLB 130;
    DLBY 83
Farah, Nuruddin 1945 **CLC 53; BLC 2; DAM**
    MULT
    See also BW 2; CA 106; DLB 125
Fargue, Leon-Paul 1876(?)-1947   **TCLC 11**
    See also CA 109
Farigoule, Louis
    See Romains, Jules
Farina, Richard 1936(?)-1966   **CLC 9**
    See also CA 81-84; 25-28R
Farley, Walter (Lorimer) 1915-1989 **CLC 17**
    See also CA 17-20R; CANR 8, 29; DLB 22;
    JRDA; MAICYA; SATA 2, 43
Farmer, Philip Jose 1918-   **CLC 1, 19**
    See also CA 1-4R; CANR 4, 35; DLB 8; MTCW
    1; SATA 93
Farquhar, George 1677-1707   **LC 21; DAM**
    DRAM
    See also DLB 84
Farrell, J(ames) G(ordon) 1935-1979 **CLC 6**
    See also CA 73-76; 89-92; CANR 36; DLB 14;
    MTCW 1
Farrell, James T(homas) 1904-1979**CLC 1, 4,**
    8, 11, 66; SSC 28
    See also CA 5-8R; 89-92; CANR 9, 61; DLB 4,
    9, 86; DLBD 2; MTCW 1
Farren, Richard J.
    See Betjeman, John
Farren, Richard M.
    See Betjeman, John
Fassbinder, Rainer Werner 1946-1982**CLC 20**
    See also CA 93-96; 106; CANR 31
Fast, Howard (Melvin) 1914- **CLC 23; DAM**

See Goebbels, (Paul) Joseph

Goethe, Johann Wolfgang von 1749-1832
**NCLC 4, 22, 34; DA; DAB; DAC; DAM
DRAM, MST, POET; PC 5; WLC**
See also DLB 94

Gogarty, Oliver St. John 1878-1957**TCLC 15**
See also CA 109; 150; DLB 15, 19

Gogol, Nikolai (Vasilyevich) 1809-1852**NCLC
5, 15, 31; DA; DAB; DAC; DAM DRAM,
MST; DC 1; SSC 4, 29; WLC**
See also DLB 198

Goines, Donald 1937(?)-1974**CLC 80; BLC 2;
DAM MULT, POP**
See also AITN 1; BW 1; CA 124; 114; DLB 33

Gold, Herbert 1924-   **CLC 4, 7, 14, 42**
See also CA 9-12R; CANR 17, 45; DLB 2;
DLBY 81

Goldbarth, Albert 1948-   **CLC 5, 38**
See also CA 53-56; CANR 6, 40; DLB 120

Goldberg, Anatol 1910-1982   **CLC 34**
See also CA 131; 117

Goldemberg, Isaac 1945-   **CLC 52**
See also CA 69-72; CAAS 12; CANR 11, 32;
HW

Golding, William (Gerald) 1911-1993**CLC 1,
2, 3, 8, 10, 17, 27, 58, 81; DA; DAB; DAC;
DAM MST, NOV; WLC**
See also AAYA 5; CA 5-8R; 141; CANR 13,
33, 54; CDBLB 1945-1960; DLB 15, 100;
MTCW 1

Goldman, Emma 1869-1940   **TCLC 13**
See also CA 110; 150

Goldman, Francisco 1954-   **CLC 76**
See also CA 162

Goldman, William (W.) 1931-   **CLC 1, 48**
See also CA 9-12R; CANR 29, 69; DLB 44

Goldmann, Lucien 1913-1970   **CLC 24**
See also CA 25-28; CAP 2

Goldoni, Carlo 1707-1793**LC 4; DAM DRAM**

Goldsberry, Steven 1949-   **CLC 34**
See also CA 131

Goldsmith, Oliver 1728-1774   **LC 2, 48; DA;
DAB; DAC; DAM DRAM, MST, NOV,
POET; DC 8; WLC**
See also CDBLB 1660-1789; DLB 39, 89, 104,
109, 142; SATA 26

Goldsmith, Peter
See Priestley, J(ohn) B(oynton)

Gombrowicz, Witold 1904-1969**CLC 4, 7, 11,
49; DAM DRAM**
See also CA 19-20; 25-28R; CAP 2

Gomez de la Serna, Ramon 1888-1963**CLC 9**
See also CA 153; 116; HW

Goncharov, Ivan Alexandrovich 1812-1891
NCLC 1, 63

Goncourt, Edmond (Louis Antoine Huot) de
1822-1896   **NCLC 7**
See also DLB 123

Goncourt, Jules (Alfred Huot) de 1830-1870
NCLC 7
See also DLB 123

Gontier, Fernande 19(?)-   **CLC 50**

Gonzalez Martinez, Enrique 1871-1952
TCLC 72
See also CA 166; HW

Goodman, Paul 1911-1972   **CLC 1, 2, 4, 7**
See also CA 19-20; 37-40R; CANR 34; CAP 2;
DLB 130; MTCW 1

Gordimer, Nadine 1923-**CLC 3, 5, 7, 10, 18, 33,
51, 70; DA; DAB; DAC; DAM MST, NOV;
SSC 17; WLCS**
See also CA 5-8R; CANR 3, 28, 56; INT CANR-
28; MTCW 1

Gordon, Adam Lindsay 1833-1870 **NCLC 21**

Gordon, Caroline 1895-1981**CLC 6, 13, 29, 83;
SSC 15**
See also CA 11-12; 103; CANR 36; CAP 1;
DLB 4, 9, 102; DLBD 17; DLBY 81; MTCW
1

Gordon, Charles William 1860-1937
See Connor, Ralph
See also CA 109

Gordon, Mary (Catherine) 1949- **CLC 13, 22**
See also CA 102; CANR 44; DLB 6; DLBY
81; INT 102; MTCW 1

Gordon, N. J.
See Bosman, Herman Charles

Gordon, Sol 1923-   **CLC 26**
See also CA 53-56; CANR 4; SATA 11

Gordone, Charles 1925-1995**CLC 1, 4; DAM
DRAM; DC 8**
See also BW 1; CA 93-96; 150; CANR 55; DLB
7; INT 93-96; MTCW 1

Gore, Catherine 1800-1861   **NCLC 65**
See also DLB 116

Gorenko, Anna Andreevna
See Akhmatova, Anna

Gorky, Maxim 1868-1936**TCLC 8; DAB; SSC
28; WLC**
See also Peshkov, Alexei Maximovich

Goryan, Sirak
See Saroyan, William

Gosse, Edmund (William) 1849-1928**TCLC 28**
See also CA 117; DLB 57, 144, 184

Gotlieb, Phyllis Fay (Bloom) 1926-   **CLC 18**
See also CA 13-16R; CANR 7; DLB 88

Gottesman, S. D.
See Kornbluth, C(yril) M.; Pohl, Frederik

Gottfried von Strassburg fl. c. 1210-   **CMLC
10**
See also DLB 138

Gould, Lois   **CLC 4, 10**
See also CA 77-80; CANR 29; MTCW 1

Gourmont, Remy (-Marie-Charles) de 1858-
1915   **TCLC 17**
See also CA 109; 150

Govier, Katherine 1948-   **CLC 51**
See also CA 101; CANR 18, 40

Goyen, (Charles) William 1915-1983**CLC 5, 8,
14, 40**
See also AITN 2; CA 5-8R; 110; CANR 6, 71;
DLB 2; DLBY 83; INT CANR-6

Goytisolo, Juan 1931-   **CLC 5, 10, 23; DAM
MULT; HLC**
See also CA 85-88; CANR 32, 61; HW; MTCW
1

Gozzano, Guido 1883-1916   **PC 10**
See also CA 154; DLB 114

Gozzi, (Conte) Carlo 1720-1806   **NCLC 23**

Grabbe, Christian Dietrich 1801-1836**NCLC
2**
See also DLB 133

Grace, Patricia 1937-   **CLC 56**

Gracian y Morales, Baltasar 1601-1658**LC 15**

Gracq, Julien   **CLC 11, 48**
See also Poirier, Louis
See also DLB 83

Grade, Chaim 1910-1982   **CLC 10**
See also CA 93-96; 107

Graduate of Oxford, A
See Ruskin, John

Grafton, Garth
See Duncan, Sara Jeannette

Graham, John
See Phillips, David Graham

Graham, Jorie 1951-   **CLC 48**

See also CA 111; CANR 63; DLB 120

Graham, R(obert) B(ontine) Cunninghame
See Cunninghame Graham, R(obert) B(ontine)
See also DLB 98, 135, 174

Graham, Robert
See Haldeman, Joe (William)

Graham, Tom
See Lewis, (Harry) Sinclair

Graham, W(illiam) S(ydney) 1918-1986 **C L C
29**
See also CA 73-76; 118; DLB 20

Graham, Winston (Mawdsley) 1910- **CLC 23**
See also CA 49-52; CANR 2, 22, 45, 66; DLB
77

Grahame, Kenneth 1859-1932**TCLC 64; DAB**
See also CA 108; 136; CLR 5; DLB 34, 141,
178; MAICYA; SATA 100; YABC 1

Granovsky, Timofei Nikolaevich 1813-1855
NCLC 75
See also DLB 198

Grant, Skeeter
See Spiegelman, Art

Granville-Barker, Harley 1877-1946**TCLC 2;
DAM DRAM**
See also Barker, Harley Granville
See also CA 104

Grass, Guenter (Wilhelm) 1927-**CLC 1, 2, 4, 6,
11, 15, 22, 32, 49, 88; DA; DAB; DAC;
DAM MST, NOV; WLC**
See also CA 13-16R; CANR 20, 75; DLB 75,
124; MTCW 1

Gratton, Thomas
See Hulme, T(homas) E(rnest)

Grau, Shirley Ann 1929-   **CLC 4, 9; SSC 15**
See also CA 89-92; CANR 22, 69; DLB 2; INT
CANR-22; MTCW 1

Gravel, Fern
See Hall, James Norman

Graver, Elizabeth 1964-   **CLC 70**
See also CA 135; CANR 71

Graves, Richard Perceval 1945-   **CLC 44**
See also CA 65-68; CANR 9, 26, 51

Graves, Robert (von Ranke) 1895-1985 **C L C
1, 2, 6, 11, 39, 44, 45; DAB; DAC; DAM
MST, POET; PC 6**
See also CA 5-8R; 117; CANR 5, 36; CDBLB
1914-1945; DLB 20, 100, 191; DLBD 18;
DLBY 85; MTCW 1; SATA 45

Graves, Valerie
See Bradley, Marion Zimmer

Gray, Alasdair (James) 1934-   **CLC 41**
See also CA 126; CANR 47, 69; DLB 194; INT
126; MTCW 1

Gray, Amlin 1946-   **CLC 29**
See also CA 138

Gray, Francine du Plessix 1930-   **CLC 22;
DAM NOV**
See also BEST 90:3; CA 61-64; CAAS 2;
CANR 11, 33, 75; INT CANR-11; MTCW 1

Gray, John (Henry) 1866-1934   **TCLC 19**
See also CA 119; 162

Gray, Simon (James Holliday) 1936- **CLC 9,
14, 36**
See also AITN 1; CA 21-24R; CAAS 3; CANR
32, 69; DLB 13; MTCW 1

Gray, Spalding 1941-**CLC 49, 112; DAM POP;
DC 7**
See also CA 128; CANR 74

Gray, Thomas 1716-1771**LC 4, 40; DA; DAB;
DAC; DAM MST; PC 2; WLC**
See also CDBLB 1660-1789; DLB 109

Grayson, David
See Baker, Ray Stannard

Grayson, Richard (A.) 1951-   **CLC 38**
See also CA 85-88; CANR 14, 31, 57
Greeley, Andrew M(oran) 1928-   **CLC 28;**
DAM POP
See also CA 5-8R; CAAS 7; CANR 7, 43, 69;
MTCW 1
Green, Anna Katharine 1846-1935 **TCLC 63**
See also CA 112; 159; DLB 202
Green, Brian
See Card, Orson Scott
Green, Hannah
See Greenberg, Joanne (Goldenberg)
Green, Hannah 1927(?)-1996   **CLC 3**
See also CA 73-76; CANR 59
Green, Henry 1905-1973   **CLC 2, 13, 97**
See also Yorke, Henry Vincent
See also DLB 15
Green, Julian (Hartridge) 1900-1998
See Green, Julien
See also CA 21-24R; 169; CANR 33; DLB 4,
72; MTCW 1
Green, Julien   **CLC 3, 11, 77**
See also Green, Julian (Hartridge)
Green, Paul (Eliot) 1894-1981 **CLC 25; DAM**
DRAM
See also AITN 1; CA 5-8R; 103; CANR 3; DLB
7, 9; DLBY 81
Greenberg, Ivan 1908-1973
See Rahv, Philip
See also CA 85-88
Greenberg, Joanne (Goldenberg) 1932- **C L C**
7, 30
See also AAYA 12; CA 5-8R; CANR 14, 32,
69; SATA 25
Greenberg, Richard 1959(?)-   **CLC 57**
See also CA 138
Greene, Bette 1934-   **CLC 30**
See also AAYA 7; CA 53-56; CANR 4; CLR 2;
JRDA; MAICYA; SAAS 16; SATA 8, 102
Greene, Gael   **CLC 8**
See also CA 13-16R; CANR 10
Greene, Graham (Henry) 1904-1991 **CLC 1, 3,**
6, 9, 14, 18, 27, 37, 70, 72; DA; DAB; DAC;
DAM MST, NOV; SSC 29; WLC
See also AITN 2; CA 13-16R; 133; CANR 35,
61; CDBLB 1945-1960; DLB 13, 15, 77,
100, 162, 201, 204; DLBY 91; MTCW 1;
SATA 20
Greene, Robert 1558-1592   **LC 41**
See also DLB 62, 167
Greer, Richard
See Silverberg, Robert
Gregor, Arthur 1923-   **CLC 9**
See also CA 25-28R; CAAS 10; CANR 11;
SATA 36
Gregor, Lee
See Pohl, Frederik
Gregory, Isabella Augusta (Persse) 1852-1932
TCLC 1
See also CA 104; DLB 10
Gregory, J. Dennis
See Williams, John A(lfred)
Grendon, Stephen
See Derleth, August (William)
Grenville, Kate 1950-   **CLC 61**
See also CA 118; CANR 53
Grenville, Pelham
See Wodehouse, P(elham) G(renville)
Greve, Felix Paul (Berthold Friedrich) 1879-
1948
See Grove, Frederick Philip
See also CA 104; 141; DAC; DAM MST
Grey, Zane 1872-1939   **TCLC 6; DAM POP**

See also CA 104; 132; DLB 9; MTCW 1
Grieg, (Johan) Nordahl (Brun) 1902-1943
TCLC 10
See also CA 107
Grieve, C(hristopher) M(urray) 1892-1978
CLC 11, 19; DAM POET
See also MacDiarmid, Hugh; Pteleon
See also CA 5-8R; 85-88; CANR 33; MTCW 1
Griffin, Gerald 1803-1840   **NCLC 7**
See also DLB 159
Griffin, John Howard 1920-1980   **CLC 68**
See also AITN 1; CA 1-4R; 101; CANR 2
Griffin, Peter 1942-   **CLC 39**
See also CA 136
Griffith, D(avid Lewelyn) W(ark) 1875(?)-1948
TCLC 68
See also CA 119; 150
Griffith, Lawrence
See Griffith, D(avid Lewelyn) W(ark)
Griffiths, Trevor 1935-   **CLC 13, 52**
See also CA 97-100; CANR 45; DLB 13
Griggs, Sutton Elbert 1872-1930(?) **TCLC 77**
See also CA 123; DLB 50
Grigson, Geoffrey (Edward Harvey) 1905-1985
CLC 7, 39
See also CA 25-28R; 118; CANR 20, 33; DLB
27; MTCW 1
Grillparzer, Franz 1791-1872   **NCLC 1**
See also DLB 133
Grimble, Reverend Charles James
See Eliot, T(homas) S(tearns)
Grimke, Charlotte L(ottie) Forten 1837(?)-1914
See Forten, Charlotte L.
See also BW 1; CA 117; 124; DAM MULT,
POET
Grimm, Jacob Ludwig Karl 1785-1863 **NCLC**
3
See also DLB 90; MAICYA; SATA 22
Grimm, Wilhelm Karl 1786-1859   **NCLC 3**
See also DLB 90; MAICYA; SATA 22
Grimmelshausen, Johann Jakob Christoffel von
1621-1676   **LC 6**
See also DLB 168
Grindel, Eugene 1895-1952
See Eluard, Paul
See also CA 104
Grisham, John 1955-   **CLC 84; DAM POP**
See also AAYA 14; CA 138; CANR 47, 69
Grossman, David 1954-   **CLC 67**
See also CA 138
Grossman, Vasily (Semenovich) 1905-1964
CLC 41
See also CA 124; 130; MTCW 1
Grove, Frederick Philip   **TCLC 4**
See also Greve, Felix Paul (Berthold Friedrich)
See also DLB 92
Grubb
See Crumb, R(obert)
Grumbach, Doris (Isaac) 1918- **CLC 13, 22, 64**
See also CA 5-8R; CAAS 2; CANR 9, 42, 70;
INT CANR-9
Grundtvig, Nicolai Frederik Severin 1783-1872
NCLC 1
Grunge
See Crumb, R(obert)
Grunwald, Lisa 1959-   **CLC 44**
See also CA 120
Guare, John 1938-   **CLC 8, 14, 29, 67; DAM**
DRAM
See also CA 73-76; CANR 21, 69; DLB 7;
MTCW 1
Gudjonsson, Halldor Kiljan 1902-1998
See Laxness, Halldor

See also CA 103; 164
Guenter, Erich
See Eich, Guenter
Guest, Barbara 1920-   **CLC 34**
See also CA 25-28R; CANR 11, 44; DLB 5,
193
Guest, Judith (Ann) 1936- **CLC 8, 30; DAM**
NOV, POP
See also AAYA 7; CA 77-80; CANR 15, 75;
INT CANR-15; MTCW 1
Guevara, Che   **CLC 87; HLC**
See also Guevara (Serna), Ernesto
Guevara (Serna), Ernesto 1928-1967
See Guevara, Che
See also CA 127; 111; CANR 56; DAM MULT;
HW
Guild, Nicholas M. 1944-   **CLC 33**
See also CA 93-96
Guillemin, Jacques
See Sartre, Jean-Paul
Guillen, Jorge 1893-1984   **CLC 11; DAM**
MULT, POET
See also CA 89-92; 112; DLB 108; HW
Guillen, Nicolas (Cristobal) 1902-1989 **C L C**
48, 79; BLC 2; DAM MST, MULT, POET;
HLC; PC 23
See also BW 2; CA 116; 125; 129; HW
Guillevic, (Eugene) 1907-   **CLC 33**
See also CA 93-96
Guillois
See Desnos, Robert
Guillois, Valentin
See Desnos, Robert
Guiney, Louise Imogen 1861-1920 **TCLC 41**
See also CA 160; DLB 54
Guiraldes, Ricardo (Guillermo) 1886-1927
TCLC 39
See also CA 131; HW; MTCW 1
Gumilev, Nikolai (Stepanovich) 1886-1921
TCLC 60
See also CA 165
Gunesekera, Romesh 1954-   **CLC 91**
See also CA 159
Gunn, Bill   **CLC 5**
See also Gunn, William Harrison
See also DLB 38
Gunn, Thom(son William) 1929- **CLC 3, 6, 18,**
32, 81; DAM POET
See also CA 17-20R; CANR 9, 33; CDBLB
1960 to Present; DLB 27; INT CANR-33;
MTCW 1
Gunn, William Harrison 1934(?)-1989
See Gunn, Bill
See also AITN 1; BW 1; CA 13-16R; 128;
CANR 12, 25
Gunnars, Kristjana 1948-   **CLC 69**
See also CA 113; DLB 60
Gurdjieff, G(eorgei) I(vanovich) 1877(?)-1949
TCLC 71
See also CA 157
Gurganus, Allan 1947-   **CLC 70; DAM POP**
See also BEST 90:1; CA 135
Gurney, A(lbert) R(amsdell), Jr. 1930- **C L C**
32, 50, 54; DAM DRAM
See also CA 77-80; CANR 32, 64
Gurney, Ivor (Bertie) 1890-1937   **TCLC 33**
See also CA 167
Gurney, Peter
See Gurney, A(lbert) R(amsdell), Jr.
Guro, Elena 1877-1913   **TCLC 56**
Gustafson, James M(oody) 1925-   **CLC 100**
See also CA 25-28R; CANR 37
Gustafson, Ralph (Barker) 1909-   **CLC 36**

See also CA 21-24R; CANR 8, 45; DLB 88

Gut, Gom
See Simenon, Georges (Jacques Christian)

Guterson, David 1956-   **CLC 91**
See also CA 132; CANR 73

Guthrie, A(lfred) B(ertram), Jr. 1901-1991
     CLC 23
See also CA 57-60; 134; CANR 24; DLB 6;
     SATA 62; SATA-Obit 67

Guthrie, Isobel
See Grieve, C(hristopher) M(urray)

Guthrie, Woodrow Wilson 1912-1967
See Guthrie, Woody
See also CA 113; 93-96

Guthrie, Woody   **CLC 35**
See also Guthrie, Woodrow Wilson

Guy, Rosa (Cuthbert) 1928-   **CLC 26**
See also AAYA 4; BW 2; CA 17-20R; CANR
     14, 34; CLR 13; DLB 33; JRDA; MAICYA;
     SATA 14, 62

Gwendolyn
See Bennett, (Enoch) Arnold

H. D.   **CLC 3, 8, 14, 31, 34, 73; PC 5**
See also Doolittle, Hilda

H. de V.
See Buchan, John

Haavikko, Paavo Juhani 1931-   **CLC 18, 34**
See also CA 106

Habbema, Koos
See Heijermans, Herman

Habermas, Juergen 1929-   **CLC 104**
See also CA 109

Habermas, Jurgen
See Habermas, Juergen

Hacker, Marilyn 1942- **CLC 5, 9, 23, 72, 91;**
     DAM POET
See also CA 77-80; CANR 68; DLB 120

Haeckel, Ernst Heinrich (Philipp August) 1834-
     1919   **TCLC 83**
See also CA 157

Haggard, H(enry) Rider 1856-1925 **TCLC 11**
See also CA 108; 148; DLB 70, 156, 174, 178;
     SATA 16

Hagiosy, L.
See Larbaud, Valery (Nicolas)

Hagiwara Sakutaro 1886-1942 **TCLC 60; PC**
18

Haig, Fenil
See Ford, Ford Madox

Haig-Brown, Roderick (Langmere) 1908-1976
     CLC 21
See also CA 5-8R; 69-72; CANR 4, 38; CLR
     31; DLB 88; MAICYA; SATA 12

Hailey, Arthur 1920-**CLC 5; DAM NOV, POP**
See also AITN 2; BEST 90:3; CA 1-4R; CANR
     2, 36, 75; DLB 88; DLBY 82; MTCW 1

Hailey, Elizabeth Forsythe 1938-   **CLC 40**
See also CA 93-96; CAAS 1; CANR 15, 48;
     INT CANR-15

Haines, John (Meade) 1924-   **CLC 58**
See also CA 17-20R; CANR 13, 34; DLB 5

Hakluyt, Richard 1552-1616   **LC 31**

Haldeman, Joe (William) 1943-   **CLC 61**
See also CA 53-56; CAAS 25; CANR 6, 70,
     72; DLB 8; INT CANR-6

Hale, Sarah Josepha (Buell) 1788-1879**NCLC**
75
See also DLB 1, 42, 73

Haley, Alex(ander Murray Palmer) 1921-1992
     CLC 8, 12, 76; BLC 2; DA; DAB; DAC;
     DAM MST, MULT, POP
See also AAYA 26; BW 2; CA 77-80; 136;
     CANR 61; DLB 38; MTCW 1

Haliburton, Thomas Chandler 1796-1865
     NCLC 15
See also DLB 11, 99

Hall, Donald (Andrew, Jr.) 1928- **CLC 1, 13,**
     37, 59; DAM POET
See also CA 5-8R; CAAS 7; CANR 2, 44, 64;
     DLB 5; SATA 23, 97

Hall, Frederic Sauser
See Sauser-Hall, Frederic

Hall, James
See Kuttner, Henry

Hall, James Norman 1887-1951   **TCLC 23**
See also CA 123; SATA 21

Hall, Radclyffe
See Hall, (Marguerite) Radclyffe

Hall, (Marguerite) Radclyffe 1886-1943
     TCLC 12
See also CA 110; 150; DLB 191

Hall, Rodney 1935-   **CLC 51**
See also CA 109; CANR 69

Halleck, Fitz-Greene 1790-1867   **NCLC 47**
See also DLB 3

Halliday, Michael
See Creasey, John

Halpern, Daniel 1945-   **CLC 14**
See also CA 33-36R

Hamburger, Michael (Peter Leopold) 1924-
     CLC 5, 14
See also CA 5-8R; CAAS 4; CANR 2, 47; DLB
     27

Hamill, Pete 1935-   **CLC 10**
See also CA 25-28R; CANR 18, 71

Hamilton, Alexander 1755(?)-1804 **NCLC 49**
See also DLB 37

Hamilton, Clive
See Lewis, C(live) S(taples)

Hamilton, Edmond 1904-1977   **CLC 1**
See also CA 1-4R; CANR 3; DLB 8

Hamilton, Eugene (Jacob) Lee
See Lee-Hamilton, Eugene (Jacob)

Hamilton, Franklin
See Silverberg, Robert

Hamilton, Gail
See Corcoran, Barbara

Hamilton, Mollie
See Kaye, M(ary) M(argaret)

Hamilton, (Anthony Walter) Patrick 1904-1962
     CLC 51
See also CA 113; DLB 10

Hamilton, Virginia 1936-   **CLC 26; DAM**
     MULT
See also AAYA 2, 21; BW 2; CA 25-28R;
     CANR 20, 37, 73; CLR 1, 11, 40; DLB 33,
     52; INT CANR-20; JRDA; MAICYA;
     MTCW 1; SATA 4, 56, 79

Hammett, (Samuel) Dashiell 1894-1961 **C L C**
     3, 5, 10, 19, 47; SSC 17
See also AITN 1; CA 81-84; CANR 42; CDALB
     1929-1941; DLBD 6; DLBY 96; MTCW 1

Hammon, Jupiter 1711(?)-1800(?)   **NCLC 5;**
     BLC 2; DAM MULT, POET; PC 16
See also DLB 31, 50

Hammond, Keith
See Kuttner, Henry

Hamner, Earl (Henry), Jr. 1923-   **CLC 12**
See also AITN 2; CA 73-76; DLB 6

Hampton, Christopher (James) 1946- **CLC 4**
See also CA 25-28R; DLB 13; MTCW 1

Hamsun, Knut   **TCLC 2, 14, 49**
See also Pedersen, Knut

Handke, Peter 1942-**CLC 5, 8, 10, 15, 38; DAM**
     DRAM, NOV
See also CA 77-80; CANR 33, 75; DLB 85, 124;

MTCW 1

Hanley, James 1901-1985   **CLC 3, 5, 8, 13**
See also CA 73-76; 117; CANR 36; DLB 191;
     MTCW 1

Hannah, Barry 1942-   **CLC 23, 38, 90**
See also CA 108; 110; CANR 43, 68; DLB 6;
     INT 110; MTCW 1

Hannon, Ezra
See Hunter, Evan

Hansberry, Lorraine (Vivian) 1930-1965**CLC**
     17, 62; BLC 2; DA; DAB; DAC; DAM
     DRAM, MST, MULT; DC 2
See also AAYA 25; BW 1; CA 109; 25-28R;
     CABS 3; CANR 58; CDALB 1941-1968;
     DLB 7, 38; MTCW 1

Hansen, Joseph 1923-   **CLC 38**
See also CA 29-32R; CAAS 17; CANR 16, 44,
     66; INT CANR-16

Hansen, Martin A(lfred) 1909-1955**TCLC 32**
See also CA 167

Hanson, Kenneth O(stlin) 1922-   **CLC 13**
See also CA 53-56; CANR 7

Hardwick, Elizabeth (Bruce) 1916- **CLC 13;**
     DAM NOV
See also CA 5-8R; CANR 3, 32, 70; DLB 6;
     MTCW 1

Hardy, Thomas 1840-1928**TCLC 4, 10, 18, 32,**
     48, 53, 72; DA; DAB; DAC; DAM MST,
     NOV, POET; PC 8; SSC 2; WLC
See also CA 104; 123; CDBLB 1890-1914;
     DLB 18, 19, 135; MTCW 1

Hare, David 1947-   **CLC 29, 58**
See also CA 97-100; CANR 39; DLB 13;
     MTCW 1

Harewood, John
See Van Druten, John (William)

Harford, Henry
See Hudson, W(illiam) H(enry)

Hargrave, Leonie
See Disch, Thomas M(ichael)

Harjo, Joy 1951-   **CLC 83; DAM MULT**
See also CA 114; CANR 35, 67; DLB 120, 175;
     NNAL

Harlan, Louis R(udolph) 1922-   **CLC 34**
See also CA 21-24R; CANR 25, 55

Harling, Robert 1951(?)-   **CLC 53**
See also CA 147

Harmon, William (Ruth) 1938-   **CLC 38**
See also CA 33-36R; CANR 14, 32, 35; SATA
     65

Harper, F. E. W.
See Harper, Frances Ellen Watkins

Harper, Frances E. W.
See Harper, Frances Ellen Watkins

Harper, Frances E. Watkins
See Harper, Frances Ellen Watkins

Harper, Frances Ellen
See Harper, Frances Ellen Watkins

Harper, Frances Ellen Watkins 1825-1911
     TCLC 14; BLC 2; DAM MULT, POET;
     PC 21
See also BW 1; CA 111; 125; DLB 50

Harper, Michael S(teven) 1938- **CLC 7, 22**
See also BW 1; CA 33-36R; CANR 24; DLB
     41

Harper, Mrs. F. E. W.
See Harper, Frances Ellen Watkins

Harris, Christie (Lucy) Irwin 1907- **CLC 12**
See also CA 5-8R; CANR 6; CLR 47; DLB 88;
     JRDA; MAICYA; SAAS 10; SATA 6, 74

Harris, Frank 1856-1931   **TCLC 24**
See also CA 109; 150; DLB 156, 197

Harris, George Washington 1814-1869**N C L C**

23
See also DLB 3, 11

Harris, Joel Chandler 1848-1908   **TCLC 2; SSC 19**
See also CA 104; 137; CLR 49; DLB 11, 23, 42, 78, 91; MAICYA; SATA 100; YABC 1

Harris, John (Wyndham Parkes Lucas) Beynon 1903-1969
See Wyndham, John
See also CA 102; 89-92

Harris, MacDonald   **CLC 9**
See also Heiney, Donald (William)

Harris, Mark 1922-   **CLC 19**
See also CA 5-8R; CAAS 3; CANR 2, 55; DLB 2; DLBY 80

Harris, (Theodore) Wilson 1921-   **CLC 25**
See also BW 2; CA 65-68; CAAS 16; CANR 11, 27, 69; DLB 117; MTCW 1

Harrison, Elizabeth Cavanna 1909-
See Cavanna, Betty
See also CA 9-12R; CANR 6, 27

Harrison, Harry (Max) 1925-   **CLC 42**
See also CA 1-4R; CANR 5, 21; DLB 8; SATA 4

Harrison, James (Thomas) 1937-   **CLC 6, 14, 33, 66; SSC 19**
See also CA 13-16R; CANR 8, 51; DLBY 82; INT CANR-8

Harrison, Jim
See Harrison, James (Thomas)

Harrison, Kathryn 1961-   **CLC 70**
See also CA 144; CANR 68

Harrison, Tony 1937-   **CLC 43**
See also CA 65-68; CANR 44; DLB 40; MTCW 1

Harriss, Will(ard Irvin) 1922-   **CLC 34**
See also CA 111

Harson, Sley
See Ellison, Harlan (Jay)

Hart, Ellis
See Ellison, Harlan (Jay)

Hart, Josephine 1942(?)-   **CLC 70; DAM POP**
See also CA 138; CANR 70

Hart, Moss 1904-1961   **CLC 66; DAM DRAM**
See also CA 109; 89-92; DLB 7

Harte, (Francis) Bret(t) 1836(?)-1902   **TCLC 1, 25; DA; DAC; DAM MST; SSC 8; WLC**
See also CA 104; 140; CDALB 1865-1917; DLB 12, 64, 74, 79, 186; SATA 26

Hartley, L(eslie) P(oles) 1895-1972   **CLC 2, 22**
See also CA 45-48; 37-40R; CANR 33; DLB 15, 139; MTCW 1

Hartman, Geoffrey H. 1929-   **CLC 27**
See also CA 117; 125; DLB 67

Hartmann, Sadakichi 1867-1944   **TCLC 73**
See also CA 157; DLB 54

Hartmann von Aue c. 1160-c. 1205   **CMLC 15**
See also DLB 138

Hartmann von Aue 1170-1210   **CMLC 15**

Haruf, Kent 1943-   **CLC 34**
See also CA 149

Harwood, Ronald 1934-   **CLC 32; DAM DRAM, MST**
See also CA 1-4R; CANR 4, 55; DLB 13

Hasegawa Tatsunosuke
See Futabatei, Shimei

Hasek, Jaroslav (Matej Frantisek) 1883-1923   **TCLC 4**
See also CA 104; 129; MTCW 1

Hass, Robert 1941-   **CLC 18, 39, 99; PC 16**
See also CA 111; CANR 30, 50, 71; DLB 105, 206; SATA 94

Hastings, Hudson

See Kuttner, Henry

Hastings, Selina   **CLC 44**

Hathorne, John 1641-1717   **LC 38**

Hatteras, Amelia
See Mencken, H(enry) L(ouis)

Hatteras, Owen   **TCLC 18**
See also Mencken, H(enry) L(ouis); Nathan, George Jean

Hauptmann, Gerhart (Johann Robert) 1862-1946   **TCLC 4; DAM DRAM**
See also CA 104; 153; DLB 66, 118

Havel, Vaclav 1936-   **CLC 25, 58, 65; DAM DRAM; DC 6**
See also CA 104; CANR 36, 63; MTCW 1

Haviaras, Stratis   **CLC 33**
See also Chaviaras, Strates

Hawes, Stephen 1475(?)-1523(?)   **LC 17**
See also DLB 132

Hawkes, John (Clendennin Burne, Jr.) 1925-1998   **CLC 1, 2, 3, 4, 7, 9, 14, 15, 27, 49**
See also CA 1-4R; 167; CANR 2, 47, 64; DLB 2, 7; DLBY 80; MTCW 1

Hawking, S. W.
See Hawking, Stephen W(illiam)

Hawking, Stephen W(illiam) 1942-   **CLC 63, 105**
See also AAYA 13; BEST 89:1; CA 126; 129; CANR 48

Hawkins, Anthony Hope
See Hope, Anthony

Hawthorne, Julian 1846-1934   **TCLC 25**
See also CA 165

Hawthorne, Nathaniel 1804-1864   **NCLC 39; DA; DAB; DAC; DAM MST, NOV; SSC 3, 29; WLC**
See also AAYA 18; CDALB 1640-1865; DLB 1, 74; YABC 2

Haxton, Josephine Ayres 1921-
See Douglas, Ellen
See also CA 115; CANR 41

Hayaseca y Eizaguirre, Jorge
See Echegaray (y Eizaguirre), Jose (Maria Waldo)

Hayashi, Fumiko 1904-1951   **TCLC 27**
See also CA 161; DLB 180

Haycraft, Anna
See Ellis, Alice Thomas
See also CA 122

Hayden, Robert E(arl) 1913-1980   **CLC 5, 9, 14, 37; BLC 2; DA; DAC; DAM MST, MULT, POET; PC 6**
See also BW 1; CA 69-72; 97-100; CABS 2; CANR 24, 75; CDALB 1941-1968; DLB 5, 76; MTCW 1; SATA 19; SATA-Obit 26

Hayford, J(oseph) E(phraim) Casely
See Casely-Hayford, J(oseph) E(phraim)

Hayman, Ronald 1932-   **CLC 44**
See also CA 25-28R; CANR 18, 50; DLB 155

Haywood, Eliza 1693(?)-1756   **LC 44**
See also DLB 39

Haywood, Eliza (Fowler) 1693(?)-1756   **LC 1, 44**

Hazlitt, William 1778-1830   **NCLC 29**
See also DLB 110, 158

Hazzard, Shirley 1931-   **CLC 18**
See also CA 9-12R; CANR 4, 70; DLBY 82; MTCW 1

Head, Bessie 1937-1986   **CLC 25, 67; BLC 2; DAM MULT**
See also BW 2; CA 29-32R; 119; CANR 25; DLB 117; MTCW 1

Headon, (Nicky) Topper 1956(?)-   **CLC 30**

Heaney, Seamus (Justin) 1939-   **CLC 5, 7, 14,**

25, 37, 74, 91; DAB; DAM POET; PC 18; WLCS
See also CA 85-88; CANR 25, 48, 75; CDBLB 1960 to Present; DLB 40; DLBY 95; MTCW 1

Hearn, (Patricio) Lafcadio (Tessima Carlos) 1850-1904   **TCLC 9**
See also CA 105; 166; DLB 12, 78, 189

Hearne, Vicki 1946-   **CLC 56**
See also CA 139

Hearon, Shelby 1931-   **CLC 63**
See also AITN 2; CA 25-28R; CANR 18, 48

Heat-Moon, William Least   **CLC 29**
See also Trogdon, William (Lewis)
See also AAYA 9

Hebbel, Friedrich 1813-1863   **NCLC 43; DAM DRAM**
See also DLB 129

Hebert, Anne 1916-   **CLC 4, 13, 29; DAC; DAM MST, POET**
See also CA 85-88; CANR 69; DLB 68; MTCW 1

Hecht, Anthony (Evan) 1923-   **CLC 8, 13, 19; DAM POET**
See also CA 9-12R; CANR 6; DLB 5, 169

Hecht, Ben 1894-1964   **CLC 8**
See also CA 85-88; DLB 7, 9, 25, 26, 28, 86

Hedayat, Sadeq 1903-1951   **TCLC 21**
See also CA 120

Hegel, Georg Wilhelm Friedrich 1770-1831   **NCLC 46**
See also DLB 90

Heidegger, Martin 1889-1976   **CLC 24**
See also CA 81-84; 65-68; CANR 34; MTCW 1

Heidenstam, (Carl Gustaf) Verner von 1859-1940   **TCLC 5**
See also CA 104

Heifner, Jack 1946-   **CLC 11**
See also CA 105; CANR 47

Heijermans, Herman 1864-1924   **TCLC 24**
See also CA 123

Heilbrun, Carolyn G(old) 1926-   **CLC 25**
See also CA 45-48; CANR 1, 28, 58

Heine, Heinrich 1797-1856   **NCLC 4, 54; PC 25**
See also DLB 90

Heinemann, Larry (Curtiss) 1944-   **CLC 50**
See also CA 110; CAAS 21; CANR 31; DLBD 9; INT CANR-31

Heiney, Donald (William) 1921-1993
See Harris, MacDonald
See also CA 1-4R; 142; CANR 3, 58

Heinlein, Robert A(nson) 1907-1988   **CLC 1, 3, 8, 14, 26, 55; DAM POP**
See also AAYA 17; CA 1-4R; 125; CANR 1, 20, 53; DLB 8; JRDA; MAICYA; MTCW 1; SATA 9, 69; SATA-Obit 56

Helforth, John
See Doolittle, Hilda

Hellenhofferu, Vojtech Kapristian z
See Hasek, Jaroslav (Matej Frantisek)

Heller, Joseph 1923-   **CLC 1, 3, 5, 8, 11, 36, 63; DA; DAB; DAC; DAM MST, NOV, POP; WLC**
See also AAYA 24; AITN 1; CA 5-8R; CABS 1; CANR 8, 42, 66; DLB 2, 28; DLBY 80; INT CANR-8; MTCW 1

Hellman, Lillian (Florence) 1906-1984   **CLC 2, 4, 8, 14, 18, 34, 44, 52; DAM DRAM; DC 1**
See also AITN 1, 2; CA 13-16R; 112; CANR 33; DLB 7; DLBY 84; MTCW 1

Helprin, Mark 1947-   **CLC 7, 10, 22, 32; DAM NOV, POP**

See also CA 81-84; CANR 47, 64; DLBY 85;
MTCW 1

Helvetius, Claude-Adrien 1715-1771 **LC 26**

Helyar, Jane Penelope Josephine 1933-
See Poole, Josephine
See also CA 21-24R; CANR 10, 26; SATA 82

Hemans, Felicia 1793-1835 **NCLC 71**
See also DLB 96

Hemingway, Ernest (Miller) 1899-1961 **C L C
1, 3, 6, 8, 10, 13, 19, 30, 34, 39, 41, 44, 50,
61, 80; DA; DAB; DAC; DAM MST, NOV;
SSC 1, 25; WLC**
See also AAYA 19; CA 77-80; CANR 34;
CDALB 1917-1929; DLB 4, 9, 102; DLBD
1, 15, 16; DLBY 81, 87, 96; MTCW 1

Hempel, Amy 1951- **CLC 39**
See also CA 118; 137; CANR 70

Henderson, F. C.
See Mencken, H(enry) L(ouis)

Henderson, Sylvia
See Ashton-Warner, Sylvia (Constance)

Henderson, Zenna (Chlarson) 1917-1983**S S C
29**
See also CA 1-4R; 133; CANR 1; DLB 8; SATA
5

Henley, Beth **CLC 23; DC 6**
See also Henley, Elizabeth Becker
See also CABS 3; DLBY 86

Henley, Elizabeth Becker 1952-
See Henley, Beth
See also CA 107; CANR 32, 73; DAM DRAM,
MST; MTCW 1

Henley, William Ernest 1849-1903 **TCLC 8**
See also CA 105; DLB 19

Hennissart, Martha
See Lathen, Emma
See also CA 85-88; CANR 64

Henry, O. **TCLC 1, 19; SSC 5; WLC**
See also Porter, William Sydney

Henry, Patrick 1736-1799 **LC 25**

Henryson, Robert 1430(?)-1506(?) **LC 20**
See also DLB 146

Henry VIII 1491-1547 **LC 10**

Henschke, Alfred
See Klabund

Hentoff, Nat(han Irving) 1925- **CLC 26**
See also AAYA 4; CA 1-4R; CAAS 6; CANR
5, 25; CLR 1, 52; INT CANR-25; JRDA;
MAICYA; SATA 42, 69; SATA-Brief 27

Heppenstall, (John) Rayner 1911-1981 **C L C
10**
See also CA 1-4R; 103; CANR 29

Heraclitus c. 540B.C.-c. 450B.C. **CMLC 22**
See also DLB 176

Herbert, Frank (Patrick) 1920-1986 **CLC 12,
23, 35, 44, 85; DAM POP**
See also AAYA 21; CA 53-56; 118; CANR 5,
43; DLB 8; INT CANR-5; MTCW 1; SATA
9, 37; SATA-Obit 47

Herbert, George 1593-1633 **LC 24; DAB;
DAM POET; PC 4**
See also CDBLB Before 1660; DLB 126

Herbert, Zbigniew 1924-1998 **CLC 9, 43;
DAM POET**
See also CA 89-92; 169; CANR 36, 74; MTCW
1

Herbst, Josephine (Frey) 1897-1969 **CLC 34**
See also CA 5-8R; 25-28R; DLB 9

Hergesheimer, Joseph 1880-1954 **TCLC 11**
See also CA 109; DLB 102, 9

Herlihy, James Leo 1927-1993 **CLC 6**
See also CA 1-4R; 143; CANR 2

Hermogenes fl. c. 175- **CMLC 6**

Hernandez, Jose 1834-1886 **NCLC 17**

Herodotus c. 484B.C.-429B.C. **CMLC 17**
See also DLB 176

Herrick, Robert 1591-1674**LC 13; DA; DAB;
DAC; DAM MST, POP; PC 9**
See also DLB 126

Herring, Guilles
See Somerville, Edith

Herriot, James 1916-1995**CLC 12; DAM POP**
See also Wight, James Alfred
See also AAYA 1; CA 148; CANR 40; SATA
86

Herrmann, Dorothy 1941- **CLC 44**
See also CA 107

Herrmann, Taffy
See Herrmann, Dorothy

Hersey, John (Richard) 1914-1993**CLC 1, 2, 7,
9, 40, 81, 97; DAM POP**
See also CA 17-20R; 140; CANR 33; DLB 6,
185; MTCW 1; SATA 25; SATA-Obit 76

Herzen, Aleksandr Ivanovich 1812-1870
NCLC 10, 61

Herzl, Theodor 1860-1904 **TCLC 36**
See also CA 168

Herzog, Werner 1942- **CLC 16**
See also CA 89-92

Hesiod c. 8th cent. B.C.- **CMLC 5**
See also DLB 176

Hesse, Hermann 1877-1962**CLC 1, 2, 3, 6, 11,
17, 25, 69; DA; DAB; DAC; DAM MST,
NOV; SSC 9; WLC**
See also CA 17-18; CAP 2; DLB 66; MTCW 1;
SATA 50

Hewes, Cady
See De Voto, Bernard (Augustine)

Heyen, William 1940- **CLC 13, 18**
See also CA 33-36R; CAAS 9; DLB 5

Heyerdahl, Thor 1914- **CLC 26**
See also CA 5-8R; CANR 5, 22, 66, 73; MTCW
1; SATA 2, 52

Heym, Georg (Theodor Franz Arthur) 1887-
1912 **TCLC 9**
See also CA 106

Heym, Stefan 1913- **CLC 41**
See also CA 9-12R; CANR 4; DLB 69

Heyse, Paul (Johann Ludwig von) 1830-1914
TCLC 8
See also CA 104; DLB 129

Heyward, (Edwin) DuBose 1885-1940 **T C L C
59**
See also CA 108; 157; DLB 7, 9, 45; SATA 21

Hibbert, Eleanor Alice Burford 1906-1993
CLC 7; DAM POP
See also BEST 90:4; CA 17-20R; 140; CANR
9, 28, 59; SATA 2; SATA-Obit 74

Hichens, Robert (Smythe) 1864-1950 **T C L C
64**
See also CA 162; DLB 153

Higgins, George V(incent) 1939-**CLC 4, 7, 10,
18**
See also CA 77-80; CAAS 5; CANR 17, 51;
DLB 2; DLBY 81; INT CANR-17; MTCW
1

Higginson, Thomas Wentworth 1823-1911
TCLC 36
See also CA 162; DLB 1, 64

Highet, Helen
See MacInnes, Helen (Clark)

Highsmith, (Mary) Patricia 1921-1995**CLC 2,
4, 14, 42, 102; DAM NOV, POP**
See also CA 1-4R; 147; CANR 1, 20, 48, 62;
MTCW 1

Highwater, Jamake (Mamake) 1942(?)- **C L C
12**
See also AAYA 7; CA 65-68; CAAS 7; CANR
10, 34; CLR 17; DLB 52; DLBY 85; JRDA;
MAICYA; SATA 32, 69; SATA-Brief 30

Highway, Tomson 1951-**CLC 92; DAC; DAM
MULT**
See also CA 151; CANR 75; NNAL

Higuchi, Ichiyo 1872-1896 **NCLC 49**

Hijuelos, Oscar 1951- **CLC 65; DAM MULT,
POP; HLC**
See also AAYA 25; BEST 90:1; CA 123; CANR
50, 75; DLB 145; HW

Hikmet, Nazim 1902(?)-1963 **CLC 40**
See also CA 141; 93-96

Hildegard von Bingen 1098-1179 **CMLC 20**
See also DLB 148

Hildesheimer, Wolfgang 1916-1991 **CLC 49**
See also CA 101; 135; DLB 69, 124

Hill, Geoffrey (William) 1932- **CLC 5, 8, 18,
45; DAM POET**
See also CA 81-84; CANR 21; CDBLB 1960
to Present; DLB 40; MTCW 1

Hill, George Roy 1921- **CLC 26**
See also CA 110; 122

Hill, John
See Koontz, Dean R(ay)

Hill, Susan (Elizabeth) 1942- **CLC 4, 113;
DAB; DAM MST, NOV**
See also CA 33-36R; CANR 29, 69; DLB 14,
139; MTCW 1

Hillerman, Tony 1925- **CLC 62; DAM POP**
See also AAYA 6; BEST 89:1; CA 29-32R;
CANR 21, 42, 65; DLB 206; SATA 6

Hillesum, Etty 1914-1943 **TCLC 49**
See also CA 137

Hilliard, Noel (Harvey) 1929- **CLC 15**
See also CA 9-12R; CANR 7, 69

Hillis, Rick 1956- **CLC 66**
See also CA 134

Hilton, James 1900-1954 **TCLC 21**
See also CA 108; 169; DLB 34, 77; SATA 34

Himes, Chester (Bomar) 1909-1984**CLC 2, 4,
7, 18, 58, 108; BLC 2; DAM MULT**
See also BW 2; CA 25-28R; 114; CANR 22;
DLB 2, 76, 143; MTCW 1

Hinde, Thomas **CLC 6, 11**
See also Chitty, Thomas Willes

Hindin, Nathan
See Bloch, Robert (Albert)

Hine, (William) Daryl 1936- **CLC 15**
See also CA 1-4R; CAAS 15; CANR 1, 20; DLB
60

Hinkson, Katharine Tynan
See Tynan, Katharine

Hinton, S(usan) E(loise) 1950- **CLC 30, 111;
DA; DAB; DAC; DAM MST, NOV**
See also AAYA 2; CA 81-84; CANR 32, 62;
CLR 3, 23; JRDA; MAICYA; MTCW 1;
SATA 19, 58

Hippius, Zinaida **TCLC 9**
See also Gippius, Zinaida (Nikolayevna)

Hiraoka, Kimitake 1925-1970
See Mishima, Yukio
See also CA 97-100; 29-32R; DAM DRAM;
MTCW 1

Hirsch, E(ric) D(onald), Jr. 1928- **CLC 79**
See also CA 25-28R; CANR 27, 51; DLB 67;
INT CANR-27; MTCW 1

Hirsch, Edward 1950- **CLC 31, 50**
See also CA 104; CANR 20, 42; DLB 120

Hitchcock, Alfred (Joseph) 1899-1980**CLC 16**
See also AAYA 22; CA 159; 97-100; SATA 27;
SATA-Obit 24

Hitler, Adolf 1889-1945   **TCLC 53**
See also CA 117; 147

Hoagland, Edward 1932-   **CLC 28**
See also CA 1-4R; CANR 2, 31, 57; DLB 6;
SATA 51

Hoban, Russell (Conwell) 1925-   **CLC 7, 25;
DAM NOV**
See also CA 5-8R; CANR 23, 37, 66; CLR 3;
DLB 52; MAICYA; MTCW 1; SATA 1, 40,
78

Hobbes, Thomas 1588-1679   **LC 36**
See also DLB 151

Hobbs, Perry
See Blackmur, R(ichard) P(almer)

Hobson, Laura Z(ametkin) 1900-1986 CLC 7,
25
See also CA 17-20R; 118; CANR 55; DLB 28;
SATA 52

Hochhuth, Rolf 1931-   **CLC 4, 11, 18; DAM
DRAM**
See also CA 5-8R; CANR 33, 75; DLB 124;
MTCW 1

Hochman, Sandra 1936-   **CLC 3, 8**
See also CA 5-8R; DLB 5

Hochwaelder, Fritz 1911-1986 CLC 36; DAM
DRAM
See also CA 29-32R; 120; CANR 42; MTCW 1

Hochwalder, Fritz
See Hochwaelder, Fritz

Hocking, Mary (Eunice) 1921-   **CLC 13**
See also CA 101; CANR 18, 40

Hodgins, Jack 1938-   **CLC 23**
See also CA 93-96; DLB 60

Hodgson, William Hope 1877(?)-1918 **T C L C
13**
See also CA 111; 164; DLB 70, 153, 156, 178

Hoeg, Peter 1957-   **CLC 95**
See also CA 151; CANR 75

Hoffman, Alice 1952-   **CLC 51; DAM NOV**
See also CA 77-80; CANR 34, 66; MTCW 1

Hoffman, Daniel (Gerard) 1923- CLC 6, 13, 23
See also CA 1-4R; CANR 4; DLB 5

Hoffman, Stanley 1944-   **CLC 5**
See also CA 77-80

Hoffman, William M(oses) 1939-   **CLC 40**
See also CA 57-60; CANR 11, 71

Hoffmann, E(rnst) T(heodor) A(madeus) 1776-
1822   **NCLC 2; SSC 13**
See also DLB 90; SATA 27

Hofmann, Gert 1931-   **CLC 54**
See also CA 128

Hofmannsthal, Hugo von 1874-1929 TCLC 11;
DAM DRAM; DC 4
See also CA 106; 153; DLB 81, 118

Hogan, Linda 1947-   **CLC 73; DAM MULT**
See also CA 120; CANR 45, 73; DLB 175;
NNAL

Hogarth, Charles
See Creasey, John

Hogarth, Emmett
See Polonsky, Abraham (Lincoln)

Hogg, James 1770-1835   **NCLC 4**
See also DLB 93, 116, 159

Holbach, Paul Henri Thiry Baron 1723-1789
LC 14

Holberg, Ludvig 1684-1754   **LC 6**

Holden, Ursula 1921-   **CLC 18**
See also CA 101; CAAS 8; CANR 22

Holderlin, (Johann Christian) Friedrich 1770-
1843   **NCLC 16; PC 4**

Holdstock, Robert
See Holdstock, Robert P.

Holdstock, Robert P. 1948-   **CLC 39**

See also CA 131

Holland, Isabelle 1920-   **CLC 21**
See also AAYA 11; CA 21-24R; CANR 10, 25,
47; JRDA; MAICYA; SATA 8, 70

Holland, Marcus
See Caldwell, (Janet Miriam) Taylor (Holland)

Hollander, John 1929-   **CLC 2, 5, 8, 14**
See also CA 1-4R; CANR 1, 52; DLB 5; SATA
13

Hollander, Paul
See Silverberg, Robert

Holleran, Andrew 1943(?)-   **CLC 38**
See also CA 144

Hollinghurst, Alan 1954-   **CLC 55, 91**
See also CA 114; DLB 207

Hollis, Jim
See Summers, Hollis (Spurgeon, Jr.)

Holly, Buddy 1936-1959   **TCLC 65**

Holmes, Gordon
See Shiel, M(atthew) P(hipps)

Holmes, John
See Souster, (Holmes) Raymond

Holmes, John Clellon 1926-1988   **CLC 56**
See also CA 9-12R; 125; CANR 4; DLB 16

Holmes, Oliver Wendell, Jr. 1841-1935 T C L C
77
See also CA 114

Holmes, Oliver Wendell 1809-1894 NCLC 14
See also CDALB 1640-1865; DLB 1, 189;
SATA 34

Holmes, Raymond
See Souster, (Holmes) Raymond

Holt, Victoria
See Hibbert, Eleanor Alice Burford

Holub, Miroslav 1923-1998   **CLC 4**
See also CA 21-24R; 169; CANR 10

Homer c. 8th cent. B.C.-   **CMLC 1, 16; DA;
DAB; DAC; DAM MST, POET; PC 23;
WLCS**
See also DLB 176

Hongo, Garrett Kaoru 1951-   **PC 23**
See also CA 133; CAAS 22; DLB 120

Honig, Edwin 1919-   **CLC 33**
See also CA 5-8R; CAAS 8; CANR 4, 45; DLB
5

Hood, Hugh (John Blagdon) 1928- CLC 15, 28
See also CA 49-52; CAAS 17; CANR 1, 33;
DLB 53

Hood, Thomas 1799-1845   **NCLC 16**
See also DLB 96

Hooker, (Peter) Jeremy 1941-   **CLC 43**
See also CA 77-80; CANR 22; DLB 40

hooks, bell   **CLC 94; BLCS**
See also Watkins, Gloria

Hope, A(lec) D(erwent) 1907-   **CLC 3, 51**
See also CA 21-24R; CANR 33, 74; MTCW 1

Hope, Anthony 1863-1933   **TCLC 83**
See also CA 157; DLB 153, 156

Hope, Brian
See Creasey, John

Hope, Christopher (David Tully) 1944-   C L C
52
See also CA 106; CANR 47; SATA 62

Hopkins, Gerard Manley 1844-1889   N C L C
17; DA; DAB; DAC; DAM MST, POET;
PC 15; WLC
See also CDBLB 1890-1914; DLB 35, 57

Hopkins, John (Richard) 1931-1998   **CLC 4**
See also CA 85-88; 169

Hopkins, Pauline Elizabeth 1859-1930 T C L C
28; BLC 2; DAM MULT
See also BW 2; CA 141; DLB 50

Hopkinson, Francis 1737-1791   **LC 25**

See also DLB 31

Hopley-Woolrich, Cornell George 1903-1968
See Woolrich, Cornell
See also CA 13-14; CANR 58; CAP 1

Horatio
See Proust, (Valentin-Louis-George-Eugene-)
Marcel

Horgan, Paul (George Vincent O'Shaughnessy)
1903-1995   **CLC 9, 53; DAM NOV**
See also CA 13-16R; 147; CANR 9, 35; DLB
102; DLBY 85; INT CANR-9; MTCW 1;
SATA 13; SATA-Obit 84

Horn, Peter
See Kuttner, Henry

Hornem, Horace Esq.
See Byron, George Gordon (Noel)

**Horney, Karen (Clementine Theodore
Danielsen)** 1885-1952   **TCLC 71**
See also CA 114; 165

Hornung, E(rnest) W(illiam) 1866-1921
TCLC 59
See also CA 108; 160; DLB 70

Horovitz, Israel (Arthur) 1939- CLC 56; DAM
DRAM
See also CA 33-36R; CANR 46, 59; DLB 7

Horvath, Odon von
See Horvath, Oedoen von
See also DLB 85, 124

Horvath, Oedoen von 1901-1938   **TCLC 45**
See also Horvath, Odon von
See also CA 118

Horwitz, Julius 1920-1986   **CLC 14**
See also CA 9-12R; 119; CANR 12

Hospital, Janette Turner 1942-   **CLC 42**
See also CA 108; CANR 48

Hostos, E. M. de
See Hostos (y Bonilla), Eugenio Maria de

Hostos, Eugenio M. de
See Hostos (y Bonilla), Eugenio Maria de

Hostos, Eugenio Maria
See Hostos (y Bonilla), Eugenio Maria de

Hostos (y Bonilla), Eugenio Maria de 1839-1903
TCLC 24
See also CA 123; 131; HW

Houdini
See Lovecraft, H(oward) P(hillips)

Hougan, Carolyn 1943-   **CLC 34**
See also CA 139

Household, Geoffrey (Edward West) 1900-1988
CLC 11
See also CA 77-80; 126; CANR 58; DLB 87;
SATA 14; SATA-Obit 59

Housman, A(lfred) E(dward) 1859-1936
TCLC 1, 10; DA; DAB; DAC; DAM MST,
POET; PC 2; WLCS
See also CA 104; 125; DLB 19; MTCW 1

Housman, Laurence 1865-1959   **TCLC 7**
See also CA 106; 155; DLB 10; SATA 25

Howard, Elizabeth Jane 1923-   **CLC 7, 29**
See also CA 5-8R; CANR 8, 62

Howard, Maureen 1930-   **CLC 5, 14, 46**
See also CA 53-56; CANR 31, 75; DLBY 83;
INT CANR-31; MTCW 1

Howard, Richard 1929-   **CLC 7, 10, 47**
See also AITN 1; CA 85-88; CANR 25; DLB 5;
INT CANR-25

Howard, Robert E(rvin) 1906-1936 TCLC 8
See also CA 105; 157

Howard, Warren F.
See Pohl, Frederik

Howe, Fanny (Quincy) 1940-   **CLC 47**
See also CA 117; CAAS 27; CANR 70; SATA-
Brief 52

Howe, Irving 1920-1993   **CLC 85**
  See also CA 9-12R; 141; CANR 21, 50; DLB
    67; MTCW 1
Howe, Julia Ward 1819-1910   **TCLC 21**
  See also CA 117; DLB 1, 189
Howe, Susan 1937-   **CLC 72**
  See also CA 160; DLB 120
Howe, Tina 1937-   **CLC 48**
  See also CA 109
Howell, James 1594(?)-1666   **LC 13**
  See also DLB 151
Howells, W. D.
  See Howells, William Dean
Howells, William D.
  See Howells, William Dean
Howells, William Dean 1837-1920**TCLC 7, 17,
  41**
    See also CA 104; 134; CDALB 1865-1917;
    DLB 12, 64, 74, 79, 189
Howes, Barbara 1914-1996   **CLC 15**
  See also CA 9-12R; 151; CAAS 3; CANR 53;
    SATA 5
Hrabal, Bohumil 1914-1997   **CLC 13, 67**
  See also CA 106; 156; CAAS 12; CANR 57
Hroswitha of Gandersheim c. 935-c. 1002
    CMLC 29
  See also DLB 148
Hsun, Lu
  See Lu Hsun
Hubbard, L(afayette) Ron(ald) 1911-1986
    CLC 43; DAM POP
  See also CA 77-80; 118; CANR 52
Huch, Ricarda (Octavia) 1864-1947**TCLC 13**
  See also CA 111; DLB 66
Huddle, David 1942-   **CLC 49**
  See also CA 57-60; CAAS 20; DLB 130
Hudson, Jeffrey
  See Crichton, (John) Michael
Hudson, W(illiam) H(enry) 1841-1922 **TCLC
  29**
    See also CA 115; DLB 98, 153, 174; SATA 35
Hueffer, Ford Madox
  See Ford, Ford Madox
Hughart, Barry 1934-   **CLC 39**
  See also CA 137
Hughes, Colin
  See Creasey, John
Hughes, David (John) 1930-   **CLC 48**
  See also CA 116; 129; DLB 14
Hughes, Edward James
  See Hughes, Ted
  See also DAM MST, POET
Hughes, (James) Langston 1902-1967**CLC 1,
  5, 10, 15, 35, 44, 108; BLC 2; DA; DAB;
  DAC; DAM DRAM, MST, MULT, POET;
  DC 3; PC 1; SSC 6; WLC**
    See also AAYA 12; BW 1; CA 1-4R; 25-28R;
    CANR 1, 34; CDALB 1929-1941; CLR 17;
    DLB 4, 7, 48, 51, 86; JRDA; MAICYA;
    MTCW 1; SATA 4, 33
Hughes, Richard (Arthur Warren) 1900-1976
    CLC 1, 11; DAM NOV
  See also CA 5-8R; 65-68; CANR 4; DLB 15,
    161; MTCW 1; SATA 8; SATA-Obit 25
Hughes, Ted 1930-1998   **CLC 2, 4, 9, 14, 37;
  DAB; DAC; PC 7**
  See also Hughes, Edward James
  See also CA 1-4R; 171; CANR 1, 33, 66; CLR
    3; DLB 40, 161; MAICYA; MTCW 1; SATA
    49; SATA-Brief 27
Hugo, Richard F(ranklin) 1923-1982 **CLC 6,
  18, 32; DAM POET**
  See also CA 49-52; 108; CANR 3; DLB 5, 206

Hugo, Victor (Marie) 1802-1885**NCLC 3, 10,
  21; DA; DAB; DAC; DAM DRAM, MST,
  NOV, POET; PC 17; WLC**
    See also DLB 119, 192; SATA 47
Huidobro, Vicente
  See Huidobro Fernandez, Vicente Garcia
Huidobro Fernandez, Vicente Garcia 1893-
  1948   **TCLC 31**
    See also CA 131; HW
Hulme, Keri 1947-   **CLC 39**
  See also CA 125; CANR 69; INT 125
Hulme, T(homas) E(rnest) 1883-1917 **TCLC
  21**
    See also CA 117; DLB 19
Hume, David 1711-1776   **LC 7**
  See also DLB 104
Humphrey, William 1924-1997   **CLC 45**
  See also CA 77-80; 160; CANR 68; DLB 6
Humphreys, Emyr Owen 1919-   **CLC 47**
  See also CA 5-8R; CANR 3, 24; DLB 15
Humphreys, Josephine 1945-   **CLC 34, 57**
  See also CA 121; 127; INT 127
Huneker, James Gibbons 1857-1921**TCLC 65**
  See also DLB 71
Hungerford, Pixie
  See Brinsmead, H(esba) F(ay)
Hunt, E(verette) Howard, (Jr.) 1918- **CLC 3**
  See also AITN 1; CA 45-48; CANR 2, 47
Hunt, Kyle
  See Creasey, John
Hunt, (James Henry) Leigh 1784-1859**NCLC
  1, 70; DAM POET**
    See also DLB 96, 110, 144
Hunt, Marsha 1946-   **CLC 70**
  See also BW 2; CA 143
Hunt, Violet 1866(?)-1942   **TCLC 53**
  See also DLB 162, 197
Hunter, E. Waldo
  See Sturgeon, Theodore (Hamilton)
Hunter, Evan 1926- **CLC 11, 31; DAM POP**
  See also CA 5-8R; CANR 5, 38, 62; DLBY 82;
    INT CANR-5; MTCW 1; SATA 25
Hunter, Kristin (Eggleston) 1931-   **CLC 35**
  See also AITN 1; BW 1; CA 13-16R; CANR
    13; CLR 3; DLB 33; INT CANR-13;
    MAICYA; SAAS 10; SATA 12
Hunter, Mollie 1922-   **CLC 21**
  See also McIlwraith, Maureen Mollie Hunter
  See also AAYA 13; CANR 37; CLR 25; DLB
    161; JRDA; MAICYA; SAAS 7; SATA 54
Hunter, Robert (?)-1734   **LC 7**
Hurston, Zora Neale 1903-1960**CLC 7, 30, 61;
  BLC 2; DA; DAC; DAM MST, MULT,
  NOV; SSC 4; WLCS**
    See also AAYA 15; BW 1; CA 85-88; CANR
    61; DLB 51, 86; MTCW 1
Huston, John (Marcellus) 1906-1987 **CLC 20**
  See also CA 73-76; 123; CANR 34; DLB 26
Hustvedt, Siri 1955-   **CLC 76**
  See also CA 137
Hutten, Ulrich von 1488-1523   **LC 16**
  See also DLB 179
Huxley, Aldous (Leonard) 1894-1963 **CLC 1,
  3, 4, 5, 8, 11, 18, 35, 79; DA; DAB; DAC;
  DAM MST, NOV; WLC**
    See also AAYA 11; CA 85-88; CANR 44;
    CDBLB 1914-1945; DLB 36, 100, 162, 195;
    MTCW 1; SATA 63
Huxley, T(homas) H(enry) 1825-1895 **NCLC
  67**
    See also DLB 57
Huysmans, Joris-Karl 1848-1907**TCLC 7, 69**
  See also CA 104; 165; DLB 123

Hwang, David Henry 1957-   **CLC 55; DAM
  DRAM; DC 4**
    See also CA 127; 132; INT 132
Hyde, Anthony 1946-   **CLC 42**
  See also CA 136
Hyde, Margaret O(ldroyd) 1917-   **CLC 21**
  See also CA 1-4R; CANR 1, 36; CLR 23; JRDA;
    MAICYA; SAAS 8; SATA 1, 42, 76
Hynes, James 1956(?)-   **CLC 65**
  See also CA 164
Ian, Janis 1951-   **CLC 21**
  See also CA 105
Ibanez, Vicente Blasco
  See Blasco Ibanez, Vicente
Ibarguengoitia, Jorge 1928-1983   **CLC 37**
  See also CA 124; 113; HW
Ibsen, Henrik (Johan) 1828-1906 **TCLC 2, 8,
  16, 37, 52; DA; DAB; DAC; DAM DRAM,
  MST; DC 2; WLC**
    See also CA 104; 141
Ibuse, Masuji 1898-1993   **CLC 22**
  See also CA 127; 141; DLB 180
Ichikawa, Kon 1915-   **CLC 20**
  See also CA 121
Idle, Eric 1943-   **CLC 21**
  See also Monty Python
  See also CA 116; CANR 35
Ignatow, David 1914-1997   **CLC 4, 7, 14, 40**
  See also CA 9-12R; 162; CAAS 3; CANR 31,
    57; DLB 5
Ihimaera, Witi 1944-   **CLC 46**
  See also CA 77-80
Ilf, Ilya   **TCLC 21**
  See also Fainzilberg, Ilya Arnoldovich
Illyes, Gyula 1902-1983   **PC 16**
  See also CA 114; 109
Immermann, Karl (Lebrecht) 1796-1840
    NCLC 4, 49
  See also DLB 133
Ince, Thomas H. 1882-1924   **TCLC 89**
Inchbald, Elizabeth 1753-1821   **NCLC 62**
  See also DLB 39, 89
Inclan, Ramon (Maria) del Valle
  See Valle-Inclan, Ramon (Maria) del
Infante, G(uillermo) Cabrera
  See Cabrera Infante, G(uillermo)
Ingalls, Rachel (Holmes) 1940-   **CLC 42**
  See also CA 123; 127
Ingamells, Reginald Charles
  See Ingamells, Rex
Ingamells, Rex 1913-1955   **TCLC 35**
  See also CA 167
Inge, William (Motter) 1913-1973 **CLC 1, 8,
  19; DAM DRAM**
    See also CA 9-12R; CDALB 1941-1968; DLB
    7; MTCW 1
Ingelow, Jean 1820-1897   **NCLC 39**
  See also DLB 35, 163; SATA 33
Ingram, Willis J.
  See Harris, Mark
Innaurato, Albert (F.) 1948(?)-   **CLC 21, 60**
  See also CA 115; 122; INT 122
Innes, Michael
  See Stewart, J(ohn) I(nnes) M(ackintosh)
Innis, Harold Adams 1894-1952   **TCLC 77**
  See also DLB 88
Ionesco, Eugene 1909-1994**CLC 1, 4, 6, 9, 11,
  15, 41, 86; DA; DAB; DAC; DAM DRAM,
  MST; WLC**
    See also CA 9-12R; 144; CANR 55; MTCW 1;
    SATA 7; SATA-Obit 79
Iqbal, Muhammad 1873-1938   **TCLC 28**
Ireland, Patrick

See O'Doherty, Brian
Iron, Ralph
See Schreiner, Olive (Emilie Albertina)
Irving, John (Winslow) 1942-**CLC 13, 23, 38, 112; DAM NOV, POP**
See also AAYA 8; BEST 89:3; CA 25-28R; CANR 28, 73; DLB 6; DLBY 82; MTCW 1
Irving, Washington 1783-1859 **NCLC 2, 19; DA; DAB; DAC; DAM MST; SSC 2; WLC**
See also CDALB 1640-1865; DLB 3, 11, 30, 59, 73, 74, 186; YABC 2
Irwin, P. K.
See Page, P(atricia) K(athleen)
Isaacs, Jorge Ricardo 1837-1895 **NCLC 70**
Isaacs, Susan 1943- **CLC 32; DAM POP**
See also BEST 89:1; CA 89-92; CANR 20, 41, 65; INT CANR-20; MTCW 1
Isherwood, Christopher (William Bradshaw) 1904-1986 **CLC 1, 9, 11, 14, 44; DAM DRAM, NOV**
See also CA 13-16R; 117; CANR 35; DLB 15, 195, DLBY 86; MTCW 1
Ishiguro, Kazuo 1954- **CLC 27, 56, 59, 110; DAM NOV**
See also BEST 90:2; CA 120; CANR 49; DLB 194; MTCW 1
Ishikawa, Hakuhin
See Ishikawa, Takuboku
Ishikawa, Takuboku 1886(?)-1912 **TCLC 15; DAM POET; PC 10**
See also CA 113; 153
Iskander, Fazil 1929- **CLC 47**
See also CA 102
Isler, Alan (David) 1934- **CLC 91**
See also CA 156
Ivan IV 1530-1584 **LC 17**
Ivanov, Vyacheslav Ivanovich 1866-1949 **TCLC 33**
See also CA 122
Ivask, Ivar Vidrik 1927-1992 **CLC 14**
See also CA 37-40R; 139; CANR 24
Ives, Morgan
See Bradley, Marion Zimmer
J. R. S.
See Gogarty, Oliver St. John
Jabran, Kahlil
See Gibran, Kahlil
Jabran, Khalil
See Gibran, Kahlil
Jackson, Daniel
See Wingrove, David (John)
Jackson, Jesse 1908 1983 **CLC 12**
See also BW 1; CA 25-28R; 109; CANR 27; CLR 28; MAICYA; SATA 2, 29; SATA-Obit 48
Jackson, Laura (Riding) 1901-1991
See Riding, Laura
See also CA 65-68; 135; CANR 28; DLB 48
Jackson, Sam
See Trumbo, Dalton
Jackson, Sara
See Wingrove, David (John)
Jackson, Shirley 1919-1965 **CLC 11, 60, 87; DA; DAC; DAM MST; SSC 9; WLC**
See also AAYA 9; CA 1-4R; 25-28R; CANR 4, 52; CDALB 1941-1968; DLB 6; SATA 2
Jacob, (Cyprien-)Max 1876-1944 **TCLC 6**
See also CA 104
Jacobs, Harriet A(nn) 1813(?)-1897**NCLC 67**
Jacobs, Jim 1942- **CLC 12**
See also CA 97-100; INT 97-100
Jacobs, W(illiam) W(ymark) 1863-1943 **TCLC 22**

See also CA 121; 167; DLB 135
Jacobsen, Jens Peter 1847-1885 **NCLC 34**
Jacobsen, Josephine 1908- **CLC 48, 102**
See also CA 33-36R; CAAS 18; CANR 23, 48
Jacobson, Dan 1929- **CLC 4, 14**
See also CA 1-4R; CANR 2, 25, 66; DLB 14, 207; MTCW 1
Jacqueline
See Carpentier (y Valmont), Alejo
Jagger, Mick 1944- **CLC 17**
Jahiz, al- c. 780-c. 869 **CMLC 25**
Jakes, John (William) 1932- **CLC 29; DAM NOV, POP**
See also BEST 89:4; CA 57-60; CANR 10, 43, 66; DLBY 83; INT CANR-10; MTCW 1; SATA 62
James, Andrew
See Kirkup, James
James, C(yril) L(ionel) R(obert) 1901-1989 **CLC 33; BLCS**
See also BW 2; CA 117; 125; 128; CANR 62; DLB 125; MTCW 1
James, Daniel (Lewis) 1911-1988
See Santiago, Danny
See also CA 125
James, Dynely
See Mayne, William (James Carter)
James, Henry Sr. 1811-1882 **NCLC 53**
James, Henry 1843-1916 **TCLC 2, 11, 24, 40, 47, 64; DA; DAB; DAC; DAM MST, NOV; SSC 8, 32; WLC**
See also CA 104; 132; CDALB 1865-1917; DLB 12, 71, 74, 189; DLBD 13; MTCW 1
James, M. R.
See James, Montague (Rhodes)
See also DLB 156
James, Montague (Rhodes) 1862-1936 **TCLC 6; SSC 16**
See also CA 104; DLB 201
James, P. D. 1920- **CLC 18, 46**
See also White, Phyllis Dorothy James
See also BEST 90:2; CDBLB 1960 to Present; DLB 87; DLBD 17
James, Philip
See Moorcock, Michael (John)
James, William 1842-1910 **TCLC 15, 32**
See also CA 109
James I 1394-1437 **LC 20**
Jameson, Anna 1794-1860 **NCLC 43**
See also DLB 99, 166
Jami, Nur al-Din 'Abd al-Rahman 1414-1492 **LC 9**
Jammes, Francis 1868-1938 **TCLC 75**
Jandl, Ernst 1925- **CLC 34**
Janowitz, Tama 1957- **CLC 43; DAM POP**
See also CA 106; CANR 52
Japrisot, Sebastien 1931- **CLC 90**
Jarrell, Randall 1914-1965**CLC 1, 2, 6, 9, 13, 49; DAM POET**
See also CA 5-8R; 25-28R; CABS 2; CANR 6, 34; CDALB 1941-1968; CLR 6; DLB 48, 52; MAICYA; MTCW 1; SATA 7
Jarry, Alfred 1873-1907 **TCLC 2, 14; DAM DRAM; SSC 20**
See also CA 104; 153; DLB 192
Jarvis, E. K.
See Bloch, Robert (Albert); Ellison, Harlan (Jay); Silverberg, Robert
Jeake, Samuel, Jr.
See Aiken, Conrad (Potter)
Jean Paul 1763-1825 **NCLC 7**
Jefferies, (John) Richard 1848-1887**NCLC 47**
See also DLB 98, 141; SATA 16

Jeffers, (John) Robinson 1887-1962**CLC 2, 3, 11, 15, 54; DA; DAC; DAM MST, POET; PC 17; WLC**
See also CA 85-88; CANR 35; CDALB 1917-1929; DLB 45; MTCW 1
Jefferson, Janet
See Mencken, H(enry) L(ouis)
Jefferson, Thomas 1743-1826 **NCLC 11**
See also CDALB 1640-1865; DLB 31
Jeffrey, Francis 1773-1850 **NCLC 33**
See also DLB 107
Jelakowitch, Ivan
See Heijermans, Herman
Jellicoe, (Patricia) Ann 1927- **CLC 27**
See also CA 85-88; DLB 13
Jen, Gish **CLC 70**
See also Jen, Lillian
Jen, Lillian 1956(?)-
See Jen, Gish
See also CA 135
Jenkins, (John) Robin 1912- **CLC 52**
See also CA 1-4R; CANR 1; DLB 14
Jennings, Elizabeth (Joan) 1926- **CLC 5, 14**
See also CA 61-64; CAAS 5; CANR 8, 39, 66; DLB 27; MTCW 1; SATA 66
Jennings, Waylon 1937- **CLC 21**
Jensen, Johannes V. 1873-1950 **TCLC 41**
See also CA 170
Jensen, Laura (Linnea) 1948- **CLC 37**
See also CA 103
Jerome, Jerome K(lapka) 1859-1927**TCLC 23**
See also CA 119; DLB 10, 34, 135
Jerrold, Douglas William 1803-1857**NCLC 2**
See also DLB 158, 159
Jewett, (Theodora) Sarah Orne 1849-1909 **TCLC 1, 22; SSC 6**
See also CA 108; 127; CANR 71; DLB 12, 74; SATA 15
Jewsbury, Geraldine (Endsor) 1812-1880 **NCLC 22**
See also DLB 21
Jhabvala, Ruth Prawer 1927-**CLC 4, 8, 29, 94; DAB; DAM NOV**
See also CA 1-4R; CANR 2, 29, 51, 74; DLB 139, 194; INT CANR-29; MTCW 1
Jibran, Kahlil
See Gibran, Kahlil
Jibran, Khalil
See Gibran, Kahlil
Jiles, Paulette 1943- **CLC 13, 58**
See also CA 101; CANR 70
Jimenez (Mantecon), Juan Ramon 1881-1958 **TCLC 4; DAM MULT, POET; HLC; PC 7**
See also CA 104; 131; CANR 74; DLB 134; HW; MTCW 1
Jimenez, Ramon
See Jimenez (Mantecon), Juan Ramon
Jimenez Mantecon, Juan
See Jimenez (Mantecon), Juan Ramon
Jin, Ha 1956- **CLC 109**
See also CA 152
Joel, Billy **CLC 26**
See also Joel, William Martin
Joel, William Martin 1949-
See Joel, Billy
See also CA 108
John, Saint 7th cent. - **CMLC 27**
John of the Cross, St. 1542-1591 **LC 18**
Johnson, B(ryan) S(tanley William) 1933-1973 **CLC 6, 9**
See also CA 9-12R; 53-56; CANR 9; DLB 14, 40

Karapanou, Margarita 1946-   **CLC 13**
See also CA 101

Karinthy, Frigyes 1887-1938   **TCLC 47**
See also CA 170

Karl, Frederick R(obert) 1927-   **CLC 34**
See also CA 5-8R; CANR 3, 44

Kastel, Warren
See Silverberg, Robert

Kataev, Evgeny Petrovich 1903-1942
See Petrov, Evgeny
See also CA 120

Kataphusin
See Ruskin, John

Katz, Steve 1935-   **CLC 47**
See also CA 25-28R; CAAS 14, 64; CANR 12;
DLBY 83

Kauffman, Janet 1945-   **CLC 42**
See also CA 117; CANR 43; DLBY 86

Kaufman, Bob (Garnell) 1925-1986 **CLC 49**
See also BW 1; CA 41-44R; 118; CANR 22;
DLB 16, 41

Kaufman, George S. 1889-1961 **CLC 38; DAM
DRAM**
See also CA 108; 93-96; DLB 7; INT 108

Kaufman, Sue   **CLC 3, 8**
See also Barondess, Sue K(aufman)

Kavafis, Konstantinos Petrou 1863-1933
See Cavafy, C(onstantine) P(eter)
See also CA 104

Kavan, Anna 1901-1968   **CLC 5, 13, 82**
See also CA 5-8R; CANR 6, 57; MTCW 1

Kavanagh, Dan
See Barnes, Julian (Patrick)

Kavanagh, Patrick (Joseph) 1904-1967 **C L C
22**
See also CA 123; 25-28R; DLB 15, 20; MTCW
1

Kawabata, Yasunari 1899-1972 **CLC 2, 5, 9,
18, 107; DAM MULT; SSC 17**
See also CA 93-96; 33-36R; DLB 180

Kaye, M(ary) M(argaret) 1909-   **CLC 28**
See also CA 89-92; CANR 24, 60; MTCW 1;
SATA 62

Kaye, Mollie
See Kaye, M(ary) M(argaret)

Kaye-Smith, Sheila 1887-1956   **TCLC 20**
See also CA 118; DLB 36

Kaymor, Patrice Maguilene
See Senghor, Leopold Sedar

Kazan, Elia 1909-   **CLC 6, 16, 63**
See also CA 21-24R; CANR 32

Kazantzakis, Nikos 1883(?)-1957 **TCLC 2, 5,
33**
See also CA 105; 132; MTCW 1

Kazin, Alfred 1915-   **CLC 34, 38**
See also CA 1-4R; CAAS 7; CANR 1, 45; DLB
67

Keane, Mary Nesta (Skrine) 1904-1996
See Keane, Molly
See also CA 108; 114; 151

Keane, Molly   **CLC 31**
See also Keane, Mary Nesta (Skrine)
See also INT 114

Keates, Jonathan 1946(?)-   **CLC 34**
See also CA 163

Keaton, Buster 1895-1966   **CLC 20**

Keats, John 1795-1821 **NCLC 8, 73; DA; DAB;
DAC; DAM MST, POET; PC 1; WLC**
See also CDBLB 1789-1832; DLB 96, 110

Keene, Donald 1922-   **CLC 34**
See also CA 1-4R; CANR 5

Keillor, Garrison   **CLC 40, 115**
See also Keillor, Gary (Edward)

See also AAYA 2; BEST 89:3; DLBY 87; SATA
58

Keillor, Gary (Edward) 1942-
See Keillor, Garrison
See also CA 111; 117; CANR 36, 59; DAM
POP; MTCW 1

Keith, Michael
See Hubbard, L(afayette) Ron(ald)

Keller, Gottfried 1819-1890 **NCLC 2; SSC 26**
See also DLB 129

Keller, Nora Okja   **CLC 109**

Kellerman, Jonathan 1949-   **CLC 44; DAM
POP**
See also BEST 90:1; CA 106; CANR 29, 51;
INT CANR-29

Kelley, William Melvin 1937-   **CLC 22**
See also BW 1; CA 77-80; CANR 27; DLB 33

Kellogg, Marjorie 1922-   **CLC 2**
See also CA 81-84

Kellow, Kathleen
See Hibbert, Eleanor Alice Burford

Kelly, M(ilton) T(erry) 1947-   **CLC 55**
See also CA 97-100; CAAS 22; CANR 19, 43

Kelman, James 1946-   **CLC 58, 86**
See also CA 148; DLB 194

Kemal, Yashar 1923-   **CLC 14, 29**
See also CA 89-92; CANR 44

Kemble, Fanny 1809-1893   **NCLC 18**
See also DLB 32

Kemelman, Harry 1908-1996   **CLC 2**
See also AITN 1; CA 9-12R; 155; CANR 6, 71;
DLB 28

Kempe, Margery 1373(?)-1440(?)   **LC 6**
See also DLB 146

Kempis, Thomas a 1380-1471   **LC 11**

Kendall, Henry 1839-1882   **NCLC 12**

Keneally, Thomas (Michael) 1935- **CLC 5, 8,
10, 14, 19, 27, 43, 117; DAM NOV**
See also CA 85-88; CANR 10, 50, 74; MTCW
1

Kennedy, Adrienne (Lita) 1931- **CLC 66; BLC
2; DAM MULT; DC 5**
See also BW 2; CA 103; CAAS 20; CABS 3;
CANR 26, 53; DLB 38

Kennedy, John Pendleton 1795-1870 **NCLC 2**
See also DLB 3

Kennedy, Joseph Charles 1929-
See Kennedy, X. J.
See also CA 1-4R; CANR 4, 30, 40; SATA 14,
86

Kennedy, William 1928-   **CLC 6, 28, 34, 53;
DAM NOV**
See also AAYA 1; CA 85-88; CANR 14, 31;
DLB 143; DLBY 85; INT CANR-31; MTCW
1; SATA 57

Kennedy, X. J.   **CLC 8, 42**
See also Kennedy, Joseph Charles
See also CAAS 9; CLR 27; DLB 5; SAAS 22

Kenny, Maurice (Francis) 1929-   **CLC 87;
DAM MULT**
See also CA 144; CAAS 22; DLB 175; NNAL

Kent, Kelvin
See Kuttner, Henry

Kenton, Maxwell
See Southern, Terry

Kenyon, Robert O.
See Kuttner, Henry

Kepler, Johannes 1571-1630   **LC 45**

Kerouac, Jack   **CLC 1, 2, 3, 5, 14, 29, 61**
See also Kerouac, Jean-Louis Lebris de
See also AAYA 25; CDALB 1941-1968; DLB
2, 16; DLBD 3; DLBY 95

Kerouac, Jean-Louis Lebris de 1922-1969

See Kerouac, Jack
See also AITN 1; CA 5-8R; 25-28R; CANR 26,
54; DA; DAB; DAC; DAM MST, NOV,
POET, POP; MTCW 1; WLC

Kerr, Jean 1923-   **CLC 22**
See also CA 5-8R; CANR 7; INT CANR-7

Kerr, M. E.   **CLC 12, 35**
See also Meaker, Marijane (Agnes)
See also AAYA 2, 23; CLR 29; SAAS 1

Kerr, Robert   **CLC 55**

Kerrigan, (Thomas) Anthony 1918- **CLC 4, 6**
See also CA 49-52; CAAS 11; CANR 4

Kerry, Lois
See Duncan, Lois

Kesey, Ken (Elton) 1935- **CLC 1, 3, 6, 11, 46,
64; DA; DAB; DAC; DAM MST, NOV,
POP; WLC**
See also AAYA 25; CA 1-4R; CANR 22, 38,
66; CDALB 1968-1988; DLB 2, 16, 206;
MTCW 1; SATA 66

Kesselring, Joseph (Otto) 1902-1967 **CLC 45;
DAM DRAM, MST**
See also CA 150

Kessler, Jascha (Frederick) 1929-   **CLC 4**
See also CA 17-20R; CANR 8, 48

Kettelkamp, Larry (Dale) 1933-   **CLC 12**
See also CA 29-32R; CANR 16; SAAS 3; SATA
2

Key, Ellen 1849-1926   **TCLC 65**

Keyber, Conny
See Fielding, Henry

Keyes, Daniel 1927- **CLC 80; DA; DAC; DAM
MST, NOV**
See also AAYA 23; CA 17-20R; CANR 10, 26,
54, 74; SATA 37

Keynes, John Maynard 1883-1946 **TCLC 64**
See also CA 114; 162, 163; DLBD 10

Khanshendel, Chiron
See Rose, Wendy

Khayyam, Omar 1048-1131 **CMLC 11; DAM
POET; PC 8**

Kherdian, David 1931-   **CLC 6, 9**
See also CA 21-24R; CAAS 2; CANR 39; CLR
24; JRDA; MAICYA; SATA 16, 74

Khlebnikov, Velimir   **TCLC 20**
See also Khlebnikov, Viktor Vladimirovich

Khlebnikov, Viktor Vladimirovich 1885-1922
See Khlebnikov, Velimir
See also CA 117

Khodasevich, Vladislav (Felitsianovich) 1886-
1939   **TCLC 15**
See also CA 115

Kielland, Alexander Lange 1849-1906 **T C L C
5**
See also CA 104

Kiely, Benedict 1919-   **CLC 23, 43**
See also CA 1-4R; CANR 2; DLB 15

Kienzle, William X(avier) 1928-   **CLC 25;
DAM POP**
See also CA 93-96; CAAS 1; CANR 9, 31, 59;
INT CANR-31; MTCW 1

Kierkegaard, Soren 1813-1855   **NCLC 34**

Killens, John Oliver 1916-1987   **CLC 10**
See also BW 2; CA 77-80; 123; CAAS 2; CANR
26; DLB 33

Killigrew, Anne 1660-1685   **LC 4**
See also DLB 131

Kim
See Simenon, Georges (Jacques Christian)

Kincaid, Jamaica 1949- **CLC 43, 68; BLC 2;
DAM MULT, NOV**
See also AAYA 13; BW 2; CA 125; CANR 47,
59; DLB 157

Leimbach, Martha 1963-
See Leimbach, Marti
See also CA 130

Leimbach, Marti   CLC 65
See also Leimbach, Martha

Leino, Eino   TCLC 24
See also Loennbohm, Armas Eino Leopold

Leiris, Michel (Julien) 1901-1990 CLC 61
See also CA 119; 128; 132

Leithauser, Brad 1953-   CLC 27
See also CA 107; CANR 27; DLB 120

Lelchuk, Alan 1938-   CLC 5
See also CA 45-48; CAAS 20; CANR 1, 70

Lem, Stanislaw 1921-   CLC 8, 15, 40
See also CA 105; CAAS 1; CANR 32; MTCW
1

Lemann, Nancy 1956-   CLC 39
See also CA 118; 136

Lemonnier, (Antoine Louis) Camille 1844-1913
TCLC 22
See also CA 121

Lenau, Nikolaus 1802-1850   NCLC 16

L'Engle, Madeleine (Camp Franklin) 1918-
CLC 12; DAM POP
See also AAYA 1; AITN 2; CA 1-4R; CANR 3,
21, 39, 66; CLR 1, 14; DLB 52; JRDA;
MAICYA; MTCW 1; SAAS 15; SATA 1, 27,
75

Lengyel, Jozsef 1896-1975   CLC 7
See also CA 85-88; 57-60; CANR 71

Lenin 1870-1924
See Lenin, V. I.
See also CA 121; 168

Lenin, V. I.   TCLC 67
See also Lenin

Lennon, John (Ono) 1940-1980 CLC 12, 35
See also CA 102

Lennox, Charlotte Ramsay 1729(?)-1804
NCLC 23
See also DLB 39

Lentricchia, Frank (Jr.) 1940-   CLC 34
See also CA 25-28R; CANR 19

Lenz, Siegfried 1926-   CLC 27; SSC 33
See also CA 89-92; DLB 75

Leonard, Elmore (John, Jr.) 1925-CLC 28, 34,
71; DAM POP
See also AAYA 22; AITN 1; BEST 89:1, 90:4;
CA 81-84; CANR 12, 28, 53; DLB 173; INT
CANR-28; MTCW 1

Leonard, Hugh   CLC 19
See also Byrne, John Keyes
See also DLB 13

Leonov, Leonid (Maximovich) 1899-1994
CLC 92; DAM NOV
See also CA 129; CANR 74; MTCW 1

Leopardi, (Conte) Giacomo 1798-1837NCLC
22

Le Reveler
See Artaud, Antonin (Marie Joseph)

Lerman, Eleanor 1952-   CLC 9
See also CA 85-88; CANR 69

Lerman, Rhoda 1936-   CLC 56
See also CA 49-52; CANR 70

Lermontov, Mikhail Yuryevich 1814-1841
NCLC 47; PC 18
See also DLB 205

Leroux, Gaston 1868-1927   TCLC 25
See also CA 108; 136; CANR 69; SATA 65

Lesage, Alain-Rene 1668-1747   LC 2, 28

Leskov, Nikolai (Semyonovich) 1831-1895
NCLC 25

Lessing, Doris (May) 1919-CLC 1, 2, 3, 6, 10,
15, 22, 40, 94; DA; DAB; DAC; DAM MST,
NOV; SSC 6; WLCS
See also CA 9-12R; CAAS 14; CANR 33, 54;
CDBLB 1960 to Present; DLB 15, 139;
DLBY 85; MTCW 1

Lessing, Gotthold Ephraim 1729-1781 LC 8
See also DLB 97

Lester, Richard 1932-   CLC 20

Lever, Charles (James) 1806-1872   NCLC 23
See also DLB 21

Leverson, Ada 1865(?)-1936(?)   TCLC 18
See also Elaine
See also CA 117; DLB 153

Levertov, Denise 1923-1997 CLC 1, 2, 3, 5, 8,
15, 28, 66; DAM POET; PC 11
See also CA 1-4R; 163; CAAS 19; CANR 3,
29, 50; DLB 5, 165; INT CANR-29; MTCW
1

Levi, Jonathan   CLC 76

Levi, Peter (Chad Tigar) 1931-   CLC 41
See also CA 5-8R; CANR 34; DLB 40

Levi, Primo 1919-1987   CLC 37, 50; SSC 12
See also CA 13-16R; 122; CANR 12, 33, 61,
70; DLB 177; MTCW 1

Levin, Ira 1929-   CLC 3, 6; DAM POP
See also CA 21-24R; CANR 17, 44, 74; MTCW
1; SATA 66

Levin, Meyer 1905-1981   CLC 7; DAM POP
See also AITN 1; CA 9-12R; 104; CANR 15;
DLB 9, 28; DLBY 81; SATA 21; SATA-Obit
27

Levine, Norman 1924-   CLC 54
See also CA 73-76; CAAS 23; CANR 14, 70;
DLB 88

Levine, Philip 1928-   CLC 2, 4, 5, 9, 14, 33;
DAM POET; PC 22
See also CA 9-12R; CANR 9, 37, 52; DLB 5

Levinson, Deirdre 1931-   CLC 49
See also CA 73-76; CANR 70

Levi-Strauss, Claude 1908-   CLC 38
See also CA 1-4R; CANR 6, 32, 57; MTCW 1

Levitin, Sonia (Wolff) 1934-   CLC 17
See also AAYA 13; CA 29-32R; CANR 14, 32;
CLR 53; JRDA; MAICYA; SAAS 2; SATA
4, 68

Levon, O. U.
See Kesey, Ken (Elton)

Levy, Amy 1861-1889   NCLC 59
See also DLB 156

Lewes, George Henry 1817-1878   NCLC 25
See also DLB 55, 144

Lewis, Alun 1915-1944   TCLC 3
See also CA 104; DLB 20, 162

Lewis, C. Day
See Day Lewis, C(ecil)

Lewis, C(live) S(taples) 1898-1963CLC 1, 3, 6,
14, 27; DA; DAB; DAC; DAM MST, NOV,
POP; WLC
See also AAYA 3; CA 81-84; CANR 33, 71;
CDBLB 1945-1960; CLR 3, 27; DLB 15,
100, 160; JRDA; MAICYA; MTCW 1; SATA
13, 100

Lewis, Janet 1899-   CLC 41
See also Winters, Janet Lewis
See also CA 9-12R; CANR 29, 63; CAP 1;
DLBY 87

Lewis, Matthew Gregory 1775-1818NCLC 11,
62
See also DLB 39, 158, 178

Lewis, (Harry) Sinclair 1885-1951 TCLC 4,
13, 23, 39; DA; DAB; DAC; DAM MST,
NOV; WLC
See also CA 104; 133; CDALB 1917-1929;
DLB 9, 102; DLBD 1; MTCW 1

Lewis, (Percy) Wyndham 1882(?)-1957TCLC
2, 9
See also CA 104; 157; DLB 15

Lewisohn, Ludwig 1883-1955   TCLC 19
See also CA 107; DLB 4, 9, 28, 102

Lewton, Val 1904-1951   TCLC 76

Leyner, Mark 1956-   CLC 92
See also CA 110; CANR 28, 53

Lezama Lima, Jose 1910-1976CLC 4, 10, 101;
DAM MULT
See also CA 77-80; CANR 71; DLB 113; HW

L'Heureux, John (Clarke) 1934-   CLC 52
See also CA 13-16R; CANR 23, 45

Liddell, C. H.
See Kuttner, Henry

Lie, Jonas (Lauritz Idemil) 1833-1908(?)
TCLC 5
See also CA 115

Lieber, Joel 1937-1971   CLC 6
See also CA 73-76; 29-32R

Lieber, Stanley Martin
See Lee, Stan

Lieberman, Laurence (James) 1935- CLC 4,
36
See also CA 17-20R; CANR 8, 36

Lieh Tzu fl. 7th cent. B.C.-5th cent. B.C.
CMLC 27

Lieksman, Anders
See Haavikko, Paavo Juhani

Li Fei-kan 1904-
See Pa Chin
See also CA 105

Lifton, Robert Jay 1926-   CLC 67
See also CA 17-20R; CANR 27; INT CANR-
27; SATA 66

Lightfoot, Gordon 1938-   CLC 26
See also CA 109

Lightman, Alan P(aige) 1948-   CLC 81
See also CA 141; CANR 63

Ligotti, Thomas (Robert) 1953-CLC 44; SSC
16
See also CA 123; CANR 49

Li Ho 791-817   PC 13

Liliencron, (Friedrich Adolf Axel) Detlev von
1844-1909   TCLC 18
See also CA 117

Lilly, William 1602-1681   LC 27

Lima, Jose Lezama
See Lezama Lima, Jose

Lima Barreto, Afonso Henrique de 1881-1922
TCLC 23
See also CA 117

Limonov, Edward 1944-   CLC 67
See also CA 137

Lin, Frank
See Atherton, Gertrude (Franklin Horn)

Lincoln, Abraham 1809-1865   NCLC 18

Lind, Jakov   CLC 1, 2, 4, 27, 82
See also Landwirth, Heinz
See also CAAS 4

Lindbergh, Anne (Spencer) Morrow 1906-
CLC 82; DAM NOV
See also CA 17-20R; CANR 16, 73; MTCW 1;
SATA 33

Lindsay, David 1878-1945   TCLC 15
See also CA 113

Lindsay, (Nicholas) Vachel 1879-1931 TCLC
17; DA; DAC; DAM MST, POET; PC 23;
WLC
See also CA 114; 135; CDALB 1865-1917;
DLB 54; SATA 40

Linke-Poot
See Doeblin, Alfred

8, 9, 11, 18, 27, 44, 78, 85; DA; DAB; DAC; DAM MST, NOV, POP; SSC 15; WLC
See also AAYA 16; CA 5-8R; 118; CABS 1; CANR 28, 62; CDALB 1941-1968; DLB 2, 28, 152; DLBY 80, 86; MTCW 1

Malan, Herman
See Bosman, Herman Charles; Bosman, Herman Charles

Malaparte, Curzio 1898-1957　　**TCLC 52**

Malcolm, Dan
See Silverberg, Robert

Malcolm X　　CLC 82, 117; BLC 2; WLCS
See also Little, Malcolm

Malherbe, Francois de 1555-1628　　**LC 5**

Mallarme, Stephane 1842-1898 **NCLC 4, 41; DAM POET; PC 4**

Mallet-Joris, Francoise 1930-　　**CLC 11**
See also CA 65-68; CANR 17; DLB 83

Malley, Ern
See McAuley, James Phillip

Mallowan, Agatha Christie
See Christie, Agatha (Mary Clarissa)

Maloff, Saul 1922-　　**CLC 5**
See also CA 33-36R

Malone, Louis
See MacNeice, (Frederick) Louis

Malone, Michael (Christopher) 1942-**CLC 43**
See also CA 77-80; CANR 14, 32, 57

Malory, (Sir) Thomas 1410(?)-1471(?)**LC 11; DA; DAB; DAC; DAM MST; WLCS**
See also CDBLB Before 1660; DLB 146; SATA 59; SATA-Brief 33

Malouf, (George Joseph) David 1934-**CLC 28, 86**
See also CA 124; CANR 50

Malraux, (Georges-)Andre 1901-1976**CLC 1, 4, 9, 13, 15, 57; DAM NOV**
See also CA 21-22; 69-72; CANR 34, 58; CAP 2; DLB 72; MTCW 1

Malzberg, Barry N(athaniel) 1939-　　**CLC 7**
See also CA 61-64; CAAS 4; CANR 16; DLB 8

Mamet, David (Alan) 1947-**CLC 9, 15, 34, 46, 91; DAM DRAM; DC 4**
See also AAYA 3; CA 81-84; CABS 3; CANR 15, 41, 67, 72; DLB 7; MTCW 1

Mamoulian, Rouben (Zachary) 1897-1987 **CLC 16**
See also CA 25-28R; 124

Mandelstam, Osip (Emilievich) 1891(?)-1938(?) **TCLC 2, 6; PC 14**
See also CA 104; 150

Mander, (Mary) Jane 1877-1949　　**TCLC 31**
See also CA 162

Mandeville, John fl. 1350-　　**CMLC 19**
See also DLB 146

Mandiargues, Andre Pieyre de　　**CLC 41**
See also Pieyre de Mandiargues, Andre
See also DLB 83

Mandrake, Ethel Belle
See Thurman, Wallace (Henry)

Mangan, James Clarence 1803-1849**NCLC 27**

Maniere, J.-E.
See Giraudoux, (Hippolyte) Jean

Mankiewicz, Herman (Jacob) 1897-1953 **TCLC 85**
See also CA 120; 169; DLB 26

Manley, (Mary) Delariviere 1672(?)-1724 **LC 1, 42**
See also DLB 39, 80

Mann, Abel
See Creasey, John

Mann, Emily 1952-　　**DC 7**
See also CA 130; CANR 55

Mann, (Luiz) Heinrich 1871-1950　　**TCLC 9**
See also CA 106; 164; DLB 66

Mann, (Paul) Thomas 1875-1955 **TCLC 2, 8, 14, 21, 35, 44, 60; DA; DAB; DAC; DAM MST, NOV; SSC 5; WLC**
See also CA 104; 128; DLB 66; MTCW 1

Mannheim, Karl 1893-1947　　**TCLC 65**

Manning, David
See Faust, Frederick (Schiller)

Manning, Frederic 1887(?)-1935　　**TCLC 25**
See also CA 124

Manning, Olivia 1915-1980　　**CLC 5, 19**
See also CA 5-8R; 101; CANR 29; MTCW 1

Mano, D. Keith 1942-　　**CLC 2, 10**
See also CA 25-28R; CAAS 6; CANR 26, 57; DLB 6

Mansfield, KatherineTCLC 2, 8, 39; DAB; SSC 9, 23; WLC
See also Beauchamp, Kathleen Mansfield
See also DLB 162

Manso, Peter 1940-　　**CLC 39**
See also CA 29-32R; CANR 44

Mantecon, Juan Jimenez
See Jimenez (Mantecon), Juan Ramon

Manton, Peter
See Creasey, John

Man Without a Spleen, A
See Chekhov, Anton (Pavlovich)

Manzoni, Alessandro 1785-1873　　**NCLC 29**

Map, Walter 1140-1209　　**CMLC 32**

Mapu, Abraham (ben Jekutiel) 1808-1867 **NCLC 18**

Mara, Sally
See Queneau, Raymond

Marat, Jean Paul 1743-1793　　**LC 10**

Marcel, Gabriel Honore 1889-1973　　**CLC 15**
See also CA 102; 45-48; MTCW 1

Marchbanks, Samuel
See Davies, (William) Robertson

Marchi, Giacomo
See Bassani, Giorgio

Margulies, Donald　　**CLC 76**

Marie de France c. 12th cent. - **CMLC 8; PC 22**
See also DLB 208

Marie de l'Incarnation 1599-1672　　**LC 10**

Marier, Captain Victor
See Griffith, D(avid Lewelyn) W(ark)

Mariner, Scott
See Pohl, Frederik

Marinetti, Filippo Tommaso 1876-1944**TCLC 10**
See also CA 107; DLB 114

Marivaux, Pierre Carlet de Chamblain de 1688-1763　　**LC 4; DC 7**

Markandaya, Kamala　　**CLC 8, 38**
See also Taylor, Kamala (Purnaiya)

Markfield, Wallace 1926-　　**CLC 8**
See also CA 69-72; CAAS 3; DLB 2, 28

Markham, Edwin 1852-1940　　**TCLC 47**
See also CA 160; DLB 54, 186

Markham, Robert
See Amis, Kingsley (William)

Marks, J
See Highwater, Jamake (Mamake)

Marks-Highwater, J
See Highwater, Jamake (Mamake)

Markson, David M(errill) 1927-　　**CLC 67**
See also CA 49-52; CANR 1

Marley, Bob　　**CLC 17**
See also Marley, Robert Nesta

Marley, Robert Nesta 1945-1981
See Marley, Bob

See also CA 107; 103

Marlowe, Christopher 1564-1593 **LC 22, 47; DA; DAB; DAC; DAM DRAM, MST; DC 1; WLC**
See also CDBLB Before 1660; DLB 62

Marlowe, Stephen 1928-
See Queen, Ellery
See also CA 13-16R; CANR 6, 55

Marmontel, Jean-Francois 1723-1799　　**LC 2**

Marquand, John P(hillips) 1893-1960**CLC 2, 10**
See also CA 85-88; CANR 73; DLB 9, 102

Marques, Rene 1919-1979　　**CLC 96; DAM MULT; HLC**
See also CA 97-100; 85-88; DLB 113; HW

Marquez, Gabriel (Jose) Garcia
See Garcia Marquez, Gabriel (Jose)

Marquis, Don(ald Robert Perry) 1878-1937 **TCLC 7**
See also CA 104; 166; DLB 11, 25

Marric, J. J.
See Creasey, John

Marryat, Frederick 1792-1848　　**NCLC 3**
See also DLB 21, 163

Marsden, James
See Creasey, John

Marsh, (Edith) Ngaio 1899-1982　　**CLC 7, 53; DAM POP**
See also CA 9-12R; CANR 6, 58; DLB 77; MTCW 1

Marshall, Garry 1934-　　**CLC 17**
See also AAYA 3; CA 111; SATA 60

Marshall, Paule 1929-　　**CLC 27, 72; BLC 3; DAM MULT; SSC 3**
See also BW 2; CA 77-80; CANR 25, 73; DLB 157; MTCW 1

Marshallik
See Zangwill, Israel

Marsten, Richard
See Hunter, Evan

Marston, John 1576-1634**LC 33; DAM DRAM**
See also DLB 58, 172

Martha, Henry
See Harris, Mark

Marti, Jose 1853-1895**NCLC 63; DAM MULT; HLC**

Martial c. 40-c. 104　　**PC 10**

Martin, Ken
See Hubbard, L(afayette) Ron(ald)

Martin, Richard
See Creasey, John

Martin, Steve 1945-　　**CLC 30**
See also CA 97-100; CANR 30; MTCW 1

Martin, Valerie 1948-　　**CLC 89**
See also BEST 90:2; CA 85-88; CANR 49

Martin, Violet Florence 1862-1915 **TCLC 51**

Martin, Webber
See Silverberg, Robert

Martindale, Patrick Victor
See White, Patrick (Victor Martindale)

Martin du Gard, Roger 1881-1958 **TCLC 24**
See also CA 118; DLB 65

Martineau, Harriet 1802-1876　　**NCLC 26**
See also DLB 21, 55, 159, 163, 166, 190; YABC 2

Martines, Julia
See O'Faolain, Julia

Martinez, Enrique Gonzalez
See Gonzalez Martinez, Enrique

Martinez, Jacinto Benavente
See Benavente (y Martinez), Jacinto

Martinez Ruiz, Jose 1873-1967
See Azorin; Ruiz, Jose Martinez

See also CA 93-96; HW

Martinez Sierra, Gregorio 1881-1947**TCLC 6**
See also CA 115

Martinez Sierra, Maria (de la O'LeJarraga)
1874-1974 **TCLC 6**
See also CA 115

Martinsen, Martin
See Follett, Ken(neth Martin)

Martinson, Harry (Edmund) 1904-1978 **C L C
14**
See also CA 77-80; CANR 34

Marut, Ret
See Traven, B.

Marut, Robert
See Traven, B.

Marvell, Andrew 1621-1678 **LC 4, 43; DA;
DAB; DAC; DAM MST, POET; PC 10;
WLC**
See also CDBLB 1660-1789; DLB 131

Marx, Karl (Heinrich) 1818-1883 **NCLC 17**
See also DLB 129

Masaoka Shiki **TCLC 18**
See also Masaoka Tsunenori

Masaoka Tsunenori 1867-1902
See Masaoka Shiki
See also CA 117

Masefield, John (Edward) 1878-1967**CLC 11,
47; DAM POET**
See also CA 19-20; 25-28R; CANR 33; CAP 2;
CDBLB 1890-1914; DLB 10, 19, 153, 160;
MTCW 1; SATA 19

Maso, Carole 19(?)- **CLC 44**
See also CA 170

Mason, Bobbie Ann 1940-**CLC 28, 43, 82; SSC
4**
See also AAYA 5; CA 53-56; CANR 11, 31,
58; DLB 173; DLBY 87; INT CANR-31;
MTCW 1

Mason, Ernst
See Pohl, Frederik

Mason, Lee W.
See Malzberg, Barry N(athaniel)

Mason, Nick 1945- **CLC 35**

Mason, Tally
See Derleth, August (William)

Mass, William
See Gibson, William

Master Lao
See Lao Tzu

Masters, Edgar Lee 1868-1950 **TCLC 2, 25;
DA; DAC; DAM MST, POET; PC 1;
WLCS**
See also CA 104; 133; CDALB 1865-1917;
DLB 54; MTCW 1

Masters, Hilary 1928- **CLC 48**
See also CA 25-28R; CANR 13, 47

Mastrosimone, William 19(?)- **CLC 36**

Mathe, Albert
See Camus, Albert

Mather, Cotton 1663-1728 **LC 38**
See also CDALB 1640-1865; DLB 24, 30, 140

Mather, Increase 1639-1723 **LC 38**
See also DLB 24

Matheson, Richard Burton 1926- **CLC 37**
See also CA 97-100; DLB 8, 44; INT 97-100

Mathews, Harry 1930- **CLC 6, 52**
See also CA 21-24R; CAAS 6; CANR 18, 40

Mathews, John Joseph 1894-1979 **CLC 84;
DAM MULT**
See also CA 19-20; 142; CANR 45; CAP 2;
DLB 175; NNAL

Mathias, Roland (Glyn) 1915- **CLC 45**
See also CA 97-100; CANR 19, 41; DLB 27

Matsuo Basho 1644-1694 **PC 3**
See also DAM POET

Mattheson, Rodney
See Creasey, John

Matthews, Greg 1949- **CLC 45**
See also CA 135

Matthews, William (Procter, III) 1942-1997
CLC 40
See also CA 29-32R; 162; CAAS 18; CANR
12, 57; DLB 5

Matthias, John (Edward) 1941- **CLC 9**
See also CA 33-36R; CANR 56

Matthiessen, Peter 1927-**CLC 5, 7, 11, 32, 64;
DAM NOV**
See also AAYA 6; BEST 90:4; CA 9-12R;
CANR 21, 50, 73; DLB 6, 173; MTCW 1;
SATA 27

Maturin, Charles Robert 1780(?)-1824**NCLC
6**
See also DLB 178

Matute (Ausejo), Ana Maria 1925- **CLC 11**
See also CA 89-92; MTCW 1

Maugham, W. S.
See Maugham, W(illiam) Somerset

Maugham, W(illiam) Somerset 1874-1965
**CLC 1, 11, 15, 67, 93; DA; DAB; DAC;
DAM DRAM, MST, NOV; SSC 8; WLC**
See also CA 5-8R; 25-28R; CANR 40; CDBLB
1914-1945; DLB 10, 36, 77, 100, 162, 195;
MTCW 1; SATA 54

Maugham, William Somerset
See Maugham, W(illiam) Somerset

Maupassant, (Henri Rene Albert) Guy de 1850-
1893**NCLC 1, 42; DA; DAB; DAC; DAM
MST; SSC 1; WLC**
See also DLB 123

Maupin, Armistead 1944-**CLC 95; DAM POP**
See also CA 125; 130; CANR 58; INT 130

Maurhut, Richard
See Traven, B.

Mauriac, Claude 1914-1996 **CLC 9**
See also CA 89-92; 152; DLB 83

Mauriac, Francois (Charles) 1885-1970 **C L C
4, 9, 56; SSC 24**
See also CA 25-28; CAP 2; DLB 65; MTCW 1

Mavor, Osborne Henry 1888-1951
See Bridie, James
See also CA 104

Maxwell, William (Keepers, Jr.) 1908-**CLC 19**
See also CA 93-96; CANR 54; DLBY 80; INT
93-96

May, Elaine 1932- **CLC 16**
See also CA 124; 142; DLB 44

Mayakovski, Vladimir (Vladimirovich) 1893-
1930 **TCLC 4, 18**
See also CA 104; 158

Mayhew, Henry 1812-1887 **NCLC 31**
See also DLB 18, 55, 190

Mayle, Peter 1939(?)- **CLC 89**
See also CA 139; CANR 64

Maynard, Joyce 1953- **CLC 23**
See also CA 111; 129; CANR 64

Mayne, William (James Carter) 1928-**CLC 12**
See also AAYA 20; CA 9-12R; CANR 37; CLR
25; JRDA; MAICYA; SAAS 11; SATA 6, 68

Mayo, Jim
See L'Amour, Louis (Dearborn)

Maysles, Albert 1926- **CLC 16**
See also CA 29-32R

Maysles, David 1932- **CLC 16**

Mazer, Norma Fox 1931- **CLC 26**
See also AAYA 5; CA 69-72; CANR 12, 32,
66; CLR 23; JRDA; MAICYA; SAAS 1;

SATA 24, 67

Mazzini, Guiseppe 1805-1872 **NCLC 34**

McAuley, James Phillip 1917-1976 **CLC 45**
See also CA 97-100

McBain, Ed
See Hunter, Evan

McBrien, William Augustine 1930- **CLC 44**
See also CA 107

McCaffrey, Anne (Inez) 1926-**CLC 17; DAM
NOV, POP**
See also AAYA 6; AITN 2; BEST 89:2; CA 25-
28R; CANR 15, 35, 55; CLR 49; DLB 8;
JRDA; MAICYA; MTCW 1; SAAS 11; SATA
8, 70

McCall, Nathan 1955(?)- **CLC 86**
See also CA 146

McCann, Arthur
See Campbell, John W(ood, Jr.)

McCann, Edson
See Pohl, Frederik

McCarthy, Charles, Jr. 1933-
See McCarthy, Cormac
See also CANR 42, 69; DAM POP

McCarthy, Cormac 1933- **CLC 4, 57, 59, 101**
See also McCarthy, Charles, Jr.
See also DLB 6, 143

McCarthy, Mary (Therese) 1912-1989**CLC 1,
3, 5, 14, 24, 39, 59; SSC 24**
See also CA 5-8R; 129; CANR 16, 50, 64; DLB
2; DLBY 81; INT CANR-16; MTCW 1

McCartney, (James) Paul 1942- **CLC 12, 35**
See also CA 146

McCauley, Stephen (D.) 1955- **CLC 50**
See also CA 141

McClure, Michael (Thomas) 1932-**CLC 6, 10**
See also CA 21-24R; CANR 17, 46; DLB 16

McCorkle, Jill (Collins) 1958- **CLC 51**
See also CA 121; DLBY 87

McCourt, Frank 1930- **CLC 109**
See also CA 157

McCourt, James 1941- **CLC 5**
See also CA 57-60

McCoy, Horace (Stanley) 1897-1955**TCLC 28**
See also CA 108; 155; DLB 9

McCrae, John 1872-1918 **TCLC 12**
See also CA 109; DLB 92

McCreigh, James
See Pohl, Frederik

McCullers, (Lula) Carson (Smith) 1917-1967
**CLC 1, 4, 10, 12, 48, 100; DA; DAB; DAC;
DAM MST, NOV; SSC 9, 24; WLC**
See also AAYA 21; CA 5-8R; 25-28R; CABS
1, 3; CANR 18; CDALB 1941-1968; DLB
2, 7, 173; MTCW 1; SATA 27

McCulloch, John Tyler
See Burroughs, Edgar Rice

McCullough, Colleen 1938(?)- **CLC 27, 107;
DAM NOV, POP**
See also CA 81-84; CANR 17, 46, 67; MTCW
1

McDermott, Alice 1953- **CLC 90**
See also CA 109; CANR 40

McElroy, Joseph 1930- **CLC 5, 47**
See also CA 17-20R

McEwan, Ian (Russell) 1948- **CLC 13, 66;
DAM NOV**
See also BEST 90:4; CA 61-64; CANR 14, 41,
69; DLB 14, 194; MTCW 1

McFadden, David 1940- **CLC 48**
See also CA 104; DLB 60; INT 104

McFarland, Dennis 1950- **CLC 65**
See also CA 165

McGahern, John 1934-**CLC 5, 9, 48; SSC 17**

Middleton, Stanley 1919- **CLC 7, 38**
See also CA 25-28R; CAAS 23; CANR 21, 46; DLB 14

Middleton, Thomas 1580-1627 **LC 33; DAM DRAM, MST; DC 5**
See also DLB 58

Migueis, Jose Rodrigues 1901- **CLC 10**

Mikszath, Kalman 1847-1910 **TCLC 31**
See also CA 170

Miles, Jack **CLC 100**

Miles, Josephine (Louise) 1911-1985 **CLC 1, 2, 14, 34, 39; DAM POET**
See also CA 1-4R; 116; CANR 2, 55; DLB 48

Militant
See Sandburg, Carl (August)

Mill, John Stuart 1806-1873 **NCLC 11, 58**
See also CDBLB 1832-1890; DLB 55, 190

Millar, Kenneth 1915-1983 **CLC 14; DAM POP**
See also Macdonald, Ross
See also CA 9-12R; 110; CANR 16, 63; DLB 2; DLBD 6; DLBY 83; MTCW 1

Millay, E. Vincent
See Millay, Edna St. Vincent

Millay, Edna St. Vincent 1892-1950 **TCLC 4, 49; DA; DAB; DAC; DAM MST, POET; PC 6; WLCS**
See also CA 104; 130; CDALB 1917-1929; DLB 45; MTCW 1

Miller, Arthur 1915- **CLC 1, 2, 6, 10, 15, 26, 47, 78; DA; DAB; DAC; DAM DRAM, MST; DC 1; WLC**
See also AAYA 15; AITN 1; CA 1-4R; CABS 3; CANR 2, 30, 54; CDALB 1941-1968; DLB 7; MTCW 1

Miller, Henry (Valentine) 1891-1980 **CLC 1, 2, 4, 9, 14, 43, 84; DA; DAB; DAC; DAM MST, NOV; WLC**
See also CA 9-12R; 97-100; CANR 33, 64; CDALB 1929-1941; DLB 4, 9; DLBY 80; MTCW 1

Miller, Jason 1939(?)- **CLC 2**
See also AITN 1; CA 73-76; DLB 7

Miller, Sue 1943- **CLC 44; DAM POP**
See also BEST 90:3; CA 139; CANR 59; DLB 143

Miller, Walter M(ichael, Jr.) 1923- **CLC 4, 30**
See also CA 85-88; DLB 8

Millett, Kate 1934- **CLC 67**
See also AITN 1; CA 73-76; CANR 32, 53; MTCW 1

Millhauser, Steven (Lewis) 1943- **CLC 21, 54, 109**
See also CA 110; 111; CANR 63; DLB 2; INT 111

Millin, Sarah Gertrude 1889-1968 **CLC 49**
See also CA 102; 93-96

Milne, A(lan) A(lexander) 1882-1956 **TCLC 6, 88; DAB; DAC; DAM MST**
See also CA 104; 133; CLR 1, 26; DLB 10, 77, 100, 160; MAICYA; MTCW 1; SATA 100; YABC 1

Milner, Ron(ald) 1938- **CLC 56; BLC 3; DAM MULT**
See also AITN 1; BW 1; CA 73-76; CANR 24; DLB 38; MTCW 1

Milnes, Richard Monckton 1809-1885 **NCLC 61**
See also DLB 32, 184

Milosz, Czeslaw 1911- **CLC 5, 11, 22, 31, 56, 82; DAM MST, POET; PC 8; WLCS**
See also CA 81-84; CANR 23, 51; MTCW 1

Milton, John 1608-1674 **LC 9, 43; DA; DAB;** **DAC; DAM MST, POET; PC 19; WLC**
See also CDBLB 1660-1789; DLB 131, 151

Min, Anchee 1957- **CLC 86**
See also CA 146

Minehaha, Cornelius
See Wedekind, (Benjamin) Frank(lin)

Miner, Valerie 1947- **CLC 40**
See also CA 97-100; CANR 59

Minimo, Duca
See D'Annunzio, Gabriele

Minot, Susan 1956- **CLC 44**
See also CA 134

Minus, Ed 1938- **CLC 39**

Miranda, Javier
See Bioy Casares, Adolfo

Mirbeau, Octave 1848-1917 **TCLC 55**
See also DLB 123, 192

Miro (Ferrer), Gabriel (Francisco Victor) 1879-1930 **TCLC 5**
See also CA 104

Mishima, Yukio 1925-1970 **CLC 2, 4, 6, 9, 27; DC 1; SSC 4**
See also Hiraoka, Kimitake
See also DLB 182

Mistral, Frederic 1830-1914 **TCLC 51**
See also CA 122

Mistral, Gabriela **TCLC 2; HLC**
See also Godoy Alcayaga, Lucila

Mistry, Rohinton 1952- **CLC 71; DAC**
See also CA 141

Mitchell, Clyde
See Ellison, Harlan (Jay); Silverberg, Robert

Mitchell, James Leslie 1901-1935
See Gibbon, Lewis Grassic
See also CA 104; DLB 15

Mitchell, Joni 1943- **CLC 12**
See also CA 112

Mitchell, Joseph (Quincy) 1908-1996 **CLC 98**
See also CA 77-80; 152; CANR 69; DLB 185; DLBY 96

Mitchell, Margaret (Munnerlyn) 1900-1949 **TCLC 11; DAM NOV, POP**
See also AAYA 23; CA 109; 125; CANR 55; DLB 9; MTCW 1

Mitchell, Peggy
See Mitchell, Margaret (Munnerlyn)

Mitchell, S(ilas) Weir 1829-1914 **TCLC 36**
See also CA 165; DLB 202

Mitchell, W(illiam) O(rmond) 1914-1998 **CLC 25; DAC; DAM MST**
See also CA 77-80; 165; CANR 15, 43; DLB 88

Mitchell, William 1879-1936 **TCLC 81**

Mitford, Mary Russell 1787-1855 **NCLC 4**
See also DLB 110, 116

Mitford, Nancy 1904-1973 **CLC 44**
See also CA 9-12R; DLB 191

Miyamoto, Yuriko 1899-1951 **TCLC 37**
See also CA 170; DLB 180

Miyazawa, Kenji 1896-1933 **TCLC 76**
See also CA 157

Mizoguchi, Kenji 1898-1956 **TCLC 72**
See also CA 167

Mo, Timothy (Peter) 1950(?)- **CLC 46**
See also CA 117; DLB 194; MTCW 1

Modarressi, Taghi (M.) 1931- **CLC 44**
See also CA 121; 134; INT 134

Modiano, Patrick (Jean) 1945- **CLC 18**
See also CA 85-88; CANR 17, 40; DLB 83

Moerck, Paal
See Roelvaag, O(le) E(dvart)

Mofolo, Thomas (Mokopu) 1875(?)-1948 **TCLC 22; BLC 3; DAM MULT**

See also CA 121; 153

Mohr, Nicholasa 1938- **CLC 12; DAM MULT; HLC**
See also AAYA 8; CA 49-52; CANR 1, 32, 64; CLR 22; DLB 145; HW; JRDA; SAAS 8; SATA 8, 97

Mojtabai, A(nn) G(race) 1938- **CLC 5, 9, 15, 29**
See also CA 85-88

Moliere 1622-1673 **LC 10, 28; DA; DAB; DAC; DAM DRAM, MST; WLC**

Molin, Charles
See Mayne, William (James Carter)

Molnar, Ferenc 1878-1952 **TCLC 20; DAM DRAM**
See also CA 109; 153

Momaday, N(avarre) Scott 1934- **CLC 2, 19, 85, 95; DA; DAB; DAC; DAM MST, MULT, NOV, POP; PC 25; WLCS**
See also AAYA 11; CA 25-28R; CANR 14, 34, 68; DLB 143, 175; INT CANR-14; MTCW 1; NNAL; SATA 48; SATA-Brief 30

Monette, Paul 1945-1995 **CLC 82**
See also CA 139; 147

Monroe, Harriet 1860-1936 **TCLC 12**
See also CA 109; DLB 54, 91

Monroe, Lyle
See Heinlein, Robert A(nson)

Montagu, Elizabeth 1720-1800 **NCLC 7**

Montagu, Mary (Pierrepont) Wortley 1689-1762 **LC 9; PC 16**
See also DLB 95, 101

Montagu, W. H.
See Coleridge, Samuel Taylor

Montague, John (Patrick) 1929- **CLC 13, 46**
See also CA 9-12R; CANR 9, 69; DLB 40; MTCW 1

Montaigne, Michel (Eyquem) de 1533-1592 **LC 8; DA; DAB; DAC; DAM MST; WLC**

Montale, Eugenio 1896-1981 **CLC 7, 9, 18; PC 13**
See also CA 17-20R; 104; CANR 30; DLB 114; MTCW 1

Montesquieu, Charles-Louis de Secondat 1689-1755 **LC 7**

Montgomery, (Robert) Bruce 1921-1978
See Crispin, Edmund
See also CA 104

Montgomery, L(ucy) M(aud) 1874-1942 **TCLC 51; DAC; DAM MST**
See also AAYA 12; CA 108; 137; CLR 8; DLB 92; DLBD 14; JRDA; MAICYA; SATA 100; YABC 1

Montgomery, Marion H., Jr. 1925- **CLC 7**
See also AITN 1; CA 1-4R; CANR 3, 48; DLB 6

Montgomery, Max
See Davenport, Guy (Mattison, Jr.)

Montherlant, Henry (Milon) de 1896-1972 **CLC 8, 19; DAM DRAM**
See also CA 85-88; 37-40R; DLB 72; MTCW 1

Monty Python
See Chapman, Graham; Cleese, John (Marwood); Gilliam, Terry (Vance); Idle, Eric; Jones, Terence Graham Parry; Palin, Michael (Edward)
See also AAYA 7

Moodie, Susanna (Strickland) 1803-1885 **NCLC 14**
See also DLB 99

Mooney, Edward 1951-
See Mooney, Ted

See also CA 130
Mooney, Ted   **CLC 25**
See also Mooney, Edward
Moorcock, Michael (John) 1939-**CLC 5, 27, 58**
See also AAYA 26; CA 45-48; CAAS 5; CANR
2, 17, 38, 64; DLB 14; MTCW 1; SATA 93
Moore, Brian 1921- **CLC 1, 3, 5, 7, 8, 19, 32,
90; DAB; DAC; DAM MST**
See also CA 1-4R; CANR 1, 25, 42, 63; MTCW
1
Moore, Edward
See Muir, Edwin
Moore, G. E. 1873-1958   **TCLC 89**
Moore, George Augustus 1852-1933**TCLC 7;
SSC 19**
See also CA 104; DLB 10, 18, 57, 135
Moore, Lorrie   **CLC 39, 45, 68**
See also Moore, Marie Lorena
Moore, Marianne (Craig) 1887-1972**CLC 1, 2,
4, 8, 10, 13, 19, 47; DA; DAB; DAC; DAM
MST, POET; PC 4; WLCS**
See also CA 1-4R; 33-36R; CANR 3, 61;
CDALB 1929-1941; DLB 45; DLBD 7;
MTCW 1; SATA 20
Moore, Marie Lorena 1957-
See Moore, Lorrie
See also CA 116; CANR 39
Moore, Thomas 1779-1852   **NCLC 6**
See also DLB 96, 144
Morand, Paul 1888-1976   **CLC 41; SSC 22**
See also CA 69-72; DLB 65
Morante, Elsa 1918-1985   **CLC 8, 47**
See also CA 85-88; 117; CANR 35; DLB 177;
MTCW 1
Moravia, Alberto 1907-1990**CLC 2, 7, 11, 27,
46; SSC 26**
See Pincherle, Alberto
See also DLB 177
More, Hannah 1745-1833   **NCLC 27**
See also DLB 107, 109, 116, 158
More, Henry 1614-1687   **LC 9**
See also DLB 126
More, Sir Thomas 1478-1535   **LC 10, 32**
Moreas, Jean   **TCLC 18**
See also Papadiamantopoulos, Johannes
Morgan, Berry 1919-   **CLC 6**
See also CA 49-52; DLB 6
Morgan, Claire
See Highsmith, (Mary) Patricia
Morgan, Edwin (George) 1920-   **CLC 31**
See also CA 5-8R; CANR 3, 43; DLB 27
Morgan, (George) Frederick 1922-   **CLC 23**
See also CA 17-20R; CANR 21
Morgan, Harriet
See Mencken, H(enry) L(ouis)
Morgan, Jane
See Cooper, James Fenimore
Morgan, Janet 1945-   **CLC 39**
See also CA 65-68
Morgan, Lady 1776(?)-1859   **NCLC 29**
See also DLB 116, 158
Morgan, Robin (Evonne) 1941-   **CLC 2**
See also CA 69-72; CANR 29, 68; MTCW 1;
SATA 80
Morgan, Scott
See Kuttner, Henry
Morgan, Seth 1949(?)-1990   **CLC 65**
See also CA 132
Morgenstern, Christian 1871-1914   **TCLC 8**
See also CA 105
Morgenstern, S.
See Goldman, William (W.)
Moricz, Zsigmond 1879-1942   **TCLC 33**

See also CA 165
Morike, Eduard (Friedrich) 1804-1875**NCLC
10**
See also DLB 133
Moritz, Karl Philipp 1756-1793   **LC 2**
See also DLB 94
Morland, Peter Henry
See Faust, Frederick (Schiller)
Morley, Christopher (Darlington) 1890-1957
TCLC 87
See also CA 112; DLB 9
Morren, Theophil
See Hofmannsthal, Hugo von
Morris, Bill 1952-   **CLC 76**
Morris, Julian
See West, Morris L(anglo)
Morris, Steveland Judkins 1950(?)-
See Wonder, Stevie
See also CA 111
Morris, William 1834-1896   **NCLC 4**
See also CDBLB 1832-1890; DLB 18, 35, 57,
156, 178, 184
Morris, Wright 1910-1998**CLC 1, 3, 7, 18, 37**
See also CA 9-12R; 167; CANR 21; DLB 2,
206; DLBY 81; MTCW 1
Morrison, Arthur 1863-1945   **TCLC 72**
See also CA 120; 157; DLB 70, 135, 197
Morrison, Chloe Anthony Wofford
See Morrison, Toni
Morrison, James Douglas 1943-1971
See Morrison, Jim
See also CA 73-76; CANR 40
Morrison, Jim   **CLC 17**
See also Morrison, James Douglas
Morrison, Toni 1931-**CLC 4, 10, 22, 55, 81, 87;
BLC 3; DA; DAB; DAC; DAM MST,
MULT, NOV, POP**
See also AAYA 1, 22; BW 2; CA 29-32R;
CANR 27, 42, 67; CDALB 1968-1988; DLB
6, 33, 143; DLBY 81; MTCW 1; SATA 57
Morrison, Van 1945-   **CLC 21**
See also CA 116; 168
Morrissy, Mary 1958-   **CLC 99**
Mortimer, John (Clifford) 1923- **CLC 28, 43;
DAM DRAM, POP**
See also CA 13-16R; CANR 21, 69; CDBLB
1960 to Present; DLB 13; INT CANR-21;
MTCW 1
Mortimer, Penelope (Ruth) 1918-   **CLC 5**
See also CA 57-60; CANR 45
Morton, Anthony
See Creasey, John
Mosca, Gaetano 1858-1941   **TCLC 75**
Mosher, Howard Frank 1943-   **CLC 62**
See also CA 139; CANR 65
Mosley, Nicholas 1923-   **CLC 43, 70**
See also CA 69-72; CANR 41, 60; DLB 14, 207
Mosley, Walter 1952- **CLC 97; BLCS; DAM
MULT, POP**
See also AAYA 17; BW 2; CA 142; CANR 57
Moss, Howard 1922-1987 **CLC 7, 14, 45, 50;
DAM POET**
See also CA 1-4R; 123; CANR 1, 44; DLB 5
Mossgiel, Rab
See Burns, Robert
Motion, Andrew (Peter) 1952-   **CLC 47**
See also CA 146; DLB 40
Motley, Willard (Francis) 1909-1965 **CLC 18**
See also BW 1; CA 117; 106; DLB 76, 143
Motoori, Norinaga 1730-1801   **NCLC 45**
Mott, Michael (Charles Alston) 1930-**CLC 15,
34**
See also CA 5-8R; CAAS 7; CANR 7, 29

Mountain Wolf Woman 1884-1960   **CLC 92**
See also CA 144; NNAL
Moure, Erin 1955-   **CLC 88**
See also CA 113; DLB 60
Mowat, Farley (McGill) 1921-**CLC 26; DAC;
DAM MST**
See also AAYA 1; CA 1-4R; CANR 4, 24, 42,
68; CLR 20; DLB 68; INT CANR-24; JRDA;
MAICYA; MTCW 1; SATA 3, 55
Mowatt, Anna Cora 1819-1870   **NCLC 74**
Moyers, Bill 1934-   **CLC 74**
See also AITN 2; CA 61-64; CANR 31, 52
Mphahlele, Es'kia
See Mphahlele, Ezekiel
See also DLB 125
Mphahlele, Ezekiel 1919-1983 **CLC 25; BLC
3; DAM MULT**
See also Mphahlele, Es'kia
See also BW 2; CA 81-84; CANR 26
Mqhayi, S(amuel) E(dward) K(rune Loliwe)
1875-1945**TCLC 25; BLC 3; DAM MULT**
See also CA 153
Mrozek, Slawomir 1930-   **CLC 3, 13**
See also CA 13-16R; CAAS 10; CANR 29;
MTCW 1
Mrs. Belloc-Lowndes
See Lowndes, Marie Adelaide (Belloc)
Mtwa, Percy (?)-   **CLC 47**
Mueller, Lisel 1924-   **CLC 13, 51**
See also CA 93-96; DLB 105
Muir, Edwin 1887-1959   **TCLC 2, 87**
See also CA 104; DLB 20, 100, 191
Muir, John 1838-1914   **TCLC 28**
See also CA 165; DLB 186
Mujica Lainez, Manuel 1910-1984   **CLC 31**
See also Lainez, Manuel Mujica
See also CA 81-84; 112; CANR 32; HW
Mukherjee, Bharati 1940-**CLC 53, 115; DAM
NOV**
See also BEST 89:2; CA 107; CANR 45, 72;
DLB 60; MTCW 1
Muldoon, Paul 1951-**CLC 32, 72; DAM POET**
See also CA 113; 129; CANR 52; DLB 40; INT
129
Mulisch, Harry 1927-   **CLC 42**
See also CA 9-12R; CANR 6, 26, 56
Mull, Martin 1943-   **CLC 17**
See also CA 105
Muller, Wilhelm   **NCLC 73**
Mulock, Dinah Maria
See Craik, Dinah Maria (Mulock)
Munford, Robert 1737(?)-1783   **LC 5**
See also DLB 31
Mungo, Raymond 1946-   **CLC 72**
See also CA 49-52; CANR 2
Munro, Alice 1931-   **CLC 6, 10, 19, 50, 95;
DAC; DAM MST, NOV; SSC 3; WLCS**
See also AITN 2; CA 33-36R; CANR 33, 53,
75; DLB 53; MTCW 1; SATA 29
Munro, H(ector) H(ugh) 1870-1916
See Saki
See also CA 104; 130; CDBLB 1890-1914; DA;
DAB; DAC; DAM MST, NOV; DLB 34, 162;
MTCW 1; WLC
Murdoch, (Jean) Iris 1919-**CLC 1, 2, 3, 4, 6, 8,
11, 15, 22, 31, 51; DAB; DAC; DAM MST,
NOV**
See also CA 13-16R; CANR 8, 43, 68; CDBLB
1960 to Present; DLB 14, 194; INT CANR-
8; MTCW 1
Murfree, Mary Noailles 1850-1922   **SSC 22**
See also CA 122; DLB 12, 74
Murnau, Friedrich Wilhelm

See Plumpe, Friedrich Wilhelm

Murphy, Richard 1927-   **CLC 41**
  See also CA 29-32R; DLB 40

Murphy, Sylvia 1937-   **CLC 34**
  See also CA 121

Murphy, Thomas (Bernard) 1935-   **CLC 51**
  See also CA 101

Murray, Albert L. 1916-   **CLC 73**
  See also BW 2; CA 49-52; CANR 26, 52; DLB 38

Murray, Judith Sargent 1751-1820 **NCLC 63**
  See also DLB 37, 200

Murray, Les(lie) A(llan) 1938-**CLC 40; DAM POET**
  See also CA 21-24R; CANR 11, 27, 56

Murry, J. Middleton
  See Murry, John Middleton

Murry, John Middleton 1889-1957 **TCLC 16**
  See also CA 118; DLB 149

Musgrave, Susan 1951-   **CLC 13, 54**
  See also CA 69-72; CANR 45

Musil, Robert (Edler von) 1880-1942 **TCLC 12, 68; SSC 18**
  See also CA 109; CANR 55; DLB 81, 124

Muske, Carol 1945-   **CLC 90**
  See also Muske-Dukes, Carol (Anne)

Muske-Dukes, Carol (Anne) 1945-
  See Muske, Carol
  See also CA 65-68; CANR 32, 70

Musset, (Louis Charles) Alfred de 1810-1857 **NCLC 7**
  See also DLB 192

My Brother's Brother
  See Chekhov, Anton (Pavlovich)

Myers, L(eopold) H(amilton) 1881-1944 **TCLC 59**
  See also CA 157; DLB 15

Myers, Walter Dean 1937-   **CLC 35; BLC 3; DAM MULT, NOV**
  See also AAYA 4, 23; BW 2; CA 33-36R; CANR 20, 42, 67; CLR 4, 16, 35; DLB 33; INT CANR-20; JRDA; MAICYA; SAAS 2; SATA 41, 71; SATA-Brief 27

Myers, Walter M.
  See Myers, Walter Dean

Myles, Symon
  See Follett, Ken(neth Martin)

Nabokov, Vladimir (Vladimirovich) 1899-1977 **CLC 1, 2, 3, 6, 8, 11, 15, 23, 44, 46, 64; DA; DAB; DAC; DAM MST, NOV; SSC 11; WLC**
  See also CA 5-8R; 69-72; CANR 20; CDALB 1941-1968; DLB 2; DLBD 3; DLBY 80, 91; MTCW 1

Nagai Kafu 1879-1959   **TCLC 51**
  See also Nagai Sokichi
  See also DLB 180

Nagai Sokichi 1879-1959
  See Nagai Kafu
  See also CA 117

Nagy, Laszlo 1925-1978   **CLC 7**
  See also CA 129; 112

Naidu, Sarojini 1879-1943   **TCLC 80**

Naipaul, Shiva(dhar Srinivasa) 1945-1985 **CLC 32, 39; DAM NOV**
  See also CA 110; 112; 116; CANR 33; DLB 157; DLBY 85; MTCW 1

Naipaul, V(idiadhar) S(urajprasad) 1932- **CLC 4, 7, 9, 13, 18, 37, 105; DAB; DAC; DAM MST, NOV**
  See also CA 1-4R; CANR 1, 33, 51; CDBLB 1960 to Present; DLB 125, 204, 206; DLBY 85; MTCW 1

Nakos, Lilika 1899(?)-   **CLC 29**

Narayan, R(asipuram) K(rishnaswami) 1906- **CLC 7, 28, 47; DAM NOV; SSC 25**
  See also CA 81-84; CANR 33, 61; MTCW 1; SATA 62

Nash, (Frediric) Ogden 1902-1971 **CLC 23; DAM POET; PC 21**
  See also CA 13-14; 29-32R; CANR 34, 61; CAP 1; DLB 11; MAICYA; MTCW 1; SATA 2, 46

Nashe, Thomas 1567-1601(?)   **LC 41**
  See also DLB 167

Nashe, Thomas 1567-1601   **LC 41**

Nathan, Daniel
  See Dannay, Frederic

Nathan, George Jean 1882-1958   **TCLC 18**
  See also Hatteras, Owen
  See also CA 114; 169; DLB 137

Natsume, Kinnosuke 1867-1916
  See Natsume, Soseki
  See also CA 104

Natsume, Soseki 1867-1916   **TCLC 2, 10**
  See also Natsume, Kinnosuke
  See also DLB 180

Natti, (Mary) Lee 1919-
  See Kingman, Lee
  See also CA 5-8R; CANR 2

Naylor, Gloria 1950-**CLC 28, 52; BLC 3; DA; DAC; DAM MST, MULT, NOV, POP; WLCS**
  See also AAYA 6; BW 2; CA 107; CANR 27, 51, 74; DLB 173; MTCW 1

Neihardt, John Gneisenau 1881-1973**CLC 32**
  See also CA 13-14; CANR 65; CAP 1; DLB 9, 54

Nekrasov, Nikolai Alekseevich 1821-1878 **NCLC 11**

Nelligan, Emile 1879-1941   **TCLC 14**
  See also CA 114; DLB 92

Nelson, Willie 1933-   **CLC 17**
  See also CA 107

Nemerov, Howard (Stanley) 1920-1991**CLC 2, 6, 9, 36; DAM POET; PC 24**
  See also CA 1-4R; 134; CABS 2; CANR 1, 27, 53; DLB 5, 6; DLBY 83; INT CANR-27; MTCW 1

Neruda, Pablo 1904-1973**CLC 1, 2, 5, 7, 9, 28, 62; DA; DAB; DAC; DAM MST, MULT, POET; HLC; PC 4; WLC**
  See also CA 19-20; 45-48; CAP 2; HW; MTCW 1

Nerval, Gerard de 1808-1855**NCLC 1, 67; PC 13; SSC 18**

Nervo, (Jose) Amado (Ruiz de) 1870-1919 **TCLC 11**
  See also CA 109; 131; HW

Nessi, Pio Baroja y
  See Baroja (y Nessi), Pio

Nestroy, Johann 1801-1862   **NCLC 42**
  See also DLB 133

Netterville, Luke
  See O'Grady, Standish (James)

Neufeld, John (Arthur) 1938-   **CLC 17**
  See also AAYA 11; CA 25-28R; CANR 11, 37, 56; CLR 52; MAICYA; SAAS 3; SATA 6, 81

Neville, Emily Cheney 1919-   **CLC 12**
  See also CA 5-8R; CANR 3, 37; JRDA; MAICYA; SAAS 2; SATA 1

Newbound, Bernard Slade 1930-
  See Slade, Bernard
  See also CA 81-84; CANR 49; DAM DRAM

Newby, P(ercy) H(oward) 1918-1997 **CLC 2,**

13; DAM NOV
  See also CA 5-8R; 161; CANR 32, 67; DLB 15; MTCW 1

Newlove, Donald 1928-   **CLC 6**
  See also CA 29-32R; CANR 25

Newlove, John (Herbert) 1938-   **CLC 14**
  See also CA 21-24R; CANR 9, 25

Newman, Charles 1938-   **CLC 2, 8**
  See also CA 21-24R

Newman, Edwin (Harold) 1919-   **CLC 14**
  See also AITN 1; CA 69-72; CANR 5

Newman, John Henry 1801-1890 **NCLC 38**
  See also DLB 18, 32, 55

Newton, (Sir)Isaac 1642-1727   **LC 35**

Newton, Suzanne 1936-   **CLC 35**
  See also CA 41-44R; CANR 14; JRDA; SATA 5, 77

Nexo, Martin Andersen 1869-1954 **TCLC 43**

Nezval, Vitezslav 1900-1958   **TCLC 44**
  See also CA 123

Ng, Fae Myenne 1957(?)-   **CLC 81**
  See also CA 146

Ngema, Mbongeni 1955-   **CLC 57**
  See also BW 2; CA 143

Ngugi, James T(hiong'o)   **CLC 3, 7, 13**
  See also Ngugi wa Thiong'o

Ngugi wa Thiong'o 1938-   **CLC 36; BLC 3; DAM MULT, NOV**
  See also Ngugi, James T(hiong'o)
  See also BW 2; CA 81-84; CANR 27, 58; DLB 125; MTCW 1

Nichol, B(arrie) P(hillip) 1944-1988 **CLC 18**
  See also CA 53-56; DLB 53; SATA 66

Nichols, John (Treadwell) 1940-   **CLC 38**
  See also CA 9-12R; CAAS 2; CANR 6, 70; DLBY 82

Nichols, Leigh
  See Koontz, Dean R(ay)

Nichols, Peter (Richard) 1927-**CLC 5, 36, 65**
  See also CA 104; CANR 33; DLB 13; MTCW 1

Nicolas, F. R. E.
  See Freeling, Nicolas

Niedecker, Lorine 1903-1970   **CLC 10, 42; DAM POET**
  See also CA 25-28; CAP 2; DLB 48

Nietzsche, Friedrich (Wilhelm) 1844-1900 **TCLC 10, 18, 55**
  See also CA 107; 121; DLB 129

Nievo, Ippolito 1831-1861   **NCLC 22**

Nightingale, Anne Redmon 1943-
  See Redmon, Anne
  See also CA 103

Nightingale, Florence 1820-1910 **TCLC 85**
  See also DLB 166

Nik. T. O.
  See Annensky, Innokenty (Fyodorovich)

Nin, Anais 1903-1977 **CLC 1, 4, 8, 11, 14, 60; DAM NOV, POP; SSC 10**
  See also AITN 2; CA 13-16R; 69-72; CANR 22, 53; DLB 2, 4, 152; MTCW 1

Nishida, Kitaro 1870-1945   **TCLC 83**

Nishiwaki, Junzaburo 1894-1982   **PC 15**
  See also CA 107

Nissenson, Hugh 1933-   **CLC 4, 9**
  See also CA 17-20R; CANR 27; DLB 28

Niven, Larry   **CLC 8**
  See also Niven, Laurence Van Cott
  See also AAYA 27; DLB 8

Niven, Laurence Van Cott 1938-
  See Niven, Larry
  See also CA 21-24R; CAAS 12; CANR 14, 44, 66; DAM POP; MTCW 1; SATA 95

See also CA 104

Rachilde 1860-1953   **TCLC 67**
  See also DLB 123, 192

Racine, Jean 1639-1699   **LC 28; DAB; DAM MST**

Radcliffe, Ann (Ward) 1764-1823 **NCLC 6, 55**
  See also DLB 39, 178

Radiguet, Raymond 1903-1923   **TCLC 29**
  See also CA 162; DLB 65

Radnoti, Miklos 1909-1944   **TCLC 16**
  See also CA 118

Rado, James 1939-   **CLC 17**
  See also CA 105

Radvanyi, Netty 1900-1983
  See Seghers, Anna
  See also CA 85-88; 110

Rae, Ben
  See Griffiths, Trevor

Raeburn, John (Hay) 1941-   **CLC 34**
  See also CA 57-60

Ragni, Gerome 1942-1991   **CLC 17**
  See also CA 105; 134

Rahv, Philip 1908-1973   **CLC 24**
  See also Greenberg, Ivan
  See also DLB 137

Raimund, Ferdinand Jakob 1790-1836 **NCLC 69**
  See also DLB 90

Raine, Craig 1944-   **CLC 32, 103**
  See also CA 108; CANR 29, 51; DLB 40

Raine, Kathleen (Jessie) 1908-   **CLC 7, 45**
  See also CA 85-88; CANR 46; DLB 20; MTCW 1

Rainis, Janis 1865-1929   **TCLC 29**
  See also CA 170

Rakosi, Carl 1903-   **CLC 47**
  See also Rawley, Callman
  See also CAAS 5; DLB 193

Raleigh, Richard
  See Lovecraft, H(oward) P(hillips)

Raleigh, Sir Walter 1554(?)-1618   **LC 31, 39**
  See also CDBLB Before 1660; DLB 172

Rallentando, H. P.
  See Sayers, Dorothy L(eigh)

Ramal, Walter
  See de la Mare, Walter (John)

Ramana Maharshi 1879-1950   **TCLC 84**

Ramon, Juan
  See Jimenez (Mantecon), Juan Ramon

Ramos, Graciliano 1892-1953   **TCLC 32**
  See also CA 167

Rampersad, Arnold 1941-   **CLC 44**
  See also BW 2; CA 127; 133; DLB 111; INT 133

Rampling, Anne
  See Rice, Anne

Ramsay, Allan 1684(?)-1758   **LC 29**
  See also DLB 95

Ramuz, Charles-Ferdinand 1878-1947 **TCLC 33**
  See also CA 165

Rand, Ayn 1905-1982 **CLC 3, 30, 44, 79; DA; DAC; DAM MST, NOV, POP; WLC**
  See also AAYA 10; CA 13-16R; 105; CANR 27, 73; MTCW 1

Randall, Dudley (Felker) 1914- **CLC 1; BLC 3; DAM MULT**
  See also BW 1; CA 25-28R; CANR 23; DLB 41

Randall, Robert
  See Silverberg, Robert

Ranger, Ken
  See Creasey, John

Ransom, John Crowe 1888-1974 **CLC 2, 4, 5, 11, 24; DAM POET**
  See also CA 5-8R; 49-52; CANR 6, 34; DLB 45, 63; MTCW 1

Rao, Raja 1909-   **CLC 25, 56; DAM NOV**
  See also CA 73-76; CANR 51; MTCW 1

Raphael, Frederic (Michael) 1931- **CLC 2, 14**
  See also CA 1-4R; CANR 1; DLB 14

Ratcliffe, James P.
  See Mencken, H(enry) L(ouis)

Rathbone, Julian 1935-   **CLC 41**
  See also CA 101; CANR 34, 73

Rattigan, Terence (Mervyn) 1911-1977 **CLC 7; DAM DRAM**
  See also CA 85-88; 73-76; CDBLB 1945-1960; DLB 13; MTCW 1

Ratushinskaya, Irina 1954-   **CLC 54**
  See also CA 129; CANR 68

Raven, Simon (Arthur Noel) 1927-   **CLC 14**
  See also CA 81-84

Ravenna, Michael
  See Welty, Eudora

Rawley, Callman 1903-
  See Rakosi, Carl
  See also CA 21-24R; CANR 12, 32

Rawlings, Marjorie Kinnan 1896-1953 **TCLC 4**
  See also AAYA 20; CA 104; 137; CANR 74; DLB 9, 22, 102; DLBD 17; JRDA; MAICYA; SATA 100; YABC 1

Ray, Satyajit 1921-1992   **CLC 16, 76; DAM MULT**
  See also CA 114; 137

Read, Herbert Edward 1893-1968   **CLC 4**
  See also CA 85-88; 25-28R; DLB 20, 149

Read, Piers Paul 1941-   **CLC 4, 10, 25**
  See also CA 21-24R; CANR 38; DLB 14; SATA 21

Reade, Charles 1814-1884   **NCLC 2, 74**
  See also DLB 21

Reade, Hamish
  See Gray, Simon (James Holliday)

Reading, Peter 1946-   **CLC 47**
  See also CA 103; CANR 46; DLB 40

Reaney, James 1926-   **CLC 13; DAC; DAM MST**
  See also CA 41-44R; CAAS 15; CANR 42; DLB 68; SATA 43

Rebreanu, Liviu 1885-1944   **TCLC 28**
  See also CA 165

Rechy, John (Francisco) 1934- **CLC 1, 7, 14, 18, 107; DAM MULT; HLC**
  See also CA 5-8R; CAAS 4; CANR 6, 32, 64; DLB 122; DLBY 82; HW; INT CANR-6

Redcam, Tom 1870-1933   **TCLC 25**

Reddin, Keith   **CLC 67**

Redgrove, Peter (William) 1932- **CLC 6, 41**
  See also CA 1-4R; CANR 3, 39; DLB 40

Redmon, Anne   **CLC 22**
  See also Nightingale, Anne Redmon
  See also DLBY 86

Reed, Eliot
  See Ambler, Eric

Reed, Ishmael 1938- **CLC 2, 3, 5, 6, 13, 32, 60; BLC 3; DAM MULT**
  See also BW 2; CA 21-24R; CANR 25, 48, 74; DLB 2, 5, 33, 169; DLBD 8; MTCW 1

Reed, John (Silas) 1887-1920   **TCLC 9**
  See also CA 106

Reed, Lou   **CLC 21**
  See also Firbank, Louis

Reeve, Clara 1729-1807   **NCLC 19**
  See also DLB 39

Reich, Wilhelm 1897-1957   **TCLC 57**

Reid, Christopher (John) 1949-   **CLC 33**
  See also CA 140; DLB 40

Reid, Desmond
  See Moorcock, Michael (John)

Reid Banks, Lynne 1929-
  See Banks, Lynne Reid
  See also CA 1-4R; CANR 6, 22, 38; CLR 24; JRDA; MAICYA; SATA 22, 75

Reilly, William K.
  See Creasey, John

Reiner, Max
  See Caldwell, (Janet Miriam) Taylor (Holland)

Reis, Ricardo
  See Pessoa, Fernando (Antonio Nogueira)

Remarque, Erich Maria 1898-1970 **CLC 21; DA; DAB; DAC; DAM MST, NOV**
  See also AAYA 27; CA 77-80; 29-32R; DLB 56; MTCW 1

Remington, Frederic 1861-1909   **TCLC 89**
  See also CA 108; 169; DLB 12, 186, 188; SATA 41

Remizov, A.
  See Remizov, Aleksei (Mikhailovich)

Remizov, A. M.
  See Remizov, Aleksei (Mikhailovich)

Remizov, Aleksei (Mikhailovich) 1877-1957 **TCLC 27**
  See also CA 125; 133

Renan, Joseph Ernest 1823-1892   **NCLC 26**

Renard, Jules 1864-1910   **TCLC 17**
  See also CA 117

Renault, Mary   **CLC 3, 11, 17**
  See also Challans, Mary
  See also DLBY 83

Rendell, Ruth (Barbara) 1930- **CLC 28, 48; DAM POP**
  See also Vine, Barbara
  See also CA 109; CANR 32, 52, 74; DLB 87; INT CANR-32; MTCW 1

Renoir, Jean 1894-1979   **CLC 20**
  See also CA 129; 85-88

Resnais, Alain 1922-   **CLC 16**

Reverdy, Pierre 1889-1960   **CLC 53**
  See also CA 97-100; 89-92

Rexroth, Kenneth 1905-1982 **CLC 1, 2, 6, 11, 22, 49, 112; DAM POET; PC 20**
  See also CA 5-8R; 107; CANR 14, 34, 63; CDALB 1941-1968; DLB 16, 48, 165; DLBY 82; INT CANR-14; MTCW 1

Reyes, Alfonso 1889-1959   **TCLC 33**
  See also CA 131; HW

Reyes y Basoalto, Ricardo Eliecer Neftali
  See Neruda, Pablo

Reymont, Wladyslaw (Stanislaw) 1868(?)-1925 **TCLC 5**
  See also CA 104

Reynolds, Jonathan 1942-   **CLC 6, 38**
  See also CA 65-68; CANR 28

Reynolds, Joshua 1723-1792   **LC 15**
  See also DLB 104

Reynolds, Michael Shane 1937-   **CLC 44**
  See also CA 65-68; CANR 9

Reznikoff, Charles 1894-1976   **CLC 9**
  See also CA 33-36; 61-64; CAP 2; DLB 28, 45

Rezzori (d'Arezzo), Gregor von 1914-1998 **CLC 25**
  See also CA 122; 136; 167

Rhine, Richard
  See Silverstein, Alvin

Rhodes, Eugene Manlove 1869-1934 **TCLC 53**

Rhodius, Apollonius c. 3rd cent. B.C.- **CMLC 28**

See also CA 105; 144; DLB 11; NNAL

Rogin, Gilbert 1929-   **CLC 18**
See also CA 65-68; CANR 15

Rohan, Koda   **TCLC 22**
See also Koda Shigeyuki

Rohlfs, Anna Katharine Green
See Green, Anna Katharine

Rohmer, Eric   **CLC 16**
See also Scherer, Jean-Marie Maurice

Rohmer, Sax   **TCLC 28**
See also Ward, Arthur Henry Sarsfield
See also DLB 70

Roiphe, Anne (Richardson) 1935-   **CLC 3, 9**
See also CA 89-92; CANR 45, 73; DLBY 80;
INT 89-92

Rojas, Fernando de 1465-1541   **LC 23**

Rolfe, Frederick (William Serafino Austin
Lewis Mary) 1860-1913   **TCLC 12**
See also CA 107; DLB 34, 156

Rolland, Romain 1866-1944   **TCLC 23**
See also CA 118; DLB 65

Rolle, Richard c. 1300-c. 1349   **CMLC 21**
See also DLB 146

Rolvaag, O(le) E(dvart)
See Roelvaag, O(le) E(dvart)

Romain Arnaud, Saint
See Aragon, Louis

Romains, Jules 1885-1972   **CLC 7**
See also CA 85-88; CANR 34; DLB 65; MTCW
1

Romero, Jose Ruben 1890-1952   **TCLC 14**
See also CA 114; 131; HW

Ronsard, Pierre de 1524-1585   **LC 6; PC 11**

Rooke, Leon 1934-   **CLC 25, 34; DAM POP**
See also CA 25-28R; CANR 23, 53

Roosevelt, Theodore 1858-1919   **TCLC 69**
See also CA 115; 170; DLB 47, 186

Roper, William 1498-1578   **LC 10**

Roquelaure, A. N.
See Rice, Anne

Rosa, Joao Guimaraes 1908-1967   **CLC 23**
See also CA 89-92; DLB 113

Rose, Wendy 1948-   **CLC 85; DAM MULT; PC**
13
See also CA 53-56; CANR 5, 51; DLB 175;
NNAL; SATA 12

Rosen, R. D.
See Rosen, Richard (Dean)

Rosen, Richard (Dean) 1949-   **CLC 39**
See also CA 77-80; CANR 62; INT CANR-30

Rosenberg, Isaac 1890-1918   **TCLC 12**
See also CA 107; DLB 20

Rosenblatt, Joe   **CLC 15**
See also Rosenblatt, Joseph

Rosenblatt, Joseph 1933-
See Rosenblatt, Joe
See also CA 89-92; INT 89-92

Rosenfeld, Samuel
See Tzara, Tristan

Rosenstock, Sami
See Tzara, Tristan

Rosenstock, Samuel
See Tzara, Tristan

Rosenthal, M(acha) L(ouis) 1917-1996 **C L C**
28
See also CA 1-4R; 152; CAAS 6; CANR 4, 51;
DLB 5; SATA 59

Ross, Barnaby
See Dannay, Frederic

Ross, Bernard L.
See Follett, Ken(neth Martin)

Ross, J. H.
See Lawrence, T(homas) E(dward)

Ross, John Hume
See Lawrence, T(homas) E(dward)

Ross, Martin
See Martin, Violet Florence
See also DLB 135

Ross, (James) Sinclair 1908-   **CLC 13; DAC;**
DAM MST; SSC 24
See also CA 73-76; DLB 88

Rossetti, Christina (Georgina) 1830-1894
NCLC 2, 50, 66; DA; DAB; DAC; DAM
MST, POET; PC 7; WLC
See also DLB 35, 163; MAICYA; SATA 20

Rossetti, Dante Gabriel 1828-1882   **NCLC 4;**
DA; DAB; DAC; DAM MST, POET; WLC
See also CDBLB 1832-1890; DLB 35

Rossner, Judith (Perelman) 1935-**CLC 6, 9, 29**
See also AITN 2; BEST 90:3; CA 17-20R;
CANR 18, 51, 73; DLB 6; INT CANR-18;
MTCW 1

Rostand, Edmond (Eugene Alexis) 1868-1918
TCLC 6, 37; DA; DAB; DAC; DAM
DRAM, MST; DC 10
See also CA 104; 126; DLB 192; MTCW 1

Roth, Henry 1906-1995   **CLC 2, 6, 11, 104**
See also CA 11-12; 149; CANR 38, 63; CAP 1;
DLB 28; MTCW 1

Roth, Philip (Milton) 1933-**CLC 1, 2, 3, 4, 6, 9,**
15, 22, 31, 47, 66, 86; DA; DAB; DAC;
DAM MST, NOV, POP; SSC 26; WLC
See also BEST 90:3; CA 1-4R; CANR 1, 22,
36, 55; CDALB 1968-1988; DLB 2, 28, 173;
DLBY 82; MTCW 1

Rothenberg, Jerome 1931-   **CLC 6, 57**
See also CA 45-48; CANR 1; DLB 5, 193

Roumain, Jacques (Jean Baptiste) 1907-1944
TCLC 19; BLC 3; DAM MULT
See also BW 1; CA 117; 125

Rourke, Constance (Mayfield) 1885-1941
TCLC 12
See also CA 107; YABC 1

Rousseau, Jean-Baptiste 1671-1741   **LC 9**

Rousseau, Jean-Jacques 1712-1778**LC 14, 36;**
DA; DAB; DAC; DAM MST; WLC

Roussel, Raymond 1877-1933   **TCLC 20**
See also CA 117

Rovit, Earl (Herbert) 1927-   **CLC 7**
See also CA 5-8R; CANR 12

Rowe, Elizabeth Singer 1674-1737   **LC 44**
See also DLB 39, 95

Rowe, Nicholas 1674-1718   **LC 8**
See also DLB 84

Rowley, Ames Dorrance
See Lovecraft, H(oward) P(hillips)

Rowson, Susanna Haswell 1762(?)-1824
NCLC 5, 69
See also DLB 37, 200

Roy, Arundhati 1960(?)-   **CLC 109**
See also CA 163; DLBY 97

Roy, Gabrielle 1909-1983   **CLC 10, 14; DAB;**
DAC; DAM MST
See also CA 53-56; 110; CANR 5, 61; DLB 68;
MTCW 1

Royko, Mike 1932-1997   **CLC 109**
See also CA 89-92; 157; CANR 26

Rozewicz, Tadeusz 1921-   **CLC 9, 23; DAM**
POET
See also CA 108; CANR 36, 66; MTCW 1

Ruark, Gibbons 1941-   **CLC 3**
See also CA 33-36R; CAAS 23; CANR 14, 31,
57; DLB 120

Rubens, Bernice (Ruth) 1923-   **CLC 19, 31**
See also CA 25-28R; CANR 33, 65; DLB 14,
207; MTCW 1

Rubin, Harold
See Robbins, Harold

Rudkin, (James) David 1936-   **CLC 14**
See also CA 89-92; DLB 13

Rudnik, Raphael 1933-   **CLC 7**
See also CA 29-32R

Ruffian, M.
See Hasek, Jaroslav (Matej Frantisek)

Ruiz, Jose Martinez   **CLC 11**
See also Martinez Ruiz, Jose

Rukeyser, Muriel 1913-1980**CLC 6, 10, 15, 27;**
DAM POET; PC 12
See also CA 5-8R; 93-96; CANR 26, 60; DLB
48; MTCW 1; SATA-Obit 22

Rule, Jane (Vance) 1931-   **CLC 27**
See also CA 25-28R; CAAS 18; CANR 12; DLB
60

Rulfo, Juan 1918-1986   **CLC 8, 80; DAM**
MULT; HLC; SSC 25
See also CA 85-88; 118; CANR 26; DLB 113;
HW; MTCW 1

Rumi, Jalal al-Din 1297-1373   **CMLC 20**

Runeberg, Johan 1804-1877   **NCLC 41**

Runyon, (Alfred) Damon 1884(?)-1946**T C L C**
10
See also CA 107; 165; DLB 11, 86, 171

Rush, Norman 1933-   **CLC 44**
See also CA 121; 126; INT 126

Rushdie, (Ahmed) Salman 1947-   **CLC 23, 31,**
55, 100; DAB; DAC; DAM MST, NOV,
POP; WLCS
See also BEST 89:3; CA 108; 111; CANR 33,
56; INT 111; MTCW 1

Rushforth, Peter (Scott) 1945-   **CLC 19**
See also CA 101

Ruskin, John 1819-1900   **TCLC 63**
See also CA 114; 129; CDBLB 1832-1890;
DLB 55, 163, 190; SATA 24

Russ, Joanna 1937-   **CLC 15**
See also CANR 11, 31, 65; DLB 8; MTCW 1

Russell, George William 1867-1935
See Baker, Jean H.
See also CA 104; 153; CDBLB 1890-1914;
DAM POET

Russell, (Henry) Ken(neth Alfred) 1927-**C L C**
16
See also CA 105

Russell, William Martin 1947-   **CLC 60**
See also CA 164

Rutherford, Mark   **TCLC 25**
See also White, William Hale
See also DLB 18

Ruyslinck, Ward 1929-   **CLC 14**
See also Belser, Reimond Karel Maria de

Ryan, Cornelius (John) 1920-1974   **CLC 7**
See also CA 69-72; 53-56; CANR 38

Ryan, Michael 1946-   **CLC 65**
See also CA 49-52; DLBY 82

Ryan, Tim
See Dent, Lester

Rybakov, Anatoli (Naumovich) 1911-**CLC 23,**
53
See also CA 126; 135; SATA 79

Ryder, Jonathan
See Ludlum, Robert

Ryga, George 1932-1987**CLC 14; DAC; DAM**
MST
See also CA 101; 124; CANR 43; DLB 60

S. H.
See Hartmann, Sadakichi

S. S.
See Sassoon, Siegfried (Lorraine)

Saba, Umberto 1883-1957   **TCLC 33**

See also CA 144; DLB 114

Sabatini, Rafael 1875-1950 **TCLC 47**
See also CA 162

Sabato, Ernesto (R.) 1911-**CLC 10, 23; DAM MULT; HLC**
See also CA 97-100; CANR 32, 65; DLB 145; HW; MTCW 1

Sa-Carniero, Mario de 1890-1916 **TCLC 83**

Sacastru, Martin
See Bioy Casares, Adolfo

Sacher-Masoch, Leopold von 1836(?)-1895 **NCLC 31**

Sachs, Marilyn (Stickle) 1927- **CLC 35**
See also AAYA 2; CA 17-20R; CANR 13, 47; CLR 2; JRDA; MAICYA; SAAS 2; SATA 3, 68

Sachs, Nelly 1891-1970 **CLC 14, 98**
See also CA 17-18; 25-28R; CAP 2

Sackler, Howard (Oliver) 1929-1982 **CLC 14**
See also CA 61-64; 108; CANR 30; DLB 7

Sacks, Oliver (Wolf) 1933- **CLC 67**
See also CA 53-56; CANR 28, 50; INT CANR-28; MTCW 1

Sadakichi
See Hartmann, Sadakichi

Sade, Donatien Alphonse Francois, Comte de 1740-1814 **NCLC 47**

Sadoff, Ira 1945- **CLC 9**
See also CA 53-56; CANR 5, 21; DLB 120

Saetone
See Camus, Albert

Safire, William 1929- **CLC 10**
See also CA 17-20R; CANR 31, 54

Sagan, Carl (Edward) 1934-1996**CLC 30, 112**
See also AAYA 2; CA 25-28R; 155; CANR 11, 36, 74; MTCW 1; SATA 58; SATA-Obit 94

Sagan, Francoise **CLC 3, 6, 9, 17, 36**
See also Quoirez, Francoise
See also DLB 83

Sahgal, Nayantara (Pandit) 1927- **CLC 41**
See also CA 9-12R; CANR 11

Saint, H(arry) F. 1941- **CLC 50**
See also CA 127

St. Aubin de Teran, Lisa 1953-
See Teran, Lisa St. Aubin de
See also CA 118; 126; INT 126

Saint Birgitta of Sweden c. 1303-1373**CMLC 24**

Sainte-Beuve, Charles Augustin 1804-1869 **NCLC 5**

Saint-Exupery, Antoine (Jean Baptiste Marie Roger) de 1900-1944 **TCLC 2, 56; DAM NOV; WLC**
See also CA 108; 132; CLR 10; DLB 72; MAICYA; MTCW 1; SATA 20

St. John, David
See Hunt, E(verette) Howard, (Jr.)

Saint-John Perse
See Leger, (Marie-Rene Auguste) Alexis Saint-Leger

Saintsbury, George (Edward Bateman) 1845-1933 **TCLC 31**
See also CA 160; DLB 57, 149

Sait Faik **TCLC 23**
See also Abasiyanik, Sait Faik

Saki **TCLC 3; SSC 12**
See also Munro, H(ector) H(ugh)

Sala, George Augustus **NCLC 46**

Salama, Hannu 1936- **CLC 18**

Salamanca, J(ack) R(ichard) 1922-**CLC 4, 15**
See also CA 25-28R

Sale, J. Kirkpatrick
See Sale, Kirkpatrick

Sale, Kirkpatrick 1937- **CLC 68**
See also CA 13-16R; CANR 10

Salinas, Luis Omar 1937- **CLC 90; DAM MULT; HLC**
See also CA 131; DLB 82; HW

Salinas (y Serrano), Pedro 1891(?)-1951 **TCLC 17**
See also CA 117; DLB 134

Salinger, J(erome) D(avid) 1919-**CLC 1, 3, 8, 12, 55, 56; DA; DAB; DAC; DAM MST, NOV, POP; SSC 2, 28; WLC**
See also AAYA 2; CA 5-8R; CANR 39; CDALB 1941-1968; CLR 18; DLB 2, 102, 173; MAICYA; MTCW 1; SATA 67

Salisbury, John
See Caute, (John) David

Salter, James 1925- **CLC 7, 52, 59**
See also CA 73-76; DLB 130

Saltus, Edgar (Everton) 1855-1921 **TCLC 8**
See also CA 105; DLB 202

Saltykov, Mikhail Evgrafovich 1826-1889 **NCLC 16**

Samarakis, Antonis 1919- **CLC 5**
See also CA 25-28R; CAAS 16; CANR 36

Sanchez, Florencio 1875-1910 **TCLC 37**
See also CA 153; HW

Sanchez, Luis Rafael 1936- **CLC 23**
See also CA 128; DLB 145; HW

Sanchez, Sonia 1934- **CLC 5, 116; BLC 3; DAM MULT; PC 9**
See also BW 2; CA 33-36R; CANR 24, 49, 74; CLR 18; DLB 41; DLBD 8; MAICYA; MTCW 1; SATA 22

Sand, George 1804-1876**NCLC 2, 42, 57; DA; DAB; DAC; DAM MST, NOV; WLC**
See also DLB 119, 192

Sandburg, Carl (August) 1878-1967**CLC 1, 4, 10, 15, 35; DA; DAB; DAC; DAM MST, POET; PC 2; WLC**
See also AAYA 24; CA 5-8R; 25-28R; CANR 35; CDALB 1865-1917; DLB 17, 54; MAICYA; MTCW 1; SATA 8

Sandburg, Charles
See Sandburg, Carl (August)

Sandburg, Charles A.
See Sandburg, Carl (August)

Sanders, (James) Ed(ward) 1939- **CLC 53**
See also CA 13-16R; CAAS 21; CANR 13, 44; DLB 16

Sanders, Lawrence 1920-1998**CLC 41; DAM POP**
See also BEST 89:4; CA 81-84; 165; CANR 33, 62; MTCW 1

Sanders, Noah
See Blount, Roy (Alton), Jr.

Sanders, Winston P.
See Anderson, Poul (William)

Sandoz, Mari(e Susette) 1896-1966 **CLC 28**
See also CA 1-4R; 25-28R; CANR 17, 64; DLB 9; MTCW 1; SATA 5

Saner, Reg(inald Anthony) 1931- **CLC 9**
See also CA 65-68

Sankara 788-820 **CMLC 32**

Sannazaro, Jacopo 1456(?)-1530 **LC 8**

Sansom, William 1912-1976 **CLC 2, 6; DAM NOV; SSC 21**
See also CA 5-8R; 65-68; CANR 42; DLB 139; MTCW 1

Santayana, George 1863-1952 **TCLC 40**
See also CA 115; DLB 54, 71; DLBD 13

Santiago, Danny **CLC 33**
See also James, Daniel (Lewis)
See also DLB 122

Santmyer, Helen Hoover 1895-1986 **CLC 33**
See also CA 1-4R; 118; CANR 15, 33; DLBY 84; MTCW 1

Santoka, Taneda 1882-1940 **TCLC 72**

Santos, Bienvenido N(uqui) 1911-1996 **C L C 22; DAM MULT**
See also CA 101; 151; CANR 19, 46

Sapper **TCLC 44**
See also McNeile, Herman Cyril

Sapphire
See Sapphire, Brenda

Sapphire, Brenda 1950- **CLC 99**

Sappho fl. 6th cent. B.C.- **CMLC 3; DAM POET; PC 5**
See also DLB 176

Sarduy, Severo 1937-1993 **CLC 6, 97**
See also CA 89-92; 142; CANR 58; DLB 113; HW

Sargeson, Frank 1903-1982 **CLC 31**
See also CA 25-28R; 106; CANR 38

Sarmiento, Felix Ruben Garcia
See Dario, Ruben

Saro-Wiwa, Ken(ule Beeson) 1941-1995**C L C 114**
See also BW 2; CA 142; 150; CANR 60; DLB 157

Saroyan, William 1908-1981**CLC 1, 8, 10, 29, 34, 56; DA; DAB; DAC; DAM DRAM, MST, NOV; SSC 21; WLC**
See also CA 5-8R; 103; CANR 30; DLB 7, 9, 86; DLBY 81; MTCW 1; SATA 23; SATA-Obit 24

Sarraute, Nathalie 1900-**CLC 1, 2, 4, 8, 10, 31, 80**
See also CA 9-12R; CANR 23, 66; DLB 83; MTCW 1

Sarton, (Eleanor) May 1912-1995**CLC 4, 14, 49, 91; DAM POET**
See also CA 1-4R; 149; CANR 1, 34, 55; DLB 48; DLBY 81; INT CANR-34; MTCW 1; SATA 36; SATA-Obit 86

Sartre, Jean-Paul 1905-1980**CLC 1, 4, 7, 9, 13, 18, 24, 44, 50, 52; DA; DAB; DAC; DAM DRAM, MST, NOV; DC 3; SSC 32; WLC**
See also CA 9-12R; 97-100; CANR 21; DLB 72; MTCW 1

Sassoon, Siegfried (Lorraine) 1886-1967**C L C 36; DAB; DAM MST, NOV, POET; PC 12**
See also CA 104; 25-28R; CANR 36; DLB 20, 191; DLBD 18; MTCW 1

Satterfield, Charles
See Pohl, Frederik

Saul, John (W. III) 1942-**CLC 46; DAM NOV, POP**
See also AAYA 10; BEST 90:4; CA 81-84; CANR 16, 40; SATA 98

Saunders, Caleb
See Heinlein, Robert A(nson)

Saura (Atares), Carlos 1932- **CLC 20**
See also CA 114; 131; HW

Sauser-Hall, Frederic 1887-1961 **CLC 18**
See also Cendrars, Blaise
See also CA 102; 93-96; CANR 36, 62; MTCW 1

Saussure, Ferdinand de 1857-1913 **TCLC 49**

Savage, Catharine
See Brosman, Catharine Savage

Savage, Thomas 1915- **CLC 40**
See also CA 126; 132; CAAS 15; INT 132

Savan, Glenn 19(?)- **CLC 50**

Sayers, Dorothy L(eigh) 1893-1957 **TCLC 2, 15; DAM POP**
See also CA 104; 119; CANR 60; CDBLB 1914-

Author Index

Siguenza y Gongora, Carlos de 1645-1700 L C 8

Sigurjonsson, Johann 1880-1919 **TCLC 27**
See also CA 170

Sikelianos, Angelos 1884-1951 **TCLC 39**

Silkin, Jon 1930- **CLC 2, 6, 43**
See also CA 5-8R; CAAS 5; DLB 27

Silko, Leslie (Marmon) 1948-**CLC 23, 74, 114; DA; DAC; DAM MST, MULT, POP; WLCS**
See also AAYA 14; CA 115; 122; CANR 45, 65; DLB 143, 175; NNAL

Sillanpaa, Frans Eemil 1888-1964 **CLC 19**
See also CA 129; 93-96; MTCW 1

Sillitoe, Alan 1928- **CLC 1, 3, 6, 10, 19, 57**
See also AITN 1; CA 9-12R; CAAS 2; CANR 8, 26, 55; CDBLB 1960 to Present; DLB 14, 139; MTCW 1; SATA 61

Silone, Ignazio 1900-1978 **CLC 4**
See also CA 25-28; 81-84; CANR 34; CAP 2; MTCW 1

Silver, Joan Micklin 1935- **CLC 20**
See also CA 114; 121; INT 121

Silver, Nicholas
See Faust, Frederick (Schiller)

Silverberg, Robert 1935- **CLC 7; DAM POP**
See also AAYA 24; CA 1-4R; CAAS 3; CANR 1, 20, 36; DLB 8; INT CANR-20; MAICYA; MTCW 1; SATA 13, 91

Silverstein, Alvin 1933- **CLC 17**
See also CA 49-52; CANR 2; CLR 25; JRDA; MAICYA; SATA 8, 69

Silverstein, Virginia B(arbara Opshelor) 1937- **CLC 17**
See also CA 49-52; CANR 2; CLR 25; JRDA; MAICYA; SATA 8, 69

Sim, Georges
See Simenon, Georges (Jacques Christian)

Simak, Clifford D(onald) 1904-1988**CLC 1, 55**
See also CA 1-4R; 125; CANR 1, 35; DLB 8; MTCW 1; SATA-Obit 56

Simenon, Georges (Jacques Christian) 1903-1989 **CLC 1, 2, 3, 8, 18, 47; DAM POP**
See also CA 85-88; 129; CANR 35; DLB 72; DLBY 89; MTCW 1

Simic, Charles 1938- **CLC 6, 9, 22, 49, 68; DAM POET**
See also CA 29-32R; CAAS 4; CANR 12, 33, 52, 61; DLB 105

Simmel, Georg 1858-1918 **TCLC 64**
See also CA 157

Simmons, Charles (Paul) 1924- **CLC 57**
See also CA 89-92; INT 89-92

Simmons, Dan 1948- **CLC 44; DAM POP**
See also AAYA 16; CA 138; CANR 53

Simmons, James (Stewart Alexander) 1933- **CLC 43**
See also CA 105; CAAS 21; DLB 40

Simms, William Gilmore 1806-1870 **NCLC 3**
See also DLB 3, 30, 59, 73

Simon, Carly 1945- **CLC 26**
See also CA 105

Simon, Claude 1913-1984 **CLC 4, 9, 15, 39; DAM NOV**
See also CA 89-92; CANR 33; DLB 83; MTCW 1

Simon, (Marvin) Neil 1927-**CLC 6, 11, 31, 39, 70; DAM DRAM**
See also AITN 1; CA 21-24R; CANR 26, 54; DLB 7; MTCW 1

Simon, Paul (Frederick) 1941(?)- **CLC 17**
See also CA 116; 153

Simonon, Paul 1956(?)- **CLC 30**

Simpson, Harriette
See Arnow, Harriette (Louisa) Simpson

Simpson, Louis (Aston Marantz) 1923-**CLC 4, 7, 9, 32; DAM POET**
See also CA 1-4R; CAAS 4; CANR 1, 61; DLB 5; MTCW 1

Simpson, Mona (Elizabeth) 1957- **CLC 44**
See also CA 122; 135; CANR 68

Simpson, N(orman) F(rederick) 1919-**CLC 29**
See also CA 13-16R; DLB 13

Sinclair, Andrew (Annandale) 1935- **CLC 2, 14**
See also CA 9-12R; CAAS 5; CANR 14, 38; DLB 14; MTCW 1

Sinclair, Emil
See Hesse, Hermann

Sinclair, Iain 1943- **CLC 76**
See also CA 132

Sinclair, Iain MacGregor
See Sinclair, Iain

Sinclair, Irene
See Griffith, D(avid Lewelyn) W(ark)

Sinclair, Mary Amelia St. Clair 1865(?)-1946
See Sinclair, May
See also CA 104

Sinclair, May 1863-1946 **TCLC 3, 11**
See also Sinclair, Mary Amelia St. Clair
See also CA 166; DLB 36, 135

Sinclair, Roy
See Griffith, D(avid Lewelyn) W(ark)

Sinclair, Upton (Beall) 1878-1968 **CLC 1, 11, 15, 63; DA; DAB; DAC; DAM MST, NOV; WLC**
See also CA 5-8R; 25-28R; CANR 7; CDALB 1929-1941; DLB 9; INT CANR-7; MTCW 1; SATA 9

Singer, Isaac
See Singer, Isaac Bashevis

Singer, Isaac Bashevis 1904-1991**CLC 1, 3, 6, 9, 11, 15, 23, 38, 69, 111; DA; DAB; DAC; DAM MST, NOV; SSC 3; WLC**
See also AITN 1, 2; CA 1-4R; 134; CANR 1, 39; CDALB 1941-1968; CLR 1; DLB 6, 28, 52; DLBY 91; JRDA; MAICYA; MTCW 1; SATA 3, 27; SATA-Obit 68

Singer, Israel Joshua 1893-1944 **TCLC 33**
See also CA 169

Singh, Khushwant 1915- **CLC 11**
See also CA 9-12R; CAAS 9; CANR 6

Singleton, Ann
See Benedict, Ruth (Fulton)

Sinjohn, John
See Galsworthy, John

Sinyavsky, Andrei (Donatevich) 1925-1997 **CLC 8**
See also CA 85-88; 159

Sirin, V.
See Nabokov, Vladimir (Vladimirovich)

Sissman, L(ouis) E(dward) 1928-1976**CLC 9, 18**
See also CA 21-24R; 65-68; CANR 13; DLB 5

Sisson, C(harles) H(ubert) 1914- **CLC 8**
See also CA 1-4R; CAAS 3; CANR 3, 48; DLB 27

Sitwell, Dame Edith 1887-1964 **CLC 2, 9, 67; DAM POET; PC 3**
See also CA 9-12R; CANR 35; CDBLB 1945-1960; DLB 20; MTCW 1

Siwaarmill, H. P.
See Sharp, William

Sjoewall, Maj 1935- **CLC 7**
See also CA 65-68; CANR 73

Sjowall, Maj
See Sjoewall, Maj

Skelton, John 1463-1529 **PC 25**

Skelton, Robin 1925-1997 **CLC 13**
See also AITN 2; CA 5-8R; 160; CAAS 5; CANR 28; DLB 27, 53

Skolimowski, Jerzy 1938- **CLC 20**
See also CA 128

Skram, Amalie (Bertha) 1847-1905 **TCLC 25**
See also CA 165

Skvorecky, Josef (Vaclav) 1924- **CLC 15, 39, 69; DAC; DAM NOV**
See also CA 61-64; CAAS 1; CANR 10, 34, 63; MTCW 1

Slade, Bernard **CLC 11, 46**
See also Newbound, Bernard Slade
See also CAAS 9; DLB 53

Slaughter, Carolyn 1946- **CLC 56**
See also CA 85-88

Slaughter, Frank G(ill) 1908- **CLC 29**
See also AITN 2; CA 5-8R; CANR 5; INT CANR-5

Slavitt, David R(ytman) 1935- **CLC 5, 14**
See also CA 21-24R; CAAS 3; CANR 41; DLB 5, 6

Slesinger, Tess 1905-1945 **TCLC 10**
See also CA 107; DLB 102

Slessor, Kenneth 1901-1971 **CLC 14**
See also CA 102; 89-92

Slowacki, Juliusz 1809-1849 **NCLC 15**

Smart, Christopher 1722-1771 **LC 3; DAM POET; PC 13**
See also DLB 109

Smart, Elizabeth 1913-1986 **CLC 54**
See also CA 81-84; 118; DLB 88

Smiley, Jane (Graves) 1949-**CLC 53, 76; DAM POP**
See also CA 104; CANR 30, 50, 74; INT CANR-30

Smith, A(rthur) J(ames) M(arshall) 1902-1980 **CLC 15; DAC**
See also CA 1-4R; 102; CANR 4; DLB 88

Smith, Adam 1723-1790 **LC 36**
See also DLB 104

Smith, Alexander 1829-1867 **NCLC 59**
See also DLB 32, 55

Smith, Anna Deavere 1950- **CLC 86**
See also CA 133

Smith, Betty (Wehner) 1896-1972 **CLC 19**
See also CA 5-8R; 33-36R; DLBY 82; SATA 6

Smith, Charlotte (Turner) 1749-1806 **N C L C 23**
See also DLB 39, 109

Smith, Clark Ashton 1893-1961 **CLC 43**
See also CA 143

Smith, Dave **CLC 22, 42**
See also Smith, David (Jeddie)
See also CAAS 7; DLB 5

Smith, David (Jeddie) 1942-
See Smith, Dave
See also CA 49-52; CANR 1, 59; DAM POET

Smith, Florence Margaret 1902-1971
See Smith, Stevie
See also CA 17-18; 29-32R; CANR 35; CAP 2; DAM POET; MTCW 1

Smith, Iain Crichton 1928-1998 **CLC 64**
See also CA 21-24R; 171; DLB 40, 139

Smith, John 1580(?)-1631 **LC 9**
See also DLB 24, 30

Smith, Johnston
See Crane, Stephen (Townley)

Smith, Joseph, Jr. 1805-1844 **NCLC 53**

Smith, Lee 1944- **CLC 25, 73**
See also CA 114; 119; CANR 46; DLB 143;

See also CA 1-4R; 85-88; CANR 3, 65; DLB 2, 173; MTCW 1; SATA-Obit 22

Stafford, William (Edgar) 1914-1993 **CLC 4, 7, 29; DAM POET**
See also CA 5-8R; 142; CAAS 3; CANR 5, 22; DLB 5, 206; INT CANR-22

Stagnelius, Eric Johan 1793-1823 **NCLC 61**

Staines, Trevor
See Brunner, John (Kilian Houston)

Stairs, Gordon
See Austin, Mary (Hunter)

Stannard, Martin 1947- **CLC 44**
See also CA 142; DLB 155

Stanton, Elizabeth Cady 1815-1902 **TCLC 73**
See also CA 171; DLB 79

Stanton, Maura 1946- **CLC 9**
See also CA 89-92; CANR 15; DLB 120

Stanton, Schuyler
See Baum, L(yman) Frank

Stapledon, (William) Olaf 1886-1950 **TCLC 22**
See also CA 111; 162; DLB 15

Starbuck, George (Edwin) 1931-1996 **CLC 53; DAM POET**
See also CA 21-24R; 153; CANR 23

Stark, Richard
See Westlake, Donald E(dwin)

Staunton, Schuyler
See Baum, L(yman) Frank

Stead, Christina (Ellen) 1902-1983 **CLC 2, 5, 8, 32, 80**
See also CA 13-16R; 109; CANR 33, 40; MTCW 1

Stead, William Thomas 1849-1912 **TCLC 48**
See also CA 167

Steele, Richard 1672-1729 **LC 18**
See also CDBLB 1660-1789; DLB 84, 101

Steele, Timothy (Reid) 1948- **CLC 45**
See also CA 93-96; CANR 16, 50; DLB 120

Steffens, (Joseph) Lincoln 1866-1936 **TCLC 20**
See also CA 117

Stegner, Wallace (Earle) 1909-1993 **CLC 9, 49, 81; DAM NOV; SSC 27**
See also AITN 1; BEST 90:3; CA 1-4R; 141; CAAS 9; CANR 1, 21, 46; DLB 9, 206; DLBY 93; MTCW 1

Stein, Gertrude 1874-1946 **TCLC 1, 6, 28, 48; DA; DAB; DAC; DAM MST, NOV, POET; PC 18; WLC**
See also CA 104; 132; CDALB 1917-1929; DLB 4, 54, 86; DLBD 15; MTCW 1

Steinbeck, John (Ernst) 1902-1968 **CLC 1, 5, 9, 13, 21, 34, 45, 75; DA; DAB; DAC; DAM DRAM, MST, NOV; SSC 11; WLC**
See also AAYA 12; CA 1-4R; 25-28R; CANR 1, 35; CDALB 1929-1941; DLB 7, 9; DLBD 2; MTCW 1; SATA 9

Steinem, Gloria 1934- **CLC 63**
See also CA 53-56; CANR 28, 51; MTCW 1

Steiner, George 1929- **CLC 24; DAM NOV**
See also CA 73-76; CANR 31, 67; DLB 67; MTCW 1; SATA 62

Steiner, K. Leslie
See Delany, Samuel R(ay, Jr.)

Steiner, Rudolf 1861-1925 **TCLC 13**
See also CA 107

Stendhal 1783-1842 **NCLC 23, 46; DA; DAB; DAC; DAM MST, NOV; SSC 27; WLC**
See also DLB 119

Stephen, Adeline Virginia
See Woolf, (Adeline) Virginia

Stephen, SirLeslie 1832-1904 **TCLC 23**

See also CA 123; DLB 57, 144, 190

Stephen, Sir Leslie
See Stephen, SirLeslie

Stephen, Virginia
See Woolf, (Adeline) Virginia

Stephens, James 1882(?)-1950 **TCLC 4**
See also CA 104; DLB 19, 153, 162

Stephens, Reed
See Donaldson, Stephen R.

Steptoe, Lydia
See Barnes, Djuna

Sterchi, Beat 1949- **CLC 65**

Sterling, Brett
See Bradbury, Ray (Douglas); Hamilton, Edmond

Sterling, Bruce 1954- **CLC 72**
See also CA 119; CANR 44

Sterling, George 1869-1926 **TCLC 20**
See also CA 117; 165; DLB 54

Stern, Gerald 1925- **CLC 40, 100**
See also CA 81-84; CANR 28; DLB 105

Stern, Richard (Gustave) 1928- **CLC 4, 39**
See also CA 1-4R; CANR 1, 25, 52; DLBY 87; INT CANR-25

Sternberg, Josef von 1894-1969 **CLC 20**
See also CA 81-84

Sterne, Laurence 1713-1768 **LC 2, 48; DA; DAB; DAC; DAM MST, NOV; WLC**
See also CDBLB 1660-1789; DLB 39

Sternheim, (William Adolf) Carl 1878-1942 **TCLC 8**
See also CA 105; DLB 56, 118

Stevens, Mark 1951- **CLC 34**
See also CA 122

Stevens, Wallace 1879-1955 **TCLC 3, 12, 45; DA; DAB; DAC; DAM MST, POET; PC 6; WLC**
See also CA 104; 124; CDALB 1929-1941; DLB 54; MTCW 1

Stevenson, Anne (Katharine) 1933- **CLC 7, 33**
See also CA 17-20R; CAAS 9; CANR 9, 33; DLB 40; MTCW 1

Stevenson, Robert Louis (Balfour) 1850-1894 **NCLC 5, 14, 63; DA; DAB; DAC; DAM MST, NOV; SSC 11; WLC**
See also AAYA 24; CDBLB 1890-1914; CLR 10, 11; DLB 18, 57, 141, 156, 174; DLBD 13; JRDA; MAICYA; SATA 100; YABC 2

Stewart, J(ohn) I(nnes) M(ackintosh) 1906-1994 **CLC 7, 14, 32**
See also CA 85-88; 147; CAAS 3; CANR 47; MTCW 1

Stewart, Mary (Florence Elinor) 1916- **CLC 7, 35, 117; DAB**
See also CA 1-4R; CANR 1, 59; SATA 12

Stewart, Mary Rainbow
See Stewart, Mary (Florence Elinor)

Stifle, June
See Campbell, Maria

Stifter, Adalbert 1805-1868 **NCLC 41; SSC 28**
See also DLB 133

Still, James 1906- **CLC 49**
See also CA 65-68; CAAS 17; CANR 10, 26; DLB 9; SATA 29

Sting 1951-
See Sumner, Gordon Matthew
See also CA 167

Stirling, Arthur
See Sinclair, Upton (Beall)

Stitt, Milan 1941- **CLC 29**
See also CA 69-72

Stockton, Francis Richard 1834-1902
See Stockton, Frank R.

See also CA 108; 137; MAICYA; SATA 44

Stockton, Frank R. **TCLC 47**
See also Stockton, Francis Richard
See also DLB 42, 74; DLBD 13; SATA-Brief 32

Stoddard, Charles
See Kuttner, Henry

Stoker, Abraham 1847-1912
See Stoker, Bram
See also CA 105; 150; DA; DAC; DAM MST, NOV; SATA 29

Stoker, Bram 1847-1912 **TCLC 8; DAB; WLC**
See also Stoker, Abraham
See also AAYA 23; CDBLB 1890-1914; DLB 36, 70, 178

Stolz, Mary (Slattery) 1920- **CLC 12**
See also AAYA 8; AITN 1; CA 5-8R; CANR 13, 41; JRDA; MAICYA; SAAS 3; SATA 10, 71

Stone, Irving 1903-1989 **CLC 7; DAM POP**
See also AITN 1; CA 1-4R; 129; CAAS 3; CANR 1, 23; INT CANR-23; MTCW 1; SATA 3; SATA-Obit 64

Stone, Oliver (William) 1946- **CLC 73**
See also AAYA 15; CA 110; CANR 55

Stone, Robert (Anthony) 1937- **CLC 5, 23, 42**
See also CA 85-88; CANR 23, 66; DLB 152; INT CANR-23; MTCW 1

Stone, Zachary
See Follett, Ken(neth Martin)

Stoppard, Tom 1937- **CLC 1, 3, 4, 5, 8, 15, 29, 34, 63, 91; DA; DAB; DAC; DAM DRAM, MST; DC 6; WLC**
See also CA 81-84; CANR 39, 67; CDBLB 1960 to Present; DLB 13; DLBY 85; MTCW 1

Storey, David (Malcolm) 1933- **CLC 2, 4, 5, 8; DAM DRAM**
See also CA 81-84; CANR 36; DLB 13, 14, 207; MTCW 1

Storm, Hyemeyohsts 1935- **CLC 3; DAM MULT**
See also CA 81-84; CANR 45; NNAL

Storm, Theodor 1817-1888 **SSC 27**

Storm, (Hans) Theodor (Woldsen) 1817-1888 **NCLC 1; SSC 27**
See also DLB 129

Storni, Alfonsina 1892-1938 **TCLC 5; DAM MULT; HLC**
See also CA 104; 131; HW

Stoughton, William 1631-1701 **LC 38**
See also DLB 24

Stout, Rex (Todhunter) 1886-1975 **CLC 3**
See also AITN 2; CA 61-64; CANR 71

Stow, (Julian) Randolph 1935- **CLC 23, 48**
See also CA 13-16R; CANR 33; MTCW 1

Stowe, Harriet (Elizabeth) Beecher 1811-1896 **NCLC 3, 50; DA; DAB; DAC; DAM MST, NOV; WLC**
See also CDALB 1865-1917; DLB 1, 12, 42, 74, 189; JRDA; MAICYA; YABC 1

Strachey, (Giles) Lytton 1880-1932 **TCLC 12**
See also CA 110; DLB 149; DLBD 10

Strand, Mark 1934- **CLC 6, 18, 41, 71; DAM POET**
See also CA 21-24R; CANR 40, 65; DLB 5; SATA 41

Straub, Peter (Francis) 1943- **CLC 28, 107; DAM POP**
See also BEST 89:1; CA 85-88; CANR 28, 65; DLBY 84; MTCW 1

Strauss, Botho 1944- **CLC 22**
See also CA 157; DLB 124

Streatfeild, (Mary) Noel 1895(?)-1986 **CLC 21**
    See also CA 81-84; 120; CANR 31; CLR 17;
    DLB 160; MAICYA; SATA 20; SATA-Obit
    48
Stribling, T(homas) S(igismund) 1881-1965
    CLC 23
    See also CA 107; DLB 9
Strindberg, (Johan) August 1849-1912 **T C L C
    1, 8, 21, 47; DA; DAB; DAC; DAM DRAM,
    MST; WLC**
    See also CA 104; 135
Stringer, Arthur 1874-1950   **TCLC 37**
    See also CA 161; DLB 92
Stringer, David
    See Roberts, Keith (John Kingston)
Stroheim, Erich von 1885-1957   **TCLC 71**
Strugatskii, Arkadii (Natanovich) 1925-1991
    CLC 27
    See also CA 106; 135
Strugatskii, Boris (Natanovich) 1933- **CLC 27**
    See also CA 106
Strummer, Joe 1953(?)-   **CLC 30**
Stuart, Don A.
    See Campbell, John W(ood, Jr.)
Stuart, Ian
    See MacLean, Alistair (Stuart)
Stuart, Jesse (Hilton) 1906-1984 **CLC 1, 8, 11,
    14, 34; SSC 31**
    See also CA 5-8R; 112; CANR 31; DLB 9, 48,
    102; DLBY 84; SATA 2; SATA-Obit 36
Sturgeon, Theodore (Hamilton) 1918-1985
    CLC 22, 39
    See also Queen, Ellery
    See also CA 81-84; 116; CANR 32; DLB 8;
    DLBY 85; MTCW 1
Sturges, Preston 1898-1959   **TCLC 48**
    See also CA 114; 149; DLB 26
Styron, William 1925- **CLC 1, 3, 5, 11, 15, 60;
    DAM NOV, POP; SSC 25**
    See also BEST 90:4; CA 5-8R; CANR 6, 33,
    74; CDALB 1968-1988; DLB 2, 143; DLBY
    80; INT CANR-6; MTCW 1
Su, Chien 1884-1918
    See Su Man-shu
    See also CA 123
Suarez Lynch, B.
    See Bioy Casares, Adolfo; Borges, Jorge Luis
Suckow, Ruth 1892-1960   **SSC 18**
    See also CA 113; DLB 9, 102
Sudermann, Hermann 1857-1928   **TCLC 15**
    See also CA 107; DLB 118
Sue, Eugene 1804-1857   **NCLC 1**
    See also DLB 119
Sueskind, Patrick 1949-   **CLC 44**
    See also Suskind, Patrick
Sukenick, Ronald 1932-   **CLC 3, 4, 6, 48**
    See also CA 25-28R; CAAS 8; CANR 32; DLB
    173; DLBY 81
Suknaski, Andrew 1942-   **CLC 19**
    See also CA 101; DLB 53
Sullivan, Vernon
    See Vian, Boris
Sully Prudhomme 1839-1907   **TCLC 31**
Su Man-shu   **TCLC 24**
    See also Su, Chien
Summerforest, Ivy B.
    See Kirkup, James
Summers, Andrew James 1942-   **CLC 26**
Summers, Andy
    See Summers, Andrew James
Summers, Hollis (Spurgeon, Jr.) 1916- **CLC 10**
    See also CA 5-8R; CANR 3; DLB 6
Summers, (Alphonsus Joseph-Mary Augustus)

Montague 1880-1948   **TCLC 16**
    See also CA 118; 163
Sumner, Gordon Matthew   **CLC 26**
    See also Sting
Surtees, Robert Smith 1803-1864   **NCLC 14**
    See also DLB 21
Susann, Jacqueline 1921-1974   **CLC 3**
    See also AITN 1; CA 65-68; 53-56; MTCW 1
Su Shih 1036-1101   **CMLC 15**
Suskind, Patrick
    See Sueskind, Patrick
    See also CA 145
Sutcliff, Rosemary 1920-1992 **CLC 26; DAB;
    DAC; DAM MST, POP**
    See also AAYA 10; CA 5-8R; 139; CANR 37;
    CLR 1, 37; JRDA; MAICYA; SATA 6, 44,
    78; SATA-Obit 73
Sutro, Alfred 1863-1933   **TCLC 6**
    See also CA 105; DLB 10
Sutton, Henry
    See Slavitt, David R(ytman)
Svevo, Italo 1861-1928 **TCLC 2, 35; SSC 25**
    See also Schmitz, Aron Hector
Swados, Elizabeth (A.) 1951-   **CLC 12**
    See also CA 97-100; CANR 49; INT 97-100
Swados, Harvey 1920-1972   **CLC 5**
    See also CA 5-8R; 37-40R; CANR 6; DLB 2
Swan, Gladys 1934-   **CLC 69**
    See also CA 101; CANR 17, 39
Swarthout, Glendon (Fred) 1918-1992 **CLC 35**
    See also CA 1-4R; 139; CANR 1, 47; SATA 26
Sweet, Sarah C.
    See Jewett, (Theodora) Sarah Orne
Swenson, May 1919-1989 **CLC 4, 14, 61, 106;
    DA; DAB; DAC; DAM MST, POET; PC
    14**
    See also CA 5-8R; 130; CANR 36, 61; DLB 5;
    MTCW 1; SATA 15
Swift, Augustus
    See Lovecraft, H(oward) P(hillips)
Swift, Graham (Colin) 1949-   **CLC 41, 88**
    See also CA 117; 122; CANR 46, 71; DLB 194
Swift, Jonathan 1667-1745   **LC 1, 42; DA;
    DAB; DAC; DAM MST, NOV, POET; PC
    9; WLC**
    See also CDBLB 1660-1789; CLR 53; DLB 39,
    95, 101; SATA 19
Swinburne, Algernon Charles 1837-1909
    **TCLC 8, 36; DA; DAB; DAC; DAM MST,
    POET; PC 24; WLC**
    See also CA 105; 140; CDBLB 1832-1890;
    DLB 35, 57
Swinfen, Ann   **CLC 34**
Swinnerton, Frank Arthur 1884-1982 **CLC 31**
    See also CA 108; DLB 34
Swithen, John
    See King, Stephen (Edwin)
Sylvia
    See Ashton-Warner, Sylvia (Constance)
Symmes, Robert Edward
    See Duncan, Robert (Edward)
Symonds, John Addington 1840-1893 **N C L C
    34**
    See also DLB 57, 144
Symons, Arthur 1865-1945   **TCLC 11**
    See also CA 107; DLB 19, 57, 149
Symons, Julian (Gustave) 1912-1994 **CLC 2,
    14, 32**
    See also CA 49-52; 147; CAAS 3; CANR 3,
    33, 59; DLB 87, 155; DLBY 92; MTCW 1
Synge, (Edmund) J(ohn) M(illington) 1871-
    1909 **TCLC 6, 37; DAM DRAM; DC 2**
    See also CA 104; 141; CDBLB 1890-1914;

DLB 10, 19
Syruc, J.
    See Milosz, Czeslaw
Szirtes, George 1948-   **CLC 46**
    See also CA 109; CANR 27, 61
Szymborska, Wislawa 1923-   **CLC 99**
    See also CA 154; DLBY 96
T. O., Nik
    See Annensky, Innokenty (Fyodorovich)
Tabori, George 1914-   **CLC 19**
    See also CA 49-52; CANR 4, 69
Tagore, Rabindranath 1861-1941 **TCLC 3, 53;
    DAM DRAM, POET; PC 8**
    See also CA 104; 120; MTCW 1
Taine, Hippolyte Adolphe 1828-1893 **N C L C
    15**
Talese, Gay 1932-   **CLC 37**
    See also AITN 1; CA 1-4R; CANR 9, 58; DLB
    185; INT CANR-9; MTCW 1
Tallent, Elizabeth (Ann) 1954-   **CLC 45**
    See also CA 117; CANR 72; DLB 130
Tally, Ted 1952-   **CLC 42**
    See also CA 120; 124; INT 124
Talvik, Heiti 1904-1947   **TCLC 87**
Tamayo y Baus, Manuel 1829-1898   **NCLC 1**
Tammsaare, A(nton) H(ansen) 1878-1940
    TCLC 27
    See also CA 164
Tam'si, Tchicaya U
    See Tchicaya, Gerald Felix
Tan, Amy (Ruth) 1952- **CLC 59; DAM MULT,
    NOV, POP**
    See also AAYA 9; BEST 89:3; CA 136; CANR
    54; DLB 173; SATA 75
Tandem, Felix
    See Spitteler, Carl (Friedrich Georg)
Tanizaki, Jun'ichiro 1886-1965 **CLC 8, 14, 28;
    SSC 21**
    See also CA 93-96; 25-28R; DLB 180
Tanner, William
    See Amis, Kingsley (William)
Tao Lao
    See Storni, Alfonsina
Tarassoff, Lev
    See Troyat, Henri
Tarbell, Ida M(inerva) 1857-1944   **TCLC 40**
    See also CA 122; DLB 47
Tarkington, (Newton) Booth 1869-1946 **TCLC
    9**
    See also CA 110; 143; DLB 9, 102; SATA 17
Tarkovsky, Andrei (Arsenyevich) 1932-1986
    CLC 75
    See also CA 127
Tartt, Donna 1964(?)-   **CLC 76**
    See also CA 142
Tasso, Torquato 1544-1595   **LC 5**
Tate, (John Orley) Allen 1899-1979 **CLC 2, 4,
    6, 9, 11, 14, 24**
    See also CA 5-8R; 85-88; CANR 32; DLB 4,
    45, 63; DLBD 17; MTCW 1
Tate, Ellalice
    See Hibbert, Eleanor Alice Burford
Tate, James (Vincent) 1943-   **CLC 2, 6, 25**
    See also CA 21-24R; CANR 29, 57; DLB 5,
    169
Tavel, Ronald 1940-   **CLC 6**
    See also CA 21-24R; CANR 33
Taylor, C(ecil) P(hilip) 1929-1981   **CLC 27**
    See also CA 25-28R; 105; CANR 47
Taylor, Edward 1642(?)-1729   **LC 11; DA;
    DAB; DAC; DAM MST, POET**
    See also DLB 24
Taylor, Eleanor Ross 1920-   **CLC 5**

See also CA 81-84; CANR 70

Taylor, Elizabeth 1912-1975   **CLC 2, 4, 29**
See also CA 13-16R; CANR 9, 70; DLB 139;
MTCW 1; SATA 13

Taylor, Frederick Winslow 1856-1915 **T C L C 76**

Taylor, Henry (Splawn) 1942-   **CLC 44**
See also CA 33-36R; CAAS 7; CANR 31; DLB 5

Taylor, Kamala (Purnaiya) 1924-
See Markandaya, Kamala
See also CA 77-80

Taylor, Mildred D.   **CLC 21**
See also AAYA 10; BW 1; CA 85-88; CANR 25; CLR 9; DLB 52; JRDA; MAICYA; SAAS 5; SATA 15, 70

Taylor, Peter (Hillsman) 1917-1994 **CLC 1, 4, 18, 37, 44, 50, 71; SSC 10**
See also CA 13-16R; 147; CANR 9, 50; DLBY 81, 94; INT CANR-9; MTCW 1

Taylor, Robert Lewis 1912-1998   **CLC 14**
See also CA 1-4R; 170; CANR 3, 64; SATA 10

Tchekhov, Anton
See Chekhov, Anton (Pavlovich)

Tchicaya, Gerald Felix 1931-1988   **CLC 101**
See also CA 129; 125

Tchicaya U Tam'si
See Tchicaya, Gerald Felix

Teasdale, Sara 1884-1933   **TCLC 4**
See also CA 104; 163; DLB 45; SATA 32

Tegner, Esaias 1782-1846   **NCLC 2**

Teilhard de Chardin, (Marie Joseph) Pierre 1881-1955   **TCLC 9**
See also CA 105

Temple, Ann
See Mortimer, Penelope (Ruth)

Tennant, Emma (Christina) 1937- **CLC 13, 52**
See also CA 65-68; CAAS 9; CANR 10, 38, 59; DLB 14

Tenneshaw, S. M.
See Silverberg, Robert

Tennyson, Alfred 1809-1892   **NCLC 30, 65; DA; DAB; DAC; DAM MST, POET; PC 6; WLC**
See also CDBLB 1832-1890; DLB 32

Teran, Lisa St. Aubin de   **CLC 36**
See also St. Aubin de Teran, Lisa

Terence 195(?)B.C.-159B.C. **CMLC 14; DC 7**

Teresa de Jesus, St. 1515-1582   **LC 18**

Terkel, Louis 1912-
See Terkel, Studs
See also CA 57-60; CANR 18, 45, 67; M T C W 1

Terkel, Studs   **CLC 38**
See also Terkel, Louis
See also AITN 1

Terry, C. V.
See Slaughter, Frank G(ill)

Terry, Megan 1932-   **CLC 19**
See also CA 77-80; CABS 3; CANR 43; DLB 7

Tertullian c. 155-c. 245   **CMLC 29**

Tertz, Abram
See Sinyavsky, Andrei (Donatevich)

Tesich, Steve 1943(?)-1996   **CLC 40, 69**
See also CA 105; 152; DLBY 83

Tesla, Nikola 1856-1943   **TCLC 88**

Teternikov, Fyodor Kuzmich 1863-1927
See Sologub, Fyodor
See also CA 104

Tevis, Walter 1928-1984   **CLC 42**
See also CA 113

Tey, Josephine   **TCLC 14**
See also Mackintosh, Elizabeth

See also DLB 77

Thackeray, William Makepeace 1811-1863 **NCLC 5, 14, 22, 43; DA; DAB; DAC; DAM MST, NOV; WLC**
See also CDBLB 1832-1890; DLB 21, 55, 159, 163; SATA 23

Thakura, Ravindranatha
See Tagore, Rabindranath

Tharoor, Shashi 1956-   **CLC 70**
See also CA 141

Thelwell, Michael Miles 1939-   **CLC 22**
See also BW 2; CA 101

Theobald, Lewis, Jr.
See Lovecraft, H(oward) P(hillips)

Theodorescu, Ion N. 1880-1967
See Arghezi, Tudor
See also CA 116

Theriault, Yves 1915-1983   **CLC 79; DAC; DAM MST**
See also CA 102; DLB 88

Theroux, Alexander (Louis) 1939- **CLC 2, 25**
See also CA 85-88; CANR 20, 63

Theroux, Paul (Edward) 1941- **CLC 5, 8, 11, 15, 28, 46; DAM POP**
See also BEST 89:4; CA 33-36R; CANR 20, 45, 74; DLB 2; MTCW 1; SATA 44

Thesen, Sharon 1946-   **CLC 56**
See also CA 163

Thevenin, Denis
See Duhamel, Georges

Thibault, Jacques Anatole Francois 1844-1924
See France, Anatole
See also CA 106; 127; DAM NOV; MTCW 1

Thiele, Colin (Milton) 1920-   **CLC 17**
See also CA 29-32R; CANR 12, 28, 53; CLR 27; MAICYA; SAAS 2; SATA 14, 72

Thomas, Audrey (Callahan) 1935- **CLC 7, 13, 37, 107; SSC 20**
See also AITN 2; CA 21-24R; CAAS 19; CANR 36, 58; DLB 60; MTCW 1

Thomas, D(onald) M(ichael) 1935- **CLC 13, 22, 31**
See also CA 61-64; CAAS 11; CANR 17, 45, 75; CDBLB 1960 to Present; DLB 40, 207; INT CANR-17; MTCW 1

Thomas, Dylan (Marlais) 1914-1953 **TCLC 1, 8, 45; DA; DAB; DAC; DAM DRAM, MST, POET; PC 2; SSC 3; WLC**
See also CA 104; 120; CANR 65; CDBLB 1945-1960; DLB 13, 20, 139; MTCW 1; SATA 60

Thomas, (Philip) Edward 1878-1917 **T C L C 10; DAM POET**
See also CA 106; 153; DLB 19

Thomas, Joyce Carol 1938-   **CLC 35**
See also AAYA 12; BW 2; CA 113; 116; CANR 48; CLR 19; DLB 33; INT 116; JRDA; MAICYA; MTCW 1; SAAS 7; SATA 40, 78

Thomas, Lewis 1913-1993   **CLC 35**
See also CA 85-88; 143; CANR 38, 60; MTCW 1

Thomas, M. Carey 1857-1935   **TCLC 89**

Thomas, Paul
See Mann, (Paul) Thomas

Thomas, Piri 1928-   **CLC 17**
See also CA 73-76; HW

Thomas, R(onald) S(tuart) 1913- **CLC 6, 13, 48; DAB; DAM POET**
See also CA 89-92; CAAS 4; CANR 30; CDBLB 1960 to Present; DLB 27; MTCW 1

Thomas, Ross (Elmore) 1926-1995   **CLC 39**
See also CA 33-36R; 150; CANR 22, 63

Thompson, Francis Clegg

See Mencken, H(enry) L(ouis)

Thompson, Francis Joseph 1859-1907 **TCLC 4**
See also CA 104; CDBLB 1890-1914; DLB 19

Thompson, Hunter S(tockton) 1939- **CLC 9, 17, 40, 104; DAM POP**
See also BEST 89:1; CA 17-20R; CANR 23, 46, 74; DLB 185; MTCW 1

Thompson, James Myers
See Thompson, Jim (Myers)

Thompson, Jim (Myers) 1906-1977(?) **CLC 69**
See also CA 140

Thompson, Judith   **CLC 39**

Thomson, James 1700-1748   **LC 16, 29, 40; DAM POET**
See also DLB 95

Thomson, James 1834-1882 **NCLC 18; DAM POET**
See also DLB 35

Thoreau, Henry David 1817-1862 **NCLC 7, 21, 61; DA; DAB; DAC; DAM MST; WLC**
See also CDALB 1640-1865; DLB 1

Thornton, Hall
See Silverberg, Robert

Thucydides c. 455B.C.-399B.C.   **CMLC 17**
See also DLB 176

Thurber, James (Grover) 1894-1961 **CLC 5, 11, 25; DA; DAB; DAC; DAM DRAM, MST, NOV; SSC 1**
See also CA 73-76; CANR 17, 39; CDALB 1929-1941; DLB 4, 11, 22, 102; MAICYA; MTCW 1; SATA 13

Thurman, Wallace (Henry) 1902-1934 **T C L C 6; BLC 3; DAM MULT**
See also BW 1; CA 104; 124; DLB 51

Ticheburn, Cheviot
See Ainsworth, William Harrison

Tieck, (Johann) Ludwig 1773-1853 **NCLC 5, 46; SSC 31**
See also DLB 90

Tiger, Derry
See Ellison, Harlan (Jay)

Tilghman, Christopher 1948(?)-   **CLC 65**
See also CA 159

Tillinghast, Richard (Williford) 1940- **CLC 29**
See also CA 29-32R; CAAS 23; CANR 26, 51

Timrod, Henry 1828-1867   **NCLC 25**
See also DLB 3

Tindall, Gillian (Elizabeth) 1938-   **CLC 7**
See also CA 21-24R; CANR 11, 65

Tiptree, James, Jr.   **CLC 48, 50**
See also Sheldon, Alice Hastings Bradley
See also DLB 8

Titmarsh, Michael Angelo
See Thackeray, William Makepeace

Tocqueville, Alexis (Charles Henri Maurice Clerel, Comte) de 1805-1859 **NCLC 7, 63**

Tolkien, J(ohn) R(onald) R(euel) 1892-1973 **CLC 1, 2, 3, 8, 12, 38; DA; DAB; DAC; DAM MST, NOV, POP; WLC**
See also AAYA 10; AITN 1; CA 17-18; 45-48; CANR 36; CAP 2; CDBLB 1914-1945; DLB 15, 160; JRDA; MAICYA; MTCW 1; SATA 2, 32, 100; SATA-Obit 24

Toller, Ernst 1893-1939   **TCLC 10**
See also CA 107; DLB 124

Tolson, M. B.
See Tolson, Melvin B(eaunorus)

Tolson, Melvin B(eaunorus) 1898(?)-1966 **CLC 36, 105; BLC 3; DAM MULT, POET**
See also BW 1; CA 124; 89-92; DLB 48, 76

Tolstoi, Aleksei Nikolaevich
See Tolstoy, Alexey Nikolaevich

Tolstoy, Alexey Nikolaevich 1882-1945 **T C L C**

18
See also CA 107; 158
Tolstoy, Count Leo
See Tolstoy, Leo (Nikolaevich)
Tolstoy, Leo (Nikolaevich) 1828-1910TCLC 4,
11, 17, 28, 44, 79; DA; DAB; DAC; DAM
MST, NOV; SSC 9, 30; WLC
See also CA 104; 123; SATA 26
Tomasi di Lampedusa, Giuseppe 1896-1957
See Lampedusa, Giuseppe (Tomasi) di
See also CA 111
Tomlin, Lily   **CLC 17**
See also Tomlin, Mary Jean
Tomlin, Mary Jean 1939(?)-
See Tomlin, Lily
See also CA 117
Tomlinson, (Alfred) Charles 1927-CLC 2, 4, 6,
13, 45; DAM POET; PC 17
See also CA 5-8R; CANR 33; DLB 40
Tomlinson, H(enry) M(ajor) 1873-1958TCLC
71
See also CA 118; 161; DLB 36, 100, 195
Tonson, Jacob
See Bennett, (Enoch) Arnold
Toole, John Kennedy 1937-1969 **CLC 19, 64**
See also CA 104; DLBY 81
Toomer, Jean 1894-1967CLC 1, 4, 13, 22; BLC
3; DAM MULT; PC 7; SSC 1; WLCS
See also BW 1; CA 85-88; CDALB 1917-1929;
DLB 45, 51; MTCW 1
Torley, Luke
See Blish, James (Benjamin)
Tornimparte, Alessandra
See Ginzburg, Natalia
Torre, Raoul della
See Mencken, H(enry) L(ouis)
Torrey, E(dwin) Fuller 1937-   **CLC 34**
See also CA 119; CANR 71
Torsvan, Ben Traven
See Traven, B.
Torsvan, Benno Traven
See Traven, B.
Torsvan, Berick Traven
See Traven, B.
Torsvan, Berwick Traven
See Traven, B.
Torsvan, Bruno Traven
See Traven, B.
Torsvan, Traven
See Traven, B.
Tournier, Michel (Edouard) 1924-CLC 6, 23,
36, 95
See also CA 49-52; CANR 3, 36, 74; DLB 83;
MTCW 1; SATA 23
Tournimparte, Alessandra
See Ginzburg, Natalia
Towers, Ivar
See Kornbluth, C(yril) M.
Towne, Robert (Burton) 1936(?)-   **CLC 87**
See also CA 108; DLB 44
Townsend, Sue   **CLC 61**
See also Townsend, Susan Elaine
See also SATA 55, 93; SATA-Brief 48
Townsend, Susan Elaine 1946-
See Townsend, Sue
See also CA 119; 127; CANR 65; DAB; DAC;
DAM MST
Townshend, Peter (Dennis Blandford) 1945-
CLC 17, 42
See also CA 107
Tozzi, Federigo 1883-1920   **TCLC 31**
See also CA 160
Traill, Catharine Parr 1802-1899 **NCLC 31**

See also DLB 99
Trakl, Georg 1887-1914   **TCLC 5; PC 20**
See also CA 104; 165
Transtroemer, Tomas (Goesta) 1931-CLC 52,
65; DAM POET
See also CA 117; 129; CAAS 17
Transtromer, Tomas Gosta
See Transtroemer, Tomas (Goesta)
Traven, B. (?)-1969   **CLC 8, 11**
See also CA 19-20; 25-28R; CAP 2; DLB 9,
56; MTCW 1
Treitel, Jonathan 1959-   **CLC 70**
Tremain, Rose 1943-   **CLC 42**
See also CA 97-100; CANR 44; DLB 14
Tremblay, Michel 1942- CLC 29, 102; DAC;
DAM MST
See also CA 116; 128; DLB 60; MTCW 1
Trevanian   **CLC 29**
See also Whitaker, Rod(ney)
Trevor, Glen
See Hilton, James
Trevor, William 1928-CLC 7, 9, 14, 25, 71, 116;
SSC 21
See also Cox, William Trevor
See also DLB 14, 139
Trifonov, Yuri (Valentinovich) 1925-1981
CLC 45
See also CA 126; 103; MTCW 1
Trilling, Lionel 1905-1975   **CLC 9, 11, 24**
See also CA 9-12R; 61-64; CANR 10; DLB 28,
63; INT CANR-10; MTCW 1
Trimball, W. H.
See Mencken, H(enry) L(ouis)
Tristan
See Gomez de la Serna, Ramon
Tristram
See Housman, A(lfred) E(dward)
Trogdon, William (Lewis) 1939-
See Heat-Moon, William Least
See also CA 115; 119; CANR 47; INT 119
Trollope, Anthony 1815-1882NCLC 6, 33; DA;
DAB; DAC; DAM MST, NOV; SSC 28;
WLC
See also CDBLB 1832-1890; DLB 21, 57, 159;
SATA 22
Trollope, Frances 1779-1863   **NCLC 30**
See also DLB 21, 166
Trotsky, Leon 1879-1940   **TCLC 22**
See also CA 118; 167
Trotter (Cockburn), Catharine 1679-1749L C
8
See also DLB 84
Trout, Kilgore
See Farmer, Philip Jose
Trow, George W. S. 1943-   **CLC 52**
See also CA 126
Troyat, Henri 1911-   **CLC 23**
See also CA 45-48; CANR 2, 33, 67; MTCW 1
Trudeau, G(arretson) B(eekman) 1948-
See Trudeau, Garry B.
See also CA 81-84; CANR 31; SATA 35
Trudeau, Garry B.   **CLC 12**
See also Trudeau, G(arretson) B(eekman)
See also AAYA 10; AITN 2
Truffaut, Francois 1932-1984   **CLC 20, 101**
See also CA 81-84; 113; CANR 34
Trumbo, Dalton 1905-1976   **CLC 19**
See also CA 21-24R; 69-72; CANR 10; DLB
26
Trumbull, John 1750-1831   **NCLC 30**
See also DLB 31
Trundlett, Helen B.
See Eliot, T(homas) S(tearns)

Tryon, Thomas 1926-1991   CLC 3, 11; DAM
POP
See also AITN 1; CA 29-32R; 135; CANR 32;
MTCW 1
Tryon, Tom
See Tryon, Thomas
Ts'ao Hsueh-ch'in 1715(?)-1763   **LC 1**
Tsushima, Shuji 1909-1948
See Dazai Osamu
See also CA 107
Tsvetaeva (Efron), Marina (Ivanovna) 1892-
1941   **TCLC 7, 35; PC 14**
See also CA 104; 128; CANR 73; MTCW 1
Tuck, Lily 1938-   **CLC 70**
See also CA 139
Tu Fu 712-770   **PC 9**
See also DAM MULT
Tunis, John R(oberts) 1889-1975   **CLC 12**
See also CA 61-64; CANR 62; DLB 22, 171;
JRDA; MAICYA; SATA 37; SATA-Brief 30
Tuohy, Frank   **CLC 37**
See also Tuohy, John Francis
See also DLB 14, 139
Tuohy, John Francis 1925-
See Tuohy, Frank
See also CA 5-8R; CANR 3, 47
Turco, Lewis (Putnam) 1934-   **CLC 11, 63**
See also CA 13-16R; CAAS 22; CANR 24, 51;
DLBY 84
Turgenev, Ivan 1818-1883   **NCLC 21; DA;
DAB; DAC; DAM MST, NOV; DC 7; SSC
7; WLC**
Turgot, Anne-Robert-Jacques 1727-1781 L C
26
Turner, Frederick 1943-   **CLC 48**
See also CA 73-76; CAAS 10; CANR 12, 30,
56; DLB 40
Tutu, Desmond M(pilo) 1931-CLC 80; BLC 3;
DAM MULT
See also BW 1; CA 125; CANR 67
Tutuola, Amos 1920-1997CLC 5, 14, 29; BLC
3; DAM MULT
See also BW 2; CA 9-12R; 159; CANR 27, 66;
DLB 125; MTCW 1
Twain, MarkTCLC 6, 12, 19, 36, 48, 59; SSC 6,
26; WLC
See also Clemens, Samuel Langhorne
See also AAYA 20; DLB 11, 12, 23, 64, 74
Tyler, Anne 1941- CLC 7, 11, 18, 28, 44, 59,
103; DAM NOV, POP
See also AAYA 18; BEST 89:1; CA 9-12R;
CANR 11, 33, 53; DLB 6, 143; DLBY 82;
MTCW 1; SATA 7, 90
Tyler, Royall 1757-1826   **NCLC 3**
See also DLB 37
Tynan, Katharine 1861-1931   **TCLC 3**
See also CA 104; 167; DLB 153
Tyutchev, Fyodor 1803-1873   **NCLC 34**
Tzara, Tristan 1896-1963   **CLC 47; DAM
POET**
See also CA 153; 89-92
Uhry, Alfred 1936-   CLC 55; DAM DRAM,
POP
See also CA 127; 133; INT 133
Ulf, Haerved
See Strindberg, (Johan) August
Ulf, Harved
See Strindberg, (Johan) August
Ulibarri, Sabine R(eyes) 1919-CLC 83; DAM
MULT
See also CA 131; DLB 82; HW
Unamuno (y Jugo), Miguel de 1864-1936
TCLC 2, 9; DAM MULT, NOV; HLC; SSC

11
See also CA 104; 131; DLB 108; HW; MTCW
1

Undercliffe, Errol
See Campbell, (John) Ramsey

Underwood, Miles
See Glassco, John

Undset, Sigrid 1882-1949**TCLC 3; DA; DAB;
DAC; DAM MST, NOV; WLC**
See also CA 104; 129; MTCW 1

Ungaretti, Giuseppe 1888-1970**CLC 7, 11, 15**
See also CA 19-20; 25-28R; CAP 2; DLB 114

Unger, Douglas 1952- **CLC 34**
See also CA 130

Unsworth, Barry (Forster) 1930- **CLC 76**
See also CA 25-28R; CANR 30, 54; DLB 194

Updike, John (Hoyer) 1932-**CLC 1, 2, 3, 5, 7,
9, 13, 15, 23, 34, 43, 70; DA; DAB; DAC;
DAM MST, NOV, POET, POP; SSC 13, 27;
WLC**
See also CA 1-4R; CABS 1; CANR 4, 33, 51;
CDALB 1968-1988; DLB 2, 5, 143; DLBD
3; DLBY 80, 82, 97; MTCW 1

Upshaw, Margaret Mitchell
See Mitchell, Margaret (Munnerlyn)

Upton, Mark
See Sanders, Lawrence

Upward, Allen 1863-1926 **TCLC 85**
See also CA 117; DLB 36

Urdang, Constance (Henriette) 1922-**CLC 47**
See also CA 21-24R; CANR 9, 24

Uriel, Henry
See Faust, Frederick (Schiller)

Uris, Leon (Marcus) 1924- **CLC 7, 32; DAM
NOV, POP**
See also AITN 1, 2; BEST 89:2; CA 1-4R;
CANR 1, 40, 65; MTCW 1; SATA 49

Urmuz
See Codrescu, Andrei

Urquhart, Jane 1949- **CLC 90; DAC**
See also CA 113; CANR 32, 68

Ustinov, Peter (Alexander) 1921- **CLC 1**
See also AITN 1; CA 13-16R; CANR 25, 51;
DLB 13

U Tam'si, Gerald Felix Tchicaya
See Tchicaya, Gerald Felix

U Tam'si, Tchicaya
See Tchicaya, Gerald Felix

Vachss, Andrew (Henry) 1942- **CLC 106**
See also CA 118; CANR 44

Vachss, Andrew H.
See Vachss, Andrew (Henry)

Vaculik, Ludvik 1926- **CLC 7**
See also CA 53-56; CANR 72

Vaihinger, Hans 1852-1933 **TCLC 71**
See also CA 116; 166

Valdez, Luis (Miguel) 1940- **CLC 84; DAM
MULT; DC 10; HLC**
See also CA 101; CANR 32; DLB 122; HW

Valenzuela, Luisa 1938- **CLC 31, 104; DAM
MULT; SSC 14**
See also CA 101; CANR 32, 65; DLB 113; HW

Valera y Alcala-Galiano, Juan 1824-1905
TCLC 10
See also CA 106

Valery, (Ambroise) Paul (Toussaint Jules) 1871-
1945 **TCLC 4, 15; DAM POET; PC 9**
See also CA 104; 122; MTCW 1

Valle-Inclan, Ramon (Maria) del 1866-1936
TCLC 5; DAM MULT; HLC
See also CA 106; 153; DLB 134

Vallejo, Antonio Buero
See Buero Vallejo, Antonio

Vallejo, Cesar (Abraham) 1892-1938**TCLC 3,
56; DAM MULT; HLC**
See also CA 105; 153; HW

Valles, Jules 1832-1885 **NCLC 71**
See also DLB 123

Vallette, Marguerite Eymery
See Rachilde

Valle Y Pena, Ramon del
See Valle-Inclan, Ramon (Maria) del

Van Ash, Cay 1918- **CLC 34**

Vanbrugh, Sir John 1664-1726 **LC 21; DAM
DRAM**
See also DLB 80

Van Campen, Karl
See Campbell, John W(ood, Jr.)

Vance, Gerald
See Silverberg, Robert

Vance, Jack **CLC 35**
See also Kuttner, Henry; Vance, John Holbrook
See also DLB 8

Vance, John Holbrook 1916-
See Queen, Ellery; Vance, Jack
See also CA 29-32R; CANR 17, 65; MTCW 1

**Van Den Bogarde, Derek Jules Gaspard Ulric
Niven** 1921-
See Bogarde, Dirk
See also CA 77-80

Vandenburgh, Jane **CLC 59**
See also CA 168

Vanderhaeghe, Guy 1951- **CLC 41**
See also CA 113; CANR 72

van der Post, Laurens (Jan) 1906-1996**CLC 5**
See also CA 5-8R; 155; CANR 35; DLB 204

van de Wetering, Janwillem 1931- **CLC 47**
See also CA 49-52; CANR 4, 62

Van Dine, S. S. **TCLC 23**
See also Wright, Willard Huntington

Van Doren, Carl (Clinton) 1885-1950 **TCLC
18**
See also CA 111; 168

Van Doren, Mark 1894-1972 **CLC 6, 10**
See also CA 1-4R; 37-40R; CANR 3; DLB 45;
MTCW 1

Van Druten, John (William) 1901-1957**TCLC
2**
See also CA 104; 161; DLB 10

Van Duyn, Mona (Jane) 1921- **CLC 3, 7, 63,
116; DAM POET**
See also CA 9-12R; CANR 7, 38, 60; DLB 5

Van Dyne, Edith
See Baum, L(yman) Frank

van Itallie, Jean-Claude 1936- **CLC 3**
See also CA 45-48; CAAS 2; CANR 1, 48; DLB
7

van Ostaijen, Paul 1896-1928 **TCLC 33**
See also CA 163

Van Peebles, Melvin 1932- **CLC 2, 20; DAM
MULT**
See also BW 2; CA 85-88; CANR 27, 67

Vansittart, Peter 1920- **CLC 42**
See also CA 1-4R; CANR 3, 49

Van Vechten, Carl 1880-1964 **CLC 33**
See also CA 89-92; DLB 4, 9, 51

Van Vogt, A(lfred) E(lton) 1912- **CLC 1**
See also CA 21-24R; CANR 28; DLB 8; SATA
14

Varda, Agnes 1928- **CLC 16**
See also CA 116; 122

Vargas Llosa, (Jorge) Mario (Pedro) 1936-
**CLC 3, 6, 9, 10, 15, 31, 42, 85; DA; DAB;
DAC; DAM MST, MULT, NOV; HLC**
See also CA 73-76; CANR 18, 32, 42, 67; DLB
145; HW; MTCW 1

Vasiliu, Gheorghe 1881-1957
See Bacovia, George
See also CA 123

Vassa, Gustavus
See Equiano, Olaudah

Vassilikos, Vassilis 1933- **CLC 4, 8**
See also CA 81-84; CANR 75

Vaughan, Henry 1621-1695 **LC 27**
See also DLB 131

Vaughn, Stephanie **CLC 62**

Vazov, Ivan (Minchov) 1850-1921 **TCLC 25**
See also CA 121; 167; DLB 147

Veblen, Thorstein B(unde) 1857-1929 **TCLC
31**
See also CA 115; 165

Vega, Lope de 1562-1635 **LC 23**

Venison, Alfred
See Pound, Ezra (Weston Loomis)

Verdi, Marie de
See Mencken, H(enry) L(ouis)

Verdu, Matilde
See Cela, Camilo Jose

Verga, Giovanni (Carmelo) 1840-1922 **T C L C
3; SSC 21**
See also CA 104; 123

Vergil 70B.C.-19B.C. **CMLC 9; DA; DAB;
DAC; DAM MST, POET; PC 12; WLCS**

Verhaeren, Emile (Adolphe Gustave) 1855-1916
TCLC 12
See also CA 109

Verlaine, Paul (Marie) 1844-1896**NCLC 2, 51;
DAM POET; PC 2**

Verne, Jules (Gabriel) 1828-1905**TCLC 6, 52**
See also AAYA 16; CA 110; 131; DLB 123;
JRDA; MAICYA; SATA 21

Very, Jones 1813-1880 **NCLC 9**
See also DLB 1

Vesaas, Tarjei 1897-1970 **CLC 48**
See also CA 29-32R

Vialis, Gaston
See Simenon, Georges (Jacques Christian)

Vian, Boris 1920-1959 **TCLC 9**
See also CA 106; 164; DLB 72

Viaud, (Louis Marie) Julien 1850-1923
See Loti, Pierre
See also CA 107

Vicar, Henry
See Felsen, Henry Gregor

Vicker, Angus
See Felsen, Henry Gregor

Vidal, Gore 1925-**CLC 2, 4, 6, 8, 10, 22, 33, 72;
DAM NOV, POP**
See also AITN 1; BEST 90:2; CA 5-8R; CANR
13, 45, 65; DLB 6, 152; INT CANR-13;
MTCW 1

Viereck, Peter (Robert Edwin) 1916- **CLC 4**
See also CA 1-4R; CANR 1, 47; DLB 5

Vigny, Alfred (Victor) de 1797-1863**NCLC 7;
DAM POET**
See also DLB 119, 192

Vilakazi, Benedict Wallet 1906-1947**TCLC 37**
See also CA 168

Villa, Jose Garcia 1904-1997 **PC 22**
See also CA 25-28R; CANR 12

Villaurrutia, Xavier 1903-1950 **TCLC 80**
See also HW

**Villiers de l'Isle Adam, Jean Marie Mathias
Philippe Auguste, Comte de** 1838-1889
NCLC 3; SSC 14
See also DLB 123

Villon, Francois 1431-1463(?) **PC 13**
See also DLB 208

Vinci, Leonardo da 1452-1519 **LC 12**

Vine, Barbara   **CLC 50**
  See also Rendell, Ruth (Barbara)
  See also BEST 90:4

Vinge, Joan (Carol) D(ennison) 1948-**CLC 30;**
  SSC 24
  See also CA 93-96; CANR 72; SATA 36

Violis, G.
  See Simenon, Georges (Jacques Christian)

Virgil
  See Vergil

Visconti, Luchino 1906-1976   **CLC 16**
  See also CA 81-84; 65-68; CANR 39

Vittorini, Elio 1908-1966   **CLC 6, 9, 14**
  See also CA 133; 25-28R

Vivekananda, Swami 1863-1902   **TCLC 88**

Vizenor, Gerald Robert 1934-**CLC 103; DAM**
  MULT
  See also CA 13-16R; CAAS 22; CANR 5, 21,
    44, 67; DLB 175; NNAL

Vizinczey, Stephen 1933-   **CLC 40**
  See also CA 128; INT 128

Vliet, R(ussell) G(ordon) 1929-1984 **CLC 22**
  See also CA 37-40R; 112; CANR 18

Vogau, Boris Andreyevich 1894-1937(?)
  See Pilnyak, Boris
  See also CA 123

Vogel, Paula A(nne) 1951-   **CLC 76**
  See also CA 108

Voigt, Cynthia 1942-   **CLC 30**
  See also AAYA 3; CA 106; CANR 18, 37, 40;
    CLR 13, 48; INT CANR-18; JRDA;
    MAICYA; SATA 48, 79; SATA-Brief 33

Voigt, Ellen Bryant 1943-   **CLC 54**
  See also CA 69-72; CANR 11, 29, 55; DLB 120

Voinovich, Vladimir (Nikolaevich) 1932-**CLC**
  10, 49
  See also CA 81-84; CAAS 12; CANR 33, 67;
    MTCW 1

Vollmann, William T. 1959-   **CLC 89; DAM**
  NOV, POP
  See also CA 134; CANR 67

Voloshinov, V. N.
  See Bakhtin, Mikhail Mikhailovich

Voltaire 1694-1778 **LC 14; DA; DAB; DAC;**
  DAM DRAM, MST; SSC 12; WLC

von Aschendrof, BaronIgnatz
  See Ford, Ford Madox

von Daeniken, Erich 1935-   **CLC 30**
  See also AITN 1; CA 37-40R; CANR 17, 44

von Daniken, Erich
  See von Daeniken, Erich

von Heidenstam, (Carl Gustaf) Verner
  See Heidenstam, (Carl Gustaf) Verner von

von Heyse, Paul (Johann Ludwig)
  See Heyse, Paul (Johann Ludwig von)

von Hofmannsthal, Hugo
  See Hofmannsthal, Hugo von

von Horvath, Odon
  See Horvath, Oedoen von

von Horvath, Oedoen
  See Horvath, Oedoen von

von Liliencron, (Friedrich Adolf Axel) Detlev
  See Liliencron, (Friedrich Adolf Axel) Detlev
    von

Vonnegut, Kurt, Jr. 1922-**CLC 1, 2, 3, 4, 5, 8,**
  12, 22, 40, 60, 111; DA; DAB; DAC; DAM
  MST, NOV, POP; SSC 8; WLC
  See also AAYA 6; AITN 1; BEST 90:4; CA 1-
    4R; CANR 1, 25, 49, 75; CDALB 1968-
    1988; DLB 2, 8, 152; DLBD 3; DLBY 80;
    MTCW 1

Von Rachen, Kurt
  See Hubbard, L(afayette) Ron(ald)

von Rezzori (d'Arezzo), Gregor
  See Rezzori (d'Arezzo), Gregor von

von Sternberg, Josef
  See Sternberg, Josef von

Vorster, Gordon 1924-   **CLC 34**
  See also CA 133

Vosce, Trudie
  See Ozick, Cynthia

Voznesensky, Andrei (Andreievich) 1933-
  CLC 1, 15, 57; DAM POET
  See also CA 89-92; CANR 37; MTCW 1

Waddington, Miriam 1917-   **CLC 28**
  See also CA 21-24R; CANR 12, 30; DLB 68

Wagman, Fredrica 1937-   **CLC 7**
  See also CA 97-100; INT 97-100

Wagner, Linda W.
  See Wagner-Martin, Linda (C.)

Wagner, Linda Welshimer
  See Wagner-Martin, Linda (C.)

Wagner, Richard 1813-1883   **NCLC 9**
  See also DLB 129

Wagner-Martin, Linda (C.) 1936- **CLC 50**
  See also CA 159

Wagoner, David (Russell) 1926- **CLC 3, 5, 15**
  See also CA 1-4R; CAAS 3; CANR 2, 71; DLB
    5; SATA 14

Wah, Fred(erick James) 1939-   **CLC 44**
  See also CA 107; 141; DLB 60

Wahloo, Per 1926-1975   **CLC 7**
  See also CA 61-64; CANR 73

Wahloo, Peter
  See Wahloo, Per

Wain, John (Barrington) 1925-1994 **CLC 2,**
  11, 15, 46
  See also CA 5-8R; 145; CAAS 4; CANR 23,
    54; CDBLB 1960 to Present; DLB 15, 27,
    139, 155; MTCW 1

Wajda, Andrzej 1926-   **CLC 16**
  See also CA 102

Wakefield, Dan 1932-   **CLC 7**
  See also CA 21-24R; CAAS 7

Wakoski, Diane 1937- **CLC 2, 4, 7, 9, 11, 40;**
  DAM POET; PC 15
  See also CA 13-16R; CAAS 1; CANR 9, 60;
    DLB 5; INT CANR-9

Wakoski-Sherbell, Diane
  See Wakoski, Diane

Walcott, Derek (Alton) 1930-**CLC 2, 4, 9, 14,**
  25, 42, 67, 76; BLC 3; DAB; DAC; DAM
  MST, MULT, POET; DC 7
  See also BW 2; CA 89-92; CANR 26, 47, 75;
    DLB 117; DLBY 81; MTCW 1

Waldman, Anne (Lesley) 1945-   **CLC 7**
  See also CA 37-40R; CAAS 17; CANR 34, 69;
    DLB 16

Waldo, E. Hunter
  See Sturgeon, Theodore (Hamilton)

Waldo, Edward Hamilton
  See Sturgeon, Theodore (Hamilton)

Walker, Alice (Malsenior) 1944- **CLC 5, 6, 9,**
  19, 27, 46, 58, 103; BLC 3; DA; DAB;
  DAC; DAM MST, MULT, NOV, POET,
  POP; SSC 5; WLCS
  See also AAYA 3; BEST 89:4; BW 2; CA 37-
    40R; CANR 9, 27, 49, 66; CDALB 1968-
    1988; DLB 6, 33, 143; INT CANR-27;
    MTCW 1; SATA 31

Walker, David Harry 1911-1992   **CLC 14**
  See also CA 1-4R; 137; CANR 1; SATA 8;
    SATA-Obit 71

Walker, Edward Joseph 1934-
  See Walker, Ted
  See also CA 21-24R; CANR 12, 28, 53

Walker, George F. 1947- **CLC 44, 61; DAB;**
  DAC; DAM MST
  See also CA 103; CANR 21, 43, 59; DLB 60

Walker, Joseph A. 1935-   **CLC 19; DAM**
  DRAM, MST
  See also BW 1; CA 89-92; CANR 26; DLB 38

Walker, Margaret (Abigail) 1915- **CLC 1, 6;**
  BLC; DAM MULT; PC 20
  See also BW 2; CA 73-76; CANR 26, 54; DLB
    76, 152; MTCW 1

Walker, Ted   **CLC 13**
  See also Walker, Edward Joseph
  See also DLB 40

Wallace, David Foster 1962- **CLC 50, 114**
  See also CA 132; CANR 59

Wallace, Dexter
  See Masters, Edgar Lee

Wallace, (Richard Horatio) Edgar 1875-1932
  TCLC 57
  See also CA 115; DLB 70

Wallace, Irving 1916-1990 **CLC 7, 13; DAM**
  NOV, POP
  See also AITN 1; CA 1-4R; 132; CAAS 1;
    CANR 1, 27; INT CANR-27; MTCW 1

Wallant, Edward Lewis 1926-1962**CLC 5, 10**
  See also CA 1-4R; CANR 22; DLB 2, 28, 143;
    MTCW 1

Walley, Byron
  See Card, Orson Scott

Walpole, Horace 1717-1797   **LC 2**
  See also DLB 39, 104

Walpole, Hugh (Seymour) 1884-1941**TCLC 5**
  See also CA 104; 165; DLB 34

Walser, Martin 1927-   **CLC 27**
  See also CA 57-60; CANR 8, 46; DLB 75, 124

Walser, Robert 1878-1956 **TCLC 18; SSC 20**
  See also CA 118; 165; DLB 66

Walsh, Jill Paton   **CLC 35**
  See also Paton Walsh, Gillian
  See also AAYA 11; CLR 2; DLB 161; SAAS 3

Walter, Villiam Christian
  See Andersen, Hans Christian

Wambaugh, Joseph (Aloysius, Jr.) 1937-**CLC**
  3, 18; DAM NOV, POP
  See also AITN 1; BEST 89:3; CA 33-36R;
    CANR 42, 65; DLB 6; DLBY 83; MTCW 1

Wang Wei 699(?)-761(?)   **PC 18**

Ward, Arthur Henry Sarsfield 1883-1959
  See Rohmer, Sax
  See also CA 108

Ward, Douglas Turner 1930-   **CLC 19**
  See also BW 1; CA 81-84; CANR 27; DLB 7,
    38

Ward, Mary Augusta
  See Ward, Mrs. Humphry

Ward, Mrs. Humphry 1851-1920 **TCLC 55**
  See also DLB 18

Ward, Peter
  See Faust, Frederick (Schiller)

Warhol, Andy 1928(?)-1987   **CLC 20**
  See also AAYA 12; BEST 89:4; CA 89-92; 121;
    CANR 34

Warner, Francis (Robert le Plastrier) 1937-
  CLC 14
  See also CA 53-56; CANR 11

Warner, Marina 1946-   **CLC 59**
  See also CA 65-68; CANR 21, 55; DLB 194

Warner, Rex (Ernest) 1905-1986 **CLC 45**
  See also CA 89-92; 119; DLB 15

Warner, Susan (Bogert) 1819-1885 **NCLC 31**
  See also DLB 3, 42

Warner, Sylvia (Constance) Ashton
  See Ashton-Warner, Sylvia (Constance)

Warner, Sylvia Townsend 1893-1978 **CLC 7, 19; SSC 23**
See also CA 61-64; 77-80; CANR 16, 60; DLB 34, 139; MTCW 1

Warren, Mercy Otis 1728-1814 **NCLC 13**
See also DLB 31, 200

Warren, Robert Penn 1905-1989 **CLC 1, 4, 6, 8, 10, 13, 18, 39, 53, 59; DA; DAB; DAC; DAM MST, NOV, POET; SSC 4; WLC**
See also AITN 1; CA 13-16R; 129; CANR 10, 47; CDALB 1968-1988; DLB 2, 48, 152; DLBY 80, 89; INT CANR-10; MTCW 1; SATA 46; SATA-Obit 63

Warshofsky, Isaac
See Singer, Isaac Bashevis

Warton, Thomas 1728-1790 **LC 15; DAM POET**
See also DLB 104, 109

Waruk, Kona
See Harris, (Theodore) Wilson

Warung, Price 1855-1911 **TCLC 45**

Warwick, Jarvis
See Garner, Hugh

Washington, Alex
See Harris, Mark

Washington, Booker T(aliaferro) 1856-1915 **TCLC 10; BLC 3; DAM MULT**
See also BW 1; CA 114; 125; SATA 28

Washington, George 1732-1799 **LC 25**
See also DLB 31

Wassermann, (Karl) Jakob 1873-1934 **T C L C 6**
See also CA 104; DLB 66

Wasserstein, Wendy 1950- **CLC 32, 59, 90; DAM DRAM; DC 4**
See also CA 121; 129; CABS 3; CANR 53; INT 129; SATA 94, 75

Waterhouse, Keith (Spencer) 1929- **CLC 47**
See also CA 5-8R; CANR 38, 67; DLB 13, 15; MTCW 1

Waters, Frank (Joseph) 1902-1995 **CLC 88**
See also CA 5-8R; 149; CAAS 13; CANR 3, 18, 63; DLBY 86

Waters, Roger 1944- **CLC 35**

Watkins, Frances Ellen
See Harper, Frances Ellen Watkins

Watkins, Gerrold
See Malzberg, Barry N(athaniel)

Watkins, Gloria 1955(?)-
See hooks, bell
See also BW 2; CA 143

Watkins, Paul 1964- **CLC 55**
See also CA 132; CANR 62

Watkins, Vernon Phillips 1906-1967 **CLC 43**
See also CA 9-10; 25-28R; CAP 1; DLB 20

Watson, Irving S.
See Mencken, H(enry) L(ouis)

Watson, John H.
See Farmer, Philip Jose

Watson, Richard F.
See Silverberg, Robert

Waugh, Auberon (Alexander) 1939- **CLC 7**
See also CA 45-48; CANR 6, 22; DLB 14, 194

Waugh, Evelyn (Arthur St. John) 1903-1966 **CLC 1, 3, 8, 13, 19, 27, 44, 107; DA; DAB; DAC; DAM MST, NOV, POP; WLC**
See also CA 85-88; 25-28R; CANR 22; CDBLB 1914-1945; DLB 15, 162, 195; MTCW 1

Waugh, Harriet 1944- **CLC 6**
See also CA 85-88; CANR 22

Ways, C. R.
See Blount, Roy (Alton), Jr.

Waystaff, Simon
See Swift, Jonathan

Webb, (Martha) Beatrice (Potter) 1858-1943 **TCLC 22**
See also Potter, (Helen) Beatrix
See also CA 117; DLB 190

Webb, Charles (Richard) 1939- **CLC 7**
See also CA 25-28R

Webb, James H(enry), Jr. 1946- **CLC 22**
See also CA 81-84

Webb, Mary (Gladys Meredith) 1881-1927 **TCLC 24**
See also CA 123; DLB 34

Webb, Mrs. Sidney
See Webb, (Martha) Beatrice (Potter)

Webb, Phyllis 1927- **CLC 18**
See also CA 104; CANR 23; DLB 53

Webb, Sidney (James) 1859-1947 **TCLC 22**
See also CA 117; 163; DLB 190

Webber, Andrew Lloyd **CLC 21**
See also Lloyd Webber, Andrew

Weber, Lenora Mattingly 1895-1971 **CLC 12**
See also CA 19-20; 29-32R; CAP 1; SATA 2; SATA-Obit 26

Weber, Max 1864-1920 **TCLC 69**
See also CA 109

Webster, John 1579(?)-1634(?) **LC 33; DA; DAB; DAC; DAM DRAM, MST; DC 2; WLC**
See also CDBLB Before 1660; DLB 58

Webster, Noah 1758-1843 **NCLC 30**

Wedekind, (Benjamin) Frank(lin) 1864-1918 **TCLC 7; DAM DRAM**
See also CA 104; 153; DLB 118

Weidman, Jerome 1913-1998 **CLC 7**
See also AITN 2; CA 1-4R; 171; CANR 1; DLB 28

Weil, Simone (Adolphine) 1909-1943 **TCLC 23**
See also CA 117; 159

Weininger, Otto 1880-1903 **TCLC 84**

Weinstein, Nathan
See West, Nathanael

Weinstein, Nathan von Wallenstein
See West, Nathanael

Weir, Peter (Lindsay) 1944- **CLC 20**
See also CA 113; 123

Weiss, Peter (Ulrich) 1916-1982 **CLC 3, 15, 51; DAM DRAM**
See also CA 45-48; 106; CANR 3; DLB 69, 124

Weiss, Theodore (Russell) 1916- **CLC 3, 8, 14**
See also CA 9-12R; CAAS 2; CANR 46; DLB 5

Welch, (Maurice) Denton 1915-1948 **TCLC 22**
See also CA 121; 148

Welch, James 1940- **CLC 6, 14, 52; DAM MULT, POP**
See also CA 85-88; CANR 42, 66; DLB 175; NNAL

Weldon, Fay 1931- **CLC 6, 9, 11, 19, 36, 59; DAM POP**
See also CA 21-24R; CANR 16, 46, 63; CDBLB 1960 to Present; DLB 14, 194; INT CANR-16; MTCW 1

Wellek, Rene 1903-1995 **CLC 28**
See also CA 5-8R; 150; CAAS 7; CANR 8; DLB 63; INT CANR-8

Weller, Michael 1942- **CLC 10, 53**
See also CA 85-88

Weller, Paul 1958- **CLC 26**

Wellershoff, Dieter 1925- **CLC 46**
See also CA 89-92; CANR 16, 37

Welles, (George) Orson 1915-1985 **CLC 20, 80**
See also CA 93-96; 117

Wellman, John McDowell 1945-
See Wellman, Mac
See also CA 166

Wellman, Mac 1945- **CLC 65**
See also Wellman, John McDowell; Wellman, John McDowell

Wellman, Manly Wade 1903-1986 **CLC 49**
See also CA 1-4R; 118; CANR 6, 16, 44; SATA 6; SATA-Obit 47

Wells, Carolyn 1869(?)-1942 **TCLC 35**
See also CA 113; DLB 11

Wells, H(erbert) G(eorge) 1866-1946 **TCLC 6, 12, 19; DA; DAB; DAC; DAM MST, NOV; SSC 6; WLC**
See also AAYA 18; CA 110; 121; CDBLB 1914-1945; DLB 34, 70, 156, 178; MTCW 1; SATA 20

Wells, Rosemary 1943- **CLC 12**
See also AAYA 13; CA 85-88; CANR 48; CLR 16; MAICYA; SAAS 1; SATA 18, 69

Welty, Eudora 1909- **CLC 1, 2, 5, 14, 22, 33, 105; DA; DAB; DAC; DAM MST, NOV; SSC 1, 27; WLC**
See also CA 9-12R; CABS 1; CANR 32, 65; CDALB 1941-1968; DLB 2, 102, 143; DLBD 12; DLBY 87; MTCW 1

Wen I-to 1899-1946 **TCLC 28**

Wentworth, Robert
See Hamilton, Edmond

Werfel, Franz (Viktor) 1890-1945 **TCLC 8**
See also CA 104; 161; DLB 81, 124

Wergeland, Henrik Arnold 1808-1845 **N C L C 5**

Wersba, Barbara 1932- **CLC 30**
See also AAYA 2; CA 29-32R; CANR 16, 38; CLR 3; DLB 52; JRDA; MAICYA; SAAS 2; SATA 1, 58

Wertmueller, Lina 1928- **CLC 16**
See also CA 97-100; CANR 39

Wescott, Glenway 1901-1987 **CLC 13**
See also CA 13-16R; 121; CANR 23, 70; DLB 4, 9, 102

Wesker, Arnold 1932- **CLC 3, 5, 42; DAB; DAM DRAM**
See also CA 1-4R; CAAS 7; CANR 1, 33; CDBLB 1960 to Present; DLB 13; MTCW 1

Wesley, Richard (Errol) 1945- **CLC 7**
See also BW 1; CA 57-60; CANR 27; DLB 38

Wessel, Johan Herman 1742-1785 **LC 7**

West, Anthony (Panther) 1914-1987 **CLC 50**
See also CA 45-48; 124; CANR 3, 19; DLB 15

West, C. P.
See Wodehouse, P(elham) G(renville)

West, (Mary) Jessamyn 1902-1984 **CLC 7, 17**
See also CA 9-12R; 112; CANR 27; DLB 6; DLBY 84; MTCW 1; SATA-Obit 37

West, Morris L(anglo) 1916- **CLC 6, 33**
See also CA 5-8R; CANR 24, 49, 64; MTCW 1

West, Nathanael 1903-1940 **TCLC 1, 14, 44; SSC 16**
See also CA 104; 125; CDALB 1929-1941; DLB 4, 9, 28; MTCW 1

West, Owen
See Koontz, Dean R(ay)

West, Paul 1930- **CLC 7, 14, 96**
See also CA 13-16R; CAAS 7; CANR 22, 53; DLB 14; INT CANR-22

West, Rebecca 1892-1983 **CLC 7, 9, 31, 50**
See also CA 5-8R; 109; CANR 19; DLB 36; DLBY 83; MTCW 1

Westall, Robert (Atkinson) 1929-1993 **CLC 17**
See also AAYA 12; CA 69-72; 141; CANR 18, 68; CLR 13; JRDA; MAICYA; SAAS 2; SATA 23, 69; SATA-Obit 75

Westermarck, Edward 1862-1939 **TCLC 87**

Westlake, Donald E(dwin) 1933- **CLC 7, 33; DAM POP**
See also CA 17-20R; CAAS 13; CANR 16, 44, 65; INT CANR-16

Westmacott, Mary
See Christie, Agatha (Mary Clarissa)

Weston, Allen
See Norton, Andre

Wetcheek, J. L.
See Feuchtwanger, Lion

Wetering, Janwillem van de
See van de Wetering, Janwillem

Wetherald, Agnes Ethelwyn 1857-1940**TCLC 81**
See also DLB 99

Wetherell, Elizabeth
See Warner, Susan (Bogert)

Whale, James 1889-1957 **TCLC 63**

Whalen, Philip 1923- **CLC 6, 29**
See also CA 9-12R; CANR 5, 39; DLB 16

Wharton, Edith (Newbold Jones) 1862-1937 **TCLC 3, 9, 27, 53; DA; DAB; DAC; DAM MST, NOV; SSC 6; WLC**
See also AAYA 25; CA 104; 132; CDALB 1865-1917; DLB 4, 9, 12, 78, 189; DLBD 13; MTCW 1

Wharton, James
See Mencken, H(enry) L(ouis)

Wharton, William (a pseudonym) **CLC 18, 37**
See also CA 93-96; DLBY 80; INT 93-96

Wheatley (Peters), Phillis 1754(?)-1784**LC 3; BLC 3; DA; DAC; DAM MST, MULT, POET; PC 3; WLC**
See also CDALB 1640-1865; DLB 31, 50

Wheelock, John Hall 1886-1978 **CLC 14**
See also CA 13-16R; 77-80; CANR 14; DLB 45

White, E(lwyn) B(rooks) 1899-1985 **CLC 10, 34, 39; DAM POP**
See also AITN 2; CA 13-16R; 116; CANR 16, 37; CLR 1, 21; DLB 11, 22; MAICYA; MTCW 1; SATA 2, 29, 100; SATA-Obit 44

White, Edmund (Valentine III) 1940-**CLC 27, 110; DAM POP**
See also AAYA 7; CA 45-48; CANR 3, 19, 36, 62; MTCW 1

White, Patrick (Victor Martindale) 1912-1990 **CLC 3, 4, 5, 7, 9, 18, 65, 69**
See also CA 81-84; 132; CANR 43; MTCW 1

White, Phyllis Dorothy James 1920-
See James, P. D.
See also CA 21-24R; CANR 17, 43, 65; DAM POP; MTCW 1

White, T(erence) H(anbury) 1906-1964 **CLC 30**
See also AAYA 22; CA 73-76; CANR 37; DLB 160; JRDA; MAICYA; SATA 12

White, Terence de Vere 1912-1994 **CLC 49**
See also CA 49-52; 145; CANR 3

White, Walter F(rancis) 1893-1955 **TCLC 15**
See also White, Walter
See also BW 1; CA 115; 124; DLB 51

White, William Hale 1831-1913
See Rutherford, Mark
See also CA 121

Whitehead, E(dward) A(nthony) 1933-**CLC 5**
See also CA 65-68; CANR 58

Whitemore, Hugh (John) 1936- **CLC 37**
See also CA 132; INT 132

Whitman, Sarah Helen (Power) 1803-1878 **NCLC 19**
See also DLB 1

Whitman, Walt(er) 1819-1892 **NCLC 4, 31; DA; DAB; DAC; DAM MST, POET; PC 3; WLC**
See also CDALB 1640-1865; DLB 3, 64; SATA 20

Whitney, Phyllis A(yame) 1903- **CLC 42; DAM POP**
See also AITN 2; BEST 90:3; CA 1-4R; CANR 3, 25, 38, 60; JRDA; MAICYA; SATA 1, 30

Whittemore, (Edward) Reed (Jr.) 1919-**CLC 4**
See also CA 9-12R; CAAS 8; CANR 4; DLB 5

Whittier, John Greenleaf 1807-1892**NCLC 8, 59**
See also DLB 1

Whittlebot, Hernia
See Coward, Noel (Peirce)

Wicker, Thomas Grey 1926-
See Wicker, Tom
See also CA 65-68; CANR 21, 46

Wicker, Tom **CLC 7**
See also Wicker, Thomas Grey

Wideman, John Edgar 1941- **CLC 5, 34, 36, 67; BLC 3; DAM MULT**
See also BW 2; CA 85-88; CANR 14, 42, 67; DLB 33, 143

Wiebe, Rudy (Henry) 1934- **CLC 6, 11, 14; DAC; DAM MST**
See also CA 37-40R; CANR 42, 67; DLB 60

Wieland, Christoph Martin 1733-1813**NCLC 17**
See also DLB 97

Wiene, Robert 1881-1938 **TCLC 56**

Wieners, John 1934- **CLC 7**
See also CA 13-16R; DLB 16

Wiesel, Elie(zer) 1928- **CLC 3, 5, 11, 37; DA; DAB; DAC; DAM MST, NOV; WLCS**
See also AAYA 7; AITN 1; CA 5-8R; CAAS 4; CANR 8, 40, 65; DLB 83; DLBY 87; INT CANR-8; MTCW 1; SATA 56

Wiggins, Marianne 1947- **CLC 57**
See also BEST 89:3; CA 130; CANR 60

Wight, James Alfred 1916-1995
See Herriot, James
See also CA 77-80; SATA 55; SATA-Brief 44

Wilbur, Richard (Purdy) 1921-**CLC 3, 6, 9, 14, 53, 110; DA; DAB; DAC; DAM MST, POET**
See also CA 1-4R; CABS 2; CANR 2, 29; DLB 5, 169; INT CANR-29; MTCW 1; SATA 9

Wild, Peter 1940- **CLC 14**
See also CA 37-40R; DLB 5

Wilde, Oscar (Fingal O'Flahertie Wills) 1854(?)-1900**TCLC 1, 8, 23, 41; DA; DAB; DAC; DAM DRAM, MST, NOV; SSC 11; WLC**
See also CA 104; 119; CDBLB 1890-1914; DLB 10, 19, 34, 57, 141, 156, 190; SATA 24

Wilder, Billy **CLC 20**
See also Wilder, Samuel
See also DLB 26

Wilder, Samuel 1906-
See Wilder, Billy
See also CA 89-92

Wilder, Thornton (Niven) 1897-1975**CLC 1, 5, 6, 10, 15, 35, 82; DA; DAB; DAC; DAM DRAM, MST, NOV; DC 1; WLC**
See also AITN 2; CA 13-16R; 61-64; CANR 40; DLB 4, 7, 9; DLBY 97; MTCW 1

Wilding, Michael 1942- **CLC 73**
See also CA 104; CANR 24, 49

Wiley, Richard 1944- **CLC 44**
See also CA 121; 129; CANR 71

Wilhelm, Kate **CLC 7**

See also Wilhelm, Katie Gertrude
See also AAYA 20; CAAS 5; DLB 8; INT CANR-17

Wilhelm, Katie Gertrude 1928-
See Wilhelm, Kate
See also CA 37-40R; CANR 17, 36, 60; MTCW 1

Wilkins, Mary
See Freeman, Mary Eleanor Wilkins

Willard, Nancy 1936- **CLC 7, 37**
See also CA 89-92; CANR 10, 39, 68; CLR 5; DLB 5, 52; MAICYA; MTCW 1; SATA 37, 71; SATA-Brief 30

William of Ockham 1285-1347 **CMLC 32**

Williams, Ben Ames 1889-1953 **TCLC 89**
See also DLB 102

Williams, C(harles) K(enneth) 1936-**CLC 33, 56; DAM POET**
See also CA 37-40R; CAAS 26; CANR 57; DLB 5

Williams, Charles
See Collier, James L(incoln)

Williams, Charles (Walter Stansby) 1886-1945 **TCLC 1, 11**
See also CA 104; 163; DLB 100, 153

Williams, (George) Emlyn 1905-1987**CLC 15; DAM DRAM**
See also CA 104; 123; CANR 36; DLB 10, 77; MTCW 1

Williams, Hank 1923-1953 **TCLC 81**

Williams, Hugo 1942- **CLC 42**
See also CA 17-20R; CANR 45; DLB 40

Williams, J. Walker
See Wodehouse, P(elham) G(renville)

Williams, John A(lfred) 1925-**CLC 5, 13; BLC 3; DAM MULT**
See also BW 2; CA 53-56; CAAS 3; CANR 6, 26, 51; DLB 2, 33; INT CANR-6

Williams, Jonathan (Chamberlain) 1929-**CLC 13**
See also CA 9-12R; CAAS 12; CANR 8; DLB 5

Williams, Joy 1944- **CLC 31**
See also CA 41-44R; CANR 22, 48

Williams, Norman 1952- **CLC 39**
See also CA 118

Williams, Sherley Anne 1944-**CLC 89; BLC 3; DAM MULT, POET**
See also BW 2; CA 73-76; CANR 25; DLB 41; INT CANR-25; SATA 78

Williams, Shirley
See Williams, Sherley Anne

Williams, Tennessee 1911-1983**CLC 1, 2, 5, 7, 8, 11, 15, 19, 30, 39, 45, 71, 111; DA; DAB; DAC; DAM DRAM, MST; DC 4; WLC**
See also AITN 1, 2; CA 5-8R; 108; CABS 3; CANR 31; CDALB 1941-1968; DLB 7; DLBD 4; DLBY 83; MTCW 1

Williams, Thomas (Alonzo) 1926-1990**CLC 14**
See also CA 1-4R; 132; CANR 2

Williams, William C.
See Williams, William Carlos

Williams, William Carlos 1883-1963**CLC 1, 2, 5, 9, 13, 22, 42, 67; DA; DAB; DAC; DAM MST, POET; PC 7; SSC 31**
See also CA 89-92; CANR 34; CDALB 1917-1929; DLB 4, 16, 54, 86; MTCW 1

Williamson, David (Keith) 1942- **CLC 56**
See also CA 103; CANR 41

Williamson, Ellen Douglas 1905-1984
See Douglas, Ellen
See also CA 17-20R; 114; CANR 39

Williamson, Jack **CLC 29**

See also Williamson, John Stewart
See also CAAS 8; DLB.8

Williamson, John Stewart 1908-
See Williamson, Jack
See also CA 17-20R; CANR 23, 70

Willie, Frederick
See Lovecraft, H(oward) P(hillips)

Willingham, Calder (Baynard, Jr.) 1922-1995
CLC 5, 51
See also CA 5-8R; 147; CANR 3; DLB 2, 44;
MTCW 1

Willis, Charles
See Clarke, Arthur C(harles)

Willy
See Colette, (Sidonie-Gabrielle)

Willy, Colette
See Colette, (Sidonie-Gabrielle)

Wilson, A(ndrew) N(orman) 1950- **CLC 33**
See also CA 112; 122; DLB 14, 155, 194.

Wilson, Angus (Frank Johnstone) 1913-1991
CLC 2, 3, 5, 25, 34; SSC 21
See also CA 5-8R; 134; CANR 21; DLB 15,
139, 155; MTCW 1

Wilson, August 1945-**CLC 39, 50, 63; BLC 3;**
DA; DAB; DAC; DAM DRAM, MST,
MULT; DC 2; WLCS
See also AAYA 16; BW 2; CA 115; 122; CANR
42, 54; MTCW 1

Wilson, Brian 1942- **CLC 12**

Wilson, Colin 1931- **CLC 3, 14**
See also CA 1-4R; CAAS 5; CANR 1, 22, 33;
DLB 14, 194; MTCW 1

Wilson, Dirk
See Pohl, Frederik

Wilson, Edmund 1895-1972**CLC 1, 2, 3, 8, 24**
See also CA 1-4R; 37-40R; CANR 1, 46; DLB
63; MTCW 1

Wilson, Ethel Davis (Bryant) 1888(?)-1980
CLC 13; DAC; DAM POET
See also CA 102; DLB 68; MTCW 1

Wilson, John 1785-1854 **NCLC 5**

Wilson, John (Anthony) Burgess 1917-1993
See Burgess, Anthony
See also CA 1-4R; 143; CANR 2, 46; DAC;
DAM NOV; MTCW 1

Wilson, Lanford 1937- **CLC 7, 14, 36; DAM**
DRAM
See also CA 17-20R; CABS 3; CANR 45; DLB
7

Wilson, Robert M. 1944- **CLC 7, 9**
See also CA 49-52; CANR 2, 41; MTCW 1

Wilson, Robert McLiam 1964- **CLC 59**
See also CA 132

Wilson, Sloan 1920- **CLC 32**
See also CA 1-4R; CANR 1, 44

Wilson, Snoo 1948- **CLC 33**
See also CA 69-72

Wilson, William S(mith) 1932- **CLC 49**
See also CA 81-84

Wilson, (Thomas) Woodrow 1856-1924**TCLC**
79
See also CA 166; DLB 47

Winchilsea, Anne (Kingsmill) Finch Counte
1661-1720
See Finch, Anne

Windham, Basil
See Wodehouse, P(elham) G(renville)

Wingrove, David (John) 1954- **CLC 68**
See also CA 133

Wintergreen, Jane
See Duncan, Sara Jeannette

Winters, Janet Lewis **CLC 41**
See also Lewis, Janet

See also DLBY 87

Winters, (Arthur) Yvor 1900-1968 **CLC 4, 8,**
32
See also CA 11-12; 25-28R; CAP 1; DLB 48;
MTCW 1

Winterson, Jeanette 1959-**CLC 64; DAM POP**
See also CA 136; CANR 58; DLB 207

Winthrop, John 1588-1649 **LC 31**
See also DLB 24, 30

Wiseman, Frederick 1930- **CLC 20**
See also CA 159

Wister, Owen 1860-1938 **TCLC 21**
See also CA 108; 162; DLB 9, 78, 186; SATA
62

Witkacy
See Witkiewicz, Stanislaw Ignacy

Witkiewicz, Stanislaw Ignacy 1885-1939
TCLC 8
See also CA 105; 162

Wittgenstein, Ludwig (Josef Johann) 1889-1951
TCLC 59
See also CA 113; 164

Wittig, Monique 1935(?)- **CLC 22**
See also CA 116; 135; DLB 83

Wittlin, Jozef 1896-1976 **CLC 25**
See also CA 49-52; 65-68; CANR 3

Wodehouse, P(elham) G(renville) 1881-1975
CLC 1, 2, 5, 10, 22; DAB; DAC; DAM
NOV; SSC 2
See also AITN 2; CA 45-48; 57-60; CANR 3,
33; CDBLB 1914-1945; DLB 34, 162;
MTCW 1; SATA 22

Woiwode, L.
See Woiwode, Larry (Alfred)

Woiwode, Larry (Alfred) 1941- **CLC 6, 10**
See also CA 73-76; CANR 16; DLB 6; INT
CANR-16

Wojciechowska, Maia (Teresa) 1927-**CLC 26**
See also AAYA 8; CA 9-12R; CANR 4, 41; CLR
1; JRDA; MAICYA; SAAS 1; SATA 1, 28,
83

Wolf, Christa 1929- **CLC 14, 29, 58**
See also CA 85-88; CANR 45; DLB 75; MTCW
1

Wolfe, Gene (Rodman) 1931- **CLC 25; DAM**
POP
See also CA 57-60; CAAS 9; CANR 6, 32, 60;
DLB 8

Wolfe, George C. 1954- **CLC 49; BLCS**
See also CA 149

Wolfe, Thomas (Clayton) 1900-1938**TCLC 4,**
13, 29, 61; DA; DAB; DAC; DAM MST,
NOV; SSC 33; WLC
See also CA 104; 132; CDALB 1929-1941;
DLB 9, 102; DLBD 2, 16; DLBY 85, 97;
MTCW 1

Wolfe, Thomas Kennerly, Jr. 1930-
See Wolfe, Tom
See also CA 13-16R; CANR 9, 33, 70; DAM
POP; DLB 185; INT CANR-9; MTCW 1

Wolfe, Tom **CLC 1, 2, 9, 15, 35, 51**
See also Wolfe, Thomas Kennerly, Jr.
See also AAYA 8; AITN 2; BEST 89:1; DLB
152

Wolff, Geoffrey (Ansell) 1937- **CLC 41**
See also CA 29-32R; CANR 29, 43

Wolff, Sonia
See Levitin, Sonia (Wolff)

Wolff, Tobias (Jonathan Ansell) 1945- **CLC**
39, 64
See also AAYA 16; BEST 90:2; CA 114; 117;
CAAS 22; CANR 54; DLB 130; INT 117

Wolfram von Eschenbach c. 1170-c. 1220

CMLC 5
See also DLB 138

Wolitzer, Hilma 1930- **CLC 17**
See also CA 65-68; CANR 18, 40; INT CANR-
18; SATA 31

Wollstonecraft, Mary 1759-1797 **LC 5**
See also CDBLB 1789-1832; DLB 39, 104, 158

Wonder, Stevie **CLC 12**
See also Morris, Steveland Judkins

Wong, Jade Snow 1922- **CLC 17**
See also CA 109

Woodberry, George Edward 1855-1930
TCLC 73
See also CA 165; DLB 71, 103

Woodcott, Keith
See Brunner, John (Kilian Houston)

Woodruff, Robert W.
See Mencken, H(enry) L(ouis)

Woolf, (Adeline) Virginia 1882-1941**TCLC 1,**
5, 20, 43, 56; DA; DAB; DAC; DAM MST,
NOV; SSC 7; WLC
See also CA 104; 130; CANR 64; CDBLB
1914-1945; DLB 36, 100, 162; DLBD 10;
MTCW 1

Woolf, Virginia Adeline
See Woolf, (Adeline) Virginia

Woollcott, Alexander (Humphreys) 1887-1943
TCLC 5
See also CA 105; 161; DLB 29

Woolrich, Cornell 1903-1968 **CLC 77**
See also Hopley-Woolrich, Cornell George

Wordsworth, Dorothy 1771-1855 **NCLC 25**
See also DLB 107

Wordsworth, William 1770-1850 **NCLC 12,**
38; DA; DAB; DAC; DAM MST, POET;
PC 4; WLC
See also CDBLB 1789-1832; DLB 93, 107

Wouk, Herman 1915-**CLC 1, 9, 38; DAM NOV,**
POP
See also CA 5-8R; CANR 6, 33, 67; DLBY 82;
INT CANR-6; MTCW 1

Wright, Charles (Penzel, Jr.) 1935-**CLC 6, 13,**
28
See also CA 29-32R; CAAS 7; CANR 23, 36,
62; DLB 165; DLBY 82; MTCW 1

Wright, Charles Stevenson 1932- **CLC 49;**
BLC 3; DAM MULT, POET
See also BW 1; CA 9-12R; CANR 26; DLB 33

Wright, Frances 1795-1852 **NCLC 74**
See also DLB 73

Wright, Jack R.
See Harris, Mark

Wright, James (Arlington) 1927-1980**CLC 3,**
5, 10, 28; DAM POET
See also AITN 2; CA 49-52; 97-100; CANR 4,
34, 64; DLB 5, 169; MTCW 1

Wright, Judith (Arandell) 1915- **CLC 11, 53;**
PC 14
See also CA 13-16R; CANR 31; MTCW 1;
SATA 14

Wright, L(aurali) R. 1939- **CLC 44**
See also CA 138

Wright, Richard (Nathaniel) 1908-1960 **C L C**
1, 3, 4, 9, 14, 21, 48, 74; BLC 3; DA; DAB;
DAC; DAM MST, MULT, NOV; SSC 2;
WLC
See also AAYA 5; BW 1; CA 108; CANR 64;
CDALB 1929-1941; DLB 76, 102; DLBD
2; MTCW 1

Wright, Richard B(ruce) 1937- **CLC 6**
See also CA 85-88; DLB 53

Wright, Rick 1945- **CLC 35**

Wright, Rowland

Literary Criticism Series
Cumulative Topic Index

This index lists all topic entries in Gale's *Classical and Medieval Literature Criticism, Contemporary Literary Criticism, Literature Criticism from 1400 to 1800, Nineteenth-Century Literature Criticism,* and *Twentieth-Century Literary Criticism.*

Topic Index

LC Cumulative Nationality Index

LC Cumulative Title Index

Title Index

Title Index

Title Index

Title Index

Title Index

Title Index

ISBN 0-7876-3263-5

90000

9 780787 632632